A Casebook on Contract

A Casebook
on Contract

ANDREW BURROWS

*MA, BCL, LLM (Harvard), QC (Hon), Honorary Bencher of Middle Temple,
Norton Rose Professor of Commercial Law in the University of Oxford and a
Fellow of St Hugh's College*

·HART·
PUBLISHING

OXFORD AND PORTLAND, OREGON
2007

Published in North America (US and Canada) by
Hart Publishing
c/o International Specialized Book Services
920 NE 58th Avenue, Suite 300
Portland, OR 97213-3786
USA
Tel: +1 503 287 3093 or toll-free: (1) 800 944 6190
Fax: +1 503 280 8832
Email: orders@isbs.com
Website: www.isbs.com

© Andrew Burrows 2007

Hart Publishing, 16C Worcester Place, Oxford, OX1 2JW
Tel: +44 (0)1865 517530 Fax: +44 (0) 1865 510710
Email: mail@hartpub.co.uk
Website: http://www.hartpub.co.uk

British Library Cataloguing in Publication Data
Data Available

ISBN: 978-1-84113-713-1 (paperback)

Typeset by Forewords, Oxford
Printed and bound in Great Britain by
TJ International Ltd, Padstow, Cornwall

IN MEMORY OF MY FATHER

Acknowledgements

The author and publisher gratefully acknowledge the authors and publishers of extracted material which appears in this book, and in particular the following for permission to reprint from the sources indicated:

Justis and the Incorporated Council of Law Reporting for England and Wales—the Law Reports, the Weekly Law Reports and the Industrial Cases Reports.

LexisNexis Butterworths—extracts from the All England Law Reports, the All England Reports Commercial Cases, Family Court Reports and Law Times Reports.

Informa UK Ltd—extracts from Lloyd's Law Reports and Building Law Reports.

Sweet & Maxwell Ltd (Westlaw)—for an extract from the Fleet Street Reports and an extract from Commercial Law Cases.

While every care has been taken to establish and acknowledge copyright, and to contact copyright owners, the publishers apologise for any accidental infringement and would be pleased to come to a suitable agreement with the rightful copyright owners in each case.

Preface

In my view, the best way for students to understand and enjoy the law of contract is by careful analysis of what the judges have said in the leading cases. It is with that in mind that I have written this book. It aims to make the cases readily accessible through a clear structure, by a succinct introductory commentary to the various sections, and by notes and questions that will enable a student to appreciate the significance of a particular case and the interesting issues raised by it. Novel features include the treatment of statutes, where I have tried to give a principled overview of the central provisions, and the summaries of academic writings either as part of the notes on a particular case or in the additional reading at the end of each chapter. Above all it is hoped that the book will convey the fascination and excitement of this central subject.

This is a casebook in the traditional sense that it is designed to be used alongside, rather than as a replacement for, a textbook. There are several excellent textbooks on contract. I have given references throughout to the three that I consider the best. As an introductory book, most usefully read at the start of a topic, I would recommend Ewan McKendrick, *Contract Law*. If the student is going to buy any other books I would recommend, as a more detailed textbook, Jack Beatson, *Anson's Law of Contract* and, as a more theoretical work, Stephen Smith, *Atiyah's Introduction to the Law of Contract*. But obviously teachers and students have their own favourites and this casebook can be used just as easily with any other textbook.

This book is aimed at all those studying contract, in particular undergraduates on law courses. The contents seek to reflect the scope of most modern university courses so that the law on illegality and incapacity is not included.

Three further particular features of the contents should be noted. The first is the prominence given to remedies. Both theoretically and in practice this topic is, arguably, the most important in contract law and yet often it is pushed to the end of a course where it is not given the attention it merits. It is to be found in the centre of this book as Part Three. The second is the recognition of the interplay between contract law and the drafting of contract terms. Lawyers need a detailed knowledge of contract law not only to advise when things go wrong but also in order to be able to draft contracts effectively. Proper attention is therefore paid at various stages of this book to interpretation and to various types of contract term. The third is the use made of the outstanding comparative work of the Commission on European Contract Law (led by Olé Lando and Hugh Beale). Their *Principles of European Contract Law* (PECL) merits greater attention by students than has traditionally been the case. What I have done here, therefore, is to set out the relevant parts of PECL at the ends of chapters (along with the page references to the detailed commentary) so that students can compare PECL with English law once they have mastered a particular topic. My own square-bracketed comments are then designed to help a student to see, and to think about, the differences. I have chosen PECL rather than the equally impressive Unidroit Principles of International Commercial Contracts because, given the ongoing talk of a European Contract Code, they are, arguably, of greater importance.

The extracts from the statutes are reproduced in the most recent form with all amendments being incorporated within square brackets.

By the time a student has worked his or her way through this book, he or she will have favourite judges who can be relied on for rational and clear exposition of contractual principles. I anticipate that most will derive the greatest illumination from the judgments of Lord Denning, Lord Wilberforce, Lord Steyn, Lord Nicholls and Lord Bingham. It is striking how much more sophisticated judicial reasoning on contract has become albeit that this coincides with ever longer judgments.

There are several people I would like to thank. Hugh Collins who, along with the late great Peter Birks, taught me contract at Brasenose College and is the author of a deservedly popular theoretical text, *The Law of Contract* (4th edn, 2004); Lyn Hambridge for her secretarial skills; my excellent research assistants, Andrew Scott (who helped with Chapter 4), Adam Rushworth (who assisted with Chapters 11–13) and Kira King (who helped on Chapters 14–15); Kate Elliott for her immaculate copy-editing; and Richard Hart and Mel Hamill at Hart Publishing for being such a great pleasure to work with and for being so encouraging and efficient from start to finish.

This book is dedicated to my father who died from cancer as I was nearing completion of it. If I can be half as good a father to my four children as he was to me, I will have done a wonderful job.

Andrew Burrows
31 March 2007

Contents

PART TWO: THE TERMS OF A CONTRACT

PART FOUR: PRIVITY OF CONTRACT AND THIRD PARTY RIGHTS

PART FIVE: FACTORS ALLOWING ESCAPE FROM A CONTRACT

11. MISREPRESENTATION   537

Table of Cases

Table of Legislation

UK Legislation

New Zealand Legislation

US Legislation

EC Legislation

International Legislation

Part One

The Formation of a Contract

Offer and Acceptance

1. INTRODUCTION

(1) What is a Contract?

In order to understand the role of offer and acceptance, one must first be clear what a contract is. In basic terms one can describe a contract as a legally binding agreement. So, for example, G Treitel, *The Law of Contract* (11th edn, 2003) at 1 begins, 'A contract is an agreement giving rise to obligations which are enforced or recognised by law.'

Most legally binding agreements comprise mutual promises. That is, each party promises to do something in return for the other party promising to do something: for example, A promises to sell his car to B and B in return promises to give A £5,000 for it. These are known as 'bilateral contracts' because each party is making a promise and each party is therefore bound to perform. But in some legally binding agreements only one party is making a promise. That is, one party may promise to do something in return for the other party doing something but without promising to do it: for example, A promises B £250 if B swims the Channel or if B finds A's lost laptop computer. B is not promising to do the swim or to find the laptop. These are referred to as 'unilateral contracts' because only one party is making a promise and only one party is therefore bound to perform.

One significant complication in describing a contract as a legally binding agreement is that this is only really apt to describe what are sometimes called 'simple' contracts. These are contracts, made in writing or orally, which are valid because of the agreement and the 'consideration' (which is the legal term describing the element of exchange between the parties: see Chapter 3 below). It is generally understood that contracts may also be made formally by deed: that is, that promises contained in a deed are contractually binding irrespective of agreement or consideration. Thus J Beatson, *Anson's Law of Contract* (28th edn, 2002) at 73, writes: 'English law does not regard a bare promise or agreement as legally enforceable but recognises only two kinds of contract, the contract made by deed, and the simple contract. A contract made by deed derives its validity neither from the fact of the agreement nor because it is an exchange but solely from the form in which it is expressed. A simple contract as a general rule need not be made in any special form, but requires the presence of consideration which…broadly means that something must be given in exchange for a promise.' G Treitel, *An Outline of the Law of Contract* (6th edn, 2004) 3, in a section discussing qualifications that need to be made to the idea that a contract is an agreement, writes the following: 'There are cases, commonly discussed under the general heading of contract, in which the obligation arises, not out of an agreement between two parties, but rather out of a promise made by one of them. This would be the position where a person made a gratuitous promise in such a form that it was legally binding: for example, in a deed. Such a promise can bind the promisor even before it is communicated to the promisee and hence without any agreement between the parties.' (But contrast G Treitel, *The Law of Contract* at 158, which seems to deny that a promise contained in a deed is a contract). M Furmston in *Cheshire, Fifoot and Furmston's Law of Contract* (15th edn, 2006) 37 writes, 'The affinity of the deed is with gift, not with bargain, and it is fair to say that the so-called "contract by deed" has little in common with agreement save its name and its history, and that it does not seem to require detailed examination in a modern book upon the law of contract.'

The important point to emphasise, therefore, is that, while it is normally accurate and illuminating to describe a contract as a legally binding agreement, contracts made by deed do not always fit that description. Strictly speaking, therefore, it may be more accurate to define a contract as a legally binding promise or set of promises. Hence the definition in section 1 of the American Law Institute's *Restatement (2d) of Contracts:* 'A contract is a promise or set of promises for the breach of which the law gives a remedy, or the performance of which the law in some way recognises as a duty.'

(2) Offer and Acceptance

Having established what a contract is, it can then be seen that offer and acceptance is the legal description of the process by which an agreement, and hence a (simple) contract, is made. Assuming that the other requirements for a valid contract are satisfied (eg the presence of consideration, as discussed in Chapter 3) a contract is formed when an offer has been accepted. The rest of this chapter is concerned with the case law on offer and acceptance.

Introductory reading: E McKendrick, *Contract Law* (7th edn, 2007) Ch 3.

2. OFFERS AND INVITATIONS TO TREAT

An offer is defined by G Treitel, *The Law of Contract,* at 8, as 'an expression of willingness to contract on specified terms, made with the intention that it is to become binding as soon as it is accepted by the person to whom it is addressed'.

An offer should be distinguished from an 'invitation to treat', which is an expression of willingness to negotiate. A person making an invitation to treat does not intend to be bound as soon as it is accepted by the person to whom the statement is addressed. There is no contract if an invitation to treat rather than an offer is accepted.

A number of cases illustrate the distinction between offers and invitations to treat. These will be examined under the following sub-headings:

(1) Two General Illustrative Cases;
(2) Display of Goods for Sale;
(3) Advertisements;
(4) Auction Sales;
(5) Tenders.

(1) Two General Illustrative Cases

Harvey v Facey [1893] AC 552, Privy Council

The claimants (who were the appellants) sent a telegram to the defendants (Facey and his wife) saying, 'Will you sell us Bumper Hall Pen? Telegraph lowest cash price.' Bumper Hall Pen was a property in Jamaica. Facey telegraphed in reply, 'Lowest price for Bumper Hall Pen £900.' In reply, the claimants telegraphed, 'We agree to buy Bumper Hall Pen for £900.' Facey made no reply to that. It was held by the Privy Council that there was no contract for the sale of Bumper Hall Pen because Facey's telegram was not an offer to sell (ie, although this terminology was not used, it was merely an invitation to treat).

Lord Morris (giving the judgment of himself, **Lord Herschell LC, Lord Watson, Lord Hobhouse, Lord Macnaghten,** and **Lord Shand**): Their Lordships cannot treat the telegram from L. M. Facey as binding him in any respect, except to the extent it does by its terms, viz., the lowest price. Everything else is left open, and the reply telegram from the appellants cannot be treated as an acceptance of an offer to sell to them; it is an offer that required to be accepted by L. M. Facey. The contract could only be completed if L. M. Facey had accepted the appellant's last telegram. It has been contended for the appellants that L. M. Facey's telegram should be read as saying "yes" to the first question put in the appellants' telegram, but there is nothing to support that contention. L. M. Facey's telegram gives a precise answer to a precise question, viz., the price. The contract must appear by the telegrams, whereas the appellants are obliged to contend that an acceptance of the first question is to be implied. Their Lordships are of opinion that the mere statement of the lowest price at which the vendor would sell contains no implied contract to sell at that price to the persons making the inquiry.

Gibson v Manchester City Council [1979] 1 WLR 294, House of Lords

The defendant city council adopted a policy of selling council houses to its tenants. The claimant, on a printed form supplied by the council, applied for details of the price of the council house he was renting and mortgage terms. In February 1971, the city treasurer replied, *'The corporation may be prepared to sell the house to you at the purchase price of £2,725 less 20% = £2,180 (freehold).'*[1] The letter then gave details of the mortgage and went on, 'This letter should not be regarded as a firm offer of a mortgage. *If you would like to make formal application to buy your Council house please complete the enclosed application form and return it to me as soon as possible.'*[1] In March 1971, the claimant completed the application form except for the purchase price and returned it to the council. In May 1971 Labour took control of the council from the Conservatives and instructed its officers not to sell council houses unless there was already a legally binding contract. It declined to sell to the claimant.

At first instance and on appeal it was held that there was a concluded contract for the sale of the council house. The defendant's appeal was allowed by the House of Lords, which held that there was no contract because the February letter was not an offer to sell (ie, although this terminology was not used, it was merely an invitation to treat).

Lord Diplock: The corporation's appeal…was dismissed by a majority of the Court of Appeal (Lord Denning M.R. and Ormrod L.J.); Geoffrey Lane L.J. dissented. Lord Denning M.R. rejected…the conventional approach of looking to see whether upon the true construction of the documents relied upon there can be discerned an offer and acceptance. One ought, he said, [1978] 1 W.L.R. 520, 523H, to "look at the correspondence as a whole and at the conduct of the parties and see therefrom whether the parties have come to an agreement on everything that was material."

…

Geoffrey Lane L.J. in a dissenting judgment, which for my part I find convincing, adopted the conventional approach. He found that upon the true construction of the documents relied upon as constituting the contract, there never was an offer by the corporation acceptance of which by Mr. Gibson was capable in law of constituting a legally enforceable contract. It was but a step in the negotiations for a contract which, owing to the change in the political complexion of the council, never reached fruition.

My Lords, there may be certain types of contract, though I think they are exceptional, which do not fit easily into the normal analysis of a contract as being constituted by offer and acceptance; but a contract alleged to have been made by an exchange of correspondence between the parties in which the successive communications other than the first are in reply to one another, is not one of these. I can see no reason in the instant case for departing from the conventional approach of looking at the handful of documents relied upon as constituting the contract sued upon and seeing whether upon their true construction there is to be found in them a contractual offer by the corporation to sell the house to Mr. Gibson and an acceptance of that offer by Mr. Gibson. I venture to think that it was by departing from this conventional approach that the majority of the Court of Appeal was led into error.

…

My Lords, the words I have italicised seem to me, as they seemed to Geoffrey Lane L.J., to make it quite impossible to construe this letter as a contractual offer capable of being converted into a legally enforceable open contract for the sale of land by Mr. Gibson's written acceptance of it. The words "may be prepared to sell" are fatal to this; so is the invitation, not, be it noted, to accept the offer, but "to make formal application to buy" upon the enclosed application form. It is, to quote Geoffrey Lane L.J., a letter setting out the financial terms on which it may be the council will be prepared to consider a sale and purchase in due course.

…

I therefore feel compelled to allow the appeal. One can sympathise with Mr. Gibson's disappointment on finding that his expectations that he would be able to buy his council

---

[1] These words were italicised by Lord Diplock in his summary of the facts.

house at 20 per cent. below its market value in the autumn of 1970 cannot be realised. Whether one thinks this makes it a hard case perhaps depends upon the political views that one holds about council housing policy. But hard cases offer a strong temptation to let them have their proverbial consequences. It is a temptation that the judicial mind must be vigilant to resist.

Lord Russell of Killowen: My Lords, I cannot bring myself to accept that a letter which says that the possible vendor "May be prepared to sell the house to you" can be regarded as an offer to sell capable of acceptance so as to constitute a contract. The language simply does not permit such a construction. Nor can the statement that the letter should not be regarded as a firm offer of a mortgage operate to turn into a firm offer to sell that which quite plainly it was not.

Lord Fraser of Tullybelton agreed with Lords Diplock and Russell. **Lord Keith of Kinkel** agreed with Lord Diplock. **Lord Edmund-Davies** gave a concurring speech.

NOTES AND QUESTIONS

1. Would the decision have been different if the council's letter of February 1971 had started, 'The corporation will sell...' or 'The corporation is prepared to sell...'?
2. The approach to the formation of a contract by Lord Denning in the Court of Appeal (as set out by Lord Diplock at the start of the extract above) was roundly rejected by the House of Lords. What was Lord Denning's approach and what are the advantages and disadvantages of that approach? See also below, 27–32.
3. Which type of exceptional contracts do you think Lord Diplock had in mind in his reference to their not fitting easily into an offer and acceptance analysis? See below, 55–56.

(2) Display of Goods for Sale

Fisher v Bell [1961] 1 QB 394, Divisional Court of the Queen's Bench

The defendant was charged with the offence of 'offering for sale' a flick knife contrary to section 1(1) of the Restriction of Offensive Weapons Act 1959. He had displayed the knife in his shop window with a ticket behind it saying 'Ejector knife—4s.' The magistrates dismissed the case. On appeal by the police to the Divisional Court, it was held that the display was an invitation to treat, not an offer for sale, so that the appeal failed.

Lord Parker CJ: The sole question is whether the exhibition of that knife in the window with the ticket constituted an offer for sale within the statute. I confess that I think most lay people and, indeed, I myself when I first read the papers, would be inclined to the view that to say that if a knife was displayed in a window like that with a price attached to it was not offering it for sale was just nonsense. In ordinary language it is there inviting people to buy it, and it is for sale; but any statute must of course be looked at in the light of the general law of the country. Parliament in its wisdom in passing an Act must be taken to know the general law. It is perfectly clear that according to the ordinary law of contract the display of an article with a price on it in a shop window is merely an invitation to treat. It is in no sense an offer for sale the acceptance of which constitutes a contract. That is clearly the general law of the country. Not only is that so, but it is to be observed that in many statutes and orders which prohibit selling and offering for sale of goods it is very common when it is so desired to insert the words "offering or exposing for sale," "exposing for sale" being clearly words which would cover the display of goods in a shop window. ...

In those circumstances I am driven to the conclusion, though I confess reluctantly, that no offence was here committed. At first sight it sounds absurd that knives of this sort cannot be manufactured, sold, hired, lent, or given, but apparently they can be displayed in shop windows; but even if this – and I am by no means saying it is – is a casus omissus it is not for this court to supply the omission. I am mindful of the strong words of Lord Simonds in *Magor and St. Mellons Rural District Council v. Newport Corporation*. [1952] A.C. 189; [1951] 2 T.L.R. 935; [1951] 2 All E.R. 839, H.L. In that case one of the Lords Justices in the Court of Appeal [1950] 2 All E.R. 1226, 1236, C.A. had, in effect, said that the court having discovered the supposed intention of Parliament must proceed to fill in the gaps – what the Legislature has not written the court must write – and in answer to that contention Lord Simonds in his speech said [1952] A.C. 189, 191 – "It appears to me to be a naked usurpation of the legislative function under the thin disguise of interpretation."

Ashworth and **Elwes JJ** concurred.

QUESTION

Do you agree that words in a criminal statute should be interpreted according to the (civil) law of contract?

Pharmaceutical Society of Great Britain v Boots Cash Chemists (Southern) Ltd [1953] 1 QB 401, Court of Appeal

Section 18(1) of the Pharmacy and Poisons Act 1933 provided that, '…it shall not be lawful (a) for a person to sell any poison listed in Part I of the Poisons List, unless…(iii) the sale is effected by, or under the supervision of, a registered pharmacist.' The defendants owned a self-service shop in which certain non-prescription drugs and medicines (listed in the Poisons List) were displayed on open shelves. Customers would select goods from the shelves, put them into a basket and pay for them at the cash till. It was not in dispute that, at the till, there was sufficient supervision by a registered pharmacist. But the question at issue was whether the defendants contravened the Act because there was no such supervision at the earlier stage when the customer selected the goods and took them to the till. The Court of Appeal, upholding Lord Goddard CJ's decision, held that the Act was not being contravened because the display was not an offer: the goods were not being sold until the customer reached the till, where it was the customer who was making an offer to buy to the cashier.

Somervell LJ: Whether the view contended for by the plaintiffs is a right view depends on what are the legal implications of this layout – the invitation to the customer. Is a contract to be regarded as being completed when the article is put into the receptacle, or is this to be regarded as a more organized way of doing what is done already in many types of shops – and a bookseller is perhaps the best example – namely, enabling customers to have free access to what is in the shop, to look at the different articles, and then, ultimately, having got the ones which they wish to buy, to come up to the assistant saying "I want this"? The assistant in 999 times out of 1,000 says "That is all right," and the money passes and the transaction is completed. I agree with what the Lord Chief Justice has said, and with the reasons which he has given for his conclusion, that in the case of an ordinary shop, although goods are displayed and it is intended that customers should go and choose what they want, the contract is not completed until, the customer having indicated the articles which he needs, the shopkeeper, or someone on his behalf, accepts that offer. Then the contract is completed. I can see no reason at all, that being clearly the normal position, for drawing any different implication as a result of this layout.

The Lord Chief Justice, I think, expressed one of the most formidable difficulties in the way of the plaintiffs' contention when he pointed out that, if the plaintiffs are right, once an article has been placed in the receptacle the customer himself is bound and would have no right, without paying for the first article, to substitute an article which he saw later of a similar kind and which he perhaps preferred. I can see no reason for implying from this self-service arrangement any implication other than that which the Lord Chief Justice found in it, namely, that it is a convenient method of enabling customers to see what there is and choose, and possibly put back and substitute, articles which they wish to have, and then to go up to the cashier and offer to buy what they have so far chosen. On that conclusion the case fails, because it is admitted that there was supervision in the sense required by the Act and at the appropriate moment of time. For these reasons, in my opinion, the appeal should be dismissed.

Birkett LJ: [T]he short point of the case is, at what point of time did the sale in this particular shop at Edgware take place? …It is said, on the one hand, that when the customer takes the package from the poison section and puts it into her basket the sale there and then takes place. On the other hand, it is said the sale does not take place until that customer, who has placed that package in the basket, comes to the exit.

The Lord Chief Justice dealt with the matter in this way, and I would like to adopt his words ([1952] 2 QB 795, 802): "It seems to me, therefore, that the transaction is in no way different from the normal transaction in a shop in which there is no self-service scheme. I am quite satisfied it would be wrong to say that the shopkeeper is making an offer to sell every article in the shop to any person who might come in and that that person can insist on buying any article by saying 'I accept your offer'." Then he went on to deal with the illustration of the bookshop, and continued: "Therefore, in my opinion, the mere fact that a customer picks up a bottle of medicine from the shelves in this case does not amount to an acceptance of an offer to sell. It is an offer by the customer to buy and there is no sale effected until the buyer's offer to buy is accepted by the acceptance of the price. The offer, the acceptance of the price, and therefore the sale take place under the supervision of the pharmacist…"

I agree with that, and I agree that this appeal ought to be dismissed.

Romer LJ delivered a concurring judgment.

NOTES AND QUESTIONS

1. An interim position between a contract being concluded by the cashier (as held by the Court of Appeal) and a contract being concluded by the customer putting an item in a basket (which was explicitly rejected) would have been to hold that the contract was concluded by the customer presenting himself at the till with the goods. That is, that the customer was at that stage accepting the shop's offer. But although such an analysis would probably have equally well meant that the defendants were not in breach of the 1933 Act (because there was accepted to be supervision by a pharmacist at the till) it would produce

other undesirable consequences for shops. For example, it would mean that a supermarket would be unable to correct a price mistakenly placed on an article on the shelves.

2.   How does this case show that, in determining the parties' intentions, courts (a) reason backwards from the end result and (b) use policy implications? See S Smith, *Atiyah's Introduction to the Law of Contract* (6th edn, 2005) 40–42.

(3) Advertisements

Partridge v Crittenden [1968] 1 WLR 1204, Queen's Bench Division

The defendant had inserted an advertisement in a periodical *Cage and Aviary Birds* which read, 'Bramblefinch cocks, Bramblefinch hens 25s each'. He was charged, in a prosecution brought by the RSPCA, with the offence of unlawfully 'offering for sale' a wild live bird contrary to the Protection of Birds Act 1954. The magistrates had held that the defendant was guilty of that offence. This was overturned by the High Court which held that the advert was an invitation to treat, not an offer for sale.

Ashworth J: A similar point arose before this court in 1960 dealing, it is true, with a different statute but with the same words, in *Fisher v. Bell* [1961] 1 Q.B. 394.

...

The words are the same here "offer for sale," and in my judgment the law of the country is equally plain as it was in regard to articles in a shop window, namely that the insertion of an advertisement in the form adopted here under the title "Classified Advertisements" is simply an invitation to treat.

That is really sufficient to dispose of this case. I should perhaps in passing observe that the editors of the publication Criminal Law Review had an article dealing with *Fisher v. Bell* [1961] 1 QB 394 in which a way round that decision was at least contemplated, suggesting that while there might be one meaning of the phrase "offer for sale" in the law of contract, a criminal court might take a stricter view, particularly having in mind the purpose of the Act, in *Fisher v. Bell* the stocking of flick knives, and in this case the selling of wild birds. But for my part that is met entirely by the quotation which appears in Lord Parker's judgment in *Fisher v. Bell*, at 400, that "It appears to me to be a naked usurpation of the legislative function under the thin disguise of interpretation."

I would allow this appeal and quash the conviction

Lord Parker CJ: I agree and with less reluctance than in *Fisher v. Bell* ...because I think when one is dealing with advertisements and circulars, unless they indeed come from manufacturers, there is business sense in their being construed as invitations to treat and not offers for sale. In a very different context in *Grainger & Son v. Gough* [1896] A.C. 325, 334, H.L.(E.) Lord Herschell said dealing with a price-list:

"The transmission of such a price-list does not amount to an offer to supply an unlimited quantity of the wine described at the price named, so that as soon as an order is given there is a binding contract to supply that quantity. If it were so, the merchant might find himself involved in any number of contractual obligations to supply wine of a particular description which he would be quite unable to carry out, his stock of wine of that description being necessarily limited."

It seems to me accordingly that not only is it the law but common sense supports it.

Blain J concurred.

This case illustrates the *general* rule that adverts are invitations to treat, not offers. What is the explanation for that general rule (see the citation by Lord Parker CJ from Lord Herschell's speech in *Grainger & Son v Gough*)?

Carlill v Carbolic Smoke Ball Company
[1893] 1 QB 256, Court of Appeal

The defendants owned a medicinal product called a 'carbolic smoke ball'. They advertised this product in various newspapers in the following terms:

> '£100 reward will be paid by the Carbolic Smoke Ball Company to any person who contracts the increasing epidemic influenza, colds, or any disease caused by taking cold, after having used the ball three times daily for two weeks according to the printed directions supplied with each ball. £1000 is deposited with the Alliance Bank Regent Street, shewing our sincerity in the matter.
>
> During the last epidemic of influenza many thousand carbolic smoke balls were sold as preventives against this disease, and in no ascertained case was the disease contracted by those using the carbolic smoke ball.
>
> One carbolic smoke ball will last a family several months making it the cheapest remedy in the world at the price, 10s., post free. The ball can be refilled at a cost of 5s. Address, Carbolic Smoke Ball Company, 27, Princess Street, Hanover Square, London.'

The claimant, relying on the advert, bought one of the balls at a chemist's and used it as directed for the specified period but then caught influenza. She sued for payment of the £100 and succeeded before Hawkins J. In dismissing the defendants' appeal, it was held by the Court of Appeal that the advert was an offer of a unilateral contract which had been accepted by the claimant.

The judgments, which are extracted below, consider not only (i) whether there was an offer but also (ii) whether it was accepted and (iii) whether there was consideration. For (ii), see below, 41, 47; and for (iii) see below, Chapter 3.

Lindley LJ: We must first consider whether this was intended to be a promise at all, or whether it was a mere puff which meant nothing. Was it a mere puff? My answer to that question is No, and I base my answer upon this passage: "1000*l.* is deposited with the Alliance Bank, shewing our sincerity in the matter." Now, for what was that money deposited or that statement made except to negative the suggestion that this was a mere puff and meant nothing at all? The deposit is called in aid by the advertiser as proof of his sincerity in the matter – that is, the sincerity of his promise to pay this 100*l.* in the event which he has specified. I say this for the purpose of giving point to the observation that we are not inferring a promise; there is the promise, as plain as words can make it.

Then it is contended that it is not binding. In the first place, it is said that it is not made with anybody in particular. Now that point is common to the words of this advertisement and to the words of all other advertisements offering rewards. They are offers to anybody who performs the conditions named in the advertisement, and anybody who does perform the condition accepts the offer. In point of law this advertisement is an offer to pay 100*l.* to anybody who will perform these conditions, and the performance of the conditions is the acceptance of the offer. ...

But then it is said, "Supposing that the performance of the conditions is an acceptance of the offer, that acceptance ought to have been notified." Unquestionably, as a general proposition, when an offer is made, it is necessary in order to make a binding contract, not only that it should be accepted, but that the acceptance should be notified. But is that so in cases of this kind? I apprehend that they are an exception to that rule, or, if not an exception, they are open to the observation that the notification of the acceptance need not precede the performance. This offer is a continuing offer. It was never revoked, and if notice of acceptance is required – which I doubt very much, for I rather think the true view is that which was expressed and explained by Lord Blackburn in the case of *Brogden v. Metropolitan Ry. Co.* 2 App Cas 666, 691 – if notice of acceptance is required, the person who makes the offer gets the notice of acceptance contemporaneously with his notice of the performance of the condition. If he gets notice of the acceptance before his offer is revoked, that in principle is all you want. I, however, think that the true view, in a case of this kind, is that the person who makes the offer shews by his language and from the nature of the transaction that he does not expect and does not require notice of the acceptance apart from notice of the performance.

We, therefore, find here all the elements which are necessary to form a binding contract enforceable in point of law, subject to two observations. First of all it is said that this advertisement is so vague that you cannot really construe it as a promise – that the vagueness of the language shews that a legal promise was never intended or contemplated. ...It is for the defendants to shew what it does mean; and it strikes me that there are two, and possibly three, reasonable constructions to be put on this advertisement, any one of which will answer the purpose of the plaintiff. ...It strikes me, I confess, that the true construction of this advertisement is that 100*l*. will be paid to anybody who uses this smoke ball three times daily for two weeks according to the printed directions, and who gets the influenza or cold or other diseases caused by taking cold within a reasonable time after so using it; and if that is the true construction, it is enough for the plaintiff.

I come now to the last point which I think requires attention – that is, the consideration. It has been argued that this is nudum pactum – that there is no consideration. We must apply to that argument the usual legal tests. Let us see whether there is no advantage to the defendants. ...It is quite obvious that in the view of the advertisers a use by the public of their remedy, if they can only get the public to have confidence enough to use it, will react and produce a sale which is directly beneficial to them. Therefore, the advertisers get out of the use an advantage which is enough to constitute a consideration.

But there is another view. Does not the person who acts upon this advertisement and accepts the offer put himself to some inconvenience at the request of the defendants? Is it nothing to use this ball three times daily for two weeks according to the directions at the request of the advertiser? Is that to go for nothing? It appears to me that there is a distinct inconvenience, not to say a detriment, to any person who so uses the smoke ball. I am of opinion, therefore, that there is ample consideration for the promise.

Bowen LJ: I am of the same opinion. We were asked to say that this document was a contract too vague to be enforced.

The first observation which arises is that the document itself is not a contract at all, it is only an offer made to the public. The defendants contend next, that it is an offer the terms of which are too vague to be treated as a definite offer, inasmuch as there is no limit of time fixed for the catching of the influenza, and it cannot be supposed that the advertisers seriously meant to promise to pay money to every person who catches the influenza at any time after the inhaling of the smoke ball. It was urged also, that if you look at this document you will find much vagueness as to the persons with whom the contract was intended to be made – that, in the first place, its terms are wide enough to include persons who may have used the smoke ball before the advertisement was issued; at all events, that it is an offer to the world in general, and, also, that it is unreasonable to suppose it to be a definite offer, because nobody in their senses would contract themselves out of the opportunity of checking the experiment which was going to be made at their own expense. It is also contended that the advertisement is rather in the nature of a puff or a proclamation than a promise or offer intended to mature into a contract when accepted. But the main point seems to be that the vagueness of the document shews that no contract whatever was intended. It seems to me that in order to arrive at a right conclusion we must read this advertisement in its plain meaning, as the public would understand it. It was intended to be issued to the public and to be read by the public. How would an ordinary person reading this document construe it? It was intended unquestionably to have some effect, and I think the effect which it was intended to have, was to make people use the smoke ball, because the suggestions and allegations which it contains are directed immediately to the use of the smoke ball as distinct from the purchase of it. It did not follow that the smoke ball was to be purchased from the defendants directly, or even from agents of theirs directly. The intention was that the circulation of the smoke ball should be promoted, and that the use of it should be increased. The advertisement begins by saying that a reward will be paid by the Carbolic Smoke Ball Company to any person who contracts the increasing epidemic after using the ball. It has been said that the words do not apply only to persons who contract the epidemic after the publication of the advertisement, but include persons who had previously contracted the influenza. I cannot so read the advertisement. It is written in colloquial and popular language, and I think that it is equivalent to this: "100*l.* will be paid to any person who shall contract the increasing epidemic after having used the carbolic smoke ball three times daily for two weeks." And it seems to me that the way in which the public would read it would be this, that if anybody, after the advertisement was published, used three times daily for two weeks the carbolic smoke ball, and then caught cold, he would be entitled to the reward. Then again it was said: "How long is this protection to endure? Is it to go on for ever, or for what limit of time?" I think that there are two constructions of this document, each of which is good sense, and each of which seems to me to satisfy the exigencies of the present action. It may mean that the protection is warranted to last during the epidemic, and it was during the epidemic that the plaintiff contracted the disease. I think, more probably, it means that the smoke ball will be a protection while it is in use. That seems to me the way in which an ordinary person would understand an advertisement about medicine, and about a specific against influenza. It could not be supposed that after you have left off using it you are still to be protected for ever, as if there was to be a stamp set upon your forehead that you were never to catch influenza because you had once used the carbolic smoke ball. I think the immunity is to last during the use of the ball. That is the way in which I should naturally read it, and it seems to me that the subsequent language of the advertisement supports that construction. It says: "During the last epidemic of influenza many thousand carbolic smoke balls were sold, and in no ascertained case was the disease contracted by those using" (not "who had used") "the carbolic smoke ball," and it concludes with saying that one smoke ball will last a family several months (which imports that it is to be efficacious while it is being used), and that the ball can be refilled at a cost of 5*s.* I, therefore, have myself no hesitation in saying that I think, on the construction of this advertisement, the protection was to enure during the time that the carbolic smoke ball was being used. ...

Was it intended that the 100*l.* should, if the conditions were fulfilled, be paid? The advertisement says that 1000*l.* is lodged at the bank for the purpose. Therefore, it cannot be said that the statement that 100*l.* would be paid was intended to be a mere puff. I think it was intended to be understood by the public as an offer which was to be acted upon.

But it was said there was no check on the part of the persons who issued the advertisement, and that it would be an insensate thing to promise 100*l.* to a person who used the smoke ball unless you could check or superintend his manner of using it. The answer to that argument seems to me to be that if a person chooses to make extravagant promises of this kind he probably does so because it pays him to make them, and, if he has made them, the extravagance of the promises is no reason in law why he should not be bound by them.

It was also said that the contract is made with all the world – that is, with everybody; and that you cannot contract with everybody. It is not a contract made with all the world. There is the fallacy of the argument. It is an offer made to all the world; and why should not an offer be made to all the world which is to ripen into a contract with anybody who comes forward and performs the condition? It is an offer to become liable to any one who, before it is retracted, performs the condition, and, although the offer is made to the world, the contract is made with that limited portion of the public who come forward and perform the condition on the faith of the advertisement. It is not like cases in which you offer to negotiate, or you issue advertisements that you have got a stock of books to sell, or houses to let, in which case there is no offer to be bound by any contract. Such advertisements are offers to negotiate – offers to receive offers – offers to chaffer, as, I think, some learned judge in one of the cases has said. If this is an offer to be bound, then it is a contract the moment the person fulfils the condition. …

Then it was said that there was no notification of the acceptance of the contract. One cannot doubt that, as an ordinary rule of law, an acceptance of an offer made ought to be notified to the person who makes the offer, in order that the two minds may come together. Unless this is done the two minds may be apart, and there is not that consensus which is necessary according to the English law – I say nothing about the laws of other countries – to make a contract. But there is this clear gloss to be made upon that doctrine, that as notification of acceptance is required for the benefit of the person who makes the offer, the person who makes the offer may dispense with notice to himself if he thinks it desirable to do so, and I suppose there can be no doubt that where a person in an offer made by him to another person, expressly or impliedly intimates a particular mode of acceptance as sufficient to make the bargain binding, it is only necessary for the other person to whom such offer is made to follow the indicated method of acceptance; and if the person making the offer, expressly or impliedly intimates in his offer that it will be sufficient to act on the proposal without communicating acceptance of it to himself, performance of the condition is a sufficient acceptance without notification.

That seems to me to be the principle which lies at the bottom of the acceptance cases, of which two instances are the well-known judgment of Mellish, L.J., in *Harris's Case* Law Rep 7 Ch 587, and the very instructive judgment of Lord Blackburn in *Brogden v. Metropolitan Ry. Co.* 2 App Cas 666, 691, in which he appears to me to take exactly the line I have indicated.

Now, if that is the law, how are we to find out whether the person who makes the offer does intimate that notification of acceptance will not be necessary in order to constitute a binding bargain? In many cases you look to the offer itself. In many cases you extract from the character of the transaction that notification is not required, and in the advertisement cases it seems to me to follow as an inference to be drawn from the transaction itself that a person is not to notify his acceptance of the offer before he performs the condition, but that if he performs the condition notification is dispensed with. It seems to me that from the point of view of common sense no other idea could be entertained. If I advertise to the world that my dog is lost, and that anybody who brings the dog to a particular place will be paid some money, are all the police or other persons whose business it is to find lost dogs to be expected to sit down and write me a note saying that they have accepted my proposal? Why, of course, they at once look after the dog, and as soon as they find the dog they have performed the condition. The essence of the transaction is that the dog should be found, and it is not necessary under such circumstances, as it seems to me, that in order to make the contract binding there should be any notification of acceptance. It follows from the nature of the thing that the performance of the condition is sufficient acceptance without the notification of it, and a person who makes an offer in an advertisement of that kind makes an offer which must be read by the light of that common sense reflection. He does, therefore, in his offer impliedly indicate that he does not require notification of the acceptance of the offer.

A further argument for the defendants was that this was a nudum pactum – that there was no consideration for the promise – that taking the influenza was only a condition, and that the using the smoke ball was only a condition, and that there was no consideration at all; in fact, that there was no request, express or implied, to use the smoke ball. …Inconvenience sustained by one party at the request of the other is enough to create a consideration. I think, therefore, that it is consideration enough that the plaintiff took the trouble of using the smoke ball. But I think also that the defendants received a benefit from this user, for the use of the smoke ball was contemplated by the defendants as being indirectly a benefit to them, because the use of the smoke balls would promote their sale.

AL Smith LJ delivered a concurring judgment.

NOTES AND QUESTIONS

1. Why was the advert in this famous case held to be an offer, contrary to the general rule that adverts are invitations to treat? Are adverts in relation to unilateral 'contracts' always offers?

2. In addition to deciding that the advert was an offer, the case is also a useful illustration of the point that there is no problem about an offer being made to more than one person. That is, the offer was valid even though made 'to all the world.'

3. It is difficult to disentangle the reasoning as to whether there was an offer in this case from the questions (i) whether the terms were sufficiently certain and (ii) whether there was an 'intention to create legal relations'. As we shall see in Chapter 2, those elements are, in the modern law, normally treated as separate requirements once one has established offer and acceptance.

4. **AWB Simpson, 'Quackery and Contract Law:** *Carlill v Carbolic Smoke Ball Company'* **in** *Leading Cases in the Common Law* **(1995) 259** examines in great detail the historical context of the case and, in particular, how 'quack medicine' was commonplace at the time. More controversially, he argues that, apart from its examination of unilateral contracts, *Carlill* is legally important because it was the first in which the courts laid down a requirement of 'intention to create legal relations'. Yet it is normally thought that that doctrine was established later in *Balfour v Balfour* [1919] 2 KB 571 (see below, 77); and in *Carlill* the discussion on intention was rather directed to whether there was an offer. Do you think *Carlill* is so well-known to lawyers because of its memorable facts (ie in Simpson's words, at 281, 'the comic and slightly mysterious object involved') or for the law applied in it or for both?

5. Is an advertisement on a website of goods for sale at a particular price an offer or an invitation to treat?

(4) Auction Sales

Barry v Davies [2000] 1 WLR 1962, Court of Appeal

Customs and Excise put up for sale by auction two brand new engine analyser machines (for use in tuning engines). Each could be obtained from the manufacturers for £14,521 but they were being sold without a reserve price. After the auctioneer failed to obtain bids of £5,000 and £3,000, the claimant bid £200 for each machine. The auctioneer refused to accept these bids and withdrew the machines from the auction. They were sold a few days later through an advert in a magazine for £750 each. The claimant brought an action against the auctioneer for breach of contract on the basis that he was the highest bidder and that, at an auction without reserve, the auctioneer had been bound to sell to him. The Court of Appeal, affirming the trial judge, held that the holding of an auction sale without reserve is an offer by the auctioneer to sell to the highest bidder so that the auctioneer was indeed contractually bound to sell to the claimant (who was entitled to damages of £27,600).

Sir Murray Stuart-Smith: The judge held that it would be the general and reasonable expectation of persons attending at an auction sale without reserve that the highest bidder would and should be entitled to the lot for which he bids. Such an outcome was in his view fair and logical. As a matter of law he held that there was a collateral contract between the auctioneer and the highest bidder constituted by an offer by the auctioneer to sell to the highest bidder which was accepted when the bid was made. In so doing he followed the views of the majority of the Court of Exchequer Chamber in *Warlow v. Harrison* (1859) 1 E. & E. 309.

He also held that this was the effect of condition 1 of the conditions of sale, which was in these terms:

> "The highest bidder to be the purchaser; but should any dispute arise between two or more bidders the same shall be determined by the auctioneers who shall have the right of withdrawing lots."

The judge concluded that the first clause meant what it said and the right of withdrawal was conditioned on there being a dispute between bidders, and there was none.

Mr. Moran on behalf of the defendant criticised this conclusion on a number of grounds. First, he submitted that the holding of an auction without reserve does not amount to a promise on the part of the auctioneer to sell the lots to the highest bidder. There are no express words to the effect, merely a statement of fact that the vendor has not placed a reserve on the lot. Such an intention, he submitted, is inconsistent with two principles of law, namely that the auctioneer's request for bids is not an offer which can be accepted by the highest bidder (*Payne v. Cave* (1789) 3 Durn. & E. 148) and that there is no completed contract of sale until the auctioneer's hammer falls and the bidder may withdraw his bid up until that time (Sale of Goods Act 1979, section 57(2), which reflects the common law). There should be no need to imply such a promise into a statement that the sale is without reserve, because there may be other valid reasons why the auctioneer should be entitled to withdraw the lot, for example if he suspected an illegal ring or that the vendor had no title to sell.

Secondly, Mr. Moran submitted that there is no consideration for the auctioneer's promise. He submitted that the bid itself cannot amount to consideration because the bidder has not promised to do anything, he can withdraw the bid until it is accepted and the sale completed by the fall of the hammer. At most the bid represents a discretionary promise, which amounts to illusory consideration, for example promising to do something "if I feel like it." The bid only had real benefit to the auctioneer at the moment the sale is completed by the fall of the hammer. Furthermore, the suggestion that consideration is provided because the auctioneer has the opportunity to accept the bid or to obtain a higher bid as the bidding is driven up depends upon the bid not being withdrawn.

Finally, Mr. Moran submitted that where an agent is acting for a disclosed principal he is not liable on the contract: *Bowstead & Reynolds on Agency*, 16th ed. (1996), p. 548, para. 9-001 and *Mainprice v. Westley* (1865) 6 B. & S. 420. If therefore there is any collateral contract it is with the principal and not the agent.

These submissions were forcefully and attractively argued by Mr. Moran. The authorities, such as they were, do not speak with one voice. The starting point is section 57 of the Sale of Goods Act 1979, which re-enacted the Sale of Goods Act 1893 (56 & 57 Vict. c. 71), itself in this section a codification of the common law. I have already referred to the effect of subsection (2). Subsections (3) and (4) are also important. They provide:

> "(3) A sale by auction may be notified to be subject to a reserve or upset price, and a right to bid may also be reserved expressly by or on behalf of the seller. (4) Where a sale by auction is not notified to be subject to the right to bid by or on behalf of the seller, it is not lawful for the seller to bid himself or to employ any person to bid at the sale, or for the auctioneer knowingly to take any bid from the seller or any such person."

Although the Act does not expressly deal with sales by auction without reserve, the auctioneer is the agent of the vendor and, unless subsection (4) has been complied with, it is not lawful for him to make a bid. Yet withdrawing the lot from the sale because it has not reached the level which the auctioneer considers appropriate is tantamount to bidding on behalf of the seller. The highest bid cannot be rejected simply because it is not high enough.

The judge based his decision on the reasoning of the majority of the Court of Exchequer Chamber in *Warlow v. Harrison*, 1 E. & E. 309. The sale was of "the three following horses, the property of a gentleman, without reserve:" see p. 314. The plaintiff bid 60 guineas for one of the horses; another person, who was in fact the owner, immediately bid 61 guineas. The plaintiff, having been informed that the bid was from the owner declined to bid higher, and claimed he was entitled to the horse. He sued the auctioneer; he based his claim on a plea that the auctioneer was his agent to complete the contract on his behalf. On that plea the plaintiff succeeded at first instance; but the verdict was set aside in the Court of Queen's Bench. The plaintiff appealed. Although the Court of Exchequer Chamber upheld the decision on the case as pleaded, all five members of the court held that if the pleadings were appropriately amended, the plaintiff would be entitled to succeed on a retrial. Martin B. gave the judgment of the majority, consisting of himself, Byles and Watson BB. He said, at pp. 316-317:

> "Upon the facts of the case, it seems to us that the plaintiff is entitled to recover. In a sale by auction there are three parties, viz. the owner of the property to be sold, the auctioneer, and the portion of the public who attend to bid, which of course includes the highest bidder. In this, as in most cases of sales by auction, the owner's name was not disclosed: he was a concealed principal. The name of the auctioneers, of whom the defendant was one, alone was published; and the sale was announced by them to be 'without reserve.' This, according to all the cases both at law and equity, means that neither the vendor nor any person in his behalf shall bid at the auction, and that the property shall be sold to the highest bidder, whether the sum bid be equivalent to the real value or not; *Thornett v. Haines* (1846) 15 M. & W. 367. We cannot distinguish the case of an auctioneer putting up property for sale upon such a condition from the case of the loser of property offering a reward, or that of a railway company publishing a timetable stating the times when, and the places to which, the trains run. It has been decided that the person giving the information advertised for, or a passenger taking a ticket, may sue as upon a contract with him; *Denton v. Great Northern Railway Co.* (1856) 5 E. & B. 860. Upon the same principle, it seems to us that the highest bona fide bidder at an auction may sue the auctioneer as upon a contract that the sale shall be without reserve. We think the auctioneer who puts

the property up for sale upon such a condition pledges himself that the sale shall be without reserve; or, in other words, contracts that it shall be so; and that this contract is made with the highest bona fide bidder; and, in case of breach of it, that he has a right of action against the auctioneer ... We entertain no doubt that the owner may, at any time before the contract is legally complete, interfere and revoke the auctioneer's authority: but he does so at his peril; and, if the auctioneer has contracted any liability in consequence of his employment and the subsequent revocation or conduct of the owner, he is entitled to be indemnified."

The two other members of the court, Willes J. and Bramwell B. reached the same conclusion, but based their decision on breach of warranty of authority.

Although therefore the decision of the majority is not strictly binding, it was the reasoned judgment of the majority and is entitled to very great respect.

...

In *Harris v. Nickerson* (1873) L.R. 8 Q.B. 286 the defendant, an auctioneer, advertised a sale by auction of certain lots including office furniture on a certain day and the two following days. But the sale of furniture on the third day was withdrawn. The plaintiff attended the sale and claimed against the defendant for breach of contract in not holding the sale, seeking to recover his expenses in attending. The claim was rejected by the Court of Queen's Bench. In the course of his judgment Blackburn J. said, at p. 288:

"in the case of *Warlow v. Harrison*, 1 E. & E. 309, 314, 318, the opinion of the majority of the judges in the Exchequer Chamber appears to have been that an action would lie for not knocking down the lot to the highest bona fide bidder when the sale was advertised as without reserve; in such a case it may be that there is a contract to sell to the highest bidder, and that if the owner bids there is a breach of the contract ..."

And Quain J. said, L.R. 8 Q.B. 286, 289:

"When a sale is advertised as without reserve, and a lot is put up and bid for, there is ground for saying, as was said in *Warlow v. Harrison*, 1 E. & E. 309, 314, that a contract is entered into between the auctioneer and the highest bona fide bidder ..."

In *Johnston v. Boyes* [1899] 2 Ch. 73, 77 Cozens-Hardy J. also accepted the majority view in *Warlow's* case as being good law.

...

So far as textbook writers are concerned both *Chitty on Contracts*, 28th ed. (1999), vol. 1, p. 94, para. 2-010 and *Benjamin's Sale of Goods*, 5th ed. (1997), p. 107, para. 2-005 adopt the view expressed by the majority of the court in *Warlow's* case.

As to consideration, in my judgment there is consideration both in the form of detriment to the bidder, since his bid can be accepted unless and until it is withdrawn, and benefit to the auctioneer as the bidding is driven up. Moreover, attendance at the sale is likely to be increased if it is known that there is no reserve.

As to the agency point, there is no doubt that, when the sale is concluded, the contract is between the purchaser and vendor and not the auctioneer. Even if the identity of the vendor is not disclosed, it is clear that the auctioneer is selling as agent. It is true that there was no such contract between vendor and purchaser. But that does not prevent a collateral agreement existing between the auctioneer and bidder. A common example of this is an action for breach of warranty of authority, which arises on a collateral contract.

For these reasons I would uphold the judge's decision on liability.

Pill LJ gave a concurring judgment.

NOTES AND QUESTIONS

1. As between the buyer and seller of the goods (where the auctioneer is acting as agent for the seller) it is clear that the auctioneer's holding of an auction and request for bids is an invitation to treat. The person making the bid is making an offer which may or may not be accepted by the auctioneer by bringing down his hammer. So the holding of an auction sale without reserve does not constitute an offer *by the seller* to sell to the highest bidder. But this case establishes, after over a century of doubt, that the majority's reasoning (albeit obiter dicta) in *Warlow v Harrison* (1859) 1 E & E 309, 316–317 was correct and that, *as between the buyer and the auctioneer*, the holding of an auction sale without reserve is an offer *by the auctioneer* to sell to the highest bidder.

2. What is the position, as between the buyer and the auctioneer, where there is an auction with reserve and the auctioneer withdraws the goods (a) before the reserve price has been reached (b) after the reserve price has been reached?

(5) Tenders

Spencer v Harding (1870) LR 5 CP 561, Court of Common Pleas

The defendants sent out a circular as follows: 'We are instructed to offer to the wholesale trade for sale by tender the stock-in-trade of Messrs G Eilbeck & Co amounting as per stock-book to £2,503 13s 1d. and which will be sold at a discount in one lot. Payment to be made in cash. The stock may be viewed on the premises…up to Thursday, the 20th instant, on which day, at 12 o'clock noon precisely, the tenders will be received and opened at our offices…' The claimants had submitted the highest tender and alleged that, in refusing to sell the goods to them, the defendants were in breach of contract. The Court of Common Pleas, rejecting that argument, held that the defendants' invitation to tender was not an offer to sell to the highest bidder.

Willes J: I am of opinion that the defendants are entitled to judgment. The action is brought against persons who issued a circular offering a stock for sale by tender, to be sold at a discount in one lot. The plaintiffs sent in a tender which turned out to be the highest, but which was not accepted. They now insist that the circular amounts to a contract or promise to sell the goods to the highest bidder, that is, in this case, to the person who should tender for them at the smallest rate of discount; and reliance is placed on the cases as to rewards offered for the discovery of an offender. In those cases, however, there never was any doubt that the advertisement amounted to a promise to pay the money to the person who first gave information. The difficulty suggested was that it was a contract with all the world. But that, of course, was soon overruled. It was an offer to become liable to any person who before the offer should be retracted should happen to be the person to fulfil the contract of which the advertisement was an offer or tender. That is not the sort of difficulty which presents itself here. If the circular had gone on, "and we undertake to sell to the highest bidder," the reward cases would have applied, and there would have been a good contract in respect of the persons. But the question is, whether there is here any offer to enter into a contract at all, or whether the circular amounts to anything more than a mere proclamation that the defendants are ready to chaffer for the sale of the goods, and to receive offers for the purchase of them. In advertisements for tenders for buildings it is not usual to say that the contract will be given to the lowest bidder, and it is not always that the contract is made with the lowest bidder. Here there is a total absence of any words to intimate that the highest bidder is to be the purchaser. It is a mere attempt to ascertain whether an offer can be obtained within such a margin as the sellers are willing to adopt.

Keating and **Montague Smith JJ** concurred.

NOTE

This case shows the general position that a tender made in response to an invitation to tender is not the acceptance of an offer but is an offer (following an invitation to treat) which can then be accepted or rejected. Tenders are most frequently encountered in the context of construction projects where an employer invites various contractors to tender for the work to be done. The employer is then free to choose between the different tenders (or indeed to reject them all).

Harvela Investments Ltd v Royal Trust Company of Canada (CI) Ltd [1986] AC 207, House of Lords

The first defendants (the Royal Trust Co) owned a block of shares in a company. By telex, they invited the claimants (Harvela) and the second defendant (Sir Leonard Outerbridge) to make offers by sealed tender for the shares. They also said, 'we bind ourselves to accept [the highest] offer.' Harvela's offer was $2,175,000 and Sir Leonard's was '$2,100,000 or $101,000 in excess of any other offer…expressed as a fixed monetary amount, whichever is higher.' The first defendants accepted Sir Leonard's bid as being the higher bid (of $2,276,000). The claimants brought an action claiming that the shares must be sold to them because there had been a binding offer to accept the highest bid and, as the 'referential bid' of Sir Leonard's was invalid, theirs was the highest bid. Peter Gibson J found for the claimants but the Court of Appeal allowed Sir Leonard's appeal. In allowing Harvela's appeal, the House of Lords held that the referential bid was invalid and that the defendants were bound to accept the only valid offer made.

Lord Diplock: The construction question turns upon the wording of the telex of 15 September 1981 referred to by Lord Templeman as "the invitation" and addressed to both Harvela and Sir Leonard. It was not a mere invitation to negotiate for the sale of the shares in Harvey & Co. Ltd. of which the vendors were the registered owners in the capacity of trustees. Its legal nature was that of a unilateral or "if" contract, or rather of two unilateral contracts in identical terms to one of which the vendors and Harvela were the parties as promisor and promisee respectively, while to the other the vendors were promisor and Sir Leonard was promisee. Such unilateral contracts were made at the time when the invitation was received by the promisee to whom it was addressed by the vendors; under neither of them did the promisee, Harvela and Sir Leonard respectively, assume any legal obligation to anyone to do or refrain from doing anything.

The vendors, on the other hand, did assume a legal obligation to the promisee under each contract. That obligation was conditional upon the happening, after the unilateral contract had been made, of an event which was specified in the invitation; the obligation was to enter into a synallagmatic contract to sell the shares to the promisee, the terms of such synallagmatic contract being also set out in the invitation. The event upon the happening of which the vendor's obligation to sell the shares to the promisee arose was the doing by the promisee of an act which was of such a nature that it might be done by either promisee or neither promisee but could not be done by both. The vendors thus did not by entering into the two unilateral contracts run any risk of assuming legal obligations to enter into conflicting synallagmatic contracts to sell the shares to each promisee.

The two unilateral contracts were of short duration; for the condition subsequent to which each was subject was the receipt by the vendors' solicitors on or before 3 p.m. on the following day, 16 September 1981, of a sealed tender or confidential telex containing an offer by the promisee to buy the shares for a single sum of money in Canadian dollars. If such an offer was received from each of the promisees under their respective contracts, the obligation of the promisor, the vendors, was to sell the shares to the promisee whose offer was the higher; and any obligation which the promisor had assumed to the promisee under the other unilateral contract came to an end, because the event the happening of which was the condition subsequent to which the vendors' obligation to sell the shares to that promisee was subject had not happened before the unilateral contract with that promisee expired.

Since the invitation in addition to containing the terms of the unilateral contract also embodied the terms of the synallagmatic contract into which the vendors undertook to enter upon the happening of the specified event, the consequence of the happening of that event would be to convert the invitation into a synallagmatic contract between the vendors and whichever promisee had offered, by sealed tender or confidential telex, the higher sum. ...

The answer to the construction question itself, however, appears to me to present no difficulties in so far as it leads to the conclusion that the condition subsequent to which the vendors' obligations under the unilateral contracts were subject was incapable of being fulfilled by either promisee except by a self-contained offer of a purchase price for the shares expressed as a fixed sum of money which did not necessitate, for its quantification, reference to offers made by any other bidders. I appreciate that this cannot be quite so obvious as I myself have thought throughout, seeing that the Court of Appeal felt compelled to come to a different conclusion.

In the case of a unilateral contract, until it is converted, if it ever is, into a synallagmatic contract between promisor and promisee, the only question of construction is: what legal obligation would the words used by the promisor reasonably convey to the promisee that it was the intention of the promisor to assume towards him?

The invitation invited each promisee to whom it was addressed to specify by a fixed hour on the following day the price at which he was willing to accept the promisor's offer to sell the shares upon the terms set out in the invitation. Such price was to be specified, not by an offer of which the other promisee could obtain knowledge, but by sealed tender or confidential telex the contents of which the promisor undertook should not be disclosed to the other promisee until it was too late for him to make a timeous offer.

The whole business purpose of unilateral contracts inviting two or more promisees to submit sealed tenders of a purchase price for property which are not to be disclosed to any competing promisee and imposing on the promisor a legal obligation to transfer the property to the promisee whose tender specifies the highest price is that each promisee should make up his mind as to the maximum sum which he estimates the property is worth to him, not a sum of money the amount of which cannot be determined except by reference to amounts specified in sealed tenders received from other promisees of which, under the terms of the unilateral contract, he is to be denied all knowledge before the time for making his own tender has expired. That business purpose would be defeated by a tender which took the form of an offer to purchase the property not for a specified fixed sum of money but for a sum greater by some specified amount than the fixed sum specified in the sealed tender lodged by some other promisee by the terms of a unilateral contract in identical terms. What other sensible reason could there be for making it a term of each unilateral contract that the promisee should be kept in ignorance of the amounts offered by any other promisees?

Lord Templeman: The argument put forward by Mr. Price on behalf of Sir Leonard was that the referential bid is an "offer" and therefore Sir Leonard was entitled to submit a referential bid. In acceding to this argument, the Court of Appeal recognised that the consequences could be unfortunate and would be unforeseeable; the Court of Appeal were inclined to blame such unfortunate and unforeseeable consequences on the vendors for binding themselves to accept the highest bid or for not expressly forbidding the submission of a referential bid. My Lords, in my opinion the argument based on the possible meaning of the word "offer" confuses definition with construction and the procedure adopted by the vendors is not open to justifiable criticism because the invitation was clear and unambiguous. The court is not concerned to define the word "offer" in isolation, without regard to its context and by reference to the widest possible meaning which can be culled from the weightiest available dictionary. The mere use by the vendors of the word "offer" was not sufficient to invoke all the frustrating dangers and uncertainties which inevitably follow from uncontrolled referential bids. The task of the court is to construe the invitation and to ascertain whether the provisions of the invitation, read as a whole, create a fixed bidding sale or an auction sale. I am content to reach a conclusion which reeks of simplicity, which does not require a draftsman to indulge in prohibitions, but which obliges a vendor to specify and control any form of auction which he seeks to combine with confidential bidding. The invitation required Sir Leonard to name his price and required Harvela to name their price and bound the vendors to accept the higher price. The invitation was not difficult to understand and the result was bound to be certain and to accord with the presumed intentions of the vendors discernible from the express provisions of the invitation. Harvela named the price of $2,175,000; Sir Leonard failed to name any price except $2,100,000 which was less than the price named by Harvela. The vendors were bound to accept Harvela's offer.

Lord Fraser of Tullybelton, Lord Edmund-Davies and **Lord Bridge of Harwich** delivered speeches concurring with Lords Diplock and Templeman.

NOTES AND QUESTIONS

1. Putting to one side the complication of the 'referential bid', the importance of this case is in showing that, contrary to the general position established in *Spencer v Harding* (above, 19), a person inviting tenders can, by the express words used, make a binding offer. Here the vendors had expressly said, 'we bind ourselves to accept [the highest] offer.'
2. Were there two contracts for sale of the shares, one with Harvela and one with Sir Leonard?
3. Was Lord Diplock correct in reasoning that there were initially two unilateral contracts with one of them subsequently being converted into a bilateral (synallagmatic) contract and the other terminating? Can one say, more simply, that there was an offer by the Royal Trust Co of a unilateral contract (to accept the highest bid) which was accepted by Harvela in making the highest bid?
4. On the true construction of the invitation to tender, 'referential bids' did not count. The position would have been different if the vendors had specified that referential bids were welcome. But in that situation it is likely that both the parties bidding would have made referential bids.

Blackpool and Fylde Aeroclub Ltd v Blackpool Borough Council
[1990] 1 WLR 1195, Court of Appeal

The defendant council owned and managed an airport and raised some revenue by granting a concession to operate pleasure flights from the airport. The claimant club had been granted the concession on three consecutive occasions since 1975. As the last concession was running out, the defendant invited the claimant and six other parties to tender for the new concession. The invitations stated that tenders were to be submitted in the envelope provided, which was not to bear any name or mark to identify the sender and that tenders received after the time specified, 12 noon on 17 March 1983, would not be considered. The claimant and two other invitees responded. The claimant's tender was put into the Town Hall letter box at 11 am on 17 March but the letter box was not cleared by council staff at 12 noon as it should have been. The claimant's tender was consequently mistakenly recorded as received late and was not considered. The concession was thereupon awarded to one of the other two tenderers. The claimant club brought an action for breach of contract against the council. The Court of Appeal, in dismissing the council's appeal, held that the invitation to tender did here contain an offer to consider tenders received by the deadline.

Bingham LJ: The judge resolved the contractual issue in favour of the club, holding that an express request for a tender might in appropriate circumstances give rise to an implied obligation to perform the service of considering that tender. Here, the council's stipulation that tenders received after the deadline would not be admitted for consideration gave rise to a contractual obligation, on acceptance by submission of a timely tender, that such tenders would be admitted for consideration.

In attacking the judge's conclusion on this issue Mr. Toulson for the council made four main submissions. First, he submitted that an invitation to tender in this form was well established to be no more than a proclamation of willingness to receive offers. Even without the first sentence of the council's invitation to tender in this case, the council would not have been bound to accept the highest or any tender. An invitation to tender in this form was an invitation to treat, and no contract of any kind would come into existence unless or until, if ever, the council chose to accept any tender or other offer. For these propositions reliance was placed on *Spencer v. Harding* (1870) L.R. 5 C.P. 561 and *Harris v. Nickerson* (1873) L.R. 8 Q.B. 286.

Second, Mr. Toulson submitted that on a reasonable reading of this invitation to tender the council could not be understood to be undertaking to consider all timely tenders submitted. The statement that later tenders would not be considered did not mean that timely tenders would. If the council had meant that they could have said it. There was, although Mr. Toulson did not put it in these words, no maxim exclusio unius, expressio alterius.

Third, the court should be no less rigorous when asked to imply a contract than when asked to imply a term in an existing contract or to find a collateral contract. A term would not be implied simply because it was reasonable to do so: *Liverpool City Council v. Irwin* [1977] A.C. 239, 253h. In order to establish collateral contracts, "Not only the terms of such contracts but the existence of an animus contrahendi on the part of all the parties to them must be clearly shewn:" *Heilbut, Symons & Co. v. Buckleton* [1913] A.C. 30, 47. No lower standard was applicable here and the standard was not satisfied.

Fourth, Mr. Toulson submitted that the warranty contended for by the club was simply a proposition "tailor-made to produce the desired result" (*per* Lord Templeman in *C.B.S. Songs Ltd. v. Amstrad Consumer Electronics Plc* [1988] A.C. 1013, 1059F) on the facts of this particular case. There was a vital distinction between expectations, however reasonable, and contractual obligations: see *per* Diplock L.J. in *Lavarack v. Woods of Colchester Ltd* [1967] 1 Q.B. 278, 294. The club here expected its tender to be considered. The council fully intended that it should be. It was in both parties' interests that the club's tender should be considered. There was thus no need for them to contract. The court should not subvert well-understood contractual principles by adopting a woolly pragmatic solution designed to remedy a perceived injustice on the unique facts of this particular case.

In defending the judge's decision Mr. Shorrock for the club accepted that an invitation to tender was normally no more than an offer to receive tenders. But it could, he submitted, in certain circumstances give rise to binding contractual obligations on the part of the invitor, either from the express words of the tender or from the circumstances surrounding the sending out of the invitation to tender or, as here, from both. The circumstances relied on here were that the council approached the club and the other invitees, all of them connected with the airport; that the club had held the concession for eight years, having successfully tendered on three previous occasions; that the council as a local authority was obliged to comply with its standing orders and owed a fiduciary duty to ratepayers to act with reasonable prudence in managing its financial affairs; and that there was a clear intention on the part of both parties that all timely tenders would be considered. If in these circumstances one asked of this invitation to tender the question posed by Bowen L.J. in *Carlill v. Carbolic Smoke Ball Co,* [1893] 1 Q.B. 256, 266, "How would an ordinary person reading this document construe it?", the answer in Mr. Shorrock's submission was clear: the council might or might not accept any particular tender; it might accept no tender; it might decide not to award the concession at all; it would not consider any tender received after the advertised deadline; but if it did consider any tender received before the deadline and conforming with the advertised conditions it would consider all such tenders.

I found great force in the submissions made by Mr. Toulson and agree with much of what he said. Indeed, for much of the hearing I was of opinion that the judge's decision, although fully in accord with the merits as I see them, could not be sustained in principle. But I am in the end persuaded that Mr. Toulson's argument proves too much. During the hearing the questions were raised: what if, in a situation such as the present, the council had opened and thereupon accepted the first tender received, even though the deadline had not expired and other invitees had not yet responded? Or if the council had considered and accepted a tender admittedly received well after the deadline? Mr. Toulson answered that although by so acting the council might breach its own standing orders, and might fairly be accused of discreditable conduct, it would not be in breach of any legal obligation because at that stage there would be none to breach. This is a conclusion I cannot accept. And if it were accepted there would in my view be an unacceptable discrepancy between the law of contract and the confident assumptions of commercial parties…

A tendering procedure of this kind is, in many respects, heavily weighted in favour of the invitor. He can invite tenders from as many or as few parties as he chooses. He need not tell any of them who else, or how many others, he has invited. The invitee may often, although not here, be put to considerable labour and expense in preparing a tender, ordinarily without recompense if he is unsuccessful. The invitation to tender may itself, in a complex case, although again not here, involve time and expense to prepare, but the invitor does not commit himself to proceed with the project, whatever it is; he need not accept the highest tender; he need not accept any tender; he need not give reasons to justify his acceptance or rejection of any tender received. The risk to which the tenderer is exposed does not end with the risk that his tender may not be the highest or, as the case may be, lowest. But where, as here, tenders are solicited from selected parties all of them known to the invitor, and where a local authority's invitation prescribes a clear, orderly and familiar procedure – draft contract conditions available for inspection and plainly not open to negotiation, a prescribed common form of tender, the supply of envelopes designed to preserve the absolute anonymity of tenderers and clearly to identify the tender in question, and an absolute deadline – the invitee is in my judgment protected at least to this extent: if he submits a conforming tender before the deadline he is entitled, not as a matter of mere expectation but of contractual right, to be sure that his tender will after the deadline be opened and considered in conjunction with all other conforming tenders or at least that his tender will be considered if others are. Had the club, before tendering, inquired of the council whether it could rely on any timely and conforming tender being considered along with others, I feel quite sure that the answer would have been "of course." The law would, I think, be defective if it did not give effect to that.

It is of course true that the invitation to tender does not explicitly state that the council will consider timely and conforming tenders. That is why one is concerned with implication. But the council do not either say that they do not bind themselves to do so, and in the context a reasonable invitee would understand the invitation to be saying, quite clearly, that if he submitted a timely and conforming tender it would be considered, at least if any other such tender were considered.

I readily accept that contracts are not to be lightly implied. Having examined what the parties said and did, the court must be able to conclude with confidence both that the parties intended to create contractual relations and that the agreement was to the effect contended for. It must also, in most cases, be able to answer the question posed by Mustill L.J. in *Hispanica de Petroleos S.A. v. Vencedora Oceanica Navegacion S.A. (No. 2) (Note)* [1987] 2 Lloyd's Rep. 321, 331: "What was the mechanism for offer and acceptance?" In all the circumstances of this case, and I say nothing about any other, I have no doubt that the parties did intend to create contractual relations to the limited extent contended for. Since it has never been the law that a person is only entitled to enforce his contractual rights in a reasonable way (*White and Carter (Councils) Ltd. v. McGregor* [1962] A.C. 413, 430A, *per* Lord Reid), Mr. Shorrock was in my view right to contend for no more than a contractual duty to consider. I think it plain that the council's invitation to tender was, to this limited extent, an offer, and the club's submission of a timely and conforming tender an acceptance.

Mr. Toulson's fourth submission is a salutary warning, but it is not a free-standing argument: if, as I hold, his first three submissions are to be rejected, no subversion of principle is involved. I am, however, pleased that what seems to me the right legal answer also accords with the merits as I see them.

I accordingly agree with the judge's conclusion on the contractual issue, essentially for the reasons which he more briefly gave.

Stocker LJ delivered a concurring judgment and **Farquharson J** concurred.

NOTES AND QUESTIONS

1. If the *Harvela* case (above, 20) illustrates an exception to *Spencer v Harding* (above, 19) because of *express* words used in the invitation to tender, this case illustrates an exception because of what was *implied* by the invitation to tender. In line with *Spencer v Harding*, the invitation to tender was not an offer to be bound by the highest (or any) tender: but a more limited offer was implied, namely an offer to consider all timely bids.

2. The most straightforward view of the contract made between the club and the council was that it was a unilateral contract by which the council made the offer of a unilateral contract (to consider all timely bids) which was accepted by the club tendering on time.

3. The trial and appeal in this case were on liability only. How would one measure the damages for breach of the contract with the club? (See below, 347–350, on damages for loss of a chance.) Would those damages be the same as for breach of a contract to grant the concession?

4. Was it of any significance in this case that the invitation to tender was made by a public body? The tendering process, in the context of public bodies, has been increasingly subjected to controls, both from European Community Law and domestic legislation. Such controls were not in force (or not in issue) in this case. For a useful succinct analysis of these rules on 'public procurement' see *Chitty on Contracts* (29th edn, 2004) paragraphs 10-024–10-030.

3. ACCEPTANCE

An acceptance may be defined as the final expression of assent to the exact terms of an offer. It is clear from this definition that the acceptance and the offer must exactly coincide: this is sometimes referred to as 'the mirror-image rule'. So, for example, in *Hyde v Wrench* (below, 53) Wrench offered to sell his farm for £1,000. Hyde responded by saying that he would give £950 for it. Clearly at that point there had been no acceptance of Wrench's offer. Rather Hyde's response was a counter-offer which Wrench was free to accept or not.

While the concept of an acceptance is easy to understand, a number of issues on acceptance have arisen in the cases. These will be examined under the following sub-headings: (1) Acceptance by Conduct; (2) 'Battle of the Forms'; (3) Communication of Acceptance; (4) Prescribed Mode of Acceptance; (5) Acceptance in Ignorance of an Offer; (6) Acceptance in Unilateral Contracts.

(1) Acceptance by Conduct

Brogden v Metropolitan Railway Co
(1877) 2 App Cas 666, House of Lords

Brogden, the defendant, had for two years supplied the claimant railway company with coal without a formal contract. Both parties wishing to regularise the situation, the claimant sent a draft contract to Brogden. Brogden added the name of an arbitrator to settle any differences and returned to the claimant the draft marked 'approved' and signed by him. The claimant's manager put the draft in a drawer and did nothing further with it. The manager then ordered, and was supplied with, coal in accordance with the terms of the draft for some two years. Then Brogden denied that it was bound to supply coal ordered and the claimant sued Brogden for breach of contract. The House of Lords held that there had been acceptance by conduct of an offer so that Brogden's argument that there was no contract for the supply of coal should be rejected.

Lord Blackburn: I have always believed the law to be this, that when an offer is made to another party, and in that offer there is a request express or implied that he must signify his acceptance by doing some particular thing, then as soon as he does that thing, he is bound. If a man sent an offer abroad saying: I wish to know whether you will supply me with goods at such and such a price, and, if you agree to that, you must ship the first cargo as soon as you get this letter, there can be no doubt that as soon as the cargo was shipped the contract would be complete, and if the cargo went to the bottom of the sea, it would go to the bottom of the sea at the risk of the orderer. So again, where, as in the case of *Ex parte Harris, In re Imperial Land Company of Marseilles*, Law Rep. 7 Ch. Ap. 587, a person writes a letter and says, I offer to take an allotment of shares, and he expressly or impliedly says, If you agree with me send an answer by the post, there, as soon as he has sent that answer by the post, and put it out of his control, and done an extraneous act which clenches the matter, and shews beyond all doubt that each side is bound, I agree the contract is perfectly plain and clear.

But when you come to the general proposition which [the judge at first instance] seems to have laid down, that a simple acceptance in your own mind, without any intimation to the other party, and expressed by a mere private act, such as putting a letter into a drawer, completes a contract, I must say I differ from that.

…

But my Lords, while… this is so upon the question of law, it is still necessary to consider this case farther upon the question of fact. I agree, and I think every Judge who has considered the case does agree… that though the parties may have gone no farther than an offer on the one side, saying, Here is the draft, – (for that I think is really what this case comes to,) – and the draft so offered by the one side is approved by the other, everything being agreed to except the name of the arbitrator, which the one side has filled in and the other has not yet assented to, if both parties have acted upon that draft and treated it as binding, they will be bound by it. …If the parties have by their conduct said, that they act upon the draft which has been approved of by Mr. *Brogden*, and which if not quite approved of by the railway company, has been exceedingly near it, if they indicate by their conduct that they accept it, the contract is binding.

Lord Cairns LC, Lord Hatherley, Lord Selborne and **Lord Gordon** delivered concurring speeches.

NOTE

While laying down that there can be acceptance by conduct, their Lordships did not make clear what constituted the offer and the acceptance on these facts. One possible analysis is that Brogden had made a counter-offer (by inserting the name of an arbitrator) which the railway company had then accepted by its conduct in ordering coal. The alternative possibility was that the offer was made by the railway company in ordering the coal in line with the terms of the draft agreement and that this was accepted by the conduct of Brogden in delivering the coal. In M Furmston's words in *Cheshire, Fifoot and Furmston's Law of Contract* (15th edn, 2007) 48, 'The House of Lords held that a contract came into existence either when the company ordered its first load of coal from Brogden upon [the] terms [of the draft] or at least when Brogden supplied it.'

(2) 'Battle of the Forms'

Butler Machine Tool Co Ltd v Ex-Cell-O Corporation (England) Ltd [1979] 1 WLR 401, Court of Appeal

On 23 May 1969 the sellers (who were the claimants) offered to sell a machine to the buyers (the defendants) for £75,535. The offer was stated to be subject to certain terms and conditions which 'shall prevail over any terms and conditions in the buyer's order'. These sellers' conditions included a price variation clause: ie a clause whereby any increase in the cost of manufacture by the date of delivery should be added to the price. On 27 May the buyers replied ordering the machine. The order was stated to be subject to the buyers' own terms and conditions, and these differed from those of the sellers, in particular in that they did not include a price variation clause. At the foot of the buyers' order there was a tear-off slip reading, 'We accept your order on the terms and conditions stated therein.' On 5 June, the sellers signed and returned this tear-off slip, accompanied by a letter stating that the buyers' order was being accepted in accordance with the quotation of 23 May. When the sellers delivered the machine they claimed, in accordance with the price variation clause, that the price had increased by a further £2,892. The buyers refused to pay the increase and the sellers sued them for it. The questions that arose were: had a contract been concluded and, if so, on whose terms? The Court of Appeal held that a contract had been concluded on the buyers' terms and therefore that they were not bound to pay any increase in price.

Lord Denning MR: This case is a "battle of forms."

...

If [the] documents are analysed in our traditional method, the result would seem to me to be this: the quotation of May 23, 1969, was an offer by the sellers to the buyers containing the terms and conditions on the back. The order of May 27, 1969, purported to be an acceptance of that offer in that it was for the same machine at the same price, but it contained such additions as to cost of installation, date of delivery and so forth that it was in law a rejection of the offer and constituted a counter-offer. That is clear from *Hyde v. Wrench* (1840) 3 Beav. 334. As Megaw J. said in *Trollope & Colls Ltd. v. Atomic Power Constructions Ltd* [1963] 1 W.L.R. 333, 337: "... the counter-offer kills the original offer." The letter of the sellers of June 5, 1969, was an acceptance of that counter-offer, as is shown by the acknowledgment which the sellers signed and returned to the buyers. The reference to the quotation of May 23 referred only to the price and identity of the machine.

To go on with the facts of the case. The important thing is that the sellers did not keep the contractual date of delivery which was March/April 1970. The machine was ready about September 1970 but by that time the buyers' production schedule had to be re-arranged as they could not accept delivery until November 1970. Meanwhile the sellers had invoked the price increase clause. They sought to charge the buyers an increase due to the rise in costs between May 27, 1969 (when the order was given), and April 1, 1970 (when the machine ought to have been delivered). It came to £2,892. The buyers rejected the claim. The judge held that the sellers were entitled to the sum of £2,892 under the price variation clause. He did not apply the traditional method of analysis by way of offer and counter-offer. He said that in the quotation of May 23, 1969, "one finds the price variation clause appearing under a most emphatic heading stating that it is a term or condition that is to prevail." So he held that it did prevail.

I have much sympathy with the judge's approach to this case. In many of these cases our traditional analysis of offer, counter-offer, rejection, acceptance and so forth is out of date. This was observed by Lord Wilberforce in *New Zealand Shipping Co. Ltd. v. A. M. Satterthwaite & Co. Ltd.* [1975] A.C. 154, 167. The better way is to look at all the documents passing between the parties – and glean from them, or from the conduct of the parties, whether they have reached agreement on all material points – even though there may be differences between the forms and conditions printed on the back of them. As Lord Cairns said in *Brogden v. Metropolitan Railway Co.* (1877) 2 App.Cas. 666, 672:

"... there may be a *consensus* between the parties far short of a complete mode of expressing it, and that *consensus* may be discovered from letters or from other documents of an imperfect and incomplete description; ..."

Applying this guide, it will be found that in most cases when there is a "battle of forms," there is a contract as soon as the last of the forms is sent and received without objection being taken to it. That is well observed in *Benjamin's Sale of Goods* , 9th ed. (1974), p. 84. The difficulty is to decide which form, or which part of which form, is a term or condition of the contract. In some cases the battle is won by the man who fires the last shot. He is the man who puts forward the latest terms and conditions: and, if they are not objected to by the other party, he may be taken to have agreed to them. Such was *British Road Services Ltd. v. Arthur V. Crutchley & Co. Ltd.* [1968] 1 Lloyd's Rep. 271, 281-282, *per* Lord Pearson; and the illustration given by Professor Guest in *Anson's Law of Contract* , 24th ed., pp. 37, 38 when he says that "the terms of the contract consist of the terms of the offer subject to the modifications contained in the acceptance.["] In some cases the battle is won by the man who gets the blow in first. If he offers to sell at a named price on the terms and conditions stated on the back: and the buyer orders the goods purporting to accept the offer – on an order form with his own different terms and conditions on the back – then if the difference is so material that it would affect the price, the buyer ought not to be allowed to take advantage of the difference unless he draws it specifically to the attention of the seller. There are yet other cases where the battle depends on the shots fired on both sides. There is a concluded contract but the forms vary. The terms and conditions of both parties are to be construed together. If they can be reconciled so as to give a harmonious result, all well and good. If differences are irreconcilable – so that they are mutually contradictory – then the conflicting terms may have to be scrapped and replaced by a reasonable implication.

In the present case the judge thought that the sellers in their original quotation got their blow in first: especially by the provision that "these terms and conditions shall prevail over any terms and conditions in the buyer's order." It was so emphatic that the price variation clause continued through all the subsequent dealings and that the buyers must be taken to have agreed to it. I can understand that point of view. But I think that the documents have to be considered as a whole. And, as a matter of construction, I think the acknowledgment of June 5, 1969, is the decisive document. It makes it clear that the contract was on the buyers' terms and not on the sellers' terms: and the buyers' terms did not include a price variation clause.

I would therefore allow the appeal and enter judgment for the defendants.

Lawton LJ: The modern commercial practice of making quotations and placing orders with conditions attached, usually in small print, is indeed likely, as in this case to produce a battle of forms. The problem is how should that battle be conducted? The view taken by Thesiger J. was that the battle should extend over a wide area and the court should do its best to look into the minds of the parties and make certain assumptions. In my judgment, the battle has to be conducted in accordance with set rules. It is a battle more on classical 18th century lines when convention decided who had the right to open fire first rather than in accordance with the modern concept of attrition.

The rules relating to a battle of this kind have been known for the past 130-odd years. They were set out by Lord Langdale M.R. in *Hyde v. Wrench*, 3 Beav. 334, 337, to which Lord Denning M.R. has already referred; and, if anyone should have thought they were obsolescent, Megaw J. in *Trollope & Colls Ltd. v. Atomic Power Constructions Ltd.* [1963] 1 W.L.R. 333, 337 called attention to the fact that those rules are still in force.

When those rules are applied to this case, in my judgment, the answer is obvious. The sellers started by making an offer. That was in their quotation. The small print was headed by the following words:

"General. All orders are accepted only upon and subject to the terms set out in our quotation and the following conditions. These terms and conditions shall prevail over any terms and conditions in the buyer's order."

That offer was not accepted. The buyers were only prepared to have one of these very expensive machines on their own terms. Their terms had very material differences in them from the terms put forward by the sellers. They could not be reconciled in any way. In the language of article 7 of the Uniform Law on the Formation of Contracts for the International Sale of Goods (see Uniform Laws on International Sales Act 1967, Schedule 2) they did "materially alter the terms" set out in the offer made by the plaintiffs.

As I understand *Hyde v. Wrench*, 3 Beav. 334, and the cases which have followed, the consequence of placing the order in that way, if I may adopt Megaw J.'s words [1963] 1 W.L.R. 333, 337, was "to kill the original offer." It follows that the court has to look at what happened after the buyers made their counter-offer. By letter dated June 4, 1969, the plaintiffs acknowledged receipt of the counter-offer, and they went on in this way:

"Details of this order have been passed to our Halifax works for attention and a formal acknowledgment of order will follow in due course."

That is clearly a reference to the printed tear-off slip which was at the bottom of the buyers' counter-offer. By letter dated June 5, 1969, the sales office manager at the plaintiffs' Halifax factory completed that tear-off slip and sent it back to the buyers.

It is true, as Mr. Scott [counsel for the sellers] has reminded us, that the return of that printed slip was accompanied by a letter which had this sentence in it: "This is being entered in accordance with our revised quotation of May 23 for delivery in 10/11 months." I agree with Lord Denning M.R. that, in business sense, that refers to the quotation as to the price and the identity of the machine, and it does not bring into the contract the small print conditions on the back of the quotation. Those small print conditions had disappeared from the story. That was when the contract was made. At that date it was a fixed price contract without a price escalation clause.

As I pointed out in the course of argument to Mr. Scott, if the letter of June 5 which accompanied the form acknowledging the terms which the buyers had specified had amounted to a counter-offer, then in my judgment the parties never were ad idem. It cannot be said that the buyers accepted the counter-offer by reason of the fact that ultimately they took physical delivery of the machine. By the time they took physical delivery of the machine, they had made it clear by correspondence that they were not accepting that there was any price escalation clause in any contract which they had made with the plaintiffs.

I agree with Lord Denning M.R. that this appeal should be allowed.

Bridge LJ: Schedule 2 to the Uniform Laws on International Sales Act 1967 is headed "The Uniform Law on the Formation of Contracts for the International Sale of Goods." To the limited extent that that Schedule is already in force in the law of this country, it would not in any event be applicable to the contract which is the subject of this appeal because that was not a contract of international sale of goods as defined in that statute.

We have heard, nevertheless, an interesting discussion on the question of the extent to which the terms of article 7 of that Schedule are mirrored in the common law of England today. No difficulty arises about paragraph 1 of the article, which provides: "An acceptance containing additions, limitations or other modifications shall be a rejection of the offer and shall constitute a counter-offer." But paragraph 2 of the article is in these terms:

"However, a reply to an offer which purports to be an acceptance but which contains additional or different terms which do not materially alter the terms of the offer shall constitute an acceptance unless the offeror promptly objects to the discrepancy; if he does not so object, the terms of the contract shall be the terms of the offer with the modifications contained in the acceptance."

For my part, I consider it both unnecessary and undesirable to express any opinion on the question whether there is any difference between the principle expressed in that paragraph 2 and the principle which would prevail in the common law of England today without reference to that paragraph, but it was presumably a principle analogous to that expressed in paragraph 2 of article 7 which the editor of *Anson's Law of Contract*, 24th ed., Professor Guest, had in mind in the passage from that work which was quoted in the judgment of Lord Denning M.R. On any view, that passage goes a good deal further than the principle expressed in article 7 of the Act of 1967, and I entirely agree with Lord Denning M.R. that it goes too far.

But when one turns from those interesting and abstruse areas of the law to the plain facts of this case, this case is nothing like the kind of case with which either the makers of the convention which embodied article 7 of Schedule 2 or the editor of *Anson*, 24th ed., had in mind in the passages referred to, because this is a case which on its facts is plainly governed by what I may call the classical doctrine that a counter-offer amounts to a rejection of an offer and puts an end to the effect of the offer.

The first offer between the parties here was the plaintiff sellers' quotation dated May 23, 1969. The conditions of sale in the small print on the back of that document, as well as embodying the price variation clause, to which reference has been made in the judgments already delivered, embodied a number of other important conditions. There was a condition providing that orders should in no circumstances be cancelled without the written consent of the sellers and should only be cancelled on terms which indemnified the sellers against loss. There was a condition that the sellers should not be liable for any loss or damage from delay however caused. There was a condition purporting to limit the sellers' liability for damage due to defective workmanship or materials in the goods sold. And there was a condition providing that the buyers should be responsible for the cost of delivery.

When one turns from that document to the buyers' order of May 27, 1969, it is perfectly clear not only that that order was a counter-offer but that it did not purport in any way to be an acceptance of the terms of the sellers' offer dated May 23. In addition, when one compares the terms and conditions of the buyers' offer, it is clear that they are in fact contrary in a number of vitally important respects to the conditions of sale in the sellers' offer. Amongst the buyers' proposed conditions are conditions that the price of the goods shall include the cost of delivery to the buyers' premises; that the buyers shall be entitled to cancel for any delay in delivery; and a condition giving the buyers a right to reject if on inspection the goods are found to be faulty in any respect.

The position then was, when the sellers received the buyers' offer of May 27, that that was an offer open to them to accept or reject. They replied in two letters dated June 4 and 5 respectively. The letter of June 4 was an informal acknowledgment of the order, and the letter of June 5 enclosed the formal acknowledgment, as Lord Denning M.R. and Lawton L.J. have said, embodied in the printed tear-off slip taken from the order itself and including the perfectly clear and unambiguous sentence "We accept your order on the terms and conditions stated thereon." On the face of it, at that moment of time, there was a complete contract in existence, and the parties were ad idem as to the terms of the contract embodied in the buyers' order.

Mr. Scott has struggled manfully to say that the contract concluded on those terms and conditions was in some way overruled or varied by the references in the two letters dated June 4 and 5 to the quotation of May 23, 1969. The first refers to the machinery being as quoted on May 23. The second letter says that the order has been entered in accordance with the quotation of May 23. I agree with Lord Denning M.R. and Lawton L.J. that that language has no other effect than to identify the machinery and to refer to the prices quoted on May 23. But on any view, at its highest, the language is equivocal and wholly ineffective to override the plain and unequivocal terms of the printed acknowledgment of order which was enclosed with the letter of June 5. Even if that were not so and if Mr. Scott could show that the sellers' acknowledgment of the order was itself a further counter-offer, I suspect that he would be in considerable difficulties in showing that any later circumstance amounted to an acceptance of that counter-offer in the terms of the original quotation of May 23 by the buyers. But I do not consider that question further because I am content to rest upon the view that there is nothing in the letter of June 5 which overrides the plain effect of the acceptance of the order on the terms and conditions stated thereon.

I too would allow the appeal and enter judgment for the defendants.

1. Lawton and Bridge LJJ applied the conventional approach of looking for an acceptance which corresponded exactly to an offer. They felt able to find it by the sellers' return of the tear-off form on 5 June: this was the acceptance of the buyers' counter-offer of 27 May. (The sellers' accompanying letter of 5 June was construed as not referring back to the price escalation term). As the contract had been concluded on the buyers' terms the contract did not include a price variation clause and the buyers were therefore not bound to pay the additional price. Here the last significant document sent was in the buyers' favour (albeit sent by the sellers). Very commonly, applying a conventional analysis, there will be no moment at which the documents exchanged correspond, and instead the contract will be regarded as constituted by the last document sent, which is then regarded as accepted by the conduct of the other party in acting in accordance with that document. In other words, the 'last shot fired' commonly wins.

2. While he came to the same conclusion, Lord Denning's approach was very different. He considered that looking for a mirror-image of offer and acceptance was not the best way of sorting out a battle of the forms. Rather one should look at whether the documents revealed 'an agreement on all material points.' If so a contract has been concluded, albeit that some terms may have to be filled out by a 'reasonable implication'. The merits of Lord Denning's approach are that it gives some flexibility to the courts, but this is at the risk of imposing terms that have not been agreed. There is also some difficulty in understanding what he meant by 'all material points'. Perhaps he had in mind a distinction between central and subsidiary terms: but one may doubt whether a price escalation clause could be regarded as subsidiary or non-material. Lord Denning's approach has won little, if any, express support in subsequent cases.

3. Do you agree with the criticism that the conventional approach of Lawton and Bridge LJJ involved a rather strained interpretation of the facts (in that it took a strained interpretation of the sellers' accompanying letter of 5 June)?

4. In a case note on *Butler v Ex-Cell-O*, **R Rawlings, 'The Battle of Forms' (1979) 42 *MLR* 715** compares the traditional offer and acceptance approach applied by the majority with Lord Denning's approach and with other approaches (eg that adopted in the US Uniform Commercial Code and Article 7 of Schedule 2 to the Uniform Laws on International Sales Act 1967). He points to the deficiencies of the non-traditional approaches and concludes that, while it does have drawbacks, the traditional analysis should be retained (at least until there has been clear empirical research on the attitudes of businessmen to the battle of the forms).

5. If it is decided that there is no contract between the parties, even though goods have been delivered or work has been done, the seller or person who has performed the work may have non-contractual restitutionary remedies for the value of the goods or work. See below, 74.

(3) Communication of Acceptance

(a) The General Rule: Acceptance must be Received by Offeror

Entores Ltd v Miles Far East Corporation
[1955] 2 QB 327, Court of Appeal

The claimants in London made an offer by telex to the agents in Amsterdam of the defendant company, which was based in New York. The agents sent their acceptance of the offer by telex which was received on the claimants' telex machine in London. The claimants sought leave to serve notice of a writ on the defendant in New York claiming damages for breach of the contract. Whether that leave could be granted turned on rules of court which required that the contract was made in England. So the question at issue was whether the contract was made where the acceptance was sent (ie Amsterdam) or where the acceptance was received (ie London). The Court of Appeal, dismissing the defendant's appeal, held that it was the latter.

Denning LJ: The question for our determination is where was the contract made?

When a contract is made by post it is clear law throughout the common law countries that the acceptance is complete as soon as the letter is put into the post box, and that is the place where the contract is made. But there is no clear rule about contracts made by telephone or by Telex. Communications by these means are virtually instantaneous and stand on a different footing.

The problem can only be solved by going in stages. Let me first consider a case where two people make a contract by word of mouth in the presence of one another. Suppose, for instance, that I shout an offer to a man across a river or a courtyard but I do not hear his reply because it is drowned by an aircraft flying overhead. There is no contract at that moment. If he wishes to make a contract, he must wait till the aircraft is gone and then shout back his acceptance so that I can hear what he says. Not until I have his answer am I bound. ...

Now take a case where two people make a contract by telephone. Suppose, for instance, that I make an offer to a man by telephone and, in the middle of his reply, the line goes "dead" so that I do not hear his words of acceptance. There is no contract at that moment. The other man may not know the precise moment when the line failed. But he will know that the telephone conversation was abruptly broken off: because people usually say something to signify the end of the conversation. If he wishes to make a contract, he must therefore get through again so as to make sure that I heard. Suppose next, that the line does not go dead, but it is nevertheless so indistinct that I do not catch what he says and I ask him to repeat it. He then repeats it and I hear his acceptance. The contract is made, not on the first time when I do not hear, but only the second time when I do hear. If he does not repeat it, there is no contract. The contract is only complete when I have his answer accepting the offer.

Lastly, take the Telex. Suppose a clerk in a London office taps out on the teleprinter an offer which is immediately recorded on a teleprinter in a Manchester office, and a clerk at that end taps out an acceptance. If the line goes dead in the middle of the sentence of acceptance, the teleprinter motor will stop. There is then obviously no contract. The clerk at Manchester must get through again and send his complete sentence. But it may happen that the line does not go dead, yet the message does not get through to London. Thus the clerk at Manchester may tap out his message of acceptance and it will not be recorded in London because the ink at the London end fails, or something of that kind. In that case, the Manchester clerk will not know of the failure but the London clerk will know of it and will immediately send back a message "not receiving." Then, when the fault is rectified, the Manchester clerk will repeat his message. Only then is there a contract. If he does not repeat it, there is no contract. It is not until his message is received that the contract is complete.

In all the instances I have taken so far, the man who sends the message of acceptance knows that it has not been received or he has reason to know it. So he must repeat it. But, suppose that he does not know that his message did not get home. He thinks it has. This may happen if the listener on the telephone does not catch the words of acceptance, but nevertheless does not trouble to ask for them to be repeated: or the ink on the teleprinter fails at the receiving end, but the clerk does not ask for the message to be repeated: so that the man who sends an acceptance reasonably believes that his message has been received. The offeror in such circumstances is clearly bound, because he will be estopped from saying that he did not receive the message of acceptance. It is his own fault that he did not get it. But if there should be a case where the offeror without any fault on his part does not receive the message of acceptance – yet the sender of it reasonably believes it has got home when it has not – then I think there is no contract.

My conclusion is, that the rule about instantaneous communications between the parties is different from the rule about the post. The contract is only complete when the acceptance is received by the offeror: and the contract is made at the place where the acceptance is received.

In a matter of this kind, however, it is very important that the countries of the world should have the same rule. I find that most of the European countries have substantially the same rule as that I have stated. Indeed, they apply it to contracts by post as well as instantaneous communications. But in the United States of America it appears as if instantaneous communications are treated in the same way as postal communications. In view of this divergence, I think that we must consider the matter on principle: and so considered, I have come to the view I have stated, and I am glad to see that Professor Winfield in this country (55 Law Quarterly Review, 514), and Professor Williston in the United States of America (Contracts, § 82, p. 239), take the same view.

Applying the principles which I have stated, I think that the contract in this case was made in London where the acceptance was received. It was, therefore, a proper case for service out of the jurisdiction.

Birkett LJ: In my opinion, the cases governing the making of contracts by letters passing through the post have no application to the making of contracts by Telex communications. The ordinary rule of law, to which the special considerations governing contracts by post are exceptions, is that the acceptance of an offer must be communicated to the offeror, and the place where the contract is made is the place where the offeror receives the notification of the acceptance by the offeree.

If a Telex instrument in Amsterdam is used to send to London the notification of the acceptance of an offer the contract is complete when the Telex instrument in London receives the notification of the acceptance (usually at the same moment that the message is being printed in Amsterdam), and the acceptance is then notified to the offeror, and the contract is made in London.

Parker LJ delivered a concurring judgment.

NOTES AND QUESTIONS

1. A telex was similar to a fax. It enabled a message typed on the sending telex machine to be almost instantaneously printed out on the receiving machine. *Entores* was applied to an acceptance by fax in *JSC Zestafoni G Nikoladze Ferroalloy Plant v Ronly Holdings Ltd* [2004] EWHC 245 (Comm), [2004] 2 Lloyd's Rep 335.

2. The exceptional rule for postal acceptances is considered below, 37–41.

3. Is there any reason to treat acceptances by e-mail differently from those by telex or fax? What about an acceptance left on a telephone answering machine?

4. What is, or should be, the law if the reason an acceptance is not received is because of the offeror's fault (eg his fax machine has run out of ink or his answering machine garbles the message)?

5. Is it important whether or not the acceptance has been read by the offeror? Say, for example, B e-mails an acceptance to A at 12 midnight which A does not read until 12 noon. Was the acceptance made at 12 midnight or 12 noon or at some other time? Although not concerning offer and acceptance, in *The Brimnes* [1975] QB 929, CA, a notice sent by telex withdrawing a ship under a charterparty for late payment of hire was held to have been effective when received during office hours on 1 April even though it was not read until 2 April.

6. **S Hill, 'Flogging a Dead Horse—The Postal Acceptance Rule and Email' (2001) 17 *JCL* 151** argues that, for the purposes of the acceptance rule, e-mail should be treated as a form of instantaneous communication. The general rule, that acceptance is valid only when received by the offeror, rather than the exceptional postal rule, should therefore apply.

Brinkibon Ltd v Stahag Stahl und Stahlwarenhandelsgesellschaft mbH [1983] 2 AC 34, House of Lords

The buyers of a quantity of steel bars were an English company and, by a telex sent from London to Vienna, they accepted the terms of sale offered by the sellers, an Austrian company. The buyers issued a writ claiming damages for breach of contract. As in the *Entores* case, the question at issue was whether leave to serve notice of the writ on the foreign company should be given; and this in turn depended on the buyers establishing that the contract was made in England. The House of Lords, approving the *Entores* decision, held that it was made in Austria where the acceptance was received.

Lord Wilberforce: The general rule, it is hardly necessary to state, is that a contract is formed *when* acceptance of an offer is communicated by the offeree to the offeror. And if it is necessary to determine *where* a contract is formed … it appears logical that this should be at the place where acceptance is communicated to the offeror. In the common case of contracts, whether oral or in writing inter praesentes, there is no difficulty; and again logic demands that even where there is not mutual presence at the same place and at the same time, if communication is instantaneous, for example by telephone or radio communication, the same result should follow.

Then there is the case – very common – of communication at a distance, to meet which the so called "postal rule" has developed. I need not trace its history: it has firmly been in the law at least since *Adams v. Lindsell* (1818) 1 B. & Ald. 681. The rationale for it, if left somewhat obscure by Lord Ellenborough C.J., has since been well explained. Mellish L.J. in *In re Imperial Land Co. of Marseilles (Harris' Case)* (1872) L.R. 7 Ch. App. 587, 594 ascribed it to the extraordinary and mischievous consequences which would follow if it were held that an offer might be revoked at any time until the letter accepting it had been actually received: and its foundation in convenience was restated by Thesiger L.J. in *Household Fire and Carriage Accident Insurance Co. Ltd. v. Grant* (1879) 4 Ex.D. 216, 223. In these cases too it seems logical to say that the place, as well as the time, of acceptance should be *where* (as *when*) the acceptance is put into the charge of the post office.

In this situation, with a general rule covering instantaneous communication inter praesentes, or at a distance, with an exception applying to non-instantaneous communication at a distance, how should communications by telex be categorised? In *Entores Ltd. v. Miles Far East Corporation* [1955] 2 Q.B. 327 the Court of Appeal classified them with instantaneous communications. Their ruling, which has passed into the textbooks, including *Williston on Contracts*, 3rd ed. (1957), appears not to have caused either adverse comment, or any difficulty to business men. I would accept it as a general rule. Where the condition of simultaneity is met, and where it appears to be within the mutual intention of the parties that contractual exchanges should take place in this way, I think it a sound rule, but not necessarily a universal rule.

Since 1955 the use of telex communication has been greatly expanded, and there are many variants on it. The senders and recipients may not be the principals to the contemplated contract. They may be servants or agents with limited authority. The message may not reach, or be intended to reach, the designated recipient immediately: messages may be sent out of office hours, or at night, with the intention, or upon the assumption, that they will be read at a later time. There may be some error or default at the recipient's end which prevents receipt at the time contemplated and believed in by the sender. The message may have been sent and/or received through machines operated by third persons. And many other variations may occur. No universal rule can cover all such cases: they must be resolved by reference to the intentions of the parties, by sound business practice and in some cases by a judgment where the risks should lie: see *Household Fire and Carriage Accident Insurance Co. Ltd. v. Grant*, 4 Ex.D. 216, 227 *per* Baggallay L.J. and *Henthorn v. Fraser* [1892] 2 Ch. 27 *per* Lord Herschell.

The present case is, as *Entores Ltd. v. Miles Far East Corporation* [1955] 2 Q.B. 327 itself, the simple case of instantaneous communication between principals, and, in accordance with the general rule, involves that the contract (if any) was made when and where the acceptance was received. This was on May 4, 1979, in Vienna.

Lord Brandon of Oakbrook: My Lords, I am not persuaded that the *Entores* case [1955] 2 Q.B. 327, was wrongly decided and should therefore be overruled. On the contrary, I think that it was rightly decided and should be approved. The general principle of law applicable to the formation of a contract by offer and acceptance is that the acceptance of the offer by the offeree must be notified to the offeror before a contract can be regarded as concluded, *Carlill v. Carbolic Smoke Ball Co.* [1893] 1 Q.B. 256, 262, *per* Lindley L.J. The cases on acceptance by letter and telegram constitute an exception to the general principle of the law of contract stated above. The reason for the exception is commercial expediency: see, for example, *Imperial Land Co. of Marseilles, In re (Harris' Case)* (1872) L.R. 7 Ch.App. 587, 692 *per* Mellish L.J. That reason of commercial expediency applies to cases where there is bound to be a substantial interval between the time when the acceptance is sent and the time when it is received. In such cases the exception to the general rule is more convenient, and makes on the whole for greater fairness, than the general rule itself would do. In my opinion, however, that reason of commercial expediency does not have any application when the means of communication employed between the offeror and the offeree is instantaneous in nature, as is the case when either the telephone or telex is used. In such cases the general principle relating to the formation of contracts remains applicable, with the result that the contract is made where and when the telex of acceptance is received by the offeror.

...

Since preparing this speech I have had the advantage of reading in draft that of my noble and learned friend, Lord Wilberforce. In it he points out that, while the present case, like the *Entores* case [1955] 2 Q.B. 327, is concerned only with instantaneous communication by telex between the principals on either side, there may in other cases be a number of variations on that simple theme. He further expresses the view that there can be no general rule capable of covering all such variations, and that, when they occur, the problems posed by them must be resolved by reference to the intention of the parties, sound business practice and in some cases a judgment where the risk shall lie. I agree entirely with these observations.

Lord Fraser of Tullybelton delivered a concurring speech and **Lord Russell of Killowen** and **Lord Bridge of Harwich** concurred.

1. Their Lordships indicated that the normal rule for instantaneous communications could be displaced where the risk (of non-receipt of an acceptance) should lie on the offeror. What sort of examples can you think of where this might be so (see question 4 on 35)?

2. Both Lord Wilberforce and Lord Brandon said that the *Entores* case was a simple case of instantaneous communication *between principals*. Is that correct factually?

(b) Acceptance by Post

Household Fire and Carriage Accident Insurance Co Ltd v Grant
(1879) 4 Ex D 216, Court of Appeal

The defendant offered to buy 100 shares from the claimant company. The claimant sent a letter of acceptance to the defendant but the letter was lost in the post and never arrived. The liquidator of the claimant sued the defendant for the money owing for the shares. The trial judge found that a valid contract had been formed. In affirming this, the majority of the Court of Appeal held that an acceptance by post is valid when sent.

Thesiger LJ: Now, whatever in abstract discussion may be said as to the legal notion of its being necessary, in order to the effecting of a valid and binding contract, that the minds of the parties should be brought together at one and the same moment, that notion is practically the foundation of English law upon the subject of the formation of contracts. Unless therefore a contract constituted by correspondence is absolutely concluded at the moment that the continuing offer is accepted by the person to whom the offer is addressed, it is difficult to see how the two minds are ever to be brought together at one and the same moment. This was pointed out by Lord Ellenborough in the case of *Adams v. Lindsell* 1 B. & A. 681, which is recognized authority upon this branch of the law. But on the other hand it is a principle of law, as well established as the legal notion to which I have referred, that the minds of the two parties must be brought together by mutual communication. An acceptance, which only remains in the breast of the acceptor without being actually and by legal implication communicated to the offeror, is no binding acceptance. How then are these elements of law to be harmonised in the case of contracts formed by correspondence through the post? I see no better mode than that of treating the post office as the agent of both parties, and it was so considered by Lord Romilly in *Hebb's Case* Law Rep. 4 Eq. at p. 12, when in the course of his judgment he said: "*Dunlop v. Higgins* 1 H. L. C. 381 decides that the posting of a letter accepting an offer constitutes a binding contract, but the reason of that is, that the post office is the common agent of both parties."...But if the post office be such common agent, then it seems to me to follow that, as soon as the letter of acceptance is delivered to the post office, the contract is made as complete and final and absolutely binding as if the acceptor had put his letter into the hands of a messenger sent by the offeror himself as his agent to deliver the offer and receive the acceptance. What other principle can be adopted short of holding that the contract is not complete by acceptance until and except from the time that the letter containing the acceptance is delivered to the offeror, a principle which has been distinctly negatived?... The contract... is actually made when the letter is posted. The acceptor, in posting the letter, has, to use the language of Lord Blackburn, in *Brogden v. Directors of Metropolitan Ry Co* 2 App. Cas. 666, 691,"put it out of his control and done an extraneous act which clenches the matter, and shews beyond all doubt that each side is bound." How then can a casualty in the post, whether resulting in delay, which in commercial transactions is often as bad as no delivery, or in non-delivery, unbind the parties or unmake the contract? To me it appears that in practice a contract complete upon the acceptance of an offer being posted, but liable to be put an end to by an accident in the post, would be more mischievous than a contract only binding upon the parties to it upon the acceptance actually reaching the offerer, and I can see no principle of law from which such an anomalous contract can be deduced.

There is no doubt that the implication of a complete, final, and absolutely binding contract being formed, as soon as the acceptance of an offer is posted, may in some cases lead to inconvenience and hardship. But such there must be at times in every view of the law. It is impossible in transactions which pass between parties at a distance, and have to be carried on through the medium of correspondence, to adjust conflicting rights between innocent parties, so as to make the consequences of mistake on the part of a mutual agent fall equally upon the shoulders of both. At the same time I am not prepared to admit that the implication in question will lead to any great or general inconvenience or hardship. An offerer, if he chooses, may always make the formation of the contract which he proposes dependent upon the actual communication to himself of the acceptance. If he trusts to the post he trusts to a means of communication which, as a rule, does not fail, and if no answer to his offer is received by him, and the matter is of importance to him, he can make inquiries of the person to whom his offer was addressed. On the other hand, if the contract is not finally concluded, except in the event of the acceptance actually reaching the offerer, the door would be opened to the perpetration of much fraud, and, putting aside this consideration, considerable delay in commercial transactions, in which despatch is, as a rule, of the greatest consequence, would be occasioned; for the acceptor would never be entirely safe in acting upon his acceptance until he had received notice that his letter of acceptance had reached its destination.

Upon balance of conveniences and inconveniences it seems to me, applying with slight alterations the language of the Supreme Court of the United States in *Tayloe v. Merchants Fire Insurance Co* 9 Howard S. Ct. Rep. 390, more consistent with the acts and declarations of the parties in this case to consider the contract complete and absolutely binding on the transmission of the notice of allotment through the post, as the medium of communication that the parties themselves contemplated, instead of postponing its completion until the notice had been received by the defendant.

Baggallay LJ delivered a concurring judgment. **Bramwell LJ** dissented, taking the view that an acceptance by post was effective only when received.

NOTES AND QUESTIONS

1.   Thesiger LJ gave a number of reasons (apart from the authority of early cases such as *Adams v Lindsell* (1818) 1 B & A 681) for preferring a rule that an acceptance by post takes effect on posting: (i) the post office is a common agent; (ii) the offeror can choose to displace the rule by requiring receipt of the acceptance; (iii) the acceptor could not otherwise safely act until receiving notice that his acceptance had been received. Which, if any, of these reasons is persuasive?

2.   Is it correct to say that the Court of Appeal here made a policy decision that, as between the offeror and offeree, the risk of loss or delay in the post should more appropriately by borne by the offeror?

3. What would be the position if the court knew that the reason for the loss of the letter of acceptance was that it was incorrectly or illegibly addressed?
4. **A Hudson, 'Retractation of Letters of Acceptance' (1966) 82 *LQR* 169** asks whether an acceptor who has posted a letter of acceptance can retract his acceptance by a speedier means of communication. He persuasively argues that, although there is no clear authority on the point, the answer should be 'yes'. 'If the offeror can be said to take the risks of delay and accidents in the post it would not seem to strain matters to say that he also assumes the risk of a letter being overtaken by a speedier means of communication' (at 170).

Holwell Securities Ltd v Hughes [1974] 1 WLR 155, Court of Appeal

On 19 October 1971, the defendant granted the claimants an option to purchase some land. Clause 2 of the agreement provided: 'The said option shall be exercisable by notice in writing to [the defendant] at any time within six months from the date hereof...' On 14 April 1972 the claimants' solicitors, on behalf of the claimants, posted a letter to the defendant purporting to exercise the option to purchase (ie accepting the offer). But that letter never arrived. In an action by the claimants seeking specific performance, it was held by the Court of Appeal (affirming Templeman J) that no contract of sale had been concluded because here the offer required notice in writing of the acceptance and that had not been given.

Russell LJ: It is not disputed that the plaintiffs' solicitors' letter dated April 14, 1972, addressed to the defendant at his residence and place of work, the house which was the subject of the option to purchase, was posted by ordinary post in a proper way, enclosing a copy of the letter of the same date delivered by hand to the defendant's solicitors. It is not disputed that the letter and enclosure somehow went astray and never reached the house nor the defendant. It is not disputed that the language of the letter and enclosure would have constituted notice of exercise of the option had they reached the defendant. ...

The plaintiffs' main contention below and before this court has been that the option was exercised and the contract for sale and purchase was constituted at the moment that the letter addressed to the defendant with its enclosure was committed by the plaintiffs' solicitors to the proper representative of the postal service, so that its failure to reach its destination is irrelevant.

It is the law in the first place that, prima facie, acceptance of an offer must be communicated to the offeror. Upon this principle the law has engrafted a doctrine that, if in any given case the true view is that the parties contemplated that the postal service might be used for the purpose of forwarding an acceptance of the offer, committal of the acceptance in a regular manner to the postal service will be acceptance of the offer so as to constitute a contract, even if the letter goes astray and is lost. Nor, as was once suggested, are such cases limited to cases in which the offer has been made by post. It suffices I think at this stage to refer to *Henthorn v. Fraser* [1892] 2 Ch. 27. In the present case, as I read a passage in the judgment below [1973] 1 W.L.R. 757, 764D, Templeman J. concluded that the parties here contemplated that the postal service might be used to communicate acceptance of the offer (by exercise of the option); and I agree with that.

But that is not and cannot be the end of the matter. In any case, before one can find that the basic principle of the need for communication of acceptance to the offeror is displaced by this artificial concept of communication by the act of posting, it is necessary that the offer is in its terms consistent with such displacement and not one which by its terms points rather in the direction of actual communication. We were referred to *Henthorn v. Fraser* and to the obiter dicta of Farwell J. in *Bruner v. Moore* [1904] 1 Ch. 305, which latter was a case of an option to purchase patent rights. But in neither of those cases was there apparently any language in the offer directed to the manner of acceptance of the offer or exercise of the option.

The relevant language here is, "The said option shall be exercised by notice in writing to the intending vendor . . . ," a very common phrase in an option agreement. There is, of course, nothing in that phrase to suggest that the notification to the defendant could not be made by post. But the requirement of "notice . . . to," in my judgment, is language which should be taken expressly to assert the ordinary situation in law that acceptance requires to be communicated or notified to the offeror, and is inconsistent with the theory that acceptance can be constituted by the act of posting, referred to by *Anson's Law of Contract,* 23rd ed. (1969), p. 47. as "acceptance *without notification.*"

It is of course true that the instrument could have been differently worded. An option to purchase within a period given for value has the characteristic of an offer that cannot be withdrawn. The instrument might have said "The offer constituted by this option may be accepted in writing within six months:" in which case no doubt the posting would have sufficed to form the contract. But that language was not used, and, as indicated, in my judgment, the language used prevents that legal outcome. Under this head of the case hypothetical problems were canvassed to suggest difficulties in the way of that conclusion. What if the letter had been delivered through the letter-box of the house in due time, but the defendant had either deliberately or fortuitously not been there to receive it before the option period expired? This does not persuade me that the artificial posting rule is here applicable. The answer might well be that in the circumstances the defendant had impliedly invited communication by use of an orifice in his front door designed to receive communications.

Lawton LJ: Mr. Macpherson on behalf of the plaintiffs submitted that the option was exercised when the letter was posted, as the rule relating to the acceptance of offers by post did apply. The foundation of his argument was that the parties to this agreement must have contemplated that the option might be, and probably would be, exercised by means of a letter sent through the post. I agree. This, submitted Mr. Macpherson, was enough to bring the rule into operation. I do not agree. In *Henthorn v. Fraser* [1892]. 2 Ch. 27, Lord Herschell stated the rule as follows, at p. 33:

> "Where the circumstances are such that it must have been within the contemplation of the parties that, according to the ordinary usages of mankind, the post might be used as a means of communicating the acceptance of an offer, the acceptance is complete as soon as it is posted."

. . .

Does the rule apply in all cases where one party makes an offer which both he and the person with whom he was dealing must have expected the post to be used as a means of accepting it? In my judgment, it does not. First, it does not apply when the express terms of the offer specify that the acceptance must reach the offeror. The public nowadays are familiar with this exception to the general rule through their handling of football pool coupons. Secondly, it probably does not operate if its application would produce manifest inconvenience and absurdity. This is the opinion set out in Cheshire and Fifoot, *Law of Contract,* 3rd ed. (1952), p. 43. It was the opinion of Lord Bramwell as is seen by his judgment in *British & American Telegraph Co. v. Colson* (1871) L.R. 6 Exch. 108, and his opinion is worthy of consideration even though the decision in that case was overruled by this court in *Household Fire and Carriage Accident Insurance Co. v. Grant* (1879) 4 Ex.D. 216. The illustrations of inconvenience and absurdity which Lord Bramwell gave are as apt today as they were then. Is a stockbroker who is holding shares to the orders of his client liable in damages because he did not sell in a falling market in accordance with the instructions in a letter which was posted but never received? Before the passing of the Law Reform (Miscellaneous Provisions) Act 1970 (which abolished actions for breach of promise of marriage), would a young soldier ordered overseas have been bound in contract to marry a girl to whom he had proposed by letter, asking her to let him have an answer before he left and she had replied affirmatively in good time but the letter had never reached him? In my judgment, the factors of inconvenience and absurdity are but illustrations of a wider principle, namely, that the rule does not apply if, having regard to all the circumstances, including the nature of the subject matter under consideration, the negotiating parties cannot have intended that there should be a binding agreement until the party accepting an offer or exercising an option had in fact communicated the acceptance or exercise to the other. In my judgment, when this principle is applied to the facts of this case it becomes clear that the parties cannot have intended that the posting of a letter should constitute the exercise of the option.

Buckley LJ agreed with the judgment of Russell LJ.

NOTE

This case clearly illustrates the point that the postal rule will not apply where the offeror has displaced it by wording to the effect that the acceptance must be received.

(c) Waiver by Offeror of the Need for Communication of Acceptance

The general rule, that (other than where the post is being used) an acceptance must be communicated to (ie received by) the offeror, may be expressly or impliedly waived by the offeror. This is usually the case as regards offers of unilateral contracts, as we have seen in *Carlill v Carbolic Smoke Ball Co* (see above, 11). Bilateral contracts in which acceptance can be constituted by conduct, as in *Brogden v Metropolitan Railway Co*, above, 26, may also be regarded as an example of this principle.

But in a bilateral contract (note that the issue of an unwilling offeree cannot arise in unilateral contracts) an offeror cannot waive the requirement of communication *against an unwilling offeree* by insisting that silence shall constitute acceptance. This was established in the following case.

Felthouse v Bindley (1862) 11 CB (NS) 869, Court of Common Pleas

The claimant was the uncle of the owner of a horse. After negotiations regarding the purchase of the horse, the claimant wrote to the nephew on 2 January 1862 offering to buy the horse for £30 15s and adding: 'If I hear no more about him, I consider the horse mine at £30 15s.' The nephew did not reply to this letter. Six weeks later (on 25 February) the defendant, an auctioneer, who was employed by the nephew to sell his farming stock and who had been directed to exclude the horse as it had already been sold, mistakenly included it in the sale and sold it to a third party. The auctioneer acknowledged his mistake in a letter to the claimant written on 26 February. On the 27th the nephew wrote to the uncle saying that he had told the auctioneer to exclude the horse because already sold but that the auctioneer had mistakenly sold it. The uncle brought an action against the auctioneer for conversion of the horse. (Conversion is a strict liability tort committed where someone has wrongfully interfered with goods that belong to another.) The claim failed, it being held that the nephew's silence did not constitute acceptance so that the uncle could not show that there had been a contract for the sale of the horse to him before it was sold by the auctioneer.

Willes J: It is clear that there was no complete bargain on the 2nd of January: and it is also clear that the uncle had no right to impose upon the nephew a sale of his horse for 30l. 15s, unless he chose to comply with the condition of writing to repudiate the offer. The nephew might, no doubt, have bound his uncle to the bargain by writing to him: the uncle might also have retracted his offer at any time before acceptance. It stood an open offer: and so things remained until the 25th February, when the nephew was about to sell his farming stock by auction. The horse in question being catalogued with the rest of the stock, the auctioneer (the defendant) was told that it was already sold. It is clear, therefore, that the nephew in his own mind intended his uncle to have the horse at the price which he (the uncle) had named, – 30l. 15s: but he had not communicated such his intention to his uncle, or done anything to bind himself. Nothing, therefore, had been done to vest the property in the horse in the plaintiff down to the 25th of February, when the horse was sold by the defendant. It appears to me that, independently of the subsequent letters, there had been no bargain to pass the property in the horse to the plaintiff, and therefore that he had no right to complain of the sale. Then, what is the effect of the subsequent correspondence? The letter of the auctioneer amounts to nothing. The more important letter is that of the nephew, of the 27th of February, which is relied on as shewing that he intended to accept and did accept the terms offered by his uncle's letter of the 2nd of January. That letter, however, may be treated either as an acceptance then for the first time made by him, or as a memorandum of a bargain complete before the 25th of February, sufficient within the statute of frauds. It seems to me that the former is the more likely construction: and, if so, it is clear that the plaintiff cannot recover. But, assuming that there had been a complete parol bargain before the 25th of February, and that the letter of the 27th was a mere expression of the terms of that prior bargain, and not a bargain then for the first time concluded, it would be directly contrary to the decision of the court of Exchequer in *Stockdale* v. *Dunlop,* 6 M. & W. 224, to hold that that acceptance had relation back to the previous offer so as to bind third persons in respect of a dealing with the property by them in the interim.

Keating J: I am of the same opinion. Had the question arisen as between the uncle and the nephew, there would probably have been some difficulty. But, as between the uncle and the auctioneer, the only question we have to consider is whether the horse was the property of the plaintiff at the time of the sale on the 25th of February. It seems to me that nothing had been done at that time to pass the property out of the nephew and vest it in the plaintiff. A proposal had been made, but there had before that day been no acceptance binding the nephew.

Byles J concurred with **Willes J**.

NOTES

1.   This decision was affirmed on appeal by the Court of Exchequer Chamber: (1863) 7 LT 835.
2.   The important point in the case is that laid down by Willes J in the first sentence of the above extract. The rule that silence does not constitute acceptance against an unwilling offeree is clearly correct. If that were not so, offers to sell goods (or goods themselves) could be sent out with a notice to the effect that they will be regarded as having been accepted unless the seller is informed to the contrary within a certain time.

3. **C Miller, 'Felthouse v Bindley Revisited' (1972) 35 *MLR* 489** persuasively argues that (leaving aside any complication flowing from the Statute of Frauds) the decision in this case was probably incorrect precisely because the evidence showed that the nephew was a willing, not an unwilling, offeree (ie he did regard himself as having accepted the offer) and there was positive conduct by him to that effect. Indeed Miller goes further in arguing that such positive conduct is unnecessary where the offeror has waived the need for communication and the offeree is a willing one: so had the horse not been sold to a third party and had the nephew been suing the uncle for the price of the horse, the nephew's silence (even without positive conduct) should have constituted a valid acceptance. (But note that subsequent to this article, albeit without direct reference to it, Kerr J in *Fairline Shipping Corp v Adamson* [1975] QB 180, 189 appeared to cast doubt on the type of approach favoured by Miller.)

(4) Prescribed Mode of Acceptance

Manchester Diocesan Council for Education v Commercial and General Investments Ltd, [1970] 1 WLR 241, Chancery Division

The claimant decided to sell some land by tender. Condition 4 of the request for tenders provided, 'The person whose tender is accepted shall be the purchaser and shall be informed of the acceptance of his tender by letter sent to him by post addressed to the address given in the tender.' On 25 August 1964, the defendant completed the form of tender and sent it (from 15 Berkeley St) to the claimant's surveyor. On 15 September 1964 the claimant's solicitor wrote *to the defendant's surveyor* informing him that the claimant had approved the sale to the defendant. But it was not until 7 January 1965, that the claimant's solicitor wrote to the defendant at 15 Berkeley St. It was alleged by the defendant that by then the offer had lapsed so that the initial question was whether there had already been a valid acceptance by the letter of 15 September. It was held that there had been because, although the acceptance should have been sent to 15 Berkeley St, acceptance sent to the defendant's surveyor was no less advantageous to the defendant.

Buckley J: The offer contained in the tender was to the effect that in the event of its being accepted in accordance with the conditions of sale on or before the day named therein for that purpose – and none was so named – the defendant would pay the price and complete the purchase. An offeror may by the terms of his offer indicate that it may be accepted in a particular manner. In the present case the conditions included condition 4... It is said, on the defendant's behalf, that that condition was not complied with until January 7, 1965; that until that date the offer was never accepted in accordance with its terms; and that consequently nothing earlier than that date can be relied on as an acceptance resulting in a binding contract. If an offeror stipulates by the terms of his offer that it may, or that it shall, be accepted in a particular manner a contract results as soon as the offeree does the stipulated act, whether it has come to the notice of the offeror or not. In such a case the offeror conditionally waives either expressly or by implication the normal requirement that acceptance must be communicated to the offeror to conclude a contract. There can be no doubt that in the present case, if the plaintiff or its authorised agent had posted a letter addressed to the defendant at 15 Berkeley Street on or about September 15 informing the defendant of the acceptance of its tender, the contract would have been complete at the moment when such letter was posted, but that course was not taken. Condition 4, however, does not say that that shall be the sole permitted method of communicating an acceptance. It may be that an offeror, who by the terms of his offer insists upon acceptance in a particular manner, is entitled to insist that he is not bound unless acceptance is effected or communicated in that precise way, although it seems probable that, even so, if the other party communicates his acceptance in some other way, the offeror may by conduct or otherwise waive his right to insist upon the prescribed method of acceptance. Where, however, the offeror has prescribed a particular method of acceptance, but not in terms insisting that only acceptance in that mode shall be binding, I am of opinion that acceptance communicated to the offeror by any other mode which is no less advantageous to him will conclude the contract. Thus in *Tinn v. Hoffman & Co.* (1873) 29 L.T. 271, where acceptance was requested by return of post, Honeyman J. said, at p. 274:

> "That does not mean exclusively a reply by letter by return of post, but you may reply by telegram or by verbal message or by any means not later than a letter written by return of post."

If an offeror intends that he shall be bound only if his offer is accepted in some particular manner, it must be for him to make this clear. Condition 4 in the present case has not, in my judgment, this effect.

Moreover, the inclusion of condition 4 in the defendant's offer was at the instance of the plaintiff, who framed the conditions and the form of tender. It should not, I think, be regarded as a condition or stipulation imposed by the defendant as offeror upon the plaintiff as offeree, but as a term introduced into the bargain by the plaintiff and presumably considered by the plaintiff as being in some way for the protection or benefit of the plaintiff. It would consequently be a term strict compliance with which the plaintiff could waive, provided the defendant was not adversely affected. The plaintiff did not take advantage of the condition which would have resulted in a contract being formed as soon as a letter of acceptance complying with the condition was posted, but adopted another course, which could only result in a contract when the plaintiff's acceptance was actually communicated to the defendant.

For these reasons, I have reached the conclusion that in accordance with the terms of the tender it was open to the plaintiff to conclude a contract by acceptance actually communicated to the defendant in any way; and, in my judgment, the letter of September 15 constituted such an acceptance. It follows that, in my judgment, and subject to a point relating to the need to obtain ministerial consent to which I will refer in a moment, the parties thereupon became contractually bound.

NOTES

1. This case is important in showing that (i) an offeror can prescribe a mode of acceptance that must be complied with but that (ii) unless, as a matter of construction, that mode is mandatory another mode of acceptance which is no less advantageous to the offeror will suffice. On these facts the mode specified was not mandatory and the mode used was equally advantageous to the offeror.

2. Buckley J went on to hold that, in any event, the offer had not lapsed before 7 January so that, even if the contract had not been concluded by the letter of 15 September, it had been concluded when the claimant wrote to the defendant at 15 Berkeley St on 7 January.

(5) Acceptance in Ignorance of an Offer

R v Clarke (1927) 40 CLR 227, High Court of Australia

A reward was offered for information leading to the conviction of persons who committed the murder of two police officers. Although Clarke was not one of the murderers, he was arrested and charged with murder. He then gave information to the police which led to the conviction of the murderers. He did so to protect himself. He accepted that, when he gave the information, he was not thinking about the reward albeit that he had previously known about it. Subsequently he sued the Crown for the reward. The High Court of Australia, in reversing the Full Court of Western Australia and refusing his claim, held that he had not accepted the offer because he had given the information without relying on the offer of reward.

Isaacs ACJ: The controlling principle, then, is that to establish the *consensus* without which no true contract can exist, acceptance is as essential as offer, even in a case of the present class where the same act is at once sufficient for both acceptance and performance. But acceptance and performance of condition, as shown by the judicial reasoning quoted, involve that the person accepting and performing must act on the offer.

...

Instances easily suggest themselves where precisely the same act done with reference to an offer would be performance of the condition, but done with reference to a totally distinct object would not be such a performance. An offer of £100 to any person who should swim a hundred yards in the harbour on the first day of the year, would be met by voluntarily performing the feat with reference to the offer, but would not in my opinion be satisfied by a person who was accidentally or maliciously thrown overboard on that date and swam the distance simply to save his life, without any thought of the offer. The offeror might or might not feel morally impelled to give the sum in such a case, but would be under no contractual obligation to do so.

...

On the question of fact whether Clarke in making his statement of 10th June acted upon the offer in the proclamation, the learned Chief Justice, who saw and heard him give his testimony, answered that question in the negative. Reading the notes of the trial, which apparently are to some extent abbreviated, and reading also the statement itself, so far from finding anything which would lead me, with all the disadvantages of an appellate Court, to reverse that finding, I quite agree with it.

Higgins J: [*Williams v Carwardine* (1833) 4 B & Ad 621] seems to me not to deal with the essential elements for a contract at all: it shows merely that the *motive* of the informer in accepting the contract offered (and the performing the conditions is usually sufficient evidence of acceptance) has nothing to do with his right to recover under the contract. The reports show (as it was assumed by the Judges after the verdict of the jury in favour of the informer), that the informer *knew* of the offer when giving the information, and meant to accept the offer though she had also a *motive* in her guilty conscience. ...The reasoning of *Woodruff* J. in *Fitch v. Snedaker* (1868) 38 N.Y. 248 seems to me to be faultless; and the decision is spoken of in *Anson* (p. 24) as being undoubtedly correct in principle:—"The motive inducing consent may be immaterial, but the consent is vital. Without that there is no contract. How then can there be consent or assent to that of which the party has never heard?" Clarke had seen the offer, indeed; but it was not present to his mind—he had forgotten it, and gave no consideration to it, in his intense excitement as to his own danger. There cannot be assent without knowledge of the offer; and ignorance of the offer is the same thing whether it is due to never hearing of it or to forgetting it after hearing. But for this candid confession of Clarke's it might fairly be presumed that Clarke, having once seen the offer, acted on the faith of it, in reliance on it; but he has himself rebutted that presumption.

...

My view is that Clarke did not act *on the faith of, in reliance upon*, the proclamation; and that although the exact fulfilment of the conditions stated in the proclamation would raise a presumption that Clarke was acting on the faith of, in reliance upon, the proclamation, that presumption is rebutted by his own express admission.

Starke J: In my opinion the true principle applicable to this type of case is that unless a person performs the conditions of the offer, acting upon its faith or in reliance upon it, he does not accept the offer and the offeror is not bound to him. ...In the present case the statements of the petitioner himself satisfied the Chief Justice that he did not act on the faith of or in reliance upon the offer and we are unable to disturb that finding.

NOTES AND QUESTIONS

1.   All the judges agreed that, while motive is irrelevant, Clarke had not accepted the offer of reward because he had not relied on that offer in giving the information. It necessarily follows that one cannot accept in the more extreme case of being ignorant of an offer. Only Higgins J went so far as to say that this was that more extreme case. On his view of the facts, Clarke had forgotten about the reward, and so was in ignorance of it, at the time of giving the information.

2.   Should the law be that one cannot accept in ignorance of an offer? Should the swimmer in Isaacs ACJ's example have a contractual entitlement to the £100? A, because he is public-spirited, gives information to the police not knowing of a reward. B, mean-spirited but knowing of the reward, gives information. Is it satisfactory that B is entitled to the reward but A is not? Why should it make any difference to the offeror whether the person accepting knows of the offer or not?

3.   Identical cross-offers do not, in themselves, constitute a binding contract: see the obiter dicta of Blackburn J in *Tinn v Hoffman & Co* (1873) 29 LT 271, 279. Is this an application, in the context of bilateral contracts, of the idea that one cannot accept in ignorance of an offer?

4.   *Williams v Carwardine* (1833) 4 B & Ad 621, referred to by all three judges, shows that, provided the 'acceptor' knew of the offer (and, arguably, provided she acted in reliance on the offer), *motive is irrelevant*: the claimant in that case was held to have accepted the offer of reward, which she knew about, albeit that her motive in giving the information was to ease her conscience. But there is no clear English authority laying down that one cannot accept in ignorance of an offer. Indeed *Gibbons v Proctor* (1891) 64 LT 594 appears to stand for the reverse proposition. Before a reward had been offered – £25 for information given to Superintendent Penn – the claimant policeman had given information to a fellow policeman for him to forward to Superintendent Penn. It was held that he was entitled to the reward. But it appears from the report in (1891) 55 JP 616 that at the time the information was actually given to Penn, which constituted the acceptance, the claimant knew of the reward. So the case is weak authority for saying that one can accept in ignorance of an offer.

5. In the light of the conflicting law reports of *Gibbons v Proctor*, **A Hudson, 'Gibbons v Proctor Revisited' (1968) 84 *LQR* 503** addresses the question of acceptance in ignorance of an offer (or, as he terms it, the 'uncommunicated offer') as a matter of principle and policy. He suggests that there are good reasons for allowing acceptances in ignorance of offers to count; for example, at 508, that it seems 'a wholly undeserved benefit to [the offeror] to free him from that legal obligation merely to preserve the formal integrity and symmetry of offer and acceptance'. He regards those arguments as particularly compelling in reward cases and therefore suggests that in those cases (but not bilateral contracts) acceptance in ignorance of an offer should be effective.

6. In a difficult article, **P Mitchell and J Phillips, 'The Contractual Nexus: Is Reliance Essential?' (2002) 22 *OJLS* 115** argue that, contrary to *R v Clarke*, an acceptance should be effective, even though the acceptor is not relying on the offer, provided he knows of the offer. They indicate that, on the correct interpretation of *Williams v Carwardine*, that is already the law in England.

(6) Acceptance in Unilateral Contracts

We have seen that an offeror of a unilateral contract usually impliedly waives the need for communication of the acceptance: *Carlill v Carbolic Smoke Ball Co* (see above, 11). That leaves the question, what does constitute acceptance in relation to unilateral contracts?

Errington v Errington [1952] 1 KB 290, Court of Appeal

A father bought a house for his son and daughter-in-law with the assistance of a mortgage. Although the father remained contractually liable to the building society to repay the mortgage instalments, he told the daughter-in-law that the house would be theirs if they paid off the mortgage. The couple began to pay off the mortgage instalments but the father died while a good deal remained to be paid off. In his will he left the house to his widow and she brought an action to eject the daughter-in-law (who had since split up from the son). In rejecting that claim, the Court of Appeal held that the father's offer of a unilateral contract could not be revoked after the couple had started to pay off the mortgage instalments.

Denning LJ: It is to be noted that the couple never bound themselves to pay the instalments to the building society; and I see no reason why any such obligation should be implied. It is clear law that the court is not to imply a term unless it is necessary; and I do not see that it is necessary here. Ample content is given to the whole arrangement by holding that the father promised that the house should belong to the couple as soon as they paid off the mortgage. The parties did not discuss what was to happen if the couple failed to pay the instalments to the building society, but I should have thought it clear that, if they did fail to pay the instalments, the father would not be bound to transfer the house to them. The father's promise was a unilateral contract – a promise of the house in return for their act of paying the instalments. It could not be revoked by him once the couple entered on performance of the act, but it would cease to bind him if they left it incomplete and unperformed, which they have not done. If that was the position during the father's lifetime, so it must be after his death. If the daughter-in-law continues to pay all the building society instalments, the couple will be entitled to have the property transferred to them as soon as the mortgage is paid off; but if she does not do so, then the building society will claim the instalments from the father's estate and the estate will have to pay them. I cannot think that in those circumstances the estate would be bound to transfer the house to them, any more than the father himself would have been.

...

[T]he couple were licensees, having a permissive occupation short of a tenancy, but with a contractual right, or at any rate, an equitable right to remain so long as they paid the instalments, which would grow into a good equitable title to the house itself as soon as the mortgage was paid. This is, I think, the right view of the relationship of the parties.

...

In the present case it is clear that the father expressly promised the couple that the property should belong to them as soon as the mortgage was paid, and impliedly promised that so long as they paid the instalments to the building society they should be allowed to remain in possession. They were not purchasers because they never bound themselves to pay the instalments, but nevertheless they were in a position analogous to purchasers. They have acted on the promise, and neither the father nor his widow, his successor in title, can eject them in disregard of it. The result is that in my opinion the appeal should be dismissed and no order for possession should be made.

Somervell and **Hodson LJJ** delivered concurring judgments.

NOTES AND QUESTIONS

1. Denning LJ's view that the offer of a unilateral contract could not be revoked once the offeree 'entered on performance of the act' (ie started to pay off the instalments) is supported by the following *obiter dicta* of Goff LJ in *Daulia Ltd v Four Mill Bank Nominees Ltd* [1978] Ch 231, 239. He said: 'Whilst I think the true view of a unilateral contract must in general be that the offeror is entitled to require full performance of the condition which he has imposed and short of that he is not bound, that must be subject to one important qualification, which stems from the fact that there must be an implied obligation on the part of the offeror not to prevent the condition becoming satisfied, which obligation it seems to me must arise as soon as the offeree starts to perform. Until then the offeror can revoke the whole thing, but once the offeree has embarked on performance it is too late for the offeror to revoke his offer.'

2. Applying the views of Denning and Goff LJJ, is the correct legal analysis that there is an *acceptance* of an offer of a unilateral contract (so that the unilateral contract is concluded) by starting performance? A difficulty with that analysis is that it would require one to say that the consideration (see Chapter 3) for the promise was starting, rather than completing, performance which may be thought unrealistic. Is it therefore preferable to say that, while the result is the same, there is a subsidiary unilateral contract whereby the offeror promises not to revoke the offer of the main unilateral contract once the offeree has started to perform?

3. A promises B £250 if he walks from London to York. Is A in breach of a unilateral contract if he seeks to revoke his offer (a) when B has walked from London to within one mile of York or (b) when B travels towards London in order to start the walk?

4. TERMINATION OF AN OFFER

An offer can terminate by revocation, rejection, lapse of time and, sometimes, by the death of the offeror. The case law primarily deals with revocation and rejection, and this is what we shall concentrate on in this section. Before doing so it should be noted, as regards lapse of time, that where the offer is stated to be open for a particular period of time, it will remain open for that period or, where no time has been specified, for a reasonable period of time (provided, in both instances, that it has not been revoked or rejected in that period of time). What constitutes a reasonable period of time depends on the facts. In *Manchester Diocesan Council for Education v Commercial and General Investments Ltd*, see above, 43, an alternative ground for the decision was that the offer made in late August 1964 had not lapsed by January 1965 and that, in deciding what constituted a reasonable period of time, the conduct of the parties, subsequent to the offer, was relevant.

(1) Revocation

An offer can be revoked at any time before it has been accepted. But once it has been validly accepted, it is then too late to withdraw. To be effective, revocation must be communicated to (ie received by) the offeree.

Byrne & Co v Van Tienhoven & Co
(1880) 5 CPD 344, Common Pleas Division

On 1 October, the defendants, in Cardiff, posted a letter to the claimants, in New York, offering to sell them 1,000 boxes of tinplates. The claimants did not receive this letter until 11 October. They telegraphed their acceptance on the same day. During the first week of October the price of tinplate had risen by some 25 per cent and so, on 8 October, the defendants posted a letter withdrawing their offer. That second letter was not received by the claimants until 20 October. The defendants denied contractual liability arguing that they had revoked the offer on 8 October. But this argument was rejected by Lindley J who held that the revocation could not be effective until received and that was after the claimants' acceptance on 11 October.

Lindley J: There is no doubt that an offer can be withdrawn before it is accepted, and it is immaterial whether the offer is expressed to be open for acceptance for a given time or not: *Routledge v. Grant*. 4 Bing. 653. For the decision of the present case, however, it is necessary to consider two other questions, viz.: 1. Whether a withdrawal of an offer has any effect until it is communicated to the person to whom the offer has been sent? 2. Whether posting a letter of withdrawal is a communication to the person to whom the letter is sent?

It is curious that neither of these questions appears to have been actually decided in this country. As regards the first question, I am aware that Pothier and some other writers of celebrity are of opinion that there can be no contract if an offer is withdrawn before it is accepted, although the withdrawal is not communicated to the person to whom the offer has been made. The reason for this opinion is that there is not in fact any such consent by both parties as is essential to constitute a contract between them. Against this view, however, it has been urged that a state of mind not notified cannot be regarded in dealings between man and man; and that an uncommunicated revocation is for all practical purposes and in point of law no revocation at all. This is the view taken in the United States: see *Tayloe v. Merchants Fire Insurance Co*, 9 How. Sup. Ct. Rep. 390 cited in Benjamin on Sales, pp. 56-58, and it is adopted by Mr. Benjamin. The same view is taken by Mr. Pollock in his excellent work on Principles of Contract, ed. ii., p. 10, and by Mr. Leake in his Digest of the Law of Contracts, p. 43. This view, moreover, appears to me much more in accordance with the general principles of English law than the view maintained by Pothier. I pass, therefore, to the next question, viz., whether posting the letter of revocation was a sufficient communication of it to the plaintiff. The offer was posted on the 1st of October, the withdrawal was posted on the 8th, and did not reach the plaintiff until after he had posted his letter of the 11th, accepting the offer. It may be taken as now settled that where an offer is made and accepted by letters sent through the post, the contract is completed the moment the letter accepting the offer is posted: *Harris' Case* Law Rep. 7 Ch. 587; *Dunlop v. Higgins*, 1 H.L. 381, even although it never reaches its destination. When, however, these authorities are looked at, it will be seen that they are based upon the principle that the writer of the offer has expressly or impliedly assented to treat an answer to him by a letter duly posted as a sufficient acceptance and notification to himself, or, in other words, he has made the post office his agent to receive the acceptance and notification of it. But this principle appears to me to be inapplicable to the case of the withdrawal of an offer. In this particular case I can find no evidence of any authority in fact given by the plaintiffs to the defendants to notify a withdrawal of their offer by merely posting a letter; and there is no legal principle or decision which compels me to hold, contrary to the fact, that the letter of the 8th of October is to be treated as communicated to the plaintiff on that day or on any day before the 20th, when the letter reached them. But before that letter had reached the plaintiffs they had accepted the offer, both by telegram and by post; and they had themselves resold the tin plates at a profit. In my opinion the withdrawal by the defendants on the 8th of October of their offer of the 1st was inoperative; and a complete contract binding on both parties was entered into on the 11th of October, when the plaintiffs accepted the offer of the 1st, which they had no reason to suppose had been withdrawn. Before leaving this part of the case it may be as well to point out the extreme injustice and inconvenience which any other conclusion would produce. If the defendants' contention were to prevail no person who had received an offer by post and had accepted it would know his position until he had waited such a time as to be quite sure that a letter withdrawing the offer had not been posted before his acceptance of it. It appears to me that both legal principles, and practical convenience require that a person who has accepted an offer not known to him to have been revoked, shall be in a position safely to act upon the footing that the offer and acceptance constitute a contract binding on both parties.

NOTES AND QUESTIONS

1.   This case shows that, contrary to the 'postal rule' for acceptance, a revocation sent by post is effective only when received by the offeree. Are these two rules inconsistent? Or is it rather the case that the policy of placing the risk of loss/delay in the post on the offeror has the consequence that both an acceptance takes effect when posted and a revocation takes effect when received?

2.   As with the rules on acceptance, the rule that a revocation must be communicated to (received by) the offeree is a general one only. So, for example, Art 2.202(1) of the *Principles of European Contract Law* states that 'an offer made to the public can be revoked by the same means as were used to make the offer.' This, no doubt, is the position in English law; and see, in the United States, *Shuey v United States* 92 US 73 (1875).

Dickinson v Dodds (1876) 2 Ch D 463, Court of Appeal

On Wednesday, 10 June 1874 the defendant (Dodds) delivered to the claimant (Dickinson) a written offer to sell certain houses for £800. Added was the following postscript, 'This offer to be left over until Friday, 9 o'clock am, June 12, 1874.' On the Thursday afternoon, the claimant was informed by a Mr Berry that the defendant had been offering the property to a Mr Allan; and in fact on that afternoon the defendant signed a formal contract for the sale of the property to Mr Allan for £800. At about 7.00 am on the Friday morning Mr Berry, acting as agent for the claimant, handed a letter of acceptance to the defendant but he refused to accept it saying that he had already sold the property. The claimant brought an action for specific performance and this was granted by the trial judge. In allowing the defendant's appeal, the Court of Appeal held that the offer had been revoked—because the claimant had notice from Berry of the defendant's withdrawal—prior to the claimant's purported acceptance.

James LJ: The document, though beginning "I hereby agree to sell," was nothing but an offer, and was only intended to be an offer, for the Plaintiff himself tells us that he required time to consider whether he would enter into an agreement or not. Unless both parties had then agreed there was no concluded agreement then made; it was in effect and substance only an offer to sell. The Plaintiff, being minded not to complete the bargain at that time, added this memorandum – "This offer to be left over until Friday, 9 o'clock A.M., 12th June, 1874." That shews it was only an offer. There was no consideration given for the undertaking or promise, to whatever extent it may be considered binding, to keep the property unsold until 9 o'clock on Friday morning; but apparently *Dickinson* was of opinion, and probably *Dodds* was of the same opinion, that he (*Dodds*) was bound by that promise, and could not in any way withdraw from it, or retract it, until 9 o'clock on Friday morning, and this probably explains a good deal of what afterwards took place. But it is clear settled law, on one of the clearest principles of law, that this promise, being a mere *nudum pactum*, was not binding, and that at any moment before a complete acceptance by *Dickinson* of the offer, *Dodds* was as free as *Dickinson* himself. Well, that being the state of things, it is said that the only mode in which *Dodds* could assert that freedom was by actually and distinctly saying to *Dickinson*, "Now I withdraw my offer." It appears to me that there is neither principle nor authority for the proposition that there must be an express and actual withdrawal of the offer, or what is called a retractation. It must, to constitute a contract, appear that the two minds were at one, at the same moment of time, that is, that there was an offer continuing up to the time of the acceptance. If there was not such a continuing offer, then the acceptance comes to nothing. Of course it may well be that the one man is bound in some way or other to let the other man know that his mind with regard to the offer has been changed; but in this case, beyond all question, the Plaintiff knew that *Dodds* was no longer minded to sell the property to him as plainly and clearly as if *Dodds* had told him in so many words, "I withdraw the offer." This is evident from the Plaintiff's own statements in the bill.

...

It is to my mind quite clear that before there was any attempt at acceptance by the Plaintiff, he was perfectly well aware that *Dodds* had changed his mind, and that he had in fact agreed to sell the property to *Allan*. It is impossible, therefore, to say there was ever that existence of the same mind between the two parties which is essential in point of law to the making of an agreement. I am of opinion, therefore, that the Plaintiff has failed to prove that there was any binding contract between *Dodds* and himself.

Mellish LJ: If an offer has been made for the sale of property, and before that offer is accepted, the person who has made the offer enters into a binding agreement to sell the property to somebody else, and the person to whom the offer was first made receives notice in some way that the property has been sold to another person, can he after that make a binding contract by the acceptance of the offer? I am of opinion that he cannot. The law may be right or wrong in saying that a person who has given to another a certain time within which to accept an offer is not bound by his promise to give that time; but, if he is not bound by that promise, and may still sell the property to some one else, and if it be the law that, in order to make a contract, the two minds must be in agreement at some one time, that is, at the time of the acceptance, how is it possible that when the person to whom the offer has been made knows that the person who has made the offer has sold the property to someone else, and that, in fact, he has not remained in the same mind to sell it to him, he can be at liberty to accept the offer and thereby make a binding contract? It seems to me that would be simply absurd. If a man makes an offer to sell a particular horse in his stable, and says, "I will give you until the day after to-morrow to accept the offer," and the next day goes and sells the horse to somebody else, and receives the purchase-money from him, can the person to whom the offer was originally made then come and say, "I accept," so as to make a binding contract, and so as to be entitled to recover damages for the non-delivery of the horse? If the rule of law is that a mere offer to sell property, which can be withdrawn at any time, and which is made dependent on the acceptance of the person to whom it is made, is a mere *nudum pactum,* how is it possible that the person to whom the offer has been made can by acceptance make a binding contract after he knows that the person who has made the offer has sold the property to some one else? It is admitted law that, if a man who makes an offer dies, the offer cannot be accepted after he is dead, and parting with the property has very much the same effect as the death of the owner, for it makes the performance of the offer impossible. I am clearly of opinion that, just as when a man who has made an offer dies before it is accepted it is impossible that it can then be accepted, so when once the person to whom the offer was made knows that the property has been sold to some one else, it is too late for him to accept the offer, and on that ground I am clearly of opinion that there was no binding contract for the sale of this property by *Dodds* to *Dickinson,* and even if there had been, it seems to me that the sale of the property to *Allan* was first in point of time. However, it is not necessary to consider, if there had been two binding contracts, which of them would be entitled to priority in equity, because there is no binding contract between *Dodds* and *Dickinson.*

Baggallay JA concurred.

NOTES AND QUESTIONS

1. The offer was stated to be open until the Friday. As is made clear, such an offer, like any other, can be revoked at any time before acceptance. This would only not be so if the offer to hold open is itself supported by consideration (ie the offeree pays for the offer to be held open) so as to comprise a separate binding 'option' contract. See also on this the opening sentence of Lindley J's judgment in *Byrne v Van Tienhoven* (see above, 49). See also below, 151, on whether 'firm offers' should be binding without the need for consideration.

2. In this case, it was held to be sufficient for a valid revocation that Dickinson had notice from a third party (Berry) of Dodds' withdrawal of the offer prior to Dickinson's acceptance. Treitel, *The Law of Contract* (11th edn, 2003) at 42 criticises this approach: 'The rule that communication of withdrawal need not come from the offeror can be a regrettable source of uncertainty. It puts on the offeree the possibly difficult task of deciding whether his source of information is reliable…Certainty would be promoted if the rule were that the withdrawal must be communicated by the offeror as well as to the offeree.'

Do you agree with that criticism? Is there anything to be said for the rule being that revocation communicated through a third party should only count if the third party is a reliable source of information (as Mr Berry appeared to be)? Or would that be a rather pointless refinement, given that the information is only relevant if it turns out to be true (that the offer has been withdrawn)?

(2) Rejection

Hyde v Wrench (1840) 3 Beav 334, Rolls Court

Wrench offered to sell his farm to Hyde for £1000. Hyde responded by saying that he would give £950 for it. Wrench wrote refusing to accept this proposal. Hyde then wrote to say that he accepted the original offer to sell at £1000. Hyde brought an action against Wrench for specific performance, but this failed. It was held by Lord Langdale MR that no contract had come into existence: once Hyde had made the counter-offer of £950 that put an end to Wrench's offer which could not therefore be accepted later.

Lord Langdale MR: Under the circumstances stated in this bill, I think there exists no valid binding contract between the parties for the purchase of the property. The Defendant offered to sell it for £1000 and if that had been at once unconditionally accepted, there would undoubtedly have been a perfect binding contract; instead of that, the Plaintiff made an offer of his own, to purchase the property for £950, and he thereby rejected the offer previously made by the Defendant. I think that it was not afterwards competent for him to revive the proposal of the Defendant, by tendering and acceptance of it; and that, therefore, there exists no obligation of any sort between the parties…

NOTE

This case shows that a counter-offer 'kills' the original offer (for this language, see *Butler Machine Tool v Ex-Cell-O*, above, 27) which is, therefore, no longer open for acceptance.

Stevenson, Jacques & Co v McLean
(1880) 5 QBD 346, Queen's Bench Division

The defendant wrote to the claimants stating that he was willing to sell a quantity of iron to the claimants for 40s per ton and that the offer was open until the following Monday. On the Monday morning, the claimants telegraphed to the defendant, 'Please wire whether you would accept forty for delivery over two months, or if not, longest limit you would give.' After receiving that telegram, the defendant sold the iron to a third party and at 1.25 pm (on the Monday) sent a telegram to the claimants telling them that the iron had been sold. Before that telegram arrived at 1.46 pm, the claimants (at 1.34 pm) telegraphed to the defendant accepting the offer to sell at 40s cash. The claimants sued the defendant for breach of contract. It was held by Lush J that a valid contract had been formed because the claimants' earlier telegram on the Monday morning was a mere inquiry and not a counter-offer so that it did not put an end to the defendant's offer.

Lush J: [I]t was contended that the telegram sent by the plaintiffs on the Monday morning was a rejection of the defendant's offer and a new proposal on the plaintiffs' part, and that the defendant had therefore a right to regard it as putting an end to the original negotiation.

Looking at the form of the telegram, the time when it was sent, and the state of the iron market, I cannot think this is its fair meaning. The plaintiff Stevenson said he meant it only as an inquiry, expecting an answer for his guidance, and this, I think, is the sense in which the defendant ought to have regarded it.

It is apparent throughout the correspondence, that the plaintiffs did not contemplate buying the iron on speculation, but that their acceptance of the defendant's offer depended on their finding some one to take the [iron] off their hands. All parties knew that the market was in an unsettled state, and that no one could predict at the early hour when the telegram was sent how the prices would range during the day. It was reasonable that, under these circumstances, they should desire to know before business began whether they were to be at liberty in case of need to make any and what concession as to the time or times of delivery, which would be the time or times of payment, or whether the defendant was determined to adhere to the terms of his letter; and it was highly unreasonable that the plaintiffs should have intended to close the negotiation while it was uncertain whether they could find a buyer or not, having the whole of the business hours of the day to look for one. Then, again, the form of the telegram is one of inquiry. It is not "I offer forty for delivery over two months," which would have likened the case to *Hyde v. Wrench* 3 Beav. 334, where one party offered his estate for 1000*l.*, and the other answered by offering 950*l.* Lord Langdale, in that case, held that after the 950*l.* had been refused, the party offering it could not, by then agreeing to the original proposal, claim the estate, for the negotiation was at an end by the refusal of his counter proposal. Here there is no counter proposal. The words are, "Please wire whether you would accept forty for delivery over two months, or, if not, the longest limit you would give." There is nothing specific by way of offer or rejection, but a mere inquiry, which should have been answered and not treated as a rejection of the offer. This ground of objection therefore fails.

NOTES AND QUESTIONS

1. Lush J, in distinguishing *Hyde v Wrench*, differentiated between a 'counter-proposal' (ie a counter-offer) which terminates the original offer and a 'mere inquiry' (ie a request for further information) which does not. Would the decision in *Hyde v Wrench* have been different if, instead of Hyde responding by saying he would give £950 for the farm, he had responded by asking if Wrench would accept £950 for the farm?

2. What would the position have been had the defendant's telegram (telling the claimant that the iron had been sold) arrived 13 minutes earlier than it did (ie at 1.33 pm instead of 1.46 pm)? (See above, 49, and *Byrne v Van Tienhoven*, which was cited by Lush J as authority for the rule that a revocation takes effect on receipt).

5. PROBLEMATIC OFFER AND ACCEPTANCE

An analysis in terms of offer and acceptance is almost always a rational and helpful way to proceed in determining whether the parties have concluded an agreement. Occasionally, however, that traditional approach has been criticised by influential judges as being out-of-date or artificial. See, eg, Lord Denning MR's comments in *Butler v Ex-Cell-O* in the context of the battle of the forms, above, 28; and Lord Wilberforce's famous statement in *New Zealand Shipping Co Ltd v AM Satterthwaite & Co Ltd* (below, 479) that, 'English law, having committed itself to a rather technical and schematic doctrine of contract, in application takes a practical approach, often at the cost of forcing the facts to fit uneasily into the marked slots of offer, acceptance and consideration.'

We here consider the classic case where, even on a traditional view, offer and acceptance was problematic.

The Satanita [1895] P 248, Court of Appeal

The claimant (Lord Dunraven) and the defendant (the owner of 'The Satanita') entered their yachts into a race. In doing so, each agreed to abide by the rules of the race. One of the rules was that if the owner of a yacht broke a rule he would be liable for 'all damages arising thereunder'. The defendant's yacht, while in breach of one of the rules, collided with, and sank, the claimant's yacht. It was held by the Court of Appeal, in allowing the claimant's appeal, that there was a contract between the claimant and defendant; and that, by that contract, the defendant was liable for the full loss of the yacht, thereby displacing the default position, laid down in statute, whereby the defendant's liability would have been limited.

Lord Esher MR: The first question raised is whether, supposing her to have broken a rule, she can be sued for that breach of the rules by the owner of the competing yacht which has been damaged; in other words, Was there any contract between the owners of those two yachts? Or it may be put thus: Did the owner of the yacht which is sued enter into any obligation to the owner of the other yacht, that if his yacht broke the rules, and thereby injured the other yacht, he would pay damages? It seems to me clear that he did; and the way that he has undertaken that obligation is this. A certain number of gentlemen formed themselves into a committee and proposed to give prizes for matches sailed between yachts at a certain place on a certain day, and they promulgated certain rules, and said: "If you want to sail in any of our matches for our prize, you cannot do so unless you submit yourselves to the conditions which we have thus laid down. And one of the conditions is, that if you do sail for one of such prizes you must enter into an obligation with the owners of the yachts who are competing, which they at the same time enter into similarly with you, that if by a breach of any of our rules you do damage or injury to the owner of a competing yacht, you shall be liable to make good the damage which you have so done." If that is so, then when they do sail, and not till then, that relation is immediately formed between the yacht owners. There are other conditions with regard to these matches which constitute a relation between each of the yacht owners who enters his yacht and sails it and the committee; but that does not in the least do away with what the yacht owner has undertaken, namely, to enter into a relation with the other yacht owners, that relation containing an obligation.

Here the defendant, the owner of the *Satanita*, entered into a relation with the plaintiff Lord Dunraven, when he sailed his yacht against Lord Dunraven's yacht, and that relation contained an obligation that if, by any breach of any of these rules, he did damage to the yacht of Lord Dunraven, he would have to pay the damages.

Lopes LJ: The questions are, first, was there a contract? Secondly, what was the contract?

...

As to the first question, I have no doubt that there was a contract. Probably a contract with the committee in certain cases, but also a contract between the owners of the competing yachts amongst themselves, and that contract was an undertaking that the owner of one competing yacht would pay the owner of any other competing yacht injured by his yacht all the damages arising from any infringement or disobedience of the rules.

In my opinion, directly any owner entered his yacht to sail, this contract arose...

Rigby LJ: The first question is that of contract or no contract. It appears to me that all that is necessary to constitute a contract between the yacht owners is to bring home to each of them the knowledge that the race is to be run under the Yacht Racing Association rules, and that they, the one and the other, deliberately enter for the race upon those terms. In this case we have a written document, signed by each yacht owner, which, if there were any doubt at all, would render it abundantly clear that he was perfectly well aware of the bargain he was entering into. In no other way than that does it appear to me to be material.

The contract did not arise with any one, other than the managing committee, at the moment that the yacht owner signed the document, which it was necessary to sign in order to be a competitor. But when the owner of the *Satanita* on the one hand, and the owner of the *Valkyrie* on the other, actually came forward and became competitors upon those terms, I think it would be idle to say that there was not then, and thereby, a contract between them, provided always that there is something in the rule which points to a bargain between the owners of yachts. Under rule 24, "If a yacht, in consequence of her neglect of any of these rules, shall foul another yacht, or compel other yachts to foul, she shall forfeit all claim to the prize, and shall pay all damages." To whom is the owner of that yacht to pay those damages? He cannot pay them to the club, nor do I think the club could recover them. The true and sensible construction is that he must pay the owner of the yacht fouled.

NOTES AND QUESTIONS

1. The decision was affirmed by the House of Lords, *sub nom Clarke v Dunraven* [1897] AC 59, without adding anything on the question of whether there was a contract between the parties.
2. It is unclear whether the judges thought that the contract was formed when sending in an entry for the race or when the yachts began to race. On either view, how could the (bilateral) contract between each yacht-owner be analysed in terms of offer and acceptance? Apart from problems over acceptance in ignorance of an offer, it would seem to require one to say, absurdly, that each yacht-owner was *at the same time* making an offer to the others and accepting their offers. As Treitel, *The Law of Contract* (11th edn, 2003) concludes, at 48, 'The competitors no doubt, reached agreement, but they did not do so by a process which can be analysed into offer and acceptance'.

J Beatson, *Anson's Law of Contract* (28th edn, 2002) 27–60
S Smith, *Atiyah's Introduction to the Law of Contract* (6th edn, 2006) 35–42, 47–65

S Gardner, 'Trashing with Trollope: A Deconstruction of the Postal Rules in Contract' (1992) 12 *OJLS* 170

In this wide-ranging article, Gardner argues that there has been no entirely convincing explanation of the rules for acceptance, and revocation, of offers by post. By examining the history of the postal service and telephones in the nineteenth century, he controversially suggests that 'the acceptance rule is explicable above all as the reflection of a popular conception about the nature of the postal service' (at 192). That is, at the time when the acceptance by post rule was first being developed, there was a popular view that, by reason of this great new invention, posting equated to delivery. Later on, when the telephone had been invented and the revocation by post rule was being developed (in 1880), the telephone had taken over as the means of instantaneous communication so that people no longer equated posting with delivery.

Principles of European Contract Law (eds O Lando and H Beale, 2000) 159–168, 171–4, 180–5

Article 2:201: Offer
(3) A proposal to supply goods or services at stated prices made by a professional supplier in a public advertisement or a catalogue, or by a display of goods, is presumed to be an offer to sell or supply at that price until the stock of goods, or the supplier's capacity to supply the service, is exhausted.

[This contrasts with English law where an advertisement for, or display of, goods is normally an invitation to treat: see above, 7–15.]

Article 2:202: Revocation of an Offer
(1) An offer may be revoked if the revocation reaches the offeree before it has dispatched its acceptance…

(2) An offer made to the public can be revoked by the same means as were used to make the offer.

(3) However, a revocation of an offer is ineffective if:

(a) the offer indicates that it is irrevocable; or

(b) it states a fixed time for its acceptance; or

(c) it was reasonable for the offeree to rely on the offer as being irrevocable and the offeree has acted in reliance on the offer.

[(1) and (2) are consistent with English law but, in contrast to (3), 'firm offers' are not binding in England: see above, 52, note 1.]

Article 2:205: Time of Conclusion of the Contract
(1) If an acceptance has been dispatched by the offeree the contract is concluded when the acceptance reaches the offeror.

[This contrasts with the English postal rule: see above, 37–41.]

Article 2:209: Conflicting General Conditions
(1) If the parties have reached agreement except that the offer and acceptance refer to conflicting general conditions of contract, a contract is nonetheless formed. The general conditions form part of the contract to the extent that they are common in substance.

(2) However, no contract is formed if one party:

(a) has indicated in advance, explicitly, and not by way of general conditions, that it does not intend to be bound by a contract on the basis of paragraph (1); or

(b) without delay, informs the other party that it does not intend to be bound by such contract.

(3) General conditions of contract are terms which have been formulated in advance for an indefinite number of contracts of a certain nature, and which have not been individually negotiated between the parties.

[This contrasts with the English approach to the 'battle of the forms': see above, 27–32.]

Certainty and Intention to Create Legal Relations

1. CERTAINTY

An agreement that is too vague or too incomplete is not legally enforceable. The standard of certainty set by the law seeks to maintain a delicate balance between giving effect to the parties' intentions while not making contracts for the parties. The leading cases are here examined under the following sub-headings: (1) Vagueness; (2) Price Not Fixed; (3) Agreements to Negotiate; (4) A Non-contractual Solution.

Introductory reading: E McKendrick, *Contract Law* (7th edn, 2007) 4.1–4.5

(1) Vagueness

Hillas & Co Ltd v Arcos Ltd (1932) 147 LT 503, House of Lords

By an agreement made on 21 May 1930, the claimants agreed to buy from the defendants '22,000 standards of softwood goods of fair specification over the season' subject to certain conditions. Clause 9 of the agreement gave them an option to buy a further 100,000 standards during the season 1931 at 5 per cent below the official list price. The claimants purported to exercise the option on 22 December 1930 but the defendants could not perform as they had already sold their supply to a third party. The claimants sued for damages for breach of contract. The defendants argued that the option agreement was too uncertain to be binding because it did not sufficiently describe the goods and contemplated a further agreement. In allowing the claimants' appeal, the House of Lords held that the option agreement was sufficiently certain so that the defendants were bound by the claimants' exercise of the option.

Lord Tomlin: In the present case one or two preliminary observations fall to be made. First, the parties were both intimately acquainted with the course of business in the Russian softwood timber trade, and had without difficulty carried out the sale and purchase of 22,000 standards under the first part of the document of May 21, 1930. Secondly, although the question here is whether Clause 9 of the document of May 21, 1930, with the letter of Dec. 22, 1930, constitutes a contract, the validity of the whole of the document of May 21, 1930, is really in question so far as the matter depends upon the meaning of the phrase "of fair specification"; and, thirdly, it is indisputable having regard to Clause 11, which provides that "this agreement cancels all previous agreements," that the parties intended by the document of May 21, 1930, to make and believed that they had made some concluded bargain. The case against the appellants is put on two grounds. First, it is said that there is in Clause 9 no sufficient description of the goods to be sold; and, secondly, it is said that Clause 9 contemplates a future bargain the terms of which remain to be settled.

As to the first point it is plain that something must necessarily be implied in Clause 9. The words "100,000 standards" without more do not even indicate that timber is the subject-matter of the clause. The implication at the least of the words "of softwood goods" is in my opinion inevitable, and if this is so I see no reason to separate the words "of fair specification" from the words "of softwood goods." In my opinion, there is a necessary implication of the words "of softwood goods of fair specification" after the words "100,000 standards" in Clause 9.

What, then, is the meaning of "100,000 standards of softwood goods of fair specification for delivery during 1931"? If the words "of fair specification" have no meaning which is certain or capable of being made certain, then not only can there be no contract under Clause 9 but there cannot have been a contract with regard to the 22,000 standards mentioned at the beginning of the document of May 21, 1930. This may be the proper conclusion, but before it is reached it is, I think, necessary to exclude as impossible all reasonable meanings which would give certainty in the words.

In my opinion, this cannot be done. The parties undoubtedly attributed to the words in connection with the 22,000 standards some meaning which was precise or capable of being made precise. ...

Reading the document of May 21, 1930, as a whole and having regard to the admissible evidence as to the course of the trade, I think that upon their true construction the words "of fair specification over the season 1930," used in connection with the 22,000 standards, mean that the 22,000 standards are to be satisfied in goods distributed over kinds, qualities and sizes in the fair proportions, having regard to the output of the season 1930 and the classifications of that output in respect of kinds, qualities and sizes. That is something which if the parties fail to agree can be ascertained just as much as the fair value of a property.

I have already expressed the view that Clause 9 must be read as "100,000 standards of fair specification for delivery during 1931," and these words, I think, have the same meaning, mutatis mutandis, as the words relating to the 22,000 standards. Thus, there is a description of the goods which if not immediately yet ultimately is capable of being rendered certain.

The second point upon Clause 9, that it contemplates a future agreement, remains to be considered. The form of the phrases "the option of entering into a contract" and "such contract to stipulate that" upon which stress has been laid by the respondents seems to me unimportant. These phrases are but an inartificial way of indicating that there is no contract till the option is exercised. The sentence that such contract is to stipulate that whatever the conditions are the buyers are to obtain the goods at a certain reduction is more difficult. The words "whatever the conditions are," being governed by the word "that" which follows the words "to stipulate," must be intended to be part of the contract. If so, the word "conditions" cannot mean terms of the contract, but must connote some extrinsic condition of affairs, and the condition of affairs referred to is, I think, the conditions as to supply and demand which may prevail during 1931. Upon this view of the matter it cannot, I think, be said that there is nothing more than an agreement to make an agreement.

...

Reference was made in the course of the arguments before your Lordships and in the judgments in the Court of Appeal to the unreported case before your Lordships' House of *May & Butcher, Ltd. v. Rex*. In the agreement there under consideration there was an express provision that the price of the goods to be sold should be subsequently fixed between the parties. Your Lordships' House reached the conclusion that there was no contract, rejecting the appellants' contention that the agreement should be construed as an agreement to sell at the fair or reasonable price or alternatively at a price to be fixed under the arbitration clause contained in the agreement. That case does not, in my opinion, afford any assistance in determining the present case, the result of which must depend upon the meaning placed upon the language employed.

Lord Thankerton: The question on which I have had doubt is whether the words "of fair specification," on their proper construction, will enable the subject to be identified by the Court. In other words, do they provide a standard by which the Court is enabled to ascertain the subject-matter of the contract, or do they involve an adjustment between the conflicting interests of the parties, which the parties have left unsettled and on which the Court is not entitled to adjudicate? Does the phrase mean a specification which is fair as between the interests, on the one hand, of the seller in respect of the stock of wood, comprising various kinds of wood and various qualities and sizes, available for sale in the season of 1931, and, on the other hand, the interests of the buyer in respect of the requirements of his trade during that season? Or does the phrase mean a fair selection from the seller's stock of wood available for sale in that season? If the former construction be the proper one, I would be of opinion that the Court would not be entitled to adjudicate between the opposing interests of the two parties. If the latter construction be the proper one, the ascertainment of a fair selection from the seller's available stock is within the province of the Court; in that case the Court is applying a standard which is provided by the contract, and is thereby merely identifying the subject-matter of the contract.

While I have had considerable doubt on this question of construction I am affected by the consideration that the contract is a commercial one and that the parties undoubtedly thought that they had concluded a contract, and I have come to the conclusion, in agreement with the noble Lord, that the second alternative construction above stated is the proper one and that there was here a concluded contract.

Lord Wright: The document of May 21, 1930, cannot be regarded as other than inartistic, and may appear repellent to the trained sense of an equity draftsman. But it is clear that the parties both intended to make a contract and thought they had done so. Business men often record the most important agreements in crude and summary fashion; modes of expression sufficient and clear to them in the course of their business may appear to those unfamiliar with the business far from complete or precise. It is accordingly the duty of the Court to construe such documents fairly and broadly, without being too astute or subtle in finding defects, but, on the contrary, the Court should seek to apply the old maxim of English law verba ita sunt intelligenda ut res magis valeat quam pereat [Words are to be understood so that the object may be carried out and not fail]. That maxim, however, does not mean that the Court is to make a contract for the parties, or to go outside the words they have used, except in so far as there are appropriate implications of law, as, for instance, the implication of what is just and reasonable to be ascertained by the Court as a matter of machinery where the contractual intention is clear but the contract is silent on some detail. Thus, in contracts for future performance over a period the parties may neither be able nor desire to specify many matters of detail, but leave them to be adjusted in the working out of the contract. Save for the legal implication I have mentioned, such contracts might well be incomplete or uncertain; with that implication in reserve they are neither incomplete nor uncertain. As obvious illustrations I may refer to such matters as prices or times of delivery in contracts for the sale of goods, or times for loading or discharging in a contract of sea carriage. Furthermore, even if the construction of the words used may be difficult, that is not a reason for holding them too ambiguous or uncertain to be enforced, if the fair meaning of the parties can be extracted.

[*Having considered the clauses in detail, and decided that none of them were too uncertain, he concluded:*]

In my judgment, the parties here did intend to enter into, and did enter into, a complete and binding agreement not dependent on any future agreement for its validity.

Lord Warrington and **Lord Macmillan** concurred.

NOTES AND QUESTIONS

1. Is it a valid criticism of *Hillas v Arcos* that it leads to the courts making contracts for the parties?
2. Is there a clear distinction in this type of case between the issue of certainty and the issue of whether the parties intended to create legal relations (see below, 77, 83)?
3. In *Baird Textiles Holdings Ltd v Marks & Spencer plc* [2001] EWCA Civ 274, [2002] 1 All ER (Comm) 737 (see also below, 136) one of the questions was whether Marks & Spencer had entered into a long-term contract to be supplied with garments by Baird. The Court of Appeal held that they had not. Rather the contracts were the seasonal contracts under which Marks & Spencer ordered particular garments. The principal reason why there was held to be no long-term contract was lack of certainty consequent on there being no objective criteria by which the court could assess what would be reasonable for Marks & Spencer to acquire either as to quantity or price. In the leading judgment, Sir Andrew Morritt V-C relied on Lord Thankerton's speech in *Hillas v Arcos*. He said at paragraphs [26]–[30]:

    'Any debate about certainty of contractual terms and implications of reasonableness to avoid uncertainty must start with the decision of the House of Lords in *Hillas & Co Ltd v Arcos Ltd*.... The distinction between those cases in which the implication of reasonableness provides for certainty and those in which it does not appears most clearly from the speech of Lord Thankerton. He distinguished [*see 61 above*] between cases where the contract provides for an objective standard which the court applies by ascertaining what is reasonable and those where, there being no such standard, the test of reasonableness is being used to make an agreement for the parties which they have not made for themselves... The alleged obligation on M&S to acquire garments from Baird is insufficiently certain to found any contractual obligation because there are no objective criteria by which the court could assess what would be reasonable either as to quantity or price. This is not a case in which, the parties having evidently sought to make a contract, the court seeks to uphold its validity by construing the terms to produce certainty. Rather it is a case in which the lack of certainty confirms the absence of any clear evidence of an intention to create legal relations.'

Scammell and Nephew Ltd v Ouston [1941] 1 AC 251, House of Lords

The claimants wished to acquire from the defendants a new van giving an old van in part exchange. They agreed the price and how much would be allowed for the old van but in their order the claimants stipulated that the balance of the purchase price should be 'on hire-purchase terms' over a period of two years. The House of Lords, allowing the defendants' appeal, held that that phrase was too vague for there to be an enforceable contract.

Viscount Simon LC: [I]t appears to me that the crucial sentence "This order is given on the understanding that the balance of purchase price can be had on hire-purchase terms over a period of two years" is so vaguely expressed that it cannot, standing by itself, be given a definite meaning – that is to say, it requires further agreement to be reached between the parties before there would be a complete consensus ad idem. If so, there was no contract and therefore no breach.

Viscount Maugham: In order to constitute a valid contract the parties must so express themselves that their meaning can be determined with a reasonable degree of certainty. It is plain that unless this can be done it would be impossible to hold that the contracting parties had the same intention; in other words the consensus ad idem would be a matter of mere conjecture. This general rule, however, applies somewhat differently in different cases. In commercial documents connected with dealings in a trade with which the parties are perfectly familiar the court is very willing, if satisfied that the parties thought that they made a binding contract, to imply terms and in particular terms as to the method of carrying out the contract which it would be impossible to supply in other kinds of contract: see *Hillas & Co. v. Arcos, Ld* . 147 L.T. 503, 511, 512, 514.

...

[W]hat do the words as to "hire-purchase terms" mean in the present case? They may indicate that the hire-purchase agreement was to be granted by the appellants or on the other hand by some finance company acting in collaboration with the appellants; they may contemplate that the appellants were to receive by instalments a sum of 168*l*. spread over a period of two years upon delivering the new van and receiving the old car, or, on the other hand, that the appellants were to receive from a third party a lump sum of 168*l*. and that the third party, presumably a finance company, was to receive from the respondents a larger sum than 168*l*. to include interest and profit spread over a period of two years. Moreover, nothing is said (except as to the two years period) as to the terms of the hire-purchase agreement, for instance, as to the interest payable, and as to the rights of the letter whoever he may be in the event of default by the respondents in payment of the instalments at the due dates. As regards the last matters there was no evidence to suggest that there are any well known "usual terms" in such a contract; and I think it is common knowledge that in fact many letters though by no means all of them insist on terms which the legislature regards as so unfair and unconscionable that it was recently found necessary to deal with the matter in the recent Act entitled the Hire-Purchase Act, 1938.

These, my Lords, are very serious difficulties, and when we find as we do in this curious case that the trial judge and the three Lords Justices, and even the two counsel who addressed your Lordships for the respondents, were unable to agree upon the true construction of the alleged agreement, it seems to me that it is impossible to conclude that a binding agreement has been established by the respondents.

Lord Russell of Killowen and **Lord Wright** gave concurring speeches.

NOTES

1. This is a rare case of the courts considering themselves unable to give a meaning to particular words used by the parties. Normally vagueness in the words used (contrast incompleteness) can be cured by the courts.
2. An alternative approach to vague or meaningless words is to sever them from the rest of the contract and to hold the rest of the contract valid. This

technique was employed in *Nicolene Ltd v Simmonds* [1953] 1 QB 543, CA. But, as Denning LJ said in that case, at 551, one must be able to sever 'without impairing the sense or reasonableness of the contract as a whole'. That was not possible in *Scammell v Ouston*.

(2) Price Not Fixed

May and Butcher Ltd v R [1934] 2 KB 17n, House of Lords

The Disposals Board looked after the disposal of goods required for the First World War but left over after it. May and Butcher Ltd alleged that they had concluded a contract with the Controller of the Disposals Board under which they agreed to buy the whole of the tentage which became available to the Board to be disposed of up to 31 March 1923. The relevant terms of the alleged agreement were as follows (note that, apparently, the Disposals Board made contracts as the Disposals and Liquidation Commission):

> '(1) The Commission agrees to sell and [May and Butcher Ltd] agree to purchase the total stock of old tentage...
> (3) The price or prices to be paid, and the date or dates on which payment is to be made by the purchasers to the Commission for such old tentage shall be agreed upon from time to time between the Commission and the purchasers as the quantities of the said old tentage become available for disposal, and are offered to the purchasers by the Commission...
> (10) It is understood that all disputes with reference to or arising out of this agreement will be submitted to arbitration in accordance with the provisions of the Arbitration Act, 1889.'

The parties could not agree on the prices to be paid for the tentage and the Disposals Board therefore wrote to May and Butcher Ltd saying that it considered itself no longer bound. The House of Lords, upholding Rowlatt J and the Court of Appeal, held that there was no binding contract because the price had still to be agreed.

Lord Buckmaster: The points that arise for determination are these: Whether or not the terms of the contract were sufficiently defined to constitute a legal binding contract between the parties. The Crown says that the price was never agreed. The [appellants] say first, that if it was not agreed, it would be a reasonable price. Secondly, they say that even if the price was not agreed, the arbitration clause in the contract was intended to cover this very question of price, and that consequently the reasonableness of the price was referred to arbitration under the contract. ...

My Lords, those being the contentions, it is obvious that the whole matter depends upon the construction of the actual words of the bargain itself. [*He looked at the terms of the alleged contract and continued:*]

What resulted was this: it was impossible to agree the prices, and unless the appellants are in a position to establish either that this failure to agree resulted out of a definite agreement to buy at a reasonable price, or that the price had become subject to arbitration, it is plain on the first two points which have been mentioned that this appeal must fail.

In my opinion there never was a concluded contract between the parties. It has long been a well recognized principle of contract law that an agreement between two parties to enter into an agreement in which some critical part of the contract matter is left undetermined is no contract at all. It is of course perfectly possible for two people to contract that they will sign a document which contains all the relevant terms, but it is not open to them to agree that they will in the future agree upon a matter which is vital to the arrangement between them and has not yet been determined. It has been argued that as the fixing of the price has broken down, a reasonable price must be assumed. That depends in part upon the terms of the Sale of Goods Act, which no doubt reproduces, and is known to have reproduced, the old law upon the matter. That provides in s. 8 that "the price in a contract of sale may be fixed by the contract, or may be left to be fixed in manner thereby agreed, or may be determined by the course of dealing between the parties. Where the price is not determined in accordance with the foregoing provisions the buyer must pay a reasonable price"; while, if the agreement is to sell goods on the terms that the price is to be fixed by the valuation of a third party, and such third party cannot or does not make such valuation, s. 9 says that the agreement is avoided. I find myself quite unable to understand the distinction between an agreement to permit the price to be fixed by a third party and an agreement to permit the price to be fixed in the future by the two parties to the contract themselves. In principle it appears to me that they are one and the same thing. ...

The next question is about the arbitration clause, and there I entirely agree with the majority of the Court of Appeal and also with Rowlatt J. The clause refers "disputes with reference to or arising out of this agreement" to arbitration, but until the price has been fixed, the agreement is not there.

The arbitration clause relates to the settlement of whatever may happen when the agreement has been completed and the parties are regularly bound. There is nothing in the arbitration clause to enable a contract to be made which in fact the original bargain has left quite open.

Viscount Dunedin: I am of the same opinion. This case arises upon a question of sale, but in my view the principles which we are applying are not confined to sale, but are the general principles of the law of contract. To be a good contract there must be a concluded bargain, and a concluded contract is one which settles everything that is necessary to be settled and leaves nothing to be settled by agreement between the parties. Of course it may leave something which still has to be determined, but then that determination must be a determination which does not depend upon the agreement between the parties. In the [Scottish] system of law in which I was brought up, that was expressed by one of those brocards of which perhaps we have been too fond, but which often express very neatly what is wanted: "Certum est quod certum reddi potest." ["If something is capable of being made certain, it should be treated as certain."] Therefore, you may very well agree that a certain part of the contract of sale, such as price, may be settled by some one else. As a matter of the general law of contract all the essentials have to be settled. What are the essentials may vary according to the particular contract under consideration. We are here dealing with sale, and undoubtedly price is one of the essentials of sale, and if it is left still to be agreed between the parties, then there is no contract. It may be left to the determination of a certain person, and if it was so left and that person either would not or could not act, there would be no contract because the price was to be settled in a certain way and it has become impossible to settle it in that way, and therefore there is no settlement. No doubt as to goods, the Sale of Goods Act, 1893, says that if the price is not mentioned and settled in the contract it is to be a reasonable price. The simple answer in this case is that the Sale of Goods Act provides for silence on the point and here there is no silence, because there is a provision that the two parties are to agree. As long as you have something certain it does not matter. For instance, with regard to price it is a perfectly good contract to say that the price is to be settled by the buyer. I have not had time, or perhaps I have not been industrious enough, to look through all the books in England to see if there is such a case; but there was such a case in Scotland in 1760, where it was decided that a sale of a landed estate was perfectly good, the price being left to be settled by the buyer himself. I have only expressed in other words what has already been said by my noble friend on the Woolsack. Here there was clearly no contract. There would have been a perfectly good settlement of price if the contract had said that it was to be settled by arbitration by a certain man, or it might have been quite good if it was said that it was to be settled by arbitration under the Arbitration Act so as to bring in a material plan by which a certain person could be put in action. The question then arises, has anything of that sort been done? I think clearly not. The general arbitration clause is one in very common form as to disputes arising out of the arrangements. In no proper meaning of the word can this be described as a dispute arising between the parties; it is a failure to agree, which is a very different thing from a dispute.

Lord Warrington of Clyffe delivered a concurring speech.

NOTES

1. The case was decided in 1929 but not reported until 1934. It is a highly controversial decision and appears to show a greater conservatism in overcoming uncertainty than was shown by their Lordships in the later case of *Hillas v Arcos* (see above, 59). The quantity and type of goods were certain and one would have thought that, as the parties had failed to agree a price, a reasonable price would have been payable and that that price could have been fixed by the courts (or by an arbitrator).

2. That criticism derives direct support from the Court of Appeal's decision in *Foley v Classique Coaches* [1934] 2 KB 1. The claimant agreed to sell some land to the defendants for a coach station on the terms that the defendants bought all their petrol from him. The petrol agreement provided that it was to be supplied 'at a price to be agreed by the parties in writing from time to time' and that any dispute on the agreement should be submitted to arbitration. The land was conveyed and the petrol agreement was acted on for three years. The defendants then repudiated the agreement. The claimant successfully brought an action for breach of contract. The Court of Appeal, in deciding that the contract was sufficiently certain, rather unconvincingly distinguished *May and Butcher Ltd v R* as dealing with the construction of a different contract. Scrutton LJ said, at 10, 'In the present case, the parties obviously believed they had a contract and they acted for three years as if they had; they had an arbitration clause which relates to the subject-matter of the agreement as to the supply of petrol, and it seems to me that this arbitration clause applies to any failure to agree as to the price. By analogy to the case of a tied house there is to be implied in this contract a term that the petrol shall be supplied at a reasonable price and shall be of reasonable quality.' And in Greer LJ's words, at 11, '[I]n order to give effect to what both parties intended the Court is justified in implying that in the absence of an agreement as to price a reasonable price must be paid, and if the parties cannot agree as to what is a reasonable price then arbitration must take place.'

3. For recent (and forceful) criticism of *May and Butcher Ltd v R*, see *Fletcher Challenge Energy Ltd v Electricity Corporation of New Zealand Ltd* [2002] 2 NZLR 433, 466–447 (New Zealand Court of Appeal).

Sudbrook Trading Estate Ltd v Eggleton
[1983] 1 AC 444, House of Lords

Under each of four leases, lessees were given an option to purchase the reversion 'at such price, not being less than twelve thousand pounds as may be agreed upon by two Valuers one to be nominated by the Lessor and the other by Lessees or in default of such agreement by an Umpire appointed by the said Valuers…'. When the lessees sought to exercise the options, the lessor claimed that the option clauses were void for uncertainty and refused to appoint a valuer. The House of Lords, in reversing the Court of Appeal, held that the contracts were sufficiently certain as the court could itself ascertain the fair value of the reversions by ordering an inquiry. As the options had been exercised by the lessees, specific performance of the contract of sale was ordered against the lessor.

Lord Diplock: What Templeman L.J. [in the Court of Appeal in this case] refers to in his summary of the effect of the authorities as the one central proposition…viz. until the price has been fixed by the method provided for in the contract "there is no complete agreement to enforce," involved a fundamental fallacy. A contract is complete as a contract as soon as the parties have reached agreement as to what each of its essential terms is or can with certainty be ascertained: for it is an elementary principle of the English law of contract id certum est quod certum reddi potest ["if something is capable of being made certain, it should be treated as certain"].

…

As regards the assessment of the fair and reasonable price to be paid by the lessees upon specific performance of the contract to convey, the lessors have clearly waived their contractual right to have that price assessed by the machinery for which the option clause provides. The lessees in their turn are content also to waive their corresponding right to use that machinery. This will leave it to the court itself to determine upon the expert evidence of valuers what is the fair and reasonable price. In these circumstances I do not find it necessary to decide whether in the absence of such waiver by the lessees the court would have jurisdiction to compel the lessors to appoint a valuer; but it must not be taken that I am accepting that it would not.

…

[W]hen honest parties to a contract for the sale of land or an option to enter into such a contract have in the past inserted provisions for the ascertainment of the purchase price similar to the italicised words included in the option clause in the instant case they must have intended to create legal rights to have those provisions acted on by both parties and not flouted by either party at his own sweet will; otherwise there is no point in inserting them at all. …

For these reasons and those given by Lord Fraser I would allow the appeal…

Lord Fraser of Tullybelton: In these proceedings the appellants seek a declaration that the options are valid, that they have been validly and effectively exercised, and that the contracts constituted by the exercise ought to be specifically performed. As regards the mode of performance, the main argument for the appellants is that the court should order such inquiries as are necessary to ascertain the value of each of the properties. Lawson J. decided the question of principle in favour of the appellants, but his decision was reversed by the Court of Appeal which held that the options were unenforceable. Templeman L.J., who delivered the judgment of the Court of Appeal, made a full review of the English authorities and the conclusion which he drew from them was, in my opinion inevitably, adverse to the appellants' contentions. The fundamental proposition upon which he relied was, in his own words, ante, p. 460A-B:

"that where the agreement on the face of it is incomplete until something else has been done, whether by further agreement between the parties or by the decision of an arbitrator or valuer, the court is powerless, because there is no complete agreement to enforce: ..."

I agree that that is the effect of the earlier decisions but, with the greatest respect, I am of opinion that it is wrong. It appears to me that, on the exercise of the option, the necessary preconditions having been satisfied, as they were in this case, a complete contract of sale and purchase of the freehold reversion was constituted. The price, which was of course an essential term of the contract, was for reasons which I shall explain, capable of being ascertained and was therefore certain. Certum est quod certum reddi potest: see *May and Butcher Ltd. v. The King (Note)* [1934] 2 K.B. 17, 21, *per* Viscount Dunedin.

The courts have applied clauses such as those in the present case in a strictly literal way and have treated them as making the completion of a contract of sale conditional upon agreement between the valuers either on the value of the property, or failing that, on the choice of an umpire. They have further laid down the principle that where parties have agreed on a particular method of ascertaining the price, and that method has for any reason proved ineffective, the court will neither grant an order for specific performance to compel parties to operate the agreed machinery, nor substitute its own machinery to ascertain the price, because either of these clauses would be to impose upon parties an agreement that they had not made.

...

While that is the general principle it is equally well established that, where parties have agreed to sell "at a fair valuation" or "at a reasonable price" or according to some similar formula, without specifying any machinery for ascertaining the price, the position is different. ... The court will order such inquiries as may be necessary to ascertain the fair price: see *Talbot v. Talbot* [1968] Ch. 1.

I recognise the logic of the reasoning which has led to the courts' refusing to substitute their own machinery for the machinery which has been agreed upon by the parties. But the result to which it leads is so remote from that which parties normally intend and expect, and is so inconvenient in practice, that there must in my opinion be some defect in the reasoning. I think the defect lies in construing the provisions for the mode of ascertaining the value as an essential part of the agreement. That may have been perfectly true early in the 19th century, when the valuer's profession and the rules of valuation were less well established than they are now. But at the present day these provisions are only subsidiary to the main purpose of the agreement which is for sale and purchase of the property at a fair or reasonable value. In the ordinary case parties do not make any substantial distinction between an agreement to sell at a fair value, without specifying the mode of ascertaining the value, and an agreement to sell at a value to be ascertained by valuers appointed in the way provided in these leases. The true distinction is between those cases where the mode of ascertaining the price is an essential term of the contract, and those cases where the mode of ascertainment, though indicated in the contract, is subsidiary and non-essential: see *Fry on Specific Performance*, 6th ed. (1921), pp. 167, 169, paragraphs 360, 364. The present case falls, in my opinion, into the latter category. Accordingly when the option was exercised there was constituted a complete contract for sale, and the clause should be construed as meaning that the price was to be a fair price. On the other hand where an agreement is made to sell at a price to be fixed by a valuer who is named, or who, by reason of holding some office such as auditor of a company whose shares are to be valued, will have special knowledge relevant to the question of value, the prescribed mode may well be regarded as essential. Where, as here, the machinery consists of valuers and an umpire, none of whom is named or identified, it is in my opinion unrealistic to regard it as an essential term. If it breaks down there is no reason why the court should not substitute other machinery to carry out the main purpose of ascertaining the price in order that the agreement may be carried out.

In the present case the machinery provided for in the clause has broken down because the respondents have declined to appoint their valuer. In that sense the breakdown has been caused by their fault, in failing to implement an implied obligation to co-operate in making the machinery work. The case might be distinguishable in that respect from cases where the breakdown has occurred for some cause outside the control of either party, such as the death of an umpire, or his failure to complete the valuation by a stipulated date. But I do not rely on any such distinction. I prefer to rest my decision on the general principle that, where the machinery is not essential, if it breaks down for any reason the court will substitute its own machinery.

...

The appropriate means for the court to enforce the present agreements is in my opinion by ordering an inquiry into the fair value of the reversions. That was the method used in *Talbot v. Talbot* [1968] Ch. 1. The alternative of ordering the respondents to appoint a valuer would not be suitable because in the event of the order not being obeyed, the only sanction would be imprisonment for contempt of court which would clearly be inappropriate.

Lord Scarman and **Lord Bridge of Harwich** gave concurring speeches. **Lord Russell of Killowen** gave a dissenting speech.

NOTES AND QUESTIONS

1. This case shows that the courts will strive to overcome uncertainty as to the price by substituting their own machinery for that provided by the parties which has broken down. But there are limits to the courts' willingness to do this. Lord Fraser's view was that they will not do so where the particular machinery provided by the parties is an essential element of the agreement. It may also have been important in the *Sudbrook* case that the person seeking to escape from the agreement had been responsible for the agreed machinery failing (by refusing to appoint a valuer). For a case distinguishing *Sudbrook* because the agreed machinery (valuation by an independent accountant) was considered essential, see *Gillatt v Sky Television Ltd* [2000] 1 All ER (Comm) 46, CA.

2. Is it accurate to say that in the *Sudbrook* case the lessor had basically agreed to sell the land to the lessee (at the lessee's option) at a reasonable price and that the particular machinery agreed for fixing that reasonable price was relatively peripheral?

3. The distinction drawn in the context of a contract for the sale *of goods* by sections 8 and 9 of the Sale of Goods Act 1979—see Lord Buckmaster's speech in *May and Butcher Ltd v R* (above, 65)—is a difficult one. It is suggested that, in the light of *Sudbrook*, section 9 should be given a narrow construction so that non-valuation by a third party should render the contract void only where valuation by a particular third party is essential.

4. Are *Sudbrook v Eggleton* and *May and Butcher v R* reconcilable?

(3) Agreements to Negotiate

Walford v Miles [1992] 2 AC 128, House of Lords

Mr and Mrs Miles, the defendants, owned a company carrying on a photographic processing business. They decided to sell it. A third party (Statusguard Ltd) made an offer of £1.9 million. The Walfords, the claimants, were also keen to buy the company and entered into negotiations with the defendants. An agreement was reached in principle for the defendants to sell the company to the claimants for £2 million. The claimants promised to provide a 'comfort letter' from their bank confirming that the bank would provide the finance and, in return for receiving that letter by a certain day, the defendants agreed that they would 'terminate negotiations with any third party or consideration of any alternative with a view to concluding agreements' with the claimants. This is known as a 'lock-out agreement'. The comfort letter was duly provided as agreed and the defendants confirmed that, subject to contract, they would sell the company to the claimants. The defendants then sold the company to the third party (Statusguard Ltd). The claimants brought an action for breach of the 'lock-out agreement' but, by an amendment to the statement of claim, also alleged that there was an implied term that the defendants would 'continue to negotiate in good faith'. This is known as a 'lock-in agreement'. The House of Lords upholding the majority of the Court of Appeal (Bingham LJ dissenting) held that the lock-out agreement and the alleged lock-in agreement were unenforceable because too uncertain.

Lord Ackner:

The pleaded case

The Walfords relied upon an oral agreement, collateral to the negotiations which were proceeding, to purchase the company and the land it occupied "subject to contract." The consideration for this oral agreement was twofold – firstly the Walfords agreeing to continue the negotiations and not to withdraw and secondly, their providing the comfort letter from their bankers in the terms requested.

For this consideration it was alleged in paragraph 5 of the statement of claim as follows:

"the first defendant on behalf of himself and the second defendant would terminate negotiations with any third party or consideration of any alternative with a view to concluding an agreement with the Plaintiffs and further that even if he received a satisfactory proposal from any third party prior to the close of business on 25 March 1987, he would not deal with that third party or give further consideration to any alternative."

As thus pleaded, the agreement purported to be what is known as a "lock-out" agreement, providing the plaintiffs with an exclusive opportunity to try and come to terms with the defendants, but without expressly providing any duration for such an opportunity.

For reasons which will become apparent hereafter, it was decided to amend this paragraph by the following addition:

"It was a term of the said collateral agreement necessarily to be implied to give business efficacy thereto that, so long as they continued to desire to sell the said property and shares, the first defendant on behalf of himself and the second defendant would continue to negotiate in good faith with the plaintiff."

Thus the statement of claim alleged that, not only were the defendants "locked-out" for some unspecified time from dealing with any third party, but were "locked-in" to dealing with the plaintiffs, also for an unspecified period.

In the statement of claim it was further alleged that by reason of the wrongful repudiation by the Miles, the Walfords lost the opportunity of completing the sale and purchase of the shares and property, and that the true market value of the shares and the property was of the order of £3m. Accordingly the Walfords claimed that they lost the difference between the price which they had agreed to pay of £2m. and the true market value.

...

The validity of the agreement alleged in paragraph 5 of the statement of claim as amended

The justification for the implied term in paragraph 5 of the amended statement of claim was that in order to give the collateral agreement "business efficacy," Mr. Miles was obliged to "continue to negotiate in good faith."

...

Mr. Naughton [counsel for the Walfords] accepted that as the law now stands and has stood for approaching 20 years, an agreement to negotiate is not recognised as an enforceable contract. This was first decided in terms in *Courtney & Fairbairn Ltd. v. Tolaini Brothers (Hotels) Ltd.* [1975] 1 W.L.R. 297, where Lord Denning M.R. said, at pp. 301–302:

> "If the law does not recognise a contract to enter into a contract (when there is a fundamental term yet to be agreed) it seems to me it cannot recognise a contract to negotiate. The reason is because it is too uncertain to have any binding force...It seems to me that a contract to negotiate, like a contract to enter into a contract, is not a contract known to the law . . . I think we must apply the general principle that where there is a fundamental matter left undecided and to be the subject of negotiation, there is no contract."

In that case, at p. 302b, Lord Denning M.R. rejected as not well founded (and Lord Diplock expressly concurred with this rejection), the dictum of Lord Wright in *Hillas and Co. Ltd. v. Arcos Ltd.* (1932) 147 L.T. 503, 515:

> "There is then no bargain except to negotiate, and negotiations may be fruitless and end without any contract ensuing; yet even then, in strict theory, there is a contract (if there is good consideration) to negotiate, though in the event of repudiation by one party the damages may be nominal, unless a jury think that the opportunity to negotiate was of some appreciable value to the injured party."

...

Before your Lordships it was sought to argue that the decision in *Courtney's* case [1975] 1 W.L.R. 297 was wrong. Although the cases in the United States did not speak with one voice your Lordships' attention was drawn to the decision of the United States' Court of Appeal, Third Circuit, in *Channel Home Centers, Division of Grace Retail Corporation v. Grossman* (1986) 795 F. 2d 291 as being "the clearest example" of the American cases in the appellants' favour. That case raised the issue whether an agreement to negotiate in good faith, if supported by consideration, is an enforceable contract. I do not find the decision of any assistance. While accepting that an agreement to agree is not an enforceable contract, the Court of Appeal appears to have proceeded on the basis that an agreement to negotiate in good faith is synonymous with an agreement to use best endeavours and as the latter is enforceable, so is the former. This appears to me, with respect, to be an unsustainable proposition. The reason why an agreement to negotiate, like an agreement to agree, is unenforceable, is simply because it lacks the necessary certainty. The same does not apply to an agreement to use best endeavours. This uncertainty is demonstrated in the instant case by the provision which it is said has to be implied in the agreement for the determination of the negotiations. How can a court be expected to decide whether, *subjectively*, a proper reason existed for the termination of negotiations? The answer suggested depends upon whether the negotiations have been determined "in good faith." However the concept of a duty to carry on negotiations in good faith is inherently repugnant to the adversarial position of the parties when involved in negotiations. Each party to the negotiations is entitled to pursue his (or her) own interest, so long as he avoids making misrepresentations. To advance that interest he must be entitled, if he thinks it appropriate, to threaten to withdraw from further negotiations or to withdraw in fact, in the hope that the opposite party may seek to reopen the negotiations by offering him improved terms. Mr. Naughton, of course, accepts that the agreement upon which he relies does not contain a duty to complete the negotiations. But that still leaves the vital question – how is a vendor ever to know that he is entitled to withdraw from further negotiations? How is the court to police such an "agreement?" A duty to negotiate in good faith is as unworkable in practice as it is inherently inconsistent with the position of a negotiating party. It is here that the uncertainty lies. In my judgment, while negotiations are in existence either party is entitled to withdraw from those negotiations, at any time and for any reason. There can be thus no obligation to continue to negotiate until there is a "proper reason" to withdraw. Accordingly a bare agreement to negotiate has no legal content.

The validity of the agreement as originally pleaded in the statement of claim

Paragraph 5 of the statement of claim, as unamended, followed the terms of the oral agreement as recorded in the penultimate paragraph of the letter of 18 March. It alleged that for good consideration (and this certainly covered the provision by the plaintiffs of the "comfort letter") Mr. Miles on behalf of himself and his wife agreed that they:

> "would terminate negotiations with any third party or consideration of any alternative with a view to concluding an agreement with the plaintiffs and, further, that even if he received the satisfactory proposal from any third party prior to the close of business on 20 March 1987 he would not deal with that third party or give further consideration to any alternative."

Despite the insistence by Mr. Naughton upon the implied term pleaded in the amendment involving the obligation to negotiate, Bingham L.J., in his dissenting judgment, considered that that obligation could be severed from the agreement. He concluded that the agreement, as originally pleaded was a valid and enforceable agreement and entitled the Walfords to recover whatever damages they could establish resulted in law from its repudiation.

Before considering the basis of Bingham L.J.'s judgment, I believe it helpful to make these observations about a so-called "lock-out" agreement. There is clearly no reason in the English contract law why A, for good consideration, should not achieve an enforceable agreement whereby B agrees for a specified period of time, not to negotiate with anyone except A in relation to the sale of his property. There are often good commercial reasons why A should desire to obtain such an agreement from B. B's property, which A contemplates purchasing, may be such as to require the expenditure of not inconsiderable time and money before A is in a position to assess what he is prepared to offer for its purchase or whether he wishes to make any offer at all. A may well consider that he is not prepared to run the risk of expending such time and money unless there is a worthwhile prospect, should he desire to make an offer to purchase, of B, not only then still owning the property, but of being prepared to consider his offer. A may wish to guard against the risk that, while he is investigating the wisdom of offering to buy B's property, B may have already disposed of it or, alternatively, may be so advanced in negotiations with a third party as to be unwilling or for all practical purposes unable, to negotiate with A. But I stress that this is a negative agreement – B by agreeing not to negotiate for this fixed period with a third party, locks himself out of such negotiations. He has in no legal sense locked himself *into* negotiations with A. What A has achieved is an exclusive opportunity, for a fixed period, to try and come to terms with B, an opportunity for which he has, unless he makes his agreement under seal, to give good consideration. I therefore cannot accept Mr. Naughton's proposition, which was the essential reason for his amending paragraph 5 of the statement of claim by the addition of the implied term, that without a positive obligation on B to negotiate with A, the lock-out agreement would be futile.

The agreement alleged in paragraph 5 of the unamended statement of claim contains the essential characteristics of a basic valid lock-out agreement, save one. It does not specify for how long it is to last. Bingham L.J. sought to cure this deficiency by holding that the obligation upon Mr. Miles and his wife not to deal with other parties should continue to bind them "for such time as is reasonable in all the circumstances." He said:

> "the time would end once the parties acting in good faith had found themselves unable to come to mutually acceptable terms . . . the defendants could not . . . bring the reasonable time to an end by procuring a bogus impasse, since that would involve a breach of the duty of reasonable good faith which parties such as these must, I think, be taken to owe to each other."

However, as Bingham L.J. recognised, such a duty, if it existed, would indirectly impose upon the Miles a duty to negotiate in good faith. Such a duty, for the reasons which I have given above, cannot be imposed. That it should have been thought necessary to assert such a duty helps to explain the reason behind the amendment to paragraph 5 and the insistence of Mr. Naughton that without the implied term, the agreement, as originally pleaded, was unworkable – unworkable because there was no way of determining for how long the Miles were locked out from negotiating with any third party.

Thus even if, despite the way in which the Walfords' case was pleaded and argued, the severance favoured by Bingham L.J. was permissible, the resultant agreement suffered from the same defect (although for different reasons), as the agreement contended for in the amended statement of claim, namely that it too lacked the necessary certainty, and was thus unenforceable.

Lord Keith of Kinkel, Lord Goff of Chieveley, Lord Jauncey of Tullichettle and **Lord Browne-Wilkinson** concurred.

NOTES AND QUESTIONS

1. The House of Lords accepted that 'lock-out agreements' are sufficiently certain to be enforceable provided they are to last for a fixed period of time. Here no period of time had been specified. For an example of a lock-out agreement that was valid because its duration was fixed see *Pitt v PHH Asset Management Ltd* [1994] 1 WLR 327, CA.
2. What would be the measure of damages for breach of a lock-out agreement?
3. The controversial aspect of their Lordships' decision was its laying down that a 'lock-in agreement', framed as an obligation to negotiate in good faith, is unenforceable. Two linked reasons were given by Lord Ackner for this. The first was that the obligation is too uncertain. The second was that negotiation in good faith is inconsistent with a negotiating party's entitlement to pursue only self-interest. But if parties have agreed (expressly or impliedly) to negotiate in good faith, why cannot one say that they have agreed to limit their pursuit of self-interest?
4. Lord Ackner drew a distinction (at 71) between an agreement to negotiate in good faith and an agreement to use best endeavours. He indicated that the latter was sufficiently certain. This is puzzling as there appears to be no real difference between an agreement to negotiate in good faith and an agreement to use best (or reasonable) endeavours *to agree*. The best interpretation of what

Lord Ackner had in mind was the uncontroversial point that an agreement to use best or reasonable endeavours to achieve a result *other than the conclusion of a contract with the other party* is sufficiently certain and enforceable; eg A and B require A to use his best endeavours to make a computer system work or to obtain planning permission. For this interpretation see *Little v Courage* (1995) 70 P & CR 469, 475.

5.   Albeit not directly mentioned by Lord Ackner, is it a further objection to the enforceability of lock-in agreements that the assessment of damages would be too speculative? In *Courtney & Fairbairn Ltd v Tolani Brothers (Hotels) Ltd* [1975] 1 WLR 297, 302, Lord Denning MR said, 'No court could estimate the damages because no one can tell whether the negotiations would be successful or would fall through: or, if successful, what the result would be.'

6.   **A Berg, 'Promises to Negotiate in Good Faith' (2003) 119 *LQR* 357** convincingly argues that the *Walford* case was incorrect to treat an agreement to negotiate in good faith as too uncertain or as unworkable in practice. Negotiation can be a problem-solving consensual process and, by agreeing to negotiate in good faith, the parties have agreed to renounce purely adversarial negotiations. He points to four clear and specific obligations (eg not to take advantage of the known ignorance of the other party) that, depending on the setting, are embraced by an undertaking to negotiate in good faith.

7.   The *Principles of European Contract Law* go one step beyond giving validity to an agreement to negotiate in good faith. Rather, reflecting the civilian tradition, Art 2:301 *imposes* an obligation to negotiate in good faith (see below, 85).

(4) A Non-contractual Solution

British Steel Corporation v Cleveland Bridge and Engineering Co Ltd
[1984] 1 All ER 504, Queen's Bench Division

The claimants manufactured steel nodes and delivered them to the defendants. The work had been carried out after the claimants had received a 'letter of intent' from the defendants stating their intention to enter into a contract on their own standard terms and requesting the claimants to start work immediately. Negotiations continued while the work was carried out but the parties were unable to agree on matters such as price, progress payments and liability for loss arising from late delivery. The defendants refused to pay for the nodes on the basis that they had a counterclaim for damages for late delivery, or delivery out of sequence, which exceeded the price. The claimants sued, arguing that, while there was no concluded contract, they had a non-contractual restitutionary claim (a quantum meruit) for the value of the work done. The defendants argued that there was a concluded contract under which they were entitled to damages for late delivery. Robert Goff J held that the claimants' argument was correct: there was no contract and the claimants were entitled in the law of restitution to the reasonable value of their work.

Robert Goff J: There can be no hard and fast answer to the question whether a letter of intent will give rise to a binding agreement: everything must depend on the circumstances of the particular case. In most cases, where work is done pursuant to a request contained in a letter of intent, it will not matter whether a contract did or did not come into existence, because, if the party who has acted on the request is simply claiming payment, his claim will usually be based on a quantum meruit, and it will make no difference whether that claim is contractual or quasi-contractual. Of course, a quantum meruit claim (like the old action for money had and received and for money paid) straddles the boundaries of what we now call contract and restitution, so the mere framing of a claim as a quantum meruit claim, or a claim for a reasonable sum, does not assist in classifying the claim as contractual or quasi contractual. But where, as here, one party is seeking to claim damages for breach of contract, the question whether any contract came into existence is of crucial importance.

As a matter of analysis the contract (if any) which may come into existence following a letter of intent may take one of two forms: either there may be an ordinary executory contract, under which each party assumes reciprocal obligations to the other; or there may be what is sometimes called an "if" contract, ie a contract under which A requests B to carry out a certain performance and promises B that, if he does so, he will receive a certain performance in return, usually remuneration for his performance. The latter transaction is really no more than a standing offer which, if acted on before it lapses or is lawfully withdrawn, will result in a binding contract.

The former type of contract was held to exist by Mr Edgar Fay QC, the official Referee, in *Turriff Construction Ltd* v. *Regalia Knitting Mills Ltd* (1971) 202 EG 169; and it is the type of contract for which counsel for CBE contended in the present case. Of course, as I have already said, everything must depend on the facts of the particular case; but certainly, on the facts of the present case (and, as I imagine, on the facts of most cases), this must be a very difficult submission to maintain. It is only necessary to look at the terms of CBE's letter of intent in the present case to appreciate the difficulties. In that letter, the request to BSC to proceed immediately with the work was stated to be "pending the preparation and issuing to you of the official form of sub-contract", being a sub-contract which was plainly in a state of negoti-ation, not least on the issue of price, delivery dates, and the applicable terms and conditions. In these circumstances, it is very difficult to see how BSC, by starting work, bound themselves to any contractual performance. No doubt it was envisaged by CBE at the time they sent the letter that negotiation had reached an advanced stage, and that a formal contract would soon be signed; but, since the parties were still in a stage of negotiation, it is impossible to say with any degree of certainty what the material terms of that contract would be. I find myself quite unable to conclude that, by starting work in these circumstances, BSC bound themselves to complete the work. In the course of argument, I put to counsel for CBE the question whether BSC were free at any time, after starting work, to cease work. His submission was that they were not free to do so, even if negotiations on the terms of the formal contract broke down completely. I find this submission to be so repugnant to common sense and the commercial realities that I am unable to accept it. It is perhaps revealing that, on 4 April 1979, BSC did indeed state that they were not prepared to proceed with the contract until they had an agreed specification, a reaction which, in my judgment, reflected not only the commercial, but also the legal, realities of the situation.

I therefore reject CBE's submission that a binding executory contract came into existence in this case. There remains the question whether, by reason of BSC carrying out work pursuant to the request contained in CBE's letter of intent, there came into existence a contract by virtue of which BSC were entitled to claim reasonable remuneration; ie whether there was an "if" contract of the kind I have described. In the course of argument, I was attracted by this alter-native (really on the basis that, not only was it analytically possible, but also that it could provide a vehicle for certain contractual obligations of BSC concerning their performance, eg implied terms as to the quality of goods supplied by them). But the more I have considered the case, the less attractive I have found this alternative. The real difficulty is to be found in the factual matrix of the transaction, and in particular the fact that the work was being done pending a formal sub-contract the terms of which were still in a state of negotiation. It is, of course, a notorious fact that, when a contract is made for the supply of goods on a scale and in circumstances such as the present, it will in all probability be subject to standard terms, usually the standard terms of the supplier. Such standard terms will frequently legislate, not only for the liability of the seller for defects, but also for the damages (if any) for which the seller will be liable in the event not only of defects in the goods but also of later delivery. It is a commonplace that a seller of goods may exclude liability for consequential loss, and may agree liquidated damages for delay. In the present case, an unresolved dispute broke out between the parties on the question whether CBS's or BSC's standard terms were to apply, the former providing no limit to the seller's liability for delay and the latter excluding such liability altogether. Accordingly, when, in a case such as the present, the parties are still in a state of negotiation, it is impossible to predicate what liability (if any) will be assumed by the seller for, eg, defective goods or late delivery, if a formal contract should be entered into. In these circumstances, if the buyer asks the seller to commence work "pending" the parties entering into a formal contract, it is difficult to infer from the buyer acting on that request that he is assuming any responsibility for his performance, except such responsibility as will rest on him under the terms of the contract which both parties confidently anticipate they will shortly enter into. It would be an extraordinary result if, by acting on such a request in such circumstances, the buyer were to assume an unlimited liability for his contractual perfor-mance, when he would never assume such liability under any contract which he entered into.

For these reasons, I reject the solution of the "if" contract. In my judgment, the true analysis of the situation is simply this. Both parties confidently expected a formal contract to eventuate. In these circumstances, to expedite performance under that anticipated contract, one requested the other to commence the contract work, and the other complied with that request. If thereafter, as anticipated, a contract was entered into, the work done as requested will be treated as having been performed under that contract; if, contrary to their expectation, no contract was entered into, then the performance of the work is not referable to any contract the terms of which can be ascertained, and the law simply imposes an obligation on the party who made the request, such an obligation sounding in quasi contract or, as we now say, in restitution.

NOTES AND QUESTIONS

1. Was Robert Goff J here laying down that letters of intent can never be contrac-tually binding?

2. A letter of intent may take a number of different forms including, eg, a 'memo-randum of understanding', a 'heads of agreement' or a 'letter of comfort'. All refer to preliminary agreements made between the negotiating parties to a contract.

3. Having decided that there was no concluded contract, because the terms were left incomplete, Robert Goff J turned to the law of restitution for a solution. In that area of law, obligations are imposed to make restitution where the defendant has been unjustly enriched at the claimant's expense. The restitutionary award— here the award of the reasonable value of the work—reverses the defendant's unjust enrichment. This case is one of numerous examples of awards of restitution in respect of work carried out under incomplete contracts. Other leading cases are *Way v Latilla* [1937] 3 All ER 759, HL, *William Lacey (Hounslow) Ltd v Davis* [1957] 1 WLR 932, and *Countrywide Communications Ltd v ICL Pathway* [2000] CLC 324, in all of which restitution was granted; and *Regalian Properties Ltd v London Docklands Development Corp* [1995] 1 WLR 212 in which restitution was

refused. For an analysis of such cases, see A Burrows, *The Law of Restitution* (2nd edn, 2002) 372–381.

4. At first sight it might appear that the restitutionary solution is defective in favouring the interests of those who have performed the work and ignoring the interests of the recipient, who may legitimately claim that, eg, the work is defective or late. That is a misleading criticism. Although the recipient may have no contractual counterclaim (for, for example, defective or late work) those considerations will be taken into account in deciding what is the reasonable value of the work: they go to reduce the value of the defendant's enrichment. As made clear later in his judgment, on the facts of this case, Robert Goff J did not think there had been any late delivery and, in any event, the amount of the quantum meruit had been agreed between the parties.

5. Another solution to the common problem of work performed under an incomplete contract might be to expand the scope of promissory estoppel (see below, 117–150) so that, contrary to the present law, it could be used as a cause of action (see below, 121–140).

2. INTENTION TO CREATE LEGAL RELATIONS

For an agreement to be legally binding, the parties must intend to create legal relations. In commercial agreements, this requirement is rarely raised once a sufficiently certain agreement has been concluded. This is because the law presumes that parties to a commercial agreement intend to create legal relations. In contrast, it is presumed that parties to a social or domestic agreement do not intend to create legal relations so that a party wishing to enforce such an agreement must rebut that presumption. In examining the cases, we will therefore distinguish between social and domestic agreements, on the one hand, and commercial agreements on the other.

Introductory reading: E McKendrick, *Contract Law* (7th edn, 2007), Ch 6.

(1) Social and Domestic Agreements

Balfour v Balfour [1919] 2 KB 571, Court of Appeal

The defendant was a civil servant stationed in Ceylon. He came to England for a period of leave with his wife, the claimant. When he had to return, his wife was advised by her doctor to stay in England temporarily because of her ill health. The husband promised to pay her £30 a month. Two years later, when the parties were still living apart, the wife sued to enforce the promise of £30 a month. Allowing the husband's appeal, the Court of Appeal held that there was no binding contract. Atkin LJ based this on there being no intention to create legal relations in agreements between spouses.

Atkin LJ: The defence to this action on the alleged contract is that the defendant, the husband, entered into no contract with his wife, and for the determination of that it is necessary to remember that there are agreements between parties which do not result in contracts within the meaning of that term in our law. The ordinary example is where two parties agree to take a walk together, or where there is an offer and an acceptance of hospitality. Nobody would suggest in ordinary circumstances that those agreements result in what we know as a contract, and one of the most usual forms of agreement which does not constitute a contract appears to me to be the arrangements which are made between husband and wife. It is quite common, and it is the natural and inevitable result of the relationship of husband and wife, that the two spouses should make arrangements between themselves – agreements such as are in dispute in this action – agreements for allowances, by which the husband agrees that he will pay to his wife a certain sum of money, per week, or per month, or per year, to cover either her own expenses or the necessary expenses of the household and of the children of the marriage, and in which the wife promises either expressly or impliedly to apply the allowance for the purpose for which it is given. To my mind those agreements, or many of them, do not result in contracts at all, and they do not result in contracts even though there may be what as between other parties would constitute consideration for the agreement. The consideration, as we know, may consist either in some right, interest, profit or benefit accruing to one party, or some forbearance, detriment, loss or responsibility given, suffered or undertaken by the other. That is a well-known definition, and it constantly happens, I think, that such arrangements made between husband and wife are arrangements in which there are mutual promises, or in which there is consideration in form within the definition that I have mentioned. Nevertheless they are not contracts, and they are not contracts because the parties did not intend that they should be attended by legal consequences. To my mind it would be of the worst possible example to hold that agreements such as this resulted in legal obligations which could be enforced in the Courts. It would mean this, that when the husband makes his wife a promise to give her an allowance of 30s. or 2l. a week, whatever he can afford to give her, for the maintenance of the household and children, and she promises so to apply it, not only could she sue him for his failure in any week to supply the allowance, but he could sue her for non-performance of the obligation, express or implied, which she had undertaken upon her part. All I can say is that the small Courts of this country would have to be multiplied one hundredfold if these arrangements were held to result in legal obligations. They are not sued upon, not because the parties are reluctant to enforce their legal rights when the agreement is broken, but because the parties, in the inception of the arrangement, never intended that they should be sued upon. Agreements such as these are outside the realm of contracts altogether. The common law does not regulate the form of agreements between spouses. Their promises are not sealed with seals and sealing wax. The consideration that really obtains for them is that natural love and affection which counts for so little in these cold Courts. The terms may be repudiated, varied or renewed as performance proceeds or as disagreements develop, and the principles of the common law as to exoneration and discharge and accord and satisfaction are such as find no place in the domestic code. The parties themselves are advocates, judges, Courts, sheriff's officer and reporter. In respect of these promises each house is a domain into which the King's writ does not seek to run, and to which his officers do not seek to be admitted. The only question in this case is whether or not this promise was of such a class or not. For the reasons given by my brethren it appears to me to be plainly established that the promise here was not intended by either party to be attended by legal consequences. I think the onus was upon the plaintiff, and the plaintiff has not established any contract. The parties were living together, the wife intending to return. The suggestion is that the husband bound himself to pay 30l. a month under all circumstances, and she bound herself to be satisfied with that sum under all circumstances, and, although she was in ill-health and alone in this country, that out of that sum she undertook to defray the whole of the medical expenses that might fall upon her, whatever might be the development of her illness, and in whatever expenses it might involve her. To my mind neither party contemplated such a result. I think that the parol evidence upon which the case turns does not establish a contract. I think that the letters do not evidence such a contract, or amplify the oral evidence which was given by the wife, which is not in dispute. For these reasons I think the judgment of the Court below was wrong and that this appeal should be allowed.

Warrington and **Duke LJJ** delivered judgments which concurred in allowing the husband's appeal (albeit that their reasoning was different from Atkin LJ's).

NOTES AND QUESTIONS

1. Of the three judgments, it is only Atkin LJ's that clearly relies on the concept of an intention to create legal relations. The other two judges stressed that there was normally no contract as between a husband and wife but did not explain precisely why, although Duke LJ, and to an extent Warrington LJ, indicated that the wife here had provided no consideration (see below, Chapter 3) for the promise.

2. Had the husband and wife already been divorced or separated at the time that the promise was made, it would appear that the presumption of there being no intention to create legal relations would have been rebutted: see *Merritt v Merritt* [1970] 1 WLR 1211, 1213, CA.

3. In focusing on the consequences for the courts and the intentions of people generally, Atkin LJ's judgment indicates that the presumption that domestic bargains are not intended to be legally binding rests on policy considerations. What precisely are those policy considerations and how convincing are they as justifications for not enforcing domestic bargains?

4. **M Freeman, 'Contracting in the Haven:** *Balfour v Balfour* **Revisited' in** *Exploring the Boundaries of Contract* **(ed R Halson, 1996) 68** argues that, from the perspective of a family lawyer, the decision in *Balfour* is now out of date. For maintenance agreements (and similar arrangements) between husbands and wives to be legally unenforceable does not reflect sound policy and is not dictated by the parties' intentions. '[The decision] no longer reflects realities nor is it in line with developments taking place in family law' (at 77).

Jones v Padavatton [1969] 1 WLR 328, Court of Appeal

A mother agreed with her daughter, a secretary in Washington DC, that if she would give up her job and read for the Bar in England the mother would provide maintenance for her. The daughter came to England and began to read for the Bar. The mother provided maintenance for her initially by monthly payments but then by providing her with a house in London which she was able to live in and also to rent out. They then quarrelled and the mother brought an action for possession of the house. The Court of Appeal held unanimously that the mother was entitled to possession. The majority arrived at that conclusion on the basis that there was no valid contract because the parties had no intention to create legal relations.

Danckwerts LJ: There is no doubt that this case is a most difficult one, but I have reached a conclusion that the present case is one of those family arrangements which depend on the good faith of the promises which are made and are not intended to be rigid, binding agreements. *Balfour v. Balfour* was a case of husband and wife, but there is no doubt that the same principles apply to dealings between other relations, such as father and son and daughter and mother. This, indeed, seems to me a compelling case. Mrs. Jones and her daughter seem to have been on very good terms before 1967. The mother was arranging for a career for her daughter which she hoped would lead to success. This involved a visit to England in conditions which could not be wholly foreseen. What was required was an arrangement which was to be financed by the mother, and was such as would be adaptable to circumstances, as it in fact was. The operation about the house was, in my view, not a completely fresh arrangement, but an adaptation of the mother's financial assistance to her daughter due to the situation which was found to exist in England. It was not a stiff contractual operation any more than the original arrangement.

Fenton Atkinson LJ: The problem is, in my view, a difficult one, because though one would tend to regard a promise by a parent to pay an allowance to a child during a course of study as no more than a family arrangement, on the facts of this case this particular daughter undoubtedly gave up a great deal on the strength of the mother's promise.

In my judgment it is the subsequent history which gives the best guide to the parties' intention at the material time. There are three matters which seem to me important: (1) The daughter thought that her mother was promising her 200 United States dollars, or £70 a month, which she regarded as the minimum necessary for her support. The mother promised 200 dollars, but she had in mind 200 British West Indian dollars, £42 a month, and that was what she in fact paid from November 1962 to December 1964. Those payments were accepted by the daughter without any sort of suggestion at any stage that the mother had legally contracted for the larger sum. (2) When the arrangements for the purchase of No. 181, Highbury Quadrant were being discussed, and the new arrangement was made for maintenance to come out of the rents, many material matters were left open: how much accommodation was the daughter to occupy; how much money was she to have out of the rents; if the rents fell below expectation, was the mother to make up the difference below £42, or £42 less the sum saved by the daughter in rent; for how long was the arrangement to continue, and so on. The whole arrangement was, in my view, far too vague and uncertain to be itself enforceable as a contract; but at no stage did the daughter bring into the discussions her alleged legal right to £42 per month until her studies were completed, and how that right was to be affected by the new arrangement. (3) It is perhaps not without relevance to look at the daughter's evidence in cross-examination. She was asked about the occasion when her mother visited the house, and she, knowing perfectly well that her mother was there, refused for some hours to open the door. She said: "I didn't open the door because a normal mother doesn't sue her daughter in court. Anybody with normal feelings would feel upset by what was happening." Those answers and the daughter's conduct on that occasion provide a strong indication that she had never for a moment contemplated the possibility of her mother or herself going to court to enforce legal obligations, and that she felt it quite intolerable that a purely family arrangement should become the subject of proceedings in a court of law.

At the time when the first arrangement was made, mother and daughter were, and always had been, to use the daughter's own words, "very close." I am satisfied that neither party at that time intended to enter into a legally binding contract, either then or later when the house was bought. The daughter was prepared to trust her mother to honour her promise of support, just as the mother no doubt trusted her daughter to study for the Bar with diligence, and to get through her examinations as early as she could.

It follows that in my view the mother's claim for possession succeeds, and her appeal should be allowed.

NOTES AND QUESTIONS

1.   Salmon LJ arrived at the same result by reasoning that (i) this was an exceptional case where the presumption against an intention to create legal relations

in a domestic agreement had been rebutted; but that (ii) that agreement was to run for a reasonable time only and that time had now run out; and (iii) there had been no intention to create legal relations in relation to the agreement to provide accommodation.

2.   What is the difference between the requirements of an intention to create legal relations and consideration (see 87, below)? What was the consideration for the mother's promise to pay maintenance? If A agrees with B to go out for dinner, A to pay for the food and B the drinks, is there a valid contract?

(2) Commercial Agreements

Esso Petroleum Co Ltd v Commissioners of Customs and Excise
[1976] 1 WLR 1, House of Lords

Esso had a sales promotion whereby it offered a World Cup coin (with a likeness on it of one of the England players in the 1970 World Cup squad) to every motorist who bought four gallons of Esso petrol. The Customs and Excise Commissioners argued that the coins were chargeable to purchase tax on the basis that they had been 'produced in quantity for general sale'. Their Lordships rejected that argument by a majority of 4–1 (Lord Fraser of Tullybelton dissenting) on the ground that it was the petrol and not the coins that were being 'sold'. But their Lordships also considered whether the coins were being given under a contractual obligation or as a mere gift and, in answering that, their Lordships held, by a three–two majority, that there was an intention to create legal relations and hence a valid contract.

Lord Simon of Glaisdale: I am…not prepared to accept that the promotion material put out by Esso was not envisaged by them as creating legal relations between the garage proprietors who adopted it and the motorists who yielded to its blandishments. In the first place, Esso and the garage proprietors put the material out for their commercial advantage, and designed it to attract the custom of motorists. The whole transaction took place in a setting of business relations. In the second place, it seems to me in general undesirable to allow a commercial promoter to claim that what he has done is a mere puff, not intended to create legal relations (cf. *Carlill v. Carbolic Smoke Ball Co.* [1893] 1 Q.B. 256). The coins may have been themselves of little intrinsic value; but all the evidence suggests that Esso contemplated that they would be attractive to motorists and that there would be a large commercial advantage to themselves from the scheme, an advantage to which the garage proprietors also would share. Thirdly, I think that authority supports the view that legal relations were envisaged. In *Rose and Frank Co. v. J. R. Crompton and Brothers Ltd.* [1923] 2 K.B. 261, 288 Scrutton L.J. said:

> "Now it is quite possible for parties to come to an agreement by accepting a proposal with the result that the agreement concluded does not give rise to legal relations. The reason of this is that the parties do not intend that their agreement shall give rise to legal relations. This intention may be implied from the subject matter of the agreement, but it may also be expressed by the parties. In social and family relations such an intention is readily implied. while in business matters the opposite result would ordinarily follow."

In the same case Atkin L.J. said, at p. 293:

"To create a contract there must be a common intention of the parties to enter into legal obligations, mutually communicated expressly or impliedly. Such an intention ordinarily will be inferred when parties enter into an agreement which in other respects conforms to the rules of law as to the formation of contracts. It may be negatived impliedly by the nature of the agreed promise or promises, as in the case of offer and acceptance of hospitality, or of some agreements made in the course of family life between members of a family as in *Balfour v. Balfour* [1919] 2 K.B. 571."

In *Edwards v. Skyways Ltd.* [1964] 1 W.L.R. 349, 355 Megaw J. quoted these passages and added:

"In the present case, the subject matter of the agreement is business relations, not social or domestic matters.... I accept the propositions ... that in a case of this nature the onus is on the party who asserts that no legal effect was intended, and the onus is a heavy one."

I respectfully agree. And I venture to add that it begs the question to assert that no motorist who bought petrol in consequence of seeing the promotion material prominently displayed in the garage forecourt would be likely to bring an action in the county court if he were refused a coin. He might be a suburban Hampden who was not prepared to forgo what he conceived to be his rights or to allow a tradesman to go back on his word.

Believing as I do that Esso envisaged a bargain of some sort between the garage proprietor and the motorist, I must try to analyse the transaction. The analysis that most appeals to me is one of the ways in which Lord Denning M.R. considered the case [1975] 1 W.L.R. 406, 409B–D, namely a collateral contract of the sort described by Lord Moulton in *Heilbut, Symons & Co. v. Buckleton* [1913] A.C. 30, 47:

"... there may be a contract the consideration for which is the making of some other contract. 'If you will make such and such a contract I will give you £100,' is in every sense of the word a complete legal contract. It is collateral to the main contract, ..."

So here. The law happily matches the reality. The garage proprietor is saying, "If you will buy four gallons of my petrol, I will give you one of these coins." None of the reasons which have caused the law to consider advertising or display material as an invitation to treat rather than an offer applies here. What the garage proprietor says by his placards is in fact and in law an offer of consideration to the motorist to enter into a contract of sale of petrol. Of course, not every motorist will notice the placard, but nor will every potential offeree of many offers be necessarily conscious that they have been made. However, the motorist who does notice the placard, and in reliance thereon drives in and orders the petrol, is in law doing two things at the same time. First, he is accepting the offer of a coin if he buys four gallons of petrol. Secondly, he is himself offering to buy four gallons of petrol: this offer is accepted by the filling of his tank.

Has there then been a sale of the coins, so that they can be said to have been "produced in quantity for general sale" within Group 25 of Schedule 1 to the Purchase Tax Act 1963? I think that the main emphasis here is on "quantity" and "general."... The primary sense of "sale" in this context is its primary meaning in ordinary legal usage. This is expressed in section 1 of the Sale of Goods Act 1893 (which codified the common law), namely "a contract whereby the seller transfers or agrees to transfer the property in goods to the buyer for a money consideration, called the price." Here the coins were not transferred for a money consideration. They were transferred in consideration of the motorist entering into a contract for the sale of petrol. The coins were therefore not produced for sale, and do not fall within the Schedule. They are exempt from purchase tax.

Viscount Dilhorne (dissenting on the issue of an intention to create legal relations): True it is that the respondents are engaged in business. True it is that they hope to promote the sale of their petrol, but it does not seem to me necessarily to follow or to be inferred that there was any intention on their part that their dealers should enter into legally binding contracts with regard to the coins; or any intention on the part of the dealers to enter into any such contract or any intention on the part of the purchaser of four gallons of petrol to do so.

If in this case on the facts of this case the conclusion is reached that there was any such intention on the part of the customer, of the dealer and of the respondents, it would seem to exclude the possibility of any dealer ever making a free gift to any of his customers however negligible its value to promote his sales.

If what was described as being a gift, which would be given if something was purchased, was something of value to the purchaser, then it could readily be inferred that there was a common intention to enter into legal relations. But here, whatever the cost of production, it is clear that the coins were of little intrinsic value.

...

The gift of a coin might lead to a motorist returning to the garage to obtain another one, but I think the facts in this case negative any contractual intention on his part and on the part of the dealer as to the coin and suffice to rebut any presumption there may be to the contrary.

Lord Wilberforce agreed with Lord Simon of Glaisdale; and **Lord Fraser of Tullybelton** delivered a speech agreeing that the parties intended to create legal relations. **Lord Russell of Killowen** delivered a speech dissenting on the issue of an intention to create legal relations.

NOTES AND QUESTIONS

1. Although the majority decided that there was an intention to create legal relations, this is a rare example of where, in relation to a *concluded* commercial agreement, there was a real question as to whether the parties intended to create legal relations. The presumption that legal relations are intended in concluded commercial agreements is a strong one: see the citation above, 82, of Megaw J's judgment in *Edwards v Skyways Ltd* [1964] 1 WLR 349. Rare examples of where the presumption is rebutted are: (i) Where the parties have expressly said that the agreement shall not be legally binding. This was held to be the position in *Rose and Frank Co v JR Crompton and Brothers Ltd* [1925] AC 445, HL where the parties had inserted an 'honour clause'. (ii) Collective agreements between trade unions and employers. By the Trade Union and Labour Relations (Consolidation) Act 1992, s 179:

    '(1) A collective agreement shall be conclusively presumed not to have been intended by the parties to be a legally enforceable contract unless the agreement –

    (a) is in writing and

    (b) contains a provision which (however expressed) states that the parties intend that the agreement shall be a legally enforceable contract.

    (2) A collective agreement which does satisfy those conditions shall be conclusively presumed to have been intended by the parties to be a legally enforceable contract.'

    What is the policy explanation for section 179?

2. The role of 'intention to create legal relations' in deciding whether 'letters of comfort' (which are commonplace in commercial banking transactions) are contractually binding was raised but not clearly answered in *Kleinwort Benson Ltd v Malaysia Mining Corporation Bhd* [1989] 1 WLR 379, CA. In that case, a

parent company had refused to give a guarantee to a bank in relation to a subsidiary company's loan from the bank and had instead given a 'letter of comfort.' That stated, 'It is our policy that [the subsidiary] is at all times in a position to meet its liabilities.' The Court of Appeal reasoned that Hirst J had been incorrect to regard the issue as being whether there was an intention to create legal relations by the comfort letter. Rather it was a matter of construing the letter of comfort to see whether the parent company had made a promise as to the future that had been broken (it was held not to have done so) rather than a warranty of existing fact (which was accurate so that there was no breach). The implication of this approach is that the letter of comfort was seen as evincing an intention to create legal relations. If so, this is in line with the approach to 'letters of intent' generally (see above, 76) which, subject to words clearly negating contractual intention, appear to be legally binding provided sufficiently complete and certain.

Additional Reading for Chapter 2

J Beatson, *Anson's Law of Contract* (28th edn, 2002) 60–72
S Smith, *Atiyah's Introduction to the Law of Contract* (6th edn, 2005) 42–7, 98–106

B Hepple, 'Intention to Create Legal Relations' [1970] *CLJ* 122

Hepple argues that there is no place for a requirement of 'intention to create legal relations' additional to offer, acceptance and consideration. Some bargains are not legally enforceable for policy reasons—and he particularly focuses on collective agreements—but that should be recognised explicitly rather than fictitiously saying that the parties had no 'intention to create legal relations'. [Note that this article was written prior to the enactment of what is now the Trade Union and Labour Relations (Consolidation) Act 1992, section 179, which deals with the enforceability of collective agreements. See above, 83, note 1.]

S Hedley, 'Keeping Contract in its Place—*Balfour v Balfour* and the Enforceability of Informal Agreements' (1985) 5 *OJLS* 391

Hedley criticises 'intention to create legal relations' as a misleading concept which conceals the true reasons for decisions made by the courts. In reality, the concept does nothing more than ensuring that commercial promises will generally be enforced while, in the domestic context, 'contractual liability will be imposed only if the party seeking enforcement has already performed one side of the bargain and is simply seeking reciprocity' (at 393).

Principles of European Contract Law (eds O Lando and H Beale, 2000) 189–193

Article 2:301: Negotiations Contrary to Good Faith
(1) A party is free to negotiate and is not liable for failure to reach an agreement.

(2) However, a party who has negotiated or broken off negotiations contrary to good faith and fair dealing is liable for the losses caused to the other party.

(3) It is contrary to good faith and fair dealing, in particular, for a party to enter into or continue negotiations with no real intention of reaching an agreement with the other party.

[This contrasts with English law which imposes no such duty to negotiate in good faith and treats an agreement to negotiate in good faith as too uncertain to be valid: see above, 69–74.]

3

Consideration and Promissory Estoppel

1. CONSIDERATION

In general, agreements or promises are contractually binding in English law only if supported by consideration. The requirement of consideration means that each party must receive or be promised something in return for giving or promising something. Consideration is, therefore, the legal description of the element of exchange and its practical effect is to ensure that gratuitous promises are not binding whereas bargains are. So if A promises B £1000, B cannot enforce that promise because B has provided no consideration (nothing in exchange) for it.

It is traditional to *define* consideration as a benefit to the promisor or a detriment to the promisee. So in *Currie v Misa* (1875) LR 10 Ex 153, 162 Lush J stated, 'A valuable consideration, in the sense of the law, may consist either in some right, interest, profit, or benefit accruing to the one party, or some forbearance, detriment, loss, or responsibility, given, suffered, or undertaken by the other.' This definition can be misleading unless one emphasises, in line with the need for an exchange, that the detriment to the promisee must be *requested* by the promisor. So if A promises B £1000 and B, in reliance on receiving that money, buys a car, that may constitute detrimental reliance by B but B has not thereby provided any consideration for A's promise. In contrast, if A promises B £1000 in return for B's car (ie A requests the car), B's transfer of the car, or promise to transfer it, is consideration for A's promise.

In a bilateral contract which has not yet been performed (ie where the consideration is 'executory') each party's promise is consideration for the other. In a unilateral contract the promisee's performance of the requested act is the consideration for the promise; and the promise is the consideration for the performance of the requested act. (For explanation of what is meant by bilateral and unilateral contracts, see above, 3.)

The main exception to the requirement of consideration is a contract made by deed (often referred to in the past as a contract under seal because, until 1989, a deed required a seal). A gratuitous promise contained in a deed is contractually binding (although, on another view—see 3–4 above—contracts made by deed are not contracts at all but are, instead, binding *outside* the law of contract). Some gratuitous promises may also be binding under the doctrine of promissory estoppel, which is examined in the second part of this chapter. The tension between consideration and promissory estoppel is as important as it is fascinating and reflects different conceptions of the scope of the law of contract.

In examining cases on the doctrine of consideration, there are three main points (leaving aside the rule, bound up with the doctrine of privity of contract, that consideration must move from the promisee: see Chapter 10). First, the consideration need not be adequate. Secondly, past consideration does not count. Thirdly, a traditionally difficult issue, where there remains some uncertainty, is whether performance of, or a promise to perform, a pre-existing duty is good consideration. The case law on each of these three points will be examined in turn.

Before we do so, this is an appropriate place to mention briefly that requirements of form play a minor role in the modern law of contract. Assuming that the contract is not being made by deed, most contracts are valid whether made orally or in writing. There are three main exceptions to this: (i) by the Statute of Frauds 1677, section 4, contracts of guarantee must be *evidenced* in writing (in *Actionstrength Ltd v International Glass Engineering SpA* [2003] UKHL 17, [2003] 2 AC 541 the House of Lords rejected the argument that estoppel could be invoked to avoid section 4); (ii) by the Law of Property (Miscellaneous Provisions) Act 1989, section 2, a contract for the sale or other disposition of an interest in land must be made in writing: (iii) by the Consumer Credit Act 1974, regulated consumer credit agreements (eg a hire-purchase agreement made by a consumer) must be in writing, in a specific form and signed. Also, by definition, contracts on, for example, a bill of exchange or promissory note (as dealt with in the Bills of Exchange Act 1882) will be in writing.

Introductory reading: E McKendrick, *Contract Law* (7th edn, 2007) 5.2–5.21, 5.29.

(1) The Consideration Need Not Be Adequate

Chappell & Co Ltd v Nestlé Co Ltd [1960] AC 87, House of Lords

The claimants owned the copyright in a piece of music called 'Rockin' Shoes'. The defendants arranged for records of this tune to be made and offered these to the public for 1s 6d plus three wrappers from their 6d chocolate bars. Section 8 of the Copyright Act 1956 permitted the making of records for retail sale provided notice was given to the owner of the copyright and a royalty was paid of 6 ¼% of the 'ordinary retail selling price'. A notice was given stating that the ordinary retail selling price was 1s 6d. The claimants refused to accept this and sought an injunction restraining the 'sale' of the records on the ground that the defendants were infringing their copyright. In determining whether section 8 had been infringed, the question at issue was whether the chocolate bar wrappers, although of trivial value, were part of the consideration for the sale of the records. By a 3–2 majority, the House of Lords held that they were and the claimants' appeal, against the overturning of an injunction granted at first instance, was therefore allowed.

Lord Reid: I can now turn to what appears to me to be the crucial question in this case: was the 1s. 6d. an "ordinary retail selling price" within the meaning of section 8? That involves two questions, what was the nature of the contract between the Nestlé Co. and a person who sent 1s. 6d. plus 3 wrappers in acceptance of their offer, and what is meant by "ordinary retail selling price" in this context. To determine the nature of the contract one must find the intention of the parties as shown by what they said and did. The Nestlé Co.'s intention can hardly be in doubt. They were not setting out to trade in gramophone records. They were using these records to increase their sales of chocolate. Their offer was addressed to everyone. It might be accepted by a person who was already a regular buyer of their chocolate; but, much more important to them, it might be accepted by people who might become regular buyers of their chocolate if they could be induced to try it and found they liked it. The inducement was something calculated to look like a bargain, a record at a very cheap price. It is in evidence that the ordinary price for a dance record is 6s. 6d. It is true that the ordinary record gives much longer playing time than the Nestlé records and it may have other advantages. But the reader of the Nestlé offer was not in a position to know that.

It seems to me clear that the main intention of the offer was to induce people interested in this kind of music to buy (or perhaps get others to buy) chocolate which otherwise would not have been bought. It is, of course, true that some wrappers might come from the chocolate which had already been bought or from chocolate which would have been bought without the offer, but that does not seem to me to alter the case. Where there is a large number of transactions – the notice mentions 30,000 records – I do not think we should simply consider an isolated case where it would be impossible to say whether there had been a direct benefit from the acquisition of the wrappers or not. The requirement that wrappers should be sent was of great importance to the Nestlé Co.; there would have been no point in their simply offering records for 1s. 6d. each. It seems to me quite unrealistic to divorce the buying of the chocolate from the supplying of the records. It is a perfectly good contract if a person accepts an offer to supply goods if he (a) does something of value to the supplier and (b) pays money: the consideration is both (a) and (b). There may have been cases where the acquisition of the wrappers conferred no direct benefit on the Nestlé Co., but there must have been many cases where it did. I do not see why the possibility that in some cases the acquisition of the wrappers did not directly benefit the Nestlé Co. should require us to exclude from consideration the cases where it did. And even where there was no direct benefit from the acquisition of the wrappers there may have been an indirect benefit by way of advertisement.

I do not think that it matters greatly whether this kind of contract is called a sale or not. The appellants did not take the point that this transaction was not a sale. But I am bound to say that I have some doubts. If a contract under which a person is bound to do something as well as to pay money is a sale, then either the price includes the obligation as well as the money, or the consideration is the price plus the obligation. And I do not see why it should be different if he has to show that he has done something of value to the seller. It is to my mind illegitimate to argue – this is a sale, the consideration for a sale is the price, price can only include money or something which can be readily converted into an ascertainable sum of money, therefore anything like wrappers which have no money value when delivered cannot be part of the consideration.

The respondents avoid this difficulty by submitting that acquiring and delivering the wrappers was merely a condition which gave a qualification to buy and was not part of the consideration for sale. Of course, a person may limit his offer to persons qualified in a particular way, e.g., members of a club. But where the qualification is the doing of something of value to the seller, and where the qualification only suffices for one sale and must be re-acquired before another sale, I find it hard to regard the repeated acquisitions of the qualification as anything other than parts of the consideration for the sales. The purchaser of records had to send 3 wrappers for each record, so he had first to acquire them. The acquisition of wrappers by him was, at least in many cases, of direct benefit to the Nestlé Co., and required expenditure by the acquirer which he might not otherwise have incurred. To my mind the acquiring and delivering of the wrappers was certainly part of the consideration in these cases, and I see no good reason for drawing a distinction between these and other cases.

...

I am of opinion that the ... notice that the ordinary retail selling price was 1s. 6d. was invalid, that there was no ordinary retail selling price in this case and that the respondents' operations were not within the ambit of section 8. They were therefore infringements of the appellants' copyright and in my judgment this appeal should be allowed.

Lord Somervell of Harrow: My Lords, section 8 of the Copyright Act, 1956, provides for a royalty of an amount, subject to a minimum, equal to $6\frac{1}{4}$ per cent. of the ordinary retail selling price of the record. This necessarily implies, in my opinion, that a sale to be within the section must not only be retail, but one in which there is no other consideration for the transfer of property in the record but the money price. Parliament would never have based the royalty on a percentage of a money price if the section was to cover cases in which part, possibly the main part, of the consideration was to be other than money. This is in no sense a remarkable conclusion, as in most sales money is the sole consideration. It was not argued that the transaction was not a sale.

The question, then, is whether the three wrappers were part of the consideration or, as Jenkins L.J. held, a condition of making the purchase, like a ticket entitling a member to buy at a co-operative store.

I think they are part of the consideration. They are so described in the offer. "They," the wrappers, "will help you to get smash hit recordings." They are so described in the record itself – all you have to do to get such new record is to send three wrappers from Nestlé's 6d. milk chocolate bars, together with postal order for 1s. 6d.' This is not conclusive but, however described, they are, in my view, in law part of the consideration. It is said that when received the wrappers are of no value to Nestlé's. This I would have thought irrelevant. A contracting party can stipulate for what consideration he chooses. A peppercorn does not cease to be good consideration if it is established that the promisee does not like pepper and will throw away the corn. As the whole object of selling the record, if it was a sale, was to increase the sales of chocolate, it seems to me wrong not to treat the stipulated evidence of such sales as part of the consideration. For these reasons I would allow the appeal.

Viscount Simonds (dissenting): In my opinion, my Lords, the wrappers are not part of the selling price. They are admittedly themselves valueless and are thrown away and it was for that reason, no doubt, that Upjohn J. was constrained to say that their value lay in the evidence they afforded of success in an advertising campaign. That is what they are. But what, after all, does that mean? Nothing more than that someone, by no means necessarily the purchaser of the record, has in the past bought not from Nestlé's but from a retail shop three bars of chocolate and that the purchaser has thus directly or indirectly acquired the wrappers. How often he acquires them for himself, how often through another, is pure speculation. The only thing that is certain is that, if he buys bars of chocolate from a retail shop or acquires the wrappers from another who has bought them, that purchase is not, or at the lowest is not necessarily, part of the same transaction as his subsequent purchase of a record from the manufacturers.

I conclude, therefore, that the objection fails, whether it is contended that (in the words of Upjohn J.) the sale "bears no resemblance at all to the transaction to which the section ... is pointing" or that the three wrappers form part of the selling price and are incapable of valuation. Nor is there any need to take what, with respect, I think is a somewhat artificial view of a simple transaction. What can be easier than for a manufacturer to limit his sales to those members of the public who fulfil the qualification of being this or doing that? It may be assumed that the manufacturer's motive is his own advantage. It is possible that he achieves his object. But that does not mean that the sale is not a retail sale to which the section applies or that the ordinary retail selling price is not the price at which the record is ordinarily sold, in this case 1s. 6d.

Lord Tucker gave a speech concurring with Lords Reid and Somervell. **Lord Keith of Avonholm** gave a dissenting speech.

NOTES AND QUESTIONS

1. As the chocolate bar wrappers, although of trivial value, were held to be part of the consideration for Nestlé's promise, the case illustrates that the courts will not assess the adequacy of the consideration: ie it does not matter that the value of what one party receives is significantly lower than what it is giving to the other party. An older, and more straightforward, example is *Thomas v Thomas* (1842) 2 QB 851 where the court accepted that a widow's promise to pay £1 a year and to keep a cottage in good repair was good consideration for the promise to allow her to live in that cottage for the rest of her life. A 'peppercorn' rent (ie rent of a trivial amount) given by a tenant to a landlord is a further illustration of this principle.

2. It is sometimes suggested that consideration must be of some economic value even if the amount of that value does not matter. However, this may be thought to be contradicted by *Chappell v Nestlé* and by, eg, *Shadwell v Shadwell* (below, 100) and *Ward v Byham* (below, 98). See also the well-known United States case of *Hamer v Sidway* 124 NY 538 (1891) where an uncle's promise to pay $5,000 to his nephew if he gave up smoking and drinking liquor was held to be supported by consideration and enforceable. (Cf *White v Bluett* (1853) 23 LJ Ex 36 where a promise of money from a father in return for his son's ceasing to complain about his unequal treatment was held not to be supported by valid consideration. Would this decision be better justified on the basis that there was no intention to create legal relations?)

3. At the margins, it is notoriously difficult to distinguish between a conditional gratuitous promise and an agreement supported by consideration. If A promises B £1000 if B goes to collect it that would normally be a conditional gratuitous promise which would not be enforceable. But the position could be different if A wants to see B who, eg, has to travel from the other side of the world. In *Chappell v Nestlé* the House of Lords decided that the sending in of the wrappers was not merely a condition for being able to purchase the records but was part of the consideration.

4. If A promises to sell his Rolls-Royce to B for a bag of sweets, and B agrees, is there a valid contract?

5. What is the policy behind the rule that the courts do not assess the adequacy of consideration?

(2) Past Consideration Does Not Count

Eastwood v Kenyon (1840) 11 Ad & E 438, Queen's Bench

The claimant was the guardian of a girl under the age of 21. He took out a loan from a Mr Blackburn for £140 to cover some of the costs of maintaining and educating the girl and improving some cottages that had been left to her. After she had come of age and on her marriage, her husband, the defendant, promised the claimant to pay off the claimant's debt to Mr Blackburn. When he failed to do so, the claimant sued him. The action failed because no present (only past) consideration had been given by the claimant for the defendant's promise.

Lord Denman CJ: The eminent counsel who argued for the plaintiff in *Lee* v. *Muggeridge* (5 Taunt. 36), spoke of Lord Mansfield as having…maintained that all promises deliberately made ought to be held binding. I do not find this language ascribed to him by any reporter, and do not know whether we are to receive it as a traditional report, or as a deduction from what he does appear to have laid down. If the latter, the note to *Wennall* v. *Adney* (3 B. & P. 249), shews the deduction to be erroneous. If the former, Lord Tenterden and this Court declared that they could not adopt it in *Littlefield* v. *Shee* (2 B. & Ad. 811). Indeed the doctrine would annihilate the necessity for any consideration at all, inasmuch as the mere fact of giving a promise creates a moral obligation to perform it.

The enforcement of such promises by law, however plausibly reconciled by the desire to effect all conscientious engagements, might be attended with mischievous consequences to society; one of which would be the frequent preference of voluntary undertakings to claims for just debts. Suits would thereby be multiplied, and voluntary undertakings would also be multiplied, to the prejudice of real creditors. The temptations *of* executors would be much increased by the prevalence of such a doctrine, and the faithful discharge of their duty be rendered more difficult.

Taking then the promise of the defendant, as stated on this record, to have been an express promise, we find that the consideration for it was past and executed long before, and yet it is not laid to have been at the request of the defendant…and the declaration really discloses nothing but a benefit voluntarily conferred by the plaintiff and received by the defendant, with an express promise by the defendant to pay money.

…

In holding this declaration bad because it states no consideration but a past benefit not conferred at the request of the defendant, we conceive that we are justified by the old common law of England.

Lampleigh v. *Brathwait* (Hob. 105), is selected by Mr. Smith (1 Smith's Leading Cases, 67), as the leading case on this subject, which was there fully discussed, though not necessary to the decision. Hobart C.J. lays it down that "a mere voluntary courtesy will not have a consideration to uphold an assumpsit. But if that courtesy were moved by a suit or request of the party that gives the assumpsit, it will bind; for the promise, though it follows, yet it is not naked, but couples itself with the suit before, and the merits of the party procured by that suit; which is the difference"; a difference brought fully out by *Hunt* v. *Bate* (Dyer, 272…) there cited from Dyer, where a promise to indemnify the plaintiff against the consequences of having bailed the defendant's servant, which the plaintiff had done without request of the defendant, was held to be made without consideration; but a promise to pay 20*l*, to plaintiff, who had married defendant's cousin, but at defendant's special instance, was held binding.

NOTES AND QUESTIONS

1. A promise to pay for what the promisee has already done is a type of gratuitous promise. The denial that past consideration is good consideration is therefore entirely consistent with consideration marking the divide between bargains and gratuitous promises. This case is historically important in making that divide and in rejecting Lord Mansfield's view that a gratuitous promise is supported by consideration where it is deliberately made so that there is a moral obligation to perform it.

2. For other examples of past consideration being held not to be good consideration, see *Roscorla v Thomas* (1842) 3 QB 234 (oral warranty as to soundness of a horse, given after the sale of the horse, held to be unenforceable) and *Re McArdle* [1951] Ch 669 (promise to reimburse a relative for work she had already done to a house held unenforceable). Jenkins LJ, in the latter case said, at 678, '[T]he true position was that, as the work had all been done and nothing remained to be done by Mrs Marjorie McArdle at all, the consideration was a wholly past consideration, and, therefore, the beneficiaries' agreement for the repayment to her of the £488 out of the estate was nudum pactum, a promise with no consideration to support it.'

3. Should past consideration be good consideration?

4. *Lampleigh v Brathwait* (1615) Hob 105, referred to in *Eastwood v Kenyon*, shows that what looks like past consideration may, on closer examination, turn out not to be. On the facts B had killed a man. He asked L to do all he could to obtain a pardon from the King. L tried to do this and incurred expenses in so doing. B later promised him £100 for what he had done. He then broke that promise and L sued him. It was held that B was liable to pay. There was valid consideration because B had requested L to do what he had later promised to pay L for. Subsequent cases, including that to be examined next, have clarified that, in addition to there being a request, there must also be an understanding throughout that the requested act was to be remunerated.

PaO On v Lau Yiu Long [1980] AC 614, Privy Council

The claimants (the Paos) owned the shares of a company called Shing On. The defendants (the Laus) were the majority shareholders in a company called Fu Chip. In February 1973 the claimants agreed with Fu Chip to sell the shares in Shing On to Fu Chip in return for an allocation of 4.2 million shares of $1 each in Fu Chip. Under that agreement, the market value of the Fu Chip shares was deemed to be $2.50 and the claimants agreed that they would retain 60 per cent of the Fu Chip shares until after 30 April 1974. This restriction was important to the defendants who were anxious to prevent the value of their own shares being depressed by heavy selling of Fu Chip shares. The claimants, however, were concerned that if the market price of the shares fell over that time, they would lose out by being unable to sell and they therefore sought protection from the defendants against a fall in the value of the shares. The form of the protection that the claimants initially accepted was that the defendants agreed to buy back at the end of April 1974 60 per cent of the shares at $2.50 a share. The claimants became unhappy about this, as being a bad bargain for them because, in the event of share prices rising, they would still be bound to sell back to the defendants 60 per cent of the shares at $2.50 a share. The claimants therefore made clear that they would not complete the main contract with Fu Chip unless the defendants agreed—which they did in a 'guarantee agreement' dated 4 May 1973—to indemnify the claimants for any loss suffered if the shares had fallen below $2.50 at the end of April 1974. Over the year, the shares slumped in value. The claimants sought to enforce that guarantee agreement which the defendants resisted on three grounds. First, that the defendants' promise to indemnify in the guarantee agreement was not supported by consideration because the consideration was past. Secondly, that the promise to indemnify was not supported by consideration because the claimants were under a pre-existing contractual duty to a third party (Fu Chip) not to sell 60 per cent of the shares. Thirdly, that the guarantee agreement had been induced by economic duress exerted on the defendants by the claimants. The Privy Council rejected each of those arguments and held that the guarantee agreement was enforceable. We are here concerned only with the first issue, in relation to which it was held that the consideration was not past.

Lord Scarman (giving the judgment of himself, **Lord Wilberforce**, **Viscount Dilhorne**, **Lord Simon of Glaisdale** and **Lord Salmon**): The first question is whether upon its true construction the written guarantee of May 4, 1973, states a consideration sufficient in law to support the defendants' promise of indemnity against a fall in value of the Fu Chip shares. ...

Mr. Neill, counsel for the plaintiffs ... contends that the consideration stated in the agreement is not in reality a past one. It is to be noted that the consideration was not on May 4, 1973, a matter of history only. The instrument by its reference to the main agreement with Fu Chip incorporates as part of the stated consideration the plaintiffs' three promises to Fu Chip: to complete the sale of Shing On, to accept shares as the price for the sale, and not to sell 60 per cent. of the shares so accepted before April 30, 1974. Thus, on May 4, 1973, the performance of the main agreement still lay in the future. Performance of these promises was of great importance to the defendants, and it is undeniable that, as the instrument declares, the promises were made to Fu Chip at the request of the defendants. It is equally clear that the instrument also includes a promise by the plaintiffs to the defendants to fulfil their earlier promises given to Fu Chip.

The Board agrees with Mr. Neill's submission that the consideration expressly stated in the written guarantee is sufficient in law to support the defendants' promise of indemnity. An act done before the giving of a promise to make a payment or to confer some other benefit can sometimes be consideration for the promise. The act must have been done at the promisors' request: the parties must have understood that the act was to be remunerated either by a payment or the conferment of some other benefit: and payment, or the conferment of a benefit, must have been legally enforceable had it been promised in advance. All three features are present in this case. The promise given to Fu Chip under the main agreement not to sell the shares for a year was at [Lau's] request. The parties understood at the time of the main agreement that the restriction on selling must be compensated for by the benefit of a guarantee against a drop in price: and such a guarantee would be legally enforceable. The agreed cancellation of the subsidiary agreement left, as the parties knew, the plaintiffs unprotected in a respect in which at the time of the main agreement all were agreed they should be protected.

Mr. Neill's submission is based on *Lampleigh v. Brathwait* (1615) Hobart 105. ...

The modern statement of the law is in the judgment of Bowen L.J. in *In re Casey's Patents* [1892] 1 Ch. 104, 115-116; Bowen L.J. said:

"Even if it were true, as some scientific students of law believe, that a past service cannot support a future promise, you must look at the document and see if the promise cannot receive a proper effect in some other way. Now, the fact of a past service raises an implication that at the time it was rendered it was to be paid for, and, if it was a service which was to be paid for, when you get in the subsequent document a promise to pay, that promise may be treated either as an admission which evidences or as a positive bargain which fixes the amount of that reasonable remuneration on the faith of which the service was originally rendered. So that here for past services there is ample justification for the promise to give the third share."

Conferring a benefit is, of course, an equivalent to payment: see *Chitty on Contracts,* 24th ed. (1977), vol. 1, para. 154.

Mr. Leggatt, for the defendants, does not dispute the existence of the rule but challenges its application to the facts of this case. He submits that it is not a necessary inference or implication from the terms of the written guarantee that any benefit or protection was to be given to the plaintiffs for their acceptance of the restriction on selling their shares. Their Lordships agree that the mere existence or recital of a prior request is not sufficient in itself to convert what is prima facie past consideration into sufficient consideration in law to support a promise: as they have indicated, it is only the first of three necessary preconditions. As for the second of those preconditions, whether the act done at the request of the promisor raises an implication of promised remuneration or other return is simply one of the construction of the words of the contract in the circumstances of its making. Once it is recognised, as the Board considers it inevitably must be, that the expressed consideration includes a reference to the plaintiffs' promise not to sell the shares before April 30, 1974 – a promise to be performed in the future, though given in the past – it is not possible to treat the defendants' promise of indemnity as independent of the plaintiffs' antecedent promise, given at [Lau's] request, not to sell. The promise of indemnity was given because at the time of the main agreement the parties intended that [Lau] should confer upon the plaintiffs the benefit of his protection against a fall in price. When the subsidiary agreement was cancelled, all were well aware that the plaintiffs were still to have the benefit of his protection as consideration for the restriction on selling. It matters not whether the indemnity thus given be regarded as the best evidence of the benefit intended to be conferred in return for the promise not to sell, or as the positive bargain which fixes the benefit on the faith of which the promise was given – though where, as here, the subject is a written contract, the better analysis is probably that of the "positive bargain." Their Lordships, therefore, accept the submission that the contract itself states a valid consideration for the promise of indemnity.

NOTES

1. Although Lord Scarman spoke of three conditions for there being good consideration even though a promise is only given later, it is the first two that defeat the 'past consideration' objection in showing that there has been consideration throughout. (The third, that the promise must be legally enforceable, is superfluous in the sense that it is applicable to all promises). The first two conditions were here satisfied because the earlier promise made by the claimants to Fu Chip not to sell the shares was made at the defendants' request; and it was understood throughout that, in return for their promise not to sell, the claimants would be protected in some way by the defendants against a drop in share price.

2. For the parts of the judgment dealing with the other two issues, see below, 103, on pre-existing duty and consideration, and 701 on economic duress.

(3) Consideration and the Promise to Perform, or Performance of, a Pre-existing Duty

(a) Pre-existing Duty Imposed by the General Law (ie a Non-contractual Duty)

Collins v Godefroy (1831) 1 B & Ad 950, King's Bench

In a trial of a civil action brought by Godefroy against Dalton, Godefroy had Collins subpoenaed to attend to give evidence as a witness and promised to pay him a guinea a day as his fee for attending. Collins brought an action against Godefroy claiming six guineas for his six days' attendance (although he was never actually called to the witness box). The claim failed on the basis that there was no consideration for the promise because Collins was bound by the general law to attend court to give evidence when subpoenaed.

Lord Tenterden CJ: If it be a duty imposed by law upon a party regularly subpoenaed, to attend from time to time to give his evidence, then a promise to give him any remuneration for loss of time incurred in such attendance is a promise without consideration. We think that such a duty is imposed by law; and on consideration of…the cases which have been decided on this subject, we are all of opinion that a party cannot maintain an action for compensation for loss of time in attending a trial as a witness. We are aware of the practice which has prevailed in certain cases, of allowing, as costs between party and party, so much per day for the attendance of professional men; but that practice cannot alter the law. What the effect of our decision may be, is not for our consideration. We think, on principle, that an action does not lie for a compensation to a witness for loss of time in attendance under a subpoena.

NOTES AND QUESTIONS

1. Leaving the issue of consideration to one side, is there any reason of public policy why one might object to a witness of fact being remunerated by a party for attending court to give evidence?
2. Under the modern law a witness of fact, required to attend court in a civil action, is entitled to be compensated but *not* remunerated by the person calling him for expenses and loss incurred, including loss of earnings; and indeed by Civil Procedure Rule 34.7 a witness must be offered or paid, at the time of service of a witness summons, a sum to cover travelling expenses to and from court and to compensate for loss of time.

Glasbrook Brothers Ltd v Glamorgan County Council
[1925] AC 270, House of Lords

During a miners' strike, the defendants' colliery manager (Mr James) requested that police should be billeted at the colliery so as to ensure that the colliery was kept open. The police superintendent thought that adequate protection could be given by having a mobile force ready, which could move quickly to the colliery in the event of trouble. But he agreed to the billeting of 70 policemen at the colliery on the terms that the defendants (the owners of the colliery) would pay for them at certain specified rates. After the strike was over, the defendants refused to pay as agreed arguing that the police had been under a duty to provide adequate policing so that there was no consideration for the promise to pay for the billeting of the police. The majority (3–2) of the House of Lords rejected that argument holding that the police had gone beyond their public duty so that there was good consideration for the promise to pay.

Viscount Cave LC: No doubt there is an absolute and unconditional obligation binding the police authorities to take all steps which appear to them to be necessary for keeping the peace, for preventing crime, or for protecting property from criminal injury; and the public, who pay for this protection through the rates and taxes, cannot lawfully be called upon to make a further payment for that which is their right. ...But it has always been recognized that, where individuals desire that services of a special kind which, though not within the obligations of a police authority, can most effectively be rendered by them, should be performed by members of the police force, the police authorities may (to use an expression which is found in the Police Pensions Act, 1890) "lend" the services of constables for that purpose in consideration of payment. Instances are the lending of constables on the occasions of large gatherings in and outside private premises, as on the occasions of weddings, athletic or boxing contests or race meetings, and the provision of constables at large railway stations. ...There may be services rendered by the police which, although not within the scope of their absolute obligations to the public, may yet fall within their powers, and in such cases public policy does not forbid their performance

...

I conclude, therefore, that the practice of lending constables for special duty in consideration of payment is not illegal or against public policy; and I pass to the second question – namely, whether in this particular case the lending of the seventy constables to be billeted in the appellants' colliery was a legitimate application of the principle. In this connection I think it important to bear in mind exactly what it was that the learned trial judge had to decide. It was no part of his duty to say – nor did he purport to say – whether in his judgment the billeting of the seventy men at the colliery was necessary for the prevention of violence or the protection of the mines from criminal injury. The duty of determining such questions is cast by law, not upon the Courts after the event, but upon the police authorities at the time when the decision has to be taken; and a Court which attempted to review such a decision from the point of view of its wisdom or prudence would (I think) be exceeding its proper functions. The question for the Court was whether on July 9, 1921, the police authorities, acting reasonably and in good faith, considered a police garrison at the colliery necessary for the protection of life and property from violence, or, in other words, whether the decision of the chief constable in refusing special protection unless paid for was such a decision as a man in his position and with his duties could reasonably take. If in the judgment of the police authorities, formed reasonably and in good faith, the garrison was necessary for the protection of life and property, then they were not entitled to make a charge for it, for that would be to exact a payment for the performance of a duty which they clearly owed to the appellants and their servants; but if they thought the garrison a superfluity and only acceded to Mr. James' request with a view to meeting his wishes, then in my opinion they were entitled to treat the garrison duty as special duty and to charge for it. Now, upon this point the Divisional Superintendent Colonel Smith, who was a highly experienced officer, gave specific and detailed evidence; and the learned judge having seen him in the witness box and heard his examination and cross-examination accepted his evidence upon the point, as the following extract from the judgment shows: "Colonel Smith says that if the matter had been left entirely to him without this requisition, he would have protected this colliery, and he would have protected it amply, but in quite a different way, and I accept his evidence that that is so. He would not have sent this garrison there..."

...

Upon the whole matter, I have come to the conclusion that the decision of the learned trial judge and of the Court of Appeal was right...

Viscount Finlay and **Lord Shaw of Dunfermline** delivered speeches concurring with Viscount Cave LC. **Lord Carson** and **Lord Blanesburgh** dissented holding that the police were doing no more than their duty in being billeted at the colliery so that the promise to pay was not supported by consideration.

NOTES AND QUESTIONS

1.   The different approaches between the judges were in relation to whether or not the police were going beyond their public duty. It was implicit in the speeches of the majority, as well as the minority, that there would have been no consideration for the promise to pay had the police merely been performing their duty to do what was necessary to protect the public.
2.   Irrespective of the concept of consideration, what is objectionable in public policy terms in a police force charging for the performance of its duty to protect the public?

Ward v Byham [1956] 1 WLR 496, Court of Appeal

When the unmarried parents of an illegitimate child, Carol, split up, the father wrote to the mother as follows: 'I am prepared to let you have Carol and pay you up to £1 a week allowance for her providing you can prove that she will be well looked after and happy and also that she is allowed to decide for herself whether or not she wishes to come and live with you.' The child went to live with the mother and the father paid the £1 a week for seven months until the mother married. She brought an action against him for the £1 a week. The action succeeded, the Court of Appeal holding that the mother's looking after the child (albeit, in Denning LJ's view, merely performing her statutory duty) constituted good consideration for the father's promise.

Denning LJ: The mother now brings this action, claiming that the father should pay her £1 per week, even though she herself has married. The only point taken before us in answer to the claim is that it is said that there was no consideration for the promise by the father to pay £1 a week: because the mother, when she looked after the child, was only doing that which she was legally bound to do, and that is no consideration in law. ...

It is quite clear that by statute the mother of an illegitimate child is bound to maintain it: whereas the father is under no such obligation. (See section 42 of the National Assistance Act, 1948.)...

I approach the case, therefore, on the footing that the mother, in looking after the child, is only doing what she is legally bound to do. Even so, I think that there was sufficient consideration to support the promise. I have always thought that a promise to perform an existing duty, or the performance of it, should be regarded as good consideration, because it is a benefit to the person to whom it is given. Take this very case. It is as much a benefit for the father to have the child looked after by the mother as by a neighbour. If he gets the benefit for which he stipulated, he ought to honour his promise; and he ought not to avoid it by saying that the mother was herself under a duty to maintain the child.

I regard the father's promise in this case as what is sometimes called a unilateral contract, a promise in return for an act, a promise by the father to pay £1 a week in return for the mother's looking after the child. Once the mother embarked on the task of looking after the child, there was a binding contract. So long as she looked after the child, she would be entitled to £1 a week.

Morris LJ: Mr. Lane [counsel for the father] submits that there was a duty on the mother to support the child; that no affiliation proceedings were in prospect or were contemplated; and that the effect of the arrangement that followed the letter was that the father was merely agreeing to pay a bounty to the mother.

It seems to me that the terms of the letter negative those submissions...

It seems to me... that the father was saying, in effect: Irrespective of what may be the strict legal position, what I am asking is that you shall prove that Carol will be well looked after and happy, and also that you must agree that Carol is to be allowed to decide for herself whether or not she wishes to come and live with you. If those conditions were fulfilled the father was agreeable to pay. Upon those terms, which in fact became operative, the father agreed to pay £1 a week. In my judgment, there was ample consideration there to be found for his promise, which I think was binding.

Parker LJ concurred.

NOTES AND QUESTIONS

1. What was the difference in approach between Denning LJ and Morris LJ?
2. Morris LJ's approach indicates again—see above, 91—that consideration need not be of economic value.

Williams v Williams [1957] 1 WLR 148, Court of Appeal

A wife deserted her husband. A few months later the parties agreed that the husband would pay the wife £1 10s a week for their joint lives so long as the wife led a chaste life. The wife promised to use that sum for her maintenance and agreed not to pledge her husband's credit. When the husband later stopped paying, the wife sued for arrears of the promised maintenance. He argued that there was no consideration for his promise because a wife who deserts her husband is not entitled to be maintained by him or to pledge his credit. The Court of Appeal rejected that argument holding that the wife was providing consideration (albeit that, in Denning LJ's view, she was merely promising to perform her legal duty to maintain herself).

Denning LJ: [I]n promising to maintain herself whilst she was in desertion, the wife was only promising to do that which she was already bound to do. Nevertheless, a promise to perform an existing duty is, I think, sufficient consideration to support a promise, so long as there is nothing in the transaction which is contrary to the public interest. Suppose that this agreement had never been made, and the wife had made no promise to maintain herself and did not do so. She might then have sought and received public assistance or have pledged her husband's credit with tradesmen: in which case the National Assistance Board might have summoned him before the magistrates, or the tradesmen might have sued him in the county court. It is true that he would have an answer to those claims because she was in desertion, but nevertheless he would be put to all the trouble, worry and expense of defending himself against them. By paying her 30s. a week and taking this promise from her that she will maintain herself and will not pledge his credit, he has an added safeguard to protect himself from all this worry, trouble and expense. That is a benefit to him which is good consideration for his promise to pay maintenance. That was the view which appealed to the county court judge: and I must say that it appeals to me also.

There is another ground on which good consideration can be found. Although the wife was in desertion, nevertheless it must be remembered that desertion is never irrevocable. It was open to her to come back at any time. Her right to maintenance was not lost by the desertion. It was only suspended. If she made a genuine offer to return which he rejected, she would have been entitled to maintenance from him. She could apply to the magistrates or the High Court for an order in her favour. If she did so, however, whilst this agreement was in force, the 30s. would be regarded as prima facie the correct figure. It is a benefit to the husband for it to be so regarded, and that is sufficient consideration to support his promise.

I construe this agreement as a promise by the husband to pay his wife 30s. a week in consideration of her promise to maintain herself during the time she is living separate from him, whether due to her own fault or not. The wife cannot throw over the agreement and seek more maintenance from him unless new circumstances arise making it reasonable to allow her to depart from it. The husband cannot throw it over unless they resume married life together (in which case it will by inference be rescinded) or they are divorced (in which case it is a post-nuptial settlement and can be varied accordingly), or perhaps other circumstances arise not envisaged at the time of the agreement. Nothing of that kind has, however, occurred here. The husband must honour his promise.

Hodson LJ: It was urged by Mr. Edmund Davies, on behalf of the wife, that …it was a valid consideration even if the wife was in desertion, because it was some benefit to the husband to be protected from the embarrassment of invalid claims against him. For my part, I would prefer not to rest my judgment upon that, because once it is conceded that there is no basis for a claim by a wife, no consideration for giving an indemnity by the wife appears to me to emerge. But it is unnecessary to express any concluded opinion upon that matter, since I am entirely in agreement with my Lord on the other point – that this desertion by the wife did not destroy her right to be maintained but only suspended it.

Morris LJ gave a judgment concurring with Hodson LJ.

NOTE

Denning LJ's approach in this case, while not supported by the other two judges, elaborates on what he said in *Ward v Byham*. He explains why, despite the pre-existing duty, there is a benefit to the promisor (ie an added safeguard of performance of the duty); and he also inserts the qualification that there must be nothing contrary to the public interest in upholding the promise (as there was in, eg, *Collins v Godefroy*).

(b) Pre-existing Duty under a Contract with a Third Party

Shadwell v Shadwell (1860) 9 CB (NS) 159, Common Bench

An uncle wrote to his nephew as follows: 'I am glad to hear of your intended marriage with Ellen Nicholl, and, as I promised to assist you at starting, I am happy to tell you that I will pay to you one hundred and fifty pounds yearly during my life, and until your annual income derived from your profession of a Chancery barrister shall amount to six hundred guineas, of which your own admission will be the only evidence that I shall receive or require.' On the uncle's death, the nephew alleged that the uncle had not paid him in full during the uncle's lifetime and he claimed the arrears from the uncle's estate. In allowing the claim, it was held that the uncle's promise was supported by good consideration constituted by the nephew marrying Ellen Nicholl.

Erle CJ: Now do these facts shew that the promise was in consideration either of a loss to be sustained by the plaintiff or a benefit to be derived from the plaintiff to the uncle, at his, the uncle's, request? My answer is in the affirmative.

First, do these facts shew a loss sustained by the plaintiff at his uncle's request? When I answer this in the affirmative, I am aware that a man's marriage with the woman of his choice is in one sense a boon, and in that sense the reverse of a loss: yet, as between the plaintiff and the party promising to supply an income to support the marriage, it may well be also a loss. The plaintiff may have made a most material change in his position, and induced the object of his affection to do the same, and may have incurred pecuniary liabilities resulting in embarrassments which would be in every sense a loss if the income which had been promised should be withheld; and, if the promise was made in order to induce the parties to marry, the promise so made would be in legal effect a request to marry.

Secondly, do these facts shew a benefit derived from the plaintiff to the uncle, at his request? In answering again in the affirmative, I am at liberty to consider the relation in which the parties stood and the interest in the settlement of his nephew which the uncle declares. The marriage primarily affects the parties thereto; but in a secondary degree it may be an object of interest to a near relative, and in that sense a benefit to him. This benefit is also derived from the plaintiff at the uncle's request. If the promise of the annuity was intended as an inducement to the marriage, and the averment that the plaintiff, relying on the promise, married, is an averment that the promise was one inducement to the marriage, this is the consideration averred in the declaration; and it appears to me to be expressed in the letter, construed with the surrounding circumstances.

Byles J (dissenting): Marriage of the plaintiff at the testator's express request would be no doubt an ample consideration. But marriage of the plaintiff without the testator's request is no consideration to the testator.

...

Was the marriage at the testator's request? Express request there was none. Can any request be implied? The only words from which it can be contended that it is to be implied, are the words "I am glad to hear of your intended marriage with Ellen Nicholl." But it appears...that the marriage had already been agreed on, and that the testator knew it. These words, therefore, seem to me to import no more than the satisfaction of the testator at the engagement,—an accomplished fact. No request can, as it seems to me, be inferred from them. And, further, how does it appear that the testator's implied request, if it could be implied, or his promise, if that promise alone would suffice, or both together, were intended to cause the marriage or did cause it, so that the marriage can be said to have taken place at the testator's request? or, in other words, in consequence of that request?

It seems to me not only that this does not appear, but that the contrary appears; for, the plaintiff before the letter had already bound himself to marry, by placing himself not only under a moral but under a legal objection to marry; and the testator knew it.

The well-known cases which have been cited at the bar in support of the position that a promise based on the consideration of doing that which a man is already bound to do is invalid, apply in this case. And it is not necessary, in order to invalidate the consideration, that the plaintiff's prior obligation to afford that consideration should have been an obligation to the defendant. It may have been an obligation to a third person...The reason why the doing what a man is already bound to do is no consideration is, not only because such a consideration is in judgment of law of no value, but because a man can hardly he allowed to say that the prior legal obligation was not his determining motive. But, whether he can be allowed to say so or not, the plaintiff does not say so here. He does, indeed, make an attempt to meet this difficulty by alleging…that he married relying on the testator's promise: but he shrinks from alleging, that, though he had promised to marry before the testator's promise to him, nevertheless he would have broken his engagement and would not have married without the testator's promise. A man may rely on encouragements to the performance of his duty, who yet is prepared to do his duty without those encouragements. At the utmost the allegation that he relied on the testator's promise seems to me to import no more than that he believed the testator would be as good as his word.

It appears to me, for these reasons, that this letter is no more than a letter of kindness, creating no legal obligation

Keating J concurred with Erle CJ.

NOTES AND QUESTIONS

1. This case is commonly cited as authority for the proposition that a promise to perform, or performance of, what one is already bound to do under a contract with a third party is good consideration for a promise (of payment). This is because, at the time, a promise to marry was a legally binding contract. Therefore the decision of the majority, in expressly accepting that the nephew's marriage was good consideration for the uncle's promise, implicitly accepted that consideration can comprise promising or doing what one is already contractually bound to a third party to do. Byles J in his dissenting judgment expressly referred to the pre-existing duty as an additional reason for there being no consideration.

2. The main point considered by the judges, and on which they disagreed, was the factual one of whether the uncle had requested the nephew to marry Ellen Nicholl. If no such request had been made, it is clear that all the judges would have decided that the promise to pay was not supported by consideration.

3. Is this case another illustration (see above, 91) of the irrelevance of the consideration being of economic value to the promisor?

4. Although not discussed by the judges, do you consider that the parties had an intention to create legal relations?

Scotson v Pegg (1861) 6 H & N 295, Court of Exchequer

The claimants had promised, under a contract with a third party (X), to deliver a cargo of coal to the defendant. The defendant then agreed with the claimants that, 'in consideration' of the claimants delivering the coal to the defendant, the defendant would unload it at a stated rate. The defendant failed to unload the coal at the stated rate as promised and the claimants sued him. The question at issue was whether the defendant's promise to unload was supported by the consideration of the claimants delivering the coal to the defendant given that the claimants were already contractually bound (under the previous contract with X) to deliver the coal. It was held that that was good consideration so that the claim succeeded.

Martin B: [T]he ordinary rule is, that any act done whereby the contracting party receives a benefit is a good consideration for a promise by him. Here the benefit is the delivery of the coals to the defendant. It is consistent with the declaration that there may have been some dispute as to the defendant's right to have the coals, or it may be that the plaintiffs detained them for demurrage, in either case there would be good consideration that the plaintiffs, who were in possession of the coals, would allow the defendant to take them out of the ship. Then is it any answer that the plaintiffs had entered into a prior contract with other persons to deliver the coals to their order upon the same terms, and that the defendant was a stranger to that contract? In my opinion it is not. We must deal with this case as if no prior contract had been entered into. Suppose the plaintiffs had no chance of getting their money from the other persons who might perhaps have become bankrupt. The defendant gets a benefit by the delivery of the coals to him, and it is immaterial that the plaintiffs had previously contracted with third parties to deliver to their order.

Wilde B: I am also of the opinion that the plaintiffs are entitled to judgment. The plaintiffs say, that in consideration that they would deliver to the defendant a cargo of coals from their ship, the defendant promised to discharge the cargo in a certain way. The defendant, in answer, says, "You made a previous contract with other persons that they should discharge the cargo in the same way, and therefore there is no consideration for my promise." But why is there no consideration? It is said, because the plaintiffs, in delivering the coals are only performing that which they were already bound to do. But to say that there is no consideration is to say that it is not possible for one man to have an interest in the performance of a contract made by another. But if a person chooses to promise to pay a sum of money in order to induce another to perform that which he has already contracted with a third person to do, I confess I cannot see why such a promise should not be binding. Here the defendant, who was a stranger to the original contract, induced the plaintiffs to part with the cargo, which they might not otherwise have been willing to do, and the delivery of it to the defendant was a benefit to him. I accede to the proposition that if a person contracts with another to do a certain thing, he cannot make the performance of it a consideration for a new promise to the same individual. But there is no authority for the proposition that where there has been a promise to one person to do a certain thing, it is not possible to make a valid promise to another to do the same thing. Therefore, deciding this matter on principle, it is plain to my mind that the delivery of the coals to the defendant was a good consideration for his promise, although the plaintiffs had made a previous contract to deliver them to the order of other persons.

NOTE

Although the consideration here was the delivery of the coal (ie the *performance* of the pre-existing duty) Wilde B makes clear that a promise to perform one's pre-existing duty under a contract with a third party would also constitute good consideration.

PaO On v Lau Yiu Long [1980] AC 614, Privy Council

The facts have been set out above, at 93–94. After dealing with the past consideration issue, Lord Scarman turned to whether there was any difficulty—he held not—if one viewed the consideration for the defendants' (the Laus') promise to indemnify the claimants (the Paos) as being the claimants' promise to the defendants not to sell even though the claimants had already made the same promise to Fu Chip (a third party).

Lord Scarman (giving the judgment of himself, **Lord Wilberforce, Viscount Dilhorne, Lord Simon of Glaisdale** and **Lord Salmon**): The extrinsic evidence in this case shows that the consideration for the promise of indemnity, while it included the cancellation of the subsidiary agreement, was primarily the promise given by the plaintiffs to the defendants, to perform their contract with Fu Chip, which included the undertaking not to sell 60 per cent. of the shares allotted to them before April 30, 1974. Thus the real consideration for the indemnity was the promise to perform, or the performance of, the plaintiffs' pre-existing contractual obligations to Fu Chip. This promise was perfectly consistent with the consideration stated in the guarantee. Indeed, it reinforces it by imposing upon the plaintiffs an obligation now owed to the defendants to do what, at [Lau's] request, they had agreed with Fu Chip to do.

Their Lordships do not doubt that a promise to perform, or the performance of, a pre-existing contractual obligation to a third party can be valid consideration. In *New Zealand Shipping Co. Ltd. v. A. M. Satterthwaite & Co. Ltd. (The Eurymedon)* [1975] A.C. 154, 168 the rule and the reason for the rule were stated:

> "An agreement to do an act which the promisor is under an existing obligation to a third party to do, may quite well amount to valid consideration ... the promisee obtains the benefit of a direct obligation... This proposition is illustrated and supported by *Scotson v. Pegg* (1861) 6 H. & N. 295 which their Lordships consider to be good law."

Unless, therefore, the guarantee was void as having been made for an illegal consideration or voidable on the ground of economic duress, the extrinsic evidence establishes that it was supported by valid consideration.

NOTES AND QUESTIONS

1. *New Zealand Shipping v Satterthwaite, The Eurymedon* [1975] AC 154, here relied on by Lord Scarman, primarily dealt with an issue on privity and is set out below, at 477. For present purposes the relevant facts were that there was a contract between a firm of stevedores and a carrier by which the stevedores were to unload a cargo from a ship. The shipper then promised whoever was unloading that it would exclude its entitlement to sue for any damage negligently caused to the cargo in the unloading. The stevedores negligently damaged the cargo while unloading it. One question was whether the shipper was bound by its promise to exclude liability. The Privy Council held that it was so bound because the consideration for that promise by the shipper was the unloading of the cargo by the stevedores. The fact that the stevedores were already bound to unload the cargo by their contract with the carrier did not invalidate the consideration.

2. The reason given for there being good consideration, even though a claimant is only doing what it was already bound to do under a contract with a third party, was that 'the promisee obtains the benefit of a direct obligation'. For similar reasoning in the context of a pre-existing non-contractual duty, see Denning LJ's judgment in *Williams v Williams* (above, 99). Can that same reasoning be applied where the pre-existing duty is owed under a contract with the promisor?

(c) Pre-existing Duty under a Contract with the Promisor

(i) Promising to pay more for a pre-existing duty

Stilk v Myrick (1809) 2 Camp 317, King's Bench

The claimant, a seaman, had contracted with the defendant, the master of a ship, to sail to the Baltic and back at a wage of £5 per month. When the ship arrived at

Cronstadt, two of the crew deserted. As the captain could not find any substitutes he promised the rest of the crew to divide the wages of the two deserters between them if they would work the ship home short-handed. After the ship had been safely brought back to England, the claimant asked for his extra wages but this was refused by the master. The claimant's action failed because the members of the crew provided no good consideration by performing what they were already contractually bound to do.

Lord Ellenborough: I think *Harris v. Watson* was rightly decided, but I doubt whether the ground of public policy, upon which Lord Kenyon is stated to have proceeded, be the true principle on which the decision is to be supported. Here, I say, the agreement is void for want of consideration. There was no consideration for the ulterior pay promised to the mariners who remained with the ship. Before they sailed from London they had undertaken to do all that they could under all the emergencies of the voyage. They had sold all their services till the voyage should be completed. If they had been at liberty to quit the vessel at Cronstadt, the case would have been quite different; or if the captain had capriciously discharged the two men who were wanting, the others might not have been compellable to take the whole duty upon themselves, and their agreeing to do so might have been a sufficient consideration for the promise of an advance of wages. But the desertion of a part of the crew is to be considered an emergency of the voyage as much as their death, and those who remain are bound by the terms of their original contract to exert themselves to the utmost to bring the ship in safety to her destined port. Therefore, without looking to the policy of this agreement, I think it is void for want of consideration, and that the plaintiff can only recover at the rate of £5 a month.

NOTES AND QUESTIONS

1. In *Harris v Watson* (1791) Peake 102, where the master had agreed to pay extra wages to a seaman to navigate the ship out of danger, the basis for the decision that the promise to pay extra was not binding was that this would open the door to duress by seamen against masters. It would appear, therefore, that in *Stilk v Myrick* Lord Ellenborough was distancing himself from that policy explanation by instead resting his decision on the lack of consideration. Unfortunately there is some doubt about this because in a different report of *Stilk v Myrick* (1809) 6 Esp 129 it is said that Lord Ellenborough 'recognised the principle of the case of *Harris v Watson* as founded on just and proper policy'. Campbell's report (which is the one we have used above) is generally regarded as more likely to be accurate than that of Espinasse. However, in a detailed examination of the two reports and of the historical background, **P Luther 'Campbell, Espinasse and the Sailors' (1999) 19** *Legal Studies* **526** argues that to ignore Espinasse's report would be over-simplistic.

2. If in this sort of case the real justification for refusing to enforce the promise is the fear of opening the door to duress, would it be clearer to distinguish consideration and duress by saying that there is a contract supported by consideration but that it may be voidable in a particular case because of duress? On the facts of *Stilk v Myrick* there was no evidence that the seamen had made any demand, express or implied, for extra wages so that it is unlikely that duress could have been established.

3. In *Stilk v Myrick* and *Harris v Watson* the members of the crew were not promising to do more than they were already bound contractually to do: ie the contract required the crew to deal with emergencies. For a case where

consideration was found because the sailors were being required to go outside their existing contract, see *Hartley v Ponsonby* (1857) 7 El & Bl 572. See also *North Ocean Shipping v Hyundai, The Atlantic Baron,* below, 699, where the promisee, a ship-builder, was agreeing to do something more than it was already bound to do in return for the promise of an extra 10 per cent payment.

Williams v Roffey Bros & Nicholls (Contractors) Ltd
[1991] 1 QB 1, Court of Appeal

The defendants had contracted to refurbish a block of 27 flats. They sub-contracted the carpentry work to the claimant for a price of £20,000 payable in instalments. After he and his men had completed some of the work and been paid £16,200, the claimant ran into financial difficulties, not least because the price was too low. The defendants were liable to a penalty clause in the head-contract with the employer if the work was not completed on time. The defendants therefore called a meeting with the claimant and (on 9 April 1986) promised to pay him an extra £10,300 at £575 per flat to complete the work on time. The claimant and his men continued with the work and substantially completed eight flats, but then the claimant refused to continue because he had received only one further payment of £1,500. The defendants brought in other carpenters to complete the work. In the claimant's action for the money he alleged was owing, the defendants denied that they had any liability to pay any part of the extra money because their promise to pay extra was not supported by any consideration. The trial judge held that the claimant was entitled to £4,600 (consisting of 8 x £575) less certain deductions for defective and incomplete items plus a reasonable proportion of the £2,200 that was outstanding from the original contract sum. In dismissing the defendants' appeal, the Court of Appeal held that the claimant had provided good consideration for the promise of extra money even though he was merely performing his pre-existing contractual duty to the defendants.

Glidewell LJ: *Was there consideration for the defendants' promise made on 9 April 1986 to pay an additional price at the rate of £575 per completed flat?*

The judge made the following findings of fact which are relevant on this issue. (i) The subcontract price agreed was too low to enable the plaintiff to operate satisfactorily and at a profit. Mr. Cottrell, the defendants' surveyor, agreed that this was so. (ii) Mr. Roffey (managing director of the defendants) was persuaded by Mr. Cottrell that the defendants should pay a bonus to the plaintiff. The figure agreed at the meeting on 9 April 1986 was £10,300.

The judge quoted and accepted the evidence of Mr. Cottrell to the effect that a main contractor who agrees too low a price with a subcontractor is acting contrary to his own interests. He will never get the job finished without paying more money. The judge therefore concluded:

"In my view where the original subcontract price is too low, and the parties subsequently agree that additional moneys shall be paid to the subcontractor, this agreement is in the interests of both parties. This is what happened in the present case, and in my opinion the agreement of 9 April 1986 does not fail for lack of consideration."

In his address to us, Mr. Evans outlined the benefits to his clients, the defendants, which arose from their agreement to pay the additional £10,300 as: (i) seeking to ensure that the plaintiff continued work and did not stop in breach of the subcontract; (ii) avoiding the penalty for delay; and (iii) avoiding the trouble and expense of engaging other people to complete the carpentry work.

However, Mr. Evans submits that, though his clients may have derived, or hoped to derive, practical benefits from their agreement to pay the "bonus," they derived no benefit in law, since the plaintiff was promising to do no more than he was already bound to do by his subcontract, i.e., continue with the carpentry work and complete it on time. Thus there was no consideration for the agreement. Mr. Evans relies on the principle of law which, traditionally, is based on the decision in *Stilk v. Myrick* (1809) 2 Camp. 317. ...In *North Ocean Shipping Co. Ltd. v. Hyundai Construction Co. Ltd* [1979] Q.B. 705, Mocatta J. regarded the general principle of the decision in *Stilk v. Myrick*, 2 Camp. 317 as still being good law. He referred to two earlier decisions of this court, dealing with wholly different subjects, in which Denning L.J. sought to escape from the confines of the rule, but was not accompanied in his attempt by the other members of the court.

[*He then considered* Ward v Byham *and concluded:*] As I read the judgment of Morris L.J., he and Parker L.J. held that, though in maintaining the child the plaintiff was doing no more than she was obliged to do by law, nevertheless her promise that the child would be well looked after and happy was a practical benefit to the father which amounted to consideration for his promise. [*After also considering* Williams v Williams *he continued:*]

It was suggested to us in argument that, since the development of the doctrine of promissory estoppel, it may well be possible for a person to whom a promise has been made, on which he has relied, to make an additional payment for services which he is in any event bound to render under an existing contract or by operation of law, to show that the promisor is estopped from claiming that there was no consideration for his promise. However, the application of the doctrine of promissory estoppel to facts such as those of the present case has not yet been fully developed: see e.g. the judgment of Lloyd J. in *Syros Shipping Co. S.A v. Elaghill Trading Co.*[1980] 2 Lloyd's Rep. 390, 392. Moreover, this point was not argued in the court below, nor was it more than adumbrated before us. Interesting though it is, no reliance can in my view be placed on this concept in the present case.

There is, however, another legal concept of relatively recent development which is relevant, namely, that of economic duress. Clearly if a subcontractor has agreed to undertake work at a fixed price, and before he has completed the work declines to continue with it unless the contractor agrees to pay an increased price, the subcontractor may be held guilty of securing the contractor's promise by taking unfair advantage of the difficulties he will cause if he does not complete the work. In such a case an agreement to pay an increased price may well be voidable because it was entered into under duress. Thus this concept may provide another answer in law to the question of policy which has troubled the courts since before *Stilk v. Myrick*, 2 Camp. 317, and no doubt led at the date of that decision to a rigid adherence to the doctrine of consideration.

This possible application of the concept of economic duress was referred to by Lord Scarman, delivering the judgment of the Judicial Committee of the Privy Council in *Pao On v. Lau Yiu Long* [1980] A.C. 614. [*He considered that case and continued:*]

Accordingly, following the view of the majority in *Ward v. Byham* [1956] 1 W.L.R. 496 and of the whole court in *Williams v. Williams* [1957] 1 W.L.R. 148 and that of the Privy Council in *Pao On* [1980] A.C. 614 the present state of the law on this subject can be expressed in the following proposition: (i) if A has entered into a contract with B to do work for, or to supply goods or services to, B in return for payment by B; and (ii) at some stage before A has completely performed his obligations under the contract B has reason to doubt whether A will, or will be able to, complete his side of the bargain; and (iii) B thereupon promises A an additional payment in return for A's promise to perform his contractual obligations on time; and (iv) as a result of giving his promise, B obtains in practice a benefit, or obviates a disbenefit; and (v) B's promise is not given as a result of economic duress or fraud on the part of A; then (vi) the benefit to B is capable of being consideration for B's promise, so that the promise will be legally binding.

As I have said, Mr. Evans accepts that in the present case by promising to pay the extra £10,300 his client secured benefits. There is no finding, and no suggestion, that in this case the promise was given as a result of fraud or duress. If it be objected that the propositions above contravene the principle in *Stilk v. Myrick*, 2 Camp. 317, I answer that in my view they do not; they refine, and limit the application of that principle, but they leave the principle unscathed e.g. where B secures no benefit by his promise. It is not in my view surprising that a principle enunciated in relation to the rigours of seafaring life during the Napoleonic wars should be subjected during the succeeding 180 years to a process of refinement and limitation in its application in the present day. It is therefore my opinion that on his findings of fact in the present case, the judge was entitled to hold, as he did, that the defendants' promise to pay the extra £10,300 was supported by valuable consideration, and thus constituted an enforceable agreement.

Russell LJ: There is no hint in [the relevant passage in the defendants'] pleading that the defendants were subjected to any duress to make the agreement or that their promise to pay the extra £10,300 lacked consideration. As the judge found, the plaintiff must have continued work in the belief that he would be paid £575 as he finished each of the 18 uncompleted flats (although the arithmetic is not precisely accurate). For their part the defendants recorded the new terms in their ledger. Can the defendants now escape liability on the ground that the plaintiff undertook to do no more than he had originally contracted to do although, quite clearly, the defendants, on 9 April 1986, were prepared to make the payment and only declined to do so at a later stage. It would certainly be unconscionable if this were to be their legal entitlement.

The submissions advanced on both sides before this court ranged over a wide field. They went far beyond the pleadings, and indeed it is worth noticing that the absence of consideration was never pleaded, although argued before the assistant recorder, Mr. Rupert Jackson Q.C. Speaking for myself – and I notice it is touched upon in the judgment of Glidewell L.J. – I would have welcomed the development of argument, if it could have been properly raised in this court, on the basis that there was here an estoppel and that the defendants, in the circumstances prevailing, were precluded from raising the defence that their undertaking to pay the extra £10,300 was not binding. For example, in *Amalgamated Investment & Property Co. Ltd. v. Texas Commerce International Bank Ltd.* [1982] Q.B. 84 Robert Goff J. said, at p. 105: "it is in my judgment not of itself a bar to an estoppel that its effect may be to enable a party to enforce a cause of action which, without the estoppel, would not exist. It is sometimes said that an estoppel cannot create a cause of action, or that an estoppel can only act as a shield, not as a sword. In a sense this is true – in the sense that estoppel is not, as a contract is, a source of legal obligation. But as Lord Denning M.R. pointed out in *Crabb v. Arun District Council* [1976] Ch. 179, 187, an estoppel may have the effect that a party can enforce a cause of action which, without the estoppel, he would not be able to do."

[*He then cited from the judgments of Lord Denning MR and Brandon LJ in the Court of Appeal in the* Amalgamated Investment *case, see below, 128, and continued:*]

These citations demonstrate that whilst consideration remains a fundamental requirement before a contract not under seal can be enforced, the policy of the law in its search to do justice between the parties has developed considerably since the early 19th century when *Stilk v. Myrick*, 2 Camp. 317 was decided by Lord Ellenborough C.J. In the late 20th century I do not believe that the rigid approach to the concept of consideration to be found in *Stilk v. Myrick* is either necessary or desirable. Consideration there must still be but, in my judgment, the courts nowadays should be more ready to find its existence so as to reflect the intention of the parties to the contract where the bargaining powers are not unequal and where the finding of consideration reflect the true intention of the parties.

What was the true intention of the parties when they arrived at the agreement pleaded by the defendants …? The plaintiff had got into financial difficulties. The defendants, through their employee Mr. Cottrell, recognised the price that had been agreed originally with the plaintiff was less than what Mr. Cottrell himself regarded as a reasonable price. There was a desire on Mr. Cottrell's part to retain the services of the plaintiff so that the work could be completed without the need to employ another subcontractor. There was further a need to replace what had hitherto been a haphazard method of payment by a more formalised scheme involving the payment of a specified sum on the completion of each flat. These were all advantages accruing to the defendants which can fairly be said to have been in consideration of their undertaking to pay the additional £10,300. True it was that the plaintiff did not undertake to do any work additional to that which he had originally undertaken to do but the terms upon which he was to carry out the work were varied and, in my judgment, that variation was supported by consideration which a pragmatic approach to the true relationship between the parties readily demonstrates.

For my part I wish to make it plain that I do not base my judgment upon any reservation as to the correctness of the law long ago enunciated in *Stilk v. Myrick.* A gratuitous promise, pure and simple, remains unenforceable unless given under seal. But where, as in this case, a party undertakes to make a payment because by so doing it will gain an advantage arising out of the continuing relationship with the promisee the new bargain will not fail for want of consideration.

Purchas LJ: The point of some difficulty which arises on this appeal is whether the judge was correct in his conclusion that the agreement reached on 9 April did not fail for lack of consideration because the principle established by the old cases of *Stilk v. Myrick,* 2 Camp. 317 approving *Harris v. Watson,* Peake 102 did not apply. Mr. Makey, who appeared for the plaintiff, was bold enough to submit that *Harris v. Watson,* albeit a decision of Lord Kenyon, was a case tried at the Guildhall at nisi prius in the Court of King's Bench and that *Stilk v. Myrick* was a decision also at nisi prius albeit a judgment of no less a judge than Lord Ellenborough C.J. and that, therefore, this court was bound by neither authority. I feel I must say at once that, for my part, I would not be prepared to overrule two cases of such veneration involving judgments of judges of such distinction except on the strongest possible grounds since they form a pillar stone of the law of contract which has been observed over the years and is still recognised in principle in recent authority: see the decision of *Stilk v. Myrick* to be found in *North Ocean Shipping Co. Ltd. v. Hyundai Construction Co. Ltd* [1979] Q.B. 705, 712 *per* Mocatta J. With respect, I agree with his view of the two judgments by Denning L.J. in *Ward v. Byham* [1956] 1 W.L.R. 496 and *Williams v. Williams* [1957] 1 W.L.R. 148 in concluding that these judgments do not provide a sound basis for avoiding the rule in *Stilk v. Myrick,* 2 Camp. 317. Although this rule has been the subject of some criticism it is still clearly recognised in current textbooks of authority: see *Chitty on Contracts,* 28th ed. (1989) and *Cheshire, Fifoot and Furmston's Law of Contract,* 11th ed. (1986). ...

In my judgment, therefore, the rule in *Stilk v. Myrick,* 2 Camp. 317 remains valid as a matter of principle, namely that a contract not under seal must be supported by consideration. Thus, where the agreement upon which reliance is placed provides that an extra payment is to be made for work to be done by the payee which he is already obliged to perform then unless some other consideration is detected to support the agreement to pay the extra sum that agreement will not be enforceable. The two cases, *Harris v. Watson,* Peake 102 and *Stilk v. Myrick,* 2 Camp. 317 involved circumstances of a very special nature, namely the extraordinary conditions existing at the turn of the 18th century under which seamen had to serve their contracts of employment on the high seas. There were strong public policy grounds at that time to protect the master and owners of a ship from being held to ransom by disaffected crews. Thus, the decision that the promise to pay extra wages even in the circumstances established in those cases, was not supported by consideration is readily understandable. Of course, conditions today on the high seas have changed dramatically and it is at least questionable, as Mr. Makey submitted, whether these cases might not well have been decided differently if they were tried today. The modern cases tend to depend more upon the defence of duress in a commercial context rather than lack of consideration for the second agreement. In the present case the question of duress does not arise. The initiative in coming to the agreement of 9 April came from Mr. Cottrell and not from the plaintiff. It would not, therefore, lie in the defendants' mouth to assert a defence of duress. Nevertheless, the court is more ready in the presence of this defence being available in the commercial context to look for mutual advantages which would amount to sufficient consideration to support the second agreement under which the extra money is paid. Although the passage cited below from the speech of Lord Hailsham of St. Marylebone L.C. in *Woodhouse A.C. Israel Cocoa Ltd. S.A. v. Nigerian Produce Marketing Co. Ltd.* [1972] A.C. 741 was strictly obiter dicta I respectfully adopt it as an indication of the approach to be made in modern times. The case involved an agreement to vary the currency in which the buyer's obligation should be met which was subsequently affected by a depreciation in the currency involved. The case was decided on an issue of estoppel but Lord Hailsham of St. Marylebone L.C. commented on the other issue, namely the variation of the original contract in the following terms, at pp. 757-758:

> "If the exchange of letters was not variation, I believe it was nothing. The buyers asked for a variation in the mode of discharge of a contract of sale. If the proposal meant what they claimed, and was accepted and acted upon, I venture to think that the vendors would have been bound by their acceptance at least until they gave reasonable notice to terminate, and I imagine that a modern court would have found no difficulty in discovering consideration for such a promise. Business men know their own business best even when they appear to grant an indulgence, and in the present case I do not think that there would have been insuperable difficulty in spelling out consideration from the earlier correspondence."

...

The question must be posed: what consideration has moved from the plaintiff to support the promise to pay the extra £10,300 added to the lump sum provision? In the particular circumstances which I have outlined above, there was clearly a commercial advantage to both sides from a pragmatic point of view in reaching the agreement of 9 April. The defendants were on risk that as a result of the bargain they had struck the plaintiff would not or indeed possibly could not comply with his existing obligations without further finance. As a result of the agreement the defendants secured their position commercially. There was, however, no obligation added to the contractual duties imposed upon the plaintiff under the original contract. Prima facie this would appear to be a classic *Stilk v. Myrick* case. It was, however, open to the plaintiff to be in deliberate breach of the contract in order to "cut his losses" commercially. In normal circumstances the suggestion that a contracting party can rely upon his own breach to establish consideration is distinctly unattractive. In many cases it obviously would be and if there was any element of duress brought upon the other contracting party under the modern development of this branch of the law the proposed breaker of the contract would not benefit. With some hesitation and comforted by the passage from the speech of Lord Hailsham of St. Marylebone L.C. in *Woodhouse A.C. Israel Cocoa Ltd. S.A. v. Nigerian Produce Marketing Co. Ltd.* [1972] A.C. 741, 757-758, to which I have referred, I consider that the modern approach to the question of consideration would be that where there were benefits derived by each party to a contract of variation even though one party did not suffer a detriment this would not be fatal to the establishing of sufficient consideration to support the agreement. If both parties benefit from an agreement it is not necessary that each also suffers a detriment. In my judgment, on the facts as found by the judge, he was entitled to reach the conclusion that consideration existed and in those circumstances I would not disturb that finding. ... For these reasons and for the reasons which have already been given by Glidewell L.J. I would dismiss this appeal.

NOTES AND QUESTIONS

1.   This is the most discussed modern case on the doctrine of consideration. It appears to lay down that a promise (by A) to perform one's existing contractual duty to the promisor (B) is good consideration for B's promise of extra money

where B thereby obtains a 'practical benefit'. On these facts the practical benefit appeared to be the greater assurance of the work being completed on time and, thereby, B's avoidance of the penalty clause (although Russell LJ did also mention as beneficial to B a more formalised payment system). But why is there not always a practical benefit to the promisor (who promises more for the promisee's performance of his existing duty) because of the greater assurance that the promisee will complete full performance of the contract? If B, a commercial party, did not think it was benefiting, why would it promise to pay more? Although the judges disputed this, it is strongly arguable that their reasoning *is* tantamount to saying that a promise to perform a pre-existing duty is good consideration for B's promise to pay more, thereby obviating the principle in *Stilk v Myrick*.

2. In a wide-ranging analysis, **M Chen-Wishart, 'Consideration: Practical Benefit and the Emperor's New Clothes' in *Good Faith and Fault in Contract Law* (eds J Beatson and D Friedmann, 1995) 123** criticises the 'illusory notion' (at 150), relied on in *Williams v Roffey*, that a 'practical benefit' is consideration.

3. An alternative approach to the problem in *Williams v Roffey*, which would have led to the same result, is to say that consideration is not needed for the variation, as opposed to the formation, of a contract. That was the approach adopted in section 2-209(1) of the United States Uniform Commercial Code. It has recently been put forward as an alternative to the *Roffey* approach, but without ultimately making a choice between them, by the New Zealand Court of Appeal in *Antons Trawling Co Ltd v Smith* [2003] 2 NZLR 23. Which is the better approach?

4. Although not disentangled in the judgments in *Williams v Roffey*, it is clearer to separate the issues of consideration and duress. That is, if the real concern is the fear of duress where B promises more for A to do what A is already bound to do, that should be tackled directly through applying the defence of duress rather than indirectly through denying that there is consideration. On the facts, there was no duress because the initiative for the extra payment came from B not A. A had made no threat and was genuinely in financial difficulties. For the law on duress, see below, Chapter 14, and for this case in that context, 709.

5. Does *Williams v Roffey* support Denning LJ's approach in *Williams v Williams* (see above, 99)?

6. *Williams v Roffey* concerned a promise to pay more for full performance of a pre-existing duty. In *Foakes v Beer*, which we shall consider next, it was laid down that a promise to accept less than full performance (ie to accept part payment of a debt in satisfaction of the whole) is not supported by consideration. *Foakes v Beer* was not mentioned in *Williams v Roffey* but there is real doubt whether the two cases can be reconciled as a matter of principle.

(ii) Promising to accept less than a pre-existing duty

Foakes v Beer (1884) 9 App Cas 605, House of Lords

In August 1875, the defendant Mrs Beer, had obtained a court judgment against Dr Foakes for £2090 19s. Mrs Beer was entitled to interest on that sum until paid off. Dr

Foakes asked for time to pay off the money and Mrs Beer agreed that, if he paid £500 immediately and £150 on two occasions each year until the whole sum had been paid, then she 'would not take any proceedings whatever on the said judgment'. Dr Foakes paid off the debt in accordance with the terms of that agreement. Mrs Beer then brought an action claiming the interest on the debt. Assuming that the true construction of the agreement was that Mrs Beer (the respondent) had promised to forgo her interest on the debt, the House of Lords nevertheless held that that promise was not binding on her because it was not supported by consideration. She was therefore entitled to the interest on the debt.

Earl of Selborne LC: But the question remains, whether the agreement is capable of being legally enforced. Not being under seal, it cannot be legally enforced against the respondent, unless she received consideration for it from the appellant, or unless, though without consideration, it operates by way of accord and satisfaction, so as to extinguish the claim for interest. What is the consideration? On the face of the agreement none is expressed, except a present payment of £500, on account and in part of the larger debt then due and payable by law under the judgment. The appellant did not contract to pay the future instalments of £150 each, at the times therein mentioned; much less did he give any new security, in the shape of negotiable paper, or in any other form. The promise de futuro was only that of the respondent, that if the half-yearly payments of £150 each were regularly paid, she would "take no proceedings whatever on the judgment." No doubt if the appellant had been under no antecedent obligation to pay the whole debt, his fulfilment of the condition might have imported some consideration on his part for that promise. But he was under that antecedent obligation; and payment at those deferred dates, by the forbearance and indulgence of the creditor, of the residue of the principal debt and costs, could not (in my opinion) be a consideration for the relinquishment of interest and discharge of the judgment, unless the payment of the £500, at the time of signing the agreement, was such a consideration. As to accord and satisfaction, in point of fact there could be no complete satisfaction, so long as any future instalment remained payable; and I do not see how any mere payments on account could operate in law as a satisfaction ad interim, conditionally upon other payments being afterwards duly made, unless there was a consideration sufficient to support the agreement while still unexecuted. Nor was anything, in fact, done by the respondent in this case, on the receipt of the last payment, which could be tantamount to an acquittance, if the agreement did not previously bind her.

The question, therefore, is nakedly raised by this appeal, whether your Lordships are now prepared, not only to overrule, as contrary to law, the doctrine stated by Sir Edward Coke to have been laid down by all the judges of the Common Pleas in *Pinnel's Case* 5 Rep. 117 a in 1602, and repeated in his note to Littleton, sect. 344 Co. Litt. 212 b, but to treat a prospective agreement, not under seal, for satisfaction of a debt, by a series of payments on account to a total amount less than the whole debt, as binding in law, provided those payments are regularly made; the case not being one of a composition with a common debtor, agreed to, inter se, by several creditors. ...The doctrine itself, as laid down by Sir Edward Coke, may have been criticised, as questionable in principle, by some persons whose opinions are entitled to respect, but it has never been judicially overruled; on the contrary I think it has always, since the sixteenth century, been accepted as law. If so, I cannot think that your Lordships would do right, if you were now to reverse, as erroneous, a judgment of the Court of Appeal, proceeding upon a doctrine which has been accepted as part of the law of England for 280 years.

The doctrine, as stated in *Pinnel's Case*, is "that payment of a lesser sum on the day" (it would of course be the same after the day), "in satisfaction of a greater, cannot be any satisfaction for the whole, because it appears to the Judges, that by no possibility a lesser sum can be a satisfaction to the plaintiff for a greater sum." As stated in Coke Littleton, 212 (b), it is, "where the condition is for payment of £20, the obligor or feoffor cannot at the time appointed pay a lesser sum in satisfaction of the whole, because it is apparent that a lesser sum of money cannot be a satisfaction of a greater;" adding (what is beyond controversy), that an acquittance under seal, in full satisfaction of the whole, would (under like circumstances) be valid and binding.

The distinction between the effect of a deed under seal, and that of an agreement by parol, or by writing not under seal, may seem arbitrary, but it is established in our law; nor is it really unreasonable or practically inconvenient that the law should require particular solemnities to give to a gratuitous contract the force of a binding obligation. If the question be (as, in the actual state of the law, I think it is), whether consideration is, or is not, given in a case of this kind, by the debtor who pays down part of the debt presently due from him, for a promise by the creditor to relinquish, after certain further payments on account, the residue of the debt, I cannot say that I think consideration is given, in the sense in which I have always understood that word as used in our law. It might be (and indeed I think it would be) an improvement in our law, if a release or acquittance of the whole debt, on payment of any sum which the creditor might be content to receive by way of accord and satisfaction (though less than the whole), were held to be, generally, binding, though not under seal; nor should I be unwilling to see equal force given to a prospective agreement, like the present, in writing though not under seal; but I think it impossible, without refinements which practically alter the sense of the word, to treat such a release or acquittance as supported by any new consideration proceeding from the debtor. …What is called "any benefit, or even any legal possibility of benefit," in Mr. Smith's notes to *Cumber v. Wane* 1 Sm. L. C. 8th ed. 366, is not (as I conceive) that sort of benefit which a creditor may derive from getting payment of part of the money due to him from a debtor who might otherwise keep him at arm's length, or possibly become insolvent, but is some independent benefit, actual or contingent, of a kind which might in law be a good and valuable consideration far any other sort of agreement not under seal.

Lord Blackburn: [I]t is necessary to consider the ground on which the Court of Appeal did base their judgment, and to say whether the agreement can be enforced. I construe it as accepting and taking £500 in satisfaction of the whole £2090 19s, subject to the condition that unless the balance of the principal debt was paid by the instalments, the whole might be enforced with interest. If, instead of £500 in money, it had been a horse valued at £500, or a promissory note for £500, the authorities are that it would have been a good satisfaction, but it is said to be otherwise as it was money.

This is a question, I think, of difficulty.

In Coke, Littleton 212 b, Lord Coke says: "where the condition is for payment of £20, the obligor or feoffor cannot at the time appointed pay a lesser sum in satisfaction of the whole, because *it is apparent* that a lesser sum of money *cannot* be a satisfaction of a greater. … If the obligor or feoffor pay a lesser sum either before the day or at another place than is limited by the condition, and the obligee or feoffee receiveth it, this is a good satisfaction." For this he cites *Pinnel's Case* 5 Rep. 117 a .That was an action on a bond for £16, conditioned for the payment of £8 10s. on the 11th of November 1600. Plea that defendant, at plaintiff's request, before the said day, to wit, on the 1st of October, paid to the plaintiff £5 2s. 2d, which the plaintiff accepted in full satisfaction of the £8 10s. The plaintiff had judgment for the insufficient pleading. But though this was so, Lord Coke reports that it was resolved by the whole Court of Common Pleas "that payment of a lesser sum on the day in satisfaction of a greater cannot be any satisfaction for the whole, because it appears to the judges that by no possibility a lesser sum can be a satisfaction to the plaintiff for a greater sum: but the gift of a horse, hawk, or robe, &c., in satisfaction is good, for it shall be intended that a horse, hawk, or robe, &c., might be more beneficial to the plaintiff than the money, in respect of some circumstance, or otherwise the plaintiff would not have accepted of it in satisfaction. But when the whole sum is due, by no intendment the acceptance of parcel can be a satisfaction to the plaintiff; but in the case at bar it was resolved that the payment and acceptance of parcel before the day in satisfaction of the whole would be a good satisfaction in regard of circumstance of time; for peradventure parcel of it before the day would be more beneficial to him than the whole at the day, and the value of the satisfaction is not material; so if I am bound in £20 to pay you £10 at Westminster, and you request me to pay you £5 at the day at York, and you will accept it in full satisfaction for the whole £10, it is a good satisfaction for the whole, for the expenses to pay it at York is sufficient satisfaction."

There are two things here resolved. First, that where a matter paid and accepted in satisfaction of a debt certain might by any possibility be more beneficial to the creditor than his debt, the Court will not inquire into the adequacy of the consideration. If the creditor, without any fraud, accepted it in satisfaction when it was not a sufficient satisfaction it was his own fault. And that payment before the day might be more beneficial, and consequently that the plea was in substance good, and this must have been decided in the case.

There is a second point stated to have been resolved, viz.: "That payment of a lesser sum on the day cannot be any satisfaction of the whole, because it appears to the judges that by no possibility a lesser sum can be a satisfaction to the plaintiff for a greater sum." This was certainly not necessary for the decision of the case; but though the resolution of the Court of Common Pleas was only a dictum, it seems to me clear that Lord Coke deliberately adopted the dictum, and the great weight of his authority makes it necessary to be cautious before saying that what he deliberately adopted as law was a mistake, and…there certainly are cases in which great judges have treated the dictum in *Pinnel's Case* as good law.

For instance, in *Sibree v. Tripp* 15 M. & W. 33, 37, Parke, B. says, "It is clear if the claim be a liquidated and ascertained sum, payment of part cannot be satisfaction of the whole, although it may, under certain circumstances, be evidence of a gift of the remainder." And Alderson, B. in the same case says, "It is undoubtedly true that payment of a portion of a liquidated demand, in the same manner as the whole liquidated demand which ought to be paid, is payment only in part, because it is not one bargain, but two; viz. payment of part, and an agreement without consideration to give up the residue. The Courts might very well have held the contrary, and have left the matter to the agreement of the parties, but undoubtedly the law is so settled." After such strong expressions of opinion, I doubt much whether any judge sitting in a Court of the first instance would be justified in treating the question as open. But as this has very seldom, if at all, been the ground of the decision even in a Court of the first instance, and certainly never been the ground of a decision in the Court of Exchequer Chamber, still less in this House, I did think it open in your Lordships' House to reconsider this question. And, notwithstanding the very high authority of Lord Coke, I think it is not the fact that to accept prompt payment of a part only of a liquidated demand, can never be more beneficial than to insist on payment of the whole. And if it be not the fact, it cannot be apparent to the judges.

…

What principally weighs with me in thinking that Lord Coke made a mistake of fact is my conviction that all men of business, whether merchants or tradesmen, do every day recognise and act on the ground that prompt payment of a part of their demand may be more beneficial to them than it would be to insist on their rights and enforce payment of the whole. Even where the debtor is perfectly solvent, and sure to pay at last, this often is so. Where the credit of the debtor is doubtful it must be more so. I had persuaded myself that there was no such long-continued action on this dictum as to render it improper in this House to reconsider the question. I had written my reasons for so thinking; but as they were not satisfactory to the other noble and learned Lords who heard the case, I do not now repeat them nor persist in them.

I assent to the judgment proposed, though it is not that which I had originally thought proper.

Lord Watson and **Lord Fitzgerald** disagreed that, on the true construction of the agreement, Mrs Beer had promised to forgo interest on the debt. But if that were the true construction, they agreed that there was no consideration for the promise to forgo interest.

1. Do you agree with Lord Blackburn's doubts about the proposition that a lesser payment than what is owed cannot be a benefit to the promisor?
2. Is it not rather artificial to say that fresh consideration would exist if a lesser payment were to be made at an earlier time or at a different place?
3. If the 'no consideration' rule here acts to protect creditors against unscrupulous debtors, is there a better way of pursuing that policy than denying that there is consideration?
4. Does *Foakes v Beer* remain good law in the light of (i) *Williams v Roffey* (on which see the next case); and (ii) the development of promissory estoppel (see below, 117–151, esp 121 notes 3–4, and 150 note 2)?
5. **J O'Sullivan, 'In Defence of *Foakes v Beer*' [1996] *CLJ* 219** controversially argues that there are good reasons to distinguish the treatment of promises to pay more from promises to accept less; they are not straightforward mirror images of each other. But if that distinction is regarded as untenable, so that either *Foakes v Beer* or *Williams v Roffey* must 'go', she tentatively argues that it should be *Roffey* that is reconsidered.

Re Selectmove Ltd [1995] 1 WLR 474, Court of Appeal

In July 1991, Selectmove Ltd owed the Inland Revenue substantial sums of income tax and national insurance contributions. At a meeting between Mr ffooks, managing director of Selectmove, and Mr Polland, a collector of taxes, Mr ffooks proposed that the company would pay future tax as it fell due and that the arrears would be paid off at a rate of £1000 per month. Mr Polland said that he would have to seek approval from his superiors for that proposal and that he would let the company know if it was unacceptable. The company heard nothing, but in October 1991 the Revenue wrote demanding payment in full of the arrears of £25,650 and threatening a winding-up petition if payment was not made. That winding-up petition was eventually made in September 1992. The company argued that the petition should be dismissed on the basis of the agreement reached in July 1991. That argument failed and the company's appeal was dismissed, the Court of Appeal taking the view that no agreement had been reached (because Mr Polland had not bound the Inland Revenue) and, in any event, there was no consideration to support that agreement.

Peter Gibson LJ: There are two elements to the consideration which the company claims was provided by it to the revenue. One is the promise to pay off its existing liability by instalments from 1 February 1992. The other is the promise to pay future P.A.Y.E. and N.I.C. as they fell due. Mr. Nugee [counsel for the company] suggested that implicit in the latter was the promise to continue trading. But that cannot be spelt out of Mr. ffooks's evidence as to what he agreed with Mr. Polland. Accordingly the second element is no more than a promise to pay that which it was bound to pay under the fiscal legislation at the date at which it was bound to make such payment. If the first element is not good consideration, I do not see why the second element should be either.

The judge held that the case fell within the principle of *Foakes v. Beer* (1884) 9 App.Cas. 605. In that case a judgment debtor and creditor agreed that in consideration of the debtor paying part of the judgment debt and costs immediately and the remainder by instalments the creditor would not take any proceedings on the judgment. The House of

Lords held that the agreement was nudum pactum, being without consideration, and did not prevent the creditor, after payment of the whole debt and costs, from proceeding to enforce payment of the interest on the judgment. Although their Lordships were unanimous in the result, that case is notable for the powerful speech of Lord Blackburn, who made plain his disagreement with the course the law had taken in and since *Pinnel's Case* (1602) 5 Co.Rep. 117a and which the House of Lords in *Foakes v. Beer*, 9 App.Cas. 605, decided should not be reversed. Lord Blackburn expressed his conviction, at p. 622, that

> "all men of business, whether merchants or tradesmen, do every day recognise and act on the ground that prompt payment of a part of their demand may be more beneficial to them than it would be to insist on their rights and enforce payment of the whole."

Yet it is clear that the House of Lords decided that a practical benefit of that nature is not good consideration in law.

Foakes v. Beer has been followed and applied in numerous cases subsequently, of which I shall mention two. In *Vanbergen v. St. Edmunds Properties Ltd.* [1933] 2 K.B. 223, 231, Lord Hanworth M.R. said:

> "It is a well established principle that a promise to pay a sum which the debtor is already bound by law to pay to the promisee does not afford any consideration to support the contract."

More recently in *D. & C. Builders Ltd. v. Rees* [1966] 2 Q.B. 617 this court also applied *Foakes v. Beer*, Danckwerts L.J. saying, at p. 626, that the case

> "settled definitely the rule of law that payment of a lesser sum than the amount of a debt due cannot be a satisfaction of the debt, unless there is some benefit to the creditor added so that there is an accord and satisfaction."

Mr. Nugee however submitted that an additional benefit to the revenue was conferred by the agreement in that the revenue stood to derive practical benefits therefrom: it was likely to recover more from not enforcing its debt against the company, which was known to be in financial difficulties, than from putting the company into liquidation. He pointed to the fact that the company did in fact pay its further P.A.Y.E. and N.I.C. liabilities and £7,000 of its arrears. He relied on the decision of this court in *Williams v. Roffey Bros. & Nicholls (Contractors) Ltd.* [1991] 1 Q.B. 1 for the proposition that a promise to perform an existing obligation can amount to good consideration provided that there are practical benefits to the promisee.

...

Mr. Nugee submitted that, although Glidewell L.J. in terms confined his remarks to a case where B is to do the work for or supply goods or services to A, the same principle must apply where B's obligation is to pay A, and he referred to an article by Adams and Brownsword, "Contract, Consideration and the Critical Path" (1990) 53 M.L.R. 536, 539-540 which suggests that *Foakes v. Beer*, 9 App.Cas. 605 might need reconsideration. I see the force of the argument, but the difficulty that I feel with it is that, if the principle of *Williams v. Roffey Bros. & Nicholls (Contractors) Ltd.* [1991] 1 Q.B. 1 is to be extended to an obligation to make payment, it would in effect leave the principle in *Foakes v. Beer*, 9 App.Cas. 605 without any application. When a creditor and a debtor who are at arm's length reach agreement on the payment of the debt by instalments to accommodate the debtor, the creditor will no doubt always see a practical benefit to himself in so doing. In the absence of authority there would be much to be said for the enforceability of such a contract. But that was a matter expressly considered in *Foakes v. Beer* yet held not to constitute good consideration in law. *Foakes v. Beer* was not even referred to in *Williams v.*

Roffey Bros. & Nicholls (Contractors) Ltd. [1991] 1 Q.B. 1, and it is in my judgment impossible, consistently with the doctrine of precedent, for this court to extend the principle of *Williams's* case to any circumstances governed by the principle of *Foakes v. Beer* 9 App.Cas. 605. If that extension is to be made, it must be by the House of Lords or, perhaps even more appropriately, by Parliament after consideration by the Law Commission.

In my judgment, the judge was right to hold that if there was an agreement between the company and the revenue it was unenforceable for want of consideration.

Stuart-Smith LJ and **Balcombe LJ** concurred.

NOTES AND QUESTIONS

1. This case clarifies that *Foakes v Beer* remains good law despite *Williams v Roffey*. But it does nothing to resolve the tension between those two cases. Are there good reasons to distinguish the treatment of promises to pay more from promises to accept less?

2. In examining *Re Selectmove*, **E Peel, 'Part Payment of a Debt is No Consideration' (1994) 100** *LQR* **353** looks at what options are open for reforming the present incoherent law on acceptance of part payment of a debt: eg, applying *Williams v Roffey*, promissory estoppel, or economic duress.

3. For a judicial view that promises to accept less (in this case, a landlord's promise to accept a reduced rent) cannot in principle be distinguished from promises to pay more, and that *Williams v Roffey* not *Foakes v Beer* is the way forward, see the decision of the Supreme Court of New South Wales (Santow J) in *Musumeci v Winadell Pty Ltd* (1994) 34 NSWLR 723. In England, see *Anangel Atlas Compania Naviera SA v Ishikawajima – Harima Heavy Industries Co Ltd (No 2)* [1990] 2 Lloyd's Rep 526: here *Williams v Roffey* was applied by Hirst J in holding that a shipbuilder's promise to reduce the price payable by the buyers was supported by the good consideration of the buyers accepting the ship's delivery on the day fixed even though the buyers were already bound to do that. However, the force of Hirst J's decision is diminished by there being no mention of *Foakes v Beer*.

2. PROMISSORY ESTOPPEL

Even though a promise is not supported by consideration, it may be binding (at least to some extent) under the doctrine of promissory estoppel. After looking at the emergence of this doctrine, we shall consider its ingredients. These may be said to be that: it is not a cause of action; the promise must be clear and unequivocal; the promisee must have relied (*quaere* detrimentally) on the promise; the promisee must not have induced the making of the promise by inequitable conduct; and that it is open to debate whether the doctrine's effect is extinctive rather than suspensory only.

Introductory reading: E McKendrick, *Contract Law* (7th edn, 2007) 5.22–5.28.

(1) The Emergence of Promissory Estoppel

Hughes v Metropolitan Rly Co (1877) 2 App Cas 439, House of Lords

In October 1874, the claimant landlord had given the defendant tenant six months' notice to repair the premises. The landlord was entitled to the forfeit of the lease if the notice was not complied with. The tenant replied agreeing to do the repairs but also suggesting that the landlord might like to buy the defendant's interest in the property and that it would defer any repairs until it heard from the landlord. On 1 December the landlord wrote back to say that it might be interested depending on the price but, on 31 December, negotiations about the price broke down. There were no further relevant communications between the parties until 19 April 1875 when the tenant wrote to say that, as negotiations had broken down, it would now be carrying out the repairs. The six months' notice expired on 22 April 1875 and, on 28 April, the landlord served a writ of ejectment on the tenant. The tenant completed the repairs in June 1875. The House of Lords, dismissing the landlord's appeal, held that the tenant was entitled to relief against forfeiture. The notice to repair was in suspension for the duration of the negotiations. It did not revive until 31 December and the tenant had carried out the repairs within six months of that date.

Lord Cairns LC: [It] is the first principle upon which all Courts of Equity proceed, that if parties who have entered into definite and distinct terms involving certain legal results – certain penalties or legal forfeiture – afterwards by their own act or with their own consent enter upon a course of negotiation which has the effect of leading one of the parties to suppose that the strict rights arising under the contract will not be enforced, or will be kept in suspense, or held in abeyance, the person who otherwise might have enforced those rights will not be allowed to enforce them where it would be inequitable having regard to the dealings which have thus taken place between the parties. My Lords, I repeat that I attribute to the Appellant no intention here to take advantage of, to lay a trap for, or to lull into false security those with whom he was dealing; but it appears to me that both parties by entering upon the negotiation which they entered upon, made it an inequitable thing that the exact period of six months dating from the month of October should afterwards be measured out as against the Respondents as the period during which the repairs must be executed.

Lords O'Hagan, Selborne, Blackburn and **Gordon** delivered concurring speeches.

NOTES AND QUESTIONS

1. This was the most important of the earlier cases relied on by Denning J in *High Trees* (see below, 119). The landlord's right to evict the tenant for non-repair was held to have been suspended because the landlord had led the tenant to believe that it would not be exercising that right while negotiations for the possible purchase of the lease by the landlord from the tenant were pending.
2. Why was the principle in this case not applied, so as to reach a different result, in *Foakes v Beer* (above, 111)?

Central London Property Trust Ltd v High Trees House Ltd
[1947] 1 KB 130, King's Bench Division

In 1937 the claimant company (the landlord) let a block of flats to the defendant company (the tenant) on a 99-year lease at an annual ground rent of £2,500. With the Second World War approaching, many people left London and the defendant was unable to sub-let all the flats. Discussions took place between the directors of the claimant and defendant companies, and in January 1940 it was agreed that the ground rent should be reduced as from the commencement of the lease to £1,250 per annum. The defendant paid the reduced ground rent until the beginning of 1945. In September 1945 the receiver of the claimant company realised that the rent stated in the lease was £2,500 and on 21 September 1945, he wrote to the defendant demanding the full amount for the future and some arrears. A friendly action was brought to test the position in law, whereby arrears of £1,250 were claimed comprising the two quarterly sums of £625 that had been due at the end of September 1945 and December 1945. While allowing that claim, Denning J held that the promise to accept less rent while war-time conditions prevailed was binding despite the absence of consideration.

Denning J: If I were to consider this matter without regard to recent developments in the law, there is no doubt that had the plaintiffs claimed it, they would have been entitled to recover ground rent at the rate of 2,500*l.* a year from the beginning of the term, since the lease under which it was payable was a lease under seal which, according to the old common law, could not be varied by an agreement by parol (whether in writing or not), but only by deed. Equity, however stepped in, and said that if there has been a variation of a deed by a simple contract (which in the case of a lease required to be in writing would have to be evidenced by writing), the courts may give effect to it as is shown in *Berry v. Berry* [1929] 2 K. B. 316. That equitable doctrine, however, could hardly apply in the present case because the variation here might be said to have been made without consideration. With regard to estoppel, the representation made in relation to reducing the rent, was not a representation of an existing fact. It was a representation, in effect, as to the future, namely, that payment of the rent would not be enforced at the full rate but only at the reduced rate. Such a representation would not give rise to an estoppel, because, as was said in *Jorden v. Money* (1854) 5 H. L. C. 185, a representation as to the future must be embodied as a contract or be nothing.

But what is the position in view of developments in the law in recent years? The law has not been standing still since *Jorden v. Money*. There has been a series of decisions over the last fifty years which, although they are said to be cases of estoppel are not really such. They are cases in which a promise was made which was intended to create legal relations and which, to the knowledge of the person making the promise, was going to be acted on by the person to whom it was made and which was in fact so acted on. In such cases the courts have said that the promise must be honoured. The cases to which I particularly desire to refer are: *Fenner v. Blake* [1900] 1 Q. B. 426, *In re Wickham* (1917) 34 T. L. R. 158, *Re William Porter & Co., Ld* [1937] 2 All E. R. 361 and *Buttery v. Pickard* [1946] W. N. 25. As I have said they are not cases of estoppel in the strict sense. They are really promises – promises intended to be binding, intended to be acted on, and in fact acted on. *Jorden v. Money* can be distinguished, because there the promisor made it clear that she did not intend to be legally bound, whereas in the cases to which I refer the proper inference was that the promisor did intend to be bound. In each case the court held the promise to be binding on the party making it, even though under the old common law it might be difficult to find any consideration for it. The courts have not gone so far as to give a cause of action in damages for the breach of such a promise, but they have refused to allow the party making it to act inconsistently with it. It is in that sense, and that sense only, that such a promise gives rise to an estoppel. The decisions are a natural result of the fusion of law and equity: for the cases of *Hughes v. Metropolitan Ry. Co* (1877) 2 App. Cas. 439, 448, *Birmingham and District Land Co. v. London & North Western Ry. Co.* (1888) 40 Ch. D. 268, 286 and *Salisbury (Marquess) v. Gilmore* [1942] 2 K. B. 38, 51, afford a sufficient basis for saying that a party would not be allowed in equity to go back on such a promise. In my opinion, the time has now come for the validity of such a promise to be recognized. The logical consequence, no doubt is that a promise to accept a smaller sum in discharge of a larger sum, if acted upon, is binding notwithstanding the absence of consideration: and if the fusion of law and equity leads to this result, so much the better. That aspect was not considered in *Foakes v. Beer* (1884) 9 App. Cas. 605. At this time of day however, when law and equity have been joined together for over seventy years, principles must be reconsidered in the light of their combined effect. It is to be noticed that in the Sixth Interim Report of the Law Revision Committee, pars. 35, 40, it is recommended that such a promise as that to which I have referred, should be enforceable in law even though no consideration for it has been given by the promisee. It seems to me that, to the extent I have mentioned that result has now been achieved by the decisions of the courts.

I am satisfied that a promise such as that to which I have referred is binding and the only question remaining for my consideration is the scope of the promise in the present case. I am satisfied on all the evidence that the promise here was that the ground rent should be reduced to 1,250*l.* a year as a temporary expedient while the block of flats was not fully, or substantially fully let, owing to the conditions prevailing. That means that the reduction in the rent applied throughout the years down to the end of 1944, but early in 1945 it is plain that the flats were fully let, and, indeed the rents received from them (many of them not being affected by the Rent Restrictions Acts), were increased beyond the figure at which it was originally contemplated that they would be let. At all events the rent from them must have been very considerable. I find that the conditions prevailing at the time when the reduction in rent was made, had completely passed away by the early months of 1945. I am satisfied that the promise was understood by all parties only to apply under the conditions prevailing at the time when it was made, namely, when the flats were only partially let, and that it did not extend any further than that. When the flats became fully let, early in 1945, the reduction ceased to apply.

In those circumstances, under the law as I hold it, it seems to me that rent is payable at the full rate for the quarters ending September 29 and December 25, 1945.

If the case had been one of estoppel, it might be said that in any event the estoppel would cease when the conditions to which the representation applied came to an end, or it also might be said that it would only come to an end on notice. In either case it is only a way of ascertaining what is the scope of the representation. I prefer to apply the principle that a promise intended to be binding, intended to be acted on and in fact acted on, is binding so far as its terms properly apply. Here it was binding as covering the period down to the early part of 1945, and as from that time full rent is payable.

I therefore give judgment for the plaintiff company for the amount claimed.

NOTES AND QUESTIONS

1. This is Lord Denning's most celebrated case. In it he lays down and applies what has subsequently been labelled the doctrine of promissory (or equitable) estoppel. As had been established in *Jorden v Money* (1854) 5 HL 185, the traditional form of estoppel—estoppel by representation—does not apply to a representation as to the future, ie a promise. But Denning J steered round that restriction by relying on an analogous promissory principle having been applied in equity in cases such as *Hughes v Metropolitan Rly Co* (above, 118).

2. Did Denning J regard the principle he was applying as suspensory or extinctive? What would the position have been if the claimant landlord in this action had been claiming arrears of rent for the period 1940–4? What would the position have been if the landlord in 1942 had given notice that it would require full rent for the future?

3. By focussing on promises (to forgo one's rights) rather than representations of fact, Denning J recognised that his principle clashed with the need for consideration laid down by the House of Lords in *Foakes v Beer* (above, 111). How did he explain away that decision? Is there any other way in which the two decisions can be reconciled?

4. It is perhaps surprising that there was no attempt to resolve the apparent conflict between *Foakes v Beer* and promissory estoppel in *Re Selectmove Ltd* (above, 115). As we have seen, *Foakes v Beer* was applied; yet the Court of Appeal also implied, in a part of the judgment not set out above, that promissory estoppel was applicable because it was only on the facts that it ruled out a separate argument based on that doctrine. (The relevant facts ruling out the doctrine were that, first, Mr Polland could not bind the Inland Revenue and, secondly, the company had not stuck by what it had itself promised it would do in paying off future tax as it fell due so it would not have been inequitable or unfair for the Revenue to withdraw from a promise to forgo some of the tax owed.)

(2) Promissory Estoppel Not a Cause of Action

Combe v Combe [1951] 2 KB 215, Court of Appeal

On a divorce, a husband (the defendant) agreed, in a solicitor's letter, to pay his wife £100 per annum free of tax. He made no payments to her at all. Several years later she sued him for the arrears of £675. Byrne J held that, while she could not recover for arrears beyond six years (because time-barred) she was entitled to six years' arrears (£600). Although she had provided no consideration for her husband's promise, the *High Trees* principle applied. This decision was overturned by the Court of Appeal which held that there was no consideration for the husband's promise and that the *High Trees* principle does not create a cause of action.

Denning LJ: Much as I am inclined to favour the principle stated in the *High Trees* case [1947] K. B. 130, it is important that it should not be stretched too far, lest it should be endangered. That principle does not create new causes of action where none existed before. It only prevents a party from insisting upon his strict legal rights, when it would be unjust to allow him to enforce them, having regard to the dealings which have taken place between the parties. That is the way it was put in *Hughes v. Metropolitan Railway* (1877) 2 App. Cas. 439, 448, the case in the House of Lords in which the principle was first stated, and in *Birmingham, etc., Land Company v. London and North-Western Railway Co* (1888) 40 Ch. D. 268, 286 the case in the Court of Appeal where the principle was enlarged. It is also implicit in all the modern cases in which the principle has been developed. Sometimes it is a plaintiff who is not allowed to insist on his strict legal rights. Thus, a creditor is not allowed to enforce a debt which he has deliberately agreed to waive, if the debtor has carried on business or in some other way changed his position in reliance on the waiver...On other occasions it is a defendant who is not allowed to insist on his strict legal rights. His conduct may be such as to debar him from relying on some condition, denying some allegation, or taking some other point in answer to the claim. Thus a government department, which had accepted a disease as due to war service, were not allowed afterwards to say it was not, seeing that the soldier, in reliance on the assurance, had abstained from getting further evidence about it: *Robertson v. Minister of Pensions* [1949] 1 K. B. 227. A buyer who had waived the contract date for delivery was not allowed afterwards to set up the stipulated time as an answer to the seller: *Charles Rickards Ld. v. Oppenhaim* [1951] 1 K. B. 149, 156. A tenant who had encroached on an adjoining building, asserting that it was comprised in the lease, was not allowed after-wards to say that it was not included in the lease: *J. F. Perrott & Co. Ld. v. Cohen* [1950] 1 K. B. 616, 621-3. A tenant who had lived in a house rent-free by permission of his landlord, thereby asserting that his original tenancy had ended, was not afterwards allowed to say that his original tenancy continued: *Foster v. Robinson* [1951] 1 K. B. 705 . In none of these cases was the defendant sued on the promise, assurance, or assertion as a cause of action in itself: he was sued for some other cause, for example, a pension or a breach of contract, and the promise, assurance or assertion only played a supplementary rôle – an important rôle, no doubt, but still a supplementary role. That is, I think, its true function. It may be part of a cause of action, but not a cause of action in itself.

The principle, as I understand it, is that, where one party has, by his words or conduct, made to the other a promise or assurance which was intended to affect the legal relations between them and to be acted on accordingly, then, once the other party has taken him at his word and acted on it, the one who gave the promise or assurance cannot afterwards be allowed to revert to the previous legal relations as if no such promise or assurance had been made by him, but he must accept their legal relations subject to the qualification which he himself has so introduced, even though it is not supported in point of law by any consider-ation but only by his word.

Seeing that the principle never stands alone as giving a cause of action in itself, it can never do away with the necessity of consideration when that is an essential part of the cause of action. The doctrine of consideration is too firmly fixed to be overthrown by a side-wind. Its ill-effects have been largely mitigated of late, but it still remains a cardinal necessity of the formation of a contract, though not of its modification or discharge. I fear that it was my failure to make this clear which misled Byrne, J., in the present case. He held that the wife could sue on the husband's promise as a separate and independent cause of action by itself, although, as he held, there was no consideration for it. That is not correct. The wife can only enforce it if there was consideration for it. That is, therefore, the real question in the case: was there sufficient consideration to support the promise?

If it were suggested that, in return for the husband's promise, the wife expressly or impliedly promised to forbear from applying to the court for maintenance – that is, a promise in return for a promise – there would clearly be no consideration, because the wife's promise was not binding on her and was therefore worth nothing. Notwithstanding her promise, she could always apply to the Divorce Court for maintenance – maybe only with leave – and no agreement by her could take away that right: *Hyman v. Hyman* [1929] A. C. 601, as inter-preted by this court in *Gaisberg v. Storr* [1950] 1 K. B. 107.

There was, however, clearly no promise by the wife, express or implied, to forbear from applying to the court. All that happened was that she did in fact forbear – that is, she did an act in return for a promise. Is that sufficient consideration? Unilateral promises of this kind have long been enforced, so long as the act or forbearance is done on the faith of the promise and at the request of the promisor, express or implied. The act done is then in itself sufficient consideration for the promise, even though it arises ex post facto, as Parker, J., pointed out in *Wigan v. English and Scottish Law Life Assurance Association* [1909] 1 Ch. 291, 298. If the findings of Byrne, J., were accepted, they would be sufficient to bring this principle into play. His finding that the husband's promise was intended to be binding, intended to be acted upon, and was, in fact, acted on – although expressed to be a finding on the *High Trees* principle – is equivalent to a finding that there was consideration within this long settled rule, because it comes to the same thing expressed in different words: see *Oliver v. Davis* [1949] 2 K. B. 727. But my difficulty is to accept the finding of Byrne, J., that the promise was "intended to be acted upon". I cannot find any evidence of any intention by the husband that the wife should forbear from applying to the court for maintenance, or, in other words, any request by the husband, express or implied, that the wife should so forbear. He left her to apply if she wished to do so. She did not do so, and I am not surprised, because it is very unlikely that the Divorce Court would have then made any order in her favour, seeing that she had a bigger income than her husband. Her forbearance was not intended by him, nor was it done at his request. It was therefore no consideration.

It may be that the wife has suffered some detriment because, after forbearing to apply to the court for seven years, she might not now be given leave to apply...The court is, however, nowadays much more ready to give leave than it used to be...and I should have thought that, if she fell on hard times, she would still obtain leave. Assuming, however, that she has suffered some detriment by her forbearance, nevertheless, as the forbearance was not at the husband's request, it is no consideration. ...

The doctrine of consideration is sometimes said to work injustice, but I see none in this case...I do not think it would be right for this wife, who is better off than her husband, to take no action for six or seven years and then come down on him for the whole 600*l.*

Asquith LJ: The judge has decided that, while the husband's promise was unsupported by any valid consideration, yet the principle in *Central London Property Trust Ld. v. High Trees House Ld.* [1947] 1 K. B. 130 entitles the wife to succeed. It is unnecessary to express any view as to the correctness of that decision, though I certainly must not be taken to be questioning it; and I would remark, in passing, that it seems to me a complete misconception to suppose that it struck at the roots of the doctrine of consideration. But assuming, without deciding, that it is good law, I do not think, however, that it helps the plaintiff at all. What that case decides is that when a promise is given which (1.) is intended to create legal relations, (2.) is intended to be acted upon by the promisee, and (3.) is in fact so acted upon, the promisor cannot bring an action against the promisee which involves the repudiation of his promise or is inconsistent with it. It does not, as I read it, decide that a promisee can sue on the promise. On the contrary, Denning, J., expressly stated the contrary. Neither in the *High Trees* case nor in *Minister of Pensions v. Robertson* [1949] 1 K. B. 227 (another decision of my Lord which is relied upon by the plaintiff) was an action brought by the promisee on the promise. In the first of those two cases the plaintiff was in effect the promisor or a person standing in the shoes of the promisor, while in the second the claim, though brought by the promisee, was brought upon a cause of action which was not the promise, but was an alleged statutory right.

[*Asquith LJ's judgment went on to deal with the question of consideration on which he concurred with Denning LJ.*]

Birkett LJ delivered a concurring judgment.

NOTES AND QUESTIONS

1.   This was the first case to make clear that, in English law, promissory estoppel does not create a cause of action. This is sometimes expressed by saying that it operates only as a defence or, in a description approved by Birkett LJ in this case, as a 'shield and not a sword'. To found a cause of action a promise must therefore be supported by consideration (or made by deed). But, as Denning LJ's judgment clarified, this is not the same as saying that promissory estoppel can be used only by defendants and not claimants. What is essentially meant is that it applies only to promises to forgo one's existing rights.

2. Assuming that Mrs Combe had detrimentally relied on Mr Combe's promise of maintenance by not seeking maintenance from the courts, why was that not good consideration?

Crabb v Arun District Council [1976] Ch 179, Court of Appeal

The claimant owned land along the side of which was a road owned by the defendant council. The claimant had a right of access to the road at point A and a right of way over the road. He wished to divide his land into two to be sold off but to do that he would need another right of access at point B. At a meeting between the claimant, his architect (Mr Alford) and the defendant's representative, an agreement in principle was reached that the claimant would be given the second access at point B. The defendant erected a boundary fence and put gates at points A and B. The claimant then sold off that part of his land which had access point A so that for the rest of his land he was dependent on access point B. However, the defendant then fenced off access point B and refused to allow the claimant access unless he paid for it. The claimant brought an action seeking, first, a declaration that he had a right of access at point B and a right of way along the road and, secondly, an injunction restraining the defendant from interfering with those rights. The Court of Appeal, applying as a cause of action a form of estoppel (which Lord Denning MR categorised as proprietary estoppel), held that the action should succeed.

Lord Denning MR: When Mr. Millett, for the plaintiff, said that he put his case on an estoppel, it shook me a little: because it is commonly supposed that estoppel is not itself a cause of action. But that is because there are estoppels and estoppels. Some do give rise to a cause of action. Some do not. In the species of estoppel called proprietary estoppel, it does give rise to a cause of action. ... The new rights and interests, so created by estoppel, in or over land, will be protected by the courts and in this way give rise to a cause of action. ...

The basis of this proprietary estoppel—as indeed of promissory estoppel—is the interposition of equity. Equity comes in, true to form, to mitigate the rigours of strict law. The early cases did not speak of it as "estoppel." They spoke of it as "raising an equity." If I may expand what Lord Cairns L.C. said in *Hughes v. Metropolitan Railway Co.* (1877) 2 App.Cas. 439, 448: "it is the first principle upon which all courts of equity proceed," that it will prevent a person from insisting on his strict legal rights – whether arising under a contract, or on his title deeds, or by statute – when it would be inequitable for him to do so having regard to the dealings which have taken place between the parties.

...

The question then is: were the circumstances here such as to raise an equity in favour of the plaintiff? True the defendants on the deeds had the title to their land, free of any access at point B. But they led the plaintiff to believe that he had or would be granted a right of access at point B. At the meeting of July 26, 1967, Mr. Alford and the plaintiff told the defendants' representative that the plaintiff intended to split the two acres into two portions and wanted to have an access at point B for the back portion; and the defendants' representative agreed that he should have this access. ...

The judge found that there was "no definite assurance" by the defendants' representative, and "no firm commitment," but only an "agreement in principle," meaning I suppose that, as Mr. Alford said, there were "some further processes" to be gone through before it would become binding. But if there were any such processes in the mind of the parties, the subsequent conduct of the defendants was such as to dispense with them. The defendants actually put up the gates at point B at considerable expense. That certainly led the plaintiff to believe that they agreed that he should have the right of access through point B without more ado.

The judge also said that, to establish this equity or estoppel, the defendants must have known that the plaintiff was selling the front portion without reserving a right of access for the back portion. I do not think this was necessary. The defendants knew that the plaintiff *intended* to sell the two portions separately and that he would need an access at point B as well as point A. Seeing that they knew of his intention – and they did nothing to disabuse him but rather confirmed it by erecting gates at point B – it was their conduct which led him to act as he did: and this raises an equity in his favour against them.

In the circumstances it seems to me inequitable that the council should insist on their strict title as they did; and to take the high-handed action of pulling down the gates without a word of warning: and to demand of the plaintiff £3,000 as the price for the easement. If he had moved at once for an injunction in aid of his equity – to prevent them removing the gates – I think he should have been granted it. But he did not do so. He tried to negotiate terms, but these failing, the action has come for trial. And we have the question: in what way now should the equity be satisfied?

Here equity is displayed at its most flexible, see *Snell's Principles of Equity*, 27th ed. (1973), p. 568, and the illustrations there given. If the matter had been finally settled in 1967, I should have thought that, although nothing was said at the meeting in July 1967, nevertheless it would be quite reasonable for the defendants to ask the plaintiff to pay something for the access at point B, perhaps – and I am guessing – some hundreds of pounds. But, as Mr. Millett pointed out in the course of the argument, because of the defendants' conduct, the back land has been landlocked. It has been sterile and rendered useless for five or six years: and the plaintiff has been unable to deal with it during that time. This loss to him can be taken into account. And at the present time, it seems to me that, in order to satisfy the equity, the plaintiff should have the right of access at point B without paying anything for it.

I would, therefore, hold that the plaintiff, as the owner of the back portion, has a right of access at point B over the verge on to Mill Park Road and a right of way along that road to Hook Lane without paying compensation. I would allow the appeal and declare that he has an easement, accordingly.

Lawton LJ: [W]hat are the legal consequences of finding as I do that there had been a firm undertaking by the defendants that access would be granted at point B? This necessitates considering principles of equity and applying them to the facts of this case. Before doing so I have reminded myself of what Harman L.J. said in *Campbell Discount Co. Ltd. v. Bridge* [1961] 1 Q.B. 445, 459:

> "Equitable principles are, I think, perhaps rather too often bandied about in common law courts as though the Chancellor still had only the length of his own foot to measure when coming to a conclusion. Since the time of Lord Eldon the system of equity for good or evil has been a very precise one, and equitable jurisdiction is exercised only on well-known principles."

...

I ask myself whether any principle of equity applies. I am grateful to Mr. Lightman [counsel for the defendant] for having drawn our attention this morning to *Ramsden v. Dyson*, L.R. 1 H.L. 129. If there had been any doubt in my mind about the application of principles of equity to the facts as I have recounted them, that case has dissipated it. As was pointed out to Mr. Lightman in the course of the argument, if one changes the parties in a passage in the speech of Lord Cranworth L.C. into the names of the parties in this case, one has a case for the intervention of equity which Lord Cranworth regarded with favour. That passage, at p. 142, is in these terms:

"... if I had come to the conclusion that Thornton, when he erected his building in 1837, did so in the belief that he had against Sir John an absolute right to the lease he claims, and that Sir John knew that he was proceeding on that mistaken notion, and did not interfere to set him right, I should have been much disposed to say that he was entitled to the relief he sought."

Mr. Lightman's answer was that the plaintiff had not got an absolute right to have the gates put up. For the reasons I have stated, I am of the opinion that he had in the sense that he had been given a firm undertaking. The defendants, knowing that the plaintiff intended to sell part of this land, stood by when he did so and without a word of warning allowed him to surround himself with a useless piece of land from which there was no exit. I would allow this appeal and grant relief in the terms indicated by Lord Denning M.R.

In conclusion I should add this: as the result of the defendants resiling from their undertaking, this piece of land which is designated for light industry has stood useless. It might well have been profitable not only to the plaintiff but to other people living nearby. In an area where employment for the young is not always easy to find, we have the spectacle of this piece of land next door to a housing estate being rendered useless at a time when it could have been of value to the community. For that the defendants are solely to blame.

In the circumstances I agree with Lord Denning M.R. that they should not be paid anything for the right of way which they should have granted as long ago as 1967.

Scarman LJ: I agree that the appeal should be allowed. The plaintiff and the defendants are adjoining landowners. The plaintiff asserts that he has a right of way over the defendants' land giving access from his land to the public highway. Without this access his land is in fact landlocked, but, for reasons which clearly appear from the narration of the facts already given by my Lords, the plaintiff cannot claim a right of way by necessity. The plaintiff has no grant. He has the benefit of no enforceable contract. He has no prescriptive right. His case has to be that the defendants are estopped by their conduct from denying him a right of access over their land to the public highway. If the plaintiff has any right, it is an equity arising out of the conduct and relationship of the parties. In such a case I think it is now well settled law that the court, having analysed and assessed the conduct and relationship of the parties, has to answer three questions. First, is there an equity established? Secondly, what is the extent of the equity, if one is established? And, thirdly, what is the relief appropriate to satisfy the equity?...Such therefore I believe to be the nature of the inquiry that the courts have to conduct in a case of this sort. In pursuit of that inquiry I do not find helpful the distinction between promissory and proprietary estoppel. This distinction may indeed be valuable to those who have to teach or expound the law; but I do not think that, in solving the particular problem raised by a particular case, putting the law into categories is of the slightest assistance.

...

I come now to consider the first of the three questions which I think in a case such as this the court have to consider. What is needed to establish an equity?...While *Ramsden v. Dyson* may properly be considered as the modern starting-point of the law of equitable estoppel, it was analysed and spelt out in a judgment of Fry J. in 1880 in *Willmott v. Barber* (1880) 15 Ch.D. 96, a decision to which Pennycuick V.-C. referred in his judgment. I agree with Pennycuick V.-C. in thinking that the passage from Fry J.'s judgment, from p. 105, is a valuable guide as to the matters of fact which have to be established in order that a plaintiff may establish this particular equity. Moreover, Mr. Lightman for the defendants sought to make a submission in reliance upon the judgment. Fry J. said, at pp. 105-106:

"It has been said that the acquiescence which will deprive a man of his legal rights must amount to fraud, and in my view that is an abbreviated statement of a very true proposition. A man is not to be deprived of his legal rights unless he has acted in such a way as would make it fraudulent for him to set up those rights. What, then, are the elements or requisites necessary to constitute fraud of that description? In the first place the plaintiff must have made a mistake as to his legal rights. Secondly, the plaintiff must have expended some money or must have done some act (not necessarily upon the defendant's land) on the faith of his mistaken belief. Thirdly, the defendant, the possessor of the legal right, must know of the existence of his own right which is inconsistent with the right claimed by the plaintiff. If he does not know of it he is in the same position as the plaintiff, and the doctrine of acquiescence is founded upon conduct with a knowledge of your legal rights. Fourthly, the defendant, the possessor of the legal right, must know of the plaintiff's mistaken belief of his rights. If he does not, there is nothing which calls upon him to assert his own rights. Lastly," – if I may digress, this is the important element as far as this appeal is concerned – "the defendant, the possessor of the legal right, must have encouraged the plaintiff in his expenditure of money or in the other acts which he has done, either directly or by abstaining from asserting his legal right."

...

I have no doubt upon the facts of this case that the first four elements referred to by Fry J. exist. The question before the judge and now in this court is whether the fifth element is present: have the defendants, as possessor of the legal right, encouraged the plaintiff in the expenditure of money or in the other acts which he has done, either directly or by abstaining from asserting their legal rights? [*Having decided that they had, Scarman LJ continued:*]

I turn now to the other two questions – the extent of the equity and the relief needed to satisfy it. There being no grant, no enforceable contract, no licence, I would analyse the minimum equity to do justice to the plaintiff as a right either to an easement or to a licence upon terms to be agreed. I do not think it is necessary to go further than that. Of course, going that far would support the equitable remedy of injunction which is sought in this action. If there is no agreement as to terms, if agreement fails to be obtained, the court can, in my judgment, and must, determine in these proceedings upon what terms the plaintiff should be put to enable him to have the benefit of the equitable right which he is held to have.

...

Had matters taken a different turn, I would without hesitation have said that the plaintiff should be put upon terms to be agreed if possible with the defendants, and, if not agreed, settled by the court. But, as already mentioned by Lord Denning M.R. and Lawton L.J., there has been a history of delay, and indeed high-handedness, which it is impossible to disregard. In January 1969 the defendants, for reasons which no doubt they thought good at the time, without consulting the plaintiff, locked up his land. They removed not only the padlocks which he had put on the gates at point B, but the gates themselves. In their place they put a fence – rendering access impossible save by breaking down the fence. I am not disposed to consider whether or not the defendants are to be blamed in moral terms for what they did. I just do not know. But the effect of their action has been to sterilise the plaintiff's land; and for the reasons which I have endeavoured to give, such action was an infringement of an equitable right possessed by the plaintiff. It has involved him in loss, which has not been measured; but, since it amounted to sterilisation of an industrial estate for a very considerable period of time, it must surpass any sort of sum of money which the plaintiff ought reasonably, before it was done, to have paid the defendants in order to obtain an enforceable legal right. I think therefore that nothing should now be paid by the plaintiff and that he should receive at the hands of the court the belated protection of the equity that he has established. Reasonable terms, other than money payment, should be agreed: or, if not agreed, determined by the court.

For those reasons I also would allow the appeal.

NOTES AND QUESTIONS

1.   Scarman LJ thought that it was unhelpful in deciding this case to categorise it as involving a proprietary, rather than a promissory, estoppel. But that is how

this case has conventionally been analysed. As Lord Denning's judgment indicates, the difficulty otherwise is that this decision would clash with promissory estoppel not being a cause of action. It is well-established that proprietary estoppel—which concerns conferring rights over one's land (or, probably, one's goods)—does create a cause of action; and the cases primarily relied on by all the judges were proprietary estoppel cases.

2.   Assuming that the law of estoppel does treat promises (and representations) as to rights over one's land (or goods) differently from other promises, can that different treatment be justified?

3.   In an infamous pair of case-notes, Professor Atiyah clashed with Peter Millett QC (counsel for Mr Crabb and later a Law Lord) on the correct interpretation of *Crabb v Arun DC.* **P Atiyah, 'When is an Enforceable Agreement not a Contract? Answer: When it is an Equity' (1976) 92** *LQR* **174** argued that the invocation in *Crabb v Arun* of estoppel to enforce a promise was unnecessary because all the elements of a binding contract were present. In particular, consideration, in Atiyah's view, embraces any good reason to enforce a promise, including unrequested detriment. The case should therefore be seen as a contract case. It is needlessly complex to have two doctrines when one alone should suffice. Pleading equitable estoppel, rather than contract, achieved no different result. Applying a conventional view in response to Atiyah's 'interesting, if intemperate, note', **P Millett, 'Crabb v Arun DC – A Riposte' (1976) 92** *LQR* **342** argued that contract and equitable estoppel are significantly different. 'The apparent similarity of the results achieved...is...deceptive. The claims [in contract and estoppel] are different, require different facts to be proved and have different consequences' (at 346).

Amalgamated Investment & Property Co Ltd v Texas Commerce International Bank Ltd [1982] QB 84, Court of Appeal

The claimant (AIP) requested the defendant bank to make a loan to AIP's subsidiary (ANPP) in the Bahamas. AIP agreed with the bank, under a guarantee, that it would pay on demand all moneys owed to the bank by ANPP. No loan was directly made by the bank to ANPP under that arrangement but $3,250,000 was loaned (the 'Nassau loan') to ANPP by the bank's subsidiary in the Bahamas (Portsoken). AIP and the bank assumed that the guarantee applied in respect of the loan by Portsoken. But when the bank sought to enforce the guarantee (by withholding other moneys owed amounting to $750,000) in respect of non-payment of money owing on the loan from Portsoken, AIP argued that it was not liable on the guarantee and sought a declaration to that effect. Robert Goff J held that, while as a matter of interpretation of the contract the guarantee did not apply to the loan by Portsoken, AIP was estopped from denying that it did so apply. The Court of Appeal disagreed on the construction of the agreement which, it held, did apply to the loan by Portsoken. However it agreed that, in any event, AIP was estopped from denying that the guarantee applied. We are here concerned solely with the estoppel point.

Lord Denning MR: When the parties to a contract are both under a common mistake as to the meaning or effect of it – and thereafter embark on a course of dealing on the footing of that mistake – thereby replacing the original terms of the contract by a conventional basis on which they both conduct their affairs, then the original contract is replaced by the conventional basis. The parties are bound by the conventional basis. Either party can sue or be sued upon it just as if it had been expressly agreed between them. ...

The doctrine of estoppel is one of the most flexible and useful in the armoury of the law. But it has become overloaded with cases. That is why I have not gone through them all in this judgment. It has evolved during the last 150 years in a sequence of separate developments: proprietary estoppel, estoppel by representation of fact, estoppel by acquiescence, and promissory estoppel. At the same time it has been sought to be limited by a series of maxims: estoppel is only a rule of evidence, estoppel cannot give rise to a cause of action, estoppel cannot do away with the need for consideration, and so forth. All these can now be seen to merge into one general principle shorn of limitations. When the parties to a transaction proceed on the basis of an underlying assumption – either of fact or of law – whether due to misrepresentation or mistake makes no difference – on which they have conducted the dealings between them – neither of them will be allowed to go back on that assumption when it would be unfair or unjust to allow him to do so. If one of them does seek to go back on it, the courts will give the other such remedy as the equity of the case demands.

That general principle applies to this case. Both the plaintiffs and the bank proceeded for years on the basis of the underlying assumption that the guarantee of the plaintiffs applied to the $3,250,000 advanced ... Their dealings in rearranging the portfolio, in releasing properties and moneys, were all conducted on that basis. On that basis the bank applied the surplus of $750,000 ... in discharge of the obligations of the plaintiffs under the guarantee. It would be most unfair and unjust to allow the liquidator to depart from that basis and to claim back now the $750,000.

Brandon LJ: Two main arguments against the existence of an estoppel were advanced on behalf of the plaintiffs both before Robert Goff J. and before us. The first argument was that, since the bank came to hold its mistaken belief in the first place as a result of its own error alone, and the plaintiffs had at most innocently acquiesced in that belief which it also held, there was no representation by the plaintiffs to the bank on which an estoppel could be founded. The second argument was that, in the present case, the bank was seeking to use estoppel not as a shield, but as a sword, and that that was something which the law of estoppel did not permit.

I consider first the argument based on the origin of the bank's mistaken belief. In my opinion this argument is founded on an erroneous view of the kind of estoppel which is relevant in this case.

The kind of estoppel which is relevant in this case is not the usual kind of estoppel in pais based on a representation made by A to B and acted on by B to his detriment. It is rather the kind of estoppel which is described in *Spencer Bower and Turner, Estoppel by Representation*, 3rd ed. (1977), at pp. 157-160, as estoppel by convention. The authors of that work say of this kind of estoppel, at p. 157:

"This form of estoppel is founded, not on a representation of fact made by a representor and believed by a representee, but on an agreed statement of facts the truth of which has been assumed, by the convention of the parties, as the basis of a transaction into which they are about to enter. When the parties have acted in their transaction upon the agreed assumption that a given state of facts is to be accepted between them as true, then as regards that transaction each will be estopped as against the other from questioning the truth of the statement of facts so assumed."

Applying that description of estoppel by convention to the present case, the situation as I see it is this. First, the relevant transactions entered into by the plaintiffs and the bank were the making of new arrangements with regard to the overall security held by the bank in relation to ... loans [including the Nassau loan]. Secondly, for the purposes of those transactions, both the bank and the plaintiffs assumed the truth of a certain state of affairs, namely that the guarantee given in relation to the Nassau loan effectively bound the plaintiffs to discharge any indebtedness of A.N.P.P. to Portsoken. The transactions took place on the basis of that assumption, and their course was influenced by it in the sense that, if the assumption had not been made, the course of the transactions would without doubt have been different.

Those facts produce, in my opinion, a classic example of the kind of estoppel called estoppel by convention as described in the passage from *Spencer Bower and Turner, Estoppel by Representation*, which I have quoted above, and so deprive the first argument advanced on behalf of the plaintiffs of any validity which, if the case were an ordinary one of estoppel by representation, it might otherwise have.

I turn to the second argument advanced on behalf of the plaintiffs, that the bank is here seeking to use estoppel as a sword rather than a shield, and that that is something which the law of estoppel does not permit. Another way in which the argument is put is that a party cannot found a cause of action on an estoppel.

In my view much of the language used in connection with these concepts is no more than a matter of semantics. Let me consider the present case and suppose that the bank had brought an action against the plaintiffs before they went into liquidation to recover moneys owed by A.N.P.P. to Portsoken. In the statement of claim in such an action the bank would have pleaded the contract of loan incorporating the guarantee, and averred that, on the true construction of the guarantee, the plaintiffs were bound to discharge the debt owed by A.N.P.P. to Portsoken. By their defence the plaintiffs would have pleaded that, on the true construction of the guarantee, the plaintiffs were only bound to discharge debts owed by A.N.P.P. to the bank, and not debts owed by A.N.P.P. to Portsoken. Then in their reply the bank would have pleaded that, by reason of an estoppel arising from the matters discussed above, the plaintiffs were precluded from questioning the interpretation of the guarantee which both parties had, for the purpose of the transactions between them, assumed to be true.

In this way the bank, while still in form using the estoppel as a shield, would in substance be founding a cause of action on it. This illustrates what I would regard as the true proposition of law, that, while a party cannot in terms found a cause of action on an estoppel, he may, as a result of being able to rely on an estoppel, succeed on a cause of action on which, without being able to rely on that estoppel, he would necessarily have failed. That, in my view, is, in substance, the situation of the bank in the present case.

It follows from what I have said above that I would reject the second argument against the existence of an estoppel put forward on behalf of the plaintiffs as well as the first. It further follows, from my rejection of both arguments against the existence of an estoppel, that I would ...[hold] that, if the plaintiffs did not, by the contract relating to the Nassau loan, undertake to the bank to discharge any indebtedness of A.N.P.P. to Portsoken, they are, nevertheless, estopped from denying that they did so by reason of the basis, accepted by both the bank and the plaintiffs, on which the transactions between them were later conducted during the period from 1974 to 1976.

Eveleigh LJ delivered a concurring judgment. But, while agreeing that estoppel here applied, he suggested, contrary to the reasoning of the other two judges, that, had the bank been bringing an action to enforce the guarantee, it could not have done so because that would be using estoppel as a cause of action.

NOTES AND QUESTIONS

1. This case concerned estoppel by convention. It is generally assumed that, like promissory estoppel, estoppel by convention does not create a cause of action. Brandon LJ's judgment is particularly helpful in showing that, while accepting that proposition, estoppel by convention (and, by analogy, promissory estoppel) can be crucial to the success of a cause of action. Had the bank been

suing on the contractual guarantee (in fact the bank had withheld other moneys owing so that the claim was being brought by AIP) the relevant cause of action would have been a standard contractual cause of action. Estoppel (by convention) would have come in not to found the cause of action but to prevent AIP applying an interpretation of that guarantee that was contrary to both parties' understanding and conduct.

2. Do you agree with Lord Denning that the various types of estoppel 'merge into one general principle shorn of limitations'? Is that consistent with his approach in *Crabb v Arun DC* (above, 124)?

Waltons Stores (Interstate) Ltd v Maher
(1988) 164 CLR 387, High Court of Australia

The defendants (Waltons) negotiated with the claimants (Mr and Mrs Maher) for the Mahers to demolish a building on their land and to construct a new one, to Waltons' specifications, which the Mahers would then lease to Waltons as retail premises. The Mahers said that they did not wish to complete all the demolition work until it was clear that there were no problems with the lease. The Mahers' solicitors sent to Waltons' solicitors 'by way of exchange' the lease which had been signed by the Mahers. Further demolition work was then carried out by the Mahers but Waltons began to have second thoughts about the deal and instructed their solicitors to go slow. Waltons knew that 40 per cent of the work had been completed when it informed the Mahers that it would not be proceeding with the lease. The trial judge found in the Mahers' favour and ordered Waltons to pay damages in lieu of specific performance. Waltons unsuccessfully appealed to the New South Wales Court of Appeal and the High Court of Australia. On appeal, the Mahers accepted that there was no formally binding contract because, as with all contracts for interests in land, the agreement was 'subject to contract' which required an exchange of contracts. The case therefore turned on estoppel, and it was held that the Mahers should succeed applying promissory estoppel as a cause of action.

Mason CJ and **Wilson J**: There has been for many years a reluctance to allow promissory estoppel to become the vehicle for the positive enforcement of a representation by a party that he would do something in the future. Promissory estoppel, it has been said, is a defensive equity: *Hughes v. Metropolitan Railway Co.* (1877) 2 App. Cas. 439, at p. 448; *Combe v. Combe* (1951) 2 K.B. 215, at pp. 219-220, and the traditional notion has been that estoppel could only be relied upon defensively as a shield and not as a sword...*High Trees* [1947] K.B. 130 itself was an instance of the defensive use of promissory estoppel. But this does not mean that a plaintiff cannot rely on an estoppel. Even according to traditional orthodoxy, a plaintiff may rely on an estoppel if he has an independent cause of action, where in the words of Denning L.J. in *Combe v. Combe*, the estoppel "may be part of a cause of action, but not a cause of action in itself".

But the respondents ask us to drive promissory estoppel one step further by enforcing directly in the absence of a pre-existing relationship of any kind a non-contractual promise on which the representee has relied to his detriment. For the purposes of discussion, we shall assume that there was such a promise in the present case. The principal objection to the enforcement of such a promise is that it would outflank the principles of the law of contract. Holmes J. expressed his objection to the operation of promissory estoppel in this situation when he said "It would cut up the doctrine of consideration by the roots, if a promisee could make a gratuitous promise binding by subsequently acting in reliance on it": *Commonwealth v. Scituate Savings Bank* (1884) 137 Mass. 301, at p. 302. Likewise, Sir Owen Dixon considered that estoppel cut across the principles of the law of contract, notably offer and acceptance and consideration: "Concerning Judicial Method" *Australian Law Journal*, vol. 29 (1956) 468, at p. 475. And Denning L.J. in *Combe v. Combe*, after noting that "The doctrine of consideration is too firmly fixed to be overthrown by a side-wind", said (at p 220) that such a promise could only be enforced if it was supported by sufficient consideration. ...

There is force in these objections and it may not be a sufficient answer to repeat the words of Lord Denning M.R. in *Crabb v. Arun District Council* [1976] Ch. 179, at p. 187, "Equity comes in, true to form, to mitigate the rigours of strict law". True it is that in the orthodox case of promissory estoppel, where the promisor promises that he will not exercise or enforce an existing right, the elements of reliance and detriment attract equitable intervention on the basis that it is unconscionable for the promisor to depart from his promise, if to do so will result in detriment to the promisee. And it can be argued...that there is no justification for applying the doctrine of promissory estoppel in this situation, yet denying it in the case of a non-contractual promise in the absence of a pre-existing relationship. The promise, if enforced, works a change in the relationship of the parties, by altering an existing legal relationship in the first situation and by creating a new legal relationship in the second. The point has been made that it would be more logical to say that when the parties have agreed to pursue a course of action, an alteration of the relationship by non-contractual promise will not be countenanced, whereas the creation of a new relationship by a simple promise will be recognized: see D. Jackson, "Estoppel as a Sword" *Law Quarterly Review*, vol. 81 (1965) 223, at p. 242.

The direct enforcement of promises made without consideration by means of promissory estoppel has proceeded apace in the United States. *The Restatement on Contracts* 2d §90 states:

> "(1) A promise which the promisor should reasonably expect to induce action or forbearance on the part of the promisee or a third person and which does induce such action or forbearance is binding if injustice can be avoided only by enforcement of the promise. The remedy granted for breach may be limited as justice requires."

...

However, we need to view the development of the doctrine in the United States with some caution. There promissory estoppel developed partly in response to the limiting effects of the adoption of the bargain theory of consideration which has not been expressly adopted in Australia or England. It may be doubted whether our conception of consideration is substantially broader than the bargain theory...though we may be willing to imply consideration in situations where the bargain theory as implemented in the United States would deny the existence of consideration: see Atiyah, *Consideration in Contracts: A Fundamental Restatement* (1971), pp 6-7, 27, f.n. 35; Treitel, "Consideration: A Critical Analysis of Professor Atiyah's Fundamental Restatement" *Australian Law Journal*, vol. 50 (1976) 439, at pp. 440 et seq. It is perhaps sufficient to say that in the United States, as in Australia, there is an obvious interrelationship between the doctrines of consideration and promissory estoppel, promissory estoppel tending to occupy ground left vacant due to the constraints affecting consideration.

The proposition stated in §90(1) of the Restatement seems on its face to reflect a closer connection with the general law of contract than our doctrine of promissory estoppel, with its origins in the equitable concept of unconscionable conduct, might be thought to allow. This is because in the United States promissory estoppel has become an equivalent or substitute for consideration in contract formation, detriment being an element common to both doctrines. Nonetheless the proposition, by making the enforcement of the promise conditional on (a) a reasonable expectation on the part of the promisor that his promise will induce action or forbearance by the promisee and (b) the impossibility of avoiding injustice by other means, makes it clear that the promise is enforced in circumstances where departure from it is unconscionable. Note that the emphasis is on the promisor's reasonable expectation that his promise will induce action or forbearance, not on the fact that he created or encouraged an expectation in the promisee of performance of the promise.

...

The foregoing review of the doctrine of promissory estoppel indicates that the doctrine extends to the enforcement of voluntary promises on the footing that a departure from the basic assumptions underlying the transaction between the parties must be unconscionable. As failure to fulfil a promise does not of itself amount to unconscionable conduct, mere reliance on an executory promise to do something, resulting in the promisee changing his position or suffering detriment, does not bring promissory estoppel into play. Something more would be required. [*Att-Gen of Hong Kong v*] *Humphreys Estate* [[1987] AC 114] suggests that this may be found, if at all, in the creation or encouragement by the party estopped in the other party of an assumption that a contract will come into existence or a promise will be performed and that the other party relied on that assumption to his detriment to the knowledge of the first party. ...

The application of these principles to the facts of the present case is not without difficulty. The parties were negotiating through their solicitors for an agreement for lease to be concluded by way of customary exchange. *Humphreys Estate* illustrates the difficulty of establishing an estoppel preventing parties from refusing to proceed with a transaction expressed to be "subject to contract". And there is the problem...that a voluntary promise will not generally give rise to an estoppel because the promisee may reasonably be expected to appreciate that he cannot safely rely upon it. This problem is magnified in the present case where the parties were represented by their solicitors.

All this may be conceded. But the crucial question remains: was the appellant entitled to stand by in silence when it must have known that the respondents were proceeding on the assumption that they had an agreement and that completion of the exchange was a formality? The mere exercise of its legal right not to exchange contracts could not be said to amount to unconscionable conduct on the part of the appellant. But there were two other factors present in the situation which require to be taken into consideration. The first was the element of urgency that pervaded the negotiation of the terms of the proposed lease. ...The respondents' solicitor had said to the appellant's solicitor on 7 November that it would be impossible for Maher to complete the building within the agreed time unless the agreement were concluded "within the next day or two". The outstanding details were agreed within a day or two thereafter, and the work of preparing the site commenced almost immediately.

The second factor of importance is that the respondents executed the counterpart deed and it was forwarded to the appellant's solicitor on 11 November. The assumption on which the respondents acted thereafter was that completion of the necessary exchange was a formality. The next their solicitor heard from the appellant was a letter from its solicitors dated 19 January, informing him that the appellant did not intend to proceed with the matter. It had known, at least since 10 December, that costly work was proceeding on the site.

It seems to us, in the light of these considerations, that the appellant was under an obligation to communicate with the respondents within a reasonable time after receiving the executed counterpart deed and certainly when it learnt on 10 December that demolition was proceeding. ...The appellant's inaction, in all the circumstances, constituted clear encouragement or inducement to the respondents to continue to act on the basis of the assumption which they had made. It was unconscionable for it, knowing that the respondents were exposing themselves to detriment by acting on the basis of a false assumption, to adopt a course of inaction which encouraged them in the course they had adopted. To express the point in the language of promissory estoppel the appellant is estopped in all the circumstances from retreating from its implied promise to complete the contract.

Brennan J: Parties who are negotiating a contract may proceed in the expectation that the terms will be agreed and a contract made but, so long as both parties recognize that either party is at liberty to withdraw from the negotiations at any time before the contract is made, it cannot be unconscionable for one party to do so. Of course, the freedom to withdraw may be fettered or extinguished by agreement but, in the absence of agreement, either party ordinarily retains his freedom to withdraw. It is only if a party induces the other party to believe that he, the former party, is already bound and his freedom to withdraw has gone that it could be unconscionable for him subsequently to assert that he is legally free to withdraw.

...

The unconscionable conduct which it is the object of equity to prevent is the failure of a party, who has induced the adoption of the assumption or expectation and who knew or intended that it would be relied on, to fulfil the assumption or expectation or otherwise to avoid the detriment which that failure would occasion. The object of the equity is not to compel the party bound to fulfil the assumption or expectation; it is to avoid the detriment which, if the assumption or expectation goes unfulfilled, will be suffered by the party who has been induced to act or to abstain from acting thereon.

If this object is kept steadily in mind, the concern that a general application of the principle of equitable estoppel would make non-contractual promises enforceable as contractual promises can be allayed.

...

A contractual obligation is created by the agreement of the parties; an equity created by estoppel may be imposed irrespective of any agreement by the party bound. A contractual obligation must be supported by consideration; an equity created by estoppel need not be supported by what is, strictly speaking, consideration. The measure of a contractual obligation depends on the terms of the contract and the circumstances to which it applies; the measure of an equity created by estoppel varies according to what is necessary to prevent detriment resulting from unconscionable conduct.

In *Combe v. Combe* [1951] 2 K.B. 215 Denning L.J. limited the application of promissory estoppel, as he expounded the doctrine, to ensure that it did not displace the doctrine of consideration. His Lordship's solution of the problem was to hold that the promise should not itself be a cause of action, but merely the foundation of a defensive equity.

...

If the object of the principle were to make a promise binding in equity, the need to preserve the doctrine of consideration would require a limitation to be placed on the remedy. But there is a logical difficulty in limiting the principle so that it applies only to promises to suspend or extinguish existing rights. If a promise by A not to enforce an existing right against B is to confer an equitable right on B to compel fulfilment of the promise, why should B be denied the same protection in similar circumstances if the promise is intended to create in B a new legal right against A? There is no logical distinction to be drawn between a change in legal relationships effected by a promise which extinguishes a right and a change in legal relationships effected by a promise which creates one. Why should an equity of the kind to which *Combe v. Combe* refers be regarded as a shield but not a sword? The want of logic in the limitation on the remedy is well exposed in Mr David Jackson's essay "Estoppel as a Sword" in *Law Quarterly Review,* vol 81 (1965) 223 at pp. 241-243.

Moreover, unless the cases of proprietary estoppel are attributed to a different equity from that which explains the cases of promissory estoppel, the enforcement of promises to create new proprietary rights cannot be reconciled with a limitation on the enforcement of other promises. If it be unconscionable for an owner of property in certain circumstances to fail to fulfil a non-contractual promise that he will convey an interest in the property to another, is there any reason in principle why it is not unconscionable in similar circumstances for a person to fail to fulfil a non-contractual promise that he will confer a non-proprietary legal right on another? It does not accord with principle to hold that equity, in seeking to avoid detriment occasioned by unconscionable conduct, can give relief in some cases but not in others.

If the object of the principle of equitable estoppel in its application to promises were regarded as their enforcement rather than the prevention of detriment flowing from reliance on promises, the courts would be constrained to limit the application of the principles of equitable estoppel in order to avoid the investing of a non-contractual promise with the legal effect of a contractual promise.

...

But the better solution of the problem is reached by identifying the unconscionable conduct which gives rise to the equity as the leaving of another to suffer detriment occasioned by the conduct of the party against whom the equity is raised. Then the object of the principle can be seen to be the avoidance of that detriment and the satisfaction of the equity calls for the enforcement of a promise only as a means of avoiding the detriment and only to the extent necessary to achieve that object. So regarded, equitable estoppel does not elevate non-contractual promises to the level of contractual promises and the doctrine of consideration is not blown away by a side-wind. Equitable estoppel complements the tortious remedies of damages for negligent mis-statement or fraud and enhances the remedies available to a party who acts or abstains from acting in reliance on what another induces him to believe.

...

In my opinion, to establish an equitable estoppel, it is necessary for a plaintiff to prove that (1) the plaintiff assumed that a particular legal relationship then existed between the plaintiff and the defendant or expected that a particular legal relationship would exist between them and, in the latter case, that the defendant would not be free to withdraw from the expected legal relationship; (2) the defendant has induced the plaintiff to adopt that assumption or expectation; (3) the plaintiff acts or abstains from acting in reliance on the assumption or expectation; (4) the defendant knew or intended him to do so; (5) the plaintiff's action or inaction will occasion detriment if the assumption or expectation is not fulfilled; and (6) the defendant has failed to act to avoid that detriment whether by fulfilling the assumption or expectation or otherwise. For the purposes of the second element, a defendant who has not actively induced the plaintiff to adopt an assumption or expectation will nevertheless be held to have done so if the assumption or expectation can be fulfilled only by a transfer of the defendant's property, a diminution of his rights or an increase in his obligations and he, knowing that the plaintiff's reliance on the assumption or expectation may cause detriment to the plaintiff if it is not fulfilled, fails to deny to the plaintiff the correctness of the assumption or expectation on which the plaintiff is conducting his affairs.

This is such a case...

Deane J and **Gaudron J** delivered concurring judgments.

NOTES AND QUESTIONS

1. The primary importance of this case is that it shows promissory estoppel being successfully used as a cause of action. The case was not one of *proprietary* estoppel because the promisor (Waltons) was not promising to confer rights over its land: rather it was promising to enter into a contract to take a lease.
2. Brennan J's judgment sought to resolve the clash between promissory estoppel as a cause of action and the doctrine of consideration by treating the former as concerned to protect the promisee's detrimental reliance rather than to enforce the promise. Do you regard that as a tenable reconciliation?
3. Despite Brennan J's words, it is unclear whether the damages actually awarded in this case protected the Mahers' expectation or reliance interest. (For explanation of the terms 'expectation' and 'reliance' interest, see below, 338, note 2.) For further consideration of whether 'Australian estoppel' protects the claimants' reliance, rather than expectation, interest, see *Commonwealth of Australia v Verwayen* (1990) 170 CLR 394; *Giumelli v Guimelli* (1999) 196 CLR 101; Edelman (1999) 15 *JCL* 179 (below, 152). There is an analogous long-standing

debate in the United States as to whether section 90 of the *Restatement of Contracts* (cited above, 132) is concerned to protect the reliance or expectation interest: see Slawson (1990) 76 *Cornell LR* 197 (below, 152).

4. *If* promissory estoppel were concerned to protect the promisee's reliance, rather than expectation interest, would it be more natural to view it as analogous to tortious misrepresentation rather than as analogous to, or part of, the law of contract?

5. Would it be acceptable to leave open the question of the appropriate remedy for promossory estoppel so as to give the courts a flexible remedial discretion? Consider the analogous question raised as to the remedies for *proprietary* estoppel: see, eg, Gardner (1999) 115 *LQR* 438 (below, 152); *Jennings v Rice* [2002] EWCA Civ 159, [2003] 1 P & CR 100; *Cobbe v Yeoman's Row Management Ltd* [2006] EWCA Civ 1139, [2006] 1 WLR 2964 (especially the judgment of Dyson LJ).

Baird Textiles Holdings Ltd v Marks & Spencer plc
[2001] EWCA Civ 274, [2002] 1 All ER (Comm) 737, Court of Appeal

The claimant had been one of the main suppliers of garments to the defendant retailer for 30 years. In October 1999 the defendant gave notice that, from the end of the current production season, they would not require any more garments from the claimant. One issue was whether the parties had entered into a long-term contract which could not be terminated by so short a period of notice. That issue was resolved in the defendant's favour as we have seen above, at 62. The claimant's alternative argument was that, even if there was no concluded long-term contract, the defendant was estopped from terminating the relationship by so short a notice period. In allowing the defendant's cross-appeal, that argument was rejected by the Court of Appeal which held that, applying the restrictions established by the English authorities, no form of estoppel (whether promissory, proprietary or estoppel by convention) could here succeed.

Sir Andrew Morritt V-C:

34 Counsel for M&S submits that the judge was wrong. He contends…that this court is, as the judge was, bound by three decisions of the Court of Appeal to conclude that the estoppel claim has no real prospect of success either. The three decisions and the propositions they respectively established are (1) a common law or promissory estoppel cannot create a cause of action (*Combe v Combe* [1951] 1 All ER 767, [1951] 2 KB 215); (2) an estoppel by convention cannot create a cause of action either (*Amalgamated Investment & Property Co. Ltd v Texas Commerce International Bank Ltd* [1981] 3 All ER 577, [1982] QB 84) and (3) accepting that a proprietary or equitable estoppel may create a cause of action it is limited to cases involving property rights, whether or not confined to land, (*Western Fish Products Ltd v Penwith District Council* [1981] 2 All ER 204 at 217).

35 Counsel for Baird did not dispute that those cases established the propositions for which M&S contended. Rather, he submitted, it is wrong to categorise particular types of estoppel and then impose limitations in each category not applicable to one or more of the other categories. He suggested that English law permits some cross-fertilisation between one category and another. He contended that English law should follow where the High Court of Australia has led in *Waltons Stores (Interstate) Ltd v Maher* (1988) 164 CLR 387 *and Commonwealth of Australia v Verwayen* (1990) 170 CLR 394 and permit estoppel to create causes of action in non-proprietary cases. In reply counsel for M&S conceded that if the Australian cases, to the effect that promissory estoppel extends to the enforcement of voluntary promises, represent the law of England then the judge was right and the cross-appeal must fail.

36 Warnings against categorisation have been given by Robert Goff J and Lord Denning MR in *Amalgamated Investment & Property Co. Ltd v Texas Commerce International Bank Ltd* [1981] All ER 923 at 935, 936 and 584, [1982] QB 84 at 103, 104, and 122, by Scarman LJ in *Crabb v Arun DC* [1975] 3 All ER 865 at 875, [1976] QB 179 at 192, 193 and by Lord Bingham of Cornhill in *Johnson v Gore Wood & Co* [2001] 1 All ER 481, [2001] 2 WLR 72. But dicta to the contrary effect are to be found in *First National Bank plc v Thompson* [1996] 1 All ER 140 at 144, [1996] Ch 231 at 236 per Millett LJ, *McIlkenny v Chief Constable of the West Midlands Police Force* [1980] 2 All ER 227 at 235, [1980] 1 QB 283 at 317 per Lord Denning MR and in *Johnson v Gore Wood & Co* [2001] 1 All ER p. 481 at 507, 508, [2001] 2 WLR 72 at 99 per Lord Goff of Chieveley.

37 As in the case of the contractual claim, it is important to appreciate exactly what is being alleged and why. The material allegation…is that M&S is estopped from denying that 'the relationship with BTH could only be determined by the giving of reasonable notice'. But by itself this claim, which has undoubted echoes of *Hughes v Metropolitan Rly Co.* (1877) 2 App Cas 439 [1874-80] All ER Rep 187 and *Central London Property Trust Ltd v High Trees House Ltd (1946)* [1956] 1 All ER 256, [1947] 1 KB 130, does not lead to the relief sought. For that purpose it is essential to establish an obligation by estoppel that, in the words of [Baird's claim], 'during the subsistence of the relationship Marks & Spencer would acquire garments from BTH in quantities and at prices which in all the circumstances were reasonable'. As counsel for Baird put it in their written argument 'BTH contends that an equity generated by estoppel can be a cause of action'. …

38 In my view English law, as presently understood, does not enable the creation or recognition by estoppel of an enforceable right of the type and in the circumstances relied on in this case. First it would be necessary for such an obligation to be sufficiently certain to enable the court to give effect to it. That such certainty is required in the field of estoppels such as is claimed in this case as well as in contract was indicated by the House of Lords in *Woodhouse AC Israel Cocoa Ltd v Nigerian Produce Marketing Co Ltd* [1972] 2 All ER 271, [1972] AC 741 and by Ralph Gibson LJ in *Troop v Gibson* [1986] 1 EGLR 1 at 6. For the reasons I have already given I do not think that the alleged obligation is sufficiently certain. Second, in my view, the decisions in the three Court of Appeal decisions on which M&S rely do establish that such an enforceable obligation cannot be established by estoppel in the circumstances relied on in this case. This conclusion does not involve the categorisation of estoppels but is a simple application of the principles established by those cases to the obligation relied on in this. …

Mance LJ:

80 Baird acknowledges that an estoppel precluding M & S from denying that the relationship with BTH could only be determined by the giving of reasonable notice would not assist, unless it also meant that M & S (and presumably Baird) were precluded from ceasing to place and honour orders for a 'reasonable' or 'appropriate' share of whatever were M & S's requirements from time to time, so as to ensure, to that extent, that the production facilities that Baird had devoted to M & S's business to date were maintained, or at least run down gradually, during such period of notice. The question presents itself how such an estoppel would differ in substance or effect (a) from the enforcement of obligations of insufficient certainty to be contractual (b) in circumstances where an intention to affect legal relations cannot objectively be imputed to either party. Baird's answer is that it does not seek to protect its expectation interest. That, it accepts, could only be done in contract. Rather it is seeking to protect its reliance interest.

83 In support of its claim based on an estoppel protecting its reliance interest, Baird argues that estoppel is or should be viewed as a flexible doctrine, that any rigid classification into different types of estoppel with differing requirements should be rejected, and that it is open

to English law to afford the protection proportionate to Baird's reliance for which Baird contends. ...Speaking generally, I accept that estoppel is a flexible doctrine, that broad equitable principles underlie its application in different fields (the concept of unconscionability being one such general principle) and that one should avoid 'rigid classification of equitable estoppel into exclusive and defined categories' (Robert Goff J's phrase in the *Amalgamated Investment* case [1981] 1 All ER 923 at 935, 936, [1982] QB 84 at 103, 104...).

84 However, not only are we bound in this court by previous authority on the scope of particular types of estoppel, but it seems to me inherent in the doctrine's very flexibility that it may take different shapes to fit the context of different fields. Throughout the passage in Robert Goff J's judgment in the *Amalgamated Investment* case [1981] 1 All ER 923 at 935-938, [1982] QB 84 at 103-107, to which Mr Field [counsel for Baird] drew our attention, careful attention was paid to context. That there are, on authority, certain distinctions between the characteristics of estoppel in different contexts is also clear. For example, it is established that to found a promissory estoppel, a representation must be clear and unequivocal: *Woodhouse AC Israel Cocoa Ltd. SA_v. Nigerian Produce Marketing Co. Ltd.* [1972] 2 All ER, [1972] AC 741. ...

85 In contrast, a proprietary estoppel may arise from promises of an 'equivocal nature': cf observations of Slade LJ in *Jones v. Watkins* [1987] CA Transcript 1200 (cited by Robert Walker LJ in *Gillett v Holt* [2000] 2 All ER 289 at 302, [2001] Ch 210 at 226). ...

86 In the present case, Baird's complaint is that M & S did not honour mutual understandings with M & S and/or assurances given by M & S. It is a 'general principle that a purely gratuitous promise is unenforceable at law or in equity' and—

'Furthermore, even if a purely gratuitous promise is acted upon by the promisee, generally speaking such conduct will not of itself give rise to an estoppel against the promissor; such an estoppel would be inconsistent with the general principle that purely gratuitous promises will not be enforced.'

87 See per Robert Goff J in the *Amalgamated Investment* case [1981] 1 All ER 923 at 937, [1982] QB 84 at 106, citing *Combe v Combe* [1951] 1 All ER 767, [1951] 2 KB 215. ...

88 How far an estoppel may assist in bringing about a cause of action, without standing alone as 'a cause of action in itself', has remained a matter of dispute over subsequent years. ...In the *Amalgamated Investment* case itself, Lord Denning MR and, on the view I would prefer, Brandon LJ held that both the company and the bank were bound by their conventional treatment of the company's guarantee of its subsidiary's indebtedness to the bank as extending to such subsidiary's indebtedness to the bank's subsidiary (Portsoken), thus entitling the bank to set up sums due under the guarantee, read in this extended sense, against the obligation that it otherwise had to account to the company for realisations which it had made.

91 In the present case, what is submitted is that the law ought to attach legal consequences to a bare assurance or conventional understanding (falling short of contract) between two parties, without any actual contract or third party being involved or affected. The suggested justification is the limitation of the relief claimed to reliance loss. On this submission, the requirements of contract (consideration, certainty and an intention to create legal relations) are irrelevant because no contract is asserted. The requirements of estoppel (eg that is an unequivocal promise to found a promissory estoppel or conventional conduct of sufficient clarity to found an estoppel by convention and, secondly, the objective intention to affect some actual or apparent pre-existing legal relationship) are bypassed by the limitation of relief. But no authority in this jurisdiction supports the submission that estoppel can here achieve so expanded an application, simply by limiting recovery to reliance loss...Any development of English law in such a direction could and should, in my view, now take place in the highest court.

92 It is also, on authority, an established feature of both promissory and conventional estoppel that the parties should have had the objective intention to make, affect or confirm a legal relationship. In *Combe v Combe*, all three judges, echoing what Denning J had said in the *High Trees* case, referred to the need for a promise or assurance 'intended to affect the legal relations between them' or 'intended to be binding' ([1951] 1 All ER 767 at 770, 772-774, [1951] 2 KB 215 at 220, 224, 225 per Denning, Birkett and Asquith LJJ respectively)…

94 As I have already said, the fact that there was never any agreement to reach or even to set out the essential principles which might govern any legally binding long-term relationship indicates that neither party can here objectively be taken to have intended to make any legally binding commitment of a long-term nature, and the law should not be ready to seek to fetter business relationships with its own view of what might represent appropriate business conduct, when parties have not chosen, or have not been willing or able, to do so in any identifiable legal terms themselves. These considerations, in my judgment, also make it wrong to afford relief based on estoppel, including relief limited to reliance loss, in the present context.

95 In support of his case, Mr Field seeks to liberate recognised principles of proprietary estoppel from the confines of that field, and use them to fertilise a more general development of equitable estoppel. …He…relied on the reasoning of the Australian cases of *Waltons Stores (Interstate) Ltd. v Maher* (1988) 164 CLR 387 and *The Commonwealth of Australia v Verwayen* (1990) 170 CLR 394 as pointing the road to development of English law.

97 There is…in this court binding authority that the scope of proprietary estoppel (leaving aside cases of mistaken belief as to the existence of current rights) does not extend beyond cases where A to the knowledge of B acts to his detriment in the expectation, encouraged by B, of acquiring a right over B's land or (probably) other property, such expectation arising from what B has said or done: *Western Fish Products v. Penwith DC* [1981] 2 All ER 204 at 217-219. In that case, it was insufficient that the plaintiffs acted to their detriment in developing their own land as a manufactury, in the belief that the District Council accepted that there was an established use for that purpose and would be prepared to give planning permission on that basis. The present case is not a case of encouragement of Baird to act to its detriment in respect of its own land or other property. It is also not a case of mistaken belief as to existing rights.

98 It does not, I think, follow axiomatically from the *Western Fish* case that this court could not and would not reach a result similar to that reached in the *Waltons Stores* case, even though not by the same reasoning. There was in the *Waltons Stores* case complete agreement on the terms of the lease. The agreement was merely unenforceable for want of compliance with the statute. It may be arguable that recognition of an estoppel here would not be to use estoppel 'as giving a cause of action in itself', and it would certainly not be to undermine the necessity of consideration. Rather, it would preclude the potential lessee from raising a collateral objection to the binding nature of the agreed lease (which was also effectively the reasoning of some of the members of the High Court of Australia: cf headnote para. (2) on (1988) 164 CLR 387 at 389). The High Court of Australia's decision in *The Commonwealth of Australia v. Verwayen* (where, after assurances by the Commonwealth that it would not plead either a limitation defence or absence of any duty of care, the Commonwealth was held estopped from later relying on either defence) could well also be reached under English law, without adopting the High Court of Australia's reasoning. I note the view of Professor Treitel to like effect in *Chitty on Contracts* (28th edn, 1999) vol. 1 paras 3-095, n 32 and 3-099, n 63.

Judge LJ delivered a concurring judgment.

1. This case firmly rejects the view that under the present English law promissory estoppel can be used as a cause of action (even if the claim is limited to the protection of the claimant's reliance interest). Yet Mance LJ suggested that *Walton Stores* might have been decided the same way in England. Do you agree with his reasoning on this point?

2. The Court of Appeal here accepted that different principles apply to different types of estoppel. Do you agree with that approach?

(3) Promissory Estoppel Requires a Clear and Unequivocal Promise

Woodhouse AC Israel Cocoa SA v Nigerian Produce Marketing Co Ltd
[1972] AC 941, House of Lords

The defendant sellers (Nigerian Produce) and the claimant buyers (Woodhouse) had entered into a contract for the sale of cocoa. This provided for payment in Nigerian pounds in Lagos. The buyers asked if the sellers would be prepared to accept payment of sterling in Lagos and the sellers, by a letter dated 30 September 1967, had replied that 'payment can be made in sterling and in Lagos'. Sterling was then devalued so that it was worth 14–15 per cent less than the Nigerian pound. The buyers argued that they were entitled to pay at the rate of one pound sterling for one Nigerian pound, which would have meant that the sellers bore the loss in the value of sterling. The buyers based their argument on the letter of 30 September being either a variation of the contract supported by consideration or as founding a promissory estoppel. In dismissing the buyers' appeal, the House of Lords held that both arguments failed because it was not clear that the promise to accept sterling meant to refer to measurement of the amount owing as opposed to the currency in which payment should be made.

Lord Hailsham of St Marylebone LC: Counsel for the appellants was asked whether he knew of any case in which an ambiguous statement had ever formed the basis of a purely promissory estoppel, as contended for here, as distinct from estoppel of a more familiar type based on factual misrepresentation. He candidly replied that he did not. I do not find this surprising, since it would really be an astonishing thing if, in the case of a genuine misunderstanding as to the meaning of an offer, the offeree could obtain by means of the doctrine of promissory estoppel something that he must fail to obtain under the conventional law of contract. I share the feeling of incredulity expressed by Lord Denning M.R. in the course of his judgment in the instant case when he said [1971] 2 Q.B. 23, 59-60:

> "If the judge be right, it leads to this extraordinary consequence: A letter which is not sufficient to *vary* a contract is, nevertheless, sufficient to work an *estoppel* – which will have the same effect as a *variation*."

There seem to me to be so many and such conclusive reasons for dismissing this appeal that it may be thought a work of supererogation to add yet another. But basically I feel convinced that there was never here any real room for the doctrine o[f] estoppel at all. If the exchange of letters was not variation, I believe it was nothing. The buyers asked for a variation in the mode of discharge of a contract of sale. If the proposal meant what they claimed, and was accepted and acted upon, I venture to think that the vendors would have been bound by their acceptance at least until they gave reasonable notice to terminate, and I imagine that a modern court would have found no difficulty in discovering consideration for such a promise. Business men know their own business best even when they appear to grant an indulgence, and in the present case I do not think that there would have been insuperable difficulty in spelling out consideration from the earlier correspondence. If, however, the two letters were insufficiently unambiguous and precise to form the basis, if accepted, for a variation in the contract I do not think their combined effect is sufficiently unambiguous or precise to form the basis of an estoppel which would produce the result of reducing the purchase price by no less than 14 per cent. against a vendor who had never consciously agreed to the proposition.

I desire to add that the time may soon come when the whole sequence of cases based on promissory estoppel since the war, beginning with *Central London Property Trust Ltd. v. High Trees House Ltd.* [1947] K.B. 130, may need to be reviewed and reduced to a coherent body of doctrine by the courts. I do not mean to say that any are to be regarded with suspicion. But as is common with an expanding doctrine they do raise problems of coherent exposition which have never been systematically explored.

Viscount Dilhorne: While I recognise that a party to a contract, while not agreeing to a variation of it, may nevertheless say that he will waive the performance by the other party of certain of its terms, and that if the other party relies on the waiver performance of the terms waived cannot be insisted on, in this case there was not a representation of the character alleged contained in or to be implied from the letter of September 30. To found an estoppel, the representation must be clear and unequivocal. In my opinion, the letter of September 30 could not reasonably be understood to contain or to imply a clear and unequivocal representation of the nature alleged.

Lord Pearson, Lord Cross of Chelsea and **Lord Salmon** delivered concurring speeches.

NOTES AND QUESTIONS

1. Does the normal law of certainty in contract (see Chapter 2 above) require promises to be 'clear and unequivocal'? Would it be better to apply the normal standard of certainty required in contract to promissory estoppel? Was there a clear and unequivocal promise in *Hughes v Metropolitan Rly Co* (above, 118)?

2. Viscount Dilhorne, as is commonplace, uses the language of 'waiver' alongside that of (promissory) estoppel. One must be careful with the language of waiver because it is broad enough to refer to, for example, a variation of a contract supported by consideration as well as to promissory estoppel. See generally Treitel, *The Law of Contract* (11th edn, 2003) 102–124.

3. More than 35 years on, Lord Hailsham's call for a judicial review and restatement of the doctrine of promissory estoppel has still not been met.

4. Just as certainty and intention to create legal relations are linked but separate doctrines in contract law so, in relation to promissory estoppel, a separate requirement from certainty is that the promisor intended to create legal relations. See Denning J's statement of the doctrine in the *High Trees* case and in *Combe v Combe* at 119 and 122 above. See also *Baird Textiles Holdings Ltd v Marks & Spencer plc*, above, 136.

(4) Does Promissory Estoppel Require Reliance or Detrimental Reliance?

WJ Alan & Co Ltd v El Nasr Export and Import Co
[1972] 2 QB 189, Court of Appeal

The sellers (WJ Alan & Co Ltd) were Kenyan producers of coffee. They contracted to sell coffee to the buyers (El Nasr Export) at 262 Kenyan shillings per hundredweight. There were to be two shipments and payment was to be made by letter of credit in Kenyan shillings. In fact the letter of credit opened by the buyers was for payment in sterling rather than Kenyan shillings. The sellers made no objection to this and presented invoices in sterling. At the time of the first shipment, this made no difference because there was parity between sterling and Kenyan currency. However, after the sellers had presented an invoice in sterling for the second shipment, sterling was devalued. Payment under the credit was made in sterling but the sellers claimed an additional sum to bring the price up to 262 Kenyan shillings per hundredweight. The Court of Appeal held that this claim should fail for two reasons: (i) the sellers had 'waived' their strict rights to insist on payment in Kenyan shillings or (ii) (per Megaw and Stephenson LJJ) there had been a variation, supported by consideration, of the contract so as to allow payment in sterling.

Lord Denning MR: [A] "conforming" letter of credit… is… one which is in accordance with the stipulations in the contract of sale. But in many cases – and our present case is one – the letter of credit does not conform. Then negotiations may take place as a result of which the letter of credit is modified so as to be satisfactory to the seller. Alternatively, the seller may be content to accept the letter of credit as satisfactory as it is, without modification. Once this happens, then the letter of credit is to be regarded as if it were a conforming letter of credit…

There are two cases on this subject. One is *Panoutsos v. Raymond Hadley Corporation of New York* [1917] 2 K.B. 473; but the facts are only to be found fully set out in 22 Com.Cas. 207. The other is *Enrico Furst & Co. v. W. E. Fischer Ltd.* [1960] 2 Lloyd's Rep. 340. In each of those cases the letter of credit did not conform to the contract of sale. In each case the non-conformity was in that it was not a confirmed credit. But the sellers took no objection to the letter of credit on that score. On the contrary, they asked for the letter of credit to be extended: and it was extended. In each case the sellers sought afterwards to cancel the contract on the ground that the letter of credit was not in conformity with the contract. In each case the court held that they could not do so.

What is the true basis of those decisions? … It is an instance of the general principle which was first enunciated by Lord Cairns L.C. in *Hughes v. Metropolitan Railway Co.* (1877) 2 App.Cas 439, and rescued from oblivion by *Central London Property Trust Ltd. v. High Trees House Ltd.* [1947] K.B. 130. The principle is much wider than waiver itself: but waiver is a good instance of its application.

The principle of waiver is simply this: If one party, by his conduct, leads another to believe that the strict rights arising under the contract will not be insisted upon, intending that the other should act on that belief, and he does act on it, then the first party will not afterwards be allowed to insist on the strict legal rights when it would be inequitable for him to do so: see *Plasticmoda Societa per Azioni v. Davidsons (Manchester) Ltd.* [1952] 1 Lloyd's Rep. 527, 539. There may be no consideration moving from him who benefits by the waiver. There may be no detriment to him by acting on it. There may be nothing in writing. Nevertheless, the one who waives his strict rights cannot afterwards insist on them. His strict rights are at any rate suspended so long as the waiver lasts. He may on occasion be able to revert to his strict legal rights for the future by giving reasonable notice in that behalf, or otherwise making it plain by his conduct that he will thereafter insist upon them: *Tool Metal Manufacturing Co. Ltd. v. Tungsten Electric Co. Ltd.* [1955] 1 W.L.R. 761. But there are cases where no withdrawal is possible. It may be too late to withdraw: or it cannot be done without injustice to the other party. In that event he is bound by his waiver. He will not be allowed to revert to his strict legal rights. He can only enforce them subject to the waiver he has made.

Instances of these principles are ready to hand in contracts for the sale of goods. A seller may, by his conduct, lead the buyer to believe that he is not insisting on the stipulated time for exercising an option: *Bruner v. Moore* [1904] 1 Ch. 305. A buyer may, by requesting delivery, lead the seller to believe that he is not insisting on the contractual time for delivery: *Charles Rickards Ltd. v. Oppenheim* [1950] 1 K.B. 616, 621. A seller may, by his conduct, lead the buyer to believe that he will not insist on a confirmed letter of credit: *Plasticmoda* [1952] 1 Lloyd's Rep. 527, but will accept an unconfirmed one instead: *Panoustsos v. Raymond Hadley Corporation of New York* [1917] 2 K.B. 473; *Enrico Furst & Co. v. W. E. Fischer* [1960] 2 Lloyd's Rep. 340. A seller may accept a less sum for his goods than the contracted price, thus inducing him to believe that he will not enforce payment of the balance: *Central London Property Trust Ltd. v. High Trees House Ltd.* [1947] K.B. 130 and *D. & C. Builders Ltd. v. Rees* [1966] 2 Q.B. 617, 624. In none of these cases does the party who acts on the belief suffer any detriment. It is not a detriment, but a benefit to him, to have an extension of time or to pay less, or as the case may be. Nevertheless, he has conducted his affairs on the basis that he has that benefit and it would not be equitable now to deprive him of it.

The judge rejected this doctrine because, he said, "there is no evidence of the buyers having acted to their detriment." I know that it has been suggested in some quarters that there must be detriment. But I can find no support for it in the authorities cited by the judge. The nearest approach to it is the statement of Viscount Simonds in the *Tool Metal* case [1955] 1 W.L.R. 761, 764, that the other must have been led "to alter his position," which was adopted by Lord Hodson in *Ajayi v. R. T. Briscoe (Nigeria) Ltd.* [1964] 1 W.L.R. 1326, 1330. But that only means that he must have been led to act differently from what he otherwise would have done. And if you study the cases in which the doctrine has been applied, you will see that all that is required is that the one should have "*acted* on the belief induced by the other party." That is how Lord Cohen put it in the *Tool Metal* case [1955] 1 W.L.R. 761, 799, and that is how I would put it myself.

Megaw LJ: In my view, if there were no variation, the buyers would still be entitled to succeed on the ground of waiver. The relevant principle is, in my opinion, that which was stated by Lord Cairns L.C., in *Hughes v. Metropolitan Railway Co.* (1877) 2 App.Cas. 439, 448. The acceptance by the sellers of the sterling credit was, as I have said, a once-for-all acceptance. It was not a concession for a specified period of time or one which the sellers could operate as long as they chose and thereafter unilaterally abrogate; any more than the buyers would have been entitled to alter the terms of the credit or to have demanded a refund from the sellers if, after this credit had been partly used, the relative values of the currencies had changed in the opposite way.

Stephenson LJ: I would leave open the question whether the action of the other party induced by the party who "waives" his contractual rights can be any alteration of his position, as Lord Denning M.R. has said, or must, as the judge thought, be an alteration to his detriment, or for the worse, in some sense. In this case the buyers did, I think, contrary to the judge's view, act to their detriment on the sellers' waiver, if that is what it was, and the contract was varied for good consideration, which may be another way of saying the same thing; so that I need not, and do not, express a concluded opinion on that controversial question.

1. The importance of this case lies in Lord Denning MR's view that for promissory estoppel (or 'waiver' as he here termed it, see above, 141, note 2) there is no need for *detrimental* reliance. Mere reliance (ie acting on) the promise is sufficient.

2. Although Stephenson LJ thought that the buyers had acted to their detriment, the facts on this are not clear. Ie there appeared to be no evidence that the buyers would be in a worse position to pay the full amount measured in Kenyan currency than they would have been had no promise to accept sterling been made by the sellers.

3. Was there any *detrimental* reliance by the tenant in the *High Trees* case?

Société Italo–Belge pour le Commerce et l'Industrie SA v Palm and Vegetable Oils (Malaysia) Sdn Bhd, The Post Chaser [1981] 2 Lloyd's Rep 695, Queen's Bench Division

The claimant sellers contracted to sell palm oil to the defendant buyers. It was a term of the contract that, as soon as possible after sailing, the sellers should notify the buyers of the name of the ship being used. In breach of contract the sellers did not notify the buyers until more than a month after the ship had sailed. The buyers made no protest about this and requested the sellers to transfer the documents covering the goods to sub-buyers. Two days later the sub-buyers rejected the documents because of the late notification of the ship's name as, on the same day, did the buyers. The sellers were therefore forced to sell the oil elsewhere at a lower price than the contract price. In an action for damages by the sellers, they argued that the buyers had 'waived' their right to reject the documents. Although Robert Goff J decided that the buyers had made an unequivocal representation that they were waiving their rights to insist on a prompt notification of the ship, he held that the sellers had not suffered any prejudice by reliance on that representation, so that the buyers could go back on it.

Robert Goff J: [T]here next arises the question whether there was any sufficient reliance by the sellers on this representation to give rise to an equitable estoppel. Here there arose a difference between [counsel for the sellers] and [counsel for the buyers] as to the degree of reliance which is required. It is plain, however, from the speech of Lord Cairns in *Hughes v Metropolitan Railway Co.*, (1877) 2 App. Cas. 439 at p 448 that the representor will not be allowed to enforce his rights "where it would be inequitable having regard to the dealings which have taken place between the parties"; accordingly there must be such action, or inaction, by the representee on the faith of the representation as will render it inequitable to permit the representor to enforce his strict legal rights

 ...

 The case therefore raises in an acute form the question...whether it is sufficient for this purpose that the representee should simply have conducted his affairs on the basis of the representation, or whether by so doing he must have suffered some form of prejudice which renders it inequitable for the representor to go back on his representation. A simple example of the latter did occur where a seller, relying upon a representation by his buyers, arranged his affairs and tendered documents to the buyer and by so doing missed an opportunity to dispose of the documents elsewhere for a price greater than that available when the buyer later rejected the documents. Such a conclusion could only be based on findings of fact as to the movements of the market over the relevant period. In [*Bremer Handelsgesellschaft mbH v Vanden Avenne-Izegem PVBA* [1978] 2 Lloyd's Rep 109] Lord Salmon felt it unnecessary to resolve this problem because, as he held, "the sellers clearly acted on the basis of waiver, and also to their detriment in spending time and money on the appropriations" which they made...

On the other hand in *WJ Alan & Co Ltd v El Nasr Export and Import Co* [1972] 1 Lloyd's Rep. 313; [1972] 2 QB 189, Lord Denning M.R. (at pp 323-324 and 213), while stating the principle of equitable estoppel in terms that it must be inequitable for the representor to be allowed to go back on his representation, nevertheless considered that it might be sufficient for that purpose that the representee had conducted his affairs on the basis of the representation, and that it was immaterial that he has suffered any detriment by doing so.

...

I approach the matter as follows. The fundamental principle is that stated by Lord Cairns, viz. that the representor will not be allowed to enforce his rights "where it would be inequitable having regard to the dealings which have thus taken place between the parties". To establish such inequity it is not necessary to show detriment; indeed, the representee may have benefited from the representation and yet it may be inequitable, at least without reasonable notice, for the representor to enforce his legal rights. Take the facts of *Central London Property Trust Ltd v High Trees House* [1947] K.B. 130, the case in which Lord ... Denning, M.R., breathed new life into the doctrine of equitable estoppel. The representation was by a letter to the effect that he would be content to accept a reduced rent. In such a case, although the lessee has benefited from the reduction in rent, it may well be inequitable for the lessor to insist upon his legal right to the unpaid rent because the lessee has conducted his affairs on the basis that he would only have to pay rent at the lower rate; and a court might well think it right to conclude that only after reasonable notice could a lessor return to charging rent at the higher rate specified in the lease. Furthermore it would be open to the court, in any particular case, to infer from the circumstances of the case that the representee must have conducted his affairs in such a way that it would be inequitable for the representor to enforce his rights, or to do so without reasonable notice. But it does not follow that in every case in which the representee has acted, or failed to act, in reliance on the representation it will be inequitable for the representor to enforce his rights; for the nature of the action, or inaction, may be sufficient to give rise to the equity, in which event a necessary requirement stated by Lord Cairns for the application of the doctrine would not have been fulfilled.

This, in my judgment, is the principle which I have to apply in the present case. Here, all that happened was that the sellers...presented the document on the same day as the buyers made their representation; and within two days the documents were rejected. Now on these simple facts, although it is plain that the sellers did actively rely on the buyers' representation, and did conduct their affairs in reliance on it, by presenting the documents, I cannot see anything which would render it inequitable for the buyers thereafter to enforce their legal right to reject the documents. In particular, having regard to the very short time which elapsed between the date of the representation, and the date of the presentation of the documents on the one hand, and the date of the rejection on the other hand, I cannot see that, in the absence of any evidence that the sellers' position had been prejudiced by reason of their action in reliance on the representation, it is possible to infer that they suffered any such prejudice. In these circumstances, a necessary element for the application of the doctrine of equitable estoppel is lacking; and I decide this point in favour of the buyers.

1.   Robert Goff J here took the view that, while detrimental reliance was needed in some cases (including this one) for equitable (ie promissory) estoppel to operate, in others (eg *High Trees*) mere reliance was sufficient. This would turn on what was equitable or inequitable on the particular facts.

2.   Is the answer to the question whether detriment is needed fact-specific or is it a policy question that the law ought to resolve once and for all?

(5) Promissory Estoppel Cannot be Founded on a Promise Induced by the Promisee's Inequitable Conduct

D & C Builders Ltd v Rees [1966] 2 QB 617, Court of Appeal

The claimants were a small firm of builders. They were engaged to do some work for Mr and Mrs Rees (the defendants). The defendants paid £250, which left a balance owing of some £483. The claimants made several requests for payment but received no reply. The claimants were by now in dire financial straits as the defendants knew. Mrs Rees, in a telephone call, offered to pay the claimants £300 in full settlement. Saying that they had no choice, the claimants accepted this and took a cheque for £300. The claimants brought this action for the balance and succeeded. The majority (Winn and Danckwerts LJJ) based their decision on *Foakes v Beer*, ie there was no consideration given by Mr and Mrs Rees for the claimants' promise to accept less. Lord Denning MR saw the case as turning on promissory estoppel and Danckwerts LJ, in obiter dicta, also touched on that approach, albeit in looking at whether there was a 'true accord'. Both decided that the equitable doctrine was inapplicable because of the intimidation by the defendants.

Lord Denning MR: This case is of some consequence: for it is a daily occurrence that a merchant or tradesman, who is owed a sum of money, is asked to take less. The debtor says he is in difficulties. He offers a lesser sum in settlement, cash down. He says he cannot pay more. The creditor is considerate. He accepts the proffered sum and forgives him the rest of the debt. The question arises: Is the settlement binding on the creditor? The answer is that, in point of law, the creditor is not bound by the settlement. He can the next day sue the debtor for the balance: and get judgment. The law was so stated in 1602 by Lord Coke in *Pinnel's Case* (1602) 5 Co.Rep. 117a – and accepted in 1889 by the House of Lords in *Foakes v. Beer* (1884) 9 App.Cas. 605.

     ...
     This doctrine of the common law has come under heavy fire. It was ridiculed by Sir George Jessel in *Couldery v. Bartram* (1881) 19 Ch.D. 394, 399. It was said to be mistaken by Lord Blackburn in *Foakes v. Beer* 9 App.Cas. 605, 622. It was condemned by the Law Revision Committee ([1937] Cmd. 5449), paras. 20 and 21. But a remedy has been found. The harshness of the common law has been relieved. Equity has stretched out a merciful hand to help the debtor. The courts have invoked the broad principle stated by Lord Cairns in *Hughes v. Metropolitan Railway Co.*(1877) 2 App.Cas. 439, 448

          "It is the first principle upon which all courts of equity proceed, that if parties, who have entered into definite and distinct terms involving certain legal results, afterwards by their own act or with their own consent enter upon a course of negotiation which has the effect of leading one of the parties to suppose that *the strict rights arising under the contract will not be enforced,* or will be kept in suspense, or held in abeyance, the person who otherwise might have enforced those rights *will not be allowed to enforce them when it would be inequitable having regard to the dealings which have taken place between the parties."*

It is worth noticing that the principle may be applied, not only so as to suspend strict legal rights, but also so as to preclude the enforcement of them.

This principle has been applied to cases where a creditor agrees to accept a lesser sum in discharge of a greater. So much so that we can now say that, when a creditor and a debtor enter upon a course of negotiation, which leads the debtor to suppose that, on payment of the lesser sum, the creditor will not enforce payment of the balance, and on the faith thereof the debtor pays the lesser sum and the creditor accepts it as satisfaction: then the creditor will not be allowed to enforce payment of the balance when it would be inequitable to do so. This was well illustrated during the last war. Tenants went away to escape the bombs and left their houses unoccupied. The landlords accepted a reduced rent for the time they were empty. It was held that the landlords could not afterwards turn round and sue for the balance, see *Central London Property Trust Ltd. v. High Trees House Ltd* [1947] 1 K.B. 130 This caused at the time some eyebrows to be raised in high places. But they have been lowered since. The solution was so obviously just that no one could well gainsay it.

In applying this principle, however, we must note the qualification: The creditor is only barred from his legal rights when it would be *inequitable* for him to insist upon them. Where there has been a true *accord,* under which the creditor voluntarily agrees to accept a lesser sum in satisfaction, and the debtor *acts upon* that accord by paying the lesser sum and the creditor accepts it, then it is inequitable for the creditor afterwards to insist on the balance. But he is not bound unless there has been truly an accord between them.

In the present case, on the facts as found by the judge, it seems to me that there was no true accord. The debtor's wife held the creditor to ransom. The creditor was in need of money to meet his own commitments, and she knew it. When the creditor asked for payment of the £480 due to him, she said to him in effect: "We cannot pay you the £480. But we will pay you £300 if you will accept it in settlement. If you do not accept it on those terms, you will get nothing. £300 is better than nothing." She had no right to say any such thing. She could properly have said: "We cannot pay you more than £300. Please accept it on account." But she had no right to insist on his taking it in settlement. When she said: "We will pay you nothing unless you accept £300 in settlement," she was putting undue pressure on the creditor. She was making a threat to break the contract (by paying nothing) and she was doing it so as to compel the creditor to do what he was unwilling to do (to accept £300 in settlement): and she succeeded. He complied with her demand. That was on recent authority a case of intimidation: see *Rookes v. Barnard* [1964] A.C. 1129, H.L.(E.) and *Stratford (J. T.) & Son Ltd. v. Lindley* [1964] 2 W.L.R. 1002, 1015, 1016, C.A. In these circumstances there was no true accord so as to found a defence of accord and satisfaction: see *Day v. McLea* (1889) 22 Q.B.D. 610, C.A. There is also no equity in the defendant to warrant any departure from the due course of law. No person can insist on a settlement procured by intimidation.

Danckwerts LJ: I agree ... that, in the circumstances of the present case, there was no true accord. The Rees really behaved very badly. They knew of the plaintiffs' financial difficulties and used their awkward situation to intimidate them. The plaintiffs did not wish to accept the sum of £300 in discharge of the debt of £482, but were desperate to get some money. It would appear also that the defendant and his wife misled the plaintiffs as to their own financial position. Rees, in his evidence, said: "In June (1964) I could have paid £700 odd. I could have settled the whole bill." There is no evidence that by August, or even by November, their financial situation had deteriorated so that they could not pay the £482.

Nor does it appear that their position was altered to their detriment by reason of the receipt given by the plaintiffs. The receipt was given on November 14, 1964. On November

23, 1964, the plaintiffs' solicitors wrote a letter making it clear that the payment of £300 was being treated as a payment on account. I cannot see any ground in this case for treating the payment as a satisfaction on equitable principles.

Winn LJ gave a concurring judgment without touching on promissory estoppel.

NOTES AND QUESTIONS

1. In deciding that there was no consideration provided by Mr and Mrs Rees, the majority (Winn and Danckwerts LJJ) overruled an earlier decision, *Goddard v O'Brien* (1882) 9 QBD 37, which held that payment by cheque, rather than cash, was good consideration for a promise to accept a lesser sum.
2. The inequitable conduct of Mr and Mrs Rees in inducing the promise was what would now be referred to as economic duress (see Chapter 14 below). What other types of conduct would equally bar promissory estoppel (see, on this, Danckwerts LJ's judgment)?
3. Danckwerts LJ indicated that, in his view, *detrimental* reliance was required for the equitable doctrine. Contrast the view of Lord Denning in this case and in other cases (see above, 142–144).

(6) Does Promissory Estoppel Extinguish or Suspend Rights?

Tool Metal Manufacturing Co Ltd v Tungsten Electric Co Ltd
[1955] 1 WLR 761, House of Lords

Tool Metal (TMMC) owned the patents over certain hard metal alloys. By a contract made in 1938 they granted Tungsten Electric (TECO) a licence until 1947 to deal in those alloys. If TECO's use of the alloys in any given month exceeded a set quota, TECO was to pay TMMC compensation. In 1942, triggered by war-time circumstances, TMMC agreed to suspend the payment of compensation until a new agreement was reached. In September 1944 TMMC submitted to TECO the draft of a proposed new agreement which contained a provision for the revival of compensation. This was rejected by TECO. In 1945 TECO brought an action against TMMC for breach of contract and fraudulent misrepresentation in relation to the 1938 agreement. TMMC counterclaimed in March 1946 for the compensation payable in respect of use of the alloys after 1 June 1945. That counterclaim failed in the Court of Appeal (reported at (1952) 69 RPC 108) on the basis that, while TMMC had promised only to suspend the payment of compensation, which could therefore be revived, the suspension was binding in equity (applying *Hughes v Metropolitan Rly*, see above, 118) until terminated by reasonable notice and reasonable notice had not been given. TMMC thereupon commenced a new action in 1950 claiming compensation as from January 1947 and arguing that the making of the counterclaim in March 1946 in the first action constituted the reasonable notice necessary to terminate the suspension of payments of compensation (ie nine months' notice had been given). The House of Lords held that that argument should succeed: the promised suspension, binding in equity, had been terminated by reasonable notice.

Lord Tucker: The sole question, therefore, before the courts on this issue in the present action has been throughout: Was the counterclaim in the first action a sufficient intimation to terminate the period of suspension which has been found to exist?

...

It has been said more than once that every case involving the application of this equitable doctrine [ie the doctrine in *Hughes v Metropolitan Rly*] must depend upon its own particular circumstances. It is, of course, clear ... that there are some cases where the period of suspension clearly terminates on the happening of a certain event or the cessation of a previously existing state of affairs or on the lapse of a reasonable period thereafter. In such cases no intimation or notice of any kind may be necessary. But in other cases where there is nothing to fix the end of the period which may be dependent upon the will of the person who has given or made the concession, equity will no doubt require some notice or intimation together with a reasonable period for readjustment before the grantor is allowed to enforce his strict rights. No authority has been cited which binds your Lordships to hold that in all such cases the notice must take any particular form or specify a date for the termination of the suspensory period. This is not surprising having regard to the infinite variety of circumstances which may give rise to this principle which was stated in broad terms and must now be regarded as of general application. It should, I think, be applied with great caution to purely creditor and debtor relationships which involve no question of forfeiture or cancellation, and it would be unfortunate if the law were to introduce into this field technical requirements with regard to notice and the like which might tend to penalise or discourage the making of reasonable concessions.

...

In my view, the counterclaim of March 26, 1946, followed by a period of nine months to January 1, 1947, from which date compensation in the present action is claimed, is sufficient to satisfy the requirements of equity and entitle T.M.M.C. to recover compensation under ... the deed as from the latter date. In the somewhat peculiar circumstances of the present case any other result would, I think, be highly inequitable.

Lord Cohen: [T]o make the principle [in *Hughes v Metropolitan Rly*] applicable the party setting up the doctrine must show that he has acted on the belief induced by the other party, but this factor is of no importance in the instant case as it has been decided in the first action that the principle is applicable. Does this principle afford a defence to the claim in the present action?

[I]n the present case equity required T.M.M.C. to give some form of notice to TECO before compensation would become payable. But it has never been decided that in every case notice should be given before a temporary concession ceases to operate. It might, for instance, cease automatically on the occurrence of a particular event. Still less has any case decided that where notice is necessary it must take a particular form.

Romer L.J. seems to have taken the view that the counterclaim could not be a notice because you cannot terminate an agreement by repudiating it. With all respect, the fallacy of this argument consists in treating the arrangement found to exist by the Court of Appeal in the first action as an agreement binding in law. It was not an agreement, it was a voluntary concession by T.M.M.C. which, for reasons of equity, the court held T.M.M.C. could not cease to allow without plain intimation to TECO of their intention so to do. The counterclaim seems to me a plain intimation of such change of intention ...

Viscount Simonds delivered a concurring speech on this matter. **Lord Oaksey** delivered a concurring speech without dealing with this matter.

NOTES AND QUESTIONS

1. This is a very difficult case to analyse. It is possible to interpret it as showing that promissory estoppel is a suspensory doctrine; or that, in relation to

periodic payments, it is suspensory as regards future, but not past, payments. However, such interpretations seem misleading because, as in *Hughes v Metropolitan Rly*, the promise in this case was intended to last for only a limited period. Ie TMMC was promising to suspend its right to compensation only pending a new agreement. When TECO rejected a new agreement, TMMC's promise ran out and, by giving reasonable notice, it could revert to its original rights from then on without breaking its promise. But during the period when the promise was operative, and until reasonable notice expired, the right to compensation was extinguished so that TMMC could not later claim compensation for that period. The implication, therefore, is that for the period during which a promise is intended to be operative, the doctrine is extinctive. What was the tenor of Denning J's judgment on this issue in the *High Trees* case (see above, 121, question 2)? In *D & C Builders v Rees* Lord Denning MR said, above, 147, 'It is worth noticing that the principle may be applied, not only so as to suspend strict legal rights, but also so as to preclude the enforcement of them.'

2. Taking the extinctive interpretation of promissory estoppel removes a possible way of partly reconciling promissory estoppel and *Foakes v Beer* (above, 111). The suspensory view would say that, even where a creditor's promise to accept less was meant to last forever (as in *Foakes v Beer*), the creditor could always revert to his right to claim the full amount by giving reasonable notice to the debtor. The extinctive view would, in contrast, say that, as the promise was intended to be permanent, the creditor's right to claim the balance forgone had been extinguished.

3. In *EA Ajayi v RT Briscoe (Nigeria) Ltd* [1964] 1 WLR 1326 the claimant owner of lorries had let them out on hire-purchase to the defendant. Some of the lorries needed repair and the owner had agreed to the hire-purchaser not paying the instalments due on those lorries while they were being repaired. However, despite the doctrine of promissory estoppel, the owner was held able to recover the full instalments due (including arrears) once the lorries had been repaired and made available to the hire-purchaser. Lord Hodson, giving the judgment of the Privy Council, rather confusingly linked the question whether promissory estoppel is suspensory or extinctive with the issue of whether the promisee had detrimentally relied (by irretrievably altering its position). In a well-known statement, he said, at 1330:

'The principle which has been described as quasi estoppel and perhaps more aptly as promissory estoppel, is that when one party to a contract in the absence of fresh consideration agrees not to enforce his rights an equity will be raised in favour of the other party. This equity is, however, subject to the qualification (a) that the other party has altered his position, (b) that the promisor can resile from his promise on giving reasonable notice, which need not be a formal notice, giving the promisee a reasonable opportunity of resuming his position, (c) the promise only becomes final and irrevocable if the promisee cannot resume his position.'

Although Lord Hodson's judgment is far from easy, he appears to have held that promissory estoppel did not here apply, so that the hire-purchaser was bound to pay all the instalments, because there had been no detrimental (ie irretrievable) alteration of position by the hire-purchaser. For the view that detrimental reliance is not needed, see Lord Denning's view in *Alan v El Nasr* above, 143, in which he contrasted Lord Hodson's words in *Ajayi v Briscoe* with those of Lord Cohen in the *Tool Metal* case.

Additional Reading for Chapter 3

J Beatson, *Anson's Law of Contract* (28th edn, 2002) 88–126
S Smith, *Atiyah's Introduction to the Law of Contract* (6th edn, 2005) 106–30

Law Revision Committee, *Sixth Interim Report (Statute of Frauds and the Doctrine of Consideration)* (1937, Cmd 5449)
While stopping short of recommending the abolition of consideration, the LRC proposed a number of reforms to the doctrine. These included that, even though not supported by consideration, the following promises should be binding: promises in writing, promises for a past consideration, promises to accept part payment as discharging a debt, promising to do what one is already bound to do, firm offers (ie offers promised to be open for a period), and promises detrimentally relied on by the promisee (where the promisor knew, or should have known, that the promisee would rely on the promise).

P Atiyah, *Consideration in Contracts: A Fundamental Restatement* (1971) reprinted (with revisions to meet the criticism of Treitel) in *Essays on Contract* (1986) 179
In this famous essay, Atiyah attacks the conventional view of the doctrine of consideration on the basis that it does not correspond with what the courts are doing. So the various propositions within the standard approach to consideration are 'deconstructed' by reference to decided cases that do not fit the propositions. On Atiyah's view, consideration means nothing more than a good reason for the enforcement of a promise and the reasons, relied on by the courts in the past, cannot be strait-jacketed into the conventional description. It is especially noteworthy that, on his view, it is a nonsense to treat 'promissory estoppel' as an exception to consideration: a promise that has been relied upon is supported by consideration because the reliance constitutes the good reason (and hence the consideration) for enforcing the promise.

G Treitel, 'Consideration: a Critical Analysis of Professor Atiyah's Fundamental Restatement' (1976) 50 *ALJ* 439
Treitel argues that Atiyah is wrong to regard consideration as meaning nothing more than a good reason for enforcing a promise. The conventional doctrine does explain

what the courts are doing and there is flexibility because courts can 'invent' consideration. In England, in contrast to the USA, only a narrow doctrine of promissory estoppel is required because of the broad definition of consideration.

W Slawson, 'The Role of Reliance in Contract Damages' (1990) 76 *Cornell LR* 197
The author examines the long-running debate in the United States as to whether promissory estoppel triggers reliance, rather than expectation, damages. He argues that, as a matter of precedent and for many reasons of principle and policy, the expectation interest is, and should be, protected for promissory estoppel.

E Cooke, 'Estoppel and the Protection of Expectations' (1997) 17 *Legal Studies* 258
Cooke argues that, in England, the primary function of estoppel (and she focuses essentially on proprietary and promissory estoppel) is, and should be, to protect and fulfil expectations and not to compensate reliance loss. Departures from that are exceptional.

S Gardner, 'The Remedial Discretion in Proprietary Estoppel' (1999) 115 *LQR* 353
This article examines what is meant when it is said that, for proprietary estoppel, relief is discretionary. Rejecting the view that this means that courts adopt whatever measure of relief they think fit, Gardner argues that the best fit with the case law is that, while protection of the expectation interest is the normal aim, this can be departed from where it is impracticable to protect that interest or for a limited range of other reasons.

J Edelman, 'Remedial Certainty or Remedial Discretion in Estoppel after Giumelli?' (1999) 15 *JCL* 179
Edelman argues that, in the light of the Australian High Court decision in *Giumelli v Giumelli* (1999) 196 CLR 101, 'Australian estoppel' rests on a 'rule-based discretion' whereby the promisee's expectation interest is protected. While such an estoppel is not enforcing a promise as a contract (in his words 'estoppel is not a contract') it does enforce a promise in the same manner as a contract.

R Halson, 'The Offensive Limits of Promissory Estoppel' [1999] *LMCLQ* 256
The author argues that, as well as being used defensively, promissory estoppel can, in various ways, assist a claimant who is asserting a recognised cause of action. However, contrary to the law in, eg, Australia, it does not create a new cause of action and there are good reasons why it should not do so.

Sir Guenter Treitel, *Some Landmarks of Twentieth Century Contract Law* (2002) Ch 1 ('Agreements to Vary Contracts')
Treitel examines the pre-existing duty rule and promissory estoppel by looking back at leading cases such as *Stilk v Myrick, Foakes v Beer, High Trees* and *Williams v Roffey Bros.* He distinguishes between 'increasing pacts' (promises to pay more), 'decreasing pacts' (promises to accept less) and 'cross-overs' (whether one can use, eg, *Williams v Roffey Bros* in a *Foakes v Beer* situation).

Principles of European Contract Law (eds **O Lando and H Beale, 2000**) 137–43, 157–8

Article 2:101: Conditions for the Conclusion of a Contract
(1) A contract is concluded if:

(a) the parties intend to be legally bound, and

(b) they reach a sufficient agreement without any further requirement.

Article 2:107: Promises Binding without Acceptance
A promise which is intended to be legally binding without acceptance is binding.

[These two provisions show that, in contrast to English law, consideration is not required under PECL.]

Part Two

The Terms of a Contract

4

Identifying the Terms

On the assumption that a contract has been formed, we are asking in this chapter, 'What are the terms of the contract?' In some situations, the answer to this is easy. This will be so, for example, where both parties have read and signed or exchanged a written legally-drafted document containing all the terms. But often matters are not so straightforward and difficulties can arise whether the contract is made in writing or orally or partly orally and partly in writing. In this chapter, we examine three discrete issues, each of which is dealt with in a separate section. First, have the statements made by one party, which have been relied on by the other in entering into the contract, become terms of the contract or are they 'mere representations' outside the contract? Secondly, have a party's written terms become incorporated into the contract? And thirdly, in addition to the express terms, are there any terms to be implied into the contract?

Before looking at those issues, we need to say something briefly about the 'parol evidence rule'. That 'rule' is so riddled with exceptions that few believe in its existence in the modern law. The basic idea is that, where there is a written contract, neither party can adduce evidence extrinsic to that contract to establish that there are other terms. Very obvious exceptions to this include implied terms (below, 197) and 'collateral warranties' (below, 161, note 2). Indeed as the 'rule' can be departed from wherever a court is satisfied that to do so accords with the parties' intentions, the better view is that there is no such rule. The so-called rule merely indicates that, where terms have been reduced to writing, there is an evidential burden of proof on a party alleging that there are other binding terms.

1. TERMS OR MERE REPRESENTATIONS?

Various statements may have been made in the course of negotiations which have been relied on by the other party in entering into the contract. It is important to know which of these statements have become incorporated as terms of the contract (ie as contractual promises) and which remain 'mere representations' outside the contract. The latter do not trigger liability in contract although, as we shall see in Chapter 11, they may trigger (as may representations incorporated as terms) liability for misrepresentation, whether in the tort of deceit or the tort of negligence or under section 2 of the Misrepresentation Act 1967.

Introductory reading: E McKendrick, *Contract Law* (7th edn, 2007) Ch 8.

Oscar Chess Ltd v Williams [1957] 1 WLR 370, Court of Appeal

The defendant's mother owned a Morris car, the registration book showing first registration on 13 April 1948. The defendant used the Morris, often giving lifts to Mr Ladd, a salesman employed by the claimants. The defendant wanted to acquire a Hillman Minx for £650, and offered the Morris to the claimants in part-exchange. In calculating an allowance of £290 for the Morris, Ladd consulted an industry guide which priced second-hand cars according to year of manufacture. When the transaction went through, the claimants issued the defendant with an invoice describing his car, for which £290 was being allowed, as a '1948 Morris 10 Saloon'. The claimants subsequently discovered that the Morris had been made in 1939. Had the claimants known of the Morris car's true age, they would have allowed only £175 for it. The claimants brought an action against the defendant to recover damages of £115 for breach of a contractual term that the Morris car was a 1948 model. The judge allowed the claim. The Court of Appeal, by a majority, overturned that decision and held that the defendant's representation as to the Morris car's age was not a term of the contract.

Denning LJ: I entirely agree with the judge that both parties assumed that the Morris was a 1948 model and that this assumption was fundamental to the contract. But this does not prove that the representation was a term of the contract.

...

[The buyer's] only remedy is in damages, and to recover these he must prove a warranty.

In saying that he must prove a warranty, I use the word "warranty" in its ordinary English meaning to denote a binding promise. Everyone knows what a man means when he says "I guarantee it" or "I warrant it" or "I give you my word on it." He means that he binds himself to it. That is the meaning it has borne in English law for 300 years from the leading case of *Chandelor v. Lopus* (1603) Cro.Jac. 4 onwards. During the last 50 years, however, some lawyers have come to use the word "warranty" in another sense. They use it to denote a subsidiary term in a contract as distinct from a vital term which they call a "condition." In so doing they depart from the ordinary meaning, not only of the word "warranty" but also of the word "condition." There is no harm in their doing this, so long as they confine this technical use to its proper sphere, namely to distinguish between a vital term, the breach of which gives the right to treat the contract as at an end, and a subsidiary term which does not. But the trouble comes when one person uses the word "warranty" in its ordinary meaning and another uses it in its technical meaning. When Holt C.J., in *Crosse v. Gardner* (1689) Carth. 90 (as glossed by Buller J. in *Pasley v. Freeman* (1789) 3 Term Rep. 51, 57) and *Medina v. Stoughton,* (1699) 1 Salk. 210, made his famous ruling that an affirmation at the time of a sale is a warranty, provided it appears on evidence to be so intended, he used the word "warranty" in its ordinary English meaning of a binding promise: and when Lord Haldane L.C. and Lord Moulton in 1913 in *Heilbut, Symons & Co. v. Buckleton* [1913] A.C. 30, 38, 50, 51 adopted his ruling, they used it likewise in its ordinary meaning. These different uses of the word seem to have been the source of confusion in the present case. The judge did not ask himself, "Was the representation (that it was a 1948 Morris) intended to be a warranty?" He asked himself, "Was it fundamental to the contract?" He answered it by saying that it was fundamental; and therefore it was a condition and not a warranty. By concentrating on whether it was fundamental, he seems to me to have missed the crucial point in the case which is whether it was a term of the contract at all. The crucial question is: was it a binding promise or only an innocent misrepresentation? The technical distinction between a "condition" and a "warranty" is quite immaterial in this case, because it is far too late for the buyer to reject the car. He can at best only claim damages. The material distinction here is between a statement which is a term of the contract and a statement which is only an innocent misrepresentation. This distinction is best expressed by the ruling of Lord Holt: Was it intended as a warranty or not? using the word warranty there in its ordinary English meaning: because it gives the exact shade of meaning that is required. It is something to which a man must be taken to bind himself.

In applying Lord Holt's test, however, some misunderstanding has arisen by the use of the word "intended." It is sometimes supposed that the tribunal must look into the minds of the parties to see what they themselves intended. That is a mistake. Lord Moulton made it quite clear that ([1913] A.C. 30, 38, 50, 51) "The intention of the parties can only be deduced from the totality of the evidence." The question whether a warranty was intended depends on the conduct of the parties, on their words and behaviour, rather than on their thoughts. If an intelligent bystander would reasonably infer that a warranty was intended, that will suffice. And this, when the facts are not in dispute, is a question of law. That is shown by *Heilbut, Symons & Co. v. Buckleton* itself, where the House of Lords upset the finding by a jury of a warranty.

It is instructive to take some recent instances to show how the courts have approached this question. When the seller states a fact which is or should be within his own knowledge and of which the buyer is ignorant, intending that the buyer should act on it, and he does so, it is easy to infer a warranty: see *Couchman v. Hill* [1947] K.B. 554; 63 T.L.R. 81; [1947] 1 All E.R. 103, where the farmer stated that the heifer was unserved, and *Harling v. Eddy* [1951] 2 K.B. 739; [1951] 2 T.L.R. 245; [1951] 2 All E.R. 212, where he stated that there was nothing wrong with her. So also if he makes a promise about something which is or should be within his own control: see *Birch v. Paramount Estates Ltd.* (unreported) decided on October 2, 1956, in this court, where the seller stated that the house would be as good as the show house. But if the seller, when he states a fact, makes it clear that he has no knowledge of his own but has got his information elsewhere, and is merely passing it on, it is not so easy to imply a warranty. Such a case was *Routledge v. McKay* [1954] 1 W.L.R. 615, 636; [1954] 1 All E.R. 855, where the seller "stated that it was a 1942 model and pointed to the corroboration found in the book," and it was held that there was no warranty.

Turning now to the present case, much depends on the precise words that were used. If the seller says "I believe it is a 1948 Morris. Here is the registration book to prove it," there is clearly no warranty. It is a statement of belief, not a contractual promise. But if the seller says "I guarantee that it is a 1948 Morris. This is borne out by the registration book, but you need not rely solely on that. I give you my own guarantee that it is," there is clearly a warranty. The seller is making himself contractually responsible, even though the registration book is wrong.

In this case much reliance was placed by the judge on the fact that the buyer looked up Glass's Guide and paid £290 on the footing that it was a 1948 model: but that fact seems to me to be neutral. Both sides believed the car to have been made in 1948 and in that belief the buyer paid £290. That belief can be just as firmly based on the buyer's own inspection of the log-book as on a contractual warranty by the seller.

Once that fact is put on one side I ask myself: What is the proper inference from the known facts? It must have been obvious to both that the seller had himself no personal knowledge of the year when the car was made. He only became owner after a great number of changes. He must have been relying on the registration book. It is unlikely that such a person would warrant the year of manufacture. The most he would do would be to state his belief, and then produce the registration book in verification of it. In these circumstances the intelligent bystander would, I suggest, say that the seller did not intend to bind himself so as to warrant that it was a 1948 model. If the seller was asked to pledge himself to it, he would at once have said "I cannot do that. I have only the log-book to go by, the same as you."

The judge seems to have thought that there was a difference between written contracts and oral contracts. He thought that the reason why the buyer failed in *Heilbut, Symons & Co. v. Buckleton* [1913] A.C. 30 and *Routledge v. McKay* [1954] 1 W.L.R. 615 was because the sales were afterwards recorded in writing, and the written contracts contained no reference to the representation. I agree that that was an important factor in those cases. If an oral representation is afterwards recorded in writing, it is good evidence that it was intended as a warranty. If it is not put into writing, it is evidence against a warranty being intended. But it is by no means decisive. There have been many cases where the courts have found an oral warranty collateral to a written contract such as *Birch v. Paramount Estates,* unreported: Oct. 2, 1956 (C.A.). But when the purchase is not recorded in writing at all it must not be supposed that every representation made in the course of the dealing is to be treated as a warranty. The question then is still: Was it intended as a warranty? In the leading case of *Chandelor v. Lopus* Cro.Jac. 4 in 1603 a man by word of mouth sold a precious stone for £100 affirming it to be a bezar stone whereas it was not. The declaration averred that the seller *affirmed* it to be a bezar stone, but did not aver that he *warranted* it to be so. The declaration was held to be ill because "the bare affirmation that it was a bezar stone, without warranting it to be so, is no cause of action." That has been the law from that day to this and it was emphatically reaffirmed by the House of Lords in *Heilbut, Symons & Co. v. Buckleton* [1913] A.C. 30, 38, 50.

One final word: It seems to me clear that the motor-dealers who bought the car relied on the year stated in the log-book. If they had wished to make sure of it, they could have checked it then and there, by taking the engine number and chassis number and writing to the makers. They did not do so at the time, but only eight months later. They are experts, and, not having made that check at the time, I do not think they should now be allowed to recover against the innocent seller who produced to them all the evidence he had, namely, the registration book. I agree that it is hard on the dealers to have paid more than the car is worth: but it would be equally hard on the seller to make him pay the difference. He would never have bought the Hillman at all unless he had got the allowance of £290 for the Morris. The best course in all these cases would be to "shunt" the difference down the train of innocent sellers until one reaches the rogue who perpetrated the fraud: but he can rarely be traced, or if he can, he rarely has the money to pay the damages. So one is left to decide between a number of innocent people who is to bear the loss. That can only be done by applying the law about representations and warranties as we know it: and that is what I have tried to do. If the rogue can be traced, he can be sued by whomsoever has suffered the loss: but if he cannot be traced, the loss must lie where it falls. It should not be inflicted on innocent sellers, who sold the car many months, perhaps many years before, and have forgotten all about it and have conducted their affairs on the basis that the transaction was concluded. Such a seller would not be able to recollect after all this length of time the exact words he used, such as whether he said "I believe it is a 1948 model," or "I warrant it is a 1948 model." The right course is to let the buyer set aside the transaction if he finds out the mistake quickly and comes promptly before other interests have irretrievably intervened; otherwise the loss must lie where it falls: and that is, I think, the course prescribed by law. I would allow this appeal accordingly.

Hodson LJ: The question is whether the statement made by the defendant that his 10-horse-power Morris car was a 1948 car was a term of the contract by which he handed over the car in part exchange for a new Hillman car or was merely an innocent misrepresentation.

The question is usually stated as being whether words are to be interpreted as giving rise to a warranty. The House of Lords in *Heilbut, Symons & Co. v. Buckleton* [1913] A.C. 30 adopted the enunciation of the true principle of law as laid down by Lord Holt C.J. in 1688:

"An affirmation at the time of the sale is a warranty provided it appears on evidence to be so intended." (Carth 90).

Where, as here, the words of the affirmation are established the question of intention remains to be determined.

Lord Haldane, in *Heilbut's* case [1913] A.C. 30, 36, expressed the opinion that, as neither the circumstances of the conversation nor its words were in dispute, the question of warranty or representation was purely one of law. Lord Moulton (at 50-51) thought that the question of intention was one for a jury and said that the intention of the parties could only be deduced from the totality of the evidence.

Treating the question of intention as one of fact proper for the determination of the county court judge, one is driven to inquire whether there was here any evidence that the statement in question went beyond an innocent misrepresentation, bearing in mind the warning contained in Lord Moulton's speech against (at 49) "attempts to extend the doctrine of warranty beyond its just limits and find that a warranty existed in cases where there was nothing more than an innocent misrepresentation."

I am of opinion that there was no evidence to support the conclusion that the statement that the Morris car was a 1948 car was a term of the contract. The registration book, showing that the car was first registered in 1948, was produced by the defendant to the plaintiffs' representative, a motor salesman, who was familiar with the car having often had lifts in it, thought it looked like a 1948 car, and checked up on the registration book.

The defendant was stating an opinion on a matter of which he had no special knowledge or on which the buyer might be expected also to have an opinion and to exercise his judgment.

This is not a decisive test, as was pointed out by Lord Moulton (in *Heilbut's* case, at 50), but it is a feature which he said may be a criterion of value in guiding a jury in coming to a decision whether or not a warranty was intended.

There is in my opinion nothing in this case to set against the criterion to which I have referred. That is to say, there is nothing to indicate that the statement as to the date of the car amounted to a promise or guarantee that the information given was accurate.

Morris LJ gave a dissenting judgment.

NOTES AND QUESTIONS

1. All the judgments in this case clarified that the test for whether a statement is a mere representation or has been incorporated as a term of the contract is whether the parties *intended* it to be a term (ie intended it to be a warranty or, put another way, intended there to be a guarantee/promise as to the accuracy of the statement). Morris LJ dissented because he considered that the application of that test to the facts meant that there was a warranty. What factors did the majority take into account in deciding that question of intention?

2. That the test is one of the parties' intentions—and that all evidence is relevant in determining that, rather than there being one decisive secondary principle—was earlier established by the House of Lords in *Heilbut Symons & Co Ltd v Buckleton* [1913] AC 30. There it was held that the defendants' statement that a company (whose shares the defendants were selling to the claimant) was a rubber company was not intended by the parties to be a warranty. A slight complication emerging from that leading case is that in the past—presumably to evade the so-called 'parol evidence rule' (above, 157)—the courts have often regarded a warranty as a separate 'collateral' contract rather than being a term of the main contract. Hence the speeches in that case were

geared towards whether the parties intended the statement to be a collateral warranty/a collateral contract. However, nothing turns on whether the warranty is a term of the main contract or a separate contract. The essential issue, to which the test of the parties' intention is addressed, is whether or not the statement has contractual force (whether as a contractual term or as a separate contract).

3.   Lord Denning MR emphasised that the usage of the term 'warranty' to mean a contractual term/promise must be carefully differentiated from a usage which contrasts warranties with conditions. The former are minor, and the latter are major, terms of the contract. The distinction between warranties and conditions is important in deciding whether the innocent party can terminate the contract for breach in addition to being entitled to damages: see Chapter 7.

4.   At the time of this case, the finding that the statement was not a term, so that there was no action for breach of contract, meant that there was no liability at all. As we shall see in Chapter 11, the defendant might today be liable under section 2 of the Misrepresentation Act 1967 or for tortious negligent misrepresentation.

5.   There was no written contract in this case. Where there is a written contract, the parties may seek to avoid arguments that there are additional terms, whether within the main contract or as collateral warranties, by including an 'entire agreement clause'. So, eg, in *Government of Zanzibar v British Aerospace (Lancaster House) Ltd*, below, 583, there was an entire agreement clause as follows: 'The parties have negotiated this contract on the basis that the terms and conditions set out herein represent the entire agreement between them relating in any way whatever to the [goods] which form the subject matter of this contract...' The effect of such a clause is to nullify the intention necessary for there to be contractual terms additional to those in the written contract. (In itself, such a clause is purely concerned with marking out the limits of contractual liability and does not prevent there being a tortious or statutory claim for misrepresentation. However, entire agreement clauses are commonly combined with clauses seeking to exclude liability for misrepresentation: see the *Government of Zanzibar* case, below, 583.)

Dick Bentley Productions Ltd v Harold Smith (Motors) Ltd
[1965] 1 WLR 623, Court of Appeal

The claimant, Dick Bentley, told the defendant, that he was looking for a well-vetted Bentley car. The defendant, who was a car dealer, found and bought a Bentley car and told the claimant that, since the car had been fitted with a replacement engine and gearbox, it had done only 20,000 miles. The claimant bought the car. It subsequently transpired that the car had in fact covered almost 100,000 miles since the engine and gearbox had been replaced. The claimant brought an action for damages against the defendant for breach of warranty. This succeeded before the trial judge. In dismissing the defendant's appeal, the Court of Appeal held that the statement as to the mileage was a contractual warranty.

Lord Denning MR: The first point is whether this representation, namely, that it had done 20,000 miles only since it had been fitted with a replacement engine and gearbox, was an innocent misrepresentation (which does not give rise to damages), or whether it was a warranty. It was said by Holt C.J., and repeated in *Heilbut, Symons & Co. v. Buckleton* [1913] A.C. 30, 49 H.L, that: "An affirmation at the time of the sale is a warranty, provided it appear on evidence to be so intended." But that word "intended" has given rise to difficulties. I endeavoured to explain in *Oscar Chess Ltd. v. Williams* [1957] 1 W.L.R. 370, 375, C.A. that the question whether a warranty was intended depends on the conduct of the parties, on their words and behaviour, rather than on their thoughts. If an intelligent bystander would reasonably infer that a warranty was intended, that will suffice. What conduct, then? What words and behaviour lead to the inference of a warranty?

Looking at the cases once more, as we have done so often, it seems to me that if a representation is made in the course of dealings for a contract for the very purpose of inducing the other party to act upon it, and actually inducing him to act upon it, by entering into the contract, that is prima facie ground for inferring that it was intended as a warranty. It is not necessary to speak of it as being collateral. Suffice it that it was intended to be acted upon and was in fact acted on. But the maker of the representation can rebut this inference if he can show that it really was an innocent misrepresentation, in that he was in fact innocent of fault in making it, and that it would not be reasonable in the circumstances for him to be bound by it. In the *Oscar Chess* case ([1957] 1 W.L.R. 370, 375) the inference was rebutted. There a man had bought a second-hand car and received with it a log-book which stated the year of the car, 1948. He afterwards resold the car. When he resold it he simply repeated what was in the log-book and passed it on to the buyer. He honestly believed on reasonable grounds that it was true. He was completely innocent of any fault. There was no warranty by him, but only an innocent misrepresentation. Whereas in the present case it is very different. The inference is not rebutted. Here we have a dealer, Smith, who was in a position to know, or at least to find out, the history of the car. He could get it by writing to the makers. He did not do so. Indeed, it was done later. When the history of this car was examined, his statement turned out to be quite wrong. He ought to have known better. There was no reasonable foundation for it.

...

The judge said "I have no hesitation [in saying] that as a matter of law the statement was a warranty. Smith stated a fact that should be within his own knowledge. He had jumped to a conclusion and stated it as a fact. A fact that a buyer would act on." That is ample foundation for the inference of a warranty.

Salmon LJ: I agree. I have no doubt at all that the judge reached a correct conclusion when he decided that Smith gave a warranty to the plaintiff and that that warranty was broken. Was what Smith said intended and understood as a legally binding promise? If so, it was a warranty and as such may be part of the contract of sale or collateral to it. In effect, Smith said: "If you will enter into a contract to buy this motor car from me for £1,850, I undertake that you will be getting a motor car which has done no more than 20,000 miles since it was fitted with a new engine and a new gearbox." I have no doubt at all that what was said by Smith was so understood and was intended to be so understood by Bentley.

Danckwerts LJ agreed with Lord Denning MR.

NOTE

Lord Denning MR's approach in this case can be criticised as placing too much importance, in purportedly ascertaining the parties' intentions, on the fault of the person making the statement. Prior to the enactment of the Misrepresentation Act 1967 (and prior to the acceptance that tortious liability for negligent misrepresentation under *Hedley Byrne & Co v Heller & Partners* [1964] AC 465 could apply to pre-contractual misrepresentations: see below, Chapter 11) Lord Denning was using the only route open to him to hold the negligent misrepresentor liable in damages. The main danger of distorting the intention test, and thereby obscuring the line between breach of contract and tortious misrepresentation, is that the measure of damages for the two causes of action is different. On these facts, it may be significant, therefore, that the claim was limited to £400 which could have been justified as a contractual (expectation) or tortious (reliance) measure. (For explanation of those terms, see below, 338, note 2; 560, note 1.)

Esso Petroleum Co Ltd v Mardon [1976] QB 801, Court of Appeal

Esso acquired a petrol station site estimating that the annual throughput of petrol at a station on that site would be 200,000 gallons. However, the planning authorities insisted that the petrol station should not be directly accessible from the main street. As built, therefore, the petrol station would attract fewer customers than Esso had originally estimated. Nevertheless Mr Mardon was induced to take a lease of the petrol station by representations made by Esso that the estimated annual throughput of petrol was 200,000 gallons. That is, Esso did not revise their estimate to take account of the changed circumstances. When, in due course, the throughput came nowhere near that figure, Mardon negotiated a lower rent from Esso (from September 1964) but continued to put money into the business. Overall, he lost considerable sums of money. On Esso's action for possession and other relief, Mardon counterclaimed, seeking damages for Esso's breach of warranty or, alternatively, for the tort of negligence applying *Hedley Byrne & Co v Heller & Partners Ltd* [1964] AC 465. Lawson J held that there was no contractual warranty and that the damages for tortious misrepresentation were limited to losses suffered before September 1964. In allowing Mardon's appeal, the Court of Appeal decided that there was a contractual warranty and that, in any event, the damages were not as limited as the judge had thought. The extract below primarily concentrates on the contractual warranty. For the reasoning on the claim for tortious negligent misrepresentation, see below, 565.

Lord Denning MR: I turn to consider the law. It is founded on the representation that the estimated throughput of the service station was 200,000 gallons. No claim can be brought under the Misrepresentation Act 1967, because that Act did not come into force until April 22, 1967: whereas this representation was made in April 1963. So the claim is put in two ways. First, that the representation was a collateral warranty. Second, that it was a negligent misrepresentation. I will take them in order.

Collateral warranty

Ever since *Heilbut, Symons & Co. v. Buckleton* [1913] A.C. 30, we have had to contend with the law as laid down by the House of Lords that an innocent misrepresentation gives no right to damages. In order to escape from that rule, the pleader used to allege – I often did it myself – that the misrepresentation was fraudulent, or alternatively a collateral warranty. At the trial we nearly always succeeded on collateral warranty. We had to reckon, of course, with the dictum of Lord Moulton, at p. 47, that "such collateral contracts must from their very nature be rare." But more often than not the court elevated the innocent misrepresentation into a collateral warranty: and thereby did justice – in advance of the Misrepresentation Act 1967. I remember scores of cases of that kind, especially on the sale of a business. A representation as to the profits that had been made in the past was invariably held to be a warranty. Besides that experience, there have been many cases since I have sat in this court where we have readily held a representation – which induces a person to enter into a contract – to be a warranty sounding in damages. I summarised them in *Dick Bentley Productions Ltd. v. Harold Smith (Motors) Ltd.* [1965] 1 W.L.R. 623, 627…

[Counsel for Esso] retaliated, however, by citing *Bisset v. Wilkinson* [1927] A.C. 177, where the Privy Council said that a statement by a New Zealand farmer that an area of land "would carry 2,000 sheep" was only an expression of opinion. He submitted that the forecast here of 200,000 gallons was an expression of opinion and not a statement of fact: and that it could not be interpreted as a warranty or promise.

Now I would quite agree with [counsel for Esso] that it was not a warranty – in this sense – that it did not *guarantee* that the throughput *would* be 200,000 gallons. But, nevertheless, it was a forecast made by a party – Esso – who had special knowledge and skill. It was the yardstick … by which they measured the worth of a filling station. They knew the facts. They knew the traffic in the town. They knew the throughput of comparable stations. They had much experience and expertise at their disposal. They were in a much better position than Mr. Mardon to make a forecast. It seems to me that if such a person makes a forecast, intending that the other should act upon it – and he does act upon it, it can well be interpreted as a warranty that the forecast is sound and reliable in the sense that they made it with reasonable care and skill. It is just as if Esso said to Mr. Mardon: "Our forecast of throughput is 200,000 gallons. You can rely upon it as being a sound forecast of what the service station should do. The rent is calculated on that footing." If the forecast turned out to be an unsound forecast such as no person of skill or experience should have made, there is a breach of warranty. …It is very different from the New Zealand case where the land had never been used as a sheep farm and both parties were equally able to form an opinion as to its carrying capacity: see particularly *Bisset v. Wilkinson* [1927] A.C. 177, 183-184.

In the present case it seems to me that there was a warranty that the forecast was sound, that is, Esso made it with reasonable care and skill. That warranty was broken. Most negligently Esso made a "fatal error" in the forecast they stated to Mr. Mardon, and on which he took the tenancy. For this they are liable in damages.

…

The measure of damages

Mr. Mardon is not to be compensated here for "loss of a bargain." He was given no bargain that the throughput *would* amount to 200,000 gallons a year. He is only to be compensated for having been induced to enter into a contract which turned out to be disastrous for him. Whether it be called breach of warranty or negligent misrepresentation, its effect was *not* to warrant the throughput, but only to induce him to enter the contract. So the damages in either case are to be measured by the loss he suffered. Just as in *Doyle v. Olby (Ironmongers) Ltd.* [1969] 2 Q.B. 158, 167 he can say: "… I would not have entered into this contract at all but for your representation. Owing to it, I have lost all the capital I put into it. I also incurred a large overdraft. I have spent four years of my life in wasted endeavour without reward: and it will take me some time to re-establish myself."

For all such loss he is entitled to recover damages. It is to be measured in a similar way as the loss due to a personal injury. You should look into the future so as to forecast what would have been likely to happen if he had never entered into this contract: and contrast it with his position as it is now as a result of entering into it. The future is necessarily problematical and can only be a rough-and-ready estimate. But it must be done in assessing the loss.

Ormrod and **Shaw LJJ** delivered concurring judgments.

1. The warranty found was *not* that the throughput would be 200,000 gallons. Rather it was a warranty that reasonable care had been taken in making that forecast. That explains why the measure of damages for breach of warranty was held to be the same as for the tortious negligent misrepresentation: had reasonable care been used in making the forecast, the forecast of 200,000 gallons would not have been given and Mardon would not have entered into the contract. In contrast, had the warranty been that the throughput would be 200,000 gallons, the contractual damages for breach of that warranty would have been significantly different from those given for the tortious negligent misrepresentation.

2. After you have read Chapter 11, ask the question, has the enactment of the Misrepresentation Act 1967 (and the recognition in this case that *Hedley Byrne* applies to pre-contractual statements) meant that fault can now be put to one side as irrelevant in deciding whether a representation has become a contractual term?

2. INCORPORATION OF A PARTY'S WRITTEN TERMS

The typical situation, with which we are here concerned, is where a contract has been largely concluded orally but one party insists that its standard written terms have been incorporated. Commonly the relevant written term in dispute is an exclusion or limitation clause (ie a clause which absolves the defendant from any liability for, eg, breach of contract or the tort of negligence or which limits the damages that can be claimed). But it would appear that the same principles of incorporation apply whatever the type of term (for example, in the *Interfoto* case, below, 179, the relevant term was one imposing a high charge for the late return of borrowed transparencies). There are four main methods by which a party's written terms are incorporated: signature, reasonable notice, course of dealing, and the parties' trade practice.

Prior to the statutory control of unfair terms (see Chapter 6 below) non-incorporation was one of the two main judicial techniques (the other being restrictive interpretation, see Chapter 5) by which exclusion and limitation clauses could be held inapplicable. The principles of incorporation are so well-established that they remain vibrant even where a court now has the power to go on, if a written term has been incorporated, to strike down that term as unreasonable/unfair under the Unfair Contract Terms Act 1977 or the Unfair Terms in Consumer Contracts Regulations 1999. An issue throughout is whether the incorporation principles should remain so vibrant. One might take the view (supported most clearly by Hobhouse LJ's dissent in *AEG (UK) Ltd v Logic Resource Ltd*, below, 182) that in the light of the statutory controls that now exist, the courts, in the event of doubt, should lean firmly in favour of incorporation.

Introductory reading: E McKendrick, *Contract Law* (7th edn, 2007) 9.3–9.5.

(1) Signature

L'Estrange v F Graucob Ltd
[1934] 2 KB 394, Divisional Court of the King's Bench

The claimant (Miss L'Estrange) agreed to purchase a cigarette vending machine from the defendants for use in her café. She signed a form printed on brown paper headed 'Sales Agreement'. The form included a clause in small print providing that: 'any express or implied condition, statement, or warranty, statutory or otherwise not stated herein is hereby excluded'. The vending machine delivered did not work properly. The claimant brought an action for damages for breach of an implied condition or warranty that the machine was reasonably fit for the purpose for which it was bought. The defendants denied liability arguing that the clause above excluded all implied conditions and warranties. The claimant counter-argued that she had known nothing of the contents of the form she had signed. In allowing the defendants' appeal, the Divisional Court held that, because the claimant had signed the form, the above clause was incorporated into the contract.

Scrutton LJ: The main question raised in the present case is whether [the] clause formed part of the contract. If it did, it clearly excluded any condition or warranty.

...

The present case is not a ticket case, and it is distinguishable from the ticket cases. ...In cases in which the contract is contained in a railway ticket or other unsigned document, it is necessary to prove that an alleged party was aware, or ought to have been aware, of its terms and conditions. These cases have no application when the document has been signed. When a document containing contractual terms is signed, then, in the absence of fraud, or, I will add, misrepresentation, the party signing it is bound, and it is wholly immaterial whether he has read the document or not.

[*Scrutton LJ found that neither fraud nor misrepresentation could be shown and continued:*]

In this case the plaintiff has signed a document headed "Sales Agreement," which she admits had to do with an intended purchase, and which contained a clause excluding all conditions and warranties. That being so, the plaintiff, having put her signature to the document and not having been induced to do so by any fraud or misrepresentation, cannot be heard to say that she is not bound by the terms of the document because she has not read them.

Maugham LJ: I regret the decision to which I have come, but I am bound by legal rules and cannot decide the case on other considerations.

The material question is whether or not there was a contract in writing between the plaintiff and the defendants in the terms contained in the brown paper document.

...

[W]here a party has signed a written agreement it is immaterial to the question of his liability under it that he has not read it and does not know its contents. That is true in any case in which the agreement is held to be an agreement in writing.

There are, however, two possibilities to be kept in view. The first is that it might be proved that the document, though signed by the plaintiff, was signed in circumstances which made it not her act. That is known as the case of Non est factum. ...The written document admittedly related to the purchase of the machine by the plaintiff. Even if she was told that it was an order form, she could not be heard to say that it did not affect her because she did not know its contents.

Another possibility is that the plaintiff might have been induced to sign the document by misrepresentation. [*Maugham LJ held that there was no misrepresentation and continued:*]

In this case it is, in my view, an irrelevant circumstance that the plaintiff did not read, or hear of, the parts of the sales document which are in small print, and that document should have effect according to its terms. I may add, however, that I could wish that the contract had been in a simpler and more usual form. It is unfortunate that the important clause excluding conditions and warranties is in such small print.

NOTES AND QUESTIONS

1. The importance of this case is in showing that terms are incorporated into a contract when the document containing them is signed even if the person signing has not read them. Two exceptions mentioned in this case are, first, where the party's signature is induced by misrepresentation (see *Curtis v Chemical Cleaning and Dyeing Co Ltd,* below, 168); and, secondly, where *non est factum* applies (below, 617–620). A third exception, not expressly mentioned here, is where the document signed does not purport to have contractual effect as in *Grogan v Robin Meredith Plant Hire* [1996] CLC 1127, CA, where the signed document was a time sheet.

2. Why is a person bound by the terms of a document which he or she has signed?

3. One can argue that Miss L'Estrange should not have been bound because the sellers knew that she was making a mistake as to the terms of the contract (so that the doctrine of unilateral mistake applied, on which see below, 597–598). For a detailed version of this argument, see **J Spencer, 'Signature, Consent, and the Rule in *L'Estrange v Graucob'* [1973] *CLJ* 104** (although note that Spencer takes a very broad view of when a unilateral mistake nullifies a contract by including wherever the other party has been at fault in causing the mistake: see below, 597, note 2.) He suggests that the refusal to apply the law on unilateral mistake where there has been a signature stems from a misunderstanding of the parol evidence and non est factum rules.

4. If the same facts arose today, the Unfair Contract Terms Act 1977 section 6 would apply (see below, 246). By this, a seller cannot exclude liability for the implied undertakings as to the goods' quality or fitness for a particular purpose as against a consumer and as against a person dealing otherwise than as consumer—such as Miss L'Estrange—the exclusion is only valid if it satisfies the test of reasonableness. On the facts, the sellers would surely not have been able to satisfy that test (ie. the term was not a fair and reasonable one to have included). So the case would now be decided differently—and Maugham LJ's concerns about fairness directly addressed—without affecting the point that the exclusion clause was incorporated.

Curtis v Chemical Cleaning and Dyeing Co
[1951] 1 KB 805, Court of Appeal

The claimant took a white satin dress to the defendants' shop for cleaning. When the shop assistant asked her to sign a document headed 'Receipt', the claimant asked why her signature was required. The assistant said that it was because the defendants would not accept responsibility for certain specified risks, including damage to the beads and sequins with which the dress was trimmed. The claimant signed the receipt which in fact contained a clause providing that the articles were accepted, 'on condition that the company is not liable for any damage howsoever arising'. The defendants returned the dress with an unexplained stain. The claimant brought an action claiming damages for negligence (whether in contract or tort). The finding by the county court judge that the defendants were negligent was not challenged on the appeal, which rather focussed on the incorporation issue. In dismissing the appeal, the Court of Appeal held that the defendants could not rely on the above clause because it was not incorporated as a term of the contract owing to the shop assistant's misrepresentation.

Somervell LJ: What was conveyed to the plaintiff, in my view, was that there were certain risks, in this case beads and sequins, which the defendants were not prepared to accept. She was asked to sign this document and she thought that its purpose was to exempt them from liability for beads and sequins, and that alone. That, I think, plainly is a misrepresentation. The words on the document purported to exempt them from all liability, howsoever arising. In those circumstances, I think, owing to that misrepresentation, this exception never became part of the contract between the parties.

Denning LJ: If the party affected signs a written document, knowing it to be a contract which governs the relations between them, his signature is irrefragable evidence of his assent to the whole contract, including the exempting clauses, unless the signature is shown to be obtained by fraud or misrepresentation: *L'Estrange v. Graucob* [1934] 2 K. B. 394. But what is a sufficient misrepresentation for this purpose? …

In my opinion any behaviour, by words or conduct, is sufficient to be a misrepresentation if it is such as to mislead the other party about the existence or extent of the exemption. If it conveys a false impression, that is enough. If the false impression is created knowingly, it is a fraudulent misrepresentation; if it is created unwittingly, it is an innocent misrepresentation; but either is sufficient to disentitle the creator of it to the benefit of the exemption. … When one party puts forward a printed form for signature, failure by him to draw attention to the existence or extent of the exemption clause may in some circumstances convey the impression that there is no exemption at all, or at any rate not so wide an exemption as that which is in fact contained in the document. The present case is a good illustration. The customer said in evidence: "When I was asked to sign the document I asked why? The assistant said I was to accept any responsibility for damage to beads and sequins. I did not read it all before I signed it". In those circumstances, by failing to draw attention to the width of the exemption clause, the assistant created the false impression that the exemption only related to the beads and sequins, and that it did not extend to the material of which the dress was made. It was done perfectly innocently, but nevertheless a false impression was created. It was probably not sufficiently precise and unambiguous to create an estoppel: *Low v. Bouverie* [1891] 3 Ch. 82; but nevertheless it was a sufficient misrepresentation to disentitle the cleaners from relying on the exemption, except in regard to beads and sequins.

In the present case the customer knew, from what the assistant said, that the document contained conditions. If nothing was said she might not have known it. In that case the document might reasonably be understood to be, like a boot repairer's receipt, only a voucher for the customer to produce when collecting the goods, and not understood to contain conditions exempting the cleaners from their common-law liability for negligence. In that case it would not protect the cleaners: see *Chapelton v. Barry Urban District Council* [1949] 1 K. B. 532. I say this because I do not wish it to be supposed that the cleaners would have been better off if the assistant had simply handed over the document to the customer without asking her to sign it; or if the customer were not so inquiring as the plaintiff, but were an unsuspecting person who signed whatever she was asked without question. In those circumstances the conduct of the cleaners might well be such that it conveyed the impression that the document contained no conditions, or, at any rate, no condition exempting them from their common-law liability, in which case they could not rely on it.

[It was argued by counsel for the defendants] that, even if there was an innocent misrepresentation, the plaintiff cannot in point of law avoid the terms of the contract. He said that an innocent misrepresentation gives no right to damages but only to rescission; that rescission was not possible because the contract was executed; and that in any case rescission was of no use to the plaintiff because, once rescission has taken place, there would be no contract to sue upon. That is an attractive argument, but I do not think that it is right. One answer to it is that an executed contract can in a proper case be rescinded for innocent misrepresentation; and if this contract was rescinded the plaintiff could sue in tort for negligence, because the defendants, having entered upon the task of cleaning the dress, were under a duty to do it carefully. I do not pursue this, however, because I prefer to put it more simply. In my opinion when the signature to a condition, purporting to exempt a person from his common-law liabilities, is obtained by an innocent misrepresentation the party who has made that misrepresentation is disentitled to rely on the exemption. Whether you call that a rule of law or equity does not matter in these days. We have got too far beyond 1873 to trouble about distinctions of that kind. Scrutton and Maugham, L.JJ., in *L'Estrange v. Graucob* treated it as plain. I therefore agree that the appeal should be dismissed.

Singleton LJ concurred.

NOTES AND QUESTIONS

1. The importance of this case is in illustrating that, contrary to the normal rule, terms are not incorporated by signature if the signature has been obtained by misrepresentation. Why is that?
2. As Denning LJ's judgment indicates, the same result could have been reached on a wider ground than non-incorporation of the clause by regarding the whole contract as having been rescinded by the claimant for innocent misrepresentation. See generally below, Chapter 11.

(2) Reasonable Notice

Parker v The South Eastern Railway Company
(1877) 2 CPD 416, Court of Appeal

The claimant deposited a bag at a cloakroom at the defendants' railway station. Having paid the clerk 2d, he received a ticket. On one side was written a number, a date, printed details of office opening hours and the words 'See back'. On the back of the ticket was printed, inter alia, the following: 'The company will not be responsible for any package exceeding the value of £10.'

When the claimant presented his ticket later that day, the defendants could not find his bag. The claimant sought damages for the loss of his bag, the value of which exceeded £10. At trial, the following questions were left to the jury: (i) Did the claimant read or was he aware of the special condition upon which the bag was deposited?; (ii) Was the claimant under the circumstances, under any obligation, in the exercise of reasonable and proper caution, to read or make himself aware of the condition? The jury answered both questions in the negative and the judge, therefore, directed judgment to be entered for the claimant. On an appeal by the defendants the Court of Appeal held that there ought to be a new trial because the judge had misdirected the jury on the second question.

Mellish LJ: In this case we have to consider whether a person who deposits in the cloak-room of a railway company, articles which are lost through the carelessness of the company's servants, is prevented from recovering, by a condition on the back of the ticket, that the company would not be liable for the loss of goods exceeding the value of 10*l*. ...

The question then is, whether the plaintiff was bound by the conditions contained in the ticket. In an ordinary case, where an action is brought on a written agreement which is signed by the defendant, the agreement is proved by proving his signature, and, in the absence of fraud, it is wholly immaterial that he has not read the agreement and does not know its contents. The parties may, however, reduce their agreement into writing, so that the writing constitutes the sole evidence of the agreement, without signing it; but in that case there must be evidence independently of the agreement itself to prove that the defendant has assented to it. In that case, also, if it is proved that the defendant has assented to the writing constituting the agreement between the parties, it is, in the absence of fraud, immaterial that the defendant had not read the agreement and did not know its contents. Now if in the course of making a contract one party delivers to another a paper containing writing, and the party receiving the paper knows that the paper contains conditions which the party delivering it intends to constitute the contract, I have no doubt that the party receiving the paper does, by receiving and keeping it, assent to the conditions contained in it, although he does not read them, and does not know what they are. ...[However] if the person receiving the ticket does not know that there is any writing upon the back of the ticket, he is not bound by a condition printed on the back. The facts in the cases before us differ ... because ...though the plaintiffs admitted that they knew there was writing on the back of the ticket, they swore not only that they did not read it, but that they did not know or believe that the writing contained conditions, and we are to consider whether, under those circumstances, we can lay down as a matter of law either that the plaintiff is bound or that he is not bound by the conditions contained in the ticket, or whether his being bound depends on some question of fact to be determined by the jury, and if so, whether, in the present case, the right question was left to the jury.

Now, I am of opinion that we cannot lay down, as a matter of law, either that the plaintiff was bound or that he was not bound by the conditions printed on the ticket, from the mere fact that he knew there was writing on the ticket, but did not know that the writing contained conditions. I think there may be cases in which a paper containing writing is delivered by one party to another in the course of a business transaction, where it would be quite reasonable that the party receiving it should assume that the writing contained in it no condition, and should put it in his pocket unread. For instance, if a person driving through a turnpike-gate received a ticket upon paying the toll, he might reasonably assume that the object of the ticket was that by producing it he might be free from paying toll at some other turnpike-gate, and might put it in his pocket unread. On the other hand, if a person who ships goods to be carried on a voyage by sea receives a bill of lading signed by the master, he would plainly be bound by it, although afterwards in an action against the shipowner for the loss of the goods, he might swear that he had never read the bill of lading, and that he did not know that it contained the terms of the contract of carriage, and that the shipowner was protected by the exceptions contained in it. Now the reason why the person receiving the bill of lading would be bound seems to me to be that in the great majority of cases persons shipping goods do know that the bill of lading contains the terms of the contract of carriage; and the shipowner, or the master delivering the bill of lading, is entitled to assume that the person shipping goods has that knowledge. It is, however, quite possible to suppose that a person who is neither a man of business nor a lawyer might on some particular occasion ship goods without the least knowledge of what a bill of lading was, but in my opinion such a person must bear the consequences of his own exceptional ignorance, it being plainly impossible that business could be carried on if every person who delivers a bill of lading had to stop to explain what a bill of lading was.

Now the question we have to consider is whether the railway company were entitled to assume that a person depositing luggage, and receiving a ticket in such a way that he could see that some writing was printed on it, would understand that the writing contained the conditions of contract, and this seems to me to depend upon whether people in general would in fact, and naturally, draw that inference. The railway company, as it seems to me, must be entitled to make some assumptions respecting the person who deposits luggage with them: I think they are entitled to assume that he can read, and that he understands the English language, and that he pays such attention to what he is about as may be reasonably expected from a person in such a transaction as that of depositing luggage in a cloak-room. The railway company must, however, take mankind as they find them, and if what they do is sufficient to inform people in general that the ticket contains conditions, I think that a particular plaintiff ought not to be in a better position than other persons on account of his exceptional ignorance or stupidity or carelessness. But if what the railway company do is not sufficient to convey to the minds of people in general that the ticket contains conditions, then they have received goods on deposit without obtaining the consent of the persons depositing them to the conditions limiting their liability. I am of opinion, therefore, that the proper direction to leave to the jury in these cases is, that if the person receiving the ticket did not see or know that there was any writing on the ticket, he is not bound by the conditions; that if he knew there was writing, and knew or believed that the writing contained conditions, then he is bound by the conditions; that if he knew there was writing on the ticket, but did not know or believe that the writing contained conditions, nevertheless he would be bound, if the delivering of the ticket to him in such a manner that he could see there was writing upon it, was, in the opinion of the jury, reasonable notice that the writing contained conditions.

I have lastly to consider whether the direction of the learned judge was correct, namely, "Was the plaintiff, under the circumstances, under any obligation, in the exercise of reasonable and proper caution, to read or to make himself aware of the condition?" I think that this direction was not strictly accurate, and was calculated to mislead the jury. The plaintiff was certainly under no obligation to read the ticket, but was entitled to leave it unread if he pleased, and the question does not appear to me to direct the attention of the jury to the real question, namely, whether the railway company did what was reasonably sufficient to give the plaintiff notice of the condition.

On the whole, I am of opinion that there ought to be a new trial.

Baggallay LJ gave a judgment concurring with Mellish LJ. **Bramwell LJ** held that the question was one of law not fact and that judgment should have been entered for the defendants.

NOTES AND QUESTIONS

1. The principal point of this case is that the excluding term would have been incorporated if the defendants had given reasonable notice of it to the claimant. The jury had not been directed to answer that critical question. Instead they had been directed to answer the different question of whether the claimant ought reasonably to have known of the term.

2. A railway company asks you for advice as to how it can ensure that it has no contractual liability for loss caused by the late running of its trains. How would you ensure that a relevant exclusion clause was incorporated into contracts with passengers?

Chapelton v Barry Urban District Council [1940] 1 KB 532, Court of Appeal

The claimant hired two deckchairs from the defendants. The chairs were in a pile beside which was this notice: 'Barry UDC...Hire of chairs 2d per session of three hours'. The claimant received two tickets from the attendant on payment of the 4d. He glanced at the tickets and slipped them into his pocket, having no idea that there were clauses on those tickets. One of the clauses read: 'The Council will not be liable for any accident or damage arising from hire of chairs.' While using one of the chairs, the claimant was injured and he brought an action claiming damages for negligence (whether in tort or contract) against the defendants. The Court of Appeal, overturning the trial judge, held that, as the ticket was a non-contractual document, the exclusion clause was not incorporated into the contract.

Slesser LJ: In the class of case where it is said that there is a term in the contract freeing railway companies, or other providers of facilities, from liabilities which they would otherwise incur at common law, it is a question as to how far that condition has been made a term of the contract and whether it has been sufficiently brought to the notice of the person entering into the contract with the railway company, or other body, and there is a large number of authorities on that point. In my view, however, the present case does not come within that category at all. I think that the contract here, as appears from a consideration of all the circumstances, was this: The local authority offered to hire chairs to persons to sit upon on the beach, and there was a pile of chairs there standing ready for use by any one who wished to use them, and the conditions on which they offered persons the use of those chairs were stated in the notice which was put up by the pile of chairs, namely, that the sum charged for the hire of a chair was 2d. per session of three hours. I think that was the whole of the offer which the local authority made in this case. They said, in effect: "We offer to provide you with a chair, and if you accept that offer and sit in the chair, you will have to pay for that privilege 2d. per session of three hours."

...

I think the learned county court judge has misunderstood the nature of this agreement. I do not think that the notice excluding liability was a term of the contract at all, and I find it unnecessary to refer to the different authorities which were cited to us, save that I would mention a passage in the judgment of Mellish L.J. in *Parker v. South Eastern Ry. Co.* 2 C.P.D. 416, 422 where he points out that it may be that a receipt or ticket may not contain terms of the contract at all, but may be a mere voucher... I think the object of the giving and the taking of this ticket was that the person taking it might have evidence at hand by which he could show that the obligation he was under to pay 2d. for the use of the chair for three hours had been duly discharged, and I think it is altogether inconsistent, in the absence of any qualification of liability in the notice put up near the pile of chairs, to attempt to read into it the qualification contended for. In my opinion, this ticket is no more than a receipt, and is quite different from a railway ticket which contains upon it the terms upon which a railway company agrees to carry the passenger. ...I think the learned county court judge as a matter of law has misconstrued this contract, and looking at all the circumstances of the case, has assumed that this condition on the ticket, or the terms upon which the ticket was issued, has disentitled the plaintiff to recover.

MacKinnon and **Goddard LJJ** delivered concurring judgments.

NOTE

In contrast to the railway ticket cases such as *Parker*, the ticket here was intended by the parties to be a receipt and not a contractual document. Even if reasonable notice had been given of the words on the ticket, they could not therefore have formed part of the contract which had already been made.

Olley v Marlborough Court Ltd [1949] 1 KB 532, Court of Appeal

Mrs Olley (the claimant) and her husband were long-term paying guests at the defendant's hotel. On first arrival they paid a week's board and lodging in advance. One afternoon, after they had been staying in the hotel for some six months, furs, jewellery and clothes belonging to Mrs Olley were stolen from their room. The claimant brought an action for damages against the defendant, alleging negligence (whether in tort or contract). The defendant denied negligence. Alternatively, it argued that its liability was excluded by a notice behind a door in each bedroom. At its head that notice contained a clause excluding liability in respect of the loss or theft of valuables from hotel rooms. The trial judge found that the defendant's negligence caused the claimant's loss and that it could not rely on the clause excluding liability. In dismissing the defendant's appeal, the Court of Appeal held that notice of the exclusion clause came too late for it to be incorporated into the contract and that, in any event, the clause did not apply as a matter of construction to what had happened.

Singleton LJ: If the defendants who would prima facie be liable for their own negligence, seek to exempt themselves by words of some kind, they must show, first, that those words form part of the contract between the parties and, secondly, that those words are so clear that they must be understood by the parties in the circumstances as absolving the defendants from the results of their own negligence. On both those points it seems to me that the defendants' argument fails. It is clear that when the plaintiff and her husband went to the hotel they had not seen the notice. Apparently, by the custom of the hotel, they were asked to pay a week in advance, and when they went to the bedroom for the first time they had not seen the notice, and the words at the head of the notice could not be part of the contract between the parties. Then when did they become so? I asked [counsel for the defendant] and I am afraid it was not a very easy question to answer; he might say it was at the end of the first week when the second payment was made and the notice was seen, although the plaintiff said she did not read the notice. But there ought to be some certainty in a matter of this kind, and there is none. ...[T]his contract when it was entered into was not a contract for a fixed period subject to renewal, but was a contract for an indeterminate period to which an end could be put by notice, and an end was not put to that contract by notice at the time this loss took place. Indeed, the conditions so far as one knows remained the same. I do not think it is open to the defendants to place reliance upon that notice in the bedroom or, at least, I do not think they are exempted by the words at the head of that notice from their liability for negligence. I agree, if I may say so, with what [Bucknill LJ] said upon the subject, and I attach even more importance to the fact that this was no part of the contract at the time when the parties first went into the bedroom; and there is no evidence to show that there was ever any alteration whatever in the terms of that contract. I agree with the submission which [counsel for the claimant] made that it is for the defendants to show that these words formed part of the contract and that they had only one clear meaning. I think they are ambiguous in more ways than one. That is all I need to say upon that side of the case.

Denning LJ: The first question is whether that notice formed part of the contract. Now people who rely on a contract to exempt themselves from their common law liability must prove that contract strictly. Not only must the terms of the contract be clearly proved, but also the intention to create legal relations – the intention to be legally bound – must also be clearly proved. The best way of proving it is by a written document signed by the party to be bound. Another way is by handing him before or at the time of the contract a written notice speci-fying its terms and making it clear to him that the contract is on those terms. A prominent public notice which is plain for him to see when he makes the contract or an express oral stipulation would, no doubt, have the same effect. But nothing short of one of these three ways will suffice. It has been held that mere notices put on receipts for money do not make a contract. (See *Chapelton v. Barry Urban District Council* [1940] 1 K.B. 532.) So, also, in my opinion, notices put up in bedrooms do not of themselves make a contract. As a rule, the guest does not see them until after he has been accepted as a guest. The hotel company no doubt hope that the guest will be held bound by them, but the hope is vain unless they clearly show that he agreed to be bound by them, which is rarely the case.

Assuming, however, that Mrs. Olley did agree to be bound by the terms of this notice, there remains the question whether on its true interpretation it exempted the hotel company from liability for their own negligence. ...In order to exempt a person from liability for negli-gence, the exemption should be clear on the face of the contract. ...Ample content can be given to the notice by construing it as a warning that the hotel company is not liable, in the absence of negligence. As such it serves a useful purpose. It is a warning to the guest that he must do his part to take care of his things himself, and, if need be, insure them. It is unnec-essary to go further and to construe the notice as a contractual exemption of the hotel company from their common law liability for negligence.

Bucknill LJ delivered a judgment which concurred on the construction point but did not consider non-incorporation.

NOTE AND QUESTIONS

1. The reasoning of the majority was that the notice in the bedroom could not constitute reasonable notice for the purposes of incorporation because the contract had been made at the reception when Mr and Mrs Olley first booked in. In any event, as a matter of construction, the notice did not cover loss caused by the hotel's negligence. For consideration of the construction of exemption clauses, see Chapter 5 below, especially 230.
2. Would it have made a difference if the same notice had been displayed at the hotel's reception?

Thornton v Shoe Lane Parking Ltd [1971] 2 QB 163, Court of Appeal

The claimant parked his car at a multi-storey automatic car park operated by the defendants. It was his first visit. The claimant drove to the entrance, took a ticket from the machine, entered the car park and parked his car. Three hours later he returned, paid the charge and went to his car. There was then an accident before he got into his car and he was badly injured. In an action in tort (for negligence or under the Occupiers' Liability Act 1957) the defendants and the claimant were held equally to blame. On appeal, the defendants argued that the judge ought to have found that the ticket was a contractual document incorporating terms that excluded their liability. The ticket recorded the time of entry and informed customers that it should be presented to the cashier in the paying office to claim their cars on departure. In small print was written, 'This ticket is issued subject to the conditions of issue as displayed on the premises'. The conditions were found inside the garage on a pillar opposite the ticket machine and at the paying office. There were many written conditions one of which excluded the defendants' liability for 'injury to the Customer…howsoever…caused'. In dismissing the defendants' appeal, the Court of Appeal held that, as insufficient notice had been given at the relevant time, the exclusion clause was not incorporated into the contract.

Lord Denning MR: We have been referred to the ticket cases of former times from *Parker v South Eastern Railway Co.* (1877) 2 C.P.D. 416 to *McCutcheon v David MacBrayne Ltd.* [1964] 1 W.L.R. 125.

…

None of those cases has any application to a ticket which is issued by an automatic machine. The customer pays his money and gets a ticket. He cannot refuse it. He cannot get his money back. He may protest to the machine, even swear at it. But it will remain unmoved. He is committed beyond recall. He was committed at the very moment when he put his money into the machine. The contract was concluded at that time. It can be translated into offer and acceptance in this way: the offer is made when the proprietor of the machine holds it out as being ready to receive the money. The acceptance takes place when the customer puts his money into the slot. The terms of the offer are contained in the notice placed on or near the machine stating what is offered for the money. The customer is bound by those terms as long as they are sufficiently brought to his notice before-hand, but not otherwise. He is not bound by the terms printed on the ticket if they differ from the notice, because the ticket comes too late. The contract has already been made: see *Olley v. Marlborough Court Ltd.* [1949] 1 K.B. 532. The ticket is no more than a voucher or receipt for the money that has been paid (as in the deckchair case, *Chapelton v. Barry Urban District Council* [1940] 1 K.B. 532) on terms which have been offered and accepted before the ticket is issued.

In the present case the offer was contained in the notice at the entrance giving the charges for garaging and saying "at owner's risk," i.e., at the risk of the owner so far as damage to the car was concerned. The offer was accepted when Mr. Thornton drove up to the entrance and, by the movement of his car, turned the light from red to green, and the ticket was thrust at him. The contract was then concluded, and it could not be altered by any words printed on the ticket itself. In particular, it could not be altered so as to exempt the company from liability for personal injury due to their negligence.

Assuming, however, that an automatic machine is a booking clerk in disguise – so that the old fashioned ticket cases still apply to it. We then have to go back to the three questions put by Mellish L.J. in *Parker v. South Eastern Railway Co.*, 2 C.P.D. 416, 423, subject to this qualification: Mellish L.J. used the word "conditions" in the plural, whereas it would be more apt to use the word "condition" in the singular, as indeed the lord justice himself did on the next page. After all, the only condition that matters for this purpose is the exempting condition. It is no use telling the customer that the ticket is issued subject to some "conditions" or other, without more: for he may reasonably regard "conditions" in general as merely regulatory, and not as taking away his rights, unless the exempting condition is drawn specifically to his attention. (Alternatively, if the plural "conditions" is used, it would be better prefaced with the word "exempting," because the exempting conditions are the only conditions that matter for this purpose.) Telescoping the three questions, they come to this: the customer is bound by the exempting condition if he knows that the ticket is issued subject to it; or, if the company did what was reasonably sufficient to give him notice of it.

Mr. Machin [counsel for the defendants] admitted here that the company did not do what was reasonably sufficient to give Mr. Thornton notice of the exempting condition. That admission was properly made. I do not pause to inquire whether the exempting condition is void for unreasonableness. All I say is that it is so wide and so destructive of rights that the court should not hold any man bound by it unless it is drawn to his attention in the most explicit way. It is an instance of what I had in mind in *J. Spurling Ltd. v. Bradshaw* [1956] 1 W.L.R. 461, 466. In order to give sufficient notice, it would need to be printed in red ink with a red hand pointing to it – or something equally startling.

But, although reasonable notice of it was not given, Mr. Machin said that this case came within the second question propounded by Mellish L.J., namely that Mr. Thornton "knew or believed that the writing contained conditions." There was no finding to that effect. The burden was on the company to prove it, and they did not do so. Certainly there was no evidence that Mr. Thornton knew of this exempting condition. He is not, therefore, bound by it.

Mr. Machin relied on a case in this court last year – *Mendelssohn v. Normand Ltd.* [1970] 1 Q.B. 177. Mr. Mendelssohn parked his car in the Cumberland Garage at Marble Arch, and was given a ticket which contained an exempting condition. There was no discussion as to whether the condition formed part of the contract. It was conceded that it did. That is shown by the report in the Law Reports at p. 180. Yet the garage company were not entitled to rely on the exempting condition for the reasons there given.

That case does not touch the present, where the whole question is whether the exempting condition formed part of the contract. I do not think it did. Mr. Thornton did not know of the condition, and the company did not do what was reasonably sufficient to give him notice of it.

I do not think the garage company can escape liability by reason of the exemption condition. I would, therefore, dismiss the appeal.

Megaw LJ: For myself, I would reserve a final view on the question at what precise moment of time the contract was concluded.

...

The essence of the decision in *Parker v. South Eastern Railway Co.*, 2 C.P.D. 416 was analysed by Lord Hodson in *McCutcheon v. David MacBrayne Ltd.* [1964] 1 W.L.R. 125, 129 as follows:

"That case, affirmed in *Hood v. Anchor Line (Henderson Brothers) Ltd.* [1918] A.C. 837, established that the appropriate questions for the jury in a ticket case were: (1) Did the passenger know that there was printing on the railway ticket? (2) Did he know that the ticket contained or referred to conditions? and (3) Did the railway company do what was reasonable in the way of notifying prospective passengers of the existence of conditions and where their terms might be considered?"

...

When the conditions sought to be attached all constitute, in Lord Dunedin's words [1918] A.C. 846, 847, "the sort of restriction ... that is usual," it may not be necessary for a defendant to prove more than that the intention to attach *some* conditions has been fairly brought to the notice of the other party. But at least where the particular condition relied on involves a sort of restriction that is not shown to be usual in that class of contract, a defendant must show that his intention to attach an unusual condition *of that particular nature* was fairly brought to the notice of the other party. How much is required as being, in the words of Mellish L.J., 2 C.P.D. 416, 424, "reasonably sufficient to give the plaintiff notice of the condition," depends upon the nature of the restrictive condition.

In the present case what has to be sought in answer to the third question is whether the defendant company did what was reasonable fairly to bring to the notice of the plaintiff, at or before the time when the contract was made, the existence of this particular condition. This condition is that part of the clause – a few words embedded in a lengthy clause – which Lord Denning M.R. has read, by which, in the midst of provisions as to damage to property, the defendants sought to exempt themselves from liability for any personal injury suffered by the customer while he was on their premises. Be it noted that such a condition is one which involves the abrogation of the right given to a person such as the plaintiff by statute, the Occupiers Liability Act 1957. True, it is open under that statute for the occupier of property by a contractual term to exclude that liability. In my view, however, before it can be said that a condition of that sort, restrictive of statutory rights, has been fairly brought to the notice of a party to a contract there must be some clear indication which would lead an ordinary sensible person to realise, at or before the time of making the contract, that a term of that sort, relating to personal injury, was sought to be included. I certainly would not accept that the position has been reached today in which it is to be assumed as a matter of general knowledge, custom, practice, or whatever is the phrase that is chosen to describe it, that when one is invited to go upon the property of another for such purposes as garaging a car, a contractual term is normally included that if one suffers any injury on those premises as a result of negligence on the part of the occupiers of the premises they shall not be liable.

Even if I were wrong in the view which I take that the third question has to be posed in relation to this particular term, it would still not avail the defendants here. In my view the judge was wholly right on the evidence in the conclusion which he reached that the defendants have not taken proper or adequate steps fairly to bring to the notice of the plaintiff at or before the time when the contract was made that any special conditions were sought to be imposed.

I think it is a highly relevant factor in considering whether proper steps were taken fairly to bring that matter to the notice of the plaintiff that the first attempt to bring to his notice the intended inclusion of those conditions was at a time when as a matter of hard reality it would have been practically impossible for him to withdraw from his intended entry upon the premises for the purpose of leaving his car there. It does not take much imagination to picture the indignation of the defendants if their potential customers, having taken their tickets and observed the reference therein to contractual conditions which, they said, could be seen in notices on the premises, were one after the other to get out of their cars, leaving the cars blocking the entrances to the garage, in order to search for, find and peruse the notices! Yet unless the defendants genuinely intended that potential customers should do just that, it would be fiction, if not farce, to treat those customers as persons who have been given a fair opportunity, before the contracts are made, of discovering the conditions by which they are to be bound.

I agree that this appeal should be dismissed.

Sir Gordon Willmer: I have reached the same conclusion, and there is very little for me to add. It seems to me that the really distinguishing feature of this case is the fact that the ticket on which reliance is placed was issued out of an automatic machine. I think it is right to say – at any rate, it is the fact so far as the cases that have been called to our attention are concerned – that in all the previous so-called "ticket cases" the ticket has been proffered by a human hand, and there has always been at least the notional opportunity for the customer to say – if he did not like the conditions – "I do not like your conditions: I will not have this ticket." But in the case of a ticket which is proffered by an automatic machine there is something quite irrevocable about the process. There can be no locus poenitentiae. I do not propose to say any more upon the difficult question which has been raised as to the precise moment when a contract was concluded in this case; but at least it seems to me that any attempt to introduce conditions after the irrevocable step has been taken of causing the machine to operate must be doomed to failure. It may be that those who operate garages of this nature, as well as those who install other types of automatic machines, should give their attention to this problem. But it seems to me that the judge below was on the right track when he said, towards the end of his judgment, that in this sort of case, if you do desire to impose upon your customers stringent conditions such as these, the least you can do is to post a prominent notice at the entrance to the premises, warning your customers that there are conditions which will apply. So far as the rest of the case is concerned, I agree with what has been said by my Lords and do not wish to add anything further.

NOTES AND QUESTIONS

1. All three judges reasoned that sufficient notice of the exclusion clause had not been given. It was too late to put an exclusion clause on a ticket in a situation

where, because issued automatically by a machine, there was in reality no opportunity for the customer to object to the exclusion. Lord Denning MR (referring back to his famous 'red-hand' example) and Megaw LJ also stressed that the more unusual or onerous the clause, the greater the degree of notice needed. What, therefore, should the defendants have done to satisfy the need to give reasonable notice?

2.   Lord Denning MR alone decided that, in any event, it was too late for words on the ticket to be incorporated because the contract had already been concluded.

3.   If these facts were to occur today, such an exclusion clause, even if incorporated, would be void under section 2(1) of the Unfair Contract Terms Act 1977 (see below, 245).

Interfoto Picture Library Ltd v Stiletto Visual Programmes Ltd
[1989] QB 433, Court of Appeal

The claimant (Interfoto) ran a library of photographic transparencies. The defendants dealt with Interfoto for the first time on 5 March when one of their directors, Mr Beeching, telephoned to enquire about the availability of certain transparencies of the 1950s for use on a client's presentation. Later that day, 47 transparencies were delivered to the defendants in a jiffy bag which also contained a delivery note. The note contained nine conditions printed fairly prominently in capitals. By condition 2, a holding charge of £5 per day was made for every transparency retained beyond 14 days of receipt. By opening the bag and telephoning Interfoto, informing it that they might be interested in a couple of the transparencies and would be in touch, the defendants entered into a contract for the holding of the transparencies. They did not get in touch with Interfoto. The transparencies were never used and were returned on 2 April. Interfoto invoiced the defendants for £3783.50 pursuant to condition 2 of the delivery note. The defendants refused to pay the sum demanded. In an action to recover the £3783.50, the judge held that Interfoto could rely on condition 2 and gave judgment for the invoiced sum. In allowing the defendants' appeal, the Court of Appeal held that, because insufficient notice was given of it, the 'holding charge' clause was not incorporated into the contract.

Dillon LJ: [T]he holding fee charged by the plaintiffs by condition 2 is extremely high, and in my view exorbitant. The judge held that on a quantum meruit a reasonable charge would have been £3.50 per transparency per week, and not £5 per day, and he had evidence before him of the terms charged by some ten other photographic libraries, most of which charged less than £3.50 per week and only one of which charged more (£4 per transparency per week). It would seem therefore that the defendants would have had a strong case for saying that condition 2 was void and unenforceable as a penalty clause; but that point was not taken in the court below or in the notice of appeal.

   ...

There was never any oral discussion of terms between the parties before the contract was made. In particular there was no discussion whatever of terms in the original telephone conversation when Mr. Beeching made his preliminary inquiry. The question is therefore whether condition 2 was sufficiently brought to the defendants' attention to make it a term of the contract which was only concluded after the defendants had received, and must have known that they had received the transparencies and the delivery note.

This sort of question was posed, in relation to printed conditions, in the ticket cases, such as *Parker v. South Eastern Railway Co.* (1877) 2 C.P.D. 416, in the last century. At that stage the printed conditions were looked at as a whole and the question considered by the courts was whether the printed conditions as a whole had been sufficiently drawn to a customer's attention to make the whole set of conditions part of the contract; if so the customer was bound by the printed conditions even though he never read them.

More recently the question has been discussed whether it is enough to look at a set of printed conditions as a whole. When for instance one condition in a set is particularly onerous does something special need to be done to draw customers' attention to that particular condition? ...

[I]n *Thornton v. Shoe Lane Parking Ltd.* [1971] 2 Q.B. 163 both Lord Denning M.R. and Megaw L.J. held as one of their grounds of decision, as I read their judgments, that where a condition is particularly onerous or unusual the party seeking to enforce it must show that that condition, or an unusual condition of that particular nature, was fairly brought to the notice of the other party.

...

Counsel for the plaintiffs submits that *Thornton v. Shoe Lane Parking Ltd.* [1971] 2 Q.B. 613 was a case of an exemption clause and that what their Lordships said must be read as limited to exemption clauses and in particular exemption clauses which would deprive the party on whom they are imposed of statutory rights. But what their Lordships said was said by way of interpretation and application of the general statement of the law by Mellish L.J. in *Parker v. South Eastern Railway Co.*, 2 C.P.D. 416, 423–424 and the logic of it is applicable to any particularly onerous clause in a printed set of conditions of the one contracting party which would not be generally known to the other party.

Condition 2 of these plaintiffs' conditions is in my judgment a very onerous clause. The defendants could not conceivably have known, if their attention was not drawn to the clause, that the plaintiffs were proposing to charge a "holding fee" for the retention of the transparencies at such a very high and exorbitant rate.

At the time of the ticket cases in the last century it was notorious that people hardly ever troubled to read printed conditions on a ticket or delivery note or similar document. That remains the case now. In the intervening years the printed conditions have tended to become more and more complicated and more and more one-sided in favour of the party who is imposing them, but the other parties, if they notice that there are printed conditions at all, generally still tend to assume that such conditions are only concerned with ancillary matters of form and are not of importance. In the ticket cases the courts held that the common law required that reasonable steps be taken to draw the other parties' attention to the printed conditions or they would not be part of the contract. It is, in my judgment, a logical development of the common law into modern conditions that it should be held, as it was in *Thornton v. Shoe Lane Parking Ltd.* [1971] 2 Q.B. 163, that, if one condition in a set of printed conditions is particularly onerous or unusual, the party seeking to enforce it must show that that particular condition was fairly brought to the attention of the other party.

In the present case, nothing whatever was done by the plaintiffs to draw the defendants' attention particularly to condition 2; it was merely one of four columns' width of conditions printed across the foot of the delivery note. Consequently condition 2 never, in my judgment, became part of the contract between the parties.

I would therefore allow this appeal and reduce the amount of the judgment which the judge awarded against the defendants to the amount which he would have awarded on a quantum meruit on his alternative findings, i.e. the reasonable charge of £3.50 per transparency per week for the retention of the transparencies beyond a reasonable period, which he fixed at 14 days from the date of their receipt by the defendants.

Bingham LJ: In many civil law systems, and perhaps in most legal systems outside the common law world, the law of obligations recognises and enforces an overriding principle that in making and carrying out contracts parties should act in good faith. This does not simply mean that they should not deceive each other, a principle which any legal system must recognise; its effect is perhaps most aptly conveyed by such metaphorical colloquialisms as "playing fair," "coming clean" or "putting one's cards face upwards on the table." It is in essence a principle of fair and open dealing. In such a forum it might, I think, be held on the facts of this case that the plaintiffs were under a duty in all fairness to draw the defendants' attention specifically to the high price payable if the transparencies were not returned in time and, when the 14 days had expired, to point out to the defendants the high cost of continued failure to return them.

English law has, characteristically, committed itself to no such overriding principle but has developed piecemeal solutions in response to demonstrated problems of unfairness. Many examples could be given. Thus equity has intervened to strike down unconscionable bargains. Parliament has stepped in to regulate the imposition of exemption clauses and the form of certain hire-purchase agreements. The common law also has made its contribution, by holding that certain classes of contract require the utmost good faith, by treating as irrecoverable what purport to be agreed estimates of damage but are in truth a disguised penalty for breach, and in many other ways.

The well known cases on sufficiency of notice are in my view properly to be read in this context. At one level they are concerned with a question of pure contractual analysis, whether one party has done enough to give the other notice of the incorporation of a term in the contract. At another level they are concerned with a somewhat different question, whether it would in all the circumstances be fair (or reasonable) to hold a party bound by any conditions or by a particular condition of an unusual and stringent nature.

[*Having referred to* Parker v. South Eastern Railway Co. *(1877) 2 CPD 416,* Hood v. Anchor Line (Henderson Brothers) Ltd. *[1918] AC 837,* J. Spurling Ltd. v. Bradshaw *[1956] 1 WLR 461,* McCutcheon v. David MacBrayne Ltd. *[1964] 1 WLR 125, and* Thornton v. Shoe Lane Parking *[1971] 2 QB 163, Bingham LJ continued:*]

The tendency of the English authorities has, I think, been to look at the nature of the transaction in question and the character of the parties to it; to consider what notice the party alleged to be bound was given of the particular condition said to bind him; and to resolve whether in all the circumstances it is fair to hold him bound by the condition in question. This may yield a result not very different from the civil law principle of good faith, at any rate so far as the formation of the contract is concerned.

Turning to the present case...[o]nce the jiffy bag was opened and the transparencies taken out with the delivery note, it is in my judgment an inescapable inference that the defendants would have recognised the delivery note as a document of a kind likely to contain contractual terms and would have seen that there were conditions printed in small but visible lettering on the face of the document. To the extent that the conditions so displayed were common form or usual terms regularly encountered in this business, I do not think the defendants could successfully contend that they were not incorporated into the contract.

The crucial question in the case is whether the plaintiffs can be said fairly and reasonably to have brought condition 2 to the notice of the defendants. The judge made no finding on the point, but I think that it is open to this court to draw an inference from the primary findings which he did make. In my opinion the plaintiffs did not do so. They delivered 47 transparencies, which was a number the defendants had not specifically asked for. Condition 2 contained a daily rate per transparency after the initial period of 14 days many times greater than was usual or (so far as the evidence shows) heard of. For these 47 transparencies there was to be a charge for each day of delay of £235 plus value added tax. The result would be that a venial period of delay, as here, would lead to an inordinate liability. The defendants are not to be relieved of that liability because they did not read the condition, although doubtless they did not; but in my judgment they are to be relieved because the plaintiffs did not do what was necessary to draw this unreasonable and extortionate clause fairly to their attention. I would accordingly allow the defendants' appeal and substitute for the judge's award the sum which he assessed upon the alternative basis of quantum meruit.

In reaching the conclusion I have expressed I would not wish to be taken as deciding that condition 2 was not challengeable as a disguised penalty clause. This point was not argued before the judge nor raised in the notice of appeal. It was accordingly not argued before us. I have accordingly felt bound to assume, somewhat reluctantly, that condition 2 would be enforceable if fully and fairly brought to the defendants' attention.

NOTES AND QUESTIONS

1.   Drawing on the majority's judgments in *Thornton v Shoe Lane Parking Ltd*, Dillon LJ here relied on the principle (sometimes subsequently referred to as 'the *Interfoto* principle') that special notice must be given where a term is 'particularly onerous or unusual'. The case is also very significant in showing that the principles of incorporation, developed primarily in relation to exclusion and limitation clauses, apply to other written terms.

2.   Bingham LJ's judgment clarifies that the incorporation of a clause by reasonable notice is closely linked to whether it is fair to hold a party to that clause.

3.   If the same facts occurred today, why could the courts *not* strike the clause down as unfair under the Unfair Terms in Consumer Contracts Regulations 1999 (set out below, 285)?

4.   Was the clause unenforceable as a penalty clause (below, 412–417)?

5.   Bingham LJ's reference to the civil law principle of good faith is of general interest: see below, 299.

AEG (UK) Ltd v Logic Resource Ltd [1996] CLC 265, Court of Appeal

Logic Resource Ltd, the defendants, placed an order with the claimants, AEG, for the purchase of cathode ray tubes for export to Iranian customers. The claimants sent a confirmation note which detailed the equipment ordered and provided in small capitals that, 'orders are subject to our conditions of sale—for extract see reverse'. The reverse extracted five conditions from the full conditions of sale and at the bottom the following was printed, 'a copy of the full conditions of sale is available on request'. The defendants never requested, and never saw, the full conditions of sale. The tubes proved to be defective and it was necessary to return them to the claimants for modification. The defendants instructed their customers to air freight the tubes to the claimants in the UK at a cost to the defendants of £4233.33. When the claimants invoiced the defendants for the price of the tubes, the defendants deducted that freight cost. The defendants disputed the deduction, having regard to their standard conditions of sale, condition 7.5 of which provided that: 'The Purchaser shall return the defective parts at his own expense to the Supplier immediately upon request of the latter.'

It was common ground that the claimants' conditions were not standard for the industry and that during negotiations the claimants had not specifically drawn condition 7 to the defendants' attention. Condition 7.5 was part of condition 7. By condition 7.1 the supplier warranted the goods to be free of defects, and by condition 7.3 the purchaser was required to give notice of defects within seven days of discovery. By condition 7.4 the purchaser was required to allow such time and opportunity as estimated by the supplier to be necessary to remedy defects. Failure to make such allowance was deemed to release the supplier from its obligations to remedy defects. Pursuant to condition 7.7 all other warranties or conditions were excluded.

In allowing the defendants' appeal, the Court of Appeal (by a majority) held that, as insufficient notice had been given of it, condition 7.5 was not incorporated into the contract.

Hirst LJ: I consider first the incorporation issue. The learned District Judge's conclusion was as follows:

> "If one can summarise the approach of the courts to the question of notice of conditions it is as follows: there must be something which puts the purchaser on notice that conditions exist and the purchaser has a reasonable opportunity of considering those conditions (whether he takes that opportunity or not) before concluding the contract. Chitty at paragraph 781 summarises the rule as to notice as follows:
> '(1) If the person receiving the document did not know that there was writing or printing on it, he is not bound.
> (2) If he knew that the writing or printing contained or referred to conditions, he is bound.
> (3) If the party tendering the document did what was reasonably sufficient to give the other party notice of the conditions, and if the other party knew that there was writing or printing on the document, but did not know it contained conditions, then the conditions will become the terms of contract between them.'
> ..."

The paragraphs which the District Judge quoted from Chitty reappear verbatim in the current 27th edition of the work and are an accurate statement of the law so far as they go. But, most importantly, they need to be read with paragraph 12-013 which comes three paragraphs after the general principles which now appear in 12-011. Paragraph 12-013 states as follows:

> "Onerous or unusual terms.
> Although the party receiving the document knows it contains conditions, if the particular condition relied on is one which is a particularly onerous or unusual term, or is one which involves the abrogation of a right given by statute, the party tendering the document must show that it has been brought fairly and reasonably to the other's attention. 'Some clauses which I have seen,' said Denning LJ, 'would need to printed in red ink on the face of the document with a red hand pointing to it before the notice could be held to be sufficient.'"

[*Hirst LJ referred to the* Interfoto *case and cited the parts of Megaw LJ's judgment in* Thornton v Shoe Lane Parking Ltd *upon which Dillon LJ had relied in* Interfoto. *He then continued:*]

On behalf of the appellants Mr Lambie's central submission in his able argument is that the present case falls into the *Interfoto* category, as described in paragraph 12-013 in Chitty, because this term is an extremely onerous and unusual one when read in its context, as he submits it must be. Taking condition 7 as a whole, he submits as follows:

1. Condition 7.7 excludes all other warranties and conditions, including of course all implied conditions and warranties under the Sale of Goods Act 1979, and therefore falls within the principle laid down by Megaw LJ in the *Thornton* case.

2. The only right available to the defendants in the case of defective goods is that prescribed by clause 7.4, namely to return them to the plaintiffs for the defects to be remedied on the rather narrow criteria laid down in the second sentence of that clause.

3. In these circumstances, to require the defendants to pay the cost of returning the goods in order to avail themselves of this one very curtailed right is extremely onerous and unusual. Put another way, he submits that condition 7 as a whole is extremely onerous and unusual, most especially condition 7.7, again in the light of Megaw's LJ reasoning in the *Thornton* case, and that, in consequence, condition 7.5, which is part and parcel of condition 7 as a whole, is similarly tainted.

Mr Norris on behalf of the plaintiffs submitted that condition 7.5 must be considered in isolation and that it is wrong to view it in the context of condition 7 as a whole. He urged us to treat the District Judge's conclusion that sufficient notice had been given as a finding of fact which should not be interfered with in this Court unless it was based on an error of principle or plainly wrong: (*George Mitchell (Chesterhall) Limited v Finney Lock Seeds* [1983] 2 AC 803). He also submitted that in any event condition 7.5 was in fact not unusual in character though he accepted that there was no evidence before the District Judge to support this contention.

...

The crucial question, to my mind, is whether condition 7.5 must be considered in its context or in isolation. In my judgment, it would be entirely wrong and wholly artificial to evaluate it in isolation.

I can illustrate that best by an example given by Hobhouse LJ during argument: let us suppose that a contract for the sale of goods did not exclude the statutory conditions and warranties in the Sale of Goods Act 1979 so that those implied terms remained in full force giving the buyers all their usual rights to recover damages in respect of breaches of contract for defective goods; but that, on top of those statutory conditions and warranties, the buyers were given an extra right, at their option, to return defective goods to the plaintiffs for repair. In those circumstances and in that context, it would, in my judgment, be by no means onerous for the contract to go on to stipulate that if the buyers chose to exercise that extra option the cost of returning the goods for repair should be borne by them. The context, which would be critical in that example, would tell strongly in favour of the sellers and against the buyers.

But in the present case the position is entirely different and, in my judgment, the context tells very strongly against the sellers and in favour the buyers. Here the statutory conditions and warranties are excluded and the option to return the defective goods for repair is imposed by the sellers in condition 7.4, confronting the buyers, in effect, with Hobson's choice, and leaving them with no other recourse in a situation where *ex hypothesi* the sellers are in breach of contract through delivery of defective goods. In that context, to impose on the buyers the obligation to pay the costs of returning the goods is extremely onerous, in my judgment, and also unusual in the absence of any evidence that it is a standard or common term.

Thus, I accept Mr Lambie's first submission and I also consider that his alternative submission is sound, namely that condition 7, taken as a whole, is extremely onerous and unusual, especially in the light of condition 7.7 excluding the statutory terms, and that, in consequence, condition 7.5 is tainted as forming part of condition 7 as a whole.

It follows that, in my judgment, this case does indeed fall within the *Interfoto* class as described in paragraph 12.013 of Chitty. I, of course, fully accept the authority of the *George Mitchell* case but, in my judgment, the question here is one of mixed fact and law.

In my judgment, the District Judge erred in two respects as a matter of law: first, by failing to apply the *Interfoto* test as described by Chitty; and, secondly, by treating condition 7.5 in isolation and not in context, and thus adopting a flawed approach to the proper construction of the condition which is also a question of law. ...

It follows that the appellants are entitled to succeed in this appeal on the incorporation ground, so that it is not necessary to consider UCTA, save to say that, in my judgment, the respondents, on whom the burden of proof lies under UCTA, must *a fortiori* fail to satisfy the UCTA reasonableness test. This is because the schedule 2 guidelines, in paragraph (c), require the Court to take into account:

"...whether the customer knew or ought reasonably to have known of the existence and extent of the term (having regard among other things to any custom of the trade and any previous course of dealing between the parties)."

This, of course, applies in circumstances where *ex hypothesi* the term has been validly incorporated in the contract, and there is therefore an additional burden on the respondent in order to make good that requirement. I would add that this is a case where paragraph (a), namely inequality of bargaining power between [the] two sides, also applies.

...

For all these reasons, I will allow this appeal...

Hobhouse LJ: I agree that the appeals should be allowed...My reasons for my decision to allow the appeal differ to some extent from those of my Lords in that I would not determine the appeal on the question of incorporation although I agree that the Unfair Contract Terms Act does preclude the plaintiffs from relying on clause 7 in this case.

...

Like my Lords, I consider that it is wrong to view clause 7.5 in isolation. It forms part of a complex clause, clause 7 which, under the heading of "Warranty", effectively excludes the greater part of the seller's obligations under the Sale of Goods Act. It is drafted in a way which one has seen in other standard terms: what it gives with one hand it takes away with the other. ...

It, therefore, is of the character of an exclusion clause, and the preceding sub clauses give a limited warranty cover. It is, in fact, a very limited warranty cover indeed because it is restricted to defects caused by faulty materials and bad workmanship and the only way in which that warranty can be taken advantage of is circumscribed by conditions.

...

The *prima facie* position is that what the plaintiffs did did comply with the ordinary requirements of English law for the incorporation of contractual conditions. They referred to them in the document; they gave the opposite party the opportunity to see the full copy of the conditions. The "acknowledgment" was a counter-offer to the defendants' offer and the defendants are to be taken – and it is not in dispute – to have accepted the counter-offer by continuing with the order. In fact, in the present case, a number of further documents were exchanged, some of which included the same references to the plaintiffs' conditions as those which I have already quoted.

The position then is conveniently summarised in the quotation from the judgment of Taylor LJ in *Circle Freight International Limited v Medeast Gulf Exports Limited* [1988] 2 Lloyd's Rep 427 at 433, already read by my Lord. It is sufficient if adequate notice is given identifying and relying upon the conditions and they are available on request. Other considerations apply if the conditions, or any of them, are particularly onerous or unusual.

Apart from the argument which is advanced and which has persuaded the other Members of the Court on the *Interfoto* case, the criteria for incorporation have been satisfied. These criteria follow from the ticket cases, typically *Parker v South Eastern Railway Company* (1877) 2 CPD 416. The opposite party has been informed that the relevant offer was subject to terms. The opposite party has been given an adequate and reasonable opportunity to inform himself of what precisely those terms are.

The point on which the plaintiffs have to rely therefore is that to be found in the *Interfoto* case. The judgment of Dillon LJ in the report at [1989] 1 QB 433 sets out the historical background to their decision. It includes references to *Parker v South Eastern Railway Company* and to the colourful dictum of Denning LJ in *Spurling v Bradshaw* [1956] 1 WLR 466 where he postulated that in certain circumstances a red hand might have to be used in order to draw a clause sufficiently to the notice of the other party.

The main authority upon which Dillon LJ and Bingham LJ founded was *Thornton v Shoe Lane Parking Limited* [1971] 2 QB 163...

...

The clause which we are concerned with here is clause 7. It is a clause which covers a topic which is commonly, and indeed normally, dealt with in the standard conditions of sellers of goods. It is in no way unusual nor is it suggested that it is unusual for standard conditions in some way to qualify the obligations of the sellers under a contract of sale. Nor is it suggested that it is unusual for such clauses to include warranty conditions, which have a limited effect both in time and obligation. In my judgment, the clauses which we find in clause 7 deal with a topic which one would expect to be dealt with in the conditions of sale of a supplier of manufactured goods and they cover the type of points which would commonly be dealt with.

The problem in the present case arises from the fact that these clauses have been unreasonably drafted. As is almost inevitable in printed standard terms, they are not related to the particular circumstances of the case and, furthermore, they stipulate for a greater protection of the seller than is reasonable, or anyway is reasonable without some special justification. In my judgment, and this is where I part company from my Lords, it is necessary before excluding the incorporation of a clause *in limine* to consider the type of clause it is. Is it a clause of the type which you would expect to find in the printed conditions? If it is, then it is only in the most exceptional circumstances that a party will be able to say that it was not adequately brought to his notice by standard words of incorporation. If a party wishes to find out precisely how a clause of a normal sort has been worded, he should ask for the actual text of the clause. This case is not analogous to either of the two cases upon which the appellant founds. The *Interfoto* case involved an extortionate clause which did not relate directly to the expected rights and obligations of the parties. In the *Shoe Lane Parking* case, it related to personal injuries and the state of the premises and not to the subject matter of the car parking contract, which would, in the view of the Court of Appeal, have been concerned with damage to property.

Therefore, in my judgment, it is necessary to consider the type of clause, and only if it is a type of clause which it is not to be expected will be found in the printed conditions referred to then to go on to question its incorporation. These conditions do include clauses which, in my judgment, do fall foul of the *Interfoto* principle, but I do not consider that clause 7 comes into that category. In my judgment, it is desirable as a matter of principle to keep what was said in the *Interfoto* case within its proper bounds. A wide range of clauses are commonly incorporated into contracts by general words. If it is to be the policy of English law that in every case those clauses are to be gone through with, in effect, a toothcomb to see whether they were entirely usual and entirely desirable in the particular contract, then one is completely distorting the contractual relationship between the parties and the ordinary mechanisms of making contracts. It will introduce uncertainty into the law of contract.

In the past there may have been a tendency to introduce more strict criteria but this is no longer necessary in view of the Unfair Contract Terms Act. The reasonableness of clauses is the subject matter of the Unfair Contract Terms Act and it is under the provisions of that Act that problems of unreasonable clauses should be addressed and the solution found. In the present case, it is my opinion that the Act provides the answer to the question which has been raised.

...

[*He then considered the Unfair Terms Act 1977, sections 3, 6(3), 11 and Schedule 2 and concluded:*]

[H]aving regard to the circumstances of this case and the effect of the provisions upon which the plaintiffs seek to rely, it is clear that on any view clause 7 must be held to be unreasonable. It therefore follows that although, in my judgment, the clause was incorporated, it is not one upon which the plaintiffs can rely. It is for this reason that I allow the appeal.

Waite LJ agreed with Hirst LJ.

NOTES AND QUESTIONS

1. Hobhouse LJ dissented on the incorporation question. More specifically, in applying the principle that special notice is needed where a written term is

particularly onerous or unusual, Hobhouse LJ differed from the majority because he did not think that the term here was unusual (or, by implication, particularly onerous). This reflected his view that the courts should lean towards treating clauses as incorporated given that, if unreasonable, they can now be struck down under the Unfair Contract Terms Act 1977.

2. For the Unfair Contract Terms Act 1977, see below, 244.

3. Was it misleading of Hirst LJ to say that the claimants 'must a fortiori fail to satisfy the UCTA reasonableness test'?

O'Brien v MGN Ltd
[2001] EWCA Civ 1279, [2002] CLC 33, Court of Appeal

MGN (the defendant) operated a scratchcard game, distributing cards with the newspapers it published. If the card revealed matching sums of money, players were to telephone a premium rate number to ascertain whether those sums also matched the mystery bonus cash amount. On 3 July 1995 Mr O'Brien, the claimant, bought a newspaper containing a card. The claimant's card revealed two sums of £50,000. He telephoned the number published and heard a recorded message announcing £50,000 as the mystery bonus cash amount. The claimant thought he had won £50,000. On the same day, he telephoned MGN to claim the money. MGN had intended to offer only one top prize of £50,000 that day and to distribute winning cards accordingly. Owing to an oversight, it had distributed many more so that 1472 people were claiming £50,000. MGN refused to pay Mr O'Brien and instead held a draw among the 1472 in which the claimant was unsuccessful. The claimant began proceedings to recover £50,000 from MGN Ltd. MGN relied upon their rules. Rule 5 authorised a draw where, as here, more prizes were claimed than were available. The question was whether those rules were incorporated into the contract. The rules were published in full in some of MGN's newspapers but not on 3 July 1995 although, in the section dealing with the game, were the words 'Normal Mirror Group rules apply' and there were similar words on the face of the scratchcard. The claimant accepted that he had seen such references. In dismissing the claimant's appeal, the Court of Appeal held that sufficient notice had been given of the competition rules which were, therefore, incorporated into the contract.

Hale LJ:

19 In my view the judge was right to hold that the contract was made on 3 July. The offer was contained in the paper that day. In my view it was accepted when the claimant telephoned to claim his prize. The offer and therefore the contract clearly incorporated the term 'Normal Mirror Group rules apply'. The words were there to be read and it makes no difference whether or not the claimant actually read or paid attention to them.

20 The question, therefore, is whether those words, in the circumstances, were enough to incorporate the Rules, including Rule 5, into the contract. In the words of Bingham LJ in *Interfoto Library Ltd. v Stiletto Ltd.*, [1989] 1 QB 433, at p 445E, can the defendant 'be said fairly and reasonably to have brought [those rules] to the notice of' the claimant? This is a question of fact. ...[O]ne has to look at the particular contract made on the particular day between the particular parties. But what is fair and reasonable notice will depend upon the nature of the transaction and upon the nature of the term. [*Hale LJ cited from Dillon and Bingham LJJ's judgments in* Interfoto Library Ltd. v. Stiletto Ltd. *[1989] 1 QB 433 and continued:*]

21 In my view, although Rule 5 does turn an apparent winner into a loser, it cannot by any normal use of language be called 'onerous' or 'outlandish'. It does not impose any extra burden upon the claimant, unlike the clause in *Interfoto*. It does not seek to absolve the defendant from liability for personal injuries negligently caused, unlike the clause in *Thornton v Shoe Lane Parking*. It merely deprives the claimant of a windfall for which he has done very little in return. He bought two newspapers, although in fact he could have acquired a card and discovered the hotline number without doing either. He made a call to a premium rate number, which will have cost him some money and gained the newspaper [by] some, but only a matter of pennies, not pounds.

22 The more difficult question is whether the rule is 'unusual' in this context. The judge found that the claimant knew that there was a limit on the number of prizes and that there were relevant rules. [There was] evidence … that these games and competitions always have rules. Indeed I would accept that this is common knowledge. This is not a situation in which players of the game would assume that the newspaper bore the risk of any mistake of any kind which might lead to more people making a claim than had been intended. Some people might assume that the 'get out' rule would provide for the prize to be shared amongst the claimants. Some might assume that it would provide for the drawing of lots. In the case of a single prize some might think drawing lots more appropriate; but it seems to me impossible to say that either solution would be 'unusual'. There is simply no evidence to that effect. Such evidence as there is was to the effect that such rules are not unusual.

23 In any event, the words 'onerous or unusual' are not terms of art. They are simply one way of putting the general proposition that reasonable steps must be taken to draw the particular term in question to the notice of those who are to be bound by it and that more is required in relation to certain terms than to others depending on their effect. In the particular context of this particular game, I consider that the defendants did just enough to bring the Rules to the claimant's attention. There was a clear reference to rules on the face of the card he used. There was a clear reference to rules in the paper containing the offer of a telephone prize. There was evidence that those rules could be discovered either from the newspaper offices or from back issues of the paper. The claimant had been able to discover them when the problem arose.

Sir Anthony Evans:

25 I agree that the appeal should be dismissed, but I do so for one reason only. I feel constrained to accept …that this Court should not interfere with the Judge's finding on an issue of fact, unless the finding is clearly wrong. The issue is whether the respondents took reasonable steps to draw the particular term to the notice of those who are to be bound by it (quoting from the judgment of Lady Justice Hale, para.23).

26 The words 'Normal Mirror Group rules apply' clearly formed part of the contract. Unless it was established that the claimant had actual knowledge of Rule 5, which it was not, it is immaterial in my judgment that he had had the opportunity to read it on previous occasions, or was aware from the earlier editions of the newspapers that some Rules did exist. If those matters were relevant, it would mean that whether he was bound by it would itself be a matter of chance in the individual case.

27 There was no obvious reason why the Rules could not appear in every edition which offered tickets for the game, except as my Lady has said the editor's wish to use the space for publishing hyperbole about the prizes to be won and the people who had won them. The reference to the Rules could have been accompanied by some indication of where they had been printed or could be found, for example 'last Friday's copy' or 'published on' a particular weekday. Instead, on Monday 3 July the only publication in the Daily Mirror during the previous month had been on 10 June and 30 June. A person reading the offer on 3 July could not be expected to have ready access to back issues, even if he or she knew what date to look for. Whether the reader could discover what the Rules were was left essentially as a matter of chance. The promise of significant riches, in my judgment, deserve more.

28 I would also have considered that a Rule which gave the 'winner' no more than a further chance to obtain the prize was sufficiently onerous, if not unusual, to require greater prominence than was given to this one. ...

29 However, the judge concluded differently, and my colleagues agree with him. I cannot say that he was clearly wrong, and so reluctantly, I must agree that the appeal should be dismissed.

Potter LJ agreed with Hale LJ.

NOTES AND QUESTIONS

1. The judgments indicate the uncertain scope of the 'particularly onerous or unusual' *Interfoto* principle. Hale LJ (with whom Potter LJ agreed) regarded the relevant competition rule as neither onerous nor unusual. In contrast, Sir Anthony Evans would have regarded the rule as sufficiently onerous to require greater notice than was given: he concurred in dismissing the appeal only because he did not think that the trial judge was clearly wrong.

2. Why did the claimant not challenge the fairness of the rule under the Unfair Terms in Consumer Contracts Regulations 1994 which, prior to the enactment of the 1999 Regulations, applied to contracts concluded after July 1 1995?

3. What would the result be today if, assuming incorporation, the 1999 Regulations were applied to the facts?

4. An argument that the contract was a gaming or wagering contract and therefore illegal or void was abandoned before the trial at first instance.

(3) Course of Dealing

McCutcheon v David MacBrayne Ltd
[1964] 1 WLR 125, House of Lords (Sc)

Mr McCutcheon, the claimant, asked his brother-in-law, Mr McSporran, to have his (the claimant's) car shipped from Islay to the mainland by the defendants (MacBrayne). The brother-in-law took the car to the port. In the defendants' office he met the purser who quoted a return price which the brother-in-law paid taking a receipt. The vessel sank owing to the defendants' negligent navigation. The claimant brought an action against the defendants to recover the value of the car. The defendants relied upon their standard terms, which purported to exclude liability in the circumstances. The defendants' usual practice was to require consignors to sign a risk note that included their terms. A risk note had been prepared for the consignment but the purser forgot to present it to Mr McSporran for signing. Mr McSporran had consigned goods by the defendants on a number of occasions. Sometimes he had signed the risk notes; on other occasions he had not. Mr McCutcheon had consigned goods by the defendant on four occasions. On each occasion he had signed a risk note. McCutcheon and McSporran admitted that they knew the risk notes to contain conditions but neither knew their specific content. The House of Lords, allowing the claimant's appeal, held that the terms were not incorporated by a course of dealing (or otherwise) so that the defendants had not excluded their liability in negligence.

Lord Reid: The only other ground on which it would seem possible to import these conditions is that based on a course of dealing. If two parties have made a series of similar contracts each containing certain conditions, and then they make another without expressly referring to those conditions it may be that those conditions ought to be implied. If the officious bystander had asked them whether they had intended to leave out the conditions this time, both must, as honest men, have said "of course not." But again the facts here will not support that ground. According to Mr. McSporran, there had been no constant course of dealing; sometimes he was asked to sign and sometimes not. And, moreover, he did not know what the conditions were. This time he was offered an oral contract without any reference to conditions, and he accepted the offer in good faith.

The respondents also rely on the appellant's previous knowledge. I doubt whether it is possible to spell out a course of dealing in his case. In all but one of the previous cases he had been acting on behalf of his employer in sending a different kind of goods and he did not know that the respondents always sought to insist on excluding liability for their own negligence. So it cannot be said that when he asked his agent to make a contract for him he knew that this or, indeed, any other special term would be included in it. He left his agent a free hand to contract, and I see nothing to prevent him from taking advantage of the contract which his agent in fact made. "The judicial task is not to discover the actual intentions of each party; it is to decide what each was reasonably entitled to conclude from the attitude of the other" (*Gloag on Contract*, 2nd ed., p. 7). In this case I do not think that either party was reasonably bound or entitled to conclude from the attitude of the other, as known to him, that these conditions were intended by the other party to be part of this contract.

Lord Hodson: Assuming in favour of the defenders that the experience of the pursuer and his brother-in-law, who acted as his agent, would establish that on previous occasions the defenders' "risk note" embodying conditions absolving them from the consequences of negligence had been regularly signed, this does not establish that the legal situation was the same on October 8, 1960, when the pursuer's car was shipped by his brother-in-law on his behalf without the risk note being signed. No question of fraud or mistake arises, and the only question is whether in some way the defenders can establish their immunity by incorporating in the contract of carriage the conditions which were present on earlier transactions but absent on the relevant occasion.

The course of dealing on earlier occasions is often relevant in determining contractual relations but does not assist when, as here, there was on the part of the defenders a departure from an earlier course in that they omitted to ask the pursuer's agent to sign the document by which they would have obtained protection.

Lord Guest: My Lords, this appeal raises a novel point in regard to the exemptions which can be claimed from a carrier's liability, namely: Whether in the absence of any contractual document a consignor of goods can by a course of previous dealing be bound by conditions of which he is generally aware but the specific terms of which he has no knowledge?

...

In a ticket case the offer is made by the company to carry the passenger or goods on the conditions referred to on the ticket and the passenger or consignor by purchasing the ticket accepts the offer with the conditions thereon incorporated. The ticket thus becomes a contractual document containing the conditions, and the passenger is bound by the conditions. It is, in my view, not legitimate to apply the tests of incorporation of conditions in such cases to a case like the present where there is no contractual document. In the present case it is incorrect to assume that the offer of carriage is made by the respondents on what are described as "standard conditions." The verbal contract is made by the consignor tendering the goods and by the carrier accepting them. A simple contract of carriage is thereby created. In this situation the respondents, upon whom lies the onus to escape liability, would have to show that exempting conditions have been incorporated into the contract. They cannot do this merely by evidence of a previous course of conduct. All that the previous dealings in the present case can show is that the appellant and his agent knew that the previous practice of the respondents was to impose special conditions. But knowledge on their part did not and could not by itself import acceptance by them of these conditions, the exact terms of which they were unaware, into a contract which was different in character from those in the previous course of dealing. The practice of the respondents was to insist on a written contract incorporated in the risk note. On the occasion in question a verbal contract was made without reference to the conditions.

Lord Devlin: In my opinion, the bare fact that there have been previous dealings between the parties does not assist the respondents at all. The fact that a man has made a contract in the same form 99 times (let alone three or four times which are here alleged) will not of itself affect the hundredth contract in which the form is not used. Previous dealings are relevant only if they prove knowledge of the terms, actual and not constructive, and assent to them. If a term is not expressed in a contract, there is only one other way in which it can come into it and that is by implication. No implication can be made against a party of a term which was unknown to him. If previous dealings show that a man knew of and agreed to a term on 99 occasions there is a basis for saying that it can be imported into the hundredth contract without an express statement. It may or may not be sufficient to justify the importation, – that depends on the circumstances; but at least by proving knowledge the essential beginning is made. Without knowledge there is nothing.

...

If a man is given a blank ticket without conditions or any reference to them, even if he knows in detail what the conditions usually exacted are, he is not, in the absence of any allegation of fraud or of that sort of mistake for which the law gives relief, bound by such conditions. It may seem a narrow and artificial line that divides a ticket that is blank on the back from one that says "For conditions see time-tables," or something of that sort, that has been held to be enough notice. I agree that it is an artificial line and one that has little relevance to everyday conditions. It may be beyond your Lordships' power to make the artificial line more natural: but at least you can see that it is drawn fairly for both sides and that there is not one law for individuals and another for organisations that can issue printed documents. If the respondents had remembered to issue a risk note in this case, they would have invited your Lordships to give a curt answer to any complaint by the appellant. He might say that the terms were unfair and unreasonable, that he had never voluntarily agreed to them, that it was impossible to read or understand them and that anyway if he had tried to negotiate any change the respondents would not have listened to him. The respondents would expect him to be told that he had made his contract and must abide by it. Now the boot is on the other foot. It is just as legitimate, but also just as vain, for the respondents to say that it was only a slip on their part, that it is unfair and unreasonable of the appellant to take advantage of it and that he knew perfectly well that they never carried goods except on conditions. The law must give the same answer: they must abide by the contract they made. What is sauce for the goose is sauce for the gander. It will remain unpalatable sauce for both animals until the legislature, if the courts cannot do it, intervenes to secure that when contracts are made in circumstances in which there is no scope for free negotiation of the terms, they are made upon terms that are clear, fair and reasonable and settled independently as such.

Lord Pearce: My Lords, at common law the defenders had a duty of care to the pursuer and a liability for negligence, unless by some special contract they have excluded that duty or liability. Usually such a special contract is achieved by the carrier producing a written contract which the customer signs, or by the carrier printing and displaying regulations to which reference is made on the ticket which the customer buys. In such a case the customer is bound by the conditions embodied in the written contract, or in the printed conditions to which the ticket refers, even if he does not read them and does not know their import, always provided that the carrier shows that he has taken reasonable steps to bring the conditions to the customer's notice (*Parker v. South Eastern Railway Co.*, 2 C.P.D. 416; *Hood v. Anchor Line (Henderson Brothers) Ltd.*, [1918] A.C. 837, 846). In the present case, however, there was no written contract or ticket. Therefore, the foundation on which the ticket cases rest is absent.

A special contract may also be made orally in express terms which set out the exclusion of liability or incorporate by reference conditions that do so. But no such express oral contract is suggested here.

It follows that the defenders must seek to rely on some implied special contract. …

The defenders rely on the course of dealing. But they are seeking to establish an oral contract by a course of dealing which always insisted on a written contract. It is the consistency of a course of conduct which gives rise to the implication that in similar circumstances a similar contractual result will follow. When the conduct is not consistent, there is no reason why it should still produce an invariable contractual result. The defenders having previously offered a written contract, on this occasion offered an oral one. The pursuer's agent duly paid the freight for which he was asked and accepted the oral contract thus offered. This raises no implication that the conditions of the oral contract must be the same as the conditions of the written contract would have been had the defenders proffered one.

Recourse is then sought to knowledge and intention. This is not a case where there was any bad faith on the part of the pursuer or his agent. Had the pursuer's agent snatched at an offer that he knew was not intended, or deliberately taken advantage of the defenders' omission to proffer their usual printed form for his signature, the situation would be different and other considerations would apply. But neither the pursuer nor his agent gave any thought to conditions. Nor had they any knowledge that [the relevant] clause …would contain, wrapped in 30 lines of small print and in language intelligible only to a lawyer or a person of education and perspicacity, a total exclusion of liability for almost every conceivable act of the defenders that might damage the pursuer's goods.

The defenders never intended to offer or make any oral contract on the terms of the printed conditions. They intended to offer a written contract and by mistake they offered an oral one. The pursuer was unaware of the mistake. He accepted an oral contract but he never intended to accept an oral contract on the printed conditions. He knew that he usually had to sign a form which he supposed contained some conditions. When he was offered an oral contract without conditions, he accepted, with no thought about its terms. Why should such intentions or knowledge on the part of the contracting parties lead the court to create a contract which neither intended? The furthest to which this argument of the defenders could lead is to the conclusion that the parties were never ad idem; in which case there was no special contract and the common law contract prevails.

Some reliance was placed on the fact that the pursuer and his agent were in no wise misled nor suffered from the absence of the written form, since they would not have read it or paid any attention to it in any event. This argument has a cynical flavour. It really amounts to saying that because the pursuer would have been bound by a harsh condition, of which he did not know, if the defenders had taken the proper legal steps, he should be likewise bound when they neglected to take those steps. The law inflicts same hardship on ignorant or careless plaintiffs who accept a ticket or sign a printed form in that it holds them bound by printed conditions which they have not read and of which they know nothing. The reasons for this are given in *Parker v South Eastern Railway Co.*, 2 C.P.D. 416. If the defenders are to have the benefit of the reasoning in *Parker's* case, they must take the necessary steps. To decide in the defenders' favour on the facts of this case would be a further extension of the protection afforded to defendants by the ticket cases. Such an extension seems to me very undesirable.

NOTES AND QUESTIONS

1. The claimant (the Scottish term being 'pursuer') through his agent (Mr McSporran) had not, on this occasion, signed a risk note, nor had notice been given of the defendants' (in Scotland, defenders') conditions. This left the possibility of incorporation by a course of dealing. This was rejected because there had been no consistent course of dealing. More specifically, as Lord Reid's speech makes clear, there was no course of dealing at all (ie no regular dealing) with the claimant himself as he had only once previously consigned goods on his own (rather than his employer's) behalf; and there was no *consistent* course of dealing with Mr McSporran because he had sometimes signed a risk note and sometimes not (as on this occasion).

2. Lords Hodson, Guest and Pearce appeared to take the view that there was no *consistent* course of dealing even with Mr McCutcheon himself because this was the first time he (through Mr McSporron) had not signed the risk note. But unless the principle of incorporation by a course of dealing is to have no real role, it is surely the consistency between the past dealings, rather than between the past and present dealings, that counts and this was Lord Reid's approach.

3. Was Lord Devlin correct in saying that actual, and not constructive, knowledge of the term is essential? (See the *Hollier* case, below).

Hollier v Rambler Motors (AMC) Ltd [1972] 2 QB 71, Court of Appeal

The claimant's car developed an oil leak and in March 1970, after telephoning the defendants, he took it for repair to the defendants' garage. Whilst it was there, a fire broke out causing substantial damage to the car. The claimant brought an action to recover damages for the defendants' negligence (ie for breach of its contractual duty of care). The trial judge found that the defendants had been negligent, but held that the oral contract between the parties incorporated a clause which validly excluded the defendants' liability for 'damage caused by fire to customers' cars on the premises'. That clause appeared on an invoice form signed by customers before repair work or servicing was done. During the five years before the fire, the claimant had had his car repaired or serviced by the defendants only three or four times, sending it elsewhere as a rule. The claimant accepted that he had signed the invoice on at least two of the three occasions, once in April 1967 and again in February 1970, on the latter occasion hurriedly and in the rain. The invoice form was never read by the claimant and had not been offered for signature when the car was deposited in March 1970. In allowing the claimant's appeal, the Court of Appeal held that the exclusion clause was not incorporated in the contract by a course of dealing (or otherwise). It also held that, in any event, the clause did not apply as a matter of construction. We deal here only with the incorporation issue (see below for the construction issue, 228).

Salmon LJ: [Counsel for Rambler Motors] says that there was a course of dealing which constituted the three or four occasions over five years – that is, on an average, not quite one dealing a year – from which it is to be implied that what he called "the condition" at the bottom of the contract should be imported into the oral agreement made in the middle of March 1970. I am bound to say that, for my part, I do not know of any other case in which it has been decided or even argued that a term could be implied into an oral contract on the strength of a course of dealing (if it can be so called) which consisted at the most of three or four transactions over a period of five years.

We have been referred to *Hardwick Game Farm v. Suffolk Agricultural Poultry Producers Association* [1969] 2 A.C. 31. That was a case in which some feeding-stuff was sold by some merchants to a farmer. The feeding-stuff was found to be defective. The farmer sued the merchants. The merchants brought in as third party the persons from whom they had purchased the feeding-stuff; they in their turn brought in their suppliers, and there was a long list of many parties brought in right down the chain. As between two of these suppliers a point arose as to whether a term that the buyer under the contract took the responsibility of any latent defects was a term which had been imported into the contract in question by reason of the course of dealing between those parties. It is to be observed that in that case there had been three or four dealings each month between the parties during the previous three years. The course of dealing had been that the feeding-stuff was ordered orally by the buyer and the order was accepted orally by the suppliers. Then on the day of the oral contract, or perhaps the next day, the suppliers sent on to the buyer a sold note. One of the terms appearing on the sold note was that the buyer under the contract took the responsibility for any latent defects. Three or four times each month, year in and year out for three years, sold notes had been sent on to the buyer, and the buyer had never raised any protest or said anything which would have led the sellers to assume that the buyers were doing anything other than accepting the terms of the contract which appeared on the sold note.

In that case, although this practice had been going on all that time, and the buyers had received well over 100 sold notes containing the condition to which I have referred, they had not actually read the condition and knew nothing about it. It was argued that therefore the condition could not be implied into the contract in question, although it had been made in exactly the same way as all the other contracts, namely, orally, with a sold note in the usual form sent on after the contract had been made. The House of Lords decided that the fact that the buyer had not read the condition on the sold notes, having had every opportunity of doing so, did not avail him, because any reasonable seller in circumstances such as those, having had no intimation from the buyer that he took any objection to the condition, would have had good cause to assume that the buyer was agreeing to the condition.

That case is obviously very different from the present case. The *Hardwick Game Farm* case seems to be a typical case where a consistent course of dealing between the parties makes it imperative for the court to read into the contract the condition for which the sellers were contending. Everything that the buyer had done, or failed to do, would have convinced any ordinary seller that the buyer was agreeing to the terms in question. The fact that the buyer had not read the term is beside the point. The seller could not be expected to know that the buyer had not troubled to acquaint himself with what was written in the form that had been sent to him so often, year in and year out during the previous three years, in transactions exactly the same as the transaction then in question.

The sellers in that case sought to rely on *McCutcheon v David MacBrayne Ltd.* [1964] 1 W.L.R. 125, which was also a decision of the House of Lords. They relied on that authority chiefly for a passage in the speech of Lord Devlin, at p. 134, which taken literally would mean that no term can be implied into a contract by a course of dealing unless it can be shown that the party charged has actual and not only constructive knowledge of the term, and with such actual knowledge has in fact assented to it. *McCutcheon v David MacBrayne Ltd.* is an example of a case in which dealings between the parties prior to the contract in question cannot be relied upon to import a term into the relevant contract.

[*He gave the facts of that case and continued:*]

The House of Lords held… that there was no previous course of dealing from which the term of exclusion could be implied into the contract which had been made on behalf of the appellant by his brother-in-law. The appellant himself…had only consigned goods on some four previous occasions, but he, the appellant, had always signed a risk note. His brother-in-law had done so many times, sometimes after signing the risk note and sometimes not.

It seems to me that if it was impossible to rely on a course of dealing in *McCutcheon v David MacBrayne Ltd.*, still less would it be possible to do so in this case, when the so-called course of dealing consisted only of three or four transactions in the course of five years. As I read the speeches of Lord Ried *[sic]*, Lord Guest and Lord Pearce, one, but only one among many, of the facts to be taken into account in considering whether there had been a course of dealing from which a term was to be implied into the contract was whether the consignor actually knew what were the terms written on the back of the risk note. Lord Devlin said that this was a critical factor. Even on the assumption that Lord Devlin's dictum went further than was necessary for the decision in that case, and was wrong – which I think is the effect of the *Hardwick Game Farm* case [1969] 2 AC 31 – I do not see how that can help the defendants here. The speeches of the other members of the House on the decision itself in *McCutcheon's* case make it plain that the clause upon which the defendants seek to rely cannot in law be imported into the oral contract they made in March 1970.

Stamp LJ and **Latey J** concurred on the incorporation issue.

NOTE

This case focuses on how *regular* the consistent dealing needs to be for incorporation by a course of dealing.. It decided that three or four transactions over five years were insufficient for incorporation of the terms on the invoice form. *Henry Kendall & Sons v William Lillico & Sons Ltd* (sub nom *Hardwick Game Farm v Suffolk Agricultural Poultry Producers Association*) [1969] 2 AC 31, HL, in which a clause was incorporated by a course of dealing comprising three or four transactions a month for three years, was distinguished.

(4) The Parties' Trade Practice

British Crane Hire Corporation Ltd v Ipswich Plant Hire Ltd
[1975] QB 303, Court of Appeal

The claimants (British Crane Hire) and the defendants (Ipswich Plant Hire) carried on plant hire businesses. They had dealt before on two occasions, once in February 1969 and again in October 1969. On both occasions a printed form was used. In June 1970 the defendants urgently required a crane and contacted the claimants. The defendants' manager was unaware of the previous dealings. Hire and transport charges were agreed by telephone and the crane was promptly delivered. The printed form was subsequently sent in accordance with the claimants' practice. The defendants would normally have signed the form, but failed to do so on this occasion. Once on site, the crane sank twice in marshland. On the second occasion, it was recovered at great expense to the claimants. They sought to recover their costs from the defendants. The claimants argued, inter alia, that the terms contained in the printed form were incorporated into the oral contract and that under those terms a hirer was obliged to indemnify the owner against all expenses in connection with the use of the plant. The trial judge held that the conditions contained in the printed form were not incorporated. The Court of Appeal, allowing the claimants' appeal, held that the conditions were incorporated by reason of the parties' trade practice.

Lord Denning MR: [*Having recited the facts, continued:*] There were thus only two transactions many months before and they were not known to the defendants' manager who ordered this crane. In the circumstances I doubt whether those two would be sufficient to show a course of dealing.

In *Hollier v Rambler Motors (AMC) Ltd*, [1972] 2 QB 71, 76, Salmon LJ said he knew of no case

> "in which it has been decided or even argued that a term could be implied into an oral contract on the strength of a course of dealing (if it can be so called) which consisted at the most of three or four transactions over a period of five years."

That was a case of a private individual who had had his car repaired by the defendants and had signed forms with conditions on three or four occasions. The plaintiff there was not of equal bargaining power with the garage company which repaired the car. The conditions were not incorporated.

But here the parties were both in the trade and were of equal bargaining power. Each was a firm of plant hirers who hired out plant. The defendants themselves knew that firms in the plant-hiring trade always imposed conditions in regard to the hiring of plant: and that their conditions were on much the same lines.

[*Lord Denning MR considered the evidence and continued:*]

From that evidence it is clear that both parties knew quite well that conditions were habitually imposed by the supplier of these machines: and both parties knew the substance of those conditions. In particular that if the crane sank in soft ground it was the hirer's job to recover it: and that there was an indemnity clause. In these circumstances, I think the conditions on the form should be regarded as incorporated into the contract. I would not put it so much on the course of dealing, but rather on the common understanding which is to be derived from the conduct of the parties, namely, that the hiring was to be on the terms of the plaintiffs' usual conditions.

As Lord Reid said in *McCutcheon v David Macbrayne Ltd.* [1964] 1 WLR 125, 128 quoting from the Scottish textbook, *Gloag on Contract*, 2nd ed (1929), p 7:

> "'The judicial task is not to discover the actual intentions of each party; it is to decide what each was reasonably entitled to conclude from the attitude of the other.'"

It seems to me that, in view of the relationship of the parties, when the defendants requested this crane urgently and it was supplied at once – before the usual form was received – the plaintiffs were entitled to conclude that the defendants were accepting it on the terms of the plaintiffs' own printed conditions – which would follow in a day or two. It is just as if the plaintiffs had said: "We will supply it on our usual conditions," and the defendants said "Of course, that is quite understood."

Applying the conditions, it is quite clear that [they] cover the second mishap. The defendants are liable for the cost of recovering the crane from the soft ground.

Megaw LJ agreed and **Sir Eric Sachs** delivered a concurring judgment.

NOTE AND QUESTION

The indemnity clause was here held to be incorporated not because of a course of dealing but rather because such terms were customarily included (ie it was 'trade practice') in the trade (hiring out plant) to which both parties belonged. Was it, therefore, irrelevant that the parties had dealt with each other, and incorporated such terms, on two previous occasions?

3. IMPLIED TERMS

In addition to express terms (ie terms that are in writing or have been spoken) terms may be implied into a contract. Terms may be implied by the courts or by statute.

Introductory reading: E McKendrick, *Contract Law* (7th edn, 2007) 9.8

(1) Terms Implied by the Courts

These may be subdivided into terms implied by fact, by law and by custom. The distinction between the first two of these reflects the idea that some implied terms are based on the intention of the particular parties, while others are based on the nature of the contract in question and therefore apply to all such types of contract (subject to the parties' contrary intention).

The possibility of implying terms by the custom or usage of the market, trade or locality in which the contract is made is long-established. The modern relevant principles for such implication—that the custom or usage must be certain, notorious, reasonable, recognised as legally binding and consistent with the express terms—were most helpfully set out by Ungoed-Thomas J in *Cunliffe-Owen v Teather & Greenwood* [1967] 1 WLR 1421, 1438–9 (which was a case dealing with the usage of the Stock Exchange). But while the importance of terms implied by custom should not be underestimated, specific case-law illustrations of such implication are rare. We shall instead, therefore, devote our attention in this subsection to terms implied by fact and law. Although we shall look at each of these two in turn, it should be recognised at the outset that some of the cases on terms implied by law also make important observations on terms implied by fact.

(a) Terms Implied by Fact

The Moorcock (1889) 14 PD 64, Court of Appeal

The claimant owned the steamship 'Moorcock' and contacted the defendants, who owned a wharf abutting on, and a jetty extending into, the River Thames. The parties agreed that the steamship would be discharged and loaded at the defendants' wharf, and moored alongside the jetty so as to be aground at low tide. No charge was made for moorings, but the claimant was to pay a charge for all goods landed on or shipped from or stored on the wharf. When aground, on mooring at the wharf, the Moorcock suffered damage caused by a ridge of hard ground on the riverbed. The defendants did not own the riverbed and admitted that they had taken no steps to ascertain whether the riverbed was suitable for the steamship. The claimant sought to recover damages for breach of contract. The Court of Appeal, affirming the trial judge, held that, since the use of the premises by the claimant required the vessel to be aground whilst moored, the defendants had impliedly warranted that reasonable care had been taken to ascertain that the bottom of the river was in such a condition as not to endanger the vessel.

Lord Esher MR: In this case the appellants made an agreement with the respondent for the use of their wharf and jetty in such a manner as to enable them to earn money from the respondent. The use of their wharf involved the use of the river adjacent to the front of their wharf, for the owner of a vessel such as the Moorcock could not use their wharf without mooring that vessel alongside the jetty. It is a necessary and an immediate step to the earning profit [sic] by the use of the wharf that the vessel should be moored to the jetty. The appellants do not charge directly for the use of their wharf, but they cannot charge anything to anybody, or, under the circumstances, earn anything until the vessel moors itself to their jetty. She is moored to the jetty in order that the wharf may be used for the loading and unloading of goods into and from the vessel, and the appellants get paid for the use of their wharf by charging in respect of the goods that lie on and cross their wharf.

Such a vessel as the Moorcock could not be moored to this wharf without taking the ground at low water on every tide; therefore, in order that the wharf may be used so that the appellants may earn profit, a vessel must be moored to their wharf, and at the front of it, under such circumstances that she must take the ground at every tide. Now the owners of the wharf and the jetty are there always, and if anything happens in front of their wharf they have the means of finding it out, but persons who come in their ships to this wharf have no reasonable means of discovering what the state of the bed of the river is until the vessel is moored and takes the ground for the first time.

What, then, is the reasonable implication in such a contract? In my opinion honest business could not be carried on between such a person as the respondent and such people as the appellants, unless the latter had impliedly undertaken some duty towards the respondent with regard to the bottom of the river at this place. If that is so, what is the least onerous duty which can be implied? In this case we are not bound to say what is the whole of the duty. All we have got to say is whether there is not at least the duty which the learned judge in the court below has held does lie on them and to be implied as part of their contract. The appellants can find out the state of the bottom of the river close to the front of their wharf without difficulty…and when they cannot honestly earn what they are desiring to earn without this, it is implied that they have undertaken to see that the bottom of the river is reasonably fit, or at all events that they have taken reasonable care to find out that the bottom of the river is reasonably fit for the purpose for which they agree that their jetty should be used, that is, they should take reasonable care to find out in what condition the bottom is, and then either have it made reasonably fit for the purpose, or inform the persons with whom they have contracted that it is not so. That I think is the least that can be implied as their duty, and this is what I understand the learned judge has implied, and then he finds as a matter of fact that they did not take reasonable means in this case, and in that view also I agree. I therefore think the appellants broke their contract, and that they are liable to the respondent for the injury which his vessel sustained.

Bowen LJ: The question which arises here is whether when a contract is made to let the use of this jetty to a ship which can only use it, as is known by both parties, by taking the ground, there is any implied warranty on the part of the owners of the jetty, and if so, what is the extent of the warranty. Now, an implied warranty, or, as it is called, a covenant in law, as distinguished from an express contract or express warranty, really is in all cases founded on the presumed intention of the parties, and upon reason. The implication which the law draws from what must obviously have been the intention of the parties, the law draws with the object of giving efficacy to the transaction and preventing such a failure of consideration as cannot have been within the contemplation of either side; and I believe if one were to take all the cases, and they are many, of implied warranties or covenants in law, it will be found that in all of them the law is raising an implication from the presumed intention of the parties with the object of giving to the transaction such efficacy as both parties must have intended that at all events it should have. In business transactions such as this, what the law desires to effect by the implication is to give such business efficacy to the transaction as must have been intended at all events by both parties who are business men; not to impose on one side all the perils of the transaction, or to emancipate one side from all the chances of failure, but to make each party promise in law as much, at all events, as it must have been in the contemplation of both parties that he should be responsible for in respect of those perils or chances.

Now what did each party in a case like this know? For if we are examining into their presumed intention we must examine into their minds as to what the transaction was. Both parties knew that this jetty was let out for hire, and knew that it could only be used under the contract by the ship taking the ground. They must have known that it was by grounding that she used the jetty; in fact, except so far as the transport to the jetty of the cargo in the ship was concerned, they must have known, both of them, that unless the ground was safe the ship would be simply buying an opportunity of danger, and that all consideration would fail unless some care had been taken to see that the ground was safe. In fact the business of the jetty could not be carried on except upon such a basis. The parties also knew that with regard to the safety of the ground outside the jetty the shipowner could know nothing at all, and the jetty owner might with reasonable care know everything. The owners of the jetty, or their servants, were there at high and low tide, and with little trouble they could satisfy themselves, in case of doubt, as to whether the berth was reasonably safe. The ship's owner, on the other hand, had not the means of verifying the state of the jetty, because the berth itself opposite the jetty might be occupied by another ship at any moment.

Now the question is how much of the peril of the safety of this berth is it necessary to assume that the shipowner and the jetty owner intended respectively to bear – in order that such a minimum of efficacy should be secured for the transaction, as both parties must have intended it to bear? Assume that the berth outside had been absolutely under the control of the owners of the jetty, that they could have repaired it and made it fit for the purpose of the unloading and the loading. If this had been the case, then the case of *The Mersey Docks Trustees v Gibbs*, Law Rep HL 93, shows that those who owned the jetty, who took money for the use of the jetty, and who had under their control the locus in quo, would have been bound to take all reasonable care to prevent danger to those who were using the jetty – either to make the berth outside good, or else not to invite ships to go there – either to make the berth safe, or to advise persons not to go there. But there is a distinction in the present instance. The berth outside the jetty was not under the actual control of the jetty owners. It is in the bed of the river, and it may be said that those who owned the jetty had no duty cast upon them by statute or common law to repair the bed of the river, and that they had no power to interfere with the bed of the river unless under the licence of the Conservators. Now it does make a difference, it seems to me, where the entire control of the locus in quo – be it canal, or be it dock, or be it river berth – is not under the control of the persons who are taking toll for accommodation which involves its user, and, to a certain extent, the view must be modified of the necessary implication which the law would make about the duties of the parties receiving the remuneration. This must be done exactly for the reason laid down by Lord Holt in his judgment in *Coggs v Bernard*, Ld Raym 909, where he says "it would be unreasonable to charge persons with a trust further than the nature of the thing puts it in their power to perform." Applying that modification, which is one of reason, to this case, it may well be said that the law will not imply that the persons who have not the control of the place have taken reasonable care to make it good, but it does not follow that they are relieved from all responsibility. They are on the spot. They must know that the jetty cannot be used unless reasonable care is taken, if not to make it safe, at all events to see whether it is safe. No one can tell whether reasonable safety has been secured except themselves, and I think if they let out their jetty for use they at all events imply that they have taken reasonable care to see whether the berth, which is the essential part of the use of the jetty, is safe, and if it is not safe, and if they have not taken such reasonable care, it is their duty to warn persons with whom they have dealings that they have not done so. This is a business transaction as to which at any moment the parties may make any bargain they please, and either side may by the contract throw upon the other the burden of the unseen and existing danger. The question is what inference is to be drawn where the parties are dealing with each other on the assumption that the negotiations are to have some fruit, and where they say nothing about the burden of this kind of unseen peril, leaving the law to raise such inferences as are reasonable from the very nature of the transaction. So far as I am concerned I do not wish it to be understood that I at all consider this is a case of any duty on the part of the owners of the jetty to see to the access to the jetty being kept clear. The difference between access to the jetty and the actual use of the jetty seems to me ... only a question of degree, but when you are dealing with implications which the law directs, you cannot afford to neglect questions of degree, and it is just that difference of degree which brings one case on the line and prevents the other from approaching it. I confess that on the broad view of the case I think that business could not be carried on unless there was an implication to the extent I have laid down, at all events in the case where a jetty like the present is so to be used, and, although the case is a novel one, and the cases which have been cited do not assist us, I feel no difficulty in drawing the inference that this case comes within the line.

Fry LJ: I agree. I will only add that the considerations which weigh much with me in coming to the conclusion that there was the implication which the learned judge had relied on, are that the Conservators were under no obligation to remove the saddle-back, or shingle, or stone, which did the injury, and that the defendants had the means of examining the bottom of the river and neglected to do so.

NOTES AND QUESTIONS

1. This case is most famous for Bowen LJ's invocation of a 'business efficacy' test for implying terms. The essence of that test is that, without the implied term, the contract will not work. He regarded this as a test based on what the parties must have intended.

2. It has sometimes been suggested (see eg Lord Wilberforce in *Liverpool CC v Irwin*, below, 202) that the test was incorrectly applied on the facts. This criticism seems misplaced. The contract could not work if the mooring was unsafe. And while the defendants would not have undertaken to make the riverbed safe (because they did not own the riverbed and so could not do work to it) there was no such objection to an undertaking that they had taken reasonable care to ascertain that the mooring was safe.

3. The other most famous test for implying a term in fact (ie a term which the parties intended) is the 'officious bystander' test. This derives from MacKinnon LJ's judgment in *Shirlaw v Southern Foundries (1927) Ltd* [1939] 2 KB 206, 227: 'I think that there is a test that may be at least as useful as [the sentences from Bowen LJ's judgment in *The Moorcock*]. If I may quote from an essay which I wrote some years ago, I then said: 'Prima facie that which in any contract is left to be implied and need not be expressed is something so obvious that it goes without saying; so that, if, while the parties were making their bargain, an officious bystander were to suggest some express provision for it in their agreement, they would testily suppress him with a common, "Oh, of course!".' See similarly *Reigate v Union Manufacturing Co (Ramsbottom) Ltd* [1918] 1 KB 592, 605 per Scrutton LJ.

4. Two modern examples of terms being implied by fact deserve mention.

(i) In *Equitable Life Assurance Society v Hyman* [2002] 1 AC 408, HL, Lord Steyn, giving the leading speech, stressed at 459, that 'The legal test for the implication of such a term is a standard of strict necessity.' He also usefully labelled what we have called terms implied by law as 'standardised implied terms' and terms implied by fact as 'individualised [implied] terms.' The case concerned 'with profit' pension policies issued by a life assurance society (which were treated as contractually binding as between the members and the directors). It was held that there was an implied term that the directors could not use their discretion in apportioning profits so as to exclude those with guaranteed annual rate policies. In Lord Steyn's words, at 459, 'In my judgment an implication precluding the use of the directors' discretion in this way is strictly necessary. The implication is essential to give effect to the reasonable expectations of the parties.'

(ii) In *Paragon Finance Plc v Nash* [2001] EWCA Civ 1466, [2002] 1 WLR 685, a loan agreement permitting the lender to vary the interest rate was held to be subject to an implied term that the rate set would not be set dishonestly, for an improper purpose, capriciously, arbitrarily or in a way that no reasonable lender, acting reasonably, would do. Dyson LJ, with whom Astill J and Thorpe LJ agreed, said at [36] and [42] that 'such an implied term is necessary in order to give effect to the reasonable expectations of the parties'.

5. Is there a difference between implying terms on the basis of the parties' intentions (including what the parties would have intended had they considered the matter) and implying terms on the basis of the reasonable expectations of the parties?

(b) Terms Implied by Law

Liverpool City Council v Irwin [1977] AC 239, House of Lords

The claimant, Liverpool City Council, owned a tower block of flats, each of which was let to tenants. A staircase and lifts provided access to the upper floors. An internal chute was available to tenants for discharging rubbish for collection at ground level. The 'Conditions of Tenancy', signed by the tenants, made detailed provision for a tenant's obligations but did not address the obligations of Liverpool City Council. The tower block suffered persistent vandalism and, in response to the claimant's inability to solve the problem, the tenants refused to pay rent. The claimant commenced proceedings for possession of the block. Mr Irwin and another of the tenants, who were the defendants, counterclaimed for damages alleging breach of an implied term requiring the claimant to keep the common parts of the block in repair. The House of Lords in dismissing the tenants' appeal held that, while the implied term alleged should be implied because necessary for the type of contract, there had been no breach of it.

Lord Wilberforce: We have then a contract which is partly, but not wholly, stated in writing. In order to complete it, in particular to give it a bilateral character, it is necessary to take account of the actions of the parties and the circumstances. As actions of the parties, we must note the granting of possession by the landlords and reservation by them of the "common parts" – stairs, lifts, chutes, etc. As circumstances we must include the nature of the premises, viz., a maisonette for family use on the ninth floor of a high block, one which is occupied by a large number of other tenants, all using the common parts and dependent upon them, none of them having any expressed obligation to maintain or repair them.

To say that the construction of a complete contract out of these elements involves a process of "implication" may be correct; it would be so if implication means the supplying of what is not expressed. But there are varieties of implications which the courts think fit to make and they do not necessarily involve the same process. Where there is, on the face of it, a complete, bilateral contract, the courts are sometimes willing to add terms to it, as implied terms: this is very common in mercantile contracts where there is an established usage: in that case the courts are spelling out what both parties know and would, if asked, unhesitatingly agree to be part of the bargain. In other cases, where there is an apparently complete bargain, the courts are willing to add a term on the ground that without it the contract will not work – this is the case, if not of *The Moorcock* (1889) 14 P.D. 64 itself on its facts, at least of the doctrine of *The Moorcock* as usually applied. This is, as was pointed out by the majority in the Court of Appeal, a strict test – though the degree of strictness seems to vary with the current legal trend – and I think that they were right not to accept it as applicable here. There is a third variety of implication, that which I think Lord Denning M.R. favours, or at least did favour in this case, and that is the implication of reasonable terms. But though I agree with many of his instances, which in fact fall under one or other of the preceding heads, I cannot go so far as to endorse his principle; indeed, it seems to me, with respect, to extend a long, and undesirable, way beyond sound authority.

The present case, in my opinion, represents a fourth category, or I would rather say a fourth shade on a continuous spectrum. The court here is simply concerned to establish what the contract is, the parties not having themselves fully stated the terms. In this sense the court is searching for what must be implied.

What then should this contract be held to be? There must first be implied a letting, that is, a grant of the right of exclusive possession to the tenants. With this there must, I would suppose, be implied a covenant for quiet enjoyment, as a necessary incident of the letting. The difficulty begins when we consider the common parts. We start with the fact that the demise is useless unless access is obtained by the staircase; we can add that, having regard to the height of the block, and the family nature of the dwellings, the demise would be useless without a lift service; we can continue that, there being rubbish chutes built into the structures and no other means of disposing of light rubbish, there must be a right to use the chutes. The question to be answered and it is the only question in this case – is what is to be the legal relationship between landlord and tenant as regards these matters.

There can be no doubt that there must be implied (i) an easement for the tenants and their licensees to use the stairs, (ii) a right in the nature of an easement to use the lifts, (iii) an easement to use the rubbish chutes.

But are these easements to be accompanied by any obligation upon the landlord, and what obligation? There seem to be two alternatives. The first, for which the council contends, is for an easement coupled with no legal obligation, except such as may arise under the Occupiers' Liability Act 1957 as regards the safety of those using the facilities, and possibly such other liability as might exist under the ordinary law of tort. The alternative is for easements coupled with some obligation on the part of the landlords as regards the maintenance of the subject of them, so that they are available for use.

My Lords, in order to be able to choose between these, it is necessary to define what test is to be applied, and I do not find this difficult. In my opinion such obligation should be read into the contract as the nature of the contract itself implicitly requires, no more, no less: a test, in other words, of necessity. The relationship accepted by the corporation is that of landlord and tenant: the tenant accepts obligations accordingly, in relation inter alia to the stairs, the lifts and the chutes. All these are not just facilities, or conveniences provided at discretion: they are essentials of the tenancy without which life in the dwellings, as a tenant, is not possible. To leave the landlord free of contractual obligation as regards these matters, and subject only to administrative or political pressure, is, in my opinion, inconsistent totally with the nature of this relationship. The subject matter of the lease (high rise blocks) and the relationship created by the tenancy demand, of their nature, some contractual obligation on the landlord.

I do not think that this approach involves any innovation as regards the law of contract. The necessity to have regard to the inherent nature of a contract and of the relationship thereby established was stated in this House in *Lister v. Romford Ice and Cold Storage Co. Ltd.* [1957] A.C. 555. That was a case between master and servant and of a search for an "implied term." Viscount Simonds, at p. 579, makes a clear distinction between a search for an implied term such as might be necessary to give "business efficacy" to the particular contract and a search, based on wider considerations, for such a term as the nature of the contract might call for, or as a legal incident of this kind of contract. If the search were for the former, he says, "... I should lose myself in the attempt to formulate it with the necessary precision." (p. 576.) We see an echo of this in the present case, when the majority in the Court of Appeal, considering a "business efficacy term" – i.e., a *"Moorcock"* term (*The Moorcock*, 14 P.D. 64) – found themselves faced with five alternative terms and therefore rejected all of them. But that is not, in my opinion, the end, or indeed the object, of the search.

...

My Lords, if, as I think, the test of the existence of the term is necessity the standard must surely not exceed what is necessary having regard to the circumstances. To imply an absolute obligation to repair would go beyond what is a necessary legal incident and would indeed be unreasonable. An obligation to take reasonable care to keep in reasonable repair and usability is what fits the requirements of the case. Such a definition involves – and I think rightly – recognition that the tenants themselves have their responsibilities. What it is reasonable to expect of a landlord has a clear relation to what a reasonable set of tenants should do for themselves.

I add one word as to lighting. In general I would accept that a grant of an easement of passage does not carry with it an obligation on the grantor to light the way. ...But the case may be different when the means of passage are constructed, and when natural light is either absent or insufficient. In such a case, to the extent that the easement is useless without some artificial light being provided, the grant should carry with it an obligation to take reasonable care to maintain adequate lighting – comparable to the obligation as regards the lifts. To impose an absolute obligation would be unreasonable; to impose some might be necessary. We have not sufficient material before us to see whether the present case on its facts meets these conditions.

I would hold therefore that the landlords' obligation is as I have described. And in agreement, I believe, with your Lordships I would hold that it has not been shown in this case that there was any breach of that obligation. On the main point therefore I would hold that the appeal fails.

My Lords, it will be seen that I have reached exactly the same conclusion as that of Lord Denning M.R., with most of whose thinking I respectfully agree. I must only differ from the passage in which, more adventurously, he suggests that the courts have power to introduce into contracts any terms they think reasonable or to anticipate legislative recommendations of the Law Commission. A just result can be reached, if I am right, by a less dangerous route.

Lord Salmon: Unless the law, in circumstances such as these, imposes an obligation upon the council at least to use reasonable care to keep the lifts working properly and the staircase lit, the whole transaction becomes inefficacious, futile and absurd. I cannot go so far as Lord Denning M.R. and hold that the courts have any power to imply a term into a contract merely because it seems reasonable to do so. Indeed, I think that such a proposition is contrary to all authority. To say, as Lord Reid said in *Young & Marten Ltd v McManus Childs Ltd* [1969] 1 AC 454, 465, that "... no warranty ought to be implied in a contract unless it is in all the circumstances reasonable" is, in my view, quite different from saying that any warranty or term which is, in all the circumstances, reasonable ought to be implied in a contract. I am confident that Lord Reid meant no more than that unless a warranty or term is in all the circumstances reasonable there can be no question of implying it into a contract, but before it is implied much else besides is necessary, for example that without it the contract would be inefficacious, futile and absurd.

...

I find it difficult to think of any term which it could be more necessary to imply than one without which the whole transaction would become futile, inefficacious and absurd as it would do if in a 15 storey block of flats or maisonettes, such as the present, the landlords were under no legal duty to take reasonable care to keep the lifts in working order and the staircases lit.

Lord Edmund-Davies: The Court of Appeal [considered] whether, in the light of *The Moorcock*, such a term [as alleged by the tenants] could be implied in the tenancy agreement. Roskill LJ (with whom Ormrod LJ .agreed) said [1976] QB 319, 337–338:

> "... I cannot agree... that it is open to us in the court at the present day to imply a term because subjectively or objectively we as individual judges think it would be reasonable so to do. It must be necessary in order to make the contract work as well as reasonable so to do, before the court can write into a contract as a matter of implication some term which the parties have themselves, assumedly deliberately, omitted to do."

Lord Denning MR, on the other hand, "with some trepidation" (p 329) (which was understandable), took a different view and, after referring to some out of the "stacks" of relevant cases, said, at p 330:

> "... in none of them did the court ask: what did both parties intend? If asked, each party would have said he never gave it a thought: or the one would have intended something different from the other. Nor did the court ask: Is it necessary to give business efficacy to the transaction? If asked, the answer would have been: 'It is reasonable, but it is not necessary.' The judgments in all those cases show that the courts implied a term according to whether or not it was reasonable in all the circumstances to do so.... This is to be decided as matter of law, not as matter of fact."

I have respectfully to say that I prefer the views of the majority in the Court of Appeal. Bowen LJ said in the well known passage in *The Moorcock*, 14 PD 64, 68:

> "In business transactions such as this, what the law desires to effect by the implication is to give such business efficacy to the transaction as must have been intended at all events by both parties who are business men;... to make each party promise in law as much, at all events, as it must have been in the contemplation of both parties that he should be responsible for..."

That is not to say, of course, that consideration of what is reasonable plays no part in determining whether or not a term should be implied. Thus, in *Hamlyn & Co v Wood & Co* [1891] 2 QB 488, decided only two years after *The Moorcock* (to which he had been a party), Lord Esher MR said, at p 491:

> "... the court has no right to imply in a written contract any such stipulation, unless, on considering the terms of the contract in a reasonable and business manner, an implication necessarily arises that the parties must have intended that the suggested stipulation should exist. It is not enough to say that it would be a reasonable thing to make such an implication. It must be a necessary implication in the sense that I have mentioned."

Bowen and Kay LJJ, who had also been members of the *Moorcock* court, delivered similar judgments. The touchstone is always necessity and not merely reasonableness: see, for example, the judgments of Scrutton LJ in *Reigate v Union Manufacturing Co (Ramsbottom) Ltd.* [1918] 1 KB 592, 605, and *In re Comptoir Commercial Anversois v Power, Son & Co* [1920] 1 KB 868, 899.

But be the test that of necessity (as I think, in common with Roskill and Ormrod L.JJ.) or reasonableness (as Lord Denning MR thought), the exercise involved is that of ascertaining the presumed intention of the parties. Whichever of these two tests one applies to the facts of the instant case, in my judgment the outcome must be the same for, in the words of Roskill LJ [1976] QB 319, 338:

> "... I find it absolutely impossible to believe that the Liverpool City Council, if asked whether it was their intention as well as that of their tenants of these flats that any of the implied terms contended for by Mr Godfrey should be written into the contract, would have given an affirmative answer. Their answers would clearly have been 'No'."

It follows that, had such continued to be the case presented on the appellants' behalf to your Lordships' House, for my part I should have rejected it. But it was not, for Mr. Godfrey [counsel for the tenants] adopted before your Lordships a previously unheralded and more attractive approach, which was very properly not objected to by Mr. Francis [counsel for the landlords] despite its late appearance on the scene. As an alternative to his argument based on *The Moorcock*, 14 PD 64, Mr Godfrey submitted before this House that an obligation is placed upon the landlords in all such lettings of multi-storey premises as are involved in this appeal by the general law, as a legal incident of this kind of contract, which the landlords must be assumed to know about as well as anyone else. This new approach was based largely upon *Lister v Romford Ice and Cold Storage Co Ltd* [1957] AC 555, a case concerning the incidents of a contract of service between master and servant ...

...

[T]here appears to be no technical difficulty in making an *express* grant of an easement coupled with an undertaking by the servient owner to maintain it. That being so, there seems to be no reason why the easement arising in the present case should not by implication carry with it a similar burden on the grantor.

[*Having considered some landlord and tenant cases, he continued:*]

I therefore conclude that the city council were under an obligation to the tenant in relation to the maintenance of stairs and lifts in Haigh Heights in such a condition as to enable them to be used as means of access to and from their maisonettes. This also involved the maintenance of reasonably adequate lighting of the staircases at such times and in such places as artificial lighting was called for.

The next question that arises is: what is the nature and extent of such obligation? In other words, is it absolute or qualified? If the former, any failure to maintain (save of a wholly minimal kind) would involve a breach of the landlord's obligation... [L]ater decisions, such as *Dunster v Hollis* [1918] 2 KB 795 and *Cockburn v Smith* [1924] 2 KB 119, treat the duty only as one of reasonable care, and such is the conclusion I have come to also. To impose an absolute duty upon the landlords in the case of buildings in multiple occupation would, I think, involve such a wide departure from the ordinary law relating to easements that it ought not to be held to exist unless expressly undertaken and should not be implied.

Lord Cross of Chelsea delivered a speech agreeing with Lords Wilberforce, Salmon and Edmund-Davies. **Lord Fraser of Tullybelton** delivered a speech agreeing with Lord Wilberforce.

NOTES AND QUESTIONS

1. All their Lordships rejected, as too wide-ranging and unsupported by authority, Lord Denning MR's test in the Court of Appeal of the courts being able to imply a term where reasonable to do so in all the circumstances. With the possible exception of Lord Salmon, who did not clearly

deal with this, they also all appeared to agree that, on the facts, applying the 'business efficacy' or 'officious bystander' tests would not result in the alleged term being implied. But applying the different test of what the nature of the contract and relationship necessarily required (see especially Lord Wilberforce's speech), the term imposing a duty of reasonable care on the landlord to keep the common parts in repair was implied. The idea, therefore, is that the law can identify particular types of contract, such as contracts of employment or for a tenancy, and that there are implied terms that are necessarily inherent in those contracts and the relationships established by them.

2.   Their Lordships regarded the 'business efficacy' and 'officious bystander' tests as concerned with the parties' intentions (ie a term implied by fact); whereas the 'necessary to the type of contract/relationship' test was for a term implied by law so that the implication was made irrespective of the parties' intentions (albeit subject to an express contrary intention).

3.   Is there a clear difference: (a) between implying a term because necessary to the particular type of contract/relationship and implying a term because reasonable in all the circumstances; (b) between implying a term because necessary to the particular type of contract/relationship and implying a term because of 'business efficacy'?

Shell UK Ltd v Lostock Garage Ltd
[1976] WLR 1187, Court of Appeal

The defendant operated a petrol station. In 1955 a 'solus' agreement was concluded by which the defendant was obliged to take petrol from the claimant (Shell) exclusively. The agreement was terminable on 12 months' notice. During the oil crisis of 1975 petrol increased sharply in price. A price war ensued. The defendant was in competition with four other petrol stations, one of which, Plumleys, was owned by the claimant. Plumleys and another of the four competitors sold the claimant's petrol; the other two did not. Each of the four competitors was able to lower its petrol prices. In contrast, had the defendant lowered its prices it would have operated at a loss owing to the fixed price of petrol under the 'solus' agreement. The claimant operated a support scheme for those who took its petrol by which it guaranteed to meet any losses which participants faced in remaining competitive, but the defendant's drop in sales was not sufficient to permit participation in the scheme. The defendant arranged to take petrol from another supplier. The claimant sought an injunction to stop the defendant doing so. The defendant found out that the claimant had supported two of the competitor stations nearby and, accordingly, one of the issues (and the only one with which we are here concerned) was whether the solus agreement contained an implied term obliging the claimant not to discriminate abnormally against the defendant in favour of the defendant's competitors so as to render the defendant's sales economically unviable. If there were such an implied term, the defendant was entitled to terminate the solus agreement for the claimant's breach. A majority of the Court of Appeal, upholding Kerr J's decision, held that there was no such implied term.

Lord Denning MR:

Implied terms

It was submitted by Mr. Kemp on behalf of the garage that there was to be implied in the solus agreement a term that Shell, as the supplier, should not abnormally discriminate against the buyer and/or should supply petrol to the buyer on terms which did not abnormally discriminate against him. He said that Shell had broken that implied term by giving support to the two Shell garages and refusing it to Lostock: that, on that ground, Shell were in breach of the solus agreement: and that Lostock were entitled to terminate it.

This submission makes it necessary once again to consider the law as to implied terms. I ventured with some trepidation to suggest that terms implied by law could be brought within one comprehensive category – in which the courts could imply a term such as was just and reasonable in the circumstances: see *Greaves & Co. (Contractors) Ltd. v. Baynham Meikle & Partners* [1975] 1 W.L.R. 1095, 1099-1100; *Liverpool City Council v. Irwin* [1976] Q.B. 319, 331-332. But, as I feared, the House of Lords in *Liverpool City Council v. Irwin* [1976] 2 W.L.R. 562, have rejected it as quite unacceptable. As I read the speeches, there are two broad categories of implied terms.

(i) The first category

The first category comprehends all those relationships which are of common occurrence. Such as the relationship of seller and buyer, owner and hirer, master and servant, landlord and tenant, carrier by land or by sea, contractor for building works, and so forth. In all those relationships the courts have imposed obligations on one party or the other, saying they are "implied terms." These obligations are not founded on the intention of the parties, actual or presumed, but on more general considerations: see *Luxor (Eastbourne) Ltd. v. Cooper* [1941] A.C. 108, 137 by Lord Wright; *Lister v. Romford Ice and Cold Storage Co. Ltd.* [1957] A.C. 555, 576 by Viscount Simonds, and at p. 594 by Lord Tucker (both of whom give interesting illustrations); and *Liverpool City Council v. Irwin* [1976] 2 W.L.R. 562, 571 by Lord Cross of Chelsea, and at p. 579 by Lord Edmund-Davies. In such relationships the problem is not to be solved by asking what did the parties intend? Or would they have unhesitatingly agreed to it, if asked? It is to be solved by asking: has the law already defined the obligation or the extent of it? If so, let it be followed. If not, look to see what would be reasonable in the general run of such cases: see by Lord Cross of Chelsea at p. 570H: and then say what the obligation shall be. The House in *Liverpool City Council v. Irwin* [1976] 2 W.L.R. 562 went through that very process. They examined the existing law of landlord and tenant, in particular that relating to easements, to see if it contained the solution to the problem: and, having found that it did not, they imposed an obligation on the landlord to use reasonable care. In these relationships the parties can exclude or modify the obligation by express words; but unless they do so, the obligation is a legal incident of the relationship which is attached by the law itself and not by reason of any implied term.

Likewise, in the general law of contract, the legal effect of frustration does not depend on an implied term. It does not depend on the presumed intention of the parties, nor on what they would have answered, if asked: but simply on what the court itself declares to amount to a frustration: see *Davis Contractors Ltd. v. Fareham Urban District Council* [1956] A.C. 696, 728 by Lord Radcliffe and *The Eugenia* [1964] 2 Q.B. 226, 238, 239.

(ii) The second category

The second category comprehends those cases which are not within the first category. These are cases – not of common occurrence – in which from the particular circumstances a term is to be implied. In these cases the implication is based on an intention imputed to the parties from their actual circumstances: see *Luxor (Eastbourne) Ltd. v. Cooper* [1941] A.C. 108, 137 by Lord Wright. Such an imputation is only to be made when it is necessary to imply a term to give efficacy to the contract and make it a workable agreement in such manner as the parties would clearly have done if they had applied their mind to the contingency which has arisen. These are the "officious bystander" types of case: see *Lister v. Romford Ice and Cold Storage Co. Ltd.* [1957] A.C. 555, 594, by Lord Tucker. In such cases a term is not to be implied on the ground that it would be reasonable: but only when it is necessary and can be formulated with a sufficient degree of precision. This was the test applied by the majority of this court in *Liverpool City Council v. Irwin* [1976] Q.B. 319, and they were emphatically upheld by the House on this point: see [1976] 2 W.L.R. 562, 571D-H by Lord Cross of Chelsea; p. 578G – 579A by Lord Edmund-Davies.

There is this point to be noted about *Liverpool City Council v. Irwin*. In this court the argument was only about an implication in the second category. In the House of Lords that argument was not pursued. It was only the first category.

Into which of the two categories does the present case come? I am tempted to say that a solus agreement between supplier and buyer is of such common occurrence nowadays that it could be put into the first category: so that the law could imply a term based on general considerations. But I do not think this would be found acceptable. Nor do I think the case can be brought within the second category. If the Shell company had been asked at the beginning: "Will you agree not to discriminate abnormally against the buyer?" I think they would have declined. It might be a reasonable term, but it is not a necessary term. Nor can it be formulated with sufficient precision. On this point I agree with Kerr J. It should be noticed that in [*Esso Petroleum Co Ltd v Harper's Garage (Stourport) Ltd*] Mocatta J. also refused to make such an implication: see [1966] 2 Q.B. 514, 536-541; and there was no appeal from his decision. In the circumstances, I do not think any term can be implied.

Ormrod LJ delivered a judgment concurring with Lord Denning MR. **Bridge LJ** delivered a dissenting judgment on the implied term issue.

NOTES AND QUESTIONS

1. Lord Denning MR here gives a useful summary of the law on implied terms as laid down in *Liverpool CC v Irwin*. His two categories refer respectively to terms implied by law and by fact. To what extent did he bring reasonableness back into the first category?

2. Lord Denning also suggests that the first category is not really concerned with implied terms at all, but rather with what the courts have imposed on the parties. This suggestion has not subsequently found favour, which is hardly surprising given English law's long-established recognition and use of terms implied by statute in addition to terms implied by law by the courts. In other words, it is simply too late in the development of implied terms in English law to argue that the only true implied terms are terms implied by fact.

3. The other issues in the case, not dealt with in the above extract, concerned whether the solus agreement was invalid as an unreasonable restraint of trade (the majority, Lord Denning dissenting, held that it was valid); and whether an injunction was an appropriate remedy to restrain breach by the defendant (Lord Denning and Ormrod LJ held that it was not because of the claimant's own bad conduct, see below, 448; Bridge LJ did not deal with this point given his view that the defendant, because of the implied term, was entitled to terminate and was hence not in breach).

Scally v Southern Health and Social Services Board
[1992] 1 AC 294, House of Lords

The claimants, including Dr Scally, were employed by the defendants. Representatives of the claimants' professional body had negotiated the terms of their contract of employment. That contract incorporated the provisions from time to time in force of regulations governing the pension entitlement of persons employed by the health services. To qualify for a full pension under those regulations, an employee was required to contribute 40 years' service. In 1975 provision was made by regulation to enable employees to purchase 'added years' of pension entitlement so as to qualify for maximum pension entitlement. The regulation required employees to take advantage of the offer within a particular period. The claimants were not made aware of the offer by the defendants. Had they been made aware of the offer, it was found that they would have taken advantage of it. They claimed damages for, inter alia, the tort of negligence and breach of contract. It was submitted that their contract of employment contained an implied term that obliged the defendants to bring the offer to their attention. The House of Lords, overturning Carswell J and the Court of Appeal, held that there was such an implied term because it was a necessary incident of the category of contractual relationship in question.

Lord Bridge of Harwich: The central question then is whether the employing boards owed any...duty [to bring the offer to the employees' attention]. Leaving aside the claim based on breach of statutory duty...it seems to me that the plaintiffs' common law claims can only succeed if the duty allegedly owed to them by their employers arose out of the contract of employment. If a duty of the kind in question was not inherent in the contractual relationship, I do not see how it could possibly be derived from the tort of negligence. [*He quoted from the judgment of Lord Scarman in* Tai Hing Cotton Mill Ltd v Liu Chong Hing Bank Ltd *[1986] AC 80, 107, and continued:*]

In the instant case I believe that an attempt to analyse the issue in terms of the law of tort may be positively misleading. If the question is framed in terms of the law of negligence, it takes the form: did the employers owe a duty of care to employees to save them from economic loss consequent on a failure to purchase added years of pensionable entitlement in due time? The strong trend of recent authority has been to narrow the range of circumstances which the law of tort will recognise as sufficient to impose on one person a duty of care to protect another from damage which consists in purely economic loss. This induced Kelly LJ to say:

> "It would be contrary to the current inclination of the law to imply a term into contracts of employment enabling a claim by an employee for purely economic loss to be brought against an employer where no express term in those contracts provided for such relief."

But if the issue is analysed in contract, the starting point is quite different. Here the express terms of the contract of employment confer a valuable right on the employee which is, however, contingent upon his taking certain action. Where that situation is known to the employer but not to the employee, will the law imply a contractual obligation on the employer to take reasonable steps to bring the existence of the contingent right to the notice of the employee? It is true that such an implication may have the consequence of sustaining a claim for purely economic loss. But this consideration would not furnish the essential reason for making the implication. If there is a basis for making the implication, it must lie rather in the consideration that the availability of the contingent right was intended by those who drew up the terms of the contract for the benefit of the employee; but if the existence of the contingent right never comes to his attention, he cannot profit by it and it might, so far as he is concerned, just as well not exist.

The problem is a novel one which could not arise in the classical contractual situation in which all the contractual terms, having been agreed between the parties, must, ex hypothesi, have been known to both parties. But in the modern world it is increasingly common for individuals to enter into contracts, particularly contracts of employment, on complex terms which have been settled in the course of negotiations between representative bodies or organisations and many details of which the individual employee cannot be expected to know unless they are drawn to his attention. The instant case presents an example of this phenomenon arising in the context of the statutory provisions which regulate the operation of the health services in Northern Ireland.

[*Lord Bridge set out these statutory provisions and rejected the submission that those provisions obliged the Department of Health to notify health service employees. He continued:*]

When the Regulations of 1974 introduced the opportunity for employees in the health services to buy added years, it was intended that this should be for their benefit. They could not, however, enjoy that benefit unless they were aware of the opportunity. There are three possible views of the legal consequences arising from this situation. The first is that it could properly be left to individual employees, knowing that they were compulsory contributors to a superannuation scheme, to make enquiries and ascertain the details of the scheme for themselves. In the light of the judge's findings, I think this view can be confidently rejected. There was no reason whatever why young doctors embarking on a career in the health services should appreciate the necessity to enquire into the details of the superannuation scheme to which they were contributors in order to be in a position to enjoy its benefits. The second view is that the law provided no means of ensuring that the intended beneficiaries of the opportunity to buy added years became aware of it, so that it would be a matter of chance whether or not, in relation to any individual employee, the relevant provision of the Regulations of 1974 achieved its intended purpose. I find this view so unattractive that I would accept it only if driven to the conclusion that there was no other legally tenable alternative. The third view is that there was an obligation on either the employing board or the department to take reasonable steps to bring the relevant provision to the notice of employees in time to avail themselves of the opportunity to buy added years if they so decided.

...

Will the law then imply a term in the contract of employment imposing such an obligation on the employer? The implication cannot, of course, be justified as necessary to give business efficacy to the contract of employment as a whole. I think there is force in the submission that, since the employee's entitlement to enhance his pension rights by the purchase of added years is of no effect unless he is aware of it and since he cannot be expected to become aware of it unless it is drawn to his attention, it is necessary to imply an obligation on the employer to bring it to his attention to render efficacious the very benefit which the contractual right to purchase added years was intended to confer. But this may be stretching the doctrine of implication for the sake of business efficacy beyond its proper reach. A clear distinction is drawn in the speeches of Viscount Simonds in *Lister v Romford Ice and Cold Storage Co Ltd* [1957] AC 555 and Lord Wilberforce in *Liverpool City Council v Irwin* [1977] AC 239 between the search for an implied term necessary to give business efficacy to a particular contract and the search, based on wider considerations, for a term which the law will imply as a necessary incident of a definable category of contractual relationship. If any implication is appropriate here, it is, I think, of this latter type. Carswell J accepted the submission that any formulation of an implied term of this kind which would be effective to sustain the plaintiffs' claims in this case must necessarily be too wide in its ambit to be acceptable as of general application. I believe however that this difficulty is surmounted if the category of contractual relationship in which the implication will arise is defined with sufficient precision. I would define it as the relationship of employer and employee where the following circumstances obtain: (1) the terms of the contract of employment have not been negotiated with the individual employee but result from negotiation with a representative body or are otherwise incorporated by reference; (2) a particular term of the contract makes available to the employee a valuable right contingent upon action being taken by him to avail himself of its benefit; (3) the employee cannot, in all the circumstances, reasonably be expected to be aware of the term unless it is drawn to his attention. I fully appreciate that the criterion to justify an implication of this kind is necessity, not reasonableness. But I take the view that it is not merely reasonable, but necessary, in the circumstances postulated, to imply an obligation on the employer to take reasonable steps to bring the term of the contract in question to the employee's attention, so that he may be in a position to enjoy its benefit. Accordingly I would hold that there was an implied term in each of the plaintiffs' contracts of employment of which the boards were in each case in breach.

Lords Roskill, Goff of Chieveley, Jauncey of Tullichettle and **Lowry** concurred.

NOTES AND QUESTIONS

1. This is an important example of the House of Lords applying the approach in *Liverpool CC v Irwin* to imply a term as a necessary incident of a definable category of contractual relationship. However, the contractual relationship was very precisely defined by Lord Bridge and was significantly narrower than simply being a contract of employment. The decision does not mean that in most contracts of employment, employers now have an implied duty to inform employees as to their rights. Having defined the relevant category of relationship narrowly, the term was then necessary in order not to defeat the purpose of giving employees the opportunity of 'buying in' extra pension years.

2. Especially in the light of his narrow definition of the relevant contractual relationship, why did Lord Bridge think that the test of 'business efficacy' was not here appropriate? Put another way, how was he maintaining the distinction between terms implied by law (as here) and terms implied by fact?

3. The implication of terms by law into contracts of employment has been considered in a number of other cases. Two deserve mention here:

(i) In *Mahmud v Bank of Credit and Commerce International SA* [1998] AC 20, HL, ex-employees of the corrupt bank, BCCI, were bringing contractual claims against the bank for stigma damages (ie damages for loss of reputation) alleging that their former employment was putting them at a serious disadvantage in finding new jobs. The central damages aspect of the case is considered below, 397. The alleged breach was of an implied term of mutual trust and confidence and the House of Lords took the opportunity authoritatively to accept the existence of that implied term. Lord Steyn, giving the leading speech, said the following at 45–6:

'The applicants do not rely on a term implied in fact. They do not therefore rely on an individualised term to be implied from the particular provisions of their employment contracts considered against their specific contextual setting. Instead they rely on a standardised term implied by law, that is, on a term which is said to be an incident of all contracts of employment: *Scally v Southern Health and Social Services Board* [1992] 1 AC 294, 307B. Such implied terms operate as default rules. The parties are free to exclude or modify them. ... The employer's primary case is based on a formulation of the implied term that has been applied at first instance and in the Court of Appeal. It imposes reciprocal duties on the employer and employee. Given that this case is concerned with alleged obligations of an employer I will concentrate on its effect on the position of employers. For convenience I will set out the term again. It is expressed to impose an obligation that the employer shall not:

"without reasonable and proper cause, conduct itself in a manner calculated and likely to destroy or seriously damage the relationship of confidence and trust between employer and employee:" ...

The evolution of the implied term of trust and confidence is a fact. It has not yet been endorsed by your Lordships' House. It has proved a workable principle in practice. It has not been the subject of adverse criticism in any decided cases and it has been welcomed in academic writings. I regard the emergence of the implied obligation of mutual trust and confidence as a sound development.'

(ii) In *Crossley v Faithful & Gould Holdings Ltd* [2004] EWCA Civ 293, [2004] 4 All ER 447, an employee, who had resigned on mental health grounds, had followed his employer's advice in backdating his resignation for tax reasons. The backdating had deprived the employee of an entitlement to benefits under the employer's insurance scheme. The employee brought a claim for damages arguing that there was a term implied by law into his employment that his employer would take reasonable care for his economic well-being. The Court of Appeal rejected the implication of such a term for two principal reasons. First, it would conflict with the narrower reasoning in, eg, the *Scally* case. Secondly, it would impose an unfair and unreasonable burden on employers. The case is particularly significant for Dyson LJ's view (with whom Thomas LJ and Sir Andrew Morritt V-C agreed) that, in implying terms by law, necessity is an unhelpful concept and that it is better to focus on questions of reasonableness, fairness and policy. While accepting that the concept of necessity was supported by the House of Lords in *Liverpool CC v Irwin* and in the *Scally* case, Dyson LJ said at paragraphs 33 and 36:

'In my view, the judge was right to reject the "portmanteau obligation"... ie an implied term of any contract of employment that the employer will take reasonable care for the economic well-being of his employee. This would be a standardised term to be implied by law, that is to say a term which, in the absence of any contrary intention, is an incident of all contracts of employment. It is not a term implied to give business efficacy to the particular contract in question which is dependent on an intention imputed to the parties from the express terms of the contract and the surrounding circumstances. ...

It seems to me that, rather than focus on the elusive concept of necessity, it is better to recognise that, to some extent at least, the existence and scope of standardised implied terms raise questions of reasonableness, fairness and the balancing of competing policy considerations: see Peden (2001) 117 LQR 459, 467-475.'

Dyson LJ's approach is reminiscent of Lord Denning MR's in *Shell v Lostock*, above, 207. While it is apparently contrary to authority to prefer reasonableness to necessity, Dyson LJ argued that, eg, the well-recognised implied terms that an employer will take reasonable care for the physical and mental health and safety of his employees is not a *necessary* feature of the employer/employee relationship and is therefore best understood as based on wider policy grounds. For the article by Peden, referred to with approval by Dyson LJ, see below, 217.

(2) Terms Implied by Statute

The implication of terms by statute is of enormous practical importance. For example, most contractual claims brought in respect of defective goods and services are based on a breach of one of the terms implied by statute. Terms have been implied by statute into many different types of contract and no attempt will be made here to try to cover the field comprehensively. Instead we shall focus on the terms implied by statute into contracts for the sale of goods (with brief reference being made to directly analogous contracts, ie contracts for hire, hire-purchase and for the supply of materials) and for the supply of services.

(a) Contracts for the Sale of Goods

Sale of Goods Act 1979, sections 12–15

12 Implied terms about title, etc
(1) In a contract of sale, other than one to which subsection (3) below applies, there is an implied [term] on the part of the seller that in the case of a sale he has a right to sell the goods, and in the case of an agreement to sell he will have such a right at the time when the property is to pass.
(2) In a contract of sale, other than one to which subsection (3) below applies, there is also an implied [term] that—

(a) the goods are free, and will remain free until the time when the property is to pass, from any charge or encumbrance not disclosed or known to the buyer before the contract is made, and
(b) the buyer will enjoy quiet possession of the goods except so far as it may be disturbed by the owner or other person entitled to the benefit of any charge or encumbrance so disclosed or known.

(3) This subsection applies to a contract of sale in the case of which there appears from the contract or is to be inferred from its circumstances an intention that the seller should transfer only such title as he or a third person may have.
(4) In a contract to which subsection (3) above applies there is an implied [term] that all charges or encumbrances known to the seller and not known to the buyer have been disclosed to the buyer before the contract is made.
(5) In a contract to which subsection (3) above applies there is also an implied [term] that none of the following will disturb the buyer's quiet possession of the goods, namely—

(a) the seller;
(b) in a case where the parties to the contract intend that the seller should transfer only such title as a third person may have, that person;
(c) anyone claiming through or under the seller or that third person otherwise than under a charge or encumbrance disclosed or known to the buyer before the contract is made.

[(5A) As regards England and Wales and Northern Ireland, the term implied by subsection (1) above is a condition and the terms implied by subsections (2), (4) and (5) above are warranties.]

...

13 Sale by description

(1) Where there is a contract for the sale of goods by description, there is an implied [term] that the goods will correspond with the description.

[(1A) As regards England and Wales and Northern Ireland, the term implied by subsection (l) above is a condition.]

(2) If the sale is by sample as well as by description it is not sufficient that the bulk of the goods corresponds with the sample if the goods do not also correspond with the description.

(3) A sale of goods is not prevented from being a sale by description by reason only that, being exposed for sale or hire, they are selected by the buyer.

...

14 Implied terms about quality or fitness

(1) Except as provided by this section and section 15 below and subject to any other enactment, there is no implied [term] about the quality or fitness for any particular purpose of goods supplied under a contract of sale.

[(2) Where the seller sells goods in the course of a business, there is an implied term that the goods supplied under the contract are of satisfactory quality.

(2A) For the purposes of this Act, goods are of satisfactory quality if they meet the standard that a reasonable person would regard as satisfactory, taking account of any description of the goods, the price (if relevant) and all the other relevant circumstances.

(2B) For the purposes of this Act, the quality of goods includes their state and condition and the following (among others) are in appropriate cases aspects of the quality of goods—

(a)   fitness for all the purposes for which goods of the kind in question are commonly supplied,
(b)   appearance and finish,
(c)   freedom from minor defects,
(d)   safety, and
(e)   durability.

(2C) The term implied by subsection (2) above does not extend to any matter making the quality of goods unsatisfactory—

(a)   which is specifically drawn to the buyer's attention before the contract is made,
(b)   where the buyer examines the goods before the contract is made, which that examination ought to reveal, or
(c)   in the case of a contract for sale by sample, which would have been apparent on a reasonable examination of the sample.]

[(2D) If the buyer deals as consumer or, in Scotland, if a contract of sale is a consumer contract, the relevant circumstances mentioned in subsection (2A) above include any public statements on the specific characteristics of the goods made about them by the seller, the producer or his representative, particularly in advertising or on labelling.

(2E) A public statement is not by virtue of subsection (2D) above a relevant circumstance for the purposes of subsection (2A) above in the case of a contract of sale, if the seller shows that—

(a)   at the time the contract was made, he was not, and could not reasonably have been, aware of the statement,

Identifying the Terms **215**

(b) before the contract was made, the statement had been withdrawn in public or, to the extent that it contained anything which was incorrect or misleading, it had been corrected in public, or

(c) the decision to buy the goods could not have been influenced by the statement.

(2F) Subsections (2D) and (2E) above do not prevent any public statement from being a relevant circumstance for the purposes of subsection (2A) above (whether or not the buyer deals as consumer or, in Scotland, whether or not the contract of sale is a consumer contract) if the statement would have been such a circumstance apart from those subsections.]

(3) Where the seller sells goods in the course of a business and the buyer, expressly or by implication, makes known—

(a) to the seller, or

(b) where the purchase price or part of it is payable by instalments and the goods were previously sold by a credit-broker to the seller, to that credit-broker,

any particular purpose for which the goods are being bought, there is an implied [term] that the goods supplied under the contract are reasonably fit for that purpose, whether or not that is a purpose for which such goods are commonly supplied, except where the circumstances show that the buyer does not rely, or that it is unreasonable for him to rely, on the skill or judgment of the seller or credit-broker.

(4) An implied [term] about quality or fitness for a particular purpose may be annexed to a contract of sale by usage.

(5) The preceding provisions of this section apply to a sale by a person who in the course of a business is acting as agent for another as they apply to a sale by a principal in the course of a business, except where that other is not selling in the course of a business and either the buyer knows that fact or reasonable steps are taken to bring it to the notice of the buyer before the contract is made.

[(6) As regards England and Wales and Northern Ireland, the terms implied by subsections (2) and (3) above are conditions.]

. . .

15 Sale by sample

(1) A contract of sale is a contract for sale by sample where there is an express or implied term to that effect in the contract.

(2) In the case of a contract for sale by sample there is an implied [term]—

(a) that the bulk will correspond with the sample in quality;

[. . .]

(c) that the goods will be free from any defect, [making their quality unsatisfactory], which would not be apparent on reasonable examination of the sample.

[(3) As regards England and Wales and Northern Ireland, the term implied by subsection (2) above is a condition.]

. . .

NOTES AND QUESTIONS

1. The first statute implying terms into contracts for the sale of goods was in 1893. This was regarded as codifying the common law (although in fact it went beyond that) so that it was the courts who first implied terms by law into contracts of sale. This highlights the close link between terms implied by law by the courts and terms implied by statute. But, although linked, there are at least two significant

differences. First, Parliament clearly does not consider itself constrained, as the courts may still do (see above, 201–213), to imply terms only where necessary to the type of contract in question. Wide-ranging policy concerns (eg to protect a party of weaker bargaining power) may underpin the statutory implication. Secondly, while terms implied by the courts are subject to the express contrary intention of the parties, this need not be so for terms implied by statute. The statutory implied terms in a contract for the sale of goods are the classic illustration of this because, by reason of the Unfair Contract Terms Act 1977 section 6 (below, 246), the implied term in section 12 is non-excludable and those in sections 13–15 are non-excludable in consumer sales.

2. There is a voluminous case law on the statutory implied terms (ie on the courts' interpretation of sections 12–15), especially the implied terms in section 14. That case law falls outside most books and courses on general contract law and is instead treated in books and courses on the sale of goods or commercial law. No attempt will therefore be made here to analyse that case law and the setting out above of the statutory provisions will, for our purposes, be considered sufficient.

3. Why has statute implied these terms into contracts for the sale of goods? Are there equivalent terms implied into contracts for the sale of land?

4. Analogous terms are implied into contracts for the hire-purchase of goods by the Supply of Goods (Implied Terms) Act 1973, sections 8–11; into contracts for the hire of goods by the Supply of Goods and Services Act 1982, sections 7–10; and into contracts for work and materials, in relation to the materials supplied, by the Supply of Goods and Services Act 1982, sections 2–5.

(b) Contracts for Services

Supply of Goods and Services Act 1982, sections 13–15

13 Implied term about care and skill
In a contract for the supply of a service where the supplier is acting in the course of a business, there is an implied term that the supplier will carry out the service with reasonable care and skill.

14 Implied term about time for performance
(1) Where, under a contract for the supply of a service by a supplier acting in the course of a business, the time for the service to be carried out is not fixed by the contract, left to be fixed in a manner agreed by the contract or determined by the course of dealing between the parties, there is an implied term that the supplier will carry out the service within a reasonable time.
(2) What is a reasonable time is a question of fact.

15 Implied term about consideration
(1) Where, under a contract for the supply of a service, the consideration for the service is not determined by the contract, left to be determined in a manner agreed by the contract or determined by the course of dealing between the parties, there is an implied term that the party contracting with the supplier will pay a reasonable charge.
(2) What is a reasonable charge is a question of fact.

J Beatson, *Law of Contract* (28th edn, 2002) 127–34, 145–59, 163–9
S Smith, *Atiyah's Introduction to the Law of Contract* (6th edn, 2005) 133–46, ch 6

M Clarke, 'Notice of Contractual Terms' [1976] *CLJ* **51**
The author examines the case law on incorporation (other than by signature) and sets
out his version of the relevant principles. Incorporation by the giving of particular
notice, by a course of dealing and by the parties' trade practice are seen as examples
of where a party is deemed to know of the existence of the other's special terms.

E Macdonald, 'Incorporation of Contract Terms by a "Consistent Course of Dealing"'
(1988) 8 *Legal Studies* **48**
The author looks at the cases on incorporation by a course of dealing, especially the
McCutcheon case, and supports Lord Reid's approach in that case as being in line
with the general principle that contractual terms are objectively ascertained. She also
points out that there is no need to take a narrow view of the consistency of a course
of dealing given that, if incorporated, courts can still strike down an exclusion clause
under UCTA 1977.

E Peden, 'Policy Concerns Behind Implication of Terms in Law' (2001) 117 *LQR* **459**
This article examines the test for terms implied by law and, in particular, focuses on
the policy concerns that appear to have been balanced by the courts. Peden divides
these into three categories (how the implied term will sit with existing law; how it will
affect parties to the relationship; and wider issues of fairness and the effect on
society) and argues that the courts should be more open about the policies that they
are balancing. She further argues that (i) implication based on custom or usage is
closely linked to the implication of terms by law; (ii) it would be helpful to recognise
overtly that a central underpinning idea in implying terms is to ensure co-operation
between the parties.

Principles of European Contract Law **(eds O Lando and H Beale, 2000) 302–5**

Article 6:102 Implied Terms
In addition to the express terms, a contract may contain implied terms which stem
from

(a) the intention of the parties,

(b) the nature and purpose of the contract, and

(c) good faith and fair dealing.

[The first two of these correspond to the implication of terms by the English courts
although the tests in English law mean that terms are not readily implied. In English
law, there is no *overt* reference to good faith and dealing as a source of implied terms.]

5

Interpreting the Terms

Until very recently, the interpretation or construction of contracts was neglected in most courses (and books) on contract. Yet, in practice, this is an area of huge importance with most modern contractual disputes turning on it. Moreover, those who draft contracts need to know how the courts will interpret them so as to avoid mistakes or omissions in the drafting. The catalyst for greater academic interest in this area was the restatement of the modern approach to construction by the House of Lords in the *Investors Compensation Scheme* case. We shall look at this first before moving on to a specific area that has been the subject of careful scrutiny by judges and commentators alike, namely the construction of exemption clauses.

1. THE MODERN APPROACH TO CONSTRUCTION

Introductory reading: E McKendrick, *Contract Law* (7th edn, 2007) 9.6

Investors Compensation Scheme Ltd v West Bromwich Building Society
[1998] 1 WLR 896, House of Lords

A number of investors had been given negligent advice and had claims (in tort or for breach of statutory duty) against their financial advisers, building societies and solicitors. A central scheme was set up by the Securities and Investments Board to ensure compensation was paid to the investors. To be entitled to compensation under that scheme, investors concluded a contract of assignment with the Investors Compensation Scheme (the claimant) whereby they assigned to the ICS their claims against their advisers, building societies and solicitors subject to a clause excluding from the assignment 'Any claim (whether sounding in rescission for undue influence or otherwise)' against a building society which would abate sums otherwise owed to that society. In an action by the ICS against the defendant building society, the central question was whether that clause meant that the investors had retained (ie had not assigned) their rights to claim damages, as well as rescission, against the building societies. In allowing the appeal and restoring the decision of the trial judge, the House of Lords (Lord Lloyd dissenting) held that the right to claim rescission had been retained but that the right to claim damages had been validly assigned.

Lord Hoffmann: In the Court of Appeal, Leggatt L.J. said, on the authority of *Through the Looking-Glass*, that the judge's interpretation was "not an available meaning of the words." "Any claim (whether sounding in rescission for undue influence or otherwise)" could not mean "Any claim sounding in rescission (whether for undue influence or otherwise)" and that was that. He was unimpressed by the alleged commercial nonsense of the alternative construction.

My Lords, I will say at once that I prefer the approach of the judge. But I think I should preface my explanation of my reasons with some general remarks about the principles by which contractual documents are nowadays construed. I do not think that the fundamental change which has overtaken this branch of the law, particularly as a result of the speeches of Lord Wilberforce in *Prenn v. Simmonds* [1971] 1 W.L.R. 1381, 1384-1386 and *Reardon Smith Line Ltd. v. Yngvar Hansen-Tangen* [1976] 1 W.L.R. 989, is always sufficiently appreciated. The result has been, subject to one important exception, to assimilate the way in which such documents are interpreted by judges to the common sense principles by which any serious utterance would be interpreted in ordinary life. Almost all the old intellectual baggage of "legal" interpretation has been discarded. The principles may be summarised as follows.

(1) Interpretation is the ascertainment of the meaning which the document would convey to a reasonable person having all the background knowledge which would reasonably have been available to the parties in the situation in which they were at the time of the contract.

(2) The background was famously referred to by Lord Wilberforce as the "matrix of fact," but this phrase is, if anything, an understated description of what the background may include. Subject to the requirement that it should have been reasonably available to the parties and to the exception to be mentioned next, it includes absolutely anything which would have affected the way in which the language of the document would have been understood by a reasonable man.

(3) The law excludes from the admissible background the previous negotiations of the parties and their declarations of subjective intent. They are admissible only in an action for rectification. The law makes this distinction for reasons of practical policy and, in this respect only, legal interpretation differs from the way we would interpret utterances in ordinary life. The boundaries of this exception are in some respects unclear. But this is not the occasion on which to explore them.

(4) The meaning which a document (or any other utterance) would convey to a reasonable man is not the same thing as the meaning of its words. The meaning of words is a matter of dictionaries and grammars; the meaning of the document is what the parties using those words against the relevant background would reasonably have been understood to mean. The background may not merely enable the reasonable man to choose between the possible meanings of words which are ambiguous but even (as occasionally happens in ordinary life) to conclude that the parties must, for whatever reason, have used the wrong words or syntax: see *Mannai Investments Co. Ltd. v. Eagle Star Life Assurance Co. Ltd.* [1997] A.C. 749.

(5) The "rule" that words should be given their "natural and ordinary meaning" reflects the common sense proposition that we do not easily accept that people have made linguistic mistakes, particularly in formal documents. On the other hand, if one would nevertheless conclude from the background that something must have gone wrong with the language, the law does not require judges to attribute to the parties an intention which they plainly could not have had. Lord Diplock made this point more vigorously when he said in *Antaios Compania Naviera S.A. v. Salen Rederierna A.B.* [1985] A.C. 191, 201:

"if detailed semantic and syntactical analysis of words in a commercial contract is going to lead to a conclusion that flouts business commonsense, it must be made to yield to business commonsense."

If one applies these principles, it seems to me that the judge must be right and, as we are dealing with one badly drafted clause which is happily no longer in use, there is little advantage in my repeating his reasons at greater length. The only remark of his which I would respectfully question is when he said that he was "doing violence" to the natural meaning of the words. This is an over-energetic way to describe the process of interpretation. Many people, including politicians, celebrities and Mrs. Malaprop, mangle meanings and syntax but nevertheless communicate tolerably clearly what they are using the words to mean. If anyone is doing violence to natural meanings, it is they rather than their listeners.

...

Finally, on this part of the case, I must make some comments upon the judgment of the Court of Appeal. Leggatt L.J. said that his construction was "the natural and ordinary meaning of the words used." I do not think that the concept of natural and ordinary meaning is very helpful when, on any view, the words have not been used in a natural and ordinary way. In a case like this, the court is inevitably engaged in choosing between competing unnatural meanings. Secondly, Leggatt L.J. said that the judge's construction was not an "available meaning" of the words. If this means that judges cannot, short of rectification, decide that the parties must have made mistakes of meaning or syntax, I respectfully think he was wrong. The proposition is not, I would suggest, borne out by his citation from *Through the Looking-Glass*. Alice and Humpty-Dumpty were agreed that the word "glory" did not mean "a nice knock-down argument." Anyone with a dictionary could see that. Humpty-Dumpty's point was that "a nice knock-down argument" was what *he* meant by using the word "glory." He very fairly acknowledged that Alice, as a reasonable young woman, could not have realised this until he told her, but once he had told her, or if, without being expressly told, she could have inferred it from the background, she would have had no difficulty in understanding what he meant.

Lord Goff of Chieveley, Lord Hope of Craighead and **Lord Clyde** concurred. **Lord Lloyd of Berwick** delivered a dissenting speech.

NOTES AND QUESTIONS

1. Lord Hoffmann's five principles of interpretation have been referred to in scores of subsequent cases, making this case already one of the most cited contract cases of all time.

2. Lord Hoffmann's modern approach, heralded by Lord Wilberforce's earlier speeches in *Prenn v Simmonds* [1971] 1 WLR 1381 and *Reardon Smith Line Ltd v Yngvar Hansen-Tangen* [1976] 1 WLR 989, is in essence that one should always construe a contract in its context. In other words, the law has moved from a literalist or dictionary approach to a contextual (or purposive) approach. Under the old approach, it was generally only if there was an ambiguity in the literal meaning that one could refer to the context.

3. Lord Hoffmann's famous statement of principles of construction should not obscure the radical nature of the decision on the facts. The exclusion from assignment clause, 'Any claim (whether sounding in rescission for undue influence or otherwise)', was interpreted as if it had read, 'Any claim sounding in rescission (whether for undue influence or otherwise)'. This construction meant that only claims for rescission (and not damages) against the building

societies were excluded from the assignment. But it would seem that a claim for rescission cannot be assigned in any event so that, as construed, the clause was superfluous and merely served to declare what was already the legal position.

4. Lord Lloyd, in his powerful dissent, could see no justification for adopting a construction that meant the courts were moving words from the inside to the outside of the brackets used by the parties. He said, at 904, 'I know of no principle of construction ...which would enable the court to take words from within the brackets, where they are clearly intended to underline the width of "any claim", and place them outside the brackets where they have the exact opposite effect. ...Purposive interpretation of a contract is a useful tool where the purpose can be identified with reasonable certainty. But creative interpretation is another thing altogether. The one must not be allowed to shade into the other.'

5. In *Bank of Credit & Commerce International v Ali* [2001] 1 AC 251 at [39], Lord Hoffmann marginally adjusted his second principle by commenting, 'I did not think it necessary to emphasise that I meant anything which a reasonable man would have regarded as *relevant.* I was merely saying that there is no conceptual limit to what can be regarded as background.'

6. The most controversial of Lord Hoffmann's principles is the third, excluding from the context or background the parties' previous negotiations and declarations of subjective intent. This exclusion—along with the exclusion of evidence of the subsequent conduct of the parties (not directly mentioned by Lord Hoffmann but laid down in *James Miller & Partners Ltd v Whitworth Street Estates (Manchester) Ltd* [1970] AC 583, HL)—has been heavily criticised by commentators. See, eg, the articles by McMeel and Lord Nicholls referred to below, 240. What are the arguments for and against the exclusion of such evidence?

7. What is the relationship between the interpretation of a contract and its rectification? On rectification, see below, 620, 645.

2. CONSTRUCTION OF EXEMPTION CLAUSES

In construing exclusion or limitation clauses, one is asking, 'Do the words of exclusion or limitation cover what has happened?'. The construction of these clauses exemplifies the long-standing 'contra proferentem' rule of construction. This means that any ambiguity in a clause will be construed 'against the person putting it forward'. Contra proferentem construction is applicable generally and is not confined to exemption clauses. However, it is in the context of such clauses that the rule has been most prominent. Indeed prior to the enactment of statutes controlling unfair terms (eg the Unfair Contract Terms Act 1977), contra proferentem construction was a major common law technique, alongside non-incorporation (see above, 166–196), by which the courts controlled unfair terms. It is a topical question whether contra proferentem construction is withering away in the light not only of the statutory controls over unfair terms but also of the modern approach to construction (and the call for a discarding of the 'old' rules of construction) in the *Investors Compensation Scheme* case.

In examining the courts' approach to construing exemption clauses, it is helpful to divide the cases into three sub-sections, where specific rules (applying the general contra proferentem approach) have been developed: (1) Excluding or Limiting Liability for Negligence; (2) Excluding or Limiting Liability for Fundamental Breach; (3) Construing *Limitation* Clauses.

Introductory reading: E McKendrick, *Contract Law* (7th edn, 2007) 11.5–11.7

(1) Excluding or Limiting Liability for Negligence

Alderslade v Hendon Laundry Ltd [1945] KB 189, Court of Appeal

The claimant sent 10 large handkerchiefs to the defendants, who ran a laundry, to be washed. The defendants lost the handkerchiefs. In the claimant's contractual action for damages of £5 to cover the replacement cost of the handkerchiefs, the defendants relied on the following term of the contract: 'The maximum amount allowed for lost or damaged articles is twenty times the charge made for laundering.' That maximum was here 11s 5½d (ie just over a tenth of what was being claimed). At first instance, the claim succeeded. In allowing the defendants' appeal, the Court of Appeal held that the limitation clause did here apply because, although it did not expressly mention negligence, the defendants could only have been liable for the loss of the handkerchiefs if they had been negligent.

Lord Greene MR: It was argued before us for the defendants that the clause did apply and was effective to limit liability for lost articles; and reliance was placed on a well-known line of authority dealing with clauses of this description. The effect of those authorities can I think be stated as follows: where the head of damage in respect of which limitation of liability is sought to be imposed by such a clause is one which rests on negligence and nothing else, the clause must be construed as extending to that head of damage, because it would otherwise lack subject-matter. Where, on the other hand, the head of damage may be based on some other ground than that of negligence, the general principle is that the clause must be confined in its application to loss occurring through that other cause, to the exclusion of loss arising through negligence. The reason is that if a contracting party wishes in such a case to limit his liability in respect of negligence, he must do so in clear terms in the absence of which the clause is construed as relating to a liability not based on negligence. A common illustration of the principle is to be found in the case of common carriers. A common carrier is frequently described, though perhaps not quite accurately, as an insurer, and his liability in respect of articles entrusted to him is not necessarily based on negligence. Accordingly if a common carrier wishes to limit his liability for lost articles and does not make it quite clear that he is desiring to limit it in respect of his liability for negligence, then the clause will be construed as extending only to his liability on grounds other than negligence. If, on the other hand, a carrier not being a common carrier, makes use of such a clause, then unless it is construed so as to cover the case of negligence there would be no content for it at all seeing that his only obligation is to take reasonable care. That, broadly speaking, is the principle which falls to be applied in this case.

...

It was said [by counsel for the plaintiff] that the loss of a customer's property might take place for one of two reasons, namely, negligence and mere breach of contract, and that in the absence of clear words referring to negligence, loss through negligence cannot be taken to be covered by the clause. In my opinion that argument fails. It is necessary to analyse the legal relationship between the customer and the defendants. What I may call the hard core of the contract, the real thing to which the contract is directed, is the obligation of the defendants to launder. That is the primary obligation. It is the contractual obligation which must be performed according to its terms, and no question of taking due care enters into it. The defendants undertake, not to exercise due care in laundering the customer's goods, but to launder them, and if they fail to launder them it is no use their saying, "We did our best, we exercised due care and took reasonable precautions, and we are very sorry if as a result the linen is not properly laundered." That is the essence of the contract, and in addition there are certain ancillary obligations into which the defendants enter if they accept goods from a customer to be laundered. The first relates to the safe custody of the goods while they are in the possession of the defendants. The customer's goods may have to wait for a time in the laundry premises to be washed, and while they are so waiting there is an obligation to take care of them, but it is in my opinion not the obligation of an insurer but the obligation to take reasonable care for the protection of the goods. If while they are waiting to be washed in the laundry a thief, through no fault of the defendants, steals them, the defendants are not liable. The only way in which the defendants could be made liable for the loss of articles awaiting their turn to be washed would, I think, quite clearly be if it could be shown that they had been guilty of negligence in performing their duty to take care of the goods. That is one ancillary obligation which is inherent in a contract of this kind. Another relates to the delivery of the goods. The laundry company in most cases, and indeed in this case, make a practice of delivering the goods to the customer, and in the ordinary way the customer expects to receive that service. But what is the precise obligation of the laundry in respect of the return of the goods after the laundering has been completed? In my opinion it stands on the same footing as the other ancillary obligation that I have mentioned, namely, the obligation to take reasonable care in looking after and safeguarding the goods. It cannot I think be suggested that the obligation of the laundry company in the matter of returning the goods after they have been laundered is the obligation of an insurer. To say that they have undertaken by contract an absolute obligation to see that they are returned seems to me to go against common sense. Supposing the defendants are returning the goods by van to their customer and while the van is on its way a negligent driver of a lorry drives into it and overturns it with the result that it is set on fire and the goods destroyed. No action would lie by the customer for damages for the loss of those goods any more than it would lie against any ordinary transport undertaking which was not a common carrier. To hold otherwise would mean that in respect of that clearly ancillary service the defendants were undertaking an absolute obligation that the goods would, whatever happened, be returned to the customer. It seems to me that the only obligation on the defendants in the matter of returning the goods is to take reasonable care.

In the present case all that we know about the goods is that they are lost. There seems to me to be no case of lost goods in respect of which it would be necessary to limit liability, unless it be a case where the goods are lost by negligence. Goods sent to the laundry will not be lost in the act of washing them. On the other hand, they may be lost while they are in the custody of the defendants before washing or after washing has been completed. They may be lost in the process of returning them to the customer after they have been washed, but in each of those two cases, if my view is right, the obligation of the defendants is an obligation to take reasonable care and nothing else. Therefore, the claim of a customer that the defendants are liable to him in respect of articles that have been lost must, I think, depend on the issue of due care on their part. If that be right, to construe this clause, so far as it relates to loss, in such a way as to exclude loss occasioned by lack of proper care, would be to leave the clause so far as loss is concerned – I say nothing about damage – without any content at all. The result is in my opinion is that the clause must be construed as applying to the case of loss through negligence. Therefore this appeal succeeds, and the appropriate reduction in damages must be made in the order.

MacKinnon LJ delivered a concurring judgment and **Uthwatt J** agreed with **Lord Greene MR.**

NOTE

Lord Greene MR's judgment helpfully differentiates the various contractual obligations of the launderer. Some are strict (eg to launder the goods) but others are merely to take reasonable care. In relation to not losing the goods, the obligation was merely one to take reasonable care. It followed that, although in breach (because they had not taken reasonable care), the defendants were able to rely on the generally-worded limitation clause: for, if it did not apply to limit liability for negligence, it would have no application at all to lost articles.

Canada Steamship Lines Ltd v R [1952] AC 192, Privy Council

The claimants' goods were stored in a shed leased from the Crown (the defendant). They were destroyed by a fire caused by the defendant's negligence. By clause 7 of the lease 'the lessee shall not have any claim…against the lessor for …damage…to… goods… being… in the said shed.' The Privy Council held that that exclusion clause did not exclude liability for the defendant's negligence because, applying the principles in the *Alderslade* case, the defendant could realistically have been strictly liable for damage to the goods (eg by breach of its strict obligation to keep the shed in repair). Their Lordships further held that an indemnity clause in the lease (clause 17) did not, on its true construction, require the lessee to indemnify the lessor for the consequences of the lessor's own negligence.

Lord Morton of Henryton, giving the judgment of the Privy Council (comprising himself, **Lord Porter, Lord Normand, Lord Asquith of Bishopstone** and **Lord Cohen**): [*he cited from Lord Greene MR's judgment in* Alderslade v Hendon Laundry Ltd *and then continued:*]
    Their Lordships think that the duty of a court in approaching the consideration of [exemption] clauses may be summarised as follows:—

(1) If the clause contains language which expressly exempts the person in whose favour it is made (hereafter called "the proferens") from the consequence of the negligence of his own servants, effect must be given to that provision. …
(2) If there is no express reference to negligence, the court must consider whether the words used are wide enough, in their ordinary meaning, to cover negligence on the part of the servants of the proferens. …
(3) If the words used are wide enough for the above purpose, the court must then consider whether "the head of damage may be based on some ground other than that of negligence," to quote again from Lord Greene in the *Alderslade* case. The "other ground" must not be so fanciful or remote that the proferens cannot be supposed to have desired protection against it; but subject to this qualification, which is no doubt to be implied from Lord Greene's words, the existence of a possible head of damage other than that of negligence is fatal to the proferens even if the words used are prima facie wide enough to cover negligence on the part of his servants.

With these principles in mind, their Lordships turn to a consideration of clause 7…

[T]he field for claims against the Crown, not based on negligence and coming within clause 7, is not a very wide one but counsel for the company has given the following instances of such claims:—

1. Claims under article 1614 of the Civil Code for "defects or faults in the thing leased which prevent or diminish its use, whether known to the lessor or not." There might be, says counsel, a defect in the construction of the roof of the shed, not known to the Crown, and as a result of this defect the roof might fall down and injure chattels in the shed which belonged to the company. A claim for damage to these chattels resulting from this breach of the lessor's obligation under article 1614 is not a claim based on negligence and it would be barred by clause 7.

2. Claims under article 1612 (3) of the Civil Code. Suppose, for example, says counsel, that the Crown were to authorize a third party to carry out some operation on adjacent land which caused damage to the shed. In that event, again, the company would have a claim for damages, not based on negligence, which would be barred by clause 7.

3. Claims for a reduction of the rent, by the joint operation of articles 1617 and 1660 of the Civil Code, if, for instance, a trespasser caused damage to the shed by setting part of it on fire, and the lessee's right of action for damages against the trespasser proved to be ineffectual. Counsel for the Crown contended that a claim for a reduction of the rent would not fall within clause 7, but their Lordships think that such a claim, although it would not be a claim for "damages" might fairly be described as "a demand against the lessor for ... damage ... of any nature ... to the said shed" within the meaning of clause 7.

It was contended on behalf of the Crown that these instances of possible claims for damages were fanciful and remote, and would not have been within the contemplation of the parties when the terms of the lease were agreed. No doubt there may be cases in which it may be difficult to draw the line. In the present case, however, their Lordships are not prepared to assume that the obligations imposed on lessors by the Civil Code were not in the minds of the parties. They think that the Crown may well have desired to protect itself from claims for damage arising out of any breach of these obligations, and yet may not have intended to go so far as to stipulate for protection from claims for damage resulting from the negligence of its servants.

[*Lord Morton went on to consider the indemnity clause, clause 17, and again concluded that, on its true construction, it did not apply to cover the Crown's negligence. He then continued:*]

If their Lordships had agreed...that clause 17 extended so far as to cover negligent acts of the Crown's servants, they might well have had to reconsider the provisional view already expressed as to clause 7, but as they have arrived at the contrary opinion, their provisional view as to clause 7, so far from being disturbed, is strengthened. It would seem unlikely that if negligent acts by the Crown's servants are outside the scope of one clause, they are within the scope of the other.

The result is that, after hearing an able argument as to the construction of the lease from both sides, their Lordships find that the Crown has failed to establish either its defence under clause 7 or its claim for indemnity under clause 17. This being so, no other question arises for decision on this appeal.

NOTES AND QUESTIONS

1. Do not be confused by the references to a civil code. Although the law being applied was the law in Quebec, which has a civil code, the relevant principles of

construction, with which we are here concerned, apply in the same way in England and Quebec.

2.   Lord Morton's statement of principles has been cited in many subsequent cases and was approved, and applied, by the House of Lords in *Smith v South Wales Switchgear Ltd* [1978] 1 WLR 165 in construing an indemnity clause.

3.   Applying *Alderslade* and *Canada Steamship,* it is clear that, to be sure that words will be construed as excluding liability for negligence, a draftsman should use the word 'negligence' or a precise synonym. Generally-worded exclusions (eg 'howsoever caused') are risky.

4.   However, a *rigid* application of the *Canada Steamship* principles appears to be out of line with the modern approach to construction, which eschews technical rules of construction. In the *Investors Compensation Scheme* case, as we have seen above at 220, Lord Hoffmann said, 'Almost all the old intellectual baggage of "legal" interpretation has been discarded'. Subsequently in *Bank of Credit and Commerce International SA v Ali* [2002] 1 AC 251 (albeit in a dissenting speech) he specifically referred to the construction of exemption clauses and continued as follows, at [62]: 'The disappearance of artificial rules for the construction of exemption clauses seems to me in accordance with the general trend in matters of construction, which has been to try to assimilate judicial techniques of construction to those which would be used by a reasonable speaker of the language in the interpretation of any serious utterance in ordinary life.' It would seem therefore that Lord Morton's principles should not be read like a statute but rather as reflecting the usual— but not invariable—position that parties do not intend liability for negligence to be excluded. This is supported by the speeches in *HIH Casualty and General Insurance Ltd v Chase Manhattan Bank* [2003] UKHL 6, [2003] 2 Lloyd's Rep 61. In that case, a generally-worded clause excluding all liability of an insured to an insurer for misrepresentation or non-disclosure of its agent was held, on its true construction, not to exclude liability (whether for damages or rescission) for the agent's fraudulent misrepresentation or fraudulent non-disclosure. But as part of the reasoning it was held that the clause did apply to exclude liability for negligent misrepresentation or non-disclosure even though a rigid application of the *Canada Steamship* principles would have led to the contrary result (because liability for innocent misrepresentation or non-disclosure was a realistic possibility). Lord Bingham, with whom Lord Steyn agreed, said at [11], 'There can be no doubting the general authority of [the *Canada Steamship*] principles, which have been applied in many cases, and the approach indicated is sound. The courts should not ordinarily infer that a contracting party has given up rights which the law confers upon him to an extent greater than the contract terms indicate he has chosen to do; and if the contract terms can take legal and practical effect without denying him the rights he would ordinarily enjoy if the other party is negligent, they will be read as not denying him those rights unless they are so expressed as to make clear that they do. But, as the insurers in argument fully recognized, Lord Morton was giving helpful guidance on the proper approach to interpretation and not laying down a code. The passage does not provide a litmus test which, applied to the terms of the contract, yields a certain and predictable result. The courts'

task of ascertaining what the particular parties intended, in their particular commercial context, remains.' See similarly Lord Hoffmann at [58]–[67]; Lord Hobhouse at [95]; and Lord Scott, albeit dissenting, at [116].

5. In the light of the modern approach to construction, are the *Canada Steamship* principles more of a hindrance than a help?

Hollier v Rambler Motors (AMC) Ltd [1972] 2 QB 71, Court of Appeal

For the facts and the incorporation issue, see above, 193. On the construction issue it was held that the clause on its proper construction did not here apply given that the defendants were seeking to exclude liability for negligence.

Salmon LJ: [I]n case I am wrong on the view that I have formed, without any hesitation, I may say, that the course of dealing did not import the so-called exclusion clause, I think I should deal with the point as to whether or not the words on the bottom of the form, had they been incorporated in the contract, would have excluded the defendants' liability to compensate the plaintiff for damage caused to the plaintiff's car by a fire which in turn had been caused by the defendants' own negligence. It is well settled that a clause excluding liability for negligence should make its meaning plain on its face to any ordinarily literate and sensible person. The easiest way of doing that, of course, is to state expressly that the garage, tradesman or merchant, as the case may be, will not be responsible for any damage caused by his own negligence. No doubt merchants, tradesmen, garage proprietors and the like are a little shy of writing in an exclusion clause quite so bluntly as that. Clearly it would not tend to attract customers, and might even put many off. I am not saying that an exclusion clause cannot be effective to exclude negligence unless it does so expressly, but in order for the clause to be effective the language should be so plain that it clearly bears that meaning. I do not think that defendants should be allowed to shelter behind language which might lull the customer into a false sense of security by letting him think – unless perhaps he happens to be a lawyer – that he would have redress against the man with whom he was dealing for any damage which he, the customer, might suffer by the negligence of that person.

The principles are stated by Scrutton L.J. with his usual clarity in *Rutter v. Palmer* [1922] 2 K.B. 87, 92:

> "For the present purposes a rougher test will serve. In construing an exemption clause certain general rules may be applied: First the defendant is not exempted from liability for the negligence of his servants unless adequate words are used; secondly, the liability of the defendant apart from the exempting words must be ascertained; then the particular clause in question must be considered; and if the only liability of the party pleading the exemption is a liability for negligence, the clause will more readily operate to exempt him."

Scrutton L.J. was far too great a lawyer, and had far too much robust common sense, if I may be permitted to say so, to put it higher than that "if the only liability of the party pleading the exemption is a liability for negligence, the clause will more readily operate to exempt him." He does not say that "if the only liability of the party pleading the exemption is a liability for negligence, the clause will necessarily exempt him." After all, there are many cases in the books dealing with exemption clauses, and in every case it comes down to a question of construing the alleged exemption clause which is then before the court. It seems to me that in *Rutter v. Palmer*, although the word "negligence" was never used in the exemption clause, the exemption clause would have conveyed to any ordinary, literate and sensible person that the garage in that case was inserting a clause in the contract which excluded their liability for the negligence of their drivers. The clause being considered in that case – and it was without any doubt incorporated in the contract – was: "Customers' cars are driven by your staff at customers' sole risk." Any ordinary man knows that when a car is damaged it is not infrequently damaged because the driver has driven it negligently. He also knows, I suppose, that if he sends it to a garage and a driver in the employ of the garage takes the car on the road for some purpose in connection with the work which the customer has entrusted the garage to do, the garage could not conceivably be liable for the car being damaged in an accident unless the driver was at fault. It follows that no sensible man could have thought that the words in that case had any meaning except that the garage would not be liable for the negligence of their own drivers. That is a typical case where, on the construction of the clause in question, the meaning for which the defendant was there contending was the obvious meaning of the clause.

The next case to which I wish to refer is the well-known case of *Alderslade v. Hendon Laundry Ltd.* [*After looking at it and discussing the facts, he continued:*] I think that the ordinary sensible housewife, or indeed anyone else who sends washing to the laundry, who saw that clause must have appreciated that almost always goods are lost or damaged because of the laundry's negligence, and therefore this clause could apply only to limit the liability of the laundry, when they were in fault or negligent.

But Mr. Tuckey [counsel for the defendants] has drawn our attention to the way in which the matter was put by Lord Greene M.R. in delivering the leading judgment in this court, and he contends that Lord Greene M.R. was in fact making a considerable extension to the law as laid down by Scrutton L.J. in the case to which I have referred. For this proposition he relies on the following passage in Lord Greene M.R.'s judgment, at p. 192:

> "The effect of those authorities can I think be stated as follows: Where the head of damage in respect of which limitation of liability is sought to be imposed by such a clause is one which rests on negligence and nothing else, the clause must be construed as extending to that head of damage, because it would otherwise lack subject matter."

If one takes that word "must" au pied de la lettre that passage does support Mr. Tuckey's contention. However, we are not here construing a statute, but a passage in an unreserved judgment of Lord Greene M.R., who was clearly intending no more than to re-state the effect of the authorities as they then stood. …I do not think that Lord Greene M.R. was intending to extend the law in the sense for which Mr. Tuckey contends. If it were so extended, it would make the law entirely artificial by ignoring that rules of construction are merely our guides and not our masters; in the end you are driven back to construing the clause in question to see what it means. Applying the principles laid down by Scrutton L.J., they lead to the result at which the court arrived in *Alderslade v. Hendon Laundry Ltd.* [1945] 1 K.B. 189. In my judgment these principles lead to a very different result in the present case. The words are: "The company is not responsible for damage caused by fire to customers' cars on the premises." What would that mean to any ordinarily literate and sensible car owner? I do not suppose that any such, unless he is a trained lawyer, has an intimate or indeed any knowledge of the liability of bailees in law. If you asked the ordinary man or woman: "Supposing you send your car to the garage to be repaired, and there is a fire, would you suppose that the garage would be liable?" I should be surprised if many of them did not answer, quite wrongly: "Of course they are liable if there is a fire." Others might be more cautious and say: "Well, I had better ask my solicitor," or, "I do not know. I suppose they may well be liable." That is the crucial difference, to my mind, between the present case and *Alderslade v. Hendon Laundry Ltd.* and *Rutter v. Palmer* [1922] 2 K.B. 87. In those two cases, any ordinary man or woman reading the conditions would have known that all that was being excluded was the negligence of the laundry, in the one case, and the garage, in the other. But here I think the ordinary man or woman would be equally surprised and horrified to learn that if the garage was so negligent that a fire was caused which damaged their car, they would be without remedy because of the words in the condition. I can quite understand that the ordinary man or woman would consider that, because of these words, the mere fact that there was a fire would not make the garage liable. Fires can occur from a large variety of causes, only one of which is negligence on the part of the occupier of the premises, and that is by no means the most frequent cause. The ordinary man would I think say to himself: "Well, what they are telling me is that if there is a fire due to any cause other than their own negligence they are not responsible for it." To my mind, if the defendants were seeking to exclude their responsibility for a fire caused by their own negligence, they ought to have done so in far plainer language than the language here used.

There is another case which I think throws some light upon the problem before us, and that is *Olley v. Marlborough Court Ltd.* [1949] 1 K.B. 532 [*see above, 174*]. ...Denning L.J. said, at p. 550:

> "Ample content can be given to the notice by construing it as a warning that the hotel company is not liable, in the absence of negligence. As such it serves a useful purpose. It is a warning to the guest that he must do his part to take care of his things himself, and, if needs be, insure them. It is unnecessary to go further and to construe the notice as a contractual exemption of the hotel company from their common law liability for negligence."

Similarly, I think, in this case the words at the bottom of this form can be given ample content by construing them as a warning in the sense that I have already indicated. It seems plain that if the notice in the bedroom of the hotel had read as follows: "Proprietors will not hold themselves responsible for articles lost or stolen, or for the damage or destruction of articles caused by fire," and then there had been a full stop, and the notice went on to say that to avoid articles being lost or stolen they should be handed to the manageress for safe custody, by a parity of reasoning the court must have come to the conclusion that the notice would not have excluded the hotel proprietors from liability for the loss of articles by a fire caused by their own negligence.

Stamp LJ: On the question of construction, I reach the same conclusion as Salmon L.J., but by, I think, a slightly different route. As I understand the law, it is settled that where in a contract such as this you find a provision excluding liability capable of two constructions, one of which will make it applicable where there is no negligence by the defendant, and the other will make it applicable where there is negligence by the defendant, it requires special words or special circumstances to make the clause exclude liability in case of negligence: see, for example, *Price & Co. v. Union Lighterage Co.* [1904] 1 K.B. 412. Similarly, I would hold that, where the words relied upon by the defendant are susceptible either to a construction under which they become a statement of fact in the nature of a warning or to a construction which will exempt the defendant from liability for negligence, the former construction is to be preferred. The words here, "the company is not responsible for damage caused by fire to customer's cars on the premises," are, in my judgment, certainly susceptible to a construction which would regard them as a mere statement in the nature of a warning, and reinforced by the principle that I have stated, I would hold that that is how they ought to be construed in this case. If this be correct, I do not find it necessary to consider the cases which have been decided upon the footing that the clause under consideration was a term of the contract excluding some liability: for on the view that I have formed, the clause on its true construction is not a clause of that nature.

Latey J delivered a concurring judgment.

NOTES AND QUESTIONS

1. Although Stamp LJ suggested that his approach was slightly different from that of Salmon LJ, both in essence reasoned that the clause did not on its true

construction exclude any liability at all. Rather it was a warning to customers as to the legal position where fire was caused without the defendants' negligence.

2.   Was Salmon LJ's distinguishing of *Alderslade v Hendon Laundry* convincing?
3.   One may regard this case as crossing the line from strict to 'hostile' construction. Subsequent to the enactment of UCTA 1977, section 2(2) (see below, 245), is there the same need for the courts to adopt such a hostile approach in order to hold such a clause inapplicable?

(2) Excluding or Limiting Liability for Fundamental Breach

Photo Production Ltd v Securicor Transport Ltd
[1980] AC 827, House of Lords

The claimants entered into a contract with the defendant to provide a night patrol service for their factory. The defendant's standard terms included the following clause: 'Under no circumstances shall the company be responsible for any injurious act or default of any employee of the company unless such act or default could have been foreseen and avoided by the exercise of due diligence on the part of the company as his employer...'. One of the defendant's employees was patrolling the factory when he deliberately started a small fire by throwing a lighted match into a cardboard box or other material. The fire spread and a large part of the claimants' factory was destroyed, causing a loss of £615,000. In the claimants' action for damages for breach of contract or the tort of negligence, the defendant sought to rely on the exclusion clause. In allowing the defendant's appeal, the House of Lords held that the defendant was able to do so because the exclusion clause as a matter of construction covered the fundamental breach that had occurred and, contrary to the Court of Appeal's reasoning, there is no rule of law preventing exclusion of a funda-mental breach.

Lord Wilberforce: It is first necessary to decide upon the correct approach to a case such as this where it is sought to invoke an exception or limitation clause in the contract. The approach of Lord Denning M.R. in the Court of Appeal was to consider first whether the breach was "fundamental." If so, he said, the court itself deprives the party of the benefit of an exemption or limitation clause ([1978] 1 W.L.R. 856, 863). Shaw and Waller L.JJ. substan-tially followed him in this argument.

   Lord Denning M.R. in this was following the earlier decision of the Court of Appeal, and in particular his own judgment in *Harbutt's Plasticine Ltd. v. Wayne Tank & Pump Co. Ltd.* [1970] 1 Q.B. 447. In that case Lord Denning M.R. distinguished two cases (a) the case where as the result of a breach of contract the innocent party has, and exercises, the right to bring the contract to an end, (b) the case where the breach automatically brings the contract to an end, without the innocent party having to make an election whether to terminate the contract or to continue it. In the first case the Master of the Rolls, purportedly applying this House's decision in *Suisse Atlantique Société d'Armement Maritime S.A. v. N.V. Rotterdamsche Kolen Centrale* [1967] 1 A.C. 361, but in effect two citations from two of their Lordships' speeches, extracted a rule of law that the "termination" of the contract brings it, and with it the exclusion clause, to an end. The *Suisse Atlantique* case in his view

"affirms the long line of cases in this court that when one party has been guilty of a fundamental breach of the contract … and the other side accepts it, so that the contract comes
to an end … then the guilty party cannot rely on an exception or limitation clause to
escape from his liability for the breach" (*Harbutt's* case [1970] 1 Q.B. 447, 467).

He then applied the same principle to the second case.

My Lords, whatever the intrinsic merit of this doctrine, as to which I shall have something
to say later, it is clear to me that so far from following this House's decision in the *Suisse
Atlantique* it is directly opposed to it and that the whole purpose and tenor of the *Suisse
Atlantique* was to repudiate it. The lengthy, and perhaps I may say sometimes indigestible
speeches of their Lordships, are correctly summarised in the headnote – holding No. 3 [1967]
1 A.C. 361, 362 – "That the question whether an exceptions clause was applicable where
there was a fundamental breach of contract was one of the true construction of the contract."
That there was any rule of law by which exceptions clauses are eliminated, or deprived of
effect, regardless of their terms, was clearly not the view of Viscount Dilhorne, Lord Hodson,
or of myself. The passages invoked for the contrary view of a rule of law consist only of short
extracts from two of the speeches – on any view a minority. But the case for the doctrine does
not even go so far as that. Lord Reid, in my respectful opinion, and I recognise that I may not
be the best judge of this matter, in his speech read as a whole, cannot be claimed as a
supporter of a rule of law.

...

I am convinced that, with the possible exception of Lord Upjohn whose critical passage,
when read in full, is somewhat ambiguous, their Lordships, fairly read, can only be taken to
have rejected those suggestions for a rule of law which had appeared in the Court of Appeal
and to have firmly stated that the question is one of construction, not merely of course of the
exclusion clause alone, but of the whole contract.

Much has been written about the *Suisse Atlantique* case. Each speech has been subjected
to various degrees of analysis and criticism, much of it constructive. Speaking for myself I am
conscious of imperfections of terminology, though sometimes in good company. But I do not
think that I should be conducing to the clarity of the law by adding to what was already too
ample a discussion a further analysis which in turn would have to be interpreted. I have no
second thoughts as to the main proposition that the question whether, and to what extent,
an exclusion clause is to be applied to a fundamental breach, or a breach of a fundamental
term, or indeed to any breach of contract, is a matter of construction of the contract. Many
difficult questions arise and will continue to arise in the infinitely varied situations in which
contracts come to be breached – by repudiatory breaches, accepted or not, by anticipatory
breaches, by breaches of conditions or of various terms and whether by negligent, or deliberate action or otherwise. But there are ample resources in the normal rules of contract law
for dealing with these without the superimposition of a judicially invented rule of law. I am
content to leave the matter there with some supplementary observations.

1. The doctrine of "fundamental breach" in spite of its imperfections and doubtful
parentage has served a useful purpose. There was a large number of problems, productive of
injustice, in which it was worse than unsatisfactory to leave exception clauses to operate. Lord
Reid referred to these in the *Suisse Atlantique* case [1967] 1 A.C. 361, 406, pointing out at the
same time that the doctrine of fundamental breach was a dubious specific. But since then
Parliament has taken a hand: it has passed the Unfair Contract Terms Act 1977. This Act
applies to consumer contracts and those based on standard terms and enables exception
clauses to be applied with regard to what is just and reasonable. It is significant that
Parliament refrained from legislating over the whole field of contract. After this Act, in
commercial matters generally, when the parties are not of unequal bargaining power, and
when risks are normally borne by insurance, not only is the case for judicial intervention
undemonstrated, but there is everything to be said, and this seems to have been Parliament's
intention, for leaving the parties free to apportion the risks as they think fit and for respecting
their decisions.

At the stage of negotiation as to the consequences of a breach, there is everything to be said for allowing the parties to estimate their respective claims according to the contractual provisions they have themselves made, rather than for facing them with a legal complex so uncertain as the doctrine of fundamental breach must be. What, for example, would have been the position of the respondents' factory if instead of being destroyed it had been damaged, slightly or moderately or severely? At what point does the doctrine (with what logical justification I have not understood) decide, ex post facto, that the breach was (factually) fundamental before going on to ask whether legally it is to be regarded as fundamental? How is the date of "termination" to be fixed? Is it the date of the incident causing the damage, or the date of the innocent party's election, or some other date? All these difficulties arise from the doctrine and are left unsolved by it.

At the judicial stage there is still more to be said for leaving cases to be decided straightforwardly on what the parties have bargained for rather than upon analysis, which becomes progressively more refined, of decisions in other cases leading to inevitable appeals. The learned judge was able to decide this case on normal principles of contractual law with minimal citation of authority. I am sure that most commercial judges have wished to be able to do the same...In my opinion they can and should.

2. The case of *Harbutt* [1970] 1 Q.B. 447 must clearly be overruled. It would be enough to put that upon its radical inconsistency with the *Suisse Atlantique* case [1967] 1 A.C. 361. But even if the matter were res integra I would find the decision to be based upon unsatisfactory reasoning as to the "termination" of the contract and the effect of "termination" on the plaintiffs' claim for damage. I have, indeed, been unable to understand how the doctrine can be reconciled with the well accepted principle of law, stated by the highest modern authority, that when in the context of a breach of contract one speaks of "termination," what is meant is no more than that the innocent party or, in some cases, both parties, are excused from further performance. Damages, in such cases, are then claimed under the contract, so what reason in principle can there be for disregarding what the contract itself says about damages – whether it "liquidates" them, or limits them, or excludes them? These difficulties arise in part from uncertain or inconsistent terminology. A vast number of expressions are used to describe situations where a breach has been committed by one party of such a character as to entitle the other party to refuse further performance: discharge, rescission, termination, the contract is at an end, or dead, or displaced; clauses cannot survive, or simply go. I have come to think that some of these difficulties can be avoided; in particular the use of "rescission," even if distinguished from rescission ab initio, as an equivalent for discharge, though justifiable in some contexts (see *Johnson v. Agnew* [1980] A.C. 367) may lead to confusion in others. To plead for complete uniformity may be to cry for the moon. But what can and ought to be avoided is to make use of these confusions in order to produce a concealed and unreasoned legal innovation: to pass, for example, from saying that a party, victim of a breach of contract, is entitled to refuse further performance, to saying that he may treat the contract as at an end, or as rescinded, and to draw from this the proposition, which is not analytical but one of policy, that all or (arbitrarily) some of the clauses of the contract lose, automatically, their force, regardless of intention.

If this process is discontinued the way is free to use such words as "discharge" or "termination" consistently with principles as stated by modern authority which *Harbutt's* case [1970] 1 Q.B. 447 disregards. I venture with apology to relate the classic passages. In *Heyman v. Darwins Ltd.* [1942] A.C. 356, 399 Lord Porter said:

> "To say that the contract is rescinded or has come to an end or has ceased to exist may in individual cases convey the truth with sufficient accuracy, but the fuller expression that the injured party is thereby absolved from future performance of his obligations under the contract is a more exact description of the position. Strictly speaking, to say that on acceptance of the renunciation of a contract the contract is rescinded is incorrect. In such a case the injured party may accept the renunciation as a breach going to the root of the whole

of the consideration. By that acceptance he is discharged from further performance and may bring an action for damages, but the contract itself is not rescinded."

And similarly Lord Macmillan at p. 373: see also *Boston Deep Sea Fishing and Ice Co. v. Ansell* (1888) 39 Ch.D. 339, 361, *per* Bowen L.J. In *Lep Air Services Ltd. v. Rolloswin Investments Ltd.* [1973] A.C. 331, 350, my noble and learned friend, Lord Diplock, drew a distinction (relevant for that case) between primary obligations under a contract, which on "rescission" generally come to an end, and secondary obligations which may then arise. Among the latter he includes an obligation to pay compensation, i.e., damages. And he states in terms that this latter obligation "is just as much an obligation arising from the contract as are the primary obligations that it replaces."

...

3. I must add to this, by way of exception to the decision not to "gloss" the *Suisse Atlantique* [1967] 1 A.C. 361 a brief observation on the deviation cases, since some reliance has been placed upon them, particularly upon the decision of this House in *Hain Steamship Co. Ltd. v. Tate and Lyle Ltd.* (1936) 155 L.T. 177 (so earlier than the *Suisse Atlantique*) in the support of the *Harbutt* doctrine. I suggested in the *Suisse Atlantique* that these cases can be regarded as proceeding upon normal principles applicable to the law of contract generally viz., that it is a matter of the parties' intentions whether and to what extent clauses in shipping contracts can be applied after a deviation, i.e., a departure from the contractually agreed voyage or adventure. It may be preferable that they should be considered as a body of authority sui generis with special rules derived from historical and commercial reasons. What on either view they cannot do is to lay down different rules as to contracts generally from those later stated by this House in *Heyman v. Darwins Ltd.* [1942] A.C. 356. ...

4. It is not necessary to review fully the numerous cases in which the doctrine of fundamental breach has been applied or discussed. Many of these have now been superseded by the Unfair Contract Terms Act 1977. Others, as decisions, may be justified as depending upon the construction of the contract (see *Levison v. Patent Steam Carpet Cleaning Co. Ltd.* [1978] Q.B. 69) in the light of well known principles such as that stated in *Alderslade v. Hendon Laundry Ltd.* [1945] K.B. 189.

In this situation the present case has to be decided. As a preliminary, the nature of the contract has to be understood. Securicor undertook to provide a service of periodical visits for a very modest charge which works out at 26p. per visit. It did not agree to provide equipment. It would have no knowledge of the value of the plaintiffs' factory: that, and the efficacy of their fire precautions, would be known to the respondents. In these circumstances nobody could consider it unreasonable, that as between these two equal parties the risk assumed by Securicor should be a modest one, and that the respondents should carry the substantial risk of damage or destruction.

The duty of Securicor was, as stated, to provide a service. There must be implied an obligation to use due care in selecting their patrolmen, to take care of the keys and, I would think, to operate the service with due and proper regard to the safety and security of the premises. The breach of duty committed by Securicor lay in a failure to discharge this latter obligation. Alternatively it could be put upon a vicarious responsibility for the wrongful act of Musgrove – viz., starting a fire on the premises: Securicor would be responsible for this upon the principle stated in *Morris v. C. W. Martin & Sons Ltd.* [1966] 1 Q.B. 716, 739. This being the breach, does condition 1 apply? It is drafted in strong terms, "Under no circumstances" ... "any injurious act or default by any employee." These words have to be approached with the aid of the cardinal rules of construction that they must be read contra proferentem and that in order to escape from the consequences of one's own wrongdoing, or that of one's servant, clear words are necessary. I think that these words are clear. The respondents in facts [*sic*] relied upon them for an argument that since they exempted from negligence they must be taken as not exempting from the consequence of deliberate acts. But this is a perversion of the rule that if a clause can cover something other than negligence, it will not be applied to negligence. Whether, in addition to negligence, it covers other, e.g., deliberate, acts, remains a matter of construction requiring, of course, clear words. I am of opinion that it does, and being free to construe and apply the clause, I must hold that liability is excluded.

Lords Diplock and **Salmon** gave concurring speeches. **Lords Keith of Kinkel** and **Scarman** agreed with **Lord Wilberforce.**

NOTES AND QUESTIONS

1. The fundamental breach 'doctrine' or 'rule of law' was an invention of the courts which, prior to the enactment of the UCTA 1977, sought to strike down extreme exclusion clauses, ie those which sought to exclude liability even for a very serious breach of contract. While producing acceptable results in consumer contracts, the doctrine was conceptually problematic (in relying on the idea that the clause was 'wiped away' on termination of the contract) and had too wide a scope because it prevented the exclusion of a fundamental breach even in freely-negotiated contracts between parties of equal bargaining power. In *Suisse Atlantique Société d'Armement Maritime SA v NV Rotterdamsche Kolen Centrale* [1967] 1 AC 361 the House of Lords appeared to have rejected fundamental breach as a rule of law, instead treating it as merely a matter of construction. However, ambiguities in the reasoning in that case allowed Lord Denning, in particular, to keep the 'rule of law' alive in the Court of Appeal; and it was not until the *Photo Production* case that it was finally laid to rest. Now the question is simply whether the exclusion clause, as a matter of construction, covers even the fundamental breach that has occurred.
2. Although now a matter of historical interest only, one should be aware that there were disputes as to the correct formulation of the fundamental breach doctrine. In its final form, it was crucial that the contract had been terminated for breach.
3. As Lord Wilberforce's speech indicates, there is continuing controversy as to whether the fundamental breach rule of law lives on in a small specialised area of the law, namely where a carrier deviates in performing a contract for the carriage of goods by sea. Even in that area, the better view is that the issue is merely one of construction of the exclusion clause.
4. Would the fundamental breach doctrine still have been alive today had UCTA 1977 (or the Unfair Terms in Consumer Contracts Regulations 1999) not been enacted?
5. For another example of the House of Lords holding that, as a matter of construction—and subject to statutory controls—a clause did apply to limit liability for a very serious breach, see *George Mitchell (Chesterhall) Ltd v Finney Lock Seeds Ltd* (below, 237).

(3) Construing *Limitation* Clauses

So far in this chapter, the approach to construing exclusion and limitation clauses has not been distinguished. Indeed, some of the cases extracted above have concerned a limitation, rather than a full exclusion, of liability (eg *Alderslade v Hendon Laundry*

Ltd). However, as we shall now see, it has been authoritatively laid down that a 'softer' approach should be taken to construing limitation, as opposed to exclusion, clauses.

Ailsa Craig Fishing Co Ltd v Malvern Fishing Co Ltd
[1983] 1 WLR 964, House of Lords (Sc)

Securicor had contracted to provide a security service in Aberdeen harbour for fishing boats moored there. By clause 2(f) of the contract, if, in respect of the services, Securicor had any liability to a customer 'whether under the express or implied terms of this contract, or at common law, or in any other way' that liability was limited to a sum '(a) Not exceeding £1000 in respect of any one claim arising from any duty assumed by the company… which involves the provision of any service not solely related to the prevention or detection of fire or theft.' On New Year's Eve 1970, a boat belonging to the claimant (ACF) was sunk when it fouled (ie while anchored, crashed against) another boat. The trial judge found that the loss had been caused by Securicor's breach of contract and negligence and awarded damages of £55,000. The damages were reduced on appeal to £1000. On ACF's appeal to the House of Lords against that reduction, it was held that, on a true construction, the limitation clause did here apply so that ACF's appeal should be dismissed.

Lord Wilberforce: Whether a clause limiting liability is effective or not is a question of construction of that clause in the context of the contract as a whole. If it is to exclude liability for negligence, it must be most clearly and unambiguously expressed, and in such a contract as this, must be construed contra proferentem. I do not think that there is any doubt so far. But I venture to add one further qualification, or at least clarification: one must not strive to create ambiguities by strained construction, as I think that the appellants have striven to do. The relevant words must be given, if possible, their natural, plain meaning. Clauses of limitation are not regarded by the courts with the same hostility as clauses of exclusion: this is because they must be related to other contractual terms, in particular to the risks to which the defending party may be exposed, the remuneration which he receives, and possibly also the opportunity of the other party to insure.

. . .

[*Having examined the terms of the contract, he continued:*]

For my part I find these clauses, though intricate, perfectly clear. …I have no doubt that subclause (*a*) applies so as to limit individual claims to £1,000 each.

Lord Fraser of Tullybelton: There are…authorities which lay down very strict principles to be applied when considering the effect of clauses of exclusion or of indemnity: see particularly the Privy Council case of *Canada Steamship Lines Ltd. v. The King* [1952] A.C. 192, 208, where Lord Morton of Henryton, delivering the advice of the Board, summarised the principles in terms which have recently been applied by this House in [*Smith v South Wales Switchgear Ltd* [1978] 1 WLR 165]. In my opinion these principles are not applicable in their full rigour when considering the effect of clauses merely limiting liability. Such clauses will of course be read contra proferentem and must be clearly expressed, but there is no reason why they should be judged by the specially exacting standards which are applied to exclusion and indemnity clauses. The reason for imposing such standards on these clauses is the inherent improbability that the other party to a contract including such a clause intended to release the proferens from a liability that would otherwise fall upon him. But there is no such high degree of improbability that he would agree to a limitation of the liability of the proferens, especially when [as here] the potential losses that might be caused by the negligence of the proferens or its servants are so great in proportion to the sums that can reasonably be charged for the services contracted for. It is enough in the present case that the clause must be clear and unambiguous.

...

Having considered...particular criticisms of clause (*f*) the question remains whether in its context it is sufficiently clear and unambiguous to receive effect in limiting the liability of Securicor for its own negligence or that of its employees. In my opinion it is. It applies to any liability "whether under the express or implied terms of this contact, or at common law, or in any other way." Liability at common law is undoubtedly wide enough to cover liability including the negligence of the proferens itself, so that even without relying on the final words 'any other way,' I am clearly of opinion that the negligence of Securicor is covered.

Lords Elwyn-Jones, **Salmon** and **Lowry** concurred.

NOTES AND QUESTIONS

1. In the light of the modern approach to construction and the recent indications that the *Canada Steamship* principles should not be applied too rigidly (see especially 227 note 4 above), is a bright-line distinction between construing limitation and exclusion clauses appropriate?
2. Irrespective of such developments, can a significantly different approach to the construction of limitation clauses, as against exclusion clauses, be justified given that some limitation clauses set a very low figure for recovery and are therefore virtually equivalent to total exclusions? Cf the High Court of Australia in *Darlington Futures Ltd v Delco Australia Pty Ltd* (1986) 161 CLR 500 which has rejected the approach in the *Ailsa Craig* case.

George Mitchell (Chesterhall) Ltd v Finney Lock Seeds Ltd
[1983] 2 AC 803, House of Lords

The defendants (the appellants) were seed merchants. The claimants were farmers who ordered Dutch winter white cabbage seeds, called 'Finney's Late Dutch Special', from the defendants. The defendants supplied the wrong type of cabbage seed so that the crop, which was planted over 63 acres, did not grow properly and had to be ploughed in as worthless. The price of the seeds was £201.60 but the damages claimed for the breach of contract were £61,513. By the conditions of sale in the contract, the defendants argued that they had limited their liability to replacement of defective seeds or a refund of the price paid. It was held by the House of Lords that, as a matter of construction, the relevant condition did so limit their liability; but that it was not fair and reasonable to allow the defendants to rely on that condition applying the then relevant statutory provision (section 55 of the Sale of Goods Act 1979). We are here solely concerned with the construction issue.

Lord Bridge of Harwich: The issues in the appeal arise from three sentences in the conditions of sale endorsed on the appellants' invoice and admittedly embodied in the terms on which the appellants contracted. For ease of reference it will be convenient to number the sentences. Omitting immaterial words they read as follows:

1. "In the event of any seeds or plants sold or agreed to be sold by us not complying with the express terms of the contract of sale ... or any seeds or plants proving defective in

varietal purity we will, at our option, replace the defective seeds or plants, free of charge to the buyer or will refund all payments made to us by the buyer in respect of the defective seeds or plants and this shall be the limit of our obligation."

2. "We hereby exclude all liability for any loss or damage arising from the use of any seeds or plants supplied by us and for any consequential loss or damage arising out of such use or any failure in the performance of or any defect in any seeds or plants supplied by us or for any other loss or damage whatsoever save for, at our option, liability for any such replacement or refund as aforesaid."

3. "In accordance with the established custom of the seed trade any express or implied condition, statement or warranty, statutory or otherwise, not stated in these conditions is hereby excluded."

I will refer to the whole as "the relevant condition" and to the parts as "clauses 1, 2 and 3" of the relevant condition.

The first issue is whether the relevant condition, on its true construction in the context of the contract as a whole, is effective to limit the appellants' liability to a refund of £201.60, the price of the seeds ("the common law issue"). The second issue is whether, if the common law issue is decided in the appellants' favour, they should nevertheless be precluded from reliance on this limitation of liability pursuant to the provisions of the modified section 55 of the Sale of Goods Act 1979 which is set out in paragraph 11 of Schedule 1 to the Act and which applies to contracts made between May 18, 1973, and February 1, 1978 ("the statutory issue").

The learned trial judge, Parker J. [1981] 1 Lloyd's Rep. 476, 480, on the basis of evidence that the seeds supplied were incapable of producing a commercially saleable crop, decided the common law issue against the appellants on the ground that "what was supplied ... was in no commercial sense vegetable seed at all" but was "the delivery of something wholly different in kind from that which was ordered and which the defendants had agreed to supply." He accordingly found it unnecessary to decide the statutory issue, but helpfully made some important findings of fact, which are very relevant if that issue falls to be decided. He gave judgment in favour of the respondents for £61,513.78 damages and £30,756.00 interest. ...

In the Court of Appeal, the common law issue was decided in favour of the appellants by Lord Denning M.R. [1983] Q.B. 284, 296 who said: "On the natural interpretation, I think the condition is sufficient to limit the seed merchants to a refund of the price paid or replacement of the seeds." Oliver L.J. [1983] Q.B. 284, 305, 306, decided the common law issue against the appellants primarily on a ground akin to that of Parker J., albeit somewhat differently expressed. Fastening on the words "agreed to be sold" in clause 1 of the relevant condition, he held that the clause could not be construed to mean "in the event of the seeds sold or agreed to be sold by us not being the seeds agreed to be sold by us." Clause 2 of the relevant condition he held to be "merely a supplement" to clause 1. He thus arrived at the conclusion that the appellants had only succeeded in limiting their liability arising from the supply of seeds which were correctly described as "Finney's Late Dutch Special" but were defective in quality. As the seeds supplied were not "Finney's Late Dutch Special," the relevant condition gave them no protection. Kerr L.J. [1983] Q.B. 284, 313, in whose reasoning Oliver L.J. also concurred, decided the common law issue against the appellants on the ground that the relevant condition was ineffective to limit the appellants' liability for a breach of contract which could not have occurred without negligence on the appellants' part, and that the supply of the wrong variety of seeds was such a breach.

The Court of Appeal, however, were unanimous in deciding the statutory issue against the appellants.

In his judgment, Lord Denning M.R. traces, in his uniquely colourful and graphic style, the history of the courts' approach to contractual clauses excluding or limiting liability, culminating in the intervention of the legislature, first by the Supply of Goods (Implied Terms) Act 1973, secondly, by the Unfair Contract Terms Act 1977. My Lords, in considering the common law issue, I will resist the temptation to follow that fascinating trail, but will content myself with references to the two recent decisions of your Lordships' House commonly called the two Securicor cases: *Photo Production Ltd. v. Securicor Transport Ltd.* [1980] A.C. 827 (*"Securicor 1"*) and *Ailsa Craig Fishing Co. Ltd. v. Malvern Fishing Co. Ltd.* [1983] 1 W.L.R. 964 (*"Securicor 2"*).

Securicor 1 gave the final quietus to the doctrine that a "fundamental breach" of contract deprived the party in breach of the benefit of clauses in the contract excluding or limiting his liability. *Securicor 2* drew an important distinction between exclusion and limitation clauses. This is clearly stated by Lord Fraser of Tullybelton...[*He cited from Lord Fraser's speech, above, 236, and continued:*]

My Lords, it seems to me, with all due deference, that the judgments of the learned trial judge and of Oliver L.J. on the common law issue come dangerously near to re-introducing by the back door the doctrine of "fundamental breach" which this House in *Securicor 1* [1980] A.C. 827, had so forcibly evicted by the front. The learned judge discusses what I may call the "peas and beans" or "chalk and cheese" cases, sc. those in which it has been held that exemption clauses do not apply where there has been a contract to sell one thing, e.g. a motor car, and the seller has supplied quite another thing, e.g. a bicycle. I hasten to add that the judge can in no way be criticised for adopting this approach since counsel appearing for the appellants at the trial had conceded "that if what had been delivered had been beetroot seed or carrot seed, he would not be able to rely upon the clause": [1981] 1 Lloyd's Rep. 476, 479. Different counsel appeared for the appellants in the Court of Appeal, where that concession was withdrawn.

In my opinion, this is not a "peas and beans" case at all. The relevant condition applies to "seeds." Clause 1 refers to seeds "sold" and "seeds agreed to be sold." Clause 2 refers to "seeds supplied." As I have pointed out, Oliver L.J. concentrates his attention on the phrase "seeds agreed to be sold." I can see no justification, with respect, for allowing this phrase alone to dictate the interpretation of the relevant condition, still less for treating clause 2 as "merely a supplement" to clause 1. Clause 2 is perfectly clear and unambiguous. The reference to "seeds agreed to be sold" as well as to "seeds sold" in clause 1 reflects the same dichotomy as the definition of "sale" in the Sale of Goods Act 1979 as including a bargain and sale as well as a sale and delivery. The defective seeds in this case were seeds sold and delivered, just as clearly as they were seeds supplied, by the appellants to the respondents. The relevant condition, read as a whole, unambiguously limits the appellants' liability to replacement of the seeds or refund of the price. It is only possible to read an ambiguity into it by the process of strained construction which was deprecated by Lord Diplock [1980] A.C. 827, 851C in *Securicor 1* and by Lord Wilberforce in *Securicor 2* [1983] 1 W.L.R. 964, 966G.

In holding that the relevant condition was ineffective to limit the appellants' liability for a breach of contract caused by their negligence, Kerr L.J. applied the principles stated by Lord Morton of Henryton giving the judgment of the Privy Council in *Canada Steamship Lines Ltd. v. The King* [1952] A.C. 192, 208. The learned Lord Justice stated correctly that this case was also referred to by Lord Fraser of Tullybelton in *Securicor 2* [1983] 1 W.L.R. 964, 970. He omitted, however, to notice that, as appears from the passage from Lord Fraser's speech which I have already cited, the whole point of Lord Fraser's reference was to express his opinion that the very strict principles laid down in the *Canada Steamship Lines* case as applicable to exclusion and indemnity clauses cannot be applied in their full rigour to limitation clauses. Lord Wilberforce's speech contains a passage to the like effect, and Lord Elwyn-Jones, Lord Salmon and Lord Lowry agreed with both speeches. Having once reached a conclusion in the instant case that the relevant condition unambiguously limited the appellants' liability, I know of no principle of construction which can properly be applied to confine the effect of the limitation to breaches of contract arising without negligence on the part of the appellants. In agreement with Lord Denning M.R., I would decide the common law issue in the appellants' favour.

Lord Diplock delivered a short concurring speech. **Lords Scarman, Roskill** and **Brightman** concurred.

NOTES

1.   On the common law construction issue, this case is important for three reasons. First, it approves the view in *Ailsa Craig Fishing Co Ltd v Malvern Fishing Co Ltd*, referred to by Lord Bridge as *Securicor 2*, that limitation clauses should be less strictly construed than exclusion clauses: see above, 235–237. Secondly, it provides a good illustration of a clause applying, as a matter of construction, to limit liability for even a 'fundamental breach': see above, 231–235. Thirdly, and more generally, it supports the view that, subsequent to UCTA 1977, there is no need to adopt a strained construction of exclusion and limitation clauses. Lord Diplock, approving Lord Denning MR's approach in the Court of Appeal in this case, said at 810 that 'the passing of the ...Unfair Contract Terms Act 1977 had removed from judges the temptation to resort to the device of ascribing to words appearing in exemption clauses a tortured meaning so as to avoid giving effect to an exclusion or limitation of liability when the judge thought that in the circumstances to do so would be unfair'.

2.   For the application of the statutory reasonableness test in this case, see below, 269.

Additional Reading for Chapter 5

J Beatson, *Anson's Law of Contract* (28th edn, 2002) 160–3, 169–77

S Smith, *Atiyah's Introduction to the Law of Contract* (6th edn, 2005) 146–54

G McMeel, 'Prior Negotiations and Subsequent Conduct—the Next Step Forward for Contractual Interpretation' (2003) 119 *LQR* 272

In the light of the *Investors Compensation Scheme* case, this article examines the arguments for and against the two well-established restrictions (prior negotiations and declarations of subjective intent; and subsequent conduct) on the evidence available in construing a contract. McMeel persuasively concludes that both restrictions should be departed from. 'The best way forward is for the matter to be one of weight rather than admissibility' (at 296).

Lord Nicholls, 'My Kingdom for a Horse: The Meaning of Words' (2005) 121 *LQR* 577

Lord Nicholls examines what is meant by the objective interpretation of contracts and, in looking at the case for and against, argues that evidence of prior negotiations and subsequent conduct should be admissible in construing a contract. He points out that evidence of prior negotiations is already admissible where rectification is sought and in cases like *The Karen Oltmann* [1976] 2 Lloyd's Rep 708 (where the parties agreed what should be meant by a word that would otherwise be ambiguous). Moreover, the courts are well-accustomed to deciding the important question of the weight to be placed on admissible evidence.

R Calnan, 'Construction of Commercial Contracts: A Practitioner's Perspective' in *Contract Terms* (eds A Burrows and E Peel, 2007) 17

In approaching the matter from the perspective of someone who drafts contracts, the author argues that the decision in *Investors Compensation Scheme* has gone too far in liberalising construction, thereby causing undesirable uncertainty. He favours a mid-position between the old literal approach and *ICS* so that it is only where, taking account of the context, the meaning of the words is ambiguous that the courts should choose a meaning. He also suggests that draftsmen should be careful about being too one-sided in their drafting lest the courts 'cut down' their clear words.

E Peel, 'Whither *Contra Proferentem?*' in *Contract Terms* (eds A Burrows and E Peel, 2007) 53

Peel argues that the courts are justified in continuing to construe exemption clauses against those who seek to rely on them. He recognises that this requires separating out exemption clauses from the primary obligations owed and argues that this is acceptable albeit that it runs counter to the thesis of Coote (that 'exemption clauses' merely go to define the primary obligations owed).

Principles of European Contract Law (eds O Lando and H Beale, 2000) 287–94

Article 5:101: General Rules of Interpretation
(1) A contract is to be interpreted according to the common intention of the parties even if this differs from the literal meaning of the words.

(2) If it is established that one party intended the contract to have a particular meaning, and at the time of the conclusion of the contract the other party could not have been unaware of the first party's intention, the contract is to be interpreted in the way intended by the first party.

(3) If an intention cannot be established according to (1) or (2), the contract is to be interpreted according to the meaning that reasonable persons of the same kind as the parties would give to it in the same circumstances.

Article 5:102: Relevant Circumstances
In interpreting the contract, regard shall be had, in particular, to:

(a) the circumstances in which it was concluded, including the preliminary negotiations;

(b) the conduct of the parties, even subsequent to the conclusion of the contract;

(c) the nature and purpose of the contract;

(d) the interpretation which has already been given to similar clauses by the parties and the practices they have established between themselves;

(e) the meaning commonly given to terms and expressions in the branch of activity concerned and the interpretation similar clauses may already have received;

(f) usages; and

(g) good faith and fair dealing

Article 5:103: Contra Proferentem Rule
Where there is doubt about the meaning of a contract term not individually negotiated, an interpretation of the term against the party which supplied it is to be preferred.

[The main contrast to the general English law on construction is that regard is to be had to preliminary negotiations and subsequent conduct (see above, 222, note 6); and good faith and fair dealing are overtly relevant.]

6

Statutory Control of Unfair Terms

Since the middle of the twentieth century the courts have been concerned with abuses that can arise where a party excludes or limits its liability. This has especially been a concern in relation to standard form contracts between businesses and consumers. At common law, the courts have had no direct techniques to knock down such clauses as being unfair. Instead, as we have seen in parts of the previous two chapters, two main methods have been relied on to control such clauses. The first has been to hold that the clause is not incorporated into the contract and therefore of no effect. The second has been to construe the clause as not applying to the particular facts. Neither of those techniques directly looks at, or responds to, the unfairness of the clause in question. They are therefore blunt 'over-inclusive' techniques which, while allowing some flexibility to the courts, can operate to strike down fair and unfair clauses alike.

It became clear in the 1970s that what was needed was a power for the judges to appraise directly the fairness or reasonableness of exclusion and limitation clauses. Following the work of the Law Commission, the Unfair Contract Terms Act 1977 was therefore passed. In addition to some clauses being rendered automatically invalid (ie irrespective of the application of a reasonableness test) this Act gives direct power to the judges to declare as invalid exclusion and limitation clauses (and indemnity clauses) that fail to pass a test of reasonableness.

More recently, the Legislature has gone even further and, in accordance with the requirements of the European Union, has implemented the Unfair Terms in Consumer Contracts Regulations 1999 (first introduced in 1994 but amended in 1999). The coverage of the regulations extends beyond exclusion, limitation and indemnity clauses to strike down all non-core unfair terms in a contract; but, in contrast to UCTA 1977, the regulations apply only to protect consumers.

This chapter primarily examines these two pieces of legislation and the courts' interpretation of them. However, it is important to bear in mind that the two common law techniques of non-incorporation and construction remain in play. It is only if a clause is incorporated and as a matter of construction applies to the facts that one needs to go on to address whether it is invalidated by statute. In considering the potential invalidity of a term, one should therefore first go through those two common law techniques. Having said that, as we have seen in Chapters 4 and 5 (see 186, note 1; 231, note 3; 240, note 1) it may be that the courts are more relaxed in ruling that a clause is incorporated, and as a matter of construction applies, given the statutory power that they now have to strike down clauses that are unreasonable or unfair.

The final short section of this chapter looks at the Law Commission's proposals for reform of the legislation on unfair terms.

Introductory reading: E McKendrick, *Contract Law* (7th edn, 2007) 11.9–11.16, 17.6

1. THE UNFAIR CONTRACT TERMS ACT 1977

The Unfair Contract Terms Act 1977, sections 1–14, 26–27, 29, Schedules 1 and 2

PART I AMENDMENT OF LAW FOR ENGLAND AND WALES AND NORTHERN IRELAND

Introductory

1 Scope of Part I

(1) For the purposes of this Part of this Act, "negligence" means the breach—

(a)   of any obligation, arising from the express or implied terms of a contract, to take reasonable care or exercise reasonable skill in the performance of the contract;

(b)   of any common law duty to take reasonable care or exercise reasonable skill (but not any stricter duty);

(c)   of the common duty of care imposed by the Occupiers' Liability Act 1957 or the Occupiers' Liability Act (Northern Ireland) 1957.

(2) This Part of this Act is subject to Part III; and in relation to contracts, the operation of sections 2 to 4 and 7 is subject to the exceptions made by Schedule 1.

(3) In the case of both contract and tort, sections 2 to 7 apply (except where the contrary is stated in section 6(4)) only to business liability, that is liability for breach of obligations or duties arising—

(a)   from things done or to be done by a person in the course of a business (whether his own business or another's); or

(b)   from the occupation of premises used for business purposes of the occupier; and references to liability are to be read accordingly [but liability of an occupier of premises for breach of an obligation or duty towards a person obtaining access to the premises for recreational or educational purposes, being liability for loss or damage suffered by reason of the dangerous state of the premises, is not a business liability of the occupier unless granting that person such access for the purposes concerned falls within the business purposes of the occupier].

(4) In relation to any breach of duty or obligation, it is immaterial for any purpose of this Part of this Act whether the breach was inadvertent or intentional, or whether liability for it arises directly or vicariously.

Avoidance of liability for negligence, breach of contract, etc

2 Negligence liability

(1) A person cannot by reference to any contract term or to a notice given to persons generally or to particular persons exclude or restrict his liability for death or personal injury resulting from negligence.

(2) In the case of other loss or damage, a person cannot so exclude or restrict his liability for negligence except in so far as the term or notice satisfies the requirement of reasonableness.

(3) Where a contract term or notice purports to exclude or restrict liability for negligence a person's agreement to or awareness of it is not of itself to be taken as indicating his voluntary acceptance of any risk.

3 Liability arising in contract

(1) This section applies as between contracting parties where one of them deals as consumer or on the other's written standard terms of business.

(2) As against that party, the other cannot by reference to any contract term—

(a)   when himself in breach of contract, exclude or restrict any liability of his in respect of the breach; or

(b)   claim to be entitled—

(i)   to render a contractual performance substantially different from that which was reasonably expected of him, or

(ii)   in respect of the whole or any part of his contractual obligation, to render no performance at all,

except in so far as (in any of the cases mentioned above in this subsection) the contract term satisfies the requirement of reasonableness.

4 Unreasonable indemnity clauses

(1) A person dealing as consumer cannot by reference to any contract term be made to indemnify another person (whether a party to the contract or not) in respect of liability that may be incurred by the other for negligence or breach of contract, except in so far as the contract term satisfies the requirement of reasonableness.

(2) This section applies whether the liability in question—

(a)   is directly that of the person to be indemnified or is incurred by him vicariously;

(b)   is to the person dealing as consumer or to someone else.

Liability arising from sale or supply of goods

5 "Guarantee" of consumer goods

(1) In the case of goods of a type ordinarily supplied for private use or consumption, where loss or damage—

(a)   arises from the goods proving defective while in consumer use; and

(b)   results from the negligence of a person concerned in the manufacture or distribution of the goods, liability for the loss or damage cannot be excluded or restricted by reference to any contract term or notice contained in or operating by reference to a guarantee of the goods.

(2) For these purposes—

(a)   goods are to be regarded as "in consumer use" when a person is using them, or has them in his possession for use, otherwise than exclusively for the purposes of a business; and

(b)   anything in writing is a guarantee if it contains or purports to contain some promise or assurance (however worded or presented) that defects will be made good by complete or partial replacement, or by repair, monetary compensation or otherwise.

(3) This section does not apply as between the parties to a contract under or in pursuance of which possession or ownership of the goods passed.

6 Sale and hire-purchase

(1) Liability for breach of the obligations arising from—

(a)   [section 12 of the Sale of Goods Act 1979] (seller's implied undertakings as to title, etc);

(b)   section 8 of the Supply of Goods (Implied Terms) Act 1973 (the corresponding thing in relation to hire-purchase),

cannot be excluded or restricted by reference to any contract term.

(2) As against a person dealing as consumer, liability for breach of the obligations arising from—

(a)   [section 13, 14 or 15 of the 1979 Act] (seller's implied undertakings as to conformity of goods with description or sample, or as to their quality or fitness for a particular purpose);

(b)   section 9, 10 or 11 of the 1973 Act (the corresponding things in relation to hire-purchase),

cannot be excluded or restricted by reference to any contract term.

(3) As against a person dealing otherwise than as consumer, the liability specified in subsection (2) above can be excluded or restricted by reference to a contract term, but only in so far as the term satisfies the requirement of reasonableness.

(4) The liabilities referred to in this section are not only the business liabilities defined by section 1(3), but include those arising under any contract of sale of goods or hire-purchase agreement.

7 Miscellaneous contracts under which goods pass

(1) Where the possession or ownership of goods passes under or in pursuance of a contract not governed by the law of sale of goods or hire-purchase, subsections (2) to (4) below apply as regards the effect (if any) to be given to contract terms excluding or restricting liability for breach of obligation arising by implication of law from the nature of the contract.

(2) As against a person dealing as consumer, liability in respect of the goods' correspondence with description or sample, or their quality or fitness for any particular purpose, cannot be excluded or restricted by reference to any such term.

(3) As against a person dealing otherwise than as consumer, that liability can be excluded or restricted by reference to such a term, but only in so far as the term satisfies the requirement of reasonableness.

[(3A) Liability for breach of the obligations arising under section 2 of the Supply of Goods and Services Act 1982 (implied terms about title etc in certain contracts for the transfer of the property in goods) cannot be excluded or restricted by references to any such term.]

(4) Liability in respect of—

(a)   the right to transfer ownership of the goods, or give possession; or

(b)   the assurance of quiet possession to a person taking goods in pursuance of the contract,

cannot [(in a case to which subsection (3A) above does not apply)] be excluded or restricted by reference to any such term except in so far as the term satisfies the requirement of reasonableness.

[(5) . . .]

Other provisions about contracts

8 Misrepresentation

[*This section inserted a new provision for section 3 of the Misrepresentation Act 1967: see below, 580.*]

9 Effect of breach

(1) Where for reliance upon it a contract term has to satisfy the requirement of reasonableness, it may be found to do so and be given effect accordingly notwithstanding that the contract has been terminated either by breach or by a party electing to treat it as repudiated.

(2) Where on a breach the contract is nevertheless affirmed by a party entitled to treat it as repudiated, this does not of itself exclude the requirement of reasonableness in relation to any contract term.

10 Evasion by means of secondary contract

A person is not bound by any contract term prejudicing or taking away rights of his which arise under, or in connection with the performance of, another contract, so far as those rights extend to the enforcement of another's liability which this Part of this Act prevents that other from excluding or restricting.

Explanatory provisions

11 The "reasonableness" test

(1) In relation to a contract term, the requirement of reasonableness for the purposes of this Part of this Act, section 3 of the Misrepresentation Act 1967 and section 3 of the Misrepresentation Act (Northern Ireland) 1967 is that the term shall have been a fair and reasonable one to be included having regard to the circumstances which were, or ought reasonably to have been, known to or in the contemplation of the parties when the contract was made.

(2) In determining for the purposes of section 6 or 7 above whether a contract term satisfies the requirement of reasonableness, regard shall be had in particular to the matters specified in Schedule 2 to this Act; but this subsection does not prevent the court or arbitrator from holding, in accordance with any rule of law, that a term which purports to exclude or restrict any relevant liability is not a term of the contract.

(3) In relation to a notice (not being a notice having contractual effect), the requirement of reasonableness under this Act is that it should be fair and reasonable to allow reliance on it, having regard to all the circumstances obtaining when the liability arose or (but for the notice) would have arisen.

(4) Where by reference to a contract term or notice a person seeks to restrict liability to a specified sum of money, and the question arises (under this or any other Act) whether the term or notice satisfies the requirement of reasonableness, regard shall be had in particular (but without prejudice to subsection (2) above in the case of contract terms) to—

(a) the resources which he could expect to be available to him for the purpose of meeting the liability should it arise; and

(b) how far it was open to him to cover himself by insurance.

(5) It is for those claiming that a contract term or notice satisfies the requirement of reasonableness to show that it does.

12 "Dealing as consumer"
(1) A party to a contract "deals as consumer" in relation to another party if—

(a) he neither makes the contract in the course of a business nor holds himself out as doing so; and

(b) the other party does make the contract in the course of a business; and

(c) in the case of a contract governed by the law of sale of goods or hire-purchase, or by section 7 of this Act, the goods passing under or in pursuance of the contract are of a type ordinarily supplied for private use or consumption.

[(1A) But if the first party mentioned in subsection (1) is an individual paragraph (c) of that subsection must be ignored.]
[(2) But the buyer is not in any circumstances to be regarded as dealing as consumer—

(a) if he is an individual and the goods are second hand goods sold at public auction at which individuals have the opportunity of attending the sale in person;

(b) if he is not an individual and the goods are sold by auction or by competitive tender.]

(3) Subject to this, it is for those claiming that a party does not deal as consumer to show that he does not.

13 Varieties of exemption clause
(1) To the extent that this Part of this Act prevents the exclusion or restriction of any liability it also prevents—

(a) making the liability or its enforcement subject to restrictive or onerous conditions;

(b) excluding or restricting any right or remedy in respect of the liability, or subjecting a person to any prejudice in consequence of his pursuing any such right or remedy;

(c) excluding or restricting rules of evidence or procedure;

and (to that extent) sections 2 and 5 to 7 also prevent excluding or restricting liability by reference to terms and notices which exclude or restrict the relevant obligation or duty.

(2) But an agreement in writing to submit present or future differences to arbitration is not to be treated under this Part of this Act as excluding or restricting any liability.

14 Interpretation of Part I
In this Part of this Act—

— "business" includes a profession and the activities of any government department or local or public authority;

— "goods" has the same meaning as in [the Sale of Goods Act 1979]:

— "hire-purchase agreement" has the same meaning as in the Consumer Credit Act 1974;

— "negligence" has the meaning given by section 1(1);

— "notice" includes an announcement, whether or not in writing, and any other communication or pretended communication; and

— "personal injury" includes any disease and any impairment of physical or mental condition.

PART III PROVISIONS APPLYING TO WHOLE OF UNITED KINGDOM

Miscellaneous

26 International supply contracts

(1) The limits imposed by this Act on the extent to which a person may exclude or restrict liability by reference to a contract term do not apply to liability arising under such a contract as is described in subsection (3) below.

(2) The terms of such a contract are not subject to any requirement of reasonableness under section 3 or 4: and nothing in Part II of this Act shall require the incorporation of the terms of such a contract to be fair and reasonable for them to have effect.

(3) Subject to subsection (4), that description of contract is one whose characteristics are the following—

(a) either it is a contract of sale of goods or it is one under or in pursuance of which the possession or ownership of goods passes; and

(b) it is made by parties whose places of business (or, if they have none, habitual residences) are in the territories of different States (the Channel Islands and the Isle of Man being treated for this purpose as different States from the United Kingdom).

(4) A contract falls within subsection (3) above only if either—

(a) the goods in question are, at the time of the conclusion of the contract, in the course of carriage, or will be carried, from the territory of one State to the territory of another; or

(b) the acts constituting the offer and acceptance have been done in the territories of different States; or

(c) the contract provides for the goods to be delivered to the territory of a State other than that within whose territory those acts were done.

27 Choice of law clauses

(1) Where the [law applicable to] a contract is the law of any part of the United Kingdom only by choice of the parties (and apart from that choice would be the law of some country outside the United Kingdom) sections 2 to 7 and 16 to 21 of this Act do not operate as part [of the law applicable to the contract].

(2) This Act has effect notwithstanding any contract term which applies or purports to apply the law of some country outside the United Kingdom, where (either or both)—

(a) the term appears to the court, or arbitrator or arbiter to have been imposed wholly or mainly for the purpose of enabling the party imposing it to evade the operation of this Act; or

(b) in the making of the contract one of the parties dealt as consumer, and he was then habitually resident in the United Kingdom, and the essential steps necessary for the making of the contract were taken there, whether by him or by others on his behalf.

(3) ...

29 Saving for other relevant legislation

(1) Nothing in this Act removes or restricts the effect of, or prevents reliance upon, any contractual provision which—

(a)   is authorised or required by the express terms or necessary implication of an enactment; or

(b)   being made with a view to compliance with an international agreement to which the United Kingdom is a party, does not operate more restrictively than is contemplated by the agreement.

(2) A contract term is to be taken—

(a)   for the purposes of Part I of this Act, as satisfying the requirement of reasonableness; ...

(b)   ...

if it is incorporated or approved by, or incorporated pursuant to a decision or ruling of, a competent authority acting in the exercise of any statutory jurisdiction or function and is not a term in a contract to which the competent authority is itself a party.

(3) In this section—

— "competent authority" means any court, arbitrator or arbiter, government department or public authority;

— "enactment" means any legislation (including subordinate legislation) of the United Kingdom or Northern Ireland and any instrument having effect by virtue of such legislation; and

— "statutory" means conferred by an enactment.

SCHEDULE 1 SCOPE OF SECTIONS 2 TO 4 AND 7

1
Sections 2 to 4 of this Act do not extend to—

(a)   any contract of insurance (including a contract to pay an annuity on human life);

(b)   any contract so far as it relates to the creation or transfer of an interest in land, or to the termination of such an interest, whether by extinction, merger, surrender, forfeiture or otherwise;

(c)   any contract so far as it relates to the creation or transfer of a right or interest in any patent, trade mark, copyright [or design right], registered design, technical or commercial information or other intellectual property, or relates to the termination of any such right or interest;

(d)   any contract so far as it relates—

(i)   to the formation or dissolution of a company (which means any body corporate or unincorporated association and includes a partnership), or

(ii)   to its constitution or the rights or obligations of its corporators or members;

(e)   any contract so far as it relates to the creation or transfer of securities or of any right or interest in securities.

2

Section 2(1) extends to—

(a)   any contract of marine salvage or towage;
(b)   any charterparty of a ship or hovercraft; and
(c)   any contract for the carriage of goods by ship or hovercraft;

but subject to this sections 2 to 4 and 7 do not extend to any such contract except in favour of a person dealing as consumer.

3

Where goods are carried by ship or hovercraft in pursuance of a contract which either—

(a)   specifies that as the means of carriage over part of the journey to be covered, or
(b)   makes no provision as to the means of carriage and does not exclude that means,

then sections 2(2), 3 and 4 do not, except in favour of a person dealing as consumer, extend to the contract as it operates for and in relation to the carriage of the goods by that means.

4

Section 2(1) and (2) do not extend to a contract of employment, except in favour of the employee.

5

Section 2(1) does not affect the validity of any discharge and indemnity given by a person, on or in connection with an award to him of compensation for pneumoconiosis attributable to employment in the coal industry, in respect of any further claim arising from his contracting that disease.

SCHEDULE 2 "GUIDELINES" FOR APPLICATION OF REASONABLENESS TEST

The matters to which regard is to be had in particular for the purposes of sections 6(3), 7(3) and (4) ... are any of the following which appear to be relevant—

(a)   the strength of the bargaining positions of the parties relative to each other, taking into account (among other things) alternative means by which the customer's requirements could have been met;
(b)   whether the customer received an inducement to agree to the term, or in accepting it had an opportunity of entering into a similar contract with other persons, but without having to accept a similar term;
(c)   whether the customer knew or ought reasonably to have known of the existence and extent of the term (having regard, among other things, to any custom of the trade and any previous course of dealing between the parties);
(d)   where the term excludes or restricts any relevant liability if some condition is not complied with, whether it was reasonable at the time of the contract to expect that compliance with that condition would be practicable;
(e)   whether the goods were manufactured, processed or adapted to the special order of the customer.

(1) Overview of the Central Scheme of UCTA 1977

As with many statutes, one can quickly become 'bogged down' in the detail of UCTA 1977. However, the Act's central scheme is relatively straightforward and can be presented in the following eight points (in which 'defendant' refers to the party seeking to rely on the clause in question):

(i)   UCTA 1977 renders invalid certain exclusion or limitation clauses. Some are rendered automatically invalid (ie irrespective of applying a reasonableness test). Most are invalid only if they are unreasonable.

(ii)   By section 1(3), the defendant's liability must be 'business liability' (other than in contracts for the sale of goods or hire purchase). This basically means that the liability must have arisen while the defendant was acting 'in the course of a business'.

(iii) By section 2(1), a clause excluding or limiting liability for negligently caused death or personal injury is invalid. By section 2(2), a clause excluding or limiting liability for other negligently caused loss is invalid unless it satisfies the test of reasonableness in section 11(1). By section 1(1), 'negligence' means the tort of negligence (or the analogous tortious liability under the Occupiers' Liability Act 1957) or breach of a contractual duty of reasonable care and skill.

(iv)   By section 3, provided the claimant is dealing as consumer or on the defendant's written standard terms of business, an exclusion or limitation of liability for breach of a strict contractual obligation is invalid unless it satisfies the test of reasonableness in section 11(1).

(v)   The reasonableness test in section 11(1) is whether the term was 'a fair and reasonable one to be included'; and by section 11(5) the burden of showing this is on the defendant. As regards exclusion clauses, there are no direct statutory guidelines for the reasonableness test but the courts have indicated that the guidelines in Schedule 2 (which directly apply to contracts of sale and other contracts in which goods pass) may be applied by analogy to other contracts. For limitation clauses, the courts in applying the reasonableness test are required under section 11(4) to have particular regard to the defendant's resources and whether it could have been insured against liability.

(vi)   Some types of contract are excluded from UCTA 1977. These include, by section 26, international supply contracts and, by Schedule 1, insurance contracts and contracts relating to the creation or transfer of an interest in land or an intellectual property right.

(vii) Contrary to what its title suggests, UCTA 1977 is not purely concerned with invalidating contract terms. Non-contractual notices are also covered. So, eg, a business occupier's notice seeking to exclude or limit its liability for injury or property damage suffered by visitors to the land is caught by section 2. For non-contractual notices, the relevant reasonableness test is that in section 11(3). This is that it should be 'fair and reasonable to allow reliance on it'.

(viii) Apart from exclusion and limitation clauses, UCTA 1977 renders certain indemnity clauses invalid. An indemnity clause is one by which a person promises to 'cover' another against that other's legal liability to the promisor or to someone else. For example, the owner of land on which a new house is being constructed may contract to indemnify the builder against the builder's liability for property damage or personal injury (whether suffered by the owner or a third party) caused by the builder's breach of contract or negligence. Provided the indemnification is against 'business liability' (section 1(3)), by section 4 a clause under which a person, dealing as consumer, is to indemnify another is invalid unless it satisfies the test of reasonableness in section 11(1).

(2) Excluding Liability for Breach of the Statutory Implied Terms in Contracts for the Sale of Goods and Analogous Contracts

We have seen at 213–216 above that terms as to title, description, quality, fitness and sample are implied by the Sale of Goods Act 1979 sections 12–15 into contracts for the sale of goods; and that analogous terms are implied into contracts for the hire-purchase of goods by the Supply of Goods (Implied Terms) Act 1973, sections 8–11; into contracts for the hire of goods by the Supply of Goods and Services Act 1982, sections 7–10; and into contracts for work and materials, in relation to the materials supplied, by the Supply of Goods and Services Act 1982, sections 2–5. Sections 6 and 7 of UCTA 1977 provide a special regime for clauses excluding or limiting liability for the breach of those implied terms. This regime is as follows:

(i)   For hire contracts and contracts for work and materials in which property passes, the defendant's liability must, as usual under UCTA 1977, be 'business liability'. By section 6(4), this is not so for sale and hire-purchase contracts: as a starting point, therefore, the person seeking to exclude liability need not be acting in the course of a business (but this has limited effect because, first, the terms as to satisfactory quality and fitness for purpose are implied only where the seller sells the goods in the course of a business; and, secondly, section 6(2) applies only where the claimant deals as consumer and the definition of deals as consumer in section 12 requires that the other party is acting in the course of a business).

(ii)   By sections 6(1) and 7(3A), a clause excluding or limiting liability for breach of the implied terms about title etc is automatically invalid in contracts of sale, hire-purchase or for work and materials. For contracts of hire, a clause excluding or restricting liability for the equivalent implied term as to title etc is invalid unless it satisfies the test of reasonableness in section 11(1) and (2).

(iii) By sections 6(2) and 7(2), a clause excluding or limiting liability for breach of the implied terms as to description, quality, fitness and sample is automatically invalid as against a person dealing as consumer.

(iv)   By sections 6(3) and 7(3), a clause excluding or limiting liability for breach of the implied terms as to description, quality, fitness and sample is invalid as against a person dealing otherwise than as consumer unless it satisfies the test of reasonableness in section 11(1) and (2).

(v)   While the reasonableness test and the burden of proof are the same as for the rest of the Act, section 11(2) lays down that, for the purposes of sections 6 and

7, regard must be paid to the guidelines for applying the reasonableness test in Schedule 2. That is, the guidelines here apply directly rather than indirectly.

(3) Cases on UCTA 1977

The major cases on UCTA 1977 have focussed on three principal issues: (a) what is meant by 'dealing as consumer'?; (b) what counts as an exclusion of liability, or as equivalent to such an exclusion, so as to fall within the Act?; and, most importantly, (c) does the clause pass or fail the reasonableness test?
    We shall examine each of these in turn.

(a) What is Meant by 'Dealing as Consumer'?

The words 'dealing as consumer' in section 3 (and elsewhere in the Act) are explained further in section 12. At heart, they require that the person in question is not making the contract in the course of a business whereas the other party is. As one can see from the Act, many of the statutory controls are not confined to protecting consumers: eg section 2(2), and section 3 in so far as the claimant was dealing on the other's written standard terms of business. That UCTA 1977 is not confined to protecting consumers represents an important contrast with the Unfair Terms in Consumer Contracts Regulations 1999 which are purely concerned with protecting consumers and do not apply in business to business contracts. Indeed, the contrast is even more pronounced than might at first sight appear because, as we shall now see, the courts have given a wide meaning to 'dealing as consumer' so that, in contrast to the 1999 Regulations, a company can be a consumer.

R & B Customs Brokers Co Ltd v United Dominions Trust Ltd
[1988] 1 WLR 321, Court of Appeal

The claimant company was in business as a shipping broker and freight forwarding agent. It had bought a car from the defendant finance company under a conditional sale agreement. This was a 'company car' to be driven by the managing director, Mr Bell. The roof leaked and it was not in dispute that there was therefore a breach of at least the implied condition in section 14(3) of the Sale of Goods Act 1979 that the car should be fit for its purpose. There was a clause in the contract excluding that liability. The Court of Appeal held that, while that exclusion would have passed the reasonableness test, section 6(2) of UCTA 1977, not section 6(3), applied. That was because the claimant company, in buying the car, was dealing as consumer. Applying section 6(2), the exclusion was, therefore, automatically invalid.

Dillon LJ: "Dealing as a consumer" is defined in section 12 of the Act of 1977...[*He set out section 12 and continued:*]
    It is accepted that the conditions (*b*) and (*c*) in section 12(1) are satisfied. This issue turns on condition (*a*). Did the company neither make the contract with the defendants in the course of a business nor hold itself out as doing so?

In the present case there was no holding out beyond the mere facts that the contract and the finance application were made in the company's corporate name, and in the finance application the section headed "Business Details" was filled in to the extent of giving the nature of the company's business as that of shipping brokers, giving the number of years trading and the number of employees, and giving the names and addresses of the directors. What is important is whether the contract was made in the course of a business.

In a certain sense, however, from the very nature of a corporate entity, where a company which carries on a business makes a contract, it makes that contract in the course of its business; otherwise the contract would be ultra vires and illegal. Thus, where a company which runs a grocer's shop buys a new delivery van, it buys it in the course of its business. Where a merchant bank buys a car as a "company car" as a perquisite for a senior executive, it buys it in the course of its business. Where a farming company buys a landrover for the personal and company use of a farm manager, it again does so in the course of its business. Possible variations are numerous. In each case it would not be legal for the purchasing company to buy the vehicle in question otherwise than in the course of its business. Section 12 does not require that the business in the course of which the one party, referred to in condition (a), makes the contract must be of the same nature as the business in the course of which the other party, referred to in condition (b), makes the contract, e.g., that they should both be motor dealers.

...

[W]e have been referred to decisions under the Trade Descriptions Act 1968, and in particular to the decision of the House of Lords in *Davies v. Sumner* [1984] 1 W.L.R. 1301.

Under the Trade Descriptions Act 1968 any person who in the course of a trade or business applies a false trade description to goods is, subject to the provisions of the Act, guilty of an offence. It is a penal Act, whereas the Act of 1977 is not, and it is accordingly submitted that decisions on the construction of the Trade Descriptions Act 1968 cannot assist on the construction of section 12 of the Act of 1977. Also the legislative purposes of the two Acts are not the same. The primary purpose of the Trade Descriptions Act 1968 is consumer protection, and the course of business referred to is the course of business of the alleged wrongdoer. But the provisions as to dealing as a consumer in the Act of 1977 are concerned with differentiating between two classes of innocent contracting party—those who deal as consumers and those who do not—for whom differing degrees of protection against unfair contract terms are afforded by the Act of 1977. Despite these distinctions, however, it would, in my judgment, be unreal and unsatisfactory to conclude that the fairly ordinary words "in the course of business" bear a significantly different meaning in, on the one hand, the Trade Descriptions Act 1968, and, on the other hand, section 12 of the Act of 1977. In particular I would be very reluctant to conclude that these words bear a significantly wider meaning in section 12 than in the Trade Descriptions Act 1968.

I turn therefore to *Davies v. Sumner* [1984] 1 W.L.R. 1301. That case was not concerned with a company, but with an individual who had used a car for the purposes of his business as a self-employed courier. When he sold the car by trading it in part exchange for a new one, he had applied a false trade description to it by falsely representing the mileage the car had travelled to have been far less than it actually was. Lord Keith of Kinkel, who delivered the only speech in the House of Lords, commented, at p. 1304F, that it was clear that the transaction—sc. of trading in the car on the purchase of a new one—was reasonably incidental to the carrying on of the business, but he went on to say, at p. 1305:

> "Any disposal of a chattel held for the purposes of a business may, in a certain sense, be said to have been in the course of that business, irrespective of whether the chattel was acquired with a view to resale or for consumption or as a capital asset. But in my opinion section 1(1) of the Act is not intended to cast such a wide net as this. The expression 'in the course of a trade or business' in the context of an Act having consumer protection as its primary purpose conveys the concept of some degree of regularity, and it is to be observed that the long title to the Act refers to 'misdescriptions of goods, services,

accommodation and facilities provided in the course of trade.' Lord Parker C.J. in the *Havering* case [1970] 1 W.L.R. 1375 clearly considered that the expression was not used in the broadest sense. The reason why the transaction there in issue was caught was that in his view it was 'an integral part of the business carried on as a car hire firm.' That would not cover the sporadic selling off of pieces of equipment which were no longer required for the purposes of a business. The vital feature of the *Havering* case appears to have been, in Lord Parker's view, that the defendant's business *as part of its normal practice* bought and disposed of cars. The need for some degree of regularity does not, however, involve that a one-off adventure in the nature of trade, carried through with a view to profit, would not fall within section 1(1) because such a transaction would itself constitute a trade."

Lord Keith then held that the requisite degree of regularity had not been established on the facts of *Davies v. Sumner* because a normal practice of buying and disposing of cars had not yet been established at the time of the alleged offence. He pointed out for good measure that the disposal of the car was not a disposal of stock in trade of the business, but he clearly was not holding that only a disposal of stock in trade could be a disposal in the course of a trade or business.

Lord Keith emphasised the need for some degree of regularity, and he found pointers to this in the primary purpose and long title of the Trade Descriptions Act 1968. I find pointers to a similar need for regularity under the Act of 1977, where matters merely incidental to the carrying on of a business are concerned, both in the words which I would emphasise, "in the course of" in the phrase "in the course of a business" and in the concept, or legislative purpose, which must underlie the dichotomy under the Act of 1977 between those who deal as consumers and those who deal otherwise than as consumers.

This reasoning leads to the conclusion that, in the Act of 1977 also, the words "in the course of business" are not used in what Lord Keith called "the broadest sense." I also find helpful the phrase used by Lord Parker C.J. and quoted by Lord Keith, "an integral part of the business carried on." The reconciliation between that phrase and the need for some degree of regularity is, as I see it, as follows: there are some transactions which are clearly integral parts of the businesses concerned, and these should be held to have been carried out in the course of those businesses; this would cover, apart from much else, the instance of a one-off adventure in the nature of trade, where the transaction itself would constitute a trade or business. There are other transactions, however, such as the purchase of the car in the present case, which are at highest only incidental to the carrying on of the relevant business; here a degree of regularity is required before it can be said that they are an integral part of the business carried on, and so entered into in the course of that business.

Applying the test thus indicated to the facts of the present case, I have no doubt that the requisite degree of regularity is not made out on the facts. Mr. Bell's evidence that the car was the second or third vehicle acquired on credit terms was in my judgment and in the context of this case not enough. Accordingly, I agree with the judge that, in entering into the conditional sale agreement with the defendants, the company was "dealing as consumer." The defendants' condition 2(a) is thus inapplicable and the defendants are not absolved from liability under section 14(3).

There is a different approach which I would wish to leave open for a future case since it was not argued before us. If the company had never been incorporated and Mr. Bell had bought the car personally for personal (or domestic) and business use, it would, I apprehend, have been difficult to argue that he had not been dealing as a consumer in buying the car. On facts such as those of the present case it would seem anomalous and in some measure disquieting if a different result were reached if the car was bought by a company for the personal and business use of its two directors. It occurs to me that in such circumstances it could well be appropriate to pierce the corporate veil and look at the realities of the situation as in *D.H.N. Food Distributors Ltd. v. Tower Hamlets London*

Borough Council [1976] 1 W.L.R. 852; see especially the comments of Lord Denning M.R., at p. 860, and Goff L.J., at p. 861.

Neill LJ delivered a concurring judgment.

NOTES AND QUESTIONS

1. The company was 'dealing as consumer' because the purchase of cars was neither clearly integral to its business nor carried out with such a degree of regularity as to go beyond being merely incidental to its business. Two criticisms might be made of this approach. First, it is strongly arguable that a company is always dealing in the course of business and can never be a consumer. Secondly, the purchase of the company car was, in any event, for purposes related to the business. Would it therefore be preferable to regard a person as 'dealing as consumer' where, first, he is a natural person who, secondly, is making the contract for purposes unrelated to his business? Is that interpretation open to the courts on the wording of UCTA 1977, section 12? Compare the definition of 'consumer' in the Unfair Terms in Consumer Contracts Regulations 1999, regulation 3(1) (below, 286).

2. Some doubt was *impliedly* cast on *R & B Customs Brokers v UDT* by the decision in *Stevenson v Rogers* [1999] QB 1028. It was there held that a trawlerman, selling his old fishing vessel, was acting 'in the course of a business' for the purpose of implying terms under section 14(2) of the Sale of Goods Act 1979 even though the sale was incidental to his business. However, this case was not concerned with UCTA 1977 as such and the Court of Appeal expressly distinguished *R & B Customs Brokers* on the basis that it was dealing with a different statutory provision.

3. An opportunity to reconsider *R & B Customs Brokers* arose, but was not taken, in *Feldarol Foundry plc v Hermes Leasing (London) Ltd* [2004] EWCA Civ 747. The claimant company, which was in the steel business, hire-purchased for their managing director an expensive company car from the defendant finance company. There was something wrong with the steering so that the defendant was in breach of the implied term as to the goods being of satisfactory quality which is implied into contracts of hire-purchase by section 10 of the Supply of Goods (Implied Terms) Act 1973. There was an exclusion of such liability, and one question was whether that exclusion was invalid, irrespective of reasonableness, by reason of section 6(2) of UCTA 1977. The Court of Appeal was urged by counsel for the defendant to reject *R & B Brokers* because inconsistent with *Stevenson v Rogers* and that it was unsatisfactory in any event for a company to be regarded as a consumer. But the Court of Appeal decided that there was no inconsistency between those decisions and held itself bound to follow *R & B Brokers* which was directly on point. The exclusion clause was therefore automatically invalid because the claimant company was dealing as consumer. Tuckey LJ said at [18], '*R & B Brokers* is binding on us. It is a reported decision that has stood unchallenged for more than 15 years, during which time the relevant provisions in the 1977 Act have stood unamended. If harmonisation of the various provisions dealing with consumer protection is

required, that is Parliament's job. If *R & B Brokers* is to be challenged, that cannot be done in this court.'

(b) What Counts as an Exclusion of Liability, or as Equivalent to such an Exclusion, so as to Fall within the Act?

One might have thought that what is meant by an exclusion or restriction of liability so as to fall within the scope of UCTA 1977 would have been a relatively straight-forward issue. In general, it is. However, in the cases extracted below, we shall see that arguments have been raised as to whether certain types of clauses are covered.

Phillips Products Ltd v Hyland [1987] 1 WLR 659, Court of Appeal

The second defendants, Hamstead, a plant hire company, hired out an excavator to the claimants together with the first defendant (Mr Hyland), a driver and operator. The excavator was for use in building an extension to the claimants' factory. While operating the excavator, the first defendant negligently damaged the claimants' building. In the claimants' action for damages for the tort of negligence, the issue was whether the second defendants could rely on condition 8 of the contract of hire. This read as follows:

> 'When a driver or operator is supplied by the owner to work the plant, he shall be under the direction and control of the hirer. Such drivers or operators shall for all purposes in connection with their employment in the working of the plant be regarded as the servants or agents of the hirer who alone shall be responsible for all claims arising in connection with the operation of the plant by the said drivers or operators...'

The trial judge decided that condition 8 was invalid to exclude liability because it was unreasonable under sections 2(2) and 11 of UCTA 1977. The second defendants were therefore liable. On their appeal, the Court of Appeal upheld the trial judge's decision. Here we look solely at the issues concerning what is meant by an exclusion of liability.

Slade LJ (giving the judgment of himself, **Neill J** and **Sir John Megaw**): The principal question arising on this appeal concerning the applicability or otherwise of the Act...itself gave rise to three issues. ...These three issues are: (i) on the admitted facts of the present case, was there on the part of Hamstead "negligence" within the definition of that word contained in section 1(1) of the Act? (ii) If the answer to (i) is "Yes," is clause 8 a contract term which, apart from the effect of the Act, can properly be said to "exclude or restrict" Hamstead's liability for negligence within the meaning of these words in section 2(2) of the Act? In considering this issue, it is necessary to bear in mind the concluding words of section 13(1) which bring within the ambit of section 2(2) terms "which exclude or restrict the relevant obligation or duty." (iii) If the answers to (i) and (ii) are both "Yes," does clause 8 satisfy the requirement of reasonableness, within the meaning of that phrase as used in the Act?

Issue (i)

As to (i), the argument for Hamstead is simple, and runs on these lines. If a claim is based on contract, "negligence" within the definition of section 1(1) (a) can have occurred only if there has been a breach of:

"any obligation, arising from the express or implied terms of a contract, to take reasonable care or exercise reasonable skill in the performance of the contract..."

So, it is said, if in the case of such a claim the contract has by its express terms excluded liability for negligence, there can ex hypothesi have been no breach of any obligation of the nature referred to in section 1(1)(*a*). The claim in the present case, as it happens, is of the nature referred to in section 1(1)(*b*); the breach of a common law duty to take reasonable care is alleged. Here, again, a similar argument is advanced. It is suggested that there can be no breach of a common law duty to take reasonable care, within the meaning of section 1(1)(*b*), by a party to a contract which contains a condition which purports to absolve him from liability for negligence.

These arguments, though superficially attractive, are in our judgment fallacious. If correct, they would make nonsense of the Act. They would mean that the very contractual term which pre-eminently is suitable to be subject to review for reasonableness under the Act would be taken out of its scope. The Act, however, is not nonsensical. Its purpose is not defeated by the wording of its first section. In our judgment, in considering whether there has been a breach of any obligation of the nature referred to in paragraph (*a*) or of any duty of the nature referred to in paragraphs (*b*) or (*c*), the court has to leave out of account, at this stage, the contract term which is relied on by the defence as defeating the plaintiffs' claim for breach of such obligation of such duty, and section 1(1) should be construed accordingly.

If any support were necessary for this construction of section 1(1), it is to be found in the concluding words of section 13(1) of the Act. For these words make it clear that section 2 is capable of negativing the effect of contract terms which purport to exclude or restrict "the relevant obligation or duty."

...

Accordingly, though the validity of clause 8 still remains to be considered, on the admitted facts of this case there was "negligence" on the part of Hamstead falling within section 1(1)(*b*) of the Act. This took the form of a breach (subject to the effect, if any, of clause 8) of Hamstead's common law duty to take reasonable care, by reason of the fact that Mr. Hyland who, subject to clause 8, was Hamstead's servant, had caused the loss to Phillips by his negligence in the performance of his duties as such servant. Issue (i) therefore has to be answered "Yes."

Issue (ii)

Issue (ii) brings us to section 2(2). Subsection (1) does not apply because there was, fortunately, no death or personal injury. Section 2(2), set out as incorporating the relevant wording of subsection (1), provides that in the case of other loss or damage a person cannot *by reference to any contract term* exclude or restrict his liability for negligence except in so far as the term satisfies the requirement of reasonableness. The argument for Hamstead is that they do not, by reference to clause 8, "*exclude or restrict*" their liability for negligence. Clause 8, it is stressed, is not an "excluding" or "restricting" clause. It may have an *effect* on the liability for negligence which would otherwise have existed if there were, as there was in the present case, negligence. (For "may" we would substitute "must" assuming that Hamstead's submission as to the validity of clause 8 is correct). Nevertheless, the clause does not, it is said, amount to an attempt by either party to the contract to "*exclude or restrict*" liability: it is simply an attempt on their part to divide and allocate the obligations or responsibilities arising in relation to the contract by *transferring* liability for the acts of the operator from the plant owners to the hirers. A transfer, it is suggested, is not an exclusion; hence the hirers fail at the section 2(2) hurdle.

[*Having examined* Spalding v Tarmac Civil Engineering Ltd *[1967] 1 WLR 1508, he continued:*] [T]here is nothing [in the *Spalding* case] which leads to the conclusion that a plant owner who uses the general conditions is not *excluding* his liability for negligence in the relevant sense by reference to the contract term clause 8. We are unable to accept that in the ordinary sensible meaning of words in the context of section 2 and the Act as a whole, the provisions of clause 8 do not fall within the scope of section 2(2). A transfer of liability from A. to B. necessarily and inevitably involves the exclusion of liability so far as A. is concerned. ...On the particular facts of this case the effect of clause 8, if valid, is to negative a common law liability in tort which would otherwise admittedly fall on the plant owner. The effect of clause 8 making "the hirer alone responsible for all claims" necessarily connotes that by the clause the plant owner's responsibility is excluded. In applying section 2(2), it is not relevant to consider whether the form of a condition is such that it can aptly be given the label of an "exclusion" or "restriction" clause. There is no mystique about "exclusion" or "restriction" clauses. To decide whether a person "excludes" liability by reference to a contract term, you look at the effect of the term. You look at its substance. The effect here is beyond doubt. Hamstead do most certainly purport to exclude their liability for negligence by *reference to* clause 8. Furthermore, clause 8 purports to "exclude or restrict the relevant obligation or duty" within the provisions of section 13(1) of the Act. Issue (ii) has to be answered "Yes."

NOTES AND QUESTIONS

1.   For the third issue—the application of the reasonableness test—see below, 271.
2.   Both the two issues in the above extract concerned the meaning of an exclusion of liability and hence went to whether section 2(2) of UCTA 1977 applied. The first raises the long-debated question of a duty-defining clause. On one extreme view, famously articulated by Professor Brian Coote, *Exception Clauses* (1964)—but rejected in this case—*all* exclusion clauses are best analysed as merely defining the relevant duty so that there is no breach. The draftsman of UCTA 1977 clearly did not subscribe to the Coote view and for the most part simply assumed the validity of the traditional two-stage 'breach and then exclusion' analysis. However, there are a few sections in the Act which directly seek to counter the 'duty-defining' analysis. One example, as referred to in this case, is section 13(1). Another example is section 3(2)(b), which ensures that duty-defining and other analogous clauses (eg a clause by which a holiday company reserves the right to substitute an alternative hotel if the original hotel booked is unavailable) are covered by section 3. For judicial consideration of the (problematic) limits of section 3(2)(b) see, eg, *Timeload Ltd v British Telecommunications plc* [1995] EMLR 459, CA; *Peninsula Business Services Ltd v Sweeney* [2004] IRLR 49, EAT.
3.   In relation to the second issue, the defendants argued that condition 8 transferred, rather than excluded, liability. Was the Court of Appeal correct to reject this argument? In considering this, it is helpful to compare the next case where the facts were different in one crucial respect.

Thompson v T Lohan (Plant Hire) Ltd [1987] 1 WLR 649, Court of Appeal

The first defendants (Lohan), a plant hire company, hired out an excavator with a driver and operator (Mr Hill) to JW Hurdiss Ltd (the third party) for use at Hurdiss' quarry. The claimant's husband was killed in an accident at the quarry caused by the operator's negligence for which the first defendants were vicariously liable. Condition 8 (set out above, 258) of the terms of the hire contract between the first defendants and Hurdiss said that the hirer (Hurdiss) alone should be responsible for all claims arising in connection with the operation of the plant by the drivers or operators.

Condition 13 provided that the hirer was to 'fully and completely indemnify the owner [the first defendants] in respect of all claims by any person whatsoever for injury to person or property caused by or in connection with or arising out of the use of the plant'. In reliance on conditions 8 and 13, the first defendants argued that their liability to the claimant (which they no longer disputed) had been transferred to Hurdiss and that Hurdiss was bound to indemnify them. So the dispute in question was between the first defendants and Hurdiss, not between the first defendants and the claimant. In upholding the trial judge, the Court of Appeal decided that the argument of the first defendants was correct and that UCTA 1977 section 2(1) had no application.

Fox LJ: It is said on behalf of the third party that, assuming clause 8 to be otherwise valid and effective according to its tenor (as I have found), it operates to exclude or restrict a liability for death or personal injury resulting from negligence; and that therefore it offends in this case the provisions of section 2(1) of the Act and is struck down.

We were referred to the decision of this court in *Phillips Products Ltd. v. Hyland (Note)* [1987] 1 W.L.R. 659. The case is concerned with the construction of the Act of 1977.

[*Having referred to the facts and arguments in that case he continued:*]

In giving the judgment of the Court of Appeal, Slade L.J. said [at] p. 665G-H.

"Certainly there is nothing which leads to the conclusion that a plant owner who uses the general conditions is not *excluding* his liability for negligence in the relevant sense by reference to the contract term clause 8. We are unable to accept that in the ordinary sensible meaning of words in the context of section 2 and the Act as a whole, the provisions of clause 8 do not fall within the scope of section 2(2). A transfer of liability from A. to B. necessarily and inevitably involves the exclusion of liability so far as A. is concerned."

It was held that, in the circumstances of that case, clause 8 could not operate, having regard to the provisions of section 2(2), to give an indemnity as claimed.

Mr. Samuels, for the third party, says that is the same in this case, and that the words from the judgment of Slade L.J. to which I have referred exactly cover the position here. It is said that there is a transfer of liability from Lohan to the third party, and that that is exactly what section 2(1) of the Act of 1977 is effective to prevent. In my view the comparison of this case with the *Phillips* case is not justified. It seems to me that the *Phillips* case was a quite different case, and the Court of Appeal was not addressing its mind to the problem which we have to determine in the present case.

In the *Phillips* case there was a tortfeasor, Hamstead, who were vicariously liable to Phillips for the damage done by their servant, Hyland. Thus Hamstead were liable to Phillips for negligence, but were seeking to exclude that liability by relying upon clause 8. If that reliance had been successful, the result in the *Phillips* case would be that the victim would be left with no remedy by virtue of the operation of clause 8. Prima facie the victim was entitled to damages for negligence against Hamstead, because Hamstead were vicariously liable in negligence for the acts of their own servant. So one starts from that point. There was a plain liability of Hamstead to Phillips. That was, as Slade L.J. said, a case of a plant owner excluding his liability for negligence in the relevant sense by reference to the contract term, clause 8. I should mention that the *Phillips* case turned upon section 2(2) of the Act, but that is of no consequence in the present case.

If one then turns to the present case, the sharp distinction between it and the *Phillips* case is this, that whereas in the *Phillips* case there was a liability in negligence of Hamstead to Phillips (and that was sought to be excluded), in the present case there is no exclusion or restriction of the liability sought to be achieved by reliance upon the provisions of clause 8. The plaintiff has her judgment against Lohan and can enforce it. The plaintiff is not prejudiced in any way by the operation sought to be established of clause 8. All that has happened is that Lohan and the third party have agreed between themselves who is to bear the consequences of Mr. Hill's negligent acts. I can see nothing in section 2(1) of the Act of 1977 to prevent that. In my opinion, section 2(1) is concerned with protecting the victim of negligence and, of course, those who claim under him. It is not concerned with arrangements made by the wrongdoer with other persons as to the sharing or bearing of the burden of compensating the victim. In such a case it seems to me there is no exclusion or restriction of the liability at all. The liability has been established by Hodgson J. It is not in dispute and is now unalterable. The circumstance that the defendants have between themselves chosen to bear the liability in a particular way does not affect that liability; it does not exclude it, and it does not restrict it. The liability to the plaintiff is the only relevant liability in the case, as it seems to me, and that liability is still in existence and will continue until discharge by payment to the plaintiff. Nothing is excluded in relation to the liability, and the liability is not restricted in any way whatever. The liability of Lohan to the plaintiff remains intact. The liability of Hamstead to Phillips was sought to be excluded.

In those circumstances it seems to me that, looking at the language of section 2(1), this case does not fall within its prohibition. I reach that conclusion on the language of section 2 itself, and without reference to section 4, to which I have referred and on which Mr. Judge, for Lohan, relied. I do not find it necessary to consider it further, having regard to the conclusion which I have reached upon the language of section 2 itself.

Dillon LJ: I entirely agree with Fox L.J. that the contract between Lohan and the third party did not and could not restrict or exclude Lohan's liability to Mr. Thompson's estate and his widow and dependants for the consequences of his death. That is sufficient to show that the contract between Lohan and the third party is outside section 2(1).

But to my mind there is great force, and I would accept Mr. Judge's submission, that there is an indication to the same effect as a result of section 4. If Mr. Samuels is right that indemnity clauses (or clauses which would have the effect of transferring the liability of the person who is primarily liable for the death or injury resulting from negligence to someone else) are within section 2(1) the clauses would be void as between Lohan and the third party. But indemnity clauses in respect of liability for negligence are dealt with in quite a different way by section 4 in that section 4 applies to invalidate those clauses except in so far as they satisfy the requirement of reasonableness, but only for the protection of persons dealing as consumers. However, Lohan and the third party, in their dealings with each other, were not dealing as consumers. So, that seems to me a strong indication that a clause of indemnity, or providing for a person who is liable to transfer his liability to someone else as between the two of them (or recoup that liability from someone else), is outside the scope of section 2 of the Act.

Woolf LJ gave a concurring judgment.

NOTES AND QUESTIONS

1. The important distinction between this and the *Phillips* case is that, on the facts of this case, conditions 8 and 13 of the terms of hire did not operate to transfer any liability from the tortfeasor *to the victim of the tort*. One was concerned with an allocation of liability (including a standard indemnity clause) as between the tortfeasor and a third party who was not the victim of the tort. Section 2 of UCTA 1977 was, therefore, not triggered because the exclusion of liability referred to in the Act is an exclusion of liability to the victim of the tort (or breach of contract).

2. If some exclusion and limitation clauses as between businesses are covered by UCTA 1977, why is section 4 on indemnity clauses confined to protecting consumers?

Smith v Eric S Bush [1990] 1 AC 831, House of Lords

A prospective purchaser of a house, the claimant, applied for a building society mortgage. The building society contracted with the defendants, a firm of surveyors, for them to carry out a valuation survey. In the application form for the mortgage it was stated that the building society would provide the claimant with a copy of the surveyor's report. It also contained a disclaimer as to the accuracy of the report by the building society or the surveyors. The surveyors' report contained a similar disclaimer. The report negligently stated that no essential repairs were needed to the house and, in reliance on that, the claimant went ahead and bought the house. Eighteen months later, part of the chimney collapsed and fell through the roof. The claimant brought an action for damages in the tort of negligence against the defendants. An initial issue, with which we are not directly concerned in this book, was whether, leaving aside the disclaimer, a duty of care in tort was owed by the surveyor to the purchaser as regards the drawing up of the report. It was held that there was such a duty of care. Two questions then arose. The first, with which we are here concerned, was whether the disclaimer fell within UCTA 1977. The second was whether the disclaimer satisfied the reasonableness test. The House of Lords held that UCTA 1977 did apply and that the disclaimer was unreasonable and, therefore, invalid.

Lord Templeman: In *Harris v. Wyre Forest District Council* [1988] Q.B. 835 [*which was the case linked with* Smith v Eric Bush *on the appeal*] the Court of Appeal (Kerr and Nourse L.JJ. and Caulfield J.) accepted an argument that the Act of 1977 did not apply because the council by their express disclaimer refused to obtain a valuation save on terms that the valuer would not be under any obligation to Mr. and Mrs. Harris to take reasonable care or exercise reasonable skill. The council did not exclude liability for negligence but excluded negligence so that the valuer and the council never came under a duty of care to Mr. and Mrs. Harris and could not be guilty of negligence. This construction would not give effect to the manifest intention of the Act but would emasculate the Act. The construction would provide no control over standard form exclusion clauses which individual members of the public are obliged to accept. A party to a contract or a tortfeasor could opt out of the Act of 1977 by declining in the words of Nourse L.J., at p. 845, to recognise "their own answerability to the plaintiff." Caulfield J. said, at p. 850, that the Act "can only be relevant where there is on the facts a potential liability." But no one intends to commit a tort and therefore any notice which excludes liability is a notice which excludes a potential liability. Kerr L.J., at p. 853, sought to confine the Act to "situations where the existence of a duty of care is not open to doubt" or where there is "an inescapable duty of care." I can find nothing in the Act of 1977 or in the general law to identify or support this distinction. In the result the Court of Appeal held that the Act does not apply to "negligent misstatements where a disclaimer has prevented a duty of care from coming into existence;" *per* Nourse L.J., at p. 848. My Lords this confuses the valuer's report with the work which the valuer carries out in order to make his report. The valuer owed a duty to exercise reasonable skill and care in his inspection and valuation. If he had been careful in his work, he would not have made a "negligent misstatement" in his report.

Section 11(3) of the Act of 1977 provides that in considering whether it is fair and reasonable to allow reliance on a notice which excludes liability in tort, account must be taken of:

"all the circumstances obtaining when the liability arose or (but for the notice) would have arisen."

Section 13(1) of the Act prevents the exclusion of any right or remedy and (to that extent) section 2 also prevents the exclusion of liability:

"by reference to . . . notices which exclude . . . the relevant obligation or duty."

Nourse L.J. dismissed section 11(3) as "peripheral" and made no comment on section 13(1). In my opinion both these provisions support the view that the Act of 1977 requires that all exclusion notices which would in common law provide a defence to an action for negligence must satisfy the requirement of reasonableness.

Lord Griffiths: [The Court of Appeal in *Harris*] held that, as the disclaimer of liability would at common law have prevented any duty to take reasonable care arising between the parties, the Act had no application. In my view this construction fails to give due weight to the provisions of [sections 11(3) and 13(1)].

[*He set out those provisions and continued:*]

I read these provisions as introducing a "but for" test in relation to the notice excluding liability. They indicate that the existence of the common law duty to take reasonable care, referred to in section 1(1)(*b*), is to be judged by considering whether it would exist "but for" the notice excluding liability. The result of taking the notice into account when assessing the existence of a duty of care would result in removing all liability for negligent misstatements from the protection of the Act. It is permissible to have regard to the second report of the Law Commission on Exemption Clauses (1975) (Law Com. No. 69) which is the genesis of the Unfair Contract Terms Act 1977 as an aid to the construction of the Act. Paragraph 127 of that report reads:

"Our recommendations in this part of the report are intended to apply to exclusions of liability for negligence where the liability is incurred in the course of a person's business. We consider that they should apply even in cases where the person seeking to rely on the exemption clause was under no legal obligation (such as a contractual obligation) to carry out the activity. This means that, for example, conditions attached to a licence to enter on to land, and disclaimers of liability made where information or advice is given, should be subject to control. . . ."

I have no reason to think that Parliament did not intend to follow this advice and the wording of the Act is, in my opinion, apt to give effect to that intention. This view of the construction of the Act is also supported by the judgment of Slade L.J. in *Phillips Products Ltd. v. Hyland (Note)* [1987] 1 W.L.R. 659, when he rejected a similar argument in relation to the construction of a contractual term excluding negligence.

Lord Jauncey gave a concurring speech. **Lord Keith of Kinkel** and **Lord Brandon of Oakbrook** concurred with Lords Templeman, Griffiths and Jauncey.

NOTES AND QUESTIONS

1. For the application of the reasonableness test in this case, see below, 275.

2. As on the first issue in *Phillips v Hyland*, the defendants' argument was, in essence, that the disclaimer operated to define the duty so that there was no breach so that section 2(2) did not apply. Again we see this type of argument being roundly rejected.
3. Why does this case illustrate that UCTA 1977 is inaptly named?

Stewart Gill Ltd v Horatio Myer & Co Ltd [1992] QB 600, Court of Appeal

The defendants (Myer) entered into a contract with the claimants (Gill) for the purchase and installation of an overhead conveyor system. Myer withheld the final 10 per cent of the price alleging breach of contract by Gill. In an action by Gill for that 10 per cent, Myer sought to exercise a set-off. This would normally have given them a defence to Gill's application for summary judgment but Gill sought to rely on condition 12.4 in the conditions of sale. This read as follows: 'The customer shall not be entitled to withhold payment of any amount due to the company under the contract by reason of any payment credit set off counterclaim allegation of incorrect or defective goods or for any other reason whatsoever which the customer may allege excuses him from performing his obligations hereunder.' Two issues arose. Did that condition fall within UCTA 1977? If so, did it fall foul of the reasonableness test? The Court of Appeal answered both in the affirmative. We are here solely concerned with the first issue.

Lord Donaldson of Lymington MR: It is a trite fact (as contrasted with being trite law) that there are more ways than one of killing a cat. Section 13 addresses this problem. On behalf of the plaintiffs it was submitted that it only did so to the extent of rendering ineffective any unreasonable term which by for example introducing restrictive or onerous conditions, indirectly achieved the exclusion or restriction of liability which, if achieved directly, would fall within the scope of other sections. The plaintiffs rightly say that clause 12.4 does not have this effect. On behalf of the defendants it was submitted that it had a wider scope.

The answer is, of course, to be found in the wording of the section, but it does not exactly leap out of the print and hit one between the eyes. Analysing the section and disregarding words which are irrelevant, it seems to deal with the matter as follows: "To the extent that this Part of this Act prevents the exclusion or restriction of any liability it also prevents . . ." This seems to me to do no more than give expression to the "cat" approach. Both sections 3 and 7 would render ineffective any clause in the plaintiffs' written standard terms of business which excluded or restricted liability in respects which are here material and section 13 extends this in some way. In order to find out in what way, one must read on:

"it also prevents—(a) making the liability or its enforcement subject to restrictive or onerous conditions; (b) excluding or restricting any right or remedy in respect of the liability . . . (c) excluding or restricting rules of . . . procedure; . . ."

Now clause 12.4 can perhaps be said to make the enforcement of the plaintiffs' liability subject to a condition that the defendants shall not have sought to set off their own claims against their liability to pay the price and this might well be said to be onerous. However, I do not think it necessary to pursue this, because it is quite clear that clause 12.4 excludes the defendants' "right" to set off their claims against the plaintiffs' claim for the price and further excludes the remedy which they would otherwise have of being able to enforce their claims against the plaintiffs by means of a set-off: see paragraph (b). It also excludes or restricts the procedural rules as to set-off: see paragraph (c). Thus far, therefore, the defendants can bring themselves within the section.

We then get to the words

> "and (to that extent) sections 2 and 5 to 7 also prevent excluding or restricting liability by reference to terms and notices which exclude or restrict the relevant obligation or duty."

Although I find this obscure, I do not think that these words restrict the ambit of the preceding words. I think that they constitute an extension and that what is intended to be covered is an exclusion or restriction of liability not by contract but by reference to notices or terms of business which are not incorporated in a contract. If this is correct, it is irrelevant to the present case.

Stuart-Smith LJ: The use of the word "also" in the introductory words [to section 13] shows that the section is intended to extend the scope of section 3 of the Act. Applying the words of section 13(1)(b) to the clause in question, the liability referred to is that of the plaintiffs, the alleged contract breaker, and the right or remedy is that of the defendant. In my judgment, but for the provisions of clause 12.4, the defendants would have a right to set off the claim for damages in respect of the plaintiffs' liability for breach of contract against the claim for the price. This is a right given by the law in the form of an equitable set-off. Does clause 12.4 exclude or restrict that right? In my judgment plainly it does, since it prevents the defendants from relying on the right of set-off.

Balcombe LJ concurred.

NOTES

1. For the application of the reasonableness test in this case, see below, 277.
2. On the first issue, it was firmly decided that, despite the obscurity of some of the wording in section 13, a 'no set-off' clause is an exemption clause within UCTA 1977.

Tudor Grange Holdings Ltd v Citibank NA
[1992] Ch 53, Chancery Division

As part of a series of agreements, relating to loans, the claimants agreed (on 13 March 1989) to release the defendant bank from 'all claims, demands and causes of action' that the claimants might have against the defendant. In the defendant bank's application to strike out the claimants' action against it for, eg, damages for misrepresentation, one issue was whether the contract of release could be challenged as being unreasonable under UCTA 1977. It was held that it could not and, in particular, that section 10 of UCTA 1977 did not here apply.

Sir Nicolas Browne-Wilkinson V-C:

The Unfair Contract Terms Act 1977

Mr. Sheridan [counsel for the claimants] accepts that the Act of 1977 is normally regarded as applying to exemption clauses in the strict sense, namely clauses in a contract exempting prospectively against a future liability. However, he submits that section 10 of the Act according to its plain meaning operates so as to make subsequent compromises and waivers of accrued claims subject to the tests of reasonableness introduced by the Act of 1977. [*He set out section 10, above, 247, and continued*:]

Mr. Sheridan puts his case in this way. He says that the banks were under contractual duties of care to the plaintiffs under the banking contracts. The release purports to take away the plaintiffs' rights to complain of breaches of the banking contracts and the duty of care contained in it. Therefore, says Mr. Sheridan, the case comes directly within the words of the section. Reading the section with the interpolation of the characters in this case, he says it would read like this: "A person (i.e. the plaintiffs) is not bound by any contract term (i.e. the release) taking away rights of the plaintiffs which arise under another contract (i.e. the banking contracts) so far as those rights (i.e. the rights under the banking contracts) extend to the enforcement of another's (i.e. the bank's) liability which this part of this Act prevents that other (i.e. the bank) from excluding or restricting." He submits, in my view correctly, that under section 2(2) of the Act, the bank could not itself by contract exclude or restrict its liability for breach of its contractual duty of care unless such exclusion or restriction was reasonable. Therefore, he says, the release is only binding if it satisfies the requirement of reasonableness, a matter which requires full investigation of all the facts and cannot be the subject matter of a striking out application.

This argument that section 10 of the Act may apply to compromises or settlement of existing disputes has been foreseen by a number of textbook writers as an unfortunate possibility. They are unanimous in their hope that the courts will be robust in resisting it. If Mr. Sheridan's construction is correct, the impact will be very considerable. The Act of 1977 is normally regarded as being aimed at exemption clauses in the strict sense, that is to say, clauses in a contract which aim to cut down prospective liability arising in the course of the performance of the contract in which the exemption clause is contained. If Mr. Sheridan's argument is correct, the Act will apply to all compromises or waivers of existing claims arising from past actions. Any subsequent agreement to compromise contractual disputes falling within sections 2 or 3 of the Act will itself be capable of being put in question on the grounds that the compromise or waiver is not reasonable. Even an action settled at the door of the court on the advice of solicitors and counsel could be re-opened on the grounds that the settlement was not reasonable within the meaning of the Act. If I am forced to that conclusion by the words of section 10 properly construed, so be it. But, in my judgment, it is improbable that Parliament intended that result: it would be an end to finality in seeking to resolve disputes.

The starting point in construing section 10 is, in my judgment, to determine the mischief aimed at by the Act itself. For this purpose, it is legitimate to look at the second report on exemption clauses of the Law Commission on Exemption Clauses (1975) (Law Com. No. 69): see *Smith v. Eric S. Bush* [1990] 1 A.C. 831, 857E, *per* Lord Griffiths. This report was the genesis of the Act of 1977. The report is wholly concerned with remedying injustices which are caused by exemption clauses in the strict sense. So far as I can see, the report makes no reference of any kind to any mischief relating to agreements to settle disputes.

Next, the marginal note to section 10 reads "Evasion by means of secondary contract." Although the marginal note to a section cannot control the language used in the section, it is permissible to have regard to it in considering what is the general purpose of the section and the mischief at which it is aimed: see *Stephens v. Cuckfield Rural District Council* [1960] 2 Q.B. 373. This sidenote clearly indicates that it is aimed at devices intended to *evade* the provisions of Part 1 of the Act of 1977 by the use of another contract. In my judgment, a contract to settle disputes which have arisen concerning the performance of an earlier contract cannot be described as an evasion of the provisions in the Act regulating exemption clauses in the earlier contract. Nor is the compromise contract "secondary" to the earlier contract.

The textbooks, to my mind correctly, identify at least one case which section 10 is designed to cover. Under contract 1, the supplier (S) contracts to supply a customer (C) with a product. Contract 1 contains no exemption clause. However, C enters into a servicing contract, contract 2, with another party (X). Under contract 2, C is precluded from exercising certain of his rights against S under contract 1. In such a case section 10 operates to preclude X from enforcing contract 2 against C so as to prevent C enforcing his rights against S under contract 1. The extent of the operation of section 10 in such circumstances may be doubtful: see *Treitel on The Law of Contract*, 7th ed. (1987), p. 206. But there is no doubt that such a case falls squarely within the terms of section 10.

In the case that I have just postulated, the references in section 10 to "another's liability" and "that other" are references to someone other than X, i.e. to the original supplier, S. On Mr. Sheridan's construction the words "another" and "that other" are taken as referring to someone other than C, the customer whose rights are restricted, so as to make the section apply to a case such as the present where there is no third party, X. Although as a matter of language the words of the section are capable of referring to anyone other than C, in my judgment, read in context and having regard to the purpose both of the Act and of the section itself, the reference to "another" plainly means someone other than X, that is to say someone other than the party to the secondary contract. In my judgment section 10 does not apply where the parties to both contacts are the same.

This view is reinforced by a further factor. If the Act were intended to apply to terms in subsequent compromise agreements between the same parties as the original contract, section 10 would be quite unnecessary. Under sections 2 and 3 there is no express requirement that the contract term excluding or restricting S's liability to C has to be contained in the same cont[r]act as that giving rise to S's liability to C. If S and C enter into two contracts, it makes no difference if the exemption clause is contained in a different contract from that under which the goods are supplied. Sections 2 and 3 by themselves will impose the test of reasonableness. Why then should Parliament have thought that in section 10 there was some possibility of evasion in such circumstances?

In my judgment, the Act is dealing solely with exemption clauses in the strict sense (i.e. clauses in a contract modifying prospective liability) and does not affect retrospective compromises of existing claims. Section 10 is dealing only with attempts to evade the Act's provisions by the introduction of such an exemption clause into a contract with a third party. This view does not in any way conflict with the construction of section 23 of the Act which has similar application to Scottish law.

My only doubt is raised by paragraph 5 of Schedule 1 to the Act. Schedule 1 provides that sections 2 to 4 of the Act are not to extend to various matters. [*He set out paragraph 5, above 251, and continued:*]

At first sight, the express exclusion from the operation of the Act of one category of compromise agreement suggests that other compromise agreements are within the Act. However, I am not persuaded of this. Paragraph 5 shows all the signs of a provision inserted at the insistence of one lobby, the coal industry, out of an abundance of caution. Why should Parliament have intended to exclude any one type of latent damage, pneumoconiosis, but leave all compromises involving other types of latent damage subject to the test of reasonableness? Moreover, paragraph 5 only excludes from the test of reasonableness the provision barring future claims. On Mr. Sheridan's construction, this would leave the other terms of settlement in the pneumoconiosis claim subject to the test of reasonableness imposed by the Act. That is not a conclusion that I think Parliament can have intended. Accordingly, for those reasons, section 10 cannot apply to the release of 13 March 1989.

NOTES AND QUESTIONS

1.   This case confirms that UCTA 1977 does not apply to a compromise or settlement or release or waiver of one's rights.

2.   Was not the argument over section 10 a 'red herring' because, if a release is not an exclusion of liability within sections 2–3 of UCTA 1977, it cannot become so by reason of section 10?

(c) Does the Clause Pass, or Fail, the Reasonableness Test?

George Mitchell (Chesterhall) Ltd v Finney Lock Seeds Ltd
[1983] 2 AC 803, House of Lords

For the facts, see above, 237. We are here concerned with the decision that the limitation clause was unreasonable.

Lord Bridge of Harwich: The statutory issue turns…on the application of the provisions of the modified section 55 of the Sale of Goods Act 1979, as set out in paragraph 11 of Schedule 1 to the Act. The Act of 1979 is a pure consolidation. The purpose of the modified section 55 is to preserve the law as it stood from May 18, 1973, to February 1, 1978, in relation to contracts made between those two dates. The significance of the dates is that the first was the date when the Supply of Goods (Implied Terms) Act 1973 came into force containing the provision now re-enacted by the modified section 55, the second was the date when the Unfair Contract Terms Act 1977 came into force and superseded the relevant provisions of the Act of 1973 by more radical and far-reaching provisions in relation to contracts made thereafter.

The relevant subsections of the modified section 55 provide as follows:

"…(4) In the case of a contract of sale of goods, any term of that or any other contract exempting from all or any of the provisions of section 13, 14 or 15 above is void in the case of a consumer sale and is, in any other case, not enforceable to the extent that it is shown that it would not be fair or reasonable to allow reliance on the term. (5) In determining for the purposes of subsection (4) above whether or not reliance on any such term would be fair or reasonable regard shall be had to all the circumstances of the case and in particular to the following matters—(a) the strength of the bargaining positions of the seller and buyer relative to each other, taking into account, among other things, the availability of suitable alternative products and sources of supply; (b) whether the buyer received an inducement to agree to the term or in accepting it had an opportunity of buying the goods or suitable alternatives without it from any source of supply; (c) whether the buyer knew or ought reasonably to have known of the existence and extent of the term (having regard, among other things, to any custom of the trade and any previous course of dealing between the parties); (d) where the term exempts from all or any of the provisions of section 13, 14, or 15 above if some condition is not complied with, whether it was reasonable at the time of the contract to expect that compliance with that condition would be practicable; (e) whether the goods were manufactured, processed, or adapted to the special order of the buyer. …"

The contract between the appellants and the respondents was not a "consumer sale," as defined for the purpose of these provisions. The effect of clause 3 of the relevant condition is to exclude, inter alia, the terms implied by sections 13 and 14 of the Act that the seeds sold by description should correspond to the description and be of merchantable quality and to substitute therefor the express but limited obligations undertaken by the appellants under clauses 1 and 2. The statutory issue, therefore, turns on the words in subsection (4) "to the extent that it is shown that it would not be fair or reasonable to allow reliance on" this restriction of the appellants' liabilities, having regard to the matters referred to in subsection (5).

This is the first time your Lordships' House has had to consider a modern statutory provision giving the court power to override contractual terms excluding or restricting liability, which depends on the court's view of what is "fair and reasonable." The particular provision of the modified section 55 of the Act of 1979 which applies in the instant case is of limited and diminishing importance. But the several provisions of the Unfair Contract Terms Act 1977 which depend on "the requirement of reasonableness," defined in section 11 by reference to what is "fair and reasonable," albeit in a different context, are likely to come before the courts with increasing frequency. It may, therefore, be appropriate to consider how an original decision as to what is "fair and reasonable" made in the application of any of these provisions should be approached by an appellate court. It would not be accurate to describe such a decision as an exercise of discretion. But a decision under any of the provisions referred to will have this in common with the exercise of a discretion, that, in having regard to the various matters to which the modified section 55 (5) of the Act of 1979, or section 11 of the Act of 1977 direct attention, the court must entertain a whole range of considerations, put them in the scales on one side or the other, and decide at the end of the day on which side the balance comes down. There will sometimes be room for a legitimate difference of judicial opinion as to what the answer should be, where it will be impossible to say that one view is demonstrably wrong and the other demonstrably right. It must follow, in my view, that, when asked to review such a decision on appeal, the appellate court should treat the original decision with the utmost respect and refrain from interference with it unless satisfied that it proceeded upon some erroneous principle or was plainly and obviously wrong.

Turning back to the modified section 55 of the Act of 1979, it is common ground that the onus was on the respondents to show that it would not be fair or reasonable to allow the appellants to rely on the relevant condition as limiting their liability. It was argued for the appellants that the court must have regard to the circumstances as at the date of the contract, not after the breach. The basis of the argument was that this was the effect of section 11 of the Act of 1977 and that it would be wrong to construe the modified section 55 of the Act as having a different effect. Assuming the premise is correct, the conclusion does not follow. The provisions of the Act of 1977 cannot be considered in construing the prior enactment now embodied in the modified section 55 of the Act of 1979. But, in any event, the language of subsections (4) and (5) of that section is clear and unambiguous. The question whether it is fair or reasonable to allow reliance on a term excluding or limiting liability for a breach of contract can only arise after the breach. The nature of the breach and the circumstances in which it occurred cannot possibly be excluded from "all the circumstances of the case" to which regard must be had.

...

My Lords, at long last I turn to the application of the statutory language to the circumstances of the case. Of the particular matters to which attention is directed by paragraphs (a) to (e) of section 55 (5), only those in (a) to (c) are relevant. As to paragraph (c), the respondents admittedly knew of the relevant condition (they had dealt with the appellants for many years) and, if they had read it, particularly clause 2, they would, I think, as laymen rather than lawyers, have had no difficulty in understanding what it said. This and the magnitude of the damages claimed in proportion to the price of the seeds sold are factors which weigh in the scales in the appellants' favour.

The question of relative bargaining strength under paragraph (a) and of the opportunity to buy seeds without a limitation of the seedsman's liability under paragraph (b) were inter-related. The evidence was that a similar limitation of liability was universally embodied in the terms of trade between seedsmen and farmers and had been so for very many years. The limitation had never been negotiated between representative bodies but, on the other hand, had not been the subject of any protest by the National Farmers' Union. These factors, if considered in isolation, might have been equivocal. The decisive factor, however, appears from the evidence of four witnesses called for the appellants, two independent seedsmen, the chairman of the appellant company, and a director of a sister company (both being wholly-owned subsidiaries of the same parent). They said that it had always been their practice, unsuccessfully attempted in the instant case, to negotiate settlements of farmers' claims for damages in excess of the price of the seeds, if they thought that the claims were "genuine" and "justified." This evidence indicated a clear recognition by seedsmen in general, and the appellants in particular, that reliance on the limitation of liability imposed by the relevant condition would not be fair or reasonable.

Two further factors, if more were needed, weight the scales in favour of the respondents. The supply of autumn, instead of winter, cabbage seeds was due to the negligence of the appellants' sister company. Irrespective of its quality, the autumn variety supplied could not, according to the appellants' own evidence, be grown commercially in East Lothian. Finally, as the trial judge found, seedsmen could insure against the risk of crop failure caused by supplying the wrong variety of seeds without materially increasing the price of seeds.

My Lords, even if I felt doubts about the statutory issue, I should not, for the reasons explained earlier, think it right to interfere with the unanimous original decision of that issue by the Court of Appeal. As it is, I feel no such doubts. If I were making the original decision, I should conclude without hesitation that it would not be fair or reasonable to allow the appellants to rely on the contractual limitation of their liability.

Lord Diplock delivered a short concurring speech. **Lords Scarman, Roskill** and **Brightman** concurred.

NOTES AND QUESTIONS

1. The statutory test of reasonableness being applied in this case, but since repealed, differed in at least three respects from section 11(1) and (2) UCTA 1977. First, its wording focussed on whether it was fair and reasonable to rely on the exemption rather than on it being fair and reasonable to include the term. Secondly, and linked to that, the nature and circumstances of the breach were, as Lord Bridge stressed, plainly relevant, whereas such matters would have to be related back to the time the contract was made to be relevant under UCTA 1977 (although this has subsequently not been regarded as problematic by the courts). Thirdly, the burden of proof in relation to reasonableness was on the claimant, not the defendant.

2. Despite those differences, the case is an excellent illustration of the factors that may be relevant in assessing reasonableness. Apart from what are now the first three guidelines in Schedule 2, the House of Lords took into account: (a) the practice of sellers of seeds to negotiate settlements above the refunding of the price paid, thus indicating that they did not regard the limitation as reasonable (this was treated as the decisive factor); (b) that the sellers could have insured against their liability; (c) that the breach was negligent.

3. Do you agree with the House of Lords that appellate courts should be very slow to interfere with decisions at first instance on whether an exemption clause is reasonable?

Phillips Products Ltd v Hyland [1987] 1 WLR 659, Court of Appeal

For the facts, and the first two issues in the case, see above, 258–260. We are here concerned with the third issue, the application of the reasonableness test and the decision that condition 8 was unreasonable.

Slade LJ:

Issue (iii)

Issue (iii) is the issue which alone, it would seem, apart from the construction of clause 8 itself, the judge was asked to decide. Does the clause, on the evidence and in the context of the contract as a whole, satisfy the "requirement of reasonableness," as defined by section 11(1) and elsewhere in the Act?

Under section 11(5) the onus falls on Hamstead to show that clause 8 satisfies the condition of reasonableness. For this purpose, having regard to section 11(1), they have to show that the condition was:

"a fair and reasonable one to be included having regard to the circumstances which were, or ought reasonably to have been, known to or in the contemplation of the parties when the contract was made."

As the judge pointed out, all the relevant circumstances were known to both parties at that time. The task which he therefore set himself was to examine all the relevant circumstances and then ask himself whether, on the balance of probabilities, he was satisfied that clause 8, in so far as it purported to exclude Hamstead's liability for Mr. Hyland's negligence, was a fair and reasonable term. As to these matters, his conclusions as set out in his judgment were:

"What then were the relevant circumstances? Firstly, the second defendants carried on the business of hiring out plant and operators. In contrast the first defendants were steel stockholders, and as such had no occasion to hire plant except on the odd occasions when they had building work to be done at their premises. There had been apparently only three such occasions: one in 1979, one in July 1980 when the drainage trench was dug and the final occasion when the damage was done in August 1980.

Secondly, the hire was to be for a very short period. It was arranged at very short notice. There was no occasion for the plaintiffs to address their mind to all the details of the hiring agreement, nor did they do so. The inclusion of condition 8 arose because it appeared in the second defendants' printed conditions. It was not the product of any discussion or agreement between the parties.

Thirdly, there was little if any opportunity for the plaintiffs to arrange insurance cover for risks arising from the first defendant's negligence. In so far as the first defendant was to be regarded as the plaintiffs' servant it might have been an easy matter to ensure that the plaintiffs' insurance policies were extended, if necessary, to cover his activities in relation to third party claims. Any businessman customarily insures against such claims. He does not usually insure against damage caused to his own property by his own employees' negligence. Thus to arrange insurance cover for the first defendant would have required time and a special and unusual arrangement with the plaintiffs' insurers.

Fourthly, the plaintiffs played no part in the selection of the first defendant as the operator of the J.C.B. They had to accept whoever the second defendant sent to drive the machine. Further, although they undoubtedly would have had to, and would have had the right to, tell the J.C.B. operator what job he was required to do, from their previous experience they knew they would be unable in any way to control the way in which the first defendant did the job that he was given. They would not have had the knowledge to exercise such control. All the expertise lay with the first defendant. I do not think condition 8 could possibly be construed as giving control of the manner of operation of the J.C.B. to the plaintiffs. Indeed in the event the first defendant made it perfectly plain to…the plaintiffs' builder that he would brook no interference in the way he operated his machine.

Those being the surrounding circumstances, was it fair and reasonable that the hire contract should include a condition which relieved the second defendants of all responsibility for damage caused, not to the property of a third party but to the plaintiff's own property, by the negligence of the second defendants' own operators? This was for the plaintiffs in a very real sense a 'take it or leave it' situation. They needed a J.C.B. for a simple job at short notice. In dealing with the second defendants they had the choice of taking a J.C.B. operator under a contract containing some 43 written conditions or not taking the J.C.B. at all. The question for me is not a general question whether *any* contract of hire of the J.C.B. could fairly and reasonably exclude such liability, but a much more limited question as to whether *this* contract of hire entered into in these circumstances fairly and reasonably included such an exemption.

I have come to the conclusion that the second defendants have failed to satisfy me that condition 8 was in this respect a fair and reasonable term."

Before reverting to the conclusions and reasoning of the judge, it is unfortunately necessary to deviate from the arguments as they were presented to us. Schedule 2 to the Act contains what are called "'Guidelines' for application of reasonableness test." [*He set out the guidelines and then continued:*]

We were told that the guidelines in Schedule 2 to the Act were not applicable in this case. It would seem, on a study of the provisions of the Act to which we were not referred in argument, that this may have been wrong. The contract here was a contract of hire. Normally in such a contract, and, it would seem consistently with the provisions of the general conditions in this case, the hirer takes possession of the article hired. Therefore, it appears to us that subsection (3) of section 7 would apply and thus render Schedule 2 applicable. On this basis the guidelines *would* fall to be considered. Fortunately, however, in view of the way in which the case has been argued on both sides, no difficulty arises on this account. Guideline (*d*) is, on any footing, irrelevant. Guidelines (*a*), (*b*) and (*c*) were argued as factors properly to be taken into account, even though not because of the guidelines themselves. Guideline (*e*) would no doubt have been mentioned in argument if counsel on either side had thought that it affected the decision as to "fair and reasonable" in this case.

In approaching the judge's reasons and conclusions on this issue, four points have, in our judgment, to be borne in mind. First, as the judge himself clearly appreciated, the question for the court is not a general question whether or not clause 8 is valid or invalid in the case of any and every contract of hire entered into between a hirer and a plant owner who uses the relevant C.P.A. conditions. The question was and is whether the exclusion of Hamstead's liability for negligence satisfied the requirement of reasonableness imposed by the Act, in relation to *this particular contract*.

Secondly, we have to bear in mind that the relevant circumstances, which were or should have been known to or contemplated by the parties, are those which existed when the contract was made. Section 11(1) is specific on that point. Hence, evidence as to what happened during the performance of the contract must, at best, be treated with great caution. As we have indicated, such evidence was adduced at the trial, apparently without objection. At best, it could probably be used to show, by evidence of conduct and absence of objection to that conduct, what the attitude of the parties would have been in that respect, what they would have contemplated, at the time when they made the contract.

Thirdly, the burden of proof falling upon the owner under section 11(5) of the Act is, in our judgment, of great significance in this case in the light, or rather in the obscurity, of the evidence and the absence of evidence on issues which were, or might have been, relevant on the issue of reasonableness. One particular example is the matter of insurance. The insurance position of all the parties was canvassed to some extent in oral evidence at the trial, but such evidence seems to us to have been singularly imprecise and inconclusive.

Finally, by way of approach to the issue of reasonableness, it is necessary to bear in mind, and strive to comply with, the clear and stern injunction issued to appellate courts by Lord Bridge of Harwich in his speech, concurred in by the other members of the House of Lords, in *George Mitchell (Chesterhall) Ltd. v. Finney Lock Seeds Ltd.* [*He set out the relevant passage, see above, 270, and continued:*]

In the context of issue (iii), criticism has been made by Mr. Thompson [counsel for Hamstead] of some parts of the judge's reasoning. It is said that in some respects he misunderstood or mis-recollected the evidence. Some of the evidence was indeed confused and not easy to follow. It is, in some passages, difficult to be confident what was really meant. It may be that the judge placed more stress than we would think right on the lack of opportunity of

Mr. Phillips [a director of Phillips] to study and understand the conditions, and in particular clause 8. But this is the very sort of point to which Lord Bridge referred in saying that there is room for a legitimate difference of judicial opinion.

Against this, there is to be set the fact, as it appeared at the trial, that the general conditions with their 43 clauses were adopted by and used by all the members of the trade association to which Hamstead belonged. ...Thus, we think he was justified in saying that in dealing with Hamstead this was for Phillips in a very real sense a "take it or leave it situation." As he said, they needed a J.C.B. for a simple job at short notice and, in dealing with Hamstead, had the choice of taking a J.C.B. operator under the general conditions or not taking the J.C.B. at all. Even if Mr. Phillips had understood and had been worried by the effect of clause 8...it is reasonable to assume, on the evidence as it stood, that he would not have thought that there was much that he could do about it, except to take the conditions offered.

It is fair to say that we were told that various changes had been made, including the alterations to some of the general conditions since the coming into force of the Act and that the position today might be very different. But Mr. Thompson necessarily and realistically accepts that we have to deal, as the judge had to deal, with the contractual terms as they were and with the facts as to the relevant considerations as they were given in evidence at the trial: not as the terms are now or as the relevant facts might have appeared to be if further evidence had been given.

As appears from the passage which we have cited, other matters which influenced the judge in his decision on unreasonableness, and which we think were clearly relevant factors to be weighed in the balance, were that the hirers could play no part in the selection of the operator who was to do the work. Nor did the general conditions contain any warranty by Hamstead as to his fitness or competence for the job. Furthermore, despite the words in clause 8, "he shall be under the direction and control of the hirer," we think it reasonable to infer that the parties, when they made the contract, would have assumed that the operator would be the expert in the management of this machine and that he would not, and could not be expected to, take any instructions from anyone representing the hirers as to the manner in which he would operate the machine to do the job, once the extent and nature of the job had been defined to him by the hirers; in short they would tell him what to do but not how to do it. If such evidence is admissible, which we do not find it necessary to decide, this inference would be strongly supported by the evidence of what actually happened on the site before the accident occurred.

It may be that in several respects this is a very special case on its facts, its evidence and its paucity of evidence. But on these facts and on the available evidence, we are wholly unpersuaded that the judge proceeded upon some erroneous principle or was plainly and obviously wrong in his conclusion that Hamstead had not discharged the burden upon them of showing that clause 8 satisfied the requirement of reasonableness in the context of this particular contract of hire. It is important therefore that our conclusion on the particular facts of this case should not be treated as a binding precedent in other cases where similar clauses fall to be considered but the evidence of the surrounding circumstances may be very different. Issue (iii) accordingly has to be answered "No" and we dismiss this appeal.

QUESTIONS

Do you agree with this decision? As between parties of relatively equal bargaining power, why should the party hiring out the equipment and driver/operator not be able to throw the risk of damage on to the hirer? Was it decisive that Hamstead was seeking to exclude for negligence liability (albeit vicarious)?

Smith v Eric S Bush [1990] 1 AC 831, House of Lords

For the facts, see above, 263. We are here solely concerned with the decision that the (non-contractual) disclaimer was unreasonable under UCTA 1977 section 11(3) and, therefore, invalid.

Lord Templeman: It is open to Parliament to provide that members of all professions or members of one profession providing services in the normal course of the exercise of their profession for reward shall be entitled to exclude or limit their liability for failure to exercise reasonable skill and care. In the absence of any such provision valuers are not, in my opinion, entitled to rely on a general exclusion of the common law duty of care owed to purchasers of houses by valuers to exercise reasonable skill and care in valuing houses for mortgage purposes.

...

The public are exhorted to purchase their homes and cannot find houses to rent. A typical London suburban house, constructed in the 1930s for less than £1,000 is now bought for more than £150,000 with money largely borrowed at high rates of interest and repayable over a period of a quarter of a century. In these circumstances it is not fair and reasonable for building societies and valuers to agree together to impose on purchasers the risk of loss arising as a result of incompetence or carelessness on the part of valuers. I agree with the speech of my noble and learned friend, Lord Griffiths, and with his warning that different considerations may apply where homes are not concerned.

Lord Griffiths: Finally, the question is whether the exclusion of liability contained in the disclaimer satisfies the requirement of reasonableness provided by section 2(2) of the Act of 1977. The meaning of reasonableness and the burden of proof are both dealt with in section 11(3) which provides:

> "In relation to a notice (not being a notice having contractual effect), the requirement of reasonableness under this Act is that it should be fair and reasonable to allow reliance on it, having regard to all the circumstances obtaining when the liability arose or (but for the notice) would have arisen."

It is clear, then, that the burden is upon the surveyor to establish that in all the circumstances it is fair and reasonable that he should be allowed to rely upon his disclaimer of liability.

I believe that it is impossible to draw up an exhaustive list of the factors that must be taken into account when a judge is faced with this very difficult decision. Nevertheless, the following matters should, in my view, always be considered.

1. Were the parties of equal bargaining power. If the court is dealing with a one-off situation between parties of equal bargaining power the requirement of reasonableness would be more easily discharged than in a case such as the present where the disclaimer is imposed upon the purchaser who has no effective power to object.

2. In the case of advice would it have been reasonably practicable to obtain the advice from an alternative source taking into account considerations of costs and time. In the present case it is urged on behalf of the surveyor that it would have been easy for the purchaser to have obtained his own report on the condition of the house, to which the purchaser replies, that he would then be required to pay twice for the same advice and that people buying at the bottom end of the market, many of whom will be young first-time buyers, are likely to be under considerable financial pressure without the money to go paying twice for the same service.

3. How difficult is the task being undertaken for which liability is being excluded. When a very difficult or dangerous undertaking is involved there may be a high risk of failure which would certainly be a pointer towards the reasonableness of excluding liability as a condition

of doing the work. A valuation, on the other hand, should present no difficulty if the work is undertaken with reasonable skill and care. It is only defects which are observable by a careful visual examination that have to be taken into account and I cannot see that it places any unreasonable burden on the valuer to require him to accept responsibility for the fairly elementary degree of skill and care involved in observing, following-up and reporting on such defects. Surely it is work at the lower end of the surveyor's field of professional expertise.

4. What are the practical consequences of the decision on the question of reasonableness. This must involve the sums of money potentially at stake and the ability of the parties to bear the loss involved, which, in its turn, raises the question of insurance. There was once a time when it was considered improper even to mention the possible existence of insurance cover in a lawsuit. But those days are long past. Everyone knows that all prudent, professional men carry insurance, and the availability and cost of insurance must be a relevant factor when considering which of two parties should be required to bear the risk of a loss. We are dealing in this case with a loss which will be limited to the value of a modest house and against which it can be expected that the surveyor will be insured. Bearing the loss will be unlikely to cause significant hardship if it has to be borne by the surveyor but it is, on the other hand, quite possible that it will be a financial catastrophe for the purchaser who may be left with a valueless house and no money to buy another. If the law in these circumstances denies the surveyor the right to exclude his liability, it may result in a few more claims but I do not think so poorly of the surveyor's profession as to believe that the floodgates will be opened. There may be some increase in surveyors' insurance premiums which will be passed on to the public...The result of denying a surveyor, in the circumstances of this case, the right to exclude liability, will result in distributing the risk of his negligence among all house purchasers through an increase in his fees to cover insurance, rather than allowing the whole of the risk to fall upon the one unfortunate purchaser.

I would not, however, wish it to be thought that I would consider it unreasonable for professional men in all circumstances to seek to exclude or limit their liability for negligence. Sometimes breathtaking sums of money may turn on professional advice against which it would be impossible for the adviser to obtain adequate insurance cover and which would ruin him if he were to be held personally liable. In these circumstances it may indeed be reasonable to give the advice upon a basis of no liability or possibly of liability limited to the extent of the adviser's insurance cover.

In addition to the foregoing four factors, which will always have to be considered, there is in this case the additional feature that the surveyor is only employed in the first place because the purchaser wishes to buy the house and the purchaser in fact provides or contributes to the surveyor's fees. No one has argued that if the purchaser had employed and paid the surveyor himself, it would have been reasonable for the surveyor to exclude liability for negligence, and the present situation is not far removed from that of a direct contract between the surveyor and the purchaser. The evaluation of the foregoing matters leads me to the clear conclusion that it would not be fair and reasonable for the surveyor to be permitted to exclude liability in the circumstances of this case. I would therefore dismiss this appeal.

It must, however, be remembered that this is a decision in respect of a dwelling house of modest value in which it is widely recognised by surveyors that purchasers are in fact relying on their care and skill. It will obviously be of general application in broadly similar circumstances. But I expressly reserve my position in respect of valuations of quite different types of property for mortgage purposes, such as industrial property, large blocks of flats or very expensive houses. In such cases it may well be that the general expectation of the behaviour of the purchaser is quite different. With very large sums of money at stake prudence would seem to demand that the purchaser obtain his own structural survey to guide him in his purchase and, in such circumstances with very much larger sums of money at stake, it may be reasonable for the surveyors valuing on behalf of those who are providing the finance either to exclude or limit their liability to the purchaser.

Lord Jauncey of Tullichettle concurred with Lord Griffiths on the application of the reasonableness test. **Lord Keith of Kinkel** and **Lord Brandon of Oakbrook** concurred with Lords Templeman, Griffiths and Jauncey.

NOTES AND QUESTIONS

1. As the disclaimer was a non-contractual notice, the relevant reasonableness test was that in section 11(3), not section 11(1). Did this make any significant difference to the factors taken into account in assessing reasonableness?
2. Nearly all the cases in which the courts have had to apply the reasonableness test have involved non-consumers. This is, therefore, a rare case where the reasonableness test was being applied to a situation in which the claimant was a consumer. What explains the rarity of consumer cases?
3. Their Lordships did not say that it is always unreasonable for a professional to exclude (let alone limit) liability for negligence in performing services. When might that be reasonable?
4. In recent times premiums for professional liability insurance have increased considerably for, eg, surveyors, architects, solicitors and accountants. This has led to them seeking ways of limiting their liability (including setting themselves up as limited liability partnerships). Should the courts take these difficulties for the professions into account in assessing the reasonableness of an exclusion clause?

Stewart Gill Ltd v Horatio Myer & Co Ltd
[1992] QB 600, Court of Appeal

For the facts, see above, 265. We are here solely concerned with the Court of Appeal's decision that condition 12.4 failed the reasonableness test.

Lord Donaldson of Lymington MR: [T]he defendants succeed because, whatever the reasonableness of a clause which excludes or restricts a right of set-off, nothing could prima facie be more unreasonable than that the defendants should not be entitled to withhold payment to the plaintiffs of any amount due to the plaintiffs under the contract by reason of a "credit" owing by the plaintiffs to the defendants and, a fortiori, a "payment" made by the defendants to the plaintiffs. In this context "payment" must I think mean overpayment under another contract and credit mean "credit note" or admitted liability again under another contract, because otherwise it would be doubtful whether it could be said by the plaintiffs that any amount was due to them under the contract. Mr. Joseph, appearing for the plaintiffs, did not seriously gainsay this, but he submitted that as the defendants were not seeking to rely upon a payment or credit, this part of the clause could be ignored. In support of my view that clause 12.4 as a whole completely fails the test of reasonableness, I gratefully adopt the additional considerations based upon its concluding words and Schedule 2 to the Act discussed in the judgment of Stuart-Smith L.J. which I have read in draft.

   Whether or not it is possible to sever parts of the clause depends upon section 11(1) *[which he set out and then continued:]* In the face of this wording it seems to me to be impossible to contend that we should look only at the part of the clause which is relied upon. The issue is whether "the term [the whole term and nothing but the term] shall have been a fair and reasonable one to be included." This has to be determined as at the time when the contract is made and without regard to what particular use one party may subsequently wish to make of it. I would unhesitatingly answer this in the negative and accordingly would dismiss the appeal.

Stuart-Smith LJ: The burden of satisfying the court that the term is reasonable rests on the plaintiffs in this case. What is it that they have to show is reasonable? Is it clause 12.4 as a whole or is it only that part of it which the plaintiffs need to rely upon in this case to defeat the defendants' set-off, namely "The customer shall not be entitled to withhold any amount due to the company under the contract by reason of . . . set off counterclaim allegation of incorrect or defective goods . . ."

If it is the former, then in my judgment the clause is plainly unreasonable. There can be no possible justification for preventing a payment or credit to be set off against the price claimed, and the width of the concluding words "or for any other reason whatsoever which the customer may allege excuses him from performing his obligations" is unlimited, and would extend for example to a defence based on fraud.

In my judgment it is the term as a whole that has to be reasonable and not merely some part of it. Throughout the Act the expression used is "by reference to any contract term," the contract "term satisfies the requirement of reasonableness:" see sections 3 and 7. And in section 11(1) the reasonableness test is laid down as *[he set out section 11(1) and continued:]* Although the question of reasonableness is primarily one for the court when the contract term is challenged, it seems to me that the parties must also be in a position to judge this at the time the contract is made. If this is so, I find it difficult to see how such an appreciation can be made if the customer has to guess whether some, and if so which, part of the term will alone be relied upon.

Section 11(2) of the Act requires the court which is determining the question of reasonableness for the purpose of sections 6 and 7 to have regard in particular to the matters specified in Schedule 2. Although Schedule 2 does not apply in the present case, the considerations there set out are usually regarded as being of general application to the question of reasonableness. Two paragraphs of these guidelines would in my judgment be unworkable unless the whole term is being considered.

Paragraph (*b*) provides:

"whether the customer received an inducement to agree to the term, or in accepting it had an opportunity of entering into a similar contract with other persons, but without having to accept a similar term; . . ."

If there was an inducement, it would I think be quite impossible in most cases to say that it related only to the words which the party seeking to establish reasonableness relies upon as opposed to those he wishes to delete. It is equally unreal to suppose that the customer could divine which part the vendor will ultimately seek to rely upon so as to decide whether other persons are willing to contract without the term.

Paragraph (c) provides:

"whether the customer knew or ought reasonably to have known of the existence and extent of the term (having regard, among other things, to any custom of the trade and any previous course of dealing between the parties); . . ."

In my judgment the customer would be most unlikely ever to know the extent of the term if the vendor is entitled, when it is questioned as to reasonableness, to rely on only part of it.

These examples in my judgment support the construction of the word term as being the whole term or clause as drafted, and not merely that part of it which may eventually be taken to be relevant to the case in point.

Nor does it appear to me to be consistent with the policy and purpose of the Act to permit [one, in relation to] a contract ... which taken as a whole is completely unreasonable to put a blue pencil through the most offensive parts and say that what is left is reasonable and sufficient to exclude or restrict his liability in a manner relied upon.

In these circumstances it is unnecessary to decide whether on the material before the court the plaintiffs had discharged the burden of showing that the particular part of clause 12.4 relied upon by them was reasonable.

Balcombe LJ concurred.

NOTES AND QUESTIONS

1. This decision means that, in applying the reasonableness test, the courts cannot sever the reasonable from the unreasonable parts of an exemption clause, even if the defendant is seeking to rely on merely the (alleged) reasonable part. Does this decision ignore the words 'in so far as' in sections 2(2) and 3(2)? How might a draftsperson seek to get round this decision?

2. In *Schenkers Ltd v Overland Shoes Ltd* [1998] 1 Lloyd's Rep 498, a 'no set-off' clause in a contract between a freight forwarder and a commercial customer was upheld as reasonable under sections 3 and 11. Factors relied on by the Court of Appeal included that there was no significant inequality of bargaining position between the parties, that the clause was in common use in the trade, and that it followed negotiations between representative bodies of freight forwarders and customers. In contrast to the *George Mitchell* case (above, 269) the fact that the clause had not been relied on in the past was not regarded as decisive because that past conduct did not indicate that those in the trade thought the clause was unreasonable.

St Albans City and District Council v International Computers Ltd
[1995] FSR 686, Queen's Bench Division

The claimants, a local authority, entered into a contract with the defendants for the supply and installation of computer software to enable the claimants to create a register for the Community Charge. Owing to an error in the software (COMCIS), the claimants gave an inaccurate, overstated, population figure to the Secretary of State. This resulted in the claimants suffering an alleged loss of £1,314,846. In an action for damages for breach of contract, the defendants sought to rely on a clause limiting their liability to £100,000. In awarding damages of £1,314,846, Scott Baker J held, as regards UCTA 1977, that: (i) sections 3 and 6 or 7 of UCTA 1977 applied (this being so as regards section 3 because the claimants were dealing on the defendants' written standard terms of business); (ii) the limitation clause was unreasonable under section 11. On appeal, [1996] 4 All ER 481, the Court of Appeal reduced the amount of damages by £484,000 but upheld, without adding anything of real significance, Scott Baker J's reasoning on UCTA 1977.

Scott Baker J: [Section 3] applies as between contracting parties, where one of them deals as consumer, or on the other's written standard terms of business. At first glance, the plaintiffs fall within the words "deals as consumer" as they did not make the contract within the course of a business (see section 12). However, that is not so because "business" is sufficiently widely defined by section 14 as to embrace the activities of a local authority.

Therefore, in order for section 3 to apply it is necessary for the plaintiffs to have dealt on the defendants' "written standard terms of business". Whether one party deals on the others' written standard terms of business is, I think, a matter to be determined on the facts of the particular case.

The terms in the present case were drawn up by the defendants for incorporation into agreements relating to their computers. In other words, they were specifically designed for their purposes, in contradistinction to the type of standard terms drawn up by, for example, a trade association where conflicting interests in a particular trade are taken into account.

In *The Flamar Pride* [1990] 1 Lloyds Rep 434, at page 438, Potter J. concluded that where there were negotiations and a number of alterations were made to the defendants' standard terms so as to fit the particular circumstances of the plaintiff, the case fell outside the section. However, I do not take it that *all* the terms have to be fixed in advance by the supplier. In many contracts there may be negotiations as to, for example, quality or price but none as to the crucial exempting terms.

What happened in the present case was this. The defendants' proposal or tender outlined how they would approach the plaintiffs' technology requirements. The defendants' eventual proposal amounted to a package containing various constituent elements. As is apparent from looking at the contract documents…there were different and particular terms and conditions for different elements in the package. But it was the 1985 General Conditions that were discussed in October 1988, and it was those conditions that I find were applicable to the problem in this case.

These conditions remained effectively untouched in the negotiations…

I am satisfied on the facts of this case that the plaintiffs dealt on the defendants' written standard terms. The negotiation that there was between the parties did not prevent this from being so.

…

The consequence of my finding that the plaintiffs dealt on the defendants' written standard terms of business is that the defendants cannot rely on the relevant term (Clause 9(c)) except in so far as it satisfies the requirement of reasonableness. By section 11(5) the burden of proof lies on the defendant, and by section 11(1) the test is that the term shall have been a fair and reasonable one to be included, having regard to the circumstances which were or ought reasonably to have been known to, or in the contemplation of, the parties when the contract was made.

In addition to section 3, either section 6 or section 7 applies, and it does not matter which because the relevant provisions are for practical purposes identical. Section 6 covers sale of goods and section 7 supply of goods. In short, the relevant terms can only be excluded or restricted if the term purporting to do so satisfies the requirement of reasonableness.

…

I refer first to the matters in section 11(4):

(a) Resources

The defendants are a very substantial company with ample resources to meet any liability. …

(b) Insurance

At the time of the contract the defendants held product liability cover in an aggregate sum of £50 million worldwide. Accordingly, when they entered the agreement the defendants had ample resources and were covered by insurance to meet any foreseeable claim. The burden of proof of reasonableness lies upon the defendants but they called no evidence to show that it was fair and reasonable to limit their liability to £100,000 or to any other sum. There are some types of agreement when ordinary risks fall within a particular sum, and there may be good reasons for limiting liability to that sum and leaving the purchaser to carry any additional risk. But this is not that kind of case. …

Turning next to the Schedule 2 matters:

(a) Bargaining Position

The defendants were one of a limited number of companies who could meet the plaintiffs [sic] requirements, all of whom dealt on similar standard conditions. The defendants were, therefore, in a very strong bargaining position. ...

[Counsel for the claimants] also draws attention to the rather special position of ... local authorit[ies]. ...Their contracts are governed by specific financial restraints, the need for public evaluation, and often competitive tendering. They do not operate in the same commercial field as a business and probably find it impractical to insure against commercial risks. The plaintiffs' bargaining position, whilst on the one hand better than, say, an individual buying a car from a motor dealer, was weaker than that of the defendants.

(b) Inducement

The defendants received no inducement and had no opportunity of entering a similar contract with anyone else without the exemption clause. The evidence...was that all the defendants' competitors operated with largely the same conditions.

(c) Knowledge of the term

The plaintiffs knew about the exemption clause and made representations about it.

...

In the present case, I take into account, as did Potter J. in *The Flamar Pride*, the schedule 2 guidelines, not only when considering section 6 and section 7 but also when applying section 3. In my judgment, the ultimately determining factors are:

(1)   the parties were of unequal bargaining power;
(2)   the defendants have not justified the figure of £100,000, which was small, both in relation to the potential risk and the actual loss;
(3)   the defendants were insured;
(4)   the practical consequences.

I make the following observations on the fourth point, which follows on in a sense from the third. On whom is it better that a loss of this size should fall, a local authority or an international computer company? The latter is well able to insure (and in this case was insured) and pass on the premium cost to the customers. If the loss is to fall the other way it will ultimately be borne by the local population either by increased taxation or reduced services. I do not think it unreasonable that he who stands to make the profit (ICL) should carry the risk. Therefore, in my view, the practical consequences count in favour of the plaintiffs.

These factors outweigh the fact that bodies such as computer companies and local authorities should be free to make their own bargain, that the plaintiffs contracted with their eyes open, that limitations of this kind are commonplace in the computer industry and that COMCIS was an area of developing technology. At the end of the day, the Act places the burden on the defendants to establish that the exclusion clause was a fair and reasonable one, and in my judgment they have not discharged that burden.

NOTES AND QUESTIONS

1.   Was Scott Baker J correct to regard the local authority as having significantly weaker bargaining power than the defendant computer company? Does his approach illustrate an excessively interventionist approach to reasonableness?
2.   The first issue in this case—were the claimants dealing on the defendants' written standard terms of business?—has generally proved non-problematic

and Scott Baker J's view on this, and that it is a question of fact, was approved by the Court of Appeal in two sentences [1996] 4 All ER 481, 491. A rare exception, where this issue did cause difficulties, was *British Fermentation Products Ltd v Compair* [1999] 2 All ER (Comm) 389 in which Judge Bowsher QC, with respect erroneously, decided that the suppliers' use of a model form of contract did not constitute contracting on the suppliers' 'standard terms of business' because the suppliers had not shown that they were their own usual terms.

Watford Electronics Ltd v Sanderson CFL Ltd
[2001] EWCA Civ 317, [2001] 1 All ER (Comm) 696, Court of Appeal

The claimant company (Watford), which was a business engaged in the mail order sale of computers, contracted with the defendant (Sanderson) for the supply of a bespoke software system for dealing with its sales, stock and accounts. The contract contained the defendant's standard terms which included a limit of liability clause of two terms, one excluding liability for any 'claims for indirect or consequential losses whether arising from negligence or otherwise' and the other limiting liability in any event to the contract price paid (which was here £104,600). The system ('Mailbrain') proved to be defective and the claimant sought damages of over £5.5M for breach of contract comprising loss of profits (of some £4.4M), the increased costs of working, and the cost of a replacement software system. On a preliminary issue, the Court of Appeal, reversing the trial judge, held that each of the two terms in the limit of liability clause was reasonable under section 11 of UCTA 1977.

Chadwick LJ:

49... I am satisfied that this is a case in which, if this Court takes a different view from that of the judge on the question whether the inclusion of the limit of liability clause in Sanderson's standard terms and conditions was fair and reasonable having regard to the circumstances which were, or ought reasonably to have been, known to or in the contemplation of the parties when the contract was made, it is entitled to give effect to its own view. That is because I am satisfied that the judge reached his conclusion on the wrong basis.

50 ...[O]n a true analysis of the limit of liability clause, it comprises two distinct contract terms in relation to which it is necessary to consider whether the requirement of reasonableness is satisfied. One (to which I shall refer for convenience as "the term excluding indirect loss") is that contained in the first sentence of the clause. The other ("the term limiting direct loss") is contained in the second sentence. It is, I think, appropriate to consider, separately in relation to each term, whether the requirement of reasonableness is satisfied; although, of course, in considering whether that requirement is satisfied in relation to each term, the existence of the other term in the contract is relevant.

51 I turn, therefore, to consider whether the requirement of reasonableness is satisfied in relation to the term excluding indirect loss. It is important to keep in mind (i) that, as a matter of construction, the term does not seek to exclude loss resulting from pre-contractual statements in relation to which a claim lies (if at all) in tort or under the Misrepresentation Act 1967 and (ii) that the term is qualified by the addenda so that it does not exclude indirect or consequential loss resulting from breach of warranty unless Sanderson has used its best endeavours to ensure that the equipment and the software does comply with the warranty.

52 I accept that the court is required to have regard, in the present case, to the 'guideline' matters set out in Sch 2 to the 1977 Act. There are factors, identified by the guidelines, which point to a conclusion that the term excluding indirect loss was a fair and reasonable one to include in this contract. The parties were of equal bargaining strength; the inclusion of the term was, plainly, likely to affect Sanderson 's decision as to the price at which [it] was prepared to sell its product; Watford must be taken to have appreciated that; Watford knew of the term, and must be taken to have understood what effect it was intended to have; the product was, to some extent, modified to meet the special needs of the customer. Other factors point in the opposite direction. The judge found that, although there were other mail order packages on the market, Mailbrain was the only one which appeared to fulfil Watford's needs…; and, further, that Watford could not reasonably have expected to have been able to have acquired a similar software package, if available, on better terms as to performance and as to the supplier's potential liability for non-performance.

53 I do not, for my part, accept that the term excluding indirect loss is a term to which s 11(4) of the 1977 Act applies. It is not, I think, properly to be regarded as a term by which a person (Sanderson) seeks to restrict liability to a specified sum of money; rather the term seeks to exclude liability for indirect or consequential loss altogether, in those circumstances in which it is intended to have effect. Nevertheless, it seems to me right to have regard, as part of the circumstances which were, or ought reasonably to have been, known to or in the contemplation of the parties when the contract was made, both to the resources which could be expected to be available to each party for the purpose of meeting indirect or consequential loss resulting from the failure of the equipment or software to perform in accordance with specification, and to the possibility that such loss could be covered by insurance.

54 It seems to me that the starting point in an enquiry whether, in the present case, the term excluding indirect loss was a fair and reasonable one to include in the contract which these parties made is to recognise (i) that there is a significant risk that a non-standard software product, 'customised' to meet the particular marketing, accounting or record-keeping needs of a substantial and relatively complex business (such as that carried on by Watford), may not perform to the customer's satisfaction, (ii) that, if it does not do so, there is a significant risk that the customer may not make the profits or savings which it had hoped to make (and may incur consequential losses arising from the product's failure to perform), (iii) that those risks were, or ought reasonably to have been, known to or in the contemplation of both Sanderson and Watford at the time when the contract was made, (iv) that Sanderson was in the better position to assess the risk that the product would fail to perform but (v) that Watford was in the better position to assess the amount of the potential loss if the product failed to perform, (vi) that the risk of loss was likely to be capable of being covered by insurance, but at a cost, and (vii) that both Sanderson and Watford would have known, or ought reasonably to have known, at the time when the contract was made, that the identity of the party who was to bear the risk of loss (or to bear the cost of insurance) was a factor which would be taken into account in determining the price at which the supplier was willing to supply the product and the price at which the customer was willing to purchase. With those considerations in mind, it is reasonable to expect that the contract will make provision for the risk of indirect or consequential loss to fall on one party or the other. In circumstances in which parties of equal bargaining power negotiate a price for the supply of product under an agreement which provides for the person on whom the risk of loss will fall, it seems to me that the court should be very cautious before reaching the conclusion that the agreement which they have reached is not a fair and reasonable one.

55 Where experienced businessmen representing substantial companies of equal bargaining power negotiate an agreement, they may be taken to have had regard to the matters known to them. They should, in my view be taken to be the best judge of the commercial fairness of the agreement which they have made; including the fairness of each of the terms in that agreement. They should be taken to be the best judge on the question whether the terms of the agreement are reasonable. The court should not assume that either is likely to commit his company to an agreement which he thinks is unfair, or which he thinks includes unreasonable terms., Unless satisfied that one party has, in effect, taken unfair advantage of the other – or

that a term is so unreasonable that it cannot properly have been understood or considered—the court should not interfere.

56 In the present case the parties did negotiate as to the price. Mr Jessa, on behalf of Watford, secured substantial concessions on price...The parties negotiated, also, as to which of them should bear the risk (or the cost of insurance against the risk) of making good the loss of profits, and other indirect or consequential loss, which Watford might suffer if the product failed to perform as intended. Mr Jessa was less successful in obtaining...the concession which he wanted. The most that he could get was an undertaking that Sanderson would use its best endeavours to allocate appropriate resources to ensuring that the product performed according to specification. But, for the reasons which I have sought to explain, that was worth something to Watford; and Mr Jessa decided that he would be content with what he could get. In my view it is impossible to hold, in the circumstances of the present case, that Sanderson took unfair advantage of Watford; or that Watford, through Mr Jessa, did not properly understand and consider the effect of the term excluding indirect loss.

57 It follows that I would hold that the term excluding indirect loss, applicable in the circumstances which I have described, was a fair and reasonable one to include in the contract.

58 In the light of that conclusion, the question whether the requirement of reasonableness is satisfied in relation to the term limiting direct loss can be answered shortly. Properly understood, all that the second sentence of the limit of liability clause seeks to do is to substitute a value equal to the price paid by the buyer for the goods for "the value which the goods would have had if they had fulfilled the warranty" for the purposes of the rule in s 53(3) of the Sale of Goods Act 1979 or the equivalent rule at common law. It seems to me impossible to hold that that is an unfair or unreasonable substitution to make in a case like the present.

Buckley J concurred and **Peter Gibson LJ** gave a concurring judgment.

NOTES AND QUESTIONS

1. This is a rare example of the Court of Appeal overturning a decision of the trial judge on reasonableness under UCTA 1977.
2. In contrast to the *Stewart Gill* case above, one was here dealing with two separate terms, albeit in a single clause. The reasonableness of each was therefore assessed separately (although the existence of the other term was relevant).
3. The non-interventionist approach to reasonableness taken here contrasts sharply with that taken in the *St Albans* computer software case (above, 279). Which approach is preferable?
4. A similarly non-interventionist approach to reasonableness was taken in *Granville Oil and Chemicals Ltd v Davies Turner and Co Ltd* [2003] EWCA Civ 570, [2003] 1 All ER (Comm) 819. The British International Freight Association's Standard Trading Conditions were there incorporated into a contract for the carriage of a consignment of paint. Those terms included a nine-month time bar for claims. The Court of Appeal held that that time bar, properly construed, did not fail the reasonableness test in section 11 of UCTA 1977. Tuckey LJ, with whom Hart J and Potter LJ agreed, said, at [31], 'The 1977 Act obviously plays a very important role in protecting vulnerable consumers from the effect of draconian contract terms. But I am less enthusiastic about its intrusion into contracts between commercial parties of equal bargaining strength, who should generally be considered capable of being

able to make contracts of their choosing and expect to be bound by their terms.'

5. The *Watford Electronics* case was distinguished in *Britvic Soft Drinks Ltd v Messer UK Ltd* [2002] EWCA Civ 548, [2002] 2 Lloyd's Rep 368. The Court of Appeal, upholding the trial judge, struck down as unreasonable a clause excluding the liability of suppliers of CO_2 for the unsatisfactory quality and non-fitness for purpose of the CO_2 in a situation where the CO_2 had been contaminated with benzene because of a manufacturing mishap. The exclusion was held to be unreasonable because the situation here was an extreme one where such contamination would not have been contemplated as a possibility by the parties.

6. Although not touched on in the extract above, the courts in *Watford Electronics* and a number of other cases have controversially taken a somewhat technical construction of the words 'indirect or consequential loss' which they have construed to mean losses falling under the second rule in *Hadley v Baxendale* (see below, 357). That is, 'direct loss' is treated as loss that follows naturally from the breach, while indirect or consequential loss is construed as loss that is recoverable only if special circumstances were brought to the defendant's attention.

2. THE UNFAIR TERMS IN CONSUMER CONTRACTS REGULATIONS 1999

The background to these regulations is the 1993 European Union Directive on Unfair Terms in Consumer Contracts (93/13/EEC of 5 April 1993 [1993] OJ L 95/29). This Directive was initially implemented in the United Kingdom by the Unfair Terms in Consumer Contracts Regulations 1994 (SI 3159/94). However, primarily in order to allow a number of other bodies (eg the Consumers' Association, and trading standards departments) to be added to the Office of Fair Trading as entitled to bring proceedings to prevent the use of unfair terms, the 1994 Regulations were replaced by the 1999 Regulations for contracts made after 1 October 1999.

Unfair Terms in Consumer Contracts Regulations 1999, SI 1999 No 2083

Preamble
Whereas the Secretary of State is a Minister designated for the purposes of section 2(2) of the European Communities Act 1972 in relation to measures relating to consumer protection:

Now, the Secretary of State, in exercise of the powers conferred upon him by section 2(2) of that Act, hereby makes the following Regulations:—

1 Citation and commencement
These Regulations may be cited as the Unfair Terms in Consumer Contracts Regulations 1999 and shall come into force on 1st October 1999.

2 Revocation
The Unfair Terms in Consumer Contracts Regulations 1994 are hereby revoked.

3 Interpretation
    (1) In these Regulations—

— "the Community" means the European Community;
— "consumer" means any natural person who, in contracts covered by these Regulations, is acting for purposes which are outside his trade, business or profession;
— "court" in relation to England and Wales and Northern Ireland means a county court or the High Court, and in relation to Scotland, the Sheriff or the Court of Session;
— "[OFT]" means [the Office of Fair Trading];
— "EEA Agreement" means the Agreement on the European Economic Area signed at Oporto on 2nd May 1992 as adjusted by the protocol signed at Brussels on 17th March 1993;
— "Member State" means a State which is a contracting party to the EEA Agreement;
— "notified" means notified in writing;
— "qualifying body" means a person specified in Schedule 1;
— "seller or supplier" means any natural or legal person who, in contracts covered by these Regulations, is acting for purposes relating to his trade, business or profession, whether publicly owned or privately owned;
— "unfair terms" means the contractual terms referred to in regulation 5.

    [(1A) The references—

(a)   in regulation 4(1) to a seller or a supplier, and
(b)   in regulation 8(1) to a seller or supplier,

include references to a distance supplier and to an intermediary.
    (1B) In paragraph (1A) and regulation 5(6)—
    "distance supplier" means—

(a)   a supplier under a distance contract within the meaning of the Financial Services (Distance Marketing) Regulations 2004, or
(b)   a supplier of unsolicited financial services within regulation 15 of those Regulations; and

    "intermediary" has the same meaning as in those Regulations.]
    (2) In the application of these Regulations to Scotland for references to an "injunction" or an "interim injunction" there shall be substituted references to an "interdict" or "interim interdict" respectively.

4 Terms to which these Regulations apply
    (1) These Regulations apply in relation to unfair terms in contracts concluded between a seller or a supplier and a consumer.
    (2) These Regulations do not apply to contractual terms which reflect—

(a)   mandatory statutory or regulatory provisions (including such provisions under the law of any Member State or in Community legislation having effect in the United Kingdom without further enactment);
(b)   the provisions or principles of international conventions to which the Member States or the Community are party.

5 Unfair Terms

(1) A contractual term which has not been individually negotiated shall be regarded as unfair if, contrary to the requirement of good faith, it causes a significant imbalance in the parties' rights and obligations arising under the contract, to the detriment of the consumer.

(2) A term shall always be regarded as not having been individually negotiated where it has been drafted in advance and the consumer has therefore not been able to influence the substance of the term.

(3) Notwithstanding that a specific term or certain aspects of it in a contract has been individually negotiated, these Regulations shall apply to the rest of a contract if an overall assessment of it indicates that it is a pre-formulated standard contract.

(4) It shall be for any seller or supplier who claims that a term was individually negotiated to show that it was.

(5) Schedule 2 to these Regulations contains an indicative and non-exhaustive list of the terms which may be regarded as unfair.

[(6) Any contractual term providing that a consumer bears the burden of proof in respect of showing whether a distance supplier or an intermediary complied with any or all of the obligations placed upon him resulting from the Directive and any rule or enactment implementing it shall always be regarded as unfair.

(7) In paragraph (6)—

— "the Directive" means Directive 2002/65/EC of the European Parliament and of the Council of 23 September 2002 concerning the distance marketing of consumer financial services and amending Council Directive 90/619/EEC and Directives 97/7/EC and 98/27/EC; and
— "rule" means a rule made by the Financial Services Authority under the Financial Services and Markets Act 2000 or by a designated professional body within the meaning of section 326(2) of that Act.]

6 Assessment of unfair terms

(1) Without prejudice to regulation 12, the unfairness of a contractual term shall be assessed, taking into account the nature of the goods or services for which the contract was concluded and by referring, at the time of conclusion of the contract, to all the circumstances attending the conclusion of the contract and to all the other terms of the contract or of another contract on which it is dependent.

(2) In so far as it is in plain intelligible language, the assessment of fairness of a term shall not relate—

(a) to the definition of the main subject matter of the contract, or
(b) to the adequacy of the price or remuneration, as against the goods or services supplied in exchange.

7 Written contracts

(1) A seller or supplier shall ensure that any written term of a contract is expressed in plain, intelligible language.

(2) If there is doubt about the meaning of a written term, the interpretation which is most favourable to the consumer shall prevail but this rule shall not apply in proceedings brought under regulation 12.

8 Effect of unfair term

(1) An unfair term in a contract concluded with a consumer by a seller or supplier shall not be binding on the consumer.

(2) The contract shall continue to bind the parties if it is capable of continuing in existence without the unfair term.

9 Choice of law clauses

These Regulations shall apply notwithstanding any contract term which applies or purports to apply the law of a non-Member State, if the contract has a close connection with the territory of the Member States.

10 Complaints—consideration by [OFT]

(1) It shall be the duty of the [OFT] to consider any complaint made to [it] that any contract term drawn up for general use is unfair, unless—

(a)   the complaint appears to the [OFT] to be frivolous or vexatious; or

(b)   a qualifying body has notified the [OFT] that it agrees to consider the complaint.

(2) The [OFT] shall give reasons for [its] decision to apply or not to apply, as the case may be, for an injunction under regulation 12 in relation to any complaint which these Regulations require [it] to consider.

(3) In deciding whether or not to apply for an injunction in respect of a term which the [OFT] considers to be unfair, [it] may, if [it] considers it appropriate to do so, have regard to any undertakings given to [it] by or on behalf of any person as to the continued use of such a term in contracts concluded with consumers.

11 Complaints—consideration by qualifying bodies

(1) If a qualifying body specified in Part One of Schedule 1 notifies the [OFT] that it agrees to consider a complaint that any contract term drawn up for general use is unfair, it shall be under a duty to consider that complaint.

(2) Regulation 10(2) and (3) shall apply to a qualifying body which is under a duty to consider a complaint as they apply to the [OFT].

12 Injunctions to prevent continued use of unfair terms

(1) The [OFT] or, subject to paragraph (2), any qualifying body may apply for an injunction (including an interim injunction) against any person appearing to the [OFT] or that body to be using, or recommending use of, an unfair term drawn up for general use in contracts concluded with consumers.

(2) A qualifying body may apply for an injunction only where—

(a)   it has notified the [OFT] of its intention to apply at least fourteen days before the date on which the application is made, beginning with the date on which the notification was given; or

(b)   the [OFT] consents to the application being made within a shorter period.

(3) The court on an application under this regulation may grant an injunction on such terms as it thinks fit.

(4) An injunction may relate not only to use of a particular contract term drawn up for general use but to any similar term, or a term having like effect, used or recommended for use by any person.

13 Powers of the [OFT] and qualifying bodies to obtain documents and information

(1) The [OFT] may exercise the power conferred by this regulation for the purpose of—

(a)   facilitating [its] consideration of a complaint that a contract term drawn up for general use is unfair; or

(b)   ascertaining whether a person has complied with an undertaking or court order as to the continued use, or recommendation for use, of a term in contracts concluded with consumers.

(2) A qualifying body specified in Part One of Schedule 1 may exercise the power conferred by this regulation for the purpose of—

(a)   facilitating its consideration of a complaint that a contract term drawn up for general use is unfair; or
(b)   ascertaining whether a person has complied with—
    (i)   an undertaking given to it or to the court following an application by that body, or
    (ii)   a court order made on an application by that body,

as to the continued use, or recommendation for use, of a term in contracts concluded with consumers.

(3) The [OFT] may require any person to supply to [it], and a qualifying body specified in Part One of Schedule 1 may require any person to supply to it—

(a)   a copy of any document which that person has used or recommended for use, at the time the notice referred to in paragraph (4) below is given, as a pre-formulated standard contract in dealings with consumers;
(b)   information about the use, or recommendation for use, by that person of that document or any other such document in dealings with consumers.

(4) The power conferred by this regulation is to be exercised by a notice in writing which may—

(a)   specify the way in which and the time within which it is to be complied with; and
(b)   be varied or revoked by a subsequent notice.

(5) Nothing in this regulation compels a person to supply any document or information which he would be entitled to refuse to produce or give in civil proceedings before the court.

(6) If a person makes default in complying with a notice under this regulation, the court may, on the application of the [OFT] or of the qualifying body, make such order as the court thinks fit for requiring the default to be made good, and any such order may provide that all the costs or expenses of and incidental to the application shall be borne by the person in default or by any officers of a company or other association who are responsible for its default.

14 Notification of undertakings and orders to [OFT]
A qualifying body shall notify the [OFT]—

(a)   of any undertaking given to it by or on behalf of any person as to the continued use of a term which that body considers to be unfair in contracts concluded with consumers;
(b)   of the outcome of any application made by it under regulation 12, and of the terms of any undertaking given to, or order made by, the court;
(c)   of the outcome of any application made by it to enforce a previous order of the court.

15 Publication, information and advice
(1) The [OFT] shall arrange for the publication in such form and manner as [it] considers appropriate, of—

(a)   details of any undertaking or order notified to [it] under regulation 14;

(b)   details of any undertaking given to [it] by or on behalf of any person as to the continued use of a term which the [OFT] considers to be unfair in contracts concluded with consumers;

(c)   details of any application made by [it] under regulation 12, and of the terms of any undertaking given to, or order made by, the court;

(d)   details of any application made by the [OFT] to enforce a previous order of the court.

(2) The [OFT] shall inform any person on request whether a particular term to which these Regulations apply has been—

(a)   the subject of an undertaking given to the [OFT] or notified to [it] by a qualifying body; or

(b)   the subject of an order of the court made upon application by [it] or notified to [it] by a qualifying body;

and shall give that person details of the undertaking or a copy of the order, as the case may be, together with a copy of any amendments which the person giving the undertaking has agreed to make to the term in question.

(3) The [OFT] may arrange for the dissemination in such form and manner as [it] considers appropriate of such information and advice concerning the operation of these Regulations as may appear to [it] to be expedient to give to the public and to all persons likely to be affected by these Regulations.

[16 The functions of the Financial Services Authority]
[The functions of the Financial Services Authority under these Regulations shall be treated as functions of the Financial Services Authority under the [Financial Services and Markets Act 2000].]

SCHEDULE 1 QUALIFYING BODIES

Regulation 3

Part One
[1   The Information Commissioner.
2   The Gas and Electricity Markets Authority.
3   The Director General of Electricity Supply for Northern Ireland.
4   The Director General of Gas for Northern Ireland.
5   [The Office of Communications].
6   [The Water Services Regulation Authority].
7   [The Office of Rail Regulation].
8   Every weights and measures authority in Great Britain.
9   The Department of Enterprise, Trade and Investment in Northern Ireland.
10   The Financial Services Authority.]

Part Two
11   Consumers' Association

SCHEDULE 2 INDICATIVE AND NON-EXHAUSTIVE LIST OF TERMS WHICH MAY BE REGARDED AS UNFAIR

Regulation 5(5)

1

Terms which have the object or effect of—

(a)   excluding or limiting the legal liability of a seller or supplier in the event of the death of a consumer or personal injury to the latter resulting from an act or omission of that seller or supplier;

(b)   inappropriately excluding or limiting the legal rights of the consumer vis-a-vis the seller or supplier or another party in the event of total or partial non-performance or inadequate performance by the seller or supplier of any of the contractual obligations, including the option of offsetting a debt owed to the seller or supplier against any claim which the consumer may have against him;

(c)   making an agreement binding on the consumer whereas provision of services by the seller or supplier is subject to a condition whose realisation depends on his own will alone;

(d)   permitting the seller or supplier to retain sums paid by the consumer where the latter decides not to conclude or perform the contract, without providing for the consumer to receive compensation of an equivalent amount from the seller or supplier where the latter is the party cancelling the contract;

(e)   requiring any consumer who fails to fulfil his obligation to pay a disproportionately high sum in compensation;

(f)   authorising the seller or supplier to dissolve the contract on a discretionary basis where the same facility is not granted to the consumer, or permitting the seller or supplier to retain the sums paid for services not yet supplied by him where it is the seller or supplier himself who dissolves the contract;

(g)   enabling the seller or supplier to terminate a contract of indeterminate duration without reasonable notice except where there are serious grounds for doing so;

(h)   automatically extending a contract of fixed duration where the consumer does not indicate otherwise, when the deadline fixed for the consumer to express his desire not to extend the contract is unreasonably early;

(i)   irrevocably binding the consumer to terms with which he had no real opportunity of becoming acquainted before the conclusion of the contract;

(j)   enabling the seller or supplier to alter the terms of the contract unilaterally without a valid reason which is specified in the contract;

(k)   enabling the seller or supplier to alter unilaterally without a valid reason any characteristics of the product or service to be provided;

(l)   providing for the price of goods to be determined at the time of delivery or allowing a seller of goods or supplier of services to increase their price without in both cases giving the consumer the corresponding right to cancel the contract if the final price is too high in relation to the price agreed when the contract was concluded;

(m)   giving the seller or supplier the right to determine whether the goods or services supplied are in conformity with the contract, or giving him the exclusive right to interpret any term of the contract;

(n)   limiting the seller's or supplier's obligation to respect commitments undertaken by his agents or making his commitments subject to compliance with a particular formality;

(o)   obliging the consumer to fulfil all his obligations where the seller or supplier does not perform his;

(p)   giving the seller or supplier the possibility of transferring his rights and obligations under the contract, where this may serve to reduce the guarantees for the consumer, without the latter's agreement;

(q)   excluding or hindering the consumer's right to take legal action or exercise any other legal remedy, particularly by requiring the consumer to take disputes exclusively to arbitration not covered by legal provisions, unduly restricting the evidence available to him or imposing on him a burden of proof which, according to the applicable law, should lie with another party to the contract.

2
Scope of paragraphs 1(g), (j) and (l)

(a) Paragraph 1(g) is without hindrance to terms by which a supplier of financial services reserves the right to terminate unilaterally a contract of indeterminate duration without notice where there is a valid reason, provided that the supplier is required to inform the other contracting party or parties thereof immediately.

(b) Paragraph 1(j) is without hindrance to terms under which a supplier of financial services reserves the right to alter the rate of interest payable by the consumer or due to the latter, or the amount of other charges for financial services without notice where there is a valid reason, provided that the supplier is required to inform the other contracting party or parties thereof at the earliest opportunity and that the latter are free to dissolve the contract immediately.

Paragraph 1(j) is also without hindrance to terms under which a seller or supplier reserves the right to alter unilaterally the conditions of a contract of indeterminate duration, provided that he is required to inform the consumer with reasonable notice and that the consumer is free to dissolve the contract.

(c) Paragraphs 1(g), (j) and (l) do not apply to:

— transactions in transferable securities, financial instruments and other products or services where the price is linked to fluctuations in a stock exchange quotation or index or a financial market rate that the seller or supplier does not control;

— contracts for the purchase or sale of foreign currency, traveller's cheques or international money orders denominated in foreign currency.

(d) Paragraph 1(l) is without hindrance to price indexation clauses, where lawful, provided that the method by which prices vary is explicitly described.

(1)   Overview of the Central Scheme of the 1999 Regulations

(i)   The Regulations apply only to unfair terms in contracts concluded between a seller or supplier and a consumer. By regulation 3(1) a consumer is defined as meaning a natural person (ie not a company) who is acting for purposes outside his business.

(ii)   The heart of the Regulations is in the definition of an unfair term in regulation 5(1). This reads as follows: 'A contractual term which has not been individually negotiated should be regarded as unfair if, contrary to the requirement of good faith, it causes a significant imbalance in the parties' rights and obligations under the contract, to the detriment of the consumer.'

(iii)   By regulation 6(2), provided in plain intelligible language, the definition of the main subject matter and the price or remuneration cannot be regarded as unfair. In other words, the core terms of a contract are outside the scope of the Regulations.

(iv)   Guidance as to the kind of terms which may be regarded as unfair is given in a list of terms in Schedule 2 to the Regulations. This is a so-called 'grey' list – that is, an indicative list – rather than being a 'black' list.

(v)   By regulation 8(1), the consequences of a term being unfair is that it shall not be binding on the consumer; and by regulation 12, the Office of Fair Trading, and the other bodies now given such power, may seek an injunction to prevent the use of the term. The leading case on the Regulations, *Director General of Fair Trading v First National Bank Plc* (below, 294) was a case involving an application for an injunction by the DGFT.

(2) What is the Relationship Between the 1999 Regulations and UCTA 1977?

(i)   The 1999 Regulations apply to a wider range of terms than does UCTA 1977. UCTA 1977 is confined to exclusion or limitation clauses and indemnity clauses. But the 1999 Regulations apply to all types of unfair term other than the core terms of a contract. In this sense the Regulations are wider.

(ii)   On the other hand, those who are protected are more narrowly defined under the 1999 Regulations than under UCTA 1977. The Regulations are confined to protecting consumers (and the definition of consumers excludes companies). UCTA 1977 is not solely concerned with the protection of consumers. Rather, as we have seen, some provisions of UCTA apply in business to business transactions (eg section 2(2), section 3 if a party is dealing on the other's written standard terms of business, and sections 6 and 7 which control the exclusion of statutorily implied terms in business to business contracts). Moreover, *R & B Customer Brokers v UDT* (above, 254) has controversially decided that the UCTA definition of consumer can include a company.

(iii) UCTA 1977 and the 1999 Regulations both apply where one is dealing with a (standard form) exclusion or limitation or indemnity clause in relation to a consumer who is a natural person. One can anticipate that the results reached under the two pieces of legislation will be the same. However, this is not inevitably the case because the two tests ('fair and reasonable' under UCTA 1977 and 'good faith' and 'significant imbalance' under the 1999 Regulations) are not identically worded. The law is in this needlessly complex state because the decision was made to implement the 1993 Directive by a 'copy-out' technique. The law would have been more coherent had the Government tried to integrate the requirements of the EU Directive with the existing law in UCTA 1977.

(3) Case-law on the 1999 Regulations

There have been very few cases on the Regulations. We shall now consider the only one of major importance. This actually concerned the 1994 Regulations but the equivalent provisions of the 1999 Regulations are, to all intents and purposes, the same.

Director General of Fair Trading v First National Bank Plc
[2001] UKHL 52, [2002] 1 AC 481, House of Lords

In its standard contract of loan, a term in condition 8 entitled the defendant bank to interest at the contractual rate 'after as well as before any judgment' until repayment (of the original loan plus outstanding interest). Under the general law, once there has been a judgment, the obligation to repay becomes merged in the judgment, so that contractually agreed interest is no longer payable albeit that statutory interest generally is by reason of, eg, the County Courts (Interest on Judgment Debts) Order 1991. However, judgment debts in respect of credit agreements regulated by the Consumer Credit Act 1974—which includes loans by banks to consumers—are excluded from the 1991 Order so that no statutory interest is payable on such judgment debts. Hence the defendant bank's inclusion of the term in condition 8 entitling it to contractual interest after judgment.

Exercising his power under what is now Regulation 12 of the 1999 Regulations, but was then Regulation 8 of the 1994 Regulations, the DGFT sought an injunction to prevent the defendant bank continuing to use the term as to post-judgment interest on the ground that it was an unfair term under the Regulations. The House of Lords held that the term was not a core term so that the Regulations applied; but that, overturning the Court of Appeal, the term satisfied the test of fairness so that the injunction should be refused.

Lord Bingham of Cornhill:

10 In reliance on regulation 3(2)(b) [of the 1994 Regulations] Lord Goodhart, on behalf of the bank, submitted that no assessment might be made of the fairness of the term because it concerns the adequacy of the bank's remuneration as against the services supplied, namely the loan of money. A bank's remuneration under a credit agreement is the receipt of interest. The term, by entitling the bank to post-judgment interest, concerns the quantum and thus the adequacy of that remuneration. ...

12 In agreement with the judge and the Court of Appeal, I do not accept the bank's submission on this issue. The Regulations, as Professor Sir Guenter Treitel QC has aptly observed (*Treitel The Law of Contract*, 10th ed (1999), p 248), "are not intended to operate as a mechanism of quality or price control" and regulation 3(2) is of "crucial importance in recognising the parties' freedom of contract with respect to the essential features of their bargain": p 249. But there is an important "distinction between the term or terms which express the substance of the bargain and 'incidental' (if important) terms which surround them": *Chitty on Contracts*, 28th ed (1999), vol 1, ch 15 "Unfair Terms in Consumer Contracts", p 747, para 15-025. The object of the Regulations and the Directive is to protect consumers against the inclusion of unfair and prejudicial terms in standard-form contracts into which they enter, and that object would plainly be frustrated if regulation 3(2)(b) were so broadly interpreted as to cover any terms other than those falling squarely within it. In my opinion the term, as part of a provision prescribing the consequences of default, plainly does not fall within it. It does not concern the adequacy of the interest earned by the bank as its remuneration but is designed to ensure that the bank's entitlement to interest does not come to an end on the entry of judgment. ... [T]he term [is] an ancillary provision and not one concerned with the adequacy of the bank's remuneration as against the services supplied. ...

[Having set out the test of unfairness in regulation 4(1) of the 1994 Regulations he continued:]

17 The test laid down by regulation 4(1), deriving as it does from article 3(1) of the Directive, has understandably attracted much discussion in academic and professional circles and helpful submissions were made to the House on it. It is plain from the recitals to the Directive that one of its objectives was partially to harmonise the law in this important field among all member states of the European Union. The member states have no common concept of fairness or good faith, and the Directive does not purport to state the law of any single member state. It lays down a test to be applied, whatever their pre-existing law, by all member states. If the meaning of the test were doubtful, or vulnerable to the possibility of differing interpretations in differing member states, it might be desirable or necessary to seek a ruling from the European Court of Justice on its interpretation. But the language used in expressing the test, so far as applicable in this case, is in my opinion clear and not reasonably capable of differing interpretations. A term falling within the scope of the Regulations is unfair if it causes a significant imbalance in the parties' rights and obligations under the contract to the detriment of the consumer in a manner or to an extent which is contrary to the requirement of good faith. The requirement of significant imbalance is met if a term is so weighted in favour of the supplier as to tilt the parties' rights and obligations under the contract significantly in his favour. This may be by the granting to the supplier of a beneficial option or discretion or power, or by the imposing on the consumer of a disadvantageous burden or risk or duty. The illustrative terms set out in Schedule 3 to the Regulations provide very good examples of terms which may be regarded as unfair; whether a given term is or is not to be so regarded depends on whether it causes a significant imbalance in the parties' rights and obligations under the contract. This involves looking at the contract as a whole. But the imbalance must be to the detriment of the consumer; a significant imbalance to the detriment of the supplier, assumed to be the stronger party, is not a mischief which the Regulations seek to address. The requirement of good faith in this context is one of fair and open dealing. Openness requires that the terms should be expressed fully, clearly and legibly, containing no concealed pitfalls or traps. Appropriate prominence should be given to terms which might operate disadvantageously to the customer. Fair dealing requires that a supplier should not, whether deliberately or unconsciously, take advantage of the consumer's necessity, indigence, lack of experience, unfamiliarity with the subject matter of the contract, weak bargaining position or any other factor listed in or analogous to those listed in Schedule 2 to the Regulations. Good faith in this context is not an artificial or technical concept; nor, since Lord Mansfield was its champion, is it a concept wholly unfamiliar to British lawyers. It looks to good standards of commercial morality and practice. Regulation 4(1) lays down a composite test, covering both the making and the substance of the contract, and must be applied bearing clearly in mind the objective which the Regulations are designed to promote.

18 In support of his contention that the term is unfair the Director adduced evidence of complaints made to him by a number of borrowers. Some of these disclose a very highly unsatisfactory state of affairs. In one case a husband and wife borrowed £3,000 plus £443.70 for insurance to finance improvements to their home. The principal was repayable over a five-year term by instalments of £84.89 plus £8.98 insurance. The borrowers fell into arrear and judgment was given for £3,953.11. The court ordered this sum to be paid by monthly instalments of £4.18, at which rate (it was calculated) the judgment debt would take 78 years to clear. Meanwhile, under the contract, interest would continue to accrue even if the instalments were fully and punctually paid. The bank's deponent described these borrowers as

"a good example of customers who demonstrated an ability easily to pay the instalments for home improvements when the credit was granted but thereafter appeared to have undertaken many other financial commitments which seriously prejudiced their ability to pay" the bank. A financial statement prepared on these borrowers some months before the county court judgment is consistent with that assertion.

19 For the Director, reliance was placed on the provisions in the 1991 Order which denied the court power to order payment of statutory interest on money judgments given under regulated agreements and precluded entitlement to interest in any case where payment by instalments had been ordered and the instalments had been fully and punctually paid. It was argued that the term was unfair because it denied the borrower the protection which those provisions afforded. ...

20 In judging the fairness of the term it is necessary to consider the position of typical parties when the contract is made. The borrower wants to borrow a sum of money, often quite a modest sum, often for purposes of improving his home. He discloses an income sufficient to finance repayment by instalments over the contract term. If he cannot do that, the bank will be unwilling to lend. The essential bargain is that the bank will make funds available to the borrower which the borrower will repay, over a period, with interest. Neither party could suppose that the bank would willingly forgo any part of its principal or interest. If the bank thought that outcome at all likely, it would not lend. If there were any room for doubt about the borrower's obligation to repay the principal in full with interest, that obligation is very clearly and unambiguously expressed in the conditions of contract. There is nothing unbalanced or detrimental to the consumer in that obligation; the absence of such a term would unbalance the contract to the detriment of the lender.

22 Should it then be said that the provisions of the 1991 Order render the term unfair, providing as it does for a continuing obligation to pay interest after judgment notwithstanding the payment of instalments by the borrower in accordance with a court order? It is, I think, pertinent that the 1974 [Consumer Credit] Act, which laid down a number of stipulations with which regulated agreements must comply, did not prohibit terms providing for post-judgment interest even though it required claims to enforce regulated agreements to be brought in the county court which could not at the time award statutory interest in any circumstances. ... I do not think that the term can be stigmatised as unfair on the ground that it violates or undermines a statutory regime enacted for the protection of consumers.

24 ...On balance, I do not consider that the term can properly be said to cause a significant imbalance in the parties' rights and obligations under the contract to the detriment of the consumer in a manner or to an extent which is contrary to the requirement of good faith.

Lord Steyn:

33 The Directive made provision for a dual system of ex casu challenges and pre-emptive or collective challenges by appropriate bodies: see article 7. This system was domestically enacted in the 1994 Regulations, with the Director General of Fair Trading as the administering official to investigate and take action on complaints... The 1999 Regulations extended the system of enforcement by including other bodies as qualified to undertake pre-emptive challenges. The system of pre-emptive challenges is a more effective way of preventing the continuing use of unfair terms and changing contracting practice than ex casu actions: see Susan Bright, "Winning the battle against unfair contract terms" (2000) 20 LS 331, 333-338. It is, however, to be noted that in a pre-emptive challenge there is not a direct lis between the consumer and the other contracting party. The Directive and the Regulations do not always distinguish between the two situations. This point is illustrated by the emphasis in article 4.1 of the Directive and regulation 4(2) on the relevance of particular circumstances affecting a contractual relationship. The Directive and the Regulations must be made to work sensibly and effectively and this can only be done by taking into account the effects of contemplated or typical relationships between the contracting parties. Inevitably, the primary focus of such a pre-emptive challenge is on issues of substantive unfairness.

34 ...Clause 8 of the contract, the only provision in dispute, is a default provision. It prescribes remedies which only become available to the lender upon the default of the consumer. For this reason the escape route of regulation 3(2) is not available to the bank. So far as the description of terms covered by regulation 3(2) as core terms is helpful at all, I would say that clause 8 of the contract is a subsidiary term. In any event, regulation 3(2) must be given a restrictive interpretation. Unless that is done regulation 3(2)(a) will enable the main purpose of the scheme to be frustrated by endless formalistic arguments as to whether a provision is a definitional or an exclusionary provision. Similarly, regulation 3(2)(b) dealing with "the adequacy of the price or remuneration" must be given a restrictive interpretation. After all, in a broad sense all terms of the contract are in some way related to the price or remuneration. That is not what is intended. Even price escalation clauses have been treated by the Director as subject to the fairness provision: see Susan Bright 20 LS 331, 345 and 349. It would be a gaping hole in the system if such clauses were not subject to the fairness requirement. For these further reasons I would reject the argument of the bank that regulation 3(2), and in particular 3(2)(b), take clause 8 outside the scope of the Regulations.

36 It is now necessary to refer to the provisions which prescribe how it should be determined whether a term is unfair. *[Having set out regulation 4(1) of the 1994 Regulations he continued:]* There are three independent requirements. But the element of detriment to the consumer may not add much. But it serves to make clear that the Directive is aimed at significant imbalance against the consumer, rather than the seller or supplier. The twin requirements of good faith and significant imbalance will in practice be determinative. Schedule 2 to the Regulations, which explains the concept of good faith, provides that regard must be had, amongst other things, to the extent to which the seller or supplier has dealt fairly and equitably with the consumer. It is an objective criterion. Good faith imports, as Lord Bingham of Cornhill has observed in his opinion, the notion of open and fair dealing: see also *Interfoto Picture Library Ltd v Stiletto Visual Programmes Ltd* [1989] QB 433. And helpfully the commentary to *Lando & Beale, Principles of European Contract Law, Parts I and II* (combined and revised 2000), p 113 prepared by the Commission of European Contract Law, explains that the purpose of the provision of good faith and fair dealing is "to enforce community standards of decency, fairness and reasonableness in commercial transactions"; a fortiori that is true of consumer transactions. Schedule 3 to the Regulations (which corresponds to the annex to the Directive) is best regarded as a check list of terms which must be regarded as potentially vulnerable. The examples given in Schedule 3 convincingly demonstrate that the argument of the bank that good faith is predominantly concerned with procedural defects in negotiating procedures cannot be sustained. Any purely procedural or even predominantly procedural interpretation of the requirement of good faith must be rejected.

37 That brings me to the element of significant imbalance. It has been pointed out by Hugh Collins that the test "of a significant imbalance of the obligations obviously directs attention to the substantive unfairness of the contract": "Good Faith in European Contract Law" (1994) 14 Oxford Journal of Legal Studies 229, 249. It is however, also right to say that there is a large area of overlap between the concepts of good faith and significant imbalance.

38 It is now necessary to turn to the application of these requirements to the facts of the present case. The point is a relatively narrow one. I agree that the starting point is that a lender ought to be able to recover interest at the contractual rate until the date of payment, and this applies both before and after judgment. On the other hand, counsel for the Director advanced a contrary argument. Adopting the test of asking what the position of a consumer is in the contract under consideration with or without clause 8, he said that the consumer is in a significantly worse position than he would have been if there had been no such provision. Certainly, the consumer is worse off. The difficulty facing counsel, however, is that this disadvantage to the consumer appears to be the consequence not of clause 8 but of the County Courts (Interest on Judgment Debts) Order 1991. Under this Order no statutory interest is payable on a county court judgment given in proceedings to recover money due under a regulated agreement: see article 2. Counsel said that for policy reasons it was decided that in such a case no interest may be recovered after judgment. He said that it is not open to the House to criticise directly or indirectly this legal context. In these circumstances he submitted that it is not legitimate for a court to conclude that fairness requires that a lender must be able to insist on a stipulation designed to avoid the statutory regime under the 1991 Order. Initially I was inclined to uphold this policy argument. On reflection, however, I have been persuaded that this argument cannot prevail in circumstances where the legislature has neither expressly nor by necessary implication barred a stipulation that interest may continue to accrue after judgment until payment in full.

39 For these reasons as well as the reasons given by Lord Bingham I agree that clause 8 is not unfair...

Lord Hope of Craighead, Lord Millett, and **Lord Rodger of Earlsferry** delivered speeches concurring with Lord Bingham.

NOTES AND QUESTIONS

1.   Regulations 3(2), 4(1), 4(2) and Schedule 3 of the 1994 Regulations correlate to what are now regulations 6(2), 5(1), 6(1) and Schedule 2 of the 1999 Regulations. Schedule 2 to the 1994 Regulations has not been re-enacted in the 1999 Regulations. This laid down, 'In making an assessment of good faith, regard shall be had in particular to (a) the strength of the bargaining positions of the parties; (b) whether the consumer had an inducement to agree to the term; (c) whether the goods or services were sold or supplied to the special order of the consumer, and (d) the extent to which the seller or supplier has dealt fairly and equitably with the consumer.'

2.   In contrast to, eg, UCTA 1977, the Regulations provide for 'pre-emptive challenges' (see Lord Steyn at [33]) by the OFT (and other appropriate bodies). Such a challenge—of which this case is an illustration—constitutes an 'administrative' or 'public law' method of controlling unfair terms additional to the traditional 'private law' method of the validity of the term being challenged in an action between the contracting parties. Even more significantly, as is stressed in Susan Bright's article referred to by Lord Steyn, the investigative powers and duties conferred on the OFT in deciding whether to seek an injunction (see regulation 10) mean that unfair terms are being effectively controlled by the OFT without any court actions.

3.   Would UCTA 1977 have been more effective in controlling unfair exclusion and limitation clauses in consumer contracts if it had provided for pre-emptive challenges by the OFT?

4.   One interpretation of the test of fairness in regulation 5(1) is that 'good faith' refers to 'open and fair dealing' (ie 'procedural fairness') and that 'significant imbalance' refers to 'substantive unfairness', so that both procedural and substantive unfairness must be present. What were the views of Lords Bingham and Steyn on this and, in your opinion, what is the best interpretation of regulation 5(1)?

5.   Ought the judiciary in this case to have shown greater deference to the views on fairness of the DGFT, given that his office has a wide everyday expertise in informally controlling unfair terms?

6.   On the first 'core term' issue in this case, the House of Lords interpreted regulation 6(2) narrowly. This was applied in *Bairstow Eves London Central Ltd v Smith* [2004] EWHC 263 (QB), [2004] 2 EGLR 25 in holding that an increase in an estate agent's commission if the sum was not paid within 10 days of completion of a sale was not a core term within regulation 6(2) so that it could

be struck down as unfair. In Gross J's words at [25], '[R]egulation 6[2] must be given a restrictive interpretation; otherwise a coach and horses could be driven through the Regulations'.

(4) A Note on Good Faith

The reference to the requirement of good faith in regulation 5(1) of the Unfair Terms in Consumer Contracts Regulations 1999 is the first *overt* recognition in English law of the civilian principle of good faith in contracting. One can argue that in many areas of English contract law such a principle is already covertly recognised: eg in the doctrine of promissory estoppel (Chapter 3), in deciding whether onerous or unusual terms are incorporated (Chapter 4, especially Bingham LJ's judgment in the *Interfoto* case, 181), in implying terms (Chapter 4), and in invalidating a contract for factors such as misrepresentation (Chapter 11), duress (Chapter 14) and undue influence and exploitation of weakness (Chapter 15). On the other hand, we have seen in Chapter 2 that in *Walford v Miles* an agreement to negotiate in good faith has been held too uncertain to be enforceable; and we shall see in Chapters 11 and 12 that there is no general duty of disclosure in English law.

The use of the concept in regulation 5(1) has brought to the fore a wide-ranging debate as to the merits, or otherwise, of overtly accepting such a principle across our law of contract. Certainly the *Principles of European Contract Law* Act 1: 201 has a basic mandatory principle running through the rest of the Principles that 'each party must act in accordance with good faith and fair dealing'. For consideration of this general debate see: E McKendrick, *Contract Law* (7th edn, 2007) 12.10; R Brownsword, *Contract Law: Themes for the Twenty First Century* (2nd edn, 2006) Ch 6; R Zimmermann and S Whittaker (eds), *Good Faith in European Contract Law* (2000) which comprises a wide-ranging survey focusing on 30 hypothetical cases.

3. REFORM OF THE LEGISLATION ON UNFAIR TERMS

In *Unfair Terms in Contracts* (Report No 292, 2005) the Law Commission has recommended a number of reforms to the present legislation on unfair terms. The most important of those recommendations are as follows:

(i)   UCTA 1977 and the 1999 Regulations should be integrated into a single piece of legislation so as to avoid the present overlapping complexity. The draft Unfair Contract Terms Bill, accompanying the Report, shows how this can be done.

(ii) Terms rendered automatically ineffective under UCTA 1977 (eg, under sections 2(1), 6 and 7) should remain so.

(iii) 'Consumer' should be defined as being a natural person who is acting (wholly or mainly) for purposes unrelated to his or her business. This would be in line with the definition in the 1999 Regulations. One effect would be to 'overrule' *R & B Customs Brokers Co Ltd v United Dominions Trust Ltd*, above, 254.

(iv) In contracts with consumers, a 'fair and reasonable' test should be applied to non-core terms. While this would basically constitute a continuation of the regime of the 1999 Regulations, individually negotiated terms would no longer be immune. As under the 1999 Regulations, core terms would continue to be immune provided transparent and in line with what the consumer reasonably expected.

(v) Subject to some exceptions (eg financial services contracts) the same protection for consumers should be extended to small businesses dealing on the other's non-negotiated written standard terms of business where the value of the contract does not exceed £500,000. Subject to some exceptions, a small business would be defined as one with nine or fewer employees.

(vi) In business to business contracts, where one business deals on the other's written standard terms of business, that other business should not be able to rely on an exclusion or limitation clause unless that clause satisfies a 'fair and reasonable' test. This would basically be a continuation of the non-consumer aspect of section 3 of UCTA 1977.

(vii) As under the present law, the 'fair and reasonable' test should be applied as at the time the contract was made (other than for non-contractual notices). In contrast to the Regulations, there should be no direct reference to good faith but it should be clarified that procedural and substantive unfairness can both be looked at and guidelines as to possible relevant factors would be set out. As under the Regulations, for consumer and small business contracts, an indicative list of terms that might be regarded as not being fair and reasonable should be contained in a Schedule. As under UCTA (but not the Regulations) the burden of satisfying that fair and reasonable test should rest on the party seeking to rely on the term.

(viii) The categories of contract currently excluded from the operation of UCTA (eg, insurance contracts, international supply contracts and shipping contracts) should continue to be exempt in business to business contracts (including contracts with small businesses).

(ix) The preventive powers of the OFT and other bodies under the Regulations should be retained in respect of consumer contracts and extended so as to include powers in relation to exclusion or limitation clauses in consumer contracts that are presently rendered automatically ineffective by UCTA 1977.

J Beatson, *Anson's Law of Contract* (28th edn, 2002) 185–202
S Smith, *Atiyah's Introduction to the Law of Contract* (6th edn, 2005) 313–331

J Adams and R Brownsword, 'The Unfair Contract Terms Act: a Decade of Discretion' (1988) 104 *LQR* 94

The authors examine how the courts, in the first decade of UCTA 1977, applied the 'reasonableness' test in commercial contracts. They argue that needless uncertainty has been caused by: (i) the view of the appellate courts that reasonableness is essentially a matter for the judge at first instance; and (ii) the conflict between Lord Wilberforce's speech in the *Photo Production* case, favouring a 'non-interventionist' approach to the reasonableness test in commercial contracts, and the more interventionist approach applied in the *George Mitchell* case. [Note that for a more recent preference for the non-interventionist approach see *Watford Electronics Ltd v Sanderson*, above 282, and 284, note 4.] They also criticise the decisive role of what they term the 'estoppel' factor (the practice of sellers of seeds) in *George Mitchell*.

E Macdonald, 'Unfair Contract Terms Act—Thirty Years On' in *Contract Terms* (eds A Burows and E Peel, 2007) 153

Macdonald argues that: (i) the courts have given an inappropriate meaning to 'deals as consumer'; (ii) greater use could be made of section 3(2)(b)(i) of the 1977 Act to cover clauses that are not standard exemption clauses (eg entire agreement clauses); (iii) since Adams and Brownsword's celebrated article in 1988, there has been greater certainty in relation to the relevant factors for determining reasonableness so that it should now be a great deal easier to draft a valid clause; (iv) there remains a need for UCTA in commercial contracts.

S Bright, 'Unfairness and the Consumer Contract Regulations' in *Contract Terms* (eds A Burrows and E Peel, 2007) 173

Following on her article in 2000 in *Legal Studies* (referred to by Lord Steyn above, 296–297), the author here brings up to date her assessment of (a) the informal 'administrative' method of controlling, and changing the use of, unfair terms by the OFT; and (b) the meaning of fairness in the Regulations. She points out that the annual reports of the Office of Fair Trading make clear that the vast majority of cases are dealt with by negotiation and through informal undertakings; and in the period 2000–5, 5000 terms were changed or abandoned following investigation by the OFT. She suggests that there may be a clash (as illustrated by the *First National Bank* case) between the approach to unfairness of the OFT and the judges. She argues that it remains unclear whether procedural or substantive unfairness alone (ie one without the other) can invalidate a term.

H Beale, 'Exclusion and Limitation Clauses in Business Contracts: Transparency' in *Contract Terms* (eds A Burrows and E Peel, 2007) 191

Beale argues that in business-to-business contracts reasonableness should generally be concerned neither with substantive unfairness alone nor with inequality of bargaining power (in the sense of 'take it or leave it'), but rather with 'unfair surprise'. However, he illustrates how difficult it is to formulate a statutory test for 'unfair surprise' and concludes that the present broad reasonableness test in UCTA cannot easily be improved upon.

Principles of European Contract Law (eds O Lando and H Beale, 2000) 266–271

Article 4.110: Unfair Terms not Individually Negotiated
(1) A party may avoid a term which has not been individually negotiated if, contrary to the requirements of good faith and fair dealing, it causes a significant imbalance in the parties' rights and obligations arising under the contract to the detriment of that party, taking into account the nature of the performance to be rendered under the contract, all the other terms of the contract and the circumstances at the time the contract was concluded.

(2) This Article does not apply to:

(a) a term which defines the main subject matter of the contract, provided the term is in plain and intelligible language; or to

(b) the adequacy in value of one party's obligations compared to the value of the obligations of the other party.

[This comprises the central provisions of the 1993 European Directive, implemented in England by the Unfair Terms in Consumer Contracts Regulations 1999, regulations 5(1) and 6 (above, 287), but it extends them to all contracts (ie including business-to-business contracts and contracts between private persons).]

Part Three

Remedies for Breach of Contract

Parties enter contracts with a view to those contracts being performed. It is therefore of great importance to know what the innocent party can do, or what the innocent party is entitled to, where the other party breaks the contract by failing to perform as promised. In other words, it is of great importance to know what are the remedies for breach of contract. In the next three chapters we examine those remedies, which are termination (Chapter 7), damages (Chapter 8) and direct enforcement (Chapter 9).

7

Termination

Where there has been a breach, the innocent party is always entitled to damages and may sometimes be granted direct enforcement of the contract. In this chapter, however, we are concerned with a remedy for breach that is available without coming to court, namely termination; and we are primarily asking, when does a breach of contract give the innocent party the right not to perform his side of the contract by putting an end to the contract? When, in other words, is an innocent party entitled to terminate the contract as well as being entitled to damages?

Let us assume, for example, that A has made a contract with B whereby A is to sell and deliver 10 computers to B on 1 March 2007 in return for B paying £5000 on delivery. A fails to deliver until 4 March 2007. A is therefore in breach of contract. B is certainly entitled to damages, even if merely nominal, for that breach. The question we are now asking is, when A fails to deliver the computers on 1 March, can B terminate the contract so that he is no longer bound to accept and pay for computers delivered by A?

Having clarified, in the first section below, what is meant by termination, we shall see in the second and main section of this chapter that (putting to one side where the contract-breaker has repudiated the contract: see 332, below) the answer to that question depends on the importance of the term broken or the seriousness of the consequences of breach. That, in turn, requires one to understand the distinction between conditions, warranties and innominate terms. The third and fourth sections of the chapter then go on to look briefly at 'anticipatory breach' and at restitution after termination for breach.

Introductory reading: E McKendrick, *Contract Law* (7th edn, 2007) Chs 10, 19, 20.5

1. THE MEANING OF TERMINATION FOR BREACH

Termination means putting an end to the contract as from the moment of termination. As was made clear in the *Photo Production* case, it wipes away the contract for the future but not for the past. Termination for breach, therefore, has to be sharply distinguished from rescission for, for example, misrepresentation or undue influence where the contract is wiped away from the start. Not surprisingly, therefore, confusion is caused when courts or commentators refer to termination for breach as rescission for breach. The preferable approach is to avoid referring to rescission for breach and instead to refer always to termination (or discharge) for breach. Note that in contrast to termination for frustration, termination for breach does not happen automatically. It is dependent on the innocent party choosing to terminate: the innocent party has an election whether to do so or not.

Photo Production Ltd v Securicor Transport Ltd
[1980] AC 827, House of Lords

For the facts and decision, see above, 231. In criticising the 'fundamental breach' doctrine, Lords Wilberforce and Diplock stressed that it was incorrect to regard a breach of contract as allowing the innocent party to wipe away the contract (including exclusion clauses) from the start.

For the relevant part of **Lord Wilberforce's** speech, see above, 233 (point 2).

Lord Diplock: A basic principle of the common law of contract, to which there are no exceptions that are relevant in the instant case, is that parties to a contract are free to determine for themselves what primary obligations they will accept. They may state these in express words in the contract itself and, where they do, the statement is determinative; but in practice a commercial contract never states all the primary obligations of the parties in full; many are left to be incorporated by implication of law from the legal nature of the contract into which the parties are entering. But if the parties wish to reject or modify primary obligations which would otherwise be so incorporated, they are fully at liberty to do so by express words.

    Leaving aside those comparatively rare cases in which the court is able to enforce a primary obligation by decreeing specific performance of it, breaches of primary obligations give rise to substituted or secondary obligations on the part of the party in default, and, in some cases, may entitle the other party to be relieved from further performance of his own primary obligations.

    ...

    Every failure to perform a primary obligation is a breach of contract. The secondary obligation on the part of the contract breaker to which it gives rise by implication of the common law is to pay monetary compensation to the other party for the loss sustained by him in consequence of the breach; but, with two exceptions, the primary obligations of both parties so far as they have not yet been fully performed remain unchanged. This secondary obligation to pay compensation (damages) for non-performance of primary obligations I will call the "general secondary obligation." It applies in the cases of the two exceptions as well.

The exceptions are: (1) Where the event resulting from the failure by one party to perform a primary obligation has the effect of depriving the other party of substantially the whole benefit which it was the intention of the parties that he should obtain from the contract, the party not in default may elect to put an end to all primary obligations of both parties remaining unperformed. (If the expression "fundamental breach" is to be retained, it should, in the interests of clarity, be confined to this exception.) (2) Where the contracting parties have agreed, whether by express words or by implication of law, that *any* failure by one party to perform a particular primary obligation ("condition" in the nomenclature of the Sale of Goods Act 1893), irrespective of the gravity of the event that has in fact resulted from the breach, shall entitle the other party to elect to put an end to all primary obligations of both parties remaining unperformed. (In the interests of clarity, the nomenclature of the Sale of Goods Act 1893, "breach of condition" should be reserved for this exception.)

Where such an election is made (a) there is substituted by implication of law for the primary obligations of the party in default which remain unperformed a secondary obligation to pay monetary compensation to the other party for the loss sustained by him in consequence of their non-performance in the future and (b) the unperformed primary obligations of that other party are discharged. This secondary obligation is additional to the general secondary obligation; I will call it "the anticipatory secondary obligation."

...

When there has been a fundamental breach or breach of condition, the coming to an end of the primary obligations of both parties to the contract at the election of the party not in default, is often referred to as the "determination" or "rescission" of the contract or, as in the Sale of Goods Act 1893 "treating the contract as repudiated." The first two of these expressions, however, are misleading unless it is borne in mind that for the unperformed primary obligations of the party in default there are substituted by operation of law what I have called the secondary obligations.

NOTES AND QUESTIONS

1. Both speeches indicate that one ought not to use the expression 'rescission for breach': termination for breach and rescission for, eg, misrepresentation are very different.

2. Do you regard Lord Diplock's analysis in terms of primary and secondary obligations helpful or confusing? Is Lord Diplock's conceptual elaboration necessary in order to make the point that, where allowed, an innocent party's termination for breach is consistent with his being awarded damages for breach because termination (unlike rescission) does not wipe away all contractual obligations.

3. Less than a year before this case, the House of Lords in *Johnson v Agnew* [1980] AC 367 had clarified that, even in relation to a contract for the sale of land, 'rescission' for breach was not 'rescission ab initio'. 'Rescission' for breach was therefore perfectly consistent with awarding damages for breach. In Lord Wilberforce's words, at 392–393, '[I]t is important to dissipate a fertile source of confusion and to make clear that although the vendor is sometimes referred to [where accepting a repudiatory breach] as "rescinding" the contract, this so-called "rescission" is quite different from rescission ab initio, such as may arise, for example, in cases of mistake, fraud or lack of consent. In those cases, the contract is treated in law as never having come into existence. ... In the case of an accepted repudiatory breach, the contract has come into existence but has been put an end to or discharged. Whatever contrary indications may be

disinterred from old authorities, it is now quite clear, under the general law of contract, that acceptance of a repudiatory breach does not bring about "rescission ab initio".'

4.   How does an innocent party terminate a contract for breach? Does one need to go to court?

5.   An innocent party who elects not to terminate is said to affirm the contract (also sometimes referred to as a 'waiver' of one's right to terminate). Once affirmed, the innocent party cannot change its mind and terminate (for the same breach).

2. CONDITIONS, WARRANTIES AND INNOMINATE TERMS

The distinction between conditions, warranties and innominate terms is often presented in textbooks as part of an examination of the terms or contents of the contract. However, as the importance of this distinction is in deciding whether an innocent party can terminate the contract for breach, it has been considered more illuminating in this book to consider it within the context of termination as a remedy for breach.

Sale of Goods Act 1979, sections 12–15

See above, 213–215.

NOTES

1.   The Sale of Goods Act, first enacted in 1893, has always drawn a distinction between conditions and warranties. By what are now sections 12(5A), 13(1A), 14(6) and 15(3) the implied terms as to title, description, quality, fitness for purpose, and sample are all conditions. By section 12(5A), the implied terms as to freedom from encumbrances and quiet enjoyment are warranties. For other terms in a contract of sale, section 11(3) lays down that it is a matter for 'the construction of the contract' whether the term is a condition or a warranty. For a modification in non-consumer contracts of the position that the implied terms are conditions, see section 15A of the Sale of Goods Act 1979, below, 324.

2.   The difference between conditions and warranties turns on the importance of the term. Major terms are conditions. Minor terms are warranties. The consequence of the distinction is that breach of a condition entitles the innocent party to terminate the contract as well as being entitled to damages; breach of a warranty entitles the innocent party merely to damages.

Hongkong Fir Shipping Co Ltd v Kawasaki Kisen Kaisha Ltd
[1962] 2 QB 26, Court of Appeal

The claimant shipowners had let out their ship under a two-year time charterparty to the defendants. By a term of the charterparty, referred to as the 'seaworthiness' term, the ship was to be 'in every way fitted for ordinary cargo service'. In fact, the members of her crew were too few and too incompetent to deal with her old-fashioned machinery. This led to serious breakdowns in the machinery with the consequence that there was a delay in the charterers' first voyage from Liverpool to Osaka. A few weeks after arriving in Osaka, when freight rates had fallen, the charterers terminated the contract for the shipowners' breach. This was so even though at that time in June it would have been unreasonable to think that the ship would not be seaworthy, with a competent and full crew, by mid-September when the charterparty would still have had 17 months to run. The shipowners brought an action for damages arguing that, in purporting to terminate the contract, the charterers were themselves in breach. The charterers' defence was that they were entitled to terminate the contract because of the admitted breach by the shipowners of the seaworthiness term. In rejecting that defence and the charterers' appeal, the Court of Appeal held that the breach of the seaworthiness term was not sufficiently serious to entitle the charterers to terminate.

Upjohn LJ: I...propose...to [say] a few words upon the two main submissions so meticulously argued before us by Mr. Ashton Roskill for the appellants.

Logically his first submission, as he recognised, was that the obligation to provide a seaworthy vessel was a condition for breach of which the charterer was at once entitled to treat the contract as repudiated.

...

Why is this apparently basic and underlying condition of seaworthiness not, in fact, treated as a condition? It is for the simple reason that the seaworthiness clause is breached by the slightest failure to be fitted "in every way" for service. Thus, to take examples from the judgments in some of the cases...if a nail is missing from one of the timbers of a wooden vessel or if proper medical supplies or two anchors are not on board at the time of sailing, the owners are in breach of the seaworthiness stipulation. It is contrary to common sense to suppose that in such circumstances the parties contemplated that the charterer should at once be entitled to treat the contract as at an end for such trifling breaches.

The classification of stipulations in a contract into conditions and warranties is familiar, and in connection with the sale of goods these phrases have statutory definition. These phrases, however, came into being in connection with the ancient system of pleadings before the Common Law Procedure Act, 1852, and when considering the remedies to which one party may be entitled today for breach of a stipulation by the other the decision whether the stipulation is a condition or warranty may not provide a complete answer.

...

In my judgment the remedies open to the innocent party for breach of a stipulation which is not a condition strictly so called, depend entirely upon the nature of the breach and its foreseeable consequences. Breaches of stipulation fall, naturally, into two classes. First there is the case where the owner by his conduct indicates that he considers himself no longer bound to perform his part of the contract; in that case, of course, the charterer may accept the repudiation and treat the contract as at an end. The second class of case is, of course, the more usual one and that is where, due to misfortune such as the perils of the sea, engine failures, incompetence of the crew and so on, the owner is unable to perform a particular stipulation precisely in accordance with the terms of the contract try he never so hard to remedy it. In that case the question to be answered is, does the breach of the stipulation go so much to the root of the contract that it makes further commercial performance of the contract impossible, or in other words is the whole contract frustrated? If yea, the innocent party may treat the contract as at an end. If nay, his claim sounds in damages only.

If I have correctly stated the principles, then as the stipulation as to the seaworthiness is not a condition in the strict sense the question to be answered is, did the initial unseaworthiness as found by the judge, and from which there has been no appeal, go so much to the root of the contract that the charterers were then and there entitled to treat the charterparty as at an end? The only unseaworthiness alleged, serious though it was, was the insufficiency and incompetence of the crew, but that surely cannot be treated as going to the root of the contract for the parties must have contemplated that in such an event the crew could be changed and augmented. In my judgment, on this part of his case Mr. Roskill neces-sarily fails.

I turn therefore to the second point: where there have been serious and repeated delays due to the inability of the owner to perform his part of the contract, is the charterer entitled to treat the contract as repudiated after a reasonable time or can he do so only if delays are such as to amount to a frustration of the contract? ...

Apart altogether from authority, it would seem to be wrong to introduce the idea that the innocent party can treat the contract as at an end for delays which, however, fall short of a frustration of the contract. Subject to the terms of the contract, of course, neither contracting party can unilaterally withdraw from the contract. If, however, one party by his conduct frustrates the contract, the law says that the other party may treat the contract as at an end. For breaches of stipulation which fall short of that, the innocent party can only sue for damages. I do not see on principle how he can have some unilateral right to withdraw from the contract when the conduct of the other falls short of frustrating the contract. References in some of the earlier cases to reasonable time and so forth are readily explained by the fact that those words were used as synonymous with a frustrating time, that is to say, a time by which the further commercial performance of the contract became impossible.

Mr. Roskill has not seriously urged that in the circumstances of this case the delays, serious though they were, were such as to amount to a frustration of the contract. I think, therefore, that his argument fails on this point also.

Diplock LJ: Every synallagmatic contract contains in it the seeds of the problem: in what event will a party be relieved of his undertaking to do that which he has agreed to do but has not yet done? The contract may itself expressly define some of these events, as in the cancellation clause in a charterparty; but, human prescience being limited, it seldom does so exhaustively and often fails to do so at all. In some classes of contracts such as sale of goods, marine insurance, contracts of affreightment evidenced by bills of lading and those between parties to bills of exchange, Parliament has defined by statute some of the events not provided for expressly in individual contracts of that class; but where an event occurs the occurrence of which neither the parties nor Parliament have expressly stated will discharge one of the parties from further performance of his undertakings, it is for the court to determine whether the event has this effect or not.

The test whether an event has this effect or not has been stated in a number of metaphors all of which I think amount to the same thing: does the occurrence of the event deprive the party who has further undertakings still to perform of substantially the whole benefit which it was the intention of the parties as expressed in the contract that he should obtain as the consideration for performing those undertakings?

This test is applicable whether or not the event occurs as a result of the default of one of the parties to the contract, but the consequences of the event are different in the two cases. Where the event occurs as a result of the default of one party, the party in default cannot rely upon it as relieving himself of the performance of any further undertakings on his part, and the innocent party, although entitled to, need not treat the event as relieving him of the further performance of his own undertakings. This is only a specific application of the fundamental legal and moral rule that a man should not be allowed to take advantage of his own wrong. Where the event occurs as a result of the default of neither party, each is relieved of the further performance of his own undertakings, and their rights in respect of under-takings previously performed are now regulated by the Law Reform (Frustrated Contracts) Act, 1943.

...

Once it is appreciated that it is the event and not the fact that the event is a result of a breach of contract which relieves the party not in default of further performance of his obliga-tions, two consequences follow. (1) The test whether the event relied upon has this consequence is the same whether the event is the result of the other party's breach of contract or not, as Devlin J. pointed out in *Universal Cargo Carriers Corporation v. Citati* [1957] 2 QB 401, 434. (2) The question whether an event which is the result of the other party's breach of contract has this consequence cannot be answered by treating all contractual undertakings as falling into one of two separate categories: "conditions" the breach of which gives rise to an event which relieves the party not in default of further performance of his obligations, and 'warranties' the breach of which does not give rise to such an event.

Lawyers tend to speak of this classification as if it were comprehensive, partly for ... historical reasons ... and partly because Parliament itself adopted it in the Sale of Goods Act, 1893, as respects a number of implied terms in contracts for the sale of goods and has in that Act used the expressions "condition" and "warranty" in that meaning. But it is by no means true of contractual undertakings in general at common law.

No doubt there are many simple contractual undertakings, sometimes express but more often because of their very simplicity ("It goes without saying") to be implied, of which it can be predicated that every breach of such an undertaking must give rise to an event which will deprive the party not in default of substantially the whole benefit which it was intended that he should obtain from the contract. And such a stipulation, unless the parties have agreed that breach of it shall not entitle the non-defaulting party to treat the contract as repudiated, is a "condition." So too there may be other simple contractual undertakings of which it can be predicated that no breach can give rise to an event which will deprive the party not in default of substantially the whole benefit which it was intended that he should obtain from the contract; and such a stipulation, unless the parties have agreed that breach of it shall entitle the non-defaulting party to treat the contract as repudiated, is a "warranty."

There are, however, many contractual undertakings of a more complex character which cannot be categorised as being "conditions" or "warranties,"... Of such undertakings all that can be predicated is that some breaches will and others will not give rise to an event which will deprive the party not in default of substantially the whole benefit which it was intended that he should obtain from the contract; and the legal consequences of a breach of such an undertaking, unless provided for expressly in the contract, depend upon the nature of the event to which the breach gives rise and do not follow automatically from a prior classifi-cation of the undertaking as a "condition" or a "warranty." For instance, to take Bramwell B.'s example in *Jackson v. Union Marine Insurance Co. Ltd* LR 10 CP 125, 142 itself, breach of an undertaking by a shipowner to sail with all possible dispatch to a named port does not neces-sarily relieve the charterer of further performance of his obligation under the charterparty, but if the breach is so prolonged that the contemplated voyage is frustrated it does have this effect.

...

As my brethren have already pointed out, the shipowners' undertaking to tender a seaworthy ship has, as a result of numerous decisions as to what can amount to "unseaworthiness," become one of the most complex of contractual undertakings. It embraces obligations with respect to every part of the hull and machinery, stores and equipment and the crew itself. It can be broken by the presence of trivial defects easily and rapidly remediable as well as by defects which must inevitably result in a total loss of the vessel.

Consequently the problem in this case is, in my view, neither solved nor soluble by debating whether the shipowner's express or implied undertaking to tender a seaworthy ship is a "condition" or a "warranty." It is like so many other contractual terms an undertaking one breach of which may give rise to an event which relieves the charterer of further performance of his undertakings if he so elects and another breach of which may not give rise to such an event but entitle him only to monetary compensation in the form of damages. It is, with all deference to Mr. Ashton Roskill's skilful argument, by no means surprising that among the many hundreds of previous cases about the shipowner's undertaking to deliver a seaworthy ship there is none where it was found profitable to discuss in the judgments the question whether that undertaking is a "condition" or a "warranty"; for the true answer, as I have already indicated, is that it is neither, but one of that large class of contractual undertakings one breach of which may have the same effect as that ascribed to a breach of "condition" under the Sale of Goods Act, 1893, and a different breach of which may have only the same effect as that ascribed to a breach of "warranty" under that Act. ...

What the judge had to do in the present case, as in any other case where one party to a contract relies upon a breach by the other party as giving him a right to elect to rescind the contract, and the contract itself makes no express provision as to this, was to look at the events which had occurred as a result of the breach at the time at which the charterers purported to rescind the charterparty and to decide whether the occurrence of those events deprived the charterers of substantially the whole benefit which it was the intention of the parties as expressed in the charterparty that the charterers should obtain from the further performance of their own contractual undertakings.

...

The question which the judge had to ask himself was, as he rightly decided, whether or not at the date when the charterers purported to rescind the contract, namely, June 6, 1957, or when the shipowners purported to accept such rescission, namely. August 8, 1957, the delay which had already occurred as a result of the incompetence of the engine-room staff, and the delay which was likely to occur in repairing the engines of the vessel and the conduct of the shipowners by that date in taking steps to remedy these two matters, were, when taken together, such as to deprive the charterers of substantially the whole benefit which it was the intention of the parties they should obtain from further use of the vessel under the charterparty.

In my view, in his judgment – on which I would not seek to improve – the judge took into account and gave due weight to all the relevant considerations and arrived at the right answer for the right reasons.

Sellers LJ gave a concurring judgment.

NOTES AND QUESTIONS

1. This case, and especially Diplock LJ's judgment, makes clear that, in deciding whether an innocent party can terminate, one cannot simply ask whether the term broken was a condition or a warranty. While that classification may sometimes be decisive, for many terms—subsequently labelled 'innominate' (or 'intermediate') terms—the answer to whether breach justifies termination will turn on the seriousness of the consequences of the breach. That is, it is the seriousness of the consequences, not the importance of the term broken, that matters.

2. In this case, the term as to seaworthiness ('in every way fitted for ordinary cargo service') was an innominate term; and the charterers' termination had not been justified because the consequences of the breach of that term (ie the delays) had not been so serious as to nullify the purpose of the contract.

3. Sir Guenter Treitel in *Some Landmarks of Twentieth Century Contract Law* (2002), at 113, writes that the judgment of Diplock LJ in this case, 'has a fair claim to being the most important judicial contribution to English contract law in the past century'. Why is it so important?

4. In deciding whether the consequences of the breach were so serious as to justify termination, the judges used the language, or the analogy, of frustration. Frustration is a separate doctrine that operates where there is no breach (see Chapter 13). It is misleading to draw too close a link between the two because the tests for, and decisions on, whether consequences are sufficiently serious to allow termination for breach (of an innominate term) and whether circumstances have so changed as to terminate the contract for frustration are similar but not identical.

5. Why might it be argued that the recognition of intermediate terms creates commercial uncertainty? How might a contract draftsman avoid this problem of uncertainty?

Maredelanto Compania Naviera SA v Bergbau – Handel GmbH, The Mihalis Angelos [1971] 1 QB 164, Court of Appeal

In a voyage charterparty, a shipowner undertook that the ship, *Mihalis Angelos,* 'expected ready to load... about July 1, 1965' would proceed to Haiphong to load a cargo of ore. If the ship was not ready to load on or before 20 July 1965, the charterer was given the option to cancel the contract. In breach of contract by the shipowner, the ship was not ready to load on about 1 July. On 17 July, the charterer cancelled the charterparty as it had been unable to obtain the cargo of ore. In the mistaken belief that the Vietnam War had made it impossible to obtain supplies of ore, it alleged that it was entitled to cancel the charterparty under a force majeure clause in the contract. The shipowner treated the cancellation as a breach of contract by the charterer and claimed damages. The Court of Appeal held that that claim should fail. The charterer had been entitled to terminate the contract, albeit not because of force majeure but rather because, by not being ready to load about 1 July, the shipowner had been in breach of a condition of the contract.

Lord Denning MR: The contest resolved itself simply into this: was the 'expected ready to load' clause a condition, such that for breach of it the charterers could throw up the charter? Or was it a mere warranty such as to give rise to damages if it was broken, but not to a right to cancel, seeing that cancellation was expressly dealt with in the cancelling clause?

Sir Frederick Pollock (*Formation of Contracts*) divided the terms of a contract into two categories: conditions and warranties. The difference between them was this: if the promisor broke a *condition* in *any* respect, however slight, it gave the other party a right to be quit of his future obligations and to sue for damages: unless he by his conduct waived the condition, in which case he was bound to perform his future obligations but could sue for the damage he suffered. If the promisor broke a *warranty* in *any* respect, however serious, the other party was not quit of his future obligations. He had to perform them. His only remedy was to sue for damages.

This division was adopted by Sir Mackenzie Chalmers when he drafted the Sale of Goods Act, 1893, and by Parliament when it passed it. It was stated by Fletcher Moulton L.J. in his celebrated dissenting judgment in *Wallis, Son & Wells v. Pratt & Haynes* [1910] 2 K.B. 1003, 1012, which was adopted in its entirety by the House of Lords in [1911] A.C. 394.

It would be a mistake, however, to look upon that division as exhaustive. There are many terms of many contracts which cannot be fitted into either category. In such cases the courts, for nigh on 200 years, have not asked themselves: was the term a condition or warranty? But rather: was the breach such as to go to the root of the contract? If it was, then the other party is entitled, at his election, to treat himself as discharged from any further performance. …The case of *Hongkong Fir Shipping Co. Ltd. v. Kawasaki Kisen Kaisha Ltd.* [1962] 2 Q.B. 26 is a useful reminder of this large category.

Although this large category exists, there is still remaining a considerable body of law by which certain stipulations have been classified as "conditions" so that any failure to perform, however slight, entitles the other to treat himself as discharged. …

The question in this case is whether the statement by the owner: "expected ready to load under this charter about July 1, 1965," is likewise a "condition." The meaning of such a clause is settled by a decision of this court. It is an assurance by the owner that he honestly expects that the vessel will be ready to load on that date and that his expectation is based on reasonable grounds: see *Samuel Sanday & Co. v. Keighley Maxted & Co.* (1922) 27 Com.Cas. 296. The clause with that meaning has been held in this court to be a "condition" which, if not fulfilled, entitled the other party to treat himself as discharged: see *Finnish Government v. H. Ford & Co. Ltd.* (1921) 6 Ll.L.Rep. 188. Those were sale of goods cases. But I think the clause should receive the same interpretation in charterparty cases. …

I hold, therefore, that on July 17, 1965, the charterers were entitled to cancel the contract on the ground that the owners had broken the "expected ready to load" clause.

Megaw LJ: It is not disputed that when a charter includes the words 'expected ready to load …' a contractual obligation on the part of the shipowner is involved. It is not an obligation that the vessel will be ready to load on the stated date, nor about the stated date, if the date is qualified, as here, by "about." The owner is not in breach merely because the vessel arrives much later, or indeed does not arrive at all. The owner is not undertaking that there will be no unexpected delay. But he is undertaking that he honestly and on reasonable grounds believes, at the time of the contract, that the date named is the date when the vessel will be ready to load. Therefore in order to establish a breach of that obligation the charterer has the burden of showing that the owner's contractually expressed expectation was not his honest expectation, or, at the least, that the owner did not have reasonable grounds for it.

In my judgment, such a term in a charterparty ought to be regarded as being a condition of the contract, in the old sense of the word "condition": that is, that when it has been broken, the other party can, if he wishes, by intimation to the party in breach, elect to be released from performance of his further obligations under the contract; and he can validly do so without having to establish that on the facts of the particular case the breach has produced serious consequences which can be treated as "going to the root of the contract" or as being "fundamental," or whatever other metaphor may be thought appropriate for a frustration case. I reach that conclusion for four interrelated reasons.

First, it tends towards certainty in the law. One of the essential elements of law is some measure of uniformity. One of the important elements of the law is predictability. At any rate in commercial law, there are obvious and substantial advantages in having, where possible, a firm and definite rule for a particular class of legal relationship: for example, as here, the legal categorisation of a particular, definable type of contractual clause in common use. It is surely much better, both for shipowners and charterers (and, incidentally, for their advisers), when a contractual obligation of this nature is under consideration, and still more when they are faced with the necessity for an urgent decision as to the effects of a suspected breach of it, to be able to say categorically: "If a breach is proved, then the charterer can put an end to the contract," rather than that they should be left to ponder whether or not the courts would be likely, in the particular case, when the evidence has been heard, to decide that in the particular circumstances the breach was or was not such as "to go to the root of the contract." Where justice does not require greater flexibility, there is everything to be said for, and nothing against, a degree of rigidity in legal principle.

Second, it would, in my opinion, only be in the rarest case, if ever, that a shipowner could legitimately feel that he had suffered an injustice by reason of the law having given to a charterer the right to put an end to the contract because of the breach by the shipowner of a clause such as this. If a shipowner has chosen to assert contractually, but dishonestly or without reasonable grounds, that he expects his vessel to be ready to load on such-and-such a date, wherein does the grievance lie?

Third, it is, as Mocatta J. held, clearly established by authority binding on this court that where a clause "expected ready to load" is included in a contract for the sale of goods to be carried by sea, that clause is a condition in the sense that any breach of it enables the buyer to reject the goods without having to show that the dishonest or unreasonable expectation of the seller has in fact been prejudicial to the buyer. The judgment of Bankes L.J., in which Warrington L.J. and Atkin L.J. concurred, in *Finnish Government v. H. Ford & Co. Ltd.* (1921) 6 Ll.L.Rep.188 is in point. The clause there was "Steamers expected ready to load February and/or March 1920." Bankes L.J. said, at p. 189: "I come to the conclusion ... that this clause is one containing a contract. It is a contract which is in its nature a condition. ..." That authority is not only binding on this court, but is, I think, completely and desirably in conformity with the line of cases which have decided – and the law in that respect is now accepted as being beyond dispute – that a statement in a contract of sale as to the loading period is a condition in the sense which I have indicated. If the contract says "loading to be during July," the buyer can reject the goods if the loading was not complete until midday on August 1. He is not limited to claiming damages; he is not obliged to show that he has suffered any damage.

It would, in my judgment, produce an undesirable anomaly in our commercial law if such a clause – "expected ready to load" – were to be held to have a materially different legal effect where it is contained in a charterparty from that which it has when it is contained in a sale of goods contract. ...

The fourth reason why I think that the clause should be regarded as being a condition when it is found in a charterparty is that that view was the view of Scrutton L.J. so expressed in his capacity as the author of *Scrutton on Charterparties*.

Edmund Davies LJ gave a concurring judgment.

NOTES AND QUESTIONS

1. How does one reconcile this decision—that the relevant term was a condition—with that in *Hongkong Fir Shipping*?

2. Was the condition that the ship would be ready to load about 1 July 1965 or that the shipowner honestly believed on reasonable grounds that the ship would be ready to load about 1 July 1965?

3. It is clear law, and was hence not in issue in this case, that if the innocent party is entitled to terminate it does not matter that it gives the wrong reason (here force majeure) for that termination. For force majeure and frustration, see below, Chapter 13.

L Schuler AG v Wickman Machine Tool Sales Ltd
[1974] AC 235, House of Lords

The claimant English company, Wickman, was for 4½ years given the sole selling rights for panel presses (used in making cars) manufactured by the defendant German company, Schuler. Clause 7(b) of the contract provided that, 'It shall be a condition of this agreement that... [Wickman] shall send its representatives to visit [the six largest UK motor manufacturers] at least once in every week for the purpose of soliciting orders for panel presses'. The clause went on to require that the same representative or an alternate, both of whom should be named, should make the visits. Clause 11 provided that either party might determine the agreement if the other party committed a 'material breach' and failed to remedy it within 60 days of being required to do so in writing. Wickman failed to carry out all the weekly visits promised. Initially that breach was waived by Schuler but when there continued to be some failures, albeit less frequent, Schuler terminated the contract forthwith. Wickman claimed damages alleging that, in terminating the contract, Schuler was itself in breach of contract. In dismissing Schuler's appeal, the House of Lords (Lord Wilberforce dissenting) held that Schuler had not been entitled to terminate the contract because clause 7(b) was not a condition (in the sense of a term, any breach of which triggered the right to terminate).

Lord Reid: In the ordinary use of the English language "condition" has many meanings, some of which have nothing to do with agreements. In connection with an agreement it may mean a pre-condition: something which must happen or be done before the agreement can take effect. Or it may mean some state of affairs which must continue to exist if the agreement is to remain in force. The legal meaning on which Schuler relies is, I think, one which would not occur to a layman; a condition in that sense is not something which has an automatic effect. It is a term the breach of which by one party gives to the other an option either to terminate the contract or to let the contract proceed and, if he so desires, sue for damages for the breach.

Sometimes a breach of a term gives that option to the aggrieved party because it is of a fundamental character going to the root of the contract, sometimes it gives that option because the parties have chosen to stipulate that it shall have that effect. Blackburn J. said in *Bettini v. Gye* (1876) 1 Q.B.D. 183, 187: "Parties may think some matter, apparently of very little importance, essential; and if they sufficiently express an intention to make the literal fulfilment of such a thing a condition precedent, it will be one; ..."

In the present case it is not contended that Wickman's failures to make visits amounted in themselves to fundamental breaches. What is contended is that the terms of clause 7 "sufficiently express an intention" to make any breach, however small, of the obligation to make visits a condition so that any breach shall entitle Schuler to rescind the whole contract if they so desire.

Schuler maintains that the use of the word "condition" is in itself enough to establish this intention. No doubt some words used by lawyers do have a rigid inflexible meaning. But we must remember that we are seeking to discover intention as disclosed by the contract as a whole. Use of the word "condition" is an indication – even a strong indication – of such an intention but it is by no means conclusive.

The fact that a particular construction leads to a very unreasonable result must be a relevant consideration. The more unreasonable the result the more unlikely it is that the parties can have intended it, and if they do intend it the more necessary it is that they shall make that intention abundantly clear.

Clause 7 (*b*) requires that over a long period each of the six firms shall be visited every week by one or other of two named representatives. It makes no provision for Wickman being entitled to substitute others even on the death or retirement of one of the named representatives. Even if one could imply some right to do this, it makes no provision for both representatives being ill during a particular week. And it makes no provision for the possibility that one or other of the firms may tell Wickman that they cannot receive Wickman's representative during a particular week. So if the parties gave any thought to the matter at all they must have realised the probability that in a few cases out of the 1,400 required visits a visit as stipulated would be impossible. But if Schuler's contention is right, failure to make even one visit entitle[s] them to terminate the contract however blameless Wickman might be.

This is so unreasonable that it must make me search for some other possible meaning of the contract. If none can be found then Wickman must suffer the consequences. But only if that is the only possible interpretation.

If I have to construe clause 7 standing by itself then I do find difficulty in reaching any other interpretation. But if clause 7 must be read with clause 11 the difficulty disappears. The word "condition" would make any breach of clause 7 (*b*), however excusable, a material breach. That would then entitle Schuler to give notice under clause 11 (*a*) (i) requiring the breach to be remedied. There would be no point in giving such a notice if Wickman were clearly not in fault but if it were given Wickman would have no difficulty in showing that the breach had been remedied. If Wickman were at fault then on receiving such a notice they would have to amend their system so that they could show that the breach had been remedied. If they did not do that within the period of the notice then Schuler would be entitled to rescind.

In my view, that is a possible and reasonable construction of the contract and I would therefore adopt it. The contract is so obscure that I can have no confidence that this is its true meaning but for the reasons which I have given I think that it is the preferable construction. It follows that Schuler was not entitled to rescind the contract as it purported to do. So I would dismiss this appeal.

Lord Wilberforce (dissenting): The use as a promissory term of "condition" is artificial, as is that of "warranty" in some contexts. But in my opinion this use is now too deeply embedded in English law to be uprooted by anything less than a complete revision. I shall not trace the development of the term through 19th-century cases, many of them decisions of Lord Blackburn, to the present time: this has been well done by academic writers. I would only add that the *Hongkong Fir* case, even if it could, did not reverse the trend. What it did decide, and I do not think that this was anything new, was that though a term (there a "seaworthiness" term) was not a "condition" in the technical sense, it might still be a term, breach of which if sufficiently serious could go to the root of the contract. Nothing in the judgments as I read them cast any doubt upon the meaning or effect of "condition" where that word is technically used.

...

Does clause 7 (*b*) amount to a "condition" or a "term"? (to call it an important or material term adds, with all respect, nothing but some intellectual assuagement). My Lords, I am clear in my own mind that it is a condition, but your Lordships take the contrary view. On a matter of construction of a particular document, to develop the reasons for a minority opinion serves no purpose. I am all the more happy to refrain from so doing because the judgments of Mocatta J., Stephenson L.J., and indeed of Edmund Davies L.J., on construction, give me complete satisfaction and I could in any case add little of value to their reasons. I would only add that, for my part, to call the clause arbitrary, capricious or fantastic, or to introduce as a test of its validity the ubiquitous reasonable man (I do not know whether he is English or German) is to assume, contrary to the evidence, that both parties to this contract adopted a standard of easygoing tolerance rather than one of aggressive, insistent punctuality and efficiency. This is not an assumption I am prepared to make, nor do I think myself entitled to impose the former standard upon the parties if their words indicate, as they plainly do, the latter. I note finally, that the result of treating the clause, so careful and specific in its requirements, as a term is, in effect, to deprive the appellants of any remedy in respect of admitted and by no means minimal breaches.

Lord Morris of Borth-y-Gest, **Lord Simon of Glaisdale** and **Lord Kilbrandon** gave speeches dismissing Schuler's appeal.

1. This case shows that, while a strong indicator, the use of the word 'condition' by the parties does not conclusively mean that the term is in law a condition. Here the majority's view was that the potential clash between clause 7(b) and clause 11, which allowed termination only on giving notice allowing remedial action, meant that clause 7(b) should be construed as not being a condition.

2. Does this decision undermine certainty or is it, rather, a predictable consequence of sloppy drafting?

3. J Adams and R Brownsword, *Understanding Contract Law* (4th edn, 2004) have famously argued that much of contract law is best viewed as a conflict between the opposed ideologies of 'market-individualism' and 'consumer-welfarism'. The first case they use in their book to illustrate this conflict (at 39–41) is *Schuler v Wickman*. They argue that Lord Wilberforce, dissenting, was applying the philosophy of market-individualism whereas the majority was applying the philosophy of consumer-welfarism. They write at 41, 'Lord Wilberforce thought it right to defer to the commercial standards and expectations of the parties as plainly expressed in their contract. ...Freedom of contract was the ruling principle, market-individualism the underlying philosophy. ...[T]he majority acted on a different principle. Central to their thinking was the idea that it is appropriate for judges to relieve parties from contracts the effects of which as things have turned out are particularly oppressive. Seen from this perspective, it is perfectly legitimate for judges to impose their standards upon the contracting parties where this is necessary to preserve reasonableness in contracting. Such ... is the philosophy of consumer-welfarism.' Do you regard this analysis as helpful (i) in understanding the different views in *Schuler v Wickman*; (ii) in understanding other contract cases?

4. Although not set out in the above extracts, this case is also well-known for its confirmation of *James Miller and Partners Ltd v Whitworth Street Estates (Manchester) Ltd* [1970] AC 583, HL, that in construing a contract one cannot take into account the subsequent conduct of the parties: see above, 222, note 6.

Cehave NV v Bremer Handelsgesellschaft mbH, The Hansa Nord
[1976] QB 44, Court of Appeal

The German sellers, who were the defendants, agreed to sell to Dutch buyers, who were the claimants, a shipment of some 3,400 tons of US citrus pulp pellets, to be used as an ingredient in cattle food. Clause 7 of the contract of sale required that 'shipment to be made in good condition'. The claimants paid the full contract price of some £100,000. The market price of pellets then fell. On arrival it was found that over a third of the pellets were damaged. The claimants rejected the whole cargo, alleging that it had not been shipped in good condition, and claimed repayment of the purchase price of £100,000. Subsequently the cargo was bought by a third party for some £30,000 who sold it on at that price to the claimants. The claimants then used the whole of that cargo, including the damaged pellets, to manufacture cattle food. It was held by the Court of Appeal that the claimants had not been entitled to reject the goods because the term 'shipment in good condition' was not a condition. The claimants were therefore not entitled to repayment of the price but were rather merely entitled to damages.

Lord Denning MR: [U]ntil the year 1893 there was much confusion in the use of the words "condition" and "warranty." But that confusion was removed by the [Sale of Goods] Act itself and by the judgment of Bowen L.J. in *Bentsen v. Taylor, Sons & Co.* [1893] 2 Q.B. 274, 280. Thenceforward those words were used by lawyers as terms of art. The difference between them was that if the promisor broke a *condition* in any respect, however slight, it gave the other party a right to be quit of his obligations and to sue for damages: unless he by his conduct waived the condition, in which case he was bound to perform his future obligations but could sue for the damage he had suffered. If the promisor broke a *warranty* in any respect, however serious, the other party was not quit of his future obligations. He had to perform them. His only remedy was to sue for damages: see *The Mihalis Angelos* [1971] 1 Q.B. 164, 193 and *Wickman Machine Tool Sales Ltd. v. L. Schuler A.G.* [1972] 1 W.L.R. 840, 851.

Now that division was not exhaustive. It left out of account the vast majority of stipulations which were neither "conditions" nor "warranties" strictly so called: but were intermediate stipulations, the effect of which depended on the breach. The cases about these stipulations were legion. ... I cannot believe that Parliament in 1893 intended to give the go-by to all these cases: or to say that they did not apply to the sale of goods. Those cases expressed the rules of the common law. They were preserved by section 61 (2) of the Act of 1893, which said:

> "The rules of the common law, including the law merchant, save in so far as they are inconsistent with the express provisions of this Act... shall continue to apply to contracts for the sale of goods."

There was nothing in the Act inconsistent with those cases. So they continued to apply.

In 1962 in the *Hongkong Fir Shipping Co. Ltd. v. Kawasaki Kisen Kaisha Ltd.* [1962] 2 Q.B. 26, the Court of Appeal drew attention to this vast body of case law. They showed that, besides conditions and warranties, strictly so called, there are many stipulations of which the effect depends on this: if the breach goes to the root of the contract, the other party is entitled to treat himself as discharged: but if it does not go to the root, he is not. In my opinion, the principle embodied in these cases applies to contracts for the sale of goods just as to all other contracts.

The task of the court can be stated simply in the way in which Upjohn L.J. stated it at p. 64. First, see whether the stipulation, on its true construction, is a condition strictly so called, that is, a stipulation such that, for any breach of it, the other party is entitled to treat himself as discharged. Second, if it is not such a condition, then look to the extent of the actual breach which has taken place. If it is such as to go to the root of the contract, the other party is entitled to treat himself as discharged: but, otherwise, not. To this may be added an anticipatory breach. If the one party, before the day on which he is due to perform his part, shows by his words or conduct that he will not perform it in a vital respect when the day comes, the other party is entitled to treat himself as discharged.

"Shipped in good condition"

This brings me back to the particular stipulation in this case: "Shipped in good condition." Was this a condition strictly so called, so that *any* breach of it entitled the buyer to reject the goods? Or was it an intermediate stipulation, so that the buyer cannot reject unless the breach is so serious as to go to the root of the contract? If there was any previous authority holding it to be a *condition* strictly so called, we should abide by it, just as we did with the clause "expected ready to load": see *Finnish Government (Ministry of Food) v. H. Ford & Co.*

Ltd. (1921) 6 L1.L.Rep. 188; *The Mihalis Angelos* [1971] 1 Q.B. 164. But, there is no such authority with the clause "shipped in good condition." I regard this clause as comparable to a clause as to quality, such as "fair average quality." If a small portion of the goods sold was a little below that standard, it would be met by commercial men by an allowance off the price. The buyer would have no right to reject the whole lot unless the divergence was serious and substantial... Likewise with the clause "shipped in good condition." If a small portion of the whole cargo was not in good condition and arrived a little unsound, it should be met by a price allowance. The buyers should not have a right to reject the whole cargo unless it was serious and substantial. ...

In my opinion, therefore, the term "shipped in good condition" was not a condition strictly so called: nor was it a warranty strictly so called. It was one of those intermediate stipulations which gives no right to reject unless the breach goes to the root of the contract.

...[T]he condition [of the goods] cannot have been very bad, seeing that all of them were in fact used for the intended purpose. The breach did not go to the root of the contract. The buyer is entitled to damages, but not to rejection.

Roskill LJ: I think the statements of law in the *Hongkong Fir Shipping Co.* case apply just as much to contracts for the sale of goods as to other contracts and the relevant law applicable to the sale of goods contracts is as there stated. ... Since I have ... held that clause 7 is not a "condition" in the strict sense of that word, the buyers can only rely upon the breach of clause 7 if they can show that that breach "deprived them of the whole of the benefit of the contract" or "went to the root of the contract" or "destroyed the consideration which the buyers gave," to use but three of the phrases canvassed in argument before us.

There is no finding that the sellers' breach of clause 7 had this effect. [Counsel for the buyers] argued that on the other facts found in the special case we should be ready to infer that that breach of clause 7 did have that effect. I am afraid that I must disagree. The other findings in the case, especially the findings on the user to which these goods were put after the buyers had bought them in ... and on merchantability strongly suggest the contrary. ... Upon the footing that the law is as I have held it to be, the buyers could only reject the goods if they could secure this finding from the tribunal of fact. This finding they have failed so to secure. They must now, as I think, accept the consequences. ...In the result, I think the buyers' contentions on this part of the case fail.

Ormrod LJ delivered a concurring judgment.

NOTES AND QUESTIONS

1. It was here decided that 'shipment in good condition' was an innominate term and not a condition; and on the facts the consequences of the breach were not sufficiently serious for the buyers to entitle them to terminate the contract. They could still have used the pellets for cattle food and indeed had done so.

2. To have allowed the buyers to reject would have allowed them to escape from a bad bargain. Although still using the pellets as intended, the buyers would have recovered the £100,000 price paid while incurring 'costs' of only £30,000 (paid to the third party) plus the losses consequent on the damage to the pellets (estimated at likely to be £20,000).

3. How does one reconcile this decision with *The Mihalis Angelos*, where the term was held to be a condition?

4. This case shattered the view that, in contracts for the sale of goods, terms must be either conditions or warranties. In this respect, the case derives support from the subsequent enactment of section 15A of the Sale of Goods Act 1979; see below, 324.

5. As is commonplace, rejection of goods and termination of a contract for the sale of goods by a buyer were treated in this case as synonymous concepts. This is in line with the fact that, normally, there is no point in distinguishing between them. Strictly speaking, however, rejection of goods is narrower and need not constitute a termination of the contract because the seller may still have the right to retender conforming goods within the contract period.

Bunge Corporation v Tradax Export SA [1981] 1 WLR 711, House of Lords

The defendant buyers (Bunge Corp) agreed to buy from the claimant sellers (Tradax) 15,000 tons of Soya bean meal to be shipped, in three shipments of 5000 tons, from a port in the Gulf of Mexico to be nominated by the sellers. One of the shipments was to be during June 1975. The sellers were to load the goods on board a ship nominated by the buyers. By clause 7 of the contract, the buyers were to 'give at least 15 consecutive days' notice' of the probable readiness of the ship for loading. In order for the goods to be shipped in June, this notice had to be given by 13 June. The buyers did not give notice until 17 June and the sellers argued that this was a breach of contract entitling them to terminate the contract and to recover damages for the difference between the contract price and the market price of the goods (which had fallen below the contract price). In dismissing an appeal by the buyers, the House of Lords held that the term in clause 7 was a condition so that the sellers had been entitled to terminate the contract and to recover damages.

Lord Wilberforce: Diplock L.J. in his seminal judgment [in *Hongkong Fir*] illuminated the existence in contracts of terms which were neither, necessarily, conditions nor warranties, but, in terminology which has since been applied to them, intermediate or innominate terms capable of operating, according to the gravity of the breach, as either conditions or warranties. Relying on this, Mr. Buckley's [counsel for the appellants'] submission was that the buyer's obligation under the clause, to "give at least [15] consecutive days' notice of probable readiness of vessel(s) and of the approximate quantity required to be loaded," is of this character. A breach of it, both generally and in relation to this particular case, might be, to use Mr. Buckley's expression, "inconsequential," i.e. not such as to make performance of the seller's obligation impossible. If this were so it would be wrong to treat it as a breach of condition: *Hongkong Fir* would require it to be treated as a warranty.

This argument, in my opinion, is based upon a dangerous misunderstanding, or misapplication, of what was decided and said in *Hongkong Fir*. That case was concerned with an obligation of seaworthiness, breaches of which had occurred during the course of the voyage. The decision of the Court of Appeal was that this obligation was not a condition, a breach of which entitled the charterer to repudiate. It was pointed out that, as could be seen in advance the breaches, which might occur of it, were various. They might be extremely trivial, the omission of a nail; they might be extremely grave, a serious defect in the hull or in the machinery; they might be of serious but not fatal gravity, incompetence or incapacity of the crew. The decision, and the judgments of the Court of Appeal, drew from these facts the inescapable conclusion that it was impossible to ascribe to the obligation, in advance, the character of a condition.

Diplock L.J. then generalised this particular consequence into the analysis which has since become classical. The fundamental fallacy of the appellants' argument lies in attempting to apply this analysis to a time clause such as the present in a mercantile contract, which is totally different in character. As to such a clause there is only one kind of breach possible, namely, to be late, and the questions which have to be asked are, first, what importance have the parties expressly ascribed to this consequence, and secondly, in the absence of expressed agreement, what consequence ought to be attached to it having regard to the contract as a whole.

The test suggested by the appellants was a different one. One must consider, they said, the breach actually committed and then decide whether that default would deprive the party not in default of substantially the whole benefit of the contract. They invoked even certain passages in the judgment of Diplock L.J. in the *Hongkong Fir* case [1962] 2 Q.B. 26 to support it. One may observe in the first place that the introduction of a test of this kind would be commercially most undesirable. It would expose the parties, after a breach of one, two, three, seven and other numbers of days to an argument whether this delay would have left time for the seller to provide the goods. It would make it, at the time, at least difficult, and sometimes impossible, for the supplier to know whether he could do so. It would fatally remove from a vital provision in the contract that certainty which is the most indispensable quality of mercantile contracts, and lead to a large increase in arbitrations. It would confine the seller – perhaps after arbitration and reference through the courts – to a remedy in damages which might be extremely difficult to quantify. These are all serious objections in practice. But I am clear that the submission is unacceptable in law. The judgment of Diplock L.J. does not give any support and ought not to give any encouragement to any such proposition; for beyond doubt it recognises that it is open to the parties to agree that, as regards a particular obligation, any breach shall entitle the party not in default to treat the contract as repudiated. Indeed, if he were not doing so he would, in a passage which does not profess to be more than clarificatory, be discrediting a long and uniform series of cases – at least from *Bowes v. Shand* (1877) 2 App.Cas. 455 onwards which have been referred to by my noble and learned friend, Lord Roskill. It remains true, as Lord Roskill has pointed out in *Cehave N.V. v. Bremer Handelsgesellschaft m.b.H. (The Hansa Nord)* [1976] Q.B. 44, that the courts should not be too ready to interpret contractual clauses as conditions. And I have myself commended, and continue to commend, the greater flexibility in the law of contracts to which *Hongkong Fir* points the way *(Reardon Smith Line Ltd. v. Yngvar Hansen-Tangen (trading as H.E. Hansen-Tangen)* [1976] 1 W.L.R. 989, 998). But I do not doubt that, in suitable cases, the courts should not be reluctant, if the intentions of the parties as shown by the contract so indicate, to hold that an obligation has the force of a condition, and that indeed they should usually do so in the case of time clauses in mercantile contracts. To such cases the "gravity of the breach" approach of the *Hongkong Fir* case [1962] 2 Q.B. 26 would be unsuitable.

...

In conclusion, the statement of the law in *Halsbury's Laws of England*, 4th ed., vol. 9 (1974), paras. 481-482, including the footnotes to paragraph 482..., appears to me to be correct, in particular in asserting (1) that the court will require precise compliance with stipulations as to time wherever the circumstances of the case indicate that this would fulfil the intention of the parties, and (2) that broadly speaking time will be considered of the essence in "mercantile" contracts...

In this present context it is clearly essential that both buyer and seller (who may change roles in the next series of contracts, or even in the same chain of contracts) should know precisely what their obligations are, most especially because the ability of the seller to fulfil his obligation may well be totally dependent on punctual performance by the buyer.

Lord Scarman: I wish ... to make a few observations upon the topic of "innominate" terms in our contract law. In *Hongkong Fir Shipping Co. Ltd. v. Kawasaki Kisen Kaisha Ltd.* [1962] 2 Q.B. 26, the Court of Appeal rediscovered and reaffirmed that English law recognises contractual terms which, upon a true construction of the contract of which they are part, are neither conditions nor warranties but are, to quote my noble and learned friend Lord Wilberforce's words in *Bremer Handelsgesellschaft m.b.H. v. Vanden Avenne-Izegem P.V.B.A.* [1978] 2 Lloyd's Rep. 109, 113, "intermediate." A condition is a term, the failure to perform which entitles the other party to treat the contract as at an end. A warranty is a term, breach of which sounds in damages but does not terminate, or entitle the other party to terminate, the contract. An innominate or intermediate term is one, the effect of non-performance of which the parties expressly or (as is more usual) impliedly agree will depend upon the nature and the consequences of breach. In the *Hongkong Fir* case the term in question provided for the obligation of seaworthiness, breach of which it is well known may be trivial (e.g. one defective rivet) or very serious (e.g. a hole in the bottom of the ship). It is inconceivable that parties when including such a term in their contract could have contemplated or intended (unless they expressly say so) that one defective rivet would entitle the charterer to end the contract or that a hole in the bottom of the ship would not. I read the *Hongkong Fir* case as being concerned as much with the construction of the contract as with the consequences and effect of breach. The first question is always, therefore, whether, upon the true construction of a stipulation and the contract of which it is part, it is a condition, an innominate term, or only a warranty. If the stipulation is one, which upon the true construction of the contract the parties have not made a condition, and breach of which may be attended by trivial, minor or very grave consequences, it is innominate, and the court (or an arbitrator) will, in the event of dispute, have the task of deciding whether the breach that has arisen is such as the parties would have said, had they been asked at the time they made their contract: "it goes without saying that, if that happens, the contract is at an end."

...

The seller needed sufficient notice to enable him to choose the loading port: the parties were agreed that the notice to be given him was 15 days: this was a mercantile contract in which the parties required to know where they stood not merely later with hindsight but at once as events occurred. Because it makes commercial sense to treat the clause in the context and circumstances of this contract as a condition to be performed before the seller takes his steps to comply with the bargain, I would hold it to be not an innominate term but a condition.

Lord Roskill: My Lords, the judgment of Diplock L.J. in the *Hongkong Fir* case is, if I may respectfully say so, a landmark in the development of one part of our law of contract in the latter part of this century. Diplock L.J. showed by reference to detailed historical analysis, contrary to what had often been thought previously, that there was no complete dichotomy between conditions and warranties and that there was a third class of term, the innominate term. But I do not believe Diplock L.J. ever intended his judgment to afford an easy escape route from the normal consequences of rescission to a contract breaker who had broken what was, upon its true construction, clearly a condition of the contract by claiming that he had only broken an innominate term.

...

In short, while recognising the modern approach and not being over-ready to construe terms as conditions unless the contract clearly requires the court so to do, none the less the basic principles of construction for determining whether or not a particular term is a condition remain as before, always bearing in mind on the one hand the need for certainty and on the other the desirability of not, when legitimate, allowing rescission where the breach complained of is highly technical and where damages would clearly be an adequate remedy.

...

To my mind the most important single factor in favour of Mr. Staughton's [counsel for the respondents'] submission is that until the requirement of the 15-day consecutive notice was fulfilled, the respondents could not nominate the "one Gulf port" as the loading port, which under the instant contract it was their sole right to do. I agree with Mr. Staughton that in a mercantile contract when a term has to be performed by one party as a condition precedent to the ability of the other party to perform another term, especially an essential term such as the nomination of a single loading port, the term as to time for the performance of the former obligation will in general fall to be treated as a condition. Until the 15 consecutive days' notice had been given, the respondents could not know for certain which loading port they should nominate so as to ensure that the contract goods would be available for loading on the ship's arrival at that port before the end of the shipment period.

Lord Fraser of Tullybelton concurred with Lords Wilberforce and Roskill. **Lord Lowry** delivered a speech concurring with Lords Wilberforce, Scarman and Roskill.

NOTES AND QUESTIONS

1. What is the important difference between the terms (held to be innominate) in *Hongkong Fir Shipping* and *The Hansa Nord* and the terms in this case and in *The Mihalis Angelos* (held to be conditions)?
2. Is this decision a welcome reassertion of the importance of certainty in the classification of terms?
3. Is it a disadvantage of certainty in classifying terms that an innocent party can use technical reasoning to justify taking advantage of market fluctuations?
4. For further decisions that particular terms are conditions see, eg, *Compagnie Commerciale Sucres et Denrées v C Czarnikow Ltd, The Naxos* [1990] 1 WLR 1337, HL (in a contract of sale, failure to have goods ready to load on arrival of the ship into port held to be a condition); *BS & N Ltd (BVI) v Micado Shipping Ltd (Malta), The Seaflower* [2001] 1 Lloyd's Rep 341, CA (in a time charterparty, failure by shipowners to obtain within 60 days Exxon's approval for the carriage of Exxon oil held to be a breach of condition).

Sale of Goods Act 1979, section 15A

[15A Modification of remedies for breach of condition in non-consumer cases]
[(1) Where in the case of a contract of sale—

(a) the buyer would, apart from this subsection, have the right to reject goods by reason of a breach on the part of the seller of a term implied by section 13, 14 or 15 above, but
(b) the breach is so slight that it would be unreasonable for him to reject them,

then, if the buyer does not deal as consumer, the breach is not to be treated as a breach of condition but may be treated as a breach of warranty.
(2) This section applies unless a contrary intention appears in, or is to be implied from, the contract.
(3) It is for the seller to show that a breach fell within subsection (1)(b) above.
(4) ...]

NOTES AND QUESTIONS

1. This provision was inserted into the 1979 Act by the Sale and Supply of Goods Act 1994. We have seen above, at 308, that the implied terms as to description, fitness for purpose, quality and sample are laid down as conditions. Is the effect of section 15A to reclassify those implied terms, where the buyer is not dealing as consumer, as innominate terms?
2. For the equivalent provisions for contracts of hire-purchase, work and materials, and hire, see Supply of Goods (Implied Terms) Act 1973 section 11A and the Supply of Goods and Services Act 1982, sections 5A and 10A.

3.   For the classic example of where section 15A would be likely to change the result, see *Arcos Ltd v Ronassen & Son* [1933] AC 470, HL. In a contract for the sale of staves of wood, the wood was to be half an inch thick. Although perfectly useable for their required purpose, the buyers rejected them on the basis that some of the staves were more than half an inch thick. It was held that they were entitled to do so because the implied term as to the goods matching their description was a condition.

3. TERMINATION CLAUSES

The two cases set out in this section focus on 'termination clauses' and their relationship with the general law on termination for breach that we have so far examined.

Lombard North Central plc v Butterworth [1987] QB 527, Court of Appeal

The claimant finance company leased a computer to the defendant for a period of five years. Clause 2 of the contract stated that time was of the essence with regard to payment of the quarterly rentals (there being 20, each being £584). Clause 5 stipulated that failure to make due and punctual payment entitled the claimant to terminate the contract. Clause 6 provided that, on termination, the claimant was entitled to all arrears of instalments, all future instalments less a discount for accelerated payment, and damages for any breach. Having paid the first two instalments on time, the defendant was late in paying the next three, although they were paid. When the sixth instalment was also delayed, the claimant wrote to the defendant terminating the contract. It subsequently repossessed the computer and sold it (for only £173). In this action, the claimant sought payment, under clause 6, of the arrears of instalments plus the future instalments or, alternatively, damages for breach. It was held by the Court of Appeal that, while clause 6 was unenforceable because a penalty clause, clause 2 meant that the claimant had been entitled to terminate the contract for breach and, in addition to the arrears on past instalments, was entitled, as damages for that breach, to the future instalments minus the proceeds of resale and a discount for acceleration.

Mustill LJ (agreed with Nicholls LJ as regards clause 6. He then continued to deal with clause 2): The reason why I am impelled to hold that the plaintiffs' contentions are well-founded can most conveniently be set out in a series of propositions.

1. Where a breach goes to the root of the contract, the injured party may elect to put an end to the contract. Thereupon both sides are relieved from those obligations which remain unperformed.

2. If he does so elect, the injured party is entitled to compensation for (a) any breaches which occurred before the contract was terminated and (b) the loss of his opportunity to receive performance of the promisor's outstanding obligations.

3. Certain categories of obligation, often called conditions, have the property that any breach of them is treated as going to the root of the contract. Upon the occurrence of any

breach of condition, the injured party can elect to terminate and claim damages, whatever the gravity of the breach.

4. It is possible by express provision in the contract to make a term a condition, even if it would not be so in the absence of such a provision.

5. A stipulation that time is of the essence, in relation to a particular contractual term, denotes that timely performance is a condition of the contract. The consequence is that delay in performance is treated as going to the root of the contract, without regard to the magnitude of the breach.

6. It follows that where a promisor fails to give timely performance of an obligation in respect of which time is expressly stated to be of the essence, the injured party may elect to terminate and recover damages in respect of the promisor's outstanding obligations, without regard to the magnitude of the breach.

7. A term of the contract prescribing what damages are to be recoverable when a contract is terminated for a breach of condition is open to being struck down as a penalty, if it is not a genuine covenanted pre-estimate of the damage, in the same way as a clause which prescribes the measure for any other type of breach. No doubt the position is the same where the clause is ranked as a condition by virtue of an express provision in the contract.

8. A clause expressly assigning a particular obligation to the category of condition is not a clause which purports to fix the damages for breaches of the obligation, and is not subject to the law governing penalty clauses.

9. Thus, although in the present case clause 6 is to be struck down as a penalty, clause 2(a)(i) remains enforceable. The plaintiffs were entitled to terminate the contract independently of clause 5, and to recover damages for loss of the future instalments.

Nicholls LJ:

The claim under clause 6

...

The ratio of the decision of this court in *Financings Ltd. v. Baldock* [1963] 2 Q.B. 104, was that when an owner determines a hire purchase agreement in exercise of a right so to do given him by the agreement, in the absence of repudiation he can recover damages for any breaches up to the date of termination but not thereafter, and a "minimum payment" clause which purports to oblige the hirer to pay larger sums than this is unenforceable as a penalty.

...

In my view, applying the principle enunciated in *Financings Ltd. v. Baldock* to this case leads inescapably to the conclusion that in the absence of a repudiatory breach clause 6(a) is a penalty insofar as it purports to oblige the hirer, regardless of the seriousness or triviality of the breach which led to the owners terminating the agreement by retaking possession of the computer, to make a payment, albeit a discounted payment, in respect of rental instalments which had not accrued due prior to [the date of termination].

The claim for damages

...

I must now consider a further submission advanced by the plaintiffs that, time of payment having been made of the essence by [clause 2(a)], it was open to the plaintiffs, once default in payment of any one instalment on the due date had occurred, to treat the agreement as having been repudiated by the defendant, and claim damages for loss of the whole transaction, even though in the absence of this provision such a default would not have had that consequence. On this, the question which arises is one of construction: on the true construction of the clause, did the "time of the essence" provision have the effect submitted by the plaintiffs? In my view, the answer to that question is "Yes." The provision in clause 2(a) has to be read and construed in conjunction with the other provisions in the agreement, including clauses 5 and 6. So read, it is to be noted that failure to pay any instalment triggers a right for the plaintiffs to terminate the agreement by re-taking possession of the goods (clause 5), with the expressed consequence that the defendant becomes liable to make payments which assume that the defendant is liable to make good to the plaintiffs the loss by them of the whole transaction (clause 6). Given that context, the "time of the essence" provision seems to me to be intended to bring about the result that default in punctual payment is to be regarded (to use a once fashionable term) as a breach going to the root of the contract and, hence, as giving rise to the consequences in damages attendant upon such a breach. I am unable to see what other purpose the "time of the essence" provision in clause 2(a) can serve or was intended to serve or what other construction can fairly be ascribed to it.

If that construction of the agreement is correct then, as at present advised, it seems to me that the legal consequence is that the plaintiffs are entitled to claim damages for loss of the whole transaction. I say "as at present advised," because on this no argument to the contrary was advanced on behalf of the defendant, and Mustill L.J.'s illuminating analysis leaves no escape from the conclusion that parties are free to agree that a particular provision in their contract shall be a condition such that a breach of it is to be regarded as going to the root of the contract and entitling the innocent party (1) to accept that breach as a repudiation, and (2) to be paid damages calculated upon that footing.

I have to say that I view the impact of that principle in this case with considerable dissatisfaction, for this reason. As already mentioned, the principle applied in *Financings Ltd. v. Baldock* [1963] 2 Q.B. 104 was that when an owner determines a hire purchase agreement in exercise of a power so to do given him by the agreement on non-payment of instalments, he can recover damages for any breaches up to the date of termination but (in the absence of repudiation) not thereafter. There is no practical difference between (1) an agreement containing such a power and (2) an agreement containing a provision to the effect that time for payment of each instalment is of the essence, so that any breach will go to the root of the contract. The difference between these two agreements is one of drafting form, and wholly without substance. Yet under an agreement drafted in the first form, the owner's damages claim arising upon his exercise of the power of termination is confined to damages for breaches up to the date of termination, whereas under an agreement drafted in the second form the owner's damages claim, arising upon his acceptance of an identical breach as a repudiation of the agreement, will extend to damages for loss of the whole transaction.

Nevertheless, as at present advised, I can see no escape from the conclusion that such is the present state of the law. This conclusion emasculates the decision in *Financings Ltd. v. Baldock,* for it means that a skilled draftsman can easily side-step the effect of that decision. Indeed, that is what has occurred here.

Lawton LJ concurred.

NOTES AND QUESTIONS

1. One way in which a contract draftsman can seek to ensure that a party is entitled to terminate for breach is to make clear that a particular term is a condition. An alternative approach is to draft a 'termination clause' by which on certain events (which need not necessarily constitute a breach) one, or both, of the parties shall have the right to terminate. This case, albeit complex, is particularly interesting because both techniques were used and examined by the court. Clause 2, by using the wording 'time is of the essence', had successfully turned what might otherwise not have been a condition into a condition. Clauses 5 and 6 together constituted a termination clause with express remedial consequences. The overall effect of the decision was that by clause 2 the claimant was able to trigger the general law on termination and damages and

thereby achieve what clause 6, because invalid as a penalty, had failed to achieve.

2.   The decision on clause 6 is important as regards termination clauses because it recognises that termination under a termination clause (ie the exercise of an express power to terminate) can have different (less beneficial) consequences than termination for breach under the general law. Here clause 6 was a penalty clause (see below, 412–417) because if one is exercising an express power to terminate one is entitled to past, but not future, instalments. Clause 6, therefore, gave the claimant too much. In contrast, if one is terminating for breach under the general law, damages do entitle one to the equivalent of the future instalments. As the Court of Appeal made clear, this is a difference that was clearly established in *Financings Ltd v Baldock* [1963] 2 QB 104, CA.

Rice v Great Yarmouth Borough Council (2001) 3 LGLR 4, Court of Appeal

The claimant (trading as 'The Garden Guardian') entered into two contracts with the defendant local authority. One was for the maintenance and management of the defendant's sports facilities (eg football pitches) and the other was for the maintenance of its parks, gardens and playgrounds. The contracts were to run for four years from 1 January 1996. The contracts provided for a system of notification to the claimant for any failure to perform his obligations to a designated council officer's satisfaction ('default notices'). The contract also contained a termination clause (23.2.1) which stated: 'If the contractor... commits a breach of any of its obligations under the Contract...the Council may... terminate the Contractor's employment under the Contract by notice in writing having immediate effect.' Between 9 May 1996 and July 1996 the defendant served a series of default notices on the claimant and on 5 August 1996 gave notice to him that it was terminating the contract under clause 23.2.1. The claimant sought damages alleging that the termination constituted a breach of contract. The Court of Appeal, dismissing the defendant's appeal, held that the claim should succeed because the defendant had not been entitled to terminate the contract.

Hale LJ:

The first issue
The council argued first that clause 23.2.1 should be applied literally so as to give them the right to terminate the contract for the breach of any of the obligations contained in it, other than the trivial. The judge was referred to a number of well-known authorities. On the one hand, 'it is open to the parties to agree that, as regards a particular obligation, any breach shall entitle the party not in default to treat the contract as repudiated': see *Bunge Corporation v Tradax Export SA* [1981] 1 WLR 711, per Lord Wilberforce at 715E. On the other hand '... if detailed semantic and syntactical analysis of words in a commercial contract is going to lead to a conclusion that flouts business commonsense, it must yield to business commonsense': see *Antaios Compania SA v Salen Rederierna* [1985] AC 191, per Lord Diplock at p 201D.
  ...
As to which line of authority should apply, [the judge] concluded:

'In the context of a contract intended to last for four years, involving substantial investment or at least substantial undertaking of financial obligations by one party and involving a myriad of obligations of differing importance and varying frequency, I have no hesitation in holding that the common sense interpretation should be imposed upon the strict words of the contract and that a repudiatory breach or an accumulation of breaches that as a whole can properly be described as repudiatory are a precondition to termination pursuant to clause 23.2.1.'

...

As is well-known, the classic position in English (but not Scottish) contract law was that the consequences of breach depended upon the importance of the term broken. A minor breach of an important term, a condition, could entitle the innocent party to terminate the contract. Breach of a less important term, a warranty, would sound only in damages. Then along came the seminal case of *Hong Kong Fir Shipping Co Ltd v Kawasaki Kisen Kaisha Ltd* [1962] 2 QB 26, in which Diplock LJ, in the words of Lord Wilberforce in *Bunge v Tradax*, above, at p 714G,

'illuminated the existence in contracts of terms which are neither, necessarily, conditions nor warranties, but in terminology which has since been applied to them, intermediate or innominate terms capable of operating, according to the gravity of the breach, as either conditions or warranties.'

Lord Wilberforce emphasised, in the words already quoted in paragraph 17 above, that it is still open to the parties to agree that a term is so important to them that it should have that effect. He continued:

'It remains true, as Lord Roskill has pointed out in *Cehave NV v Bremer Handelsgesellshaft m b H (The Hansa Nord)* [1976] QB 44, that courts should not be too ready to interpret contractual clauses as conditions ... But I do not doubt that, in suitable cases, the courts should not be reluctant, if the intentions of the parties as shown by the contract so indicate, to hold that an obligation has the force of a condition.'

The problem with the council's argument in this case is that clause 23.2.1 does not characterise any particular term as a condition or indicate which terms are to be considered so important that any breach will justify termination. It appears to visit the same draconian consequences upon any breach, however small, of any obligation, however small. In this it is unlike cases, such as *Bunge*, which concerned an obviously vital time clause that can only be broken in one way, and much closer to the cases, such as *Hong Kong Fir Shipping* and *The Antaios*, concerning multi-faceted obligations, which can be broken in many different ways.

The comparable term in *The Antaios* provided that 'on any breach of this charterparty, the owners shall be at liberty to withdraw the vessel...' The owners sought to do so on discovering that inaccurate bills of lading had been issued. As Lord Diplock observed, the dispute

'was a typical case of a shipowner seeking to find an excuse to bring a long term time charter to a premature end in a rising market. Stripped to its essentials the shipowners were seeking to rely upon the charterer's breach of an innominate term in the charterparty relating to the charterer's rights to issue bills of lading as constituting "any other breach of this charterparty"...'

Lord Diplock agreed entirely with the arbitrators' view that 'the owner's construction is wholly unreasonable, totally uncommercial and in total contradiction to the whole purpose of the NYPE time charter form.' The contract should not be interpreted in such a way as to defeat its commercial purpose.

Mr Mann [counsel for the defendant] seeks to distinguish clause 23.2.1 from the clause in *The Antaios* on the basis that the latter referred to 'any breach of this charterparty', while clause 23.2.1 refers to the 'breach of any of its obligations under this contract'. While the *Antaios* term might be limited to a breach defeating the whole contract, the term here might refer to any material or non-trivial breach. The judge characterised this distinction as a semantic one and I agree with him. For the reasons which the judge gave, the notion that this term would entitle the council to terminate a contract such as this at any time for any breach of any term flies in the face of commercial common sense.

However, Mr Mann also argues that the judge should first have considered which terms of the contract had been broken and whether they were such important terms as to give rise to a right to terminate. He identified a core obligation in each contract, either in the exact terms of clause 6.1 or something very similar to it:

> 'During the contract period the contractor shall provide the Service in a proper skilful and workmanlike manner, to the contract standard and to the entire satisfaction of the authorised officer.'

The difficulty with that argument is that this is a classic example of an innominate term: one which can be broken in so many different ways and with such varying consequences that the parties cannot be taken to have intended that any breach should entitle the innocent party to terminate the whole contract. In the words of Diplock LJ in the *Hong Kong Fir Shipping* case, at p 71:

> 'It is like so many other contractual terms an undertaking one breach of which may give rise to an event which relieves the charterer of further performance of his undertakings if he so elects and another breach of which may not give rise to such an event but entitle him only to monetary compensation in the form of damages.'

...

In my view the judge was entirely right to reach the conclusion he did on this aspect of the case and for the reasons he gave.

The second issue

The council argued that, in any event, the totality of breaches found by the judge were sufficient to justify it in terminating the contract. It was argued on behalf of the contractor that the appropriate test of a repudiatory breach was that derived from the *Hong Kong Fir Shipping* case, at p 66:

> '... does the occurrence of the event deprive the party who has further undertakings still to perform of substantially the whole benefit which it was the intention of the parties as expressed in the contract that he should obtain as the consideration for performing those undertakings?'

...

The question for the court (and indeed the contracting parties) in any case like this is whether the cumulative effect of the breaches of contract complained of is so serious as to justify the innocent party in bringing the contract to a premature end. The technical term is 'repudiatory' but that is just a label to describe the consequence which may flow. It is not always an entirely satisfactory label, if it implies that the conduct itself must always be such as to demonstrate an intention to abandon contractual obligations: while this will sometimes be so it is not an invariable requirement. As the judge indicated, there are in effect three categories: (1) those cases in which the parties have agreed either that the term is so important that any breach will justify termination or that the particular breach is so important that it will justify termination; (2) those contractors who simply walk away from their obligations thus clearly indicating an intention no longer to be bound; and (3) those cases in which the cumulative effect of the breaches which have taken place is sufficiently serious to justify the innocent party in bringing the contract to a premature end.

It is clear that the test of what is sufficiently serious to bring the case within the third of these categories is severe. No case has been cited to us which addresses this question in the context of a long running contract to provide public services such as this. There are some parallels with a charterparty, but that is a somewhat less complex undertaking than these. There are also some parallels with building contracts, in the number and variety of the obligations involved and the varying gravity of the breaches which may be committed, some of which may be remediable and some not.

...

Building contracts differ from these contracts in that there will, it is hoped, be an end product. Defects may or should be remedied during or, in some cases, after completion. Delay in completion can be compensated. These contracts contemplated a multitude of different results at different times, from cricket pitches ready for the summer season, football pitches ready for the autumn, flower beds in full bloom at the appropriate times, properly mown grass on lawns and bowling greens, raked bunkers in a pitch and putt course, edged and weeded rose beds, pruned shrubs, cleared litter, and so on and so on. Mr Smith [counsel for the claimant] accepted that in the case of a four year contract such as this, the court is entitled to look at the contractor's performance over a year, the most important part of which is the spring and summer, but it must still ask itself whether the council was deprived of substantially the whole benefit of what it had contracted for during that period.

These contracts are, however, like building contracts in that the accumulation of past breaches is relevant, not only for its own sake, but also for what it shows about the future. In my view, the judge was right to ask himself whether the cumulative breaches were such as to justify an inference that the contractor would continue to deliver a substandard performance. However, I would agree with Mr Smith that the inference should be that the council would thereby be deprived of a substantial part of the totality of that which it had contracted for that year, subject to the additional possibility that some aspects of the contract were so important that the parties are to be taken to have intended that depriving the council of that part of the contract would be sufficient in itself. That is not what the judge found in this case.

Once it is accepted that the proven breaches are relevant to show what will happen in the future, it is clear that the judge was entitled to take both the drought and the knock on effect of the council's own behaviour in relation to the summer bedding into account. He examined the facts of this case in great detail over a trial lasting some 13 days. He was well placed to evaluate the true importance of the proven breaches in the context of the contracts as a whole and all the circumstances of the case. He had a judgment to make. If anything, the test which he applied was somewhat more favourable to the council than the test which, in my judgment, he should have applied. He was undoubtedly entitled to reach the conclusion that he did.

I would dismiss this appeal.

May LJ and **Peter Gibson LJ** concurred.

NOTES AND QUESTIONS

1. This decision has been heavily criticised as undermining certainty and as producing the effect that the termination clause added nothing to the legal position that would have applied in any event. See, eg, Whittaker, below, 336.
2. Would the judges have been able to construe away the termination clause if it had said that the council could terminate 'for any breach, however trivial'?
3. Was this case an example, reminiscent of the pre-UCTA 1977 approach to exclusion clauses (above, Chapter 6), of hostile construction being used to

nullify an unreasonable clause? Is there any conceivable argument that the termination clause in this case fell within UCTA 1977?

4. In consumer contracts, termination clauses that are unfair to consumers may be struck down under the Unfair Terms in Consumer Contracts Regulations 1999 (see especially Schedule 2 clause 1(1)(g), above, 291).

4. ANTICIPATORY BREACH

We have seen in the last section that an innocent party can terminate a contract for a serious breach (of an innominate term) or for breach of a condition. Without having to classify the terms precisely, a party can also terminate for breach where the other party repudiates (or renounces) the contract by making clear that it is not going to perform its main obligations under the contract. Commonly, such a repudiation (or renunciation) will occur prior to the due time for performance: together with the situation where it is otherwise clear that the defendant will not be able to perform on the due date, this is referred to as 'anticipatory breach'. The most important feature of the law on anticipatory breach is that the innocent party is entitled to terminate *now*—and to recover damages *at once*—by accepting the anticipatory breach. He does not have to wait for an actual breach at the due date of performance. This is classically illustrated by the following case.

Hochster v De La Tour (1853) 2 E & B 678, Court of Queen's Bench

On 12 April 1852, the defendant agreed to employ the claimant as a travel courier for three months starting on 1 June 1852. On 11 May the defendant wrote to the claimant stating that he had changed his mind and would not require his services. On 22 May the claimant commenced an action claiming damages for breach of contract. It was held by the Court of Queen's Bench that he was entitled to terminate the contract and to claim damages in advance of the date of performance.

Lord Campbell CJ (delivering the judgment of the court comprising himself, **Coleridge J, Erle J** and **Croughton J**): [I]t cannot be laid down as a universal rule that, where by agreement an act is to be done on a future day, no action can be brought for a breach of the agreement till the day for doing the act has arrived. If a man promises to marry a woman on a future day, and before that day marries another woman, he is instantly liable to an action for breach of promise of marriage; *Short v Stone* (8 Q. B. 358). If a man contracts to execute a lease on and from a future day for a certain term, and, before that day, executes a lease to another for the same term, he may be immediately sued for breaking the contract; *Ford v Tiley* (6 B. & C. 325). So, if a man contracts to sell and deliver specific goods on a future day, and before the day he sells and delivers them to another, he is immediately liable to an action at the suit of the person with whom he first contracted to sell and deliver them; *Bowdell v Parsons* (10 East, 359). ...

  If the plaintiff has no remedy for breach of the contract unless he treats the contract as in force, and acts upon it down to the 1st June 1852, it follows that, till then, he must enter into no employment which will interfere with his promise "to start with the defendant on such travels on the day and year," and that he must then be properly equipped in all respects as a courier for a three months' tour on the continent of Europe. But it is surely much more rational, and more for the benefit of both parties, that, after the renunciation of the agreement by the defendant, the plaintiff should be at liberty to consider himself absolved from any future performance of it, retaining his right to sue for any damage he has suffered from the breach of it. Thus, instead of remaining idle and laying out money in preparations which must be useless, he is at liberty to seek service under another employer, which would go in mitigation of the damages to which he would otherwise be entitled for a breach of the contract. It seems strange that the defendant, after renouncing the contract, and absolutely declaring that be will never act under it, should be permitted to object that faith is given to his assertion, and that an opportunity is not left to him of changing his mind. If the plaintiff is barred of any remedy by entering into an engagement inconsistent with starting as a courier with the defendant on the lst June, he is prejudiced by putting faith in the defendant's assertion: and it would be more consonant with principle, if the defendant were precluded from saying that he had not broken the contract when he declared that he entirely renounced it. Suppose that the defendant, at the time of his renunciation, had embarked on a voyage for Australia, so as to render it physically impossible for him to employ the plaintiff as a courier on the continent of Europe in the months of June, July and August 1852: according to decided cases, the action might have been brought before the lst June; but the renunciation may have been founded on other facts, to be given in evidence, which would equally have rendered the defendant's performance of the contract impossible. The man who wrongfully renounces a contract into which he has deliberately entered cannot justly complain if he is immediately sued for a compensation in damages by the man whom he has injured: and it seems reasonable to allow an option to the injured party, either to sue immediately, or to wait till the time when the act was to be done, still holding it as prospectively binding for the exercise of this option, which may be advantageous to the innocent party, and cannot be prejudicial to the wrongdoer. An argument against the action before the lst of June is urged from the difficulty of calculating the damages: but this argument is equally strong against an action before the lst of September, when the three months would expire. In either case, the Jury in assessing the damages would be justified in looking to all that had happened, or was likely to happen, to increase or mitigate the loss of the plaintiff down to the day of trial. ...If it should be held that, upon a contract to do an act on a future day, a renunciation of the contract by one party dispenses with a condition to be performed in the meantime by the other, there seems no reason for requiring that other to wait till the day arrives before seeking his remedy by action: and the only ground on which the condition can be dispensed with seems to be, that the renunciation may be treated as a breach of the contract

NOTES

1. Another old, but clear, illustration of anticipatory breach is *Frost v Knight* (1872) LR 7 Ex 111. There the defendant promised to marry the claimant on the death of his father, who objected to the marriage. In those days, an engagement was a legally binding contract. The defendant broke off the engagement while his father was still alive. It was held by the Exchequer Chamber that, applying *Hochster v De La Tour*, the claimant was entitled to accept that repudiatory breach and sue for damages while the father was still alive.

2. As with an actual breach, the innocent party is not bound to accept an anticipatory breach as terminating the contract. Rather it has an election (as is most starkly shown where the innocent party continues with its own unwanted performance so as to claim the agreed price payable under the contract: see, eg, *White & Carter (Councils) Ltd v McGregor*, below, 424). If it chooses not to

accept the anticipatory breach, the contract continues in force. The continuation of the contract may be beneficial to the innocent party because the other party may properly perform. However, the continuation also carries risks for the innocent party. For example, the contract may become frustrated so that the right to claim any damages for breach is lost (as in *Avery v Bowden* (1855) 5 Ex B 714, QB); or the innocent party may commit a breach of its own obligations so that the (original) contract-breaker is entitled to terminate the contract and to recover damages (as in *Fercometal SARL v Mediterranean Shipping Co SA*, [1989] AC 788, HL).

5. RESTITUTION AFTER TERMINATION FOR BREACH

We have seen that termination does not wipe away a contract from the start. The question therefore arises as to what, if anything, is to happen to the benefits that the parties have conferred on each other prior to the date of termination. The basic answer is that on termination, the innocent party, and sometimes the contract-breaker, is entitled to restitutionary remedies, in particular the recovery of money had and received for a (total) failure of consideration or a quantum meruit for services rendered. (A total failure of consideration, as laid down by the House of Lords in *Stocznia Gdanska SA v Latvian Shipping Co* [1988] 1 WLR 574, means that there has been none of the performance that the other party was paying for.)

These restitutionary remedies are triggered not by the cause of action of breach of contract but by the cause of action of unjust enrichment. They therefore belong outside the law of contract and within the law of restitution (sometimes alternatively referred to as the law of unjust enrichment). That they are not remedies for breach of contract explains a number of their features:

(i)   They are not available in respect of a breach until a contract has been terminated; and traditionally there has been the further restriction on the recovery of money that the failure of consideration must have been total rather than merely partial.

(ii) They are analogous to the restitutionary remedies available where there has never been a valid contract; for example where an alleged contract is too uncertain to be binding (see above, 74–77).

(iii) Even the party in breach may sometimes be entitled to these restitutionary remedies.

(iv) It is possible that by claiming restitution an innocent party can escape from a known bad bargain, which is difficult to explain if one views the remedy as one for the breach of contract. Say, for example, the claimant contracts to buy a car from the defendant for £900 and pays £100 in advance; the defendant fails to deliver the car; and the market price is £700. The claimant can recover £100 in an action for money had and received for total failure of consideration (see, eg,

Wilkinson v Lloyd [1845] 7 QB 27). This cannot be sensibly explained if the recovery is regarded as a remedy for the breach of contract. Had the contract been performed, the claimant would have lost the £100. Moreover, one cannot regard the £100 as stripping a gain made by the defendant by the breach (as in *Attorney General v Blake*, below, 401) because the defendant would still have made that gain had there been no breach: one is therefore concerned not with restitution for a wrong (the breach of contract) but rather with restitution of an unjust enrichment.

The law of restitution/unjust enrichment is a recently discovered and developing area of the law. It was only clearly detached from contract (hence the old label 'quasi-contract') in the 1990s by the House of Lords in cases such as *Lipkin Gorman v Karpnale Ltd* [1991] 2 AC 548 and *Westdeutsche Landesbank Girozentrale v Islington London Borough Council* [1996] AC 669. The whole subject bristles with issues of interest and controversy. In the context of restitution after termination for breach, unresolved issues include the following. First, is it, and should it be, necessary to show that a failure of consideration is total rather than partial in order to recover money paid? Secondly, can one recover a quantum meruit for the reasonable value of work done that is higher than the (pro-rata) contract price? Thirdly, when is the party in breach entitled to restitution? For analysis of these and other related issues, see A Burrows, *The Law of Restitution* (2nd edn, 2002) 322–59.

Additional Reading for Chapter 7

J Beatson, *Anson's Law of Contract* (28th edn, 2002) 134–45, 642–52, Ch 15
S Smith, *Atiyah's Introduction to the Law of Contract* (6th edn, 2005) 196–205, 408–11

J C Smith, 'Anticipatory Breach of Contract' in *Contemporary Issues in Commercial Law* (eds E Lomnicka and C Morse, 1997) 175

The author attempts to dispel some myths about anticipatory breach. For example, he argues that: an unaccepted repudiation should be viewed as a breach; that acceptance of a repudiation equates to electing to terminate and not to acceptance of an offer; that an insistence on a construction of the contract entitling one not to perform, which proves to be wrong, does constitute a repudiatory breach; and that the innocent party, having accepted the repudiation, must remain ready and willing to perform.

S Whittaker, 'Termination Clauses' in *Contract Terms* (eds A Burrows and E Peel, 2007) 253

The author looks at the functions of termination clauses (for breach) and at the particular ways in which such termination clauses are restricted or controlled. These include by directly invalidating the clause (eg under the Unfair Terms in Consumer Contracts Regulations 1999) and by judicial construction. The judicial technique of 'reading down' such clauses is examined with particular reference to *Rice v Great Yarmouth DC* (above, 328) which, it is persuasively argued, was incorrectly decided.

Principles of European Contract Law (eds O Lando and H Beale, 2000) 364–8, 409–11, 416–19

Article 8:103: Fundamental Non-Performance
A non-performance of an obligation is fundamental to the contract if:

(a) strict compliance with the obligation is of the essence of the contract; or

(b) the non-performance substantially deprives the aggrieved party of what it was entitled to expect under the contract, unless the other party did not foresee and could not reasonably have foreseen that result; or

(c) the non-performance is intentional and gives the aggrieved party reason to believe that it cannot rely on the other party's future performance.

Article 9:301: Right to Terminate the Contract
(1) A party may terminate the contract if the other party's non-performance is fundamental.

Article 9:304: Anticipatory Non-Performance
Where prior to the time for performance by a party it is clear that there will be a fundamental non-performance by it the other party may terminate the contract.

[These articles in PECL are worth examining not because they contrast with English law but rather because they elegantly match, very closely, English law (albeit that they are intended to apply to termination for frustration as well as for breach). The distinctions in Article 8:103 correspond to conditions, innominate terms with serious consequences, and repudiation.]

8

Damages

There is a fundamental distinction between compensatory damages and non-compensatory damages. Compensatory damages are the normal type of damages and if one simply refers to 'damages' this is what one has in mind. They are concerned to cover—to provide a financial equivalent for—the claimant's loss caused by the breach of contract whether that loss is pecuniary or non-pecuniary. In other words, they are concerned to compensate the claimant's loss. Exceptionally, however, non-compensatory (eg restitutionary) damages can be awarded for a breach of contract. These will be looked at after we have considered normal compensatory damages. A final section will consider agreed ('liquidated') damages, which differ fundamentally from compensatory or non-compensatory (unliquidated) damages because they are fixed by the parties in the contract rather than being assessed by the courts.

1. COMPENSATORY DAMAGES

It is convenient to examine compensatory damages under two main heads. First, basic issues in applying the compensatory aim (and we here examine the precise aim, whether the difference in value of property or the cost of cure is awarded, assessment according to the chances, and whether contractual damages can protect the reliance interest); and, secondly, limitations on compensation (that is, the extent to which the compensatory aim is cut back by remoteness, intervening cause, the duty to mitigate, contributory negligence, and where the loss is non-pecuniary such as mental distress or a loss of reputation).

Introductory reading: E McKendrick, *Contract Law* (7th edn, 2007) 20.1–20.3, 20.7 20.14.

(1) Basic Issues in Applying the Compensatory Aim

(a) The Precise Aim of Contractual Compensation: Protecting the Expectation Interest

Robinson v Harman (1848) 1 Exch 850, Court of Exchequer

The defendant agreed in writing to grant a 21-year lease of a house to the claimant for an annual rent of £110. The defendant, in breach of contract, failed to grant the lease and indeed knew that he was not in a position to do so because the legal title to the house was vested in trustees. The premises were worth considerably more than £110 a year so that the claimant had made a good bargain. The defendant argued that the claimant was merely entitled to the £20 expenses wasted because of the breach. But the trial judge had awarded the claimant £200 damages for the loss of his bargain. In dismissing the defendants' appeal, the Court of Exchequer held that the claimant was entitled to be put into as good a position as if the contract had been performed.

Parke B: [W]hat damages is the plaintiff entitled to recover? The rule of the common law is, that where a party sustains a loss by reason of a breach of contract, he is, so far as money can do it, to be placed in the same situation, with respect to damages, as if the contract had been performed. The case of *Flureau v Thornhill* 2 W Bla 1078 qualified that rule of the common law. It was there held, that contracts for the sale of real estate are merely on condition that the vendor has a good title; so that, when a person contracts to sell real property, there is an implied understanding that, if he fail to make a good title, the only damages recoverable are the expenses which the vendee may be put to in investigating the title. The present case comes within the rule of the common law, and I am unable to distinguish it from *Hopkins v Grazebrook* 6 B & C 31.

Alderson, B: I am of the same opinion. The damages have been assessed according to the general rule of law, that where a person makes a contract and breaks it, he must pay the whole damage sustained. Upon that general rule an exception was engrafted by the case of *Flureau v Thornhill*, and upon that exception the case of *Hopkins v Grazebrook* engrafted another exception. This case comes within the latter, by which the old common-law rule has been restored. Therefore the defendant, having undertaken to grant a valid lease, not having any colour of title, must pay the loss which the plaintiff has sustained by not having that for which he contracted.

Platt B concurred.

NOTES AND QUESTIONS

1. The second sentence of the extract from Parke B's judgment has been cited in scores of cases since. It is the classic authority for the aim of (compensatory) damages for breach of contract being to put the claimant into as good a position as if the contract had been performed.

2. Adopting the terminology used by L Fuller and W Perdue (1936) 46 *Yale LJ* 52, 373 (below, 417) the above aim has commonly been described as the protection of the claimant's 'expectation interest'. More recently, D Friedmann (1995) 111 *LQR* 628 (below, 418) has suggested that the preferable (albeit

synonymous) term is the protection of the claimant's 'performance interest'. The protection of the expectation or performance interest is to be contrasted with the protection of the claimant's 'reliance interest' which, as explained by Fuller and Perdue, aims to put the claimant into as good a position as if no contract had been entered into.

3. What is the justification for the law protecting the claimant's expectation, rather than reliance, interest for breach of contract? (On this, see the articles by Fuller and Perdue and by Friedmann, below, 417–418.) Note that the aim of damages for a tortious misrepresentation inducing a contract is to protect the claimant's reliance interest. What is the justification for that difference?

4. A complication on the facts of *Robinson v Harman* was that contracts for the sale or letting of land, where title was defective, were subject to an exception to the general rule of damages so that the claimant could only be awarded damages to cover certain expenses. That anomalous exception (established in *Flureau v Thornhill* (1776) 2 Wm Bl 1078) was confirmed by the House of Lords in *Bain v Fothergill* (1874) LR 7 HL 158 and remained good law, albeit controversial, until statutorily abolished by the Law of Property (Miscellaneous Provisions) Act 1989, section 3. In *Robinson v Harman* the judges were able to rely on the exception to *Flureau v Thornhill*, established in *Hopkins v Grazebrook* (1826) 6 B & C 31, that the exceptional rule of damages did not apply where the defendant knew that his title was defective.

(b) Difference in the Value of Property or Cost of Cure?

Radford v de Froberville [1977] 1 WLR 1262, Chancery Division

The claimant owned a house which was split into flats and rented out. It had a large garden. He obtained planning permission for a house to be built on a part of the garden and sold that plot to the defendant. The defendant covenanted to build a wall on her side of the boundary so as to separate the two properties. In breach of contract, she failed to build that wall and sold the land on to a third party (against whom the defendant sought an indemnity for any damages awarded against her). The question arose as to what was the correct measure of damages. The cost of erecting a wall of the agreed specification at the date when it should have been erected was £1200 and, at the time of trial, £3400. The difference in (letting) value of the claimant's property, with and without the wall on the boundary, was considered to be nil. Oliver J held that the cost of cure (ie the cost of the claimant building the wall on his own side of the boundary) was the appropriate measure.

Oliver J: As to principle, I take my starting point from what, I think, is the universal starting point in any inquiry of this nature – that is to say, the well known statement of Parke B. in *Robinson v. Harman* (1848) 1 Exch. 850, 855 which is in these terms:

"The rule of common law is, that where a party sustains a loss by reason of a breach of contract, he is, so far as money can do it, to be placed in the same situation, with respect to damages, as if the contract had been performed."

Mr. Sher [counsel for the third party] rationalises this by asking "What is the loss sustained by reason of the breach of contract" and answering that question thus: "Where the contract is a contract for the provision of an amenity the loss occasioned is the monetary value of that amenity, no more and no less. And the only way in which the monetary value of an amenity can be quantified is by asking 'What (if anything) is the amount by which the value of the land intended to enjoy the amenity would be enhanced by its presence or is lessened by its absence?'" So, he submits, if I sell a plot of land adjoining my house and stipulate for the erection on it of some ornamental feature (for instance a pool and a fountain), all that I lose by the breach of that stipulation is the view of the pool and fountain, the economic measure of which is the amount by which its presence next-door would enhance the value of my premises.

I can follow him thus far along the road down which he seeks to lead me. The point at which I cease to follow him is the point at which he seeks to apply that analogy to the facts of the instant case. True it is that what was covenanted to be built in this case was to be built entirely on adjoining land; and true it is that its constructional details were, no doubt, arrived at, in some measure at least, with an eye to artistic or aesthetic considerations. But where, as it seems to me, the present case differs from the example postulated is that the edifice in the instant case was clearly intended to fulfil a purpose for the plaintiff which was functional as well as artistic, namely, that of enclosing and preserving the privacy of the plaintiff's land by a permanent boundary feature constructed in an acceptable architectural style. Its purpose, to put it another way, was to provide for the plaintiff in a form acceptable to him, but at the defendant's expense, that which otherwise the plaintiff would have been bound to provide for himself on his own land. He could, of course, when he parted with his adjoining land, have reserved a right of entry and liberty to construct a wall himself, and extracted a covenant from the defendant to reimburse him the cost or charged it on the land. If that had been done and the defendant had failed to pay there could, I think, be no doubt that the plaintiff would have recovered the cost from him. In the event, he trusted the defendant to do the work herself and extracted a covenant from her to do it. But, in either case, viewed realistically, the answer to the question "What has the plaintiff actually lost by the breach?" seems to me to be, as a practical matter, the same. The plaintiff contracted for the supply of a wall bounding his property as part of the consideration for the transfer and the effect of the transaction was that he paid for it in advance, because he transferred his land before the work was done. That price cannot, of course, be restored to him nor can the defendant's part of the bargain be specifically performed, because she has sold the land to a stranger to the contract. Why should he not now be compensated by awarding him the sum which is required to enable him to carry out, as nearly as possible, for himself what the defendant has failed to do for him?

...

Now, it may be that, viewed objectively, it is not to the plaintiff's financial advantage to be supplied with the article or service which he has stipulated. It may be that another person might say that what the plaintiff has stipulated for will not serve his commercial interests so well as some other scheme or course of action. And that may be quite right. But that, surely, must be for the plaintiff to judge. Pacta sunt servanda. If he contracts for the supply of that which he thinks serves his interests – be they commercial, aesthetic or merely eccentric – then if that which is contracted for is not supplied by the other contracting party I do not see why, in principle, he should not be compensated by being provided with the cost of supplying it through someone else or in a different way, subject to the proviso, of course, that he is seeking compensation for a genuine loss and not merely using a technical breach to secure an uncovenanted profit.

...

In the instant case, the plaintiff says in evidence that he wishes to carry out the work on his own land and there are, as it seems to me, three questions that I have to answer. First, am I satisfied on the evidence that the plaintiff has a genuine and serious intention of doing the work? Secondly, is the carrying out of the work on his own land a reasonable thing for the plaintiff to do? Thirdly, does it make any difference that the plaintiff is not personally in occupation of the land but desires to do the work for the benefit of his tenants? I see no reason to disbelieve the plaintiff's evidence, but in any event [counsel for the claimant] is prepared, as I understand it, to protect the position by a suitable form of undertaking. ...

I have to acknowledge my debt to Megarry V.-C. who has dealt with this point...in the course of his judgment in *Tito v. Waddell (No. 2)* [1977] Ch. 106. He said, at p. 333:

> "In other cases, if the circumstances fail to indicate sufficiently that the work will be done, the court might accept an undertaking by the plaintiff to do the work; and this, as in the business tenancy cases, would surely 'compel fixity of intention'. Whatever the circumstances, if the plaintiff establishes that the contractual work has been or will be done, then in all normal circumstances it seems to me that he has shown that the cost of doing it is, or is part of, his loss, and is recoverable as damages."

...

In the instant case, I am entirely satisfied that the plaintiff genuinely wants this work done and that he intends to expend any damages awarded on carrying it out. In my judgment, therefore, the damages ought to be measured by the cost of the work, unless there are some other considerations which point to a different measure.

That brings me to the second question, which is really one of mitigation. Mr. Sher submits that the purpose of the wall is to keep out weeds and trespassers, these being the matters of which the plaintiff specifically complains in his evidence. A pre-fabricated boundary fence would, he submits, be just as effective for that purpose and would cost much less, This would, therefore, he submits, be the reasonable way of mitigating the plaintiff's loss and the damages ought to be measured by the cost of this cheaper substitute. ...A plaintiff may be willing to accept a less expensive method of performance but I see nothing unreasonable in his wishing to adhere to the contract specification.

Finally, Mr. Sher argues that since the plaintiff does not himself occupy the property, he cannot be said, in any real sense, to have lost... the cost of the wall, because he will not, at any rate while the leases of the flats subsist, be there to enjoy it. ...As it seems to me, the fact that his motive may be to confer what he conceives to be a benefit on persons who have no contractual rights to demand it cannot alter the genuineness of his intentions. The recent case of *Jackson v. Horizon Holidays Ltd.* [1975] 1 W.L.R. 1468 demonstrates that the plaintiff may obtain damages for breach of a contract entered into for the benefit of himself and other persons not parties to the contract.

In the circumstances of this case, therefore, the correct measure of damages is, in my judgment, the cost to the plaintiff of carrying out the work on his own land.

NOTES AND QUESTIONS

1. It is important to appreciate that difference in value and cost of cure are both measures of the claimant's expectation (or performance) interest. The former assesses the value of the claimant's property with and without the contracted-for work. The latter assesses what it will cost the claimant to have the (contracted-for) work done.

2. In awarding the cost of cure, Oliver J did not need to decide the precise date at which that cost should be assessed. However, he did say (in a passage not set out above) that it should be assessed at the date when the claimant should reasonably have brought the case to trial.

3. As can be seen, Oliver J relied on *Tito v Waddell*. In that case, a British phosphate company had failed to replant, after mining, an island in the Pacific Ocean (Ocean Island) as it had contracted to do. Megarry V-C clarified that

the higher cost of cure (replanting the island) would be the correct measure if the claimants had already effected cure or intended to do so (see the passage cited by Oliver J, above, 341). But the claimants, the islanders, had left Ocean Island and moved to another island and it was therefore clear that they had no intention of replanting their former home. The appropriate measure of damages was therefore the trivial difference in value between the island with and without the trees.

4.   Contrary to the suggestions of Megarry V-C and Oliver J, the House of Lords in the *Ruxley* case (below, 346) rejected as irrelevant an undertaking from the claimant that, if awarded, he or she would use higher cost of cure damages to effect the cure. Even if one could show that relevant, would there nevertheless be overwhelming practical problems with such an undertaking?

Ruxley Electronics and Construction Ltd v Forsyth
[1996] AC 344, House of Lords

The claimants agreed to build a swimming pool for the defendant in his garden. It was agreed that the depth at the deep end of the pool would be seven feet six inches. When built, the pool was in fact only six feet nine inches. Nevertheless, it was still perfectly safe for swimming and diving so that the resale value of the property was not affected by the admitted breach of contract (ie the difference in the property's value, with and without the extra nine inches, was nil). To increase the depth of the pool to the agreed depth would cost £21,560 (nearly a third of the total price of the pool). The trial judge had held that the claimants were entitled to the price agreed (which they were suing for) and that the damages on the defendant's counterclaim should not be assessed by the cost of cure. Rather £2500 damages for loss of amenity were awarded. The Court of Appeal allowed the defendant's appeal and awarded him the cost of cure of £21,500. In overturning that decision, and restoring the trial judge's award of £2500, the House of Lords held that the defendant was not entitled to the cost of cure, taking into account the unreasonableness of effecting the cure and that he did not intend to cure.

Lord Jauncey of Tullichettle: Damages are designed to compensate for an established loss and not to provide a gratuitous benefit to the aggrieved party from which it follows that the reasonableness of an award of damages is to be linked directly to the loss sustained. If it is unreasonable in a particular case to award the cost of reinstatement it must be because the loss sustained does not extend to the need to reinstate.

...

I take the example suggested during argument by my noble and learned friend, Lord Bridge of Harwich. A man contracts for the building of a house and specifies that one of the lower courses of brick should be blue. The builder uses yellow brick instead. In all other respects the house conforms to the contractual specification. To replace the yellow bricks with blue would involve extensive demolition and reconstruction at a very large cost. It would clearly be unreasonable to award to the owner the cost of reconstructing because his loss was not the necessary cost of reconstruction of his house, which was entirely adequate for its design purpose, but merely the lack of aesthetic pleasure which he might have derived from the sight of blue bricks. Thus in the present appeal the respondent has acquired a perfectly serviceable swimming pool, albeit one lacking the specified depth. His loss is thus not the lack of a useable pool with consequent need to construct a new one. Indeed were he to receive the cost of building a new one and retain the existing one he would have recovered not compensation for loss but a very substantial gratuitous benefit, something which damages are not intended to provide.

What constitutes the aggrieved party's loss is in every case a question of fact and degree. Where the contract breaker has entirely failed to achieve the contractual objective it may not be difficult to conclude that the loss is the necessary cost of achieving that objective. Thus if a building is constructed so defectively that it is of no use for its designed purpose the owner may have little difficulty in establishing that his loss is the necessary cost of reconstructing. Furthermore in taking reasonableness into account in determining the extent of loss it is reasonableness in relation to the particular contract and not at large. Accordingly if I contracted for the erection of a folly in my garden which shortly thereafter suffered a total collapse it would be irrelevant to the determination of my loss to argue that the erection of such a folly which contributed nothing to the value of my house was a crazy thing to do.

...

My Lords, the trial judge found that it would be unreasonable to incur the cost of demolishing the existing pool and building a new and deeper one. In so doing he implicitly recognised that the respondent's loss did not extend to the cost of reinstatement. He was, in my view, entirely justified in reaching that conclusion. It therefore follows that the appeal must be allowed.

It only remains to mention two further matters. The appellant argued that the cost of reinstatement should only be allowed as damages where there was shown to be an intention on the part of the aggrieved party to carry out the work. Having already decided that the appeal should be allowed I no longer find it necessary to reach a conclusion on this matter. However I should emphasise that in the normal case the court has no concern with the use to which a plaintiff puts an award of damages for a loss which has been established. Thus irreparable damage to an article as a result of a breach of contract will entitle the owner to recover the value of the article irrespective of whether he intends to replace it with a similar one or to spend the money on something else. Intention, or lack of it, to reinstate can have relevance only to reasonableness and hence to the extent of the loss which has been sustained. Once that loss has been established intention as to the subsequent use of the damages ceases to be relevant.

The second matter relates to the award of £2,500 for loss of amenity made by the trial judge. The respondent argued that he erred in law in making such award. However as the appellant did not challenge it, I find it unnecessary to express any opinion on the matter.

Lord Mustill: My Lords, I agree that this appeal should be allowed for the reasons stated by my noble and learned friends, Lord Jauncey of Tullichettle and Lord Lloyd of Berwick. I add some observations of my own on the award by the trial judge of damages in a sum intermediate between, on the one hand, the full cost of reinstatement, and on the other the amount by which the malperformance has diminished the market value of the property on which the work was done: in this particular case, nil. ...

The proposition that these two measures of damage represent the only permissible bases of recovery lie [sic] at the heart of the employer's case. From this he reasons that there is a presumption in favour of the cost of restitution, since this is the only way in which he can be given what the contractor had promised to provide. Finally, he contends that there is nothing in the facts of the present case to rebut this presumption.

The attraction of this argument is its avoidance of the conclusion that, in a case such as the present, unless the employer can prove that the defects have depreciated the market value of the property the householder can recover nothing at all. This conclusion would be unacceptable to the average householder, and it is unacceptable to me. It is a common feature of small building works performed on residential property that the cost of the work is not fully reflected by an increase in the market value of the house, and that comparatively minor deviations from specification or sound workmanship may have no direct financial effect at all. Yet the householder must surely be entitled to say that he chose to obtain from the builder a promise to produce a particular result because he wanted to make his house more comfortable, more convenient and more conformable to his own particular tastes; not because he had in mind that the work might increase the amount which he would receive if, contrary to expectation, he thought it expedient in the future to exchange his home for cash. To say that in order to escape unscathed the builder has only to show that to the mind of the average onlooker, or the average potential buyer, the results which he has produced seem just as good as those which he had promised would make a part of the promise illusory, and unbalance the bargain. In the valuable analysis contained in *Radford v. De Froberville* [1977] 1 W.L.R. 1262, Oliver J. emphasised, at p. 1270, that it was for the plaintiff to judge what performance he required in exchange for the price. The court should honour that choice. Pacta sunt servanda. If the appellant's argument leads to the conclusion that in all cases like the present the employer is entitled to no more than nominal damages, the average householder would say that there must be something wrong with the law.

In my opinion there would indeed be something wrong if, on the hypothesis that cost of reinstatement and the depreciation in value were the only available measures of recovery, the rejection of the former necessarily entailed the adoption of the latter; and the court might be driven to opt for the cost of reinstatement, absurd as the consequence might often be, simply to escape from the conclusion that the promisor can please himself whether or not to comply with the wishes of the promise which, as embodied in the contract, formed part of the consideration for the price. Having taken on the job the contractor is morally as well as legally obliged to give the employer what he stipulated to obtain, and this obligation ought not to be devalued. In my opinion however the hypothesis is not correct. There are not two alternative measures of damage, at opposite poles, but only one; namely, the loss truly suffered by the promisee. In some cases the loss cannot be fairly measured except by reference to the full cost of repairing the deficiency in performance. In others, and in particular those where the contract is designed to fulfil a purely commercial purpose, the loss will very often consist only of the monetary detriment brought about by the breach of contract. But these remedies are not exhaustive, for the law must cater for those occasions where the value of the promise to the promisee exceeds the financial enhancement of his position which full performance will secure. This excess, often referred to in the literature as the "consumer surplus" (see for example the valuable discussion by Harris, Ogus and Philips (1979) 95 L.Q.R. 581) is usually incapable of precise valuation in terms of money, exactly because it represents a personal, subjective and non-monetary gain. Nevertheless where it exists the law should recognise it and compensate the promisee if the misperformance takes it away. The lurid bathroom tiles, or the grotesque folly instanced in argument by my noble and learned friend, Lord Keith of Kinkel, may be so discordant with general taste that in purely economic terms the builder may be said to do the employer a favour by failing to install them. But this is too narrow and materialistic a view of the transaction. Neither the contractor nor the court has the right to substitute for the employer's individual expectation of performance a criterion derived from what ordinary people would regard as sensible. As my Lords have shown, the test of reasonableness plays a central part in determining the basis of recovery, and will indeed be decisive in a case such as the present when the cost of reinstatement would be wholly disproportionate to the non-monetary loss suffered by the employer. But it would be equally unreasonable to deny all recovery for such a loss. The amount may be small, and since it cannot be quantified directly there may be room for difference of opinion about what it should be. But in several fields the judges are well accustomed to putting figures to intangibles, and I see no reason why the imprecision of the exercise should be a barrier, if that is what fairness demands.

My Lords, once this is recognised the puzzling and paradoxical feature of this case, that it seems to involve a contest of absurdities, simply falls away. There is no need to remedy the injustice of awarding too little, by unjustly awarding far too much. The judgment of the trial judge acknowledges that the employer has suffered a true loss and expresses it in terms of money. Since there is no longer any issue about the amount of the award, as distinct from the principle, I would simply restore his judgment by allowing the appeal.

Lord Lloyd of Berwick:

Reasonableness

The starting point is *Robinson v. Harman*, 1 Exch. 850, where Parke B. said, at p. 855:

> "The rule of the common law is, that where a party sustains a loss by reason of a breach of contract, he is, so far as money can do it, to be placed in the same situation, with respect to damages, as if the contract had been performed."

This does not mean that in every case of breach of contract the plaintiff can obtain the monetary equivalent of specific performance. It is first necessary to ascertain the loss the plaintiff has in fact suffered by reason of the breach. If he has suffered no loss, as sometimes happens, he can recover no more than nominal damages. For the object of damages is always to compensate the plaintiff, not to punish the defendant.

...

In building cases, the pecuniary loss is almost always measured in one of two ways; either the difference in value of the work done or the cost of reinstatement. Where the cost of reinstatement is less than the difference in value, the measure of damages will invariably be the cost of reinstatement. By claiming the difference in value the plaintiff would be failing to take reasonable steps to mitigate his loss. In many ordinary cases, too, where reinstatement presents no special problem, the cost of reinstatement will be the obvious measure of damages, even where there is little or no difference in value, or where the difference in value is hard to assess. This is why it is often said that the cost of reinstatement is the ordinary measure of damages for defective performance under a building contract.

But it is not the only measure of damages. Sometimes it is the other way round.

...

If the court takes the view that it would be unreasonable for the plaintiff to insist on reinstatement, as where, for example, the expense of the work involved would be out of all proportion to the benefit to be obtained, then the plaintiff will be confined to the difference in value. If the judge had assessed the difference in value in the present case at, say, £5,000, I have little doubt that the Court of Appeal would have taken that figure rather than £21,560. The difficulty arises because the judge has, in the light of the expert evidence, assessed the difference in value as nil. But that cannot make reasonable what he has found to be unreasonable.

So I cannot accept that reasonableness is confined to the doctrine of mitigation. It has a wider impact...

Intention

I fully accept that the courts are not normally concerned with what a plaintiff does with his damages. But it does not follow that intention is not relevant to reasonableness, at least in those cases where the plaintiff does not intend to reinstate. Suppose in the present case Mr. Forsyth had died and the action had been continued by his executors. Is it to be supposed that they would be able to recover the cost of reinstatement, even though they intended to put the property on the market without delay?

There is, as Staughton L.J. observed, a good deal of authority to the effect that intention may be relevant to a claim for damages based on cost of reinstatement. The clearest decisions on the point are those of Sir Robert Megarry V.-C. in *Tito v Waddell (No 2)* [1977] Ch. 106, and Oliver J. in *Radford v De Froberville* [1977] 1 W.L.R. 1262. ...In the present case the judge found as a fact that Mr. Forsyth's stated intention of rebuilding the pool would not persist for long after the litigation had been concluded. In these circumstances it would be "mere pretence" to say that the cost of rebuilding the pool is the loss which he has in fact suffered. This is the critical distinction between the present case, and the example given by Staughton L.J. of a man who has had his watch stolen. In the latter case, the plaintiff is entitled to recover the value of the watch, because that is the true measure of his loss. He can do what he wants with the damages. But if, as the judge found, Mr. Forsyth had no intention of rebuilding the pool, he has lost nothing except the difference in value, if any.

The relevance of intention to the issue of reasonableness is expressly recognised by the respondent in his case [at] paragraph 37...

> "The respondent accepts that the genuineness of the parties' indicated predilections can be a factor which the court must consider when deciding between alternative measures of damage. Where a plaintiff is contending for a high as opposed to a low cost measure of damages the court must decide whether in the circumstances of the particular case such high cost measure is reasonable. One of the factors that may be relevant is the genuineness of the plaintiff's desire to pursue the course which involves the higher cost. Absence of such desire (indicated by untruths about intention) may undermine the reasonableness of the higher cost measure."

I can only say that I find myself in complete agreement with that approach, in contrast to the approach taken by the majority of the Court of Appeal.

Does Mr. Forsyth's undertaking to spend any damages which he may receive on rebuilding the pool make any difference? Clearly not. He cannot be allowed to create a loss, which does not exist, in order to punish the defendants for their breach of contract. The basic rule of damages, to which exemplary damages are the only exception, is that they are compensatory not punitive.

Loss of Amenity

...

Addis v. Gramophone Co. Ltd. established the general rule that in claims for breach of contract, the plaintiff cannot recover damages for his injured feelings. But the rule, like most rules, is subject to exceptions. One of the well established exceptions is when the object of the contract is to afford pleasure, as, for example, where the plaintiff has booked a holiday with a tour operator. If the tour operator is in breach of contract by failing to provide what the contract called for, the plaintiff may recover damages for his disappointment: see *Jarvis v. Swans Tours Ltd.* [1973] Q.B. 233 and *Jackson v. Horizon Holidays Ltd.* [1975] 1 W.L.R. 1468.

This was, as I understand it, the principle which Judge Diamond applied in the present case. He took the view that the contract was one "for the provision of a pleasurable amenity." In the event, Mr. Forsyth's pleasure was not so great as it would have been if the swimming pool had been 7 feet 6 inches deep. This was a view which the judge was entitled to take. If it involves a further inroad on the rule in *Addis v. Gramophone Co. Ltd.* [1909] A.C. 488, then so be it. But I prefer to regard it as a logical application or adaptation of the existing exception to a new situation.

...

I would therefore allow the appeal and restore the judgment of Judge Diamond.

Lord Keith of Kinkel concurred and **Lord Bridge of Harwich** gave a concurring speech.

NOTES AND QUESTIONS

1. The House of Lords took account both of reasonableness and of Mr Forsyth's intentions, although the emphasis given to each of these differed as between their Lordships. On the facts both pointed in the same direction. Mr Forsyth did not intend to have the pool rebuilt and it was thought unreasonable for him to do so given the disparity between the cost of cure and the difference in value. The more difficult question is, what would the correct measure have been if Mr Forsyth had already rebuilt the pool to the specified depth or intended to do

so? In that situation, intention and reasonableness might be thought to pull in opposite directions and one would therefore need to decide which is the dominant concept. *Radford v de Froberville,* above, 339, suggests that the dominant concept is 'intention' and that, if Mr Forsyth had already rebuilt or intended to do so, he would have been entitled to the higher cost of cure. It is arguable that reasonableness should only come in to qualify intention where, for reasons other than the disparity in amount between the cost of cure and the difference in value, it would be unreasonable for the claimant to effect the cure. For example, it would have been unreasonable if Mr Forsyth had been a property speculator (rather than a consumer wanting to use the pool) who insisted on rebuilding the pool to the required depth even though that made no difference to the property's value.

2. It is sometimes suggested that placing priority on the innocent party's intention to effect cure undermines the normal rule that the courts are not concerned with the use to which damages are put. Is that a valid objection? (See A Burrows, *Remedies for Torts and Breach of Contract* (3rd edn, 2004) 222).

3. What was the precise justification for the £2500 damages? Are they an example of an award of damages for mental distress where the predominant object of the contract was mental satisfaction (see below, 389)?

4. Was it of any relevance in assessing the damages that the builders must have saved themselves expense in not building the pool to the correct depth (see below, 401–402)?

(c) Assessment According to the Chances

Chaplin v Hicks [1911] 2 KB 786, Court of Appeal

The defendant, a theatre manager, ran a newspaper beauty competition in which the prizes were 'theatrical engagements' for the 12 winners. At the first stage of the competition, 50 of the women were to be chosen by the readers of the newspaper from the photographs printed. At the second stage, the defendant was to interview the 50 and to choose the 12 winners from them. Six thousand women entered the contest and the claimant succeeded in being voted as one of the 50 to be interviewed. However, because of the defendant's breach of contract, she was not informed of the interview in time and the 12 winners were chosen in her absence. The claimant sought damages for the loss of the chance of winning the competition and the jury awarded her damages of £100. This award was upheld by the Court of Appeal on the basis that substantial damages for the loss of the chance were appropriate.

Vaughan Williams LJ: It was said that the plaintiff's chance of winning a prize turned on such a number of contingencies that it was impossible for any one, even after arriving at the conclusion that the plaintiff had lost her opportunity by the breach, to say that there was any assessable value of that loss. It is said that in a case which involves so many contingencies it is impossible to say what was the plaintiff's pecuniary loss. I am unable to agree with that contention. I agree that the presence of all the contingencies upon which the gaining of the prize might depend makes the calculation not only difficult but incapable of being carried out with certainty or precision. The proposition is that, whenever the contingencies on which the result depends are numerous and difficult to deal with, it is impossible to recover any damages for the loss of the chance or opportunity of winning the prize. In the present case I understand that there were fifty selected competitors, of whom the plaintiff was one, and twelve prizes, so that the average chance of each competitor was about one in four. Then it is said that the questions which might arise in the minds of the judges are so numerous that it is impossible to say that the case is one in which it is possible to apply the doctrine of averages at all. I do not agree with the contention that, if certainty is impossible of attainment, the damages for a breach of contract are unassessable. I agree, however, that damages might be so unassessable that the doctrine of averages would be inapplicable because the necessary figures for working upon would not be forthcoming; there are several decisions, which I need not deal with, to that effect. I only wish to deny with emphasis that, because precision cannot be arrived at, the jury has no function in the assessment of damages.

...[T]he fact that damages cannot be assessed with certainty does not relieve the wrong-doer of the necessity of paying damages for his breach of contract. I do not wish to lay down any such rule as that a judge can in every case leave it to the jury to assess damages for a breach of contract. There are cases, no doubt, where the loss is so dependent on the mere unrestricted volition of another that it is impossible to say that there is any assessable loss resulting from the breach. In the present case there is no such difficulty. It is true that no market can be said to exist. None of the fifty competitors could have gone into the market and sold her right; her right was a personal right and incapable of transfer. But a jury might well take the view that such a right, if it could have been transferred, would have been of such a value that every one would recognize that a good price could be obtained for it. My view is that under such circumstances as those in this case the assessment of damages was unquestionably for the jury. The jury came to the conclusion that the taking away from the plaintiff of the opportunity of competition, as one of a body of fifty, when twelve prizes were to be distributed, deprived the plaintiff of something which had a monetary value. I think that they were right and that this appeal fails.

Fletcher Moulton LJ: Mr. McCardie [for the defendant]...contends that the plaintiff can only recover nominal damages, say one shilling. To start with, he puts it thus: where the expectation of the plaintiff depends on a contingency, only nominal damages are recoverable. Upon examination, this principle is obviously much too wide; everything that can happen in the future depends on a contingency, and such a principle would deprive a plaintiff of anything beyond nominal damages for a breach of contract where the damages could not be assessed with mathematical accuracy. The learned counsel admitted that it was very difficult to formulate his proposition, but he ultimately said that where the volition of another comes between the competitor and what he hopes to get under the contract, no damages can, as matter of law, be given. ...I do not think that any such distinction as that suggested by Mr. McCardie can be drawn. The Common Law Courts never enforced contracts specifically, as was done in equity; if a contract was broken, the common law held that an adequate solatium was to be found in a pecuniary sum, that is, in the damages assessed by a jury. But there is no other universal principle as to the amount of damages than that it is the aim of the law to ensure that a person whose contract has been broken shall be placed as near as possible in the same position as if it had not. The assessment is sometimes a matter of great difficulty.

...

[Mr McCardie] says that the damages are difficult to assess, because it is impossible to say that the plaintiff would have obtained any prize. ...Is expulsion from a limited class of competitors an injury? To my mind there can be only one answer to that question; it is an injury and may be a very substantial one. Therefore the plaintiff starts with an unchallengeable case of injury, and the damages given in respect of it should be equivalent to the loss. But it is said that the damages cannot be arrived at because it is impossible to estimate the quantum of the reasonable probability of the plaintiff's being a prize-winner. I think that, where it is clear that there has been actual loss resulting from the breach of contract, which it is difficult to estimate in money, it is for the jury to do their best to estimate; it is not necessary that there should be an absolute measure of damages in each case. ...Is there any such rule as that, where the result of a contract depends on the volition of an independent party, the law shuts its eyes to the wrong and says that there are no damages? Such a rule, if it existed, would work great wrong. Let us take the case of a man under a contract of service to serve as a second-class clerk for five years at a salary of 200*l.* a year, which expressly provides that, at the end of that period, out of every five second-class clerks two first-class clerks will be chosen at a salary of 500*l.* a year. If such a clause is embodied in the contract, it is clear that a person thinking of applying for the position would reckon that he would have the advantage of being one of five persons from whom the two first-class clerks must be chosen, and that that might be a very substantial portion of the consideration for his appointment. If, after he has taken the post and worked under the contract of service, the employers repudiate the obligation, is he to have no remedy? He has sustained a very real loss, and there can be no possible reason why the law should not leave it to the jury to estimate the value of that of which he has been deprived. Where by contract a man has a right to belong to a limited class of competitors, he is possessed of something of value, and it is the duty of the jury to estimate the pecuniary value of that advantage if it is taken from him. The present case is a typical one. From a body of six thousand, who sent in their photographs, a smaller body of fifty was formed, of which the plaintiff was one, and among that smaller body twelve prizes were allotted for distribution; by reason of the defendant's breach of contract she has lost all the advantage of being in the limited competition, and she is entitled to have her loss estimated. I cannot lay down any rule as to the measure of damages in such a case; this must be left to the good sense of the jury. They must of course give effect to the consideration that the plaintiff's chance is only one out of four and that they cannot tell whether she would have ultimately proved to be the winner. But having considered all this they may well think that it is of considerable pecuniary value to have got into so small a class, and they must assess the damages accordingly.

Farwell LJ gave a concurring judgment.

NOTES AND QUESTIONS

1. This is the classic case showing that damages for breach of contract can be given for the loss of a chance of making a gain (or of avoiding a loss). There are many other illustrations. For example, damages compensating a claimant's loss of profits will very commonly be proportionate to what the chances are proved to be (see, eg, the damages, diminishing over time, awarded for the loss of profits in *Jackson v Royal Bank of Scotland plc,* below, 372). And damages, based on what the chances of success in an action would have been, have commonly been awarded against solicitors for breach of contract (or tortious negligence) in allowing a client's claim to become time-barred (see, eg, *Kitchen v Royal Air Forces Association* [1958] 1 WLR 563, CA).

2. However, assessment according to the chances has not always been thought appropriate. In *Allied Maples Group Ltd v Simmons & Simmons* [1995] 1 WLR 1602 CA, which was a professional negligence claim against a solicitor brought in contract and tort in relation to the drawing up of a contract, the uncertainty was as to whether the claimant client would have acted on the solicitor's advice, had proper advice been given, and whether the other party to the contract (the third party) would then have agreed to the different clauses in the contract. The Court of Appeal drew a distinction between the hypothetical conduct of the third party to which the normal chances approach applied; and the hypothetical conduct of the claimant to which it was held that an all or nothing

'balance of probabilities' approach should apply. No explanation for that distinction was offered. *McGregor on Damages* (17th edn, 2003) para 8-035 explains it on the basis that the claimant can be expected to satisfy the court (on the all or nothing balance of probabilities civil standard of proof) as to how it would itself have behaved if it wished to have damages assessed on the basis that it would have behaved in that way. He writes,

'At first glance it may seem somewhat strange to have different tests applicable to hypothetical acts of the claimant and hypothetical acts of third parties. But it can be seen to make sense. For a claimant can hardly claim for loss of a chance that he himself may have acted in a particular way: he must show that he would have done.'

3. One should also bear in mind that a chances approach to the assessment of damages is normally not taken in relation to the *defendant's* hypothetical conduct. By aiming to put the claimant into as good a position *as if the contract had been performed* the starting assumption for assessment is that the defendant would not have broken the contract. Moreover, where the defendant had a choice of different modes of performance, the courts have traditionally assessed damages by applying the principle that the defendant would have performed in the way most favourable to itself, often referred to as the 'minimum obligation' principle. Does *Chaplin v Hicks* illustrate that the minimum obligation may sometimes coincide with the most accurate assessment of the chances? Or was the Court of Appeal incorrect on these facts (where the uncertainty was essentially as to who the *defendant* would have chosen after the interviews) to apply a 'chances' approach?

4. Where the issue is whether a personal injury has been caused by a breach of duty, which will normally be a tort duty but could be a contractual duty, the law appears not to apply a chances approach. Instead an all or nothing balance of probabilities approach is applied so that one cannot recover for the lost chance of avoiding a particular injury or illness. So, for example, in *Gregg v Scott* [2005] UKHL 2, [2005] 2 AC 176, the House of Lords (by a 3–2 majority) held that no substantial damages should be awarded to a claimant who had been deprived of a 17 per cent chance of being cured of cancer by the defendant's negligent failure to diagnose that cancer. Can *Chaplin v Hicks* be sensibly reconciled with *Gregg v Scott*?

(d) Contractual Damages Protecting the Reliance Interest?

Anglia TV v Reed [1972] 1 QB 60, Court of Appeal

The claimants, a television company, with the intention of making a film of a play for television, entered into a contract with the defendant, Robert Reed, for the main part. At the time when that contract was entered into they had already incurred expenses for the purposes of the production and they incurred further expenses subsequently. A few days after the contract was concluded, the defendant repudiated the contract and, as they could not find a suitable substitute, the claimants accepted that repudiation as terminating the contract. The claimants were held entitled to the £2750 expenses that they had incurred (both before and after the contract was made) which would now be wasted.

Lord Denning MR: Anglia Television do not claim their profit. They cannot say what their profit would have been on this contract if Mr. Reed had come here and performed it. So, instead of claim[ing] for loss of profits, they claim for the wasted expenditure. They had incurred the director's fees. the designer's fees, the stage manager's and assistant manager's fees, and so on. It comes in all to £2,750. Anglia Television say that all that money was wasted because Mr. Reed did not perform his contract.

Mr. Reed's advisers take a point of law. They submit that Anglia Television cannot recover for expenditure incurred *before* the contract was concluded with Mr. Reed. They can only recover the expenditure *after* the contract was concluded. They say that the expenditure *after* the contract was only £854.65, and that is all that Anglia Television can recover.

The master rejected that contention: he held that Anglia Television could recover the whole £2,750; and now Mr. Reed appeals to this court.

...

It seems to me that a plaintiff in such a case as this has an election: he can either claim for loss of profits; or for his wasted expenditure. But he must elect between them. He cannot claim both. If he has not suffered any loss of profits – or if he cannot prove what his profits would have been – he can claim in the alternative the expenditure which has been thrown away, that is, wasted, by reason of the breach. That is shown by *Cullinane v. British"Rema" Manufacturing Co. Ltd.* [1954] 1 Q.B. 292, 303, 308.

If the plaintiff claims the wasted expenditure, he is not limited to the expenditure incurred *after* the contract was concluded. He can claim also the expenditure incurred *before* the contract, provided that it was such as would reasonably be in the contemplation of the parties as likely to be wasted if the contract was broken. Applying that principle here, it is plain that, when Mr. Reed entered into this contract, he must have known perfectly well that much expenditure had already been incurred on director's fees and the like. He must have contemplated – or, at any rate, it is reasonably to be imputed to him – that if he broke his contract, all that expenditure would be wasted, whether or not it was incurred before or after the contract. He must pay damages for all the expenditure so wasted and thrown away. This view is supported by the recent decision of Brightman J. in *Lloyd v. Stanbury* [1971] 1 W.L.R. 535. There was a contract for the sale of land. In anticipation of the contract – and before it was concluded – the purchaser went to much expense in moving a caravan to the site and in getting his furniture there. The seller afterwards entered into a contract to sell the land to the purchaser, but afterwards broke his contract. The land had not increased in value, so the purchaser could not claim for any loss of profit. But Brightman J. held, at p. 547, that he could recover the cost of moving the caravan and furniture, because it was "within the contemplation of the parties when the contract was signed." That decision is in accord with the correct principle, namely, that wasted expenditure can be recovered when it is wasted by reason of the defendant's breach of contract. It is true that, if the defendant had never entered into the contract, he would not be liable, and the expenditure would have been incurred by the plaintiff without redress; but, the defendant having made his contract and broken it, it does not lie in his mouth to say he is not liable, when it was because of his breach that the expenditure has been wasted.

I think the master was quite right and this appeal should be dismissed.

Phillimore and **Megaw LJJ** concurred.

NOTES AND QUESTIONS

1. This case is important as showing both that the claimant can elect to seek damages for wasted expenditure as opposed to seeking directly damages for lost profits; and that pre-contractual expenses can be recovered.
2. Does the fact that pre-contractual expenses can be recovered show that it is misleading to analyse these damages as concerned to protect the claimant's

reliance interest (the aim of which would be to put the claimant into as good a position as if no contract had been made)?

C & P Haulage v Middleton [1983] 1 WLR 1461, Court of Appeal

The claimants granted the defendant a contractual licence to occupy premises for use in his business on a renewable six-month basis. The defendant incurred expenses in making the premises suitable (eg by building a wall and putting in electricity) even though the lease expressly provided that fixtures put in by him were not to be removed at the expiry of the licence. Ten weeks before the end of a six-month period, the defendant was unlawfully ejected from the premises by the claimants. However, he was able to transfer his work place temporarily to the garage of his home, having managed to secure temporary permission from the local authority to use that garage as his place of work until well after the six-month period would have expired. The claimants brought an action against the defendant for unpaid rent and the defendant counterclaimed for damages for breach of contract to compensate for the expenses he had incurred in improving the property. The Court of Appeal held that he was entitled to only nominal damages because to compensate his expenses would put him into a better position than if the contract had been performed (ie than if the claimants had lawfully terminated the contract after the six months).

Ackner LJ: The judge approached the case essentially on this basis, that the accepted principle in relation to the assessment of damages for breach of contract was to put the plaintiff in the same position, as far as one could, as he would have been in if the contract had been performed; and in order to evaluate whether if the contract had been performed what was the nature, if any, of the damages that he should be entitled to claim, one had to look at the consequences of the breach of contract.

The consequences of this breach of contract were that so far from the defendant suffering any damage as a result of being excluded from the premises ten weeks earlier than would lawfully have been the case, thanks to the tolerance of the local authority he had in effect been saved the payment, which was likely to be between £60 and £100 a week, which he would have had to have paid for the use of the plaintiffs' premises. He accordingly came to the conclusion that if he was to award the damages claimed, he would be putting the defendant in a better position than would have been the case if the contract had been lawfully determined.

The case which was at the forefront of Mr. Keogh's submissions [for the defendant] before the judge and before us as well is that of *Anglia Television Ltd. v. Reed* [1972] 1 Q.B. 60.

...

[The defendant] is not claiming for the loss of his bargain, which would involve being put in the position that he would have been in if the contract had been performed. He is not asking to be put in that position. He is asking to be put in the position he would have been in if the contract had never been made at all. If the contract had never been made at all, then he would not have incurred these expenses, and that is the essential approach he adopts in mounting this claim; because if the right approach is that he should be put in the position in which he would have been had the contract been performed, then it follows that he suffered no damage. He lost his entitlement to a further ten weeks of occupation after October 5, and during that period he involved himself in no loss of profit because he found other accommodation, and in no increased expense – in fact the contrary – because he returned immediately to his own garage, thereby saving whatever would have been the agreed figure which he would have to have paid the plaintiffs.

…

The case which I have found of assistance – and I am grateful to counsel for their research – is a case in the British Columbia Supreme Court: *Bowlay Logging Ltd. v. Domtar Ltd.* [1978] 4 W.W.R. 105. Berger J., in a very careful and detailed judgment, goes through various English and American authorities and refers to the leading textbook writers, and I will only quote a small part of his judgment. At the bottom of p. 115 he refers to the work of Professor L.L. Fuller and William R. Perdue, Jr., in "The Reliance Interest in Contract Damages: 1" (1936), 46 Yale Law Jour. 52 and their statement, at p. 79:

"We will not in a suit for reimbursement for losses incurred in reliance on a contract knowingly put the plaintiff in a better position than he would have occupied had the contract been fully performed."

Berger J., at p. 116, then refers to *L. Albert & Son v. Armstrong Rubber Co.* (1949) 178 F. 2d 182 in which Learned Hand C.J., speaking for the Circuit Court of Appeals, Second Circuit:

"held that on a claim for compensation for expenses in part performance the defendant was entitled to deduct whatever he could prove the plaintiff would have lost if the contract had been fully performed."

What Berger J. had to consider was this, p. 105:

"The parties entered into a contract whereby the plaintiff would cut timber under the defendant's timber sale, and the defendant would be responsible for hauling the timber away from the site of the timber sale. The plaintiff claimed the defendant was in breach of the contract as the defendant had not supplied sufficient trucks to make the plaintiff's operation, which was losing money, viable, and claimed not for loss of profits but for compensation for expenditures. The defendant argued that the plaintiff's operation lost money not because of a lack of trucks but because of the plaintiff's inefficiency, and, further, that even if the defendant had breached the contract the plaintiff should not be awarded damages because its operation would have lost money in any case."

This submission was clearly accepted because the plaintiff was awarded only nominal damages, and Berger J. said, at p. 117:

"The law of contract compensates a plaintiff for damages resulting from the defendant's breach; it does not compensate a plaintiff for damages resulting from his making a bad bargain. Where it can be seen that the plaintiff would have incurred a loss on the contract as a whole, the expenses he has incurred are losses flowing from entering into the contract, not losses flowing from the defendant's breach. In these circumstances, the true consequence of the defendant's breach is that the plaintiff is released from his obligation to complete the contract – or in other words, he is saved from incurring further losses. If the law of contract were to move from compensating for the consequences of breach to compensating for the consequences of entering into contracts, the law would run contrary to the normal expectations of the world of commerce. The burden of risk would be shifted from the plaintiff to the defendant. The defendant would become the insurer of the plaintiff's enterprise. Moreover, the amount of the damages would increase not in relation to the gravity or consequences of the breach but in relation to the inefficiency with which the plaintiff carried out the contract. The greater his expenses owing to inefficiency, the greater the damages. The fundamental principle upon which damages are measured under the law of contract is restitutio in integrum. The principle contended for here by the plaintiff would entail the award of damages not to compensate the plaintiff but to punish the defendant."

It is urged here that the garage itself was merely an element in the defendant's business; it was not a profit-making entity on its own. Nevertheless, if as a result of being kept out of these premises the defendant had found no other premises to go to for a period of time, his claim would clearly have been a claim for such loss of profit as he could establish his business suffered.

In my judgment, the approach of Berger J. is the correct one. It is not the function of the courts where there is a breach of contract knowingly, as this would be the case, to put a plaintiff in a better financial position than if the contract had been properly performed. In this case the defendant who is the plaintiff in the counterclaim, if he was right in his claim, would indeed be in a better position because, as I have already indicated, had the contract been lawfully determined as it could have been in the middle of December, there would have been no question of his recovering these expenses.

...

I do not consider that a plaintiff is entitled in an action for damages for breach of contract to ask to be put in the position in which he would have been if the contract had never been made. Accordingly, save in the respect to which I have already made reference, namely that there should be judgment for the defendant for nominal damages of £10, I would dismiss the appeal.

Fox LJ: The present case seems to me to be quite different both from *Anglia Television Ltd. v. Reed* [1972] 1 Q.B. 60 and from *Lloyd v. Stanbury* [1971] 1 W.L.R. 535 in that while it is true that the expenditure could in a sense be said to be wasted in consequence of the breach of contract, it was equally likely to be wasted if there had been no breach, because the plaintiffs wanted to get the defendant out and could terminate the licence at quite short notice. A high risk of waste was from the very first inherent in the nature of the contract itself, breach or no breach. The reality of the matter is that the waste resulted from what was, on the defendant's side, a very unsatisfactory and dangerous bargain.

I agree with Ackner L.J. that the appeal must be dismissed.

NOTES AND QUESTION

1. This case established that in a claim for wasted expenditure the courts will not knowingly put the 'claimant' into a better position than if the contract had been performed. That is, they will not knowingly allow the 'claimant' to escape from a bad bargain.

2. Does this indicate that it is misleading to view these damages as protecting the reliance interest rather than the expectation (or performance) interest?

CCC Films (London) Ltd v Impact Quadrant Films Ltd
[1985] QB 16, Queen's Bench Division

The defendants had granted a licence to the claimants to exploit three films and the claimants had paid the agreed consideration of $12,000 for that licence. By the contract the defendants were to send to the claimants tapes of the films but, in breach of contract, they failed to do so, with the result that the claimants were unable to exploit the films. The claimants did not seek to prove any loss of profit but instead claimed damages of $12,000 as wasted expenditure. It was held that the claim should succeed because the defendants had not proved that the expenses would not have been recouped had the contract been performed.

Hutchison J: On th[e] crucial question of where the onus of proof lies in relation to whether or not the exploitation of the subject matter of the contract would or would not have recouped the expenditure…Mr. Willer, on behalf of the plaintiffs, submits that *C. & P. Haulage v. Middleton* [1983] 1 W.L.R. 1461 is binding English authority for the view that the onus is on the defendant. … He relies on the terms in which Ackner L.J. cites the judgment of Berger J. in *Bowlay Logging Ltd. v. Domtar Ltd.* [1978] 4 W.W.R. 105, and that of Learned Hand C.J. in *L. Albert & Son v. Armstrong Rubber Co.* (1949) 178 F. 2d 182. But Ackner L.J. was citing those passages as authority for the proposition that expenditure cannot be recovered in cases where, if the contract had been performed, the plaintiff would not have recouped his expenditure. He was in no way concerned with the question of burden of proof. The most that can be said is that, given that both cases contain clear statements to the effect that the onus was on the defendant and that the passage cited by Ackner L.J. from *L. Albert & Son v. Armstrong Rubber Co.* contained an express assertion to that effect, the proposition is obviously one which did not strike Ackner L.J. as being plainly erroneous, for he would otherwise presumably have said as much. To that extent *C. & P. Haulage v. Middleton* [1983] 1 W.L.R. 1461 assists Mr. Willer, but it is not in my judgment English authority for the proposition that in these circumstances the onus lies on the defendant.

I turn, therefore, to the Canadian and American cases. In the *Bowlay Logging* case [1978] 4 W.W.R. 105 Berger J. held that the onus of showing that the exploitation of the contract would have lost money lay on the defendant. In doing so, he based himself on the American cases *L. Albert & Son v. Armstrong Rubber Co.*, 178 F. 2d 182 and *Dade County v. Palmer & Baker Engineers Inc.* (1965) 339 F. 2d 208, so it is those cases that I must consider.

In the former case, where a claim for damages for breach of contract in relation to the sale of some machines designed to recondition old rubber was advanced on the wasted expenditure rather than the loss of profit basis, Learned Hand C.J. held that the onus was on the defendants and said, at p. 189:

"In cases where the venture would have proved profitable to the promisee there is no reason why he should not recover his expenses. On the other hand, on those occasions in which the performance would not have covered the promisee's outlay, such a result imposes the risk of the promisee's contract upon the promisor. We cannot agree that the promisor's default in performance should under this guise make him an insurer of the promisee's venture; yet it does not follow that the breach should not throw upon him the duty of showing that the value of the performance would in fact have been less than the promisee's outlay. It is often very hard to learn what the value of the performance would have been; and it is a common expedient, and a just one, in such situations to put the peril of the answer upon that party who by his wrong has made the issue relevant to the rights of the other. On principle, therefore, the proper solution would seem to be that the promisee may recover his outlay in preparation for the performance, subject to the privilege of the promisor to reduce it by as much as he can show that the promisee would have lost, if the contract had been performed."

The judgment in the *Dade County* case, 339 F. 2d 208, while again being direct authority on the point, again favourable to Mr. Willer, is very brief and contains the bare statement: "The burden is on the defendant to prove that full performance would have resulted in a net loss."

I am, of course, not bound by any of these cases, but plainly they are of great persuasive authority. I am impressed by, and respectfully adopt, the reasoning of Learned Hand C.J. in *L. Albert & Son v Armstrong Rubber Co.* (1949) 178 F. 2d 182 and I do so the more readily because, as I have already mentioned, that case and *Bowlay Logging Ltd. v. Domtar Ltd* [1978] 4 W.W.R. 105 were relied upon by Ackner L.J. in *C. & P. Haulage v. Middleton* [1983] 1 W.L.R. 1461 in a different context without eliciting from Ackner L.J. any adverse comment on this point. Even without the assistance of such authorities, I should have held on principle that the onus was on the defendant. It seems to me that at least in those cases where the plaintiff's decision to base his claim on abortive expenditure was dictated by the practical impossibility of proving loss of profit rather than by unfettered choice, any other rule would largely, if not entirely, defeat the object of allowing this alternative method of formulating the claim. This is because, notwithstanding the distinction...between proving a loss of net profit and proving in general terms the probability of sufficient returns to cover expenditure, in the majority of contested cases impossibility of proof of the first would probably involve like impossibility in the case of the second. It appears to me to be eminently fair that in such cases where the plaintiff has by the defendant's breach been prevented from exploiting the chattel or the right contracted for and, therefore, putting to the test the question of whether he would have recouped his expenditure, the general rule as to the onus of proof of damage should be modified in this manner.

It follows that, the onus being on the defendants to prove that the expenditure incurred by the plaintiffs is irrecoverable because they would not have recouped their expenditure (and that onus admittedly not having been discharged), the plaintiffs are entitled to recover such expenditure as was wasted as a result of such breach or breaches of contract as they have proved.

...

I therefore find: (1) that the foreseeable result of the breach of their obligations imposed by one or more of the subsidiary contracts to deliver any of the tapes was that the expenditure incurred by the plaintiffs in acquiring the licence to exploit the tapes would be wasted; (2) that in the event that expenditure was wasted because, given that the receipt of the tapes was a necessary prerequisite to any exploitation, the plaintiffs were, by the breaches of the subsidiary contracts, prevented from undertaking any sort of exploitation of the rights for which they had paid $12,000; (3) that the onus of proving that, had the tapes been received, the plaintiffs would not have succeeded in recouping their expenditure, i.e., the $12,000 and any other exploitation expenditure, lay on the defendants and has not been discharged; (4) that accordingly the plaintiffs are entitled to judgment for $12,000.

NOTES AND QUESTIONS

1. This case makes clear that the advantage to the claimant of framing its claim as one for reliance expenses—rather than *directly* seeking to be put into as good a position as if the contract had been performed—is that the onus of proving what is needed to protect the claimant's expectation (or performance) interest is reversed. Put another way, the claimant is given the benefit of a rebuttable factual presumption that, had the contract been performed, it would have recouped its reliance expenses. The justification for that reversal of the burden of proof is, it would seem, that the reason why there is doubt about whether the claimant would have recouped its expenses is the defendant's breach. It is only fair and proper that the problems of establishing whether the claimant would have recouped its reliance loss should fall on the contract-breaker and not on the innocent party.

2. In *Dataliner Ltd v Vehicle Builders & Repairers Association* (1995) Independent, 30 August, the Court of Appeal confusingly appeared to limit the reversal of the burden of proof to cases where the claimant has an impossible burden. With respect, the judgment is best interpreted as saying merely that where the claimant can prove that it would have made sufficient profits to recoup its expenses, it has no need to rely on the presumption.

3. Are compensatory damages for breach of contract best viewed as always being concerned to protect the claimant's expectation (or performance) interest? Is the recovery of wasted reliance expense merely an indirect method, supported

by a reverse burden of proof, of protecting that expectation interest? See A Burrows, *Remedies for Torts and Breach of Contract* (3rd edn, 2004) 70–2.

(2) Limitations on Compensation

(a) Remoteness

Hadley v Baxendale (1854) 9 Exch 341, Court of Exchequer

The claimant's mill in Gloucester was brought to a standstill by a broken crank-shaft. The claimant engaged the defendant carriers to take it to a firm of engineers in Greenwich to act as a pattern for the engineers to make a new crank-shaft. In breach of contract the defendants delayed in delivering the crank-shaft so that, instead of being delivered the next day at Greenwich, it was delivered several days later. This delay resulted in the mill being kept idle for five days longer than would otherwise have been the case. The claimants sought damages for the loss of profits for those five days. In ordering a new trial (by jury), the Court of Exchequer laid down a two-rule test of remoteness and, applying it, held that that loss of profit was too remote and therefore irrecoverable.

Alderson B (giving the judgment of the court, comprising himself, **Parke B** and **Martin B**): Now we think the proper rule in such a case as the present is this:—Where two parties have made a contract which one of them has broken, the damages which the other party ought to receive in respect of such breach of contract should be such as may fairly and reasonably be considered either arising naturally, i.e., according to the usual course of things, from such breach of contract itself, or such as may reasonably be supposed to have been in the contemplation of both parties, at the time they made the contract, as the probable result of the breach of it. Now, if the special circumstances under which the contract was actually made were communicated by the plaintiffs to the defendants, and thus known to both parties, the damages resulting from the breach of such a contract, which they would reasonably contemplate, would be the amount of injury which would ordinarily follow from a breach of contract under these special circumstances so known and communicated. But, on the other hand, if these special circumstances were wholly unknown to the party breaking the contract, he, at the most, could only be supposed to have had in his contemplation the amount of injury which would arise generally, and in the great multitude of cases not affected by any special circumstances, from such a breach of contract. For, had the special circumstances been known, the parties might have specially provided for the breach of contract by special terms as to the damages in that case; and of this advantage it would be very unjust to deprive them. Now the above principles are those by which we think the jury ought to be guided in estimating the damages arising out of any breach of contract. …Now, in the present case, if we are to apply the principles above laid down, we find that the only circumstances here communicated by the plaintiffs to the defendants at the time the contract was made, were, that the article to be carried was the broken shaft of a mill, and that the plaintiffs were the millers of that mill. But how do these circumstances shew reasonably that the profits of the mill must be stopped by an unreasonable delay in the delivery of the broken shaft by the carrier to the third person? Suppose the plaintiffs had another shaft in their possession put up or putting up at the time, and that they only wished to send back the broken shaft to the engineer who made it; it is clear that this would be quite consistent with the above circumstances, and yet the unreasonable delay in the delivery would have no effect upon the intermediate profits of the mill. Or, again, suppose that, at the time of the delivery to the carrier, the machinery of the mill had been in other respects defective, then, also, the same results would follow. Here it is true that the shaft was actually sent back to serve as a model for a new one, and that the want of a new one was the only cause of the stoppage of the mill, and that the loss of profits really arose from not sending down the new shaft in proper time, and that this arose from the delay in delivering the broken one to serve as a model. But it is obvious that, in the great multitude of cases of millers sending off broken shafts to third persons by a carrier under ordinary circumstances, such consequences would not, in all probability, have occurred; and these special circumstances were here never communicated by the plaintiffs to the defendants. It follows, therefore, that the loss of profits here cannot reasonably be considered such a consequence of the breach of contract as could have been fairly and reasonably contemplated by both the parties when they made this contract. For such loss would neither have flowed naturally from the breach of this contract in the great multitude of such cases occurring under ordinary circumstances, nor were the special circumstances, which, perhaps, would have made it a reasonable and natural consequence of such breach of contract, communicated to or known by the defendants. The Judge ought, therefore, to have told the jury, that, upon the facts then before them, they ought not to take the loss of profits into consideration at all in estimating the damages. There must therefore be a new trial in this case.

NOTES AND QUESTIONS

1. This is probably the most famous, and most-cited, case in English contract law. The two rules of remoteness laid down by Alderson B were said by Lord Hope in *Jackson v Royal Bank of Scotland plc* (see below, 373) to be 'very familiar to every student of contract law. Most would claim to be able to recite them by heart.'

2. Why was it that, on the facts, neither of the two rules was held to be satisfied? (Note that Alderson B took it that the defendant carriers did not know that the mill was stopped, although the head-note and summary of apparent facts in the report indicates that the defendant's clerk was told that the mill was stopped: see the criticism of the head-note and summary in the next case).

Victoria Laundry (Windsor) Ltd v Newman Industries Ltd
[1949] 2 KB 528, Court of Appeal

The claimants, launderers and dyers, decided to expand their business and contracted to buy from the defendants a larger boiler than they already had. The defendants knew that the claimants wanted the boiler for immediate use in their business but, in breach of contract, delivered the boiler five months late. The claimants sought damages under two heads for their loss of profit during those months. First, for what might be termed the 'ordinary loss of profit', they claimed £16 a week for the new customers they could have taken on. Secondly, for what might be termed the 'exceptional loss of profit', they claimed £262 a week for the highly lucrative dyeing contracts with the Ministry of Supply that they would have taken on. Streatfeild J had refused damages for any of those loss of profits but, in ordering a reassessment by an Official Referee, the Court of Appeal held that, applying *Hadley v Baxendale*, the ordinary loss of profits was not too remote albeit that the exceptional loss of profits was.

Asquith LJ (giving the judgment of the court, comprising himself, **Tucker LJ** and **Singleton LJ**): Three of the authorities call for more detailed examination. First comes *Hadley v. Baxendale* 9 Exch. 341 itself. Familiar though it is, we should first recall the memorable sentence in which the main principles laid down in this case are enshrined: "Where two parties have made a contract which one of them has broken, the damages which the other party ought to receive in respect of such breach of contract should be such as may fairly and reasonably be considered as either arising naturally, i.e. according to the usual course of things, from such breach of contract itself, or such as may reasonably be supposed to have been in the contemplation of both parties, at the time they made the contract, as the probable result of the breach of it." The limb of this sentence prefaced by "either" embodies the so-called "first" rule; that prefaced by "or" the "second." In considering the meaning and application of these rules, it is essential to bear clearly in mind the facts on which *Hadley v. Baxendale* proceeded. The head-note is definitely misleading in so far as it says that the defendant's clerk, who attended at the office, was told that the mill was stopped and that the shaft must be delivered immediately. The same allegation figures in the statement of facts which are said on page 344 to have "appeared" at the trial before Crompton J. If the Court of Exchequer had accepted these facts as established, the court must, one would suppose, have decided the case the other way round; must, that is, have held the damage claimed was recoverable under the second rule. But it is reasonably plain from Alderson B's judgment that the court rejected this evidence, for on page 355 he says: "We find that the only circumstances here communicated by the plaintiffs to the defendants at the time when the contract was made were that the article to be carried was the broken shaft of a mill and that the plaintiffs were the millers of that mill," and it is on this basis of fact that he proceeds to ask, "How do these circumstances show reasonably that the profits of the mill must be stopped by an unreasonable delay in the delivery of the broken shaft by the carrier to the third person?"

[*He then considered* British Columbia Sawmills v Nettleship *(1868) LR 3 CP 409 and* Cory v Thomas Ironworks Co *(1868) LR 3 QB 181 and continued*:]

What propositions applicable to the present case emerge from the authorities as a whole, including those analysed above? We think they include the following:—

(1.) It is well settled that the governing purpose of damages is to put the party whose rights have been violated in the same position, so far as money can do so, as if his rights had been observed: *(Sally Wertheim v. Chicoutimi Pulp Company* [1911] A. C. 301). This purpose, if relentlessly pursued, would provide him with a complete indemnity for all loss de facto resulting from a particular breach, however improbable, however unpredictable. This, in contract at least, is recognized as too harsh a rule. Hence,

(2.) In cases of breach of contract the aggrieved party is only entitled to recover such part of the loss actually resulting as was at the time of the contract reasonably foreseeable [*sic*] as liable to result from the breach.

(3.) What was at that time reasonably so foreseeable depends on the knowledge then possessed by the parties or, at all events, by the party who later commits the breach.

(4.) For this purpose, knowledge "possessed" is of two kinds; one imputed, the other actual. Everyone, as a reasonable person, is taken to know the "ordinary course of things" and consequently what loss is liable to result from a breach of contract in that ordinary course. This is the subject matter of the "first rule" in *Hadley v. Baxendale*. But to this knowledge, which a contract-breaker is assumed to possess whether he actually possesses it or not, there may have to be added in a particular case knowledge which he actually possesses, of special circumstances outside the "ordinary course of things," of such a kind that a breach in those special circumstances would be liable to cause more loss. Such a case attracts the operation of the "second rule" so as to make additional loss also recoverable.

(5.) In order to make the contract-breaker liable under either rule it is not necessary that he should actually have asked himself what loss is liable to result from a breach. As has often been pointed out, parties at the time of contracting contemplate not the breach of the contract, but its performance. It suffices that, if he had considered the question, he would as a reasonable man have concluded that the loss in question was liable to result (see certain observations of Lord du Parcq in the recent case of *A/B Karlshamns Oljefabriker v. Monarch Steamship Company Limited* [1949] A. C. 196.)

(6.) Nor, finally, to make a particular loss recoverable, need it be proved that upon a given state of knowledge the defendant could, as a reasonable man, foresee that a breach must necessarily result in that loss. It is enough if he could foresee it was likely so to result. It is indeed enough, to borrow from the language of Lord du Parcq in the same case, at page 158, if the loss (or some factor without which it would not have occurred) is a "serious possibility" or a "real danger." For short, we have used the word "liable" to result. Possibly the colloquialism "on the cards" indicates the shade of meaning with some approach to accuracy.

[*After referring to Streatfeild J's reasoning, he continued that, in answer to it, the court wished to make the following points:*] First,...the learned judge appears to infer that because certain "special circumstances" were, in his view, not "drawn to the notice of" the defendants and therefore, in his view, the operation of the "second rule" was excluded, ergo nothing in respect of loss of business can be recovered under the "first rule." This inference is, in our view, no more justified in the present case than it was in the case of *Cory v. Thames Ironworks Company*. Secondly, that while it is not wholly clear what were the "special circumstances" on the non-communication of which the learned judge relied, it would seem that they were, or included, the following:—(a) the "circumstance" that delay in delivering the boiler was going to lead "necessarily" to loss of profits. But the true criterion is surely not what was bound "necessarily" to result, but what was likely or liable to do so, and we think that it was amply conveyed to the defendants by what was communicated to them (plus what was patent without express communication) that delay in delivery was likely to lead to "loss of business"; (b) the "circumstance" that the plaintiffs needed the boiler "to extend their business." It was surely not necessary for the defendants to be specifically informed of this, as a precondition of being liable for loss of business. Reasonable, persons in the shoes of the defendants must be taken to foresee without any express intimation, that a laundry which, at a time when there was a famine of laundry facilities, was paying 2,000*l.* odd for plant and intended at such a time to put such plant "into use" immediately, would be likely to suffer in pocket from five months' delay in delivery of the plant in question, whether they intended by means of it to extend their business, or merely to maintain it, or to reduce a loss; (c) the "circumstance" that the plaintiffs had the assured expectation of special contracts, which they could only fulfil by securing punctual delivery of the boiler. Here, no doubt, the learned judge had in mind the particularly lucrative dyeing contracts to which the plaintiffs looked forward and which they mention in para. 10 of the statement of claim. We agree that in order that the plaintiffs should recover specifically and as such the profits expected on these contracts, the defendants would have had to know, at the time of their agreement with the plaintiffs, of the prospect and terms of such contracts. We also agree that they did not in fact know these things. It does not, however, follow that the plaintiffs are precluded from recovering some general (and perhaps conjectural) sum for loss of business in respect of dyeing contracts to be reasonably expected, any more than in respect of laundering contracts to be reasonably expected.

Thirdly, the other point on which Streatfeild J. largely based his judgment was that there is a critical difference between the measure of damages applicable when the defendant defaults in supplying a self-contained profit-earning whole and when he defaults in supplying a part of that whole. In our view, there is no intrinsic magic, in this connexion, in the whole as against a part. The fact that a part only is involved is only significant in so far as it bears on the capacity of the supplier to foresee the consequences of non-delivery.

NOTES AND QUESTIONS

1.   In his proposition (2), we see Asquith LJ formulating a single rule centring on 'reasonable foreseeability' as underpinning the two rules of *Hadley v Baxendale*. Does anything of substance turn on whether one formulates the

test of remoteness in two rules or one? Have the courts in subsequent cases preferred to think in terms of two rules or one? See, eg, Lord Reid in *The Heron II,* below, 361; *The Pegase* [1981] 1 Lloyd's Rep 175, 182; *Kpohraror v Woolwich Building Society* [1996] 4 All ER 119, CA.

2.   Is there any difference between saying that a loss must have been 'reasonably foreseeable' (the term used by Asquith LJ) or 'reasonably contemplated' (the term used by Alderson B in *Hadley v Baxendale*)?

Koufos v C Czarnikow Ltd, The Heron II [1969] 1 AC 350, House of Lords

The claimant had chartered a ship from the defendant shipowner for the carriage of sugar by the defendant from Constanza to Basrah. In breach of contract, the ship arrived in Basrah nine days late. During those nine days, 8,000 tons of sugar had arrived at Basrah with the result that the market price for sugar there had fallen from £32 10s per ton to £31 2s 9d per ton. The defendant had not known that the charterer intended to sell the sugar as soon as it reached Basrah but had known that there was a market for sugar at Basrah. The loss of profit from the fall in the market was held to be too remote by the judge at first instance but this was overturned by the Court of Appeal. In affirming the decision of the Court of Appeal, the House of Lords held that the loss of profit was not too remote because, at the time of the contract, it was reasonably contemplated as sufficiently likely to result from such a breach.

Lord Reid: So the question for decision is whether a plaintiff can recover as damages for breach of contract a loss of a kind which the defendant, when he made the contract, ought to have realised was not unlikely to result from a breach of contract causing delay in delivery. I use the words "not unlikely" as denoting a degree of probability considerably less than an even chance but nevertheless not very unusual and easily foreseeable.

   ...

   In cases like *Hadley v. Baxendale* 9 Exch. 341, or the present case it is not enough that in fact the plaintiff's loss was directly caused by the defendant's breach of contract. It clearly was so caused in both. The crucial question is whether, on the information available to the defendant when the contract was made, he should, or the reasonable man in his position would, have realised that such loss was sufficiently likely to result from the breach of contract to make it proper to hold that the loss flowed naturally from the breach or that loss of that kind should have been within his contemplation.

   The modern rule of tort is quite different and it imposes a much wider liability. The defendant will be liable for any type of damage which is reasonably foreseeable as liable to happen even in the most unusual case, unless the risk is so small that a reasonable man would in the whole circumstances feel justified in neglecting it. And there is good reason for the difference. In contract, if one party wishes to protect himself against a risk which to the other party would appear unusual, he can direct the other party's attention to it before the contract is made, and I need not stop to consider in what circumstances the other party will then be held to have accepted responsibility in that event. But in tort there is no opportunity for the injured party to protect himself in that way, and the tortfeasor cannot reasonably complain if he has to pay for some very unusual but nevertheless foreseeable damage which results from his wrongdoing. I have no doubt that today a tortfeasor would be held liable for a type of damage as unlikely as was the stoppage of Hadley's Mill for lack of a crankshaft: to anyone with the knowledge the carrier had that may have seemed unlikely but the chance of it happening would have been seen to be far from negligible. But it does not at all follow that *Hadley v. Baxendale* would today be differently decided.

...

It is true that in some later cases opinions were expressed that the measure of damages is the same in tort as it is in contract, but those were generally cases where it was sought to limit damages due for a tort and not cases where it was sought to extend damages due for breach of contract, and I do not recollect any case in which such opinions were based on a full consideration of the matter. In my view these opinions must now be regarded as erroneous.

...

But then it has been said that the liability of defendants has been further extended by *Victoria Laundry (Windsor) Ltd. v. Newman Industries Ltd.* [1949] 2 K.B. 528. I do not think so.

...

[W]hat is said to create a "landmark" is the statement of principles by Asquith L.J. This does to some extent go beyond the older authorities and in so far as it does so, I do not agree with it. In paragraph (2) it is said (at 539) that the plaintiff is entitled to recover "such part of the loss actually resulting as was at the time of the contract reasonably foreseeable as liable to result from the breach." To bring in reasonable foreseeability appears to me to be confusing measure of damages in contract with measure of damages in tort. A great many extremely unlikely results are reasonably foreseeable: it is true that Lord Asquith may have meant foreseeable as a likely result, and if that is all he meant I would not object further than to say that I think that the phrase is liable to be misunderstood. For the same reason I would take exception to the phrase (at 540) "liable to result" in paragraph (5). Liable is a very vague word but I think that one would usually say that when a person foresees a very improbable result he foresees that it is liable to happen.

I agree with the first half of paragraph (6). For the best part of a century it has not been required that the defendant could have foreseen that a breach of contract must necessarily result in the loss which has occurred. But I cannot agree with the second half of that paragraph. It has never been held to be sufficient in contract that the loss was foreseeable as "a serious possibility" or "a real danger" or as being "on the cards." It is on the cards that one can win £100,000 or more for a stake of a few pence – several people have done that. And anyone who backs a hundred to one chance regards a win as a serious possibility – many people have won on such a chance. And the *Wagon Mound (No. 2)* [1967] 1 A.C. 617. could not have been decided as it was unless the extremely unlikely fire should have been foreseen by the ship's officer as a real danger. It appears to me that in the ordinary use of language there is [a] wide gulf between saying that some event is not unlikely or quite likely to happen and saying merely that it is a serious possibility, a real danger, or on the cards. Suppose one takes a well-shuffled pack of cards, it is quite likely or not unlikely that the top card will prove to be a diamond: the odds are only 3 to 1 against. But most people would not say that it is quite likely to be the nine of diamonds for the odds are then 51 to 1 against. On the other hand I think that most people would say that there is a serious possibility or a real danger of its being turned up first and of course it is on the cards. If the tests of "real danger" or "serious possibility" are in future to be authoritative then the *Victoria Laundry* case [1949] 2 K.B. 528 would indeed be a landmark because it would mean that *Hadley v. Baxendale* 9 Ex. 341 would be differently decided today. I certainly could not understand any court deciding that, on the information available to the carrier in that case, the stoppage of the mill was neither a serious possibility nor a real danger. If those tests are to prevail in future then let us cease to pay lip service to the rule in *Hadley v. Baxendale* . But in my judgment to adopt these tests would extend liability for breach of contract beyond what is reasonable or desirable.

...

It appears to me that, without relying in any way on the *Victoria Laundry* case, and taking the principle that had already been established, the loss of profit claimed in this case was not too remote to be recoverable as damages.

Lord Morris of Borth-y-Gest: I regard the illuminating judgment of the Court of Appeal in *Victoria Laundry (Windsor) Ltd. v. Newman Industries Ltd.* [1949] 2 K.B. 528 as a most valuable analysis of the rule. It was there pointed out (at 540) that in order to make a contract-breaker liable under what was called "either rule" in *Hadley v. Baxendale* 9 Exch. 341 it is not necessary that he should actually have asked himself what loss is liable to result from a breach but that it suffices that if he had considered the question he would as a reasonable man have concluded that the loss in question was liable to result. Nor need it be proved, in order to recover a particular loss, that upon a given state of knowledge he could, as a reasonable man, foresee that a breach must necessarily result in that loss. Certain illustrative phrases are employed in that case. They are valuable by way of exposition but for my part I doubt whether the phrase "on the cards" has a sufficiently clear meaning or possesses such a comparable shade of meaning as to qualify it to take its place with the various other phrases which line up as expositions of the rule.

If the problem in the present case is that of relating accepted principle to the facts which have been found, I entertain no doubt that if at the time of their contract the parties had considered what the consequence would be if the arrival of the ship at Basrah was delayed they would have contemplated that some loss to the respondents was likely or was liable to result. The appellant at the time that he made his contract must have known that if in breach of contract his ship did not arrive at Basrah when it ought to arrive he would be liable to pay damages. He would not know that a loss to the respondents was certain or inevitable but he must, as a reasonable business man, have contemplated that the respondents would very likely suffer loss, and that it would be or would be likely to be a loss referable to market price fluctuations at Basrah. I cannot think that he should escape liability by saying that he would only be aware of a possibility of loss but not of a probability or certainty of it. He might have used any one of many phrases. He might have said that a loss would be likely: or that a loss would not be unlikely: or that a loss was liable to result: or that the risk that delay would cause loss to the respondents was a serious possibility: or that there would be a real danger of a loss: or that the risk of his being liable to have to pay for the loss was one that he ought commercially to take into account. As a practical business man he would not have paused to reflect on the possible nuances of meaning of any one of these phrases. Nor would he have sent for a dictionary.

Lord Hodson: A close study of the rule [in *Hadley v Baxendale*] was made by the Court of Appeal in the case of the *Victoria Laundry (Windsor) Ltd. v. Newman Industries Ltd.* [1949] 2 K.B. 528, 540. ...Asquith LJ...suggested the phrase "liable to result" as appropriate to describe the degree of probability required. This may be a colourless expression but I do not find it possible to improve on it. If the word "likelihood" is used it may convey the impression that the chances are all in favour of the thing happening, an idea which I would reject.

Lord Pearce: I do not think that there was anything startling or novel about [the judgment of the Court of Appeal in the case of *Victoria Laundry (Windsor) Ltd. v. Newman Industries Ltd.* [1949] 2 K.B. 528]. In my opinion it represented (in felicitous language) the approximate view of *Hadley v. Baxendale* 9 Exch. 341 taken by many judges in trying ordinary cases of breach of contract.

It is argued that it was an erroneous departure from *Hadley v. Baxendale* in that it allowed damages where the loss was "a serious possibility" or "a real danger" instead of maintaining that the loss must be "probable," in the sense that it was more likely to result than not.

...

[I]n my opinion the expressions used in the *Victoria Laundry* case [1949] 2 K.B. 528 were right. I do not however accept the colloquialism "on the cards" as being a useful test because I am not sure just what nuance it has either in my own personal vocabulary or in that of others. I suspect that it owes its attraction, like many other colloquialisms, to the fact that one may utter it without having the trouble of really thinking out with precision what one means oneself or what others will understand by it, a spurious attraction which in general makes colloquialism unsuitable for definition, though it is often useful as shorthand for a collection of definable ideas. It was in this latter convenient sense that the judgment uses the ambiguous words "liable to result." They were not intended as a further or different test from "serious possibility" or "real danger."

Lord Upjohn: Asquith L.J. in *Victoria Laundry* [1949] 2 K.B. 528, 540 used the words "likely to result" and he treated that as synonymous with a serious possibility or a real danger. He went on to equate that with the expression "on the cards" but like all your Lordships I deprecate the use of that phrase which is far too imprecise and to my mind is capable of denoting a most improbable and unlikely event, such as winning a prize on a premium bond on any given drawing.

...

It is clear that on the one hand the test of foreseeability as laid down in the case of tort is not the test for breach of contract; nor on the other hand must the loser establish that the loss was a near certainty or an odds-on probability. I am content to adopt as the test a "real danger" or a "serious possibility." There may be a shade of difference between these two phrases but the assessment of damages is not an exact science and what to one judge or jury will appear a real danger may appear to another judge or jury to be a serious possibility. I do not think that the application of that test would have led to a different result in *Hadley v. Baxendale*. 9 Exch. 341. I cannot see why [the carriers] in the absence of express mention should have contemplated as a real danger or serious possibility that work at the factory would be brought to a halt while the shaft was away.

NOTES AND QUESTIONS

1.   The focus of this case was on the degree of likelihood of the loss occurring that is required to be reasonably contemplated under the contract remoteness test. All their Lordships agreed that a higher degree of likelihood of the loss occurring is required in contract than under the tort remoteness test of reasonable foreseeability laid down in the *Wagon Mound* [1961] 1 AC 388, PC, so that losses may be too remote in contract that would not be too remote in tort. Also very important is the policy explanation for the difference in tests put forward by Lord Reid. Does that explanation justify always applying different remoteness tests in contract and tort?

2.   Unfortunately there was no clear consensus as to how the degree of likelihood required in contract should be expressed. In this respect, Lord Reid was out of line with the other Lords. For while Lords Morris, Pearce and Upjohn were content with 'real danger' or 'serious possibility' and Lord Hodson thought 'liable to result' could not be improved upon, Lord Reid thought those phrases expressed the degree of likelihood at too low a level. Taking the majority's view it is submitted that the clearest way to express the degree of likelihood in contract is to talk of the loss being a 'serious possibility' which can then be contrasted with the lower 'slight possibility' applied in tort.

Parsons (Livestock) Ltd v Uttley Ingham & Co Ltd
[1978] QB 791, Court of Appeal

The claimants were pig farmers and bought from the defendants, who were manufacturers of bulk food storage hoppers, a hopper which the defendants agreed to install at the claimants' farm. The hopper was fitted with a ventilator top but this was sealed for the purposes of carriage and the defendants forgot to unseal it when erecting it. As the ventilator was 28 feet high, the claimants did not notice that the ventilator was closed. Owing to the lack of ventilation, the pignuts stored in the hopper became mouldy. At first the claimants continued to feed the nuts to the pigs thinking that they would not do them any harm. Many of the pigs suffered a rare intestinal disease, E coli, from eating the nuts and 254 of them died. The claimants brought an action against the defendants for breach of contract in which they claimed damages for the loss of the pigs. The defendants argued that the loss of the pigs was too remote but this was rejected by the trial judge. In upholding this decision, the majority of the Court of Appeal held that it is the type of loss, rather than the actual loss, that is relevant in applying the contract remoteness test. Lord Denning MR, while agreeing that the loss was not too remote, reasoned differently in drawing a distinction between contract remoteness tests for loss of profit and physical damage.

Lord Denning MR:

The law as to remoteness

Remoteness of damage is beyond doubt a question of law. In *C. Czarnikow Ltd. v. Koufos* [1969] A.C. 350 the House of Lords said that, in remoteness of damage, there is a difference between contract and tort. In the case of a *breach of contract*, the court has to consider whether the consequences were of such a kind that a reasonable man, at the time of making the contract, would *contemplate* them as being of a very substantial degree of probability. (In the House of Lords various expressions were used to describe this degree of probability, such as, not merely "on the cards" because that may be too low: but as being "not unlikely to occur" (see pp. 383 and 388); or "likely to result or at least not unlikely to result" (see p. 406); or "liable to result" (see p. 410); or that there was a "real danger" or "serious possibility" of them occurring (see p. 415).)

In the case of a *tort*, the court has to consider whether the consequences were of such a kind that a reasonable man, at the time of the tort committed, would *foresee* them as being of a much lower degree of probability. (In the House of Lords various expressions were used to describe this, such as, it is sufficient if the consequences are "liable to happen in the most unusual case" (see p. 385); or in a "very improbable" case (see p. 389); or that "they may happen as a result of the breach, however unlikely it may be, unless it can be brushed aside as far-fetched" (see p. 422).)

I find it difficult to apply those principles universally to all cases of contract or to all cases of tort: and to draw a distinction between what a man "contemplates" and what he "foresees." I soon begin to get out of my depth. I cannot swim in this sea of semantic exercises – to say nothing of the different degrees of probability – especially when the cause of action can be laid either in contract or in tort. I am swept under by the conflicting currents. I go back with relief to the distinction drawn in legal theory by Professors Hart and Honoré in their book *Causation in the Law* (1959), at pp. 281-287. They distinguish between those cases in contract in which a man has suffered no damage to person or property, but only *economic loss*, such as, loss of profit or loss of opportunities for gain in some future transaction: and those in which he claims damages for an *injury actually done* to his person or *damage actually done* to his property (including his livestock) or for ensuing expense (damnum emergens) to which he has actually been put. In the law of tort, there is emerging a distinction between economic loss and physical damage: see *Spartan Steel & Alloys Ltd. v. Martin & Co. (Contractors) Ltd.* [1973] Q.B. 27, 36-37. ...

It seems to me that in the law of contract, too, a similar distinction is emerging. It is between loss of profit consequent on a breach of contract and physical damage consequent on it.

Loss of profit cases

I would suggest as a solution that in the former class of case – loss of profit cases – the defaulting party is only liable for the consequences if they are such as, at the time of the contract, he ought reasonably to have *contemplated* as a *serious* possibility or real danger. You must assume that, at the time of the contract, he had the very kind of breach in mind – such a breach as afterwards happened, as for instance, delay in transit – and then you must ask: ought he reasonably to have *contemplated* that there was a *serious* possibility that such a breach would involve the plaintiff in loss of profit? If yes, the contractor is liable for the loss unless he has taken care to exempt himself from it by a condition in the contract – as, of course, he is able to do if it was the sort of thing which he could reasonably contemplate. The law on this class of case is now covered by the three leading cases of *Hadley v. Baxendale*, 9 Exch. 341; *Victoria Laundry (Windsor) Ltd. v. Newman Industries Ltd.* [1949] 2 K.B. 528; and *C. Czarnikow Ltd. v. Koufos* [1969] 1 A.C. 350. These were all "loss of profit" cases: and the test of "reasonable contemplation" and "serious possibility" should, I suggest, be kept to that type of loss or, at any rate, to economic loss.

Physical damage cases

In the second class of case – the physical injury or expense case – the defaulting party is liable for any loss or expense which he ought reasonably to have *foreseen* at the time of the breach as a possible consequence, even if it was only a *slight* possibility. You must assume that he was aware of his breach, and then you must ask: ought he reasonably to have foreseen, at the time of the breach, that something of this kind might happen in consequence of it? This is the test which has been applied in cases of tort ever since *The Wagon Mound* cases [1961] A.C. 388 and [1967] 1 A.C. 617. But there is a long line of cases which support a like test in cases of contract.

One class of case which is particularly apposite here concerns latent defects in goods: in modern words "product liability." In many of these cases the manufacturer is liable in contract to the immediate party for a breach of his duty to use reasonable care and is liable in tort to the ultimate consumer for the same want of reasonable care. The ultimate consumer can either sue the retailer in contract and pass the liability up the chain to the manufacturer, or he can sue the manufacturer in tort and thus by-pass the chain. The liability of the manufacturer ought to be the same in either case. In nearly all these cases the defects were outside the range of anything that was in fact contemplated, or could reasonably have been contemplated, by the manufacturer or by anyone down the chain to the retailers. Yet the manufacturer and others in the chain have been held liable for the damage done to the ultimate user, as for instance the death of the young pheasants in *Hardwick Game Farm v. Suffolk Agricultural Poultry Producers Association* [1969] 2 A.C. 31 and of the mink in *Christopher Hill Ltd. v. Ashington Piggeries Ltd.* [1972] A.C. 441. Likewise, the manufacturers and retailers were held liable for the dermatitis caused to the wearer in the woollen underwear case of *Grant v. Australian Knitting Mills Ltd.* [1936] A.C. 85, even though they had not the faintest suspicion of any trouble. So were the manufacturers down the chain to the sub-contractors for the disintegrating roofing tiles in *Young & Marten Ltd. v. McManus Childs Ltd.* [1969] 1 A.C. 454.

...

Instances could be multiplied of injuries to persons or damage to property where the defendant is liable for his negligence to one man in contract and to another in tort. Each suffers like damage. The test of remoteness is, and should be, the same in both.

Coming to the present case, we were told that in some cases the makers of these hoppers supply them direct to the pig farmer under contract with him, but in other cases they supply them through an intermediate dealer – who buys from the manufacturer and resells to the pig farmer on the self-same terms – in which the manufacturer delivers direct to the pig farmer. In the one case the pig farmer can sue the manufacturer in contract. In the other in tort. The test of remoteness should be the same. It should be the test in tort.

Conclusion

The present case falls within the class of case where the breach of contract causes physical damage. The test of remoteness in such cases is similar to that in tort. The contractor is liable for all such loss or expense as could reasonably have been foreseen, at the time of the breach, as a possible consequence of it. Applied to this case, it means that the makers of the hopper are liable for the death of the pigs. They ought reasonably to have foreseen that, if the mouldy pignuts were fed to the pigs, there was a possibility that they might become ill. Not a serious possibility. Nor a real danger. But still a slight possibility. On that basis the makers were liable for the illness suffered by the pigs. They suffered from diarrhoea at the beginning. This triggered off the deadly E. coli. That was a far worse illness than could then be foreseen. But that does not lessen this liability. The type or kind of damage was foreseeable even though the extent of it was not: see *Hughes v. Lord Advocate* [1963] A.C. 837. The makers are liable for the loss of the pigs that died and of the expenses of the vet and such like, but not for loss of profit on future sales or future opportunities of gain: see *Simon v. Pawson and Leafs Ltd.* (1932) 38 Com.Cas. 151.

So I reach the same result as the judge, but by a different route. I would dismiss the appeal.

Scarman LJ: My conclusion in the present case is the same as that of Lord Denning M.R. but I reach it by a different route. I would dismiss the appeal. I agree with him in thinking it absurd that the test for remoteness of damage should, in principle, differ according to the legal classification of the cause of action, though one must recognise that parties to a contract have the right to agree on a measure of damages which may be greater, or less, than the law would offer in the absence of agreement. I also agree with him in thinking that, notwithstanding the interpretation put on some dicta in *C. Czarnikow Ltd. v. Koufos* [1969] A.C. 350, the law is not so absurd as to differentiate between contract and tort save in situations where the agreement, or the factual relationship, of the parties with each other requires it in the interests of justice. I differ from him only to this extent: the cases do not, in my judgment, support a distinction in law between loss of profit and physical damage. Neither do I think it necessary to develop the law judicially by drawing such a distinction. Of course (and this is a reason for refusing to draw the distinction in law) the type of consequence – loss of profit or market or physical injury – will always be an important matter of fact in determining whether in all the circumstances the loss or injury was of a type which the parties could reasonably be supposed to have in contemplation.

In *C. Czarnikow Ltd. v. Koufos* [1969] 1 A.C. 350 (a case of a contract of carriage of goods by sea) the House of Lords resolved some of the difficulties in this branch of the law. The law which the House in that case either settled or recognised as already settled may be stated as follows. (1) The general principle regulating damages for breach of contract is that "where a party sustains a loss by reason of a breach of contract, he is, so far as money can do it, to be placed in the same situation ... as if the contract had been performed": see *per* Lord Pearce, at p. 414, quoting Parke B. in *Robinson v. Harman* (1848) 1 Exch. 850, 855. (2) The formulation of the remoteness test is not the same in tort and in contract because the relationship of the parties in a contract situation differs from that in tort: see *per* Lord Reid, at pp. 385-386. (3) The two rules formulated by Alderson B. in *Hadley v. Baxendale*, 9 Exch. 341 are but two aspects of one general principle – that to be recoverable in an action for damages for breach of contract the plaintiff's loss must be such as may reasonably be supposed would have been in the contemplation of the parties as a serious possibility had their attention been directed to the possibility of the breach which has, in fact, occurred.

Two problems are left unsolved by *C. Czarnikow Ltd. v. Koufos*: (1) the law's reconciliation of the remoteness principle in contract with that in tort where, as, for instance, in some product liability cases, there arises the danger of differing awards, the lesser award going to the party who has a contract, even though the contract is silent as to the measure of damages and all parties are, or must be deemed to be, burdened with the same knowledge, or enjoying the same state of ignorance; and (2) what is meant by "serious possibility" or its synonyms: is it a reference to the type of consequence which the parties might be supposed to contemplate as possible though unlikely, or must the chance of it happening appear to be likely? (see the way Lord Pearce puts it, at pp. 416-417).

As to the first problem, I agree with Lord Denning M.R. in thinking that the law must be such that, in a factual situation where all have the same actual or imputed knowledge and the contract contains no term limiting the damages recoverable for breach, the amount of damages recoverable does not depend upon whether, as a matter of legal classification, the plaintiff's cause of action is breach of contract or tort. It may be that the necessary reconciliation is to be found, notwithstanding the strictures of Lord Reid at pp. 389-390, in holding that the difference between "reasonably foreseeable" (the test in tort) and "reasonably contemplated" (the test in contract) is semantic, not substantial. Certainly, Asquith L.J, in *Victoria Laundry (Windsor) Ltd. v. Newman Industries Ltd* [1949] 2 K.B. 528, 535 and Lord Pearce in *C. Czarnikow Ltd. v. Koufos* [1969] 1 A.C. 350, 414 thought so; and I confess I think so too.

The second problem – what is meant by a "serious possibility" – is, in my judgment, ultimately a question of fact. I shall return to it, therefore, after analysing the facts, since I believe it requires of the judge no more – and no less – than the application of common sense in the particular circumstances of the case.

Finally, there are two legal rules relevant to the present case which were not considered in *C. Czarnikow Ltd. v. Koufos.* The first relates to sale of goods. Section 53 (2) of the Sale of Goods Act 1893 provides that "The measure of damages for breach of warranty is the estimated loss directly and naturally resulting, in the ordinary course of events, from the breach of warranty." The subsection, clearly a statutory formulation of the first rule in *Hadley v. Baxendale,* is not, however, intended to oust the second rule, where appropriate: see section 54. Nevertheless, it vindicates the judge's approach to this case, always assuming that the facts are such as to make the application of the first rule appropriate.

Secondly, the breach does not have to be foreseen, or contemplated. In a breach of warranty case the point may be put in this way: it does not matter if the defect is latent. It may be unknown, even unknowable: see *Grant v. Australian Knitting Mills Ltd.* [1936] A.C. 85. The court has to assume, though it be contrary to the fact, that the parties had in mind the breach that has occurred. Thus, whenever a question of remoteness of damage arises in a contract case, its solution involves the court in making a hypothesis, which may, or may not, correspond with fact.

The court's task, therefore, is to decide what loss to the plaintiffs it is reasonable to suppose would have been in the contemplation of the parties as a serious possibility had they had in mind the breach when they made their contract.

...

[The judge] held that the assumption, or hypothesis, to be made is that the parties had in mind at the time of contract not a breach of warranty limited to the delivery of mouldy nuts but a warranty as to the fitness of the hopper for its purpose. The assumption is of the parties asking themselves not what is likely to happen if the nuts are mouldy but what is likely to happen to the pigs if the hopper is unfit for storing nuts suitable to be fed to them. ...

I would agree with *McGregor on Damages,* 13th ed. (1972), pp. 131-132 that

"... in contract as in tort, it should suffice that, if physical injury or damage is within the contemplation of the parties, recovery is not to be limited because the degree of physical injury or damage could not have been anticipated."

This is so, in my judgment, not because there is, or ought to be, a specific rule of law governing cases of physical injury but because it would be absurd to regulate damages in such cases upon the necessity of supposing the parties had a prophetic foresight as to the exact nature of the injury that does in fact arise. It is enough if upon the hypothesis predicated physical injury must have been a serious possibility. Though in loss of market or loss of profit cases the factual analysis will be very different from cases of physical injury, the same principles, in my judgment, apply. Given the situation of the parties at the time of contract, was the loss of profit, or market, a serious possibility, something that would have been in their minds had they contemplated breach?

It does not matter, in my judgment, if they thought that the chance of physical injury, loss of profit, loss of market, or other loss as the case may be, was slight, or that the odds were against it, provided they contemplated as a serious possibility the type of consequence, not necessarily the specific consequence, that ensued upon breach. Making the assumption as to breach that the judge did, no more than common sense was needed for them to appreciate that food affected by bad storage conditions might well cause illness in the pigs fed upon it.

As I read the judgment under appeal, this was how the judge, whose handling of the issues at trial was such that none save one survives for our consideration, reached this decision. In my judgment, he was right, upon the facts as found, to apply the first rule in *Hadley v. Baxendale,* or, if the case be one of breach of warranty, as I think it is, the rule in section 53 (2) of the Sale of Goods Act 1893 without inquiring as to whether, upon a juridical analysis, the rule is based upon a presumed contemplation. At the end of a long and complex dispute the judge allowed common sense to prevail. I would dismiss the appeal.

Orr LJ delivered a judgment concurring with Scarman LJ.

NOTES AND QUESTIONS

1.   By emphasising that it is the type of loss that must be reasonably contemplated as a serious possibility, the majority brought the contract remoteness test closer to that in tort. But it still differs significantly both as to the degree of likelihood required and the time at which one assesses the defendant's state of knowledge. It was, therefore, misleading of Scarman LJ to suggest that the 'necessary reconciliation' between the tests is to regard 'reasonably foreseeable' and 'reasonably contemplated' as semantically, and not substantially, different.

2.   Had the claimants brought their claim for loss of the pigs in the tort of negligence, and had they established negligence by the defendants on the facts, what would the test of remoteness have been? See below, 372, note 2.

3.   How does one reconcile the majority's emphasis on the type of loss with the decision in the *Victoria Laundry* case? That is, if illness to pigs and death of 254 pigs are the same type of loss, merely differing in degree, why are not ordinary and exceptional loss of profits the same type of loss?

4.   Lord Denning's division in remoteness tests, turning on whether the loss in question is loss of profit or physical damage, did not find favour with the majority and has not been supported in subsequent cases. It has therefore been unnecessary to clarify the exact nature of his division. Given his reasoning—and in particular that he treated the claim as one for physical damage despite a substantial sum being claimed for loss of profit—it is tolerably clear that he meant by 'loss of profit' pure loss of profit and not loss of profit directly consequent on physical damage.

Brown v KMR Services Ltd [1995] 4 All ER 598, Court of Appeal

The claimant was an underwriter at Lloyd's (a 'Name' at Lloyd's). He brought an action for breach of contract and the tort of negligence against the defendants, his members' agents, alleging that they had negligently failed to warn him of the risks of joining the high reward/high risk syndicates that he had joined. The defendants were held to have been negligent and one issue that then arose was whether the loss claimed was too remote. The defendants' argument was that the magnitude of the financial disasters that had struck, and the consequent scale of the claimant's underwriting loss, was too remote: no-one would have predicted such a run of major catastrophes as had occurred in the relevant years (1987–90). In affirming the trial judge's decision that the loss was not too remote, the Court of Appeal held that it was the type of loss—not the actual scale of loss suffered—that had to be reasonably contemplated/foreseen.

Stuart-Smith LJ:

Remoteness

The judge found that no one anticipated the size and frequency of the various disasters that occurred between 1987 and 1990 (see [1994] 4 All ER 385 at 390); and that it was most unlikely that any professional member of Lloyd's foresaw the magnitude of the financial disasters that struck in the middle to late 1980s (see [1994] 4 All ER 385 at 398). Basing himself on these findings and the evidence which supported them, Mr Simon [counsel for the defendants] submitted to the judge that the losses actually incurred were too remote to be recoverable in law. The judge rejected this submission. Relying on *H Parsons (Livestock) Ltd v Uttley Ingham & Co Ltd* [1978] 1 All ER 525, [1978] QB 791, he concluded that losses of the type that occurred were undoubtedly foreseeable and foreseen, even though their scale was not. That was sufficient.

Mr Simon submitted that the judge was in error. In cases of financial loss, as opposed to physical damage, he submitted that concentration on type or kind of loss was of little or no assistance. He relied upon the decision in the case of *Victoria Laundry (Windsor) Ltd v Newman Industries Ltd (Coulsdon & Co Ltd (third party))* [1949] 1 All ER 997, [1949] 2 KB 528. In that case the court was dealing with the same kind or type of loss, namely loss of profit due to delay in delivery. Ordinary loss of profit was recoverable; but because the defendants had no knowledge of a specially profitable contract, loss of profit on that contract was not. ...I accept that difficulty in practice may arise in categorisation of loss into types or kinds, especially where financial loss is involved. But I do not see any difficulty in holding that loss of ordinary business profits is different in kind from that flowing from a particular contract which gives rise to very high profits, the existence of which is unknown to the other contracting party who therefore does not accept the risk of such loss occurring. The law relating to remoteness of damage in contract is laid down in three cases, all of which deal with financial loss, namely *Hadley v Baxendale*, *Victoria Laundry* and *The Heron II, Koufos v C Czarnikow Ltd* [1967] 3 All ER 686, [1969] 1 AC 350. The effect of these decisions is, in my judgment, accurately summarised in *Chitty on Contracts* (27th edn, 1994) vol 1, para 26-023, p 1218:

> 'A type or kind of loss is not too remote a consequence of a breach of contract if, at the time of contracting (and on the assumption that the parties actually foresaw the breach in question), it was within their reasonable contemplation as a not unlikely result of that breach',

and para 26-024, pp 1219-1220:

'The reference to "the loss" in the formulations of the test for remoteness of damage is to be interpreted as the type or kind of loss in question. The "party who has suffered damage does not have to show that the contract-breaker ought to have contemplated, as being not unlikely, the precise detail of the damage or the precise manner of its happening. It is enough if he should have contemplated that damage of *that kind* is not unlikely." ... The application of the test for remoteness to a particular set of facts therefore depends largely on the judicial discretion to categorise losses into broad categories, without requiring any contemplation of the precise manner in which the loss was caused, or of the precise details of the loss.' (Authors' emphasis.)

The difficulty in Mr Simon's argument is clearly illustrated in my view by his inability to differentiate between those underwriting losses on [some] syndicates which are not too remote and those which he submitted were. ... I agree with the judge's succinct analysis of the losses in this case: the fact that the scale or amount of the losses was not foreseeable does not make them too remote. I would dismiss this ground of appeal.

Hobhouse LJ:

Remoteness

Reduced to its essentials [the defendants' argument] amounts to the following. The reasonable person in the position of the contracting parties would not have predicted that in the years 1988, 1989 and 1990 there would have been such a concatenation of major catastrophes as in fact occurred. The expectation and prediction of the reasonable man would have been that only one or two catastrophes would occur in any of those years. It follows that the reasonable man would not have foreseen losses on anything like the scale which was subsequently suffered. It is therefore said that the recoverable damages should be limited to such losses as would reasonably have been foreseen.

In support of this argument Mr Simon cited cases such as *Victoria Laundry (Windsor) Ltd v Newman Industries Ltd (Coulsdon & Co Ltd (third party))* [1949] 1 All ER 997, [1949] 2 KB 528. ...

This and similar cases relate to indirect or consequential losses. The primary head of recovery is the loss liable to result from the breach in the ordinary course. In the present case the potential direct consequence of the defendants' breach was, and must always have been foreseen to be, that Mr Brown would be a member of an excessive number of high risk syndicates with excessive allocations of premium to those syndicates. Accordingly, the direct and wholly foreseeable consequence would be that Mr Brown would be liable for the losses made by those syndicates to an excessive extent, whatever those losses might turn out to be. Having identified that the natural, direct and foreseeable consequence of inadequate or improper advice was that Mr Brown would incur a liability as a member of high risk syndicates, Mr Brown has established what he needs to show — that the damages he is seeking to recover are not too remote.

Gatehouse J rejected the defendants' argument (which was raised in both of the actions before him). He said ([1994] 4 All ER 385 at 398-399):

'It is most unlikely that any professional member of Lloyd's foresaw the magnitude of the financial disasters that struck in the middle-to-late 1980s. Certainly those who gave evidence before me were all agreed on this. But losses of the *type* that occurred were undoubtedly foreseeable and in fact foreseen, even though their scale was not. That is enough for the plaintiff (see eg *H Parsons (Livestock) Ltd v Uttley Ingham & Co Ltd* [1978] 1 All ER 525, [1978] QB 791). The plaintiff's losses were the natural and obvious result of his being a member of the "disaster" syndicates.' (My emphasis.)

In my judgment the judge was right. His conclusion is amply supported by authority besides that of the case he cited. In *Banque Bruxelles Lambert SA v Eagle Star Insurance Co Ltd* [1995] 2 All ER 769 at 841, [1995] 2 WLR 607 at 620 Sir Thomas Bingham MR delivering the judgment of the Court of Appeal said:

> 'The test is whether, at the date of the contract or tort, damage of the kind for which the plaintiff claims compensation was a reasonably foreseeable consequence of the breach of contract or tortious conduct of which the plaintiff complains. If the kind of damage was reasonably foreseeable it is immaterial that the extent of the damage was not.'

> ...

The submission of the defendants is not only wrong in law but also remarkable in its consequences. For example, if a reinsurer improperly declines to pay a claim under a reinsurance contract, is it to be said, when the reassured sues him for damages for failing to indemnify him in respect of the loss, that at the time of the making of the reinsurance contract the reasonable man would not have predicted a claim under the policy of the scale in fact made and therefore the damages payable should be limited to what the reasonable person would have predicted as likely to occur? The argument which concentrates upon the quantification as opposed to the character and causation of the plaintiff's loss is mistaken and wrong in law. It is also manifestly unjust. If it was the duty of the defendants to protect the plaintiff from losses of the kind which he subsequently suffers, how can it be just or appropriate to say that, because those losses are larger than either party anticipated, the plaintiff must bear those losses not the defendants?

Peter Gibson LJ concurred with Hobhouse LJ.

NOTES AND QUESTIONS

1. This decision approved and applied the majority's approach in *Parsons v Uttley Ingham* which emphasises that it is the type of loss, and not the actual loss, that needs to have been reasonably contemplated. How then did the judges reconcile the decision in *Brown* with that in *Victoria Laundry*?

2. It would appear that the contract remoteness test was applied not only to the claim for breach of contract but also to the claim in the tort of negligence. As a matter of policy this would seem correct. Lord Reid's rationale in *The Heron II* for there being a stricter test in contract than in tort—that the claimant has the opportunity to inform the other party of unusual risks—applies equally to a tort claim where the parties are in a contractual relationship. See A Burrows, *Remedies for Torts and Breach of Contract* (3rd edn, 2004) 92–4.

Jackson v Royal Bank of Scotland plc
[2005] UKHL 3, [2005] 1 WLR 377, House of Lords

The claimant firm, Samson, had as its principal customer a firm called Economy Bag, which sold dog biscuits. Samson bought dog biscuits from Thailand and sold them on to Economy Bag. Economy Bag paid Samson by letter of credit issued by the defendant bank. The price included what Samson had to pay to its Thailand supplier (Pet Products) plus Samson's mark-up. Economy Bag did not know what Samson's mark-up was. This arrangement continued for some two-and-a-half years. Then in breach of its contractual duty of confidence to Samson, the defendant bank on one occasion mistakenly sent the completion statement and other documents to Economy Bag rather than to Samson. This revealed to Economy Bag that Samson's mark-up was 19 per cent which was far higher than Economy Bag had thought. Angered by this, Economy Bag refused to enter into future contracts with Samson and instead dealt directly with the Thailand suppliers. This termination of their relationship was disastrous for Samson, which had to cease trading. Samson brought an action against the bank for breach of contract claiming damages for loss of profit. The trial judge, Judge Kershaw QC, held that, but for the breach of contract, there was a significant chance that Economy Bag would have continued trading with Samson for a further four years. He did not think that that loss was too remote and he therefore awarded damages for loss of profit for a period of four years, albeit on a reducing basis because of the uncertainties. The Court of Appeal overturned that on the basis that all loss of profit after one year was too remote. In restoring the decision of the trial judge, the House of Lords criticised the Court of Appeal's misunderstanding of *Hadley v Baxendale*.

Lord Hope of Craighead:

The issues relating to damages

25 The way in which the Court of Appeal dealt with the case suggests it misunderstood the effect of the rules that were identified in *Hadley v Baxendale* (1854) 9 Exch 341, 354. They are very familiar to every student of contract law. Most would claim to be able to recite them by heart. [*He set out the two rules in Alderson B's judgment and continued:*] The first rule, prefaced by the word "either", is the rule that applies in this case. It is the ordinary rule. Everyone is taken to know the usual course of things and consequently to know what loss is liable to result from a breach of the contract if things take their usual course. But the way the second rule is expressed, prefaced by the word "or", shows the principle that underlies both limbs. It refers to what was in the contemplation of the parties at the time they made their contract.

26 As Asquith LJ said in *Victoria Laundry (Windsor) Ltd v Newman Industries Ltd* [1949] 2 KB 528, 539 in cases of breach of contract the aggrieved party is only entitled to recover such part of the loss actually resulting as was at the time of the contract reasonably foreseeable as likely to result from the breach. In tort, the question whether loss was reasonably foreseeable is addressed to the time when the tort was committed. In contract, the question is addressed to the time when the parties made their contract. Where knowledge of special circumstances is relied on, the assumption is that the defendant undertook to bear any special loss which was referable to those special circumstances. It is assumed too that he had the opportunity to seek to limit his liability under the contract for ordinary losses in the event that he was in breach of it.

27 The bank's primary argument on damages was that the loss of the repeat business on which Samson based its claim was too remote. This was because it was not in the bank's reasonable contemplation that the disclosure of the profit that Samson was making would lead to the termination by Economy Bag of its trading relationship with Samson. Their relationship, it was said, was based on mutual trust and confidence. There was no reason for the bank to think that breach of its duty of confidence to Samson would result in any loss at all. The real reason for the loss of repeat business was Mr Taylor's [of Economy Bag] anger when he detected the amount of the mark-up. This was something that could not have been predicted.

28 The trial judge rejected that argument, and the Court of Appeal did so too for the reasons explained by Potter LJ [2002] CLC 1457, paras 25 and 26. ...

30 But at the end of para 31 and the beginning of para 32, in a passage where he identified the approach that he then took to this issue, Potter LJ said:

> "31 ... That principle however, properly regarded is a principle or method of *quantification*, and not a rule as to *remoteness*, of damage. It is thus subject to, and may be constrained by, the rules as to remoteness laid down in *Hadley v Baxendale*, so that, whatever the judge's view of the percentage chance that, but for the bank's breach, Samson would *in fact* have been Economy Bag's supplier in the respect of the transactions in the following years, the cut-off point for the bank's liability was the end of such period as was within the reasonable contemplation of the bank at the time of breach. [emphasis in the original]
>
> 32. As to that, the bank's knowledge of the background and details of Samson's trading relationship was limited to the period of time and the individual transactions conducted *prior to breach*." (Emphasis added.)

31 In para 33 Potter LJ said that it seemed to him that there was no sufficient basis on which the judge could or should have predicated his award covering a period anything like as long as four years. In para 34 he said that the judge could and should have approached the case on the broad basis that, while it could reasonably be contemplated that the established relationship of Samson and Economy Bag would have continued for a time, and thus that some award of damages for future business fell to be made, that time should in all the circumstances be limited to a period of one year from the date of the breach, all loss thereafter being regarded as too remote. ...

32 Miss Andrews [counsel for Samson] submitted that the Court of Appeal fell into error at this point. All that the claimant had to show was that at the time of the contract the contract-breaker should have contemplated that damage of the kind suffered would have occurred as a result of his breach. Once it had decided, correctly, that it was a natural and probable consequence of the bank's breach that Samson would suffer a loss of repeat business, there was no cut-off point. The bank's liability was open-ended, as it had not limited its liability by the contract to any particular period. The restriction which the Court of Appeal had imposed ex post facto on the bank's liability cut across the rules in *Hadley v Baxendale*,9 Exch 341 which allocated risk between the parties at the time of the contract when they were still in a position to make provision for it in their bargain if they wished to do so.

How is that loss to be quantified?

35 The first question is whether the Court of Appeal was wrong to limit the period for which damages were recoverable by reference to what was within the reasonable contemplation of the bank at the time of the breach. Potter LJ said [2000] CLC 1457, para 31, that, whatever the judge's view was of the percentage chance that Samson would in fact in the following years have been Economy Bag's supplier of dog chews, the bank's reasonable contemplation at the date of the breach introduced a cut-off point beyond which the bank was not liable. He said that this was the effect of the rule as to remoteness in *Hadley v Baxendale* 9 Exch 341.

36 In my opinion there are two errors in this approach to the assessment of damages. This first may appear to be the somewhat technical point, that it is the date of the making of the contract, not the date of the breach, that was identified as the relevant date in *Hadley v Baxendale*. I say that it may appear to be somewhat technical because in this case the date of the making of the contract and the date of the breach were only about two months apart. There is no evidence that the facts that were relevant to what the bank had in reasonable contemplation changed to any significant extent between 22 January 1993 when the letter of credit was issued and 15 March 1993 when the bank sent Pet Products' invoice to Economy Bag. But the error was an error of principle. The choice of dates is more important than the differences, if any, in those facts. The parties have the opportunity to limit their liability in damages when they are making their contract. They have the opportunity at that stage to draw attention to any special circumstances outside the ordinary course of things which they ought to have in contemplation when entering into the contract. If no cut-off point is provided by the contract, there is no arbitrary limit that can be set to the amount of the damages once the test of remoteness according to one or other of the rules in *Hadley v Baxendale* has been satisfied.

37 The second error flows from the first. The bank did not include any provision in the letter of credit limiting its liability for the loss of repeat business to any particular period. So the only limit on the period of its liability is that which the trial judge identified. This is when, on the facts, the question whether any loss has been sustained has become too speculative to permit the making of any award. ...

38 These errors lie at the heart of the Court of Appeal's decision to limit the bank's liability to a period of one year. For this reason I would hold that its decision cannot stand. I would allow the appeal and set aside its assessment of the amount to be awarded to the appellants as damages.

Lord Walker of Gestingthorpe delivered a concurring speech. **Lord Nicholls of Birkenhead, Lord Hoffmann** and **Lord Brown of Eaton-Under-Heywood** concurred.

NOTES AND QUESTIONS

1. By judicial standards, Lord Hope's criticism of Potter LJ's misunderstanding of remoteness in contract is scathing. Would you be able to recite the *Hadley v Baxendale* rules by heart?
2. Although it made no difference on the facts, this case stressed that the contract remoteness test looks at the defendant's knowledge at the date the contract is made and not at the date of breach. Echoing Lord Reid in *Heron II* Lord Hope also made clear why this should be so.

(b) Intervening Cause

Even though the defendant's breach of contract is a cause of the claimant's loss, the claimant will not recover damages for the loss where an intervening cause (whether a natural event or a third party's conduct or the claimant's conduct) is regarded as breaking the chain of causation between the defendant's breach of contract and the loss. In that situation, the causal potency of the breach of contract is nullified. However, no clear test, or set of principles, has emerged from the cases to determine whether the chain of causation has been broken or not and the language used by the courts has been unhelpfully vague. Two examples will suffice to illustrate the point.

Quinn v Burch Bros (Builders) Ltd [1966] 2 QB 370, Court of Appeal

The defendants, in breach of contract, failed to supply a step-ladder to the claimant, who was a sub-contracting plasterer. The claimant instead used an unfooted trestle which collapsed so that the claimant fell and injured his heel. The trial judge dismissed his claim for substantial damages, and this was upheld by the Court of Appeal because the breach did not cause the injury.

Sellers LJ: [T]his cannot be said to be an accident which was caused by the defendants' breach of contract. No doubt that circumstance was the occasion which brought about this conduct of the plaintiff but it in no way caused it.

Danckwerts LJ: I can express my judgment in four propositions which I believe to be established by the facts and the law relating to the matter: (1) Assuming that the defendants were in breach of contract by not providing the equipment reasonably necessary for the work, there was no obligation on the plaintiff to do the work without suitable equipment. (2) The plaintiff voluntarily and without the defendants' knowledge chose to use the trestle, which was unsuitable and subject to the risk of slipping. (3) The cause of the plaintiff's accident was the choice by the plaintiff to use the unsuitable equipment. (4) The failure of the defendants to provide the equipment required may have been the occasion of the accident but was not the cause of the accident.

Salmon LJ: I am quite satisfied that the breach of contract cannot, in the circumstances of this case, be said to have caused the plaintiff's injury.

NOTES AND QUESTIONS

1. The failure to supply the ladder in breach of contract was clearly a 'but for' cause of the injury. What, then, did the judges mean when they said that the breach did not cause, or was not the cause of, the injury?
2. The claimant was awarded no substantial damages for his injury. Would a preferable solution have been to have awarded him some damages albeit reduced for his contributory negligence? Was that an option open to the judges (see below, 380–387)?

Galoo Ltd v Bright Grahame Murray [1994] 1 WLR 1360, Court of Appeal

A claim was brought for trading losses by the claimant companies (Galoo and Gamine) against the defendant auditors. The claimants argued that, had the auditors drawn up their accounts using reasonable care, they would have revealed that the claimants were insolvent. The claimants would thereupon have stopped trading. The auditors were therefore, so it was argued, liable in contract and tort for the companies' continued trading loss after that time. The trial judge struck out that claim as disclosing no reasonable cause of action. This striking out was upheld by the Court of Appeal because the auditors' breach had not caused the trading losses.

Glidewell LJ: The second head of damage claimed by Galoo and Gamine is that they incurred trading losses as a result of relying on the negligent auditing by B.G.M. and thus continued to trade when they would otherwise not have done. The claim under this head is for damages for trading losses of approximately £25m. incurred in and between 1986 and 1990 and for making a dividend payment of £500,000 in 1988...

[The claim] can be expressed as follows: (a) if they had not acted in breach of their duty in contract or tort, B.G.M. would have detected the fraud during their audit of the 1985 accounts; (b) in that case, Galoo and Gamine would have been put into liquidation in mid-1986 and thus ceased to trade at that date; (c) if the companies had ceased to trade, they would neither have incurred any further trading losses nor paid the dividend in 1988; (d) therefore the trading losses and the loss caused by the dividend payment were caused by the breach of duty by B.G.M.

This argument depends upon the nature of the causation necessary to establish liability for breach of duty, whether in contract or in tort. There is no doubt that this is one of the most difficult areas of the law. Both counsel are agreed that, at least in the context of this case, the principles applicable to liability in either contract or tort are the same.

Mr. Hunter, for the defendants, submits that the plaintiff's case depends upon the adoption of the "but for" test of causation which, at least in contract, is not the proper test in English law. This is causation of the kind which has sometimes been referred to as a "causa sine qua non". In *Chitty on Contracts*, 26th ed. (1989), vol. 2, pp. 1128-1129, para. 1785, the editors say:

> "The important issue in remoteness of damage in the law of contract is whether a particular loss was within the reasonable contemplation of the parties, but causation must also be proved: there must be a causal connection between the defendant's breach of contract and the plaintiff's loss. The courts have avoided laying down any formal tests for causation: they have relied on common sense to guide decisions as to whether a breach of contract is a sufficiently substantial cause of the plaintiff's loss. (It need not be the sole cause)."

For these propositions the editors quote three authorities, including the decision of the House of Lords in *Monarch Steamship Co. Ltd. v. Karlshamns Oljefabriker (A/B)* [1949] A.C. 196 and *Quinn v. Burch Bros. (Builders) Ltd.* [1966] 2 Q.B. 370.

In the *Monarch Steamship* case [1949] A.C. 196, the defendants' ship was chartered to carry a cargo from Manchuria to Sweden. The ship should have reached Sweden in July 1939 but the boilers were defective, which resulted in the defendants breaking their contractual duty to provide a seaworthy ship. She was delayed and did not leave Port Said, at the north end of the Suez canal, until 24 September 1939. By that date the Second World War had broken out. The British Admiralty prohibited the ship from proceeding to Sweden and ordered her to proceed to and discharge at Glasgow. The cargo was eventually transshipped and delivered to Sweden at extra cost. The purchasers of the cargo sued the ship owners for damages. The ship owners by their defence claimed that the cause of the additional expense was the order from the Admiralty, not their breach of contract in failing to provide a seaworthy ship. The House of Lords rejected this argument, and held that the damages were recoverable.

However, in the course of the speeches in the House of Lords, their Lordships considered what test to apply in order to decide whether the defendants' breach of contract was causative of the plaintiffs' loss. In particular Lord Porter said, at p. 212, that it had to be determined whether the breach of contract was "the effective cause." Lord Wright said, at pp. 227-228:

> "There is, however, in this case a contention of a more general nature, which is that the delay which resulted from the defective boilers did not in any legal sense cause the diversion of the vessel. It is said that the relation of cause and effect cannot be postulated here between the unseaworthiness and the restraints of princes or the delay. As to such a contention it may be said at once that all the judges below have rejected it. . . . If a man is too late to catch a train, because his car broke down on the way to the station, we should all naturally say, that he lost the train because of the car breaking down. We recognise that the two things or events are causally connected. Causation is a mental concept, generally based on inference or induction from uniformity of sequence as between two events that there is a causal connection between them. . . . The common law however is not concerned with philosophic speculation, but is only concerned with ordinary everyday life and thoughts and expressions, and would not hesitate to think and say that, because it caused the delay, unseaworthiness caused the Admiralty order diverting the vessel. I think the common law would be right in picking out unseaworthiness from the whole complex of circumstances as the dominant cause."

[*Glidewell LJ then considered* Quinn v Burch *and two Australian cases,* Alexander v Cambridge Credit Corp *(1987) 9 NSWLR 310 and* March v E & MH Stramare Pty Ltd *(1991) 171 CLR 506 and continued:*]

The passages which I have cited from the speeches in *Monarch Steamship Co. Ltd. v. Karlshamns Oljefabriker A/B* [1949] A.C. 196 make it clear that if a breach of contract by a defendant is to be held to entitle the plaintiff to claim damages, it must first be held to have been an "effective" or "dominant" cause of his loss. The test in *Quinn v. Burch Bros. (Builders) Ltd.* [1966] 2 Q.B. 370 that it is necessary to distinguish between a breach of contract which causes a loss to the plaintiff and one which merely gives the opportunity for him to sustain the loss, is helpful but still leaves the question to be answered "How does the court decide whether the breach of duty was the cause of the loss or merely the occasion for the loss?"

The answer in my judgment is supplied by the Australian decisions to which I have referred, which I hold to represent the law of England as well as of Australia, in relation to a breach of a duty imposed on a defendant whether by contract or in tort in a situation analogous to breach of contract. The answer in the end is "By the application of the court's common sense."

Doing my best to apply this test, I have no doubt that the deputy judge arrived at a correct conclusion on this issue. The breach of duty by the defendants gave the opportunity to Galoo and Gamine to incur and to continue to incur trading losses; it did not cause those trading losses, in the sense in which the word "cause" is used in law.

Evans and **Waite LJJ** concurred.

QUESTIONS

Behind the opaque reliance on unarticulated 'common sense', what do you think explains the court's decision that the chain of causation from the auditor's breach of contract to the companies' trading losses was broken? Was it because the claimants' own poor decisions were primarily responsible? Or was the court making a specific policy decision to limit an auditor's liability?

(c) The Duty to Mitigate and Mitigation

British Westinghouse Electric v Underground Electric Railways Co of London Ltd [1912] AC 673, House of Lords

The claimants in breach of contract supplied to the defendants turbines which were defective. The defendants subsequently replaced them with other turbines. The replacement turbines turned out to be more efficient and profitable than the old turbines would have been even if non-defective. In the claimants' action for sums owing under the contract, the defendants counterclaimed for damages for breach of contract. The question was whether the greater efficiency of the replacement turbines should be taken into account in reducing the defendants' damages for the claimants' breach of contract. In allowing the claimants' appeal, the House of Lords held that the greater efficiency of the replacements should be taken into account as mitigating the defendants' loss.

Viscount Haldane LC: I think that there are certain broad principles which are quite well settled. The first is that, as far as possible, he who has proved a breach of a bargain to supply what he contracted to get is to be placed, as far as money can do it, in as good a situation as if the contract had been performed.

The fundamental basis is thus compensation for pecuniary loss naturally flowing from the breach; but this first principle is qualified by a second, which imposes on a plaintiff the duty of taking all reasonable steps to mitigate the loss consequent on the breach, and debars him from claiming any part of the damage which is due to his neglect to take such steps. In the words of James L.J. in *Dunkirk Colliery Co. v. Lever* (1878) 9 Ch. D. at p 25, "The person who has broken the contract is not to be exposed to additional cost by reason of the plaintiffs not doing what they ought to have done as reasonable men, and the plaintiffs not being under any obligation to do anything otherwise than in the ordinary course of business."

As James L.J. indicates, this second principle does not impose on the plaintiff an obligation to take any step which a reasonable and prudent man would not ordinarily take in the course of his business. But when in the course of his business he has taken action arising out of the transaction, which action has diminished his loss, the effect in actual diminution of the loss he has suffered may be taken into account even though there was no duty on him to act.

...

Recent illustrations of the way in which this principle has been applied, and the facts have been allowed to speak for themselves, are to be found in the decisions of the Judicial Committee of the Privy Council in *Erie County Natural Gas and Fuel Co. v. Carroll* [1911] A.C. 105 and *Wertheim v. Chicoutimi Pulp Co.* [1911] A.C. 301. The subsequent transaction, if to be taken into account, must be one arising out of the consequences of the breach and in the ordinary course of business. This distinguishes such cases from a quite different class illustrated by *Bradburn v. Great Western Ry. Co.* L. R. 10 Ex. 1, where it was held that, in an action for injuries caused by the defendants' negligence, a sum received by the plaintiff on a policy for insurance against accident could not be taken into account in reduction of damages. The reason of the decision was that it was not the accident, but a contract wholly independent of the relation between the plaintiff and the defendant, which gave the plaintiff his advantage.

...

I think the principle which applies here is that which makes it right for the jury or arbitrator to look at what actually happened, and to balance loss and gain. The transaction was not res inter alios acta, but one in which the person whose contract was broken took a reasonable and prudent course quite naturally arising out of the circumstances in which he was placed by the breach. Apart from the breach of contract, the lapse of time had rendered the appellants' machines obsolete, and men of business would be doing the only thing they could properly do in replacing them with new and up-to-date machines.

Lords Ashbourne, Macnaghten and **Atkinson** concurred.

NOTES AND QUESTIONS

1. This decision illustrates that the courts in assessing compensatory damages will normally deduct benefits that have accrued to the claimant as a result of the breach. Put another way, losses that have been actually mitigated (ie avoided) will not be compensated. To do otherwise would overcompensate the claimant. But not all such benefits are deducted. For example, Viscount Haldane LC referred to the non-deduction of the proceeds of a personal accident insurance in a claim for personal injuries. How does one decide whether benefits accruing as a result of the breach should, or should not, be deducted?

2. Viscount Haldane LC's speech also makes clear that, apart from taking account of actual mitigation of losses, there is a 'duty to mitigate' on claimants. Although the language of 'duty' may be thought misleading (because breach of a duty to mitigate is not a civil wrong triggering an award of damages) what is meant is that losses will not be compensated if they should

reasonably have been avoided. Whether a loss should reasonably have been avoided depends on the particular facts in question, but certain principles have emerged from past cases. For example, the claimant need not take action which will put its commercial reputation at risk (*James Finlay & Co Ltd v Kwik Hoo Tong* [1929] 1 KB 400, CA); the claimant need not take steps which would involve it in complicated litigation (*Pilkington v Wood* [1953] 1 Ch 770); it will generally be unreasonable for the claimant to turn down an offer of alternative performance of a contract of sale, if acceptance would reduce its loss (*Payzu Ltd v Saunders* [1919] 2 KB 581, CA). The burden of proof in relation to the duty to mitigate is on the defendant and it is a heavy one because the courts tend to treat unsympathetically arguments from those who created the predicament that the claimant could have reasonably taken steps, or steps different from those it did take, to avoid the loss (see, eg, *Banco de Portugal v Waterlow & Sons Ltd* [1932] AC 452, HL).

3. **M Bridge, 'Mitigation of Damages in Contract and the Meaning of Avoidable Loss' (1989) 105 *LQR* 398** explores the policies underlying the principle of mitigation and criticises the decisions, such as *Payzu Ltd v Saunders* (see above), in which it was held that the claimant had failed in its duty to mitigate in turning down an offer of alternative performance by the defendant seller of goods.

(d) Contributory Negligence

Law Reform (Contributory Negligence) Act 1945 sections 1(1) and 4

1 Apportionment of liability in case of contributory negligence
(1) Where any person suffers damage as the result partly of his own fault and partly of the fault of any other person or persons, a claim in respect of that damage shall not be defeated by reason of the fault of the person suffering the damage, but the damages recoverable in respect thereof shall be reduced to such extent as the court thinks just and equitable having regard to the claimant's share in the responsibility for the damage…

4 Interpretation
'fault' means negligence, breach of statutory duty or other act or omission which gives rise to liability in tort or would, apart from this Act, give rise to the defence of contributory negligence.

(i) Overview of sections 1(1) and 4 of the 1945 Act

Sections 1(1) and 4 are the basis of the law on contributory negligence in both tort and contract. If contributory negligence applies, it operates to reduce the claimant's damages to the extent that the court considers it just 'having regard to the claimant's share in the responsibility for the damage'. In deciding on the appropriate reduction the courts look at the comparative blameworthiness and causal potency of the parties' conduct. However, the major issue in respect of breach of contract is whether contributory negligence can apply at all to reduce a claimant's damages and, if so, when. One might have thought that, as the meaning of 'fault' in section 4 does not mention breach of contract, contributory negligence is applicable to tort but never to breach of contract. That is not the interpretation that has been taken in the cases which, as we shall see, have held that contributory negligence can apply to the breach of a contractual duty of care where there is concurrent liability in the tort of negligence.

(ii) Cases on the applicability of the 1945 Act to contract

Forsikringsaktieselskapet Vesta v Butcher
[1988] 3 WLR 565, Court of Appeal

The claimants were insurers who had given insurance to the owners of a fish farm in Norway in respect of lost fish. The claimants asked their brokers, who were the defendants, to sort out for them reinsurance of that underlying insurance. They specifically told them in a telephone call that they did not want one of the terms in the underlying insurance (requiring a 24-hour watch over the fish) to be relevant to the reinsurance contract. In breach of their contractual (and tortious) duty of care to the claimants, the defendants failed to delete that term in the offer of reinsurance. Ultimately it was held by the Court of Appeal, and upheld by the House of Lords [1989] AC 852, that the reinsurers were liable to pay the claimants for what they had had to pay out in respect of a loss of fish irrespective of the '24-hour watch' term. The defendants' breach of contract did not therefore cause the claimants any loss. But if that term had been crucial the claimants would have been entitled to substantial damages against the defendants for breach of contract. It was in relation to that entitlement that contributory negligence was discussed, albeit as *obiter dicta*, by the Court of Appeal (there was no examination of the point by the House of Lords). The defendants argued that the claimants were contributorily negligent in relying on just the one telephone call to bring about the deletion of an important contract term, especially as the claimants had asked for confirmation that the deletion was acceptable to the reinsurers and the defendants had never given that confirmation. The Court of Appeal accepted that argument and concluded that, had the breach of contract caused loss, contributory negligence would have here applied so that, as Hobhouse J had held, the damages would have been reduced by 75 per cent.

O'Connor LJ: The important issue of law is whether on the facts of this case there is power to apportion under the Law Reform (Contributory Negligence) Act 1945 and thus reduce the damages recoverable by Vesta.

I start by pointing out that Vesta pleaded its claim against the brokers in contract and tort. This is but a recognition of what I regard as a clearly established principle that where under the general law a person owes a duty to another to exercise reasonable care and skill in some activity, a breach of that duty gives rise to a claim in tort notwithstanding the fact that the activity is the subject matter of a contract between them. In such a case the breach of duty will also be a breach of contract. The classic example of this situation is the relationship between doctor and patient.

Since the decision of the House of Lords in *Hedley Byrne & Co. Ltd. v. Heller & Partners Ltd.* [1964] A.C. 465 the relationship between the brokers and Vesta is another example. Mr. Longmore for Vesta accepts that this is so but he submits that if a plaintiff makes his claim in contract contributory negligence cannot be relied on by the defendant, whereas it is available if the claim is made in tort. If this contention is sound then the law has been sadly adrift for a very long time for it would mean that in employers' liability cases an injured employee could debar the employer from relying on any contributory negligence by framing his action in contract. ...The judge dealt with this submission and said [1986] 2 All E.R. 488, 508:

> "The question whether the 1945 Act applies to claims brought in contract can arise in a number of classes of case. Three categories can conveniently be identified. (1) Where the defendant's liability arises from some contractual provision which does not depend on negligence on the part of the defendant. (2) Where the defendant's liability arises from a contractual obligation which is expressed in terms of taking care (or its equivalent) but does not correspond to a common law duty to take care which would exist in the given case independently of contract. (3) Where the defendant's liability in contract is the same as his liability in the tort of negligence independently of the existence of any contract."

The present case fell fairly and squarely within the judge's category (3). He said, at p. 509:

> "The category (3) question has arisen in very many different types of case and the answer is treated as so obvious that it passes without any comment. It is commonplace that actions are brought by persons who have suffered personal injuries as the result of the negligence of the person sued and that there is a contractual as well as tortious relationship. In such cases apportionment of blame is invariably adopted by the court notwithstanding that the plaintiff could sue in contract as well as in tort. The example normally cited in the present context is the decision of the Court of Appeal in *Sayers v. Harlow Urban District Council* [1958] 2 All E.R. 342; [1958] 1 W.L.R. 623, which concerned a contractual visitor to premises (a lady who had paid to use a public lavatory). The Court of Appeal said it did not matter whether the cause of action was put in tort or in contract and proceeded to apportion blame awarding her three-quarters of her damages. This was a decision on a category (3) case. The power to make an apportionment was part of the ratio decidendi and is binding on me. There are innumerable similar decisions to the same effect which could be cited, very many by appellate courts."

...

I will return to *Sayers v. Harlow Urban District Council* but first I will consider the true construction of the Act of 1945. [*He set out sections 1(1) and 4 and continued:*] When considering the "fault of any other person or persons" it is the first part of the definition in section 4 that applies: "negligence, breach of statutory duty or other act or omission which gives rise to a liability in tort". In my judgment the phrase "which gives rise to a liability in tort" defines the kind or type of negligence etc. which is to rank as "fault" when considering "the fault of any other person or persons".

When considering the fault of the person who suffers damage both parts of the definition apply. The second part is necessary because, whereas the defendant cannot be at fault unless in breach of duty owed to the plaintiff, the plaintiff's contributory negligence may or may not involve a breach of duty owed to the defendant. Thus the drivers of two motor cars which collide at crossroads because both failed to keep a good look out are both within the first part of the definition, regardless of which is plaintiff and which defendant. In contrast, the injured front seat passenger not wearing a seat belt is at fault only within the second part of the definition. ...

I appreciate that, when considering the fault of the plaintiff, if the fault is within the first part of the definition it will also be within the second part.

...

In my judgment *Sayers v. Harlow Urban District Council* is a category (3) case and the decision of the Court of Appeal that there is power to apportion was not only right but is binding on us just as the judge held it was binding on him.

...

I am satisfied that the judge came to the right conclusion on this topic and in respect of it I would dismiss Vesta's appeal.

Neill LJ and **Sir Roger Ormrod** delivered concurring judgments.

NOTES AND QUESTIONS

1. The tripartite classification of cases, devised by Hobhouse J and here affirmed by the Court of Appeal, has become the standard way of analysing the law in relation to contributory negligence in contract. The Court of Appeal further accepted here (albeit that all the discussion of contributory negligence was obiter dicta) that contributory negligence applies in a category three case. For a subsequent *decision* to that effect, see *UCB Bank plc v Hepherd Winstanley & Pugh* [1999] Lloyd's Rep PN 963, CA.
2. Whether a contract imposes a strict obligation or one to use reasonable care depends on its construction and on implied terms. Most contractual obligations are strict but some (eg, some obligations undertaken by a professional in relation to services for a client) impose merely an obligation to use reasonable care. For a helpful discussion, see Treitel, *The Law of Contract* (11th edn, 2003) 838–41. See also above, 223–225.
3. Since the authoritative acceptance in *Henderson v Merrett Syndicates* [1995] 2 AC 145, HL, that there can be concurrent liability in contract and tort, it will be rare for a case to fall within category two rather than category three. For such a rare category two case—in which contributory negligence was therefore held inapplicable—see *Raflatec Ltd v Eade* [1999] 1 Lloyd's Rep 506.

Barclays Bank Plc v Fairclough Building Ltd
[1995] QB 214, Court of Appeal

The defendant, in breach of contract, had failed to take proper precautions in cleaning the roofs of the claimant bank's storage warehouse. The roofs were made of asbestos cement sheeting. As a result of the way in which the work was done, the warehouse was contaminated with asbestos fibres and dust which necessitated remedial work of £4 million. The defendant alleged that the claimant bank was partly responsible, through its property division, for proper precautions not having been taken and that therefore there should be a reduction for contributory negligence. That argument succeeded before the trial judge who reduced damages by 40 per cent for contributory negligence. In allowing an appeal by the claimant, it was held that contributory negligence could not here be applied so as to reduce damages.

Beldam LJ: It is generally agreed that the first part of the definition [of fault in section 4 of the 1945 Act] relates to the defendant's fault and the second part to the plaintiff's but debate has focused on the words "or other act or omission which gives rise to a liability in tort" in the first part and "other act or omission which . . . would, apart from this Act, give rise to the defence of contributory negligence" in the second part. It has been argued that, merely because the plaintiff frames his cause of action as a breach of contract, if the acts or omissions on which he relies could equally well give rise to a liability in tort the defendant is entitled to rely on the defence of contributory negligence. Examples frequently cited are claims for damages against an employer or by a passenger against a railway or bus company where the plaintiff may frame his action either in tort or in contract and the duty relied on in either case is a duty to take reasonable care for the plaintiff's safety. Contributory negligence has been a defence in such actions for many years. So it is argued that, in all cases in which the contractual duty broken by a defendant is the same as and is coextensive with a similar duty in tort, the defendant may now rely on the defence. An opposing view based on the second part of the definition is that, if the plaintiff framed his action for breach of contract, contributory negligence at common law was never regarded as a defence to his claim and so cannot be relied on under the Act of 1945.

Under the first part of the definition, if the plaintiff claims damages for breach of a contractual term which does not correspond with a duty in tort to take reasonable care, the defendant's acts or omissions would not give rise to a liability in tort and accordingly no question of contributory negligence could arise.

These arguments have led courts to classify contractual duties under three headings: (i) where a party's liability arises from breach of a contractual provision which does not depend on a failure to take reasonable care; (ii) where the liability arises from an express contractual obligation to take care which does not correspond to any duty which would exist independently of the contract; (iii) where the liability for breach of contract is the same as, and coextensive with, a liability in tort independently of the existence of a contract. This analysis was adopted by Hobhouse J. in *Forsikringsaktieselskapet Vesta v. Butcher* [1986] 2 All E.R. 488 and by the Court of Appeal in the same case [1989] A.C. 852, 860, 862, 866-867. The judgments in the Court of Appeal in that case assert that in category (iii) cases the Court of Appeal is bound by the decision in *Sayers v. Harlow Urban District Council* [1958] 1 W.L.R. 623 to admit the availability of the defence.

Since I do not regard the case before the court as being in that category, I am content to accept that decision. To regard the definition of fault in section 4 as extending to cases such as employer's liability places no great strain on the construction of the words used. In 1945 actions brought by an employee whether framed in contract or tort were usually regarded as actions in negligence and the defence of contributory negligence was by no means uncommon.

On the other hand, in category (i) cases there is no decision in which contributory negligence has been held to be a partial defence. There are powerful dicta to the effect that it cannot be: see the judgment of the court in *Tennant Radiant Heat Ltd. v. Warrington Development Corporation* [1988] 1 E.G.L.R. 41, in *Bank of Nova Scotia v. Hellenic Mutual War Risks Association (Bermuda) Ltd.* [1990] 1 Q.B. 818, 904, and the observations of Nolan L.J. in *Schering Agrochemicals Ltd. v. Resibel N.V. S.A.*(unreported), 26 November 1992; Court of Appeal (Civil Division) Transcript No. 1298 of 1992, noted in (1993) 109 L.Q.R. 175, 177.

. . .

[I]n the present case the defendant was in breach of two conditions which required strict performance and did not depend on a mere failure to take reasonable care. Nevertheless it was argued by Mr. Butcher in support of the respondent's notice that the defendant could have been held liable in tort for the same acts or omissions. By creating the asbestos dust it was guilty of nuisance. Further the settling of the dust on the storage racks and floors of the plaintiff's building amounted to trespass. I would reject these submissions.

On the other hand, Mr. Elliott addressed arguments to the court that the defendant would not have been found liable to the plaintiff in negligence, for the only damage proved was economic loss. These arguments amply justified the fears expressed by the Law Commission in its 1993 report (Law Com. No. 219) that actions for breach of a strict contractual obligation would become unduly complex if contributory negligence were admitted as a partial defence by introducing an element of uncertainty into many straightforward commercial disputes and increasing the issues to be determined.

In my judgment therefore in the present state of the law contributory negligence is not a defence to a claim for damages founded on breach of a strict contractual obligation. I do not believe the wording of the Law Reform (Contributory Negligence) Act 1945 can reasonably sustain an argument to the contrary. Even if it did, in the present case the nature of the contract and the obligation undertaken by the skilled contractor did not impose on the plaintiff any duty in its own interest to prevent the defendant from committing the breaches of contract. To hold otherwise would, I consider, be equivalent to implying into the contract an obligation on the part of the plaintiff inconsistent with the express terms agreed by the parties. The contract clearly laid down the extent of the obligations of the plaintiff as architect and of the defendant. It was the defendant who was to provide appropriate supervision on site, not the architect.

Simon Brown LJ: The central issue raised by this appeal is clearly one of some importance: when does section 1(1) of the Law Reform (Contributory Negligence) Act 1945 apply to actions in contract? Although I agree entirely with the judgment of Beldam L.J., I wish, in deference to the skilful arguments presented on both sides, to indicate something of my own approach.

...

The argument by which Mr. Butcher seeks to uphold the judge's finding that the plaintiff here was 40 per cent. contributorily negligent proceeded, as I understand it, essentially as follows. (i) There is no challenge (save only as to the sufficiency of the defendant's pleading) to the judge's finding that the damage suffered by the plaintiff was the result partly of its own fault. (ii) Accepting, as the judge found, that the defendant's liability for that damage arose from breaches of one or more strict contractual terms, i.e. provisions which did not depend on negligence on the defendant's part, and so fall into category 1 of the three categories identified by Hobhouse J. in *Forsikringsaktieselskapet Vesta v. Butcher* [1986] 2 All E.R. 488, 508, nevertheless the defendant was entitled to the benefit of apportionment under section 1(1) provided only and always that it established that the damage resulted not only from its contractual breach but also from some "fault," i.e. tortious liability, on its part. (iii) Such tortious "fault" here consisted in (a) its own breach of a duty of care at common law, (b) its own nuisance, (c) its own trespass.

Although Mr. Butcher's argument is clearly vulnerable at all three stages ... I prefer to focus on stage (ii) because it is there that I believe as a matter of principle the argument should fail.

Why should it fail? Not, let me acknowledge, for any failure to bring the defendant's case within the language of section 1(1). I for my part would accept that the defendant here – assuming it could make good stage (iii) of its argument – would thereby establish that the relevant damage was the result equally and concurrently of its tortious fault as of its breaches of contract.

...

Let it therefore be assumed, as Mr. Butcher submitted, that the defendant was in breach of an exactly parallel obligation in tort coterminous with its duty in contract to avoid the damage that in the result occurred; I would nevertheless reject its claim to be entitled to apportionment. I would, however, do so by reference rather to the proper construction of the contract than of the statute itself.

I for my part would accept Hobhouse J.'s view expressed in *Forsikringsaktieselskapet Vesta v. Butcher* [1986] 2 All E.R. 488, 509-510, that apportionment of blame and liability is open to the court in any ordinary category (iii) case, unless the parties by their contract have varied that position, because, as he explained:

"there is independently of contract a status or common law relationship which exists between the parties and which can then give rise to tortious liabilities which fall to be adjusted in accordance with the Act of 1945."

In short, the contract in such cases really adds nothing to the common law position...

But when, as in a category (i) case, the contractual liability is by no means immaterial, when rather it is a strict liability arising independently of any negligence on the defendant's part, then there seem to me compelling reasons why the contract, even assuming it is silent as to apportionment, should be construed as excluding the operation of the Act of 1945. The very imposition of a strict liability on the defendant is to my mind inconsistent with an apportionment of the loss. And not least because of the absurdities that the contrary approach carries in its wake. Assume a defendant, clearly liable under a strict contractual duty. Is his position to be improved by demonstrating that besides breaching that duty he was in addition negligent? Take this very case. Is this contract really to be construed so that the defendant is advantaged by an assertion of its own liability in nuisance or trespass as well as in contract? Are we to have trials at which the defendant calls an expert to implicate him in tortious liability, whilst the plaintiff's expert seeks paradoxically to exonerate him? The answer to all these questions is surely "No." Whatever arguments exist for apportionment in other categories of case – and these are persuasively deployed in the 1993 Law Commission Report (Law Com. No. 219) – to my mind there are none in the present type of case and I for my part would construe the contract accordingly.

Nourse LJ: I am in complete agreement with the judgment of Beldam L.J.

It ought to be a cause of general concern that the law should have got into such a state that a contractor who was in breach of two of the main obligations expressly undertaken by him in a standard form building contract was able to persuade the judge in the court below that the building owner's damages should be reduced by 40 per cent. because of its own negligence in not preventing the contractor from committing the breaches. In circumstances such as these release, waiver, forbearance or the like are the only defences available to a party to a contract who wishes to assert that the other party's right to recover damages for its breach has been lost or diminished. It ought to have been perfectly obvious that the Law Reform (Contributory Negligence) Act 1945 was never intended to obtrude the defence of contributory negligence into an area of the law where it has no business to be.

NOTES AND QUESTIONS

1. Do you find convincing the judges' reasons for rejecting contributory negligence in a category one case? Can the approach here be reconciled with the acceptance that contributory negligence applies to torts of strict liability? If the claimant's unreasonable conduct can sometimes result in its recovering no damages, through the principles of intervening cause or the duty to mitigate, would it not be sensible for there to be a mid-position where its negligence results in a mere reduction of damages? Consider, for example, whether contributory negligence would have been a better way of dealing with *Quinn v Burch* (above, 375)?

2. The judges referred to the Law Commission's project on contributory negligence in contract (undertaken when Beldam LJ was Chairman of the Law Commission). In its Report No 219, *Contributory Negligence as a Defence in Contract* (1993) it recommended the minor reform (so minor that there is no prospect of it being implemented) that contributory negligence should be extended to category two. Why did it reject applying contributory negligence to category one cases?

3. Prior to its Report, in its Working Paper No 114, paragraphs 2.9, 5.2, the Law Commission gave the following example to consider. 'A customer, P, buys an iron from retailer, D. When taking it out of the package, he notices that the heat dial has fallen off and that it is defective in several other ways. Nevertheless he uses it and ruins a shirt. Assuming no negligence on D's part, P sues D for breach of its strict contractual obligation that the iron will be of

[satisfactory] quality and reasonably fit for its purpose.' At that stage in its thinking (prior to backtracking in its Report) the Law Commission provisionally recommended that contributory negligence should be extended to all three categories and argued that the law would be unnecessarily inflexible in dictating that P would recover either in full for the ruined shirt or not at all.

(e) Mental Distress

Addis v Gramophone Co Ltd [1909] AC 488, House of Lords

The claimant was employed as a manager by the defendants at a salary of £15 per week plus commission. He could be dismissed by being given six months' notice. The defendants gave him the requisite six months' notice but, at the same time, appointed his replacement and took steps to prevent the claimant acting as manager. He therefore left after three months. In his action for wrongful dismissal, the jury awarded £600 damages plus £340 in respect of lost commission. The House of Lords held that the claimant was entitled to his lost salary during the six months (which was less than the £600) plus £340 lost commission but was not entitled to damages for, inter alia, mental distress.

Lord Loreburn LC: To my mind it signifies nothing in the present case whether the claim is to be treated as for wrongful dismissal or not. In any case there was a breach of contract in not allowing the plaintiff to discharge his duties as manager, and the damages are exactly the same in either view. They are, in my opinion, the salary to which the plaintiff was entitled for the six months between October, 1905, and April, 1906, together with the commission which the jury think he would have earned had he been allowed to manage the business himself. I cannot agree that the manner of dismissal affects these damages. Such considerations have never been allowed to influence damages in this kind of case. ...

If there be a dismissal without notice the employer must pay an indemnity; but that indemnity cannot include compensation either for the injured feelings of the servant, or for the loss he may sustain from the fact that his having been dismissed of itself makes it more difficult for him to obtain fresh employment.

Lord Atkinson: The damages plaintiff sustained by this illegal dismissal were (1.) the wages for the period of six months during which his formal notice would have been current; (2.) the profits or commission which would, in all reasonable probability, have been earned by him during the six months had he continued in the employment; and possibly (3.) damages in respect of the time which might reasonably elapse before he could obtain other employment. He has been awarded a sum possibly of some hundreds of pounds, not in respect of any of these heads of damage, but in respect of the harsh and humiliating way in which he was dismissed, including, presumably, the pain he experienced by reason, it is alleged, of the imputation upon him conveyed by the manner of his dismissal. This is the only circumstance which makes the case of general importance, and this is the only point I think it necessary to deal with.

...

In many...cases of breach of contract there may be circumstances of malice, fraud, defamation, or violence, which would sustain an action of tort as an alternative remedy to an action for breach of contract. If one should select the former mode of redress, he may, no doubt, recover exemplary damages, or what is sometimes styled vindictive damages; but if he should choose to seek redress in the form of an action for breach of contract, he lets in all the consequences of that form of action...One of these consequences is, I think, this: that he is to be paid adequate compensation in money for the loss of that which he would have received had his contract been kept, and no more.

I can conceive nothing more objectionable and embarrassing in litigation than trying in effect an action of libel or slander as a matter of aggravation in an action for illegal dismissal, the defendant being permitted, as he must in justice be permitted, to traverse the defamatory sense, rely on privilege, or raise every point which he could raise in an independent action brought for the alleged libel or slander itself.

In my opinion, exemplary damages ought not to be, and are not according to any true principle of law, recoverable in such an action as the present, and the sums awarded to the plaintiff should therefore be decreased by the amount at which they have been estimated, and credit for that item should not be allowed in his account

Lord James of Hereford, Lord Gorell, and **Lord Shaw of Dunfermline** gave concurring speeches. **Lord Collins** delivered a dissenting speech.

NOTES AND QUESTIONS

1. Although not relevant to the general law on damages it should be noted that wrongful dismissal (which was the cause of action in *Addis* itself) has recently been treated as requiring special restrictions on damages (including the denial of damages for psychiatric illness or mental distress or a pecuniary loss of reputation) so as to avoid undermining the statutory regime of unfair dismissal: see *Johnson v Unisys Ltd* [2001] UKHL 13, [2003] 1 AC 518.

2. *Addis* has traditionally been interpreted as laying down that, in general, damages for mental distress, damages for loss of reputation and exemplary (or punitive) damages cannot be awarded for breach of contract. Do those three types of damages raise distinct issues so that, contrary to their treatment in this case, they should be clearly separated from each other?

3. As regards damages for mental distress, *Addis* largely remains good law (and in *Johnson v Gore Wood & Co* [2002] AC 1, 37-38, HL it was confirmed as laying down the general rule). But two important exceptions to it, where mental distress damages are recoverable, have been recognised in subsequent cases: (i) where the very, or predominant, object of the contract from the claimant's point of view was to obtain mental satisfaction; and (ii) where the claimant's mental distress is directly consequent on physical inconvenience caused by the defendant's breach of contract. We shall look at an important illustration of each before turning to the leading case of *Farley v Skinner* which has since loosened both those exceptional categories.

Jarvis v Swan's Tours Ltd [1973] QB 233, Court of Appeal

The claimant booked a Christmas skiing holiday with the defendants for £63.45. The defendants' brochure described the hotel as being a 'House Party Centre' so that the price included welcome party, afternoon tea and cake, fondue party, yodeller evening and chalet farewell party. In fact there were only 13 people in the hotel in the first week and in the second week the claimant was the only guest. Nor did the skiing correspond to what was said in the brochure. In an action for breach of contract, the claimant at trial was awarded as damages half of what he paid (ie £31.72). On the claimant's appeal on the amount of damages, it was held that the sum of damages should be increased to cover his mental distress as this was an exceptional case where mental distress damages could be awarded.

Lord Denning MR: What is the right way of assessing damages? It has often been said that on a breach of contract damages cannot be given for mental distress. Thus in *Hamlin v. Great Northern Railway Co.* (1856) 1 H. & N. 408, 411 Pollock C.B. said that damages cannot be given "for the disappointment of mind occasioned by the breach of contract." And in *Hobbs v. London & South Western Railway Co.* (1875) L.R. 10 Q.B. 111, 122, Mellor J. said that

> "for the mere inconvenience, such as annoyance and loss of temper, or vexation, or for being disappointed in a particular thing which you have set your mind upon, without real physical inconvenience resulting, you cannot recover damages."

The courts in those days only allowed the plaintiff to recover damages if he suffered physical inconvenience, such as having to walk five miles home, as in *Hobbs'* case; or to live in an over-crowded house, *Bailey v. Bullock* [1950] 2 All E.R. 1167.

I think that those limitations are out of date. In a proper case damages for mental distress can be recovered in contract, just as damages for shock can be recovered in tort. One such case is a contract for a holiday, or any other contract to provide entertainment and enjoyment. If the contracting party breaks his contract, damages can be given for the disappointment, the distress, the upset and frustration caused by the breach. I know that it is difficult to assess in terms of money, but it is no more difficult than the assessment which the courts have to make every day in personal injury cases for loss of amenities. Take the present case. Mr. Jarvis has only a fortnight's holiday in the year. He books it far ahead, and looks forward to it all that time. He ought to be compensated for the loss of it.

A good illustration was given by Edmund Davies L.J. in the course of the argument. He put the case of a man who has taken a ticket for Glyndebourne. It is the only night on which he can get there. He hires a car to take him. The car does not turn up. His damages are not limited to the mere cost of the ticket. He is entitled to general damages for the disappointment he has suffered and the loss of the entertainment which he should have had. Here, Mr. Jarvis's fortnight's winter holiday has been a grave disappointment. It is true that he was conveyed to Switzerland and back and had meals and bed in the hotel. But that is not what he went for. He went to enjoy himself with all the facilities which the defendants said he would have. He is entitled to damages for the lack of those facilities, and for his loss of enjoyment.

...

I think the judge was in error in taking the sum paid for the holiday £63.45 and halving it. The right measure of damages is to compensate him for the loss of entertainment and enjoyment which he was promised, and which he did not get.

Looking at the matter quite broadly, I think the damages in this case should be the sum of £125. I would allow the appeal, accordingly.

Edmund Davies LJ and **Stephenson LJ** delivered concurring judgments.

NOTE

For other examples of cases falling within the first exceptional category where the predominant object is mental satisfaction, see *Diesen v Samson* 1971 SLT 49 (photographer failing to appear at a wedding); *Heywood v Wellers* [1976] QB 446, CA (solicitor's failure to obtain injunction to stop molestation of the claimant by her former boyfriend); and the *Ruxley Electronics* case (above, 342).

Watts v Morrow [1991] 1 WLR 1421, Court of Appeal

The claimants bought a second home in the country in reliance on a survey prepared by the defendant surveyor. That survey was negligently prepared and failed to mention some substantial defects which required urgent repair, including the renewal of the roof, windows and floor boards. In an action by the claimants for breach of the defendant's contractual and tortious duty of care, the trial judge awarded each claimant £4,000 as damages for distress and inconvenience (in addition to the damages for their pecuniary loss). On appeal by the defendant against the amount of damages, the Court of Appeal confirmed that contractual damages for mental distress are recoverable in two exceptional categories—distress consequent on inconvenience being one—but reduced the amount here awarded for distress and inconvenience to £750 for each claimant.

Ralph Gibson LJ: It is clear, I think, that the judge was regarding the contract between Mr. and Mrs. Watts and the defendant as a contract in which the subject matter was to provide peace of mind or freedom [from] distress within the meaning of Dillon L.J.'s phrase in *Bliss v. South East Thames Regional Health Authority* [1987] I.C.R. 700, 718 cited by Purchas L.J. in *Hayes v. James & Charles Dodd* [1990] 2 All E.R. 815, 826. That, with respect, seems to me to be an impossible view of the ordinary surveyor's contract. No doubt house buyers hope to enjoy peace of mind and freedom from distress as a consequence of the proper performance by a surveyor of his contractual obligation to provide a careful report, but there was no express promise for the provision of peace of mind or freedom from distress and no such implied promise was alleged. In my view, in the case of the ordinary surveyor's contract, damages are only recoverable for distress caused by physical consequences of the breach of contract. Since the judge did not attempt to assess the award on that basis this court must reconsider the award and determine what it should be.

...

The right course, in my view, is for this court, accepting and applying the principle that damages for mental distress resulting from the physical consequence of such a breach of contract should be modest, to accept the judge's finding that, during the weekends over a period of eight months, there was discomfort from the physical circumstances of living in the house caused by the presence of Mr. and Mrs. Watts during the carrying out of repairs in respect of unreported defects. ...

I would award to each plaintiff, since it has not been suggested that there is any basis for distinguishing between them, general damages in the sum of £750.

Bingham LJ: A contract-breaker is not in general liable for any distress, frustration, anxiety, displeasure, vexation, tension or aggravation which his breach of contract may cause to the innocent party. This rule is not, I think, founded on the assumption that such reactions are not foreseeable, which they surely are or may be, but on considerations of policy.

But the rule is not absolute. Where the very object of a contract is to provide pleasure, relaxation, peace of mind or freedom from molestation, damages will be awarded if the fruit of the contract is not provided or if the contrary result is procured instead. If the law did not cater for this exceptional category of case it would be defective. A contract to survey the condition of a house for a prospective purchaser does not, however, fall within this exceptional category.

In cases not falling within this exceptional category, damages are in my view recoverable for physical inconvenience and discomfort caused by the breach and mental suffering directly related to that inconvenience and discomfort. If those effects are foreseeably suffered during a period when defects are repaired I am prepared to accept that they sound in damages even though the cost of the repairs is not recoverable as such. But I also agree that awards should be restrained, and that the awards in this case far exceeded a reasonable award for the injury shown to have been suffered. I agree with the figures which Ralph Gibson L.J. proposes to substitute.

Sir Stephen Brown P delivered a concurring judgment.

NOTES AND QUESTIONS

1. Bingham LJ's judgment sets out clearly the general rule that mental distress damages cannot be awarded in contract and the two exceptions. But in the next case, both those exceptions were widened.
2. Bingham LJ said that the general rule rested on 'considerations of policy'. What are those policy considerations?

Farley v Skinner [2001] UKHL 49, [2002] 2 AC 732, House of Lords

The claimant was considering buying a house (Riverside House) 15 miles from Gatwick Airport. He engaged the defendant to survey the property and specifically asked him to investigate whether the property was affected by aircraft noise. In breach of his contractual duty of care, the defendant reported that it was unlikely that the property would suffer greatly from aircraft noise. After buying the property and moving in, the claimant discovered that aircraft bound for Gatwick flew directly over, or nearly over, the house and that the noise substantially affected the property and was 'a confounded nuisance'. Nevertheless he decided not to sell. Moreover, he was found to have suffered no financial loss in that he had paid the market value of the property where that value took into account the aircraft noise. Nevertheless he sought mental distress damages for the defendant's breach of contract because his enjoyment of the property was detrimentally affected. The House of Lords, in restoring the first instance judge's award of £10,000 for his mental distress, held that these facts fell within both of the exceptional categories where such damages can be awarded.

Lord Steyn:

14 The judgments in the Court of Appeal and the arguments before the House took as their starting point the propositions enunciated by Bingham LJ in *Watts v Morrow* [1991] 1 WLR 1421. ...

15 But useful as the observations of Bingham LJ undoubtedly are, they were never intended to state more than broad principles. In *Broome v Cassell & Co Ltd* [1972] AC 1027 Lord Reid commented, at p 1085:...

> "it is not the function of ... judges to frame definitions or to lay down hard and fast rules. It is their function to enunciate principles and much that they say is intended to be illustrative or explanatory and not to be definitive."

Bingham LJ would have had this truth about judicial decision making well in mind. So interpreted the passage cited is a helpful point of departure for the examination of the issues in this case. Specifically, it is important to bear in mind that *Watts v Morrow* [1991] 1 WLR 1421 was a case where a surveyor negligently failed to discover defects in a property. The claim was not for breach of a specific undertaking to investigate a matter important for the buyer's peace of mind. It was a claim for damages for inconvenience and discomfort resulting from breach. In *Watts v Morrow* therefore there was no reason to consider the case where a surveyor is in breach of a distinct and important contractual obligation which was intended to afford the buyer information.

17 I reverse the order in which the Court of Appeal considered the two issues. I do so because the issue whether the present case falls within the exceptional category governing cases where the very object of the contact is to give pleasure, and so forth, focuses directly on the terms actually agreed between the parties. It is concerned with the reasonable expectations of the parties under the specific terms of the contract. Logically, it must be considered first.

18 It is necessary to examine the case on a correct characterisation of the plaintiff's claim. Stuart-Smith LJ [2000] Lloyd's Rep PN 516, 521 thought that the obligation undertaken by the surveyor was "one relatively minor aspect of the overall instructions". What Stuart-Smith and Mummery LJJ would have decided if they had approached it on the basis that the obligation was a major or important part of the contract between the plaintiff and the surveyor is not clear. But the Court of Appeal's characterisation of the case was not correct. The plaintiff made it crystal-clear to the surveyor that the impact of aircraft noise was a matter of importance to him. Unless he obtained reassuring information from the surveyor he would not have bought the property. That is the tenor of the evidence. It is also what the judge found. The case must be approached on the basis that the surveyor's obligation to investigate aircraft noise was a major or important part of the contract between him and the plaintiff. It is also important to note that, unlike in *Addis v Gramophone Co Ltd* [1909] AC 488, the plaintiff's claim is not for injured feelings caused by the breach of contract. Rather it is a claim for damages flowing from the surveyor's failure to investigate and report, thereby depriving the buyer of the chance of making an informed choice whether or not to buy resulting in mental distress and disappointment.

19 The broader legal context of *Watts v Morrow* [1991] 1 WLR 1421 must be borne in mind. The exceptional category of cases where the very object of a contract is to provide pleasure, relaxation, peace of mind or freedom from molestation is not the product of Victorian contract theory but the result of evolutionary developments in case law from the 1970s. ...

20 At their Lordships' request counsel for the plaintiff produced a memorandum based on various publications which showed the impact of the developments already described on litigation in the county courts. Taking into account the submissions of counsel for the surveyor and making due allowance for a tendency of the court sometimes not to distinguish between the cases presently under consideration and cases of physical inconvenience and discomfort, I am satisfied that in the real life of our lower courts non-pecuniary damages are regularly awarded on the basis that the defendant's breach of contract deprived the plaintiff of the very object of the contract, viz pleasure, relaxation, and peace of mind. The cases arise in diverse contractual contexts, e g the supply of a wedding dress or double glazing, hire purchase transactions, landlord and tenant, building contracts, and engagements of estate agents and solicitors. The awards in such cases seem modest. For my part what happens on the ground casts no doubt on the utility of the developments since the 1970s in regard to the award of non-pecuniary damages in the exceptional categories. But the problem persists of the precise scope of the exceptional category of case involving awards of non-pecuniary damages for breach of contract where the very object of the contract was to ensure a party's pleasure, relaxation or peace of mind.

21 An important development for this branch of the law was *Ruxley Electronics and Construction Ltd v Forsyth* [1996] AC 344. ...I draw attention to the fact that the majority in the Court of Appeal, at p 521, regarded the relevant observations of Lord Mustill and Lord Lloyd as obiter dicta. I am satisfied that the principles enunciated in *Ruxley's* case in support of the award of £2,500 for a breach of respect of the provision of a pleasurable amenity have been authoritatively established. ...

22 Counsel for the surveyor advanced three separate arguments each of which he said was sufficient to defeat the plaintiff's claim. First, he submitted that even if a major or important part of the contract was to give pleasure, relaxation and peace of mind, that was not enough.

It is an indispensable requirement that the object of the entire contract must be of this type. Secondly, he submitted that the exceptional category does not extend to a breach of a contractual duty of care, even if imposed to secure pleasure, relaxation and peace of mind. It only covers cases where the promiser guarantees achievement of such an object. Thirdly, he submitted that by not moving out of Riverside House the plaintiff forfeited any right to recover non-pecuniary damages.

23 The first argument fastened onto a narrow reading of the words "the very object of [the] contract" as employed by Bingham LJ in *Watts v Morrow* [1991] 1 WLR 1421, 1445. Cases where a major or important part of the contract was to secure pleasure, relaxation and peace of mind were not under consideration in *Watts v Morrow*. It is difficult to see what the principled justification for such a limitation might be. ...Counsel was, however, assisted by the decision of the Court of Appeal in *Knott v Bolton* (1995) 11 Const LJ 375 which in the present case the Court of Appeal treated as binding on it. In *Knott v Bolton* an architect was asked to design a wide staircase for a gallery and impressive entrance hall. He failed to do so. The plaintiff spent money in improving the staircase to some extent and he recovered the cost of the changes. The plaintiff also claimed damages for disappointment and distress at the lack of an impressive staircase. In agreement with the trial judge the Court of Appeal disallowed this part of his claim. Reliance was placed on the dicta of Bingham LJ in *Watts v Morrow* [1991] 1 WLR 1421, 1445.

24 Interpreting the dicta of Bingham LJ in *Watts v Morrow* narrowly the Court of Appeal in *Knott v Bolton* ruled that the central object of the contract was to design a house, not to provide pleasure to the occupiers of the house. It is important, however, to note that *Knott v Bolton* was decided a few months before the decision of the House in *Ruxley Electronics and Construction Ltd v Forsyth* [1996] AC 344. In any event, the technicality of the reasoning in *Knott v Bolton*, and therefore in the Court of Appeal judgments in the present case, is apparent. It is obvious, and conceded, that if an architect is employed only to design a staircase, or a surveyor is employed only to investigate aircraft noise, the breach of such a distinct obligation may result in an award of non-pecuniary damages. Logically the same must be the case if the architect or surveyor, apart from entering into a general retainer, concludes a separate contract, separately remunerated, in respect of the design of a staircase or the investigation of aircraft noise. If this is so the distinction drawn in *Knott v Bolton* and in the present case is a matter of form and not substance. David Capper, "Damages for Distress and Disappointment—The Limits of *Watts v Morrow*" (2000) 116 LQR 553, 556 has persuasively argued:

> "A ruling that intangible interests only qualify for legal protection where they are the 'very object of the contract' is tantamount to a ruling that contracts where these interests are merely important, but not the central object of the contract, are in part unenforceable. It is very difficult to see what policy objection there can be to parties to a contract agreeing that these interests are to be protected via contracts where the central object is something else. If the defendant is unwilling to accept this responsibility he or she can say so and either no contract will be made or one will be made but including a disclaimer."

There is no reason in principle or policy why the scope of recovery in the exceptional category should depend on the object of the contract as ascertained from all its constituent parts. It is sufficient if a major or important object of the contract is to give pleasure, relaxation or peace of mind. In my view *Knott v Bolton* 11 Const LJ 375 was wrongly decided and should be overruled. To the extent that the majority in the Court of Appeal relied on *Knott v Bolton* their decision was wrong.

[*He then rejected the second and third of the surveyor's arguments and continued:*]

28 In the surveyor's written case it was submitted that the award of £10,000 was excessive. It was certainly high. Given that the plaintiff is stuck indefinitely with a position which he sought to avoid by the terms of his contract with the surveyor I am not prepared to interfere with the judge's evaluation on the special facts of the case. On the other hand, I have to say that the size of the award appears to be at the very top end of what could possibly be regarded as appropriate damages. Like Bingham LJ in *Watts v Morrow* [1991] 1 WLR 1421, 1445H I consider that awards in this area should be restrained and modest. It is important that logical and beneficial developments in this corner of the law should not contribute to the creation of a society bent on litigation.

30 It is strictly unnecessary to discuss the question whether the judge's decision can be justified on the ground that the breach of contract resulted in inconvenience and discomfort. It is, however, appropriate that I indicate my view. ...[A]ircraft noise is capable of causing inconvenience and discomfort within the meaning of Bingham LJ's relevant proposition. It is a matter of degree whether the case passes the threshold. It is sufficient to say that I have not been persuaded that the judge's decision on this point was not open to him on the evidence which he accepted. For this further reason ... I would rule that the decision of the Court of Appeal was wrong.

Lord Scott of Foscote:

75 In my opinion, the issue can and should be resolved by applying the well known principles laid down in *Hadley v Baxendale* (1854) 9 Exch 341 (as restated in *Victoria Laundry (Windsor) Ltd v Newman Industries Ltd* [1949] 2 KB 528) in the light of the recent guidance provided by Bingham LJ in *Watts v Morrow* [1991] 1 WLR 1421 and by this House in *Ruxley Electronics and Construction Ltd v Forsyth* [1996] AC 344.

76 The basic principle of damages for breach of contract is that the injured party is entitled, so far as money can do it, to be put in the position he would have been in if the contractual obligation had been properly performed. He is entitled, that is to say, to the benefit of his bargain: see *Robinson v Harman* (1848) 1 Exch 850, 855.

79 *Ruxley's* case establishes, in my opinion, that if a party's contractual performance has failed to provide to the other contracting party something to which that other was, under the contract, entitled, and which, if provided, would have been of value to that party, then, if there is no other way of compensating the injured party, the injured party should be compensated in damages to the extent of that value. Quantification of that value will in many cases be difficult and may often seem arbitrary. In *Ruxley's* case the value placed on the amenity value of which the pool owner been deprived was £2,500. By that award, the pool owner was placed, so far as money could do it, in the position he would have been in if the diving area of the pool had been constructed to the specified depth.

80 In *Ruxley's* case the breach of contract by the builders had not caused any consequential loss to the pool owner. He had simply been deprived of the benefit of a pool built to the depth specified in the contract. It was not a case where the recovery of damages for consequential loss consisting of vexation, anxiety or other species of mental distress had to be considered.

81 In *Watts v Morrow*, [1991] 1 WLR 1421 however, that matter did have to be considered. [*He set out the passage from Bingham LJ's judgment, set out above, 390, and continued:*]

82 In the passage I have cited, Bingham LJ was dealing with claims for consequential damage consisting of the intangible mental states and sensory experiences to which he refers. Save for the matters referred to in the first paragraph, all of which reflect or are brought about by the injured party's disappointment at the contract breaker's failure to carry out his contractual obligations, and recovery for which, if there is nothing more, is ruled out on policy grounds, Bingham LJ's approach is, in my view, wholly consistent with established principles for the recovery of contractual damages.

83 There are, however, two qualifications that I would respectfully make to the proposition in the final paragraph of the cited passage that damages "for physical inconvenience and discomfort caused by the breach" are recoverable.

84 First, there will, in many cases, be an additional remoteness hurdle for the injured party to clear. Consequential damage, including damage consisting of inconvenience or discomfort, must, in order to be recoverable, be such as, at the time of the contract, was reasonably foreseeable as liable to result from the breach: see *McGregor on Damages*, 16th ed, pp 159-160, para 250.

85 Second, the adjective "physical", in the phrase "physical inconvenience and discomfort", requires, I think, some explanation or definition. The distinction between the "physical" and the "non-physical" is not always clear and may depend on the context. Is being awoken at night by aircraft noise "physical"? If it is, is being unable to sleep because of worry and anxiety "physical"? What about a reduction in light caused by the erection of a building under a planning permission that an errant surveyor ought to have warned his purchaser-client about but had failed to do so? In my opinion, the critical distinction to be drawn is not a distinction between the different types of inconvenience or discomfort of which complaint may be made but a distinction based on the cause of the inconvenience or discomfort. If the cause is no more than disappointment that the contractual obligation has been broken, damages are not recoverable even if the disappointment has led to a complete mental breakdown. But, if the cause of the inconvenience or discomfort is a sensory (sight, touch, hearing, smell etc) experience, damages can, subject to the remoteness rules, be recovered.

86 In summary, the principle expressed in *Ruxley Electronics and Construction Ltd v Forsyth* [1996] AC 344 should be used to provide damages for deprivation of a contractual benefit where it is apparent that the injured party has been deprived of something of value but the ordinary means of measuring the recoverable damages are inapplicable. The principle expressed in *Watts v Morrow* [1991] 1 WLR 1421 should be used to determine whether and when contractual damages for inconvenience or discomfort can be recovered.

105 It is time for me to turn to the present case and apply the principles expressed in *Ruxley Electronics and Construction Ltd v Forsyth* [1996] AC 344 and *Watts v Morrow* [1991] 1 WLR 1421. In my judgment, Mr Farley is entitled to be compensated for the "real discomfort" that the judge found he suffered. He is so entitled on either of two alternative bases.

106 First, he was deprived of the contractual benefit to which he was entitled. He was entitled to information about the aircraft noise from Gatwick-bound aircraft that Mr Skinner, through negligence, had failed to supply him with. If Mr Farley had, in the event, decided not to purchase Riverside House, the value to him of the contractual benefit of which he had been deprived would have been nil. But he did buy the property. And he took his decision to do so without the advantage of being able to take into account the information to which he was contractually entitled. If he had had that information he would not have bought. So the information clearly would have had a value to him. Prima facie, in my opinion, he is entitled to be compensated accordingly.

107 In these circumstances, it seems to me, it is open to the court to adopt a *Ruxley Electronics and Construction Ltd v Forsyth* [1996] AC 344 approach and place a value on the contractual benefit of which Mr Farley has been deprived. In deciding on the amount, the discomfort experienced by Mr Farley can, in my view, properly be taken into account. If he had had the aircraft noise information he would not have bought Riverside House and would not have had that discomfort.

108 Alternatively, Mr Farley can, in my opinion, claim compensation for the discomfort as consequential loss. Had it not been for the breach of contract, he would not have suffered the discomfort. It was caused by the breach of contract in a causa sine qua non sense. Was the discomfort a consequence that should reasonably have been contemplated by the parties at the time of contract as liable to result from the breach? In my opinion, it was. It was obviously within the reasonable contemplation of the parties that, deprived of the information about aircraft noise that he ought to have had, Mr Farley would make a decision to purchase that he would not otherwise have made. Having purchased, he would, having become aware of the noise, either sell—in which case at least the expenses of the resale would have been recoverable as damages—or he would keep the property and put up with the noise. In the latter event, it was within the reasonable contemplation of the parties that he would experience discomfort from the noise of the aircraft. And the discomfort was "physical" in the sense that Bingham LJ in *Watts v Morrow* [1991] 1 WLR 1421, 1445 had in mind. In my opinion, the application of *Watts v Morrow* principles entitles Mr Farley to damages for discomfort caused by the aircraft noise.

109 I would add that if there had been an appreciable reduction in the market value of the property caused by the aircraft noise, Mr Farley could not have recovered both that difference in value and damages for discomfort. To allow both would allow double recovery for the same item.

110 Whether the approach to damages is on *Ruxley Electronics and Construction Ltd v Forsyth* [1996] AC 344 lines, for deprivation of a contractual benefit, or on *Watts v Morrow* [1991] 1 WLR 1421 lines, for consequential damage within the applicable remoteness rules, the appropriate amount should, in my opinion, be modest. The degree of discomfort experienced by Mr Farley, although "real", was not very great. I think £10,000 may have been on the high side. But in principle, in my opinion, the judge was right to award damages and I am not, in the circumstances, disposed to disagree with his figure.

111 For the reasons I have given and for the reasons contained in the opinion of my noble and learned friend, Lord Steyn, I would allow the appeal and restore the judge's order.

Lord Clyde and **Lord Hutton** delivered concurring speeches. **Lord Browne-Wilkinson** agreed with Lords Steyn and Scott.

NOTES AND QUESTIONS

1. This decision lays down that it is sufficient to bring a case within the first exceptional category that mental satisfaction was *an important* object of the contract even though not the predominant, or very, object of the contract. In this case the predominant object of the survey contract was, presumably, to ensure that the claimant was not paying too much for the property. But it was an important object for Mr Farley to be satisfied that the aircraft noise at the house was not excessive.

2. Could one say that it is always an important object of a consumer contract to receive mental satisfaction (whether, for example, through a new kitchen or double glazing or even financial advice)? Or did their Lordships' clarification that an ordinary survey contract, as in *Watts v Morrow*, does not fall within the first exceptional category show that, to be an important object, one sometimes needs a specific request/specific undertaking relating to the mental satisfaction (see especially [15])?

3. A subsequent case falling within the first category, as expanded by *Farley v Skinner*, was *Hamilton Jones v David & Snape* [2003] EWHC 3147 (Ch), [2004] 1 All ER 657. Here a claim was brought against solicitors in contract and tort for having negligently failed to renew 'agency notifications' of the risk of the claimant's twin sons being taken out of England by her former husband. The children had been taken to Tunisia by the ex-husband and, as a consequence, the mother had lost custody of them. Neuberger J held that the claimant was entitled to £20,000 mental distress damages for breach of contract (and concurrently for the tort of negligence). While the primary object of the contract between the claimant and her solicitors was the welfare of the children, an important factor was to ensure, so far as possible, that the claimant retained custody of the children for her own satisfaction and peace of

mind. Applying the approach to the first category taken in *Farley v Skinner*, damages for the mental distress consequent on losing custody of her children were therefore held to be recoverable.

4. In interpreting noise as causing inconvenience, it would appear that their Lordships have also loosened the second exceptional category. Previously the emphasis was on 'physical' inconvenience. Now it would appear that any inconvenience or discomfort (whether physical or not), and the mental distress directly consequent on it, is compensatable (provided other limiting principles, such as remoteness, are not infringed).

5. Lord Scott took the novel approach of seeking to distinguish between loss of expected mental benefits and mental distress as a consequential loss. Although this has proved attractive to some commentators, it is an unworkable distinction not least because, where one has lost a mental benefit, there is an inevitable consequential suffering of mental distress. Lord Scott's attempt to explain past cases using this approach not surprisingly, therefore, produced forced classifications (eg he regarded *Hobbs v London and South Western Rly Co* (1875) LR 10 QB 111, see above, 389, as a loss of expected benefit case).

6. What are the arguments for and against the law on mental distress damages moving to the position whereby mental distress consequent on a breach of contract is always recoverable, subject to normal limiting principles like remoteness and the duty to mitigate? See A Burrows, *Remedies for Torts and Breach of Contract* (3rd edn, 2004) 332–3.

(f) Loss of Reputation

Mahmud v Bank of Credit and Commerce International SA
[1998] AC 20, House of Lords

The claimants were former employees of the defendant bank, BCCI, which had collapsed as a result of a massive and notorious fraud perpetrated by those controlling the bank. The claimants brought an action for breach by the bank of its implied term not to undermine its employees' trust and confidence; and they claimed 'stigma damages' for that breach (that is, damages for their financial loss of reputation and hence handicap in the labour market, flowing from the stigma of dishonesty attaching to BCCI's employees). On the trial of a preliminary issue, it was held by the House of Lords, overturning the Court of Appeal, that such damages are recoverable in contract.

Lord Nicholls of Birkenhead: The liquidators submitted that injury to reputation is protected by the law of defamation. The boundaries set by the tort of defamation are not to be side-stepped by allowing a claim in contract that would not succeed in defamation...Here, it was submitted, a claim in defamation would not succeed: the bank made no defamatory statements, either referring to the applicants or at all. This submission is misconceived.

I agree that the cause of action known to the law in respect of injury to reputation is the tort of defamation. With certain exceptions this tort provides a remedy, where the necessary ingredients are present, whether or not the injury to a person's reputation causes financial loss. No proof of actual damage is necessary, and damages are at large. If, as a result of the injury to his reputation the plaintiff does in fact suffer financial loss, this may be recoverable in a defamation action as "special damage."

All this is commonplace. It by no means follows, however, that financial loss which may be recoverable as special damage in a defamation action is irrecoverable as damages for breach of contract. If a breach of contract gives rise to financial loss which on ordinary principles would be recoverable as damages for breach of contract, those damages do not cease to be recoverable because they might also be recoverable in a defamation action. There can be no justification for artificially excising from the damages recoverable for breach of contract that part of the financial loss which might or might not be the subject of a successful claim in defamation. Hallett J. summarised the position in *Foaminol Laboratories Ltd. v. British Artid Plastics Ltd.* [1941] 2 All E.R. 393, 399-400:

> "a claim for mere loss of reputation is the proper subject of an action for defamation, and cannot ordinarily be sustained by means of any other form of action . . . However . . . if pecuniary loss can be established, the mere fact that the pecuniary loss is brought about by the loss of reputation caused by a breach of contract is not sufficient to preclude the plaintiffs from recovering in respect of that pecuniary loss."

Furthermore, the fact that the breach of contract injures the plaintiff's reputation in circumstances where no claim for defamation would lie is not, by itself, a reason for excluding from the damages recoverable for breach of contract compensation for financial loss which on ordinary principles would be recoverable. An award of damages for breach of contract has a different objective: compensation for financial loss suffered by a breach of contract, not compensation for injury to reputation.

Sometimes, in practice, the distinction between damage to reputation and financial loss can become blurred. Damage to the reputation of professional persons, or persons carrying on a business, frequently causes financial loss. None the less, the distinction is fundamentally sound, and when awarding damages for breach of contract courts take care to confine the damages to their proper ambit: making good financial loss. In *Herbert Clayton and Jack Waller Ltd. v. Oliver* [1930] A.C. 209, 220, when considering an award of damages to an actor who should have been billed to appear at the London Hippodrome, Lord Buckmaster regarded loss of publicity rather than loss of reputation as the preferable expression. In *Aerial Advertising Co. v. Batchelors Peas Ltd. (Manchester)* [1938] 2 All E.R. 788, 796-797, where aerial advertising ("Eat Batchelors Peas") took place during Armistice Day services, Atkinson J. was careful to confine damages to the financial loss flowing from public boycotting of the defendant's goods and to exclude damages for loss of reputation. Lord Denning M.R. drew the same distinction in *G.K.N. Centrax Gears Ltd. v. Matbro Ltd.* [1976] 2 Lloyd's Rep. 555, 573.

Lord Steyn: In considering the availability of the remedy of damages it is important to bear in mind that the applicants claim damages for financial loss. That is the issue. It will be recalled that the Court of Appeal decided the case against the applicants on the basis that there is a positive rule debarring the recovery of damages in contract for injury to an existing reputation, and that in truth the two applicants were claiming damages for injury to their previously existing reputations. For this conclusion the Court of Appeal relied on three decided cases, namely *Addis v. Gramophone Co. Ltd.* [1909] A.C. 488; *Withers v. General Theatre Corporation Ltd.* [1933] 2 K.B. 536 and *O'Laoire v. Jackel International Ltd. (No. 2)* [1991] I.C.R. 718. It will be necessary to examine each of these authorities.

The true ratio decidendi of the House of Lords' decision in *Addis v. Gramophone Co. Ltd.* has long been debated. Some have understood it as authority for the proposition that an employee may not recover damages even for pecuniary loss caused by a breach of contract of the employer which damages the employment prospects of an employee. If *Addis's* case establishes such a rule it is an inroad on traditional principles of contract law. And any such restrictive rule has been criticised by distinguished writers: *Treitel, The Law of Contract*, 9th ed. (1995), p. 893; *Burrows, Remedies for Torts and Breach of Contract*, 2nd ed. (1994), pp. 221–225. Moreover, it has been pointed out that *Addis's* case was decided in 1909 before the development of modern employment law, and long before the evolution of the implied mutual obligation of trust and confidence. Nevertheless, it is necessary to take a closer look at *Addis's* case so far as it affects the issues in this case. A company had dismissed an overseas manager in a harsh and oppressive manner. The House of Lords held that the employee was entitled to recover his direct pecuniary loss, such as loss of salary and commission. But the jury had been allowed to take into account the manner in which the employee had been dismissed and to reflect this in their award. The House of Lords, with Lord Collins dissenting, held that this was wrong. The headnote to the case states that in a case of wrongful dismissal the award of damages may not include compensation for the manner of his dismissal, for his injured feelings, or for the loss he may suffer from the fact that the dismissal of itself makes it more difficult to obtain fresh employment. Lord Collins was apparently alone in wanting time to consider the matter. The majority would apparently have dealt with the matter summarily. And the majority did not find it necessary to analyse the matter in any depth. The speeches are not always easy to follow. Thus Lord Atkinson observed, at p. 496:

"I can conceive nothing more objectionable and embarrassing in litigation than trying in effect an action of libel or slander as a matter of aggravation in an action for illegal dismissal, the defendant being permitted, as he must in justice be permitted, to traverse the defamatory sense, rely on privilege, or raise every point which he could raise in an independent action brought for the alleged libel or slander itself."

That is a misconception: ex hypothesi liability has been established and only the assessment of damages is at stake. Moreover, Lord Gorell apparently arrived at his conclusion on the basis of ordinary principles of remoteness: p. 501. Depending on the facts those principles would not necessarily in all cases debar an award of damages for loss of employment prospects. I would accept, however, that Lord Loreburn L.C. and the other Law Lords in the majority apparently thought they were applying a special rule applicable to awards of damages for wrongful dismissal. It is, however, far from clear how far the ratio of *Addis's* case extends. It certainly enunciated the principle that an employee cannot recover exemplary or aggravated damages for wrongful dismissal. That is still sound law. The actual decision is only concerned with wrongful dismissal. It is therefore arguable that as a matter of precedent the ratio is so restricted. But it seems to me unrealistic not to acknowledge that *Addis's* case is authority for a wider principle. There is a common proposition in the speeches of the majority. That proposition is that damages for breach of contract may only be awarded for breach of contract, and not for loss caused by the manner of the breach. No Law Lord said that an employee may not recover financial loss for damage to his employment prospects caused by a breach of contract. And no Law Lord said that in breach of contract cases compensation for loss of reputation can never be awarded, or that it can only be awarded in cases falling in certain defined categories. *Addis's* case simply decided that the loss of reputation in that particular case could not be compensated because it was not caused by a breach of contract: Nelson Enonchong, "Contract Damages for Injury to Reputation" (1996) 59 M.L.R. 592, 593. So analysed *Addis's* case does not bar the claims put forward in the present case.

Withers v. General Theatre Corporation Ltd. [1933] 2 KB 536 may rule out a claim such as is under consideration in the present case. The case concerned an artist engaged to appear and perform at the London Palladium. The defendant refused to allow him to perform at the London Palladium. It was held to be a breach of contract. The Court of Appeal drew a distinction. It was held that the plaintiff was entitled to damages for the loss of reputation which the plaintiff would have acquired if the defendant had not committed the breach of contract. But the Court of Appeal held that the plaintiff was not entitled as a matter of law to damages to his existing reputation. Nothing in *Addis's* case supported this distinction. It is difficult as a matter of principle to justify it. A rule that damages can never be recovered in respect of loss of reputation caused by a breach of contract is also out of line with ordinary principles of contract law. Moreover, the *Withers* case is in conflict with *Marbe v. George Edwardes (Daly's Theatre) Ltd.* [1928] 1 K.B. 269. In *Marbe's* case on similar facts the Court of Appeal came to the opposite conclusion: damages in respect of loss of an existing reputation was expressly held to be recoverable: see Bankes L.J., at p. 281, Atkin L.J., at p. 288 and Lawrence L.J., at p. 290. But in the *Withers* case Scrutton L.J. erroneously considered that *Marbe's* case was inconsistent with the House of Lords decision in *Herbert Clayton and Jack Waller Ltd. v. Oliver* [1930] A.C. 209. The latter case did not involve a claim for loss of existing reputation: p. 214. Moreover, as the headnote states, in *Herbert Clayton v. Oliver* the House of Lords approved *Marbe's* case. The House of Lords did so expressly. The *Withers* decision was based on a misunderstanding. In any event, I am persuaded that the distinction drawn in the *Withers* case, and the rule applied, is contrary to principle and unsound. In my judgment the decision in the *Withers* case was wrong on this point. Ordinary contract law principles govern.

O'Laoire v. Jackel International Ltd. (No. 2) [1991] I.C.R. 718, involved a claim by a dismissed employee for loss "due to the manner and nature of his dismissal." It was held that such a claim is excluded by *Addis's* case. But that does not affect the present case which is based not on the manner of a wrongful dismissal but on a breach of contract which is separate from and independent of the termination of the contract of employment.

In my judgment therefore the authorities relied on by Morritt L.J. do not on analysis support his conclusion. Moreover, the fact that in appropriate cases damages may in principle be awarded for loss of reputation caused by breach of contract is illustrated by a number of cases which Morritt L.J. discussed: *Aerial Advertising Co. v. Batchelors Peas Ltd. (Manchester)* [1938] 2 All E.R. 788; *Foaminol Laboratories Ltd. v. British Artid Plastics Ltd.* [1941] 2 All E.R. 393 and *Anglo-Continental Holidays Ltd. v. Typaldos Lines (London) Ltd.* [1967] 2 Lloyd's Rep. 61. But, unlike Morritt L.J., I regard these cases not as exceptions but as the application of ordinary principles of contract law. Moreover, it is clear that a supplier who delivers contaminated meat to a trader can be sued for loss of commercial reputation involving loss of trade: see *Cointax v. Myham & Son* [1913] 2 K.B. 220 and *G.K.N. Centrax Gears Ltd. v. Matbro Ltd.* [1976] 2 Lloyd's Rep. 555. Rhetorically, one may ask, why may a bank manager not sue for loss of professional reputation, if it causes financial loss flowing from a breach of the contract of employment? ...The principled position is as follows. Provided that a relevant breach of contract can be established, and the requirements of causation, remoteness and mitigation can be satisfied, there is no good reason why in the field of employment law recovery of financial loss in respect of damage to reputation caused by breach of contract is necessarily excluded.

...It is...improbable that many employees would be able to prove "stigma compensation." The limiting principles of causation, remoteness and mitigation present formidable practical obstacles to such claims succeeding. But difficulties of proof cannot alter the legal principles which permit, in appropriate cases, such claims for financial loss caused by breach of contract being put forward for consideration.

Lord Goff of Chieveley and **Lord Mackay of Clashfern** agreed with Lords Nicholls and Steyn. **Lord Mustill** agreed with Lord Steyn.

NOTES AND QUESTIONS

1. This case establishes that, contrary to earlier doubts, there is no special restriction on the recoverability of damages for a *pecuniary* loss of reputation.

2. It would appear that *Addis v Gramophone Co* (above, 387) continues to rule out, at least generally, damages for a *non-pecuniary* loss of reputation. This is

closely linked to the general non-recoverability of mental distress damages. What are the reasons for denying contractual damages for a non-pecuniary loss of reputation? Does recognition of the first exceptional category of mental distress damages suggest that damages for a non-pecuniary loss of reputation might be awarded where an important object of the contract was, eg, to enhance the claimant's reputation?

2. RESTITUTIONARY DAMAGES/AN ACCOUNT OF PROFITS

Introductory reading: E McKendrick, *Contract Law* (7th edn, 2007) 20.6

Attorney General v Blake [2001] 1 AC 268, House of Lords

George Blake, the notorious Russian spy and British traitor, had written his autobiography in 1989. The Crown wished to stop him profiting from that book. Its claims were brought in both public and private law. The public law claim ultimately failed in the House of Lords and does not concern us here. As regards private law, it had been conceded at first instance that, by the time of publication, the information in the book was in the public domain and no longer confidential so that the standard remedy of an account of profits for the equitable wrong of breach of confidence was not available. Moreover, the Court of Appeal had upheld the trial judge's decision that there could be no account of profits for breach of fiduciary duty (which is again a standard remedy for that equitable wrong) because there was no fiduciary duty owed by an ex-employee to the Crown. Nevertheless in publishing the book without the Crown's consent, Blake had committed a breach of his contractual undertaking to the Crown, signed when he joined the Secret Service, that he would not publish, during or after his employment, any official information gained from his employment. So the question arose in the House of Lords whether an account of profits (often alternatively referred to as 'restitutionary damages') could be awarded for a breach of contract. It was held (Lord Hobhouse dissenting) that, while the normal remedy for breach of contract is damages compensating for loss, exceptionally, as here, an account of profits aimed at a disgorgement of the gains made from the breach of contract can be, and here should be, awarded.

Lord Nicholls of Birkenhead [*He set the scene by referring to, eg, (i) damages measured exceptionally by the benefit gained by the tortfeasor in cases of interference with rights of property (for torts of trespass to land or conversion); and (ii) the award of an account of profits as a standard award for intellectual property torts, breach of confidence and breach of fiduciary duty. He continued:*]
Against this background I turn to consider the remedies available for breaches of contract. The basic remedy is an award of damages. In the much quoted words of Baron Parke, the rule of the common law is that where a party sustains a loss by reason of a breach of contract, he is, so far as money can do it, to be placed in the same position as if the contract had been

performed: *Robinson v Harman* (1848) 1 Exch 850, 855. Leaving aside the anomalous exception of punitive damages, damages are compensatory. That is axiomatic. It is equally well established that an award of damages, assessed by reference to financial loss, is not always "adequate" as a remedy for a breach of contract. The law recognises that a party to a contract may have an interest in performance which is not readily measurable in terms of money. On breach the innocent party suffers a loss. He fails to obtain the benefit promised by the other party to the contract. To him the loss may be as important as financially measurable loss, or more so. An award of damages, assessed by reference to financial loss, will not recompense him properly. For him a financially assessed measure of damages is inadequate.

The classic example of this type of case, as every law student knows, is a contract for the sale of land. The buyer of a house may be attracted by features which have little or no impact on the value of the house. An award of damages, based on strictly financial criteria, would fail to recompense a disappointed buyer for this head of loss. The primary response of the law to this type of case is to ensure, if possible, that the contract is performed in accordance with its terms. The court may make orders compelling the party who has committed a breach of contract, or is threatening to do so, to carry out his contractual obligations. To this end the court has wide powers to grant injunctive relief. The court will, for instance, readily make orders for the specific performance of contracts for the sale of land, and sometimes it will do so in respect of contracts for the sale of goods. In *Beswick v Beswick* [1968] AC 58 the court made an order for the specific performance of a contract to make payments of money to a third party. The law recognised that the innocent party to the breach of contract had a legitimate interest in having the contract performed even though he himself would suffer no financial loss from its breach. Likewise, the court will compel the observance of negative obligations by granting injunctions. This may include a mandatory order to undo an existing breach, as where the court orders the defendant to pull down building works carried out in breach of covenant.

All this is trite law. In practice, these specific remedies go a long way towards providing suitable protection for innocent parties who will suffer loss from breaches of contract which are not adequately remediable by an award of damages. But these remedies are not always available. For instance, confidential information may be published in breach of a non-disclosure agreement before the innocent party has time to apply to the court for urgent relief. Then the breach is irreversible. Further, these specific remedies are discretionary. Contractual obligations vary infinitely. So do the circumstances in which breaches occur, and the circumstances in which remedies are sought. The court may, for instance, decline to grant specific relief on the ground that this would be oppressive.

An instance of this nature occurred in *Wrotham Park Estate Co Ltd v Parkside Homes Ltd* [1974] 1 WLR 798. For social and economic reasons the court refused to make a mandatory order for the demolition of houses built on land burdened with a restrictive covenant. Instead, Brightman J made an award of damages under the jurisdiction which originated with Lord Cairns's Act. The existence of the new houses did not diminish the value of the benefited land by one farthing. The judge considered that if the plaintiffs were given a nominal sum, or no sum, justice would manifestly not have been done. He assessed the damages at 5% of the developer's anticipated profit, this being the amount of money which could reasonably have been demanded for a relaxation of the covenant.

In reaching his conclusion the judge applied by analogy the cases mentioned above concerning the assessment of damages when a defendant has invaded another's property rights but without diminishing the value of the property. I consider he was right to do so. Property rights are superior to contractual rights in that, unlike contractual rights, property rights may survive against an indefinite class of persons. However, it is not easy to see why, as between the parties to a contract, a violation of a party's contractual rights should attract a lesser degree of remedy than a violation of his property rights. As Lionel D Smith has pointed out in his article "Disgorgement of the profits of Breach of Contract: Property, Contract and 'Efficient Breach'" (1995) 24 Can BLJ 121, it is not clear why it should be any more permissible to expropriate personal rights than it is permissible to expropriate property rights.

I turn to the decision of the Court of Appeal in *Surrey County Council v Bredero Homes Ltd* [1993] 1 WLR 1361. A local authority had sold surplus land to a developer and obtained a covenant that the developer would develop the land in accordance with an existing planning permission. The sole purpose of the local authority in imposing the covenant was to enable it to share in the planning gain if, as happened, planning permission was subsequently granted for the erection of a larger number of houses. The purpose was that the developer would have to apply and pay for a relaxation of the covenant if it wanted to build more houses. In breach of covenant the developer completed the development in accordance with the later planning permission, and the local authority brought a claim for damages. The erection of the larger number of houses had not caused any financial loss to the local authority. The judge awarded nominal damages of £2, and the Court of Appeal dismissed the local authority's appeal.

This is a difficult decision. It has attracted criticism from academic commentators and also in judgments of Sir Thomas Bingham MR and Millett LJ in *Jaggard v Sawyer* [1995] 1 WLR 269. I need not pursue the detailed criticisms. In the *Bredero* case Dillon LJ himself noted, at p 1364, that had the covenant been worded differently, there could have been provision for payment of an increased price if a further planning permission were forthcoming. That would have been enforceable. But, according to the *Bredero* decision, a covenant not to erect any further houses without permission, intended to achieve the same result, may be breached with impunity. That would be a sorry reflection on the law. Suffice to say, in so far as the *Bredero* decision is inconsistent with the approach adopted in the *Wrotham Park* case, the latter approach is to be preferred.

The *Wrotham Park* case, therefore, still shines, rather as a solitary beacon, showing that in contract as well as tort damages are not always narrowly confined to recoupment of financial loss. In a suitable case damages for breach of contract may be measured by the benefit gained by the wrongdoer from the breach. The defendant must make a reasonable payment in respect of the benefit he has gained. In the present case the Crown seeks to go further. The claim is for all the profits of Blake's book which the publisher has not yet paid him. This raises the question whether an account of profits can ever be given as a remedy for breach of contract. The researches of counsel have been unable to discover any case where the court has made such an order on a claim for breach of contract. In *Tito v Waddell (No 2)* [1977] Ch 106, 332, a decision which has proved controversial, Sir Robert Megarry V-C said that, as a matter of fundamental principle, the question of damages was "not one of making the defendant disgorge" his gains, in that case what he had saved by committing the wrong, but "one of compensating the plaintiff". In *Occidental Worldwide Investment Corporation v Skibs A/S Avanti* [1976] 1 Lloyd's Rep 293, 337, Kerr J summarily rejected a claim for an account of profits when ship owners withdrew ships on a rising market.

There is a light sprinkling of cases where courts have made orders having the same effect as an order for an account of profits, but the courts seem always to have attached a different label. A person who, in breach of contract, sells land twice over must surrender his profits on the second sale to the original buyer. Since courts regularly make orders for the specific performance of contracts for the sale of land, a seller of land is, to an extent, regarded as holding the land on trust for the buyer: *Lake v Bayliss* [1974] 1 WLR 1073. In *Reid-Newfoundland Co v Anglo-American Telegraph Co Ltd* [1912] AC 555 a railway company agreed not to transmit any commercial messages over a particular telegraph wire except for the benefit and account of the telegraph company. The Privy Council held that the railway company was liable to account as a trustee for the profits it wrongfully made from its use of the wire for commercial purposes. In *British Motor Trade Association v Gilbert* [1951] 2 All ER 641 the plaintiff suffered no financial loss but the award of damages for breach of contract effectively stripped the wrongdoer of the profit he had made from his wrongful venture into the black market for new cars.

These cases illustrate that circumstances do arise when the just response to a breach of contract is that the wrongdoer should not be permitted to retain any profit from the breach. In these cases the courts have reached the desired result by straining existing concepts. Professor Peter Birks has deplored the "failure of jurisprudence when the law is forced into this kind of abusive instrumentalism"; see "Profits of Breach of Contract" (1993) 109 LQR 518, 520. Some years ago Professor Dawson suggested there is no inherent reason why the technique of equity courts in land contracts should not be more widely employed, not by granting remedies as the by-product of a phantom "trust" created by the contract, but as an alternative form of money judgment remedy. That well known ailment of lawyers, a hardening of the categories, ought not to be an obstacle: see "Restitution or Damages" (1959) 20 Ohio SLJ 175.

My conclusion is that there seems to be no reason, *in principle*, why the court must in all circumstances rule out an account of profits as a remedy for breach of contract. I prefer to avoid the unhappy expression "restitutionary damages". Remedies are the law's response to a wrong (or, more precisely, to a cause of action). When, exceptionally, a just response to a breach of contract so requires, the court should be able to grant the discretionary remedy of requiring a defendant to account to the plaintiff for the benefits he has received from his breach of contract. In the same way as a plaintiff's interest in performance of a contract may render it just and equitable for the court to make an order for specific performance or grant an injunction, so the plaintiff's interest in performance may make it just and equitable that the defendant should retain no benefit from his breach of contract.

The state of the authorities encourages me to reach this conclusion, rather than the reverse. The law recognises that damages are not always a sufficient remedy for breach of contract. This is the foundation of the court's jurisdiction to grant the remedies of specific performance and injunction. Even when awarding damages, the law does not adhere slavishly to the concept of compensation for financially measurable loss. When the circumstances require, damages are measured by reference to the benefit obtained by the wrongdoer. This applies to interference with property rights. Recently, the like approach has been adopted to breach of contract. Further, in certain circumstances an account of profits is ordered in preference to an award of damages. Sometimes the injured party is given the choice: either compensatory damages or an account of the wrongdoer's profits. Breach of confidence is an instance of this. If confidential information is wrongfully divulged in breach of a non-disclosure agreement, it would be nothing short of sophistry to say that an account of profits may be ordered in respect of the equitable wrong but not in respect of the breach of contract which governs the relationship between the parties. With the established authorities going thus far, I consider it would be only a modest step for the law to recognise openly that, exceptionally, an account of profits may be the most appropriate remedy for breach of contract. It is not as though this step would contradict some recognised principle applied consistently throughout the law to the grant or withholding of the remedy of an account of profits. No such principle is discernible.

The main argument against the availability of an account of profits as a remedy for breach of contract is that the circumstances where this remedy may be granted will be uncertain. This will have an unsettling effect on commercial contracts where certainty is important. I do not think these fears are well founded. I see no reason why, *in practice*, the availability of the remedy of an account of profits need disturb settled expectations in the commercial or consumer world. An account of profits will be appropriate only in exceptional circumstances. Normally the remedies of damages, specific performance and injunction, coupled with the characterisation of some contractual obligations as fiduciary, will provide an adequate response to a breach of contract. It will be only in exceptional cases, where those remedies are inadequate, that any question of accounting for profits will arise. No fixed rules can be prescribed. The court will have regard to all the circumstances, including the subject matter of the contract, the purpose of the contractual provision which has been breached, the circumstances in which the breach occurred, the consequences of the breach and the circumstances in which relief is being sought. A useful general guide, although not exhaustive, is whether the plaintiff had a legitimate interest in preventing the defendant's profit-making activity and, hence, in depriving him of his profit.

It would be difficult, and unwise, to attempt to be more specific. In the Court of Appeal [1998] Ch 439 Lord Woolf MR suggested there are at least two situations in which justice requires the award of restitutionary damages where compensatory damages would be inadequate: see p 458. Lord Woolf MR was not there addressing the question of when an account of profits, in the conventional sense, should be available. But I should add that, so far as an account of profits is concerned, the suggested categorisation would not assist. The first suggested category was the case of "skimped" performance, where the defendant fails to provide the full extent of services he has contracted to provide. He should be liable to pay back the amount of expenditure he saved by the breach. This is a much discussed problem. But a part refund of the price agreed for services would not fall within the scope of an account of profits as ordinarily understood. Nor does an account of profits seem to be needed in this context. The resolution of the problem of cases of skimped performance, where the plaintiff does not get what was agreed, may best be found elsewhere. If a shopkeeper supplies inferior and cheaper goods than those ordered and paid for, he has to refund the difference in price. That would be the outcome of a claim for damages for breach of contract. That would be so, irrespective of whether the goods in fact served the intended purpose. There must be scope for a similar approach, without any straining of principle, in cases where the defendant provided inferior and cheaper services than those contracted for.

The second suggested category was where the defendant has obtained his profit by doing the very thing he contracted not to do. This category is defined too widely to assist. The category is apt to embrace all express negative obligations. But something more is required than mere breach of such an obligation before an account of profits will be the appropriate remedy.

Lord Woolf MR [1998] Ch 439, 457, 458, also suggested three facts which should not be a sufficient ground for departing from the normal basis on which damages are awarded: the fact that the breach was cynical and deliberate; the fact that the breach enabled the defendant to enter into a more profitable contract elsewhere; and the fact that by entering into a new and more profitable contract the defendant put it out of his power to perform his contract with the plaintiff. I agree that none of these facts would be, by itself, a good reason for ordering an account of profits.

The present case

The present case is exceptional. The context is employment as a member of the security and intelligence services.

...

In considering what would be a just response to a breach of Blake's undertaking the court has to take these considerations into account. The undertaking, if not a fiduciary obligation, was closely akin to a fiduciary obligation, where an account of profits is a standard remedy in the event of breach. Had the information which Blake has now disclosed still been confidential, an account of profits would have been ordered, almost as a matter of course. In the special circumstances of the intelligence services, the same conclusion should follow even though the information is no longer confidential. That would be a just response to the breach. I am reinforced in this view by noting that most of the profits from the book derive indirectly from the extremely serious and damaging breaches of the same undertaking committed by Blake in the 1950s. As already mentioned, but for his notoriety as an infamous spy his autobiography would not have commanded royalties of the magnitude Jonathan Cape agreed to pay.

Lord Steyn gave a concurring speech. **Lord Goff of Chieveley** and **Lord Browne-Wilkinson** concurred with Lord Nicholls. **Lord Hobhouse of Woodborough** gave a dissenting speech.

NOTES AND QUESTIONS

1. Did Lord Nicholls lay down any clear guide as to when an account of profits will be awarded for breach of contract? A breaks his contract with B in order

to make a much more lucrative contract with C. Can B recover from A the profits made by A on the contract with C?

2.   Lord Nicholls regarded the *Wrotham Park* case as a bridge to the (full) account of profits awarded in *Blake*. In that case, damages stripping 5 per cent of the defendant's profits were awarded for breach of a restrictive covenant. Brightman J applied a 'hypothetical bargain' test in calculating the damages by which he asked what sum would have been reasonably demanded by the claimant for releasing the defendant from the covenant. He accepted, however, that in reality the claimant would not have released the defendant. There is on-going debate as to whether the damages in that case were compensatory or restitutionary.

3.   Would *Surrey County Council v Bredero Homes Ltd* (referred to above, 403) be decided differently after *Blake*? In *Lane v O'Brien Homes Ltd* [2004] EWCH 303 (QB) a defendant developer built four houses, instead of three, in breach of a collateral contract with the claimant seller of the land. David Clarke J upheld an award of damages of £150,000 based on the defendant's estimated profit from building the extra house of £280,000. The *Wrotham Park* case was applied and the damages were treated as compensating the claimant's loss of opportunity to bargain.

4.   There is an important difference between restitution (or disgorgement) of gains made by a breach of contract and restitution of an unjust enrichment after a contract has been terminated for breach. For this distinction, see above, 334–335. The cause of action for the former, with which *Blake* was concerned, is breach of contract. The cause of action for the latter is unjust enrichment and, specifically, failure of consideration. Put another way, the former concerns 'restitution for a wrong' and the latter 'restitution of an unjust enrichment'.

5.   An account of profits or restitutionary damages is non-compensatory. However, it is to be distinguished from another type of non-compensatory damages, namely punitive (sometimes called exemplary) damages, which are concerned to punish the defendant. As we have seen, *Addis v Gramophone Co Ltd*, above, 387–388, has laid down that punitive damages cannot be awarded for breach of contract. While the power to strip gains recognised in *Blake* may, in one sense, have reduced the pressure to introduce punitive damages in contract, the recognition that contract law has moved away from just compensation may be thought to have opened the door to punitive damages also being made available, albeit exceptionally, for breach of contract. Certainly punitive damages are available for torts in limited categories of case: see *Rookes v Barnard* [1964] AC 1129, HL; *Kuddus v Chief Constable of Leicestershire Constabulary* [2001] UKHL 29, [2002] 2 AC 122. See on this debate the articles by McKendrick and Cunnington, below, 419–420.

6.   It should be noted that another example of non-compensatory damages is nominal damages. These comprise a trivial sum of money, usually about £2–£10, and serve to declare that there has been a breach of contract (ie that the claimant's rights have been infringed) in a situation where no other remedy is to be awarded. For an example, see *C & P Haulage v Middleton*, above, 352.

Experience Hendrix LLC v PPX Enterprises Inc
[2003] EWCA Civ 323, [2003] 1 All ER (Comm) 830, Court of Appeal

This case followed from a settlement in 1973 of a dispute between the rock star Jimi Hendrix and the defendant record company. By the terms of that contractual settlement, it was agreed that certain master tapes could be used for recording purposes by the defendant but that the rest ('non-Schedule A material') should be delivered up to Jimi Hendrix. In breach of that contract, the defendant used master tapes that should have been delivered up. The claimant, the estate of Jimi Hendrix, sought damages or an account of profits for that breach of contract. The Court of Appeal, allowing the claimant's appeal, held that substantial damages, albeit not an account of profits, should be awarded.

Mance LJ:

14 At the outset of the trial before Buckley J, Mr Jones representing the appellant made clear that he had no evidence, and he said that he did not imagine that he could ever possibly get any evidence, to show or quantify any financial loss suffered by the appellant as a result of PPX's breaches. So it was accepted that, if this was the only available measure, then no (or perhaps strictly only a nominal) award of damages could be made. However, Mr Jones obtained leave to amend to introduce claims for (i) damages consisting of such sums as could reasonably have been demanded by the appellant for relaxing the prohibitions contained in clause 3(b) of the settlement agreement or, alternatively, (ii) the entire profit attributable to PPX's exploitation of the non-Schedule A material. It was agreed that the trial should concern itself with the points of principle raised by this claim, and that the quantification of any such claims for damages and/or profit should be stood over. ...

16 The inspiration for the appellant's amendment of its case was the House of Lords decision in *A-G v Blake (Jonathan Cape Ltd, third party)* [2000] 2 All ER (Comm) 487, [2001] 1 AC 268. This marks a new start in this area of law. The exposition by counsel before us of prior authority threw light on considerations which may still be relevant to its future development. But, as I see the decision in *Blake*'s case, it freed us from some constraints that prior authority in this court (particularly *Surrey CC v Bredero Homes Ltd.* [1993] 3 All ER 705, [1993] 1 WLR 1361 and some of the reasoning in *Jaggard v. Sawyer* [1995] 2 All ER 189, [1995] 1 WLR 269) would have imposed. To apply Lord Steyn's words, *Blake*'s case leaves future courts with the task of 'hammering out on the anvil of decided cases' when and how far remedies such as the appellant now seeks should be available. The original Nibelungen produced a powerful image of restitution. The appellant invites us to fashion a modern and more deliberate equivalent on Jimi Hendrix's legacy.

26...In a case such as the *Wrotham Park* case the law gives effect to the instinctive reaction that, whether or not the appellant would have been better off if the wrong had not been committed, the wrongdoer ought not to gain an advantage for free, and should make some reasonable recompense. In such a context it is natural to pay regard to any profit made by the wrongdoer (although a wrongdoer surely cannot always rely on avoiding having to make reasonable recompense by showing that despite his wrong he failed, perhaps simply due to his own incompetence, to make any profit). The law can in such cases act either by ordering payment over of a percentage of any profit or, in some cases, by taking the cost which the wrongdoer would have had to incur to obtain (if feasible) equivalent benefit from another source.

31 As to subsequent authority [after *Blake*], we were referred to *Esso Petroleum Co. Ltd. v. Niad Ltd.* [2001] All ER (D) 324 (Nov), where Sir Andrew Morritt V-C ordered an account of profits as a remedy for breach of a contractual scheme called "Pricewatch" operated by Esso with its dealers. Dealers agreed to report competitors' prices and to abide by prices set daily by Esso which were intended to match the competition. Dealers received financial support by

Esso to assist them to do this. The defendant failed to maintain prices as agreed on four occasions, despite giving repeated assurances that he would do so. Damages were an inadequate remedy, since it was impossible for Esso to attribute lost sales to breach by one dealer. Yet the obligation to observe Pricewatch was fundamental to its operation, and failure to do so gave the lie to Esso's advertising campaign to support it. Account was also taken of the defendant's repetition of its breaches, and of Esso's legitimate interest in preventing the defendant profiting. Sir Andrew Morritt V-C regarded an account of profits as particularly appropriate when the defendant had been receiving financial support from Esso to maintain Pricewatch.

34 It was argued before us by Mr Englehart [for PPX] that any order for the payment of damages or a fortiori an account of profits must in a case such as the present be precluded by the judge's grant of an injunction. …The decision in *Blake's* case in my view avoids the need to consider Mr Englehart's submissions on these points at length. …

35 I can take the example put in argument of breach of a restrictive covenant not to use land for a pop concert, committed in circumstances where the beneficiary was out of the country and suffered no discomfort at all. Why should he not obtain an injunction to restrain repetition and a reasonable sum having regard to the financial benefit obtained by the neighbouring landowner from the infringement? Likewise, if a breach of contract occurs in such circumstances that there is no possibility at all of obtaining an injunction (eg because the interests of a third party have intervened), I see no reason why that should, since *Blake's* case, present any insuperable bar, in appropriate circumstances, to an order for payment of a reasonable sum having regard to any benefit made by the infringement, even though the appellant cannot prove any financial loss…Lord Nicholls in *Blake's* case [2000] 2 All ER (Comm) 487 at 500, [2001] 1 AC 268 at 285 took as 'A useful general guide, although not exhaustive' of circumstances in which an account of profit might be appropriate, 'whether the plaintiff had a legitimate interest in preventing the defendant's profit-making activity'. Those are precisely the circumstances in which an injunction for the future is likely to be granted. It would be paradoxical if its granting in the light of a continuing future risk were at the same time to deprive the appellant of any claim to strip, or seek a reasonable sum taking account of, the defendant's profit from past infringement. And if Lord Nicholls' general guide is a useful starting point in respect of an account of profits, it must be all the more so in respect of the lesser claim to a reasonable sum taking account of the defendant's profitable infringement.

36 I turn to apply these principles to the present facts. As in *Blake's* case we are concerned with a breach of a negative obligation, and PPX did do the very thing it had contracted not to do. Further, as in *Blake's* case so here on the Judge's findings, PPX through Mr Chalpin knew that it was doing something which it had contracted not to do, and in 1995 and 1999 well knew that the appellant would not consent thereto. Further, as in *Wrotham Park Estate Co v Parkside Homes Ltd* [1974] 2 All ER 321, [1974] 1 WLR 798, it can be said that the restriction against use of PPX's property of which PPX was in breach was imposed to protect the appellant's property, although there is the distinction that PPX's property did not ever belong to the appellant or appellant's predecessor. Finally, the grant of an injunction for the future shows that the appellants had a legitimate interest in preventing PPX's profit-making activity (cf Lord Nicholls in *Blake's* case [2000] 2 All ER (Comm) 487 at 500, [2001] 1 AC 268 at 285). But, since we are concerned with past profits, it is too late for either specific performance or an injunction to offer any effective remedy, and it is not suggested that this was or is the appellant's fault.

37 On the other hand, there are also obvious distinctions from *Blake's* case. First, we are not concerned with a subject anything like as special or sensitive as national security. The state's special interest in preventing a spy benefiting by breaches of his contractual duty of secrecy, and so removing at least part of the financial attraction of such breaches, has no parallel in this case. Second, the notoriety which accounted for the magnitude of Blake's royalty-earning capacity derived from his prior breaches of secrecy, and that too has no present parallel. Third, there is no direct analogy between PPX's position and that of a fiduciary.

38 The case of *Esso Petroleum Co Ltd v Niad Ltd* presents a similar feature to the present, in so far as damages may be said to be an inadequate remedy, because of the practical impossibility in each case of demonstrating the effect of a defendant's undoubted breaches on the appellant's general programme of promoting their product. But...it is not shown that the present defendant's breaches went to the root of the appellant's programme or gave the lie to its integrity. Nor is the present a case where the defendant can be said to have profited directly, by receipt under the agreement which it broke of monies that it ought in fairness to restore.

39 The present case does however arise out of a particular background, which has no direct parallel in these prior cases. ...

42 In the light of this background and in the light of the terms of the settlement agreement itself, I consider that any reasonable observer of the situation would conclude that, as a matter of practical justice, PPX should make (at the least) reasonable payment for its use of masters in breach of the settlement agreement. The intention of the agreement is clear. Consent to extensions or renewals was only contemplated in the case of existing licences. Even then, if it was given at all, it would no doubt only be given on terms requiring payment of a royalty. In relation to masters not on Sch A and not subject to any existing licences, the appellant's dominant interest was to remove them from the market. ...

Conclusions

43 It would in these circumstances be anomalous and unjust, if PPX could, by simply breaching the agreement, avoid paying royalties or any sum, when they have to pay royalties in respect of Sch A masters and they would have expected that, even if consent to the extension or renewal of existing licences of non-Sch A masters was forthcoming at all, it would only be on terms as to payment of further royalties. As it is, this case is concerned with fresh licences of non-Sch A masters to different licensees, so that the incongruity of allowing PPX free user to its own profit is yet more obvious.

44 However, I do not regard this case as exceptional to the point where the Court should order a full account of all profits which have been or may be made by PPX by its breaches. I have already drawn attention to significant features of *Blake*'s case which have no counterpart in this case (see [37], above). Here, the breaches, though deliberate, took place in a commercial context. PPX, though knowingly and deliberately breaching its contract, acted as it did in the course of a business, to which it no doubt gave some expenditure of time and effort and probably the use of connections and some skill (although how much is evidently in issue, and is not a matter on which we can at this stage reach any view). An account of profits would involve a detailed assessment of such matters, which, as is very clear from *Blake*'s case, should not lightly be ordered.

45... The injunction that [the appellant] has obtained will protect it for the future. For the past, in the absence of any proven loss, I would confine any financial remedy to an order that PPX pay a reasonable sum for its use of material in breach of the settlement agreement. That sum can properly be described as being 'such sum as might reasonably have been demanded' by Jimi Hendrix's estate 'as a quid pro quo for agreeing to permit the two licences into which PPX entered in breach of the settlement agreement', which was the approach adopted by Brightman J in the *Wrotham Park* case (see [22], above). This involves an element of artificiality, if, as in the *Wrotham Park* case, no permission would ever have been given on any terms. And, where no injunction is possible, even the value of a bargaining opportunity depends on the value which the court puts on the right infringed (see [19], above, citing Lord Nicholls in *Blake*'s case). That said, the approach adopted by Brightman J has the merit of directing the court's attention to the commercial value of the right infringed and of enabling it to assess the sum payable by reference to the fees that might in other contexts be demanded and paid between willing parties. It points in the present case towards orders that PPX pay over, by way of damages, a proportion of each of the advances received to date and (subject to deduction of such proportion) an appropriate royalty rate on retail selling prices. I would therefore allow the appeal against the judge's decision on the first point and declare accordingly.

46 Counsel were also agreed that we should in that event go as far as we could to give guidance to the parties regarding the appropriate proportion. I do not consider that it is possible on the present state of information to reach any final conclusions as [to] the appropriate sum(s) or the appropriate royalty rate(s) on retail selling prices which might be used to arrive at such sums. ...But it may assist if I express my present view (albeit one reached without the benefit of any expert evidence that might be available hereafter) that I would be surprised if the appropriate rate in respect of non-Sch A masters was less than twice that agreed in respect of Sch A masters, or was in other words less than one-third of PPX's royalties on the retail selling price of records.

Peter Gibson LJ:

53 ...*Blake*'s case builds on the recognition in one case on compensation for a breach of a contractual obligation as well as on authorities in other areas of the law that financial loss to the claimant is not always the appropriate or just measure of damages to compensate the claimant for the wrong done to him. A claimant's interest in the performance of a contract may render it just and equitable that the defendant should not benefit from his breach but should account for the profits made by that breach. But it is made abundantly clear in *Blake*'s case that this is a remedy to be granted only in exceptional circumstances.

55 However, like Mance L.J., I do not think the present case an appropriate one for ordering an account of profits. He has drawn attention at paragraph [37], above to the features of the present case which distinguish it from the circumstances in *Blake*'s case. No doubt deliberate breaches of contract occur frequently in the commercial world; yet something more is needed to make the circumstances exceptional enough to justify ordering an account of profits, particularly when another remedy is available.

56 It is apparent from Lord Nicholls' speech that he regarded the decision of Brightman J. in *Wrotham Park Estate Co v Parkside Homes Ltd* [1974] 2 All ER 321, [1974] 1 WLR 798 as a crucial stepping-stone in his reasoning as to why the absence of financially measurable loss flowing from a breach of contract was not necessarily fatal to a claimant's claim for compensation. ...

57 Lord Nicholls was clearly of the view that Brightman J was right not to decide the case on the basis that the breach of covenant did not diminish the value of the houses in the estate at all. As Lord Nicholls said ([2000] 2 All ER (Comm) 487 at 497, [2001] 1 AC 268 at 283), if the estate company was given a nominal or no sum by way of compensation, justice would manifestly not have been done. The same in my judgment applies to the present case. Buckley J thought it relevant that the claimant would never have agreed to PPX's exploitation of the non-Sch A masters, and he rejected a wholly fictional approach. But the *Wrotham Park* case itself demonstrated that it is irrelevant, in assessing compensation on the basis adopted by Brightman J, that in reality there would have been no relaxation of the relevant obligation because of the opposition of the person entitled to the benefit of that obligation. As Brightman J said:

> 'On the facts of this particular case the plaintiffs, rightly conscious of their obligations towards existing residents, would clearly not have granted any relaxation, but for present purposes I must assume that it could have been induced to do so.' (See [1974] 2 All ER 321 at 341, [1974] 1 WLR 798 at 815.)

58 In my judgment, because (1) there has been a deliberate breach by PPX of its contractual obligations for its own reward, (2) the claimant would have difficulty in establishing financial loss therefrom, and (3) the claimant has a legitimate interest in preventing PPX's profit-making activity carried out in breach of PPX's contractual obligations, the present case is a suitable one (as envisaged by Lord Nicholls: [2000] 2 All ER (Comm) 487 at 498, [2001] 1 AC 268 at 283-284) in which damages for breach of contract may be measured by the benefits gained by the wrongdoer from the breach. To avoid injustice I would require PPX to make a reasonable payment in respect of the benefit it has gained. I agree with the guidance suggested by Mance L.J. for the court assessing the damages.

60 For these as well as the reasons given by Mance L.J. I too would allow the appeal.

Hooper J concurred.

NOTES AND QUESTIONS

1. The Court of Appeal was not required to assess the reasonable sum to be awarded as damages but, at [46] above, Mance LJ thought that one-third of the defendant's royalties on the retail selling price of records made from the forbidden tapes would probably be an appropriate reasonable sum. Were these damages compensatory or restitutionary?

2. Was Sir Andrew Morritt V-C correct to order an account of profits in *Esso Petroleum Co Ltd v Niad* [2001] All ER (D) 324, a case referred to by Mance LJ (at [31])?

3. Did the Court of Appeal in part apply *Blake* and in part distinguish *Blake*? See A Burrows, *Remedies for Torts and Breach of Contract* (3rd edn, 2004) 406–7.

4. Is it correct to say that two factors that were influential in the decisions in *Blake* and *Experience Hendrix* were that the breach of contract was cynical and that normal compensatory damages were inadequate?

5. In *WWF–World Wide Fund for Nature v World Wrestling Federation Entertainment Inc* [2007] EWCA Civ 286 it was decided that, having been refused permission to amend its claim to seek an account of profits for breach of contract, it would be an abuse of process for the claimant now to be given permission to claim 'damages on the *Wrotham Park* basis'. In reaching that decision, the Court of Appeal reasoned that damages on that basis and an account of profits are compensatory and not 'gains-based'. Chadwick LJ said at [59]:

    'The circumstances in which an award of damages on the *Wrotham Park* basis may be an appropriate response, and those in which the appropriate response is an account of profits, may differ in degree. But the underlying feature, in both cases, is that the court recognises the need to compensate the claimant in circumstances where he cannot demonstrate identifiable financial loss. To label an award of damages on the *Wrotham Park* basis as a "compensatory" remedy and an order for an account of profits as a "gains-based" remedy does not assist an understanding of the principles on which the court acts. The two remedies should, I think, each be seen as a flexible response to the need to compensate the claimant for the wrong which has been done to him.'

    Whatever the best analysis of 'damages on a *Wrotham Park* basis', can it possibly be correct to regard an account of profits as compensatory and not restitutionary?

3. AGREED/LIQUIDATED DAMAGES

Introductory reading: E McKendrick, *Contract Law* (7th edn, 2007) 21.5–21.6

Dunlop Pneumatic Tyre Ltd v New Garage and Motor Co Ltd
[1915] AC 79, House of Lords

The claimants (Dunlop) were manufacturers of tyres. In a contract with the defendant dealer, the claimants agreed to supply tyres for a discounted price in return for the defendant agreeing that it would not sell the tyres for a price which was lower than the list price. By a further clause of the contract it was agreed that for every tyre sold in breach of the agreement the dealer would pay Dunlop £5 'by way of liquidated damages and not as a penalty'. On discovering a breach by the defendant in selling at below list price a tyre supplied by the claimants, the claimants brought an action for liquidated damages. The trial judge held that the £5 per tyre was liquidated damages but the Court of Appeal reversed this and held that the clause imposed a penalty so that the claimants were entitled to nominal damages only. In overturning the Court of Appeal's decision, the House of Lords held that the clause did not impose a penalty because it was a genuine pre-estimate of loss.

Lord Dunedin: I do not think it advisable to attempt any detailed review of the various cases, but I shall content myself with stating succinctly the various propositions which I think are deducible from the decisions which rank as authoritative:—

1. Though the parties to a contract who use the words "penalty" or "liquidated damages" may prima facie be supposed to mean what they say, yet the expression used is not conclusive. The Court must find out whether the payment stipulated is in truth a penalty or liquidated damages. This doctrine may be said to be found passim in nearly every case.

2. The essence of a penalty is a payment of money stipulated as in terrorem of the offending party; the essence of liquidated damages is a genuine covenanted pre-estimate of damage (*Clydebank Engineering and Shipbuilding Co. v. Don Jose Ramos Yzquierdo y Castaneda* [1905] A. C. 6).

3. The question whether a sum stipulated is penalty or liquidated damages is a question of construction to be decided upon the terms and inherent circumstances of each particular contract, judged of as at the time of the making of the contract, not as at the time of the breach (*Public Works Commissioner v. Hills* [1906] A. C. 368 and *Webster v. Bosanquet* [1912] A. C. 394).

4. To assist this task of construction various tests have been suggested, which if applicable to the case under consideration may prove helpful, or even conclusive. Such are:

(a) It will be held to be penalty if the sum stipulated for is extravagant and unconscionable in amount in comparison with the greatest loss that could conceivably be proved to have followed from the breach. (Illustration given by Lord Halsbury in *Clydebank Case*).

(b) It will be held to be a penalty if the breach consists only in not paying a sum of money, and the sum stipulated is a sum greater than the sum which ought to have been paid (*Kemble v. Farren* 6 Bing. 141). This though one of the most ancient instances is truly a corollary to the last test. …

(c) There is a presumption (but no more) that it is penalty when "a single lump sum is made payable by way of compensation, on the occurrence of one or more or all of several events, some of which may occasion serious and others but trifling damage" (Lord Watson in *Lord Elphinstone v. Monkland Iron and Coal Co.*, 11 App. Cas. 332).

On the other hand:

(*d*) It is no obstacle to the sum stipulated being a genuine pre-estimate of damage, that the consequences of the breach are such as to make precise pre-estimation almost an impossibility. On the contrary, that is just the situation when it is probable that pre-estimated damage was the true bargain between the parties (*Clydebank Case,* Lord Halsbury at p. 11; *Webster v. Bosanquet,* Lord Mersey at p. 398).

Turning now to the facts of the case, it is evident that the damage apprehended by the appellants owing to the breaking of the agreement was an indirect and not a direct damage. So long as they got their price from the respondents for each article sold, it could not matter to them directly what the respondents did with it. Indirectly it did. Accordingly, the agreement is headed "Price Maintenance Agreement," and the way in which the appellants would be damaged if prices were cut is clearly explained in evidence by Mr. Baisley [the appellants' manager], and no successful attempt is made to controvert that evidence. But though damage as a whole from such a practice would be certain, yet damage from any one sale would be impossible to forecast. It is just, therefore, one of those cases where it seems quite reasonable for parties to contract that they should estimate that damage at a certain figure, and provided that figure is not extravagant there would seem no reason to suspect that it is not truly a bargain to assess damages, but rather a penalty to be held in terrorem.

...

On the whole matter, therefore,...I move your Lordships that the appeal be allowed...

Lord Atkinson, Lord Parker of Waddington and **Lord Parmoor** delivered concurring speeches.

NOTES AND QUESTIONS

1. Lord Dunedin's principles are the traditional guide to determining whether the agreed damages are enforceable as liquidated damages or unenforceable as a penalty. If construed as a penalty, normal (unliquidated) damages will be awarded instead.

2. In some recent cases (eg *Murray v Leisureplay plc* [2005] EWCA Civ 963, [2005] IRLR 946) Colman J's words in *Lordsvale Finance plc v Bank of Zambia* [1996] QB 752 have been treated as a useful modern summary of what underpins the approach in the *Dunlop* case. He said at 762 (in deciding that a clause allowing an increase in the interest rate for default on a loan was not a penalty): '[W]hether a provision is to be treated as a penalty is a matter of construction to be resolved by asking whether, at the time the contract was entered into, the predominant contractual function of the provision was to deter a party from breaking the contract or to compensate the innocent party for breach. That the contractual function is deterrent rather than compensatory can be deduced by comparing the amount that would be payable on breach with the loss that might be sustained if breach occurred.' Do you regard this as a helpful gloss on Lord Dunedin's speech?

3. The 'price maintenance' agreement in the *Dunlop* case might now be void under the Competition Act 1998 (which is the latest in a line of legislation dealing with anti-competitive agreements and practices dating back to the (repealed) Restrictive Trade Practices Act 1956).

4. The advantages of upholding liquidated damages include certainty for the parties and the saving of judicial time and expense in assessing damages. Less obvious is why penalties should be struck down even though the term is otherwise a valid one. See on this the articles by Goetz and Scott, and

Downes, below, 418–419. Do you think it would improve the law if penalties were upheld subject to the operation of standard factors invalidating a contract including the Unfair Terms in Consumer Contracts Regulations 1999 (above, 285)? See, in particular, Schedule 2, paragraph 1(e) to those Regulations, which includes on the indicative list of unfair terms a term 'requiring any consumer who fails to fulfil his obligation to pay a disproportionately high sum in compensation'. Assuming, therefore, that consumers are in any event protected, the central question concerning the justification of penalties is whether there is good reason for striking down penalties in a contract between commercial parties.

5.   The law on penalty clauses was extended to a clause to transfer shares rather than to pay money in *Jobson v Johnson* [1989] 1 WLR 1026, CA.

6.   Although this may be thought to encourage the drawing of arbitrary distinctions, the law on liquidated damages and penalties applies only to payments that are to be made in the event of a breach of contract. For examples of the penalty rules not applying to payments on events other than breach (and other than the standard payment of an agreed price or remuneration) see, eg, *Alder v Moore* [1961] 2 QB 57, CA; *Export Credits Guarantee Department v Universal Oil Products Co* [1983] 1 WLR 399, HL.

7.   The courts' power to relieve against a forfeiture clause, requiring the forfeiture of money paid, raises somewhat analogous problems to that raised by penalties and liquidated damages. The obvious difference is that the money has already been paid whereas, in relation to penalties and liquidated damages, the dispute is as to a payment that has yet to be made. This leads to the important point that the underlying cause of action is generally different because, in relation to the forfeiture of money paid, one is generally concerned with restitution for the cause of action of unjust enrichment rather than breach of contract. It would not therefore be appropriate in this book to deal with the forfeiture of money paid in any detail. But it is important to appreciate that, after some dispute in earlier cases, the Privy Council in *Workers Trust and Merchant Bank Ltd v Dojap Investment Ltd* [1993] AC 573 decided that a clause allowing the forfeiture of money paid could be and, on the facts, would be struck down as a 'penalty'; and, in this context, given that deposits do not generally pre-estimate loss, the test applied to decide whether the sum to be forfeited was penal or not was one of reasonableness. One should further note that the courts' long-established power to relieve against unfair forfeiture clauses in contracts extends beyond the forfeiture of money paid to the forfeiture of property: see, eg, *Scandinavian Trading Tanker Co AB v Flota Petrolera Ecuatoriana, The Scaptrade* [1983] 2 AC 694, HL.

Philips Hong Kong Ltd v Attorney General of Hong Kong
(1993) 61 BLR 41, Privy Council

The claimant ('Philips') commenced proceedings to ascertain whether an agreed damages clause, in a contract between the claimant and the Government of Hong Kong for the construction of a road, was penal. The clause in question required the claimant to pay to the Government a sum of money per day 'as liquidated damages … and not as a penalty' for late completion of the work. At first instance the clause was held to be penal but this was overturned by the Court of Appeal of Hong Kong. The claimant's appeal to the Privy Council was unsuccessful, it being held that the clause was a genuine pre-estimate of loss.

Lord Woolf (delivering the judgment of the Privy Council comprising himself, **Lord Templeman, Lord Goff of Chieveley** and **Lord Browne-Wilkinson**): This appeal…raises the issue as to the approach which the courts should adopt in determining whether a clause in a commercial contract is unenforceable as being penal in effect.

…

At this stage Mr Nicholas Dennys QC does not suggest on behalf of Philips that the sum claimed by the Government by way of liquidated damages is in fact exorbitant in view of the very substantial delay which in fact occurred in the execution of this contract by Philips. Instead he bases his argument on what could have happened in a number of different hypothetical situations. He suggests that if one or more of those situations had happened, the sum which would then be payable by way of liquidated damages would be wholly out of proportion to any loss which the Government was likely to suffer in that situation and that this is sufficient to establish that the provisions are penal in effect. If Philips' approach is correct this would be unsatisfactory. It would mean that it would be extremely difficult to devise any provision for the payment of liquidated damages in the case of a contract of this sort which would not be open to attack as being penal. As is the case with most commercial contracts, there is always going to be a variety of different situations in which damage can occur and even though long and detailed provisions are contained in a contract it will often be virtually impossible to anticipate accurately and provide for all the possible scenarios. Whatever the degree of care exercised by the draftsman it will still be almost inevitable that an ingenious argument can be developed for saying that in a particular hypothetical situation a substantially higher sum will be recovered than would be recoverable if the plaintiff was required to prove his actual loss in that situation. Such a result would undermine the whole purpose of parties to a contract being able to agree beforehand what damages are to be recoverable in the event of a breach of contract. This would not be in the interest of either of the parties to the contract since it is to their advantage that they should be able to know with a reasonable degree of certainty the extent of their liability and the risks which they run as a result of entering into the contract. This is particularly true in the case of building and engineering contracts. In the case of those contracts provision for liquidated damages should enable the employer to know the extent to which he is protected in the event of the contractor failing to perform his obligations.

As for the contractor, by agreeing to a provision for liquidated damages, he is seeking to remove the uncertainty as to the extent of his liability under the contract if he is unable to comply with his contractual obligations. That he may be unable to comply with those obligations is always a risk which a contractor has to face and there are substantial advantages from his point of view in being able to quantify accurately the amount of his liability if matters do not proceed according to plan. As [counsel for the Attorney General of Hong Kong] submitted, the liquidated damages clause enables the contractor when quoting for a contract to take account of the possible liability which he may be under in determining a price which he quotes for undertaking the contract, particularly where the amount of loss actually suffered by the employer will be difficult to quantify. It therefore makes commercial sense for both sides of the contract to remove the uncertainty by including a liquidated damages clause in the contract. However this will only be the result if the inclusion of a clause providing for liquidated damages will reduce and not increase the risk of a dispute and possible litigation in the event of the contractor failing to fulfil his contractual obligations.

What then is the position? Is it sufficient for a contractor to identify hypothetical situations where the effect of the application of the clause may be to produce a sum payable to the employer substantially in excess of the damage which the employer is likely to suffer in order to defeat the intended effect of a clause freely entered into by the parties providing for the payment of liquidated damages?...

Although there is a good deal of disagreement as to how the penalty jurisdiction grew up (see the Law Commission Working Paper No 61, *Penalty Clauses and Forfeiture of Monies Paid*) it is recorded in the judgment of Kay LJ in *Law v Local Board of Redditch* [1892] 1 QB 127 at page 133 that originally it was by the Courts of Equity that relief was granted. They did so where a sum of money was agreed to be paid as a penalty for non-performance of a collateral contract where the actual damage which would be sustained could be estimated. In such circumstances the Courts would limit the sum recoverable to the actual loss suffered. The principle would be applied in particular where the penalty was agreed to be paid for the non-payment of a sum of money under a bond. This limited application of the principle was subsequently extended to other situations by the courts of common law, but the principle was always recognised as being subject to fairly narrow constraints and the courts have always avoided claiming that they have any general jurisdiction to rewrite the contracts that the parties have made.

Guidance as to what are the constraints is authoritatively set out in the speech of Lord Dunedin in *Dunlop Pneumatic Tyre Co Ltd v New Garage & Motor Co* [1915] AC 79, at page 86
...

Except possibly in the case of situations where one of the parties to the contract is able to dominate the other as to the choice of the terms of a contract, it will normally be insufficient to establish that a provision is objectionably penal to identify situations where the application of the provision could result in a larger sum being recovered by the injured party than his actual loss. Even in such situations so long as the sum payable in the event of non-compliance with the contract is not extravagant, having regard to the range of losses that it could reasonably be anticipated it would have to cover at the time the contract was made, it can still be a genuine pre-estimate of the loss that would be suffered and so a perfectly valid liquidated damage provision. The use in argument of unlikely illustrations should therefore not assist a party to defeat a provision as to liquidated damages. As the Law Commission stated in Working Paper No 61 (page 30):-

> "The fact that in certain circumstances a party to a contract might derive a benefit in excess of his loss does not . . . outweigh the very definite practical advantages of the present rule upholding a genuine estimate, formed at the time the contract was made of the probable loss."

A difficulty can arise where the range of possible loss is broad. Where it should be obvious that, in relation to part of the range, the liquidated damages are totally out of proportion to certain of the losses which may be incurred, the failure to make special provision for those losses may result in the "liquidated damages" not being recoverable. ...However the court has to be careful not to set too stringent a standard and bear in mind that what the parties have agreed should normally be upheld. Any other approach will lead to undesirable uncertainty especially in commercial contracts. ...

In seeking to establish that the sum described in the Philips contract as liquidated damages was in fact a penalty, Philips has to surmount the strong inference to the contrary resulting from its agreement to make the payments as liquidated damages and the fact that it is not suggesting in these proceedings that the sum claimed is excessive in relation to the actual loss suffered by the Government. The fact that the issue has to be determined objectively, judged at the date the contract was made, does not mean what actually happens subsequently is irrelevant. On the contrary it can provide valuable evidence as to what could reasonably be expected to be the loss at the time the contract was made. Likewise the fact that two parties who should be well capable of protecting their respective commercial interests agreed the allegedly penal provision suggests that the formula for calculating liquidated damages is unlikely to be oppressive.

[*Applying the above principles to the particular facts in this case, he concluded that the particular clause was a genuine pre-estimate of law and not a penalty and therefore dismissed the appeal.*]

NOTES AND QUESTIONS

1. The importance of this case is its refreshing recognition that, in commercial contracts, agreed damages clauses should normally be upheld. More specifically it was stressed that a clause can be a genuine pre-estimate of loss even though hypothetical situations could be presented in which the claimant's actual loss would have been substantially lower. To hold otherwise would be to render it very difficult to draw up valid liquidated damages clauses in complex commercial contracts.
2. Was the case made easier to decide because Philips was not alleging that the agreed damages exceeded the Government's actual loss?

Additional Reading for Chapter 8

J Beatson, *Anson's Law of Contract* (28th edn, 2002) 589–620, 624–9, 653–5
S Smith, *Atiyah's Introduction to the Law of Contract* (6th edn, 2005) 396–408, 412–23

L Fuller and W Perdue, 'The Reliance Interest in Contract Damages' (1936) 46 *Yale LJ* 52

This is the most cited law journal article of all time. In it the authors explore the purposes behind contract damages. They distinguish three such purposes, which they label the protection of the claimant's restitution interest, reliance interest and expectation interest. They principally argue that, contrary to the traditional view that damages are solely concerned with protection of the expectation interest—which aims to put the claimant into as good a position as if the contract had been performed—damages should often be, and on close inspection often are, concerned to protect the reliance interest, which aims to put the claimant into as good a position as he was in before the contract was made. The article therefore seeks to ensure that greater recognition is given to the reliance interest. In seeking to explain why the law ever protects the expectation interest they suggest (at 60–2) that, for bargain promises, the expectation interest may be best justified as: (1) really seeking to protect the claimant's reliance interest because the reliance interest is difficult to prove particularly with regard to the forgoing of opportunities to enter into other bargains; (2) encouraging reliance on bargains thereby ensuring that goods and services find their way to where they are most wanted.

C Goetz and R Scott, 'Liquidated Damages, Penalties and the Just Compensation Principle' (1977) 77 *Col LR* 554

The authors argue that, in the absence of process unfairness in bargaining, economic efficiency will be enhanced by the enforcement of penalties. This is because penalties represent the most efficient means by which parties can insure against what would otherwise not be compensated by damages (eg because the party has idiosyncratic values). Furthermore, the distinction between liquidated damages and penalties involves a costly re-examination of agreements.

D Harris, A Ogus and J Phillips, 'Contract Remedies and the Consumer Surplus' (1979) 95 *LQR* 581

The authors argue that, in respect of remedies for breach of contract, the courts should pay more attention to what economists call the 'consumer surplus', that is, the subjective value of a 'good' over and above its market value. Recognition of this would clarify and rationalise present judicial intuitions in deciding whether to award consumers specific performance, cost of cure damages, and mental distress damages.

P Atiyah, 'Executory Contracts, Expectation Damages, and the Economic Analysis of Contract' in his *Essays on Contract* (1986) 150

Atiyah has long expressed the view that expectation damages are difficult to justify especially in executory contracts. Here he returns to that theme primarily so as to refute the argument that such damages are economically efficient. He concludes, at 178, 'I remain troubled and uncertain about the extent to which executory contracts should be enforced, and the extent to which the expectation damages measure is appropriate, both in wholly executory contracts ...and in partly performed or relied-upon contracts.'

D Friedmann, 'The Performance Interest in Contract Damages' (1995) 111 *LQR* 628

This constitutes a penetrating attack on Fuller and Perdue's 'Reliance Interest' article. Terminologically, it is argued that it is better to talk of the 'performance interest' than the 'expectation interest' (not least because the latter implies, incorrectly, that one has no legal right to it). More importantly, the article goes on to show that the law is justified in protecting the performance interest and has expanded, rather than weakened, that protection in recent years (eg by being more willing to order specific performance and cost of cure damages). The author therefore argues that Fuller and Perdue's thesis favouring reliance damages and attacking the 'performance interest' is fundamentally flawed.

T Downes, 'Rethinking Penalty Clauses' in *Wrongs and Remedies in the Twenty-First Century* (ed P Birks, 1996) 249

The author argues that the law on penalty clauses (and related clauses) can be, and should be, realigned with the general law on 'unconscionability'. This would mean that freely-negotiated penalty clauses would be valid. In contrast, penalty clauses that fall foul of the Unfair Terms in Consumer Contracts Regulations or which constitute unfair advantage-taking of a weaker party (see Chapter 15 below) would be invalid.

J Cartwright, 'Remoteness of Damage in Contract and Tort: a Reconsideration' [1996] *CLJ* 488

Cartwright argues that, while 'foreseeability of consequences' plays an important role in the tests of remoteness in both contract and tort, its precise meaning differs according to the basis for the imposition of the duty with which one is concerned. That is, the rule of remoteness must be consistent with the reasons for the cause of action. So in contract, and in tort where one is concerned with a duty of care based on an 'assumption of responsibility', one is concerned with the scope of the risks agreed or assumed; but in most tort cases, concerned with the claimant's physical interest, 'the courts tend to look more towards ensuring compensation for the plaintiff than protecting the defendant from a liability wider than he can be taken to have agreed' (at 514).

B Coote, 'Contract Damages, Ruxley and the Performance Interest' [1997] *CLJ* 537

Coote takes Friedmann's 'performance interest' terminology and equates it with 'cost of cure' damages. He contrasts this with what he calls 'mere compensation for the economic consequences of breach' which has more conventionally been called 'difference in value' damages. He then goes on to argue, in the light of the *Ruxley* case, that the courts should be more willing to award damages protecting the performance interest (ie cost of cure) provided reasonable to do so. He favours 'downgrading' the importance of the claimant's intention to cure. In contracts for the benefit of third parties his approach would lead to 'cost of cure' damages being naturally recoverable by the contracting party as his own loss, irrespective of whether that party has cured or intends to cure. [Note that Coote's approach to contracts for the benefit of third parties was especially influential on Lord Goff in his minority reasoning in the *Alfred McAlpine* case (see below, 491). For criticism of Coote's article see A Burrows, *Remedies for Torts and Breach of Contract* (3rd edn, 2004, 210–11).]

E McKendrick, 'Breach of Contract, Restitution for Wrongs, and Punishment' in *Commercial Remedies* (eds A Burrows and E Peel, 2003) 93

The author explores the decision in, and consequences of, *AG v Blake*. He emphasises the exceptional nature of an account of profits for breach of contract and criticises *Esso Petroleum Co Ltd v Niad* (above, 408) for taking too wide a view of when such an award can be made. He also assesses the argument, in the light of the tort case of *Kuddus v Chief Constable of Leicestershire Constabulary* (above, 406, note 5), that punitive damages should be available for breach of contract. He suggests that they should be, albeit only in a very exceptional case. Overall he points out that the impact of these decisions is to make the remedial regime for breach of contract potentially more complex and, in the short term, uncertain. [For a practitioner's comment on McKendrick's paper and for a review of a discussion on the issues in it, see *Commercial Remedies* 125–30.]

R Cunnington, 'Should Punitive Damages be Part of the Judicial Arsenal in Contract Cases?' (2006) 26 *Legal Studies* 369

The author recommends that punitive damages should be exceptionally awarded to deter outrageous breaches of contract where compensatory damages are inadequate and where restitutionary damages are unavailable. He argues that the *Addis* case is weak authority for the non-availability of such damages; that the main arguments against punitive damages in civil cases are unpersuasive; that there is no good reason for retaining punitive damages in tort while denying them for breach of contract; and that the efficient breach theory is unconvincing.

***Principles of European Contract Law* (eds O Lando and H Beale, 2000) 434–48**

Article 9:501: Right to Damages

(1) The aggrieved party is entitled to damages for loss caused by the other party's non-performance which is not excused under Article 8:108.

(2) The loss for which damages are recoverable includes:

(a) non-pecuniary loss; and

(b) future loss which is reasonably likely to occur.

[This is very similar to English law but there appears to be no possibility of non-compensatory damages; and there is no limit expressed on the availability of damages for non-pecuniary loss: see above, 401–412 and 389–397. For Article 8:108, see below, 694.]

Article 9:502: General Measure of Damages

The general measure of damages is such sum as will put the aggrieved party as nearly as possible into the position in which it would have been if the contract had been duly performed. Such damages cover the loss which the aggrieved party has suffered and the gain of which it has been deprived.

[This is the same as English law's protection of the expectation (or performance) interest: see above, 338–339.]

Article 9:503: Foreseeability

The non-performing party is liable only for loss which it foresaw or could reasonably have foreseen at the time of conclusion of the contract as a likely result of its non-performance, unless the non-performance was intentional or grossly negligent.

[This is similar to the English law on remoteness, leaving aside the exception: see above, 357–375.]

Article 9:504: Loss Attributable to Aggrieved Party
The non-performing party is not liable for loss suffered by the aggrieved party to the extent that the aggrieved party contributed to the non-performance or its effects.

[This is similar to the English law but appears to differ in envisaging that contributory negligence can apply to all types of breach of contract: see above, 380–387.]

Article 9:505: Reduction of Loss
(1) The non-performing party is not liable for loss suffered by the aggrieved party to the extent that the aggrieved party could have reduced its loss by taking reasonable steps.

(2) The aggrieved party is entitled to recover any expenses reasonably incurred in attempting to reduce its loss.

[This precisely matches the English law on mitigation: see above, 378–380.]

Article 9:509: Agreed Payment for Non-performance
(1) Where the contract provides that a party who fails to perform is to pay a specified sum to the aggrieved party for such non-performance, the aggrieved party shall be awarded that sum irrespective of its actual loss.

(2) However, despite any agreement to the contrary the specified sum may be reduced to a reasonable amount where it is grossly excessive in relation to the loss resulting from the non-performance and the other circumstances.

[This differs from the English approach to liquidated damages in eg looking, after the event, at whether those damages grossly exceed the actual loss: see above, 412–417.]

9

Direct Enforcement

In the last chapter we examined damages, which are a substitutionary remedy for a breach of contract. They do not purport to enforce directly the defendant's contractual promise. Put another way, they constitute the enforcement of a secondary obligation triggered by the breach rather than enforcing the primary contractual obligation. In this chapter, we turn to look at remedies which enforce directly the contractual promise/the primary contractual obligation. They require the defendant to do, or not to do, what he promised to do or not to do. There are three such remedies.

The first, the award of an agreed sum (commonly referred to as an action in debt) is a common law monetary remedy. It is the commonest claim brought in respect of a breach of contract. It is the appropriate remedy, for example, for the price of goods sold, for remuneration for work done, for the repayment of a loan, or for a landlord's rent.

The second and third remedies are specific performance and (prohibitory) injunctions. These are equitable and, normally, non-monetary remedies which, respectively, require the promisor to do (specific performance) or not to do (prohibitory injunction) what he contractually promised to do or not to do.

Introductory reading: E McKendrick, *Contract Law* (7th edn, 2007) 21.4 (and 19.9), 21.9–21.10.

1. THE AWARD OF AN AGREED SUM

The award of an agreed sum is a very straightforward remedy. It simply orders the defendant to pay the sum that it contracted to pay. In general, all that the claimant needs to show is that the sum claimed is due. So, for example, subject to an express term for advance payment or for payment at another time, a seller of goods is entitled to the agreed price once property in the goods has passed to the buyer (as laid down in section 49(1) of the Sale of Goods Act 1979); and, subject to a term to the contrary, a builder is entitled to the agreed price once he has substantially completed the stage of the building to which the payment relates (a leading case on substantial performance being *Hoenig v Isaacs* [1952] 2 All ER 176, CA, in which the claimant, who had decorated and furnished a flat, was held entitled to the agreed price of £750 subject to a set-off of some £56 damages enabling the owner to rectify some defects in the workmanship).

In contrast to (unliquidated) damages, an award of an agreed sum requires no assessment by the courts; and limitations, such as remoteness, intervening cause and contributory negligence, are inapplicable. The one burning issue of controversy—as we shall see in the cases below—is whether the duty to mitigate ever applies to bar the award of an agreed sum.

It should be emphasised that we are not examining in this chapter liquidated damages, albeit that liquidated damages are enforceable by an award of the agreed sum. Liquidated damages have instead been considered in Chapter 8. In contrast to the agreed sums covered in this chapter, an award of liquidated damages does not seek to enforce the primary contractual obligation. It rather enforces the agreed secondary obligation for breach of the primary contractual obligation.

White and Carter (Councils) Ltd v McGregor
[1962] AC 413, House of Lords (Sc)

The claimants supplied to local authorities litterbins on which they let advertising space. The defendants contracted to pay for the display of adverts on litterbins, advertising their garage business, but later that day they repudiated the contract, which had been concluded by their sales manager contrary to the wishes of the proprietor. The claimants refused to accept the repudiation, went ahead and displayed the adverts for the three-year period of the contract and claimed the agreed price of £196 4s. The House of Lords, allowing an appeal from the Court of Session, held, by a 3–2 majority, that they were entitled to the agreed price.

Lord Reid: The general rule cannot be in doubt. It was settled in Scotland at least as early as 1848 and it has been authoritatively stated time and again in both Scotland and England. If one party to a contract repudiates it in the sense of making it clear to the other party that he refuses or will refuse to carry out his part of the contract, the other party, the innocent party, has an option. He may accept that repudiation and sue for damages for breach of contract, whether or not the time for performance has come; or he may if he chooses disregard or refuse to accept it and then the contract remains in full effect.

   ...

I need not refer to the numerous authorities. They are not disputed by the respondent but he points out that in all of them the party who refused to accept the repudiation had no active duties under the contract. The innocent party's option is generally said to be to *wait* until the date of performance and then to claim damages estimated as at that date. There is no case in which it is said that he may, in face of the repudiation, go on and incur useless expense in performing the contract and then claim the contract price. The option, it is argued, is merely as to the date as at which damages are to be assessed.

Developing this argument, the respondent points out that in most cases the innocent party cannot complete the contract himself without the other party doing, allowing or accepting something, and that it is purely fortuitous that the appellants can do so in this case. In most cases by refusing co-operation the party in breach can compel the innocent party to restrict his claim to damages. Then it was said that, even where the innocent party can complete the contract without such co-operation, it is against the public interest that he should be allowed to do so. An example was developed in argument. A company might engage an expert to go abroad and prepare an elaborate report and then repudiate the contract before anything was done. To allow such an expert then to waste thousands of pounds in preparing the report cannot be right if a much smaller sum of damages would give him full compensation for his loss. It would merely enable the expert to extort a settlement giving him far more than reasonable compensation.

...

It may well be that, if it can be shown that a person has no legitimate interest, financial or otherwise, in performing the contract rather than claiming damages, he ought not to be allowed to saddle the other party with an additional burden with no benefit to himself. If a party has no interest to enforce a stipulation, he cannot in general enforce it: so it might be said that, if a party has no interest to insist on a particular remedy, he ought not to be allowed to insist on it. And, just as a party is not allowed to enforce a penalty, so he ought not to be allowed to penalise the other party by taking one course when another is equally advantageous to him. If I may revert to the example which I gave of a company engaging an expert to prepare an elaborate report and then repudiating before anything was done, it might be that the company could show that the expert had no substantial or legitimate interest in carrying out the work rather than accepting damages: I would think that the de minimis principle would apply in determining whether his interest was substantial, and that he might have a legitimate interest other than an immediate financial interest. But if the expert had no such interest then that might be regarded as a proper case for the exercise of the general equitable jurisdiction of the court. But that is not this case. Here the respondent did not set out to prove that the appellants had no legitimate interest in completing the contract and claiming the contract price rather than claiming damages; there is nothing in the findings of fact to support such a case, and it seems improbable that any such case could have been proved. It is, in my judgment, impossible to say that the appellants should be deprived of their right to claim the contract price merely because the benefit to them, as against claiming damages and re-letting their advertising space, might be small in comparison with the loss to the respondent: that is the most that could be said in favour of the respondent. Parliament has on many occasions relieved parties from certain kinds of improvident or oppressive contracts, but the common law can only do that in very limited circumstances. Accordingly, I am unable to avoid the conclusion that this appeal must be allowed...

Lord Hodson: In *Howard v. Pickford Tool Co. Ltd.* [1951] 1 K.B. 417, 421 Asquith L.J. said: "An unaccepted repudiation is a thing writ in water and of no value to anybody: it confers no legal rights of any sort or kind." [This is an] English [case] but that the law of Scotland is the same is, I think, clear from the authorities...

It follows that, if, as here, there was no acceptance, the contract remains alive for the benefit of both parties and the party who has repudiated can change his mind but it does not follow that the party at the receiving end of the proffered repudiation is bound to accept it before the time for performance and is left to his remedy in damages for breach.

Mr. Bennett, for the respondent, did not seek to dispute the general proposition of law to which I have referred but sought to argue that if at the date of performance by the innocent party the guilty party maintains his refusal to accept performance and the innocent party does not accept the repudiation, although the contract still survives, it does not survive so far as the right of the innocent party to perform it is concerned but survives only for the purpose of enforcing remedies open to him by way of damages or specific implement.

This produces an impossible result; if the innocent party is deprived of some of his rights it involves putting an end to the contract except in cases, unlike this, where, in the exercise of the court's discretion, the remedy of specific implement is available.

The true position is that the contract survives and does so not only where specific implement is available. When the assistance of the court is not required the innocent party can choose whether he will accept repudiation and sue for damages for anticipatory breach or await the date of performance by the guilty party. Then, if there is failure in performance, his rights are preserved.

It may be unfortunate that the appellants have saddled themselves with an unwanted contract causing an apparent waste of time and money. No doubt this aspect impressed the Court of Session but there is no equity which can assist the respondent. It is trite that equity will not rewrite an improvident contract where there is no disability on either side. There is no duty laid upon a party to a subsisting contract to vary it at the behest of the other party so as to deprive himself of the benefit given to him by the contract. To hold otherwise would be to introduce a novel equitable doctrine that a party was not to be held to his contract unless the court in a given instance thought it reasonable so to do. In this case it would make an action for debt a claim for a discretionary remedy. This would introduce an uncertainty into the field of contract which appears to be unsupported by authority either in English or Scottish law save for the one case upon which the Court of Session founded its opinion and which must, in my judgment, be taken to have been wrongly decided.

Lord Morton of Henryton (dissenting): My Lords, I think that this is a case of great importance, although the claim is for a comparatively small sum. If the appellants are right, strange consequences follow in any case in which, under a repudiated contract, services are to be performed by the party who has not repudiated it, so long as he is able to perform these services without the co-operation of the repudiating party. Many examples of such contracts could be given. One, given in the course of the argument and already mentioned by my noble and learned friend, Lord Reid, is the engagement of an expert to go abroad and write a report on some subject for a substantial fee plus his expenses. If the appellants succeed in the present case, it must follow that the expert is entitled to incur the expense of going abroad, to write his unwanted report, and then to recover the fee and expenses, even if the other party has plainly repudiated the contract before any expense has been incurred.

It is well established that repudiation by one party does not put an end to a contract. The other party can say "I hold you to your contract, which still remains in force." What then is his remedy if the repudiating party persists in his repudiation and refuses to carry out his part of the contract? The contract has been broken. The innocent party is entitled to be compensated by damages for any loss which he has suffered by reason of the breach, and in a limited class of cases the court will decree specific implement. The law of Scotland provides no other remedy for a breach of contract and there is no reported case which decides that the innocent party may act as the appellants have acted. The present case is one in which specific implement could not be decreed, since the only obligation of the respondent under the contract was to pay a sum of money for services to be rendered by the appellants. Yet the appellants are claiming a kind of inverted specific implement of the contract. They first insist on performing their part of the contract, against the will of the other party, and then claim that he must perform his part and pay the contract price for unwanted services. In my opinion, my Lords, the appellants' only remedy was damages, and they were bound to take steps to minimise their loss, according to a well-established rule of law. Far from doing this, having incurred no expense at the date of the repudiation, they made no attempt to procure another advertiser, but deliberately went on to incur expense and perform unwanted services with the intention of creating a money debt which did not exist at the date of the repudiation.

Lord Keith of Avonholm (dissenting): I find the argument advanced for the appellants a somewhat startling one. If it is right it would seem that a man who has contracted to go to Hongkong at his own expense and make a report, in return for remuneration of £10,000, and who, before the date fixed for the start of the journey and perhaps before he has incurred any expense, is informed by the other contracting party that he has cancelled or repudiates the contract, is entitled to set off for Hongkong and produce his report in order to claim in debt the stipulated sum. Such a result is not, in my opinion, in accordance with principle or authority, and cuts across the rule that where one party is in breach of contract the other must take steps to minimise the loss sustained by the breach.

Lord Tucker agreed with Lord Hodson.

1. This is the leading case establishing that, at least in general, the duty to mitigate does not apply to restrict the award of an agreed sum. It is also authority for the proposition that an innocent party has an election whether or not to accept an anticipatory repudiation (see above, 332, note 2).

2. The decision serves to mark off the award of an agreed sum not only from damages but also from specific performance (which is referred to in this case by its Scottish name 'specific implement'). This is because the primary bar to specific performance is where damages are adequate and adequacy includes where the claimant can go out into the market and acquire a substitute, thereby mitigating its loss.

3. Even if one agrees with the *White & Carter* principle, it can only apply, as emphasised by Lord Reid, where the innocent party can earn the agreed sum without the other party's co-operation. In many cases, this will not be possible. In obiter dicta in *Hounslow London BC v Twickenham Garden Developments Ltd* [1971] Ch 233 Megarry J said that co-operation included passive co-operation and that a builder working on another's land could not ignore the owner's repudiation, and go on with performance of the contract so as to claim the agreed sum, because the builder required the owner's co-operation in allowing him to enter his land.

4. Do you agree with the decision in *White & Carter?* Can it be correct for the courts to encourage economic efficiency, through the duty to mitigate, in the context of damages while abandoning that policy in the context of an award of an agreed sum?

5. Lord Reid, while allowing the appeal, qualified the innocent party's right to hold the contract open and to claim the agreed sum by saying that it might be that that would not apply where it could be shown that the claimant had 'no legitimate interest' in performing the contract rather than claiming damages. It is not entirely clear what he meant by this. It would seem that he had extreme facts in mind given that in this case he held that that qualification was not made out. In *Attica Sea Carriers Corporation v Ferrostaal, The Puerto Buitrago* [1976] 1 Lloyd's Rep 250, *White and Carter* was distinguished on facts that were extreme. The charterers chartered a ship from the shipowners for 17 months. The ship developed engine trouble. Repairs were estimated to cost four times ($2 million) as much as the difference between the value of the ship with and without the repairs. Although the charterers admitted liability for $400,000, the owners refused to accept redelivery of the ship until repaired and claimed the continuing agreed hire. The Court of Appeal held that, even if the charterers were contractually bound to repair the ship before redelivery (the Court of Appeal thought they were not so bound) the owners could not insist on holding the contract open and claiming the agreed hire. Lord Denning MR mounted a full-scale attack on *White & Carter.* Orr and Browne LJJ, while saying that they

agreed with Lord Denning, distinguished *White & Carter* on the grounds that the owners here needed the co-operation of the charterers and, applying Lord Reid's qualification, that the charterers had set out to show that the owners had 'no legitimate interest' in holding the contract open. But it should be stressed that the facts of *The Puerto Buitrago* were extreme. The owners' approach was clearly unreasonable given that repairing the ship would have been so economically wasteful.

6. In contrast, *White & Carter* was applied in *Gator Shipping Corp v Trans-Asiatic Oil Co Ltd SA and Occidental Shipping Establishment, The Odenfeld* [1978] 2 Lloyd's Rep 357, another charterparty case, in which there were no such extreme facts. Charterers had repudiated a charterparty but the owners had refused to accept this and had kept the vessel at their disposal. The claimants, who were assignees of money due under the charterparty, now claimed the agreed hire for the period in question. Kerr J distinguished *The Puerto Buitrago* and considered that it was only in extreme cases like that that *White & Carter* did not apply. In a statement resembling Lord Reid's, Kerr J said, at 374, '... any fetter on the innocent party's right of election whether or not to accept a repudiation will only be applied in extreme cases, viz where damages would be an adequate remedy *and* where an election to keep the contract alive would be wholly unreasonable'. Kerr J went on to say that on the facts of the case there was doubt about the adequacy of damages because of the difficulty in their assessment and that, since the owners had obligations to the claimants to keep the charterparty in existence, they were not acting unreasonably in refusing to accept the repudiation.

Clea Shipping Corporation v Bulk Oil International Ltd, The Alaskan Trader [1983] 2 Lloyd's Rep 645, Queen's Bench Division

The owners of a ship time-chartered it to the charterers for a period of two years. After about a year the ship had an engine breakdown which required repair. The charterers indicated that they had no further use for the ship but the owners went ahead with the repairs (which took some months), and from April 1981 until the expiry of the charter in December 1981 kept the ship at the charterers' disposal. No orders were given by the charterers (ie no use was made of the ship). The charterers paid the hire during that eight-month period but now sought to recover it on the ground that the owners should have accepted their repudiation and were restricted to damages. Lloyd J held that the charterers were entitled to recover the hire because the arbitrator had found on the evidence—and it could not be said that no reasonable arbitrator could so have found—that the owners had no legitimate interest in holding the contract open and claiming the hire.

Lloyd J: The owners argued that they were entitled to retain the hire, since they had kept the vessel at the disposal of the charterers throughout the period. They relied on the decision of the House of Lords in *White and Carter (Councils) Ltd. v. McGregor*, [1962] 2 A.C. 413, and the decision of Mr. Justice Kerr in *The Odenfeld*, [1978] 2 Lloyd's Rep. 357. The charterers on the other hand argued that the owners ought, in all reason, to have accepted the charterers' conduct as a repudiation of the charter, and claimed damages. Even if no alternative employment could be found for the vessel, it would have been a great deal cheaper to lay the vessel up, rather than maintain her with a full crew on board. They relied on the decision of the Court of Appeal in *Attica Sea Carriers Corporation v. Ferrostaal Poseidon Bulk Reederei G.m.b.H. (The Puerto Buitrago)*, [1976] 1 Lloyd's Rep. 250.

[*Having considered those authorities, Lloyd J continued:*]

...Whether one takes Lord Reid's language, which was adopted by Lords Justices Orr and Browne in *The Puerto Buitrago*, or Lord Denning M.R.'s language in that case ("in all reason"), or Mr. Justice Kerr's language in *The Odenfeld* ("wholly unreasonable, quite unrealistic, unreasonable and untenable"), there comes a point at which the Court will cease, on general equitable principles, to allow the innocent party to enforce his contract according to its strict legal terms. How one defines that point is obviously a matter of some difficulty; for it involves drawing a line between conduct which is merely unreasonable (see per Lord Reid in *White and Carter v. McGregor* criticizing the Lord President in *Langford Co. Ltd. v. Dutch*) and conduct which is *wholly* unreasonable: see per Mr. Justice Kerr in *The Odenfeld*. But however difficult it may be to define the point, that there *is* such a point seems to me to have been accepted both by the Court of Appeal in *The Puerto Buitrago* and by Mr. Justice Kerr in *The Odenfeld*.

...I appreciate, too, that the importance of certainty was one of the main reasons urged by Lord Hodson in *White and Carter v. McGregor* in upholding the innocent party's unfettered right to elect. But for reasons already mentioned, it seems to me that this Court is bound to hold that there is some fetter, if only in extreme cases; and for want of a better way of describing that fetter, it is safest for this Court to use the language of Lord Reid, which, as I have already mentioned, was adopted by a majority of the Court of Appeal in *The Puerto Buitrago*.

...

On the facts of *The Odenfeld*, Mr. Justice Kerr held on various grounds that the owners had ample justification for enforcing their claim for hire, at least until September, 1976, although he went on to hold that the owners must be taken to have accepted the charterers' repudiation when they laid up the vessel in July, 1976. Mr. Justice Kerr did not use the language of "legitimate interest". But he must be taken to have found that the charterers had failed to prove absence of legitimate interest on the part of the owners in claiming hire. One of the grounds on which Mr. Justice Kerr so found was the difficulty in calculating damages.

In the present case, by contrast, the arbitrator has found, and found clearly, that the owners had *no* legitimate interest in pursuing their claim for hire. In my view that finding is conclusive of this appeal. Mr. Colman argued that the finding must be wrong in law. The arbitrator must have misunderstood what was said by Lord Reid, or applied the wrong test. But I could only accept that submission if the conclusion reached by the arbitrator was one which no reasonable arbitrator could have reached applying the right test. I cannot take that view. Indeed I can well understand why the arbitrator reached the conclusion he did. It is of course quite unnecessary for me to say whether I would have reached the same conclusion on the facts myself; nor by saying even that, do I mean to imply that I would have reached a different conclusion. It was the arbitrator who heard the evidence over many days; not me. It was for him to decide.

NOTES AND QUESTIONS

1. It is hard to see why this was regarded as an 'extreme' case. While purporting to follow *White and Carter*, was Lloyd J in substance, if not in form, approving a departure from it?

2. In another charterparty case, *Ocean Marine Navigation Ltd v Koch Carbon Inc, The Dynamic* [2003] EWHC 1936 (Comm), [2003] 2 Lloyd's Rep 693, Simon J, in remitting the case back to the arbitrator, summarised the *White and Carter v McGregor* line of cases as follows at [23]:

'These cases establish the following exception to the general rule that the innocent party has an option whether or not to accept a repudiation: (i) The burden is on the *contract-breaker* to show that the innocent party has no legitimate interest in performing the contract rather than claiming damages. (ii) The burden is not discharged merely by showing that the benefit to the other party is small in comparison to the loss to the contract-breaker. (iii) The exception to the general rule applies only in extreme cases: where damages would be an adequate remedy and where an election to keep the contract alive would be unreasonable.'

In the previous paragraph, he said, 'Although the use of the qualifying word *wholly* in the expression *wholly unreasonable* in *The Odenfeld* properly emphasises that the rule is general and the exception only applies in extreme cases, it adds nothing to the test …' Do you agree?

Reichman v Beveridge [2006] EWCA Civ 1659, Court of Appeal

The claimants let out offices to the defendant solicitors (Beveridge and Gauntlett) on a five-year lease. About half-way through, the defendants ceased to practise and, having no need for the offices, stopped paying rent (in March 2003). Nine months later the claimants sued for the arrears of rent then due. Although the claimants knew of the defendants' circumstances, they had not instructed agents to find new tenants, had refused an offer of a prospective new tenant, and had refused the defendants' offer to negotiate a payment for surrender of the lease. The defendants argued that the claimants had therefore failed in their duty to mitigate and so were not entitled to the arrears. In dismissing the defendants' appeal, that argument was rejected by the Court of Appeal. It held that, applying Lord Reid's speech in *White and Carter v McGregor*, as developed in later cases, damages were not adequate because a landlord was probably not entitled to damages from a tenant who had given up a lease, and the claimants had not acted wholly unreasonably.

Lloyd LJ [*After first examining* White and Carter v McGregor *and the four charterparty cases, mentioned above, 427–430, he continued:*]

17 There is, therefore, a very limited category of cases in which, although the innocent party to a contract has not accepted a repudiation by the other party, and although the innocent party is able to continue to perform all his obligations under the contract despite the absence of co-operation from the other party, nevertheless the court will not allow the innocent party to enforce his full contractual right to maintain the contract in force and sue for the contract price. The characteristics of such cases are that an election to keep the contract alive would be wholly unreasonable and that damages would be an adequate remedy, or that the landlord would have no legitimate interest in making such an election. Mr Gauntlett seeks to establish that a case where the tenant has not only failed to pay rent and all other sums due under the lease, but has also abandoned the demised premises is, or may be, within this category of cases.

28 If it is still the law of England that damages for the loss of future rent cannot be recovered after the landlord has taken back possession of the premises following a tenant's default, as seems to me to be the case, then damages cannot be an adequate remedy for the landlord…and one of the conditions for the intervention of equity so as to fetter the landlord's ability to hold the tenant to the lease is not satisfied. Even if it is not clear that this is the position under English law, the uncertainty of the position at law would be relevant to the reasonableness or otherwise of the landlord's conduct. The landlord could not be

criticised for wishing to avoid embarking on litigation which might have to go to the House of Lords before the point was settled.

39 Mr Gauntlett urged on us a modern approach to the relationship between landlord and tenant, focussing on principles of contract law, and a policy approach which would not leave premises empty, after the tenants had abandoned them and while the landlord waited for the end of the lease, so as to avoid the waste of useful space and to ensure that property is put to beneficial use. As to the latter factor, if there is enough demand for the space, the market rent may exceed that payable under the lease in which case the landlord will no doubt terminate the lease and re-let at a profit. Equally, the tenant can attempt to find an assignee or sub-tenant to use the premises; it is not only the landlord who can take steps to fill the space.

40 Leaving aside policy issues of that kind, it seems to me that Mr Gauntlett's submissions fail to take account of the present state of English law as to the consequences of the premature termination of a tenancy, or of the very limited scope for the intervention of equity as explained in *White and Carter* and subsequent cases. Having regard to the way in which that has been explored and explained in the cases, in particular *The Odenfeld* ...it seems to me impossible to say that a tenant could successfully invoke equity in that way. First, it seems to me very far from clear, to say the least, that the landlords were acting unreasonably in not taking their own steps to find a new tenant, rather than leaving it to the tenants to propose one, or in rejecting a proposal made by the tenants. Given the extremely limited nature of the test ('wholly unreasonable'), it would have to be a most extraordinary case for a tenant to be able to show that the landlord's conduct could properly be characterised in this way. Secondly, if it be the case that in 2003 the market rent was lower than that reserved by the lease, damages would not be an adequate remedy for the landlords if they terminated the lease by way of forfeiture and then re-let at a lower rent, because under English law as it stands they could not recover damages to compensate for the loss of rent. If, on the other hand the market rent was the same or higher, it should have been possible for the tenants to take their own steps to find an assignee. ...

41 It is also to be noted that it is for the party in breach to establish that the innocent party's conduct is wholly unreasonable and that damages would be an adequate remedy. Mr Gauntlett's position seems to be that any landlord, knowing that the tenants have abandoned the premises, ought to take steps to re-let, and therefore to terminate the tenancy, and look to the tenant for damages to cover any resulting loss. It does not seem to me that this could be right. It cannot follow from what Lord Reid said in *White and Carter*. It is clear from that and the later cases that it would be extremely rare for this principle to apply, whereas Mr Gauntlett seeks to apply it to what must be a very common set of circumstances.

42 ...There is...no case in English law that shows that a landlord can recover damages from a former tenant in respect of loss of future rent after termination, and there is at least one case which decides that he cannot. In those circumstances, either damages are not an adequate remedy for the landlord, or at least the landlord would be acting reasonably in taking the view that he should not terminate the lease because he may well not be able to recover such damages. In principle, moreover, if the landlord chooses to regard it as up to the tenant to propose an assignee, sub-tenant or, if he wishes, a substitute tenant under a new tenancy, rather than take the initiative himself, that is not unreasonable, still less wholly unreasonable.

Auld and **Rix LJJ** concurred.

NOTE AND QUESTION

This is an interesting application of *White & Carter* to the common situation of a tenant giving up an unexpired lease. It seems very odd that damages are not available to a landlord in that situation and it is a pity that the Court of Appeal was not willing to develop the law of landlord and tenant in that respect. Had damages been available, what do you think the decision would then have been?

2. SPECIFIC PERFORMANCE

Specific performance is an equitable remedy which directly enforces a defendant's positive contractual obligations: that is, it orders the defendant to do what he or she promised to do. Prohibitory injunctions also directly enforce contractual promises but differ in that the promises in question are negative. However, if what is in form a prohibitory injunction in substance orders specific performance, or if the courts consider that in practice the injunction amounts to specific performance, it is governed by specific performance principles and is dealt with in this section. For example, if a prohibitory injunction orders the defendant, in accordance with his contract, not to work for anyone other than the claimant, this will generally in practice force the defendant to carry on working for the claimant and the principles applicable to specific performance should therefore apply.

In contrast to damages, specific performance is not available for every breach of contract. Indeed the law on specific performance is best approached by examining the numerous restrictions on its availability. It then follows that, if the remedy is not barred by such restrictions, a claimant who applies for it will succeed.

One can list the bars/restrictions on specific performance as follows: adequacy of damages, the constant supervision objection, contracts for personal service, want of mutuality, uncertainty, contracts not supported by valuable consideration, contracts unfairly obtained, impossibility, severe hardship, and the claimant's conduct. We shall confine our examination of the cases to the first four of these bars which are the most interesting. For a full consideration of all the bars, see A Burrows, *Remedies for Torts and Breach of Contract* (3rd edn, 2004) Chapter 20.

One may detect in the cases a general trend towards specific performance being easier to obtain today than in the past. For consideration of this, see Burrows, 504–5.

(1) The Primary Restriction—Adequacy of Damages

Falcke v Gray (1859) 4 Drew 651, Court of Chancery

The defendant, Mrs Gray, contracted to sell to Mr Falcke, who was a dealer in curiosities and china, two china jars for £40. He knew that they were worth a lot more than £40. Subsequent to the contract, Mrs Gray, now realising that the jars were worth far more than £40, refused to deliver them to Mr Falcke and sold them for £200 to a third party. Mr Falcke sought specific performance against Mrs Gray (and delivery up for the tort of conversion against the third party). The claim for specific performance failed (as did the claim against the third party) because the contract had been unfairly obtained. But the court would otherwise have ordered specific performance because, given the rarity and beauty of the goods, damages were inadequate.

Vice-Chancellor Kindersley: The first ground of defence is that, this being a bill for the specific performance of a contract for the purchase of chattels, this Court will not interfere. But I am of opinion that the Court will not refuse to interfere simply because the contract relates to chattels, and that if there were no other objection the contract in this case is such a contract as the Court would specifically perform.

What is the difference in the view of the Court between realty and personalty in respect to the question whether the Court will interfere or not? Upon what principle does the Court decree specific performance of any contract whatever?...A Court of law gives damages for the non-performance, but a Court of Equity says "that is not sufficient – justice is not satisfied by that remedy;" and, therefore, a Court of Equity will decree specific performance, because a mere compensation in damages is not a sufficient remedy and satisfaction for the loss of the performance of the contract.

Now why should that principle apply less to chattels? If in a contract for chattels damages will be a sufficient compensation, the party is left to that remedy. Thus if a contract is for the purchase of a certain quantity of coals, stock, &c. this Court will not decree specific performance, because a person can go into the market and buy similar articles, and get damages for any difference in the price of the articles in a Court of law. But if damages would not be a sufficient compensation, the principle, on which a Court of Equity decrees specific performance, is just as applicable to a contract for the sale and purchase of chattels, as to a contract for the sale and purchase of land.

In the present case the contract is for the purchase of articles of unusual beauty, rarity and distinction, so that damages would not be an adequate compensation for non-performance; and I am of opinion that a contract for articles of such a description is such a contract as this Court will enforce; and, in the absence of all other objection, I should have no hesitation in decreeing specific performance.

NOTE

Specific performance will not be ordered unless damages are inadequate. Damages are inadequate if money cannot buy a substitute. In relation to contracts of sale, this leads to the idea that specific performance will only be ordered if the subject-matter is unique. Contracts for the sale of land have traditionally been specifically enforceable on the ground that each piece of land is unique and cannot be replaced in the market. In *Falcke v Gray* we see recognition of the same idea in relation to goods. The china jars were physically unique.

Sky Petroleum Ltd v VIP Petroleum Ltd
[1974] 1 WLR 576, Chancery Division

The defendant agreed for 10 years to supply to the claimant for its filling stations at fixed prices (subject to variation clauses) all the petrol needed by the claimant. After three-and-a-half years, the defendant purported to terminate the contract, alleging that the claimant was in breach. The claimant sought an interim injunction (amounting to temporary specific performance) to enforce the supply of petrol by the defendant. In granting that injunction, Goulding J held that in the circumstances, where petrol was in such short supply, damages were inadequate.

Goulding J: Now I come to the most serious hurdle in the way of the plaintiffs which is the well known doctrine that the court refuses specific performance of a contract to sell and purchase chattels not specific or ascertained. That is a well-established and salutary rule, and I am entirely unconvinced by Mr. Christie, for the plaintiffs, when he tells me that an injunction in the form sought by him would not be specific enforcement at all. The matter is one of substance and not of form, and it is, in my judgment, quite plain that I am, for the time being, specifically enforcing the contract if I grant an injunction. However, the ratio behind the rule is, as I believe, that under the ordinary contract for the sale of non-specific goods, damages are a sufficient remedy. That, to my mind, is lacking in the circumstances of the present case. The evidence suggests, and indeed it is common knowledge that the petroleum market is in an unusual state in which a would-be buyer cannot go out into the market and contract with another seller, possibly at some sacrifice as to price. Here, the defendants appear for practical purposes to be the plaintiffs' sole means of keeping their business going, and I am prepared so far to depart from the general rule as to try to preserve the position under the contract until a later date. I therefore propose to grant an injunction.

NOTES AND QUESTIONS

1.   Clearly petrol is not physically unique. This case is, therefore, best interpreted as accepting that specific performance can be granted where goods are *commercially* unique: that is, where buying substitutes would be so difficult or would cause such delay that the claimant's business would be seriously disrupted. While theoretically damages for the substantial disruption to a business are adequate, since it is ultimately only money that the claimant is losing, in practice in this situation, an accurate assessment of the claimant's losses is so difficult that the claimant is likely to be incorrectly compensated.

2.   The case is a particularly radical one because the goods were not even 'specific or ascertained'. Section 52(1) of the Sale of Goods Act 1979 reads, 'In any action for breach of a contract to deliver specific or ascertained goods, the court may, if it thinks fit, on the plaintiff's application, by its judgment or decree direct that the contract shall be performed specifically...' As this case shows, that subsection does not prevent specific performance of unascertained goods: but nor does it mean that specific performance will be granted if goods are specific or ascertained because the case law requires the goods to be unique. Would it be fair to say, therefore, that section 52(1) serves no useful purpose?

3.   This decision has not been approved or applied; and whatever the policy merits for accepting 'commercial uniqueness', that concept was apparently rejected by the Court of Appeal in *Société des Industries Métallurgiques SA v Bronx Engineering Co Ltd* [1975] 1 Lloyd's Rep 465. It was there held that an interim injunction restraining the sellers from removing certain machinery from the jurisdiction should be refused because, even if the sellers were in breach of contract, there was no likelihood of the claimant buyers being granted specific performance at the trial, as damages were adequate. This was held to be so, even though the court accepted that the delay of nine to 12 months in obtaining substitute machinery might substantially disrupt the claimants' business.

Beswick v Beswick [1968] AC 58, House of Lords

For the facts and speeches, see below, 468–473.

1. This decision is principally well known for laying down that specific performance can be granted to avoid the injustice that the privity rule can produce. The reasoning was as follows: if a party sues on a contract made for the benefit of a third party his damages, which are assessed according to his own loss, are usually going to be nominal; where this produces injustice, as here where the nephew had got the business and would end up paying almost nothing for it, nominal damages should be regarded as inadequate; in the light of that inadequacy of damages, specific performance should be granted to enforce the defendant's promise. Only Lord Pearce thought that the administratrix could have recovered substantial damages but, even then, he regarded specific performance as the 'more appropriate remedy' (see below, 472).

2. The administratrix could have brought a common law action for the agreed sums payable under the annuity. However, as recognised by their Lordships, specific performance was a better remedy because it avoided the inconvenience of bringing numerous actions to recover the agreed sum.

3. A radical interpretation of this case (taken by eg FH Lawson, *Remedies of English Law* (2nd edn, 1980) 223–4)) is that, in the light of the terminology used by their Lordships of specific performance being the appropriate or apt or just remedy, specific performance may have replaced damages as the primary contractual remedy. Has that interpretation been borne out in cases subsequent to *Beswick v Beswick*? And what precisely is meant when one says that, conventionally in English law, damages, not specific performance, is the primary contractual remedy?

4. Is it satisfactory to maintain an adequacy of damages bar to specific performance? See on this A Burrows, *Remedies for Torts and Breach of Contract* (3rd edn, 2004) 472–5.

5. Sections 48A–48F of the Sale of Goods Act 1979, inserted by the Sale and Supply of Goods to Consumers Regulations 2002, give a buyer, who is a consumer, a right to the repair or replacement, within a reasonable time, of goods which do not conform to the contract terms unless repair or replacement is impossible or disproportionate to a price reduction or rescission (ie termination) of the contract. By section 48E(2), the courts are expressly given the power to enforce this right to repair or replacement by an order of specific performance. As **D Harris, 'Specific Performance—a Regular Remedy for Consumers' (2003) 119 *LQR* 541** has argued, the structure of the provisions militates against the courts applying the normal common law approach of denying specific performance unless damages are inadequate. Rather it appears that courts should only refuse specific performance (ordering repair or replacement) if repair or replacement would be impossible or disproportionate to a price reduction or rescission. This therefore appears to mark a move in favour of specific performance being the primary judicial remedy for consumers in sale contracts. Given that those Regulations implement an EC

Directive it is perhaps not surprising that, in the primacy apparently afforded to specific performance, they reflect a civilian rather than a common law approach.

(2) The Constant Supervision Objection

Co-operative Insurance Society Ltd v Argyll Stores (Holdings) Ltd
[1998] AC 1, House of Lords

The defendants were the lessees of the largest shopping unit, which they used for a supermarket, in the claimants' shopping centre. A covenant in the lease required the defendants to keep their premises open for retail trade during usual hours of business. Sixteen years of the 35-year lease had expired, when the defendants gave notice that they were closing, and then did close, their supermarket. The claimants, concerned that the closure would have an adverse effect on the remaining businesses in the shopping centre, sought specific performance of the above covenant. The majority of the Court of Appeal made that order (albeit that it was suspended for three months) but the House of Lords, allowing the defendants' appeal, held that one could not have specific performance of a covenant to keep open a business.

Lord Hoffmann: The judge refused to order specific performance. He said that there was on the authorities a settled practice that orders which would require a defendant to run a business would not be made. …

The settled practice

There is no dispute about the existence of the settled practice to which the judge referred. It is sufficient for this purpose to refer to *Braddon Towers Ltd. v. International Stores Ltd.* [1987] 1 E.G.L.R. 209, 213, where Slade J. said:

> "Whether or not this may be properly described as a rule of law, I do not doubt that for many years practitioners have advised their clients that it is the settled and invariable practice of this court never to grant mandatory injunctions requiring persons to carry on business. "

But the practice has never, so far as I know, been examined by this House and it is open to C.I.S. to say that it rests upon inadequate grounds or that it has been too inflexibly applied.

Specific performance is traditionally regarded in English law as an exceptional remedy, as opposed to the common law damages to which a successful plaintiff is entitled as of right. There may have been some element of later rationalisation of an untidier history, but by the 19th century it was orthodox doctrine that the power to decree specific performance was part of the discretionary jurisdiction of the Court of Chancery to do justice in cases in which the remedies available at common law were inadequate. This is the basis of the general principle that specific performance will not be ordered when damages are an adequate remedy. By contrast, in countries with legal systems based on civil law, such as France, Germany and Scotland, the plaintiff is prima facie entitled to specific performance. The cases in which he is confined to a claim for damages are regarded as the exceptions. In practice, however, there is less difference between common law and civilian systems than these general statements might lead one to suppose. The principles upon which English judges exercise the discretion to grant specific performance are reasonably well settled and depend upon a number of considerations, mostly of a practical nature, which are of very general application. I have made no investigation of civilian systems, but a priori I would expect that judges take much the same matters into account in deciding whether specific performance would be inappropriate in a particular case.

The practice of not ordering a defendant to carry on a business is not entirely dependent upon damages being an adequate remedy. In *Dowty Boulton Paul Ltd. v. Wolverhampton Corporation* [1971] 1 W.L.R. 204, Sir John Pennycuick V.-C. refused to order the corporation to maintain an airfield as a going concern because: "It is very well established that the court will not order specific performance of an obligation to carry on a business:" see p. 211. He added: "It is unnecessary in the circumstances to discuss whether damages would be an adequate remedy to the company:" see p. 212. Thus the reasons which underlie the established practice may justify a refusal of specific performance even when damages are not an adequate remedy.

The most frequent reason given in the cases for declining to order someone to carry on a business is that it would require constant supervision by the court. In *J. C. Williamson Ltd. v. Lukey and Mulholland* (1931) 45 C.L.R. 282, 297-298, Dixon J. said flatly: "Specific performance is inapplicable when the continued supervision of the court is necessary in order to ensure the fulfilment of the contract."

There has, I think, been some misunderstanding about what is meant by continued superintendence. It may at first sight suggest that the judge (or some other officer of the court) would literally have to supervise the execution of the order. In *C.H. Giles & Co. Ltd. v. Morris* [1972] 1 W.L.R. 307, 318 Megarry J. said that "difficulties of constant superintendence" were a "narrow consideration" because:

> "there is normally no question of the court having to send its officers to supervise the performance of the order . . . Performance . . . is normally secured by the realisation of the person enjoined that he is liable to be punished for contempt if evidence of his disobedience to the order is put before the court; . . ."

This is, of course, true but does not really meet the point. The judges who have said that the need for constant supervision was an objection to such orders were no doubt well aware that supervision would in practice take the form of rulings by the court, on applications made by the parties, as to whether there had been a breach of the order. It is the possibility of the court having to give an indefinite series of such rulings in order to ensure the execution of the order which has been regarded as undesirable.

Why should this be so? A principal reason is that, as Megarry J. pointed out in the passage to which I have referred, the only means available to the court to enforce its order is the quasi-criminal procedure of punishment for contempt. This is a powerful weapon; so powerful, in fact, as often to be unsuitable as an instrument for adjudicating upon the disputes which may arise over whether a business is being run in accordance with the terms of the court's order. The heavy-handed nature of the enforcement mechanism is a consideration which may go to the exercise of the court's discretion in other cases as well, but its use to compel the running of a business is perhaps the paradigm case of its disadvantages and it is in this context that I shall discuss them.

The prospect of committal or even a fine, with the damage to commercial reputation which will be caused by a finding of contempt of court, is likely to have at least two undesirable consequences. First, the defendant, who ex hypothesi did not think that it was in his economic interest to run the business at all, now has to make decisions under a sword of Damocles which may descend if the way the business is run does not conform to the terms of the order. This is, as one might say, no way to run a business. In this case the Court of Appeal made light of the point because it assumed that, once the defendant had been ordered to run the business, self-interest and compliance with the order would thereafter go hand in hand. But, as I shall explain, this is not necessarily true.

Secondly, the seriousness of a finding of contempt for the defendant means that any application to enforce the order is likely to be a heavy and expensive piece of litigation. The possibility of repeated applications over a period of time means that, in comparison with a once-and-for-all inquiry as to damages, the enforcement of the remedy is likely to be expensive in terms of cost to the parties and the resources of the judicial system.

This is a convenient point at which to distinguish between orders which require a defendant to carry on an activity, such as running a business over a more or less extended period of time, and orders which require him to achieve a result. The possibility of repeated applications for rulings on compliance with the order which arises in the former case does not exist to anything like the same extent in the latter. Even if the achievement of the result is a complicated matter which will take some time, the court, if called upon to rule, only has to examine the finished work and say whether it complies with the order. This point was made in the context of relief against forfeiture in *Shiloh Spinners Ltd. v. Harding* [1973] A.C. 691. If it is a condition of relief that the tenant should have complied with a repairing covenant, difficulty of supervision need not be an objection. As Lord Wilberforce said, at p. 724:

> "what the court has to do is to satisfy itself, ex post facto, that the covenanted work has been done, and it has ample machinery, through certificates, or by inquiry, to do precisely this."

This distinction between orders to carry on activities and orders to achieve results explains why the courts have in appropriate circumstances ordered specific performance of building contracts and repairing covenants: see *Wolverhampton Corporation v. Emmons* [1901] 1 K.B. 515 (building contract) and *Jeune v. Queens Cross Properties Ltd.* [1974] Ch. 97 (repairing covenant). It by no means follows, however, that even obligations to achieve a result will always be enforced by specific performance. There may be other objections, to some of which I now turn.

One such objection, which applies to orders to achieve a result and a fortiori to orders to carry on an activity, is imprecision in the terms of the order. If the terms of the court's order, reflecting the terms of the obligation, cannot be precisely drawn, the possibility of wasteful litigation over compliance is increased. So is the oppression caused by the defendant having to do things under threat of proceedings for contempt. The less precise the order, the fewer the signposts to the forensic minefield which he has to traverse. The fact that the terms of a contractual obligation are sufficiently definite to escape being void for uncertainty, or to found a claim for damages, or to permit compliance to be made a condition of relief against forfeiture, does not necessarily mean that they will be sufficiently precise to be capable of being specifically enforced. So in *Wolverhampton Corporation v. Emmons,* Romer L.J. said, at p. 525, that the first condition for specific enforcement of a building contract was that

> "the particulars of the work are so far definitely ascertained that the court can sufficiently see what is the exact nature of the work of which it is asked to order the performance."

Similarly in *Morris v. Redland Bricks Ltd.* [1970] A.C. 652, 666, Lord Upjohn stated the following general principle for the grant of mandatory injunctions to carry out building works:

> "the court must be careful to see that the defendant knows exactly in fact what he has to do and this means not as a matter of law but as a matter of fact, so that in carrying out an order he can give his contractors the proper instructions."

Precision is of course a question of degree and the courts have shown themselves willing to cope with a certain degree of imprecision in cases of orders requiring the achievement of a result in which the plaintiffs' merits appeared strong; like all the reasons which I have been discussing, it is, taken alone, merely a discretionary matter to be taken into account: see *Spry, Equitable Remedies*, 4th ed. (1990), p. 112. It is, however, a very important one.

I should at this point draw attention to what seems to me to have been a misreading of certain remarks of Lord Wilberforce in *Shiloh Spinners Ltd. v. Harding*, at p. 724. He pointed out, as I have said, that to grant relief against forfeiture subject to compliance with a repairing covenant involves the court in no more than the possibility of a retrospective assessment of whether the covenanted work has been done. For this reason, he said:

> "Where it is necessary, and, in my opinion, right, to move away from some 19th century authorities, is to reject as a reason against granting relief, the impossibility for the courts to supervise the doing of work."

This is plainly a remark about cases involving the achievement of a result, such as doing repairs, and, within that class, about making compliance a condition of relief against forfeiture. But in *Tito v. Waddell (No. 2)* [1977] Ch. 106, 322 Sir Robert Megarry V.-C. took it to be a generalisation about specific performance and, in particular, a rejection of difficulty of supervision as an objection, even in cases of orders to carry on an activity. Sir Robert Megarry V.-C. regarded it as an adoption of his own views (based, as I have said, on incomplete analysis of what was meant by difficulty of supervision) in *C.H. Giles & Co. Ltd. v. Morris* [1972] 1 W.L.R. 307, 318. In the present case [1996] Ch. 286, 292-293, Leggatt L.J. took this claim at face value. In fact, Lord Wilberforce went on to say that impossibility of supervision "is a reality no doubt, and explains why specific performance cannot be granted of agreements to this effect ..." Lord Wilberforce was in my view drawing attention to the fact that the collection of reasons which the courts have in mind when they speak of difficulty of supervision apply with much greater force to orders for specific performance, giving rise to the possibility of committal for contempt, than they do to conditions for relief against forfeiture. While the paradigm case to which such objections apply is the order to carry on an activity, they can also apply to an order requiring the achievement of a result.

There is a further objection to an order requiring the defendant to carry on a business, which was emphasised by Millett L.J. in the Court of Appeal. This is that it may cause injustice by allowing the plaintiff to enrich himself at the defendant's expense. The loss which the defendant may suffer through having to comply with the order (for example, by running a business at a loss for an indefinite period) may be far greater than the plaintiff would suffer from the contract being broken. As Professor R. J. Sharpe explains in "Specific Relief for Contract Breach," ch. 5 of *Studies in Contract Law* (1980), edited by Reiter and Swan, p. 129:

> "In such circumstances, a specific decree in favour of the plaintiff will put him in a bargaining position vis-à-vis the defendant whereby the measure of what he will receive will be the value to the defendant of being released from performance. If the plaintiff bargains effectively, the amount he will set will exceed the value to him of performance and will approach the cost to the defendant to complete."

This was the reason given by Lord Westbury L.C. in *Isenberg v. East India House Estate Co. Ltd.* (1863) 3 De G.J. & S. 263, 273 for refusing a mandatory injunction to compel the defendant to pull down part of a new building which interfered with the plaintiff's light and exercising instead the Court of Chancery's recently-acquired jurisdiction under Lord Cairns's Act 1858 (21 & 22 Vict. c. 27) to order payment of damages:

> ". . . I hold it . . . to be the duty of the court in such a case as the present not, by granting a mandatory injunction, to deliver over the defendants to the plaintiff bound hand and foot, in order to be made subject to any extortionate demand that he may by possibility make,

but to substitute for such mandatory injunction an inquiry before itself, in order to ascertain the measure of damage that has been actually sustained."

It is true that the defendant has, by his own breach of contract, put himself in such an unfortunate position. But the purpose of the law of contract is not to punish wrongdoing but to satisfy the expectations of the party entitled to performance. A remedy which enables him to secure, in money terms, more than the performance due to him is unjust. From a wider perspective, it cannot be in the public interest for the courts to require someone to carry on business at a loss if there is any plausible alternative by which the other party can be given compensation. It is not only a waste of resources but yokes the parties together in a continuing hostile relationship. The order for specific performance prolongs the battle. If the defendant is ordered to run a business, its conduct becomes the subject of a flow of complaints, solicitors' letters and affidavits. This is wasteful for both parties and the legal system. An award of damages, on the other hand, brings the litigation to an end. The defendant pays damages, the forensic link between them is severed, they go their separate ways and the wounds of conflict can heal.

The cumulative effect of these various reasons, none of which would necessarily be sufficient on its own, seems to me to show that the settled practice is based upon sound sense. Of course the grant or refusal of specific performance remains a matter for the judge's discretion. There are no binding rules, but this does not mean that there cannot be settled principles, founded upon practical considerations of the kind which I have discussed, which do not have to be re-examined in every case, but which the courts will apply in all but exceptional circumstances. As Slade J. said, in the passage which I have quoted from *Braddon Towers Ltd. v. International Stores Ltd.* [1987] 1 E.G.L.R. 209, 213, lawyers have no doubt for many years advised their clients on this basis. In the present case, Leggatt L.J. [1996] Ch. 286, 294 remarked that there was no evidence that such advice had been given. In my view, if the law or practice on a point is settled, it should be assumed that persons entering into legal transactions will have been advised accordingly. I am sure that Leggatt L.J. would not wish to encourage litigants to adduce evidence of the particular advice which they received. Indeed, I doubt whether such evidence would be admissible.

... The decision of the Court of Appeal

I must now examine the grounds upon which the majority of the Court of Appeal [1996] Ch. 286 thought it right to reverse the judge. In the first place, they regarded the practice which he followed as outmoded and treated Lord Wilberforce's remarks about relief against forfeiture in *Shiloh Spinners Ltd. v. Harding* [1973] A.C. 691, 724 as justifying a rejection of the arguments based on the need for constant supervision. Even Millett L.J., who dissented on other grounds, said, at p. 303, that such objections had little force today. I do not agree. As I have already said, I think that Lord Wilberforce's remarks do not support this proposition in relation to specific performance of an obligation to carry on an activity and that the arguments based on difficulty of supervision remain powerful.

The Court of Appeal said that it was enough if the contract defined the tenant's obligation with sufficient precision to enable him to know what was necessary to comply with the order. Even assuming that this to be right, I do not think that the obligation in clause 4(19) can possibly be regarded as sufficiently precise to be capable of specific performance. It is to "keep the demised premises open for retail trade." It says nothing about the level of trade, the area of the premises within which trade is to be conducted, or even the kind of trade, although no doubt the tenant's choice would be restricted by the need to comply with the negative covenant in clause 4(12)(a) not to use the premises "other than as a retail store for the sale of food groceries provisions and goods normally sold from time to time by a retail grocer food supermarkets and food superstores . . ." This language seems to me to provide ample room for argument over whether the tenant is doing enough to comply with the covenant.

...

Conclusion

I think that no criticism can be made of the way in which Judge Maddocks exercised his discretion. All the reasons which he gave were proper matters for him to take into account. In my view the Court of Appeal should not have interfered and I would allow the appeal and restore the order which he made.

Lord Browne-Wilkinson, Lord Slynn of Hadley, Lord Hope of Craighead, and **Lord Clyde** agreed.

NOTES AND QUESTIONS

1. While the decision to refuse specific performance was probably correct, Lord Hoffmann's reasoning is controversial for at least two reasons. First, and most importantly, he breathed new life into the constant supervision objection that other cases had indicated was no longer a valid bar. As a matter of policy that bar seems flawed because (i) in almost all cases defendants do obey court orders; (ii) even if supervision were required, this need not involve full judicial machinery but could be carried out by, eg, an officer of the court; and (iii) even if judicial time and expense were involved, this seems merited where justice otherwise requires such an order. Moreover, Lord Hoffmann has introduced a problematic distinction in relation to constant supervision between orders to carry on activities and orders to achieve results. Secondly, he thought that, on the facts, an order could not be drawn up with sufficient precision so as to avoid arguments over whether it was being complied with. Do you agree that that was a problem?

2. The preferable approach would perhaps have been to say that specific performance will not be ordered of an obligation to carry on a business either because that falls foul of the well-established hardship bar to specific performance (especially where the business is losing money); or because there is a separate bar against specific performance of such an obligation which is justified by the need to maintain managerial discretion (analogous to the best justification for why specific performance is not available against an employer to compel performance of an employment contract).

3. In *Rainbow Estates Ltd v Tokenhold Ltd* [1999] Ch 64, at 73, Lawrence Collins QC, in holding that, exceptionally, a tenant's (as well as a landlord's) repairing obligation can be specifically enforced, said the following, '[T]he problems of defining the work and the need for supervision can be overcome by ensuring that there is sufficient definition of what has to be done in order to comply with the order of the court.' Although he cited *Co-operative Insurance Society Ltd v Argyll Stores (Holdings) Ltd,* that sentence indicates that Lawrence Collins QC did not regard constant supervision as an objection separate from uncertainty.

(3) Contracts for Personal Service

Trade Union and Labour Relations (Consolidation) Act 1992, section 236

236 No compulsion to work
No court shall, whether by way of –

   (a)   an order for specific performance… of a contract of employment, or
   (b)   an injunction… restraining a breach or threatened breach of such a contract,

compel an employee to do any work or attend at any place for the doing of any work.

NOTE

This is a statutory embodiment of the rule, long-established in the case law, that specific performance will not be ordered *against* an employee. The main justification for this was given by Fry LJ in refusing specific performance in *De Francesco v Barnum* (1890) 45 Ch D 430, 438. He said that the courts were afraid of turning 'contracts of service into contracts of slavery'.

Powell v Brent London Borough Council
[1988] ICR 176, Court of Appeal

The claimant was appointed principal benefits officer for the defendant local authority. A few days after starting work, she was told by Mr Connell (the Assistant Director of Housing) that her appointment was invalid because there might have been a breach of the defendant's equal opportunity code of practice in appointing her. She sought an interim injunction requiring the defendant to treat her as if she was properly employed as principal benefits officer. Even though that injunction would amount to temporary specific performance, the Court of Appeal granted it because the employer still had sufficient confidence in the employee.

Ralph Gibson LJ: Having regard to the decision in *Hill v. C. A. Parsons & Co. Ltd.* [1972] Ch. 305 and to the long-standing general rule of practice to which *Hill v. C. A. Parsons & Co. Ltd.* was an exception, the court will not by injunction require an employer to let a servant continue in his employment, when the employer has sought to terminate that employment and to prevent the servant carrying out his work under the contract, unless it is clear on the evidence not only that it is otherwise just to make such a requirement but also that there exists sufficient confidence on the part of the employer in the servant's ability and other necessary attributes for it to be reasonable to make the order. Sufficiency of confidence must be judged by reference to the circumstances of the case, including the nature of the work, the people with whom the work must be done and the likely effect upon the employer and the employer's operations if the employer is required by injunction to suffer the plaintiff to continue in the work.

   …

   [T]here is now the uncontradicted fact that she has, for over four months, done the job satisfactorily and without complaint. There is no rational ground, in my view, for the council to lack confidence in the plaintiff's competence to do the job pending trial. I decline to attribute to them or their officers an irrational belief in her incompetence. …

As to confidence in the happiness of the relationship, in the phrase used by [the judge] I have formed the same view. There is clearly a good working relationship of mutual respect between the plaintiff and Mr. Connell and Mr. Wilson, who was her higher superior. There is no basis for supposing that there is any defect in the relationship between her and any other person with whom she works in this post or with whom she may be expected to have to work.

...

In my judgment, accordingly, the plaintiff...has a good arguable case and a real prospect of obtaining at the trial the injunction which she seeks.

Nicholls LJ and **Sir Roger Ormrod** delivered concurring judgments.

NOTES AND QUESTIONS

1. What is the justification for the general rule that specific performance will not be granted against an employer? Does the 'sufficiency of confidence' exception tie in with that justification?

2. In the earlier case of *Hill v CA Parsons & Co Ltd* [1972] Ch 305 the claimant had been wrongfully dismissed by being given only one month's notice that he must join a trade union (in accordance with a closed shop agreement between the employer and the trade union). The majority (Lord Denning MR and Sachs LJ) thought that an exception to the general rule barring specific performance against an employer was justified because the employee would then remain an employee until the coming into effect of the Industrial Relations Act 1971 by which he would be protected if dismissed for not joining a union: ie it would constitute unfair dismissal (which is a statutory wrong similar, but not identical, to wrongful dismissal at common law). Sachs LJ also stressed that there was no breakdown in mutual confidence between employer and employee. It is Sachs LJ's influential judgment that was built upon by the Court of Appeal in the *Powell* case.

3. In most cases (but not *Powell*) in which the sufficiency of confidence exception has been applied, the courts have required the defendant employer to pay the employee and to retain the employee but have not actually required the employer to provide work: see, eg, *Irani v Southampton and South West Hampshire Area Health Authority* [1985] ICR 590.

4. The statutory unfair dismissal regime is now embodied in the Employment Rights Act 1996 sections 113–117. Under those provisions employment tribunals can order the reinstatement or re-engagement of an employee who has been unfairly dismissed although they usually prefer to award compensation.

5. Office-holders (ie those in public employment) have always been able to gain a measure of specific protection of their positions through the application of public law principles (eg judicial review for breach of natural justice leading to a quashing order). Those principles were not discussed (as there was no application for judicial review) in the *Powell* case.

6. A particularly controversial decision is *Robb v Hammersmith and Fulham London Borough Council* [1991] ICR 514 in which an injunction was granted requiring the defendants to continue to employ and pay the claimant unless and until the proper disciplinary procedures had been complied with. This was so even though Morland J accepted that the employee had lost the trust and confidence of his employers.

(4) Want of Mutuality

Price v Strange [1978] Ch 337, Court of Appeal

The defendant, Mrs Strange, was the head-lessee of some flats in a house. She agreed to grant the claimant, Mr Price, a new underlease of his flat in return for the claimant's promise to carry out certain repairs to the house. The claimant did half the repairs but the defendant refused to allow him to complete them, had them done at her own expense, and refused to grant the underlease. The claimant brought an action for specific performance of the promise to grant him the underlease. At first instance the judge refused the claim because, at the date of the contract, the remedies of the parties were not mutual, given that the claimant's obligation to carry out repairs was not specifically enforceable. This was overturned by the Court of Appeal, which held that mutuality was not here a bar to specific performance. Specific performance was therefore ordered (subject to the claimant compensating the defendant for the expense she had incurred in having the remaining repair work done).

Goff LJ: The judge accepted as good law certain statements in *Fry on Specific Performance*, 6th ed. (1921), and quoting from *Fry* he said:

> "My understanding of the law is that it is correctly stated in *Fry on Specific Performance*, 6th ed., at pp. 219 and 222, and also p. 223. *Fry* says, at p. 219: 'A contract to be specifically enforced by the court must, as a general rule, be mutual, – that is to say, such that it might, at the time it was entered into, have been enforced by either of the parties against the other of them.' At p. 222 in paragraph 463 he says: 'The mutuality of a contract is, as we have seen, to be judged of at the time it is entered into.' At p. 223 *Fry* says: 'From the time of the execution of the contract being the time to judge of its mutuality it further follows, that the subsequent performance by one party of terms which could not have been enforced by the other will not prevent the objection which would arise from the presence of such terms.' ...I hold accordingly."

> ...

The plaintiff's main case is that the statement in *Fry on Specific Performance* that mutuality has to be determined at the date of the contract is not good law, and that on the contrary the question of mutuality is simply one of the factors, which like hardship, mistake and delay has to be considered in the exercise of a judicial discretion when the court is considering whether or not to order specific performance, and, therefore, the relevant time is that of the hearing, and, he argues, if that be the proper rule, then having regard to all the circumstances this is a proper case for an order, especially as the work has now been finished and complete justice can be done by a monetary adjustment.

> ...

The proposition in paragraphs 460 and 463 of *Fry* has...been much criticised. Thus, in *Hanbury and Maudsley, Modern Equity*, 10th ed. (1976) there is a section, at p. 50, headed "Criticisms of Fry's Rule" followed by a section headed "An Alternative Rule" which reads, at pp. 51-52:

> "These matters, among others, are considered in a famous article by James Barr Ames in which he offers as an alternative to Fry's rule of mutuality a principle that 'Equity will not compel specific performance by a defendant if, after performance, the common law remedy of damages would be his sole security for the performance of the plaintiff's side of the contract.' Such a formulation has not satisfied everyone, but it is the basis of the rule accepted by the Restatement of Contracts. In England, Fry's rule is often still stated in its wide form. It is submitted that Ames' principle is much to be preferred."

...

Surely the defence of want of mutuality should be governed by the state of affairs as seen at the hearing, since one is dealing not with a question affecting the initial validity of the contract, but with whether or not the discretionary remedy of specific performance should be granted. ...

In my judgment, therefore, the proposition in *Fry* is wrong and the true principle is that one judges the defence of want of mutuality on the facts and circumstances as they exist at the hearing, albeit in the light of the whole conduct of the parties in relation to the subject matter, and in the absence of any other disqualifying circumstances the court will grant specific performance if it can be done without injustice or unfairness to the defendant. ...

If, therefore, the plaintiff had been allowed to finish the work and had done so, I am clearly of opinion that it would have been right to order specific performance, but we have to consider what is the proper order, having regard to the fact that he was allowed to do an appreciable part and then not allowed to finish. Even so, in my judgment, the result is still the same for the following reasons.

First, the defendant by standing by and allowing the plaintiff to spend time and money in carrying out an appreciable part of the work created an equity against herself. ...

Secondly, the work has in fact been finished. The court will not be deterred from granting specific performance in a proper case, even though there remain obligations still to be performed by the plaintiff if the defendant can be properly protected. ...Still more readily should it act where the work has been done so that the defendant is not at risk of being ordered to grant the underlease and having no remedy except in damages for subsequent non-performance of the plaintiff's agreement to put the premises in repair.

Thirdly, the defendant can be fully recompensed by a proper financial adjustment for the work she has had carried out.

...

For these reasons I would allow this appeal and order specific performance but upon terms that the plaintiff do pay to the defendant proper compensation for the work done by her. ...[A]nd it may well be possible, and certainly in the best interests of the parties, for them to agree a figure...

Buckley LJ: It is easy to understand that as the equitable jurisdiction to enforce specific performance of contractual obligations developed it should have become an accepted rule that equity would not compel one party to perform his obligations specifically in accordance with the terms of the contract unless it could also ensure that any unperformed obligations of the other party would also be performed specifically. For breaches of some kinds of contract, pre-eminently contracts for the sale of land, the common law remedy of damages was inadequate. The courts of equity consequently supplemented the common law by introducing the equitable remedy of specific performance, compelling the defendant to carry out his contract instead of penalising him in damages for failing to do so.

Considering the position a priori and apart from authority, it would seem that the questions which should be asked by any court which is invited to enforce specific performance of a contractual obligation should be: (1) is the plaintiff entitled to a remedy of some kind in respect of the alleged breach of contract? (2) If so, would damages be an adequate remedy? (3) If not, would specific performance be a more adequate remedy for the plaintiff? (4) If so, would it be fair to the defendant to order him to perform his part of the contract specifically? The first question goes to the validity and enforceability of the contract. Only if it is answered affirmatively do the subsequent questions arise. If the second question is answered affirmatively there is no occasion for equity to interfere, so that again the subsequent questions do not arise. If the second question is answered in the negative it will not necessarily follow that the third question must be answered affirmatively. For instance, the circumstances may not be such as to admit of specific performance, as where the subject matter of the contract no longer exists. Only in the event of the third question arising and being answered in the affirmative can the fourth question arise. It is here, as it seems to me, that the alleged principle of mutuality comes in.

If one party were compelled to perform his obligations in accordance with the terms of the contract while the obligations of the other party under the contract, or some of them, remained unperformed, it might be unfair that the former party should be left to his remedy in damages if the latter party failed to perform any of his unperformed obligations. This is a consideration which bears upon the appropriateness of specific performance as a remedy in the particular case: it has no bearing on the validity or enforceability of the contract, that is to say, upon whether the plaintiff has a cause of action. A contract of which mutual specific performance cannot be enforced may yet afford a good cause of action for a remedy in damages at law. It would seem, therefore, that the appropriate time at which to consider the fourth question, and the appropriate circumstances to consider, must be the date of judgment and the circumstances then existing. And yet Sir Edward Fry said in very clear terms in *Fry on Specific Performance*, 3rd ed., p. 215 (6th ed., p. 219):

> "A contract to be specifically enforced by the court must, as a general rule, be mutual, that is to say, such that it might, at the time it was entered into, have been enforced by either of the parties against the other of them."

...

It is a remarkable thing that, in spite of what might justly be called a chorus of academic criticism and dissent, the *Fry* proposition has occasioned virtually no judicial comment. In only one of the cases to which our attention has been called has any direct judicial reference been made to it and then only in circumstances in which it was unnecessary for the decision...

...

I can discover nothing in principle to recommend the *Fry* proposition and authority seems to me to be strongly against it. Accordingly, in my judgment, it should be regarded as wrong. The time at which the mutual availability of specific performance and its importance must be considered is, in my opinion, the time of judgment, and the principle to be applied can I think be stated simply as follows: the court will not compel a defendant to perform his obligations specifically if it cannot at the same time ensure that any unperformed obligations of the plaintiff will be specifically performed, unless, perhaps, damages would be an adequate remedy to the defendant for any default on the plaintiff's part.

...

The present case differs from any decided case to which I have referred in this respect, that, although all the agreed repairs have been done, they have not all been done by the plaintiff. In my judgment, however, this is no bar to the plaintiff's right to a grant of a sublease in accordance with the contract. That the plaintiff did not do all the work was not due to any default of his: it was due to the defendant's unjustified repudiation of the contract. She was, in my opinion, clearly under an implied obligation not to prevent the plaintiff from performing his part of the contract, but she did so. This was an incident of her wrongful repudiation of her obligation to grant him a sublease. The financial consequences of the defendant's having carried out at her own expense work which under the contract should have been done by the plaintiff at his expense could be adjusted by appropriate accounts, inquiries and adjustments under the court's order. If, as Goff L.J. has said, this part of the case can be dealt with by agreement, so much the better.

For these reasons I agree that in this case specific performance should be ordered on the lines proposed by Goff L.J.

Scarman LJ agreed.

NOTES AND QUESTIONS

1.   The Court of Appeal firmly rejected Fry's formulation of the want of mutuality bar to specific performance. What then is the correct way to express this bar?

2. The mutuality bar protects the defendant against the risk of the claimant (who is being granted specific performance) subsequently not performing. But why should the courts be concerned with that risk given that it is a risk which the defendant accepted by entering into a contract where the claimant's performance follows the defendant's?

3. The problem of mutuality in this case arose because it was thought that the tenant's obligation to carry out the repairs could not be specifically enforced. But subsequently the rule that a tenant's repairing obligations cannot be specifically enforced was departed from in *Rainbow Estates Ltd v Tokenhold Ltd* [1999] Ch 64, above, 441, note 3.

4. The order in *Price v Strange* is a good illustration of the point that specific performance is a flexible remedy that can be granted *on terms*. To have ordered the granting of the underlease to the claimant, without his paying for the repair work that he had not done, would have left the claimant better off, and the defendant worse off, than if there had been no breach.

3. INJUNCTIONS

Injunctions can be classified according to whether they are granted at trial (final injunctions) or pre-trial (interim injunctions, which are to last until trial at the latest); and whether they order the defendant to do something (mandatory injunctions) or not to do something (prohibitory injunctions). Our focus here is on prohibitory injunctions. This is because, in the context of contract, the role of mandatory injunctions at trial (leaving aside mandatory 'restorative' injunctions ordering the 'undoing' of what has been done) is entirely supplanted by specific performance (although this is not true pre-trial because specific performance is a final remedy only so that the equivalent pre-trial remedy is an interim mandatory injunction).

The prohibitory injunction is the appropriate remedy for restraining the breach of a negative contractual duty. So it belongs on the reverse side of the coin from specific performance which enforces a positive contractual duty. However, in contrast to specific performance, and presumably because the law considers it less of an infringement of individual liberty to be ordered not to do something than to be ordered to do something, a prohibitory injunction is much easier to obtain than specific performance. In particular, while there is technically an adequacy of damages bar, it is very easily overcome. In other words, damages are in this context hardly ever considered adequate and one can rightly regard the prohibitory injunction as the primary remedy as against compensatory damages. The classic 'authority' on the primacy afforded to the prohibitory injunction is the obiter dictum of Lord Cairns LC in *Doherty v Allman* (1878) 3 App Cas 709, 720. He said, '…if there had been a negative covenant, I apprehend, according to well-settled practice, a Court of Equity would have no discretion to exercise. If parties, for valuable consideration, with their eyes open, contract that a particular thing shall not be done, all that a Court of Equity has to do is to say, by way of injunction that which the parties have already said by way of covenant, that the thing shall not be done; and in such case, the injunction does nothing more than give the sanction of the process of the Court to that which already is the contract between the parties. It is not then a question of the balance of convenience or inconvenience, or the amount of damage or of injury – it is the specific performance by the Court, of that negative bargain which the parties have made, with their eyes open, between themselves.'

To say that the prohibitory injunction is the primary remedy, as against damages, for breach of a negative contractual duty does not of course mean that it will never be refused. Two main grounds for refusal are that the claimant has acted inequitably or that he has delayed too long in seeking the injunction so as to be barred by the doctrine of laches. But indisputably the most discussed ground for refusal is that to grant the prohibitory injunction would amount to indirect specific performance of a contractual promise for which specific performance would not be directly ordered under the principles we have looked at earlier. This will now be examined in relation to express negative promises in contracts for personal service, which is the main area where the problem has arisen.

Lumley v Wagner (1852) 1 De GM & G 604, Lord Chancellor's Court

Mlle Johanna Wagner undertook that for three months from 1 April 1852 she would sing at Mr Lumley's theatre (Her Majesty's Theatre) in Drury Lane on two nights a week and not use her talents at any other theatre without Mr Lumley's written consent. She then agreed to sing for Mr Gye at Covent Garden for more money. On Mr Lumley's application, on 9 May 1852, Sir James Parker granted an injunction restraining her for the rest of the contract period from singing except for Mr Lumley. In dismissing the appeal, the Lord Chancellor held that the injunction did not constitute indirect specific performance of Mlle Wagner's obligation to sing at Mr Lumley's theatre.

Lord St Leonards LC: Wherever this Court has not proper jurisdiction to enforce specific performance, it operates to bind men's consciences, as far as they can be bound, to a true and literal performance of their agreements; and it will not suffer them to depart from their contracts at their pleasure, leaving the party with whom they have contracted to the mere chance of any damages which a jury may give. The exercise of this jurisdiction has, I believe, had a wholesome tendency towards the maintenance of that good faith which exists in this country to a much greater degree perhaps than in any other; and although the jurisdiction is not to be extended, yet a Judge would desert his duty who did not act up to what his predecessors have handed down as the rule for his guidance in the administration of such an equity.

It was objected that the operation of the injunction in the present case was mischievous, excluding the Defendant J. Wagner from, performing at any other theatre while this Court had no power to compel her to perform at Her Majesty's Theatre. It is true that I have not the means of compelling her to sing, but she has no cause of complaint if I compel her to abstain from the commission of an act which she has bound herself not to do, and thus possibly cause her to fulfil her engagement. The jurisdiction which I now exercise is wholly within the power of the Court, and being of opinion that it is a proper case for interfering, I shall leave nothing unsatisfied by the judgment I pronounce. The effect, too, of the injunction in restraining J. Wagner from singing elsewhere may, in the event of an action being brought against her by the Plaintiff, prevent any such amount of vindictive damages being given against her as a jury might probably be inclined to give if she had carried her talents and exercised them at the rival theatre: the injunction may also, as I have said, tend to the fulfilment of her engagement; though, in continuing the injunction, I disclaim doing indirectly what I cannot do directly.

QUESTIONS

Do you agree with Lord St Leonards that the granting of the injunction did not constitute indirect specific performance of Mlle Wagner's obligation to sing for Mr Lumley? Is it relevant that the contract had less than two months left to run?

Warner Bros Pictures Inc v Nelson
[1937] 1 KB 209, King's Bench Division

The defendant, Bette Davis, a film actress, agreed that she would render her exclusive services as an actress to the claimants, who were film producers, for one year, renewable annually at the claimants' option for a further seven years. The contract also contained a negative stipulation that, amongst other things, she would not, without the claimants' written consent, render any similar services to any other person. During the second year of the agreement, the defendant, in breach of contract, entered into an agreement to appear for another film company. The claimants sought an injunction to restrain her from appearing for any other film company during the currency of the contract. This was granted (albeit limited to three years) on the ground that it did not constitute indirect specific performance of the obligation to perform as an actress for the claimants.

Branson J: I turn then to the consideration of the law applicable to this case on the basis that the contract is a valid and enforceable one. It is conceded that our Courts will not enforce a positive covenant of personal service; and specific performance of the positive covenants by the defendant to serve the plaintiffs is not asked in the present case. The practice of the Court of Chancery in relation to the enforcement of negative covenants is stated on the highest authority by Lord Cairns in the House of Lords in *Doherty v. Allman* 3 App Cas 709, 719. [*He then quoted the passage set out above, 447–448, and continued:*]

That was not a case of a contract of personal service; but the same principle had already been applied to such a contract by Lord St. Leonards in *Lumley v. Wagner* 1 De G.M.& G. 604, 619. ...

The defendant, having broken her positive undertakings in the contract without any cause or excuse which she was prepared to support in the witness-box, contends that she cannot be enjoined from breaking the negative covenants also. The mere fact that a covenant which the Court would not enforce, if expressed in positive form, is expressed in the negative instead, will not induce the Court to enforce it. ...The Court will attend to the substance and not to the form of the covenant. Nor will the Court, true to the principle that specific performance of a contract of personal service will never be ordered, grant an injunction in the case of such a contract to enforce negative covenants if the effect of so doing would be to drive the defendant either to starvation or to specific performance of the positive covenants: see *Whitwood Chemical Co. v. Hardman* [1891] 2 Ch. 416, 427, where Lindley L.J. said: "What injunction can be granted in this particular case which will not be, in substance and effect, a decree for specific performance of this agreement?"; *Ehrman v. Bartholomew* [1898] 1 Ch. 671 where the injunction was refused, firstly, on the ground that it was doubtful whether the covenant applied at all, and, secondly, on the ground that to grant it would compel the defendant wholly to abstain from any business whatsoever; and *Mortimer v. Beckett* [1920] 1 Ch. 615 where there was also no negative stipulation.

...

The conclusion to be drawn from the authorities is that, where a contract of personal service contains negative covenants the enforcement of which will not amount either to a decree of specific performance of the positive covenants of the contract or to the giving of a decree under which the defendant must either remain idle or perform those positive covenants, the Court will enforce those negative covenants; but this is subject to a further consideration. An injunction is a discretionary remedy, and the Court in granting it may limit it to what the Court considers reasonable in all the circumstances of the case.

...

The case before me is, therefore, one in which it would be proper to grant an injunction unless to do so would in the circumstances be tantamount to ordering the defendant to perform her contract or remain idle or unless damages would be the more appropriate remedy.

With regard to the first of these considerations, it would, of course, be impossible to grant an injunction covering all the negative covenants in the contract. That would, indeed, force the defendant to perform her contract or remain idle; but this objection is removed by the restricted form in which the injunction is sought. It is confined to forbidding the defendant, without the consent of the plaintiffs, to render any services for or in any motion picture or stage production for any one other than the plaintiffs.

It was also urged that the difference between what the defendant can earn as a film artiste and what she might expect to earn by any other form of activity is so great that she will in effect be driven to perform her contract. That is not the criterion adopted in any of the decided cases. The defendant is stated to be a person of intelligence, capacity and means, and no evidence was adduced to show that, if enjoined from doing the specified acts otherwise than for the plaintiffs, she will not be able to employ herself both usefully and remuneratively in other spheres of activity, though not as remuneratively as in her special line. She will not be driven, although she may be tempted, to perform the contract, and the fact that she may be so tempted is no objection to the grant of an injunction. This appears from the judgment of Lord St. Leonards in *Lumley v. Wagner* ...

With regard to the question whether damages is not the more appropriate remedy, I have the uncontradicted evidence of the plaintiffs as to the difficulty of estimating the damages which they may suffer from the breach by the defendant of her contract.

...

I think ...that an injunction should be granted in regard to the specified services.

Then comes the question as to the period for which the injunction should operate. ...The main difficulty that the plaintiffs apprehend is that the defendant might appear in other films whilst the films already made by them and not yet shown are in the market for sale or hire and thus depreciate their value. I think that if the injunction is in force during the continuance of the contract or for three years from now, whichever period is the shorter, that will substantially meet the case.

QUESTIONS

Was it at all likely that, if the injunction was granted, Bette Davis would for three years take up employment other than as a film actress? If that was very unlikely, was not the injunction indirectly ordering specific performance of a contract for personal service?

Page One Records v Britton [1968] 1 WLR 157, Chancery Division

The members of 'The Troggs' pop group, the defendants, employed the first claimant as their sole agent and manager for five years, and agreed not to make records for anyone else during that time. In breach of that contract they then entered into an agreement to be managed by someone else. The first claimant sought an interim injunction to restrain this breach. Stamp J refused to grant it because he thought that it would amount to indirect specific performance of the defendants' personal obligations. (An analogous injunction was also unsuccessfully sought by the second claimant who was the 'publisher' of the Troggs' music.)

Stamp J: [*Having discussed want of mutuality, Stamp J continued:*] [T]his present case, in my judgment, fails, on the facts at present before me, on a more general principle, the converse of which was conveniently stated in the judgment of Branson J. in *Warner Brothers Pictures, Inc. v. Nelson* [1937] 1 K.B. 209, 217. Branson J. stated the converse of the proposition and the proposition, correctly stated, is, I think, this, that where a contract of personal service contains negative covenants the enforcement of which will amount either to a decree of specific performance of the positive covenants of the contract or to the giving of a decree under which the defendant must either remain idle or perform those positive covenants, the court will not enforce those negative covenants.

In the *Warner Brothers* case Branson J. felt able to find that the injunction sought would not force the defendant to perform his contract or remain idle. ... So it was said in this case that if an injunction is granted the Troggs could, without employing any other manager or agent, continue as a group on their own or seek other employment of a different nature. So far as the former suggestion is concerned, in the first place I doubt whether consistently with the terms of the agreements which I have read, the Troggs could act as their own managers; and, in the second place, I think I can, and should, take judicial notice of the fact that these groups, if they are to have any great success, must have managers. Indeed, it is the plaintiffs' own case that the Troggs are simple persons, of no business experience, and could not survive without the services of a manager. As a practical matter on the evidence before me, I entertain no doubt that they would be compelled, if the injunction was granted, on the terms that the plaintiffs seek, to continue to employ the first plaintiff as their manager and agent. ...

On the facts before me on this interlocutory motion, I should, if I granted the injunction, be enforcing a contract for personal services in which personal services are to be performed by the first plaintiff. In *Lumley v. Wagner* (1852) 1 De G.M. & G. 604, Lord St. Leonards, in his judgment, disclaimed doing indirectly what he could not do directly: and in the present case, by granting an injunction I would, in my judgment, be doing precisely that. I must, therefore, refuse the injunction which the first plaintiff seeks.

NOTES AND QUESTIONS

1. Stamp J thought that 'as a practical matter' to grant the injunction would constitute specific performance of the Troggs' personal obligation to employ the first claimant as their manager and agent. Do you agree?
2. Is this decision reconcilable with *Warner Brothers v Nelson*?

Warren v Mendy [1989] 1 WLR 853, Court of Appeal

This concerned a dispute over the management of the boxer, Nigel Benn. The case differed from the usual restrictive covenant case in that the injunction being sought by the claimant (Warren) was not against Benn for breach of contract but against another manager (Mendy) in a tort action for inducing breach of Benn's contract with the claimant. But the Court of Appeal felt that, as the claimant would seek an injunction against anyone who arranged to manage Benn, the same principles should be applied as if the injunction had been sought against Benn for breach of contract. The injunction was refused on the ground that to grant it would constitute indirect specific performance of Benn's contract to be exclusively managed by the claimant for the three-year contract period.

Nourse LJ (giving the judgment of himself, **Purchas LJ** and **Stuart-Smith LJ**): It is well settled that an injunction to restrain a breach of contract for personal services ought not to be granted where its effect will be to decree performance of the contract. Speaking generally, there is no comparable objection to the grant of an injunction restraining the performance of particular services for a third party, because, by not prohibiting the performance of other services, it does not bind the servant to his contract. But a difficulty can arise, usually in the entertainment or sporting worlds, where the services are inseparable from the exercise of some special skill or talent, whose continued display is essential to the psychological and material, and sometimes to the physical, well-being of the servant. The difficulty does not reside in any beguilement of the court into looking more tenderly on such who breach their contracts, glamorous though they often are. It is that the human necessity of maintaining the skill or talent may practically bind the servant to the contract, compelling him to perform it.

The best known of the authorities on this subject are *Lumley v. Wagner* (1852) 1 De G.M. & G. 604 (impressario and opera singer) and *Warner Brothers Pictures Inc. v. Nelson* [1937] 1 K.B. 209 (film producer and actress), where injunctions were granted, and *Page One Records Ltd. v. Britton* [1968] 1 W.L.R. 157 (manager and pop group), where an injunction was refused. Here we have the case of manager and boxer. It is in one respect unusual, in that the manager has brought the action not against the boxer but against a third party who seeks to replace him, at all events in some respects. The manager claims that the third party has induced a breach of his contract with the boxer. He seeks an injunction only against the third party.

...

The question posed by the judge was formulated after a consideration of the more recent authorities in the line which starts with *Lumley v. Wagner,* 1 De G.M. & G. 604. We were helpfully referred to most, if not quite all, of the authorities in that line, some 20 in number, by Mr. Burnett, for the plaintiff. The more important of these were fully considered in the judgment of Oliver J. in *Nichols Advanced Vehicle Systems Inc. v. De Angelis* (unreported), 21 December 1979, of which we were given copies of the unrevised transcript and to which we would also express our indebtedness. It is now possible to dispense with a lengthy citation of authority, to refer only to those decisions which bear directly on the issues arising in this case and to state the principles, so far as they can be stated. Then they must be applied to the facts which are before us.

[*After considering* Lumley v Wagner, Warner Bros v Nelson *and* Page One Records v Britton *he continued:*] In *Nichols Advanced Vehicle Systems Inc. v. De Angelis* (unreported), 21 December 1979, the first defendant, an Italian Formula 1 racing driver aged 21, agreed to drive one of the plaintiffs' "Shadow" motor cars in Grand Prix events for part of 1979 and for the years 1980 and 1981 as well. He also agreed not to use or compete in any racing car other than a Shadow car in any of the Grand Prix events during the years in question. However, on 1 November 1980 he entered into a contract to drive for the second defendant, Team Lotus Ltd., in the 1980 season, subject to his obtaining before the 15 November a release from his contract with the plaintiffs. That not having been obtained, on 16 November the first defendant entered into an exclusive driver's contract with a foreign associated company of Lotus for the year 1980, renewable at the option of Lotus for 1981 and 1982. The plaintiffs thereupon commenced proceedings and applied for an interlocutory injunction to enforce the first defendant's negative obligation. Although he took an extremely unfavourable view of the first defendant's conduct, Oliver J. refused to grant an injunction against him. Having fully considered the more important of the earlier authorities, he recognised that there was a conflict between the approach of Branson J. in *Warner Brothers Pictures Inc. v. Nelson* [1937] 1 K.B. 209 and that of Stamp J. in *Page One Records Ltd. v. Britton* [1968] 1 W.L.R. 157. He described the former decision as representing the high watermark of the application of *Lumley v. Wagner* and said that up to that point no such injunction had been granted, at any rate so far as the reported cases went, in relation to anything but short-term engagements. Later he said that the injunction in that case appeared to him to be coming extremely close to specific performance. He said:

> "I do not find *Warner Brothers Pictures Inc. v. Nelson* and *Page One Records Ltd. v. Britton* easy to reconcile, but I am bound to say that the approach of Stamp J. in his consideration of what in substance amounts to specific performance seems to me, if I may say so respectfully, to be the more realistic one. It simply does not, with respect, seem to me to be realistic to say that nothing short of idleness and starvation is compulsive, and therefore no injunction which involves anything less than that can be said to infringe the principle that the court will not specifically enforce a contract of personal services. The injunction in *Warner Brothers Pictures Inc. v. Nelson* did not in practice leave the defendant in that case much freedom of choice if she wanted to pursue her chosen profession. No doubt it might have been quite otherwise if, as in the other previous cases in which similar injunctions had been granted, the contract had been a very short-term one."

In that case the plaintiff company had evinced a clear intention to force the first defendant back to drive for it and the evidence on both sides assumed that that would be the effect of an injunction. Oliver J. concluded that an injunction would force the first defendant either to drive for the plaintiffs or to give up his career for so long as the injunction continued. He refused relief accordingly.

With the exception of Branson J., no significant inconsistency of approach is discoverable amongst the judges who decided these cases. On a first consideration, that judge's view that Miss Bette Davis might employ herself both usefully and remuneratively in other spheres of activity for a period of up to three years appears to have been extraordinarily unrealistic. It could hardly have been thought to be a real possibility that an actress of her then youth and soaring talent would be able to forego screen and stage for such a period. (Although the injunction operated only within the jurisdiction of the English court, it must, we think, have been assumed that the negative covenants could and would be enforced in California. The 1930s was the high period of the studio contract system in Hollywood. We believe that the Warner Brothers' studio was markedly forthright in enforcing its contracts.) But then it is to be observed that Miss Davis did not give evidence, a feature of the case which made a great impression on the judge: see [1937] 1 K.B. 209, 215-216. In the absence of evidence from her, the judge no doubt thought that it was not for the court to assume that she could not or would not employ herself both usefully and remuneratively in other spheres of activity. From what can be gathered from the report it cannot be said with confidence that the injunction was wrongly granted.

Special considerations apart, we are firmly with Oliver J. in preferring the approach of Stamp J. to that of Branson J., both on grounds of realism and practicality and because that approach is more consistent with the earlier authorities. Any of these cases can be explained by the particular considerations which there arose, but we agree with Oliver J. in thinking that the most significant feature of each of those in which an injunction was granted before *Warner Brothers Pictures Inc. v. Nelson* was that the term of the engagement was short, in none of them exceeding 20 weeks. In *Lumley v. Wagner* itself the contractual period was three months, of which there were less than two to run when the injunction was granted. That was the maximum period for which Miss Wagner would have had to remain idle in England. It might even not have been too late for her to return to Berlin and sing there during the summer season. Although it is impossible to state in general terms where the line between short and long term engagements ought to be drawn, it is obvious that an injunction lasting for two years or more (the period applicable in the present case) may practically compel performance of the contract.

...

Having thus far considered only the more common case where the injunction is sought directly against the servant, we must now introduce the unusual feature of this case, which is that an injunction is not sought against the servant but only against a third party who must for present purposes be taken to have induced a breach of the contract between master and servant.

...

[W]e are all of the opinion that the court ought usually to refuse the grant of an injunction against a third party who induces a breach of the contract if on the evidence its effect would be to compel performance of the contract. If that were not so, the master could...obtain by the back door relief which he could not obtain through the front. The material considerations will not be exactly the same as in a case where the relief is sought directly against the servant. Most significantly, the court must take account not only of other third parties with whom the servant may be able to contract but also the likelihood or not that the plaintiff will take similar proceedings against them.

This consideration of the authorities has led us to believe that the following general principles are applicable to the grant or refusal of an injunction to enforce performance of the servant's negative obligations in a contract for personal services inseparable from the exercise of some special skill or talent. (We use the expressions "master" and "servant" for ease of reference and not out of any regard for the reality of the relationship in many of these cases.) In such a case the court ought not to enforce the performance of the negative obligations if their enforcement will effectively compel the servant to perform his positive obligations under the contract. Compulsion is a question to be decided on the facts of each case, with a realistic regard for the probable reaction of an injunction on the psychological and material, and sometimes the physical, need of the servant to maintain the skill or talent. The longer the term for which an injunction is sought, the more readily will compulsion be inferred. Compulsion may be inferred where the injunction is sought not against the servant but against a third party if either the third party is the only other available master or if it is likely that the master will seek relief against anyone who attempts to replace him. An injunction will less readily be granted where there are obligations of mutual trust and confidence, more especially where the servant's trust in the master may have been betrayed or his confidence in him has genuinely gone.

In stating the principles as we have, we are not to be taken as intending to pay anything less than a full and proper regard to the sanctity of contract. No judge would wish to detract from his duty to enforce the performance of contracts to the very limit which established principles allow him to go. Nowhere is that duty better vindicated than in the words of Lord St. Leonards L.C. in *Lumley v. Wagner*, 1 De G.M. & G. 604, 619. To that end the judge will scrutinise most carefully, even sceptically, any claim by the servant that he is under the human necessity of maintaining the skill or talent and thus will be compelled to perform the contract, or that his trust in the master has been betrayed or that his confidence in him has genuinely gone. But if, having done that, the judge is satisfied that the grant of an injunction will effectively compel performance of the contract, he ought to refuse it.

...

With these considerations in mind we return to the judgment of Pill J. In dealing with the law, he ...said that, as to the principles to be applied, he agreed with the reasoning and conclusion of Oliver J. in *Nichols Advanced Vehicle Systems Inc. v. De Angelis*. The question which he asked himself is now shown to have been correct. He said that in reaching his conclusion he bore in mind that the trade of a professional boxer was a very specialist one, requiring dedication, extensive training and expertise and that his professional life was comparatively short. He readily accepted that a high degree of mutual trust and confidence was required between boxer and manager. There were duties of a personal and fiduciary nature to be performed by the manager. Later, he completely rejected the suggestion that the covenant was not compulsive because Benn could get work, for example, as a security guard.

...

[T]he judge had the correct principles in mind when considering whether an injunction should be granted against the defendant as opposed to Nigel Benn. On the case as a whole, he did not take into account anything which he ought not to have taken into account, nor did he leave out of account anything which he ought to have taken into account. He exercised his discretion and he did not exercise it in a manner which was plainly wrong. His decision is not one with which this court can interfere and we affirm it on that ground.

NOTE AND QUESTION

The Court of Appeal here preferred the approach in *Page One Records* to that in *Warner Bros v Nelson* on grounds of 'realism and practicality'. Why, then, did it think *Lumley v Wagner* was correctly decided?

LauritzenCool AB v Lady Navigation Inc
[2005] EWCA Civ 579, [2005] 1 WLR 3686, Court of Appeal

In 1998 the defendant owners chartered two ships to the claimant charterers under a time charter that was due to run until 2010. The ships were part of a 'pool' managed by the claimants. Following a dispute the owners informed the charterers that they wished to withdraw the two ships from the pool: that is, they wished to pull out of the charterparty in respect of the two ships. Pending final arbitration, the charterers sought an interim injunction to restrain that alleged breach. At first instance Cooke J granted the following injunctions: that the defendants would not 'employ [the two ships] in a manner inconsistent with the time charters'; and would not 'fix [the ships] with any third party for employment' until the expiry of the charters in 2010. On appeal by the owners, the Court of Appeal, in upholding Cooke J, reasoned that the injunctions did not contradict Lord Diplock's speech in *The Scaptrade* [1983] 2 AC 694. Lord Diplock had there clarified that specific performance will not be ordered of a time charter because it is a contract for personal services (the owner being required to provide the ship and the services of the crew).

Mance LJ:

9 [I]t is common ground before us that *The Scaptrade* stands as authority for the proposition that specific performance will not be ordered of a time charter. Mr Berry for the claimants reserves his clients' right to ask the House to review this proposition, should the matter go that far. Mr Popplewell [for the appellants] submits that the House of Lords' classification of a time charter as a contract of services brings it within a category of case where the courts will not order negative injunctive relief, if the practical effect will be to compel its performance. He submits that there is, in this context at least, no sustainable distinction between an order which amounts in law to an order to perform and an order which has that practical effect. Mr Berry submits that there is a great difference, and that it is only in certain cases having special characteristics that the practical effect of injunctive relief may preclude its grant.

10 I start by noting that, in [*The Scaptrade*], Lord Diplock was addressing or presupposing a very different type of injunctive relief to that granted by Cooke J. Lord Diplock was concerned, at p 701c with "an injunction restraining the shipowner from exercising his right of withdrawal of the vessel from the service of the charterer" which he said was "though negative in form ... pregnant with an affirmative order to the shipowner to perform the contract" and "juristically ... indistinguishable from a decree of specific performance of a contract to render services". One can well understand why an injunction restraining a right of withdrawal would be regarded as pregnant with an affirmative order, and as juristically indistinguishable from an order for specific performance. But it is not now suggested that the relief granted by Cooke J was pregnant with any affirmative order. Further, it was, whatever its practical effect, juristically distinct from a decree of specific performance.

12 [T]he question is whether there is any principle that the English courts will – either invariably or absent exceptional circumstances – refuse to grant negative injunctive relief, when this would not juristically amount to an order of specific performance, but would as a matter of practical reality compel the other party to perform. In his speech in *The Scaptrade* [1983] 2 AC 694 Lord Diplock said nothing at all about the possibility of negative injunctive relief not, juristically, amounting to an order of specific performance. Nor, with one exception, did he refer to any of the cases to which Cooke J referred, in which negative injunctive relief had previously been contemplated or granted. We should therefore be cautious before concluding that it was either the intention or the effect of the House of Lords' decision in *The Scaptrade* to alter established principles or to depart from any of such cases in relation to such relief.

13 The one exception was *Lumley v Wagner* 1 De G M & G 604, to which Lord Diplock referred [1983] 2 AC 694, 701 for the principle that a court would never grant specific performance of a contract for services. But the fact that he only referred to it in this context confirms the narrow ambit of the first reason for the House's decision in *The Scaptrade* [1983] 2 AC 694. Lord Diplock would have regarded *Lumley v Wagner* as horn-book law, and the actual outcome *was* the grant of negative injunctive relief. ...

19 This brings me to Mr Popplewell's submission that there is a general principle that injunctive relief will not be given in respect of [a] contract for services if the practical effect would be to compel performance. He suggests that this derives from the nature of the relationship of trust and confidence which exists in relation to such contracts, and is, he submits, of particular importance in time charters. If so, the point must have been overlooked by Lord Chelmsford LC in *De Mattos v Gibson* 4 De G & J 276 and by the Court of Appeal in *The Georgios C* [1971] 1 QB 488, in so far as it is general, and by the Privy Council in *The Lord Strathcona* [1926] AC 108 and by the Court of Appeal in *The Georgios C* if and in so far as it is suggested that it is specific to time charters. However, I cannot, for my part, see what there is in *The Scaptrade* to suggest that any of these courts was wrong or to alter the pre-established principles stated in them.

20 Even if one is considering a contract for services far more easily described as personal in nature than the present, there is no inflexible principle precluding negative injunctive relief which prevents activity outside the contract contrary to its terms.

21 Mr Popplewell referred to *Warren v Mendy* [1989] 1 WLR 853. ...

22 ... The case was particularly concerned with the problem that can arise even in relation to [purely negative] injunctions where "the human necessity" of maintaining "some special skill or talent, whose continued display is essential to the psychological and material, and sometimes to the physical, well-being of the servant" may "practically bind the servant to the contract, compelling him to perform". It is an obvious non sequitur to derive from this reasoning a conclusion that, whenever the practical effect of negative injunctive relief would be to bind any party to any contract for services to the contract, compelling him to perform it, the court will or should refuse such relief.

24 The case thus bears no similarity on the facts to the present. I doubt whether Nourse LJ had in mind at all the present type of contract, when speaking of a contract for personal services. But, however the present contract may be described, it is very far from the particular sub-category of contract for personal services involving very special personal skills, talent and other features which *Warren v Mendy* [1989] 1 WLR 853 concerned and which Nourse LJ identified. Nor does the present case bear any factual similarity to *Page One Records Ltd v Britton* [1968] 1 WLR 157, which was among the cases cited by Nourse LJ. ...

33 In conclusion, neither the fact that the contracts involved were for services in the form of a time charter nor the existence under such contracts of a fiduciary relationship of mutual trust and confidence represents in law any necessary or general objection in principle to the grant of injunctive relief precluding the defendants from employing their vessels outside the pool pending the outcome of the current arbitration. Nor does it afford any such objection to the grant of such relief that the only realistic commercial course which it left to the defendants was, as I am prepared to assume, to do what they have done, namely to continue to provide the vessels to the pool and to perform the charters. In my judgment, therefore, the present appeal by the defendants should be dismissed.

Thomas and **Judge LJJ** concurred.

NOTES AND QUESTIONS

1. With respect to Mance LJ (a highly respected commercial judge) his reasoning in this case is, uncharacteristically, unpersuasive. He draws a distinction between a prohibitory injunction that juristically would amount to specific performance (eg an injunction restraining the defendant from taking any step which would prevent performance of the contract) and one that would *as a practical matter* amount to specific performance. But if one knows as a practical matter that the effect of the injunction is that the defendant will be compelled to perform, the decision to grant or refuse the injunction should surely be governed by specific performance principles as was recognised by the Court of Appeal in *Warren v Mendy*. No doubt it is correct to say that the personal service element involved in a time charter is far less significant than in a close working relationship between, eg, a boxing manager and a boxer. The correct way to deal with that point is to attack directly the rule, accepted by Lord Diplock in *The Scaptrade*, that specific performance cannot be ordered of a time charter. It is unsatisfactory to attack it indirectly by pretending that what was here ordered did not, in substance, constitute specific performance.
2. Do you agree with Mance LJ's description of the generalisation of the approach in *Warren v Mendy* as 'an obvious non sequitur'?

Additional Reading for Chapter 9

J Beatson, *Anson's Law of Contract* (28th edn, 2002) Ch 18
S Smith, *Atiyah's Introduction to the Law of Contract* (6th edn, 2005) 377–88

A Kronman, 'Specific Performance' (1978) 45 *U Chicago LR* 351
Applying an economic analysis, the author argues that: (i) the present mix of contract rights being sometimes protected, under the 'uniqueness' test, by specific performance (a 'property rule') but usually by damages (a 'liability rule') generally makes

economic sense and represents what rational parties would, in advance, have chosen; but that (ii) courts should be willing to enforce clauses under which the parties have actually agreed that the remedy should be specific performance.

G Schwartz, 'The Case for Specific Performance' (1979) 89 *Yale LJ* 271

Using economic analysis, Schwartz argues that, contrary to the present law, specific performance should be as routinely available as damages. Such a reform would not give promisees an incentive to exploit 'breaching promisors' and is unlikely to result in the efficiency losses predicted by some other commentators (eg Kronman). In particular, it would not result in more costly pre- or post-breach negotiations than damages and would produce efficiency gains (such as avoiding undercompensation and the costs of calculating damages).

Principles of European Contract Law (eds O Lando and H Beale, 2000) 391–402

Article 9:101: Monetary Obligations
(1) The creditor is entitled to recover money which is due.

(2) Where the creditor has not yet performed its obligation and it is clear that the debtor will be unwilling to receive performance, the creditor may nonetheless proceed with its performance and may recover any sum due under the contract unless:

(a) it could have made a reasonable substitute transaction without significant effort or expense; or

(b) performance would be unreasonable in the circumstances.

[This appears to match English law: see above, 423–432.]

Article 9:102: Non-monetary Obligations
(1) The aggrieved party is entitled to specific performance of an obligation other than one to pay money, including the remedying of a defective performance.

(2) Specific performance cannot, however, be obtained where:

(a) performance would be unlawful or impossible; or

(b) performance would cause the obligor unreasonable effort or expense; or

(c) the performance consists in the provision of services or work of a personal character or depends upon a personal relationship, or

(d) the aggrieved party may reasonably obtain performance from another source.

(3) The aggrieved party will lose the right to specific performance if it fails to seek it within a reasonable time after it has or ought to have become aware of the non-performance.

[While there are similarities, this fundamentally differs from English law in giving the aggrieved party a right to specific performance: see above, 432–447.]

Part Four

Privity of Contract and Third Party Rights

10

Privity of Contract and Third Party Rights

1. INTRODUCTION

The privity of contract doctrine lays down that a contract can only be enforced by, and is only enforceable against, the parties to that contract. So, for example, if A contracts with B to confer a benefit on C, C cannot enforce the contract against A even though C is the intended beneficiary of that contract. C is not a party to the contract but is rather a third party.

It is essential from the outset to keep clearly in mind the distinction between enforcement by third parties to the contract (the benefit side of the privity doctrine) and enforcement against third parties to the contract (the burden side of the privity doctrine). If A contracts with B that C shall do something for A (eg that C shall mow A's lawn or that C shall pay A £1000) it is obvious that, in general, C should not be bound to do that thing. The contract should not be enforceable against C. The reason is that a burden should not be imposed on a person by contract unless that person has agreed to that burden. There would otherwise be an unacceptable interference with individual liberty. There are a few exceptions to the burden side of privity which we shall briefly consider at the end of this chapter. But the privity doctrine on its burden side is plainly justified and there have been no calls for reform of it.

In contrast, the rule against enforcement of a contract *by* third parties—the benefit side of privity—is much harder to justify. There is no question here of enforcement undermining the third party's individual liberty because it is the third party's choice whether to enforce the contract or not. On the face of it, the privity of contract doctrine, on its benefit side, appears to conflict with the intentions of the contracting parties that the third party should benefit and, furthermore, appears to disappoint the reasonable expectations of the third party beneficiary. It is therefore not surprising that it is in relation to this side of the doctrine that over many years there have been calls for reform. It is solely with this benefit aspect of privity that, as its name suggests, the Contracts (Rights of Third Parties) Act 1999 is concerned; and it is with this benefit side of privity that this chapter is principally concerned.

Introductory reading: E McKendrick, *Contract Law* (7th edn, 2007) Ch 7.

2. FOUR CASES ESTABLISHING OR CONFIRMING THE PRIVITY DOCTRINE (ON ITS BENEFIT SIDE)

Tweddle v Atkinson (1861) 1 B & S 393, Court of Queen's Bench

The fathers of a bride and groom, on the occasion of their offspring's marriage, contracted with each other for each to pay a sum of money to the groom. The groom was William Tweddle, his father was John Tweddle, and the father of the bride was William Guy. The contract was made in writing and included the following clause: 'it is hereby further agreed by the aforesaid William Guy and the said John Tweddle that the said William Tweddle has full power to sue the said parties in any Court of law or equity for the aforesaid sums hereby promised and specified'. William Guy broke the contract and failed to pay William Tweddle the promised money. William Tweddle brought an action against William Guy's estate (William Guy had died) for the promised sum of £200. His claim failed because he was a stranger to the consideration/consideration did not move from him.[1]

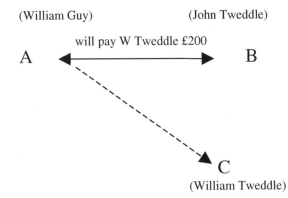

(William Guy)   (John Tweddle)

will pay W Tweddle £200

A   B

C
(William Tweddle)

Wightman J: Some of the old decisions appear to support the proposition that a stranger to the consideration of a contract may maintain an action upon it, if he stands in such a near relationship to the party from whom the consideration proceeds, that he may be considered a party to the consideration. The strongest of those cases is that cited in *Bourne v Mason*

---

[1] **Key**
A is the relevant promisor and contract-breaker
B is the promisee (ie the other party to the contract)
C is the third party beneficiary who wishes to enforce A's promise
◄──────►   mutual contractual obligations
┈┈┈┈┈┈►   intended factual beneficiary of A's promise
──N──►   obligation in the tort of negligence
──U──►   obligation under a unilateral contract

(1 Ventr. 6), in which it was held that the daughter of a physician might maintain assumpsit upon a promise to her father to give her a sum of money if he performed a certain cure. But there is no modern case in which the proposition has been supported. On the contrary, it is now established that no stranger to the consideration can take advantage of a contract, although made for his benefit.

Crompton J: The modern cases have, in effect, overruled the old decisions; they shew that the consideration must move from the party entitled to sue upon the contract. It would be a monstrous proposition to say that a person was a party to the contract for the purpose of suing upon it for his own advantage, and not a party to it for the purpose of being sued. It is said that the father in the present case was agent for the son in making the contract, but that argument ought also to make the son liable upon it. I am prepared to overrule the old decisions, and to hold that, by reason of the principles which now govern the action of assumpsit, the present action is not maintainable.

Blackburn J: Mr. Mellish [counsel for the claimant] admits that in general no action can be maintained upon a promise, unless the consideration moves from the party to whom it is made. But he says that there is an exception; namely, that when the consideration moves from a father, and the contract is for the benefit of his son, the natural love and affection between the father and son gives the son the right to sue as if the consideration had proceeded from himself. And *Dutton and Wife v Poole* 2 Lev. 21; 1 Ventr. 318 was cited for this. We cannot overrule a decision of the Exchequer Chamber; but there is a distinct ground on which that case cannot be supported. The cases…shew that natural love and affection are not a sufficient consideration whereon an action of assumpsit may be founded.

NOTE AND QUESTION

The judges said that William Tweddle could not sue because he was a stranger to the consideration or that consideration did not move from him. Is that merely an alternative way of saying that William Tweddle could not enforce the contract because he was not a party to it?

Dunlop Pneumatic Tyre Co Ltd v Selfridge
[1915] AC 847, House of Lords

This case concerned an attempt by Dunlop, a manufacturer of tyres, to ensure that its tyres were not sold below their list price. Every time it supplied tyres to a dealer Dunlop insisted, as a term of the contract of sale to that dealer, that that dealer's sales of the tyres should not be at a price below the list price and that, if they were, the dealer would pay £5 per tyre liquidated damages to Dunlop; and that the dealer would in turn extract the same undertaking from its purchaser. In this instance, the dealer was Dew & Co. In line with the agreement with Dunlop, when Dew & Co sold to Selfridge, the purchaser, it was a term of the agreement with Selfridge (made on 2 January 1912) that Selfridge would not sell on the tyres at below the list price and that, if it did so, it would pay Dunlop £5 liquidated damages. Selfridge did sell on at below the list price and Dunlop brought an action for liquidated damages of £5 per tyre against Selfridge. This action failed before the Court of Appeal, and the House of Lords dismissed Dunlop's appeal because it had not provided the consideration for Selfridge's promise.

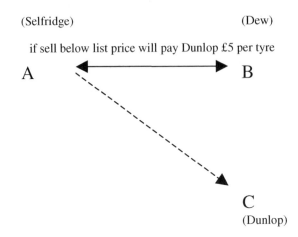

For key see 462.

Viscount Haldane LC: My Lords, in the law of England certain principles are fundamental. One is that only a person who is a party to a contract can sue on it. Our law knows nothing of a jus quaesitum tertio arising by way of contract. Such a right may be conferred by way of property, as, for example, under a trust, but it cannot be conferred on a stranger to a contract as a right to enforce the contract in personam. A second principle is that if a person with whom a contract not under seal has been made is to be able to enforce it consideration must have been given by him to the promisor or to some other person at the promisor's request. These two principles are not recognized in the same fashion by the jurisprudence of certain Continental countries or of Scotland, but here they are well established. A third proposition is that a principal not named in the contract may sue upon it if the promisee really contracted as his agent. But again, in order to entitle him so to sue, he must have given consideration either personally or through the promisee, acting as his agent in giving it.

My Lords, in the case before us, I am of opinion that the consideration, the allowance of what was in reality part of the discount to which Messrs. Dew, the promisees, were entitled as between themselves and the appellants, was to be given by Messrs. Dew on their own account, and was not in substance, any more than in form, an allowance made by the appellants. ...

No doubt it was provided as part of these terms that the appellants should acquire certain rights, but these rights appear on the face of the contract as jura quaesita tertio, which the appellants could not enforce. Moreover, even if this difficulty can be got over by regarding the appellants as the principals of Messrs. Dew in stipulating for the rights in question, the only consideration disclosed by the contract is one given by Messrs. Dew, not as their agents, but as principals acting on their own account.

Lord Dunedin: My Lords, I confess that this case is to my mind apt to nip any budding affection which one might have had for the doctrine of consideration. For the effect of that doctrine in the present case is to make it possible for a person to snap his fingers at a bargain deliberately made, a bargain not in itself unfair, and which the person seeking to enforce it has a legitimate interest to enforce. Notwithstanding these considerations I cannot say that I have ever had any doubt that the judgment of the Court of Appeal was right.

My Lords, I am content to adopt from a work of Sir Frederick Pollock, to which I have often been under obligation, the following words as to consideration: "An act or forbearance of one party, or the promise thereof, is the price for which the promise of the other is bought, and the promise thus given for value is enforceable." (Pollock on Contracts, 8th ed., p. 175.)

Now the agreement sued on is an agreement which on the face of it is an agreement between Dew and Selfridge. But speaking for myself, I should have no difficulty in the circumstances of this case in holding it proved that the agreement was truly made by Dew as agent for Dunlop, or in other words that Dunlop was the undisclosed principal, and as such can sue on the agreement. None the less, in order to enforce it he must show consideration, as above defined, moving from Dunlop to Selfridge.

In the circumstances, how can he do so? The agreement in question is not an agreement for sale. It is only collateral to an agreement for sale; but that agreement for sale is an agreement entirely between Dew and Selfridge. The tyres, the property in which upon the bargain is transferred to Selfridge, were the property of Dew, not of Dunlop, for Dew under his agreement with Dunlop held these tyres as proprietor, and not as agent. What then did Dunlop do, or forbear to do, in a question with Selfridge? The answer must be, nothing. He did not do anything, for Dew, having the right of property in the tyres, could give a good title to any one he liked, subject, it might be, to an action of damages at the instance of Dunlop for breach of contract, which action, however, could never create a vitium reale in the property of the tyres. He did not forbear in anything, for he had no action against Dew which he gave up, because Dew had fulfilled his contract with Dunlop in obtaining, on the occasion of the sale, a contract from Selfridge in the terms prescribed.

To my mind, this ends the case. That there are methods of framing a contract which will cause persons in the position of Selfridge to become bound, I do not doubt. But that has not been done in this instance; and as Dunlop's advisers must have known of the law of consideration, it is their affair that they have not so drawn the contract.

I think the appeal should be dismissed.

Lords Atkinson, **Parker of Waddington**, **Sumner** and **Parmoor** delivered concurring speeches.

NOTES AND QUESTIONS

1. As in *Tweddle v Atkinson* the judges' central reasoning was that Dunlop could not succeed because it had not provided consideration for Selfridge's promise. Rather the consideration had been provided by Dew & Co. Viscount Haldane did explicitly refer to the privity rule—that only a party to a contract can enforce it—but he appeared to think that privity and consideration moving from the claimant were separate principles. Are they?
2. There is a difference between saying that consideration must move from the claimant and saying that consideration must move from the promisee (although the latter is often interpreted to mean the same as the former). Strictly speaking, the latter says nothing about who can enforce the contract and simply reiterates that, other than for contracts made by deed, consideration is a necessary requirement for a promise to be contractually binding.
3. Much of the discussion in the speeches examined whether the well-recognised exception to privity of undisclosed agency (see below, 475) could here be established. It was held that it could not be because Dew & Co was acting (and providing consideration) on its own behalf and not on behalf of Dunlop.

4.   For the decision that the £5 clause was liquidated damages and not a penalty see *Dunlop Pneumatic Tyre Ltd v New Garage and Motor Co Ltd*, above, 412.

Scruttons Ltd v Midland Silicones Ltd [1962] AC 446, House of Lords

The claimants were the owners (and consignees) of a drum of chemicals and they entered into a contract with carriers for the carriage of the drum by sea to England from the United States. Under that contract, there was a term limiting the carriers' liability to $500 for loss of, or damage to, the goods. The carriers contracted with the defendant stevedores to unload the drum of chemicals in London. In doing so, the stevedores negligently damaged the drum. The claimants sued the stevedores in the tort of negligence for the damage to their drum. The stevedores argued that they were entitled to rely on the limitation clause in the contract between the claimants and the carriers so that their liability in tort was limited to $500. In rejecting that argument, and upholding the decisions of the trial judge and the Court of Appeal, the House of Lords affirmed and applied the privity doctrine.

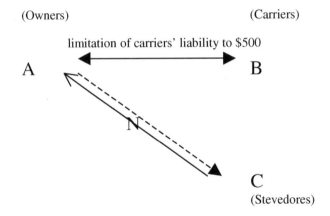

For key see 462.

Lord Reid: In considering the various arguments for the appellants, I think it is necessary to have in mind certain established principles of the English law of contract. Although I may regret it, I find it impossible to deny the existence of the general rule that a stranger to a contract cannot in a question with either of the contracting parties take advantage of provisions of the contract, even where it is clear from the contract that some provision in it was intended to benefit him. That rule appears to have been crystallised a century ago in *Tweddle v. Atkinson* (1861) 1 B & S 393 and finally established in this House in *Dunlop Pneumatic Tyre Co. Ltd. v. Selfridge & Co. Ltd.* [1915] A.C. 847. There are, it is true, certain well-established exceptions to that rule – though I am not sure that they are really exceptions and do not arise from other principles. But none of these in any way touches the present case.

   The actual words used by Lord Haldane in the *Dunlop* case at 853 were made the basis of an argument that, although a stranger to a contract may not be able to sue for any benefit under it, he can rely on the contract as a defence if one of the parties to it sues him in breach of his contractual obligation – that he can use the contract as a shield though not as a sword. I can find no justification for that. If the other contracting party can prevent the breach of contract well and good, but if he cannot I do not see how the stranger can. As was said in *Tweddle v. Atkinson,* at 398, the stranger cannot "take advantage" from the contract.

It may be that in a roundabout way the stranger could be protected. If A, wishing to protect X, gives to X an enforceable indemnity, and contracts with B that B will not sue X, informing B of the indemnity, and then B does sue X in breach of his contract with A, it may be that A can recover from B as damages the sum which he has to pay X under the indemnity, X having had to pay it to B. But there is nothing remotely resembling that in the present case.

The appellants in this case seek to get round this rule in three different ways. In the first place, they say that the decision in *Elder, Dempster & Co. Ltd. v. Paterson, Zochonis & Co. Ltd.* [1924] A.C. 522 establishes an exception to the rule sufficiently wide to cover the present case. I shall later return to consider this case. Secondly, they say that through the agency of the carrier they were brought into contractual relation with the shipper and that they can now found on that against the consignees, the respondents. And thirdly, they say that there should be inferred from the facts an implied contract, independent of the bill of lading, between them and the respondents. It was not argued that they had not committed a tort in damaging the respondents' goods.

I can see a possibility of success of the agency argument if (first) the bill of lading makes it clear that the stevedore is intended to be protected by the provisions in it which limit liability, (secondly) the bill of lading makes it clear that the carrier, in addition to contracting for these provisions on his own behalf, should apply to the stevedore, (thirdly) the carrier has authority from the stevedore to do that, or perhaps later ratification by the stevedore would suffice, and (fourthly) that any difficulties about consideration moving from the stevedore were overcome. And then to affect the consignee it would be necessary to show that the provisions of the Bills of Lading Act, 1855, apply.

But again there is nothing of that kind in the present case. I agree with your Lordships that "carrier" in the bill of lading does not include stevedore, and if that is so I can find nothing in the bill of lading which states or even implies that the parties to it intended the limitation of liability to extend to stevedores. Even if it could be said that reasonable men in the shoes of these parties would have agreed that the stevedores should have this benefit, that would not be enough to make this an implied term of the contract. And even if one could spell out of the bill of lading an intention to benefit the stevedore, there is certainly nothing to indicate that the carrier was contracting as agent for the stevedore in addition to contracting on his own behalf. So it appears to me that the agency argument must fail.

And the implied contract argument seems to me to be equally unsound. From the stevedores' angle, they are employed by the carrier to deal with the goods in the ship. They can assume that the carrier is acting properly in employing them and they need not know whom the goods belong to. There was in their contract with the carrier a provision that they should be protected, but that could not by itself bind the consignee. They might assume that the carrier would obtain protection for them against the consignee and feel aggrieved when they found that the carrier did not or could not do that. But a provision in the contract between them and the carrier is irrelevant in a question between them and the consignee. Then from the consignees' angle they would know that stevedores would be employed to handle their goods, but if they read the bill of lading they would find nothing to show that the shippers had agreed to limit the liability of the stevedores. There is nothing to show that they ever thought about this or that if they had they would have agreed or ought as reasonable men to have agreed to this benefit to the stevedores. I can find no basis in this for implying a contract between them and the stevedores. It cannot be said that such a contract was in any way necessary for business efficiency.

So this case depends on the proper interpretation of the *Elder, Dempster* case. What was there decided is clear enough. The ship was under time charter, the bill of lading made by the shippers and the charterers provided for exemption from liability in the event which happened and this exemption was held to enure to the benefit of the shipowners who were not parties to the bill of lading but whose servant[,] the master[,] caused damage to the shippers' goods by his negligence. The decision is binding on us but I agree that the decision by itself will not avail the present appellants because the facts of this case are very different from those in the *Elder, Dempster* case.

...

...I do not think that it is my duty to pursue the unrewarding task of seeking to extract a ratio decidendi from what was said in this House in *Elder, Dempster*. Nor is it my duty to seek to rationalise the decision by determining in any other way just how far the scope of the decision should extend. I must treat the decision as an anomalous and unexplained exception to the general principle that a stranger cannot rely for his protection on provisions in a contract to which he is not a party. The decision of this House is authoritative in cases of which the circumstances are not reasonably distinguishable from those which gave rise to the decision. The circumstances in the present case are clearly distinguishable in several respects. Therefore I must decide this case on the established principles of the law of England apart from that decision, and on that basis I have no doubt that this appeal must be dismissed.

Viscount Simonds, **Lord Keith of Avonholme** and **Lord Morris of Borth-y-Gest** gave concurring speeches. **Lord Denning** gave a dissenting speech.

NOTES AND QUESTIONS

1. The importance of this case lies not only in its clear confirmation of the privity doctrine but also in its application of that doctrine to *negative* (rather than the usual positive) rights. That is, in contrast to *Tweddle v Atkinson* and *Dunlop v Selfridge*, the third party was here seeking to avail itself of a limitation clause rather than trying to sue for breach of contract.
2. In the light of subsequent common law developments, it is crucial to realise that the contract of carriage did not expressly say that stevedores were to enjoy the protection of the limitation clause.
3. Prior to this case, in *Elder Dempster & Co Ltd v Paterson, Zochonis & Co Ltd* [1924] AC 522, HL, third party shipowners, who were being sued in the tort of negligence by cargo-owners for damage to their goods, were held able to rely on an exclusion of liability in the contract of carriage between the cargo-owners and the charterers. But the majority of their Lordships in *Scruttons v Midland Silicones* regarded *Elder Dempster* as anomalous and to be confined to its own facts.
4. Had the Contracts (Rights of Third Parties) Act 1999 been in force would the result in *Scruttons v Midland Silicones* have been any different? See below, 508.

Beswick v Beswick [1968] AC 58, House of Lords

Old Peter Beswick had entered into a contract with his nephew. By this he transferred his coal business to his nephew in consideration of the nephew agreeing to employ Peter Beswick as a consultant at £6 10s a week for the rest of his life and agreeing to pay £5 a week to Peter Beswick's widow for the rest of her life after his death. Peter Beswick died but the nephew failed to pay the widow the money as promised. The widow sued the nephew. She did so in two capacities: first, in her personal capacity as widow; and, secondly, in her capacity as Peter Beswick's personal representative (ie as his administratrix). She succeeded in both capacities in the Court of Appeal. On appeal by the nephew to the House of Lords, she was held able to succeed as administratrix but, applying the privity doctrine, not in her personal capacity.

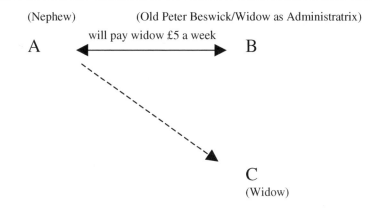

(Nephew)   (Old Peter Beswick/Widow as Administratrix)

A   will pay widow £5 a week   B

C
(Widow)

For key see 462.

Lord Reid: For clarity I think it best to begin by considering a simple case where, in consideration of a sale by A to B, B agrees to pay the price of £1,000 to a third party X. Then the first question appears to me to be whether the parties intended that X should receive the money simply as A's nominee so that he would hold the money for behoof of A and be accountable to him for it, or whether the parties intended that X should receive the money for his own behoof and be entitled to keep it. That appears to me to be a question of construction of the agreement read in light of all the circumstances which were known to the parties. …In the present case I think it clear that the parties to the agreement intended that the respondent should receive the weekly sums of £5 in her own behoof and should not be accountable to her deceased husband's estate for them. Indeed the contrary was not argued.

Reverting to my simple example the next question appears to me to be: Where the intention was that X should keep the £1,000 as his own, what is the nature of B's obligation and who is entitled to enforce it? It was not argued that the law of England regards B's obligation as a nullity, and I have not observed in any of the authorities any suggestion that it would be a nullity. There may have been a time when the existence of a right depended on whether there was any means of enforcing it, but today the law would be sadly deficient if one found that, although there is a right, the law provides no means for enforcing it. So this obligation of B must be enforceable either by X or by A. I shall leave aside for the moment the question whether section 56 (1) of the Law of Property Act, 1925, has any application to such a case, and consider the position at common law.

Lord Denning's view, expressed in this case not for the first time, is that X could enforce this obligation. But the view more commonly held in recent times has been that such a contract confers no right on X and that X could not sue for the £1,000. Leading counsel for the respondent based his case on other grounds, and as I agree that the respondent succeeds on other grounds, this would not be an appropriate case in which to solve this question. It is true that a strong Law Revision Committee recommended so long ago as 1937 (Cmd. 5449):

> "That where a contract by its express terms purports to confer a benefit directly on a third party it shall be enforceable by the third party in his own name …" (p. 31).

And, if one had to contemplate a further long period of Parliamentary procrastination, this House might find it necessary to deal with this matter. But if legislation is probable at any early date I would not deal with it in a case where that is not essential. So for the purposes of this case I shall proceed on the footing that the commonly accepted view is right.

What then is A's position? I assume that A has not made himself a trustee for X, because it was not argued in this appeal that any trust had been created. So, if X has no right, A can at any time grant a discharge to B or make some new contract with B. If there were a trust the position would be different. X would have an equitable right and A would be entitled and, indeed, bound to recover the money and account for it to X. And A would have no right to grant a discharge to B. If there is no trust and A wishes to enforce the obligation, how does he set about it? He cannot sue B for the £1,000 because under the contract the money is not payable to him, and, if the contract were performed according to its terms, he would never have any right to get the money. So he must seek to make B pay X.

The argument for the appellant is that A's only remedy is to sue B for damages for B's breach of contract in failing to pay the £1,000 to X. Then the appellant says that A can only recover nominal damages of 40s. because the fact that X has not received the money will generally cause no loss to A: he admits that there may be cases where A would suffer damage if X did not receive the money but says that the present is not such a case.

Applying what I have said to the circumstances of the present case, the respondent in her personal capacity has no right to sue, but she has a right as administratrix of her husband's estate to require the appellant to perform his obligation under the agreement. He has refused to do so and he maintains that the respondent's only right is to sue him for damages for breach of his contract. If that were so, I shall assume that he is right in maintaining that the administratrix could then only recover nominal damages because his breach of contract has caused no loss to the estate of her deceased husband.

If that were the only remedy available the result would be grossly unjust. It would mean that the appellant keeps the business which he bought and for which he has only paid a small part of the price which he agreed to pay. He would avoid paying the rest of the price, the annuity to the respondent, by paying a mere 40s. damages.

The respondent's first answer is that the common law has been radically altered by section 56 (1) of the Law of Property Act, 1925, and that that section entitles her to sue in her personal capacity and recover the benefit provided for her in the agreement although she was not a party to it. ...

Section 56 was obviously intended to replace section 5 of the Real Property Act, 1845 (8 and 9 Vict. c. 106). That section provided:

> "That, under an indenture, executed after October 1, 1845, an immediate estate or interest, in any tenements or hereditaments, and the benefit of a condition or covenant, respecting any tenements or hereditaments, may be taken, although the taker thereof be not named a party to the same indenture. ..."

Section 56 (1) now provides:

> "A person may take an immediate or other interest in land or other property, or the benefit of any condition, right of entry covenant or agreement over or respecting land or other property, although he may not be named as a party to the conveyance or other instrument: ..."

If the matter stopped there it would not be difficult to hold that section 56 does not substantially extend or alter the provisions of section 5 of the Act of 1845. But more difficulty is introduced by the definition section of the Act of 1925 (section 205) which provides:

> "(1) In this Act unless the context otherwise requires, the following expressions have the meanings hereby assigned to them respectively, that is to say:— ... (xx) 'Property' includes any thing in action, and any interest in real or personal property."

...

By express provision in the definition section a definition contained in it is not to be applied to the word defined if in the particular case the context otherwise requires. If application of that definition would result in giving to section 56 a meaning going beyond that of the old section, then, in my opinion, the context does require that the definition of "property" shall not be applied to that word in section 56. The context in which this section occurs is a consolidation Act. If the definition is not applied the section is a proper one to appear in such an Act because it can properly be regarded as not substantially altering the pre-existing law. But if the definition is applied the result is to make section 56 go far beyond the pre-existing law. Holding that the section has such an effect would involve holding that the invariable practice of Parliament has been departed from *per incuriam* so that something has got into this consolidation Act which neither the draftsman nor Parliament can have intended to be there. I am reinforced in this view by two facts. The language of section 56 is not at all what one would have expected if the intention had been to bring in all that the application of the definition would bring in. And, secondly, section 56 is one of 25 sections which appear in the Act under the cross-heading "Conveyances and other Instruments." The other twenty-four sections come appropriately under that heading and so does section 56 if it has a limited meaning: but, if its scope is extended by the definition of property, it would be quite inappropriately placed in this part of the Act. For these reasons I am of opinion that section 56 has no application to the present case.

The respondent's second argument is that she is entitled in her capacity of administratrix of her deceased husband's estate to enforce the provision of the agreement for the benefit of herself in her personal capacity, and that a proper way of enforcing that provision is to order specific performance. That would produce a just result, and, unless there is some technical objection, I am of opinion that specific performance ought to be ordered. For the reasons given by your Lordships I would reject the arguments submitted for the appellant that specific performance is not a possible remedy in this case. I am therefore of opinion that the Court of Appeal reached a correct decision and that this appeal should be dismissed.

Lord Hodson: Like my noble and learned friend, Lord Reid, whose opinion I have had the opportunity of reading, I am of opinion that section 56, one of 25 sections in the Act appearing under the cross-heading "Conveyances and other Instruments," does not have the revolutionary effect claimed for it, appearing as it does in a consolidation Act. I think, as he does, that the context does otherwise require a limited meaning to be given to the word "property" in the section.

...

The peculiar feature of this case is that the plaintiff is not only the personal representative of the deceased but also his widow and the person beneficially entitled to the money claimed. Although the widow cannot claim specific performance in her personal capacity, there is no objection to her doing so in her capacity as administratrix, and when the moneys are recovered they will be in this instance held for the benefit of herself as the person for whom they are intended.

...

In such a case as this, there having been an unconscionable breach of faith, the equitable remedy sought is apt.

Lord Pearce: It is argued that the estate can only recover nominal damages and that no other remedy is open, either to the estate or to the personal plaintiff. Such a result would be wholly repugnant to justice and commonsense. And if the argument were right it would show a very serious defect in the law.

In the first place, I do not accept the view that damages must be nominal. ...I agree with the comment of Windeyer J. in the case of *Coulls v. Bagot's Executor and Trustee Co. Ltd.* (1967) 40 A.L.J.R. 471, 486 in the High Court of Australia...

"I can see no reason why in such cases the damages which A would suffer upon B's breach of his contract to pay C $500 would be merely nominal: I think that in accordance with the ordinary rules for the assessment of damages for breach of contract they could be substantial. They would not necessarily be $500; they could I think be less or more."

In the present case I think that the damages, if assessed, must be substantial. It is not necessary, however, to consider the amount of damages more closely since this is a case in which, as the Court of Appeal rightly decided, the more appropriate remedy is that of specific performance.

The administratrix is entitled, if she so prefers, to enforce the agreement rather than accept its repudiation, and specific performance is more convenient than an action for arrears of payment followed by separate actions as each sum falls due. Moreover, damages for breach would be a less appropriate remedy since the parties to the agreement were intending an annuity for a widow; and a lump sum of damages does not accord with this. And if (contrary to my view) the argument that a derisory sum of damages is all that can be obtained be right, the remedy of damages in this case is manifestly useless.

[*On the section 56 point, he held that the section had no relevance in this case and he was inclined to the view of section 56 expressed by Lord Upjohn.*]

Lord Upjohn: As it is necessary to keep clear and distinct the rights of the widow as administratrix of her husband and personally, I think it will be convenient to use letters: letter A represents the deceased and A1 the widow, as personal representative, B the widow in her personal capacity and C the appellant. And in other examples I shall give, these letters will serve the same purpose.

...

Counsel for the respondent has not felt able to support the view, expressed by Lord Denning M.R., that apart from section 56 of the Law of Property Act, 1925, B is entitled to sue C at common law. I think that he was right to make this concession, for whatever may have been the state of the law before *Tweddle v. Atkinson* 1 B. & S. 393 it is difficult to see how your Lordships can go back over 100 years in view of the decisions in this House of *Dunlop Pneumatic Tyre Co. Ltd. v. Selfridge & Co. Ltd.* [1915] A.C. 847 and *Scruttons Ltd. v. Midland Silicones Ltd.* [1962] A.C. 496.

...

[W]hen the money payment is not made once and for all but in the nature of an annuity there is an even greater need for equity to come to the assistance of the common law. Equity is to do true justice to enforce the true contract that the parties have made and to prevent the trouble and expense of a multiplicity of actions.

...

[E]quity comes to the aid of the common law and it is sufficiently flexible to meet and satisfy the justice of the case in the many different circumstances that arise from time to time.

To sum up this matter: had C repudiated the contract in the lifetime of A the latter would have had a cast iron case for specific performance. Can it make any difference that by the terms of the agreement C is obliged to pay the annuity after A's death to B? Of course not. On the principle I have just stated it is clear that there can be nothing to prevent equity in A's specific performance action making an appropriate decree for specific performance directing payment of the annuity to A but during his life and thereafter to B for her life.

[*On section 56, he held that it did not help the widow and was not intended to alter the rule laid down in* Tweddle v Atkinson. *But he tended to think that its scope was wider than just applying to real property.*]

Lord Guest gave a concurring speech.

1.   All their Lordships accepted that, subject to the argument (which they ultimately all rejected) that the common law had been altered by section 56 of the Law of Property Act 1925, the widow in her personal capacity could not succeed because of the privity doctrine. As made clear in the extract from Lord Reid's speech, this was a rejection of Lord Denning MR's anti-privity views put forward in the Court of Appeal in this case and in several other cases. In *Smith & Snipes Hall Farm Ltd v River Douglas Catchment Board* [1949] 2 KB 500, 514, Denning LJ had said, 'A man who makes a deliberate promise which is intended to be binding, that is to say, under seal, or for good consideration, must keep his promise; and the court will hold him to it, not only at the suit of the party who gave the consideration but also at the suit of one who was not a party to the contract, provided that it was made for his benefit and that he has a sufficient interest to entitle him to enforce it, subject always, of course, to any defences that may be open on the merits.' And in the Court of Appeal in this case, Lord Denning MR said [1966] Ch 538, 557, 'Where a contract is made for the benefit of a third person who has a legitimate interest to enforce it, it can be enforced by the third person in the name of the contracting party or jointly with him or, if he refuses to join, by adding him as a defendant. In that sense, and it is a very real sense, the third person has a right arising by way of contract.' Assuming that Lord Denning was incorrect as to what the law was, do you nevertheless agree with him that that was what the law ought to have been?

2.   While rejecting Lord Denning's views, Lord Reid indicated that, if Parliament did not reform privity within the near future, the House of Lords might have to do so judicially. See similarly Lord Scarman's comments in *Woodar v Wimpey*, below, 487. This is characteristic of the judicial approach to privity: a recognition that the doctrine is, or may be, flawed but an unwillingness (with the exception of Lord Denning) to do anything fundamental about it. Parliament procrastinated for a further 30 years after *Beswick v Beswick* before the Contracts (Rights of Third Parties) Act 1999 was passed.

3.   The case is also important for its acceptance that the promisee (here the widow as administratrix) may sometimes be granted the remedy of specific performance which precisely orders the defendant to perform, as promised, for the benefit of the third party. On this, see above, 435, and below, 482.

3. EXCEPTIONS TO PRIVITY (ON ITS BENEFIT SIDE)

Putting to one side the Contracts (Rights of Third Parties) Act 1999 (below, 501), there can be said to be seven main exceptions to privity: agency, assignment, trusts of the promise, statutory exceptions, covenants concerning land, some examples of the recovery of pure economic loss in the tort of negligence, and the enforcement by third parties of exemption clauses.

In order to understand the general principles of the law of contract, all but the last of these exceptions to privity can be dealt with very briefly. Exploration of their details can be found in specialist chapters or books. What is important for our purposes is knowing how, in general terms, the exceptions work; and, in particular, why they are exceptions.

Before turning to those exceptions, there are two additional introductory points. First, it is often suggested that *collateral contracts* constitute an exception to privity. This is misleading. While collateral contracts can be used as a way of avoiding the privity problem, collateral contracts are normally true contracts so that one can say, without artificiality, that the 'third party' and the promisor are in a real contractual relationship. Take the well-known case of *Shanklin Pier v Detel Products Ltd* [1951] 2 KB 854. Here the owner of a pier (C) instructed painters of the pier (B) to use paint manufactured by A in reliance on A's assurance that the paint would last for seven years. When the paint lasted only three months, C was held able to sue A for breach of contract even though the main contract for the purchase of the paint was between A and B. This may look like a third party (C) being held able to enforce a contract made for its benefit between two other parties (A and B). However, there is no artificiality in saying that there was a collateral contract between A and C with the consideration for A's promise being C's instruction to B to buy A's paint. In other words, there is no artificiality in saying that A and C were in a direct contractual relationship.[2] It is submitted, therefore, that normally collateral contracts are not a real exception to privity. They will only be so if the finding of the collateral contract is artificial based on illusory consideration. We will examine an example of this artificiality below in the context of the enforcement of exemption clauses (see *The Eurymedon,* below, 477).

Secondly, it is likely that a *joint promisee* can enforce a contract (even though it has not itself provided consideration and the contract was not made by deed). Say, eg, A promises B and C to pay C £1000 if B will do certain work for A. If B does the work and A refuses to pay the £1000 to C, can C sue A? Although there is no clear English authority, the High Court of Australia in *Coulls v Bagot's Executor and Trustee Co Ltd* (1967) 119 CLR 461 suggested that the answer is in the affirmative. Assuming that that is correct, is the 'joint promisee principle' an exception to privity? That depends on what one means by a 'party' to a contract (not made by deed). One view (taken by Coote: see below, 532) is that to be a party to a contract one must provide consideration: C is therefore not a party to the contract and the joint promisee principle is an exception to privity (as it is to the synonymous rule that consideration must move from the claimant). The alternative view is that a party is someone to whom the promise was made. On that view, C is a party to the contract, because the promise was made to him, and the joint promisee principle is not an exception to privity although it is an exception to the rule that consideration must move from the claimant.

---

[2]   It is now laid down by statutory instrument that a consumer guarantee takes effect as a contractual obligation owed by the guarantor to the consumer: see Sale and Supply of Goods to Consumers Regs 2002, reg 15.

(1) Agency

In the law of contract, an agent can act on behalf of his principal in making contracts with other parties. To do so, the agent must have the principal's authority, whether actual or apparent. Where a (bilateral) contract is concluded by an agent for his principal, the principal can both sue and be sued on the contract. So, one *could* argue that the whole law of agency in contract is an exception to privity. The principal, albeit in one sense a third party to the contract concluded by his agent, is able to sue and be sued on that contract. However, in most circumstances, one can say without any fiction that the principal, not the agent, is the real party to the contract concluded by his agent. Indeed in most circumstances the agent will not be named in the contract and will drop out of the picture once the contract has been concluded. However, that is not the case where one has an undisclosed agency. That is, where the other party is not informed that he is dealing with an agent rather than with a principal. In an undisclosed agency, the agent does not drop out of the picture: in general, the agent, as well as the principal, can sue and be sued on the contract. Therefore, it is artificial to say that the principal, not the agent, is the real party to the contract. In an undisclosed agency, the other party has no knowledge of the principal's existence and may find that he is in a contractual relationship with someone of whom he has never heard and with whom he never intended to contract. It follows that, whatever one says about disclosed agency, undisclosed agency is a true exception to privity. One should note that it is an exception not only to the benefit side of privity but also to the burden side. In other words, the undisclosed principal can both sue the other party and be sued by him.

(2) Assignment

By the law of assignment, the benefit of (that is, the right to enforce) most types of contract can be transferred to a third party. The assignment is brought about by a separate contract of assignment between the promisee under the main contract, who is called the assignor, and the third party, who is called the assignee. The effect is that the third party assignee can sue the promisor under the main contract. Two points are especially noteworthy. First, only benefits and not burdens can be assigned. Secondly, the assignment takes effect irrespective of the wishes of the promisor so that the promisor can find itself bound to perform for someone it did not intend to perform for. However, there are some protections for promisors: in particular, a promisor can validly prohibit an assignment unless its consent is given; and so-called personal contracts (eg an agreement to perform personal services) cannot be assigned.

(3) Trusts of the Promise

A trust of the promise is established where, instead of there being merely a contract for the benefit of a third party, the promise to benefit the third party is regarded as being held by the promisee on trust for the third party. That is, there is a fully constituted trust where the subject-matter is the promise itself. This draws on the well-established principle that a contractual promise is a form of personal property, namely a chose in action. It can therefore be held on trust like any other form of property. Applying normal trust rules the third party, exercising the normal rights of a beneficiary under a trust, is then able to enforce the promise. At first sight, this appears to be a very wide-ranging exception to the privity doctrine. But in order for a trust to be established, one must be satisfied that the contracting parties did intend to create a trust rather than merely to set up a contractual relationship. In some cases in the past the courts have been satisfied that there was that intention by implication. A famous example of this is the decision of the House of Lords in *Les Affreteurs Réunis Société Anonyme v Leopold Walford* [1919] AC 801 in which it was held that a promise in a charterparty to pay commission to the third party chartering broker created a trust of the promise enforceable by that third party. However, in the modern law that approach to intention is no longer adhered to and, in practice, it will only be where the parties have expressly stated that they are creating a trust for the third party that the necessary intention will be found. Nevertheless, the trust of the promise has remained an important method open to those drafting contracts to ensure that a third party to a contract is given enforceable rights. One should note that, if this exception applies, there can be no variation or rescission of the contract by the contracting parties without the third party's consent. One cannot unwind a trust, once constituted, without the beneficiaries' consent.

(4) Statutory Exceptions

Over the years, a wide number of specific exceptions to the privity doctrine— applicable to particular types of contract—have been embodied in various statutes. Three important examples are as follows. First, by section 11 of the Married Women's Property Act 1882, a life insurance policy is enforceable against the insurer by a spouse or child named in the policy. Secondly, by the Bills of Exchange Act 1882, a negotiable instrument (such as a bill of exchange) is enforceable by the holder even though that person is a third party to the original contract containing the payment obligation. Thirdly, by the Carriage of Goods by Sea Act 1992, replacing the Bills of Lading Act 1855, the holder of a bill of lading is able to sue the carrier on the contract for the carriage of goods by sea evidenced or contained in the bill of lading even though the holder is not a party to that contract.

(5) Covenants Concerning Land

The law allows certain covenants, whether positive or restrictive, to run with land so as to benefit (or burden) persons other than the original contracting parties. The relevant covenant may relate to freehold or leasehold land. This area of the law was developed at common law, an early famous case being *Tulk v Moxhay* (1848) 2 Ph 774, which concerned a restrictive covenant. However, the law is now largely embodied in statute whether under section 78 of the Law of Property Act 1925, as regards freehold covenants, or the Landlord and Tenant (Covenants) Act 1995, as regards leasehold covenants.

(6) The Tort of Negligence

There are a few examples of liability being imposed for pure economic loss in the tort of negligence which one can regard as tantamount to enforcement of a contract by a third party beneficiary. The most important example of this is *White v Jones* [1995] 2 AC 207, HL. In this case, solicitors were held to be negligent and liable to a prospective beneficiary of a will for loss of the intended legacy when they negligently failed to draw up the will before the testator died. One can argue that the prospective beneficiaries under the will were third party beneficiaries of the contract between the solicitor and the testator and that the tortious negligence action that succeeded amounted to enforcement by those third parties of the solicitor's contractual duty of care.

(7) Enforcement by Third Parties of Exemption Clauses

New Zealand Shipping Co Ltd v AM Satterthwaite & Co Ltd,
The Eurymedon
[1975] AC 154, Privy Council

A contract for the carriage by sea of a drilling machine was made between the claimant shipper and the carrier. The machine was damaged during unloading by the negligence of the defendant stevedores engaged by the carrier. A provision in the contract of carriage excluded the carrier from all liability unless an action was brought within one year after delivery of the goods. By a further term of the contract the benefit of that limitation clause was said to protect not only the carrier but also every servant or agent or independent contractor of the carrier while acting in the course of its employment by the carrier. More than one year after the delivery of the goods, the claimant shipper brought an action in the tort of negligence against the defendant stevedores for damage to the machine. The stevedores argued that they were entitled to take the benefit of the one-year time limitation clause in the contract of carriage. Reversing the New Zealand Court of Appeal and restoring the judgment of Beattie J, the Privy Council, by a majority, held that, applying unilateral contract reasoning to bypass the privity objection, the stevedores were so entitled.

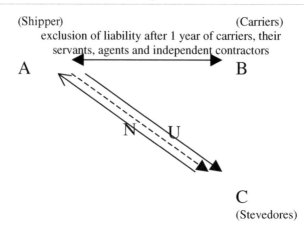

(Shipper)   (Carriers)

exclusion of liability after 1 year of carriers, their servants, agents and independent contractors

A   B

N   U

C

(Stevedores)

For key see 462.

Lord Wilberforce (delivering the opinion of himself, **Lord Hodson** and **Lord Salmon**): The question in the appeal is whether the stevedore can take the benefit of the time limitation provision. The starting point, in discussion of this question, is provided by the House of Lords decision in *Midland Silicones Ltd. v. Scruttons Ltd.* [1962] A.C. 446. There is no need to question or even to qualify that case in so far as it affirms the general proposition that a contract between two parties cannot be sued on by a third person even though the contract is expressed to be for his benefit. …But *Midland Silicones* left open the case where one of the parties contracts as agent for the third person: in particular Lord Reid's speech spelt out, in four propositions, the prerequisites for the validity of such an agency contract. [*He quoted the relevant part of that speech, set out above, 467, and continued:*] The question in this appeal is whether the contract satisfies these propositions.

Clause 1 of the bill of lading, whatever the defects in its drafting, is clear in its relevant terms. The carrier, on his own account, stipulates for certain exemptions and immunities: among these is that conferred by article III, rule 6, of the Hague Rules which discharges the carrier from all liability for loss or damage unless suit is brought within one year after delivery. In addition to these stipulations on his own account, the carrier as agent for, inter alios, independent contractors stipulates for the same exemptions.

Much was made of the fact that the carrier also contracts as agent for numerous other persons; the relevance of this argument is not apparent. It cannot be disputed that among such independent contractors, for whom, as agent, the carrier contracted, is the appellant company which habitually acts as stevedore in New Zealand by arrangement with the carrier and which is, moreover, the parent company of the carrier. The carrier was, indisputably, authorised by the appellant to contract as its agent for the purposes of clause 1. All of this is quite straightforward and was accepted by all the judges in New Zealand. The only question was, and is, the fourth question presented by Lord Reid, namely that of consideration.

It was on this point that the Court of Appeal differed from Beattie J., holding that it had not been shown that any consideration for the shipper's promise as to exemption moved from the promisee, i.e., the appellant company.

If the choice, and the antithesis, is between a gratuitous promise, and a promise for consideration, as it must be in the absence of a tertium quid, there can be little doubt which, in commercial reality, this is. The whole contract is of a commercial character, involving service on one side, rates of payment on the other, and qualifying stipulations as to both. The relations of all parties to each other are commercial relations entered into for business reasons of ultimate profit. To describe one set of promises, in this context, as gratuitous, or nudum pactum, seems paradoxical and is prima facie implausible. It is only the precise analysis of this complex of relations into the classical offer and acceptance, with identifiable consideration, that seems to present difficulty, but this same difficulty exists in many situations of daily life, e.g., sales at auction; supermarket purchases; boarding an omnibus; purchasing a train ticket; tenders for the supply of goods; offers of rewards; acceptance by post; warranties of authority by agents; manufacturers' guarantees; gratuitous bailments; bankers' commercial credits. These are all examples which show that English law, having committed itself to a rather technical and schematic doctrine of contract, in application takes a practical approach, often at the cost of forcing the facts to fit uneasily into the marked slots of offer, acceptance and consideration.

In their Lordships' opinion the present contract presents much less difficulty than many of those above referred to. It is one of carriage from Liverpool to Wellington. The carrier assumes an obligation to transport the goods and to discharge at the port of arrival. The goods are to be carried and discharged, so the transaction is inherently contractual. It is contemplated that a part of this contract, viz. discharge, may be performed by independent contractors – viz. the appellant. By clause 1 of the bill of lading the shipper agrees to exempt from liability the carrier, his servants and independent contractors in respect of the performance of this contract of carriage. Thus, if the carriage, including the discharge, is wholly carried out by the carrier, he is exempt. If part is carried out by him, and part by his servants, he and they are exempt. If part is carried out by him and part by an independent contractor, he and the independent contractor are exempt. The exemption is designed to cover the whole carriage from loading to discharge, by whomsoever it is performed: the performance attracts the exemption or immunity in favour of whoever the performer turns out to be. There is possibly more than one way of analysing this business transaction into the necessary components; that which their Lordships would accept is to say that the bill of lading brought into existence a bargain initially unilateral but capable of becoming mutual, between the shipper and the appellant, made through the carrier as agent. This became a full contract when the appellant performed services by discharging the goods. The performance of these services for the benefit of the shipper was the consideration for the agreement by the shipper that the appellant should have the benefit of the exemptions and limitations contained in the bill of lading. The conception of a "unilateral" contract of this kind was recognised in *Great Northern Railway Co. v. Witham* (1873) L.R. 9 C.P. 16 and is well established. This way of regarding the matter is very close to if not identical to that accepted by Beattie J. in the Supreme Court: he analysed the transaction as one of an offer open to acceptance by action such as was found in *Carlill v. Carbolic Smoke Ball Co.* [1893] 1 Q.B. 256. But whether one describes the shipper's promise to exempt as an offer to be accepted by performance or as a promise in exchange for an act seems in the present context to be a matter of semantics. The words of Bowen L.J. in *Carlill v. Carbolic Smoke Ball Co.* [1893] 1 Q.B. 256, 268: "why should not an offer be made to all the world which is to ripen into a contract with anybody who comes forward and performs the condition?" seem to bridge both conceptions: he certainly seems to draw no distinction between an offer which matures into a contract when accepted and a promise which matures into a contract after performance, and, though in some special contexts (such as in connection with the right to withdraw) some further refinement may be needed, either analysis may be equally valid. On the main point in the appeal, their Lordships are in substantial agreement with Beattie J.

The following points require mention. 1. In their Lordships' opinion, consideration may quite well be provided by the appellant, as suggested, even though (or if) it was already under an obligation to discharge to the carrier. (There is no direct evidence of the existence or nature of this obligation, but their Lordships are prepared to assume it.) An agreement to do an act which the promisor is under an existing obligation to a third party to do, may quite well amount to valid consideration and does so in the present case: the promisee obtains the benefit of a direct obligation which he can enforce. This proposition is illustrated and supported by *Scotson v. Pegg* (1861) 6 H. & N. 295 which their Lordships consider to be good law.

...

4. A clause very similar to the present was given effect by a United States District Court in *Carle & Montanari Inc. v. American Export Isbrandtsen Lines Inc.* [1968] 1 Lloyd's Rep. 260. The carrier in that case contracted, in an exemption clause, as agent, for, inter alios, all stevedores and other independent contractors, and although it is no doubt true that the law in the United States is more liberal than ours as regards third party contracts, their Lordships see no reason why the law of the Commonwealth should be more restrictive and technical as regards agency contracts. Commercial considerations should have the same force on both sides of the Pacific.

In the opinion of their Lordships, to give the appellant the benefit of the exemptions and limitations contained in the bill of lading is to give effect to the clear intentions of a commercial document, and can be given within existing principles. They see no reason to strain the law or the facts in order to defeat these intentions. It should not be overlooked that the effect of denying validity to the clause would be to encourage actions against servants, agents and independent contractors in order to get round exemptions (which are almost invariable and often compulsory) accepted by shippers against carriers, the existence, and presumed efficacy, of which is reflected in the rates of freight. They see no attraction in this consequence.

Viscount Dilhorne and **Lord Simon of Glaisdale** delivered dissenting opinions.

NOTES AND QUESTIONS

1. The reasoning of the majority was that the shipper made the offer of a unilateral contract to the stevedores; that that offer was received by the carriers acting as agents in this respect for the stevedores; and that the terms of the unilateral contract were that, in return for the stevedores unloading the goods, the shipper excluded the stevedores from liability for negligently damaging the goods (unless the action was brought within one year). This reasoning produced the desired result that the stevedores were protected by the exclusion clause because they were parties to that unilateral contract (rather than merely being third parties to the contract of carriage). Was the reasoning artificial in (i) regarding the unloading of the goods as consideration for the exclusion of liability and (ii) treating the carriers as agents for the stevedores in receiving the offer of a unilateral contract?

2. Why have the courts been unwilling to apply the *Eurymedon* principle outside the context of a carriage of goods by sea? For example, it was held inapplicable to enable a sub-contractor to take the benefit of an exclusion clause in the head construction contract between the employer and the main contractor in *Southern Water Authority v Carey* [1985] 2 All ER 1077. (But note that a different method of enabling such a third party to take the benefit of such an exemption clause was found in *Norwich City Council v Harvey* [1989] 1 WLR 828, CA.)

3. Why is the clause in the contract of carriage extending the benefit of the exemption clause to servants, agents and independent contractors of the carrier commonly referred to as a Himalaya clause? See, on this, *Adler v Dickson* [1955] 1 QB 158, CA.

4. *The Eurymedon* was subsequently affirmed by the Privy Council in *Port Jackson Stevedoring Pty Ltd v Salmond & Spraggon Pty (Australia) Ltd, The New York Star* [1981] 1 WLR 138 in holding that stevedores continued to be protected even where the loss had occurred after the unloading of the goods (they had been negligently delivered by the stevedores to thieves). Support was expressed for the reasoning of Barwick CJ in his (dissenting) judgment in the High Court of Australia in this case. Yet confusingly, he had referred to the

relevant contract between the shipper and the stevedores as 'bilateral' rather than 'unilateral'. This seems false labelling. The stevedores were not promising *the shipper* to unload the goods. So, if, for example, the stevedores had justifiably terminated their contract with the carriers, they could not have been sued by the shipper for a failure to unload the goods.

5. *The Eurymedon* was further approved by the Privy Council in *The Mahkutai* [1996] AC 650 (although Lord Goff of Chieveley, giving the opinion of the Privy Council, indicated that, in line with Barwick CJ's analysis, the contract could be described as 'bilateral'). In this case, the relevant clause was not an exclusion or limitation clause but rather an exclusive jurisdiction clause. It was held that such a clause was not a benefit to the 'third party' to the contract of carriage and was therefore not covered by the Himalaya clause because an exclusive jurisdiction clause imposes burdens as well as benefits. Lord Goff, after pointing out that criticism had been made of *The Eurymedon* principle, said the following at 664–665

'Nevertheless there can be no doubt of the commercial need of some such principle as this, and not only in cases concerned with stevedores; and the bold step taken by the Privy Council in *The Eurymedon*, and later developed in *The New York Star*, has been widely welcomed. But it is legitimate to wonder whether that development is yet complete. Here their Lordships have in mind not only Lord Wilberforce's discouragement of fine distinctions, but also the fact that the law is now approaching the position where, provided that the bill of lading contract clearly provides that (for example) independent contractors such as stevedores are to have the benefit of exceptions and limitations contained in that contract, they will be able to enjoy the protection of those terms as against the cargo owners. ... Though these solutions are now perceived to be generally effective for their purpose, their technical nature is all too apparent; and the time may well come when, in an appropriate case, it will fall to be considered whether the courts should take what may legitimately be perceived to be the final, and perhaps inevitable, step in this development, and recognise in these cases a fully-fledged exception to the doctrine of privity of contract, thus escaping from all the technicalities with which courts are now faced in English law.'

6. Even more importantly, the *Eurymedon* principle was approved by the House of Lords in *Homburg Houtimport BV v Agrosin Private Ltd, The Starsin* [2003] UKHL 12, [2004] 1 AC 715. Although Lord Bingham, at [34], again confusingly talks of a bilateral contract, there is a clear analysis by Lord Hoffmann at [93], by Lord Hobhouse at [149]–[153] and, especially helpful, by Lord Millett at [196]–[197]. However, the principle was held inapplicable on the facts because the third party was the actual performing carrier and to allow it to take the benefit of an exemption clause in the contract of carriage would undermine the policy of the Hague-Visby Rules (given legislative force by the Carriage of Goods Act 1971) which invalidated the exemption clause in question.

7. Under the Contracts (Rights of Third Parties) Act 1999 the stevedores on the facts in *The Eurymedon* would now straightforwardly be able to rely on the exclusion clause without any need to resort to the common law's convoluted reasoning.

8. Lord Wilberforce's comments on consideration in relation to a pre-existing contract with a third party have already been referred to in Chapter 3 (above,

104); and his point about the occasional artificiality of slotting facts into the concepts of offer and acceptance (and consideration) has been referred to in Chapter 1 (above, 55).

4. THE PROMISEE'S REMEDIES IN A CONTRACT MADE FOR THE BENEFIT OF A THIRD PARTY

(1) Specific Performance and Injunctions

Beswick v Beswick [1968] AC 58, House of Lords

For the facts and speeches, see above, 468–473.

NOTES AND QUESTIONS

1. Specific performance is, in general, an exceptional remedy in English law which can only be granted where damages are inadequate (see above, 432–436). Why were damages in this case inadequate? Note that, even if one were to say that in a contract made for a third party's benefit, damages will always be inadequate, this does not mean that specific performance will always be available because performance may no longer be possible and, even if it were, there are a number of bars, apart from the adequacy of damages, to that remedy (for example, where the contract is one of personal service or would require constant supervision: see above, 432).

2. A prohibitory injunction, in contrast to specific performance, is a readily available remedy to enforce negative contractual promises (see above, 447–448). In *Snelling v John G Snelling Ltd* [1973] 1 QB 87 it was therefore accepted in principle that the promisees could obtain an injunction to prevent the promisor breaking his promise not to demand repayment of a loan from the family company (that company being the third party beneficiary of the contract between the directors who were all brothers). As the promisor had already broken the contract by commencing proceedings for repayment against the company, Ormrod J held that the appropriate relief on the facts was a dismissal of the promisor's action for repayment against the company.

(2) Damages

Jackson v Horizon Holidays Ltd [1975] 1 WLR 1468, Court of Appeal

The claimant entered into a contract with the defendant, a travel company, for a package holiday in Ceylon for himself, his wife and two children. The price including air fares was £1200. The accommodation, food and facilities at the hotel were unsatisfactory and did not comply with the description given by the defendant in important respects. In an action for breach of contract, the trial judge awarded Mr Jackson £1100 damages including mental distress damages following *Jarvis v Swans Tours Ltd* (above, 388). The defendant appealed on the amount of damages. In dismissing the appeal, the majority held that Mr Jackson was able to recover damages for the loss suffered by the third parties (his wife and children) as well as for his own loss.

Lord Denning MR: The judge said that he could only consider the mental distress to Mr. Jackson himself, and that he could not consider the distress to his wife and children. He said:

> "The damages are the plaintiff's. ... I can consider the effect upon his mind of the wife's discomfort, vexation, and the like, although I cannot award a sum which represents her own vexation."

Mr. Davies, for Mr. Jackson, disputes that proposition. He submits that damages can be given not only for the leader of the party – in this case, Mr. Jackson's own distress, discomfort and vexation – but also for that of the rest of the party.

We have had an interesting discussion as to the legal position when one person makes a contract for the benefit of a party. In this case it was a husband making a contract for the benefit of himself, his wife and children. Other cases readily come to mind. A host makes a contract with a restaurant for a dinner for himself and his friends. The vicar makes a contract for a coach trip for the choir. In all these cases there is only one person who makes the contract. It is the husband, the host or the vicar, as the case may be. Sometimes he pays the whole price himself. Occasionally he may get a contribution from the others. But in any case it is he who makes the contract. It would be a fiction to say that the contract was made by all the family, or all the guests, or all the choir, and that he was only an agent for them. Take this very case. It would be absurd to say that the twins of three years old were parties to the contract or that the father was making the contract on their behalf as if they were principals. It would equally be a mistake to say that in any of these instances there was a trust. The transaction bears no resemblance to a trust. There was no trust fund and no trust property. No, the real truth is that in each instance, the father, the host or the vicar, was making a contract himself for the benefit of the whole party. In short, a contract by one for the benefit of third persons.

What is the position when such a contract is broken? At present the law says that the only one who can sue is the one who made the contract. None of the rest of the party can sue, even though the contract was made for their benefit. But when that one does sue, what damages can he recover? Is he limited to his own loss? Or can he recover for the others? Suppose the holiday firm puts the family into a hotel which is only half built and the visitors have to sleep on the floor? Or suppose the restaurant is fully booked and the guests have to go away, hungry and angry, having spent so much on fares to get there? Or suppose the coach leaves the choir stranded halfway and they have to hire cars to get home? None of them individually can sue. Only the father, the host or the vicar can sue. He can, of course, recover his own damages. But can he not recover for the others? I think he can. The case comes within the principle stated by Lush L.J. in *Lloyd's v. Harper* (1880) 16 Ch.D. 290, 321:

> "I consider it to be an established rule of law that where a contract is made with A. for the benefit of B., A. can sue on the contract for the benefit of B., and recover all that B. could have recovered if the contract had been made with B. himself."

It has been suggested that Lush L.J. was thinking of a contract in which A was trustee for B. But I do not think so. He was a common lawyer speaking of common law. His words were quoted with considerable approval by Lord Pearce in *Beswick v. Beswick* [1968] A.C. 58, 88. I have myself often quoted them. I think they should be accepted as correct, at any rate so long as the law forbids the third persons themselves from suing for damages. It is the only way in which a just result can be achieved. Take the instance I have put. The guests ought to recover from the restaurant their wasted fares. The choir ought to recover the cost of hiring the taxis home. Then is no one to recover from them except the one who made the contract for their benefit? He should be able to recover the expense to which he has been put, and pay it over to them. Once recovered, it will be money had and received to their use. (They might even, if desired, be joined as plaintiffs). If he can recover for the expense, he should also be able to recover for the discomfort, vexation and upset which the whole party have suffered by reason of the breach of contract, recompensing them accordingly out of what he recovers.

Applying the principles to this case, I think that the figure of £1,100 was about right. It would, I think, have been excessive if it had been awarded only for the damage suffered by Mr. Jackson himself. But when extended to his wife and children, I do not think it is excessive. People look forward to a holiday. They expect the promises to be fulfilled. When it fails, they are greatly disappointed and upset. It is difficult to assess in terms of money; but it is the task of the judges to do the best they can. I see no reason to interfere with the total award of £1,100. I would therefore dismiss the appeal.

James LJ: In this case Mr. Jackson, as found by the judge on the evidence, was in need of a holiday at the end of 1970. He was able to afford a holiday for himself and his family. According to the form he completed, which was the form of Horizon Holidays Ltd., he booked what was a family holiday. The wording of that form might in certain circumstances give rise to a contract in which the person signing the form is acting as his own principal and as agent for others. In the circumstances of this case, as indicated by Lord Denning M.R., it would be wholly unrealistic to regard this contract as other than one made by Mr. Jackson for a family holiday. The judge found that he did not get a family holiday. The costs were some £1,200. When he came back he felt no benefit. His evidence was to the effect that, without any exaggeration, he felt terrible. He said: "The only thing, I was pleased to be back, very pleased, but I had nothing at all from that holiday." For my part, on the issue of damages in this matter, I am quite content to say that £1,100 awarded was the right and proper figure in those circumstances. I would dismiss the appeal.

Orr LJ agreed with Lord Denning.

NOTES AND QUESTIONS

1. We have seen (above, 473) that Lord Denning did not like the privity doctrine. In this case, he launched an attack not on the privity rule itself but on the linked traditional rule that, in a contract made for a third party's benefit, the promisee recovers damages for its own loss and not the loss of the third party.
2. Is the reasoning of James LJ consistent with the damages being awarded for the claimant's *own* mental distress (and financial loss)?

Woodar Investment Development Ltd v Wimpey Construction UK Ltd
[1980] 1 WLR 277, House of Lords

Wimpey contracted to buy some land from Woodar for a purchase price of £850,000 but with a further condition that, on completion of the purchase, Wimpey would pay an additional £150,000 to a third party, Transworld Trade Ltd. Wimpey had terminated the contract alleging that they were entitled to do so under a clause allowing termination where a statutory authority had commenced compulsory purchase proceedings. Woodar alleged that, by so doing, Wimpey had committed a repudiatory breach of the contract and claimed as damages, inter alia, the £150,000 that Wimpey had agreed to pay Transworld. The majority of the House of Lords (Lord Salmon and Lord Russell of Killowen dissenting) held that there had been no repudiatory breach by Wimpey so that Woodar was not entitled to damages. But, as obiter dicta, all of their Lordships went on to discuss, without deciding, whether, as the Court of Appeal had held, Woodar could have recovered the £150,000 as damages if Wimpey had been in breach.

Lord Wilberforce: The second issue in this appeal is one of damages. Both courts below have allowed Woodar to recover substantial damages in respect of condition I under which £150,000 was payable by Wimpey to Transworld Trade Ltd. on completion. On the view which I take of the repudiation issue, this question does not require decision, but in view of the unsatisfactory state in which the law would be if the Court of Appeal's decision were to stand I must add three observations:

1. The majority of the Court of Appeal followed, in the case of Goff L.J. with expressed reluctance, its previous decision in *Jackson v. Horizon Holidays Ltd.* [1975] I W.L.R. 1468. I am not prepared to dissent from the actual decision in that case. It may be supported either as a broad decision on the measure of damages (*per* James L.J.) or possibly as an example of a type of contract – examples of which are persons contracting for family holidays, ordering meals in restaurants for a party, hiring a taxi for a group – calling for special treatment. As I suggested in *New Zealand Shipping Co. Ltd. v. A. M. Satterthwaite & Co. Ltd.* [1975] A.C. 154, 167, there are many situations of daily life which do not fit neatly into conceptual analysis, but which require some flexibility in the law of contract. *Jackson's* case may well be one.

I cannot however agree with the basis on which Lord Denning M.R. put his decision in that case. The extract on which he relied from the judgment of Lush L.J. in *Lloyd's v. Harper* (1880) 16 Ch.D. 290, 321 was part of a passage in which the Lord Justice was stating as an "established rule of law" that an agent (sc. an insurance broker) may sue on a contract made by him on behalf of the principal (sc. the assured) if the contract gives him such a right, and is no authority for the proposition required in *Jackson's* case, still less for the proposition, required here, that, if Woodar made a contract for a sum of money to be paid to Transworld, Woodar can, without showing that it has itself suffered loss or that Woodar was agent or trustee for Transworld, sue for damages for nonpayment of that sum. That would certainly not be an established rule of law, nor was it quoted as such authority by Lord Pearce in *Beswick v. Beswick* [1968] A.C. 58.

2. Assuming that *Jackson's* case was correctly decided (as above), it does not carry the present case, where the factual situation is quite different. I respectfully think therefore that the Court of Appeal need not, and should not have followed it.

3. Whether in a situation such as the present – viz. where it is not shown that Woodar was agent or trustee for Transworld, or that Woodar itself sustained any loss, Woodar can recover any damages at all, or any but nominal damages, against Wimpey, and on what principle, is, in my opinion, a question of great doubt and difficulty – no doubt open in this House – but one on which I prefer to reserve my opinion.

Lord Salmon: [T]he interesting question in relation to damages in respect of the claim for £150,000 does not now arise. I do, however, agree with what my noble and learned friend, Lord Wilberforce, has said about the finding of the majority of the Court of Appeal (Goff L.J. with reluctance) on this topic. I would add that, in my opinion, the law as it stands at present in relation to damages of this kind is most unsatisfactory; and I can only hope that your Lordships' House will soon have an opportunity of reconsidering it unless in the meantime it is altered by statute.

Lord Russell of Killowen: If it were necessary to decide the point, which in the light of the views of the majority of your Lordships on the first point it is not, I would have concluded that no more than nominal damages had been established by Woodar as a consequence of the refusal by Wimpey to pay Transworld in the light of the law of England as it now stands. I would not have thought that the reasoning of Oliver J. in *Radford v. De Froberville* [1977] 1 W.L.R. 1262 supported Woodar's case for substantial damages. Nor do I think that on this point the Court of Appeal was correct in thinking it was constrained by *Jackson v. Horizon Holidays Ltd.* [1975] 1 W.L.R. I468 to award substantial damages. I do not criticize the outcome of that case: the plaintiff had bought and paid for a high class family holiday: he did not get it, and therefore he was entitled to substantial damages for the failure to supply him with one. It is to be observed that the order of the Court of Appeal as drawn up did not suggest that any part of the damages awarded to him were "for the use and benefit of" any member of his family. It was a special case quite different from the instant case on the Transworld point.

I would not, my Lords, wish to leave the *Jackson* case without adverting with respectful disapproval to the reliance there placed by Lord Denning M.R. – not for the first time – on an extract taken from the judgment of Lush L.J. in *Lloyd's v. Harper,* 16 Ch.D. 290. That case was plainly a case in which a trustee or agent was enforcing the rights of a beneficiary or principal, there being therefore a fiduciary relationship.

...

I venture to suggest that the brief quotation should not be used again as support for a proposition which Lush L.J. cannot have intended to advance.

In summary therefore, in disagreement with the majority of your Lordships, I would have dismissed this appeal on repudiation. Had I been correct I would, as at present advised, have allowed the appeal on the Transworld point, and awarded only nominal damages on that point to Woodar, and not substantial damages to be paid to Woodar "for the use and benefit of" Transworld, a form of order which I cannot see was justified.

Lord Keith of Kinkel: In the circumstances the issue regarding the respondents' right to damages in respect of alleged breach of the appellants' obligation under the contract to pay £150,000 to Transworld does not arise for decision. It is desirable, however, that I should express my agreement with my noble and learned friend, Lord Wilberforce, that the decision in favour of the respondents upon this issue, arrived at by the majority of the Court of Appeal, was not capable of being supported by *Jackson v. Horizon Holidays Ltd.* [1975] 1 W.L.R. 1468. That case is capable of being regarded as rightly decided upon a reasonable view of the measure of damages due to the plaintiff as the original contracting party, and not as laying down any rule of law regarding the recovery of damages for the benefit of third parties. There may be a certain class of cases where third parties stand to gain indirectly by virtue of a contract, and where their deprivation of that gain can properly be regarded as no more than a consequence of the loss suffered by one of the contracting parties. In that situation there may be no question of the third parties having any claim to damages in their own right, but yet it may be proper to take into account in assessing the damages recoverable by the contracting party an element in respect of expense incurred by him in replacing by other means benefits of which the third parties have been deprived or in mitigating the consequences of that deprivation. The decision in *Jackson v. Horizon Holidays Ltd.* is not, however, in my opinion, capable of being supported upon the basis of the true ratio decidendi in *Lloyd's v. Harper,* 16 Ch.D. 29, which rested entirely on the principles of agency.

I would also associate myself with the observations of my noble and learned friend, Lord Scarman, as to the desirability of this House having an opportunity of reviewing, in some appropriate future case, the general attitude of English law towards the topic of jus quaesitum tertio.

Lord Scarman: B, in breach of his contract with A, has failed to pay C. C, it is said, has no remedy, because the English law of contract recognises no "jus quaesitum tertio": *Tweddle v.*

Atkinson (1861) 1 B. & S. 393. No doubt, it was for this reason that Transworld Trade is not a party to the suit. A, it is acknowledged, could in certain circumstances obtain specific performance of the promise to pay C: *Beswick v. Beswick* [1968] A.C. 58. But, since the contract in the present case is admitted (for reasons which do not fall to be considered by the House) to be no longer in existence, specific performance is not available. A's remedy lies only in an award of damages to himself. It is submitted that, in the absence of any evidence that A has suffered loss by reason of B's failure to pay C, A is only entitled to nominal damages.

I wish to add nothing to what your Lordships have already said about the authorities which the Court of Appeal cited as leading to the conclusion that the plaintiff company is entitled to substantial damages for the defendants' failure to pay Transworld Trade. I agree that they do not support the conclusion. But I regret that this House has not yet found the opportunity to reconsider the two rules which effectually prevent A or C recovering that which B, for value, has agreed to provide.

First, the "jus quaesitum tertio." I respectfully agree with Lord Reid that the denial by English law of a "jus quaesitum tertio" calls for reconsideration. In *Beswick v. Beswick* [1968] A.C. 58, 72 Lord Reid, after referring to the Law Revision Committee's recommendation in 1937 (Cmnd. 5449) p. 31 that the third party should be able to enforce a contractual promise taken by another for his benefit, observed:

> "And, if one had to contemplate a further long period of Parliamentary procrastination, this House might find it necessary to deal with this matter."

The committee reported in 1937: *Beswick v. Beswick* was decided in 1967. It is now 1979: but nothing has been done. If the opportunity arises, I hope the House will reconsider *Tweddle v. Atkinson* and the other cases which stand guard over this unjust rule.

Likewise, I believe it open to the House to declare that, in the absence of evidence to show that he has suffered no loss, A, who has contracted for a payment to be made to C, may rely on the fact that he required the payment to be made as prima facie evidence that the promise for which he contracted was a benefit to him and that the measure of his loss in the event of non-payment is the benefit which he intended for C but which has not been received. Whatever the reason, he must have desired the payment to be made to C and he must have been relying on B to make it. If B fails to make the payment, A must find the money from other funds if he is to confer the benefit which he sought by his contract to confer upon C. Without expressing a final opinion on a question which is clearly difficult, I think the point is one which does require consideration by your Lordships' House.

Certainly the crude proposition for which the defendants contend, namely that the state of English law is such that neither C for whom the benefit was intended nor A who contracted for it can recover it, if the contract is terminated by B's refusal to perform, calls for review: and now, not forty years on.

NOTES AND QUESTIONS

1. All their Lordships indicated that the traditional rule is that the promisee (here Woodar) recovers for its own loss and not for the third party's (here Transworld's) loss. Lord Denning's general reasoning to the contrary in *Jackson v Horizon Holidays* (above, 483–484), and his reliance to that effect on Lush LJ in *Lloyd's v Harper*, was firmly rejected. On what basis, then, was it thought that the *Jackson* case had been correctly decided?

2. Did their Lordships accept that, applying the traditional rule, the promisee's damages are necessarily nominal?

3. In *Beswick v Beswick*, above, 435, 468, all their Lordships accepted the traditional rule that the promisee is suing for its own loss and all, except Lord

Pearce, thought that on those facts the promisee's (the administratrix's) damages would be nominal.

Darlington Borough Council v Wiltshier Northern Ltd
[1995] 1 WLR 68, Court of Appeal

Darlington BC (Darlington) owned land on which they wanted a recreation centre (the Dolphin centre) to be built. In order to avoid restrictions on a local authority's borrowing powers, it was arranged that Morgan Grenfell (MG) would enter into a contract for the building of the centre with Wiltshier (the builders); that Darlington would enter into a contract with MG whereby it would reimburse MG for monies paid under the building contract; and that MG would assign to Darlington its rights against Wiltshier for defects in the building work. The work went ahead in accordance with those contracts including MG's assignment of its rights against Wiltshier to Darlington. Darlington claimed that there were defects in Wiltshier's building work. It is a principle of the law of assignment that an assignor cannot assign better rights than it itself has; so when Darlington, as assignee, sued Wiltshier for damages for breach of the building contract, the question became one of what damages could MG have recovered under its contract with Wiltshier. At first instance it was held that, as MG would not own the centre and would not be paying for repairs, it could have recovered only nominal damages. Darlington successfully appealed, the Court of Appeal holding that, as MG could here recover damages for Darlington's loss, MG (and hence Darlington, as assignee) was entitled to substantial damages.

Dillon LJ: [T]he general position is that if a plaintiff contracts with a defendant for the defendant to make a payment or confer some other benefit on a third party who was not a party to the contract, the plaintiff cannot recover substantial damages from the defendant for breach of that obligation on the part of the defendant: see *Woodar Investment Development Ltd. v. Wimpey Construction U.K. Ltd.* [1980] 1 W.L.R. 277. The plaintiff can, prima facie, only recover for his own loss.

> ...
>
> One exception, recognised in the *Woodar Investment* case, is where the plaintiff made the contract as agent or trustee for the third party and was enforcing the rights of a beneficiary, there being a fiduciary relationship: see *per* Lord Wilberforce, at p. 284A-B and *per* Lord Russell of Killowen, at p. 293H. This is recognised in the decision of this court in *Lloyd's v. Harper* (1880) 16 Ch.D. 290, where it was held that the corporation of Lloyd's, as successors to the committee of Lloyd's, were entitled to enforce a guarantee of the liabilities of an underwriting member which had been given to the committee, which had itself suffered no loss, for the benefit of all persons, whether members or not, with whom the member had contracted engagements as underwriting member. A further exception is to be found, in the law as to the carriage of goods by sea, in the recognition by the House of Lords in *The Albazero* [1977] A.C. 774 of the continuing validity in such a context of the earlier decision of the House in *Dunlop v. Lambert* (1839) 6 Cl. & F. 600.
>
> It is unnecessary to go into details of the circumstances in *The Albazero* and *Dunlop v. Lambert*, since what Lord Diplock referred to in *The Albazero* [1977] A.C. 774, 846 as the rule laid down by the House in *Dunlop v. Lambert* was applied by the House in a building contract context in *St. Martin's Property Corporation Ltd. v. Sir Robert McAlpine Ltd.*, reported with *Linden Gardens Trust Ltd. v. Lenesta Sludge Disposals Ltd.* [1994] A.C. 85. The key passage giving the ratio in the *McAlpine* case is in the speech of Lord Browne-Wilkinson with which all other members of the House agreed, at pp. 114-115:

"In my judgment the present case falls within the rationale of the exceptions to the general rule that a plaintiff can only recover damages for his own loss. The contract was for a large development of property which, to the knowledge of both Corporation and McAlpine, was going to be occupied, and possibly purchased, by third parties and not by Corporation itself. Therefore it could be foreseen that damage caused by a breach would cause loss to a later owner and not merely to the original contracting party, Corporation. As in contracts for the carriage of goods by land, there would be no automatic vesting in the occupier or owners of the property for the time being who sustained the loss of any right of suit against McAlpine. On the contrary, McAlpine had specifically contracted that the rights of action under the building contract *could* not without McAlpine's consent be transferred to third parties who became owners or occupiers and might suffer loss. In such a case, it seems to me proper, as in the case of the carriage of goods by land, to treat the parties as having entered into the contract on the footing that Corporation would be entitled to enforce contractual rights for the benefit of those who suffered from defective perfor-mance but who, under the terms of the contract, could not acquire any right to hold McAlpine liable for breach. It is truly a case in which the rule provides 'a remedy where no other would be available to a person sustaining loss which under a rational legal system ought to be compensated by the person who caused it.' "

The present case is, in my judgment, a fortiori since, so far from there being a prohibition on the assignment of Morgan Grenfell's rights against Wiltshier under the building contracts, the covenant agreement, of which Wiltshier was aware, gave the council the right to call for an assignment of such rights. ...

Mr. Blackburn [counsel for Wiltshier] also sought to distinguish the decision in the *McAlpine* case on the ground that in the present case Morgan Grenfell never acquired or transmitted to the council any proprietary interest in the Dolphin Centre. I do not see that that matters as the council had the ownership of the site of the Dolphin Centre all along. It was plainly obvious to Wiltshier throughout that the Dolphin Centre was being constructed for the benefit of the council on the council's land.

Accordingly, I would allow this appeal by direct application of the rule in *Dunlop v. Lambert* as recognised in a building contract context in Lord Browne-Wilkinson's speech in the *McAlpine* case.

Lord Steyn: In order lawfully to avoid the financial constraints of the Local Government Act 1972 Morgan Grenfell acted as financier to the council in connection with the construction of the Dolphin Centre in Darlington. Morgan Grenfell entered into building contracts with Wiltshier for the benefit of the council. That is how the transaction was structured and that is how all three parties saw it. And it is, of course, manifest that the council, as the third party, accepted the benefit of the building contract. But for the rule of privity of contract the council could simply have sued on the contract made for its benefit.

The case for recognising a contract for the benefit of a third party is simple and straight-forward. The autonomy of the will of the parties should be respected. The law of contract should give effect to the reasonable expectations of contracting parties. Principle certainly requires that a burden should not be imposed on a third party without his consent. But there is no doctrinal, logical or policy reason why the law should deny effectiveness to a contract for the benefit of a third party where that is the expressed intention of the parties. Moreover, often the parties, and particularly third parties, organise their affairs on the faith of the contract. They rely on the contract. It is therefore unjust to deny effectiveness to such a contract. I will not struggle further with the point since nobody seriously asserts the contrary...

The judge regarded it as fatal to the claim that Morgan Grenfell had not paid for the cost of remedying the defects and had no intention of doing so. Mr. Blackburn supports the judge's reasoning. He says that a prima facie meritorious claim has indeed disappeared down a legal blackhole. He says that if Morgan Grenfell had done the repairs or had undertaken to do so, or if there was evidence that it intended to do so, Morgan Grenfell would have been able effectively to assign a claim for substantial damages to the council. As a mere financier of the transaction Morgan Grenfell, of course, had no interest in taking such action. Accordingly, Mr. Blackburn submits that Morgan Grenfell, the party in contractual relationship with Wiltshier, suffered no loss and could transfer no claim for substantial damages; and the council, which suffered the loss, is precluded by the privity rule from claiming the damages which it suffered. He submits that established doctrine deprives the council of a remedy and allows the contract-breaker to go scot-free. Recognising that this is hardly an attractive result, he reminds us of our duty to apply the law as it stands.

That brings me to the speech of Lord Browne-Wilkinson in the *Linden Gardens* case [1994] A.C. 85. In his speech Lord Browne-Wilkinson rested his decision on the exception to the rule that a plaintiff can only recover damages for his own loss which was enunciated in *The Albazero* [1977] A.C. 774 in the context of carriage of goods by sea, bills of lading and bailment. The relevant passage from Lord Diplock's speech in *The Albazero* reads, at p. 847:

> "The only way in which I find it possible to rationalise the rule in *Dunlop v. Lambert* so that it may fit into the pattern of the English law is to treat it as an application of the principle, accepted also in relation to policies of insurance upon goods, that in a commercial contract concerning goods where it is in the contemplation of the parties that the proprietary interests in the goods may be transferred from one owner to another after the contract has been entered into and before the breach which causes loss or damage to the goods, an original party to the contract, if such be the intention of them both, is to be treated in law as having entered into the contract for the benefit of all persons who have or may acquire an interest in the goods before they are lost or damaged, and is entitled to recover by way of damages for breach of contract the actual loss sustained by those for whose benefit the contract is entered into."

Clearly, this passage did not exactly fit the material facts in the *Linden Gardens* case. But Lord Browne-Wilkinson extracted the rationale of the decision and by analogy applied it to the purely contractual situation in *Linden Gardens.* He particularly justified this extension of the exception in *The Albazero* by invoking Lord Diplock's words in *The Albazero:*

> "there may still be occasional cases in which the rule would provide a remedy where no other would be available to a person sustaining loss which under a rational legal system ought to be compensated by the person who has caused it."

Lord Browne-Wilkinson's conclusion was supported by all members of the House of Lords, although, it is right to say, Lord Griffiths wished to go further. Relying on the exception recognised in the *Linden Gardens* case, as well as on the need to avoid a demonstrable unfairness which no rational legal system should tolerate, I would rule that the present case is within the rationale of Lord Browne-Wilkinson's speech. I do not say that the relevant passages in his speech precisely fit the material facts of the present case. But it involves only a very conservative and limited extension to apply it by analogy to the present case. For these reasons I would hold that the present case is covered by an exception to the general rule that a plaintiff can only recover damages for his own loss.

Waite LJ: I agree with both Dillon L.J. and Steyn L.J. that this appeal should be allowed by direct application of the rule in *Dunlop v. Lambert,* 6 Cl. & F. 600 as recognised in a building contract context in the speech of Lord Browne-Wilkinson in the *McAlpine* case [1994] A.C. 85.

NOTES

1. The Court of Appeal here recognised and developed an exception to the normal rule that a promisee can recover only for its own loss. The exception is

derived from contracts for the carriage of goods (as recognised in *Dunlop v Lambert* (1839) 6 Cl & Fin 600, HL and *The Albazero* [1977] AC 774, HL) and was extended to building contracts by the House of Lords in *Linden Gardens Trust Ltd v Lenesta Sludge Disposals Ltd* [1994] 1 AC 85. The key passage in the leading speech of Lord Browne-Wilkinson in *Linden Gardens* is set out in full above by Dillon LJ (albeit that he refers to the *Linden Gardens* case as the *McAlpine* case). The fully developed exception (often referred to as *The Albazero* exception) may be expressed as follows: a promisee can recover a third party's loss (and, it would seem, is bound to pay over those damages to the third party) on a contract relating to property (whether goods or land) where the parties contemplated that the property in question would be transferred to the third party or where the parties otherwise contemplated that loss in respect of that property would be suffered by the third party. On the facts this exception applied. Although there was to be no transfer to the third party of the land, which always belonged to Darlington, it was contemplated from the start that any loss in respect of the property would be borne by Darlington as its owner.

2. Dillon and Waite LJJ alternatively relied on (in passages not set out above) the controversial idea that Morgan Grenfell were constructive trustees for Darlington. Fortunately this fictional invocation of a trust has not been taken up in subsequent cases and is best ignored.

Alfred McAlpine Construction Ltd v Panatown Ltd
[2001] 1 AC 518, House of Lords

Panatown entered into a construction contract with McAlpine for McAlpine to design and construct an office building on land owned by Unex Investment Properties Ltd (UIPL). The building was defective and delayed and Panatown sought damages for the cost of repair, loss of use and delay. These losses were actually suffered by UIPL not by Panatown so that, at least on the face of it, the claim was by a promisee to recover damages suffered by a third party. It should be noted that Panatown was in the same group of companies—the Unex Group—as UIPL; and that the reason the contract was made with Panatown rather than UIPL was as a means of avoiding value added tax. Judge Thornton QC, as official referee, had held that Panatown could recover only nominal and not substantial damages. The Court of Appeal had overturned that and, by applying the *Albazero* exception (see above, 491) to the normal rule that a promisee can recover only its own loss, had held that Panatown was entitled to substantial damages for UIPL's loss. By a 3–2 majority, the House of Lords restored Judge Thornton's decision. Panatown was not here entitled to substantial damages because, as a duty of care deed gave UIPL direct contractual rights against McAlpine, the *Albazero* exception did not apply.

Lord Clyde: I find no reason to question the general principle that a plaintiff may only recover damages for a loss which he has himself suffered. But there are exceptions to that principle. ...

The exception which is invoked by the respondents, Panatown, is the one which was identified in *The Albazero* [1977] AC 774. ...

In *The Albazero* [1977] AC 774, 847 Lord Diplock sought to "rationalise the rule in *Dunlop v Lambert*" so that it might fit into the pattern of English law. [*Lord Clyde cited the relevant passage from Lord Diplock's speech set out above, 490, in Lord Steyn's speech in* Darlington v Wiltshier *and continued:*]

It is particularly this passage in Lord Diplock's speech which has given rise to a question discussed in the present appeal whether *The Albazero* exception is a rule of law or is based upon the intention of the parties. ...The problem arises from two phrases in the speech of Lord Diplock the mutual relationship between which may not be immediately obvious. The two phrases, in the reverse order than that in which they appear, are "is to be treated in law as having entered into the contract" and "if such be the intention of the parties". In my view it is preferable to regard it as a solution imposed by the law and not as arising from the supposed intention of the parties, who may in reality not have applied their minds to the point. On the other hand if they deliberately provided for a remedy for a third party it can readily be concluded that they have intended to exclude the operation of the solution which would otherwise have been imposed by law. The terms and provisions of the contract will then require to be studied to see if the parties have excluded the operation of the exception.

...

The Albazero exception will plainly not apply where the parties contemplate that the carrier will enter into separate contracts of carriage with the later owners of the goods, identical to the contract with the consignor. Even more clearly, as Lord Diplock explained [1977] AC 774, 848, will the exception be excluded if other contracts of carriage are made in terms different from those in the original contract. In *The Albazero* the separate contracts which were mentioned were contracts of carriage. That is understandable in the context of carriage by sea involving a charterparty and bills of lading. But the counterpart in a building contract to a right of suit under a bill of lading should be the provision of a direct entitlement in a third party to sue the contractor in the event of a failure in the contractor's performance. In the context of a building contract one does not require to look for a second building contract to exclude the exception. It would be sufficient to find the provision of a right to sue.

...

I have no difficulty in holding in the present case that the exception cannot apply. As part of the contractual arrangements entered into between Panatown and McAlpine there was a clear contemplation that separate contracts would be entered into by McAlpine, the contracts of the deed of duty of care and the collateral warranties. The duty of care deed and the collateral warranties were of course not in themselves building contracts. But they did form an integral part of the package of arrangements which the employer and the contractor agreed upon and in that respect should be viewed as reflecting the intentions of all the parties engaged in the arrangements that the third party should have a direct cause of action to the exclusion of any substantial claim by the employer, and accordingly that the exception should not apply. There was some dispute upon the difference in substance between the remedies available under the contract and those available under the duty of care deed. Even if it is accepted that in the circumstances of the present case where the eventual issue may relate particularly to matters of reasonable skill and care, the remedies do not absolutely coincide, the express provision of the direct remedy for the third party is fatal to the application of *The Albazero* exception. On a more general approach the difference between a strict contractual basis of claim and a basis of reasonable care makes the express remedy more clearly a substitution for the operation of the exception. Panatown cannot then in the light of these deeds be treated as having contracted with McAlpine for the benefit of the owner or later owners of the land and the exception is plainly excluded.

I turn accordingly to what was referred to in the argument as the broader ground. But the label requires more careful definition. The approach under *The Albazero* exception has been one of recognising an entitlement to sue by the innocent party to a contract which has been breached, where the innocent party is treated as suing on behalf of or for the benefit of some other person or persons, not parties to the contract, who have sustained loss as a result of the breach. In such a case the innocent party to the contract is bound to account to the person suffering the loss for the damages which the former has recovered for the benefit of the latter. But the so-called broader ground involves a significantly different approach. What it proposes is that the innocent party to the contract should recover damages for himself as a compensation for what is seen to be his own loss. In this context no question of accounting to anyone else arises. This approach however seems to me to have been developed into two formulations.

The first formulation, and the seeds of the second, are found in the speech of Lord Griffiths in the *St Martins* case [1994] 1 AC 85, 96. At the outset his Lordship expressed the opinion that Corporation, faced with a breach by McAlpine of their contractual duty to perform the contract with sound materials and with all reasonable skill and care, would be entitled to recover from McAlpine the cost of remedying the defect in the work as the normal measure of damages. He then dealt with two possible objections. First, it should not matter that the work was not being done on property owned by Corporation. Where a husband instructs repairs to the roof of the matrimonial home it cannot be said that he has not suffered damage because he did not own the property. He suffers the damage measured by the cost of a proper completion of the repair:

"In cases such as the present the person who places the contract has suffered financial loss because he has to spend money to give him the benefit of the bargain which the defendant had promised but failed to deliver." (See p 97.)

The second objection, that Corporation had in fact been reimbursed for the cost of the repairs, was answered by the consideration that the person who actually pays for the repairs is of no concern to the party who broke the contract. But Lord Griffiths added, at p 97:

"The court will of course wish to be satisfied that the repairs have been or are likely to be carried out but if they are carried out the cost of doing them must fall upon the defendant who broke his contract."

In the first formulation this approach can be seen as identifying a loss upon the innocent party who requires to instruct the remedial work. That loss is, or may be measured by, the cost of the repair. The essential for this formulation appears to be that the repair work is to be, or at least is likely to be, carried out. This consideration does not appear to be simply relevant to the reasonableness of allowing the damages to be measured by the cost of repair. It is an essential condition for the application of the approach, so as to establish a loss on the part of the plaintiff. Thus far the approach appears to be consistent with principle, and in particular with the principle of privity. It can cover the case where A contracts with B to pay a sum of money to C and B fails to do so. The loss to A is in the necessity to find other funds to pay to C and provided that he is going to pay C, or indeed has done so, he should be able to recover the sum by way of damages for breach of contract from B. If it was evident that A had no intention to pay C, having perhaps changed his mind, then he would not be able to recover the amount from B because he would have sustained no loss, and his damages would at best be nominal.

But there can also be found in Lord Griffiths's speech the idea that the loss is not just constituted by the failure in performance but indeed consists in that failure. This is the "second formulation". In relation to the suggestion that the husband who instructs repair work to the roof of his wife's house and has to pay for another builder to make good the faulty repair work has sustained no damage Lord Griffiths observed, at p 97:

"Such a result would in my view be absurd and the answer is that the husband has suffered loss because he did not receive the bargain for which he had contracted with the first builder and the measure of damages is the cost of securing the performance of that bargain by completing the roof repairs properly by the second builder."

That is to say that the fact that the innocent party did not receive the bargain for which he contracted is itself a loss. As Steyn LJ put it in *Darlington Borough Council v Wiltshier Northern Ltd* [1995] 1 WLR 68, 80: "He suffers a loss of bargain or of expectation interest." In this more radical formulation it does not matter whether the repairs are or are not carried out, and indeed in the *Darlington* case that qualification is seen as unnecessary. In that respect the disposal of the damages is treated as res inter alios acta. Nevertheless on this approach the intention to repair may cast light on the reasonableness of the measure of damages adopted. In order to follow through this aspect of the second formulation in Lord Griffiths's speech it would be necessary to understand his references to the carrying out of the repairs to be relevant only to that consideration.

I find some difficulty in adopting the second formulation as a sound way forward. First, if the loss is the disappointment at there not being provided what was contracted for, it seems to me difficult to measure that loss by consideration of the cost of repair. A more apt assessment of the compensation for the loss of what was expected should rather be the difference in value between what was contracted for and what was supplied. Secondly, the loss constituted by the supposed disappointment may well not include all the loss which the breach of contract has caused. It may not be able to embrace consequential losses, or losses falling within the second head of *Hadley v Baxendale* 9 Exch 341. The inability of the wife to let one of the rooms in the house caused by the inadequacy of the repair, does not seem readily to be something for which the husband could claim as his loss. Thirdly, there is no obligation on the successful plaintiff to account to anyone who may have sustained actual loss as a result of the faulty performance. Some further mechanism would then be required for the court to achieve the proper disposal of the monies awarded to avoid a double jeopardy. Alternatively, in order to achieve an effective solution, it would seem to be necessary to add an obligation to account on the part of the person recovering the damages. But once that step is taken the approach begins to approximate to *The Albazero* exception. Fourthly, the "loss" constituted by a breach of contract has usually been recognised as calling for an award of nominal damages, not substantial damages.

The loss of an expectation which is here referred to seems to me to be coming very close to a way of describing a breach of contract. A breach of contract may cause a loss, but is not in itself a loss in any meaningful sense. ...

Both of these two formulations seek to remedy the problem of the legal black hole. At the heart of the problem is the doctrine of privity of contract which excludes the ready development of a solution along the lines of a jus quaesitum tertio. It might well be thought that such a solution would be more direct and simple. In the context of the domestic and familial situations, such as the husband instructing the repairs to the roof of his wife's house, or the holiday which results in disappointment to all the members of the family, the jus quaesitum tertio may provide a satisfactory means of redress, enabling compensation to be paid to the people who have suffered the loss. Such an approach is available in Germany: see W Lorenz, "Contract Beneficiaries in German Law" in *The Gradual Convergence: Foreign Ideas, Foreign Influences, and English Law on the Eve of the 21st Century*, edited by Markesinis (1994), pp 65, 78, 79. It may also be available in Scotland (*Carmichael v Carmichael's Executrix*, 1920 SC(HL) 195). But we were not asked to adopt it in the present case and so radical a step cannot easily be achieved without legislative action. Since Parliament has recently made some inroad into the principle of privity but has stopped short of admitting a solution to a situation such as the present, it would plainly be inappropriate to enlarge the statutory provision by judicial innovation. The alternative has to be the adoption of what Lord Diplock in *Swain v The Law Society* [1983] 1 AC 598, 611 described as a juristic subterfuge "to mitigate the effect of the lacuna resulting from the non-recognition of a jus quaesitum tertio". The solution, achieved by the operation of law, may carry with it some element of artificiality and may not be supportable on any clear or single principle. If the entitlement to sue is not to be permitted to the party who has suffered the loss, the law has to treat the person who is entitled to sue as doing so on behalf of the third party. As Lord Wilberforce observed in *Woodar Investment Development Ltd v Wimpey Construction UK Ltd* [1980] 1 WLR 277, 283, "there are many situations of daily life which do not fit neatly into conceptual analysis, but which require some flexibility in the law of contract".

It seems to me that a more realistic and practical solution is to permit the contracting party to recover damages for the loss which he and a third party ha[ve] suffered, being duly accountable to them in respect of their actual loss, than to construct a theoretical loss in law on the part of the contracting party, for which he may be under no duty to account to anyone since it is to be seen as his own loss. The solution is required where the law will not tolerate a loss caused by a breach of contract to go uncompensated through an absence of privity between the party suffering the loss and the party causing it. In such a case, to avoid the legal black hole, the law will deem the innocent party to be claiming on behalf of himself and any others who have suffered loss. It does not matter that he is not the owner of the property affected, nor that he has not himself suffered any economic loss. He sues for all the loss which has been sustained and is accountable to the others to the extent of their particular losses. While it may be that there is no necessary right in the third party to compel the innocent employer to sue the contractor, in the many cases of the domestic or familial situation that consideration should not be a realistic problem. In the commercial field, in relation to the interests of such persons as remoter future proprietors who are not related to the original employer, it may be that a solution by way of collateral warranty would still be required. If there is an anxiety lest the exception would permit an employer to receive excessive damages, that should be set at rest by the recognition of the basic requirement for reasonableness which underlies the quantification of an award of damages.

The problem which has arisen in the present case is one which is most likely to arise in the context of the domestic affairs of a family group or the commercial affairs of a group of companies. How the members of such a group choose to arrange their own affairs among themselves should not be a matter of necessary concern to a third party who has undertaken to one of their number to perform services in which they all have some interest. It should not be a ground of escaping liability that the party who instructed the work should not be the one who sustained the loss or all of the loss which in whole or part has fallen on another member or members of the group. But the resolution of the problem in any particular case has to be reached in light of its own circumstances. In the present case the decision that Panatown should be the employer under the building contract although another company in the group owned the land was made in order to minimise charges of VAT. No doubt thought was given as to the mechanics to be adopted for the building project in order to achieve the course most advantageous to the group. Where for its own purposes a group of companies decides which of its members is to be the contracting party in a project which is of concern and interest to the whole group I should be reluctant to refuse an entitlement to sue on the contract on the ground simply that the member who entered the contract was not the party who suffered the loss on a breach of the contract. But whether such an entitlement is to be admitted must depend upon the arrangements which the group and its members have decided to make both among themselves and with the other party to the contract. In the present case there was a plain and deliberate course adopted whereby the company with the potential risk of loss was given a distinct entitlement directly to sue the contractor and the professional advisers. In the light of such a clear and deliberate course I do not consider that an exception can be admitted to the general rule that substantial damages can only be claimed by a party who has suffered substantial loss.

Lord Jauncey of Tullichettle: The DCD [duty of care deed] in favour of UIPL was executed by McAlpine in pursuance of an obligation contained in the building contract. In these circumstances Mr Pollock for McAlpine argued that the *Dunlop v Lambert* rule had no application and the general rule that a plaintiff can only recover damages (other than nominal) for his own loss applied. Mr Friedman countered this by pointing out that the remedies available to UIPL under the DCD were different from and less effective than those available under the building contract. He referred to the arbitration clause in the building contract which was absent in the DCD, and to the facts that McAlpine's duty of compliance with the contractual provisions of the building contract under the DCD were merely to exercise reasonable care and skill whereas the duty under the building contract was absolute and that the provision for liquidated damages for delay in the building contract was absent in the DCD. ...Mr Friedman also urged upon your Lordships that the DCD was granted, not for the benefit of UIPL, but to enable that company to assign the benefit thereof to a future purchaser. Be that as it may there can be no doubt that UIPL were, and indeed are, entitled to sue McAlpine under the DCD and this cannot be ignored.

My Lords it is of course correct that the DCD is not coterminous with the building contract but does that necessarily mean that the exception to the *Dunlop v Lambert* rule above referred to has no application? That rule provides a remedy where no other would be available for breach of a contract in circumstances where it is within the contemplation of contracting parties that breach by one is likely to cause loss to an identified or identifiable stranger to the contract, rather than to the other contracting party. It prevents the claim to damages falling into what Lord Keith of Kinkel in *GUS Property Management Ltd v Littlewoods Mail Stores Ltd*, 1982 SC(HL) 157, 177 so graphically described as "some legal black hole". ...What is important, as I see it, is that the third party should as a result of the main contract have the right to recover substantial damages for breach under his contract even if those damages may not be identical to those which would have been recovered under the main contract in the same circumstances. In such a situation the need for an exception to the general rule ceases to apply. I therefore conclude that in this case the general rule is not displaced by the rule in *Dunlop v Lambert* and that Mr Pollock's submissions are correct. ...

The broader ground

For the purposes of his argument Mr Friedman limited the application of the broader ground to contracts for the supply of services and defined it as recovery on the basis that the promisee suffers a loss if there is a breach of a contract to confer a benefit on a third party. The promisee suffers that loss because he has not received the benefit of the bargain for which he contracted. Since Panatown had not received what they had contracted for, namely the construction of a building conform to contract, it followed that they had suffered loss, which was the cost of achieving that objective.

The basis for the foregoing proposition was the speech of Lord Griffiths in the *St Martins* case [1994] 1 AC 85...

The greater part of Lord Griffiths's reasoning was directed to reject the proposition that entitlement to more than nominal damages was dependent upon the plaintiff having a proprietary interest in the subject matter. His examples predicated that the husband/employer required to pay for repairs rendered necessary by the breach. He did not require to address the situation where, as here, Panatown has neither spent money in entering into the contract nor intends to do so in remedying the breach and has therefore suffered no loss thereby. Had he had to do so I very much doubt whether he would have expressed the same views in relation thereto.

...

However, there is a further matter to be considered in this case, namely the DCD in favour of UIPL. This, in my view, is equally relevant to the broader as to the narrow ground. The former as does the latter seeks to find a rational way of avoiding the "black hole". What is the justification for allowing A to recover from B as his own a loss which is truly that of C when C has his own remedy against B? I would submit none. The complications and anomalies to which Lord Diplock referred in *The Albazero* [1977] AC 774, 848F as arising from two contracts of carriage for the same goods could arise equally if not more sharply were Panatown entitled to claim substantial damages on the broader ground. If Panatown have a claim for loss of expectation of interest measured by the cost of achieving what they contracted for and UIPL have a separate claim in relation to the same defects McAlpine cannot be mulcted twice over in damages. Panatown's claim for loss of expectation of interest can have only nominal value when UIPL has an enforceable claim and Panatown has no intention of taking steps to remedy the breach. Were it otherwise the great practical difficulties referred to by my noble and learned friend, Lord Browne-Wilkinson, at the end of his speech would arise. Lord Griffiths [1994] 1 AC 85, 97E in a passage to which I have already referred accepted that A should not have a remedy for loss of cargo which had caused him no financial loss when C had a direct right of action. It would be surprising if he had taken a different view of the position of Panatown and UIPL. I therefore consider that Panatown is not entitled to recover under Mr Friedman's broader ground not only because they have suffered no financial loss but also because UIPL have a direct right of action against McAlpine under the DCD. As I have come to the conclusion that neither the narrow nor the broader ground is applicable to the facts of this case I would allow the appeal.

Lord Browne-Wilkinson: In my judgment the direct cause of action which UIPL has under the DCD is fatal to any claim to substantial damages made by Panatown against McAlpine based on the narrower ground. First, the principle in *The Albazero* [1977] AC 774 as applied to building contracts by the *St Martins* case [1994] 1 AC 85 is based on the fact that it provides a remedy to the third party "where no other would be available to a person sustaining loss which under a rational legal system ought to be compensated by the person who has caused it": see *The Albazero* [1977] AC 774, 847B and the *St Martins* case [1994] 1 AC 85, 114G. If the contractual arrangements between the parties in fact provide the third party with a direct remedy against the wrongdoer the whole rationale of the rule disappears. Moreover...both the decision in *The Albazero* case itself and dicta in the *St Martins* case, at p 115F, state that where the third party (C) has a direct claim against the builder (B) the promisee under the building contract (A) cannot claim for the third party's damage.

I turn now to the broader ground on which Lord Griffiths decided the *St Martins* case. He held that the building contractor (B) was liable to the promisee (A) for more than nominal damages even though A did not own the land at the date of breach. He held in effect that by reason of the breach A had himself suffered damage, being the loss of the value to him of the performance of the contract. On this view even though A might not be legally liable to C to provide him with the benefit which the performance of the contract by B would have provided, A has lost his "performance interest" and will therefore be entitled to substantial damages being, in Lord Griffiths's view, the cost to A of providing C with the benefit. In the *St Martins* case Lord Keith of Kinkel, Lord Bridge of Harwich and I all expressed sympathy with Lord Griffiths's broader view. However, I declined to adopt the broader ground until the possible consequences of so doing had been examined by academic writers. That has now happened and no serious difficulties have been disclosed. However, there is a division of opinion as to whether the contracting party, A, is accountable to the third party, C, for the damages recovered or is bound to expend the damages on providing for C the benefit which B was supposed to provide. Lord Griffiths in the *St Martins* case, at p 97G, took that view. But as I understand them Lord Goff of Chieveley and Lord Millett in the present case...would hold that, in the absence of the specific circumstances of the present case[,] A...is not accountable to C for any damages recovered by A from B.

I will assume that the broader ground is sound in law and that in the ordinary case where the third party (C) has no direct cause of action against the building contractor (B) A can recover damages from B on the broader ground. Even on that assumption, in my judgment Panatown has no right to substantial damages in this case because UIPL (the owner of the land) has a direct cause of action under the DCD.

The essential feature of the broader ground is that the contracting party A, although not himself suffering the physical or pecuniary damage sustained by the third party C, has suffered his own damage being the loss of his performance interest, i e the failure to provide C with the benefit that B had contracted for C to receive. In my judgment it follows that the critical factor is to determine what interest A had in the provision of the service for the third party C. If, as in the present case, the whole contractual scheme was designed, inter alia, to give UPIL and its successors a legal remedy against McAlpine for failure to perform the building contract with due care, I cannot see that Panatown has suffered any damage to its performance interests: subject to any defence based on limitation of actions, the physical and pecuniary damage suffered by UPIL can be redressed by UPIL exercising its own cause of action against McAlpine. It is not clear to me why this has not occurred in the present case: but, subject to questions of limitation which were not explored, there is no reason even now why UPIL should not be bringing the proceedings against McAlpine. The fact that the DCD may have been primarily directed to ensuring that UPIL's successors in title should enjoy a remedy in tort against McAlpine is nothing to the point: the contractual provisions were directed to ensuring that UPIL and its successors in title did have the legal right to sue McAlpine direct. So long as UPIL enjoys this right Panatown has suffered no failure to satisfy its performance interest.

The theoretical objection to giving the contracting party A substantial damages for breach of the contract by B for failing to provide C with a benefit which C itself can enforce against B is further demonstrated by great practical difficulties which such a view would entail. Let me illustrate this by postulating a case where, before the breach occurred, UPIL had with consent assigned the benefit of the DCD to a purchaser of the site, X. What if Panatown itself was entitled to, and did, sue for and recover damages from McAlpine? Presumably McAlpine could not in addition be liable to X for breach of the DCD: yet Panatown would not be liable to account to X for the damages it had recovered from McAlpine. The result would therefore be another piece of legal nonsense: the party who had suffered real, tangible damage, X, could recover nothing but Panatown which had suffered no real loss could recover damages. Again, suppose that X agrees with McAlpine certain variations of McAlpine's liability under the building contract. What rights would Panatown then have against McAlpine? The Law Commission in its Report, Privity of Contract: Contracts for the Benefit of Third Parties (1996) (Law Com No 242), considered at length questions like these (see in particular paragraphs 11.14, 11.21 and 11.22) and many other problems such as set off and counter-claims. The Law Commission recommended that in certain defined circumstances third parties should be entitled to enforce the contract. But in the draft Bill annexed to the Report and in the Act of Parliament which enacted the recommendations, the Contracts (Rights of Third Parties) Act 1999, specific statutory provisions were included to deal with the difficulties arising. Although both the Law Commission's Report (paragraphs 5.10 and 5.11) and sections 4 and 6(1) of the Act make it clear that the Act is not intended to discourage the courts from developing the rights of third parties when it is appropriate to do so, in my judgment there is little inducement in a case such as the present where a third party has himself the right to enforce the contract against the contract breaker, to extend the law so as to give both the promisee and the third party concurrent rights of enforcement.

For these reasons I would allow the appeal.

Lord Goff of Chieveley (dissenting): [T]he invocation of the rule in *Dunlop v Lambert* 6 Cl & F 600 in the present context is, I believe, inapposite. This is because we are not here addressing a problem of privity of contract. The problem is not that UIPL had no enforceable rights against McAlpine arising under the building contract: it was the evident intention that UIPL should not have such rights, its rights against McAlpine being restricted to different rights under a separate contract, the DCD. That the rule in *Dunlop v Lambert* is inapposite in the present context is illustrated in particular by the irrelevance, in this context, of any contemplation that the property of the contracting party should be transferred to a third party—a feature which was regarded by Lord Diplock as a prerequisite of the application of the rule in *Dunlop v Lambert*, and was fortuitously present in the *St Martins* case [1994] 1 AC 85. An indication that any such prerequisite is irrelevant in the present context may be derived from the fact that, in the next case in which the *St Martins* case was applied, *Darlington Borough Council v Wiltshier Northern Ltd* [1995] 1 WLR 68, there was no such feature and yet its absence was ignored by the Court of Appeal, no doubt because they felt that it did not matter. The same applies to the judgment of the Court of Appeal in the present case. In truth, what we are concerned with here is the effectiveness of the rights conferred on Panatown under the building contract itself. In expressing this opinion I wish to stress that I fully understand, and indeed sympathise with, the hesitation of the majority in the *St Martins* case to follow Lord Griffiths down the route which he preferred. But, with the passage of time and the benefit of much useful academic writing, I feel more hesitant about adopting the rule in *Dunlop v Lambert* in what I consider to be an inappropriate context than I do about adopting Lord Griffiths's approach. That the latter approach itself involves certain difficulties, I freely recognise; but I regard my appropriate course in the present case as being not to reject Lord Griffiths's approach, but to identify and confront these difficulties in order to reach a solution which is in accordance with principle and also does practical justice between the parties, without leaving too great a legacy of problems for the future. To that task I now address myself.

I start with the proposition that the interest of a contracting party (A) in the performance by the other party (B) of his contractual obligations to A has long been recognised, and is protected as such by a remedy by A against B in damages. The protection of this "performance interest" or "expectation interest" is today placed at the forefront of their treatment of damages by both Professor Treitel (see *Treitel on Contract,* 10th ed (1999), pp 973 et seq) and Professor Beatson (see *Anson on Contract,* 27th ed (1998), pp 364 et seq). The question raised by McAlpine's argument in the present case is said to arise in circumstances in which the plaintiff attempts to enforce his right to damages where the "loss" has been suffered by a third party: see, e g, *Anson on Contract,* 27th ed, pp 412 et seq.

The argument advanced by McAlpine in the present case appears more compelling in cases where the plaintiff is claiming damages in respect of loss of, or damage to a third party's property, than in cases such as the present, where the plaintiff is claiming damages in respect of failure by the defendant to carry out, or to carry out properly, work of improvement (or repair) on the land (or chattel) of a third party. It is in the former case that it can more readily be said that the third party has suffered loss, and indeed that the loss has fallen on the third party rather than on the plaintiff. It is in such cases that we have seen the development of the specific exception identified by Lord Diplock in *The Albazero* [1977] AC 774. In the latter case, however, it is difficult to see why the fact that the land (or chattel) is owned by a third party should of itself prevent the plaintiff from recovering damages in respect of the failure by the other contracting party to fulfil his side of the bargain with the plaintiff (for which the plaintiff has ex hypothesi furnished consideration). Indeed, if the law should in such circumstances deny the plaintiff a remedy in damages, it can be said with force that his performance or expectation interest is insufficiently protected in law. Historically this may have been the position; but, if so, it appears that this defect in the law has, in recent years, been addressed and remedied in cases in which the point has arisen for decision and furthermore that those decisions have been generally welcomed by the academic legal community.

I add that, if Lord Griffiths's approach was to be rejected, it would follow that, for example, the employer under a building contract for work on another's property would have no remedy in damages if the builder was to repudiate the contract or to fail altogether to perform the contractual work. In other words, the builder could repudiate with impunity. It is no answer, or an insufficient answer, to this point that money paid in advance by the employer may be recoverable on the ground of failure of consideration, any more than it is an answer to other cases that there may be an abatement of the price.

In the light of this preamble I wish to state that I find persuasive the reasoning and conclusion expressed by Lord Griffiths in his opinion in the *St Martins* case [1994] 1 AC 85 that the employer under a building contract may in principle recover substantial damages from the building contractor, because he has not received the performance which he was entitled to receive from the contractor under the contract, notwithstanding that the property in the building site was vested in a third party. The example given by Lord Griffiths of a husband contracting for repairs to the matrimonial home which is owned by his wife is most telling. It is not difficult to imagine other examples, not only within the family, but also, for example, where work is done for charitable purposes—as where a wealthy man who lives in a village decides to carry out at his own expense major repairs to, or renovation or even reconstruction of, the village hall, and himself enters into a contract with a local builder to carry out the work to the existing building which belongs to another, for example to trustees, or to the parish council. Nobody in such circumstances would imagine that there could be any legal obstacle in the way of the charitable donor enforcing the contract against the builder by recovering damages from him if he failed to perform his obligations under the building contract, for example because his work failed to comply with the contract specification.

At this stage I find it necessary to return to the opinion of Lord Griffiths in the *St Martins* case. In the passage from his opinion [1994] 1 AC 85, 96-97 which I have already quoted, he gave the example of a husband placing a contract with a builder for the replacement of the roof of the matrimonial home which belonged to his wife. The work proved to be defective. Lord Griffiths expressed the opinion that, in such a case, it would be absurd to say that the husband has suffered no damage because he does not own the property. I wish now to draw attention to the fact that, in his statement of the facts of his example, Lord Griffiths included the fact that the husband had to call in and pay another builder to complete the work. It might perhaps be thought that Lord Griffiths regarded that fact as critical to the husband's cause of action against the builder, on the basis that the husband only has such a cause of action in respect of defective work on another person's property if he himself has actually sustained financial loss, in this example by having paid the second builder. In my opinion, however, such a conclusion is not justified on a fair reading of Lord Griffiths's opinion. This is because he stated the answer to be that

> "the husband has suffered loss because he did not receive the bargain for which he had contracted with the first builder and the measure of damages is the cost of securing the performance of that bargain by completing the roof repairs properly by the second builder."

It is plain, therefore, that the payment to the second builder was not regarded by Lord Griffiths as essential to the husband's cause of action.

The point can perhaps be made more clearly by taking a different example, of the wealthy philanthropist who contracts for work to be done to the village hall. The work is defective; and the trustees who own the hall suggest that he should recover damages from the builder and hand the damages over to them, and they will then instruct another builder, well known to them, who, they are confident, will do the work well. The philanthropist agrees, and starts an action against the first builder. Is it really to be suggested that his action will fail, because he does not own the hall, and because he has not incurred the expense of himself employing another builder to do the remedial work? Echoing the words of Lord Griffiths, I regard such a conclusion as absurd. The philanthropist's cause of action does not depend on his having actually incurred financial expense; as Lord Griffiths said of the husband in his example, he "has suffered loss because he did not receive the bargain for which he had contracted with the first builder".

> ...

It follows, in my opinion, that the principal argument advanced on behalf of McAlpine is inconsistent with authority and established principle. This conclusion may involve a fuller recognition of the importance of the protection of a contracting party's interest in the performance of his contract than has occurred in the past. But not only is it justified by authority, but the principle on which it is based is supported by a number of distinguished writers, notably Professor Brian Coote [[1997] CLJ 537] and Mr Duncan Wallace QC [(1994) 110 LQR 42 and (1999) 115 LQR 394].

Lord Millett delivered a dissenting speech.

NOTES AND QUESTIONS

1.   The majority held that the *Albazero* exception (as developed in *Darlington v Wiltshier*) did not here apply even though McAlpine and Panatown contemplated that any loss in relation to the building would be suffered by UIPL and

not Panatown. This was because UIPL had been given a direct contractual right against McAlpine. Was this a good reason for knocking out the exception? Note that the relevant terms of the main contract and of the duty of care deed were not co-extensive; and that the duty of care deed would seem to have been conceived of as a contractual replacement for the liability in the tort of negligence that would have been imposed on McAlpine prior to the decision of the House of Lords in *Murphy v Brentwood DC* [1991] 1 AC 398.

2. The minority (Lord Goff of Chieveley and Lord Millett) reasoned that Panatown was entitled to recover substantial damages *for its own loss.* They derived support for this from what was termed Lord Griffiths' 'broad ground' in the *Linden Gardens* case. (Lord Goff also referred to, and was clearly influenced by, an article by Coote [1997] CLJ 537, see above, 419). But as Lords Clyde and Jauncey persuasively argued, it was fictional to regard Panatown as having itself suffered a financial loss (other than the reliance loss constituted by the contract price paid). Panatown had not itself paid for the cost of repairs nor did it intend to do so. Moreover, the loss of use and delay were suffered by UIPL, not Panatown. The minority's approach also appears to produce problems of double liability: if the loss was Panatown's, and yet UIPL had direct contractual rights under the duty of care deed, it is hard to see how one can avoid saying that both Panatown and UIPL were entitled to substantial damages.

3. **A Burrows, 'No Damages for a Third Party's Loss' (2001) 1 *OUCLJ* 107** argues that all of their Lordships' reasoning was flawed. The minority's view that Panatown had suffered the loss was fictional; and the majority should not have knocked out the *Albazero* exception. That exception should have applied so that Panatown should have been awarded substantial damages on behalf of UIPL for which it was bound to account to UIPL. See also A Burrows, *Remedies for Torts and Breach of Contract* (3rd edn, 2004) 226–9.

5. THE CONTRACTS (RIGHTS OF THIRD PARTIES) ACT 1999

This Act, which effects a wide-ranging reform of privity of contract on its benefit side, implements (with some modifications) the recommendations of the Law Commission in *Privity of Contract: Contracts for the Benefit of Third Parties,* Report No 242 (1996). The Act came into force on 11 November 1999 and by section 10(2) applies to contracts entered into six months or more after that date (ie contracts made on or after 11 May 2000). After setting out the Act, we shall examine its main elements under eight sub-headings: most importantly, the tests of enforceability; variation and rescission by the contracting parties; defences available to the promisor; the promisee's rights; exclusions from the Act; existing exceptions; the relationship with the Unfair Contract Terms Act 1977; and the meaning of 'contract' under the

Act. Throughout you should be considering whether you regard the 1999 Act as having effected a welcome reform or whether, on the contrary, you believe that it has created more problems than it has solved.

Contracts (Rights of Third Parties) Act 1999

1 Right of third party to enforce contractual term

(1) Subject to the provisions of this Act, a person who is not a party to a contract (a "third party") may in his own right enforce a term of the contract if—

(a)　the contract expressly provides that he may, or
(b)　subject to subsection (2), the term purports to confer a benefit on him.

(2) Subsection (1)(b) does not apply if on a proper construction of the contract it appears that the parties did not intend the term to be enforceable by the third party.

(3) The third party must be expressly identified in the contract by name, as a member of a class or as answering a particular description but need not be in existence when the contract is entered into.

(4) This section does not confer a right on a third party to enforce a term of a contract otherwise than subject to and in accordance with any other relevant terms of the contract.

(5) For the purpose of exercising his right to enforce a term of the contract, there shall be available to the third party any remedy that would have been available to him in an action for breach of contract if he had been a party to the contract (and the rules relating to damages, injunctions, specific performance and other relief shall apply accordingly).

(6) Where a term of a contract excludes or limits liability in relation to any matter references in this Act to the third party enforcing the term shall be construed as references to his availing himself of the exclusion or limitation.

(7) In this Act, in relation to a term of a contract which is enforceable by a third party—

— "the promisor" means the party to the contract against whom the term is enforceable by the third party, and
— "the promisee" means the party to the contract by whom the term is enforceable against the promisor.

2 Variation and rescission of contract

(1) Subject to the provisions of this section, where a third party has a right under section 1 to enforce a term of the contract, the parties to the contract may not, by agreement, rescind the contract, or vary it in such a way as to extinguish or alter his entitlement under that right, without his consent if—

(a)　the third party has communicated his assent to the term to the promisor,
(b)　the promisor is aware that the third party has relied on the term, or
(c)　the promisor can reasonably be expected to have foreseen that the third party would rely on the term and the third party has in fact relied on it.

(2) The assent referred to in subsection (1)(a)—

(a)　may be by words or conduct, and
(b)　if sent to the promisor by post or other means, shall not be regarded as communicated to the promisor until received by him.

(3) Subsection (1) is subject to any express term of the contract under which—

(a) the parties to the contract may by agreement rescind or vary the contract without the consent of the third party, or

(b) the consent of the third party is required in circumstances specified in the contract instead of those set out in subsection (1)(a) to (c).

(4) Where the consent of a third party is required under subsection (1) or (3), the court or arbitral tribunal may, on the application of the parties to the contract, dispense with his consent if satisfied—

(a) that his consent cannot be obtained because his whereabouts cannot reasonably be ascertained, or

(b) that he is mentally incapable of giving his consent.

(5) The court or arbitral tribunal may, on the application of the parties to a contract, dispense with any consent that may be required under subsection (1)(c) if satisfied that it cannot reasonably be ascertained whether or not the third party has in fact relied on the term.

(6) If the court or arbitral tribunal dispenses with a third party's consent, it may impose such conditions as it thinks fit, including a condition requiring the payment of compensation to the third party.

(7) The jurisdiction conferred on the court by subsections (4) to (6) is exercisable by both the High Court and a county court.

3 Defences etc available to promisor

(1) Subsections (2) to (5) apply where, in reliance on section 1, proceedings for the enforcement of a term of a contract are brought by a third party.

(2) The promisor shall have available to him by way of defence or set-off any matter that—

(a) arises from or in connection with the contract and is relevant to the term, and

(b) would have been available to him by way of defence or set-off if the proceedings had been brought by the promisee.

(3) The promisor shall also have available to him by way of defence or set-off any matter if—

(a) an express term of the contract provides for it to be available to him in proceedings brought by the third party, and

(b) it would have been available to him by way of defence or set-off if the proceedings had been brought by the promisee.

(4) The promisor shall also have available to him—

(a) by way of defence or set-off any matter, and

(b) by way of counterclaim any matter not arising from the contract,

that would have been available to him by way of defence or set-off or, as the case may be, by way of counterclaim against the third party if the third party had been a party to the contract.

(5) Subsections (2) and (4) are subject to any express term of the contract as to the matters that are not to be available to the promisor by way of defence, set-off or counterclaim.

(6) Where in any proceedings brought against him a third party seeks in reliance on section 1 to enforce a term of a contract (including, in particular, a term purporting to exclude or limit liability), he may not do so if he could not have done so (whether by reason of any particular circumstances relating to him or otherwise) had he been a party to the contract.

4 Enforcement of contract by promisee
Section 1 does not affect any right of the promisee to enforce any term of the contract.

5 Protection of party promisor from double liability
Where under section 1 a term of a contract is enforceable by a third party, and the promisee has recovered from the promisor a sum in respect of—

(a)   the third party's loss in respect of the term, or

(b)   the expense to the promisee of making good to the third party the default of the promisor,

then, in any proceedings brought in reliance on that section by the third party, the court or arbitral tribunal shall reduce any award to the third party to such extent as it thinks appropriate to take account of the sum recovered by the promisee.

6 Exceptions
(1) Section 1 confers no rights on a third party in the case of a contract on a bill of exchange, promissory note or other negotiable instrument.

(2) Section 1 confers no rights on a third party in the case of any contract binding on a company and its members under section 14 of the Companies Act 1985.

[(2A) Section 1 confers no rights on a third party in the case of any incorporation document of a limited liability partnership or any limited liability partnership agreement as defined in the Limited Liability Partnerships Regulations 2001 (SI No 2001/1090).]

(3) Section 1 confers no right on a third party to enforce—

(a)   any term of a contract of employment against an employee,

(b)   any term of a worker's contract against a worker (including a home worker), or

(c)   any term of a relevant contract against an agency worker.

(4) In subsection (3)—

(a)   "contract of employment", "employee", "worker's contract", and "worker" have the meaning given by section 54 of the National Minimum Wage Act 1998,

(b)   "home worker" has the meaning given by section 35(2) of that Act,

(c)   "agency worker" has the same meaning as in section 34(1) of that Act, and

(d)   "relevant contract" means a contract entered into, in a case where section 34 of that Act applies, by the agency worker as respects work falling within subsection (1)(a) of that section.

(5) Section 1 confers no rights on a third party in the case of—

(a)   a contract for the carriage of goods by sea, or

(b)   a contract for the carriage of goods by rail or road, or for the carriage of cargo by air, which is subject to the rules of the appropriate international transport convention,

except that a third party may in reliance on that section avail himself of an exclusion or limitation of liability in such a contract.

(6) In subsection (5) "contract for the carriage of goods by sea" means a contract of carriage—

(a)   contained in or evidenced by a bill of lading, sea waybill or a corresponding electronic transaction, or

(b) under or for the purposes of which there is given an undertaking which is contained in a ship's delivery order or a corresponding electronic transaction.

(7) For the purposes of subsection (6)—

(a) "bill of lading", "sea waybill" and "ship's delivery order" have the same meaning as in the Carriage of Goods by Sea Act 1992, and
(b) a corresponding electronic transaction is a transaction within section 1(5) of that Act which corresponds to the issue, indorsement, delivery or transfer of a bill of lading, sea waybill or ship's delivery order.

(8) In subsection (5) "the appropriate international transport convention" means—

(a) in relation to a contract for the carriage of goods by rail, the Convention which has the force of law in the United Kingdom under section 1 of the International Transport Conventions Act 1983 [regulation 3 of the Railways (Convention on International Carriage by Rail) Regulations 2005],
(b) in relation to a contract for the carriage of goods by road, the Convention which has the force of law in the United Kingdom under section 1 of the Carriage of Goods by Road Act 1965, and
(c) in relation to a contract for the carriage of cargo by air—
    (i) the Convention which has the force of law in the United Kingdom under section 1 of the Carriage by Air Act 1961, or
    (ii) the Convention which has the force of law under section 1 of the Carriage by Air (Supplementary Provisions) Act 1962, or
    (iii) either of the amended Conventions set out in Part B of Schedule 2 or 3 to the Carriage by Air Acts (Application of Provisions) Order 1967.

7 Supplementary provisions relating to third party

(1) Section 1 does not affect any right or remedy of a third party that exists or is available apart from this Act.

(2) Section 2(2) of the Unfair Contract Terms Act 1977 (restriction on exclusion etc of liability for negligence) shall not apply where the negligence consists of the breach of an obligation arising from a term of a contract and the person seeking to enforce it is a third party acting in reliance on section 1.

(3) In sections 5 and 8 of the Limitation Act 1980 the references to an action founded on a simple contract and an action upon a specialty shall respectively include references to an action brought in reliance on section 1 relating to a simple contract and an action brought in reliance on that section relating to a specialty.

(4) A third party shall not, by virtue of section 1(5) or 3(4) or (6), be treated as a party to the contract for the purposes of any other Act (or any instrument made under any other Act).

8 Arbitration provisions

(1) Where—

(a) a right under section 1 to enforce a term ("the substantive term") is subject to a term providing for the submission of disputes to arbitration ("the arbitration agreement"), and
(b) the arbitration agreement is an agreement in writing for the purposes of Part I of the Arbitration Act 1996,

the third party shall be treated for the purposes of that Act as a party to the arbitration agreement as regards disputes between himself and the promisor relating to the enforcement of the substantive term by the third party.

(2) Where—

(a)   a third party has a right under section 1 to enforce a term providing for one or more descriptions of dispute between the third party and the promisor to be submitted to arbitration ("the arbitration agreement"),

(b)   the arbitration agreement is an agreement in writing for the purposes of Part I of the Arbitration Act 1996, and

(c)   the third party does not fall to be treated under subsection (1) as a party to the arbitration agreement,

the third party shall, if he exercises the right, be treated for the purposes of that Act as a party to the arbitration agreement in relation to the matter with respect to which the right is exercised, and be treated as having been so immediately before the exercise of the right.

9 Northern Ireland

(1) In its application to Northern Ireland, this Act has effect with the modifications specified in subsections (2) and (3).

(2) In section 6(2), for "section 14 of the Companies Act 1985" there is substituted "Article 25 of the Companies (Northern Ireland) Order 1986".

(3) In section 7, for subsection (3) there is substituted—

"(3) In Articles 4(a) and 15 of the Limitation (Northern Ireland) Order 1989, the references to an action founded on a simple contract and an action upon an instrument under seal shall respectively include references to an action brought in reliance on section 1 relating to a simple contract and an action brought in reliance on that section relating to a contract under seal.".

(4) In the Law Reform (Husband and Wife) (Northern Ireland) Act 1964, the following provisions are hereby repealed—

(a)   section 5, and

(b)   in section 6, in subsection (1)(a), the words "in the case of section 4" and "and in the case of section 5 the contracting party" and, in subsection (3), the words "or section 5".

10 Short title, commencement and extent

(1) This Act may be cited as the Contracts (Rights of Third Parties) Act 1999.

(2) This Act comes into force on the day on which it is passed but, subject to subsection (3), does not apply in relation to a contract entered into before the end of the period of six months beginning with that day.

(3) The restriction in subsection (2) does not apply in relation to a contract which—

(a)   is entered into on or after the day on which this Act is passed, and

(b)   expressly provides for the application of this Act.

(4) This Act extends as follows—

(a)   section 9 extends to Northern Ireland only;

(b)   the remaining provisions extend to England and Wales and Northern Ireland only.

(1) The Tests of Enforceability

We are here seeking to answer the central question, 'Under the Act, when does a third party have the right to enforce a term of a contract?'

The Act lays down two separate tests. The first and simpler is in section 1(1)(a) and 1(3). A third party has the right to enforce a term where the contract expressly provides that he may. This will be satisfied where the contract contains words such as 'and C shall have the right to enforce the contract' or 'C shall have the right to enforce clauses 11 and 12 of the contract' or 'C shall have the right to sue on the contract'. Section 1(3) clarifies that, provided there is express identification, the third party does not have to be named. It is sufficient if the third party is expressly identified in the contract as a member of a class (eg stevedores, subsequent tenants) or as answering a particular description (eg 'person living at 3 Coronation Street'). Section 1(3) also clarifies that the third party does not need to be in existence when the contract is made so that contracting parties may confer third party rights on, for example, an unborn child or a future spouse or a company that has not yet been incorporated.

Less straightforward is the second test of enforceability which is in section 1(1)(b), 1(2) and 1(3). One can say that this second test is concerned with the *implied* conferral of rights on a third party, as opposed to the express conferral of rights under the first test. The second test is satisfied if three conditions (two positive and one negative) are met. If the term purports to confer a benefit on the third party (section 1(1)(b)) and he is expressly identified by name, class or description (section 1(3)), the third party will have a right of enforceability unless, on a proper construction of the contract, the parties did not intend the term to be enforceable by him (section 1(2)). It can be seen that the second test, through its two positive conditions in section 1(1)(b) and section 1(3), sets up a rebuttable presumption of intention. So if money is to be paid by A not to B but to an expressly identified third party, C, the presumption is that C has the right to enforce that payment term. But that will be rebutted under section 1(2) where, for example, there is an express term of the contract laying down that C shall have no right of enforceability; or where there are other terms inconsistent with C having that right (for example, the existence of a term prohibiting assignment of B's right to enforce the payment term to a third party without A's written consent would indicate that the contracting parties did not intend C to have an immediate right of enforceability).

An important point to add on this second test is that the words 'purport to confer a benefit on [the third party]' were intended by the Law Commission to convey the idea that the presumption is triggered only where the third party is to receive the benefit *directly* from the promisor. Say, for example, A was engaged by B 'to cut B's hedge adjoining C's land'. Even though performance might be of benefit to C, and C is expressly identified, the term would not 'purport to confer a benefit on [C]'. Similarly the Law Commission's view was that a solicitor's contractual obligation to a testator to use reasonable care in drawing up a will does not purport to confer a benefit on the proposed beneficiaries of the will under section 1(1)(b). The benefit is conferred, if at all, by the testator not the solicitor. The role of the solicitor, and hence the purpose of the contractual duty, is to enable the testator, at his or her discretion, to confer a benefit on the beneficiaries.

There are four additional points on the two tests looked at together.

First, a contract draftsman can make the position on third party rights absolutely clear one way or the other. He can do this either by giving a third party an express right within the first test; or by expressly negating any third party rights so that neither test can be satisfied. An example of the latter would be a clause which said, 'A person who is not a party to this contract shall have no rights under the Contracts (Rights of Third Parties) Act 1999 to enforce any of its terms'.

Secondly, what does the right of enforceability mean? This is laid down in section 1(5). The third party is to have the same judicial remedies for breach of contract as he would have had 'if he had been a party to the contract'. So the third party is entitled to expectation damages for its own loss (subject to normal restrictions, such as remoteness) and to an award of the agreed sum, specific performance and injunctions subject to the normal rules applying to those remedies. The phrase '[as] if he had been a party to the contract' allows the court the flexibility to reach a sensible solution by treating the third party's position as analogous to, but not identical with, that of the promisee.

Thirdly, section 1(6) clarifies that the tests of enforceability apply not only to positive rights but also to negative rights (that is, exclusion and limitation clauses). Generally speaking, if an exclusion or limitation clause is expressed to be for the benefit of an expressly identified third party, this will satisfy the first test because a clause expressed in that way will almost always mean that the parties intended the third party's *rights* to be affected. But if there is any doubt about that, the second test will, in any event, be satisfied by such a clause.

Fourthly, it is a useful exercise to 'play the game' of considering whether the facts of some of the leading past cases would have satisfied the tests of enforceability. It is submitted that, for example, *Tweddle v Atkinson* (above, 462) and *New Zealand Shipping v Satterthwaite* (above, 477) would have satisfied the first test; that *Beswick v Beswick*, *Jackson v Horizon Holidays* and *Woodar v Wimpey* (above, 468, 482, 484) would have satisfied the second test; but that *Scruttons v Midland Silicones* (above, 466), *White v Jones* (above, 477) and *McAlpine v Panatown* (above, 491) would have satisfied neither test.

We can now turn to examine the two most important reported cases on the 1999 Act in both of which the second test of enforceability was held to be satisfied.

Nisshin Shipping Co Ltd v Cleaves & Co Ltd
[2003] EWHC 2602, [2004] 1 Lloyd's Rep 38,
Queen's Bench Division

A chartering broker (Cleaves) had negotiated a number of charterparties on behalf of the shipowners (Nisshin). In each of the charterparties, Nisshin agreed with the charterers to pay Cleaves its commission. In each charterparty, there was also an arbitration clause by which the parties agreed to refer all disputes arising out of the contract to arbitration. Colman J held that Cleaves had the right, as a third party under the 1999 Act, to enforce Nisshin's promise to pay it commission; and that it was entitled, and indeed bound (as a condition of enforcement), to enforce that right by arbitration.

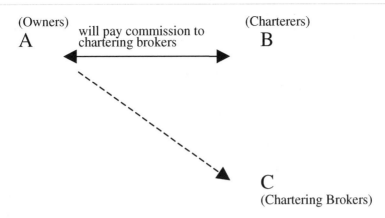

For key see 462.

Colman J:

Introduction

1 In 1999, following an admirable report by the Law Commission, Parliament dealt a long overdue body blow to the doctrine of privity of contract. It enacted the Contracts (Rights of Third Parties) Act 1999. That broadly had the purpose of enabling a third party to a contract under which one party had promised to confer a benefit on that third party to enforce that promise direct against the promisor. That facility is of particular importance to chartering brokers...and to others who create contracts under which one party promises to pay them commission.

2 This case is, I understand, the first time that the 1999 Act has been before the courts. It raises questions highly relevant to the shipping industry as to how a third party may enforce a promise of a benefit for him where there is an arbitration clause in the underlying contract.

Do Cleaves fall within s. 1 of the 1999 Act?

10 It is accepted on behalf of Cleaves that in none of the charters did the commission clauses expressly provide that Cleaves could enforce such clauses directly against the owners. However the real issues are (i) whether those clauses purported to confer a benefit on Cleaves within sub-s. (1)(b) of s. 1 and (ii) whether sub-s. 1(b) is disapplied by sub-s. (2) because "on a proper construction of the contact it appears that the parties did not intend the term to be enforceable by the third party".

11 It is argued by Mr Michael Ashcroft, on behalf of Nisshin, that under four of the charter-parties – those numbered (ii), (iii), (iv) and (v) in the arbitration award – the commission clauses did not purport to confer a benefit on Cleaves alone. Although there was an issue before the arbitrators as to whether certain words had been deleted from numbers (iv) and (v) before or after the contract was entered into, it is common ground that, for the purposes of this application only, I should disregard deletions of part of these clauses which were made at some stage. The relevant wording for all four charter-parties is thus as follows:

> "A commission of two per cent for equal division is payable by the vessel and owners to Messrs Ifchor S.A. Lausanne and Messrs Cleaves and Company Ltd., London on hire earned and paid under this Charter, and also upon any continuation or extension of this charter".

12 It is argued that the phraseology is such that the benefit conferred by the clause is to be subsequently divided between the two firms as distinct from a provision which specifies that a particular percentage should be paid to a particular broker.

13 I cannot accept this argument. These provisions leave no doubt as to the identity of the broker to whom payment is to be made and as to the amount to be paid. It is in substance exactly the same as if the clause had provided that there was to be a commission of two per cent of which one per cent was to be paid to Ifchor and one per cent to Cleaves. There is nothing in this clause to suggest that the total two per cent commission is to be paid to Ifchor and that Ifchor will then pay half of that to Cleaves. The words "for division" do not, in my judgment, bear that connotation in the absence of any indication as to the broker to whom payment is first to be made. Nor do the words support the submission that the obligation to pay commission can only be enforced jointly by both the firms of brokers. There is no conceivable commercial purpose in a construction which creates a joint and indivisible right of enforcement. Absent of much clearer wording than this, I do not consider that the clause should be thus construed.

14 Accordingly, I hold that the effect of the clause was to confer a benefit to the extent of one per cent commission on Cleaves alone.

15 It is then further argued by Mr Ashcroft, on behalf of Nisshin, that on the proper construction of the charter-parties the parties to them did not intend the commission clause to be enforceable by Cleaves and accordingly s. 1(1)(b) of the 1999 Act is disapplied by s. 1(2).

16 In support of this argument Nisshin relies on three distinct points.

17 First, it is argued that the arbitration clauses in all of the charter-parties do not make express provision for enforcement by a broker of a claim for commission. All except those numbered (viii) and (ix) include substantially the standard New York Produce Exchange arbitration clause:

> "Should any dispute arise between Owners and the Charterers, the matter in dispute shall be referred to three persons at London, one to be appointed by each of the parties hereto, and the third by the two so chosen."

18 Those charter-parties numbered (viii) and (ix) which substantially incorporated the Shelltime 4 standard claims provided as follows:

> "41(a) This charter shall be construed and the relations between the parties determined in accordance with the laws of England. (b) Any dispute arising under this charter shall be decided by the English Courts to whose jurisdiction the parties hereby agree. See also LMAA Arbitration Clause. See additional Clause 48. (c) Notwithstanding the foregoing, but without prejudice to any party's right to arrest or maintain the arrest of any maritime property, either party may, by giving written notice of election to the other party, elect to have any such dispute referred to the arbitration of a single arbitrator in London in accordance with the provisions of the Arbitration Act 1950, or any statutory modification or re-enactment thereof for the time being in force."

19 The relevant part of the LMAA arbitration clause provided:

> "48. LMAA Arbitration Clause. All disputes or differences arising out of this contract which cannot be amicably resolved shall be referred to arbitration in London. Unless the parties agree upon a sole arbitrator, one arbitrator to be appointed by each party .. This contract is governed and construed by English law both in regards to substance and procedure, and there shall apply to all proceedings under this Clause the terms of the London [Maritime] Arbitrators Association current at the time when the arbitration proceedings were commenced ..."

20 The references to "owners and charterers" and to two arbitrators to be appointed by "the parties hereto" in the NYPE form are thus expressly inconsistent with the brokers being obliged to utilise that arbitration agreement in order to enforce their rights to commission: the only parties being obliged or entitled to arbitrate are the owners and charterers; similarly the reference in the Shelltime 4 clause to "either party" is a reasonably clear indication that its application is confined to disputes between owners and charterers.

21 It is accepted by Miss Philippa Hopkins, on behalf of Cleaves, that the brokers were not parties to the arbitration agreements as a matter of construction of those clauses. Her case is that the effect of s. 8 of the 1999 Act is to impose the arbitration clauses on the owners and the brokers as the means of enforcement of the commission benefit conferred by the commission clause. I shall have to consider this submission more fully when I come to discuss the effect of s. 8. However, for the purposes of the submission in relation to absence of intention to confer a benefit, the wording of the arbitration clauses is, in my judgment, of little or no materiality. Firstly, although the parties to the charter-parties clearly expressed their mutual intention that their disputes should be arbitrated, that mutual intention is entirely consistent with a mutual intention that the brokers should be obliged to recover their commission by court action rather than by arbitration. Secondly, if, on the proper construction of the 1999 Act, the third party is obliged to enforce the commission benefit by arbitration, even where the agreement does not on its proper construction provide for any participants in an arbitration other than the parties to the main contract, identification of the intention to be imputed to the parties as to enforceability of the third party commission benefit clearly has to take this into account. That is to say, if, as a matter of law, it makes no difference to the broker's ability to enforce his right to commission benefit that no express provision is made for this in the arbitration agreement, the strength of any inference derived from the absence of such express provision could be little more than negligible.

22 Secondly, it is argued by Mr Ashcroft on behalf of Nisshin that there is no positive indication in the charter-parties that the parties did intend the brokers to have enforceable rights. There is no suggestion in those contracts that the owners and charterers were mutually in agreement that the brokers should be entitled to claim against the owners as if they were parties to the contract.

23 It is to be noted that s. 1(2) of the 1999 Act does not provide that sub-s. 1(b) is disapplied unless on a proper construction of the contract it appears that the parties intended that the benefit term should be enforceable by the third party. Rather it provides that sub-s. 1(b) is disapplied if, on a proper construction, it appears that the parties did not intend third party enforcement. In other words, if the contract is neutral on this question, sub-s. (2) does not disapply sub-s. 1(b). Whether the contract does express a mutual intention that the third party should not be entitled to enforce the benefit conferred on him or is merely neutral is a matter of construction having regard to all relevant circumstances. The purpose and background of the Law Commission's recommendations in relation to sub-s. (2) are explained in a paper by Professor Andrew Burrows who, as a member of the Law Commission, made a major contribution to the drafting of the bill as enacted. He wrote at [2000] L.M.C.L.Q. 540 at p. 544:

> "The second test therefore uses a rebuttable presumption of intention. In doing so, it copies the New Zealand Contracts (Privity) Act 1982, s. 4, which has used the same approach. It is this rebuttable presumption that provides the essential balance between sufficient certainty for contracting parties and the flexibility required for the reform to deal fairly with a huge range of different situations. The presumption is based on the idea that, if you ask yourself, 'When is it that parties are likely to have intended to confer rights on a third party to enforce a term, albeit that they have not expressly conferred that right', the answer will be: 'Where the term purports to confer a benefit on an expressly identified third party'. That then sets up the presumption. But the presumption can be rebutted if, as

a matter of ordinary contractual interpretation, there is something else indicating that the parties did not intend such a right to be given."

24 In the present case, apart from Mr Ashcroft's third point, the charterparties are indeed neutral in the sense that they do not express any intention contrary to the entitlement of the brokers to enforce the commission term.

25 Thirdly, Mr Ashcroft submits that the parties' mutual intention on the proper construction of the contracts was to create a trust of a promise in favour of the brokers – a trust enforceable against the owners at the suit of the charterers as trustees. That being the proper construction of the contracts by reference to the state of the law at the time when the 1999 Act came into force, the very same contract wording did not, subsequently to that, evidence a different mutual intention. Accordingly, the mutual intention evidenced by the contracts was that the enforcement of the promise to pay commission would be at the suit of the charterers who must be joined by the brokers as co-claimants.

26 The starting point for consideration of this point is *Les Affreteurs Reunis S.A. v. Leopold Walford (London) Ltd.*, [1919] AC 801. The House of Lords in that case confirmed the decision in *Robertson v. Wait*, (1853) 8 Ex. 299. In relation to that authority Lord Birkenhead LC said this at pp. 806-807:

> "My Lords, so far as I am aware, that case has not before engaged the attention of this House, and I think it right to say plainly that I agree with that decision and I agree with the reasoning, shortly as it is expressed, upon which the decision was founded. In this connection I would refer to the well-known case of *In re Empress Engineering Company*. In the judgment of Sir George Jessel MR the principle is examined which, in my view, underlies and is the explanation of the decision in *Robertson v. Wait*. The Master of the Rolls uses this language: 'So, again, it is quite possible that one of the parties to the agreement may be the nominee or trustee of the third person. As Lord Justice James suggested to me in the course of the argument, a married woman may nominate somebody to contract on her behalf, but then the person makes the contract really as trustee for somebody else, and it is because he contracts in that character that the cestui que trust can take the benefit of the contract.'
>
> It appears to me plain that for convenience, and under long established practice, the broker in such cases, in effect, nominates the charterer to contract on his behalf, influenced probably by the circumstance that there is always a contract between charterer and owner in which this stipulation, which is to enure to the benefit of the broker, may very conveniently be inserted. In these cases the broker, on ultimate analysis, appoints the charterer to contract on his behalf. I agree therefore with the conclusion arrived at by all the learned judges in *Robertson v. Wait*, that in such cases charterers can sue as trustees on behalf of the broker."

27 Viscount Finlay and Lords Atkinson and Wrenbury adopted identical reasoning.

28 Accordingly, the position in 1853 and 1919 was that when a charter-party was entered into and incorporated a term that the owners could pay commission to the brokers the only means of enforcement of that promise was an action by the charterers and the brokers as co-plaintiff because, the charterer having contracted for commission on behalf of the broker, once the contract had been signed, the charterer became trustee of the broker's right to recover that commission, the broker being unable to enforce the promise direct and without the charterer's intervention because he was not a party to the contract and therefore had no cause of action available to him against the owner. With regard to this trustee relationship it could then be said that when the charter-party was entered into neither owners nor charterers contemplated that the brokers could sue the owners direct.

29 What is the position arising from the contract itself following the coming into force of the 1999 Act? As a matter of analysis of the underlying relationship between the parties, it must

be precisely the same. Thus, the charterer is no less the trustee of the owners' promise to pay the commission, having regard to the fact that the charterer contracts for payment of the commission on behalf of a non-contracting party. Indeed, the only thing that has changed is the coming into force of the 1999 Act and the introduction of the statutory facility of a direct right of action for a non-contracting party on whom a contract purports to confer a benefit.

30 Accordingly, the argument advanced by the owners can only succeed if it is to be inferred from the existence of the underlying trustee relationship that it was the mutual intention of owners and charterers that the broker beneficiary should not be entitled to avail himself of the facility of direct action by the 1999 Act.

31 This proposition is, in my judgment, entirely unsustainable. The fact that prior to the 1999 Act it would be the mutual intention that the only available facility for enforcement would be deployed by the broker does not lead to the conclusion that, once an additional statutory facility for enforcement had been introduced, the broker would not be entitled to use it, but would instead be confined to the use of the pre-existing procedure. Indeed, quite apart from the complete lack of any logical basis for such an inference, the very cumbersome and inconvenient nature of the procedure based on the trustee relationship (described by Lord Wright as a "cumbrous fiction") would point naturally to the preferred use by the broker of the right to sue directly provided by the 1999 Act. Not only would that original procedure be inconvenient, but it might involve risk that the broker would be prevented from recovering his commission, for example, in a case where the charterer had been dissolved in its place of incorporation or where, in the absence of co-operation by the charterer, proceedings had to be served on it outside the jurisdiction and service could not be effected. There are therefore very strong grounds pointing against any mutual intention to confine the brokers to the old procedure and to deny them the right to rely on the Act.

32 I therefore reject the third ground relied upon by Nisshin. In so doing I reach the same conclusion as the arbitrators.

33 It follows that Cleaves are entitled to enforce the commission clauses in their own right by reason of s. 1 of the 1999 Act.

Is the enforcement of those rights subject to the arbitration agreements in the charter-parties?

34 It is conceded by Ms Hopkins that, given that the arbitration agreements are between and only between owners and charterers, they do not confer rights or impose obligations on the brokers unless the effect of s. 8 of the 1999 Act is to deem the brokers to be bound by and entitled to the benefit of the arbitration clauses for the specific purpose of enforcement against the owners of their entitlement to commission.

36 Section 8 of the Act has an unusual legislative history. Although the text of the bill originally recommended by the Law Commission included s. 1(4) and so reflected the principle of conditional benefit, there was no provision dealing expressly with arbitration. The Report excluded its application to arbitration agreements. When the bill was first introduced before the House of Lords it contained no specific provision as to arbitration. The background to the addition of s. 8 is described by Professor Burrows in his most helpful article on the Act at Lloyd's Maritime and Commercial Law Quarterly, [2000] p. 540. Eventually, s. 8 was introduced by way of Government amendment at the Report stage in the House of Commons. The Lord Chancellor's Department issued Explanatory Notes which were made available to members of Parliament and peers before the debates. In respect of s. 8 those Notes contained the following advice:

> "33. Section 8 ensures that, where appropriate, the provisions of the Arbitration Act 1996 apply in relation to third party rights under this Act. Without this section, the main provisions of the Arbitration Act 1996 would not apply because a third party is not a party to the arbitration agreement between the promisor and the promisee.
> 34. Subsection (1) deals with what is likely to be the most common situation. The third

party's substantive right (for example, to payment by the promisor) is conferred subject to disputes being referred to arbitration (see s. 1(4)). This section is based on a 'conditional benefit' approach. It ensures that a third party who wishes to take action to enforce his substantive right is not only able to enforce effectively his right to arbitrate, but is also 'bound' to enforce his right by arbitration (so that, for example, a stay of proceedings can be ordered against him under s. 9 of the Arbitration Act 1996). This approach is analogous to that applied to assignees who may be prevented from unconscionably taking a substantive benefit free of its procedural burden (see, for example, *DVA v. Voest Alpine, The Jay Bola* [1997] 2 Lloyd's Rep. 279). 'Disputes ... relating to the enforcement of the substantive term by the third party' is intended to have a wide ambit and to include disputes between the third party (who wishes to enforce the term) and the promisor as to the validity, interpretation, existence or performance of the term; the third party's entitlement to enforce the term; the jurisdiction of the arbitral tribunal; or the recognition and enforcement of an arbitration award. But to avoid imposing a 'pure' burden on the third party, it does not cover, for example, a separate dispute in relation to a tort claim by the promisor against the third party for damages.

35. Subsection (2) is likely to be of rarer application. It deals with situations where the third party is given a right to arbitrate under s. 1 but the 'conditional benefit' approach underpinning subs. (1) is inapplicable. For example, where the contracting parties give the third party a unilateral right to arbitrate or a right to arbitrate a dispute other than one concerning a right conferred on the third party under s. (1). To avoid imposing a pure burden on the third party (in a situation where, for example, the contracting parties give the third party a right to arbitrate a tort claim made by the promisor against the third party) the subsection requires the third party to have chosen to exercise the right. The timing point at the end of the subsection is designed to ensure that a third party who chooses to exercise his right to go to arbitration by, for example, applying for a stay of proceedings under s. 9 of the Arbitration Act 1996, can do so. Under s. 9 of the Arbitration Act 1996, the right to apply for a stay of proceedings can only be exercised by someone who is already a party to the arbitration agreement."

37 Although these Notes clearly do not have the force of law, they occupy a position in relation to the Act similar to that of the statement by a minister introducing a bill. The courts are entitled to construe the wording of the Act on the assumption that, if the precise meaning of the words used is in doubt, when Parliament enacted those words it did so with some regard to the ministerial explanation.

38 The reference in the Explanatory Notes to the decision of the Court of Appeal in *The Jay Bola* [1997] 2 Lloyd's Rep. 279 and to the approach of s. 8(1) being "analogous to that applied to assignees who may be prevented from unconscionably taking a substantive benefit free of its procedural burden" is of some importance. It is quite clearly directed to the meaning to be given to the words "a right under section 1... is *subject to* an arbitration agreement" (emphasis added).

39 The introduction into these Notes of the assignment analogy directs attention to the concept that under the contract the promisee could not enforce the substantive term unless he had resort to arbitration if the scope of the agreement to arbitrate were wide enough to cover the dispute about such enforcement. Once the latter condition is satisfied an assignee from the promisee stands in the shoes of the promisee as regards enforcement of that term.
...

42 It is against this background that one must consider the words in sub-s. (1) "... the third party shall be treated for the purposes of that Act as a party to the arbitration agreement ...". In my judgment these words clearly reflect and are entirely consistent with the assignment analogy. The third party never was expressed to be a party to the arbitration agreement but, in view of the fact that he has in effect become a statutory assignee of the promisee's right of action against the promisor and because, by reason of the underlying policy of the 1999 Act

expressed in s. 1(4) he is confined to the means of enforcement provided by the contract to the promisee, namely arbitration, he is to be treated as standing in the shoes of that promisee for the purpose only of the enforcement of the substantive term. Thus although the wording of sub-s. (1)(a) – "is subject to a term" – is capable of having a range of possible meanings, one of those meanings is that which I have described and, having regard to the further words of the sub-section, entirely reflects the assignment analogy referred to in the Explanatory Notes

44 Since, as I have held, the scope of the disputes covered by all nine arbitration agreements is wide enough to embrace a dispute between owners and charterers about payment of the brokers' commission, I conclude that in the present case Cleaves were entitled and, indeed, obliged to refer those disputes to arbitration and that the arbitrators had jurisdiction to determine them.

NOTES AND QUESTIONS

1. Prior to the 1999 Act, by what reasoning had third party chartering brokers been held entitled to payment of commission? Was that reasoning artificial? See above, 476.
2. In holding that the second test of enforceability was satisfied, the most difficult argument facing Colman J was that, as the contract had not provided for arbitration by the third party, so the parties could not have intended the third party to have a right of enforceability. The contracting parties could only have intended either a right of enforceability by arbitration (which they had not) or no right of enforceability at all. Colman J rejected that argument at [21] by accepting that the parties could have intended the third party to have a right of enforceability by court action. In any event, in the second part of the judgment, he went on to hold that the third party, by reason of section 8 of the 1999 Act, *did* have the right to enforce payment of the commission by arbitration (and indeed was bound to do so, applying the 'conditional benefit' analysis).
3. Colman J's interpretation of section 8(1) (and 1(4)) is to be supported. Where one is relying on the second test of enforceability, which rests on implied intention, a clause referring disputes to arbitration can be presumed to be intended to apply to enforceability by the third party unless, on a true construction of the contract, the parties had the contrary intention. There was no such contrary intention here. However, while assignment was a useful analogy to make in this context, that analogy must not be pushed too far because the 1999 Act does not make the third party a statutory assignee of the promisee's right of action. The basis of the Act (see below, 521) is that the third party is given an independent right separate from that of the promisee.

Laemthong International Lines Company Ltd v Artis,
The Laemthong Glory (No 2)
[2005] EWCA Civ 519, [2005] 1 Lloyd's Rep 688, Court of Appeal

By a contractual letter of indemnity (LOI) given by the receivers (ie buyers) of sugar to the charterers of the ship carrying the sugar, the receivers promised to indemnify the charterers against loss sustained by them. Under clause 1 of the letter of indemnity, the promise was to indemnify the charterers and their 'servants and agents' against loss caused by releasing the goods without the bill of lading. Under clause 3 the promise was to provide security for the ship's release, and to indemnify the charterers against loss caused, if the ship was arrested in connection with the delivery of the cargo. The ship was arrested by a bank for non-payment to it in relation to the cargo. The question at issue was whether the third party shipowners could enforce clause 3 of the letter of indemnity given by the receivers to the charterers. In dismissing an appeal from Cooke J, the Court of Appeal held that, applying section 1 of the 1999 Act, they could.

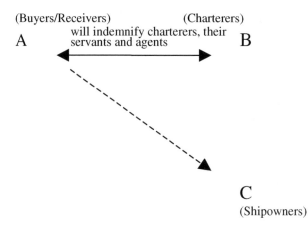

(Buyers/Receivers)   (Charterers)

will indemnify charterers, their

A   servants and agents   B

C

(Shipowners)

For key see 462.

Clarke LJ (giving the judgment of himself, **Sir Andrew Morritt V-C** and **Neuberger LJ**):

22 It is common ground that two issues potentially arise under section 1. In order to satisfy the section, the claimant must show that the term of the contract relied upon purports to confer a benefit upon him. If the claimant succeeds in showing that the term purports to confer a benefit upon him, he is entitled to enforce the term directly against the defendant unless the defendant persuades the court that the parties did not intend the term to be enforceable by him: see *Nisshin Shipping Co Ltd v Cleaves & Co Ltd,* [2004] 1 Lloyd's Rep 38, per Mr Justice Colman.

The first issue

24 The owners' case is that each of the terms of the receivers' LOI was for their benefit. They say that they were agents of the charterers for the limited purpose of delivering the cargo to the receivers. ...

27 ...The charterers needed the assistance of the owners because the only way they could procure the delivery of the cargo to the receivers was through the owners or, to put it another way and in ordinary language, through the agency of the owners. The owners were accordingly the agents of the charterers for the purpose of complying with the receivers' request in the receivers' LOI, namely to deliver the cargo to them under the receivers' LOI, and were thus properly to be regarded as falling within the category of "agents" whom the receivers promised to indemnify in clause 1 of the LOI.

28 The owners' case is as straightforward as that and, as we read his judgment, the Judge accepted it as both simple and correct. ...

45 The Judge expressed his conclusions with regard to clause 3 in these terms:

> "41. It was suggested that cl. 3 might fall into a different category. Clause 3 makes provision for two different types of obligation. First the provision of bail, or surety, or security, in order to release the ship; and secondly, for an indemnity to the addressee. The context of the clause is, however, 'the ship and any other ship in the same or associated ownership', so that attention is immediately directed to the owners of the ship who, as already mentioned, are the party with the primary liability to deliver and against whom proceedings would normally be taken. ...
> 42. Although there is no reference to 'servants or agents' in cl. 3, the clause plainly purports to confer a benefit, namely the release of the vessel, which is primarily a benefit to the owners and only secondarily a benefit to the charterers in respect of any liability which they may have to the owners. The wording of the indemnity in cl. 3 must, in my judgment, be taken to be commensurate with that in cl. 1. And although there is no express reference to 'servants or agents', it is plain that the indemnity must operate in the same way, and so the difference in wording adds nothing to the arguments advanced by charterers. ...
> 44. Clause 3 not only has to be read in the context of the letter of indemnity as a whole, which is to benefit the owners or their agents, but also on its own terms it purports to confer benefit both on charterers and owners."

We entirely agree with the conclusions and reasoning of the judge in those paragraphs.

48 In all these circumstances, we have reached the clear conclusion...that the Judge was right in holding that the terms of the receivers' LOI relied upon by the owners purport to confer a benefit upon the owners within the meaning of s. 1(1)(b) of the 1999 Act, essentially for the reasons he gave...

The second issue

49 The second issue is whether the Judge was right to hold that the receivers had failed to discharge the burden of showing that the parties did not intend the terms of the receivers' LOI to be enforceable by the third party. It is plain that there is a considerable overlap between the considerations relevant to this question and those relevant to the first issue.

50 Mr Berry [counsel for the receivers] submitted that the Judge was wrong to reach the conclusion he did. He relied in particular upon the fact that there was here a chain of LOIs (albeit a short chain) in the sense that the charterers provided an LOI to the owners and the receivers in turn provided an LOI to the charterers. The owners could have but did not ask for an LOI directly from the receivers. The result was that the parties all proceeded on the express basis that the owners' contractual rights against and obligations to the charterers were contained in the charter-party and in the charterers' LOI, which was provided under cl. 42 of the charter-party. The owners had contractual obligations to the indorsees of the bills of lading, namely the Yemen Bank, to whom they had been indorsed by the shippers. They would no doubt have owed such obligations to the receivers if and when they became indorsees or holders of the bills of lading but that had not happened by the time of the relevant events. By contrast the rights and obligation of the charterers and the receivers as between themselves were contained in the contract for the sale of the sugar and in the receivers' LOI.

51 Mr Berry submitted that the chain of contracts in this case is similar to the chain of contracts common in the construction industry to which the Law Commission referred in par. 7.18 of its Report No. 242 where it considered the proposed 1999 Act. In that paragraph, having observed that the parties can of course include an express clause, the Commission said:

> "But to allay the fears of the construction industry we should clarify that, even if there is no express contracting out of our proposed reform, we do not see our second limb [ie what became s. 1(2)] as cutting across the chain of sub-contracts that have traditionally been a feature of that industry. For example, we do not think that in normal circumstances an owner would be able to sue a sub-contractor for breach of the latter's contract with the head-contractor. This is because, even if the sub-contractor has promised to confer a benefit on the expressly designated owner, the parties have deliberately set up a chain of contracts which are well understood in the construction industry as ensuring that a party's remedies lie against the other contracting party only. In other words, for breach of the promisor's obligation, the owners' remedies lie against the head-contractor who in turn has the right to sue the sub-contractor. On the assumption that that deliberately created chain of liability continues to thrive subsequent to our reform, our reform would not cut across it because on a proper construction of the contract – construed in the light of the surrounding circumstances (that is, the existence of the connected head-contract and the background practice and understanding of the construction industry) – the contracting parties (for example, the sub-contractor and the head-contractor) did not intend the third party to have the right of enforceability. Rather the third party's rights of enforcement in relation to the promised benefit were intended to lie against the head-contractor only and not against the promisor. For similar reasons we consider that the second limb of our test would not normally give a purchaser of goods from a retailer a right to sue the manufacturer (rather than the retailer) for breach of contract as regards the quality of the goods."

52 Mr Berry submitted that similar considerations apply to the chain of LOIs here. He recognised that this was not a chain of quite the kind which commonly exists in the construction industry but he drew attention to the fact that the report referred to chains of sale contracts and submitted that chains of charter-parties are common in the maritime industry, as for example a time charter, a sub-time charter, a voyage charter and a sub-voyage charter, and that similar considerations should apply both to them and to these two LOIs. His essential point was that, as in the case of other chain contracts, the parties had expressly set up the contractual arrangements as described above, namely between the owners and the charterers and between the charterers and the receivers.

53 The Judge did not accept those submissions when they were made to him. In para. 45 of his judgment he referred to the two examples of chains in the Law Commission Report, said that the contents of the Report did not assist the receivers any more under this head than they had done under s. 1(1)(a) of the 1999 Act, and added:

> "Those situations are well-known and provide a commercial background of practice to contracts which are unlikely to cut across the legal framework customarily employed. Here there is no such background. Letters of indemnity take a number of different forms and have given rise to a wealth of arguments between parties as to their terms. Each has to be construed according to its own terms."

54 We agree with the Judge. We say nothing about the position on the case of a chain of charter-parties but we agree that there is no tradition of chain LOIs similar to the examples given in the report. All depends upon the construction of the receivers' LOI. The reasons we have given in reaching our conclusion under the first issue also point to the correct resolution of this issue. If we are right in agreeing with the judge that both cll. 1 and 3 of the LOI were intended to be for the benefit of the owners, it makes no sense to hold that it was nevertheless intended that the receivers' liability should not be directly to the owners. For example, as pointed out earlier, it was the owners who needed the benefit of cl. 3 in order to secure the release of the vessel from arrest. They needed the bail or other security, not the charterers. We see nothing in the LOI to lead to the conclusion that the parties did not intend cll. 1 and 3 to be enforceable by the owners. The whole purpose of the receivers' LOI was on the one hand to ensure that the receivers received the cargo from the ship without production of the original bills of lading and on the other hand to ensure that the owners were fully protected from the consequences of arrest or other action which might be taken by the holders of the original bills of lading. In short, in our judgment, the Judge was correct on this second issue as well as the first.

Conclusion

55 For these reasons the appeal must be dismissed.

NOTES AND QUESTIONS

1. In deciding that the letter of indemnity purported to confer a benefit upon the shipowners, the term 'agents' was construed as referring to the shipowners. Although not mentioned, this also satisfied the need under section 1(3) for the shipowners to be expressly identified (the identification here being 'by class').
2. The charterers had also given a direct letter of indemnity to the shipowners. There was therefore a chain of contracts. Why did the Court of Appeal think that that chain of contracts, in contrast to the commonplace chain of contracts in a construction project, did not rebut the presumption under section 1(1)(b)?
3. There has been one other noteworthy case on the 1999 Act. In *Avraamides v Colwill* [2006] EWCA Civ 1533, A agreed to 'pay any liabilities properly incurred' by B. C, to whom B (now insolvent) had a liability, was held unable to claim from A under the second test of enforceability. This was not least because C had not been *expressly* identified as required by section 1(3) of the Act.

(2) Variation and Rescission by the Contracting Parties

Section 2(1) sets up a default position. By this, if the third party has a right of enforceability under section 1, the contracting parties cannot take away that right, without the third party's consent, by subsequently varying or rescinding the contract by agreement once the 'crystallisation point' (as the Law Commission called it) has been reached. That point is where the third party has communicated his assent to the term to the promisor (section 2(1)(a)) or has relied on that term and the promisor knew of that reliance or ought reasonably to have foreseen it (section 2(1)(b) and (c)).

The justification for that default position is that, where the third party has communicated its assent or relied, the injustice to the third party, in disappointing its expectations of having a right of enforceability, outweighs the importance of respecting the contracting parties' changed intentions.

However, that is a default position only. By section 2(3) the contracting parties can expressly agree in the contract that the third party's right is more or less secure than under the default position. Under section 2(3)(a) the third party's right can be made less secure by expressly providing that the third party's consent is never needed prior to rescission or variation. Under section 2(3)(b) the third party's right can be made more secure by expressly providing that the third party's consent is always needed for rescission or variation irrespective of the third party's communication of assent or reliance.

The one minor qualification on the above is that, where the third party's consent is, or may be, required, a court or arbitral tribunal has a discretion under section 2(4)–(7) to authorise variation or rescission without the need for the third party's consent. This discretion is conferred in very limited circumstances to avoid the contracting parties being unreasonably locked in to a contract that they cannot escape from. The limited circumstances are where the third party cannot reasonably be found (section 2(4)(a)) or where the third party is mentally incapable of giving consent (section 2(4)(b)) or where it cannot be reasonably ascertained whether the third party has relied on the term (section 2(5)).

(3) Defences Available to the Promisor

These are covered by section 3. Although the basic ideas underpinning this section are relatively straightforward, the drafting is extremely complex. One can strongly argue that much of the complexity could have been avoided by leaving some of these matters to the general law. There are four main points:

(i) Most importantly, the default position, as laid down in section 3(2), is that defences that would have been available to the promisor had the promisee been suing are also available as defences to the third party's action (provided the defence arises from or in connection with the contract and is relevant to the term the third party is seeking to enforce). This can be illustrated by two examples:

(a) Where a contract is void or unenforceable or has been discharged for breach or frustration it cannot be enforced by the third party any more than it could have been by the promisee.

(b) A and B contract that B will sell goods to A but that A will pay the contract price to C. In breach of contract, B delivers to A goods that are not of the quality contracted for. In an action for the price by C against A, A is able to abate the price (ie to reduce or extinguish the price) by reason of the damages for breach of contract (just as A would have been able to do in an action for the price by B).

(ii) By section 3(3), the parties can depart from the above default position by an express term whereby the range of defences is expanded so that a defence does not need to arise from or in connection with the contract. This can be illustrated by the following example. A and B contract that A will pay C if B transfers his car to A. B owes A money under a different contract. A and B agree to an express term in the contract which provides that A can raise against a claim by C the set-off (which may be a partial or total defence) arising from that other contract which A would have had in an action by B.

(iii) By section 3(5), the parties can depart from the above default position by an express term whereby the range of defences is narrowed. This can be illustrated as follows. B agrees with A to purchase a painting, the painting to be delivered by A to C, who is expressly given a right to enforce the delivery obligation. B is also bound to pay A considerable sums for other art works purchased under the same contract. B wishes to ensure that C's right is not affected by the agreement in relation to those other art works. A and B expressly agree that A may not raise against C defences (eg set-offs) relating to those other art works that would have been available to A in an action by B.

(iv) Section 3(4) is a clarificatory provision dealing with defences and counter-claims that are specific to the third party ie that would not have been available to the promisor in an action by the promisee. It lays down, as would be the obvious position under the general law in any event, that those defences and counterclaims that are specific to the third party apply. Say, for example, A contracts with B to pay C £1000. C already owes A £600. By section 3(4), A has a set-off to C's claim so that A is only bound to pay C £400. But again this is a default position only and while it cannot be widened (it is already as wide as it could be) section 3(5) allows the parties by an express term to narrow it. So in the above example, A and B may include an express term that any defence or counterclaim that A would otherwise have had against C shall not apply in relation to the exercise of C's right under the 1999 Act. C would then be able to assert its right to payment of £1000 from A free of A's defence or counterclaim relating to the £600.

(4) Promisee's Rights

By section 4, a promisee retains its rights to sue on the contract even though it is also enforceable by the third party. The third party's right is, therefore, additional to, and does not replace, the promisee's rights: nor is there a statutory assignment of the promisee's rights to the third party (albeit that the *analogy* of assignment has proved useful in interpreting section 8 of the Act: see the *Nisshin* case, above, 508).

A consequence of section 4 is that, prima facie, the promisor may face unacceptable double liability (ie being liable to pay substantial damages to both the promisee and the third party for the same loss). Section 5 seeks to remove that objection by enabling the court to reduce the third party's award to take account of a sum recovered (in relation to the same loss) by the promisee.

It should be noted, however, that section 5(a) appears to have been rendered unnecessary by the subsequent decision of the majority of the House of Lords in *Alfred McAlpine v Panatown* (above, 491). That subsection was concerned to cover *The Albazero* exception where a promisee can recover the third party's loss (above, 491, note 1). But in *Alfred McAlpine* it was laid down that that exception does not apply where a third party has its own contractual right against the promisor: and, of course, that is precisely what is given to the third party under the 1999 Act.

(5) Exclusions from the Act

By section 6, certain types of contract are excluded from the operation of the Act. This is primarily because, in relation to some types of contract, statute has already conferred third party rights in a way that would clash with the conferral of third party rights under the 1999 Act. So by section 6(1), contracts on a bill of exchange, promissory note or other negotiable instrument are excluded. Here third party rights are conferred under the Bills of Exchange Act 1882. By section 6(5)(a) contracts for the carriage of goods by sea, governed by the Carriage of Goods by Sea Act 1992, are excluded; as, by section 6(5)(b), are contracts for the international carriage of goods by road, rail or air, where the relevant statutes conferring third party rights are those giving force to various international transport conventions.

It is important to notice, however, that there is an exception to the exclusion in section 6(5) so that exemption clauses in contracts for the carriage of goods by sea, or for the international carriage of goods by road, rail or air, *do* fall within the 1999 Act. As we have seen (above, 477–482) the enforcement of such clauses by third parties has created serious problems for the common law, and allowing third parties to use the 1999 Act would not clash with the third party regime laid down in other statutes. So by reason of the exception in section 6(5), a Himalaya clause would be rendered straightforwardly enforceable by an expressly identified third party without the need to rely on the complex reasoning used in, eg, *The Eurymedon* (above, 477).

There are two other types of contracts excluded from the operation of the 1999 Act. Neither exclusion was recommended by the Law Commission and instead reflected particular policy concerns voiced by the Department of Trade and Industry. By section 6(2), the contract that comprises the memorandum and articles of a company (and is binding by reason of section 14 of the Companies Act 1985) cannot confer third party rights under the 1999 Act (so that, eg, third party non-members cannot be given rights to sue). (Analogously, by section 6(2A) limited liability partnership agreements have also been excluded.) And by section 6(3), contracts of employment (and analogous contracts) cannot confer rights on third parties (eg customers of the employer) to enforce the contract against an employee or other worker.

(6) Existing Exceptions

Section 7(1) makes clear that existing statutory and common law exceptions to privity are preserved (for these exceptions, see above, 473–482). The Law Commission anticipated that some of the more artificial exceptions would wither away. We have seen a good example of this in the *Nisshin* case, above, 508. Prior to the 1999 Act, the common law allowed a third party chartering broker to enforce a promise of commission by fictitiously finding an intention by the contracting parties to create a trust of the promise. Under the 1999 Act, reliance on that strained exception to privity is rendered unnecessary as the chartering broker will straightforwardly have third party rights under the second test of enforceability.

The relationship with the existing exceptions is, perhaps, best understood if one recognises, as the Law Commission stressed at paragraph 13.2 of its Report, that the 1999 Act does not *abolish* privity. Rather it creates a new very wide-ranging exception which sits alongside, and renders it unnecessary to rely on some of, the existing exceptions.

(7) The Relationship with the Unfair Contract Terms Act 1977

Say a third party is given a right under the 1999 Act but there is an exclusion or limitation clause in the contract (valid as between the promisor and promisee) which excludes or limits the promisor's contractual liability to the third party. Might that exclusion or limitation clause be struck down as unreasonable under the Unfair Contract Terms Act 1977? To ensure that the answer to this question is 'no'—which the Law Commission thought important in reassuring contracting parties that their intentions do govern—section 7(2) of the 1999 Act lays down that section 2(2) of UCTA 1977 does not apply in this situation. It was thought unnecessary to curtail the operation of any other section of UCTA or of the Unfair Terms in Consumer Contracts Regulations 1999 because they could not apply in any event where a third party is seeking to enforce its rights.

(8) The Meaning of 'Contract' under the 1999 Act

The term 'contract' was not defined in the 1999 Act. The better view is that, in accordance with our general understanding of what a contract is (see above, 3–4), it includes both simple contracts (contracts supported by consideration) and contracts made by deed. This is supported by section 7(3) of the 1999 Act in the references made to the Limitation Act 1980. If this is correct, it means, eg, that covenants to settle after-acquired property (raised in cases such as *Re Pryce* [1917] 1 Ch 234 and *Re Kay* [1939] Ch 329, considered in trusts courses and books) would now be affected, and the problems solved, by the 1999 Act.

6. EXCEPTIONS TO THE PRIVITY DOCTRINE ON ITS BURDEN SIDE

As we have explained above (461), there is good reason for the general rule being that burdens should not be imposed on third parties by contract. We have also noted that there are some well-established exceptions to this, eg agency (in the sense that a principal is bound by a contract concluded by his authorised agent with another party, even if the agent is undisclosed: see above, 475); and covenants concerning land (476). We here consider two further exceptions: bailment or sub-bailment on terms and burden running with goods.

(1) Bailment or Sub-bailment on Terms

Morris v C W Martin & Sons Ltd [1966] 1 QB 716, Court of Appeal

The claimant sent her mink stole to Mr Beder, a furrier, for cleaning. He did not do cleaning, so agreed with her to send the stole to the defendants for cleaning. By the terms of the contract between the defendants and Mr Beder, goods belonging to customers on the defendants' premises were held at the customer's risk and the defendants were not to be responsible for 'loss of or damage to the goods during processing'. The defendants' employee, who was supposed to clean the fur, in fact stole it. The claimant sued the defendants for the tort of conversion. The Court of Appeal held that the defendants were vicariously liable for the tortious conversion by their employee. It was further unanimously held that, even if the claimant was bound by the terms of the contract between the defendants and the furrier, the words did not, as a matter of construction, apply. But in important obiter dicta Lord Denning MR reasoned that, subject to the construction point, the claimant would have been bound by the terms of the contract, to which she was not a party, because she had impliedly consented to the sub-bailment on terms.

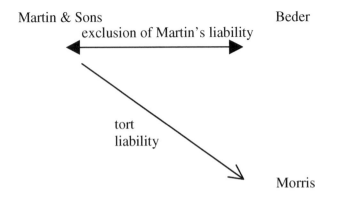

Is Morris bound by the exclusion of liability?

Lord Denning MR: Can the defendants rely, as against the plaintiff, on the exempting conditions although there was no contract directly between them and her? There is much to be said on each side. On the one hand, it is hard on the plaintiff if her just claim is defeated by exempting conditions of which she knew nothing and to which she was not a party. On the other hand, it is hard on the defendants if they are held liable to a greater responsibility than they agreed to undertake. As long ago as 1601 Lord Coke advised a bailee to stipulate specially that he would not be responsible for theft, see *Southcote's* case (1601) 4 Co.Rep. 83b, a case of theft by a servant. It would be strange if his stipulation was of no avail to him. The answer to the problem lies, I think, in this: the owner is bound by the conditions if he has expressly or impliedly consented to the bailee making a sub-bailment containing those conditions, but not otherwise. Suppose the owner of goods lets them out on hire, and the hirer sends them for repair, and the repairer holds them for a lien. The owner is bound by the lien because he impliedly consented to the repairs being done, since they were reasonably incidental to use of the car: see *Tappenden v. Artus* [1964] 2 Q.B. 185. So also if the owner of a ship accepts goods for carriage on a bill of lading containing exempting conditions (i.e., a "bailment upon terms") the owner of the goods (although not a party to the contract) is bound by those conditions if he impliedly consented to them as being in "the known and contemplated form," see the words of Lord Sumner in *Elder, Dempster & Co. v. Paterson, Zochonis & Co. Ltd.* [1924] A.C, 522, 564...

In this case the plaintiff agreed that Beder should send the fur to the defendants, and by so doing I think she impliedly consented to his making a contract for cleaning on the terms usually current in the trade. But when I come to study the conditions I do not think they are sufficient to protect the cleaners. We always construe such conditions strictly. Clause 9 applies only to "goods belonging to customers," that is, goods belonging to Beder, and not to goods belonging to his customers such as the plaintiff. The conditions themselves draw a distinction between "customer" and "his own customer," see clause 16. Clause 14 only applies to "the loss of or damage to the goods during processing." The loss here was not during processing. It was before or after processing.

Seeing that the conditions do not protect the defendants, I am of opinion that they are liable for the loss due to the theft by their servant.

Diplock and **Salmon LJJ** concurred on vicarious liability and construction of the terms but expressed no concluded view on Lord Denning's obiter dicta on sub-bailment on terms.

NOTES AND QUESTIONS

1. Bailment is the legal term used to describe the situation where one person (the bailee) is in possession of goods which belong to another (the bailor). It can arise in a wide range of ways. Eg the hirer of a car is a bailee, as is a dry-cleaner of clothes, as is a pledgee (eg a pawnbroker) of a watch, or the finder of another's ring. A bailee may owe contractual duties, as well as tortious duties, to the bailor. Although the best view is that this is an unnecessary complication, it is argued by some that there are duties owed 'in bailment' as if this were a cause of action separate from contract and tort.
2. One might have thought that 'implied consent' to be bound by particular terms would be sufficient in itself to form an exception to the burden side of privity. However, the courts have so far accepted this as an exception only in the context of a bailment of one's goods. Why is that?

KH Enterprise v Pioneer Container, The Pioneer Container
[1994] 2 AC 324, Privy Council

The claimants contracted with freight carriers for the carriage of their goods by sea from Taiwan to Hong Kong. That contract contained terms which allowed the carriers to sub-contract the carriage 'on any terms'. The carriers duly sub-contracted the carriage to the defendant shipowners. That sub-contract included an exclusive jurisdiction clause whereby disputes in relation to the carriage of the goods were to be exclusively determined in Taiwan. The ship was involved in a collision and all the claimants' goods on board were lost. The claimants commenced proceedings in Hong Kong seeking damages (in tort) against the defendant shipowners for the loss of the cargo. The defendants sought a stay of the proceedings arguing that the claimants were bound by the exclusive jurisdiction clause in the contract of carriage between the freight-carriers and the defendant shipowners so that the proceedings should have been commenced in Taiwan, not Hong Kong. This argument succeeded before the Court of Appeal of Hong Kong. In dismissing the appeal, the Privy Council held that the claimants were bound because they had consented to the terms of the sub-bailment.

Lord Goff of Chieveley (delivering the judgment of the Privy Council comprising himself, **Lord Lowry, Lord Slynn of Hadley, Lord Lloyd of Berwick** and **Sir Thomas Eichelbaum**): In *Morris v. C. W. Martin & Sons Ltd*. Lord Denning M.R. expressed his opinion on this point in clear terms, though on the facts of the case his opinion was obiter. He said, at p. 729: "The answer to the problem lies, I think, in this: the owner is bound by the conditions if he has expressly or impliedly consented to the bailee making a sub-bailment containing those conditions, but not otherwise."

...

In order to decide whether...to accept the principle so stated by Lord Denning M.R., it is necessary to consider the relevance of the concept of "consent" in this context. It must be assumed that, on the facts of the case, no direct contractual relationship has been created between the owner and the sub-bailee, the only contract created by the sub-bailment being that between the bailee and the sub-bailee. Even so, if the effect of the sub-bailment is that the sub-bailee voluntarily receives into his custody the goods of the owner and so assumes towards the owner the responsibility of a bailee, then to the extent that the terms of the sub-bailment are consented to by the owner, it can properly be said that the owner has authorised the bailee so to regulate the duties of the sub-bailee in respect of the goods entrusted to him, not only towards the bailee but also towards the owner. ...

Such a conclusion, finding its origin in the law of bailment rather than the law of contract, does not depend for its efficacy either on the doctrine of privity of contract or on the doctrine of consideration.

...

[O]nce it is recognised that the sub-bailee, by voluntarily taking the owner's goods into his custody, ipso facto becomes the bailee of those goods vis-à-vis the owner, it must follow that the owner's rights against the sub-bailee will only be subject to terms of the sub-bailment if he has consented to them, i.e., if he has authorised the bailee to entrust the goods to the sub-bailee on those terms. Such consent may, as Lord Denning pointed out, be express or implied...

NOTE

The importance of this case lies in its approval of Lord Denning's obiter dicta in *Morris v Martin*.

(2) Burden Running with Goods

Lord Strathcona Steamship Company Ltd v Dominion Coal Company Ltd
[1926] AC 108, Privy Council

The owners of a steamship, the *Lord Strathcona*, chartered her to the claimants (the Dominion Coal Co Ltd) for 10 successive seasons on the St Lawrence River from 1915, with an option to extend the charterparty for another five years. The ship was sold a couple of times before it was bought in 1920 by the defendants. The defendants had notice of the terms of the charterparty and had covenanted with the sellers to perform the obligations under it. However, the defendants refused to adhere to the charterparty for the 1920 season. The claimants sought a declaration that the defendants were bound to perform the charterparty and an injunction restraining the defendants from using the ship in any way that was inconsistent with the charterparty. The judge at first instance ordered that the injunction be granted, and this was upheld by the Supreme Court of Nova Scotia. In dismissing the defendants' appeal, the Privy Council held that the defendants were bound because the principle that applied to restrictive covenants over land could be applied by analogy to covenants in respect of goods.

Lord Shaw (giving the judgment of himself, **Viscount Haldane, Lord Wrenbury, Lord Carson** and **Lord Blanesburgh**): The proposal of the appellants and the argument submitted by them is to the effect that they are not bound to respect and carry forward this charterparty either in law or in equity, but that, upon the contrary, they can, in defiance of its terms, of which they had knowledge, use the vessel at their will in any other way. It is accordingly, when the true facts are shown, a very simple case raising the question of whether an obligation affecting the user of the subject of sale, namely, a ship, can be ignored by the purchaser so as to enable that purchaser, who has bought a ship notified to be not a free ship but under charter, to wipe out the condition of purchase and use the ship as a free ship. It was not bought or paid for as a free ship, but it is maintained that the buyer can thus extinguish the charterer's rights in the vessel, of which he had notice, and that the charterer has no means, legal or equitable, of preventing this in law.

In the opinion of the Board the case is ruled by *De Mattos v. Gibson*, 4 De G & J 276, also a shipping case, the case of the user of a piece of property by a third person (e.g., the respondent company in this case) of "the property for a particular purpose in a specified manner." Their Lordships think that the judgment of Knight Bruce L.J. at 282 plainly applies to the present case: "Reason and justice seem to prescribe that, at least as a general rule, where a man, by gift or purchase, acquires property from another, with knowledge of a previous contract, lawfully and for valuable consideration made by him with a third person, to use and employ the property for a particular purpose in a specified manner, the acquirer shall not to the material damage of the third person, in opposition to the contract and inconsistently with it, use and employ the property in a manner not allowable to the giver or seller." A principle, not without analogy, had previously been laid down in reference to the user of land.

In the opinion of their Lordships the case of *De Mattos v. Gibson* still remains, notwithstanding many observations and much criticism of it in subsequent cases, of outstanding authority.

The general character of the principle on which a Court of equity acts was explained in *Tulk v. Moxhay* (1848) 2 Ph. 774, 776, 779. The plaintiff there was owner in fee of Leicester Square, and several houses forming the Square. He sold the property to one Elms in fee, and the deed of conveyance contained a covenant obliging Elms, his heirs and assigns, to "keep and maintain the said piece of ground and Square Garden .... in its then form .... in an open state, uncovered with any buildings." Elms sold to others, and the property came into the hands of the defendant, who admitted that he had purchased with notice of the covenant. The defendant, "having manifested an intention to alter the character of the Square Garden, and asserted a right, if he thought fit, to build upon it," the plaintiff, who still remained owner of several houses in the Square, [successfully] filed a bill for an injunction. ...

It has sometimes been considered that *Tulk v. Moxhay* and *De Mattos v. Gibson* carried forward to and laid upon the shoulders of an alienee with notice the obligations of the alienor, and, therefore, that the former is liable to the covenantee in specific performance as by the law of contract, and under a species of implied privity. This is not so; the remedy is a remedy in equity by way of injunction against acts inconsistent with the covenant, with notice of which the land was acquired.

...

Tulk v. Moxhay is important for a further and vital consideration – namely, that it analyses the true situation of a purchaser who having bought upon the terms of the restriction upon free contract existing, thereafter when vested in the lands, attempts to divest himself of the condition under which he had bought: "it is said that the covenant being one which does not run with the land, this Court cannot enforce it; but the question is, not whether the covenant runs with the land, but whether a party shall be permitted to use the land in a manner inconsistent with the contract entered into by his vendor, and with notice of which he purchased. Of course, the price would be affected by the covenant, and nothing could be more inequitable than that the original purchaser should be able to sell the property the next day for a greater price, in consideration of the assignee being allowed to escape from the liability which he had himself undertaken."

In the opinion of the Board these views, much expressive of the justice and good faith of the situation, are still part of English equity jurisprudence, and an injunction can still be granted thereunder to compel, as in a court of conscience, one who obtains a conveyance or grant sub conditione from violating the condition of his purchase to the prejudice of the original contractor. Honesty forbids this; and a Court of equity will grant an injunction against it.

...

[T]he person seeking to enforce such a restriction must, of course, have, and continue to have, an interest in the subject matter of the contract. For instance, in the case of land he must continue to hold the land in whose favour the restrictive covenant was meant to apply. That was clearly the state of matters in the case of *Tulk v. Moxhay* applicable to the possession of real estate in Leicester Square. It was also clearly the case in *De Mattos v. Gibson*, in which the person seeking to enforce the injunction had an interest in the user of the ship. In short, in regard to the user of land or of any chattel, an interest must remain in the subject matter of the covenant before a right can be conceded to an injunction against the violation by another of the covenant in question.

...

[T]he present is, as has been seen, a case as to the user of a ship, with regard to the subject matter of which, namely, the vessel, the respondent has, and will have during the continuance of the period covered by the charterparty, a plain interest so long as she is fit to go to sea. Again, to adopt the language of Knight Bruce L.J. in the *De Mattos v. Gibson* case at 283: "Why should it (the Court) not prevent the commission or continuance of a breach of such a contract, when, its subject being valuable, as for instance, a trading ship or some costly machine, the original owner and possessor, or a person claiming under him, with notice and standing in his right, having the physical control of the chattel, is diverting it from the agreed object, that object being of importance to the other? A system of laws in which such a power does not exist must surely be very defective. I repeat that, in my opinion, the power does exist here."

...

If a man acquires from another rights in a ship which is already under charter, with notice of rights which required the ship to be used for a particular purpose and not inconsistently with it, then he appears to be plainly in the position of a constructive trustee with obligations which a Court of equity will not permit him to violate. It does not matter that this Court cannot enforce specific performance. It can proceed, if there is expressed or clearly implied a negative stipulation. ...

For the reasons already fully set forth the Board is of opinion that the injunction granted by Mellish J. in cl. 7 of his order of June 20, 1922, was correct, and was properly affirmed by the Supreme Court for the reasons set forth by Chisholm J. The fundamental point indicated is thus determined.

NOTES AND QUESTIONS

1.   While granting the injunction, the Privy Council accepted that it could not order specific performance requiring the defendant to perform the charterparty. For that tenuous distinction, see above, 448–457.

2.   Although this has been overlooked in some subsequent cases, the Privy Council appeared to go on to decide that the claimants were also entitled to damages

albeit that their assessment was remitted back to the Supreme Court of Nova Scotia.

3.   Arguably, the analogy with *Tulk v Moxhay* was misplaced. There the person seeking to enforce the restrictive covenant had acquired a proprietary interest in the land. But a time-charterer acquires no proprietary interest in the ship. What, then, was the precise basis for the granting of the injunction (and damages) against the defendants, given that there was no contract between the defendants and the claimants? Although not mentioned, might it be best explained as resting on the economic tort of wrongfully interfering with a claimant's contractual rights?

4.   In *Port Line Ltd v Ben Line Steamers Ltd* [1958] 2 QB 146 Diplock J had to decide who was entitled to compensation under a statutory scheme when a ship was requisitioned by the Crown. He held that, even if *Strathcona* was rightly decided, as it only entitled the time-charterer to an injunction and did not mean that the charterer had positive rights against the new owner, the time-charterer was not entitled to compensation under the terms of the statutory scheme. However, he expressed the firm view that, in any event, the *Strathcona* case was wrongly decided. This was essentially because a time-charterer, like a voyage charterer (and unlike a demise charterer), has no proprietary interest in the ship and, in his view, the basis for an injunction against the new owner of the ship, even one with notice of the charter, was therefore lacking. He said of the *Strathcona* case, at 168, 'The difficulty that I have found in ascertaining its ratio decidendi, the impossibility which I find of reconciling the actual decision with well-established principles of law, the unsolved and, to me, insoluble problems which that decision raises combine to satisfy me that it was wrongly decided.'

5.   If a charterer were to have proprietary rights in a ship, which is then sold to another, the buyer would take the ship subject to those proprietary rights. This would be to apply the standard law on proprietary rights (including the maxim *nemo dat quod non habet,* 'one cannot give what one does not have'). The primary causes of action protecting those with proprietary rights in goods against wrongful interference are the torts of conversion and trespass to goods.

Swiss Bank Corporation v Lloyds Bank Ltd
[1979] Ch 548, Chancery Division

The claimant bank agreed to loan money to Israel Financial Trust Ltd (IFT) for the purchase of securities in a new bank in Israel called First International Bank of Israel Ltd (FIBI). Under the terms of the loan, the FIBI securities were in effect to be used for the repayment of the loan to the claimant. In breach of that contract, IFT granted a charge over the FIBI securities to the defendant bank. The securities were sold by the defendant bank as charge-holder. The claimant now brought a claim, inter alia, for an injunction to restrain the defendant applying the proceeds of sale to satisfy IFT's debts owed to the defendant. It was held that, in order to restrain the tort of wrongful interference with another's contract, which was made out because the defendant bank's charge was invalid as illegal, that injunction should be granted.

But had the charge been valid, there would have been no tort committed because the defendant did not have actual knowledge of the claimant's rights when it became a charge-holder.

Browne-Wilkinson J: I can turn to the *De Mattos v. Gibson* principle itself. When that case was decided, it had already been recognised at common law that it was a legal wrong or tort for someone knowingly to interfere with the contractual rights of others: *Lumley v. Gye* (1853) 2 E. & B. 216. It has subsequently been established that equity will intervene to restrain such a tort and such jurisdiction is frequently exercised at the present day: see for example *Sefton v. Tophams Ltd.* [1965] Ch. 1140 as to the injunction against the second defendants. It follows that, if at the date of the Lloyds charge, Lloyds had had *actual* notice of the plaintiff's rights in relation to the F.I.B.I. securities and the plaintiff had been informed of I.F.T.'s intention to grant the Lloyds charge, the plaintiff could in my judgment have obtained an injunction restraining Lloyds from taking the charge since by so doing they would have been committing the tort. If Lloyds had taken the charge with actual knowledge of the plaintiff's rights – no injunction having been applied for in time because of the plaintiff's ignorance of what was going on – in my judgment Lloyds could not be in any better position. The taking of the charge with that state of knowledge being itself a tort by Lloyds could not put Lloyds in a better position just because the charge had been completed before the threat of the tort was known to the plaintiff: a man cannot rely on his own wrong.

...But Lloyds did not have actual notice of the plaintiff's rights when it took its charge and therefore committed no legal wrong by so doing since actual knowledge of the other contract is an essential ingredient of the tort. Having acquired its charge otherwise than by means of a legal wrong, I can see no ground in principle for saying that Lloyds is not entitled to rely on its rights under the charge as justification at the present time for applying the proceeds of the F.I.B.I. securities in paying its own secured debt, even though to Lloyds' knowledge that involves a breach of the contract between the plaintiff and I.F.T. To say, as [counsel for the claimant] urges, that a person acquiring a property right with constructive notice of a contract affecting it cannot rely on such property right to justify future interference with that contract is to introduce into the question "has a legal tort been committed?" equitable concepts of notice designed to regulate the priority of conflicting property interests. Unless there are compelling authorities requiring me to do so, I would not be prepared to bedevil the tort with such equitable refinements.

How then do the authorities stand? In *De Mattos v. Gibson,* 4 De G. & J. 276, the plaintiff had chartered a ship from its owner Curry. Curry had subsequently charged the ship to Gibson, who had actual notice of the charterparty. Curry got into financial difficulties and was unable to continue the voyage. Gibson was proposing to sell the ship of which he had taken possession. In the action the plaintiff claimed an injunction against Gibson restraining him from interfering with the charterparty. The plaintiff applied for an interim injunction which was granted, on appeal. ... [I]n my judgment the *De Mattos v. Gibson* principle is merely the equitable counterpart of the tort. But two points have to be emphasised about the decision in *De Mattos v. Gibson:* first, the ship was acquired with actual knowledge of the plaintiff's contractual rights; secondly, that no such injunction will be granted against the third party if it is clear that the original contracting party cannot in any event perform his contract. It is this second point which in my judgment accounts for the fact that the *De Mattos v. Gibson* principle is not applicable to restrictive covenants: the original contracting party – even if traceable – could not carry out his contract relating to the land or the chattel once he had parted with it.

...

There are parts of the judgment in the *Strathcona* case [1926] A.C. 108 which I find difficult to follow but in my judgment it certainly decides (a) that *De Mattos v. Gibson* is good law and (b) that an injunction can be granted to restrain a subsequent purchaser of a chattel from using it so as to cause a breach of a contract of which he has express notice.

In *Port Line Ltd. v. Ben Line Steamers Ltd.* [1958] 2 Q.B. 146, Diplock J. – sitting as a judge of first instance – stated that he thought the *Strathcona* case [1926] A.C. 108 was wrongly decided and refused to follow it. ...It is important to notice that Port could only succeed if it showed either that it had a positive right to possession of the vessel or that Ben was accountable for the compensation as constructive trustee. Diplock J. was not concerned with the question whether Port was entitled to a negative injunction to restrain the tort.

It is not necessary for me to express any view as to whether the *Strathcona* case was rightly decided so far as it was a decision based on constructive trusteeship, which was all that Diplock J. was concerned with: the *Strathcona* case itself decided that there was no right to specific performance of the charterparty. However, although I of course differ from Diplock J. with diffidence, in my judgment the *Strathcona* case was rightly decided on the basis that Dominion was entitled to an injunction against Strathcona to prevent Strathcona from interfering with the contract between Dominion and the original charterer. Diplock J. at p. 165, explained *De Mattos v. Gibson*, on that ground, and at p. 168, gave as an alternative ground for his decision that actual, as opposed to constructive, notice was necessary in such a case. To that extent his decision supports my own view.

Therefore, in my judgment the authorities establish the following propositions. (1) The principle stated by Knight Bruce L.J. in *De Mattos v. Gibson* is good law and represents the counterpart in equity of the tort of knowing interference with contractual rights. (2) A person proposing to deal with property in such a way as to cause a breach of a contract affecting that property will be restrained by injunction from so doing if when he acquired that property he had actual knowledge of that contract. (3) A plaintiff is entitled to such an injunction even if he has no proprietary interest in the property: his right to have his contract performed is a sufficient interest. (4) There is no case in which such an injunction has been granted against a defendant who acquired the property with only constructive, as opposed to actual, notice of the contract. In my judgment constructive notice is not sufficient, since actual knowledge of the contract is a requisite element in the tort.

Accordingly, on this argument I conclude that, even assuming that Lloyds had constructive notice of the plaintiff's claim when the Lloyds charge was granted, no injunction lies against Lloyds to restrain the application of the F.I.B.I. securities in payment of the debt from I.F.T. to Lloyds in reliance on the rights granted by the charge: Lloyds did not at the date of the charge have actual knowledge. Therefore if the charge is valid, no injunction lies against Lloyds on this ground since they can properly rely on the charge to justify interfering with the plaintiff's rights. However, if the Lloyds charge is invalid (on the grounds of illegality) an injunction should be granted against Lloyds since, at this stage, to apply the moneys in paying Lloyds' debt will amount to a knowing interference with the plaintiff's rights without any lawful justification.

[*He went on to hold that, as the charge was invalid, an injunction should be granted.*]

NOTES

1. On appeal, Browne-Wilkinson J's decision was overturned by the Court of Appeal and the House of Lords [1982] AC 584 on the ground that the charge was valid. The correctness or otherwise of Browne-Wilkinson J's general reasoning on the *De Mattos v Gibson* point was not discussed.

2. The importance of Browne-Wilkinson J's reasoning is twofold. First, he regarded the *Strathcona* case as correctly decided, contrary to Diplock J's views in the *Port Line* case. Secondly, the *De Mattos v Gibson* principle and the *Strathcona* case were explained as illustrating the tort of knowing interference with another's contract; and the knowledge required for the tort neatly justified the need for actual, rather than constructive, notice. The injunction granted was therefore to restrain that tort (and this explanation could also explain an

award of damages). But note Treitel's view, *The Law of Contract* (11th edn, 2003) 622–3, that the tortious explanation of the *Strathcona* case runs into difficulties because the cause of the failure to perform the charterparty was the shipowners' poverty.

3. In the complex case of *Law Debenture Trust Corp plc v Ural Caspian Oil Corp Ltd* [1993] 1 WLR 138 Hoffmann J took a rather different approach from Browne-Wilkinson J. Rather than treating the *De Mattos v Gibson* principle as absorbed within the tort of wrongful interference with contract, he saw that principle as existing separately alongside that tort. In his view, however, at 144, 'the *De Mattos* principle permits no more than the grant of a negative injunction to restrain the third party from doing acts which would be inconsistent with performance of the contract by the original contracting party. The terms of the injunction must be such that refraining altogether from action would constitute compliance.' The principle was therefore held to be inapplicable on the facts of the case where the claimants were seeking a remedy based on positive performance of the covenants. And while Hoffmann J went on to hold that the economic tort could be made out on the facts, provided one extended its ambit to include wrongful interference with contractual remedies, there was a successful appeal against that decision on the ground that the tort was not as wide as Hoffmann J thought: see [1995] Ch 152, CA.

Additional Reading for Chapter 10

J Beatson, *Anson's Law of Contract* (28th edn, 2002) Ch 10, 620–4
S Smith, *Atiyah's Introduction to the Law of Contract* (6th edn, 2005) Ch 13

B Coote, 'Consideration and the Joint Promisee' [1978] *CLJ* 301

Coote rejects the joint promisee principle suggested in the Australian case of *Coulls v Bagot's Executor and Trustee Co Ltd* (see above, 474). He argues that in a bilateral contract, the joint promisee can only be regarded as having provided consideration if it has undertaken an obligation to the promisor; and that to be a party to a contract (other than one made by deed) one must have provided consideration. The joint promisee principle therefore infringes privity/the rule that consideration must move from the claimant.

R Flannigan, 'Privity—the End of an Era (Error)' (1987) 103 *LQR* 564

The author argues that the doctrine of privity, preventing a third party enforcing a contract made for its benefit, was an error and is inconsistent with all descriptive and normative theories conceptualising contract law (will theory, bargain theory, promise theory, relational contract law, economic analysis, critical analysis, detrimental reliance, unconscionability). The era of its operation should therefore be ended. [This was written before the 1999 Act].

Law Commission Report No 242, *Privity of Contract: Contracts for the Benefit of Third Parties* (1996)
This was the report which led to the Contracts (Rights of Third Parties) Act 1999. See, particularly, Part III giving the arguments for reform; Part VI on the relationship between privity and consideration; paragraphs 7.28–7.44 giving 17 examples of the application of the second test of enforceability; and Part XV summarising the Law Commission's recommendations.

S Smith, 'Contracts for the Benefit of Third Parties: in Defence of the Third Party Rule' (1997) 17 *OJLS* 643
Smith argues that the privity rule can be defended because it recognises that, morally, a promisor's obligation to perform is owed only to the person to whom the promise is made (the promisee). He controversially suggests that the apparent injustice of privity in reality stems from legal obstacles to, eg, properly protecting the promisee's expectation interest, or the third party's reliance interest, or preventing the promisor's unjust enrichment. [See also *Atiyah's Introduction to the Law of Contract,* 338–41.]

A Burrows, 'The Contracts (Rights of Third Parties) Act 1999 and its Implications for Commercial Contracts' [2000] *LMCLQ* 540
The author (who worked on the reform of privity while a Law Commissioner) examines the background to the 1999 Act and its main provisions (especially the tests of enforceability). He also considers some possible uses that may be made of the Act by those drafting contracts of insurance, construction contracts, and contracts for the issue of securities.

C MacMillan, 'A Birthday Present for Lord Denning: The Contracts (Rights of Third Parties) Act 1999' (2000) 63 *MLR* 721
MacMillan examines, and welcomes, the provisions of the 1999 Act. She argues that, as a result of the Act, 'The intentions of the parties to a contract can operate unencumbered by the privity rule and without the necessity of artificial devices' (at 738).

T Roe, 'Contractual Intention under Section 1(1)(b) and 1(2) of the Contracts (Rights of Third Parties) Act 1999' (2000) 63 *MLR* 887
Roe argues that there is uncertainty as to how the second test of enforceability will be applied. Rather than there being any strong presumption in favour of the test being satisfied where a contract purports to confer a benefit on an expressly identified third party, Roe argues that 'the significance of a failure to exclude or to include third party rights expressly ought to be assessed in context on a case by case basis' (at 892).

Sir Guenter Treitel, *Some Landmarks of Twentieth Century Contract Law* (2002) Ch 2 ('The Battle over Privity')
Treitel examines the privity doctrine and some exceptions to it with especial reference to the *Midland Silicones* case and *Beswick v Beswick*. He espouses general support for the 1999 Act on the grounds that experience in some other jurisdictions (eg USA) indicates that a general judicially-created right of a third party beneficiary to sue would create undesirable uncertainty.

R Stevens, 'The Contract (Rights of Third Parties) Act 1999' (2004) 120 *LQR* 292
In this characteristically robust and controversial attack on the reform of privity by the 1999 Act, Stevens's thesis is 'that the arguments in favour of reform were not as overwhelming as they appeared and that the problems created may be as great as those solved' (at 292). He argues that, as a third party is not a promisee and has not provided consideration, there is no justification for his acquiring rights under a contract (at 322); that each of the nine reasons given by the Law Commission for reform is inadequate; and that there are a number of problems raised in applying the 1999 Act not all of which, in his opinion, can be readily solved.

Principles of European Contract Law **(eds O Lando and H Beale, 2000) 317–22**

Article 6:110: Stipulation in Favour of a Third Party
(1) A third party may require performance of a contractual obligation when its right to do so has been expressly agreed upon between the promisor and the promisee, or when such agreement is to be inferred from the purpose of the contract or the circumstances of the case. The third party need not be identified at the time the agreement is concluded.

(2) If the third party renounces the right to performance the right is treated as never having accrued to it.

(3) The promisee may by notice to the promisor deprive the third party of the right to performance unless:

(a) the third party has received notice from the promisee that the right has been made irrevocable, or

(b) the promisor or the promisee has received notice from the third party that the latter accepts the right.

[Although drafted at a higher level of generality and therefore less specific than the 1999 Act this is similar to the position in English law under the Contracts (Rights of Third Parties) Act 1999. But the approach to the third party being deprived of that right differs from that in section 2 of the 1999 Act.]

Part Five

Factors Allowing Escape from a Contract

11

Misrepresentation

A misrepresentation inducing a contract may have two important, but different, sets of consequences. First, it may allow the misrepresentee to escape from the contract. That is, a misrepresentation, even if purely innocent, allows the misrepresentee to rescind the contract. In this respect, misrepresentation sits alongside duress (Chapter 14) and undue influence and exploitation of weakness (Chapter 15) which similarly allow rescission. Secondly, instead of or in addition to rescission, the misrepresentation may allow the misrepresentee to recover damages in tort or under the Misrepresentation Act 1967. A fraudulent misrepresentation triggers liability in the tort of deceit; and a negligent misrepresentation triggers liability either in the tort of negligence, as recognised in *Hedley, Byrne and Co Ltd v Heller and Partners Ltd* [1964] AC 465, or under section 2(1) of the Misrepresentation Act 1967. Damages cannot be awarded for a purely innocent misrepresentation unless given *in lieu of* rescission under section 2(2) of the Misrepresentation Act 1967.

Both those sets of consequences must be distinguished from where the representation inducing a contract becomes incorporated as a term of the contract (ie as a contractual promise). Where so incorporated the innocent party has remedies for breach of contract as well as for misrepresentation. We have seen in Chapter 4 (157–166) how the law decides whether a representation remains a 'mere representation' outside the contract or becomes incorporated as a term of the contract. In this chapter, although we are concerned with both mere representations and representations that have become incorporated as terms, we are concerned only with liability for misrepresentation as such, whether rescission or damages in tort or under the Misrepresentation Act 1967, and not with liability for breach of contract.

Students must be aware, however, that as in real life so in answering problem questions on misrepresentation in exams, *if* the representation has become incorporated as a term, one will have to advise on liability and remedies for both misrepresentation and breach of contract. For the purposes of clarity in analysis it is essential to keep the two distinct. It is often easiest to do this by looking first at misrepresentation (what is a misrepresentation and the remedies of rescission and damages for misrepresentation as dealt with in this chapter) before going on later to the possibility of incorporation as a term (as dealt with at 157–166) triggering remedies for breach of contract. Note in particular that, although in principle there is no objection to combining remedies for misrepresentation and for breach of contract, one cannot assert both where it is inconsistent to do so: eg one cannot rescind for misrepresentation and recover damages for breach of contract because rescission wipes away the contract from the start so that there can be no possible breach of contract.

We will examine the cases on misrepresentation in four sections: (1) the requirements of misrepresentation (ie what constitutes a misrepresentation); (2) rescission for misrepresentation (which is a remedy available whatever the type of misrepresentation); (3) damages for misrepresentation (where one must distinguish between fraudulent, negligent and purely innocent misrepresentation); and (4) exclusion of liability for misrepresentation.

Introductory reading: McKendrick, *Contract Law* (7th edn, 2007) Ch 13

1. REQUIREMENTS OF MISREPRESENTATION

An actionable misrepresentation is basically (1) a false statement of fact or law that (2) is relied on by the other party in entering into the contract. (There may, of course, be reliance, triggering tort liability for a misrepresentation, in ways other than 'entering into the contract' but that is all we are concerned with in a book on contract.)

(1) False Statement of Fact or Law

Formerly, and peculiarly, incorrect statements of law, as opposed to fact, did not count as misrepresentations. In the law of restitution the mistake of law bar was abolished in *Kleinwort Benson Ltd v Lincoln City Council* [1999] 2 AC 349, HL. It seemed an inevitable consequence that the law on misrepresentation (and mistake) in contract would likewise abandon the law/fact distinction, and so it has proved. For mistake, see below, 638–640. As regards misrepresentation it was held in *Pankhania v Hackney London Borough Council* [2002] EWHC 2441 (Ch) that, particularly in the light of *Kleinwort Benson*, there was liability in damages for a misrepresentation of law under section 2(1) of the Misrepresentation Act 1967 where the agents of a seller of land had incorrectly represented to the purchaser that those running a car park on part of the property were mere contractual licensees whereas they were actually protected business tenants.

The main cases have focused on three areas where the requirement of a statement of fact (or law) has proved problematic: statements of opinion, statements of intention, and silence.

(a) Statements of Opinion

Smith v Land and House Property Corporation
(1884) 28 Ch D 7, Court of Appeal

The defendant company entered into a contract with the claimants to buy a hotel that had been advertised by the claimants as being let to Mr Fleck, 'a most desirable tenant'. It subsequently transpired that, at the time of the representation, Mr Fleck was overdue with his rent and had only just paid the previous term's rent, six months after it was due. After the making of the contract, but before the transfer of title, Mr Fleck became bankrupt. The defendant refused to complete the purchase. When the claimants brought an action seeking specific performance, the defendant counter-claimed for rescission for misrepresentation. In dismissing the claimants' appeal, the Court of Appeal held that there had been a misrepresentation that had been relied on by the defendant.

Bowen LJ: In considering whether there was a misrepresentation, I will first deal with the argument that the particulars only contain a statement of opinion about the tenant. It is material to observe that it is often fallaciously assumed that a statement of opinion cannot involve the statement of a fact. In a case where the facts are equally well known to both parties, what one of them says to the other is frequently nothing but an expression of opinion. The statement of such opinion is in a sense a statement of a fact, about the condition of the man's own mind, but only of an irrelevant fact, for it is of no consequence what the opinion is. But if the facts are not equally known to both sides, then a statement of opinion by the one who knows the facts best involves very often a statement of a material fact, for he impliedly states that he knows facts which justify his opinion. Now a landlord knows the relations between himself and his tenant, other persons either do not know them at all or do not know them equally well, and if the landlord says that he considers that the relations between himself and his tenant are satisfactory, he really avers that the facts peculiarly within his knowledge are such as to render that opinion reasonable. Now are the statements here statements which involve such a representation of material facts? They are statements on a subject as to which prima facie the vendors know everything and the purchasers nothing. The vendors state that the property is let to a most desirable tenant, what does that mean? I agree that it is not a guarantee that the tenant will go on paying his rent, but it is to my mind a guarantee of a different sort, and amounts at least to an assertion that nothing has occurred in the relations between the landlords and the tenant which can be considered to make the tenant an unsatisfactory one. That is an assertion of a specific fact. Was it a true assertion?...I think that it was not. In my opinion a tenant who has paid his last quarter's rent by driblets under pressure must be regarded as an undesirable tenant.

Treating this then as a misrepresentation, did it induce the purchasers to buy? ...The chairman of the company was called and swore in the most distinct and positive way that it did influence him...and the Judge believed him. ...I think we ought not to differ from his conclusion.

Baggallay LJ and **Fry LJ** gave concurring judgments.

NOTES AND QUESTIONS

1. This case shows that what appears to be a statement of opinion may contain an actionable statement of fact.
2. What was held to be the statement of fact implicit in the statement 'a most desirable tenant'?

3.   Was it relevant in deciding whether there was a statement of fact to examine whether the claimants believed, or had reasonable grounds for believing, that the tenant was desirable?

Bisset v Wilkinson [1927] AC 177, Privy Council

The claimant (Bisset) owned two adjoining areas of land ('Homestead' and 'Hogan's') in New Zealand which he intended to sell. During negotiations with the defendant (Wilkinson), who wanted the land for sheep farming, the claimant stated that if the plots were properly worked they had a carrying capacity of 2000 sheep. As both parties knew, the claimant had not previously carried on sheep-farming on the land. The defendant agreed to buy the land and paid the first instalment but then refused to pay the rest. When the claimant brought an action for the money due under the contract, the defendant sought to have the contract rescinded for misrepresentation, arguing that the land could not support 2000 sheep. In allowing the claimant's appeal, the Privy Council held that the statement was one of opinion and not fact and was therefore not actionable.

Lord Merrivale (giving the judgment of the Privy Council comprising himself, **Viscount Dunedin**, **Lord Atkinson**, **Lord Phillimore** and **Lord Carson**): A representation of fact may be inherent in a statement of opinion and, at any rate, the existence of the opinion in the person stating it is a question of fact. …In *Smith v. Land and House Property Corporation* (1884) 28 Ch D 7, 15 there came in question a vendor's description of the tenant of the property sold as "a most desirable tenant" – a statement of his opinion, as was argued on his behalf in an action to enforce the contract of sale. This description was held by the Court of Appeal to be a misrepresentation of fact, which, without proof of fraud, disentitled the vendor to specific performance of the contract of purchase. [*He cited from Bowen LJ's judgment set out above, 539, and continued:*] The kind of distinction which is in question is illustrated again in a well known case of *Smith v. Chadwick* (1884) 9 App Cas 187. There the words under consideration involved the inquiry in relation to the sale of an industrial concern whether a statement of "the present value of the turnover or output" was of necessity a statement of fact that the produce of the works was of the amount mentioned, or might be and was a statement that the productive power of the works was estimated at so much. The words were held to be capable of the second of these meanings. The decisive inquiries came to be: what meaning was actually conveyed to the party complaining; was he deceived, and, as the action was based on a charge of fraud, was the statement in question made fraudulently?

In the present case, as in those cited, the material facts of the transaction, the knowledge of the parties respectively, and their relative positions, the words of representation used, and the actual condition of the subject-matter spoken of, are relevant to the two inquiries necessary to be made: What was the meaning of the representation? Was it true?

In ascertaining what meaning was conveyed to the minds of the now respondents by the appellant's statement as to the two thousand sheep, the most material fact to be remembered is that, as both parties were aware, the appellant had not and, so far as appears, no other person had at any time carried on sheep-farming upon the unit of land in question. That land as a distinct holding had never constituted a sheep-farm. …As was said by Sim J.: "In ordinary circumstances, any statement made by an owner who has been occupying his own farm as to its carrying capacity would be regarded as a statement of fact… This, however, is not such a case. The defendants knew all about Hogan's block and knew also what sheep the farm was carrying when they inspected it. In these circumstances… the defendants were not justified in regarding anything said by the plaintiff as to the carrying capacity as being anything more than an expression of his opinion on the subject." In this view of the matter their Lordships concur.

...If a reasonable man with the appellant's knowledge could not have come to the conclusion he stated, the description of that conclusion as an opinion would not necessarily protect him against rescission for misrepresentation. But what was actually the capacity in competent hands of the land the respondents purchased had never been, and never was, practically ascertained.

...

It is of dominant importance that Sim J. negatived the respondents' charge of fraud.

After attending to the close and very careful examination of the evidence which was made by learned counsel for each of the parties their Lordships entirely concur in the view which was expressed by the learned judge who heard the case. The defendants failed to prove that the farm if properly managed was not capable of carrying two thousand sheep.

NOTES AND QUESTIONS

1. This is the best-known illustration of the principle that a statement of mere opinion is not an actionable misrepresentation. However, note that in the last sentence the Privy Council indicated that, in any event, it had not been proved that the statement was false.

2. How does one distinguish this decision from that in *Smith v Land and House Property Corp* (above, 539)? Is it of central importance that Bisset's statement was made honestly and non-negligently?

3. In *Esso Petroleum Co Ltd v Mardon*, see above, 164, an estimate as to the throughput of petrol of a service station was held actionable as a tortious negligent misrepresentation (and as a contractual warranty). *Bisset v Wilkinson* was distinguished (albeit in the parts of the judgments dealing with the warranty rather than the negligent misstatement) apparently because, in contrast to the facts in *Esso*, the 'opinion' was not being put forward by someone who professed to have special expertise, as against the other party, in relation to the matter stated.

(b) Statements of Intention

Edgington v Fitzmaurice (1885) 29 Ch D 459, Court of Appeal

The defendants, who were the directors of a company, sent to its shareholders a prospectus inviting subscriptions for debenture bonds. The prospectus stated that the money raised would be used to complete alterations to the company's buildings, to purchase horses and vans, and to expand its business into supplying fish. In fact the real purpose in raising the money was to pay off the pressing liabilities of the company, which was in financial trouble. Having read the prospectus and under the mistaken belief that the debenture-holders would be given a first charge on the company's property, the claimant went ahead and bought some of the bonds. He admitted that he would not have entered into the transaction had he known that he would not be granted a charge. When the company later went into liquidation, the claimant sought to recover the money paid as damages for the tort of deceit. In dismissing the defendants' appeal against the award of damages, the Court of Appeal held that, first, the statement of purpose in the prospectus constituted a (fraudulent) misrepresentation; and, secondly, that the claimant had sufficiently relied on that misrepresentation in entering into the contract despite his admission about the charge. We are here solely concerned with the first point. For the second, see below, 547.

Cotton LJ: I allude to statements respecting the objects for which the loan was effected: [*His Lordship read the passage from the prospectus in which the objects of the issue of the debentures were stated, and continued:*] It was argued that this was only the statement of an intention, and that the mere fact that an intention was not carried into effect could not make the Defendants liable to the Plaintiff. I agree that it was a statement of intention, but it is nevertheless a statement of fact, and if it could not be fairly said that the objects of the issue of the debentures were those which were stated in the prospectus the Defendants were stating a fact which was not true; and if they knew that it was not true, or made it recklessly, not caring whether it was true or not, they would be liable. …I cannot but come to the conclusion that however hopeful the directors may have been of the ultimate success of the company, this statement was such as ought not to have been made.

Bowen LJ: A mere suggestion of possible purposes to which a portion of the money might be applied would not have formed a basis for an action of deceit. There must be a misstatement of an existing fact: but the state of a man's mind is as much a fact as the state of his digestion. It is true that it is very difficult to prove what the state of a man's mind at a particular time is, but if it can be ascertained it is as much a fact as anything else. A misrepresentation as to the state of a man's mind is, therefore, a misstatement of fact. Having applied as careful consideration to the evidence as I could, I have reluctantly come to the conclusion that the true objects of the Defendants in raising the money were not those stated in the circular. I will not go through the evidence, but looking only to the cross-examination of the Defendants, I am satisfied that the objects for which the loan was wanted were misstated by the Defendants, I will not say knowingly, but so recklessly as to be fraudulent in the eye of the law.

Fry LJ: [W]ith respect to the statement of the objects for which the debentures were issued, I have come to the conclusion that there was a misstatement of fact, that the statement contained in the circular was false in fact and false to the knowledge of the Defendants.

NOTES AND QUESTIONS

1. What is the false statement of fact implicit in a dishonest statement of intention?
2. Does an honest but negligent statement of intention constitute a false statement of existing fact?
3. If A sells a business to B representing that he has no intention of starting up another business which would compete with the one sold to B, which is true at the time of making the representation, can he change his mind?
4. In an exam, as when advising a client, one should beware of spending excessive time considering whether a changed statement of intention gives rise to a claim for a misrepresentation where there is an obvious claim for breach of contract.

(c) Silence: No Duty of Disclosure

While a misrepresentation can be made by conduct as well as by words, staying silent does not in itself constitute a misrepresentation. Moreover, as is classically shown by the mistake case of *Smith v Hughes* (below, 592), English law does not generally require a party to disclose to the other that it is making a mistake in entering into a contract. That is, there is no law requiring disclosure sitting alongside misrepresentation (although, exceptionally, there is such a duty in contracts *uberrimae fidei*—'of utmost good faith'—such as insurance contracts and in contracts between a fiduciary and his beneficiary). However, as shown in the next case, there is a misrepresentation where one fails to correct one's earlier representation which has been falsified by a subsequent change of circumstances during the negotiations.

With v O'Flanagan [1936] Ch 575, Court of Appeal

The defendant vendor represented to the claimant purchaser that the medical practice being sold had takings of £2000 per annum. That was true at the time the representation was made. Five months later, when the contract was signed, the takings of the practice had dwindled to an average of £5 per week due to the illness of the defendant. The claimant subsequently sought rescission of the contract. In allowing the claimant's appeal, it was held by the Court of Appeal that the claimant should be allowed to rescind either because the defendant had a duty to point out the change of circumstances or because the representation continued from the time he made it to the point where the contract was signed and thus the contract was entered into on the basis of a misrepresentation.

Lord Wright MR: I take the law to be as it was stated by Fry J. in *Davies v. London and Provincial Marine Insurance Co* 8 Ch D 469... The learned judge points out, at 474: "Where parties are contracting with one another, each may, unless there be a duty to disclose, observe silence even in regard to facts which he believes would be operative upon the mind of the other; and it rests upon those who say that there was a duty to disclose, to shew that the duty existed." Then the learned judge points out that in many cases there is such a duty as between persons in a confidential or a fiduciary relationship where the preexisting relationship involves the duty of entire disclosure. Then his Lordship says: "In the next place, there are certain contracts which have been called contracts uberrimae fidei where, from their nature, the Court requires disclosure from one of the contracting parties." The learned judge refers to contracts of partnership and marine insurance. Then he goes on, at 475: "Again, in ordinary contracts the duty may arise from circumstances which occur during the negotiation. Thus, for instance, if one of the negotiating parties has made a statement which is false in fact, but which he believes to be true and which is material to the contract, and during the course of the negotiation he discovers the falsity of that statement, he is under an obligation to correct his erroneous statement; although if he had said nothing he very likely might have been entitled to hold his tongue throughout." Then he adds what was material in that case and what is material in this case: "So, again, if a statement has been made which is true at the time, but which during the course of the negotiations becomes untrue, then the person who knows that it has become untrue is under an obligation to disclose to the other the change of circumstances."...In [this case]... the position is based upon the duty to communicate the change of circumstances.

The matter, however, may be put in another way though with the same effect, and that is on the ground that a representation made as a matter of inducement to enter into a contract is to be treated as a continuing representation. ...

On these grounds, with great respect to the learned judge, I think he ought to have come to the conclusion that the plaintiffs have established their case and there ought to be a declaration rescinding the contract with the consequences which follow upon such a declaration.

Romer LJ delivered a concurring judgment. **Clauson J** concurred.

NOTES AND QUESTIONS

1. There seems to be no practical difference, as regards rescission, between the two bases of the decision: (i) failing in a duty to disclose that the change of circumstances had rendered the initially true statement untrue or (ii) misrepresentation *at the time the contract was entered into.* However, it is arguable that analysis (ii) may be required if a claimant is seeking damages. This is because, as shown in *Banque Financière de la Cité SA v Westgate Insurance Co Ltd, sub nom Banque Keyser Ullmann SA v Skandia (UK) Insurance Co Ltd* [1990] 1 AC 665, CA, affirmed [1991] 2 AC 249, HL, the exceptional duty of disclosure in insurance contracts triggers rescission but not damages; and the same should arguably apply to any other duty of disclosure.

2. On the facts of *With v O'Flanagan* the defendant knew that the representation had been falsified by subsequent events. Would rescission still have been allowed if the defendant had not been fraudulent but merely negligent or purely innocent (ie if he had not known that the representation had become falsified)?

3. For an interesting application of this case, see *Spice Girls Ltd v Aprilla World Service BV* [2002] EWCA Civ 15, [2002] EMLR 27. Contrary to earlier and, at the time, true representations by conduct made by Spice Girls Ltd, it knew at the time it entered into a contract with the claimant that Geri Halliwell had stated an intention to leave the group. It was held that, as the representations continued until the making of the contract, by which time they were untrue, and as they had induced the claimant to enter into the contract, the claimant was entitled to damages under section 2(1) of the Misrepresentation Act 1967.

4. One should also note that a half-truth can constitute a misrepresentation. For example, in *Dimmock v Hallett* (1866) LR 2 Ch App 21 a vendor of land told a purchaser that two farms on the land were fully let but failed to inform him that the tenants had given notice to quit. This was held to be a misrepresentation. Similarly, in *Notts Patent Brick and Tile Co v Butler* (1866) 16 QBD 778 a purchaser of land asked the vendor's solicitors whether there were any restrictive covenants over the land. The solicitor replied that he was not aware of any. Although that statement was literally true, it was held to be a misrepresentation because there were restrictive covenants and the reason for the solicitor's ignorance was that he had not bothered to check.

(2) Reliance

Redgrave v Hurd (1881) 20 Ch D 1, Court of Appeal

The claimant (Redgrave) was an elderly solicitor. He advertised for a partner to join his business and to buy the accompanying house. During an interview with the defendant (Hurd), the claimant stated that the practice brought in about £300 per annum (or on another version of the evidence, £300–£400 per annum). This was untrue because the actual returns of the business were only about £200 per annum. A couple of days later, the defendant sent a letter asking how much the average per annum value of the practice was over the previous three years. The claimant produced financial summaries ('bills of costs') giving the value at a little under £200. When they met, the defendant queried the difference between the earlier (£300) representation and the summaries. In response, the claimant pointed to a quantity of papers saying that other business in them made up the difference. The defendant did not inspect the papers, which showed only a trifling amount of extra business. The contract of sale of the house was concluded but, before the transaction was completed, the defendant realised the true facts and refused to complete. The claimant brought an action for specific performance. The defendant counterclaimed that the contract should be rescinded for misrepresentation as to the value of the business and that he was entitled to damages for deceit. The Court of Appeal, overruling Fry J and allowing the defendant's appeal as regards rescission, held that it was sufficient for rescission that the defendant had relied on the misrepresentation so that it did not matter that he had not taken the opportunity presented to discover the truth.

Jessel MR: As regards the Defendant's counter-claim, we consider that it fails so far as damages are concerned, because he has not pleaded knowledge on the part of the Plaintiff that the allegations made by the Plaintiff were untrue, nor has he pleaded the allegations themselves in sufficient detail to found an action for deceit. It only remains to consider the claim of the Plaintiff for specific performance, and so much of the counter-claim of the Defendant as asks to have the contract rescinded.

...As regards the rescission of a contract, there was no doubt a difference between the rules of Courts of Equity and the rules of Courts of Common Law – a difference which of course has now disappeared by the operation of the *Judicature Act*, which makes the rules of equity prevail. According to the decisions of Courts of Equity it was not necessary, in order to set aside a contract obtained by material false representation, to prove that the party who obtained it knew at the time when the representation was made that it was false. It was put in two ways, either of which was sufficient. One way of putting the case was, "A man is not to be allowed to get a benefit from a statement which he now admits to be false. He is not to be allowed to say, for the purpose of civil jurisdiction, that when he made it he did not know it to be false; he ought to have found that out before he made it." The other way of putting it was this: "Even assuming that moral fraud must be shewn in order to set aside a contract, you have it where a man, having obtained a beneficial contract by a statement which he now knows to be false, insists upon keeping that contract. To do so is a moral delinquency: no man ought to seek to take advantage of his own false statements." The rule in equity was settled, and it does not matter on which of the two grounds it was rested. ...

There is another proposition of law of very great importance which I think it is necessary for me to state, because, with great deference to the very learned Judge from whom this appeal comes, I think it is not quite accurately stated in his judgment. If a man is induced to enter into a contract by a false representation it is not a sufficient answer to him to say, "If you had used due diligence you would have found out that the statement was untrue. You had the means afforded you of discovering its falsity, and did not choose to avail yourself of them."... Nothing can be plainer, I take it, on the authorities in equity than that the effect of false representation is not got rid of on the ground that the person to whom it was made has been guilty of negligence. One of the most familiar instances in modern times is where men issue a prospectus in which they make false statements of the contracts made before the formation of a company, and then say that the contracts themselves may be inspected at the offices of the solicitors. It has always been held that those who accepted those false statements as true were not deprived of their remedy merely because they neglected to go and look at the contracts. Another instance with which we are familiar is where a vendor makes a false statement as to the contents of a lease, as, for instance, that it contains no covenant preventing the carrying on of the trade which the purchaser is known by the vendor to be desirous of carrying on upon the property. Although the lease itself might be produced at the sale, or might have been open to the inspection of the purchaser long previously to the sale, it has been repeatedly held that the vendor cannot be allowed to say, "You were not entitled to give credit to my statement." It is not sufficient, therefore, to say that the purchaser had the opportunity of investigating the real state of the case, but did not avail himself of that opportunity. It has been apparently supposed by the learned Judge in the Court below that the case of *Attwood v. Small* (1838) 6 Cl & F 232 conflicts with that proposition. [*He considered* Attwood v Small, *concluded that it did not conflict with the above proposition, and continued:*] In no way, as it appears to me, does the decision, or any of the grounds of decision, in *Attwood v. Small*, support the proposition that it is a good defence to an action for rescission of a contract on the ground of fraud that the man who comes to set aside the contract inquired to a certain extent, but did it carelessly and inefficiently, and would, if he had used reasonable diligence, have discovered the fraud. ...

[T]he learned Judge came to the conclusion either that the Defendant did not rely on the statement, or that if he did rely upon it he had shewn such negligence as to deprive him of his title to relief from this Court. As I have already said, the latter proposition is in my opinion not founded in law, and the former part is not founded in fact; I think also it is not founded in law, for when a person makes a material representation to another to induce him to enter into a contract, and the other enters into that contract, it is not sufficient to say that the party to whom the representation is made does not prove that he entered into the contract, relying upon the representation. If it is a material representation calculated to induce him to enter into the contract, it is an inference of law that he was induced by the representation to enter into it, and in order to take away his title to be relieved from the contract on the ground that the representation was untrue, it must be shewn either that he had knowledge of the facts contrary to the representation, or that he stated in terms, or shewed clearly by his conduct, that he did not rely on the representation. If you tell a man, "You may enter into partnership with me, my business is bringing in between £300 and £400 a year," the man who makes that representation must know that it is a material inducement to the other to enter into the partnership, and you cannot investigate as to whether it was more or less probable that the inducement would operate on the mind of the party to whom the representation was made. Where you have neither evidence that he knew facts to shew that the statement was untrue, or that he said or did anything to shew that he did not actually rely upon the statement, the inference remains that he did so rely, and the statement being a material statement, its being untrue is a sufficient ground for rescinding the contract. For these reasons I am of opinion that the judgment of the learned Judge must be reversed and the appeal allowed.

Baggallay and **Lush LJJ** delivered concurring judgments.

NOTES AND QUESTIONS

1. Which of these is the better way of expressing the ratio of this case: (i) contributory negligence does not bar rescission where one has relied on a misrepresentation; or (ii) a failure to check the truth does not constitute contributory negligence where one has relied on a misrepresentation? If (ii) is correct, the case affects damages for misrepresentation as well as rescission. For while it is clear that damages for the tort of deceit cannot be reduced for contributory negligence (*Standard Chartered Bank v Pakistan National Shipping Corpn (No 2)* [2002] UKHL 43, [2003] 1 AC 959) it is equally clear that damages for tortious negligent misrepresentation can be so reduced (*Gran*

Gelato Ltd v Richcliff (Group) Ltd [1992] QB 560, which also decided that contributory negligence can apply to damages under section 2(1) of the Misrepresentation Act 1967).

2. This case is one of many in which the judges indicate that the misrepresentation needs to be 'material'. Is that a requirement additional to reliance? If so, what does it mean?

3. *Attwood v Small* (1838) 6 Cl & F 232, referred to by Jessel MR, is a long and difficult case. It involved the sale of mines and steelworks from the defendant to the claimants. The defendant made several representations about the 'capabilities' of the property and the claimant agreed to purchase subject to verifying those statements. An inquiry into the statements was undertaken by the claimants' agents, who reported that the defendant's statements were true. It later turned out that they were untrue. The House of Lords found that there was no actionable misrepresentation. The reasoning is not entirely clear but the standard interpretation is that that there was no reliance on the misrepresentations because the claimants had relied instead on their agents. The different point stressed in *Redgrave v Hurd* is that, contrary to Fry J's interpretation at first instance, *Attwood v Small* does not support the view that a rejected opportunity to check the truth bars rescission.

4. The second paragraph above of Jessel MR's judgment on rescission shows that one can rescind even for a purely innocent misrepresentation (although on the facts, the misprepresentation was surely at least negligent albeit that fraud had not been proved). In Chapter 12 we shall see that, in contrast to this wide-ranging willingness to intervene in relation to mistakes induced by misrepresentation, English law has a narrow doctrine of (non-induced) mistake.

Edgington v Fitzmaurice (1885) 29 Ch D 459, Court of Appeal

For the facts, see above, 541. We are here solely concerned with the second (the reliance) point.

Cotton LJ: It is true that if he had not supposed he would have a charge he would not have taken the debentures; but if he also relied on the misstatement in the prospectus, his loss none the less resulted from that misstatement. It is not necessary to shew that the misstatement was the sole cause of his acting as he did. If he acted on that misstatement, though he was also influenced by an erroneous supposition, the Defendants will be still liable. Did he act upon that misstatement? He states distinctly in his evidence that he did rely on the Defendants' statements, and the learned Judge found, as a fact, that he did, and it would be wrong for this Court, without seeing or hearing the witness, to reverse that finding of the Judge. We must therefore come to the conclusion that the statements in the prospectus as to the objects of the issue of the debentures were false in fact, and were relied upon by the Plaintiff.

Bowen LJ: Then the question remains – Did this misstatement contribute to induce the Plaintiff to advance his money. ... [Counsel for the defendant, Fitzmaurice] contended that the Plaintiff admits that he would not have taken the debentures unless he had thought they would give him a charge on the property, and therefore he was induced to take them by his own mistake, and the misstatement in the circular was not material. But such misstatement was material if it was actively present to his mind when he decided to advance his money. The real question is, what was the state of the Plaintiff's mind, and if his mind was disturbed by the misstatement of the Defendants, and such disturbance was in part the cause of what he did, the mere fact of his also making a mistake himself could make no difference. It resolves itself into a mere question of fact. I have felt some difficulty about the pleadings, because in the statement of claim this point is not clearly put forward... But the balance of my judgment is weighed down by the probability of the case. What is the first question which a man asks when he advances money? It is, what is it wanted for? Therefore I think that the statement is material, and that the Plaintiff would be unlike the rest of his race if he was not influenced by the statement of the objects for which the loan was required. The learned Judge in the Court below came to the conclusion that the misstatement did influence him, and I think he came to a right conclusion.

Fry LJ: The next inquiry is whether this statement materially affected the conduct of the Plaintiff in advancing his money. He has sworn that it did, and the learned Judge who tried the action has believed him. On such a point I should not like to differ from the Judge who tried the action, even though I were not myself convinced, but in this case the natural inference from the facts is in accordance with the Judge's conclusion. The prospectus was intended to influence the mind of the reader. Then this question has been raised: the Plaintiff admits that he was induced to make the advance not merely by this false statement, but by the belief that the debentures would give him a charge on the company's property, and it is admitted that this was a mistake of the Plaintiff. Therefore it is said that the Plaintiff was the author of his own injury. It is quite true that the Plaintiff was influenced by his own mistake, but that does not benefit the Defendants' case. The Plaintiff says: I had two inducements, one my own mistake, the other the false statement of the Defendants. The two together induced me to advance the money. But in my opinion if the false statement of fact actually influenced the Plaintiff, the Defendants are liable, even though the Plaintiff may have been also influenced by other motives. I think, therefore, the Defendants must be held liable.

NOTES AND QUESTIONS

1. The claimant was held entitled to damages for deceit even though he entered the contract relying on both the misrepresentation as to the company's purposes in raising the loan and his own mistaken belief that debenture-holders would be given a charge over the company's property. So the misrepresentation does not need to be the sole cause. Does a claimant need nonetheless to establish that the misrepresentation was a 'but for' cause? Are the tests of whether the misrepresentation 'influenced' the claimant or was 'actively present in his mind' different from establishing 'but for' causation?

2. Compare the law on 'causation' in the context of duress: below, 698, 715. Should there be consistency on the approach to this issue as between misrepresentation and duress?

2. RESCISSION FOR MISREPRESENTATION

We have seen that *Redgrave v Hurd* (above, 547 note 4) shows that one can rescind for even a purely innocent misrepresentation. Here we examine cases on what is meant by rescission, bars to rescission, and how one rescinds.

One should note that an issue that can arise on rescission for misrepresentation but more usually arises in relation to rescission for undue influence—and our consideration of it is therefore postponed until Chapter 15 (see below, 729, 737)—is whether a claimant can rescind a contract for the misrepresentation of a third party that has been relied on by the claimant in making a contract with the defendant.

(1) What Does Rescission Mean?

Rescission (or, as it is sometimes referred to, 'setting aside') wipes away a contract from the start. It is the remedy that goes with a contract being 'voidable'. Rescission therefore differs from *termination* of a contract for breach which discharges only future obligations. Where a contract has been partly or fully performed, the rescinding party will want (and is prima facie entitled to) restitution of the benefits it has conferred on the other party. So, for example, if a buyer is rescinding it will want restitution of the purchase price paid; and if a seller is rescinding it will want restitution of the property transferred or its value. Rescission is normally understood to refer to both the wiping away of the contract and the consequential restitution. In the case set out in this subsection, *Whittington v Seale-Hayne*, we see the court distinguishing between, on the one hand, rescission and consequential restitution, and on the other hand, damages.

There is on-going controversy as to whether there can be 'partial rescission'. In *TSB Bank plc v Camfield* [1995] 1 WLR 430, CA, a wife entered into a contract with a bank in which she guaranteed the repayment of a loan to her husband's partnership secured by a charge over her home. She was induced to do so by the innocent misrepresentation of her husband that the maximum liability under the charge was £15,000. Applying *Barclays Bank plc v O'Brien* (below, 729) she was held able to rescind the guarantee and charge. The argument was rejected that the contract and charge could, and should, be partly rescinded on the terms that there remained in place a charge securing £15,000. *Camfield* was subsequently applied by Colman J in *De Molestina v Ponton* [2002] 1 Lloyd's Rep 271 who said at 286: 'There can be no doubt that, according to the present state of development of English law, this Court is bound by the general principle that a misrepresentee is permitted to rescind the whole of a contract but not part of it.' This inflexibility seems surprising (perhaps not least because rescission is an equitable remedy). Cf the different approach of the High Court of Australia in *Vadasz v Pioneer Concrete (SA) Pty Ltd* (1995) 184 CLR 102.

Whittington v Seale-Hayne (1900) 82 LT 49, Chancery Division

The claimants entered into a lease of a farm which they wished to use for breeding prize poultry. They were induced to take the lease by the defendant's non-fraudulent misrepresentation that the premises were in a thoroughly sanitary condition and in a good state of repair. Owing to the condition of the premises, the water supply was poisoned. As a result, the claimants' manager became seriously ill and the poultry either died or became valueless. The claimants sought rescission of the lease plus an indemnity for all losses that had been suffered as a result of the misrepresentation (including, under paragraph 11 of the statement of claim, the loss of the poultry, the consequent loss of profits, and the medical expenses incurred on behalf of the manager). It was not in dispute that the claimants were entitled to repayment of the rent paid to the defendant and to an indemnity for the rates paid and for the cost of the repairs carried out in compliance with a local authority order. Farwell J held that they were not entitled to the other losses claimed because they fell outside the ambit of an indemnity. They could only be compensated if damages could be awarded, which they could not as the representation was non-fraudulent.

Farwell J: The plaintiffs' action is one for the rescission of a lease on the ground of innocent misrepresentation, and the claim also asks for damages and an indemnity against all costs and charges incurred by the plaintiffs in respect of the lease and the insanitary condition of the premises. The suggestion was made that I should assume for the purpose of argument that innocent misrepresentations were made sufficient to entitle the plaintiffs to rescission. The question then arises to what extent the doctrine, that a plaintiff who succeeds in an action for rescission on the ground of innocent misrepresentation is entitled to be placed *in statu quo ante*, is to be applied. Counsel for the plaintiffs say that in such a case the successful party is to be placed in exactly the same position as if he had never entered into the contract. The defendant admits liability so far as regards anything which was paid under the contract, but not in respect of any damages incurred by reason of the contract; and I think the defendant's view is the correct one. ...When the plaintiffs say they are entitled to have the misrepresentations made good, it may mean one of two things. It may mean that they are entitled to have the whole of the injury incurred by their entering into the contract made good, or that they are entitled to be repaid what they have paid under their contract... but to make good by way of compensation for the consequences of the misrepresentations is the same thing as asking for damages. ... [T]he point I have here to consider is what is the limit of the liabilities which are within the indemnity. [Counsel for the defendant] admits that the rents, rates, and repairs under the covenants in the lease ought to be made good; but he disputes, and I agree with him, that the plaintiff is entitled to what is claimed by paragraph 11 of the statement of claim, which is really damages pure and simple.

NOTES AND QUESTIONS

1. This case illustrates that, as an aspect of restitution consequent on rescission, an indemnity can be given for expenses that have necessarily been incurred which the other party would itself have had to incur. But the other losses claimed were not of benefit to the defendant. They therefore fell outside the scope of the (restitutionary) indemnity and could only have been compensated by an award of damages.
2. It is likely that the claimants on similar facts would now have a claim for damages either at common law applying *Hedley Byrne & Co Ltd v Heller & Partners Ltd* or under section 2(1) of the Misrepresentation Act 1967 (see below, 564, 567). When, therefore, does the distinction between an indemnity and damages remain important?

(2) Bars to Rescission

Although rescission is available for any type of misrepresentation (whether fraudulent, negligent or innocent) there are four bars to it. These are: (i) affirmation (ie where the misrepresentee has continued with the contract after knowing of the misrepresentation); (ii) third party rights (ie where a third party has acquired rights to property transferred under the contract, as illustrated by mistaken identity cases such as *Cundy v Lindsay* , see below, 598–599 especially note 1); (iii) lapse of time; and (iv) counter-restitution impossible. We now consider the leading case on each of the last two bars.

Leaf v International Galleries [1950] 2 KB 86, Court of Appeal

The defendants sold the claimant a painting called 'Salisbury Cathedral', representing that it was a Constable. Five years later, the claimant tried to auction the painting. The auction house informed the claimant that it was not a Constable and the claimant sought to rescind the contract with the defendants on the ground of innocent (ie non-fraudulent) misrepresentation. The Court of Appeal, disallowing the claimant's appeal, held that rescission was barred by the length of time that had passed.

Denning LJ: The way in which the case is put by Mr. Weitzman, on behalf of the plaintiff, is this: he says that this was an innocent misrepresentation and that in equity he is, or should be, entitled to claim rescission even of an executed contract of sale on that account. He points out that the judge has found that it is quite possible to restore the parties to their original position. It can be done by simply handing back the picture to the defendants.

In my opinion, this case is to be decided according to the well known principles applicable to the sale of goods. This was a contract for the sale of goods. There was a mistake about the quality of the subject-matter, because both parties believed the picture to be a Constable; and that mistake was in one sense essential or fundamental. But such a mistake does not avoid the contract: there was no mistake at all about the subject-matter of the sale. It was a specific picture, "Salisbury Cathedral." The parties were agreed in the same terms on the same subject-matter, and that is sufficient to make a contract...

There was a term in the contract as to the quality of the subject-matter: namely, as to the person by whom the picture was painted – that it was by Constable. That term of the contract was, according to our terminology, either a condition or a warranty. If it was a condition, the buyer could reject the picture for breach of the condition at any time before he accepted it, or is deemed to have accepted it; whereas, if it was only a warranty, he could not reject it at all but was confined to a claim for damages.

I think it right to assume in the buyer's favour that this term was a condition, and that, if he had come in proper time he could have rejected the picture; but the right to reject for breach of condition has always been limited by the rule that, once the buyer has accepted, or is deemed to have accepted, the goods in performance of the contract, then he cannot thereafter reject, but is relegated to his claim for damages: see s. 11, sub-s. 1 (c), of the Sale of Goods Act, 1893, and *Wallis, Son & Wells v. Pratt & Haynes* [1910] 2 KB 1003.

The circumstances in which a buyer is deemed to have accepted goods in performance of the contract are set out in s. 35 of the Act, which says that the buyer is deemed to have accepted the goods, amongst other things, "when, after the lapse of a reasonable time, he retains the goods without intimating to the seller that he has rejected them." In this case the buyer took the picture into his house and, apparently, hung it there, and five years passed before he intimated any rejection at all. That, I need hardly say, is much more than a reasonable time. It is far too late for him at the end of five years to reject this picture for breach of any condition. His remedy after that length of time is for damages only, a claim which he has not brought before the court.

Is it to be said that the buyer is in any better position by relying on the representation, not as a condition, but as an innocent misrepresentation? I agree that on a contract for the sale of goods an innocent material misrepresentation may, in a proper case, be a ground for rescission even after the contract has been executed.

...

Although rescission may in some cases be a proper remedy, it is to be remembered that an innocent misrepresentation is much less potent than a breach of condition; and a claim to rescission for innocent misrepresentation must at any rate be barred when a right to reject for breach of condition is barred. A condition is a term of the contract of a most material character, and if a claim to reject on that account is barred, it seems to me *a fortiori* that a claim to rescission on the ground of innocent misrepresentation is also barred.

Jenkins LJ: It is true that the plaintiff bought the picture on the faith of the representation, innocently made, that it was a painting by Constable. It is true that this was a representation of great importance, which went to the root of the contract and induced him to buy. Clearly if, before he had taken delivery of the picture, he had obtained other advice and come to the conclusion that the picture was not a Constable, it would have been open to him to rescind. It may be that if, having taken delivery of the picture on the faith of the representation and having taken it home, he had, within a reasonable time, taken other advice and satisfied himself that it was not a Constable, he might have been able to make good his claim to rescission notwithstanding the delivery. That point I propose to leave open. What in fact happened was that he took delivery of the picture, kept it for some five years, and took no steps to obtain any further evidence as to its authorship; and that, finally, when he was minded to sell the picture at the end of a matter of five years, the untruth of the representation was brought to light.

In those circumstances, it seems to me to be quite out of the question that a court of equity should grant relief by way of rescission. It is perfectly true that the county court judge held that there had been no laches, and, of course, it may be said that the plaintiff had no occasion to obtain any further evidence as to the authorship of the picture until he wanted to sell; but in my judgment contracts such as this cannot be kept open and subject to the possibility of rescission indefinitely. Assuming that completion is not fatal to his claim, I think that, at all events, it behoves the purchaser either to verify or, as the case may be, to disprove the representation within a reasonable time, or else stand or fall by it. If he is allowed to wait five, ten, or twenty years and then reopen the bargain, there can be no finality at all. I, for my part, do not think that equity will intervene in such a case, more especially as in the present case it cannot be said that, apart from rescission, the plaintiff would have been without remedy. The county court judge was of opinion, and it seems to me that he was clearly right, that the representation that the picture was a Constable amounted to a warranty. If it amounted to a warranty, and that was broken, as on the findings of the county court judge it was, then the plaintiff had a right at law in the shape of damages for breach of warranty. That remedy he did not choose to exercise, and, although he was invited at the hearing to amend his claim so as to include a claim for breach of warranty, he declined that opportunity. That being so, it seems to me that he has no justification at all for now coming to equity five years after the event and claiming rescission. Accordingly, it seems to me that this is not a case in which the equitable remedy of rescission, assuming it to be available in the absence of fraud in respect of a completed sale of chattels, should be allowed to the plaintiff. For these reasons, I agree that the appeal fails and should be dismissed.

Evershed MR delivered a concurring speech.

NOTES AND QUESTIONS

1.   Was Denning LJ correct to say that rescission for innocent misrepresentation must be barred (by lapse of time) if the different remedy (of termination, and rejection of goods, for breach of contract) is barred (by lapse of time)? More

generally, can one assimilate the law on losing the right to rescind for misrepresentation with the law on losing the right to terminate for breach?

2. Jenkins LJ's apparent agreement with the trial judge's view that there had been no 'laches' is puzzling as that is simply the terminology traditionally used in equity to refer to the lapse of time bar.

3. Laches is a somewhat uncertain doctrine but it is normally assumed that the innocent party must have known of its right (to rescind), or that it ought reasonably to have known of that right, before time starts to run (see, eg, *Lindsay Petroleum Company v Hurd* (1874) LR 5 PC 221). Yet this case appears to contradict that.

4. The judges accepted that the claimant had an action for damages for breach of contract which, at the time of this case and today, would be subject to a limitation period of six years from the date of breach (Limitation Act 1980, section 5). It is unclear why the claimant failed to bring such a claim in this case.

5. The judges assumed, without having to decide, that there was no problem about rescinding for a non-fraudulent misrepresentation even though the representation had been incorporated as a term of the contract and even though the contract had been fully executed. Although there were authorities appearing to cast doubt on that, the position has subsequently been made absolutely clear by the **Misrepresentation Act 1967 section 1**:

1 Removal of certain bars to rescission for innocent misrepresentation

Where a person has entered into a contract after a misrepresentation has been made to him, and—

(a) the misrepresentation has become a term of the contract; or

(b) the contract has been performed;

or both, then, if otherwise he would be entitled to rescind the contract without alleging fraud, he shall be so entitled … notwithstanding the matters mentioned in paragraphs (a) and (b) of this section.

Erlanger v New Sombrero Phosphate Co
(1878) 3 App Cas 1218, House of Lords

The defendants, who were the promoters of the claimant company, sold an island for phosphate mining to the claimant for £110,000. After mining for a period of time, the claimant sought to rescind the contract of sale on the ground that the defendants, in breach of their fiduciary duty of disclosure, had failed to disclose to the claimant that they had bought the mine for £55,000 a few days before the sale to the claimant. The House of Lords held that, because of the non-disclosure, the claimant was entitled to rescission of the sale contract and restitution of the contract price in return for giving back the mine and accounting for profits made from working it. While their Lordships decided that delay (laches) did not here bar rescission, Lord Blackburn also examined the bar of restitution being impossible. We are here solely concerned with that.

Lord Blackburn: The contract was not void, but only voidable at the election of the company.

In *Clough v. The London and North Western Railway Company Law Rep.* 7 Ex. 34, 35, in the judgment of the Exchequer Chamber, it is said, "We agree that the contract continues valid till the party defrauded has determined his election by avoiding it. In such cases, (*i.e.*, of fraud) the question is, Has the person on whom the fraud was practised, having notice of the fraud, elected not to avoid the contract? Or, Has he elected to avoid it? Or, Has he made no election? We think that so long as he has made no election he retains the right to determine it either way; subject to this, that if, in the interval whilst he is deliberating, an innocent third party has acquired an interest in the property, or if, *in consequence of his delay the position even of the wrongdoer is affected,* it will preclude him from exercising his right to rescind." It is, I think, clear on principles of general justice, that as a condition to a rescission there must be a *restitutio in integrum.* The parties must be put *in statu quo.* ...It is a doctrine which has often been acted upon both at law and in equity. But there is a considerable difference in the mode in which it is applied in Courts of Law and Equity, owing, as I think, to the difference of the machinery which the Courts have at command. ...

It would be obviously unjust that a person who has been in possession of property under the contract which he seeks to repudiate should be allowed to throw that back on the other party's hands without accounting for any benefit he may have derived from the use of the property, or if the property, though not destroyed, has been in the interval deteriorated, without making compensation for that deterioration. But as a Court of Law has no machinery at its command for taking an account of such matters, the defrauded party, if he sought his remedy at law, must in such cases keep the property and sue in an action for deceit, in which the jury, if properly directed, can do complete justice by giving as damages a full indemnity for all that the party has lost...

But a Court of Equity could not give damages, and, unless it can rescind the contract, can give no relief. And, on the other hand, it can take accounts of profits, and make allowance for deterioration. And I think the practice has always been for a Court of Equity to give this relief whenever, by the exercise of its powers, it can do what is practically just, though it cannot restore the parties precisely to the state they were in before the contract. And a Court of Equity requires that those who come to it to ask its active interposition to give them relief, should use due diligence, after there has been such notice or knowledge as to make it inequitable to lie by. And any change which occurs in the position of the parties or the state of the property after such notice or knowledge should tell much more against the party *in morâ*, than a similar change before he was *in morâ* should do.

Lord Penzance, Lord Hatherley, Lord O'Hagan, Lord Selborne and **Lord Gordon** delivered speeches concurring in ordering rescission. **Lord Cairns LC,** while ultimately not willing to dissent, delivered a speech expressing the view that laches should have here barred rescission.

NOTES AND QUESTIONS

1. Although this was a non-disclosure case, the requirement that counter-restitution must be possible if rescission is to be granted applies in exactly the same way to rescission for misrepresentation.

2. There is normally no duty of disclosure in English law but, as we have noted (above, 543) an exception, as here, is where there is a fiduciary relationship between the parties. The promoters of a company are in a fiduciary relationship with that company.

3. The rationale for counter-restitution having to be possible is that a party seeking rescission and restitution must not itself be left unjustly enriched. As Lord Wright said in *Spence v Crawford* [1939] 3 All ER 271, 288–9, HL, in which the claimant misrepresentee was held able to rescind a contract for the sale of shares on repayment of the purchase price received (plus an agreed sum of compensation): '[I]f a plaintiff who has been defrauded seeks to have the contract annulled and his money or property returned to him, it would be

inequitable if he did not also restore what he had got under the contract from the defendant. Though the defendant has been fraudulent, he must not be robbed, nor must the plaintiff be unjustly enriched, as he would be if he both got back what he had parted with and kept what he had received in return.'

4.   The importance of the *Erlanger* case is that it recognised that the correct approach is not to insist on precise specific counter-restitution. Rather the courts should apply the equitable approach of aiming for 'practical justice' by making flexible use of monetary counter-restitution for benefits that cannot be directly returned.

5.   Given that the courts now apply the more flexible *Erlanger* approach, are there likely to be many cases in which rescission and consequential restitution will be denied because counter-restitution is impossible? Rather than talking of a bar, would it be better simply to say that counter-restitution is always a requirement for rescission?

(3) How Does One Rescind?

Car and Universal Finance Co Ltd v Caldwell
[1965] 1 QB 525, Court of Appeal

The defendant (Caldwell) was the owner of a Jaguar car. A rogue (Norris) convinced the defendant to sell and give him the car on the faith of a cheque for £965 and a deposit of £10. When the defendant went to the bank the next day (13 January) the cheque was dishonoured and the defendant immediately informed the police and the Automobile Association of the fraudulent transaction. Norris subsequently sold the car to a firm of dealers and it was subsequently sold on a number of times and ultimately to the claimants, who bought in good faith and without any notice of the defect in title. In interpleader proceedings to determine whether the claimants or the defendant owned the car, the central question at issue was whether the defendant had validly rescinded the contract on 13 January before the car had been acquired by a bona fide purchaser for value without notice. The Court of Appeal, in dismissing an appeal by the claimant from the first instance decision of Lord Denning MR (sitting, unusually, as an additional judge of the Queen's Bench Division), held that the contract had been validly rescinded by the defendant informing the police and AA.

Sellers LJ: This appeal raises a primary point in the law of contract. The question has arisen whether a contract which is voidable by one party can in any circumstances be terminated by that party without his rescission being communicated to the other party. Lord Denning M.R. has held in the circumstances of this case that there can be rescission without communication where the seller of a motor car, who admittedly had the right to rescind the contract of sale on the ground of fraudulent misrepresentation, terminated the contract by an unequivocal act of election which demonstrated clearly that he had elected to rescind it and to be no longer bound by it. The general rule, no doubt, is that where a party is entitled to rescind a contract and wishes to do so the contract subsists until the opposing party is informed that the contract has been terminated. The difficulty of the seller in this case was that, when he learnt of the fraud and, therefore, ascertained his right to terminate the bargain, he could not without considerable delay find either the fraudulent buyer or the car which had been sold.

Such circumstances would not appear to be so rare in transactions in motor cars (or horses in earlier days) that they would not, it might be thought, have given rise to litigation and an authoritative decision, but it seems that over the years the point in issue has not been decided in any reported cases in similar or comparable circumstances. ...

...Where a contracting party could be communicated with, and modern facilities make communication practically world-wide and almost immediate, it would be unlikely that a party could be held to have disaffirmed a contract unless he went so far as to communicate his decision so to do. It would be what the other contracting party would normally require and unless communication were made the party's intention to rescind would not have been unequivocally or clearly demonstrated or made manifest. But in circumstances such as the present case, the other contracting party, a fraudulent rogue who would know that the vendor would want his car back as soon as he knew of the fraud, would not expect to be communicated with as a matter of right or requirement, and would deliberately, as here, do all he could to evade any such communication being made to him. In such exceptional contractual circumstances, it does not seem to me appropriate to hold that a party so acting can claim any right to have a decision to rescind communicated to him before the contract is terminated. To hold that he could would involve that the defrauding party, if skilful enough to keep out of the way, could deprive the other party to the contract of his right to rescind, a right to which he was entitled and which he would wish to exercise, as the defrauding party would well know or at least confidently suspect. The position has to be viewed, as I see it, between the two contracting parties involved in the particular contract in question. That another innocent party or parties may suffer does not in my view of the matter justify imposing on a defrauded seller an impossible task. He has to establish, clearly and unequivocally, that he terminates the contract and is no longer to be bound by it. If he cannot communicate his decision he may still satisfy a judge or jury that he had made a final and irrevocable decision and ended the contract.

Upjohn LJ: If one party, by absconding, deliberately puts it out of the power of the other to communicate his intention to rescind which he knows the other will almost certainly want to do, I do not think he can any longer insist on his right to be made aware of the election to determine the contract. In these circumstances communication is a useless formality. I think that the law must allow the innocent party to exercise his right of rescission otherwise than by communication or repossession. To hold otherwise would be to allow a fraudulent contracting party by his very fraud to prevent the innocent party from exercising his undoubted right. I would hold that in circumstances such as these the innocent party may evince his intention to disaffirm the contract by overt means falling short of communication or repossession.

We heard much interesting argument on the position where one party makes an innocent misrepresentation which entitles the other to elect to rescind and then innocently so acts that the other cannot find him to communicate his election to him. I say nothing about that case and would leave it to be decided if and when it arises. I am solely concerned with the fraudulent rogue who deliberately makes it impossible for the other to communicate with him or to retake the property.

Davies LJ: On the facts of this case Norris must be taken to have known that the defendant might, on ascertaining the fraud, wish to rescind the contract. Norris disappeared; and so did the car. The defendant could, therefore, neither communicate with Norris nor retake the car. It must, therefore, I think, be taken to be implied in the transaction between Norris and the defendant that in the event of the defendant's wishing to rescind he should be entitled to do so by the best other means possible. Lex non ogit ad impossibilia. [The law does not compel the impossible.] It is true that it was conceivably possible that the defendant might decide not to rescind but to sue on the cheque instead; but it is most doubtful whether on the facts of this case such a possibility could have occurred to Norris as a real one. The fact that Norris knew that he was a rogue and that, therefore, the defendant was likely to be after him distinguishes this case from that of an innocent misrepresentor. It would not occur to the latter that the other party to the contract would have any right or desire to rescind, so that there would be no such implication as that which I have suggested arose in the present case.

It was argued that the defendant's action in going to the police and the Automobile Association was not an unequivocal act, since it was open to him to have changed his mind on the next day if, to use [counsel for the claimants'] phrase, Norris had suddenly won a football pool and so have become a worthwhile defendant to an action on the cheque. That again, in my opinion, is an unrealistic view of the facts. The defendant was, as I think, declaring to the world: "I have been swindled and I want my car back." He was declaring his intention as clearly as if he had seen the car in the street and seized it.

NOTES AND QUESTIONS

1. This case lays down that, while communication to the other contracting party that one is rescinding the contract is normally required, an overt act showing that one is rescinding the contract is sufficient where communication is not possible, at least where the other contracting party is a fraudster.
2. Why was it confusing of Sellers LJ to refer to 'termination' of the contract?
3. It might be argued that, as both the claimants and the defendant were innocent, the loss should have stayed where it fell so that Caldwell should not have got his car back. But on that argument, one would never be able to rescind as against a bona fide purchaser for value without notice even by prior communication to the misrepresentor.
4. It is implicit in this decision that rescission is a self-help remedy which is available without coming to court. This is not to deny that commonly a claimant wishing to rescind will come to court because, eg, it is seeking consequential restitution.
5. **W Swadling, 'Rescission, Property and the Common Law' (2005) 121** *LQR* **123** very controversially suggests that the reasoning on the recovery of property in this and numerous other cases (both on rescission for misrepresentation and on mistakes making contracts void) is flawed in merging the issues of the validity of a contract and of the transfer of title. The truth, in his view, is that the two are separate: the rights in property are passed by delivery and intent to pass title, which is not dependent on the validity of the contract. Therefore, Caldwell should not have got his car back even though he had validly rescinded the contract. **B Hacke, 'Rescission of Contract and Revesting of Title: A Reply to Mr Swadling' [2006]** *RLR* **106,** in a persuasive rebuttal of that argument, defends the orthodox view that *Caldwell* and other cases are correct in their approach to proprietary rights.

3. DAMAGES FOR MISREPRESENTATION

In contrast to rescission, which is available whatever the type of misrepresentation, it is important in relation to damages to distinguish between fraudulent, negligent and purely innocent misrepresentations. This is not least because the causes of action in play differ. Note that because fraudulent and negligent misrepresentations trigger liability for damages in tort it is in this section, more than in any other in this book, that we see the interaction of tort and contract (and students should recognise some of the cases from their tort courses).

(1) Fraudulent Misrepresentation: the Tort of Deceit

Derry v Peek (1889) 14 App Cas 337, House of Lords

Legislation incorporating a tram company provided that the company's tramways were to be horse-powered unless it was given the consent of the Board of Trade to use steam power. The company issued a prospectus stating that the benefit of its tramways (as opposed to those of other companies) was that it had the right to use steam power. On the strength of that prospectus, the claimant bought shares in the company. The Board of Trade refused the company's application to use steam power except on certain portions of the tramways. The company was later wound up and the claimant brought an action for damages in the tort of deceit against the defendant directors of the company. The House of Lords, in allowing the defendants' appeal, held that the defendants were not liable in deceit because they had not made the statements in the prospectus fraudulently. They honestly believed the statements to be true (because they thought the consent needed was a mere formality) and fraud does not encompass a statement made without reasonable care by someone who honestly believes it to be true.

Lord Herschell: I think it important that it should be borne in mind that such an action differs essentially from one brought to obtain rescission of a contract on the ground of misrepresentation of a material fact. The principles which govern the two actions differ widely. Where rescission is claimed it is only necessary to prove that there was misrepresentation; then, however honestly it may have been made, however free from blame the person who made it, the contract, having been obtained by misrepresentation, cannot stand. In an action of deceit, on the contrary, it is not enough to establish misrepresentation alone; it is conceded on all hands that something more must be proved to cast liability upon the defendant, though it has been a matter of controversy what additional elements are requisite.

...

I think the authorities establish the following propositions: First, in order to sustain an action of deceit, there must be proof of fraud, and nothing short of that will suffice. Secondly, fraud is proved when it is shewn that a false representation has been made (1) knowingly, or (2) without belief in its truth, or (3) recklessly, careless whether it be true or false. Although I have treated the second and third as distinct cases, I think the third is but an instance of the second, for one who makes a statement under such circumstances can have no real belief in the truth of what he states. To prevent a false statement being fraudulent, there must, I think, always be an honest belief in its truth. And this probably covers the whole ground, for one who knowingly alleges that which is false, has obviously no such honest belief. Thirdly, if fraud be proved, the motive of the person guilty of it is immaterial. It matters not that there was no intention to cheat or injure the person to whom the statement was made.

...

In my opinion making a false statement through want of care falls far short of, and is a very different thing from, fraud, and the same may be said of a false representation honestly believed though on insufficient grounds. ...

At the same time I desire to say distinctly that when a false statement has been made the questions whether there were reasonable grounds for believing it, and what were the means of knowledge in the possession of the person making it, are most weighty matters for consideration. The ground upon which an alleged belief was founded is a most important test of its reality. I can conceive many cases where the fact that an alleged belief was destitute of all reasonable foundation would suffice of itself to convince the Court that it was not really entertained, and that the representation was a fraudulent one. So, too, although means of knowledge are, as was pointed out by Lord Blackburn in *Brownlie v Campbell* 5 App Cas 592, a very different thing from knowledge, if I thought that a person making a false statement had shut his eyes to the facts, or purposely abstained from inquiring into them, I should hold that honest belief was absent, and that he was just as fraudulent as if he had knowingly stated that which was false.

...

It now remains for me to apply what I believe to be the law to the facts of the present case. [*He reviewed the facts and continued:*]

Adopting the language of Jessel M.R. in *Smith v. Chadwick* 20 Ch D 67, I conclude by saying that on the whole I have come to the conclusion that the statement, "though in some respects inaccurate and not altogether free from imputation of carelessness, was a fair, honest and bonâ fide statement on the part of the defendants, and by no means exposes them to an action for deceit."

I think the judgment of the Court of Appeal should be reversed.

Lords Halsbury LC, Watson, Bramwell and **Fitzgerald** gave concurring speeches (the first two expressly concurring with Lord Herschell).

NOTES AND QUESTIONS

1. This is the leading case on the definition of a fraudulent misrepresentation. It establishes that a fraudulent misrepresentation is one made knowing that it is false or reckless as to whether it is true or false. In contrast if one makes a statement merely negligently, in the honest belief that it is true, there is no fraud.

2. Now that there is liability in the tort of negligence for negligent misrepresentation at common law and liability under section 2(1) of the Misrepresentation Act 1967, why would a claimant ever wish to establish the tort of deceit? Remember to ask yourself this question again when you have read all the cases in this section on damages.

Doyle v Olby (Ironmongers) Ltd [1969] 2 QB 158, Court of Appeal

The claimant bought a business from the defendant company. He was induced to do so by fraudulent representations made on behalf of the defendant. In particular he was told that the business was 'all over the counter'. In fact half of it was obtained by a travelling salesman. The claimant made a heavy loss from the business and brought an action for damages in the tort of deceit. The trial judge awarded damages of £1500. On appeal by the claimant, the Court of Appeal held that the amount of damages should be increased to £5500.

Lord Denning MR: The judge awarded Mr. Doyle £1,500 damages. Mr. Doyle appeals against that award. He says it is far too small. ...

It appears... that the plaintiff's counsel submitted, and the judge accepted, that the proper measure of damages was the "cost of making good the representation," or what came to the same thing, "the reduction in value of the goodwill" due to the misrepresentation. In so doing, he treated the representation as if it were a contractual promise, that is, as if there were a contractual term to the effect "The trade is all over the counter. There is no need to employ a traveller." I think it was the wrong measure. Damages for fraud and conspiracy are assessed differently from damages for breach of contract.

...

The second question is what is the proper measure of damages for fraud, as distinct from damages for breach of contract. ...

On principle the distinction seems to be this: in contract, the defendant has made a promise and broken it. The object of damages is to put the plaintiff in as good a position, as far as money can do it, as if the promise had been performed. In fraud, the defendant has been guilty of a deliberate wrong by inducing the plaintiff to act to his detriment. The object of damages is to compensate the plaintiff for all the loss he has suffered, so far, again, as money can do it. In contract, the damages are limited to what may reasonably be supposed to have been in the contemplation of the parties. In fraud, they are not so limited. The defendant is bound to make reparation for all the actual damages directly flowing from the fraudulent inducement. The person who has been defrauded is entitled to say:

> "I would not have entered into this bargain at all but for your representation. Owing to your fraud, I have not only lost all the money I paid you, but, what is more, I have been put to a large amount of extra expense as well and suffered this or that extra damages."

All such damages can be recovered: and it does not lie in the mouth of the fraudulent person to say that they could not reasonably have been foreseen. For instance, in this very case Mr. Doyle has not only lost the money which he paid for the business, which he would never have done if there had been no fraud: he put all that money in and lost it; but also he has been put to expense and loss in trying to run a business which has turned out to be a disaster for him. He is entitled to damages for all his loss, subject, of course to giving credit for any benefit that he has received. There is nothing to be taken off in mitigation: for there is nothing more that he could have done to reduce his loss. He did all that he could reasonably be expected to do.

...I will not go into the details myself as to the figures. It is a case for assessing damages at large, much as a jury would do. Winn LJ has considered the matter carefully and he will deal with it; but I say in advance that I agree with the figure which he is going to propose, that the damages should be in the sum of £5,500.

Winn LJ delivered a judgment concurring with Lord Denning but in which he went on to work out the damages as being £5,500. **Sachs LJ** delivered a judgment concurring with both the other two judges.

NOTES AND QUESTIONS

1. This case clarifies two points on the principles of damages for the tort of deceit. (i) The measure of damages is the tort 'reliance' measure which seeks to put the claimant into as good a position as if no representation had been made; it is *not* the contractual expectation measure which seeks to put the claimant into as good a position as if the representation had been true. (ii) The remoteness test for the tort of deceit is not 'reasonable forseeability' as in the tort of negligence (as established in *The Wagon Mound* [1961] AC 388, PC) but rather the wider test of 'directness'.

2. Why is the reliance measure the correct measure for the tort of deceit? Does this reflect the difference between lying and breach of promise?

3. After you have also read the next case, consider why there is a wider test of remoteness for the tort of deceit than for the tort of negligence.

Smith New Court Ltd v Scrimgeour Vickers (Asset Management) Ltd
[1997] AC 254, House of Lords

The claimant was interested in buying shares in FIS Inc that were pledged to the defendant bank. In reliance on fraudulent misrepresentations by Roberts, a representative of the bank, that there were close rival bids, the claimant bought shares at 82.25p per share at a total price of over £23.1 million. A couple of months later, FIS Inc revealed that it had been the victim of a massive fraud (unrelated to the fraudulent misrepresentations in this case and referred to as the 'Guerin' fraud) and, as a consequence, its share price dropped dramatically. The claimant sold the shares over several months at prices of between 30p and 49p per share for £11,788,204 (at a loss of £11,353,220). In the claimant's action in the tort of deceit, the Court of Appeal limited the damages to £1,196,010 as being the difference between the price paid for the shares and the market value of the shares at the date of purchase. In allowing the claimant's appeal on the quantum of damages, the House of Lords held that they were entitled to their full loss of £11,353,220 (albeit that, as they had not appealed against the trial judge's award of £10,764,005, the claim should be limited to that sum).

Lord Browne-Wilkinson: In sum, in my judgment the following principles apply in assessing the damages payable where the plaintiff has been induced by a fraudulent misrepresentation to buy property: (1) the defendant is bound to make reparation for all the damage directly flowing from the transaction; (2) although such damage need not have been foreseeable, it must have been directly caused by the transaction; (3) in assessing such damage, the plaintiff is entitled to recover by way of damages the full price paid by him, but he must give credit for any benefits which he has received as a result of the transaction; (4) as a general rule, the benefits received by him include the market value of the property acquired as at the date of acquisition; but such general rule is not to be inflexibly applied where to do so would prevent him obtaining full compensation for the wrong suffered; (5) although the circumstances in which the general rule should not apply cannot be comprehensively stated, it will normally not apply where either (a) the misrepresentation has continued to operate after the date of the acquisition of the asset so as to induce the plaintiff to retain the asset or (b) the circumstances of the case are such that the plaintiff is, by reason of the fraud, locked into the property. (6) In addition, the plaintiff is entitled to recover consequential losses caused by the transaction; (7) the plaintiff must take all reasonable steps to mitigate his loss once he has discovered the fraud. …

How then do those principles apply in the present case? First, there is no doubt that the total loss incurred by Smith was caused by the Roberts fraud, unless it can be said that Smith's own decision to retain the shares until after the revelation of the Guerin fraud was a causative factor. The Guerin fraud had been committed before Smith acquired the shares on 21 July 1989. Unknown to everybody, on that date the shares were already pregnant with disaster. Accordingly when, pursuant to the Roberts fraud, Smith acquired the…shares they were induced to purchase a flawed asset. This is not a case of the difficult kind that can arise where the depreciation in the asset acquired between the date of acquisition and the date of realisation may be due to factors affecting the market which have occurred after the date of the defendant's fraud. In the present case the loss was incurred by reason of the purchasing of the shares which were pregnant with the loss and that purchase was caused by the Roberts fraud.

Can it then be said that the loss flowed not from Smith's acquisition but from Smith's decision to retain the shares? In my judgment it cannot. The judge found that the shares were acquired as a market-making risk and at a price which Smith would only have paid for an acquisition as a market-making risk. As such, Smith could not dispose of them on 21 July 1989 otherwise than at a loss. Smith were in a special sense locked into the shares having bought them for a purpose and at a price which precluded them from sensibly disposing of them. It was not alleged or found that Smith acted unreasonably in retaining the shares for as long as they did or in realising them in the manner in which they did.

...

In my judgment, this is one of those cases where to give full reparation to Smith, the benefit which Smith ought to bring into account to be set against its loss for the total purchase price paid should be the actual resale price achieved by Smith when eventually the shares were sold.

Lord Steyn: [I now turn] to the question of policy whether there is a justification for differentiating between the extent of liability for civil wrongs depending on where in the sliding scale from strict liability to intentional wrongdoing the particular civil wrong fits in. It may be said that logical symmetry and a policy of not punishing intentional wrongdoers by civil remedies favour a uniform rule. On the other hand, it is a rational and defensible strategy to impose wider liability on an intentional wrongdoer. ... Such a policy of imposing more stringent remedies on an intentional wrongdoer serves two purposes. First it serves a deterrent purpose in discouraging fraud. ... Secondly, as between the fraudster and the innocent party, moral considerations militate in favour of requiring the fraudster to bear the risk of misfortunes directly caused by his fraud. I make no apology for referring to moral considerations. The law and morality are inextricably interwoven.

...

The logic of the decision in *Doyle v. Olby (Ironmongers) Ltd.* justifies the following propositions. (1) The plaintiff in an action for deceit is not entitled to be compensated in accordance with the contractual measure of damage, i.e. the benefit of the bargain measure. He is not entitled to be protected in respect of his positive interest in the bargain. (2) The plaintiff in an action for deceit is, however, entitled to be compensated in respect of his negative interest. The aim is to put the plaintiff into the position he would have been in if no false representation had been made. (3) The practical difference between the two measures was lucidly explained in a contemporary case note on *Doyle v. Olby (Ironmongers) Ltd:* G. H. Treitel, "Damages for Deceit" (1969) 32 M.L.R. 556, 558-559. The author said:

> "If the plaintiff's bargain would have been a bad one, even on the assumption that the representation was true, he will do best under the tortious measure. If, on the assumption that the representation was true, his bargain would have been a good one, he will do best under the first contractual measure (under which he may recover something even if the actual value of what he has recovered is greater than the price)."

(4) Concentrating on the tort measure, the remoteness test whether the loss was reasonably foreseeable had been authoritatively laid down in *The Wagon Mound* in respect of the tort of negligence a few years before *Doyle v. Olby (Ironmongers) Ltd.* was decided: *Overseas Tankship (U.K.) Ltd. v. Morts Dock & Engineering Co. Ltd. (The Wagon Mound)* [1961] A.C. 388. *Doyle v. Olby (Ironmongers) Ltd.* settled that a wider test applies in an action for deceit. (5) The dicta in all three judgments, as well as the actual calculation of damages in *Doyle v. Olby (Ironmongers) Ltd.*, make clear that the victim of the fraud is entitled to compensation for all the actual loss directly flowing from the transaction induced by the wrongdoer. That includes heads of consequential loss. (6) Significantly in the present context the rule in the previous paragraph is not tied to any process of valuation at the date of the transaction. It is squarely based on the overriding compensatory principle, widened in view of the fraud to cover all direct consequences. The legal measure is to compare the position of the plaintiff as it was before the fraudulent statement was made to him with his position as it became as a result of his reliance on the fraudulent statement.

Doyle v. Olby (Ironmongers) Ltd. was subsequently applied by the Court of Appeal in two Court of Appeal decisions: *East v. Maurer* [1991] 1 W.L.R. 461 and *Smith Kline & French Laboratories Ltd. v. Long* [1989] 1 W.L.R. 1. *East v. Maurer* is of some significance since it throws light on a point which arose in argument. Counsel for [the defendant] argued that in the case of a fraudulently induced sale of a business, loss of profits is only recoverable on the basis of the contractual measure and never on the basis of the tort measure applicable to fraud. This is an oversimplification. The plaintiff is not entitled to demand that the defendant must pay to him the profits of the business as represented. On the other hand, *East v. Maurer* shows that an award based on the hypothetical profitable business in which the plaintiff would have engaged but for deceit is permissible: it is classic consequential loss. Turning to the *Smith Kline* case it has been suggested that the *Doyle v. Olby (Ironmongers) Ltd.* rule was wrongly applied: *Burrows, Remedies for Torts and Breach of Contract*, 2nd ed. (1994), pp. 173-174. The correctness of that comment I need not examine. In my view it is sufficient to say that the principles emerging from *Doyle v. Olby (Ironmongers) Ltd.* are good law.

...

In the actual circumstances of this case I am satisfied that there was a sufficient causal link between the fraud and Smith's loss. Moreover, for substantially the same reasons, I would hold that Smith's losses, calculated on the basis of the difference between the price paid and the proceeds of subsequent realisations, flow directly from the fraud. In my view Smith would on this basis be entitled to recover the sum of about £11.3m. Smith merely seeks restoration of the order for payment of £10,764,005 which Chadwick J. made on a different basis. In law Smith are entitled to succeed on this appeal to that extent.

Lord Keith of Kinkel and **Lord Slynn of Hadley** concurred with Lord Browne-Wilkinson and Lord Steyn. **Lord Mustill** delivered a speech concurring with Lord Browne-Wilkinson and Lord Steyn.

NOTES

1. The importance of this case lies in: first, its clear confirmation that *Doyle v Olby* had been correct in what it had said on the aim of, and remoteness test for, damages in the tort of deceit; and, secondly, its rejection of any rigid rule that a court has to assess the value of shares (or other property) bought at the date when bought. Both the trial judge and the Court of Appeal had wrongly thought that one should assess the damages at that date albeit that they had radically differed as to what the correct valuation at that date should be (the trial judge, but not the Court of Appeal, thought that one should take into account the impact on the share value that knowledge of the Guerin fraud would have had).

2. On the facts, all the loss on the shares was held recoverable because it was not too remote (applying the wider directness test for deceit) and because the claimant had not acted unreasonably in holding onto the shares and selling them at the low prices ultimately realised.

3. While Lord Steyn stressed the difference between the tortious and contractual measures of damages, he also recognised, giving *East v Maurer* as an example, that it is incorrect to think that loss of profits can only be recovered in contract. In the *East* case, the claimant had been induced to buy a hair salon by the vendor's fraudulent misrepresentation that he would not be continuing to run a competing salon. In an action for the tort of deceit, the claimant was awarded not only the price paid minus the selling price, plus the trading losses, plus the expenses incurred in buying and selling and carrying out

improvements, but also £10,000 for profits forgone. However, it was emphasised by the Court of Appeal that the profits forgone that were recoverable in tort were what the claimant might have been expected to make in another similar hairdressing business. The profits that would have been made in this particular business, had the vendor's representation been true, could only have been recovered had there been the breach of a contractual warranty.

4.   Subsequent to *Smith New Court*, there was an interesting example of the recovery of lost profits in the tort of deceit in *Clef Acquitaine SARL v Laporte Materials (Barrow) Ltd* [2001] QB 488, CA. The claimant had entered into two profitable distributorship contracts with the defendant. The defendant had induced the claimant to agree to the particular terms by a fraudulent misrepresentation. Had that fraudulent misrepresentation not been made, the claimant would have entered into the contracts with the defendant on more favourable terms and would have made greater profits than it in fact did make. In an action in deceit, it was held that the claimant was entitled to those gains foregone (that is, the greater profits lost). It was no bar to awarding damages for those lost profits that the claimant had still entered into profitable, rather than loss-making, contracts with the defendant.

(2) Negligent Misrepresentation Actionable in the Tort of Negligence

Hedley Byrne & Co Ltd v Heller & Partners Ltd
[1964] AC 465, House of Lords

The claimants were advertising agents. A customer, Easipower Ltd, placed a large order and before carrying out the order the claimants wished to check Easipower's financial standing. They instructed their bank to request a bankers' report from Easipower's bank, the defendant. The defendant stated on a letter headed 'without responsibility on the part of this bank' that Easipower was 'considered good for its ordinary business engagements'. Relying on this, the claimants proceeded with Easipower's order. Easipower later went into liquidation and the claimants lost £17,000 on the contracts with them. As there had been no contract between the claimants and the defendant, the claimants brought an action in the tort of negligence against the defendant. The defendant argued that there was no duty of care owed as regards statements or, alternatively, that they had excluded any liability by virtue of the heading in the letter. In dismissing the claimants' appeal, the House of Lords held that where, as here, there was a special relationship between the parties, there was a duty of care owed in the making of the statement (so that the tort of negligence applied) but that liability had been excluded by the heading.

Lord Morris of Borth-y-Gest:
My Lords, I consider that it…should now be regarded as settled that if someone possessed of a special skill undertakes, quite irrespective of contract, to apply that skill for the assistance of another person who relies upon such skill, a duty of care will arise. The fact that the service is to be given by means of or by the instrumentality of words can make no difference. Furthermore, if in a sphere in which a person is so placed that others could reasonably rely upon his judgment or his skill or upon his ability to make careful inquiry, a person takes it

upon himself to give information or advice to, or allows his information or advice to be passed on to, another person who, as he knows or should know, will place reliance upon it, then a duty of care will arise.

...

[I]n my judgment, the bank in the present case, by the words which they employed, effectively disclaimed any assumption of a duty of care. They stated that they only responded to the inquiry on the basis that their reply was without responsibility. If the inquirers chose to receive and act upon the reply they cannot disregard the definite terms upon which it was given. They cannot accept a reply given with a stipulation and then reject the stipulation. Furthermore, within accepted principles...the words employed were apt to exclude any liability for negligence.

Lords Reid, Hodson, Devlin and **Pearce** all delivered speeches dismissing the appeal.

NOTES AND QUESTIONS

1. This is one of the most famous cases in the law of tort. Both the case and the subsequent refinements of it are extensively analysed in tort courses and, for this reason, the above extract is a short one and we will not explore the many cases subsequently applying or distinguishing it. For that, see H Rogers, *Winfield and Jolowicz on Tort* (17th edn, 2006) 11-16–11-32.

2. For the purposes of contract law, *Hedley Byrne* is relevant only in so far as a negligent misrepresentation induces the making of a contract between the parties (which was not the case in *Hedley Byrne* itself). It was *Esso v Mardon*, below, that made clear that *Hedley Byrne* is applicable to a pre-contractual negligent misrepresentation.

3. The non-contractual disclaimer in this case would now be subject to the Unfair Contract Terms Act 1977 sections 2(2) and 11(3): see analogously *Smith v Eric Bush*, above, 275. Do you think it would now fail the reasonableness test?

Esso Petroleum Co Ltd v Mardon [1976] QB 801, Court of Appeal

For the facts, see above, 164.

Lord Denning MR [*having decided that there was a collateral warranty, see above, 164–165, he went on to consider the alternative claim in tort:*]

Negligent misrepresentation

Assuming that there was no warranty, the question arises whether Esso are liable for negligent misstatement under the doctrine of *Hedley Byrne & Co. Ltd. v. Heller & Partners Ltd.* [1964] A.C. 465. It has been suggested that *Hedley Byrne* cannot be used so as to impose liability for negligent pre-contractual statements: and that, in a pre-contract situation, the remedy (at any rate before the Act of 1967) was only in warranty or nothing.

In arguing this point, [counsel for Esso] took his stand in this way. He submitted that when the negotiations between two parties resulted in a contract between them, their rights and duties were governed by the law of contract and not by the law of tort. There was, therefore, no place in their relationship for *Hedley Byrne* [1964] A.C. 465, which was solely on liability in tort. He relied particularly on *Clark v. Kirby-Smith* [1964] Ch. 506 where Plowman J. held that the liability of a solicitor for negligence was a liability in contract and not in tort, following the observations of Sir Wilfrid Greene M.R. in *Groom v. Crocker* [1939] 1 K.B. 194, 206. [Counsel for Esso] might also have cited *Bagot v. Stevens Scanlan & Co. Ltd.* [1966] 1 Q.B. 197, about an architect; and other cases too. But I venture to suggest that those cases are in conflict with other decisions of high authority which were not cited in them. These decisions show that, in the case of a professional man, the duty to use reasonable care arises not only in contract, but is also imposed by the law apart from contract, and is therefore actionable in tort. It is comparable to the duty of reasonable care which is owed by a master to his servant, or vice versa. It can be put either in contract or in tort: see *Lister v. Romford Ice and Cold Storage Co. Ltd.* [1957] A.C. 555, 587 by Lord Radcliffe and *Matthews v. Kuwait Bechtel Corporation* [1959] 2 Q.B. 57.

...

It follows that I cannot accept [counsel for Esso's] proposition. It seems to me that *Hedley Byrne & Co. Ltd. v. Heller & Partners Ltd.* [1964] A.C. 465, properly understood, covers this particular proposition: if a man, who has or professes to have special knowledge or skill, makes a representation by virtue thereof to another – be it advice, information or opinion – with the intention of inducing him to enter into a contract with him, he is under a duty to use reasonable care to see that the representation is correct, and that the advice, information or opinion is reliable. If he negligently gives unsound advice or misleading information or expresses an erroneous opinion, and thereby induces the other side to enter into a contract with him, he is liable in damages. ...

Applying this principle, it is plain that Esso professed to have – and did in fact have – special knowledge or skill in estimating the throughput of a filling station. They made the representation – they forecast a throughput of 200,000 gallons – intending to induce Mr. Mardon to enter into a tenancy on the faith of it. They made it negligently. It was a "fatal error." And thereby induced Mr. Mardon to enter into a contract of tenancy that was disastrous to him. For this misrepresentation they are liable in damages.

[*He went on to consider the measure of damages, for both breach of warranty and negligent misrepresentation, as set out above, 165.*]

NOTES AND QUESTIONS

1. This case made clear that *Hedley Byrne* is applicable to a negligent misrepresentation inducing the misrepresentee to enter a contract with the misrepresentor. But, as we shall see, in that situation *Hedley Byrne* has in practice been rendered largely redundant by section 2(1) of the Misrepresentation Act 1967. Why was the Act inapplicable in *Esso v Mardon*? (See above, 164.)

2. On the face of it, a problem with the claim for the tortious negligent misrepresentation was that the forecast was an opinion (being a statement as to the future) rather than a statement of fact. Although the judges did not make clear precisely how this objection was overcome, it would appear that, consistently with their approach to the contractual warranty (see above, 165), the relevant false fact was treated as being that reasonable care had been exercised in making the forecast (or, similarly, that there were reasonable grounds for that forecast). On the distinction between *Bisset v Wilkinson* and *Esso v Mardon* see above, 541, note 3.

(3) Negligent and Purely Innocent Misrepresentation under the Misrepresentation Act 1967

Misrepresentation Act 1967, section 2

2 Damages for misrepresentation

(1) Where a person has entered into a contract after a misrepresentation has been made to him by another party thereto and as a result thereof he has suffered loss, then, if the person making the misrepresentation would be liable to damages in respect thereof had the misrepresentation been made fraudulently, that person shall be so liable notwithstanding that the misrepresentation was not made fraudulently, unless he proves that he had reasonable ground to believe and did believe up to the time the contract was made that the facts represented were true.

(2) Where a person has entered into a contract after a misrepresentation has been made to him otherwise than fraudulently, and he would be entitled, by reason of the misrepresentation, to rescind the contract, then, if it is claimed, in any proceedings arising out of the contract, that the contract ought to be or has been rescinded the court or arbitrator may declare the contract subsisting and award damages in lieu of rescission, if of opinion that it would be equitable to do so, having regard to the nature of the misrepresentation and the loss that would be caused by it if the contract were upheld, as well as to the loss that rescission would cause to the other party.

(3) Damages may be awarded against a person under subsection (2) of this section whether or not he is liable to damages under subsection (1) thereof, but where he is so liable an award under the said subsection (2) shall be taken into account in assessing his liability under the said subsection (1).

(a) Overview of Section 2

(i)   In the context of misrepresentations inducing a contract between the parties, section 2(1) is similar to *Hedley Byrne* liability, but with a reversed burden of proof as regards the negligence. That is, it is for the misrepresentor to prove that it had reasonable grounds for making the statement (ie that it was non-negligent). Provided one always remembers that there is a reverse burden of proof, it can be regarded as creating a statutory tort of negligent misrepresentation. As we shall see, the 'fiction of fraud' wording has caused problems.

(ii)   Section 2(2) allows a court, in its discretion, to award damages instead of rescission for a negligent or a purely innocent misrepresentation. As we shall see, the precise purpose of this has been a matter of dispute.

(b) Cases on Section 2(1) of the Misrepresentation Act 1967

Howard Marine and Dredging Co Ltd v A Ogden & Sons (Excavations) Ltd [1978] QB 574, Court of Appeal

The defendants (Ogden) wished to hire barges to transport excavated clay from a building site to be dumped at sea. They approached the claimants (Howards) whose employee, Mr O'Loughlin, in the course of negotiations represented to Mr Redpath (of Ogdens) that their two barges had a carrying capacity of about 1600 tonnes deadweight. This figure was based on the Lloyd's Register entry for the relevant barges, which was incorrect. In fact the barges had a carrying capacity of about 1055 tonnes. Mr O'Loughlin had seen the correct figure for the capacity in the German shipping documents (the barges were German-built) but had preferred to rely on the Lloyd's Register entry. In the hire contracts (the charterparties) entered into, there was a clause saying that the defendants' acceptance of the barges was conclusive that they were in every way satisfactory to them. After difficulties with the barges, the defendants refused to pay the greater part of the contract price. The claimants terminated the contracts and brought an action for the outstanding payments. The defendants counterclaimed for damages (i) for breach of a collateral warranty (ii) under section 2(1) of the Misrepresentation Act 1967 and (iii) for negligent misrepresentation under *Hedley Byrne v Heller*. It was contended by the claimants that they had a reasonable ground to believe that their representation was true as it was based on the Lloyd's Register, the shipping trade's 'bible'. While all three judges in the Court of Appeal held that the representation was not a contractual collateral warranty, Bridge and Shaw LJJ (Lord Denning MR dissenting) held that there was liability under section 2(1) and that it had not been validly excluded. This made it unnecessary to decide whether there was also liability under *Hedley Byrne* (although Shaw LJ held that there was such liability, Lord Denning MR held that there was not, and Bridge LJ doubted that there was). The extract below is purely concerned with liability under section 2(1).

Bridge LJ: The first question … is whether Howards would be liable in damages in respect of Mr. O'Loughlin's misrepresentation if it had been made fraudulently, that is to say, if he had known that it was untrue. An affirmative answer to that question is inescapable. The judge found in terms that what Mr. O'Loughlin said about the capacity of the barges was said with the object of getting the hire contract for Howards, in other words, with the intention that it should be acted on. This was clearly right. Equally clearly the misrepresentation was in fact acted on by Ogdens. It follows, therefore, on the plain language of the statute that, although there was no allegation of fraud, Howards must be liable unless they proved that Mr. O'Loughlin had reasonable ground to believe what he said about the barges' capacity.

It is unfortunate that the judge never directed his mind to the question whether Mr. O'Loughlin had any reasonable ground for his belief. The question he asked himself, in considering liability under the Misrepresentation Act 1967, was whether the innocent misrepresentation was negligent. He concluded that if Mr. O'Loughlin had given the inaccurate information in the course of the April telephone conversations he would have been negligent to do so but that in the circumstances obtaining at the Otley interview in July there was no negligence. I take it that he meant by this that on the earlier occasions the circumstances were such that he would have been under a duty to check the accuracy of his information, but on the later occasions he was exempt from any such duty. I appreciate the basis of this distinction, but it seems to me, with respect, quite irrelevant to any question of liability under the statute. If the representee proves a misrepresentation which, if fraudulent, would have sounded in damages, the onus passes immediately to the representor to prove that he had reasonable ground to believe the facts represented. In other words the liability of the representor does not depend upon his being under a duty of care the extent of which may vary according to the circumstances in which the representation is made. In the course of negotiations leading to a contract the statute imposes an absolute obligation not to state facts which the representor cannot prove he had reasonable ground to believe.

…

[I]t is to be assumed that Mr. O'Loughlin was perfectly honest throughout. But the question remains whether his evidence, however benevolently viewed, is sufficient to show that he had an objectively reasonable ground to disregard the figure in the ship's documents and to prefer the Lloyd's Register figure. I think it is not. The fact that he was more interested in cubic capacity could not justify reliance on one figure of deadweight capacity in preference to another. The fact that the deadweight figure in the ship's documents was a freshwater figure was of no significance since, as he knew, the difference between freshwater and sea water deadweight capacity was minimal. Accordingly I conclude that Howards failed to prove that Mr. O'Loughlin had reasonable ground to believe the truth of his misrepresentation to Mr. Redpath.

Shaw LJ gave a judgment concurring with Bridge LJ in respect of section 2(1). **Lord Denning MR** dissented.

NOTES AND QUESTIONS

1. The above extract stresses the burden of proof advantage in claiming for negligent misrepresentation under section 2(1) rather than at common law under *Hedley Byrne*.
2. The further possible advantage of section 2(1) is that it obviates the need to establish that a duty of care is owed in making the statement. That is, it is arguable that not every representation by a contracting party to the other that induces the contract triggers a *Hedley Byrne* duty of care. Rather it is arguable that the 'special relationship' needed for a *Hedley Byrne* duty of care requires something more than that the parties are negotiating a contract. Bridge LJ's judgment is a practical illustration because he went on to say, at 598, 'I doubt if the circumstances surrounding the misrepresentation ... were such as to impose on Howards a common law duty of care for the accuracy of the statement.'
3. In the light of the above advantages of section 2(1) of the Misrepresentation Act 1967 over *Hedley Byrne*, should we simply ignore *Hedley Byrne* in the context of misrepresentations inducing a contract between the parties?
4. For the reasoning on exclusion of liability in this case, see below, 585.

Royscot Trust Ltd v Rogerson [1991] 2 QB 297, Court of Appeal

The defendant car dealer agreed to sell a car on hire purchase to Rogerson for £7600 of which £1200 was to be paid as a deposit. In its proposal to the claimant finance company for it to finance this deal (which would involve the claimant paying the defendant the balance of £6400 and then being repaid a higher sum in instalments by Rogerson) the defendant non-fraudulently misrepresented that the price was £8000 and the deposit £1600. The claimant would only finance hire-purchases if the deposit was at least 20 per cent of the purchase price. That was not the case on the true figures but, as the deal as represented had a deposit of 20 per cent, the claimant went ahead. Rogerson paid the claimant instalments of £2,774.76 but then stopped paying and informed the claimant that he had wrongfully sold the car. The claimant brought an action against the defendant for damages for misrepresentation under section 2(1) of the Misrepresentation Act 1967 claiming the difference (£3,625.24) between the sum it had paid to the defendant (£6400) and the amount of the instalments received from Rogerson (£2,774.76). The defendant argued that the claimant had suffered no recoverable loss, as the wrongful sale of the car either was too remote or broke the chain of causation. The trial judge awarded damages of £1600 on a basis that neither party sought to uphold. In allowing the claimant's appeal, the Court of Appeal held that, as the wrongful sale of the car was not too remote, the claimant was entitled to damages for its full loss of £3,625.24.

Balcombe LJ: As a result of some dicta by Lord Denning M.R. in two cases in the Court of Appeal – *Gosling v. Anderson* [1972] E.G.D. 709 and *Jarvis v. Swans Tours Ltd.* [1973] Q.B. 233, 237 – and the decision at first instance in *Watts v. Spence* [1976] Ch. 165, there was some doubt whether the measure of damages for an innocent misrepresentation giving rise to a cause of action under the Act of 1967 was the tortious measure, so as to put the representee in the position in which he would have been if he had never entered into the contract, or the contractual measure, so as to put the representee in the position in which he would have been if the misrepresentation had been true, and thus in some cases give rise to a claim for damages for loss of bargain. ...However, there is now a number of decisions which make it clear that the tortious measure of damages is the true one. ... One at least, *Chesneau v. Interhome Ltd.* (1983) 134 N.L.J. 341; Court of Appeal (Civil Division) Transcript No. 238 of 1983, is a decision of this court. The claim was one under section 2(1) of the Act of 1967 and the appeal concerned the assessment of damages. In the course of his judgment Eveleigh L.J. said:

> "[Damages] should be assessed in a case like the present one on the same principles as damages are assessed in tort. The subsection itself says: 'if the person making the misrepresentation would be liable to damages in respect thereof had the misrepresentation been made fraudulently, that person shall be so liable . . .' By 'so liable' I take it to mean liable as he would be if the misrepresentation had been made fraudulently."

In view of the wording of the subsection it is difficult to see how the measure of damages under it could be other than the tortious measure and, despite the initial aberrations referred to above, that is now generally accepted. Indeed counsel before us did not seek to argue the contrary.

The first main issue before us was: accepting that the tortious measure is the right measure, is it the measure where the tort is that of fraudulent misrepresentation, or is it the measure where the tort is negligence at common law? The difference is that in cases of fraud a plaintiff is entitled to any loss which flowed from the defendant's fraud, even if the loss could not have been foreseen: see *Doyle v. Olby (Ironmongers) Ltd.* [1969] 2 Q.B. 158. In my judgment the wording of the subsection is clear: the person making the innocent misrepresentation shall be "so liable," i.e., liable to damages as if the representation had been made fraudulently. ...

This was also the original view of the academic writers. In an article, "The Misrepresentation Act 1967" (1967) 30 M.L.R. 369 by P. S. Atiyah and G. H. Treitel, the authors say, at pp. 373-374:

> "The measure of damages in the statutory action will apparently be that in an action of deceit . . . But more probably the damages recoverable in the new action are the same as those recoverable in an action of deceit . . ."

Professor Treitel has since changed his view. In *Treitel, The Law of Contract*, 7th ed. (1987), p. 278, he says:

> "Where the action is brought under section 2(1) of the Misrepresentation Act, one possible view is that the deceit rule will be applied by virtue of the fiction of fraud. But the

preferable view is that the severity of the deceit rule can only be justified in cases of actual fraud and that remoteness under section 2(1) should depend, as in actions based on negligence, on the test of foreseeability."

The only authority cited in support of the "preferable" view is *Shepheard v. Broome* [1904] A.C. 342, a case under section 38 of the Companies Act 1867, which provided that in certain circumstances a company director, although not in fact fraudulent, should be "deemed to be fraudulent." As Lord Lindley said, at p. 346: "To be compelled by Act of Parliament to treat an honest man as if he were fraudulent is at all times painful," but he went on to say:

"but the repugnance which is naturally felt against being compelled to do so will not justify your Lordships in refusing to hold the appellant responsible for acts for which an Act of Parliament clearly declares he is to be held liable."

The House of Lords so held.

It seems to me that that case, far from supporting Professor Treitel's view, is authority for the proposition that we must follow the literal wording of section 2(1), even though that has the effect of treating, so far as the measure of damages is concerned, an innocent person as if he were fraudulent.

Chitty on Contracts, 26th ed. (1989), vol. 1, p. 293, para. 439, says:

"it is doubtful whether the rule that the plaintiff may recover even unforeseeable losses suffered as the result of fraud would be applied; it is an exceptional rule which is probably justified only in cases of actual fraud."

No authority is cited in support of that proposition save a reference to the passage in Professor Treitel's book cited above.

Professor Furmston in *Cheshire, Fifoot and Furmston's Law of Contract*, 11th ed. (1986), p. 286, says:

"It has been suggested" – and the reference is to the passage in Atiyah and Treitel's article cited above – "that damages under section 2(1) should be calculated on the same principles as govern the tort of deceit. This suggestion is based on a theory that section 2(1) is based on a 'fiction of fraud.' We have already suggested that this theory is misconceived. On the other hand the action created by section 2(1) does look much more like an action in tort than one in contract and it is suggested that the rules for negligence are the natural ones to apply."

The suggestion that the "fiction of fraud" theory is misconceived occurs at p. 271, in a passage which includes:

"Though it would be quixotic to defend the drafting of the section, it is suggested that there is no such 'fiction of fraud' since the section does not say that a negligent misrepresentor shall be treated for all purposes as if he were fraudulent. No doubt the wording seeks to incorporate by reference some of the rules relating to fraud but, for instance, nothing in the wording of the subsection requires the measure of damages for deceit to be applied to the statutory action."

With all respect to the various learned authors whose works I have cited above, it seems to me that to suggest that a different measure of damage applies to an action for innocent misrepresentation under the section than that which applies to an action for fraudulent misrepresentation (deceit) at common law is to ignore the plain words of the subsection and is inconsistent with the cases to which I have referred. In my judgment, therefore, the finance company is entitled to recover from the dealer all the losses which it suffered as a result of its entering into the agreements with the dealer and the customer, even if those losses were unforeseeable, provided that they were not otherwise too remote.

[*Balcombe LJ went on to consider whether the sale of the car broke the chain of causation (see above, 375–378) and decided that it had not done so, an important factor being that the sale was reasonably foreseeable.*]

Ralph Gibson LJ gave a concurring judgment.

NOTES AND QUESTIONS

1. The case is highly controversial in laying down that the remoteness test for damages under section 2(1) of the Misrepresentation Act 1967 is the same as that applicable to the tort of deceit. That is, all loss directly caused is recoverable even if not reasonably foreseeable (although note that the judges thought that the sale of the car was in any event reasonably foreseeable). In terms of policy this is bizarre. The wider test for deceit is based on the fact that the tort is intentional and that the moral fault involved is higher than for negligence: see, eg, Lord Steyn in *Smith New Court*, above, 562. That does not apply to section 2(1) where the misrepresentation is merely negligent and indeed has a reversed burden of proof. The judges thought that they were bound so to hold because of the wording of section 2(1). Do you agree? While the 'fiction of fraud' used in section 2(1) does necessitate that damages must be available, does it necessitate that every aspect of the law on damages for deceit must apply to damages under section 2(1)? In addition to remoteness, consider, eg, contributory negligence which is inapplicable to the tort of deceit: see above, 546 note 1.

2. **R Hooley, 'Damages and the Misrepresentation Act 1967' (1991) 107 *LQR* 547**, in a persuasive criticism of the Court of Appeal's reasoning, argues that 'the subsection establishes liability in damages but not their quantum' (at 549); and goes on to say (at 550), 'Even if the arguments against this alternative interpretation prevail it is submitted that there is a strong case for Parliament to intervene and remove the reference to fraudulent misrepresentation from s 2(1). Fraudulent misrepresentation is an intentional tort where the public policy of deterring deliberate wrongdoing dictates the shift in emphasis from foreseeability to causation. No such considerations dictate that the same emphasis apply under section 2(1).' Note that, although Parliamentary intervention is most unlikely, a judicial departure from *Royscot* may be thought to be encouraged by Lord Steyn's comments in the *Smith New Court* case [1997] AC 254, 283, in which, after referring to Hooley's casenote, his Lordship said, 'Since this point does not directly arise in this case, I express no concluded view on the correctness of the *Royscot* case.' See also the article by Brown and Chandler, below, 588.

3. *If Royscot* is correct, it provides yet another advantage to a claimant (see above, 569) in basing a claim for a negligent misrepresentation on section 2(1) rather than on *Hedley Byrne v Heller*. Furthermore, it would seem to render the tort of deceit largely redundant in the context of representations inducing a contract: would there be any point in a claimant taking on the difficult burden of proving fraud, if the same damages were going to be awarded in a claim under section 2(1)?

4. One good feature of Balcombe LJ's reasoning is in clarifying that the tortious and not the contractual measure applies under section 2(1). The aim is to put the claimant into as good a position as if the representation had not been made, not into as good a position as if the representation had been true.

(c) Cases on Section 2(2) of the Misrepresentation Act 1967

William Sindall Plc v Cambridgeshire County Council
[1994] 1 WLR 1016, Court of Appeal

The claimants (Sindall) agreed to purchase land for development from the defendants (Cambridgeshire CC). In reply to an inquiry by the claimants regarding easements over the land, the defendants stated that they were not aware of any. A private sewer built 20 years before the transaction was found under the development site after the sale had been completed. The claimants brought an action for a declaration that the contract was validly rescinded on the grounds of misrepresentation and common mistake. As regards the latter, it was held that the contract had allocated the risk of the unknown sewer to the buyer so that there was no possibility of rescission for common mistake (rescission for common mistake has since been removed as a possibility by *The Great Peace*: see Chapter 12). With regard to misrepresentation, the Court of Appeal held that there was no misrepresentation. But in *obiter dicta*, set out in the extracts below, the judges went on to consider how they would have exercised their section 2(2) discretion had there been a misrepresentation.

Hoffmann LJ: My conclusion that there are no grounds for rescission, either for misrepresentation or mistake, mean that it is unnecessary to consider whether the judge correctly exercised his discretion under section 2(2) of the Misrepresentation Act 1967 not to award damages in lieu of rescission. But in case this case goes further, I should say that in my judgment the judge approached this question on a false basis, arising from his mistake about the seriousness of the defect. ...

The discretion conferred by section 2(2) is a broad one, to do what is equitable. But there are three matters to which the court must in particular have regard.

The first is the nature of the misrepresentation. It is clear from the Law Reform Committee's report that the court was meant to consider the importance of the representation in relation to the subject matter of the transaction. ...[I]n my view, in the context of a £5m. sale of land, a misrepresentation which would have cost £18,000 to put right and was unlikely seriously to have interfered with the development or resale of the property was a matter of relatively minor importance.

The second matter to which the court must have regard is "the loss that would be caused by [the misrepresentation] if the contract were upheld." The section speaks in terms of loss suffered rather than damages recoverable but clearly contemplates that if the contract is upheld, such loss will be compensated by an award of damages. Section 2(2) therefore gives a power to award damages in circumstances in which no damages would previously have been recoverable. Furthermore, such damages will be compensation for loss caused by the misrepresentation, whether it was negligent or not. This is made clear by section 2(3), which provides:

"Damages may be awarded under subsection (2) of this section whether or not he is liable to damages under subsection (1) thereof, but where he is so liable any award under subsection (2) shall be taken into account in assessing his liability under the said subsection (1)."

Damages under section 2(2) are therefore damages for the misrepresentation as such. What would be the measure of such damages? This court is not directly concerned with quantum, which would be determined at an inquiry. But since the court, in the exercise of its discretion, needs to know whether damages under section 2(2) would be an adequate remedy and to be able to compare such damages with the loss which rescission would cause to Cambridgeshire, it is necessary to decide in principle how the damages would be calculated.

...

Under section 2(1), the measure of damages is the same as for fraudulent misrepresentation, i.e. all loss caused by the plaintiff having been induced to enter into the contract: *Cemp Properties (UK) Ltd. v. Dentsply Research & Development Corporation* [1991] 2 E.G.L.R. 197. This means that the misrepresentor is invariably deprived of the benefit of the bargain (e.g. any difference between the price paid and the value of the thing sold) and may have to pay additional damages for consequential loss suffered by the representee on account of having entered into the contract. In my judgment, however, it is clear that this will not necessarily be the measure of damages under section 2(2).

First, section 2(1) provides for damages to be awarded to a person who "has entered into a contract after a misrepresentation has been made to him by another party and as a result thereof" – sc. of having entered into the contract – "he has suffered loss." In contrast, section 2(2) speaks of "the loss which would be caused by it" – sc. the misrepresentation – "if the contract were upheld." In my view, section 2(1) is concerned with the damage flowing from having entered into the contract, while section 2(2) is concerned with damage caused by the property not being what it was represented to be.

Secondly, section 2(3) contemplates that damages under section 2(2) may be less than damages under section 2(1) and should be taken into account when assessing damages under the latter subsection. This only makes sense if the measure of damages may be different.

Thirdly, the Law Reform Committee report makes it clear that section 2(2) was enacted because it was thought that it might be a hardship to the representor to be deprived of the whole benefit of the bargain on account of a minor misrepresentation. It could not possibly have intended the damages in lieu to be assessed on a principle which would invariably have the same effect.

The Law Reform Committee drew attention to the anomaly which already existed by which a minor misrepresentation gave rise to a right of rescission whereas a warranty in the same terms would have grounded no more than a claim for modest damages. It said that this anomaly would be exaggerated if its recommendation for abolition of the bar on rescission after completion were to be implemented. I think that section 2(2) was intended to give the court a power to eliminate this anomaly by upholding the contract and compensating the plaintiff for the loss he has suffered on account of the property not having been what it was represented to be. In other words, damages under section 2(2) should never exceed the sum which would have been awarded if the representation had been a warranty. It is not necessary for present purposes to discuss the circumstances in which they may be less.

If one looks at the matter when Sindall purported to rescind, the loss which would be caused if the contract were upheld was relatively small: the £18,000 it would have cost to divert the sewer, the loss of a plot and interest charges on any consequent delay at the rate of £2,000 a day. If one looks at the matter at the date of trial, the loss would have been nil because the sewer had been diverted.

The third matter to be taken into account under section 2(2) is the loss which would be caused to Cambridgeshire by rescission. This is the loss of the bargain at the top of the market (cf. *The Lucy* [1983] 1 Lloyd's Rep. 188) having to return about £8m. in purchase price and interest in exchange for land worth less than £2m.

Having regard to these matters, and in particular the gross disparity between the loss which would be caused to Sindall by the misrepresentation and the loss which would be caused to Cambridgeshire by rescission, I would have exercised my discretion to award damages in lieu of rescission.

Evans LJ: Section 2(3) makes it clear that the statutory power to award damages under section 2(2) is distinct from the plaintiff's right to recover damages under section 2(1). Quoting from section 2(2) itself, such damages are awarded "in lieu of rescission" and the court has to have regard to three factors in particular, namely, the nature of the misrepresentation, the loss that would be caused by it (sc. the misrepresentation) if the contract was upheld, and the loss that rescission would cause to the other party (sc. the non-fraudulent author of the misrepresentation). It has not been suggested that these three are the only factors which the court may take into account. The discretion is expressed in broad terms – "if of opinion that it would be equitable to do so." The three factors, however, in all but an exceptional case, are likely to be the ones to which most weight would be given, even if the subsection were silent in this respect.

No real difficulty arises in the present case as regards the nature of the misrepresentation, if any was made, nor as regards the loss which would be caused to the council, if rescission were upheld. There was no blameworthiness, on the judge's findings, so far as the council's officers in 1988-89 were concerned. The fault, if there was any, lay in their predecessors' failure to note the title deeds in 1970. The consequences of the misrepresentation were not negligible, but they were small in relation to the purchase and the project as a whole. The loss caused to the council by rescission would be very great. They would repay in excess of £5m., together with interest, and would have restored to them land worth only a fraction of that amount. In other words, they would suffer the decline in market values which has occurred since 1988. And, even if the easement had been discovered immediately and the contract had been rescinded then, the council would have suffered significant loss, simply by reason of the need to repeat the tendering process and find another buyer.

There is, however, much room for debate as to the "loss that would be caused if the contract were upheld." The subsection assumes, as I read it, that this loss will be compensated by the damages awarded, if the contract is upheld. But if the measure is the same as those awarded in respect of a fraudulent misrepresentation (*Doyle v. Olby (Ironmongers) Ltd.* [1969] 2 Q.B. 158) or under section 2(1) *(Cemp Properties (UK) Ltd. v. Dentsply Research and Development Corporation* [1991] 2 E.G.L.R. 197; cf. *Royscott Trust Ltd. v. Rogerson* [1991] 2 Q.B. 297) in cases where the contract continues in force, then two consequences seem to follow. First damages under section 2(2) are co-extensive with those under section 2(1), whereas section 2(3) suggests that they are or may be different. Secondly, an innocent and non-negligent defendant will be liable under section 2(2) for damages which he is specifically excused under section 2(1). Furthermore, if the plaintiff recovers full compensation under section 2(2), if the contract is upheld, then he will not suffer any net loss, assuming that the damages are paid.

...

In my judgment, it is not correct that the measure of damages under section 2(2) for the loss that would be caused by the misrepresentation if the contract were upheld is the same measure as under section 2(1). The latter is established by the common law and it is the amount required to compensate the party to whom the misrepresentation was made for all the losses which he has sustained by reason of his acting upon it at the time when he did. But the damages contemplated by section 2(2) are damages in lieu of rescission. The starting point for the application of the sub-section is the situation where a plaintiff has established a right to rescind the contract on grounds of innocent misrepresentation: its object is to ameliorate for the innocent misrepresentor the harsh consequences of rescission for a wholly innocent (meaning, non-negligent as well as non-fraudulent) misrepresentor, in a case where it is fairer to uphold the contract and award damages against him. Such an award of damages was not permitted in law or equity before 1967. The court, therefore, exercises a statutory jurisdiction and it does so having regard to the circumstances at the date of the hearing, when otherwise rescission would be ordered. ...

[I]t would be substantially unjust, in my judgment, to deprive Cambridgeshire of the bargain which it made in 1988, albeit that the bargain was induced by a misrepresentation innocently made, but which was of little importance in relation to the contract as a whole. That misrepresentation apart, Sindall made what has proved to be so far an unfortunate bargain for them (although they remain owners of an important potential development site in what is a notoriously cyclical market). To permit them to transfer the financial consequences to Cambridgeshire, in the circumstances of this case, could properly be described as a windfall for them.

For the above reasons, and taking into account the nature of the alleged representation and the history of the matter generally, including Sindall's deliberate failure to make any serious attempt to find a solution to the difficulty which arose when the sewer was discovered, the equitable balance, in my judgment, lies in favour of upholding the contract and awarding damages in lieu of rescission in this case. If there were a live issue under section 2(2), I would award damages in lieu of rescission and order the amount of such damages to be assessed.

There remains the question of whether these damages should include the decline in the market value of the land since the contract was made. ...[I]n my judgment they should not. This conclusion may be inconsistent with the view expressed in *McGregor on Damages*, 15th. ed. (1988), para. 1752, and in deference to the distinguished author I should explain my reasons briefly. He suggests that the measure to be adopted is

> "the same as the normal measure of damages in tort where the plaintiff has been induced to contract by fraudulent or negligent misrepresentation. . . . The overall result, therefore, is that the damages will be held to be the difference between the value transferred and the value received . . . no recovery being possible for consequential losses."

If the "value transferred" (meaning the price paid by the plaintiff, to whom the representation was made) was the market value of the property, then there is no difference between this formula and what *McGregor* calls the contract measure, that is to say, the difference between the actual value received and the value which the property would have had, if the representation had been true: see paragraph 1718. By adopting the tort measure, therefore, as he does in paragraph 1752 in the paragraph already quoted, the author impliedly rejects the contract measure, whereas in my judgment that becomes the correct measure in circumstances where the plaintiff is entitled to an order for rescission, but rescission is refused under section 2(2) of the Act. This is because the difference in value between what the plaintiff was misled into believing that he was acquiring, and the value of what he in fact received, seems to me to be the measure of the loss caused to him by the misrepresentation in a case where he cannot rescind the contract and therefore retains the property which he received. ...

It is unnecessary to explore the wider questions whether a tortious measure should ever include damages for a fall in market values, and whether this measure, as described by Lord Denning M.R. in *Doyle v. Olby (Ironmongers) Ltd.* [1969] 2 Q.B. 158, 166, is necessarily exclusive of or inconsistent with the contractual measure to the extent which has been suggested. The recovery of such damages in the present case, even if the tortious measure under section 2(2) applies, appears to be barred...

Russell LJ concurred.

NOTES AND QUESTIONS

1. While parts of this reasoning are helpful—especially the recognition that the main purpose of section 2(2) is to protect a misrepresentor against a contract being rescinded for a trivial or wholly innocent misrepresentation—some of what was said on the measure of damages under section 2(2) is puzzling. Evans

LJ explicitly said that the contract measure applies and Hoffmann LJ also saw a close link to the measure for breach of warranty. It surely cannot be correct that damages under section 2(2), which can be given for a wholly innocent misrepresentation, can go beyond the tort measure that applies for the tort of deceit and for a negligent misrepresentation at common law or under section 2(1). That ought to be the maximum that can be awarded and the real question should be whether even that full tort measure is merited under section 2(2). The reasoning may have become distorted because of the court's desire to disallow damages for the sharp fall in the market value of the land (an issue that, in a series of subsequent claims for damages against negligent valuers in tort and contract, led to the controversial decision in *South Australia Asset Management Corpn v York Montague Ltd ('SAAMCO')* [1997] AC 191, HL: see A Burrows, *Remedies for Torts and Breach of Contract* (3rd edn, 2004) 109–22)).

2.   The references to the Law Reform Committee are to its Tenth Report, *Innocent Misrepresentation* (1962) (Cmnd. 1782) which led to the Misrepresentation Act 1967.

3.   Do you agree with G Treitel, *The Law of Contract* (11th edn, 2003) 366 that damages under section 2(2) are *sui generis*?

4.   **H Beale, 'Damages in Lieu of Rescission for Misrepresentation' (1995) 111** *LQR* **60** comments on the different approaches to the measure of damages under section 2(2) taken in this case. He criticises Evans LJ's view that the measure should be the contractual measure. He argues that Evans LJ's suggestion (in the final paragraph set out above) of awarding reliance loss, but ignoring any post-contract fall in the market, is to be preferred as being consistent with the principle of section 2(2) and with Hoffmann LJ's speech.

Government of Zanzibar v British Aerospace (Lancaster House) Ltd
[2000] 1 WLR 2333, Queen's Bench Division

The claimant contracted to purchase an executive aircraft from the defendant. As a means of financing the deal, the claimant and the defendant then entered into a contract with a finance company whereby the finance company purchased the aircraft and leased it back to the claimant. The aircraft had serious faults and it was returned to the defendant to repair. The faults continued and the claimant stopped the lease payments to the finance company, whereupon the finance company took possession of the aircraft and sold it. The claimant brought an action against the defendant for rescission of the purchase agreement, or alternatively damages under section 2(1) or section 2(2), on the ground of misrepresentations that the aircraft was airworthy, reliable and without design or construction defects. In dismissing the claim it was held that, as the contract could not have been rescinded because the aircraft had been sold (ie counter-restitution was impossible), section 2(2) damages were unavailable. A further issue in the case concerned an exclusion of liability under section 2(1) and that is dealt with below, 583.

Judge Raymond Jack QC: I am satisfied that, if [the claimant] had a right by reason of misrepresentations to rescind the purchase contract after it was made, that right has now been lost. ...The aircraft has been sold.

Does that mean that any claim to damages under section 2(2) has also been lost? There has been some previous debate whether the right to damages under section 2(2) is dependent on a right to rescission still existing at the time the matter comes before the court. ...

To my mind the wording of section 2(2) shows clearly enough that the effect of the subsection is to give the court an alternative to rescission where a right to rescission has been established but the court considers that damages would be a more equitable solution. I refer in particular to "and he would be entitled," "if it is claimed ... that the contract ought to be or has been rescinded," "the court ... may declare the contract subsisting and award damages in lieu of rescission" and "as well as to the loss that rescission would cause to the other party." The last part of the section contemplates a balancing exercise between the situation if damages are awarded and that if rescission were granted: this supposes that rescission is an option open to the court. So I would disagree with the editors of *Chitty on Contracts*, 28th ed. (1999), vol. 1, pp. 383-384, para. 6-097 where it is stated that the words are far from clear.

The scheme of the section is thus in my view that section 2(1) gives a right to damages for non-fraudulent misrepresentation subject to the defence that the representor had reasonable grounds to believe his representation true, whereas section 2(2) gives the court power to award damages where this would be more equitable than making an order for rescission or upholding a previous rescission by act of party. Because it is no defence to a claim for rescission that the representor had reasonable grounds to believe the representation true, that is not a defence where the court is considering damages under section 2(2). In this way, where rescission remains an option, a claimant may do better under section 2(2) because that defence is not available against him. That is no doubt why Zanzibar seeks to rely on it in addition to section 2(1). It is also stated in *Chitty*, pp. 383-384, para. 6-097 that, if the power to award damages under section 2(2) is restricted to situations in which rescission remains possible, then it would be strange because there would be no power to award damages in situations where the right has been lost, for example, because a car which has been misrepresented has been resold. The answer to that point is the claim to damages under section 2(1), though here as a matter of policy it has been enacted that there should be the reasonable-grounds-of-belief defence.

...

In *William Sindall Plc. v. Cambridgeshire County Council* [1994] 1 W.L.R. 1016 the Court of Appeal held that no misrepresentation or mistake to found a claim for rescission had been made out. Having, however, heard full argument the court went on to consider what claim might otherwise have been made under section 2(2). The court was mainly concerned to explore the remedy in damages and did not consider the point which concerns me. It did however refer to the origin of the Act, namely the Tenth Report of the Law Reform Committee, *Innocent Misrepresentation* (1962) (Cmnd. 1782). The Report recommended the abolition of the bar to rescission which the law then imposed once a contract had been completed or performed. That abolition was given effect to by section 1 of the Act. In paragraph 11 of its report the committee considered that this wider right to rescission could work injustice in some situations, as where, for example, the misrepresentation was as to something of minor importance so rescission would be harsh on the representor. It therefore recommended in paragraph 12 that:

> "wherever the court has power to order rescission it should, as an alternative, have a discretionary power to award damages if it is satisfied that these would afford adequate compensation to the plaintiff, having regard to the nature of the misrepresentation and the fact that the injury suffered by the plaintiff is small compared with what rescission would involve."

The issue was considered and decided by Jacob J. in *Thomas Witter Ltd. v. T.B.P. Industries Ltd.* [1996] 2 All E.R. 573. He had held that rescission was no longer available because it was not possible to restore the parties to their positions before the contract. He held that the wording of section 2(2) was sufficiently ambiguous to justify reference to the proceedings in Parliament at the Act's passing. He referred to a reply given by the Solicitor-General (Hansard (H.C. Debates), 20 February 1967, cols. 1388-1389). He held that this showed that it was the Solicitor-General's view that damages could be awarded under section 2(2) where rescission was no longer possible. He accordingly held, at p. 590, that the power to award damages under section 2(2) did not depend on an extant right to rescission—it only depended on a right having existed in the past. I accept that the reply taken by itself does suggest that that was the Solicitor-General's view, though it may not be absolutely clear. But, given that this was an extempore answer given a little after 3 o'clock in the morning, I question how much weight should be given to it where it does not accord with other statements. In introducing the Bill in the House of Lords Lord Gardiner L.C. stated (Hansard (H.L. Debates), 17 May 1966, cols. 921 et seq.):

> "My Lords, this Bill implements the recommendations of the committee under five heads ... Thirdly, it empowers the court to award damages instead of ordering rescission of the contract ... I now come to damages as an alternative to rescission. The committee recommended that a discretionary power should be conferred on the court to award damages in lieu of ordering rescission where damages would afford adequate compensation to the victim of an innocent misrepresentation, whether it was made negligently or not. They thought that there would be a number of cases where the remedy of rescission might be too drastic in the circumstances. This is the recommendation which is implemented by clause 2(2)."

I conclude that both the report of the Law Reform Committee and the manner in which clause 2(2) of the Bill was introduced in the House of Lords make clear that section 2(2) gives the court a discretionary power to hold the contract to be subsisting and to award damages where it would otherwise be obliged to grant rescission or to hold that the contract had been rescinded by the representee. The court does not have that power, and does not need to have that power, where rescission is no longer available. In short, the power to award damages is an alternative to an order for rescission or the upholding of a prior rescission by the representee if that has occurred. So, if, contrary to my view, the wording of section 2(2) is unclear on this point, the matter is to be resolved in this way in accordance with the report and what was said by the Lord Chancellor. I should not follow the decision in *Thomas Witter Ltd. v. T.B.P. Industries Ltd.* I should not leave this point without mentioning the helpful discussion provided by Professor Beale, "Points on Misrepresentation" (1995) 111 L.Q.R. 385.

As rescission is no longer available as a remedy to Zanzibar, it is not open to Zanzibar to claim damages under section 2(2) of the Act.

NOTE

This reasoning—that damages cannot be awarded under section 2(2) if rescission is barred—is to be preferred to the rejected view of Jacob J in the *Thomas Witter* case (which was challenged on this point by Beale in the casenote referred to by Judge Raymond Jack QC). This is essentially because the purpose of section 2(2) was not to add to the misrepresentee's remedies but to give the courts a discretion to *cut back* the remedy of rescission where the misrepresentation has been, for example, trivial or wholly innocent and rescission would cause undue hardship to the misrepresentor.

4. EXCLUSION OF LIABILITY FOR MISREPRESENTATION: MISREPRESENTATION ACT 1967, SECTION 3

Contractual clauses excluding liability for misrepresentation raise the same issues of incorporation and construction that have been considered in relation to exemption clauses generally in Chapters 4 and 5. They will not be repeated here. On construction, see in particular 227, note 4, referring to *HIH Casualty General Insurance Ltd v Chase Manhattan Bank* [2003] UKHL 6, [2003] 2 Lloyd's Rep 61, in which a generally-worded clause excluding all liability of an insured to an insurer for misrepresentation or non-disclosure of its agent was held, on its true construction, not to exclude liability for the agent's fraudulent misrepresentation or fraudulent non-disclosure. Note also that it was clarified in that case (at [16], [24], [76], [122]) that, *as a matter of public policy,* one cannot exclude liability for one's own fraudulent misrepresentation.

In this section we are therefore solely concerned with the statutory control of contractual clauses excluding liability for misrepresentation. Moreover, there is nothing specific that needs to be said about the application of the Unfair Terms in Consumer Contracts Regulations 1999 (see above, 285) to such clauses: for, although not mentioned in the indicative list of unfair terms in Schedule 2, it is clear that the Regulations will apply in the normal way to invalidate unfair exclusions of liability for misrepresentations in *consumer* contracts. This leaves us to focus on section 3 of the Misrepresentation Act 1967 which, because of its sole concern with the exclusion of liability for misrepresentation, is more conveniently discussed here than in Chapter 6.

Misrepresentation Act 1967, section 3
(as substituted by Unfair Contract Terms Act 1977 section 8)

3 Avoidance of provision excluding liability for misrepresentation
If a contract contains a term which would exclude or restrict—

    (a)   any liability to which a party to a contract may be subject by reason of any misrepresentation made by him before the contract was made; or

    (b)   any remedy available to another party to the contract by reason of such a misrepresentation,

that term shall be of no effect except in so far as it satisfies the requirement of reasonableness as stated in section 11(1) of the Unfair Contract Terms Act 1977; and it is for those claiming that the term satisfies that requirement to show that it does.

Section 3 is concerned with the contractual exclusion or restriction of liability or remedies for a misrepresentation made by one party to the contract to the other inducing the other to enter into that contract. Mirroring issues raised on UCTA 1977 generally (above, 258–285), the cases on section 3 have considered two main questions: (1) what counts as an exemption clause so as to fall within section 3?; (2) does the clause pass, or fail, the reasonableness test?

(1) What Counts as an Exemption Clause Falling Within Section 3?

Overbrooke Estates Ltd v Glencombe Properties Ltd
[1974] 1 WLR 1335, Chancery Division

The defendant buyers successfully bid for the claimants' property in London at auction. One of the conditions of sale (R(b)) stated, 'The vendors do not make or give and neither the auctioneers nor any person in the employment of the auctioneers has any authority to make or give any representation or warranty in relation to [the property].' In response to an inquiry from the defendants, the auctioneers (Wilmotts) had represented to them that the relevant local authority had no plans for the property and were not interested in compulsory purchase of it. In the week following their successful bid, the defendants were informed by the local authority that there was a chance the property would shortly be included in a slum clearance programme. The defendants therefore refused to pay for the property and the claimants sought specific performance. The defendants argued that they were entitled to escape from the contract because of Wilmotts' misrepresentation. On the assumption that there had been a misrepresentation by the auctioneers inducing the contract, it was held that, because of the above condition, the claimants were not liable for the misrepresentation. The condition negated the ostensible authority of the agent (the auctioneers) to make representations on behalf of its principal (the claimants) and section 3 of the Misrepresentation Act 1967 did not apply. Specific performance was therefore granted.

Brightman J: [Counsel for the defendants'] argument is as follows. The words in section 3 (a), "... misrepresentation made by him before the contract was made; . . ." must include a misrepresentation made by the contracting party's agent. The authority of the contracting party's agent in such a case is a necessary ingredient of any liability sought to be imposed on such contracting party. Therefore a provision restricting the ostensible authority of the agent is a provision which restricts the liability of the contracting party for the misrepresentation. Therefore, if such a provision is relied upon to negative the principal's liability for the misrepresentation, the court has to consider what is fair and reasonable in the circumstances of the case and that can only be done in the course of the trial of the action.

To put the matter more shortly, condition R(b) excludes or restricts liability because it excludes or restricts an essential ingredient of liability, namely, the ostensible authority of Willmotts.

In my judgment section 3 of the Act will not bear the load which [counsel for the defendants] seeks to place upon it. In my view the section only applies to a provision which would exclude or restrict liability for a misrepresentation made by a party or his duly authorised agent, including of course an agent with ostensible authority. The section does not, in my judgment, in any way qualify the right of a principal publicly to limit the otherwise ostensible authority of his agent. The defendants'...argument fails.

NOTES AND QUESTIONS

1. This case lays down that a clause in a contract by which a principal denies responsibility for the representations of its agent—that is, by which a principal limits the authority of its agent—is outside section 3.
2. Although this would not have enabled the buyers to escape from the contract, they would presumably have had an action for damages against the auctioneers

in tort for negligent misrepresentation (assuming they could establish that the statement was negligently made).
3.   Had the buyers been consumers, could the clause defining the agent's authority now be struck down under the Unfair Terms in Consumer Contracts Regulations 1999?
4.   The test of reasonableness briefly referred to in this case was the test under the old section 3 of the 1967 Act.

Cremdean Properties Ltd v Nash (1977) 244 EG 547, Court of Appeal

The claimants contracted to buy a property in Bristol from the defendant. They were intending to develop it and therefore relied on the representation in the defendant's invitation to tender document that there was planning permission for approximately 17, 900 square feet of offices at the property. That was significantly higher than the true figure. The claimants sought rescission of the contract, or alternatively damages, on the grounds of that misrepresentation. The defendant sought to rely on a footnote clause in the invitation to tender document which said:

'(a) These particulars are prepared for the convenience of an intending purchaser... and although they are believed to be correct their accuracy is not guaranteed and any error, omission or misdescription shall not annul the sale or be grounds on which compensation may be claimed and neither do they constitute any part of an offer of a contract.
(b) Any intending purchaser...must satisfy himself by inspection of otherwise as to the correctness of each of the statements contained in these particulars.'

In refusing the defendant's appeal on a preliminary issue as to the applicability of section 3, the Court of Appeal held that the footnote clause was an exclusion of liability for misrepresentation so that it fell within section 3 of the 1967 Act.

Bridge LJ: Mr Newsom's able argument on behalf of the defendant can really be summarised very shortly. In effect what he says is this. The terms of the footnote are not simply, if contractual at all, a contractual exclusion either of any liability to which the defendant would otherwise be subject for any misrepresentation in the document, or of any remedy otherwise available on that ground to the plaintiff. The footnote is effective, so the argument runs, to nullify any representation in the document altogether; it is effective, so it is said, to bring about a situation in law as if no representation at all had ever been made. For my part, I am quite unable to accept that argument. I reject it primarily on the simple basis that on no reading of the language of the footnote could it have the remarkable effect contended for.
[*He referred to* Overbrooke Estates v Glencombe *and continued:*]
I respectfully agree entirely with the whole of [Brightman J's] reasoning. With respect to Mr Newsom's argument I am unable to see that it has any application at all to the facts of the present case, because there never was any question here but that the agents acting for the first defendant and the other defendants, when they published the document on which the plaintiffs rely as embodying the relevant misrepresentation, had the full authority of their principals to say what they did say in the document. It is one thing to say that section 3 does not inhibit a principal from publicly giving notice limiting the ostensible authority of his agents; it is quite another thing to say that a principal can circumvent the plainly intended effect of section 3 by a clause excluding his own liability for a representation which he has undoubtedly made.

I am quite content to found my judgment in this case on the proposition that the language of the footnote relied upon by Mr Newsom simply does not, on its true interpretation, have the effect contended for. But I would go further and say that if the ingenuity of a draftsman could devise language which would have that effect, I am extremely doubtful whether the court would allow it to operate so as to defeat section 3. Supposing the vendor included a clause which the purchaser was required to, and did, agree to in some such terms as "notwithstanding any statement of fact included in these particulars the vendor shall be conclusively deemed to have made no representation within the meaning of the Misrepresentation Act 1967," I should have thought that that was only a form of words the intended and actual effect of which was to exclude or restrict liability, and I should not have thought that the courts would have been ready to allow such ingenuity in forms of language to defeat the plain purpose at which section 3 is aimed.

Scarman LJ: [T]he case for the appellant does have an audacity and a simple logic which I confess I find attractive. It runs thus: a statement is not a representation unless it is also a statement that what is stated is true. If in context a statement contains no assertion, express or implied, that its content is accurate, there is no representation. Ergo, there can be no misrepresentation; ergo, the Misrepresentation Act 1967 cannot apply to it. Humpty Dumpty would have fallen for this argument. If we were to fall for it, the Misrepresentation Act would be dashed to pieces which not all the King's lawyers could put together again.

Buckley LJ concurred.

NOTE

This decision is clearly correct. The clause in effect said 'we have made no representations' or 'any representation we have made does not count'. A decision that such a clause was outside section 3 would have 'driven a coach and horses' through the section.

Government of Zanzibar v British Aerospace (Lancaster House) Ltd
[2000] 1 WLR 2333, Queen's Bench Division

For the main facts, see above, 577. We are here concerned solely with the clause (clause 23) in the contract for the purchase of the aircraft which, according to the defendant, excluded its liability for misrepresentation under section 2 of the Misrepresentation Act 1967. It was held that, while the second and third parts, but not the first part, of clause 23 fell within section 3 of the 1967 Act, there was insufficient evidence to determine whether those parts of the clause passed or failed the reasonableness test.

Judge Raymond Jack QC: It is the case of BAeLH that Zanzibar's claims for damages for misrepresentation under both section 2(1) and (2) of the Act are barred by clause 23 of the purchase contract. The clause is set out in the contract as a single paragraph. For ease of reference I will set it out in three parts, which I will head A, B and C:

"[A] The parties have negotiated this contract on the basis that the terms and conditions set out herein represent the entire agreement between them relating in any way whatsoever to the aircraft and the initial and continuing spares which form the subject matter of this contract and [B] accordingly they agree that all liabilities for and remedies in respect of any representations made are excluded save in so far as provided in this contract. [C] The parties further agree that neither party has placed any reliance whatsoever on any representations agreements statements or understandings whether oral or in writing made prior to the date of this contract other than those expressly incorporated or recited in this contract."

Part A is what is often called an entire agreement clause. The wording of this part of clause 23 does not affect Zanzibar's right to rely on any misrepresentations. I refer to *Alman v. Associated Newspapers Group Ltd.*, 20 June 1980 and to the Court of Appeal's judgment in *Deepak Fertilisers and Petrochemicals Corporation v. ICI Chemicals & Polymers Ltd.* [1999] 1 Lloyd's Rep. 387, 395, para. 34. Part B clearly excludes liability for misrepresentations unless the misrepresentation has become a term of the contract – which is not the case here. Section 3 of the Misrepresentation Act 1967 as amended provides that such a clause shall be of no effect except in so far as it satisfies the requirement of reasonableness as stated in section 11(1) of the Unfair Contract Terms Act 1977. The burden of showing that it does is laid by the section on BAeLH.

...

[T]he court must consider the particular facts. They include the nature and circumstances of the negotiations which led to the agreement in question. I am not in a position to conduct that inquiry. Nor is it an appropriate exercise on applications such as the present. I conclude that it is not shown that Zanzibar has no real prospect [of] resisting the case to be made by BAeLH that part B of clause 23 is reasonable within the terms of section 3.

Part C of clause 23 was described by Mr. Hollander [counsel for BAeLH] as a warranty that Zanzibar has not relied on any representations. He submitted alternatively that it provided an estoppel. There is a discussion of how a somewhat similar term may operate in *E. A. Grimstead & Son Ltd. v. McGarrigan* [27 October 1999]. But, however the present term operates, in my view it comes within section 3 of the Act. I assume that a representation was made, and I assume that it was in fact relied on by Zanzibar. Part C is then "a term [of the contract] which would exclude or restrict—(a) any liability to which a party to [the] contract may be subject by reason of any misrepresentation made by him before the contract was made:" section 3 of the Act of 1967 as substituted by section 8(1) of the Act of 1977.

A term which negates a reliance which in fact existed is a term which excludes a liability which the representor would otherwise be subject to by reason of the representation. If that were wrong, it would mean that section 3 could always be defeated by including an appropriate non-reliance clause in the contract, however unreasonable that might be. So I consider that part C of clause 23 has to satisfy the requirement of reasonableness. In that respect it stands in no different position to part B: I cannot determine the issue.

NOTES AND QUESTIONS

1.   Clause 23 was divided into three. Following *Deepak Fertilisers and Petrochemicals Corp v ICI Chemicals & Polymers Ltd* [1999] 1 Lloyd's Rep 387, 395, CA, the first 'entire agreement' clause was held not to be an exclusion of liability for misrepresentation. It therefore fell outside section 3 of the 1967 Act. Such a clause sets out that the terms of the written contract are the 'entire agreement' between them. It has the effect of limiting the contractual force of what has been said in negotiations but it does not seek to exclude liability for misrepresentation. See above, 162 note 5.

2.   In contrast, the second and third clauses were excluding liability for misrepresentation and therefore fell within section 3 of the 1967 Act. This is obvious in relation to part B but not so clear in relation to part C. Indeed there is obiter dicta of Chadwick LJ in *Watford Electronics Ltd v Sanderson CFL Ltd* [2001] EWCA Civ 317 at [40] (set out above, 282, but not on this point) that a

non-reliance clause is outside section 3. Although Judge Raymond Jack QC's contrary approach is to be preferred, it is not entirely clear how one explains the operation of a 'no reliance' clause, which depends for its effectiveness on the parties denying the truth of what has happened. While it has been suggested that the claimant is estopped from asserting that he has relied on the misrepresentation, a problem with that analysis is that the defendant can hardly be said to have relied on the 'no reliance' representation; and reliance is essential for the usual type of estoppel. In *Peekay Intermark Ltd v Australia and New Zealand Banking Group Ltd* [2006] EWCA Civ 386, [2006] 2 Lloyd's Rep 511, at [56]–[57] Moore-Bick LJ in obiter dicta suggested that, in order to avoid that problem, the relevant estoppel should be seen not as an estoppel by representation but rather as an estoppel by convention. Is that a neat solution?

(2) Does the Clause Pass or Fail the Reasonableness Test?

Howard Marine & Dredging Co v A Ogden & Sons (Excavations) Ltd [1978] QB 574, Court of Appeal

For the facts, see above, 567. We are here solely concerned with the validity of the exclusion clause. Bridge and Shaw LJJ (Lord Denning MR dissenting) held that, as a matter of construction, the clause did not here apply; but that, even if it did, the judge's decision that the exemption failed the reasonableness test in section 3 of the 1967 Act should not be disturbed.

Bridge LJ: There remains the question whether Howards can escape from their liability under the statute in reliance on clause 1 of the charterparty which provides:

> "On handing over by the owners the vessel shall be tight, staunch and strong but charterers' acceptance of handing over the vessel shall be conclusive that they have examined the vessel and found her to be in all respects seaworthy, in good order and condition and in all respects fit for the intended and contemplated use by the charterers and in every other way satisfactory to them."

A clause of this kind is to be narrowly construed. It can only be relied on as conclusive evidence of the charterers' satisfaction in relation to such attributes of the vessel as would be apparent on an ordinary examination of the vessel. I do not think deadweight capacity is such an attribute. It can only be ascertained by an elaborate calculation or by an inspection of the ship's documents. But even if, contrary to this view, the clause can be read as apt to exclude liability for the earlier misrepresentation, Howards still have to surmount the restriction imposed by section 3 of the Misrepresentation Act 1967...

What the judge said in this matter was: "If the wording of the clause is apt to exempt from responsibility for negligent misrepresentation as to carrying capacity, I hold that such exemption is not fair and reasonable." The judge having asked himself the right question and answered it as he did in the exercise of the discretion vested in him by the Act, I can see no ground on which we could say that he was wrong.

Lord Denning MR (dissenting): In the old days we used to construe such an exception clause strictly against the party relying on it: but there is no need – and I suggest no warrant – any longer for construing it so strictly. The reason is that now by section 3 of the

Misrepresentation Act 1967 the provision is of no effect except to the extent that the court may allow reliance on it as being fair and reasonable in the circumstances of the case. Under this section the question is not whether the provision itself is reasonable: but only whether "reliance on it [is] fair and reasonable in the circumstances of the case."

If the clause itself is reasonable, that goes a long way towards showing that reliance on it is fair and reasonable. It seems to me that the clause was itself fair and reasonable. The parties here were commercial concerns and were of equal bargaining power. The clause was not foisted by one on the other in a standard printed form. It was contained in all the drafts which passed between them, and it was no doubt given close consideration by both sides, like all the other clauses, some of which were amended and others not. It was a clause common in charterparties of this kind: and is familiar in other commercial contracts ... It is specially applicable in cases where the contractor has the opportunity of checking the position for himself. It tells him that he should do so: and that he should not rely on any information given beforehand, for it may be inaccurate. Thus it provides a valuable safeguard against the consequences of innocent misrepresentation.

Even if the clause were somewhat too wide (I do not think it is), nevertheless this is, I think, a case where it would be fair and reasonable to allow reliance on it. Here is a clause by which Ogdens accepted that the barges were "in all respects fit for the intended and contemplated use by the charterers." Ogdens had had full inspection and examination of the barges. They had had an on-hire survey by their surveyors. Any expert could have given them a reliable estimate as to the deadweight capacity. Yet they seek to say that the barges were not fit for the use for which they intended them – in that they were of too low carrying capacity. And in support of this case they have no written representation to go upon. They only have two telephone conversations and one interview – as to which there is an acute conflict of evidence. It is just such conflicts which commercial men seek to avoid by such a clause as this. I would do nothing to impair its efficacy. I would allow Howards to rely on it.

Shaw LJ agreed with Bridge LJ on the exclusion of liability.

NOTES AND QUESTIONS

1.   The judges were applying the then version of section 3 of the 1967 Act but the same or similar reasoning would presumably have applied under the present version of section 3.

2.   Lord Denning MR dissenting thought that, even if there was liability for misrepresentation (he held not, see above, 568), the exemption clause applied and was reasonable applying section 3 of the 1967 Act. Do you agree with his dissent?

3.   On the preliminary construction question, would you have expected the judges to have referred to *Canada Steamship v R* (above, 225)?

Walker v Boyle [1982] 1 WLR 495, Chancery Division

The claimant negotiated for the purchase of property from the defendant. During these negotiations the claimant had sent preliminary enquiries to the defendant including the question, 'Is the vendor aware of any disputes regarding the boundaries, easements, covenants or other matters relating to the property or its use?' The defendant passed the question on to her husband, who simply answered 'no'. In fact, there had been a long running dispute over the border between the property and a neighbour's property, though the defendant's husband incorrectly thought that it had been settled. The final contract included the National Conditions of Sale. Condition

17(1) stated that, 'no error, misstatement or omission in any preliminary answer concerning the property... shall annul the sale...' When the claimant brought an action for rescission of the contract for misrepresentation, the defendant sought to rely on the above condition. It was held that the condition fell foul of section 3 of the Misrepresentation Act 1967.

Dillon J: If condition 17 has any validity or relevance in the circumstances of this case, it is a term which would exclude liabilities to which Mrs. Boyle would be subject by reason of misrepresentation, and so section 3 is applicable. The requirement of reasonableness in section 11 of the Unfair Contract Terms Act 1977 is that the term shall have been a fair and reasonable one to be included, having regard to the circumstances which were or ought reasonably to have been known to or in the contemplation of the parties when the contract was made. I do not regard condition 17 as satisfying that requirement in the circumstances of this case. Another way of putting it is that Mrs. Boyle has not shown that it does satisfy that requirement.

It has been submitted by Mr. Seymour [counsel for the defendant] that, as there were solicitors acting for both parties, it would be a very strong thing to say that any term of the contract which resulted is not a fair and reasonable one in the circumstances. That argument would have great force, no doubt, if the solicitors had specifically directed their minds to the problem and had evolved the clause which was under attack. In fact, however, neither solicitor directed his mind to condition 17, and they have both told me, and they are men of not inconsiderable experience as conveyancing solicitors, that they have never come across a case where any question under condition 17 has arisen. It was submitted that it was the duty of the purchaser's solicitor to advise his client, Mr. Walker, of the implications of condition 17 and of the other terms of the contract, which Mr. Walker was going to enter into, and he must be taken to have discharged that duty and satisfied himself and Mr. Walker that the terms were reasonable. It is, of course, the duty of a solicitor to advise his client about any abnormal or unusual term in a contract, but I think it is perfectly normal and proper for a solicitor to use standard forms of conditions of sale such as the National Conditions of Sale. I do not think he is called on to go through the small print of those somewhat lengthy conditions with a toothcomb every time he is advising a purchaser to draw the purchaser's attention to every problem which on a careful reading of the conditions might in some circumstance or other conceivably arise. I cannot believe that purchasers of house property throughout the land would be overjoyed at having such lengthy explanations of the National Conditions of Sale ritually foisted upon them.

It has also been submitted by Mr. Seymour that the court should be very slow to hold that a common form clause like condition 17 is not fair and reasonable. Of course it is true that there are common form clauses which have been evolved by negotiation between trade associations, associations of merchants or associations of growers or trade unions or other such bodies concerned to protect the rights of their members, which can be regarded as representing what consensus in the trade regards as fair and reasonable. ... [T]he National Conditions of Sale are not the product of negotiation between such bodies...

NOTES AND QUESTIONS

1. Both parties were represented by solicitors in the drawing up of the contract. Why did that not lead to the conclusion that the term was reasonable?
2. Dillon J indicated that a standard term is more likely to be regarded as reasonable if has been negotiated between representative bodies. Is that a helpful approach in applying the reasonableness test?

Additional Reading for Chapter 11

J Beatson, *Anson's Law of Contract* (28th edn, 2002) Ch 6
S Smith, *Atiyah's Introduction to the Law of Contract* (6th edn, 2005) Ch 10

P Atiyah and G Treitel, 'Misrepresentation Act 1967' (1967) 30 *MLR* 369
This is the classic in-depth analysis of the Misrepresentation Act 1967. It looks in particular at the consequences of the 'fiction of fraud' wording in section 2(1); and at the uncertainty of section 2(2). [Note that this should be read bearing in mind developments since 1967, eg, the change in wording of section 3.]

R Taylor, 'Expectation, Reliance and Misrepresentation' (1982) 45 *MLR* 139
This article examines the correct measure of damages under the Misrepresentation Act 1967, section 2(1). It draws the distinction between expectation and reliance damages. In the former, the representee is awarded damages to put him in the position he would have been in had the representation been true, whilst the latter awards damages to put him into the position as if no representation had been made. Taylor gives the following example of the difference. A buys from B for £1000 an article which is represented to have quality X; it would have been worth £1200 with quality X but in fact as it is without quality X it is worth only £900. The contractual expectation measure would be £300, whereas the tortious reliance measure would be £100. It is argued that, although at the time of writing, the authorities were inconclusive, section 2(1) damages should be reliance damages. [More recent cases have clarified that damages under section 2(1) should indeed protect the reliance, not the expectation, interest.]

I Brown and A Chandler, 'Deceit, Damages and the Misrepresentation Act 1967, s 2(1)' [1992] *LMCLQ* 40
This article principally rejects the argument that the 'fiction of fraud' wording should be given weight. The use of 'fraudulently' in section 2(1) was merely a way of saying, at a time when deceit was the only tort triggering damages, that tortious damages for the misrepresentation should be given. The authors make six specific points as to why no greater significance should be afforded to the fraud analogy. (i) *Derry v Peek* makes it absolutely clear that an honest mind discharges an allegation of fraud; (ii) a defendant cannot exclude his liability for fraud, but section 3 surely allows one to exclude liability under section 2(1); (iii) the Legislature surely did not intend to attach the 'moral opprobrium' of fraud to a defendant liable for negligent misrepresentation; (iv) the Act does not say in section 2(1) that one is liable 'in deceit'; (v) section 2(2) permits damages where the misrepresentation was non-fraudulent which clearly suggests that the Act still separates between fraudulent misrepresentations and non-fraudulent ones; (vi) the higher evidentiary standard of proof for fraud would surely be inappropriate under section 2(1).

J O'Sullivan, 'Rescission as a Self-Help Remedy: a Critical Analysis' [2000] *CLJ* 509
The author argues that rescission (whether for misrepresentation or duress or undue influence) should be viewed as a court order and not as a self-help remedy. This would avoid problems caused by the idea that a judicial order for rescission is

backdated to the date of the party's election. It would also mean that, until a court order for rescission, bona fide purchasers for value without notice would take good title. [Although she does not clarify this point, presumably she would need to concede that, like termination for breach, an election to avoid a contract would be a self-help remedy as regards *discharging future obligations.*]

J Cartwright, 'Excluding Liability for Misrepresentation' in *Contract Terms* **(eds A Burrows and E Peel, 2007), 213**
Reflecting the complexity of the law on misrepresentation, Cartwright identifies several types of relevant exclusion clause and explores how each of them works, with especial focus on the 'estoppel' explanation of a 'no-reliance' clause. He points out that while an 'entire agreement' clause is not an exclusion of liability for misrepresentation as such, and therefore falls outside section 3 of the 1967 Act, the other types of clause examined all fall within section 3. He thinks it unfortunate that section 3 has never been fully integrated into the regime of UCTA 1977 and was excluded from the scope of the Law Commission's recent review of Unfair Terms.

Principles of European Contract Law **(eds O Lando and H Beale) 252–6, 279–284**
Article 4:107: Fraud
(1) A party may avoid a contract when it has been led to conclude it by the other party's fraudulent representation, whether by words or conduct, or fraudulent non-disclosure of any information which in accordance with good faith and fair dealing it should have disclosed.

(2) A party's representation or non-disclosure is fraudulent if it was intended to deceive.

(3) In determining whether good faith and fair dealing required that a party disclose particular information, regard should be had to all the circumstances, including:

(a) whether the party had special expertise;

(b) the cost to it of acquiring the relevant information;

(c) whether the other party could reasonably acquire the information for itself; and

(d) the apparent importance of the information to the other party.

Article 4:116: Partial Avoidance
If a ground of avoidance affects only particular terms of a contract, the effect of an avoidance is limited to those terms unless, giving due consideration to all the circumstances of the case, it is unreasonable to uphold the remaining contract.

Article 4:117: Damages
(1) A party who avoids a contract under this Chapter may recover from the other party damages so as to put the avoiding party as nearly as possible into the same position as if it had not concluded the contract, provided that the other party knew

or ought to have known of the mistake, fraud, threat or taking of excessive benefit or unfair advantage.

(2) If a party has the right to avoid a contract under this Chapter, but does not exercise its right or has lost its right..., it may recover, subject to paragraph (1), damages limited to the loss caused to it by the mistake, fraud, threat or taking of excessive benefit or unfair advantage. ...

[These articles contrast with English law in recognising a general duty of disclosure and in accepting that avoidance of the contract may be partial: see above, 543, 549. For PECL provisions on mistake, including induced mistake, see below, 651–652.]

12

Mistake

Mistake is often regarded by students as the hardest of the topics within contract law. This is reflected in, and reinforced by, the very different ways in which contract textbooks and commentators approach the topic. Four particular difficulties should be noted at the outset.

First, where both parties make the same mistake, this is now most frequently referred to as 'common mistake'. However, J Beatson, *Anson's Law of Contract* (28th edn, 2002) Chapter 8, persists in calling it 'mutual mistake'. This might not in itself be a serious problem were it not for the fact that other books, eg M Furmston, *Cheshire, Fifoot and Furmston's Law of Contract* (15th edn, 2007) Chapter 8, use 'mutual mistake' to refer to something different, namely where each party is making a different mistake. The commentary in this casebook seeks to avoid this terminological confusion by avoiding the term 'mutual mistake'.

A second difficulty is that in some textbooks (eg E McKendrick, *Contract Law*) the discussion of mistake is spread over two or three different chapters. In particular, unilateral mistake is discussed in a separate chapter from common mistake; and the complex question of whether the parties' intentions are assessed objectively or subjectively, which is crucial to understanding unilateral mistake, is discussed in detail at the very start of the book as a prelude to offer and acceptance. While acknowledging that unilateral mistake and common mistake are very different, and that unilateral mistake is closely tied in with whether any agreement has been reached and with whether offer and acceptance coincide, it has been thought more helpful and less off-putting for students if the objective/subjective debate is looked at through the prism of mistake.

A third difficulty, closely tied to the second, is that a theme of much academic writing on mistake is that English law has no doctrine of mistake. Rather the law in this chapter is explained away as based on other grounds (eg offer and acceptance or implied terms). The approach taken in this book is that, while those reductionist arguments constitute a possible analysis, the better, more illuminating, view is that English law does have a doctrine of mistake (for both unilateral and common mistakes), albeit that it is narrow.

A final difficulty is that in the context of mistake one still needs to be acutely conscious of the historical, albeit irrational, divide between the treatment of mistakes at common law and in equity. Prior to the *Great Peace* case (below, 643) it was very hard to describe the law on common mistake without drawing a sharp distinction between the position at common law and the position in equity. One effect of that decision is that no such sharp division needs to be drawn. But some differences remain. In particular, mistake at common law renders the contract void, whereas the main role of mistake in equity is to render a written contract rectifiable.

Introductory reading: E McKendrick, *Contract Law* (7th edn, 2007) 4.6, 14.2–14.7

1. UNILATERAL MISTAKE

By unilateral mistake we mean a mistake of one party which is not shared by the other party and which may, or may not, be known about by the other party. The general position, as classically laid down in *Smith v Hughes* (below), is that a unilateral mistake, even if known about by the other party, does not invalidate a contract provided that viewing their intentions objectively (that is, through the eyes of a reasonable observer) there is agreement between the parties. That one of the parties is mistaken and, subjectively therefore (that is, through his own eyes), has a different intention from the other is, in general, irrelevant. So in a contract for the sale of a painting between A and B, unless something is specifically said about the quality of the painting, it is irrelevant that A mistakenly thinks he is buying an original and B knows that the painting is a copy and not worth what A is paying for it. The contract is valid, not void.

There are four main exceptions to that general position.

(i)   There is the very rare case where, objectively, there is ambiguity as to what has been agreed, so that the contract is void (below, 595–597).

(ii)   Where there is a mistake as to terms or as to the identity of the other party—and the other party knows of that mistake—the contract is void (below, 597–617).

(iii) Where a written contract has been mistakenly signed, the doctrine of non est factum may mean that the contract is void (below, 617–620).

(iv)   Where one party knows that the other party is making a mistake, in circumstances where it is unconscionable for him to remain silent, a written contract may (in equity) be rectifiable (below, 620–625).

(1) The General Position: No Escape for Unilateral Mistake

Smith v Hughes (1871) LR 6 QB 597, Court of Queen's Bench

After having inspected a sample, the defendant racehorse trainer agreed to buy 16 quarters of oats from the claimant farmer. When the first portion of the oats was delivered, the defendant refused to pay, stating that the oats delivered were new oats and he had intended to buy old oats. The claimant brought an action for the price of the oats already delivered, and damages for breach of contract for the oats to be delivered. At trial, the jury was directed that it must find for the defendant if the claimant believed that the defendant believed that he was contracting for the purchase of old oats. The jury found for the defendant. On the claimant's appeal, the Court of Queen's Bench held that that had been a misdirection so that there must be a new trial.

Cockburn CJ: I take the true rule to be, that where a specific article is offered for sale, without express warranty, or without circumstances from which the law will imply a warranty – as where, for instance, an article is ordered for a specific purpose – and the buyer has full opportunity of inspecting and forming his own judgment, if he chooses to act on his own judgment, the rule caveat emptor applies.

...

It only remains to deal with an argument which was pressed upon us, that the defendant in the present case intended to buy old oats, and the plaintiff to sell new, so the two minds were not ad idem; and that consequently there was no contract. This argument proceeds on the fallacy of confounding what was merely a motive operating on the buyer to induce him to buy with one of the essential conditions of the contract. Both parties were agreed as to the sale and purchase of this particular parcel of oats. The defendant believed the oats to be old, and was thus induced to agree to buy them, but he omitted to make their age a condition of the contract. All that can be said is, that the two minds were not ad idem as to the age of the oats; they certainly were ad idem as to the sale and purchase of them. Suppose a person to buy a horse without a warranty, believing him to be sound, and the horse turns out unsound, could it be contended that it would be open to him to say that, as he had intended to buy a sound horse, and the seller to sell an unsound one, the contract was void, because the seller must have known from the price the buyer was willing to give, or from his general habits as a buyer of horses, that he thought the horse was sound? The cases are exactly parallel.

Blackburn J: In this case I agree that on the sale of a specific article, unless there be a warranty making it part of the bargain that it possesses some particular quality, the purchaser must take the article he has bought though it does not possess that quality. And I agree that even if the vendor was aware that the purchaser thought that the article possessed that quality, and would not have entered into the contract unless he had so thought, still the purchaser is bound, unless the vendor was guilty of some fraud or deceit upon him, and that a mere abstinence from disabusing the purchaser of that impression is not fraud or deceit; for, whatever may be the case in a court of morals, there is no legal obligation on the vendor to inform the purchaser that he is under a mistake, not induced by the act of the vendor. ...

I apprehend that if one of the parties intends to make a contract on one set of terms, and the other intends to make a contract on another set of terms, or, as it is sometimes expressed, if the parties are not ad idem, there is no contract, unless the circumstances are such as to preclude one of the parties from denying that he has agreed to the terms of the other. ... If, whatever a man's real intention may be, he so conducts himself that a reasonable man would believe that he was assenting to the terms proposed by the other party, and that other party upon that belief enters into the contract with him, the man thus conducting himself would be equally bound as if he had intended to agree to the other party's terms.

...

I think that, if from [the] direction the jury would understand that they were first to consider whether they were satisfied that the defendant intended to buy this parcel of oats on the terms that it was part of his contract with the plaintiff that they were old oats, so as to have the warranty of the plaintiff to that effect, they were properly told that, if that was so, the defendant could not be bound to a contract without any such warranty unless the plaintiff was misled. But I doubt whether the direction would bring to the minds of the jury the distinction between agreeing to take the oats under the belief that they were old, and agreeing to take the oats under the belief that the plaintiff contracted that they were old.

The difference is the same as that between buying a horse believed to be sound, and buying one believed to be warranted sound; but I doubt if it was made obvious to the jury, and I doubt this the more because I do not see much evidence to justify a finding for the defendant on this latter ground if the word "old" was not used. There may have been more evidence than is stated in the case; and the demeanour of the witnesses may have strengthened the impression produced by the evidence there was; but it does not seem a very satisfactory verdict if it proceeded on this latter ground. I agree, therefore, in the result that there should be a new trial.

Hannen J delivered a concurring judgment.

NOTES AND QUESTIONS

1. Blackburn J's speech contains (at the end of the second paragraph set out above) the classic exposition of the objective approach to intention. He further made clear that, absent misrepresentation, it was insufficient that the claimant knew that the defendant intended to buy old oats. Ie in general, a unilateral mistake, even though serious and known to the other party, is insufficient to render a contract invalid. There is no general duty of disclosure. The exception referred to was significantly different and narrower. It required that the claimant knew that the defendant mistakenly thought that it was a term of the contract that the oats were old: ie the unilateral mistake, known to the other party, must be one as to the terms of the contract. The rationale for this distinction is the desire not to allow mistakes to invalidate contracts too readily.

2. Caveat emptor means 'buyer beware', and indicates that the buyer in a sale of goods contract must rely on his own judgment.

3. Supposing that the seller did know that the buyer thought that there was a warranty that the oats were old as part of the contract. Would the buyer be restricted to arguing that the contract alleged by the seller was invalid for mistake or could the buyer hold the seller to the contractual terms as he believed them to be?

4. An excellent example of the objective approach being applied is *Centrovincial Estates plc v Merchant Investors Assurance Company Ltd* [1983] Com LR 158, CA. The claimant landlords let offices to the defendant tenants. For the purposes of a rent review the claimants mistakenly offered for agreement by the tenants the figure of £65,000 per annum (instead of £126,000) as the current market rental value of the offices. The defendants accepted that figure. On the claimants' application for summary judgment, it was held that the claimants were not entitled to a declaration that there was no valid contract based on the £65,000 figure. Objectively that was the figure agreed and, although the claimants had made a mistake as to the terms, on the assumed facts the defendants did not know, nor ought reasonably to have known, of that mistake.

(2) Exceptions where Unilateral Mistake Invalidates the Contract

(a) Objective Ambiguity

Raffles v Wichelhaus (1864) 2 H & C 906, Court of Exchequer

The defendants agreed to purchase bales of Surat cotton from the claimant which would arrive 'ex *Peerless*' from Bombay. There were two vessels named *Peerless* leaving Bombay, one in October and one in December. The defendants intended to purchase the cotton on the October *Peerless*, not the December *Peerless*, and they therefore refused to pay for the cotton delivered from the December *Peerless*. The claimant brought an action for breach of contract. Counsel for the defendants argued that there was a 'latent ambiguity' as to which ship was meant and that oral evidence would show that the claimant intended one ship and the defendants intended another. That being so, he argued, there was no consensus ad idem and therefore no binding contract. The Court of Exchequer (Pollock CB, Martin B and Pigott B) simply stated 'There must be judgment for the defendants'.

NOTES

1. This was a claim brought to recover the price due on goods. The claim was rejected but no reasons were given. On the assumption that the court was holding that there was no valid contract, the best explanation is that the buyers' mistake (in thinking that the seller meant the October *Peerless*) was an excuse because, objectively, there was ambiguity as to which *Peerless* shipment was being contracted for. A reasonable observer could not say which 'ex *Peerless*' applied and the contract was therefore too uncertain to be valid. For general examples of uncertainty rendering a contract invalid (albeit not involving mistakes of this kind) see above, Chapter 2.

2. Some commentators treat this case as one of mutual rather than unilateral mistake because each party was mistaken as to the other's intentions (that is, they were at cross-purposes). We have seen at the start of this chapter, however, that the language of a mutual mistake is confusing and best avoided. One can treat the *relevant* mistake as being that of the buyers—so that this can be treated as a case of unilateral mistake—because it was the seller's terms that the buyers were trying to escape from by reason of their mistake.

Scriven Brothers & Co v Hindley & Co
[1913] 3 KB 564, King's Bench Division

The claimants instructed an auctioneer to sell 47 bales of Russian hemp and 176 bales of Russian tow. The auction catalogue separated the hemp and tow into two lots but without stating that one was hemp and the other was tow. Both lots carried the same shipping mark 'S.L.'. The showroom had samples of the lots on display with the respective lot numbers in front of the hemp and the tow. The defendants' manager, Mr Gill, was then shown two bales of hemp as samples of the 'S.L.' goods by the showroom foreman, Calman. Mr Gill instructed his buyer, Macgregor, to bid for both lots, which he successfully did. The price bid for the lot of tow was extravagant. When the defendants realised that one lot was tow, they refused to pay stating that they thought it was hemp. The claimants brought an action for the price. The findings of fact by the jury were as follows: (1) That hemp and tow are different commodities in commerce. (2) That the auctioneer intended to sell 176 bales of tow. (3) That Macgregor intended to bid for 176 bales of hemp. (4) That the auctioneer believed that the bid was made under a mistake when he knocked down the lot. (5) That the auctioneer had reasonable ground for believing that the mistake was merely one as to value. (6) That the form of the catalogue and the conduct of Calman, or one of them, contributed to cause the mistake that occurred. (7) That Mr Gill's 'negligence' in not taking his catalogue to Cutler Street and more closely examining and identifying the bales with the lots contributed to cause Macgregor's mistake. It was held that the defendants were not bound to pay for the lot of tow.

A T Lawrence J: I think that the findings of the jury determine what my judgment should be in this case.

The jury have found that hemp and tow are different commodities in commerce. I should suppose that no one can doubt the correctness of this finding. The second and third findings of the jury shew that the parties were never ad idem as to the subject-matter of the proposed sale; there was therefore in fact no contract of bargain and sale. The plaintiffs can recover from the defendants only if they can shew that the defendants are estopped from relying upon what is now admittedly the truth. Mr. Hume Williams for the plaintiffs argued very ingeniously that the defendants were estopped; for this he relied upon findings 5 and 7, and upon the fact that the defendants had failed to prove the allegation in paragraph 4 of the defence to the effect that Northcott knew at the time he knocked down the lot that Macgregor was bidding for hemp and not for tow.

I must, of course accept for the purposes of this judgment the findings of the jury, but I do not think they create any estoppel. Question No. 7 was put to the jury as a supplementary question, after they had returned into Court with their answers to the other questions, upon the urgent insistence of the learned junior counsel for the plaintiffs. It begs an essential question by using the word "negligence" and assuming that the purchaser has a duty towards the seller to examine goods that he does not wish to buy, and to correct any latent defect there may be in the sellers' catalogue.

Once it was admitted that Russian hemp was never before known to be consigned or sold with the same shipping marks as Russian tow from the same cargo, it was natural for the person inspecting the "S. L." goods and being shewn hemp to suppose that the "S. L." bales represented the commodity hemp. Inasmuch as it is admitted that some one had perpetrated a swindle upon the bank which made advances in respect of this shipment of goods it was peculiarly the duty of the auctioneer to make it clear to the bidder either upon the face of his catalogue or in some other way which lots were hemp and which lots were tow.

In my view it is clear that the finding of the jury upon the sixth question prevents the plaintiffs from being able to insist upon a contract by estoppel. Such a contract cannot arise when the person seeking to enforce it has by his own negligence or by that of those for whom he is responsible caused, or contributed to cause, the mistake.

NOTES AND QUESTIONS

1. This is a very difficult case to interpret. The buyers were not bound to pay for the lot of tow because they thought it was hemp. But why was that an excuse, given the normal objective approach to intention? One interpretation is that there was objective ambiguity as in *Raffles v Wichelhaus*.

2. Alternatively, one might argue that objectively there was no ambiguity and that the agreement was one for the lot of tow. Hence the sellers' estoppel argument that the buyers could not now deny that they were agreeing to buy the lot bid for. The reason that that objective agreement could not stand (and why the estoppel argument failed) was that the sellers had been at fault in contributing to the buyers' mistake. A difficulty with this is that, even if one could say that the sellers had misrepresented the contents of the lot, misrepresentation renders a contract voidable, not void.

(b) Unilateral Mistake as to Terms or Identity Known to the Other Party

(i) Mistake as to terms

We have seen that in *Smith v Hughes* (above, 592) it was accepted that a mistake as to an important term, known about by the other party, makes the contract void. We now consider a case that is best explained on that basis.

Hartog v Colin & Shields [1939] 3 All ER 566, King's Bench Division

The claimant was in negotiation with the defendants for the purchase of 30,000 Argentine hare skins. All the negotiations until the final offer and acceptance had been in terms of price per piece rather than price per pound. The defendants mistakenly quoted the price as per pound instead of per piece in an offer letter which the claimant immediately accepted. The consequence of this was that the price was a third of that intended by the defendants. The defendants refused to deliver the goods and the claimant brought an action for damages for breach of contract. It was held that, as the claimant must have known that the offer was mistaken, he could not enforce the contract.

Singleton J: In this case, the plaintiff, a Belgian subject, claims damages against the defendants because he says they broke a contract into which they entered with him for the sale of Argentine hare skins. The defendants' answer to that claim is: 'There really was no contract, because you knew that the document which went forward to you, in the form of an offer, contained a material mistake. You realised that, and you sought to take advantage of it.'

Counsel for the defendants took upon himself the onus of satisfying me that the plaintiff knew that there was a mistake and sought to take advantage of that mistake. In other words, realising that there was a mistake, the plaintiff did that which James LJ, in *Tamplin v James* (1880) 15 Ch D 215, 2[2]1, described as 'snapping up the offer'.

…

I cannot help thinking that, when [the] quotation in pence per pound reached Mr Hartog, the plaintiff, he must have realised…that there was a mistake. Otherwise I cannot understand the quotation. There was an absolute difference from anything which had gone before – a difference in the manner of quotation, in that the skins are offered per pound instead of per piece.

I am satisfied that it was a mistake on the part of the defendants or their servants which caused the offer to go forward in that way, and I am satisfied that anyone with any knowledge of the trade must have realised that there was a mistake. …I have seen the witnesses and heard them, and in this case can form no other view than that there was an accident. The offer was wrongly expressed, and the defendants by their evidence, and by the correspondence, have satisfied me that the plaintiff could not reasonably have supposed that that offer contained the offerers' real intention. Indeed, I am satisfied to the contrary. That means that there must be judgment for the defendants.

NOTES AND QUESTIONS

1. Was it crucial (i) that the offeree realised that the offeror had made a mistake? (ii) that the offeree had 'snapped up the offer'?
2. Allowing the offeror to escape for mistake by holding that there was no contract at the stated price 'per pound' did not of course entail that there was a valid contract at the stated price 'per piece'. On what basis might one argue that there was indeed such a contract at the stated price 'per piece'?
3. *Hartog v Colin & Shields* was applied, in a modern context, by the Singapore Court of Appeal in *Chwee Kin Keong v Digilandmall.com Pte Ltd* [2005] 1 SLR 502. Owing to an employee's mistake, a particular type of commercial laser printer was advertised for sale on the defendant's web-site for $66 instead of $3,854. Before the mistake was detected, 784 individuals had placed orders for more than 4000 printers. The orders had been accepted by the defendant's automated responses. The six claimants had between them ordered 1606 printers. They sought to enforce the contracts. It was held that the contracts were void for the defendant's unilateral mistake as to terms (ie on these facts, the price) known about by the claimants.

(ii) Mistake as to identity

Cundy v Lindsay (1878) 3 App Cas 459, House of Lords

A third party rogue, Alfred Blenkarn, hired a room overlooking Wood Street. He wrote a letter to the claimant linen manufacturers, Lindsay, stating his intention to purchase handkerchiefs from them. He put his address as 37, Wood Street and signed the letter to look like 'Blenkiron & Co', similar to the name of a very respectable firm, Blenkiron & Son, which carried on business at 123, Wood Street. The claimants sent the goods to the rogue and then, later, the invoice for the goods. The rogue sold the goods to various people including 250 handkerchiefs to the defendant purchasers, Cundy, before the fraud was discovered. The claimants brought an action for the tort of conversion against the defendants, arguing that they still owned the handkerchiefs as their property rights had not passed to the rogue. Their action succeeded, the House of Lords holding, in dismissing Cundy's appeal, that property had not passed from the claimants to the rogue as there had been no valid contract between them.

Lord Cairns LC: [H]ow is it possible to imagine that in that state of things any contract could have arisen between the Respondents and Blenkarn, the dishonest man? Of him they knew nothing, and of him they never thought. With him they never intended to deal. Their minds never, even for an instant of time rested upon him, and as between him and them there was no consensus of mind which could lead to any agreement or any contract whatever. As between him and them there was merely the one side to a contract, where, in order to produce a contract, two sides would be required. With the firm of *Blenkiron & Co.* of course there was no contract, for as to them the matter was entirely unknown, and therefore the pretence of a contract was a failure.

The result, therefore, my Lords, is this, that your Lordships have not here to deal with one of those cases in which there is de facto a contract made which may afterwards be impeached and set aside, on the ground of fraud; but you have to deal with a case which ranges itself under a completely different chapter of law, the case namely in which the contract never comes into existence. My Lords, that being so, it is idle to talk of the property passing. The property remained, as it originally had been, the property of the Respondents, and the title which was attempted to be given to the Appellants was a title which could not be given to them.

Lord Hatherley: We have been pressed very much with an ingenious mode of putting the case on the part of the counsel who have argued with eminent ability for the Appellants in this case, namely, suppose this fraudulent person had gone himself to the firm from whom he wished to obtain the goods, and had represented that he was a member of one of the largest firms in London. Suppose on his making that representation the goods had been delivered to him. Now I am very far, at all events on the present occasion, from seeing my way to this, that the goods being sold to him as representing that firm he could be treated in any other way than as an agent of that firm, or suppose he had said: "I am as rich as that firm. I have transactions as large as those of that firm. I have a large balance at my bankers;" then the sale would have been a sale to a fraudulent purchaser on fraudulent representations, and a sale which would have been capable of being set aside, but still a sale would have been made to the person who made those false representations; and the parting with the goods in that case might possibly – I say no more – have passed the property.

But this case is an entirely different one. The whole case, as represented here is this; from beginning to end the Respondents believed they were dealing with *Blenkiron & Co.*, they made out their invoices to *Blenkiron & Co.*, they supposed they sold to *Blenkiron & Co.*, they never sold in any way to *Alfred Blenkarn*; and therefore *Alfred Blenkarn* cannot, by so obtaining the goods, have by possibility made a good title to a purchaser, as against the owners of the goods, who had never in any shape or way parted with the property nor with anything more than the possession of it.

Lord Penzance delivered a concurring speech and **Lord Gordon** concurred.

NOTES AND QUESTIONS

1. The importance of there being no contract or a void contract, as opposed to there being a contract voidable for Blenkarn's fraudulent misrepresentation, was that, under the latter, title to the goods would have passed to Cundy as a bona fide purchaser for value without notice: ie Lindsay could not rescind as against a bona fide purchaser for value without notice. In contrast, no title to the goods passed to Cundy if there was no contract at all. This is an important point in relation to nearly all the mistake as to identity cases as the real contest is between two innocent parties rather than between an innocent party and a rogue.

2. As in several of the mistake as to identity cases, the relevant cause of action was the tort of conversion. This is the appropriate tort where a person is wrongfully interfering with a person's right to possession of goods. So, eg, if a person steals my car, he commits the tort of conversion against me (as well as committing the crime of theft). I will be entitled to damages (or, if he still has it, the return of the car) for that tort.

3. There was no contract between Blenkarn and Lindsay because, as Blenkarn knew, Lindsay intended to deal with Blenkiron not Blenkarn: ie it had made a mistake as to the identity of the other party, known to the other party. Although objectively one might say that there was an agreement between Lindsay and the person at 37, Wood Street, the subjective intention of Lindsay to deal with Blenkiron, as known to Blenkarn, meant that the contract was void.

4. Supposing Blenkarn could have been found and had been solvent, could Lindsay have sued Blenkarn in contract for the price of the goods? Were there any possible non-contractual claims for the value of the goods?

5. In *King's Norton Metal Co Ltd v Edridge* (1897) 14 TLR 98, CA, the claimants, who were metal manufacturers, received a letter purporting to come from Hallam & Co in Sheffield. At the head of the letter was a representation of a large factory and there was a printed statement that the company had depots and agencies in Belfast, Lille and Ghent. The letter requested a quotation of prices for wire which the claimants sent. Hallam & Co then sent a written order for goods which were despatched to them but never paid for. It transpired that Hallam & Co did not exist but was the name being used by a rogue called Wallis. Having received the goods he sold them on to the defendants, who were innocent purchasers. The claimants brought an action against the defendants for damages for the tort of conversion. The claim failed. The contract was held not to be void for a mistake as to identity because there were not two people, Hallam & Co and Wallis, but only one, Wallis, albeit dealing under an alias. The claimant intended to deal with the writer of the letter. The central passage of AL Smith LJ's leading judgment was reported as follows, at 99: 'The question was, With whom, upon this evidence, which was all one way, did the plaintiffs contract to sell the goods? Clearly with the writer of the letters. If it could have been shown that there was a separate entity called Hallam and Co and another entity called Wallis then the case might have come within the decision in *Cundy v Lindsay*. In his opinion there was a contract by the plaintiffs with the person who wrote the letters, by which the property passed to him. There was only one entity, trading it might be under an alias, and there was a contract by which the property passed to him.'

6. **C Macmillan, 'Rogues, Swindlers and Cheats: the Development of Mistake of Identity in English Contract Law' [2005] *CLJ* 711** examines the historical background to the early leading cases on mistake as to identity. Controversially she argues that the approach in *Cundy v Lindsay* was heavily influenced by the criminal law which, prior to amendments in 1893 and 1916, restored property in goods obtained by false pretences to the original owner. '[The] case must be understood as one where the proprietary consequences of nineteenth century criminal law seemingly compelled a void result in contract law' (at 743).

Phillips v Brooks Ltd [1919] 2 KB 243, King's Bench Division

A customer walked into the claimant jeweller's shop and selected some pearls and a ring to purchase. He wrote a cheque for the goods, signing himself as Sir George

Bullough and told the claimant that he was Sir George Bullough of St James's Square. The claimant looked up Sir George Bullough in the directory and upon finding his address to be in St James's Square asked the customer if he would like to take the articles with him. The customer told the claimant that he would wait until the cheque cleared for the pearls but would like to take the ring to give to his wife for her birthday the following day. The claimant gave the customer the ring. It transpired that the customer was not Sir George Bullough but in fact a rogue by the name of North, who then pawned the ring at the defendant's pawnbroker shop. On realising this, the claimant sued the defendant in the tort of conversion for the return of the ring. It was held that there was a contract between the claimant and the rogue and thus the rights in the property had passed to the rogue who had passed on good title to the defendant. The claim therefore failed.

Horridge J: I have carefully considered the evidence of the plaintiff, and have come to the conclusion that, although he believed the person to whom he was handing the ring was Sir George Bullough, he in fact contracted to sell and deliver it to the person who came into his shop, and who was not Sir George Bullough, but a man of the name of North, who obtained the sale and delivery by means of the false pretence that he was Sir George Bullough. It is quite true the plaintiff in re-examination said he had no intention of making any contract with any other person than Sir George Bullough; but I think I have myself to decide what is the proper inference to draw where a verbal contract is made and an article delivered to an individual describing himself as somebody else.

After obtaining the ring the man North pledged it in the name of Firth with the defendants, who bona fide and without notice advanced 350l. upon it. The question, therefore, in this case is whether or not the property had so passed to the swindler as to entitle him to give a good title to any person who gave value and acted bona fide without notice. This question seems to have been decided in an American case of *Edmunds v. Merchants' Despatch Transportation Co.* 135 Mass 283, 284. The headnote in that case contains two propositions, which I think adequately express my view of the law. They are as follows: (1.) "If A., fraudulently assuming the name of a reputable merchant in a certain town, buys, in person, goods of another, the property in the goods passes to A." (2.) "If A., representing himself to be a brother of a reputable merchant in a certain town, buying for him, buys, in person, goods of another, the property in the goods does not pass to A."

The following expressions used in the judgment of Morton C.J. seem to me to fit the facts in this case: "The minds of the parties met and agreed upon all the terms of the sale, the thing sold, the price and time of payment, the person selling and the person buying. The fact that the seller was induced to sell by fraud of the buyer made the sale voidable, but not void. He could not have supposed that he was selling to any other person; his intention was to sell to the person present, and identified by sight and hearing; it does not defeat the sale because the buyer assumed a false name or practised any other deceit to induce the vendor to sell." Further on, Morton C.J. says: "In the cases before us, there was a de facto contract, purporting, and by which the plaintiffs intended, to pass the property and possession of the goods to the person buying them; and we are of opinion that the property did pass to the swindler who bought the goods."

...

It was argued before me that the principle quoted from Pothier (Traité des Obligations, 19), in *Smith v. Wheatcroft* 9 Ch D 223, 230, namely, "Whenever the consideration of the person with whom I am willing to contract enters as an element into the contract which I am willing to make, error with regard to the person destroys my consent and consequently annuls the contract" applies. I do not think, however, that that passage governs this case, because I think the seller intended to contract with the person present, and there was no error as to the person with whom he contracted, although the plaintiff would not have made the contract if there had not been a fraudulent misrepresentation.

1. In contrast to *Cundy v Lindsay*, the parties here were dealing face to face. In such transactions, this case indicates that it is particularly difficult for the innocent party to establish that he was making a mistake as to the identity, rather than as to the creditworthiness, of the other party.
2. Why is it that it is only a mistake as to identity, and not as to creditworthiness, that counts?

Ingram v Little [1961] 1 QB 31, Court of Appeal

The three claimant sisters advertised their car in the newspaper. A man phoned asking to come and view the car, calling himself Hutchinson. When he arrived, he offered to purchase the car by cheque, which the claimants rejected, demanding cash only. Hutchinson tried to convince the claimants that he was a reputable person and stated that he was PGM Hutchinson living at Stanstead House, Stanstead Road, Caterham. Whilst this discussion was going on with the first claimant, the second claimant went to the post office and looked up the name in the telephone directory, which had the entry 'Hutchinson, PGM, Stanstead House, Stanstead Road, Caterham 4665'. The second claimant informed the first claimant of this and they accepted payment by cheque. The man was not PGM Hutchinson but a swindler. He disappeared after selling the car to the defendant motor dealers. The claimants sued the defendants in the tort of conversion and succeeded at trial. In dismissing the defendants' appeal, a majority of the Court of Appeal (Devlin LJ dissenting) held that there had been no contract as the claimants had intended to contract with the named Hutchinson rather than the person in front of them. Therefore property in the car did not pass.

Sellers LJ: [*Phillips v Brooks Ltd*] is not an authority to establish that where an offer or acceptance is addressed to a person (although under a mistake as to his identity) who is present in person, then it must in all circumstances be treated as if actually addressed to him. I would regard the issue as a question of fact in each case depending on what was said and done and applying the elementary principles of offer and acceptance in the manner in which [the trial judge] Slade J directed himself.

...

Phillips v Brooks Ltd is the closest authority on which the defendant relies. Once that is distinguished on its facts, without going so far as to say it is wrong, authority leans strongly in favour of the judgment appealed from.

Pearce LJ: I agree. The question here is whether there was any contract, whether offer and acceptance met.

...

The real problem in the present case is whether the plaintiffs were in fact intending to deal with the person physically present, who had fraudulently endowed himself with the attributes of some other identity, or whether they were intending only to deal with that other identity. If the former, there was a valid but voidable contract and the property passed. If the latter, there was no contract and the property did not pass.

...

The mere fact that the offeror is dealing with a person bearing an alias or false attributes does not create a mistake which will prevent the formation of a contract: *King's Norton Metal Co. Ltd. v. Edridge, Merrett & Co. Ltd.* 14 T.L.R. 98. For in such a case there is no other identity for which the identity of the offeree is mistaken. ...

But where a cheat passes himself off as another identity (e.g., as someone with whom the other party is accustomed to deal), it is otherwise.

...

An apparent contract made orally inter praesentes raises particular difficulties. The offer is apparently addressed to the physical person present. Prima facie, he, by whatever name he is called, is the person to whom the offer is made. ... Yet clearly, though difficult, it is not impossible to rebut the prima facie presumption that the offer can be accepted by the person to whom it is physically addressed. To take two extreme instances. If a man orally commissions a portrait from some unknown artist who had deliberately passed himself off, whether by disguise or merely by verbal cosmetics, as a famous painter, the impostor could not accept the offer. For though the offer is made to him physically, it is obviously, as he knows, addressed to the famous painter. The mistake in identity on such facts is clear and the nature of the contract makes it obvious that identity was of vital importance to the offeror. At the other end of the scale, if a shopkeeper sells goods in a normal cash transaction to a man who misrepresents himself as being some well-known figure, the transaction will normally be valid. For the shopkeeper was ready to sell goods for cash to the world at large and the particular identity of the purchaser in such a contract was not of sufficient importance to override the physical presence identified by sight and hearing. Thus the nature of the proposed contract must have a strong bearing on the question of whether the intention of the offeror (as understood by his offeree) was to make his offer to some other particular identity rather than to the physical person to whom it was orally offered.

In our case, the facts lie in the debatable area between the two extremes. At the beginning of the negotiations, always an important consideration, the name or personality of the false Hutchinson were of no importance and there was no other identity competing with his physical presence. The plaintiffs were content to sell the car for cash to any purchaser. The contractual conversation was orally addressed to the physical identity of the false Hutchinson. The identity was the man present, and his name was merely one of his attributes. Had matters continued thus, there would clearly have been a valid but voidable contract.

...

Each case must be decided on its own facts. The question in such cases is this. Has it been sufficiently shown in the particular circumstances that, contrary to the prima facie presumption, a party was not contracting with the physical person to whom he uttered the offer, but with another individual whom (as the other party ought to have understood) he believed to be the physical person present. The answer to that question is a finding of fact.

...

Although I appreciate the force of [counsel for the defendants'] very full and fair argument, he has failed to persuade me that the judge could not properly arrive at his conclusion. I agree that the appeal should be dismissed.

Devlin LJ (*dissented on the basis that there was a presumption, not here rebutted, that the ladies intended to contract with the person before them. He added the following passage at the end of his judgment:*) There can be no doubt, as all this difference of opinion shows, that the dividing line between voidness and voidability, between fundamental mistake and incidental deceit, is a very fine one. That a fine and difficult distinction has to be drawn is not necessarily any reproach to the law. But need the rights of the parties in a case like this depend on such a distinction? ...Why should the question whether the defendant should or should not pay the plaintiff damages for conversion depend upon voidness or voidability, and upon inferences to be drawn from a conversation in which the defendant took no part? ...For the doing of justice, the relevant question in this sort of case is not whether the contract was void or voidable, but which of two innocent parties shall suffer for the fraud of a third. The plain answer is that the loss should be divided between them in such proportion as is just in all the circumstances. If it be pure misfortune, the loss should be borne equally; if the fault or imprudence of either party has caused or contributed to the loss, it should be borne by that party in the whole or in the greater part. In saying this, I am suggesting nothing novel, for this sort of observation has often been made. But it is only in comparatively recent times that the idea of giving to a court power to apportion loss has found a place in our law. I have in mind particularly the Law Reform Acts of 1935, 1943 and 1945, that dealt respectively with joint tortfeasors, frustrated contracts and contributory negligence. These statutes, which I believe to have worked satisfactorily, show a modern inclination towards a decision based on a just apportionment rather than one given in black or in white according to the logic of the law. I believe it would be useful if Parliament were now to consider whether or not it is practicable by means of a similar act of law reform to provide for the victims of a fraud a better way of adjusting their mutual loss than that which has grown out of the common law.

NOTES AND QUESTIONS

1. Can this decision be reconciled with *Phillips v Brooks Ltd*? Is there not a strong presumption in face to face dealings that one intends to deal with the person in front of one and not someone else? If so, do you agree that it was rebutted on these facts?

2. The Law Reform Committee, 'Transfer of Title to Chattels' (1966, Cmnd. 2598), looked at Devlin LJ's comments but decided that apportionment would lead to too much uncertainty in the law and would occasion too many procedural and practical difficulties (imagine, eg, the difficulties of apportionment where goods have been resold several times). However, it did recommend that, where there is a mistake as to identity, the contract should be voidable rather than void. What would be the impact of such a reform on innocent third parties?

Lewis v Averay [1972] 1 QB 198, Court of Appeal

Responding to a newspaper car advert placed by the claimant, Lewis, a man telephoned asking to view the car. The man test-drove it with the claimant to the claimant's fiancée's flat where, during conversation, the man led the claimant to believe that he was the well-known actor Richard Greene of the Robin Hood television series. When the man began to write out a cheque, the claimant asked for proof of identity. The man showed a special Pinewood Studios admission pass with an official stamp on it, bearing the name Richard Green with a photograph of the man. Relying on that proof of identity, the claimant agreed to let him have the car. The car was then sold to the defendant, Averay, three days later where the same man represented himself to be Lewis. Upon realising the fraud the claimant brought an action for conversion against the defendant. In allowing the defendant's appeal, it was held by the Court of Appeal that there was no operative mistake rendering the contract void as between the claimant and the rogue. Property had therefore passed to the rogue.

Lord Denning MR: Who is entitled to the goods? Original seller? Or the ultimate buyer? The courts have given different answers. In *Phillips v Brooks,* the ultimate buyer was held to be entitled to the ring. In *Ingram v Little* the original seller was held to be entitled to the car. In the present case the deputy county court judge has held the original seller entitled.

It seems to me that the material facts in each case are quite indistinguishable the one from the other. In each case there was, to all outward appearance, a contract: but there was a mistake by the seller as to the identity of the buyer. This mistake was fundamental. In each case it led to the handing over of the goods. Without it the seller would not have parted with them.

This case therefore raises the question: What is the effect of a mistake by one party as to the identity of the other? It has sometimes been said that if a party makes a mistake as to the identity of the person with whom he is contracting there is no contract, or, if there is a contract, it is a nullity and void, so that no property can pass under it.

...

Again it has been suggested that a mistake as to the identity of a person is one thing: and a mistake as to his attributes is another. A mistake as to identity, it is said, avoids a contract: whereas a mistake as to attributes does not. But this is a distinction without a difference. A man's very name is one of his attributes. It is also a key to his identity. If then, he gives a false name, is it a mistake as to his identity? or a mistake as to his attributes? These fine distinctions do no good to the law.

As I listened to the argument in this case, I felt it wrong that an innocent purchaser (who knew nothing of what passed between the seller and the rogue) should have his title depend on such refinements. After all, he has acted with complete circumspection and in entire good faith: whereas it was the seller who let the rogue have the goods and thus enabled him to commit the fraud. I do not, therefore, accept the theory that a mistake as to identity renders a contract void. ... When two parties have come to a contract – or rather what appears, on the face of it, to be a contract – the fact that one party is mistaken as to the identity of the other does not mean that there is no contract or that the contract is a nullity and void from the beginning. It only means that the contract is voidable, that is, liable to be set aside at the instance of the mistaken person, so long as he does so before third parties have in good faith acquired rights under it.

...

In this case Mr. Lewis made a contract of sale with the very man, the rogue, who came to the flat. I say that he "made a contract" because in this regard we do not look into his intentions, or into his mind to know what he was thinking or into the mind of the rogue. We look to the outward appearances. On the face of the dealing, Mr. Lewis made a contract under which he sold the car to the rogue, delivered the car and the logbook to him, and took a cheque in return. The contract is evidenced by the receipts which were signed. It was, of course, induced by fraud. The rogue made false representations as to his identity, But it was still a contract, though voidable for fraud. It was a contract under which this property passed to the rogue, and in due course passed from the rogue to Mr. Averay, before the contract was avoided.

Though I very much regret that either of these good and reliable gentlemen should suffer, in my judgment it is Mr. Lewis who should do so. I think the appeal should be allowed and judgment entered for the defendant.

Phillimore LJ: I share the regret expressed by Lord Denning M.R. I think the law was conveniently stated by Pearce L.J. in the course of his judgment in *Ingram v. Little* [1961] 1 Q.B. 31 to which reference has already been made. He said, at p. 61:

> "Each case must be decided on its own facts. The question in such cases is this. Has it been sufficiently shown in the particular circumstances that, contrary to the prima facie presumption" – and I would emphasise those words – "a party was not contracting with the physical person to whom he uttered the offer, but with another individual whom (as the other party ought to have understood) he believed to be the physical person present. The answer to that question is a finding of fact."

Now, in that particular case the Court of Appeal, by a majority and in the very special and unusual facts of the case, decided that it had been sufficiently shown in the particular circumstances that, contrary to the prima facie presumption, the lady who was selling the motor car was not dealing with the person actually present. But in the present case I am bound to say that I do not think there was anything which could displace the prima facie presumption that Mr. Lewis was dealing with the gentleman present there in the flat – the rogue.

Megaw LJ: ...I find it difficult to understand the basis, either in logic or in practical consider-ations, of the test laid down by the majority of the court in *Ingram v. Little* [1961] 1 Q.B. 31. That test is, I think, accurately recorded in the headnote, as follows:

> "- where a person physically present and negotiating to buy a chattel fraudulently assumed the identity of an existing third person, the test to determine to whom the offer was addressed was how ought the promisee to have interpreted the promise."

The promisee, be it noted, is the rogue. The question of the existence of a contract and therefore the passing of property, and therefore the right of third parties, if this test is correct, is made to depend upon the view which some rogue should have formed, presumably knowing that he is a rogue, as to the state of mind of the opposite party to the negotiation, who does not know that he is dealing with a rogue.

However that may be, and assuming that the test so stated is indeed valid, in my view this appeal can be decided on a short and simple point. It is the point which was put at the outset of his argument by Mr. Titheridge on behalf of the defendant appellant. The well-known textbook *Cheshire and Fifoot on the Law of Contract* 7th ed. (1969), 213 and 214, deals with the question of invalidity of a contract by virtue of unilateral mistake, and in particular unilateral mistake relating to mistaken identity. The editors describe what in their submission are certain facts that must be established in order to enable one to avoid a contract on the basis of unilateral mistake by him as to the identity of the opposite party. The first of those facts is that at the time when he made the offer he regarded the identity of the offeree as a matter of vital importance. To translate that into the facts of the present case, it must be established that at the time of offering to sell his car to the rogue, Mr. Lewis regarded the identity of the rogue as a matter of vital importance. In my view, Mr. Titheridge is abundantly justified, on the notes of the evidence and on the findings of the judge, in his submission that the mistake of Mr. Lewis went no further than a mistake as to the attributes of the rogue. It was simply a mistake as to the creditworthiness of the man who was there present and who described himself as Mr. Green. ...When one looks at the evidence of the plaintiff...there was not here any evidence that would justify the finding that [the claimant] regarded the identity of the man who called himself Mr. Green as a matter of vital importance.

I agree that the appeal should be allowed.

NOTES AND QUESTIONS

1. Can this decision be reconciled with *Ingram v Little*? If not, which is correct?
2. Although Lord Denning MR agreed with the result and allowed the appeal, his reasoning was different from that of the other two judges. In line with what the Law Reform Committee in 1966 had recommended, he thought that a mistake as to identity (and he appeared to say that here there was such a mistake) renders a contract voidable not void.

Shogun Finance Ltd v Hudson
[2003] UKHL 62, [2004] 1 AC 919, House of Lords

A rogue acquired by dishonest means the driving licence of Mr Durlabh Patel. The rogue then entered the showrooms of a motor dealer in Leicester, introduced himself as Mr Patel, and gave Mr Patel's address. The rogue agreed to hire-purchase a car subject to obtaining finance. The motor dealer faxed through to the claimant finance company (Shogun Finance Ltd) a copy of the presented driving licence and hire-purchase agreement form with the forged signature of Mr Patel. The finance company, after carrying out several credit checks, entered into a hire-purchase agreement with 'Mr Patel' and the rogue took away the car. The rogue then sold the car to the defendant, Mr Hudson, and disappeared. The claimant finance company brought an action for the tort of conversion against Hudson, contending that there had been a mistake as to identity so that there was no contract of hire-purchase between it and the rogue. The exception for bona fide purchasers of hire-purchased cars in section 27 of the Hire Purchase Act 1964 did not therefore apply and the car remained the claimant's property. By a 3–2 majority the House of Lords (dismissing the defendant's appeal) held that there was indeed no contract of hire-purchase between the claimant and the rogue so that the property remained the claimant's and the action succeeded.

Lord Nicholls of Birkenhead (dissenting):

1 My Lords, this appeal raises a difficult problem about the effect of fraudulent misrepresentation on the formation of a contract. If a crook (C) fraudulently represents to the owner of goods (O) that he is another identifiable person (X) and on that basis O parts with goods to C by way of sale, is there in law a contract between O and C? Does the answer to this question differ according to whether O and C communicated face-to-face, or by correspondence, or over the telephone, or by e-mail? The law on cases involving this type of fraudulent conduct, euphemistically described as cases of "mistaken identity", is notoriously unsatisfactory. The reported decisions are few in number and they are not reconcilable. In the present case Sedley LJ said the law has tied itself into a Gordian knot. Brooke LJ said the law is in a "sorry condition" which only Parliament or your Lordships' House can remedy: see [2002] QB 834, 847, 855, paras [23], [51].

2 Two features are usually present when cases of this type come before the court. The first feature is that a seller of goods is concerned with the creditworthiness of the proposed buyer. The seller wants to be sure he will be paid for the goods he is handing over. Here the common law seems to have drawn a distinction between two kinds of fraudulent misrepresentation. The common law distinguished between a case (1) where a crook fraudulently asserts he is creditworthy and a case (2) where a crook fraudulently asserts he is someone else known to be creditworthy. One might suppose there is no difference of substance between these two cases. These are merely two ways a crook may assert a spurious creditworthiness. But, historically, the law seems to have been otherwise. In case (1), when the seller parts with his goods he does so pursuant to a *voidable* contract. This is said to be a case of mistake as to a person's attributes. In case (2), in some circumstances but not all, the seller has been held to part with his goods pursuant to a *void* contract, that is, no contract at all. This is said to be a case of mistake as to a person's identity.

3 The second feature usually present in cases of this type is that the crook then sells the goods to an innocent third party. This feature explains why the distinction between a voidable and a void contract matters. Having fraudulently acquired the goods from their owner, the crook then sells them to an unsuspecting third party. The rights of this innocent third party may depend upon the nice distinction between a voidable contract and a void contract. In case (1), where the crook fraudulently misrepresents his own financial standing, the loss falls on the unfortunate owner of the goods who was tricked into parting with them to the crook. *King's Norton Metal Co Ltd v Edridge, Merrett & Co Ltd* (1897) 14 TLR 98 [*see above, 600*] is an instance of this. ...

4 This outcome is to be contrasted with case (2), where the crook asserts he is someone else. In such a case the loss sometimes, but not always, falls upon the unfortunate third party who also was a victim of the crook's trickery. The third party paid for the goods in all honesty, but he must return them to their original owner or pay their value. Thus in *Cundy v Lindsay* (1878) 3 App Cas 459 Cundy had to pay the linen manufacturers Lindsay & Co for the 250 dozen cambric handkerchiefs the crook acquired from Lindsay by fraudulently representing he was the respectable business firm of Blenkiron.

5 The distinction in outcome thus drawn between these two kinds of fraudulent misrepresentation, one as to "attributes" and the other as to "identity", is unconvincing. It has been described as a reproach to the law. To a considerable extent the distinction has now been eroded. *Cundy v Lindsay* 3 App Cas 459 was decided over a century ago, and since then there have been significant developments in this area of case law. Unfortunately these developments have left the law in a state of disarray. The question before the House on this appeal is whether this distinction, so far as it remains, should still be regarded as good law.

12 …The factual postulate now under consideration, as mentioned at the outset, is that a crook (C) fraudulently misrepresents to the owner of goods (O) that he, C, is another identifiable person (X) whom O believes to be creditworthy. In reliance on this representation O agrees to sell the goods and he hands them over to C. Is this pursuant to a voidable contract between O and C? Or is there no contract between them at all? As between O and C the answer is of no moment. Either way O has ample remedies against C, assuming C has some money and can be traced. As already noted, however, the answer to these question may be of crucial importance to a third party who subsequently bought the goods in good faith from C.

13 In cases of this type there are two innocent parties, O and the third party purchaser. Striking the right balance when one of two innocent parties must sustain a loss is seldom easy. In 1960 Devlin LJ suggested that in this type of case the loss should be divided between O and the third party in such proportion as is just in all the circumstances: see *Ingram v Little* [1961] 1 QB 31, 73-74. Lord Gardiner LC then referred this problem to the Law Reform Committee. In its Twelfth Report, on the Transfer of Title to Chattels (1966) (Cmnd 2958) the committee rejected Devlin LJ's apportionment suggestion as impracticable. The committee recommended that where goods are sold under a mistake as to the buyer's identity the contract should, so far as third parties are concerned, be voidable and not void: paragraphs 9-12 and 15.

Fraudulent misrepresentation: face-to-face dealings

18 I can now turn to the effect of a fraudulent misrepresentation made by a person about his identity. In cases of face-to-face dealings the law, as declared by the preponderance of authority, is tolerably clear. The owner of the goods believes the person in front of him is X, and in that belief he contracts with the person in front of him. The fraudulent misrepresentation by the crook C regarding his identity [does not] negative…O's intention to contract with C. …O believes C, the person in front of him, to be X *and he deals with C in that belief*. The fraud entitles O to avoid the contract, but it does not negative the formation of a contract with C.

> *[He considered* Phillips v Brooks, Ingram v Little *and* Lewis v Averay *and continued:]*

24 Sometimes in these cases the transaction is evidenced in writing. This can make no difference to the outcome. Clearly there is no magic attaching to a misrepresentation made in writing rather than by word of mouth. The presence or absence of a written record of a transaction negotiated face to face, such as an invoice or receipt made out in favour of Sir George Bullough, with or without his address, or a cheque ostensibly signed by Sir George Bullough, is neither here nor there for present purposes. Writings such as these are no more than stark contemporary confirmation that the misrepresentation was made and that the seller believed it.

25 Similarly the contractual position between O and C must be the same if they meet face-to-face and the deal arranged by them is later embodied in a written agreement. This further step does not relevantly change the legal position. The written contract is expressed to be made between O and X. But C, the person with whom O was physically dealing, asserted he was X, and O believed him. So the description of C in the contract as X was a fraudulent misnomer. C used a false name and address, and the written contract is to be construed accordingly.

Fraudulent misrepresentation: dealing by correspondence

26 But what of the case where a fraudulent misrepresentation is made in writing but O and C do not meet each other? C writes to O saying he is X and the deal proceeds on that basis. O parts with his goods to the person with whom he is in fact dealing, namely, C, in the belief he is X.

27 At first sight it seems counter-intuitive to speak of a contract between O and C in cases of this type. It seems counter-intuitive because on its face a contract in writing or in correspondence expressed to be made between O and X is inconsistent, agency apart, with its being a contract between O and C. But this intuitive response is not a sound guide if it leaves out of account, as all too easily it may, the vitally important underlying fraudulent misrepresentation. In his dealings with O the crook C represented he was X, and O proceeded to *deal with him (C)* in that belief.

28 When this feature is kept in mind it readily becomes apparent that in principle cases of this type are no different from cases of face-to-face dealings. The existence of physical immediacy in one case, and the absence of it in the other, is immaterial. The physical immediacy of C in face-to-face cases tends to emphasise O's intention to deal with the person in front of him. With other forms of communication such as the telephone or correspondence this physical immediacy is lacking. But in each case, whatever the mode of communication, what matters is *whether* O agreed to sell his goods to the person with whom he was dealing, not *why* he did so or under what name. The latter is relevant to remedy, not to formation of a contract.

29 In this regard mention must be made of reasoning sometimes advanced here, along the lines that the identity of the person to whom a written offer is made is a question solely of construction of the document. The offer, it is said, is made to the person identified in the document and no one else. A written offer made by O to X is not capable of acceptance by C. Hence, it is said that, whatever the position in face-to-face dealings, in cases of written contracts or contracts made by correspondence there can be no contract between O and C, contradicting as this would the terms of the document.

30 The flaw in this reasoning is that it begs the crucial question: to whom was the offer made? The reasoning assumes this is a straightforward case of an offer made to the person named. Indeed the person named is X. But that is only part of the picture. O believes that X, the person to whom he is writing and to whom he addressed the offer, is one and the same person as the person with whom he is dealing. In fact he is not dealing with X. He is dealing with C. O's misapprehension in this regard, induced by C's fraud, is no different in principle from a case where C's misrepresentation is made orally in the course of the face-to-face meeting. The legal problem is the same in both cases. The presence or absence of writing does not constitute a principled ground of distinction.

    [After looking at Cundy v Lindsay *he continued:]*

The choice

33 In my view this decision is not reconcilable with *Phillips v Brooks Ltd* [1919] 2 KB 243 or with *Lewis v Averay* [1972] 1 QB 198 or with the starting point "presumption" formulated by Devlin LJ in *Ingram v Little* [1961] 1 QB 31. The legal principle applicable in these cases cannot sensibly differ according to whether the transaction is negotiated face-to-face, or by letter, or by fax, or by e-mail, or over the telephone or by video link or video telephone. Typically today a purchaser pays for goods with a credit or debit card. He produces the card in person in a shop or provides details of the card over the telephone or by e-mail or by fax. When a credit or debit card is fraudulently misused in this way the essence of the transaction is the same in each case. It does not differ from one means of communication to the next. The essence of the transaction in each case is that the owner of the goods agrees to part with his goods on the basis of a fraudulent misrepresentation made by the other regarding his identity. Since the essence of the transaction is the same in each case, the law in its response should apply the same principle in each case, irrespective of the precise mode of communication of offer and acceptance.

34 Accordingly, if the law of contract is to be coherent and rescued from its present unsatisfactory and unprincipled state, the House has to make a choice: either to uphold the approach adopted in *Cundy v Lindsay* and overrule the decisions in *Phillips v Brooks Ltd* and *Lewis v Averay*, or to prefer these later decisions to *Cundy v Lindsay*.

35 I consider the latter course is the right one, for a combination of reasons. It is in line with the direction in which, under the more recent decisions, the law has now been moving for some time. It accords better with basic principle regarding the effect of fraud on the formation of a contract. It seems preferable as a matter of legal policy. As between two innocent persons the loss is more appropriately borne by the person who takes the risks inherent in parting with his goods without receiving payment. This approach fits comfortably with the intention of Parliament in enacting the limited statutory exceptions to the proprietary principle of nemo dat quod non habet. Thus, by section 23 of the 1979 Act Parliament protected an innocent buyer from a seller with a voidable title. The classic instance of a person with a voidable title is a person who acquired the goods by fraud: see per Bramwell LJ in *Babcock v Lawson* (1880) 5 QBD 284, 286. Further, this course is supported by writers of the distinction of Sir Jack Beatson: see *Anson's Law of Contract*, 28th ed (2002), p 332. It is consistent with the approach adopted elsewhere in the common law world, notably in the United States of America in the Uniform Commercial Code, 14th ed (1995), section 2-403. And this course makes practical sense. In a case such as the present the owner of goods has no interest in the identity of the buyer. He is interested only in creditworthiness. It is little short of absurd that a subsequent purchaser's rights depend on the precise manner in which the crook seeks to persuade the owner of his creditworthiness and permit him to take the goods away with him. This ought not to be so. The purchaser's rights should not depend upon the precise form the crook's misrepresentation takes.

36 *Cundy v Lindsay* has stood for a long time. But I see no reason to fear that adopting this conclusion will unsettle the law of contract. In practice the problems surrounding *Cundy v Lindsay* arise only when third parties' rights are in issue. To bring the law here into line with the law already existing in "face-to-face" cases will rid the law of an anomaly. Devlin LJ's starting point presumption is a workable foundation which should apply in all cases. A person is presumed to intend to contract with the person with whom he is actually dealing, whatever be the mode of communication.

37 Although expressed by Devlin LJ as a presumption, it is not easy to think of practical circumstances where, once in point, the presumption will be displaced. The factual postulate necessary to bring the presumption into operation is that a person (O) believes that the person with whom he is dealing is the person the latter has represented himself to be. Evidence that the other's identity was of importance to O, and evidence of the steps taken to check the other's identity, will lead nowhere if the transaction proceeds on the basis of the underlying factual postulate.

The present case

38 It follows that I would allow this appeal. The principles applicable to the formation of a contract of sale are equally applicable to the formation of a hire-purchase agreement. The document submitted to Shogun Finance, and signed by the crook in the name of Mr Patel, does of course refer unequivocally to Mr Patel. The document identifies him with some particularity: his full name and address, his date of birth, his driving licence number, and his employer's name and address. These details were of prime importance to Shogun Finance

because they identified the person whose credit rating it had checked and approved. The company intended to contract with this person. But it is clear from the evidence that Shogun Finance, as much as the dealer in the car showroom, thought this was one and the same person as the individual in the showroom. Shogun Finance proceeded in this (fraud-induced) belief.

41 One further point may be noted. Some time was taken up in this case with arguments on whether the dealer was an agent for the finance company and for what purposes. This was in an endeavour to bring the case within the "face-to-face" principle. The need for such singularly sterile arguments underlines the practical absurdity of a principle bounded in this way. The practical reality is that in the instant case the presence or absence of a representative of the finance company in the dealer's showroom made no difference to the course of events. Had an authorised representative of the finance company been present no doubt he would have inspected the driving licence himself and himself obtained the information needed by his company. As it was, a copy of the licence, together with the necessary information, were faxed to the finance company. I can see no sensible basis on which these different modes of communication should affect the outcome of this case. I would set aside the orders of the assistant recorder and the Court of Appeal, and dismiss this action. Mr Hudson acquired a good title to the car under section 27 of the 1964 Act.

Lord Hobhouse of Woodborough:

48 ...Mr Durlabh Patel is the sole hirer under this written agreement. No one else acquires any rights under it; no one else can become the bailee of the motor car or the "debtor" "under the agreement". It is not in dispute that R [the rogue] was not Mr Durlabh Patel nor that R had no authority from Mr Patel to enter into the agreement or take possession of the motor car.

49 Mr Hudson seeks to escape from this conclusion by saying: "but the rogue was the person who came into the dealer's office and negotiated a price with the dealer and signed the form in the presence of the dealer who then witnessed it." ... The gist of the argument is that oral evidence may be adduced to contradict the agreement contained in a written document which is the only contract to which the finance company was a party. The agreement is a written agreement with Mr Durlabh Patel. The argument seeks to contradict this and make it an agreement with the rogue. It is argued that other evidence is always admissible to show who the parties to an agreement are. Thus, if the contents of the document are, without more, insufficient unequivocally to identify the actual individual referred to or if the identification of the party is non-specific, evidence can be given to fill any gap. Where the person signing is also acting as the agent of another, evidence can be adduced of that fact. None of this involves the contradiction of the document: *Young v Schuler* (1883) 11 QBD 651, which was a case of an equivocal agency signature and it was held that evidence was admissible that the signature was also a personal signature—"evidence that he intended to sign in both capacities ... does not contradict the document, and is admissible": per Cotton LJ, at p 655. But it is different where the party is, as here, specifically identified in the document: oral or other extrinsic evidence is not admissible. Further, the rogue was no one's agent (nor did he ever purport to be). The rule that other evidence may not be adduced to contradict the provisions of a contract contained in a written document is fundamental to the mercantile law of this country; the bargain is the document; the certainty of the contract depends on it. The relevant principle is well summarised in *Phipson on Evidence* 15th ed (2000), pp 1165-1166, paras 42-11 and 42-12:

> "when the parties have deliberately put their agreement into writing, it is conclusively presumed between themselves and their privies that they intend the writing to form a full and final statement of their intentions, and one which should be placed beyond the reach of future controversy, bad faith or treacherous memory."

(See also *Bank of Australasia v Palmer* [1897] AC 540, 545, per Lord Morris.) This rule is one of the great strengths of English commercial law and is one of the main reasons for the international success of English law in preference to laxer systems which do not provide the same certainty. *Hector v Lyons* 58 P & CR 156 is simply an application of this basic and long established principle. The father was claiming to be able to enforce a contract of sale of land. The father had conducted the negotiations. Woolf LJ said, at pp 160-161:

> "In this case there is no dispute as to who, according to the written contract, are the parties. The son was described in the contract as one of the parties. He does exist and, in so far as there was a contract at all, it was between him and the other party identified in the contract, Mrs Pamela Doris Lyons."

Sir Nicolas Browne-Wilkinson V-C delivered a judgment to the same effect. He referred, at p 159, to the cases "entirely concerned with transactions between two individuals face to face entering into oral agreement", saying:

> "In my judgment the principle there enunciated has no application to a case such as the present where there is a contract and wholly in writing. There the identity of the vendor and of the purchaser is established by the names of the parties included in the written contract."

Mr Hudson submitted, as he had to, that this decision was wrong and should be overruled. In my opinion the Court of Appeal's decision was clearly correct and correctly reasoned in accordance with well established principles.

50 The argument also fails on another ground. There was no consensus ad idem between the finance company and the rogue. Leaving on one side the fact that the rogue never had any intention himself to contract with the finance company, the hire-purchase "agreement" to which Mr Hudson pins his argument was one purportedly made by the acceptance by the finance company, by signing the creditor's box in the form, of a written offer by Mr Durlabh Patel to enter into the hire-purchase agreement. This faces Mr Hudson with a dilemma: either the contract created by that acceptance was a contract with Mr Durlabh Patel or there was no consensus ad idem, the rogue having no honest belief or contractual intent whatsoever and the finance company believing that it was accepting an offer by Mr Durlabh Patel. On neither alternative was there a hire-purchase agreement with the rogue.

54 It follows that the appeal must be dismissed and the majority judgment of the Court of Appeal affirmed.

55 But, before I leave this case, I should shortly summarise why the argument of the appellant's counsel was so mistaken. The first reason was that they approached the question as if it was simply a matter of sorting out the common law authorities relating to the sale of goods. They did not treat it as a matter of applying a statutory exception to the basic common law rule, nemo dat quod non habet. Further, they did not analyse the structure of the overall transaction and the consumer credit agreement within it. Accordingly, they misrepresented the role of the dealer, wrongly treating him as the contracting agent of the finance company which he was not. They never analysed the terms of the written document and had no regard at all to the offer and acceptance clause it contained which, if there was any contract between a "debtor" and the finance company, governed their relationship and which expressly set out the *only* way in which such a contract could come into existence. They made submissions which contradicted the express written contract and were therefore contrary to principle and long established English mercantile law. They submitted that *Cundy v Lindsay* 3 App Cas 459 was wrongly decided and should be overruled, substituting for it a general rule which, in disregard of the document or documents which constitute the agreement (if any), makes everything depend upon a factual inquiry into extraneous facts not known to both of the parties thus depriving documentary contracts of their certainty. They sought to convert a direct documentary contract with the finance company into a face-to-face oral contract made through the dealer as the contracting agent of the finance company, notwithstanding that the dealer was never such an agent of the finance company. Finally they sought, having bypassed the written contract, to rely upon authorities on oral contracts for the sale of goods, made face-to-face and where the title to the goods had passed to the "buyer", notwithstanding that this was a documentary consumer credit transaction not a sale and, on any view, no title had ever passed to R. In the result they have invited a review of those authorities by reference to the particular facts of each of them. They have sought to draw your Lordships into a discussion of the evidential tools, e g, rebuttable presumptions of fact and the so-called face-to-face "principle", used by judges in those cases to assist them in making factual decisions…notwithstanding that the present case concerns the construction of a written contract. They forget that the, presently relevant, fundamental principles of law to be applied—consensus ad idem, the correspondence of the contractual offer and the contractual acceptance, the legal significance of the use of a written contract—are clear and are not in dispute. Inevitably over the course of time there have been decisions on the facts of individual "mistaken identity" cases which seem now to be inconsistent; the further learned, but ultimately unproductive, discussion of them will warm academic hearts. But what matters is the principles of law. They are clear and sound and need no revision. To cast doubt upon them can only be a disservice to English law. Similarly, to attempt to use this appeal to advocate, on the basis of continental legal systems which are open to cogent criticism, the abandonment of the soundly based nemo dat quod non habet rule (statutorily adopted) would be not only improper but even more damaging.

Lord Millett (dissenting):

81 In my opinion, once one accepts that there are two questions involved: (i) did a contract come into existence at all? and (ii) if so was the contract vitiated by fraud or mistake? there is only one principled conclusion. Whatever the medium of communication, a contract comes into existence if, on an objective appraisal of the facts, there is sufficient correlation between offer and acceptance to make it possible to say that the impostor's offer has been accepted by the person to whom it was addressed. While a person cannot intercept and accept an offer made to some one else, he should normally be treated as intending to contract with the person with whom he is dealing. Provided that the offer is made to him, then whether his acceptance of the offer is obtained by deception or mistake, and whether his mistake is as to the identity of the offeror or some material attribute of his, the transaction should result in a contract, albeit one which is voidable.

83 In the Court of Appeal [2002] QB 834 both Sedley LJ (who dissented) and Brooke LJ, at p 855, para [51], expressed disquiet at "the sorry condition" of the law. In the former's view, with which I agree, the decision in *Cundy v Lindsay* 3 App Cas 459 stands in the way of a coherent development of this branch of the law. We have the opportunity to restate the law, and cannot shirk the duty of putting it on a basis which is both just and principled, even if it means deciding that we should no longer follow a previous decision of the House.

84 We cannot leave the law as it is. It is neither fair nor principled, and not all the authorities from which it is derived can be reconciled; some, at least, must be overruled if it is to be extricated from the present quagmire. If the law is to be rationalised and placed on a proper footing, the formulation which I have proposed has the merit of according with the recommendations made in the Twelfth Report of the Law Reform Committee on the Transfer of Title to Chattels (Cmnd 2958) and in *Anson's Law of Contract*, 28th ed, p 332. It would also bring English law into line with the law both in the United States and in Germany. …

87 Where does this leave the authorities? Most of those which are concerned with face-to-face transactions can stand with the exception of the decision of the majority of the Court of Appeal in *Ingram v Little* [1961] 1 QB 31, which is inconsistent with *Lewis v Averay* [1972] 1 QB 198 and should be overruled. …

107 ...The claimant and the dealer both believed that the customer who was hiring the car and Mr Durlabh Patel were one and the same; but the claimant did not make that a condition of the dealer's authority to part with the car. From first to last it believed that the impostor who attended the dealer's showroom, gave his name as Mr Durlabh Patel, and signed the agreement in that name, was indeed Mr Durlabh Patel; in that belief it entered into a hiring agreement and authorised the dealer to deliver possession of the car to the customer who had so identified himself. In my opinion, the claimant not only took a credit risk, but also took the risk that the customer who was hiring the car was not Mr Durlabh Patel and that its credit inquiries had been fraudulently misdirected. I would hold that there was a hiring, and the impostor was the hirer.

108 This conclusion involves a departure from *Cundy v Lindsay* 3 App Cas 459, a decision of this House which has stood for more than 120 years. But its reasoning is unsound. It is vitiated by its subjective approach to the formation of contract and the necessary correlation between offer and acceptance; which may be why textbook writers treat it as an example of unilateral mistake even though this was not the basis on which it was decided. For the same reason it cannot be regarded as authoritative on the question whether a contract otherwise properly entered into is void for mistake rather than voidable. It has had an unfortunate influence on the development of the law, leading to an unprincipled distinction between face-to-face transactions and others and the indefensible conclusion that an innocent purchaser's position depends on the nature of the mistake of a third party or the precise mechanics of the fraud which had been perpetrated on him. In my view it should now be discarded and the law put on a simpler and more principled and defensible basis.

109 In my opinion only the decision in *Cundy v Lindsay* stands in the way of a rational and coherent restatement of the law. My noble and learned friend, Lord Phillips of Worth Matravers, has expressed the view that the conclusion to which Lord Nicholls and I have come conflicts not only with that case but with the approach in almost all the numerous cases which he has cited. If they had preceded *Cundy v Lindsay*, that would be a strong reason for not adopting it. But they were merely following a decision of this House by which they were bound. Far from applying it generally, they attempted to distinguish it by carving out an unprincipled exception from it which Lord Nicholls has shown cannot be supported. While departing from *Cundy v Lindsay* would make obsolete the reasoning in those cases, dictated as it was by that decision, it would undermine the actual decision in very few cases. There is no long line of authority to be overruled. Indeed, only two cases need to be overruled; and neither of them can be supported even on the view that *Cundy v Lindsay* was rightly decided.

110 In my opinion *Cundy v Lindsay* 3 App Cas 459 should no longer be followed and *Ingram v Little* [1961] 1 QB 31 and *Hector v Lyons* 58 P & CR 156 should be overruled. I would allow the appeal.

Lord Phillips of Worth Matravers:

167 I have had the advantage of reading in draft the opinions of my noble and learned friends who have sat with me on this appeal. Lord Hobhouse of Woodborough and Lord Walker of Gestingthorpe have concluded that, as the contract was a written document, the identity of the hirer falls to be ascertained by construing that document. Adopting that approach, the hirer was, or more accurately purported to be, Mr Patel. As he had not authorised the conclusion of the contract, it was void.

168 Lord Nicholls of Birkenhead and Lord Millett have adopted a different approach. They point out the illogicality of applying a special approach to face-to-face dealings. What of dealings on the telephone, or by videolink? There also it could be said that each of the parties to the dealings is seeking to make a contract with the other party to the dealings. And this can even be said when the dealings are conducted by correspondence. If A writes to B making an offer and B writes back responding to that offer, B is intending to contract with the person who made that offer. If a contract is concluded in face-to-face dealings, notwithstanding that

one party is masquerading as a third party, why should the result be different when the dealings are by letter?

169 Lord Nicholls of Birkenhead and Lord Millett propose an elegant solution to this illogicality. Where two individuals *deal with each other,* by whatever medium, and agree terms of a contract, then a contract will be concluded between them, notwithstanding that one has deceived the other into thinking that he has the identity of a third party. In such a situation the contract will be voidable but not void. While they accept that this approach cannot be reconciled with *Cundy v Lindsay* 3 App Cas 459, they conclude that *Cundy v Lindsay* was wrongly decided and should no longer be followed.

170 While I was strongly attracted to this solution, I have found myself unable to adopt it. *Cundy v Lindsay* exemplifies the application by English law of the same approach to identifying the parties as is applied to identifying the terms of the contract. In essence this focuses on deducing the intention of the parties from their words and conduct. Where there is some form of personal contact between individuals who are conducting negotiations, this approach gives rise to problems. In such a situation I would favour the application of a strong presumption that each intends to contract with the other, with whom he is dealing. Where, however, the dealings are exclusively conducted in writing, there is no scope or need for such a presumption. This can be illustrated by a slight adaption of the facts of the present case. Assume that the rogue had himself filled in the application form and sent it and a photocopy of Mr Patel's driving licence to Shogun. Assume further that he had been authorised to do so by Mr Patel. There can be no doubt that a contract would have been concluded between Shogun and Mr Patel. Mr Patel would have intended to contract with Shogun; Shogun would have intended to contract with Mr Patel; and this would have been demonstrated by the application form.

171 Assume now that the rogue had wrongly understood that he had been requested by Mr Patel to fill in and submit the application form on his behalf, but in fact had no authority to do so. In this situation, according to established principles of the law of agency, an apparent contract would have been concluded between Shogun and Mr Patel but, being concluded without the latter's authority, it would be a nullity. Shogun might have a claim against the rogue for breach of warranty of authority, but could not have demonstrated that a contract had been concluded with the rogue.

172 Turning to the true position—that the rogue knew he had no authority to conclude a contract in the name of Mr Patel, but fraudulently wished to induce Shogun to believe that they were entering into such a contract—I do not see by what legal principle this change in the mental attitude of the rogue could result in a binding contract being concluded with him.

173 The position is not, of course, as simple as that. Negotiations between the rogue and Shogun were not conducted exclusively by written correspondence. They were conducted with the aid of the dealer and the use of fax and telephone communications. Acceptance of the offer was conveyed by telephone via the dealer—and this might have been capable of concluding a contract, notwithstanding that clause 1 of the standard terms provided for acceptance by signature: see the discussion in *Chitty on Contracts*, 28th ed, vol 1, p 117, para 2-062. ...

176 ...I have not found the assessment of the law easy, but nor is the application of the law to the facts. Shogun's representatives were aware of the presence of the prospective hirer in the dealer's showrooms in Leicester. To an extent the dealings were interpersonal through the medium of the dealer. Should one treat them as comparable to face-to-face dealings and conclude that there was a presumption that Shogun intended to contract with the man with whom they were dealing? Should one treat the written agreement as no more than peripheral to the dealings and conclude that it does not override that presumption? I have concluded that the answer to these questions is "no".

177 Shogun had, on the evidence, set up a formal system under which contracts would be concluded in writing on a standard form. This form was designed to cater for both regulated and non-regulated hire-purchase agreements. In order to be suitable for the former it had to

comply with the requirements of the Consumer Credit (Agreements) Regulations 1983 (SI 1983/1553). Schedule 1 to these Regulations, under the heading *"Parties to agreement"*, requires the agreement to set out "The name and a postal address of the creditor" and "The name and a postal address of the debtor". The agreement with which this appeal is concerned was not a regulated agreement, for the purchase price of the vehicle exceeded what was, at the time, the maximum to which the relevant provisions of the 1974 Act applied. I do not see, however, that the approach to the identification of the parties to the putative agreement can turn on whether or not the agreement was subject to the Regulations. Shogun put in place a system for concluding contracts that required both regulated and unregulated agreements to be entered into in writing in a form which provided essential information, including the identity of the parties to the agreement.

178 These considerations lead me to conclude that the correct approach in the present case is to treat the agreement as one concluded in writing and to approach the identification of the parties to that agreement as turning upon its construction. The particulars given in the agreement are only capable of applying to Mr Patel. It was the intention of the rogue that they should identify Mr Patel as the hirer. The hirer was so identified by Shogun. Before deciding to enter into the agreement they checked that Mr Patel existed and that he was worthy of credit. On that basis they decided to contract with him and with no one else. Mr Patel was the hirer under the agreement. As the agreement was concluded without his authority, it was a nullity. The rogue took no title under it and was in no position to convey any title to Mr Hudson.

179 For these reasons I would dismiss this appeal.

Lord Walker of Gestingthorpe delivered a speech concurring with Lord Hobhouse.

NOTES AND QUESTIONS

1. Assessing the overall impact of this case is not straightforward because Lord Hobhouse, giving the leading speech of the majority, approached the issue in such a very different way from the minority. He did not see this case as raising the issue of principle of how to reconcile the different approaches taken in past cases to mistakes of identity. Rather he saw the minority's approach as an attack on the certainty that should result from written terms.

2. As regards mistake as to identity, the majority's reasoning entrenches in the law a distinction between the approach to a contract concluded face to face and a contract concluded by correspondence. In the former, there is a presumption that the parties intended to deal with each other and that there is no mistake as to identity. This case concerned the latter. *Cundy v Lindsay* was firmly approved, there was an operative mistake as to identity, and there was no contract between the hire-purchase company and the rogue.

3. The majority rejected the notion (favoured by the minority and by Lord Denning in *Lewis v Averay*) that a mistake as to identity makes the contract voidable, not void.

4. As we have seen, *Ingram v Little* appears to be out of line with the other face-to-face cases. Although Lords Nicholls, Hobhouse and Phillips did not expressly indicate that it was wrong, Lord Walker (at [185] which is not set out above) and Lord Millett (at [110]) expressly said that it was incorrect.

5. The fact that the immediate issue raised was one concerning section 27 of the Hire Purchase Act 1964 should not mislead one into seeing the issue as a narrow one confined to that statutory exception in favour of third party

purchasers. On the contrary, the same issue would have arisen irrespective of that provision because of the differing impact on third parties of whether a contract is non-existent/void or voidable.

6. Has the emergence of new forms of communication made the distinction between face-to-face and other dealings difficult to apply?

7. Counsel for Mr Hudson argued that the dealership was acting as agent for the finance company, and thus the transaction was a 'face-to-face' transaction. This was rejected by their Lordships. Do you agree with Lord Nicholls' comment at [41] that the fact that counsel was trying to put to their Lordships such a 'sterile' argument demonstrates the 'practical absurdity' of the law?

8. In the light of what Lord Millett said at [83], do you consider that this was a missed opportunity and that the majority shirked the duty of putting the law on a just and principled basis?

(c) Non Est Factum

Saunders v Anglia Building Society (sub nom Gallie v Lee) [1971] AC 1004, House of Lords

The claimant, a widow aged 78, owned a house. Knowing that this would enable her nephew to raise money, she intended to make a gift of the house to him on condition that she could live there for the rest of her life. Her nephew and his business associate, Mr Lee, went round to the claimant's house and asked her to sign a document. The claimant had broken her spectacles and could not read it. Lee told her that it was a deed of gift of the house to her nephew. In fact, as the nephew wanted to sell the house on to Lee, it was an assignment of her interest in the house direct to Lee for £3000 (which was never intended to be paid to her). The claimant signed the document. Lee then mortgaged the house for £2000 to the defendant building society. He used the money to pay off his debts and then defaulted on the mortgage. The claimant sought a declaration that the assignment was void on the basis of non est factum so that the defendant had no right to the house enforceable against her. It was held by the House of Lords in dismissing her appeal that, as the document was not fundamentally different from what she thought, she did not satisfy the requirements for non est factum.

Lord Reid: My Lords, I am in general agreement with the speech of my noble and learned friend, Lord Pearson. In my opinion, this appeal must fail, however one states the law. The existing law seems to me to be in a state of some confusion. I do not think it is possible to reconcile all the decisions, let alone all the reasons given for them. ...

The plea of non est factum obviously applies when the person sought to be held liable did not in fact sign the document. But at least since the sixteenth century it has also been held to apply in certain cases so as to enable a person who in fact signed a document to say that it is not his deed. Obviously any such extension must be kept within narrow limits if it is not to shake the confidence of those who habitually and rightly rely on signatures when there is no obvious reason to doubt their validity. Originally this extension appears to have been made in favour of those who were unable to read owing to blindness or illiteracy and who therefore had to trust someone to tell them what they were signing. I think it must also apply in favour of those who are permanently or temporarily unable through no fault of their own to have without explanation any real understanding of the purport of a particular document, whether that be from defective education, illness or innate incapacity.

But that does not excuse them from taking such precautions as they reasonably can. The matter generally arises where an innocent third party has relied on a signed document in ignorance of the circumstances in which it was signed, and where he will suffer loss if the maker of the document is allowed to have it declared a nullity. So there must be a heavy burden of proof on the person who seeks to invoke this remedy. He must prove all the circumstances necessary to justify its being granted to him, and that necessarily involves his proving that he took all reasonable precautions in the circumstances. I do not say that the remedy can never be available to a man of full capacity. But that could only be in very exceptional circumstances: certainly not where his reason for not scrutinising the document before signing it was that he was too busy or too lazy. In general I do not think he can be heard to say that he signed in reliance on someone he trusted. But, particularly when he was led to believe that the document which he signed was not one which affected his legal rights, there may be cases where this plea can properly be applied in favour of a man of full capacity.

The plea cannot be available to anyone who was content to sign without taking the trouble to try to find out at least the general effect of the document. Many people do frequently sign documents put before them for signature by their solicitor or other trusted advisers without making any inquiry as to their purpose or effect. But the essence of the plea non est factum is that the person signing believed that the document he signed had one character or one effect whereas in fact its character or effect was quite different. He could not have such a belief unless he had taken steps or been given information which gave him some grounds for his belief. The amount of information he must have and the sufficiency of the particularity of his belief must depend on the circumstances of each case. ...

Finally, there is the question as to what extent or in what way must there be a difference between that which in fact he signed and that which he believed he was signing. In an endeavour to keep the plea within bounds there have been many attempts to lay down a dividing line.

...

There must, I think, be a radical difference between what he signed and what he thought he was signing – or one could use the words "fundamental" or "serious" or "very substantial." But what amounts to a radical difference will depend on all the circumstances. If he thinks he is giving property to A whereas the document gives it to B, the difference may often be of vital importance, but in the circumstances of the present case I do not think that it is. I think that it must be left to the courts to determine in each case in light of all the facts whether there was or was not a sufficiently great difference. The plea non est factum is in a sense illogical when applied to a case where the man in fact signed the deed. But it is none the worse for that if applied in a reasonable way.

Lord Wilberforce: How, then, ought the principle, on which a plea of non est factum is admissible, to be stated? In my opinion, a document should be held to be void (as opposed to voidable) only when the element of consent to it is totally lacking, that is, more concretely, when the transaction which the document purports to effect is essentially different in substance or in kind from the transaction intended. Many other expressions, or adjectives, could be used – "basically" or "radically" or "fundamentally."...

To this general test it is necessary to add certain amplifications. First, there is the case of fraud. The law as to this is best stated in the words of the judgment in *Foster v. Mackinnon* (1869) L.R. 4 C.P. 704, 711 where it is said that a signature obtained by fraud

"is invalid not merely on the ground of fraud, where fraud exists, but on the ground that the mind of the signer did not accompany the signature; in other words, that he never intended to sign, and therefore in contemplation of law never did sign, the contract to which his name is appended."

In other words, it is the lack of consent that matters, not the means by which this result was brought about. Fraud by itself may do no more than make the contract voidable.

Secondly, a man cannot escape from the consequences, as regards innocent third parties, of signing a document if, being a man of ordinary education and competence, he chooses to sign it without informing himself of its purport and effect. ...

Thirdly, there is the case where the signer has been careless in not taking ordinary precautions against being deceived. This is a difficult area. ...

In my opinion, the correct rule...is that, leaving aside negotiable instruments to which special rules may apply, a person who signs a document, and parts with it so that it may come into other hands, has a responsibility, that of the normal man of prudence, to take care what he signs, which, if neglected, prevents him from denying his liability under the document according to its tenor. I would add that the onus of proof in this matter rests upon him, i.e., to prove that he acted carefully, and not upon the third party to prove the contrary. ...

The preceding paragraphs contemplate persons who are adult and literate: the conclusion as to such persons is that, while there are cases in which they may successfully plead non est factum these cases will, in modern times, be rare.

As to persons who are illiterate, or blind, or lacking in understanding, the law is in a dilemma. On the one hand, the law is traditionally, and rightly, ready to relieve them against hardship and imposition. On the other hand, regard has to be paid to the position of innocent third parties who cannot be expected, and often would have no means, to know the condition or status of the signer. I do not think that a defined solution can be provided for all cases. The law ought, in my opinion, to give relief if satisfied that consent was truly lacking but will require of signers even in this class that they act responsibly and carefully according to their circumstances in putting their signature to legal documents.

This brings me to the present case. Mrs. Gallie was a lady of advanced age, but, as her evidence shows, by no means incapable physically or mentally. It certainly cannot be said that she did not receive sympathetic consideration or the benefit of much doubt from the judge as to the circumstances in which the assignment was executed. But accepting all of this, I am satisfied, with Russell L.J., that she fell short, very far short, of making the clear and satisfactory case which is required of those who seek to have a legal act declared void and of establishing a sufficient discrepancy between her intentions and her act.

Lord Pearson: Russell L.J. carefully examined the facts of the case and made ... comments on the plaintiff's evidence, and these were in effect his grounds of decision. He said...:

> '...At first sight, of course, it is easy to see the difference between a voluntary assignment of a leasehold property to A and an assignment for value of that property to B. But what upon the plaintiff's own evidence was the essential character of the document she was intending to execute? It was a document intended by her to divest herself of her leasehold property by transferring it to another, not as mere trustee for her, but so that the transferee should be in a position to deal with the property and in particular by borrowing money on the security of the property. Her evidence in my view makes it plain that she understood that Lee and Parkin were jointly concerned in a project of raising money on security of the property and this was her intention. In those circumstances I do not consider that it is correct to say that, for the purposes of the plea of non est factum, a transfer by her to Lee is to be regarded as of a totally different character or nature from a transfer to Parkin. ...'

I respectfully agree with the reasoning of Russell L.J. ...

In my opinion, the plea of non est factum ought to be available in a proper case for the relief of a person who for permanent or temporary reasons (not limited to blindness or illiteracy) is not capable of both reading and sufficiently understanding the deed or other document to be signed. By "sufficiently understanding" I mean understanding at least to the point of detecting a fundamental difference between the actual document and the document as the signer had believed it to be. There must be a proper case for such relief. There would not be a proper case if (a) the signature of the document was brought about by negligence of the signer in failing to take precautions which he ought to have taken, or (b) the actual document was not fundamentally different from the document as the signer believed it to be.

Lord Hodson and **Viscount Dilhorne** gave concurring speeches.

NOTES AND QUESTIONS

1. It was decided that the document was not fundamentally different than the widow thought because she knew that her nephew and Lee were jointly interested in raising money on the house. Against that background, a transfer to Lee rather than to her nephew was not so very different.
2. It would appear that their Lordships did not think that the widow fell foul of the negligence bar. Lord Pearson, in a passage not extracted above, expressly said, at 1034, 'I do not think that a reasonable jury would have found that she was negligent.'
3. The deed was voidable for Lee's fraudulent misrepresentation. Why was that of no real help to the widow?
4. Non est factum ('it is not my deed') is an extreme doctrine. It renders a contract void for a unilateral mistake irrespective of whether the other party knew of that mistake. Not surprisingly, therefore, its requirements are strict. Since the above leading case, there appears to have been no reported case in which the plea has succeeded. In contrast, see *United Dominions Trust Ltd v Western BS Romanay* [1976] QB 513, CA, *Avon Finance Co Ltd v Bridger* [1985] 2 All ER 281, CA, *Norwich & Peterborough Building Society v Steed* [1993] Ch 116, CA, in each of which the plea failed.
5. **J Stone, 'The Limits of Non Est Factum After Gallie v Lee' (1972) 88 *LQR* 190** provides an in-depth analysis of when a *non est factum* plea is available in the light of *Gallie v Lee*. At 216–19, the law is represented as being a policy battle between, on the one hand, protecting an innocent signor and, on the other hand, protecting those who honestly rely on the document. Their Lordships in *Gallie v Lee* used the burdens of proof to delineate the policy battle. The party pleading *non est factum* must prove that there is a fundamental discrepancy, that he was not negligent and, according to Stone but quaere, that he is not 'estopped' from denying that his signature should bind him.

(d) Equitable Rectification for Unilateral Mistake

Rectification is an equitable remedy by which the court alters the words that have been used in a written contact in order to reflect the actual intentions of both parties (common mistake rectification), or one party where the mistake was known to the other (unilateral mistake rectification). Common mistake rectification was traditionally all that was permitted and is dealt with below, 645–649. It has more recently been accepted that unilateral mistake rectification is also possible, although its precise requirements are not as easy to state as those for common mistake rectification.

Thomas Bates & Son Ltd v Wyndham's (Lingerie) Ltd
[1981] 1 WLR 505, Court of Appeal

The defendant tenants leased a property from the claimant landlords in 1956. By the terms of the lease the tenants had the option to renew the lease, after seven years, for a further seven or 14 years 'at a rent to be agreed between the landlords and the tenants but in default of such agreement at a rent to be fixed by [an] arbitrator'. The lease was renewed in 1963 on similar terms, and in 1970 the tenants exercised the option of entering into a 14-year lease with rent reviews every five years. The 1970 lease was drawn up by the landlords but, by mistake, omitted reference to the fixing of rent by arbitration in default of agreement at a rent review. So the relevant clause simply said that the rent was such 'as shall have been agreed between the parties'. The tenants when signing the lease realised that there had been that drafting mistake but did not bring it to the landlords' attention. The consequence, detrimental to the landlords and beneficial to the tenants, was that, if a new rent could not be agreed at a rent review, the old rent would continue. It was held by the Court of Appeal that because of the landlords' mistake (made by their managing director, Mr Bates), known to the tenants (through their relevant director, Mr Avon), the landlords were entitled to rectification of the 1970 lease to include a clause to the effect that the rent would be fixed by an arbitrator in default of agreement.

Buckley LJ: The landlords claim rectification in the present case on the basis of a principle enunciated by Pennycuick J. in *A. Roberts & Co. Ltd. v. Leicestershire Council* [1961] Ch. 555, 570 where he said: "The second ground rests upon the principle that a party is entitled to rectification of a contract upon proof that he believed a particular term to be included in the contract, and that the other party concluded the contract with the omission or a variation of that term in the knowledge that the first party believed the term to be included. ...The principle is stated in *Snell on Equity*, 25th ed. (1960), p. 569 as follows: 'By what appears to be a species of equitable estoppel, if one party to a transaction knows that the instrument contains a mistake in his favour but does nothing to correct it, he (and those claiming under him) will be precluded from resisting rectification on the ground that the mistake is unilateral and not common.'"

Of course if a document is executed in circumstances in which one party realises that in some respect it does not accurately reflect what down to that moment had been the common intention of the parties, it cannot be said that the document is executed under a common mistake, because the party who has realised the mistake is no longer labouring under the mistake. There may be cases in which the principle enunciated by Pennycuick J. applies although there is no prior common intention, but we are not, I think, concerned with such a case here, for it seems to me, upon the facts that I have travelled through, that it is established that the parties had a common intention down to the time when Mr. Avon realised the mistake in the terms of the lease, a common intention that the rent in respect of any period after the first five years should be agreed or, in default of agreement, fixed by an arbitrator.

The principle so enunciated by Pennycuick J. was referred to, with approval, in this court in *Riverlate Properties Ltd. v. Paul* [1975] Ch. 133, where Russell L.J., reading the judgment of the court, said, at p. 140:

"It may be that the original conception of reformation of an instrument by rectification was based solely upon common mistake: but certainly in these days rectification may be based upon such knowledge on the part of the lessee: see, for example, *A. Roberts & Co. Ltd. v. Leicestershire County Council* [1961] Ch. 555. Whether there was in any particular case knowledge of the intention and mistake of the other party must be a question of fact to be decided upon the evidence. Basically it appears to us that it must be such as to involve the lessee in a degree of sharp practice."

In that case the lessee against whom the lessor sought to rectify a lease was held to have had no such knowledge as would have brought the doctrine into play. The reference to "sharp practice" may thus be said to have been an obiter dictum. Undoubtedly I think in any such case the conduct of the defendant must be such as to make it inequitable that he should be allowed to object to the rectification of the document. If this necessarily implies some measure of "sharp practice", so be it; but for my part I think that the doctrine is one which depends more upon the equity of the position. The graver the character of the conduct involved, no doubt the heavier the burden of proof may be; but, in my view, the conduct must be such as to affect the conscience of the party who has suppressed the fact that he has recognised the presence of a mistake.

For this doctrine – that is to say the doctrine of *A. Roberts & Co. Ltd. v. Leicestershire County Council* – to apply I think it must be shown: first, that one party A erroneously believed that the document sought to be rectified contained a particular term or provision, or possibly did not contain a particular term or provision which, mistakenly, it did contain; secondly, that the other party B was aware of the omission or the inclusion and that it was due to a mistake on the part of A; thirdly, that B has omitted to draw the mistake to the notice of A. And I think there must be a fourth element involved, namely, that the mistake must be one calculated to benefit B. If these requirements are satisfied, the court may regard it as inequitable to allow B to resist rectification to give effect to A's intention on the ground that the mistake was not, at the time of execution of the document, a mutual mistake.

... [I]t seems to me, as I have already said, that the omission from the review clause of any reference to arbitration was one which was clearly contrary to the landlords' interests, one which must have occurred as a result of a mistake, and one which Mr. Avon, on his own evidence, recognised, and must I think be taken to have recognised, as having been the result of a mistake on the part of Mr. Bates.

...

For these reasons I think that the judge...reached the right conclusion on the matter relating to rectification.

Brightman LJ delivered a judgment concurring with Buckley LJ. **Eveleigh LJ** gave a concurring judgment.

NOTES AND QUESTIONS

1. As explained in Buckley LJ's judgment, unilateral mistake rectification was first applied in *Roberts & Co Ltd v Leicestershire CC* [1961] Ch 555. There the date for the completion of a building contract was rectified to reflect the intention of the builder in a situation where, during the negotiations, the owner had known that the builder was making a mistake as to that date.

2. On the facts of *Bates*, there was a common intention right until the execution of the lease, and hence there was a unilateral mistake in the drawing up of the contract known to the other party. However, in the normal case of unilateral mistake rectification, as illustrated by the *Roberts* case, the objection is not that the written contract inaccurately reflects a prior common intention. On the contrary, the written contract accurately reflects the fact that, in the prior negotiations, one party was mistaken and that mistake was known about by the other.

3. While the essence of common mistake rectification is that the written contract does not reflect the prior common intention of the parties, the rationale of

unilateral mistake rectification is here expressed to rest on the unconscionability of one party in knowing of the other's mistake and saying nothing.

4. Buckley LJ appeared to distinguish between conduct 'affecting the conscience' and 'sharp practice'. Is there any real difference between them?

5. What is the relationship between unilateral mistake rectification and unilateral mistake as to an important term of a contract (above, 597–598)? Could the landlords in the *Bates* case have successfully argued that the lease was void? Might the mistaken offeror in *Hartog v Colin & Shields* (above, 597) have been entitled to rectification so that there was a contract at the stated price 'per piece'?

Commission for the New Towns v Cooper (GB) Ltd
[1995] Ch 259, Court of Appeal

Milton Keynes Development Corporation (MK) sub-let land to Edison Halo Ltd (EHL). MK entered into an agreement with EHL whereby, inter alia: MK were to carry out certain building works for EHL; MK granted to EHL an option requiring MK to take an assignment of the underlease after five years or on any fifth anniversary ('the put-option'); and MK granted an option to EHL allowing EHL to acquire a lease of an adjoining site ('the side land option'). In 1987, CoopInd UK Ltd (the predecessor of the defendant) acquired the business of EHL. By 1991, CoopInd wanted to get out of the underlease. But it could not exercise the 'put option' because that was an option personal to EHL, as was the side land option. So under the pretence of sorting out other matters and of being interested in acquiring the side land option, CoopInd entered into an agreement with MK that MK should treat CoopInd as having the same rights as EHL had had.

The terms of the contract, which were set out in a letter confirming what had been agreed at a meeting, included the following: 'You will treat CoopInd (UK) Ltd in all respects as having the same rights and benefits under the original documentation as Edison Halo Ltd...CoopInd (UK) Ltd will continue to have all such rights previously granted to Edison Halo Ltd.' It did not cross the mind of MK that it was thereby agreeing to grant the put option to CoopInd. Shortly after the contract was entered into, CoopInd purported to exercise that put option. MK resisted that and argued that, as a matter of construction, a put option had not been granted to CoopInd or, if that was incorrect, that there should be rectification of the contract so that no put option was granted by it. Both arguments succeeded in the Court of Appeal. As regards rectification, this was held to be within the ambit of unilateral mistake rectification because of CoopInd's unconscionable conduct.

Stuart-Smith LJ: The commonest circumstance in which rectification is granted is where the written contract does not accurately record the parties' joint agreement. In other words, there is a mistake common to both parties. In the case of unilateral mistake, that is to say where only one party is mistaken as to the meaning of the contract, rectification is not ordinarily appropriate. This follows from the ordinary rule that it is the objective intention of the parties which determines the construction of the contract and not the subjective intention of one of them. Also, it would generally be inequitable to compel the other party to execute a contract, which he had no intention of making, simply to accord with the mistaken interpretation of the other party: see *Olympia Sauna Shipping Co. S.A. v. Shinwa Kaiun Kaisha Ltd.* [1985] 2 Lloyd's Rep. 364, 371, *per* Bingham J. But the court will intervene if there are "additional circumstances that render unconscionable reliance on the document by the party who has intended that it should have effect according to its terms:" *Spry, Equitable Remedies,* 4th ed. (1990), p. 599. The debate in this case turns on what amounts to unconscionable conduct. The judge held that nothing less than actual knowledge of M.K.'s mistake was sufficient, and although CoopInd's representatives suspected that it was mistaken, it was not proved that it actually did.

...

[Mr Wood, counsel for the plaintiff] submits, even if there was no actual knowledge and no false representation, CoopInd was guilty of such sharp and unconscionable practice that rectification should be granted. Mr. Wood relies upon a dictum of Buckley L.J. in *Thomas Bates and Son Ltd. v. Wyndham's (Lingerie) Ltd.* [1981] 1 W.L.R. 505, 515. [*He quoted most of what is set out above, 622, as the fourth paragraph of that judgment and continued:*]

...

But Mr. Neuberger [counsel for CoopInd] submits that it is not open to the court to adopt this approach. Nothing short of actual knowledge of the mistake, which creates an estoppel against the party with knowledge of the mistake or fraud, will suffice, though in this context fraud includes equitable fraud in the sense of undue influence of abuse of a fiduciary relationship.

...

[W]ere it necessary to do so in this case, I would hold that where A intends B to be mistaken as to the construction of the agreement, so conducts himself that he diverts B's attention from discovering the mistake by making false and misleading statements, and B in fact makes the very mistake that A intends, then notwithstanding that A does not actually know, but merely suspects, that B is mistaken, and it cannot be shown that the mistake was induced by any misrepresentation, rectification may be granted. A's conduct is unconscionable and he cannot insist on performance in accordance to the strict letter of the contract; that is sufficient for rescission. But it may also not be unjust or inequitable to insist that the contract be performed according to B's understanding, where that was the meaning that A intended that B should put upon it. That is so here because, although on the assumption that CoopInd's construction is correct and the put option was included, the contract appeared to be a whole package; in truth CoopInd thought it was getting something for nothing.

...

Here the [implied] representation was made for the purpose of concealing from M.K.'s representative that the language used was wide enough to cover the put option. It would be likely to have that intended effect and it is impossible to say what M.K. might have thought but for the smokescreen. It is no answer to a claim for fraudulent misrepresentation that, if the plaintiff or his agent, who was deceived, had taken proper care, he would not have been misled.

For all these reasons, in my judgment CoopInd's conduct was unconscionable and the circumstances are such that equity requires that the contract be rectified, if in truth it is to be construed as CoopInd contend it should be.

Evans LJ: In my judgment, [CoopInd's] conduct was "unconscionable" and beyond the boundaries of fair dealing even in an arm's length commercial negotiation. It ventured into territory where, in my judgment, the court is entitled to intervene; and there is nothing unfair in holding them to the agreement which, to its knowledge, was the only one which M.K.'s representatives intended to make. I would have no hesitation, if necessary, in holding that "knowledge" in this context includes "shut-eye" knowledge...

Given an agreement reached in these terms and in these circumstances, it comes as no surprise that the scope of the agreement is the same, whether as a matter of construction in accordance with common law principles or after rectification by equity of those terms which read literally and in isolation from their context might be said to support CoopInd's unconscionable claim.

Farquharson LJ concurred.

NOTES AND QUESTIONS

1. Even if CoopInd did not have actual knowledge of the claimant's mistake, they had acted unconscionably (ie dishonestly or in bad faith) in failing to point out that the agreement would give them the 'put option'. In these circumstances, where they had created a smokescreen by misleading statements, mere suspicion that the other party was mistaken, rather then actual knowledge, was sufficient for rectification.

2. In *Riverlate Properties Ltd v Paul* [1975] Ch 133, CA (where a landlord mistakenly thought that a lease required the tenant to pay half for external and structural repairs) and *George Wimpey (UK) Ltd v VI Construction Ltd* [2005] EWCA Civ 77, [2005] BLR 135, CA (where a purchaser of land made a mistake as to the formula for working out extra payments due if the sale price of flats to be built exceeded a particular figure) rectification was refused essentially because the defendant did not know of the claimant's mistake.

3. In *Littman v Aspen Oil (Broking) Ltd* [2005] EWCA Civ 1579, [2006] 2 P & CR 2, unilateral mistake rectification would have been granted, substituting the word 'tenant' for 'landlord' in a break clause in a lease, had it not already been decided that, as a matter of construction, 'landlord' should be read as 'tenant'.

4. What is the relationship between construction of a contract (above, 219–222) and rectification for unilateral mistake?

5. Can a contract be rescinded for a unilateral mistake known to (or suspected by) the other party or is the contract either void or rectifiable?

2. COMMON MISTAKE

A common mistake is one where both parties make the same mistake in entering into a contract. Just as the ambit of unilateral mistake is narrow, so is the ambit of common mistake. In examining the main cases we shall see in the first subsection that it is essentially only mistakes where on the true state of affairs performance is impossible ('possibility mistakes')—for example, mistakes as to the existence of the subject matter—that render a contract void for common mistake. In the following subsection we shall see that Lord Denning's attempt to develop a wider doctrine of common mistake in equity, rendering the contract voidable, was controversially and momentously erased by the Court of Appeal in the *Great Peace* case. In the final subsection, we examine equitable rectification of a written contract for common mistake.

(1) The Narrow Scope of Common Mistake Rendering a Contract Void

Couturier v Hastie (1856) 5 HLC 673, House of Lords

In February 1848, the claimants chartered a vessel to ship corn from Salonica to London. They engaged the defendants to sell the corn for them in return for commission. On 15 May 1848 the defendants sold the corn, along with the benefit of insurance, to Mr Callander. At the time that that contract of sale was made, the cargo of corn no longer existed: the corn had been deteriorating because of heat during the voyage and had been sold off at Tunis. Callander therefore refused to pay the defendants for the goods. The claimants brought an action for the price against the defendants which they were entitled to if Callander had been bound to pay for the goods under his contract with the defendants. So the question was whether Callander had been in breach of contract by failing to pay the defendants. It was held by the House of Lords, affirming the decision of the Exchequer Chamber, that, on the construction of the contract between the defendants and Callander, Callander had not been bound to pay the defendants.

Lord Cranworth LC: ...I may state shortly that the whole question turns upon the construction of the contract which was entered into between the parties. I do not mean to deny that many plausible and ingenious arguments have been pressed by both the learned counsel who have addressed your Lordships, showing that there might have been a meaning attached to that contract different from that which the words themselves impart. If this had depended not merely upon the construction of the contract but upon evidence, which, if I recollect rightly, was rejected at the trial, of what mercantile usage had been, I should not have been prepared to say that a long-continued mercantile usage interpreting such contracts might not have been sufficient to warrant, or even to compel your Lordships to adopt a different construction. But in the absence of any such evidence, looking to the contract itself alone, it appears to me clearly that what the parties contemplated, those who bought and those who sold, was that there was an existing something to be sold and bought, and if sold and bought, then the benefit of insurance should go with it. ...The contract plainly imports that there was something which was to be sold at the time of the contract, and something to be purchased. No such thing existing, I think the Court of Exchequer Chamber has come to the only reasonable conclusion upon it, and consequently there must be judgment given by your Lordships for the Defendants...

NOTES AND QUESTIONS

1. This case is often cited in support of the view that, where the parties are mistaken as to the existence of the subject matter, the contract is void. However, there was no express reference in the reasoning to mistake or to the contract being void. Instead Lord Cranworth saw the issue as turning on the construction of the sale contract. How might one argue that the emphasis on construction is compatible with saying that the contract was void? Could one say, for example, that the contract requiring payment in return for transfer of property in the goods was conditional on the goods existing?

2. The decision was the inspiration for what is now section 6 of the Sale of Goods Act 1979 (first enacted in 1893). That reads: 'Where there is a contract for the sale of specific goods, and the goods without the knowledge of the seller have perished at the time when the contract is made, the contract is void'.

Bell v Lever Brothers Ltd [1932] AC 161, House of Lords

The claimant company, Lever Brothers, owned the Niger Company, a West African subsidiary dealing in African products, including cocoa. The claimant company employed the first defendant, Mr Bell, as Chairman of the Niger Company, and the second defendant, Mr Snelling, as Vice-Chairman. When the Niger Company merged with another African company, the claimant decided that the services of the defendants were no longer required. The claimant entered into severance agreements with the defendants under which they paid the first defendant £30,000 and the second defendant £20,000. The claimant then discovered that, while employees, the defendants had been secretly involved in transactions in cocoa on their own account, which would have given the claimant the right to terminate their employment without compensation. The claimant brought an action for rescission of the severance contracts on the grounds of fraudulent misrepresentation and/or concealment. The jury found that, at the time of the severance contracts, the defendants had not been fraudulent and had forgotten about the cocoa speculations. However, the trial judge and the Court of Appeal held that the contracts were void for common mistake. In allowing the defendants' appeal, the House of Lords held, by a 3–2 majority, that the mutual (ie common) mistake was not such as to make the contract void. Although not of direct concern to us here, it was also held that there was no duty of disclosure.

Lord Atkin: My Lords, the rules of law dealing with the effect of mistake on contract appear to be established with reasonable clearness. If mistake operates at all it operates so as to negative or in some cases to nullify consent. The parties may be mistaken in the identity of the contracting parties, or in the existence of the subject-matter of the contract at the date of the contract, or in the quality of the subject-matter of the contract. These mistakes may be by one party, or by both, and the legal effect may depend upon the class of mistake above mentioned. Thus a mistaken belief by A. that he is contracting with B., whereas in fact he is contracting with C., will negative consent where it is clear that the intention of A. was to contract only with B. So the agreement of A. and B. to purchase a specific article is void if in fact the article had perished before the date of sale. In this case, though the parties in fact were agreed about the subject-matter, yet a consent to transfer or take delivery of something not existent is deemed useless, the consent is nullified. As codified in the Sale of Goods Act the contract is expressed to be void if the seller was in ignorance of the destruction of the specific chattel. ...Corresponding to mistake as to the existence of the subject-matter is mistake as to title in cases where, unknown to the parties, the buyer is already the owner of that which the seller purports to sell to him. The parties intended to effectuate a transfer of ownership: such a transfer is impossible: the stipulation is naturali ratione inutilis. This is the case of *Cooper v. Phibbs* L.R. 2 H.L. 149, where A. agreed to take a lease of a fishery from B., though contrary to the belief of both parties at the time A. was tenant for life of the fishery and B. appears to have had no title at all. To such a case Lord Westbury applied the principle that if parties contract under a mutual mistake and misapprehension as to their relative and respective rights the result is that the agreement is liable to be set aside as having proceeded upon a common mistake. Applied to the context the statement is only subject to the criticism that the agreement would appear to be void rather than voidable. Applied to mistake as to rights generally it would appear to be too wide. Even where the vendor has no title, though both parties think he has, the correct view would appear to be that there is a contract: but that the vendor has either committed a breach of a stipulation as to title, or is not able to perform his contract. The contract is unenforceable by him but is not void.

Mistake as to quality of the thing contracted for raises more difficult questions. In such a case a mistake will not affect assent unless it is the mistake of both parties, and is as to the existence of some quality which makes the thing without the quality essentially different from the thing as it was believed to be. Of course it may appear that the parties contracted that the article should possess the quality which one or other or both mistakenly believed it to possess. But in such a case there is a contract and the inquiry is a different one, being whether the contract as to quality amounts to a condition or a warranty, a different branch of the law.

...

We are now in a position to apply to the facts of this case the law as to mistake so far as it has been stated. ...[O]n the whole, I have come to the conclusion that it would be wrong to decide that an agreement to terminate a definite specified contract is void if it turns out that the agreement had already been broken and could have been terminated otherwise. The contract released is the identical contract in both cases, and the party paying for release gets exactly what he bargains for. It seems immaterial that he could have got the same result in another way, or that if he had known the true facts he would not have entered into the bargain. A. buys B.'s horse; he thinks the horse is sound and he pays the price of a sound horse; he would certainly not have bought the horse if he had known as the fact is that the horse is unsound. If B. has made no representation as to soundness and has not contracted that the horse is sound, A. is bound and cannot recover back the price. A. buys a picture from B.; both A. and B. believe it to be the work of an old master, and a high price is paid. It turns out to be a modern copy. A. has no remedy in the absence of representation or warranty. A. agrees to take on lease or to buy from B. an unfurnished dwelling-house. The house is in fact uninhabitable. A. would never have entered into the bargain if he had known the fact. A. has no remedy, and the position is the same whether B. knew the facts or not, so long as he made no representation or gave no warranty. A. buys a roadside garage business from B. abutting on a public thoroughfare: unknown to A., but known to B., it has already been decided to construct a byepass road which will divert substantially the whole of the traffic from passing A.'s garage. Again A. has no remedy. All these cases involve hardship on A. and benefit B., as most people would say, unjustly. They can be supported on the ground that it is of paramount importance that contracts should be observed, and that if parties honestly comply with the essentials of the formation of contracts – i.e., agree in the same terms on the same subject-matter – they are bound, and must rely on the stipulations of the contract for protection from the effect of facts unknown to them.

This brings the discussion to the alternative mode of expressing the result of a mutual mistake. It is said that in such a case as the present there is to be implied a stipulation in the contract that a condition of its efficacy is that the facts should be as understood by both parties – namely, that the contract could not be terminated till the end of the current term. The question of the existence of conditions, express or implied, is obviously one that affects not the formation of contract, but the investigation of the terms of the contract when made. A condition derives its efficacy from the consent of the parties, express or implied. They have agreed, but on what terms. One term may be that unless the facts are or are not of a particular nature, or unless an event has or has not happened, the contract is not to take effect. With regard to future facts such a condition is obviously contractual. Till the event occurs the parties are bound. Thus the condition (the exact terms of which need not here be investigated) that is generally accepted as underlying the principle of the frustration cases is contractual, an implied condition. Sir John Simon [counsel for Lever Brothers] formulated for the assistance of your Lordships a proposition which should be recorded: "Whenever it is to be inferred from the terms of a contract or its surrounding circumstances that the consensus has been reached upon the basis of a particular contractual assumption, and that assumption is not true, the contract is avoided: i.e., it is void ab initio if the assumption is of present fact and it ceases to bind if the assumption is of future fact."

I think few would demur to this statement, but its value depends upon the meaning of "a contractual assumption," and also upon the true meaning to be attached to "basis," a metaphor which may mislead. When used expressly in contracts, for instance, in policies of insurance, which state that the truth of the statements in the proposal is to be the basis of the contract of insurance, the meaning is clear. The truth of the statements is made a condition of the contract, which failing, the contract is void unless the condition is waived. The proposition does not amount to more than this that, if the contract expressly or impliedly contains a term that a particular assumption is a condition of the contract, the contract is avoided if the assumption is not true. But we have not advanced far on the inquiry how to ascertain whether the contract does contain such a condition. Various words are to be found to define the state of things which make a condition. "In the contemplation of both parties fundamental to the continued validity of the contract," "a foundation essential to its existence," "a fundamental reason for making it," are phrases found in the important judgment of Scrutton L.J. in the present case. The first two phrases appear to me to be unexceptionable. They cover the case of a contract to serve in a particular place, the existence of which is fundamental to the service, or to procure the services of a professional vocalist, whose continued health is essential to performance. But "a fundamental reason for making a contract" may, with respect, be misleading. The reason of one party only is presumedly not intended, but in the cases I have suggested above, of the sale of a horse or of a picture, it might be said that the fundamental reason for making the contract was the belief of both parties that the horse was sound or the picture an old master, yet in neither case would the condition as I think exist. Nothing is more dangerous than to allow oneself liberty to construct for the parties contracts which they have not in terms made by importing implications which would appear to make the contract more businesslike or more just. The implications to be made are to be no more than are "necessary" for giving business efficacy to the transaction, and it appears to me that, both as to existing facts and future facts, a condition would not be implied unless the new state of facts makes the contract something different in kind from the contract in the original state of facts. Thus, in *Krell v. Henry* [1903] 2 K.B. 740, 754, Vaughan Williams L.J. finds that the subject of the contract was "rooms to view the procession": the postponement, therefore, made the rooms not rooms to view the procession. This also is the test finally chosen by Lord Sumner in *Bank Line v. Arthur Capel & Co.* [1919] A.C. 435, agreeing with Lord Dunedin in *Metropolitan Water Board v. Dick Kerr* [1918] A.C.119, 128, where, dealing with the criterion for determining the effect of interruption in "frustrating" a contract, he says: "An interruption may be so long as to destroy the identity of the work or service, when resumed, with the work or service when interrupted." We therefore get a common standard for mutual mistake, and implied conditions whether as to existing or as to future facts. Does the state of the new facts destroy the identity of the subject-matter as it was in the original state of facts? To apply the principle to the infinite combinations of facts that arise in actual experience will continue to be difficult, but if this case results in establishing order into what has been a somewhat confused and difficult branch of the law it will have served a useful purpose.

I have already stated my reasons for deciding that in the present case the identity of the subject-matter was not destroyed by the mutual mistake, if any, and need not repeat them.

Lord Thankerton: The phrase "underlying assumption by the parties," as applied to the subject-matter of a contract, may be too widely interpreted so as to include something which one of the parties had not necessarily in his mind at the time of the contract; in my opinion it can only properly relate to something which both must necessarily have accepted in their minds as an essential and integral element of the subject-matter. In the present case, however probable it may be, we are not necessarily forced to that assumption.

...

In the present case the terms of the contracts throw no light on the question, and, as already indicated, I do not find sufficient material to compel the inference that the appellants, at the time of the contract, regarded the indefeasibility of the service agreements as an essential and integral element in the subject-matter of the bargain.

Accordingly, I am of opinion that the appellants are entitled to succeed in their appeal.

Lord Warrington of Clyffe (dissenting): The real question, therefore, is whether the erroneous assumption on the part of both parties to the agreements that the service contracts were undeterminable except by agreement was of such a fundamental character as to constitute an underlying assumption without which the parties would not have made the contract they in fact made, or whether it was only a common error as to a material element, but one not going to the root of the matter and not affecting the substance of the consideration.

With the knowledge that I am differing from the majority of your Lordships, I am unable to arrive at any conclusion except that in this case the erroneous assumption was essential to the contract which without it would not have been made.

It is true that the error was not one as to the terms of the service agreements, but it was one which, having regard to the matter on which the parties were negotiating – namely, the terms on which the service agreements were to be prematurely determined and the compensation to be paid therefor, was in my opinion as fundamental to the bargain as any error one can imagine.

Viscount Hailsham, dissenting, agreed with Lord Warrington of Clyffe. **Lord Blanesburgh** refused to allow the claimants to amend their pleadings to include 'mutual mistake' but, if he was wrong on that pleading issue, he concurred with Lords Atkin and Thankerton on mistake.

NOTES AND QUESTIONS

1. This is the leading case on common mistake (referred to by their Lordships as 'mutual mistake'). Although the precise ambit of common mistake rendering a contract void is not articulated, the general thrust is clear. Using Lord Atkin's categories, a common mistake as to the existence or ownership of the subject-matter counts; a common mistake as to quality rarely counts. On the facts, one was dealing with a quality mistake. The subject matter of each severance contract was an employment contract. That employment contract existed. The fact that it was terminable without compensation rather than, as the parties mistakenly believed, terminable only with compensation, did not make the subject matter of the severance contract 'essentially different' from what the parties believed it to be.

2. Just as the words 'essentially different' are open to interpretation—and it was clear that Lord Atkin intended them to be taken narrowly—many commentators have interpreted this case as recognising a doctrine of fundamental common mistake, albeit that 'fundamental' has to be narrowly construed (given that, on the facts, the mistake was clearly a very important one and yet did not count).

3. In policy terms, the courts are anxious not to expand the range of common mistakes for fear of undermining contractual certainty whereby parties must be held to even bad bargains. Does that policy necessitate a very narrow doctrine of common mistake?

4. Lord Atkin recognised that an alternative way of expressing the result in cases of common mistake is to think of there being an implied term of the contract that, eg, the subject matter exists.

5. **C MacMillan, 'How Temptation Led to Mistake: an Explanation of *Bell v Lever Brothers Ltd*' (2003) 119 *LQR* 625** explores in detail the interesting historical background to the case. Controversially she suggests that the analysis of mistake may be regarded as unsatisfactory because the case was fought by the

claimant company not as a mistake case but in order to admonish the two employees for their unacceptable conduct as managers.

McRae v Commonwealth Disposals Commission
(1951) 84 CLR 377, High Court of Australia

The defendant commission invited tenders for the purchase of a wrecked oil tanker on 'Journmaund Reef'. The claimant made the successful tender. Upon consulting a map the claimant realised that there was no Journmaund Reef and thus requested the longitude and latitude of the vessel from the defendant. This was provided and the claimant expended a large sum of money trying to locate the tanker. It transpired that there was no such oil tanker at, or anywhere near, the location specified. The claimant brought an action for breach of contract. The defendant argued that the contract was void for common mistake as both parties had incorrectly thought the vessel existed. The Australian High Court held that the contract was not void and that the claimant was entitled to damages for breach of contract as the defendant had promised that the vessel existed.

Dixon and Fullagar JJ: [T]he case of *Couturier v Hastie* does not compel one to say that the contract in the present case was void. But, even if the view that *Couturier v Hastie* was a case of a void contract be correct, we would still think that it could not govern the present case. …[I]t must be true to say that a party cannot rely on mutual mistake where the mistake consists of a belief which is, on the one hand, entertained by him without any reasonable ground, and, on the other hand, deliberately induced by him in the mind of the other party. …

It was not decided in *Couturier v. Hastie* that the contract in that case was void. The question whether it was void or not did not arise. If it had arisen, as in an action by the purchaser for damages, it would have turned on the ulterior question whether the contract was subject to an implied condition precedent. Whatever might then have been held on the facts of *Couturier v. Hastie*, it is impossible in this case to imply any such term. The terms of the contract and the surrounding circumstances clearly exclude any such implication. The buyers relied upon, and acted upon, the assertion of the seller that there was a tanker in existence. It is not a case in which the parties can be seen to have proceeded on the basis of a common assumption of fact so as to justify the conclusion that the correctness of the assumption was intended by both parties to be a condition precedent to the creation of contractual obligations. The officers of the Commission made an assumption, but the plaintiffs did not make an assumption in the same sense. They knew nothing except what the Commission had told them. If they had been asked, they would certainly not have said: "Of course, if there is no tanker, there is no contract". They would have said: "We shall have to go and take possession of the tanker. We simply accept the Commission's assurance that there is a tanker and the Commission's promise to give us that tanker." The only proper construction of the contract is that it included a promise by the Commission that there was a tanker in the position specified. The Commission contracted that there was a tanker there. …If, on the other hand, the case of *Couturier v. Hastie* and this case ought to be treated as cases raising a question of "mistake", then the Commission cannot in this case rely on any mistake as avoiding the contract, because any mistake was induced by the serious fault of their own servants, who asserted the existence of a tanker recklessly and without any reasonable ground. There was a contract, and the Commission contracted that a tanker existed in the position specified. Since there was no such tanker, there has been a breach of contract, and the plaintiffs are entitled to damages for that breach.

McTiernan J concurred.

NOTES

1. On the face of it, this well-known Australian decision is problematic because, according to *Bell v Lever Bros* (and on one interpretation of *Couturier v Hastie*), a contract is void where both parties mistakenly believe that the subject-matter exists but it does not. See also section 6 of the Sale of Goods Act 1979, above, 626.

2. The judges suggest two main ways of explaining why the contract was not void. The first is that the seller had promised that the tanker existed. Explained more fully, one can say that mistake only applies where the parties have not contractually allocated the risk of the non-existence of the subject-matter. Here they had done so because the seller had promised that the tanker existed. The second is that a party cannot rely on a mistake where it has been at fault in making that mistake and /or inducing that mistake in the other party.

3. Alternatively, and more radically, one might argue that the court was using breach of contract to effect what was in reality a remedy for negligent misrepresentation prior to the recognition in *Hedley Byrne v Heller* (above, 564) that that can trigger a claim in the tort of negligence. Although not dealt with in the extract above, the contractual damages awarded covered the claimant's wasted expenses, which is consistent with the reliance measure of damages for tortious misrepresentation.

Associated Japanese Bank International Ltd v Credit du Nord SA [1989] 1 WLR 255, Queen's Bench Division

Bennett concluded an agreement with the claimant bank (AJB) concerning four textile compression packaging machines. This agreement involved Bennett selling the machines to the claimant, and the claimant then leasing them back to Bennett. This was done as a means of Bennett raising money for his business. The claimant wanted Bennett's quarterly lease payments guaranteed, and the defendant bank agreed to guarantee the payments. Bennett defaulted on his payments and was declared bankrupt. It transpired that Bennett had been acting fraudulently and that the machines had never existed. The claimant brought an action under the guarantee against the defendant. That claim failed. It was held that there was a condition precedent, express or implied, in the guarantee that it only applied in respect of a lease of existing machines. Had that not been so, the common mistake as to the existence of the machines would have meant that, in any event, the guarantee was void. We here confine ourselves to the judge's reasoning on mistake.

Steyn J: No one could fairly suggest that in this difficult area of the law there is only one correct approach or solution. But a narrow doctrine of common law mistake (as enunciated in *Bell v. Lever Brothers Ltd.* [1932] A.C. 161), supplemented by the more flexible doctrine of mistake in equity (as developed in *Solle v. Butcher* [1950] 1 K.B. 671 and later cases), seems to me to be an entirely sensible and satisfactory state of the law: see *Sheikh Bros. Ltd. v. Ochsner* [1957] A.C. 136. And there ought to be no reason to struggle to avoid its application by artificial interpretations of *Bell v. Lever Brothers Ltd.*

It might be useful if I now summarised what appears to me to be a satisfactory way of approaching this subject. Logically, before one can turn to the rules as to mistake, whether at common law or in equity, one must first determine whether the contract itself, by express or implied condition precedent or otherwise, provides who bears the risk of the relevant mistake. It is at this hurdle that many pleas of mistake will either fail or prove to have been unnecessary. Only if the contract is silent on the point, is there scope for invoking mistake. That brings me to the relationship between common law mistake and mistake in equity. Where common law mistake has been pleaded, the court must first consider this plea. If the contract is held to be void, no question of mistake in equity arises. But, if the contract is held to be valid, a plea of mistake in equity may still have to be considered: see *Grist v. Bailey* [1967] Ch. 532 and the analysis in *Anson's Law of Contract*, 26th ed. (1984), p. 290. Turning now to the approach to common law mistake, it seems to me that the following propositions are valid although not necessarily all [are] entitled to be dignified as propositions of law.

The first imperative must be that the law ought to uphold rather than destroy apparent contracts. Secondly, the common law rules as to a mistake regarding the quality of the subject matter, like the common law rules regarding commercial frustration, are designed to cope with the impact of unexpected and wholly exceptional circumstances on apparent contracts. Thirdly, such a mistake in order to attract legal consequences must substantially be shared by both parties, and must relate to facts as they existed at the time the contract was made. Fourthly, and this is the point established by *Bell v. Lever Brothers Ltd.* [1932] A.C. 161, the mistake must render the subject matter of the contract essentially and radically different from the subject matter which the parties believed to exist. While the civilian distinction between the substance and attributes of the subject matter of a contract has played a role in the development of our law (and was cited in speeches in *Bell v. Lever Brothers Ltd.*), the principle enunciated in *Bell v. Lever Brothers Ltd.* is markedly narrower in scope than the civilian doctrine. It is therefore no longer useful to invoke the civilian distinction. The principles enunciated by Lord Atkin and Lord Thankerton represent the ratio decidendi of *Bell v. Lever Brothers Ltd.* Fifthly, there is a requirement which was not specifically discussed in *Bell v. Lever Brothers Ltd.* What happens if the party, who is seeking to rely on the mistake, had no reasonable grounds for his belief? An extreme example is that of the man who makes a contract with minimal knowledge of the facts to which the mistake relates but is content that it is a good speculative risk. In my judgment a party cannot be allowed to rely on a common mistake where the mistake consists of a belief which is entertained by him without any reasonable grounds for such belief: cf. *McRae v. Commonwealth Disposals Commission* (1951) 84 C.L.R. 377, 408. That is not because principles such as estoppel or negligence require it, but simply because policy and good sense dictate that the positive rules regarding common mistake should be so qualified. Curiously enough this qualification is similar to the civilian concept where the doctrine of error in substantia is tempered by the principles governing culpa in contrahendo. More importantly, a recognition of this qualification is consistent with the approach in equity where fault on the part of the party adversely affected by the mistake will generally preclude the granting of equitable relief: *Solle v. Butcher* [1950] 1 K.B. 671, 693.

Applying the law to the facts

It is clear, of course, that in this case both parties – the creditors and the guarantors – acted on the assumption that the lease related to existing machines. If they had been informed that the machines might not exist, neither the plaintiffs nor the defendants would for one moment have contemplated entering into the transaction. That by itself, I accept, is not enough to sustain the plea of common law mistake. I am also satisfied that the defendants had reasonable grounds for believing that the machines existed. That belief was based on the defendants' discussions with Mr. Bennett, information supplied by National Leasing, a respectable firm of lease brokers, and the confidence created by the fact that the plaintiffs were the lessors. The real question is whether the subject matter of the guarantee (as opposed to the sale and lease) was essentially different from what it was reasonably believed to be. The real security of the guarantors was the machines. The existence of the machines, being profit-earning chattels, made it more likely that the debtor would be able to service the debt. More importantly, if the debtor defaulted, and the creditors repossessed the machines the creditors had to give credit for 97 ½ per cent. of the value of the machines. If the creditors sued the guarantors first, and the guarantors paid, the guarantors were entitled to be subrogated to the creditors' rights in respect of recovery against the debtor: see Goff and Jones, *The Law of Restitution*, 3rd ed. (1986), p. 533 et seq. No doubt the guarantors relied to some extent on the creditworthiness of Mr. Bennett. But I find that the prime security to which the guarantors looked was the existence of the four machines as described to both parties. For both parties the guarantee of obligations under a lease with non-existent machines was essentially different from a guarantee of a lease with four machines which both parties at the time of the contract believed to exist. The guarantee is an accessory contract. The non-existence of the subject matter of the principal contract is therefore of fundamental importance. Indeed the analogy of the classic res extincta cases, so much discussed in the authorities, is fairly close. In my judgment the stringent test of common law mistake is satisfied: the guarantee is void ab initio.

NOTES AND QUESTIONS

1. Steyn J clarified that, at common law, the doctrine of common mistake is a narrow one; and that logically one should first construe the contract to see whether the risk of mistake has been dealt with expressly or impliedly.

2. Steyn J was therefore of the view that the doctrine of mistake comes in where the contract 'runs out'. Some commentators (see , eg, the articles by Slade and JC Smith referred to below, 649, 650) would dispute this and argue that the implication of a term swallows up the need for a doctrine of common mistake so that Steyn J's second stage is never reached. Does that argument rely, however, on the courts' adopting a strained approach to implying terms?

3. The most brilliant part of Steyn J's judgment was his 'reconciliation' of *Bell v Lever Bros* with *Solle v Butcher* to the effect that the common law doctrine is supplemented by a wider doctrine rendering the contract voidable (on terms) in equity. However, that reconciliation is now merely of historical interest because, as we shall see below, 634, the *Great Peace* case has subsequently overruled *Solle v Butcher*.

Great Peace Shipping Ltd v Tsavliris Salvage (International) Ltd, The Great Peace [2002] EWCA Civ 1407, [2003] QB 679, Court of Appeal

The Cape Providence suffered structural damage in the South Indian Sea. The defendants offered their salvage services which were accepted. The defendants tried to find a merchant vessel which could assist an evacuation. They approached an organisation which receives reports about vessels at sea and were given the names of four vessels reported to be in the area. The nearest was supposedly *The Great Peace*, approximately 35 miles away. The defendants chartered *The Great Peace* from the claimant owners but, soon after, realised that it was actually 410 miles from *The Cape Providence*. The defendants agreed a contract with a nearer vessel (*The Nordfarer*) and cancelled the contract with the claimants. That contract expressly entitled the defendants to cancel the contract subject to paying a cancellation fee of five days' hire (which here amounted to $82,500). The defendants refused to pay that fee and the claimants brought a contractual action to recover it. The defendants argued that the contract was void at common law, or voidable in equity, for common mistake. In dismissing the defendants' appeal from the decision of Toulson J, the Court of Appeal held that the common mistake did not fall within the narrow doctrine recognised at common law so as to render the contract void; and that there is no doctrine of equitable common mistake. We here deal solely with the examination of the common law doctrine.

Lord Phillips of Worth Matravers MR (giving the judgment of himself, **May LJ** and **Laws LJ**):

50 ...The first step is to identify the nature of the common law doctrine of mistake that was identified, or established, by *Bell v Lever Bros Ltd*.

51 Lord Atkin and Lord Thankerton were breaking no new ground in holding void a contract where, unknown to the parties, the subject matter of the contract no longer existed at the time that the contract was concluded. The Sale of Goods Act 1893 (56 & 57 Vict c 71) was a statute which set out to codify the common law. Section 6, to which Lord Atkin referred, provided: "When there is a contract for the sale of specific goods, and the goods without the knowledge of the seller have perished at the time when the contract is made, the contract is void."

52 Judge Chalmers, the draftsman of the Act, commented in the first edition of his book on the Act, *The Sale of Goods Act 1893* (1894), p 17:

> "The rule may be based either on the ground of mutual mistake, or on the ground of impossibility of performance."

53 He put at the forefront of the authorities that he cited in support *Couturier v Hastie* (1856) 5 HL Cas 673. That case involved the sale of a cargo of corn which, unknown to the parties, no longer existed at the time that the contract was concluded. Other decisions where agreements were held not to be binding were *Strickland v Turner* (1852) 7 Exch 208—the sale of an annuity upon the life of a person who, unknown to the parties, had died—and *Pritchard v Merchant's and Tradesman's Mutual Life Assurance Society* (1858) 3 CBNS 622—an insurance policy renewed in ignorance of the fact that the assured had died.

55 Where that which is expressly identified as the subject of a contract does not exist, the contract will necessarily be one which cannot be performed. Such a situation can readily be identified. The position is very different where there is "a mistake as to the existence of some quality of the subject matter which makes the thing without the quality essentially different from the thing as it was believed to be". In such a situation it may be possible to perform the letter of the contract. In support of the proposition that a contract is void in such circumstances, Lord Atkin cited two authorities, in which he said that the principles to be applied were to be found. The first was *Lord Kennedy v Panama, New Zealand and Australian Royal Mail Co Ltd* LR 2 QB 580. ...

60 The other case to which Lord Atkin referred was *Smith v Hughes* (1871) LR 6 QB 597. ...

61 We conclude that the two authorities to which Lord Atkin referred provided an insubstantial basis for his formulation of the test of common mistake in relation to the quality of the subject matter of a contract. Lord Atkin advanced an alternative basis for his test: the implication of a term of the same nature as that which was applied under the doctrine of frustration, as it was then understood. In so doing he adopted the analysis of Scrutton LJ in the Court of Appeal. It seems to us that this was a more solid jurisprudential basis for the test of common mistake that Lord Atkin was proposing. At the time of *Bell v Lever Bros Ltd* [1932] AC 161 the law of frustration and common mistake had advanced hand in hand on the foundation of a common principle. Thereafter frustration proved a more fertile ground for the development of this principle than common mistake, and consideration of the development of the law of frustration assists with the analysis of the law of common mistake.

[*He then considered the doctrine of frustration and continued:*]

73 What do these developments in the law of frustration have to tell us about the law of common mistake? First that the theory of the implied term is as unrealistic when considering common mistake as when considering frustration. Where a fundamental assumption upon which an agreement is founded proves to be mistaken, it is not realistic to ask whether the parties impliedly agreed that in those circumstances the contract would not be binding. The avoidance of a contract on the ground of common mistake results from a rule of law under which, if it transpires that one or both of the parties have agreed to do something which it is impossible to perform, no obligation arises out of that agreement.

74 In considering whether performance of the contract is impossible, it is necessary to identify what it is that the parties agreed would be performed. This involves looking not only at the express terms, but at any implications that may arise out of the surrounding circumstances. In some cases it will be possible to identify details of the "contractual adventure" which go beyond the terms that are expressly spelt out, in others it will not.

75 Just as the doctrine of frustration only applies if the contract contains no provision that covers the situation, the same should be true of common mistake. If, on true construction of the contract, a party warrants that the subject matter of the contract exists, or that it will be possible to perform the contract, there will be no scope to hold the contract void on the ground of common mistake.

76 If one applies the passage from the judgment of Lord Alverstone CJ in *Blakeley v Muller & Co* 19 TLR 186, [*a frustration case*]... to a case of common mistake, it suggests that the following elements must be present if common mistake is to avoid a contract: (i) there must be a common assumption as to the existence of a state of affairs; (ii) there must be no warranty by either party that that state of affairs exists; (iii) the non-existence of the state of affairs must not be attributable to the fault of either party; (iv) the non-existence of the state of affairs must render performance of the contract impossible; (v) the state of affairs may be the existence, or a vital attribute, of the consideration to be provided or circumstances which must subsist if performance of the contractual adventure is to be possible.

77 The second and third of these elements are well exemplified by the decision of the High Court of Australia in *McRae v Commonwealth Disposals Commission* (1951) 84 CLR 377. ...

79 [In the leading judgment Dixon and Fullagar JJ] held, at p 410, that, on its proper construction, the contract included a promise by the Commission that the tanker existed in the position specified. Alternatively, they held that if the doctrine of mistake fell to be applied

> "then the Commission cannot in this case rely on any mistake as avoiding the contract, because any mistake was induced by the serious fault of their own servants, who asserted the existence of a tanker recklessly and without any reasonable ground."

80 This seems, if we may say so, an entirely satisfactory conclusion and one that can be reconciled with the English doctrine of mistake. That doctrine fills a gap in the contract where it transpires that it is impossible of performance without the fault of either party and the parties have not, expressly or by implication, dealt with their rights and obligations in that eventuality. In *Associated Japanese Bank (International) Ltd v Crédit du Nord SA* [1989] 1 WLR 255, 268 Steyn J observed:

> "Logically, before one can turn to the rules as to mistake, whether at common law or in equity, one must first determine whether the contract itself, by express or implied condition precedent or otherwise, provides who bears the risk of the relevant mistake. It is at this hurdle that many pleas of mistake will either fail or prove to have been unnecessary. Only if the contract is silent on the point, is there scope for invoking mistake."

82 Thus, while we do not consider that the doctrine of common mistake can be satisfactorily explained by an implied term, an allegation that a contract is void for common mistake will often raise important issues of construction. Where it is possible to perform the letter of the contract, but it is alleged that there was a common mistake in relation to a fundamental assumption which renders performance of the essence of the obligation impossible, it will be necessary, by construing the contract in the light of all the material circumstances, to decide whether this is indeed the case. ...

84 Once the court determines that unforeseen circumstances have, indeed, resulted in the contract being impossible of performance, it is next necessary to determine whether, on true construction of the contract, one or other party has undertaken responsibility for the subsistence of the assumed state of affairs. This is another way of asking whether one or other party has undertaken the risk that it may not prove possible to perform the contract, and the answer to this question may well be the same as the answer to the question of whether the impossibility of performance is attributable to the fault of one or other of the parties.

85 Circumstances where a contract is void as a result of common mistake are likely to be less common than instances of frustration. Supervening events which defeat the contractual adventure will frequently not be the responsibility of either party. Where, however, the parties agree that something shall be done which is impossible at the time of making the agreement, it is much more likely that, on true construction of the agreement, one or other will have undertaken responsibility for the mistaken state of affairs. This may well explain why cases where contracts have been found to be void in consequence of common mistake are few and far between.

86 Lord Atkin himself gave no examples of cases where a contract was rendered void because of a mistake as to quality which made "the thing without the quality essentially different from the thing as it was believed to be". He gave a number of examples of mistakes which did not satisfy this test, which served to demonstrate just how narrow he considered the test to be. Indeed this is further demonstrated by the result reached on the facts of *Bell v Lever Bros Ltd* [1932] AC 161 itself.

[*He considered* Associated Japanese Bank v Crédit du Nord *and Steyn LJ's summary of the law (above, 633) and continued:*]

91 The detailed analysis that we have carried out leads us to concur in this summary, subject to the proviso that the result in *McRae*'s case can, we believe, be explained on the basis of construction, as demonstrated above. ...

94 Our conclusions have marched in parallel with those of Toulson J. We admire the clarity with which he has set out his conclusions, which emphasise the importance of a careful analysis of the contract and of the rights and obligations created by it as an essential precursor to consideration of the effect of an alleged mistake. We agree with him that, on the facts of the present case, the issue in relation to common mistake turns on the question of whether the mistake as to the distance apart of the two vessels had the effect that the services that the *Great Peace* was in a position to provide were something essentially different from that to which the parties had agreed. We shall defer answering that question until we have considered whether principles of equity provide a second string to the defendants' bow.

[*He considered common mistake in equity (below, 643–645) and continued:*]

162 We revert to the question that we left unanswered at paragraph 94. It was unquestionably a common assumption of both parties when the contract was concluded that the two vessels were in sufficiently close proximity to enable the *Great Peace* to carry out the service that she was engaged to perform. Was the distance between the two vessels so great as to confound that assumption and to render the contractual adventure impossible of performance? If so, the defendants would have an arguable case that the contract was void under the principle in *Bell v Lever Bros Ltd* [1932] AC 161.

165 ...[T]he fact that the vessels were considerably further apart than the defendants had believed did not mean that the services that the *Great Peace* was in a position to provide were essentially different from those which the parties had envisaged when the contract was concluded. The *Great Peace* would arrive in time to provide several days of escort service. The defendants would have wished the contract to be performed but for the adventitious arrival on the scene of a vessel prepared to perform the same services. The fact that the vessels were further apart than both parties had appreciated did not mean that it was impossible to perform the contractual adventure.

166 The parties entered into a binding contract for the hire of the *Great Peace*. That contract gave the defendants an express right to cancel the contract subject to the obligation to pay the "cancellation fee" of five days' hire. When they engaged the *Nordfarer* they cancelled the *Great Peace*. They became liable in consequence to pay the cancellation fee. There is no injustice in this result.

167 For the reasons that we have given, we would dismiss this appeal.

NOTES AND QUESTIONS

1. Was the Court of Appeal any clearer than the House of Lords in *Bell v Lever Bros* in explaining precisely when a common mistake renders a contract void?
2. An analogy was drawn between common mistake and frustration. What is the relationship between the two and how close is the analogy?
3. The Court of Appeal stressed at [80] that, while the doctrine of common mistake is not explicable by there being an implied term, common mistake only applies if the contract has not already dealt with the eventuality. See also 634, note 2 above.
4. For the treatment in this case of equitable common mistake, see below, 643.

Brennan v Bolt Burdon
[2005] QB 303 [2004] EWCA Civ 1017, Court of Appeal

The claimant, Miss Brennan, brought a claim against her landlord (the second defendants, Islington Council) for personal injuries allegedly caused by leaking carbon monoxide from a faulty boiler. A contract of compromise was entered into. Both parties believed (and the defendants had successfully had the claim struck out) that the claim was time-barred because the claim form had not been validly served in time. Although served on a Saturday, just within the requisite four months, the (unreported) first instance decision in *Anderton v Clwyd County Council (No 2)* had laid down that the service was deemed to be on the Monday which was outside the four months. Subsequent to the compromise, the Court of Appeal in *Anderton* [2002] 1 WLR 3174 reversed the decision at first instance which meant that the service on the Saturday had been valid. The claimant now wished to withdraw from the contract of compromise arguing that it was void for a common mistake as to law. In allowing the defendants' appeal, the Court of Appeal held that, while common mistakes of law as well as fact now count, that mistake did not invalidate the compromise.

Maurice Kay LJ:

17...What principles relevant to the resolution of the present appeal can be extracted from [the] authorities? In my judgment, the following propositions emerge. (1) As with any other contracts, compromises or consent orders may be vitiated by a common mistake of law. (2) It is initially a question of construction as to whether the alleged mistake has that consequence. (3) Whilst a general release executed in a prospective or nascent dispute requires clear language to justify an inference of an intention to surrender rights of which the releasor was unaware and could not have been aware ..., different considerations arise in relation to the compromise of litigation which the parties have agreed to settle on a give-and-take basis ...

(4) For a common mistake of fact or law to vitiate a contract of any kind, it must render the performance of the contract impossible: see *Great Peace Shipping Co Ltd v Tsavliris Salvage Ltd* [2003] QB 679.

22 Another way of looking at all this is on the basis of risk in the context of impossibility of performance. As Lord Phillips of Worth Matravers MR said in *Great Peace Shipping Co Ltd v Tsavliris Salvage Ltd* [2003] QB 679, 705, para 84: [*he set out [84], above, 637, and continued:*] In my judgment, this passage resonates in the present case for a number of reasons. First, this is quite simply not a case of impossibility of performance. The compromise has at all times remained performable, albeit to the disadvantage of Miss Brennan. It seems to me that, in the light of the *Great Peace* case, that is in itself sufficient to put it beyond the reach of common mistake of law. Secondly, although [counsel for the claimant] submits that it was for Islington to bargain for a term whereby the compromise would survive subsequent legal change (or, to be consistent with the declaratory theory of the common law which attracted the majority in the *Kleinwort Benson* case [1999] 2 AC 349, further judicial consideration), I do not accept that that is the correct approach to the construction of compromises. Their essence is finality. There is a real difference between the situation where the compromise is agreed in ignorance of significant facts and the law which would be applicable to them (as in *Bank of Credit and Commerce International SA v Ali* [2002] 1 AC 251) and the situation in which the compromise is agreed with no misapprehension of the facts at all (as in the present case), just an erroneous assumption about the law. This is not to reintroduce the distinction between mistake of fact and mistake of law. It is to require that, where a party wishes to reserve his rights in the event of subsequent judicial decision in a future case to which he is not a party, it is he who should seek and secure a term to that effect, not his opponent who should have to stipulate for protection notwithstanding the possibility of such a subsequent decision. Such a requirement is consistent with the policy of encouraging settlements and respecting their finality. I do not consider it to be in conflict with *Ali*'s case [2002] 1 AC 251. Thirdly, turning to what Lord Phillips of Worth Matravers MR said about fault, it is my view that, for the reasons I have given, in the present case the fault was on the side of [the claimant's solicitor] who agreed the compromise without inquiry as to any appeal in *Anderton*'s case, without appealing the decision of the Recorder and without defending an application on behalf of Islington. No fault lay at the door of Islington.

Conclusion

23 It follows from what I have said that I would allow Islington's appeal on the grounds that the evidence does not establish a true mistake of law at all, more a state of doubt; that Miss Brennan's solicitor was at fault in not inquiring about any appeal in *Anderton*'s case; that the compromise was a matter of give-and-take which ought not lightly to be set aside; that it is not impossible to perform; and that, as a matter of construction, the risk of a future judicial decision affecting matters to Miss Brennan's advantage was impliedly accepted and bargained away by her solicitor. In deciding the appeal on these grounds I have remained within the parameters of the submissions of counsel, [counsel for the defendant] having disavowed a simple submission to the effect that a compromise in the course of litigation, entered into on professional advice, should never be vitiated by a subsequent judicial decision in a case to which the instant litigants are not parties, unless the compromise contains a suitable express provision. For my part I suspect that there is scope for a substantive exception to the ambit of mistake of law as a matter of policy in such circumstances and that it could live with what was said in the *Kleinwort Benson* case but, as we have heard no submissions about such an approach, this is not the case in which to say anything further about it.

Sedley LJ:

58 A ... problem, in my view, lies in the formulation of the elements of common mistake set out in the *Great Peace* case, at p 703, para 76. The fourth element is that "the non-existence of the state of affairs must render contractual performance impossible". Where the mistake is

as to the existence of goods, or (as in the *Great Peace* case) as to the location of a vessel, this is straightforward. But what is the analogue in a case of mutual mistake of law?

59 The only kind of common mistake of law which is such that the true legal position renders performance of the contract impossible is, it seems to me, a mistake as to the legality of the contract. But [counsel for the defendants]…has accepted, as I would do, the broader proposition that a common mistake of law may vitiate an agreement by which litigation is compromised. The difficulty is in seeing how the effect of such a mistake can be equiparated with the impossibility of a contractual venture.

60 I think that in cases of mutual mistake of law a different test may be necessary. The equivalent question needs to be whether, had the parties appreciated that the law was what it is now known to be, there would still have been an intelligible basis for their agreement. This seems to me to come as close as one can come to what was identified as being at issue in the *Great Peace* case, at p 691, para 32: a common mistaken assumption (in that case one of fact) which renders the service that will be provided if the contract is performed something different from the performance that the parties contemplated. It also echoes the question posed by Lord Atkin in *Bell v Lever Bros* [1932] AC 161, 227. "Does the state of the new facts destroy the identity of the subject-matter as it was in the original state of facts?", if for "facts" one reads "law".

64 …[L]ike Maurice Kay LJ and Bodey J, I see no choice in the present case. The law must be taken to have been what it was only later declared to be, but the putative mistake created by this shift cannot be allowed to undo a compromise of litigation entered into in the knowledge both of how the law now stood and of the fact—for it is always a fact—that it might not remain so. While I am not happy about translating such knowledge into an implied term that the settlement is to stand notwithstanding any future change in the understanding of the law, I have less difficulty in recognising it as part of the matrix of fact in which a litigation compromise is cast.

65 On this footing and without satisfaction, I agree that the appeal must be allowed.

Bodey J delivered a judgment concurring with Maurice Kay LJ.

NOTES AND QUESTIONS

1.   The most important aspect of this case is the extension of mistake to cover a mistake of law as well as fact. That mistakes of law, as well as of fact, entitle a payor to restitution of money paid by mistake was first accepted in *Kleinwort Benson Ltd v Lincoln City Council* [1999] 2 AC 349, HL. The *Brennan* case therefore represents the inevitable extension of that decision in the law of restitution to the law of contract.

2.   The case further illustrates how reluctant the courts are to allow common mistakes to render void contracts of compromise. Why is that?

3.   Maurice Kay LJ interpreted the *Great Peace* case as saying that it is only possibility mistakes that count. Sedley LJ took a slightly wider interpretation. Who is correct?

(2) A Wider Equitable Doctrine of Common Mistake Rejected

After the very narrow formulation of common mistake in *Bell v Lever Bros* (above, 627), the Court of Appeal in *Solle v Butcher* (below) 'introduced' a wider, more flexible, doctrine of equitable common mistake. This allowed the courts to rescind the contract where there was a common mistake that was fundamental (although not quite as fundamental as *Bell v Lever Bros* fundamental!) and the party asking for rescission was faultless. It was also possible to rescind 'on terms'. However, in *The Great Peace* (below, 643) *Solle v Butcher* was overruled as incompatible with *Bell v Lever Bros* and rescission for equitable common mistake was erased from the law.

Solle v Butcher [1950] 1 KB 671, Court of Appeal

The claimant (who became the tenant) and the defendant (who became the landlord) were partners in an estate agent business. In 1947, the defendant purchased a block of five flats, damaged during the war, with the intention of renovating them for the purposes of letting them out. In 1939, the first flat had been leased to a third party for £140 per annum. After the renovation, the defendant leased the first flat to the claimant for £250 per annum, the claimant and the defendant both believing that the defendant was free to fix a new rent for the renovated flat. In reality, the Rent Acts applied which meant that, unless the landlord had gone through particular procedures before letting the flat, the rent was fixed at the previous amount of £140. When relations between the two deteriorated, the claimant sued the defendant for restitution of overpaid rent, alleging that the Rent Acts did apply. The defendant, by way of counterclaim, brought an action for rescission of the lease on the ground of common mistake. It was held by a majority of the Court of Appeal that there should be no order for restitution of the overpaid rent and that the contract should be rescinded on the terms that the claimant tenant be allowed to choose whether to have a lease of the flat for £250 per annum or to leave.

Bucknill LJ: In my opinion…there was a common mistake of fact on a matter of fundamental importance, namely, as to the identity of the flat with the dwelling-house previously let at a standard rent of 140l. a year, and that the principle laid down in *Cooper v. Phibbs* L.R. 2 H.L. 249 applies.

…

Subject to arguments by counsel on the point, I agree with the terms proposed by Denning L.J., on which the present lease should be set aside.

Denning LJ: It is quite plain that the parties were under a mistake. They thought that the flat was not tied down to a controlled rent, whereas in fact it was. In order to see whether the lease can be avoided for this mistake it is necessary to remember that mistake is of two kinds: first, mistake which renders the contract void, that is, a nullity from the beginning, which is the kind of mistake which was dealt with by the courts of common law; and, secondly, mistake which renders the contract not void, but voidable, that is, liable to be set aside on such terms as the court thinks fit, which is the kind of mistake which was dealt with by the courts of equity. Much of the difficulty which has attended this subject has arisen because, before the fusion of law and equity, the courts of common law, in order to do justice in the case in hand, extended this doctrine of mistake beyond its proper limits and held contracts to be void which were really only voidable, a process which was capable of being attended with much injustice to third persons who had bought goods or otherwise committed themselves on the faith that there was a contract. In the well-known case of *Cundy v. Lindsay* 3 App. Cas. 459, Cundy suffered such an injustice. He bought the handkerchiefs from the rogue, Blenkarn, before the Judicature Acts came into operation. Since the fusion of law and equity, there is no reason to continue this process, and it will be found that only those contracts are now held void in which the mistake was such as to prevent the formation of any contract at all.

Let me first consider mistakes which render a contract a nullity. All previous decisions on this subject must now be read in the light of *Bell v. Lever Bros. Ld.*[1932] A.C.161, 222, 224, 225-7, 236. The correct interpretation of that case, to my mind, is that, once a contract has been made, that is to say, once the parties, whatever their inmost states of mind, have to all outward appearances agreed with sufficient certainty in the same terms on the same subject matter, then the contract is good unless and until it is set aside for failure of some condition on which the existence of the contract depends, or for fraud, or on some equitable ground. Neither party can rely on his own mistake to say it was a nullity from the beginning, no matter that it was a mistake which to his mind was fundamental, and no matter that the other party knew that he was under a mistake. A fortiori if the other party did not know of the mistake, but shared it. The cases where goods have perished at the time of sale, or belong to the buyer, are really contracts which are not void for mistake, but are void by reason of an implied condition precedent, because the contract proceeded on the basic assumption that it was capable of performance. ...

Applying these principles, it is clear that here there was a contract. The parties agreed in the same terms on the same subject-matter. It is true that the landlord was under a mistake which was to him fundamental: he would not for one moment have considered letting the flat for seven years if it meant that he could only charge 140l. a year for it. He made the fundamental mistake of believing that the rent he could charge was not tied down to a controlled rent; but, whether it was his own mistake or a mistake common to both him and the tenant, it is not a ground for saying that the lease was from the beginning a nullity.

Let me next consider mistakes which render a contract voidable, that is, liable to be set aside on some equitable ground. Whilst presupposing that a contract was good at law, or at any rate not void, the court of equity would often relieve a party from the consequences of his own mistake, so long as it could do so without injustice to third parties. The court, it was said, had power to set aside the contract whenever it was of opinion that it was unconscientious for the other party to avail himself of the legal advantage which he had obtained: *Torrance v. Bolton* per James L.J. (1872) L.R. 8 Ch.118, 124.

The court had, of course, to define what it considered to be unconscientious, but in this respect equity has shown a progressive development. It is now clear that a contract will be set aside if the mistake of the one party has been induced by a material misrepresentation of the other, even though it was not fraudulent or fundamental; or if one party, knowing that the other is mistaken about the terms of an offer, or the identity of the person by whom it is made, lets him remain under his delusion and concludes a contract on the mistaken terms instead of pointing out the mistake. That is, I venture to think, the ground on which the defendant in *Smith v. Hughes* (1871) L.R. 6 Q.B. 597 would be exempted nowadays, and on which, according to the view by Blackburn J. of the facts, the contract in *Lindsay v. Cundy*, was voidable and not void; and on which the lease in *Sowler v. Potter* [1940] 1 K.B.271, was, in my opinion, voidable and not void.

A contract is also liable in equity to be set aside if the parties were under a common misapprehension either as to facts or as to their relative and respective rights, provided that the misapprehension was fundamental and that the party seeking to set it aside was not himself at fault.

... [T]he House of Lords in 1867 in the great case of *Cooper v. Phibbs* (1867) L.R. 2 H.L. 149, 170, affirmed the doctrine... It is in no way impaired by *Bell v. Lever Bros. Ld.*, which was treated in the House of Lords as a case at law depending on whether the contract was a nullity or not. If it had been considered on equitable grounds, the result might have been different. ...

Applying that principle to this case, the facts are that the plaintiff... wants to take advantage of the mistake to get the flat at 140l. a year for seven years instead of the 250l. a year, which is not only the rent he agreed to pay but also the fair and economic rent; and it is also the rent permitted by the Acts on compliance with the necessary formalities. If the rules of equity have become so rigid that they cannot remedy such an injustice, it is time we had a new equity, to make good the omissions of the old. But, in my view, the established rules are amply sufficient for this case...

If the lease were set aside without any terms being imposed, it would mean that the tenant would have to go out and would have to pay a reasonable sum for his use and occupation. That would, however, not be just to the tenant.

...

If the mistake here had not happened a proper notice of increase would have been given and the lease would have been executed at the full permitted rent. I think this court... should impose terms which will enable the tenant to choose either to stay on at the proper rent or to go out.

Jenkins LJ dissented on the ground that the mistake was a mistake of law.

NOTES AND QUESTIONS

1. Was the mistake one of fact or law? Does that now matter?
2. Denning LJ took the view that, in relation to mistakes, equity has taken over the common law so that unilateral and common mistake render a contract voidable and not void. This ties in with his approach to mistakes as to identity, above, 604. Is what he said compatible with *Bell v Lever Bros*?
3. *Solle v Butcher* was followed in respect of common mistake by several first instance and Court of Appeal decisions, including *Laurence v Lexcourt Holdings Ltd* [1978] 1 WLR 1128, *Grist v Bailey* [1967] Ch 532, *Magee v Pennine Insurance Co Ltd* [1969] 2 QB 507. However, this line of authority was treated as bad law and momentously overruled in the next case.

Great Peace Shipping Ltd v Tsavliris Salvage (International) Ltd, The Great Peace [2002] EWCA Civ 1407, [2003] QB 679, Court of Appeal

For the facts, see above, 634. We are here solely concerned with common mistake in equity.

Lord Phillips of Worth Matravers MR (giving the judgment of himself, **May LJ** and **Laws LJ**):

98 The following issues fall to be considered in relation to the effect of common mistake in equity. (1) Prior to *Bell v Lever Bros Ltd* was there established a doctrine under which equity permitted rescission of a contract on grounds of common mistake in circumstances where the contract was valid at common law? (2) Could such a doctrine stand with *Bell v Lever Bros Ltd*? (3) Is this court none the less bound to find that such a doctrine exists having regard to *Solle v Butcher* and subsequent decisions?

118...[T]he House of Lords in *Bell v Lever Bros Ltd* [1932] AC 161 considered that the intervention of equity, as demonstrated in *Cooper v Phibbs* LR 2 HL 149, took place in circumstances where the common law would have ruled the contract void for mistake. We do not find it conceivable that the House of Lords overlooked an equitable right in *Lever Bros* to rescind the agreement, notwithstanding that the agreement was not void for mistake at common law. The jurisprudence established no such right. Lord Atkin's test for common mistake that avoided a contract, while narrow, broadly reflected the circumstances where equity had intervened to excuse performance of a contract assumed to be binding in law.

126 Toulson J described [the *Solle v Butcher*] decision by Denning LJ as one which "sought to outflank *Bell v Lever Bros Ltd* [1932] AC 161". We think that this was fair comment. It was not

realistic to treat the House of Lords in *Bell v Lever Bros Ltd* as oblivious to principles of equity, nor to suggest that "if it had been considered on equitable grounds the result might have been different"...[W]e do not consider that *Cooper v Phibbs* LR 2 HL 149 demonstrated or established an equitable jurisdiction to grant rescission for common mistake in circumstances that fell short of those in which the common law held a contract void. In so far as this was in doubt, the House of Lords in *Bell v Lever Bros Ltd* delimited the ambit of operation of *Cooper v Phibbs* by holding, rightly or wrongly, that on the facts of that case the agreement in question was void at law and by holding that, on the facts in *Bell v Lever Bros Ltd*, the mistake had not had the effect of rendering the contract void.

129 Nor was it accurate to state that *Cooper v Phibbs* afforded ample authority for saying that the lease could be set aside "on such terms as the court thinks fit". ...[T]he terms imposed by the House of Lords in *Cooper v Phibbs* were no more than necessary to give effect to the rights and interests of those involved.

130 In *Bell v Lever Bros Ltd* the House of Lords equated the circumstances which rendered a contract void for common mistake with those which discharged the obligations of the parties under the doctrine of frustration. Denning LJ rightly concluded that the facts of *Solle v Butcher* [1950] 1 KB 671 did not amount to such circumstances. The equitable jurisdiction that he then asserted was a significant extension of any jurisdiction exercised up to that point and one that was not readily reconcilable with the result in *Bell v Lever Bros Ltd*.

156 The effect of *Solle v Butcher* [1950] 1 KB 671 is not to supplement or mitigate the common law: it is to say that *Bell v Lever Bros Ltd* was wrongly decided.

157 Our conclusion is that it is impossible to reconcile *Solle v Butcher* with *Bell v Lever Bros Ltd*. The jurisdiction asserted in the former case has not developed. It has been a fertile source of academic debate, but in practice it has given rise to a handful of cases that have merely emphasised the confusion of this area of our jurisprudence. In paras 110 to 121 of his judgment, Toulson J has demonstrated the extent of that confusion. If coherence is to be restored to this area of our law, it can only be by declaring that there is no jurisdiction to grant rescission of a contract on the ground of common mistake where that contract is valid and enforceable on ordinary principles of contract law. That is the conclusion of Toulson J. Do the principles of case precedent permit us to endorse it? What is the correct approach where this court concludes that a decision of the Court of Appeal cannot stand with an earlier decision of the House of Lords? There are two decisions which bear on this question.

[*Lord Phillips considered two cases indicating that the law laid down by the House of Lords, not a later Court of Appeal decision, could be followed and continued:*]

160 We have been in some doubt as to whether this line of authority goes far enough to permit us to hold that *Solle v Butcher* [1950] 1 KB 671 is not good law. We are very conscious that we are not only scrutinising the reasoning of Lord Denning MR in *Solle v Butcher* and in *Magee v Pennine Insurance Co Ltd* [1969] 2 QB 507 but are also faced with a number of later decisions in which Lord Denning MR's approach has been approved and followed. Further, a division of this court has made it clear in *West Sussex Properties Ltd v Chichester District Council* 28 June 2000 that they felt bound by *Solle v Butcher*. However, it is to be noticed that while junior counsel in the court below in the *West Sussex Properties* case had sought to challenge the correctness of *Solle v Butcher*, in the Court of Appeal leading counsel accepted that it was good law unless and until overturned by their Lordships' House. In this case we have heard full argument, which has provided what we believe has been the first opportunity in this court for a full and mature consideration of the relation between *Bell v Lever Bros Ltd* [1932] AC 161 and *Solle v Butcher*. In the light of that consideration we can see no way that *Solle v Butcher* can stand with *Bell v Lever Bros Ltd*. In these circumstances we can see no option but so to hold.

161 We can understand why the decision in *Bell v Lever Bros Ltd* did not find favour with Lord Denning MR. An equitable jurisdiction to grant rescission on terms where a common fundamental mistake has induced a contract gives greater flexibility than a doctrine of common law which holds the contract void in such circumstances. Just as the Law Reform (Frustrated

Contracts) Act 1943 was needed to temper the effect of the common law doctrine of frustration, so there is scope for legislation to give greater flexibility to our law of mistake than the common law allows.

NOTES AND QUESTIONS

1. The decision to overrule the *Solle v Butcher* line of authority was a radical and controversial one. With respect, the Court of Appeal seemed to underplay the enormity of what it was doing. *Solle v Butcher* had stood for 50 years and had been applied several times not only here but in other jurisdictions (eg Canada). One might think that Steyn J's 'reconciliation' in the *Associated Japanese Bank* case, above, 632, was a better approach than overruling *Solle v Butcher.*

2. Had *Solle v Butcher* been good law, would it have applied on the facts to render the contract voidable? **FMB Reynolds, 'Reconsider the Contract Textbooks'** **(2003) 119 *LQR* 177** persuasively argues that, through the provision on cancellation, the parties had allocated the risk of the ship being further away than thought so that there was no scope for common mistake, whether equitable or common law. In other words, the overruling of *Solle v Butcher* was unnecessary to the decision.

3. Paragraph [161] is odd. Having gone to great lengths to overrule Lord Denning, the Court of Appeal suggests that he may have been justified after all. Why call for legislation to give the very flexibility that one has just wiped out?

4. **S Midwinter, 'The Great Peace and Precedent' (2003) 119 *LQR* 180** deals with the problem of the Court of Appeal overruling itself. The Court of Appeal is bound by its own decisions with three exceptions: (i) when there are two irreconcilable Court of Appeal judgments, the Court must choose one and ignore the other; (ii) when the earlier Court of Appeal judgment is inconsistent with a subsequent decision of the House of Lords the latter is binding; (iii) where the earlier Court of Appeal judgment was *per incuriam* ('through lack of care' ie unaware of binding authority). It cannot be said that *Solle v Butcher* fell into any of these categories and thus, applying the standard rules of precedent, it would seem that the Court of Appeal in *The Great Peace* did not have the authority to overrule *Solle v Butcher.* The next Court of Appeal case to come along, however, will fall under exception (i).

5. Whatever the technical position as regards precedent, it is surely inconceivable that, after such a detailed examination of the issue, *Great Peace* would not be followed.

(3) Equitable Rectification for Common Mistake

Rose (Frederick E) (London) v Pim (William H) Junior & Co
[1953] 2 QB 450, Court of Appeal

The claimants had been asked by Egyptian buyers to supply 'feveroles'. Not knowing precisely what these were, they asked the defendants who told them that they were ordinary horsebeans. That was incorrect because 'feveroles' were a particular type of medium-size horsebean. The claimants, acting on that information, contracted to buy 'horsebeans' from the defendants, which they then sold on to the Egyptian buyers. The Egyptian buyers claimed damages from the claimants for delivering ordinary horsebeans and not feveroles. The claimants now sought to rectify their contract with the defendant sellers so that the word horsebeans would be replaced by feveroles. This would then entitle the claimants to damages for the defendants' breach of contract. In allowing the defendants' appeal, rectification was refused because the written contract accurately reflected the parties' oral agreement/common intention.

Denning LJ: The buyers now, after accepting the goods, seek to rectify the contract. Instead of it being a contract for "horsebeans" simpliciter, they seek to make it a contract for "horsebeans described in Egypt as feveroles" or, in short, a contract for "feveroles." The judge has granted their request. He has found that there was "a mutual and fundamental mistake" and that the defendants and the plaintiffs, through their respective market clerks, "intended to deal in horsebeans of the feverole type"; and he has held that, because that was their intention – their "continuing common intention" – the court could rectify their contract to give effect to it. In this I think he was wrong. Rectification is concerned with contracts and documents, not with intentions. In order to get rectification it is necessary to show that the parties were in complete agreement on the terms of their contract, but by an error wrote them down wrongly; and in this regard, in order to ascertain the terms of their contract, you do not look into the inner minds of the parties – into their intentions – any more than you do in the formation of any other contract. You look at their outward acts, that is, at what they said or wrote to one another in coming to their agreement, and then compare it with the document which they have signed. If you can predicate with certainty what their contract was, and that it is, by a common mistake, wrongly expressed in the document, then you rectify the document; but nothing less will suffice. It is not necessary that all the formalities of the contract should have been executed so as to make it enforceable at law (see *Shipley Urban District Council v. Bradford Corporation* [1936] Ch 375); but, formalities apart, there must have been a concluded contract. There is a passage in *Crane v. Hegeman-Harris Co. Inc.* [1939] 1 All ER 662, 664 which suggests that a continuing common intention alone will suffice; but I am clearly of opinion that a continuing common intention is not sufficient unless it has found expression in outward agreement. There could be no certainty at all in business transactions if a party who had entered into a firm contract could afterwards turn round and claim to have it rectified on the ground that the parties intended something different. He is allowed to prove, if he can, that they *agreed something different*: see *Lovell & Christmas v. Wall*, per Lord Cozens-Hardy M.R., and *per* Buckley L.J., 104 LT 88 and 93; but not that they *intended* something different.

    The present case is a good illustration of the distinction. The parties no doubt intended that the goods should satisfy the inquiry of the Egyptian buyers, namely, "horsebeans described in Egypt as feveroles." They assumed that they would do so, but they made no contract to that effect. Their agreement, as outwardly expressed, both orally and in writing, was for "horsebeans." That is all that the defendants ever committed themselves to supply, and all they should be bound to. There was, no doubt, an erroneous assumption underlying the contract – an assumption for which it might have been set aside on the ground of misrepresentation or mistake – but that is very different from an erroneous expression of the contract, such as to give rise to rectification.

Singleton and **Morris LJJ** delivered concurring judgments.

NOTES AND QUESTIONS

1.   As Denning LJ's judgment recognises, the main requirements for common mistake rectification are (i) a continuing common intention (ii) that is

outwardly manifested and (iii) a common mistake *in the drawing up of the contract*. This case is an excellent illustration of (iii). The written contract accurately reflected the parties' common intention/oral agreement to buy and sell horsebeans. Although they were making a serious common mistake in thinking that feveroles were ordinary horsebeans, that was not enough: there was no common mistake in the drawing up of the contract.

2. Say the written contract had said 'feveroles', the oral agreement had been for the buying and selling of 'ordinary horsebeans', and both parties mistakenly believed that feveroles were ordinary horsebeans. Would rectification then have been granted so that the written contract read 'ordinary horsebeans' instead of 'feveroles'?

3. Applying *Bell v Lever Bros,* could the claimants have argued that the contract was void for common mistake?

4. The contract was voidable for the defendants' misrepresentation. But rescission was barred because the Egyptian buyers—as bona fide purchasers for value without notice—had taken good title to the horsebeans. In contrast, the claimants' purpose in seeking rectification was not to revest title in the beans in the claimants but to enable them to recover damages for breach of contract from the defendants for supplying the wrong type of horsebeans.

Joscelyn v Nissen [1970] 2 QB 86, Court of Appeal

A father had agreed, in a written contract, to transfer his car hire business to his daughter. In negotiations between them, it had been orally agreed that the consideration for the transfer would be that the daughter would pay the father a weekly pension, would permit him (and the mother) to occupy the ground floor of the daughter's house ('Martindale'), and would pay the gas, electricity and coal bills for the parents' part of the house and the cost for them of home help. In the written contract between them, there was no express mention of those bills or of the home help. Clause 6 said that the daughter 'shall discharge all expenses in connection with the whole premises "Martindale"... and shall indemnify [the father] from and against any claim in respect of the same.' Clause 7 read that the daughter should permit the father 'to occupy the ground floor of "Martindale"... free of all rent and outgoings of every kind in any event.' The Court of Appeal rectified clause 6 so that it instead read that the daughter 'shall discharge ... [the father's] expenses in respect of gas, coal, electricity and home help incurred by him while occupying "Martindale"...' It was held that rectification could be granted even though no oral *contract* had been concluded prior to the written agreement.

Russell LJ (giving the judgment of himself, **Sachs** and **Phillimore LJJ**): For the daughter it is argued that the law says that the father cannot get rectification of the written instrument save to accord with a complete antecedent concluded oral contract with the daughter, and, as was found by the judge, there was none such here. For the father it is argued that if in the course of negotiation a firm accord has been expressly reached on a particular term of the proposed contract, and both parties continue minded that the contract should contain appropriate language to embrace that term, it matters not that the accord was not part of a complete antecedent concluded oral contract.

...

[*Russell LJ set out the following passage from Simonds J in* Crane v. Hegeman-Harris Co. Inc. *[1939] 1 All E.R. 662:*]

'I am clear that I must follow the decision of Clauson J., as he then was, in *Shipley Urban District Council v. Bradford Corpn.* [1936] 1 Ch. 375, the point of which is that, in order that this court may exercise its jurisdiction to rectify a written instrument, it is not necessary to find a concluded and binding contract between the parties antecedent to the agreement which it is sought to rectify. The judge held, and I respectfully concur with his reasoning and his conclusion, that it is sufficient to find a common continuing intention in regard to a particular provision or aspect of the agreement. If one finds that, in regard to a particular point, the parties were in agreement up to the moment when they executed their formal instrument, and the formal instrument does not conform with that common agreement, then this court has jurisdiction to rectify, although it may be that there was, until the formal instrument was executed, no concluded and binding contract between the parties. That is what the judge decided, and, as I say, with his reasoning I wholly concur, and I can add nothing to his authority in the matter, except that I would say that, if it were not so, it would be a strange thing, for the result would be that two parties binding themselves by a mistake to which each had equally contributed, by an instrument which did not express their real intention, would yet be bound by it. That is a state of affairs which I hold is not the law, and, until a higher court tells me it is the law, I shall continue to exercise the jurisdiction which Clauson J., as I think rightly, held might be entertained by this court.

Secondly, I want to say this upon the principle of the jurisdiction. It is a jurisdiction which is to be exercised only upon convincing proof that the concluded instrument does not represent the common intention of the parties. That is particularly the case where one finds prolonged negotiations between the parties eventually assuming the shape of a formal instrument in which they have been advised by their respective skilled legal advisers. The assumption is very strong in such a case that the instrument does represent their real intention, and it must be only upon proof which Lord Eldon, I think, in a somewhat picturesque phrase described as 'irrefragable' that the court can act. I would rather, I think, say that the court can only act if it is satisfied beyond all reasonable doubt that the instrument does not represent their common intention, and is further satisfied as to what their common intention was. For let it be clear that it is not sufficient to show that the written instrument does not represent their common intention unless positively also one can show what their common intention was.'

...

In our judgment the law is as expounded by Simonds J. in *Crane*'s case with the qualification that some outward expression of accord is required. We do not wish to attempt to state in any different phrases that with which we entirely agree, except to say that it is in our view better to use only the phrase "convincing proof" without echoing an old-fashioned word such as "irrefragable" and without importing from the criminal law the phrase "beyond all reasonable doubt." Remembering always the strong burden of proof that lies on the shoulders of those seeking rectification, and that the requisite accord and continuance of accord of intention may be the more difficult to establish if a complete antecedent concluded contract be not shown, it would be a sorry state of affairs if when that burden is discharged a party to a written contract could, on discovery that the written language chosen for the document did not on its true construction reflect the accord of the parties on a particular point, take advantage of the fact.

The contention in law for the daughter would, we apprehend, involve this proposition, that if all the important terms of an agreement were set out in correspondence with clarity, but expressly "subject to contract," and the contract by a slip of the copyist unnoticed by either party departed from what had been "agreed," there could not be rectification.

NOTES AND QUESTIONS

1. This is the leading case showing that common mistake rectification does not require a prior oral contract provided that there was an outwardly manifested continuing common intention. On the facts, it would appear that there was no prior oral binding contract because there was insufficient certainty as to the terms.

2. What is the relationship between common mistake rectification and interpretation of a contract? Would it have been permissible for the court to have looked at evidence of the parties' prior negotiations had it been construing the contract (see above, 222, note 6)? See generally on this issue, the article by Burrows, below, 651.

Additional Reading for Chapter 12

J Beatson, *Anson's Law of Contract* (28th edn, 2002) Ch 8 (but note that this was written before the *Great Peace* case and that 'common mistake' is referred to as 'mutual mistake').

S Smith, *Atiyah's Introduction to the Law of Contract* (6th edn, 2005) 76–85, 172–82

C Slade, 'The Myth of Mistake in the English Law of Contract' (1954) 70 *LQR* 385

This article argues that there is no doctrine of mistake in English law. Cases said to be examples of unilateral mistake are better explained as ones where there is no coincidence of offer and acceptance (including, where one party knows of the other's true intention, no subjective coincidence). In a situation where both parties are under the same mistaken assumption, the contract can only be void where there is an express or implied condition precedent preventing the contract arising if the said assumption is incorrect. In other words, express and implied terms explain the cases of so-called common mistake. Moreover, it is argued that Denning LJ's reasoning in *Solle v Butcher* invoking a separate equitable jurisdiction was unsound.

P Atiyah and F Bennion, 'Mistake in the Construction of Contracts' (1961) 24 *MLR* 421

The authors argue that there is no doctrine of common mistake (and they agree with Slade that unilateral and mutual mistake relate to offer and acceptance). Common mistake should be seen as resting on the construction of the contract. One must ask whether there is an express term or implied term rendering the contractual obligations of the parties inoperative if a certain fact is untrue: if there is no such term, then the contractual obligations exist in full force. By deciding that the obligations of the parties are inoperative, one is construing the contract as placing the risk of matters being different than the parties believed them to be on neither party. Denning LJ's reasoning in *Solle v Butcher* is argued to be incorrect.

P Atiyah, 'Judicial Techniques and Contract Law' in *Essays on Contract* (1986) 244
This essay puts forward the view that many of the theoretical arguments surrounding mistake (and frustration) are not arguments about the basis of the doctrines, but are actually arguments over the *techniques* used to apply those doctrines. The technique of using 'fundamental mistake' is contrasted with the technique of construing contracts. Although construction has the disadvantage of uncertainty and can involve some artificiality, it has the great advantage of flexibility which allows the courts to achieve what is just in the individual case without having to fit within the established parameters of a doctrine of mistake.

J Cartwright, 'Solle v Butcher and the Doctrine of Mistake in Contract' (1987) 103 *LQR* 594
Cartwright argues that the reasoning of Denning LJ in *Solle v Butcher* was unsound in terms of authority and doubtful in terms of principle. Other interventions of equity—(i) a mistake induced by a misrepresentation and (ii) a mistake which one party knows the other is making but fails to point out—involve some form of unconscientiousness by the non-mistaken party. But the category invoked in *Solle v Butcher* involves no such unconscientiousness.

JC Smith, 'Contract, Mistake, Frustration and Implied Terms' (1994) 110 *LQR* 400
The central thesis of this article is that there is no room for the application of a distinct doctrine of mistake additional to the principles of the formation of contract and of implied terms. Where a common mistake has occurred, one asks whether there is an express, or implied, condition precedent that the mistaken fact was in fact true. There is no room for a further inquiry. There is no closed list of implied terms, as they arise out of the facts of the case. However, there are some standard ones such as *res extincta* (the item being bought and sold actually exists) and *res sua* (the item being bought is not already owned by the buyer). The latter means that *Bell v Lever Bros* itself was wrongly decided because the right to terminate the employment of Mr Bell was bought for £30,000 by Lever Bros when they already owned that right by virtue of the illegal transactions Mr Bell had been involved in. Finally, *Solle v Butcher* is irreconcilable with *Bell v Lever Bros* and with the long-established principles of *caveat emptor*.

R Stevens, 'Objectivity, Mistake and the Parol Evidence Rule' in *Contract Terms* (eds A Burrows and E Peel, 2007) 101
Stevens looks generally at objectivity and mistake in the formation of contracts before examining *Shogun v Hudson*. He regards the majority's reasoning in that case as 'unimpeachable'. In his view, it was clear that there was no contract of hire-purchase between the finance company and the rogue because the finance company was only intending to deal with Mr Patel and not with the rogue. The hirer's

identity was an essential term of the agreement and the only possible agreement was that evidenced in the written agreement.

A Burrows, 'Construction and Rectification' in *Contract Terms* **(eds A Burrows and E Peel, 2007) 77**
Having clarified aspects of the modern law of construction and especially rectification (with particular emphasis on the distinction between 'common mistake' rectification and 'unilateral mistake' rectification) this essay analyses the modern relationship between the two. The author's radical conclusion is that, in the context of the rectification of contracts for mistakes of fact, rectification is on the point of being rendered largely superfluous by modern developments in the law of construction.

Principles of European Contract Law **(eds O Lando and H Beale, 2000) 228–41, 246–8**

Article 4:102: Initial Impossibility
A contract is not invalid merely because at the time it was concluded performance of the obligation assumed was impossible, or because a party was not entitled to dispose of the assets to which the contract relates.

Article 4:103: Fundamental Mistake as to Facts or Law
(1) A party may avoid a contract for mistake of fact or law existing when the contract was concluded if:

(a)(i)   the mistake was caused by information given by the other party; or

(ii)   the other party knew or ought to have known of the mistake and it was contrary to good faith and fair dealing to leave the mistaken party in error; or

(iii) the other party made the same mistake, and

(b) the other party knew or ought to have known that the mistaken party, had it known the truth, would not have entered the contract or would have done so only on fundamentally different terms.

(2) However a party may not avoid the contract if:

(a) in the circumstances its mistake was inexcusable, or

(b) the risk of the mistake was assumed, or in the circumstances should be borne, by it.

Article 4:105: Adaptation of Contract
(1) If a party is entitled to avoid the contract for mistake but the other party indicates that it is willing to perform, or actually does perform, the contract as it was understood by the party entitled to avoid it, the contract is to be treated as if it had been concluded as the *[sic]* that party understood it. The other party must indicate its

willingness to perform, or render such performance, promptly after being informed of the manner in which the party entitled to avoid it understood the contract and before that party acts in reliance on any notice of avoidance.

(2) After such indication or performance the right to avoid is lost and any earlier notice of avoidance is ineffective.

(3) Where both parties have made the same mistake, the court may at the request of either party bring the contract into accordance with what might reasonably have been agreed had the mistake not occurred.

Article 4:116: Partial Avoidance
See above, 589.

Article 4:117: Damages
See above, 589.

[This contrasts with the English law on mistake in several respects: eg the requirement that the mistake was inexcusable; in the approach to unilateral mistake especially the test of good faith and fair dealing; that the contract is not rendered void or rectifiable but instead can be avoided and may be reformulated by the courts in cases of common mistake; and that damages may be awarded to the mistaken party, if the other party should have known of that mistake, irrespective of misrepresentation.]

13

Frustration

Where a contract has been concluded and a subsequent event occurs which alters the basis of the contract, it is often the case that one party will wish to escape from what is now, for him, a bad bargain (or, at least, a less beneficial bargain than anticipated). The doctrine of frustration deals with whether there can be an escape because of a change in circumstances.

Originally, as exemplified by *Paradine v Jane* (below, 654), there was no such escape. Although a doctrine of frustration has since been developed, the kinds of event which amount to frustration may be regarded as rather narrow. Moreover, the doctrine does not apply where the subsequent event was the party's own fault ('self-induced frustration') or, very importantly, where the parties have dealt with the subsequent event in the contract. The latter explains why, in practice, frustration is rarely invoked: commercial parties tend to include in their contracts 'force majeure' clauses dealing with supervening events.

If made out, the effect of frustration is to terminate the contract automatically. This raises the question as to what is to happen to benefits that have already been conferred prior to the frustrating event. As we shall see, the Law Reform (Frustrated Contracts) Act 1943 was enacted to reform the common law on restitution after the frustration of a contract.

Two other central issues are the juristic basis of (that is, how the courts explain) the doctrine of frustration; and the relationship between common mistake and frustration (both being linked in that they deal with the circumstances being different from what the parties thought, albeit that common mistake covers the state of affairs prior to, or at the time of, the contract, whereas frustration covers events subsequent to the contract).

Our examination of the cases is divided according to the following sub-headings. (1) The early approach of absolute liability. (2) The kinds of events that amount to frustration. (3) Factors excluding frustration. (4) The juristic basis of frustration. (5) The effects of frustration. (6) The relationship between common mistake and frustration.

Introductory reading: E McKendrick, *Contract Law* (7th edn, 2007) 14.8–14.18

1. THE EARLY APPROACH OF ABSOLUTE LIABILITY

Paradine v Jane (1647) Aleyn 26, King's Bench

The claimant lessor claimed rent due from the defendant lessee. The defendant argued that, as he had been evicted from the land by Prince Rupert, a German Prince who was an enemy of the King, he ought not to be liable for the rent. The court rejected that argument.

Judgment of the court:
[W]hen the party by his own contract creates a duty or charge upon himself, he is bound to make it good, if he may, notwithstanding any accident by inevitable necessity, because he might have provided against it by his contract. And therefore if the lessee covenant to repair a house, though it be burnt by lightning, or thrown down by enemies, yet he ought to repair it. ... Now the rent is a duty created by the parties upon the reservation, and had there been a covenant to pay it, there had been no question but the lessee must have made it good, notwithstanding the interruption by enemies, for the law would not protect him beyond his own agreement, no more then [sic] in the case of reparations; this reservation then being a covenant in law, and whereupon an action of covenant hath been maintained (as Roll said) it is all one as if there had been an actual covenant.

NOTES AND QUESTIONS

1. Do not be confused by the antiquated language. While there were some excep-
    tions (eg death), this case provides the classic illustration of the old approach
    ('no doctrine of frustration') to a change of circumstances.
2. Why is it an unsatisfactory argument against a doctrine of frustration to say
    that it is always open to the parties to provide for a possible change of circum-
    stances in the contract?

2. THE KINDS OF EVENTS THAT AMOUNT TO FRUSTRATION

(1) Physical Impossibility

Taylor v Caldwell (1863) 3 B & S 826, Queen's Bench

The claimants hired the Surrey Gardens and Music Hall from the defendants for the purposes of putting on four concerts. Six days before the first of the concerts, the Music Hall was destroyed by an accidental fire. The claimants sought damages for breach of contract to cover their expenses incurred in preparing for the concerts. It was held by the Queen's Bench that there was no liability to pay damages: both parties were excused because the contract was impossible to perform.

Blackburn J (giving the judgment of himself, **Cockburn CJ, Wightman J** and **Crompton J**):
There seems no doubt that where there is a positive contract to do a thing, not in itself unlawful, the contractor must perform it or pay damages for not doing it, although, in consequence of unforeseen accident, the performance of his contract has become unexpectedly burdensome, or even impossible. …But this rule is only applicable when the contract is positive and absolute and not subject to any condition either expressed or implied; and there are authorities which, as we think, establish the principle that where, from the nature of the contract, it appears that the parties must from the beginning have known that it could not be fulfilled unless, when the time for the fulfilment of the contract arrived, some particular specified thing continued to exist, so that when entering into the contract they must have contemplated such continued existence as the foundation of what was to be done, there, in the absence of any expressed or implied warranty that the thing shall exist, the contract is not to be construed as a positive contract, but as subject to an implied condition that the parties shall be excused in case, before breach, performance becomes impossible from the perishing of the thing without default of the contractor.

There seems little doubt that this implication tends to further the great object of making the legal construction such as to fulfil the intention of those who enter into the contract, for, in the course of affairs, men, in making such contracts, in general, would, if it were brought to their minds, say that there should be such a condition.

[*Having referred to civil law and to English cases on death and the perishing of goods subsequent to a contract of sale or hire, he continued:*]

The principle seems to us to be that in contracts in which the performance depends on the continued existence of a given person or thing, a condition is implied that the impossibility of performance arising from the perishing of the person or thing shall excuse the performance.

In none of these cases is the promise in words other than positive, nor is there any express stipulation that the destruction of the person or thing shall excuse the performance; that excuse is by law implied, because from the nature of the contract it is apparent that the parties contracted on the basis of the continued existence of the particular person or chattel. In the present case, looking at the whole contract, we find that the parties contracted on the basis of the continued existence of the music hall at the time when the concerts were to be given, that being essential to their performance.

We think, therefore, that, the music hall having ceased to exist without fault of either party, both parties are excused, the plaintiffs from taking the gardens and paying the money, the defendants from performing their promise to give the use of the hall and gardens, and other things. Consequently the rule must be absolute to enter the verdict for the defendants.

NOTES

1. This decision is generally considered to mark the start of the modern doctrine of frustration (albeit that, as in many of the earlier cases, as we shall see, the word 'frustration' was not used).

2. Although in one sense the impossibility was partial and not total, because the Surrey Gardens could still have been provided and used, that was irrelevant. The claimants did not want to use the Gardens alone as this would not enable them to go ahead with the concerts as planned. In any event, the question in issue was whether the defendants were in breach of contract in failing to provide the Music Hall.

3. Blackburn J justifies excusing the parties by reference to there being an implied condition in the contract apparently derived from the parties' intentions. It will be seen throughout the extracts, but particularly in the section on the juristic basis (674–677), that there has been a long-running debate between two main justifications for frustration. One treats the intention of the parties as the

justification for the doctrine. The other argues from broader notions of justice and fairness and sees the doctrine as being imposed where the contract has 'run out'.

Jackson v Union Marine Insurance Co Ltd
(1879) LR 10 CP 125, Exchequer Chamber

In November 1871, the claimant owner of a ship entered into a charterparty with a third party charterer. Under the charterparty, the ship was to proceed with 'all possible despatch (dangers and accidents of navigation excepted)' from Liverpool to Newport where it was to take on board a cargo of iron rails. The ship was to proceed to San Francisco with that cargo. The ship left Liverpool on 2 January 1872 but ran aground the next day before reaching Newport. The ship was refloated in February but needed repairs which took until the end of August. Meanwhile, on 18 February 1872, the third party charterer pulled out of the charterparty and chartered another vessel. The claimant brought an action against its insurer (the defendant) for the loss of freight. It was entitled to recover under the insurance if the freight was lost by a 'peril of the sea' but not if it was lost because the charterer had been in breach of contract. Affirming the lower court, it was held by the majority of the Court of Exchequer Chamber (Cleasby J dissenting) that the charterer had been excused by the non-availability of the ship which had made the intended early-year shipment to San Francisco impossible. The freight was therefore lost by a peril of the sea and was recoverable under the insurance.

Bramwell B: I understand that the jury have found that the voyage the parties contemplated had become impossible; that a voyage undertaken after the ship was sufficiently repaired would have been a different voyage, not, indeed, different as to the ports of loading and discharge, but different as a different adventure, – a voyage for which at the time of the charter the plaintiff had not in intention engaged the ship, nor the charterers the cargo; a voyage as different as though it had been described as intended to be a spring voyage, while the one after the repair would be an autumn voyage.

> ...
> The question turns on the construction and effect of the charter. By it the vessel is to sail to Newport with all possible dispatch, perils of the seas excepted. It is said this constitutes the only agreement as to time, and, provided all possible dispatch is used, it matters not when she arrives at Newport. I am of a different opinion. If this charterparty be read as a charter for a definite voyage or adventure, then it follows that there is *necessarily* an implied condition that the ship shall arrive at Newport in time for it. ...
> [I]t seems to me that, in this case, the shipowner undertook to use all possible dispatch to arrive at the port of loading, and also agreed that the ship should arrive there "at such a time that in a commercial sense the commercial speculation entered into by the shipowner and charterers should not be at an end, but in existence." That latter agreement is also a condition precedent. Not arriving at such a time puts an end to the contract; though, as it arises from an excepted peril, it gives no cause of action.
> The same result is arrived at by what is the same argument differently put. Where no time is named for the doing of anything, the law attaches a reasonable time.
> ...
> There is, then, a condition precedent that the vessel shall arrive in a reasonable time. On failure of this, the contract is at an end and the charterers discharged, though they have no cause of action, as the failure arose from an excepted peril. The same result follows, then,

whether the implied condition is treated as one that the vessel shall arrive in time for that adventure, or one that it shall arrive in a reasonable time, that time being, in time for the adventure contemplated. And in either case…non-arrival and incapacity by that time ends the contract…

Mellor and **Lush JJ** and **Amphlett B** concurred with Bramwell B. **Cleasby J** dissented on the ground that the charterers were bound to perform the contract despite the delay and that to imply a term excusing the charterers would introduce unacceptable uncertainty.

NOTES AND QUESTIONS

1. This case shows that impossibility must be assessed in the light of the purpose of the contract. Although the ship would have been ready by August 1872 that delay was too long for the charterers, who wanted the ship before then in order to make the shipment of iron rails.
2. How did Bramwell B explain why the charterers were excused?

(2) Legal Impossibility (ie Subsequent Illegality)

Metropolitan Water Board v Dick Kerr and Co Ltd
[1918] AC 119, House of Lords

The claimant water board entered into a contract with the defendant contractors for the purposes of building a reservoir near Staines, Middlesex. The reservoir was to be built in six years, commencing in July 1914. On 21 February 1916, the Ministry of Munitions used its wartime powers to prevent work on the contract continuing, and to disperse and sell the plant as directed by the Ministry. The claimant sought a declaration that the contract was still continuing. In dismissing an appeal by the claimant, the House of Lords held that, because the illegality and the delay consequent on it were indefinite, the contract had ceased to be binding (and that, although there was a clause—condition 32—expressly dealing with delay caused by difficulties, it did not cover delay of this kind).

Lord Finlay LC: It is admitted that the prosecution of the works became illegal in consequence of the action of the Minister of Munitions. It became illegal on February 21, 1916, and remains illegal at the present time. This is not a case of a short and temporary stoppage, but of a prohibition in consequence of war, which has already been in force for the greater part of two years, and will, according to all appearances, last as long as the war itself, as it was the result of the necessity of preventing the diversion to civil purposes of labour and material required for purposes immediately connected with the war. Condition 32 provides for cases in which the contractor has, in the opinion of the engineer, been unduly delayed or impeded in the completion of his contract by any of the causes therein enumerated or by any other causes, so that an extension of time was reasonable. Condition 32 does not cover the case in which the interruption is of such a character and duration that it vitally and fundamentally changes the conditions of the contract, and could not possibly have been in the contemplation of the parties to the contract when it was made.

It was not disputed, as I understand the argument for the appellants, that in the case of a commercial contract, as for the sale of goods or agency, such a prohibition would have brought it to an end. It was sought to distinguish the present case on the ground that the contract was for the construction of works of a permanent character, which would last for a very long time, and that a delay, even of years, might be disregarded. This contention ignores the fact that, though the works when constructed may last for centuries, the process of construction was to last for six years only. It is obvious that the whole character of such a contract for construction may be revolutionized by indefinite delay, such as that which has occurred in the present case, in consequence of the prohibition.

Lord Atkinson: [A] condition should by implication be read into the contract to the effect that the obligation to perform it should cease if by vis major, such as the action of the Executive Government of this country, [the parties] should be deprived to a very substantial extent of their freedom of action. Well, the respondents have been for a considerable time deprived of all freedom of action. The Executive Government, acting no doubt legally and within its powers, has for objects of State made it illegal and impossible for the respondents to do that which they promised to do. No one can tell how long it may continue to be invaded. In my opinion they are entitled to be absolved from the further performance of that promise. In addition it may well be that in this case, just as in that of *Jackson v. Union Marine Insurance Co.* L.R. 10 C.P. 125, the delay may render the adventure the respondents embarked upon as different from what it would have been if completed without interruption, as was the summer voyage which the parties contemplated in that case from the winter voyage which the delay would have necessitated. The conditions after the war may be entirely changed and the work already done may be deteriorated by the delay. I think the decision of the Court of Appeal was right, therefore, and should be upheld, and this appeal be dismissed.

Lords Dunedin and **Parmoor** gave concurring speeches.

NOTES

1. In deciding whether subsequent illegality/legal impossibility frustrates a contract, one must consider its impact on the contract. A short delay because of a prohibition is unlikely to mean that the contract is terminated; but the facts of this case, where the delay had already been substantial and was indefinite, clearly fell on the other side of the line. For a case going the other way, see *National Carriers Ltd v Panalpina (Northern) Ltd*, below, 674 (legal impossibility constituted by temporary closure of a road to the defendants' warehouse, held not to amount to frustration of the 10-year lease).
2. As to the express term on delays not covering the frustrating event, see below, 672.
3. For another well-known example of subsequent illegality amounting to frustration, see the *Fibrosa* case, below, 677.

(3) Cancellation of Events

Krell v Henry [1903] 2 KB 740, Court of Appeal

The claimant advertised by a notice in the window of his flat that windows to view the procession route of King Edward VII's coronation were to be let. The defendant agreed to hire the third floor flat for the two days (26 and 27 June), but not the nights, that the procession was scheduled to take place. He paid a £25 deposit with £50 due on 24 June. The offer and acceptance letters made no mention of the procession. Owing to the illness of the King, the procession was cancelled on 24 June before the

£50 was due. The defendant refused to pay the £50 balance and the claimant brought an action to recover it. In dismissing the claimant's appeal, the Court of Appeal held that the principle of *Taylor v Caldwell* applied so that the £50 did not have to be paid.

Vaughan Williams LJ: The real question in this case is the extent of the application in English law of the principle of the Roman law which has been adopted and acted on in many English decisions, and notably in the case of *Taylor v. Caldwell* 3 B. & S. 826. ...The doubt in the present case arises as to how far this principle extends. ... I do not think that the principle of the civil law as introduced into the English law is limited to cases in which the event causing the impossibility of performance is the destruction or non-existence of some thing which is the subject-matter of the contract or of some condition or state of things expressly specified as a condition of it. I think that you first have to ascertain, not necessarily from the terms of the contract, but, if required, from necessary inferences, drawn from surrounding circumstances recognised by both contracting parties, what is the substance of the contract, and then to ask the question whether that substantial contract needs for its foundation the assumption of the existence of a particular state of things. If it does, this will limit the operation of the general words, and in such case, if the contract becomes impossible of performance by reason of the non-existence of the state of things assumed by both contracting parties as the foundation of the contract, there will be no breach of the contract thus limited. ...[I]n my judgment the taking place of those processions on the days proclaimed along the proclaimed route, which passed [the flat], was regarded by both contracting parties as the foundation of the contract; and I think that it cannot reasonably be supposed to have been in the contemplation of the contracting parties, when the contract was made, that the coronation would not be held on the proclaimed days, or the processions not take place on those days along the proclaimed route; and I think that the words imposing on the defendant the obligation to accept and pay for the use of the rooms for the named days, although general and unconditional, were not used with reference to the possibility of the particular contingency which afterwards occurred. It was suggested in the course of the argument that if the occurrence, on the proclaimed days, of the coronation and the procession in this case were the foundation of the contract, and if the general words are thereby limited or qualified, so that in the event of the non-occurrence of the coronation and procession along the proclaimed route they would discharge both parties from further performance of the contract, it would follow that if a cabman was engaged to take some one to Epsom on Derby Day at a suitable enhanced price for such a journey, say 10l., both parties to the contract would be discharged in the contingency of the race at Epsom for some reason becoming impossible; but I do not think this follows, for I do not think that in the cab case the happening of the race would be the foundation of the contract. No doubt the purpose of the engager would be to go to see the Derby, and the price would be proportionately high; but the cab had no special qualifications for the purpose which led to the selection of the cab for this particular occasion. Any other cab would have done as well. Moreover, I think that, under the cab contract, the hirer, even if the race went off, could have said, "Drive me to Epsom; I will pay you the agreed sum; you have nothing to do with the purpose for which I hired the cab," and that if the cabman refused he would have been guilty of a breach of contract, there being nothing to qualify his promise to drive the hirer to Epsom on a particular day. Whereas in the case of the coronation, there is not merely the purpose of the hirer to see the coronation procession, but it is the coronation procession and the relative position of the rooms which is the basis of the contract as much for the lessor as the hirer; and I think that if the King, before the coronation day and after the contract, had died, the hirer could not have insisted on having the rooms on the days named. It could not in the cab case be reasonably said that seeing the Derby race was the foundation of the contract, as it was of the licence in this case. Whereas in the present case, where the rooms were offered and taken, by reason of their peculiar suitability from the position of the rooms for a view of the coronation procession, surely the view of the coronation procession was the foundation of the contract, which is a very different thing from the purpose of the man who engaged the cab – namely, to see the race – being held to be the foundation of the contract. Each case must be judged by its own circumstances. In each case one must ask oneself, first, what, having regard to all the circumstances, was the foundation of the contract? Secondly, was the performance of the contract prevented? Thirdly, was the event which prevented the performance of the contract of such a character that it cannot reasonably be said to have been in the contemplation of the parties at the date of the contract? If all these questions are answered in the affirmative (as I think they should be in this case), I think both parties are discharged from further performance of the contract.

Romer LJ, while ultimately agreeing with Vaughan Williams LJ, had some doubts as to whether or not the defendant had taken the risk of the procession not taking place. **Stirling LJ** concurred with Vaughan Williams LJ.

NOTES AND QUESTIONS

1. This decision takes the law one step further on from *Taylor v Caldwell* because it was clearly *possible* for the flat to be let and used on those days. What led to the contract being frustrated was that the performance of the contract on those days would not achieve the purpose of the contract, which was to view the procession.
2. In deciding whether the purpose was frustrated, was it relevant that the rent agreed was inflated because of the procession?
3. Was Vaughan Williams LJ correct to distinguish his Epsom Derby example?
4. One might think that the claimant's case was not an appealing one on the merits. He kept the deposit (£25)—which was presumably non-refundable—and was free to hire out the flat (at an inflated rate) for any rearranged coronation procession on that route.
5. A hires a coach from B to take supporters to watch an away football match. The day before the match, it is cancelled because of bad weather. Assuming no express provisions in the contract to deal with this, is the contract of hire frustrated?

Herne Bay Steam Boat Company v Hutton
[1903] 2 KB 683, Court of Appeal

The defendant, Mr Hutton, agreed, in writing, to hire the claimant's vessel for two days. It was stated in the contract that the purpose of the hire, on the first day, was to take out a party to view the royal naval review at Spithead and to enjoy a day's cruise around the fleet; and on the second day, 'for similar purposes'. The price was £250 and the defendant paid a £50 deposit. The naval review was subsequently cancelled because of the King's illness, although the fleet remained at Spithead. The defendant then stated that he did not require the vessel and refused to pay the agreed balance. The claimant sued for £110 which was that balance minus the profits it had made from using the ship during those two days. Allowing the claimant's appeal, the Court of Appeal held that it was entitled to £110 damages because the defendant was in breach. The contract had not been discharged by reason of the cancellation of the naval review.

Vaughan Williams LJ: Mr Hutton, in hiring this vessel, had two objects in view: first, of taking people to see the naval review, and, secondly, of taking them round the fleet. Those, no doubt, were the purposes of Mr Hutton, but it does not seem to me that because, as it is said, those purposes became impossible, it would be a very legitimate inference that the happening of the naval review was contemplated by both parties as the basis and foundation of this contract, so as to bring the case within the doctrine of *Taylor v Caldwell* 3 B. & S. 826. On the contrary, when the contract is properly regarded, I think the purpose of Mr Hutton, whether of seeing the naval review or of going round the fleet with a party of paying guests, does not lay the foundation of the contract within the authorities.

Having expressed that view, I do not know that there is any advantage to be gained by going on in any way to define what are the circumstances which might or might not constitute the happening of a particular contingency as the foundation of a contract. I will content myself with saying this, that I see nothing that makes this contract differ from a case where, for instance, a person has engaged a brake to take himself and a party to Epsom to see the races there, but for some reason or other, such as the spread of an infectious disease, the races are postponed. In such a case it could not be said that he could be relieved of his bargain. So in the present case it is sufficient to say that the happening of the naval review was not the foundation of the contract.

Romer LJ: I may point out that this case is not one in which the subject-matter of the contract is a mere licence to the defendant to use a ship for the purpose of seeing the naval review and going round the fleet. In my opinion, as my Lord has said, it is a contract for the hiring of a ship by the defendant for a certain voyage, though having, no doubt, a special object, namely, to see the naval review and the fleet; but it appears to me that the object was a matter with which the defendant, as hirer of the ship, was alone concerned, and not the plaintiffs, the owners of the ship.

…

The ship (as a ship) had nothing particular to do with the review or the fleet except as a convenient carrier of passengers to see it: any other ship suitable for carrying passengers would have done equally as well. Just as in the case of the hire of a cab or other vehicle, although the object of the hirer might be stated, that statement would not make the object any the less a matter for the hirer alone, and would not directly affect the person who was letting out the vehicle for hire. In the present case I may point out that it cannot be said that by reason of the failure to hold the naval review there was a total failure of consideration. That cannot be so. Nor is there anything like a total destruction of the subject-matter of the contract. Nor can we, in my opinion, imply in this contract any condition in favour of the defendant which would enable him to escape liability. A condition ought only to be implied in order to carry out the presumed intention of the parties, and I cannot ascertain any such presumed intention here. It follows that, in my opinion, so far as the plaintiffs are concerned, the objects of the passengers on this voyage with regard to sight-seeing do not form the subject-matter or essence of this contract.

Stirling LJ: It is said that, by reason of the reference in the contract to the "naval review," the existence of the review formed the basis of the contract, and that as the review failed to take place the parties became discharged from the further performance of the contract, in accordance with the doctrine of *Taylor v. Caldwell*. I am unable to arrive at that conclusion. It seems to me that the reference in the contract to the naval review is easily explained; it was inserted in order to define more exactly the nature of the voyage, and I am unable to treat it as being such a reference as to constitute the naval review the foundation of the contract so as to entitle either party to the benefit of the doctrine in *Taylor v. Caldwell*. I come to this conclusion the more readily because the object of the voyage is not limited to the naval review, but also extends to a cruise round the fleet. The fleet was there, and passengers might have been found willing to go round it. It is true that in the event which happened the object of the voyage became limited, but, in my opinion, that was the risk of the defendant whose venture the taking the passengers was.

1. The decision in this case was given a few days before that in *Krell v Henry* but, although the same judges were sitting, no reference was made to this case in *Krell*. On the face of it, the two cases are difficult to reconcile.

2. One might argue that a crucial difference was that, in this case, the fleet could still be viewed so that one of the purposes of the contract was unaffected. In contrast, the only purpose of hiring the flat in *Krell* was for the viewing of the procession.

3. **R Brownsword, 'Henry's Lost Spectacle and Hutton's Lost Speculation: a Classic Riddle Solved?' (1985) 129 *SJ* 860** argues that the difference between *Krell v Henry* and *Herne Bay v Hutton* is that Mr Henry was a consumer and Mr Hutton was acting in a business capacity. The courts do not as readily release a commercial party, as opposed to a consumer, from what has turned out to be a bad bargain. Do you find this convincing? Would it have made any difference in *Krell* if the hirer had been a company that had wished to use the occasion of the royal procession to entertain a client?

(4) No Frustration merely because Performance made more Onerous/ Expensive

Davis Contractors Ltd v Fareham Urban District Council
[1956] AC 696, House of Lords

The claimant building contractors agreed with the defendant local authority to build 78 houses over an eight-month period for a fixed fee of £92,425. The building work ended up taking 22 months, owing to a shortage of labour and materials, and cost the claimants £115,233. The claimants' main submission was that the contract was frustrated and therefore they should not be restricted to the contract sum but should instead be entitled to a *quantum meruit* (which is a non-contractual restitutionary remedy) for the value of the work they had done. An alternative argument, which was rejected and with which we are not here concerned, was that incorporated into the contract was an express term whereby the agreed price was binding only if there were adequate supplies of labour and material. The House of Lords, dismissing the claimants' appeal, held that, although the delays had made performance more onerous for the claimants, the contract was not frustrated.

Lord Reid: Frustration has often been said to depend on adding a term to the contract by implication…I find great difficulty in accepting this as the correct approach, because it seems to me hard to account for certain decisions of this House in this way.

   …

   I think that there is much force in Lord Wright's criticism in *Denny, Mott & Dickson Ltd. v. James B. Fraser & Co. Ltd.* [1944] A.C. 265, 275: "The parties did not anticipate fully and completely, if at all, or provide for what actually happened. It is not possible, to my mind, to say that, if they had thought of it, they would have said: 'Well, if that happens, all is over between us.' On the contrary, they would almost certainly on the one side or the other have sought to introduce reservations or qualifications or compensations."

It appears to me that frustration depends, at least in most cases, not on adding any implied term, but on the true construction of the terms which are in the contract read in light of the nature of the contract and of the relevant surrounding circumstances when the contract was made. ... On this view there is no need to consider what the parties thought or how they or reasonable men in their shoes would have dealt with the new situation if they had foreseen it. The question is whether the contract which they did make is, on its true construction, wide enough to apply to the new situation: if it is not, then it is at an end.

...

The appellant's case must rest on frustration, the termination of the contract by operation of law on the emergence of a fundamentally different situation. ...In most cases the time when the new situation emerges is clear; there has been some particular event which makes all the difference. It may be that frustration can occur as a result of gradual change, but, if so, the first question I would be inclined to ask would be when the frustration occurred and when the contract came to an end. It has been assumed in this case that it does not matter at what point during the progress of the work the contract came to an end, and that, whatever the time may have been, if the contract came to an end at some time the whole of the work must be paid for on a quantum meruit basis. I do not pursue this matter because the respondents have admitted that if there was frustration at any time the appellants are entitled to the sum awarded. But, even so, I think one must see whether there was any time at which the appellants could have said to the respondents that the contract was at an end, and that if the work was to proceed there must be a new contract, and I cannot find any time from first to last at which they would have been entitled to say that the job had become a job of a different kind which the contract did not contemplate.

...

It may be that delay could be of a character so different from anything contemplated that the contract was at an end, but in this case, in my opinion, the most that could be said is that the delay was greater in degree than was to be expected. It was not caused by any new and unforeseeable factor or event: the job proved to be more onerous but it never became a job of a different kind from that contemplated in the contract.

Lord Radcliffe: The theory of frustration belongs to the law of contract and it is represented by a rule which the courts will apply in certain limited circumstances for the purpose of deciding that contractual obligations, ex facie binding, are no longer enforceable against the parties. The description of the circumstances that justify the application of the rule and, consequently, the decision whether in a particular case those circumstances exist are, I think, necessarily questions of law.

It has often been pointed out that the descriptions vary from one case of high authority to another. Even as long ago as 1918 Lord Sumner was able to offer an anthology of different tests directed to the factor of delay alone, and delay, though itself a frequent cause of the principle of frustration being invoked, is only one instance of the kind of circumstance to which the law attends (see *Bank Line Ltd. v. Arthur Capel & Co.* [1919] A.C. 435, 457-460). A full current anthology would need to be longer yet. But the variety of description is not of any importance so long as it is recognized that each is only a description and that all are intended to express the same general idea. I do not think that there has been a better expression of that general idea than the one offered by Lord Loreburn in *F. A. Tamplin Steamship Co. Ltd. v. Anglo-Mexican Petroleum Products Co. Ltd.* [1916] 2 A.C. 397, 403. It is shorter to quote than to try to paraphrase it: "... a court can and ought to examine the contract and the circumstances in which it was made, not of course to vary, but only to explain it, in order to see whether or not from the nature of it the parties must have made their bargain on the footing that a particular thing or state of things would continue to exist. And if they must have done so, then a term to that effect will be implied, though it be not expressed in the contract. ... no court has an absolving power, but it can infer from the nature of the contract and the surrounding circumstances that a condition which is not expressed was a foundation on which the parties contracted." So expressed, the principle of frustration, the origin of which seems to lie in the development of commercial law, is seen to be a branch of a wider principle which forms part of the English law of contract as a whole. But, in my opinion, full weight ought to be given to the requirement that the parties "must have made" their bargain on the particular footing. Frustration is not to be lightly invoked as the dissolvent of a contract.

Lord Loreburn ascribes the dissolution to an implied term of the contract that was actually made. This approach is in line with the tendency of English courts to refer all the consequences of a contract to the will of those who made it. But there is something of a logical difficulty in seeing how the parties could even impliedly have provided for something which ex hypothesi they neither expected nor foresaw; and the ascription of frustration to an implied term of the contract has been criticized as obscuring the true action of the court which consists in applying an objective rule of the law of contract to the contractual obligations that the parties have imposed upon themselves. So long as each theory produces the same result as the other, as normally it does, it matters little which theory is avowed (see *British Movietonews Ltd. v. London and District Cinemas Ltd.*, [1952] A.C. 166, 184 *per* Viscount Simon). But it may still be of some importance to recall that, if the matter is to be approached by way of implied term, the solution of any particular case is not to be found by inquiring what the parties themselves would have agreed on had they been, as they were not, forewarned. It is not merely that no one can answer that hypothetical question: it is also that the decision must be given "irrespective of the individuals concerned, their temperaments and failings, their interest and circumstances" (*Hirji Mulji v. Cheong Yue Steamship Co. Ltd.* [1926] A.C. 497, 510). The legal effect of frustration "does not depend on their intention or their opinions, or even knowledge, as to the event." [1926] A.C. 497, 509. On the contrary, it seems that when the event occurs "the meaning of the contract must be taken to be, not what the parties did intend (for they had neither thought nor intention regarding it), but that which the parties, as fair and reasonable men, would presumably have agreed upon if, having such possibility in view, they had made express provision as to their several rights and liabilities in the event of its occurrence" (*Dahl v. Nelson* (1886) 6 App. Cas. 38, *per* Lord Watson).

By this time it might seem that the parties themselves have become so far disembodied spirits that their actual persons should be allowed to rest in peace. In their place there rises the figure of the fair and reasonable man. And the spokesman of the fair and reasonable man, who represents after all no more than the anthropomorphic conception of justice, is and must be the court itself. So perhaps it would be simpler to say at the outset that frustration occurs whenever the law recognizes that without default of either party a contractual obligation has become incapable of being performed because the circumstances in which performance is called for would render it a thing radically different from that which was undertaken by the contract. Non haec in foedera veni. It was not this that I promised to do.

There is, however, no uncertainty as to the materials upon which the court must proceed. "The data for decision are, on the one hand, the terms and construction of the contract, read in the light of the then existing circumstances, and on the other hand the events which have occurred" (*Denny, Mott & Dickson Ltd. v. James B. Fraser & Co. Ltd.* [1944] A.C. 265, 274-275, *per* Lord Wright). In the nature of things there is often no room for any elaborate inquiry. The court must act upon a general impression of what its rule requires. It is for that reason that special importance is necessarily attached to the occurrence of any unexpected event that, as it were, changes the face of things. But, even so, it is not hardship or inconvenience or material loss itself which calls the principle of frustration into play. There must be as well such a change in the significance of the obligation that the thing undertaken would, if performed, be a different thing from that contracted for.

I am bound to say that, if this is the law, the appellants' case seems to me a long way from a case of frustration. Here is a building contract entered into by a housing authority and a big firm of contractors in all the uncertainties of the post-war world. Work was begun shortly before the formal contract was executed and continued, with impediments and minor stoppages but without actual interruption, until the 78 houses contracted for had all been built. After the work had been in progress for a time the appellants raised the claim, which they repeated more than once, that they ought to be paid a larger sum for their work than the contract allowed; but the respondents refused to admit the claim and, so far as appears, no conclusive action was taken by either side which would make the conduct of one or the other a determining element in the case. That is not in any obvious sense a frustrated contract.

...

Two things seem to me to prevent the application of the principle of frustration to this case. One is that the cause of the delay was not any new state of things which the parties could not reasonably be thought to have foreseen. On the contrary, the possibility of enough labour and materials not being available was before their eyes and could have been the subject of special contractual stipulation. It was not made so. The other thing is that, though timely completion was no doubt important to both sides, it is not right to treat the possibility of delay as having the same significance for each. The owner draws up his conditions in detail, specifies the time within which he requires completion, protects himself both by a penalty clause for time exceeded and by calling for the deposit of a guarantee bond and offers a certain measure of security to a contractor by his escalator clause with regard to wages and prices. In the light of these conditions the contractor makes his tender, and the tender must necessarily take into account the margin of profit that he hopes to obtain upon his adventure and in that any appropriate allowance for the obvious risks of delay. To my mind, it is useless to pretend that the contractor is not at risk if delay does occur, even serious delay. And I think it a misuse of legal terms to call in frustration to get him out of his unfortunate predicament

Viscount Simonds and **Lords Morton** and **Somervell** delivered concurring speeches.

NOTES AND QUESTIONS

1. Although the contract had clearly become a bad bargain for the builders, the shortage of labour and materials and hence delays did not frustrate the contract. They are the risks that a builder takes when it agrees to do work for a particular price. If it wishes to be protected against those risks, it is for the builder to cover itself by express terms in the contract. The case therefore indicates that the courts are astute to ensure that frustration does not allow a party a simple way out of a bad bargain.

2. Parties often do include express terms dealing with the risk of changed circumstances. Apart from 'force majeure clauses' (see below, 672, 693), there are so-called 'hardship clauses' which specifically deal with changes in economic circumstances and which tend to provide for the parties to renegotiate the terms and the intervention of experts to adjust the contract if no renegotiated deal can be agreed. For an example, see *Superior Overseas Development Corporation v British Gas Corporation* [1982] 1 Lloyd's Rep 262, 264–5, CA.

3. Of the cases we have set out, this is the first in which the courts expressly referred to a theory or principle of 'frustration'.

4. In examining the basis of frustration, the 'implied term' justification was criticised by Lords Reid and Radcliffe. Why?

5. Lord Radcliffe's test for frustration of whether the change of circumstances has made the contractual obligation to perform 'radically different from that which was undertaken' has proved very influential. It has been approved and applied many times since and is now the courts' preferred test (see, eg, *National Carriers Ltd v Panalpina (Northern) Ltd*, below, 674).

Ocean Tramp Tankers Corporation v V/O Sovfracht, The Eugenia
[1964] 2 QB 226, Court of Appeal

The defendants chartered a vessel (under a trip time charter) from the claimant owners for the carriage of iron and steel from Genoa to 'India via Black Sea'. At the time the charterparty was made, it was obvious to the parties that the Suez Canal—which was the standard route to India—might soon be closed as a result of military activity. However, the parties could not reach an agreement on a clause to deal with that possibility and, as a consequence, the contract was silent on the point. A general 'war clause' in the contract prohibited the charterers ordering, or allowing, the ship to sail into a zone that was dangerous because of war. Despite the fact that hostilities had broken out, the charterers ordered the ship, or allowed her to continue, into the Suez Canal on 31 October 1956. She became trapped in the canal until January 1957 when she was able to return the way she had come. The charterers then abandoned the charterparty, claiming that it had been frustrated by the closure of the Suez Canal as the alternative route would have been round the Cape of Good Hope which would have taken a lot longer. A first question, with which we are not here directly concerned, was whether the charterers were in breach of the 'war clause'. It was held that they were. On the frustration question, it was held that the charterparty had not been frustrated because the trip via the Cape would not have been radically different.

Lord Denning MR: The second question is whether the charterparty was frustrated by what took place. The arbitrator has held it was not. The judge has held that it was. Which is right? One thing that is obvious is that the charterers cannot rely on the fact that the *Eugenia* was trapped in the canal; for that was their own fault. They were in breach of the war clause in entering it. They cannot rely on a self-induced frustration, see *Maritime National Fish Ltd. v. Ocean Trawlers Ltd.* [1935] A.C. 524. But they seek to rely on the fact that the canal itself was blocked. They assert that even if the *Eugenia* had never gone into the canal, but had stayed outside (in which case she would not have been in breach of the war clause), nevertheless she would still have had to go round by the Cape. And that, they say, brings about a frustration, for it makes the venture fundamentally different from what they contracted for. ...This means that once again we have had to consider the authorities on this vexed topic of frustration. But I think the position is now reasonably clear. It is simply this: if it should happen, in the course of carrying out a contract, that a fundamentally different situation arises for which the parties made no provision – so much so that it would not be just in the new situation to hold them bound to its terms – then the contract is at an end.

It was originally said that the doctrine of frustration was based on an implied term. In short, that the parties, if they had foreseen the new situation, would have said to one another: "If that happens, of course, it is all over between us." But the theory of an implied term has now been discarded by everyone, or nearly everyone, for the simple reason that it does not represent the truth. The parties would not have said: "It is all over between us." They would have differed about what was to happen. Each would have sought to insert reservations or qualifications of one kind or another. Take this very case. The parties realised that the canal might become impassable. They tried to agree on a clause to provide for the contingency. But they failed to agree. So there is no room for an implied term.

It has frequently been said that the doctrine of frustration only applies when the new situation is "unforeseen" or "unexpected" or "uncontemplated," as if that were an essential feature. But it is not so. The only thing that is essential is that the parties should have made no provision for it in their contract. The only relevance of it being "unforeseen" is this: If the parties did not foresee anything of the kind happening, you can readily infer they have made no provision for it: whereas, if they did foresee it, you would expect them to make provision for it. But cases have occurred where the parties have foreseen the danger ahead, and yet made no provision for it in the contract. Such was the case in the Spanish Civil War when a ship was let on charter to the republican government. The purpose was to evacuate refugees. The parties foresaw that she might be seized by the nationalists. But they made no provision for it in their contract. Yet, when she was seized, the contract was frustrated, see *W. J. Tatem Ltd. v. Gamboa.* [1939] 1 K.B. 132. So here the parties foresaw that the canal might become impassable: it was the very thing they feared. But they made no provision for it. So there is room for the doctrine to apply if it be a proper case for it.

We are thus left with the simple test that a situation must arise which renders performance of the contract "a thing radically different from that which was undertaken by the contract," see *Davis Contractors Ltd. v. Fareham Urban District Council* [1956] A.C. 696, 729 by Lord Radcliffe. To see if the doctrine applies, you have first to construe the contract and see whether the parties have themselves provided for the situation that has arisen. If they have provided for it, the contract must govern. There is no frustration. If they have not provided for it, then you have to compare the new situation with the situation for which they did provide. Then you must see how different it is. The fact that it has become more onerous or more expensive for one party than he thought is not sufficient to bring about a frustration. It must be more than merely more onerous or more expensive. It must be positively unjust to hold the parties bound. It is often difficult to draw the line. But it must be done. And it is for the courts to do it as a matter of law: see *Tsakiroglou & Co. Ltd. v. Noblee Thorl G.m.b.H.* [1962] A.C. 93, 116, 119 by Lord Simonds and by Lord Reid.

Applying these principles to this case, I have come to the conclusion that the blockage of the canal did not bring about a "fundamentally different situation" such as to frustrate the venture. My reasons are these: (1) The venture was the whole trip from delivery at Genoa, out to the Black Sea, there load cargo, thence to India, unload cargo, and redelivery. The time for this vessel from Odessa to Vizagapatam via the Suez Canal would be 26 days, and via the Cape, 56 days. But that is not the right comparison. You have to take the whole venture from delivery at Genoa to redelivery at Madras. We were told that the time for the whole venture via the Suez Canal would be 108 days and via the Cape 138 days. The difference over the whole voyage is not so radical as to produce a frustration. (2) The cargo was iron and steel goods which would not be adversely affected by the longer voyage, and there was no special reason for early arrival. The vessel and crew were at all times fit and sufficient to proceed via the Cape. (3) The cargo was loaded on board at the time of the blockage of the canal. If the contract was frustrated, it would mean, I suppose, that the ship could throw up the charter and unload the cargo wherever she was, without any breach of contract. (4) The voyage round the Cape made no great difference except that it took a good deal longer and was more expensive for the charterers than a voyage through the canal.

Donovan LJ delivered a concurring judgment. **Danckwerts LJ** concurred.

NOTES AND QUESTIONS

1.   As is made clear by Lord Denning MR, there was no prospect of the contract being frustrated *by being trapped in the canal* because that constituted 'self-induced frustration' (ie breach): see below, 668–672. The question was rather whether the contract would have been frustrated by the canal's closure had the ship not yet entered the canal. Even on that basis, there was no frustration because the trip via the Cape, while more expensive, was not radically different from the trip via the Suez Canal (ie the trip was still from Genoa to India via the Black Sea).

2.   Lord Denning MR's judgment is especially interesting for its firm rejection of the often-cited proposition (favoured subject to qualifications by, eg, Treitel, *The Law of Contract* (11th edn, 2003) 901–4) that frustration can only apply where the event was unforeseen or unexpected. Is it at all convincing to argue against Lord Denning's reasoning that, if the parties foresaw an event, but did not expressly provide for it, they must have intended that the occurrence of that event would *not* provide an excuse for non-performance? What is the best view as to the relevance of an event having been foreseen by the parties?

3.   This and the last case illustrate the point that the mere fact that a performance is made more onerous and expensive does not constitute frustration. Another example is that the failure of a seller's intended source of supply of goods (eg, because of war) does not generally frustrate a sale contract even though it may be very difficult and expensive to find an alternative supplier: see, eg, *Blackburn Bobbin Co v TW Allen & Sons* [1918] 2 KB 467, CA (outbreak of First World War cut off seller's normal supply of Finland birch timber).

3. FACTORS EXCLUDING FRUSTRATION

(1) Self-induced Frustration

Maritime National Fish Ltd v Ocean Trawlers Ltd
[1935] AC 524, Privy Council

The defendants chartered a steam trawler, the *St Cuthbert*, from the claimant owners. The vessel was fitted with, and could only operate as a trawler for catching fish with, an 'otter trawl'. By a Canadian statute it was illegal to leave a Canadian port with the intent to use an otter trawl without a licence from the Minister of Fisheries. The defendants applied for five licences for the five trawlers they operated, including the *St Cuthbert*. The Minister agreed to grant a licence for only three, asking the defendants to nominate which three. The three nominated by the defendants excluded the *St Cuthbert*. When the claimants sued for the hire, the defendants refused to pay, arguing that the charterparty was frustrated. The Privy Council, dismissing the defendants' appeal, held that the defendants were in breach because of self-induced frustration and were therefore liable to pay the hire.

Lord Wright (giving the judgment of himself and **Lords Atkin, Tomlin** and **Macmillan**):
[I]t was the act and election of the appellants which prevented the *St. Cuthbert* from being licensed for fishing with an otter trawl. It is clear that the appellants were free to select any three of the five trawlers they were operating and could, had they willed, have selected the *St. Cuthbert* as one, in which event a licence would have been granted to her. It is immaterial to speculate why they preferred to put forward for licences the three trawlers which they actually selected. Nor is it material, as between the appellants and the respondents, that the appellants were operating other trawlers to three of which they gave the preference. What matters is that they could have got a licence for the *St. Cuthbert* if they had so minded. If the case be figured as one in which the *St. Cuthbert* was removed from the category of privileged

trawlers, it was by the appellants' hand that she was so removed, because it was their hand that guided the hand of the Minister in placing the licences where he did and thereby excluding the *St. Cuthbert*. The essence of "frustration" is that it should not be due to the act or election of the party. ... [T]heir Lordships are of opinion that the loss of the *St. Cuthbert*'s licence can correctly be described, quoad the appellants, as a "self-induced frustration".

NOTES AND QUESTIONS

1. In the report of the decision of the lower court (the Supreme Court of Nova Scotia, [1934] 1 DLR 621), albeit not in the report of the appeal to the Privy Council, it is made clear that the defendants owned two of the five trawlers they operated and had chartered the other three. When awarded the three licences they chose to nominate the two vessels they owned and one of the chartered vessels, but not the one owned by the claimants. With those facts in mind, the case was more clearly one of self-induced frustration because, on the face of it, the defendants could have fulfilled all its contracts by allocating one of the three licences to the *St Cuthbert* rather than to one of their own trawlers. However, Lord Wright suggests that those particular facts would be irrelevant. In other words, it would appear that the decision would have been the same even if the defendants had been chartering all five vessels. Should the frustration be treated as self-induced in that situation?

2. For another example of self-induced frustration, see *The Eugenia*, above, 666 (as regards being trapped in the Suez Canal).

J Lauritzen AS v Wijsmuller BV, The Super Servant Two
[1990] 1 Lloyd's Rep 1, Court of Appeal

The defendants (Wijsmuller) entered into a contract with the claimants (Lauritzen) to carry a drilling rig (named the *Dan King*) from Japan to Rotterdam using, at the defendants' option, either the *Super Servant One* or the *Super Servant Two*. Before the collection of the drilling rig was due, the *Super Servant Two* sank. The defendants had already entered into a contract for the use of the *Super Servant One*. Two weeks after the sinking, they gave notice to the claimants that they would not be able to perform the contract. The claimants sued for breach of contract for losses suffered. At the time of judgment it was not known whether the sinking was caused by the negligence of the defendants. One issue, with which we are not here concerned, was whether a force majeure clause in the contract entitled the defendants to cancel it. It was held by the Court of Appeal that, on its true construction, it did do so unless the sinking was caused by the negligence of the defendants. On the issue of frustration, with which we are here concerned, it was held that, even assuming that the defendants had not been negligent in relation to the sinking, the frustration was self-induced so that they were in breach of contract because they had elected not to use the *Super Servant One* to fulfil the contract with the claimants.

Bingham LJ: The argument in this case raises important issues on the English law of frustration. Before turning to the specific questions I think it helpful to summarize the established law so far as relevant to this case.

The classical statement of the modern law is that of Lord Radcliffe in *Davis Contractors Ltd v Fareham Urban District Council*, [1956] AC 696 at p 729.

'...frustration occurs whenever the law recognises that without default of either party a contractual obligation has become incapable of being performed because the circumstances in which performance is called for would render it a thing radically different from that which was undertaken by the contract. Non haec in foedera veni. It was not this that I promised to do.'

As Lord Reid observed in the same case (at p 721):

'...there is no need to consider what the parties thought or how they or reasonable men in the shoes would have dealt with the new situation if they had foreseen it. The question is whether the contract which they did make is, on its true construction, wide enough to apply to the new situation: if it is not, then it is at an end.'

Certain propositions, established by the highest authority, are not open to question:

1. The doctrine of frustration was evolved to mitigate the rigour of the common law's insistence on literal performance of absolute promises...The object of the doctrine was to give effect to the demands of justice, to achieve a just and reasonable result, to do what is reasonable and fair, as an expedient to escape from injustice where such would result from enforcement of a contract in its literal terms after a significant change in circumstances...

2. Since the effect of frustration is to kill the contract and discharge the parties from further liability under it, the doctrine is not to be lightly invoked, must be kept within very narrow limits and ought not to be extended...

3. Frustration brings the contract to an end forthwith, without more and automatically...

4. The essence of frustration is that it should not be due to the act or election of the party seeking to rely on it...

5. A frustrating event must take place without blame or fault on the side of the party seeking to rely on it...

Had the *Dan King* contract provided for carriage by *Super Servant Two* with no alternative, and that vessel had been lost before the time for performance, then assuming no negligence by Wijsmuller (as for purposes of this question we must), I feel sure the contract would have been frustrated. The doctrine must avail a party who contracts to perform a contract of carriage with a vessel which, through no fault of his, no longer exists. But that is not this case. The *Dan King* contract did provide an alternative. When that contract was made one of the contracts eventually performed by *Super Servant One* during the period of contractual carriage of *Dan King* had been made, the other had not, at any rate finally. Wijsmuller have not alleged that when the *Dan King* contract was made either vessel was earmarked for its performance. That, no doubt, is why an option was contracted for. Had it been foreseen when the *Dan King* contract was made that *Super Servant Two* would be unavailable for performance, whether because she had been deliberately sold or accidentally sunk, Lauritzen at least would have thought it no matter since the carriage could be performed with the other. I accordingly accept [counsel for the claimants'] submission that the present case does not fall within the very limited class of cases in which the law will relieve one party from an absolute promise he has chosen to make.

But I also accept [counsel for the claimants'] submission that Wijsmuller's argument is subject to other fatal flaws. If, as was argued, the contract was frustrated when Wijsmuller made or communicated their decision on Feb. 16, it deprives language of all meaning to describe the contract as coming to an end automatically. It was, indeed, because the contract did not come to an end automatically on Jan. 29, that Wijsmuller needed a fortnight to review their schedules and their commercial options. I cannot, furthermore, reconcile Wijsmuller's argument with the reasoning or the decision in *Maritime National Fish Ltd*. [[1935] A.C. 524]. In that case the Privy Council declined to speculate why the charterers selected three of the five vessels to be licensed but, as I understand the case, regarded the interposition of human choice after the allegedly frustrating event as fatal to the plea of frustration. If Wijsmuller are entitled to succeed here, I cannot see why the charterers lost there. The cases on frustrating delay do not, I think, help Wijsmuller since it is actual and prospective delay (whether or not recognized as frustrating by a party at the time) which frustrates the contract, not a party's election or decision to treat the delay as frustrating. I have no doubt that force majeure clauses are, where their terms permit, to be construed and applied as in the commodity cases on which Wijsmuller relied, but it is in my view inconsistent with the doctrine of frustration as previously understood on high authority that its application should depend on any decision, however reasonable and commercial, of the party seeking to rely on it.

Dillon LJ: Was the contract frustrated by the sinking of *Super Servant Two* or by that event coupled with the subsequent election by the defendants to use *Super Servant One* on other voyages and not for carrying the *Dan King*? The important factor, common to both issues, is that under the contract the defendants could have satisfied their obligation by using *Super Servant One* to carry the rig, after *Super Servant Two* had sunk, but they elected not to do so.

In this respect, the present case appears to be a direct parallel to that described by Lord Wright in *Maritime National Fish Ltd. v. Ocean Trawlers Ltd*...

The parallel seems to be even closer, if, as some of the documents seem to suggest, the defendants, after the loss of the *Super Servant Two*, negotiated extra fees with the parties with whom they had other contracts of carriage before finally allocating the *Super Servant One* to perform those other contracts.

It is the view of Professor Treitel...that where a party has entered into a number of contracts with other parties and an uncontemplated supervening event has the result that he is deprived of the means of satisfying all those contracts, he can, provided he acts "reasonably" in making his election, elect to use such means as remains available to him to perform some of the contracts, and claim that the others, which he does not perform, have been frustrated by the supervening event. The reasoning depends on the proposition that if it is known to those concerned that the party will have entered into commitments with others and if he acts "reasonably" in his allocation of his remaining means to his commitments, the chain of causation between the uncontemplated supervening event and the non-performance of those of his contracts which will not have been performed will not have been broken by the election to apply his remaining means in a "reasonable" way.

Such an approach is however inconsistent to my mind with the view expressed by Lord Wright in that passage in *Maritime National Fish* ..., where he said:

'It is immaterial to speculate why they preferred to put forward for licences the three trawlers which they actually selected.'

It is also, as my Lord has pointed out, inconsistent with the long accepted view that frustration brings the contract to an end forthwith, without more ado automatically. Plainly the sinking of *Super Servant Two* did not do that, since even after that sinking the defendants could have used *Super Servant One* to perform the contract.

NOTES AND QUESTIONS

1. At first sight, this may appear a harsh decision. The defendants had no choice other than to break one contract or the other and they appeared to have acted reasonably in making the choice between the contracts. However, one may counterargue that defendants in this situation deserve no sympathy because they can deal with the risk of subsequent events by a force majeure clause.

Indeed the defendants in this case had agreed a force majeure clause and the actual decision was that, unless the defendants had been negligent in relation to the sinking, they were entitled to cancel under the force majeure clause. It should also be stressed that, as Bingham LJ recognised, the problem stemmed from the defendants having been given an option. Had the contract simply said that the transportation would be by the *Super Servant Two*, the contract would have been frustrated (assuming that the sinking was not caused by the defendants' fault). So the message coming from the judges is that, as the parties are free to allocate risks in the contract, there is no justification for anything other than a narrow doctrine of frustration.

2. A further issue on self-induced frustration, considered by the Court of Appeal but not set out above, is what is meant by fault in this context. It was held that it was not confined to acting deliberately or in breach of an actionable duty but includes carelessness. Bingham LJ said the following, at 10, '[T]he real question… is whether the frustrating event relied upon is truly an outside event or extraneous change of situation or whether it is an event which the party seeking to rely on it had the means and opportunity to prevent but nevertheless caused or permitted to come about. A fine test of legal duty is inappropriate; what is needed is a pragmatic judgment whether a party seeking to rely on an event as discharging him from a contractual promise was himself responsible for the occurrence of that event.'

3. What consequences follow from deciding that a frustration is self-induced?

(2) Express Provision

The point cannot be overstated that the parties are free to deal with subsequent events in the contract and, where they have done so, the doctrine of frustration is excluded. Hence the important role played by force majeure clauses. We have already looked at cases in which the courts have construed clauses which arguably dealt with the relevant subsequent event (see, eg, *The Super Servant Two* above in relation to cancellation under the force majeure clause). We confine ourselves here to an illustration from another case that we have already examined.

Metropolitan Water Board v Dick Kerr and Co Ltd
[1918] AC 119, House of Lords

See above, 657, for the facts. It was argued by the claimant water board that clause 32 of the contract covered the delay that had occurred and thus precluded frustration.

Lord Atkinson: Have the respondents contracted themselves out of all claim to be absolved from the performance of their promises, no matter how prolonged the enforced suspension of their work may be, or how absolute the deprivation of their freedom of action, and have they limited themselves to the relief the engineer may, under that condition, accord to them in the shape of extending the time for completion of the work? If so…the express provisions of the contract would then be inconsistent with the terms of the implied condition under which they would be relieved from the further performance of their promises. As I understood Mr. Lawrence [counsel for the appellants], he contended that condition No. 32 did contain a provision covering the action of the Ministry of Munitions. It is to be found, he said, in the proviso following the clause requiring that the works are to be completed and delivered up in clean and perfect condition within six years from the date of the engineer's order to commence them. In this clause it is provided that if, in the opinion of the engineer (which is to be final), the respondents should be unduly delayed or impeded in the completion of the contract by any one of a great number of things previously enumerated, the engineer might at any time or times extend the time, and fix such other day or days for completion as to him should seem reasonable without thereby prejudicing or in any way affecting the validity of the contract or the adequacy of the contract prices, &c. The several things enumerated which may cause this undue delay are additional or enlarged works or any just cause arising with the Board or engineer, bad weather, strikes, want or deficiency of orders, drawings or directions, or any difficulties, impediments, obstructions, oppositions, doubts, disputes, or differences whatsoever or howsoever caused. Mr. Lawrence contended that the word "difficulties" used in this condition in a contract made on July 24, 1914, covered the action of the Ministry of Munitions. It is obvious that as the attempt to continue working in defiance of this order of the Ministry would be a crime for which the respondents and the members of their staff employed on the works could be imprisoned, the order did impose difficulties in the respondents' way; but it is only necessary to read the clause to see that difficulties arising from the exercise by the Executive of their most unprecedented and arbitrary powers, not conferred on them till long after the date of the contract, could never have been within the contemplation of the parties at the time they entered into the contract. The difficulties they referred to must have been difficulties arising in the execution of the works somewhat analogous in kind and character to those things they had enumerated, or which at least the engineer might adjudge had unduly delayed or impeded the completion of the contract. It would be absurd to leave it in the power of the engineer to decide that the removal of all the plant, coupled with the making it a crime to proceed with the works, had not unduly delayed the completion of the contract. Yet if the argument be sound that would be in his power. I am clearly of opinion, therefore, that the provisions of this condition do not apply to the action of the Ministry of Munitions or its result, and that the case must be decided as if it did not form any part in the contract.

Lord Finlay LC and **Lords Dunedin** and **Parmoor** gave concurring speeches.

NOTES AND QUESTIONS

1. This case shows that, if the subsequent event would otherwise fall within the doctrine of frustration, the courts take a strict approach in construing a clause that would oust that doctrine.
2. As regards the long-running debate as to whether frustration is best regarded as resting on implied terms or on the court's imposition of a just solution, does the strict interpretation of express terms provide support for the latter?
3. While it is important for students to understand the law on frustration, that law constitutes the default position and, in practice, is rarely invoked because commercial parties deal with subsequent events by clauses (most obviously force majeure and 'hardship' clauses) in their contracts. The English law of frustration has been criticised for being narrow and inflexible; but there is little incentive for the courts to modify that law given that the parties are essentially free to deal in advance with subsequent events as they choose.

4. THE JURISTIC BASIS OF FRUSTRATION

We have seen that in the early cases, above, 654–662, the courts relied on there being an implied term to explain the discharge of a contract because of a subsequent event and they did not expressly refer to frustration at all. *Davis Contractors Ltd v Fareham UDC*, above, 662, marked something of a turning point, with Lords Reid and Radcliffe being critical of the implied term approach. Although no-one would today dispute that there is a doctrine of frustration (compare the continuing debate as to whether there is a doctrine of mistake) it is arguable that the best explanation for the doctrine remains a matter of dispute and a version of the implied term theory may not necessarily be dead. The juristic basis of frustration was comprehensively analysed in the next case.

National Carriers v Panalpina (Northern) Ltd
[1981] AC 675, House of Lords

In 1974, the defendants leased a warehouse from the claimants for 10 years. In 1979, owing to the dangerous condition of a derelict warehouse opposite, the only vehicular access to the leased warehouse was temporarily closed by the local authority. This was to enable the derelict warehouse to be demolished and, as it was a listed building, that required Ministerial consent. Initially, it was thought that the road would be closed for a year although, by the time of judgment, the total period of closure was likely to be about 20 months. In 1979, the defendants stopped paying rent and argued that the lease was frustrated. In the claimants' action for unpaid rent, the issues for their Lordships were whether a lease could ever be frustrated and, if so, whether the lease on these facts had been frustrated. In dismissing the defendants' appeal, it was held (Lord Russell of Killowen expressing doubts) that, exceptionally, a lease could be frustrated; but (unanimously) that the interruption here was not sufficiently grave to constitute frustration (there would be three of the 10 years still left to run once the road was reopened and under two years would have been lost). The claimants were therefore entitled to the unpaid rent. In the course of their speeches, all of their Lordships except Lord Russell of Killowen thought it helpful to consider the juristic basis of frustration and it is this that we here focus on.

Lord Hailsham of St Marylebone LC: At least five theories of the basis of the doctrine of frustration have been put forward at various times, and, since the theoretical basis of the doctrine is clearly relevant to the point under discussion, I enumerate them here. The first is the "implied term" or "implied condition" theory on which Blackburn J. plainly relied in *Taylor v. Caldwell* [(1863) 3 B & S 826], as applying to the facts of the case before him. To these it is admirably suited. The weakness, it seems to me, of the implied term theory is that it raises once more the spectral figure of the officious bystander intruding on the parties at the moment of agreement. In the present case, had the officious bystander pointed out to the parties in July 1974 the danger of carrying on the business of a commercial warehouse opposite a listed building of doubtful stability and asked them what they would do in the event of a temporary closure of Kingston Street pending a public local inquiry into a proposal for demolition after the lease had been running for over five years, I have not the least idea what they would have said, or whether either would have entered into the lease at all. In *Embiricos v. Sydney Reid & Co.* [1914] 3 KB 45, 54 Scrutton J. appears to make the estimate of what constitutes a frustrating event something to be ascertained only at the time when the parties to a contract are called on to make up their minds, and this I would think to be right, both as to the inconclusiveness of hindsight which Scrutton J. had primarily in mind and as to the inappropriateness of the intrusion of an officious bystander immediately prior to the conclusion of the agreement.

Counsel for the respondent sought to argue that *Taylor v. Caldwell* could as easily have been decided on the basis of a total failure of consideration. This is the second of the five theories. But *Taylor v. Caldwell* was clearly not so decided, and in any event many, if not most, cases of frustration which have followed *Taylor v. Caldwell* have occurred during the currency of a contract partly executed on both sides, when no question of total failure of consideration can possibly arise.

In *Hirji Mulji v. Cheong Yue Steamship Co. Ltd.* [1926] AC 497, 510 Lord Sumner seems to have formulated the doctrine as a "... device [sic], by which the rules as to absolute contracts are reconciled with a special exception which justice demands" and Lord Wright in *Denny, Mott & Dickson Ltd. v. James B. Fraser & Co. Ltd.* [1944] AC 265, 275 seems to prefer this formulation to the implied condition view. The weakness of the formulation, however, if the implied condition theory, with which Lord Sumner coupled it, be rejected, is that, though it admirably expresses the purpose of the doctrine, it does not provide it with any theoretical basis at all.

Hirji Mulji v. Cheong Yue Steamship Co. Ltd. is, it seems to me, really an example of the more sophisticated theory of "frustration of the adventure" or "foundation of the contract" formulation, said to have originated with *Jackson v. Union Marine Insurance Co. Ltd.* (1874) LR 10 CP 125, compare also, for example, per Goddard J. in *W. J. Tatem Ltd. v. Gamboa* [1939] 1 KB 132, 138. This, of course, leaves open the question of what is, in any given case, the foundation of the contract or what is "fundamental" to it, or what is the "adventure." Another theory, of which the parent may have been Earl Loreburn in *F. A. Tamplin Steamship Co. Ltd. v. Anglo-Mexican Petroleum Products Co. Ltd.* [1916] 2 AC 397 is that the doctrine is based on the answer to the question: "What in fact is the true meaning of the contract?": see p. 404. This is the "construction theory." In *Davis Contractors Ltd. v. Fareham Urban District Council* [1956] AC 696, 729 Lord Radcliffe put the matter thus, and it is the formulation I personally prefer:

> "... frustration occurs whenever the law recognises that without default of either party a contractual obligation has become incapable of being performed because the circumstances in which performance is called for would render it a thing radically different from that which was undertaken by the contract. Non haec in foedera veni. It was not this that I promised to do."

Incidentally, it may be partly because I look at frustration from this point of view that I find myself so much in agreement with my noble and learned friends that the appellants here have failed to raise any triable issue as to frustration by the purely temporary, though prolonged, and in 1979 indefinite, interruption, then expected to last about a year, in the access to the demised premises. In all fairness, however, I must say that my approach to the question involves me in the view that whether a supervening event is a frustrating event or not is, in a wide variety of cases, a question of degree, and therefore to some extent at least of fact, whereas in your Lordships' House in *Tsakiroglou & Co. Ltd. v. Noblee Thorl G.m.b.H.* [1962] AC 93 the question is treated as one at least involving a question of law, or, at best, a question of mixed law and fact.

Lord Wilberforce: The doctrine of frustration of contracts made its appearance in English law in answer to the proposition, which since *Paradine v Jane* Aleyn 26 had held the field, that an obligation expressed in absolute and unqualified terms, such as an obligation to pay rent, had to be performed and could not be excused by supervening circumstances. Since *Taylor v Caldwell* 3 B & S 826, it has been applied generally over the whole field of contract.

...Various theories have been expressed as to its justification in law: as a device by which the rules as to absolute contracts are reconciled with a special exception which justice demands, as an implied term, as a matter of construction of the contract, as related to removal of the foundation of the contract, as a total failure of consideration. It is not necessary to attempt selection of any one of these as the true basis: my own view would be that they shade into one another and that a choice between them is a choice of what is most appropriate to the particular contract under consideration. One could see, in relation to the present contract, that it could provisionally be said to be appropriate to refer to an implied term, in view of the grant of the right of way, or to removal of the foundation of the contract – viz. use as a warehouse.

In any event, the doctrine can now be stated generally as part of the law of contract; as all judicially evolved doctrines it is, and ought to be, flexible and capable of new applications.

Lord Simon of Glaisdale: [A] number of theories have been advanced to clothe the doctrine of frustration in juristic respectability, the two most in favour being the "implied term theory" (which was potent in the development of the doctrine and which still provides a satisfactory explanation of many cases) and the "theory of a radical change in obligation" or "construction theory" (which appears to be the one most generally accepted today). My noble and learned friends who have preceded me have enumerated the various theories; and the matter is discussed in *Chitty on Contracts*, 24th ed. (1977), vol. I, paras. 1401-1411, pp. 656-663. Of all the theories put forward the only one, I think, incompatible with the application of the doctrine to a lease is that which explains it as based on a total failure of consideration. Though such may be a feature of some cases of frustration, it is plainly inadequate as an exhaustive explanation: there are many cases of frustration where the contract has been partly executed. (I shall deal later with the argument that "the foundation of the contract" in a lease is the conveyance of the term of years, which is accomplished once for all and can never be destroyed.)

Lord Roskill: My Lords, I do not find it necessary to examine in detail the jurisprudential foundation upon which the doctrine of frustration supposedly rests. At least five theories have been advanced at different times. At one time without doubt the implied term theory found most favour, and there is high authority in its support. But weighty judicial opinion has since moved away from that view. What is sometimes called the construction theory has found greater favour. But, my Lords, if I may respectfully say so, I think the most satisfactory explanation of the doctrine is that given by Lord Radcliffe in *Davis Contractors Ltd. v. Fareham Urban District Council* [1956] AC 696, 728. There must have been by reason of some supervening event some such fundamental change of circumstances as to enable the court to say: "this was not the bargain which these parties made and their bargain must be treated as at an end" – a view which Lord Radcliffe himself tersely summarised in a quotation of five words from the Aeneid: "non haec in foedera veni." Since in such a case the crucial question must be answered as one of law – see the decision of your Lordships' House in *Tsakiroglou & Co. Ltd. v. Noblee Thorl G.m.b.H.* [1962] AC 93 – by reference to the particular contract which the parties made and to the particular facts of the case in question, there is, I venture to think, little difference between Lord Radcliffe's view and the so-called construction theory.

NOTES AND QUESTIONS

1. Of the five juristic theories considered (implied terms, total failure of consideration, a just solution, removal of the foundation, construction) the construction theory—as articulated by Lord Radcliffe in *Davis Contractors v Fareham UDC*, above, 664—is preferred by Lords Hailsham and Roskill. It was further approved by the House of Lords in *Pioneer Shipping Ltd v BTP Tioxide, The Nema* [1982] AC 724. It should be noted, however, that Lord

Radcliffe's classic statement is not merely an explanation of the juristic basis but also sets out a helpful, workable test—the 'radically different' test—and this may explain why it has proved particularly popular.

2. Is there a difference between the construction theory and implying terms? Does the answer depend on what test for implying terms one is adopting? Does the real debate as to the juristic basis boil down to whether it is a court-imposed or intention-based doctrine? Do any practical consequences turn on which juristic basis one adopts?

3. Why, in relation to frustration, do we debate these issues in terms of juristic basis, whereas in relation to (common) mistake we debate them in terms of whether there is a doctrine at all?

5. THE EFFECTS OF FRUSTRATION

If a contract is frustrated, the effect is to *terminate* (or, as it is commonly alternatively referred to, to *discharge*) the contract automatically. Frustration therefore sits alongside (serious or repudiatory) breach as having the effect of terminating the contract—that is, wiping it away for the future but not for the past—in contrast to, for example, misrepresentation or duress or undue influence which make the contract voidable (that is, liable to be wiped away the from the start by rescission: see above, Chapter 11, and below, Chapters 14–15). It also of course differs from the effect of mistake which, if operative at common law, renders the contract void (see above, Chapter 12). However, the major difference from termination for breach is that, as we have seen in, eg, *The Super Servant Two*, above, 669, termination for frustration occurs automatically and does not depend on the election of a party.

The question then arises as to what is to happen to benefits that have been conferred under the contract prior to its frustration. It might be thought from what has been said above (that the contract is wiped away only for the future) that nothing should happen and that benefits (and losses) should lie where they fall. However, the law of restitution comes into play at this point to reverse a party's unjust enrichment. For other references to this area of the law, see 76–77, 334–335 above. The relevant part of the law of restitution dealing with the effects of frustration is now almost entirely based on statute, namely the Law Reform (Frustrated Contracts) Act 1943.

Prior to the 1943 Act, the common law of restitution was underdeveloped and only went so far as to allow the recovery of *money* paid under a frustrated contract where there had been a *total failure of consideration*. The leading case was *Fibrosa Spolka Akcyjna v Fairbairn Lawson Combe Barbour Ltd* [1943] AC 32, HL. Here the claimant buyers (who were Polish) agreed to purchase machines from the defendant sellers (who were English). The machines were to be delivered to Poland. The contract required an advance payment of £1600 and the claimants had paid £1000. The contract was then frustrated by the outbreak of the Second World War. That is, delivery of the goods to Poland was now made illegal so that performance was legally impossible. The claimants were held able to recover the £1000 because there had been a total failure of consideration. Total failure of consideration refers to the performance, not the making, of a promise and requires that no part of the contracted-for performance has been carried out. So in this case there was a total failure of consideration because none of the machines had been delivered.

While the *Fibrosa* case went some way towards ensuring that frustration did not leave a party unjustly enriched, the law was regarded as defective in three main respects.

First, the restitution of money was ordered only if there had been a total failure of consideration. So, eg, in *Whincup v Hughes* (1871) LR 6 CP 78, where a claimant had paid to have his son apprenticed to a watchmaker for six years and the watchmaker died after one year, restitution of the money paid was denied because the consideration had only partly failed.

Secondly, the law did not take into account losses that the recipient of the money had incurred. In *Fibrosa*, if the defendants had incurred considerable loss in manufacturing the machines (on the facts it appears that there was no such loss because, although two machines had been completed, they could be sold without loss) that would have afforded them no defence to the claim for restitution of the money.

Thirdly, restitution was given only in respect of money paid and was not given for the value of other types of benefit conferred, in particular work done. For example, in *Appleby v Myers* (1867) LR 2 CP 651 the claimant had contracted to erect certain machinery on the defendant's premises. The price was to be paid upon completion of the whole. After some of the work had been finished, the premises with all the machinery and materials were destroyed by an accidental fire which frustrated the contract. It was held that the claimant was not entitled to a *quantum meruit* for the value of the work done.

The Law Reform (Frustrated Contracts) Act 1943 was enacted essentially to deal with those three defects in the law as it then stood.

Law Reform (Frustrated Contracts) Act 1943

1 Adjustment of rights and liabilities of parties to frustrated contracts
(1) Where a contract governed by English law has become impossible of performance or been otherwise frustrated, and the parties thereto have for that reason been discharged from the further performance of the contract, the following provisions of this section shall, subject to the provisions of section two of this Act, have effect in relation thereto.

(2) All sums paid or payable to any party in pursuance of the contract before the time when the parties were so discharged (in this Act referred to as "the time of discharge") shall, in the case of sums so paid, be recoverable from him as money received by him for the use of the party by whom the sums were paid, and, in the case of sums so payable, cease to be so payable:

Provided that, if the party to whom the sums were so paid or payable incurred expenses before the time of discharge in, or for the purpose of, the performance of the contract, the court may, if it considers it just to do so having regard to all the circumstances of the case, allow him to retain or, as the case may be, recover the whole or any part of the sums so paid or payable, not being an amount in excess of the expenses so incurred.

(3) Where any party to the contract has, by reason of anything done by any other party thereto in, or for the purpose of, the performance of the contract, obtained a valuable benefit (other than a payment of money to which the last foregoing subsection applies) before the

time of discharge, there shall be recoverable from him by the said other party such sum (if any), not exceeding the value of the said benefit to the party obtaining it, as the court considers just, having regard to all the circumstances of the case and, in particular,—

(a) the amount of any expenses incurred before the time of discharge by the benefited party in, or for the purpose of, the performance of the contract, including any sums paid or payable by him to any other party in pursuance of the contract and retained or recoverable by that party under the last foregoing subsection, and

(b) the effect, in relation to the said benefit, of the circumstances giving rise to the frustration of the contract.

(4)   In estimating, for the purposes of the foregoing provisions of this section, the amount of any expenses incurred by any party to the contract, the court may, without prejudice to the generality of the said provisions, include such sum as appears to be reasonable in respect of overhead expenses and in respect of any work or services performed personally by the said party.

(5) In considering whether any sum ought to be recovered or retained under the foregoing provisions of this section by any party to the contract, the court shall not take into account any sums which have, by reason of the circumstances giving rise to the frustration of the contract, become payable to that party under any contract of insurance unless there was an obligation to insure imposed by an express term of the frustrated contract or by or under any enactment.

(6) Where any person has assumed obligations under the contract in consideration of the conferring of a benefit by any other party to the contract upon any other person, whether a party to the contract or not, the court may, if in all the circumstances of the case it considers it just to do so, treat for the purposes of subsection (3) of this section any benefit so conferred as a benefit obtained by the person who has assumed the obligations as aforesaid.

2 Provision as to application of this Act

(1) This Act shall apply to contracts, whether made before or after the commencement of this Act, as respects which the time of discharge is on or after the first day of July, nineteen hundred and forty-three, but not to contracts as respects which the time of discharge is before the said date.

(2) This Act shall apply to contracts to which the Crown is a party in like manner as to contracts between subjects.

(3) Where any contract to which this Act applies contains any provision which, upon the true construction of the contract, is intended to have effect in the event of circumstances arising which operate, or would but for the said provision operate, to frustrate the contract, or is intended to have effect whether such circumstances arise or not, the court shall give effect to the said provision and shall only give effect to the foregoing section of this Act to such extent, if any, as appears to the court to be consistent with the said provision.

(4) Whether it appears to the court that a part of any contract to which this Act applies can properly be severed from the remainder of the contract, being a part wholly performed before the time of discharge, or so performed except for the payment in respect of that part of the contract of sums which are or can be ascertained under the contract, the court shall treat that part of the contract as if it were a separate contract and had not been frustrated and shall treat the foregoing section of this Act as only applicable to the remainder of that contract.

(5) This Act shall not apply—

(a) to any charterparty, except a time charterparty or a charterparty by way of demise, or to any contract (other than a charterparty) for the carriage of goods by sea; or

(b) to any contract of insurance, save as is provided by subsection (5) of the foregoing section; or

(c) to any contract to which [section 7 of the Sale of Goods Act 1979] (which avoids contracts for the sale of specific goods which perish before the risk has passed to the buyer) applies, or to any other contract for the sale, or for the sale and delivery, of specific goods, where the contract is frustrated by reason of the fact that the goods have perished.

(1) Overview of the 1943 Act

(i)   The central provisions of the Act are section 1(2) and 1(3). Section 1(2) deals with the restitution of money and section 1(3) with the restitution of non-money benefits (eg, the value of work done).

(ii)   Section 1(2) lays down that, on termination for frustration, all sums paid are prima facie recoverable (and sums payable prior to termination, but not yet paid, cease to be payable). This goes beyond *Fibrosa*, above, 677, because it is not a requirement that there has been a total failure of consideration. On the contrary, money can also be recovered for a partial failure of consideration. *Whincup v Hughes*, above, 678, is therefore no longer good law.

(iii) However, there is a proviso or qualification added to section 1(2). By this the payee, to the extent that the court considers it just, can recover its expenses—provided incurred prior to termination in, or for the purpose of, performing the contract—by setting them off against, or recovering compensation for them up to a maximum of, the sums paid or payable prior to termination. So there are three main elements. First, the expenses must have been incurred prior to termination in, or for the purpose of, performing the contract. A defendant who, in reliance on the money paid, buys a holi-day, which he would otherwise not have done, is outside section 1(2). In contrast, the expenses of manufacturing the machines in *Fibrosa* would be covered. Secondly, the amount of the sums paid or payable prior to dis-charge is the maximum that can be retained or recovered in respect of expenses incurred. In *Fibrosa*, the buyers were bound to pay £1600 in advance (of which £1000 had been paid). The maximum the sellers could have recovered was therefore £1600 even if their expenses incurred in or for the purpose of performance exceeded that sum. Thirdly, the court has an overall discretion, to be exercised according to what it considers is just, in deciding how much, if any, of the expenses are recoverable. The *Gamerco* case, below, 688, gives some assistance as to how a court will decide what is just in this context.

(iv)   Section 1(3) lays down that a party who, in or for the purpose of performing the contract and prior to the time of discharge, has conferred a valuable non-money benefit on the other party can recover a just sum up to the maxi-mum value of that benefit. In deciding the amount of the just sum, a court is particularly required (analogously to the proviso to section 1(2)) to consider the expenses incurred in or for the purpose of performing the contract by the party who has received the non-money benefit; and the effect on the non-money ben-efit of the frustrating event. The operation of this subsection was considered in detail in *BP Exploration Co (Libya) v Hunt (No 2)*, below, 681.

(v)   The other most important sections of the Act are section 2(3) and section 2(5). Section 2(3) recognises that the parties are free to contract out of or round sec-tion 1(2) and (3). Section 2(5) lists the four types of contracts which are excluded from the Act. They are voyage charterparties, contracts for the car-riage of goods by sea, contracts of insurance, and contracts for the sale of goods where the goods have perished. If one of these types of contracts has been terminated for frustration, the common law of restitution will apply.

(2) Cases on the 1943 Act

BP Exploration Co (Libya) v Hunt (No 2)
[1979] 1 WLR 783, Queen's Bench Division

The defendant, Mr Hunt, was the owner of an oil concession in Libya. As he did not have the resources to exploit the concession himself, he entered into a contract with the claimant oil company, BP. Under that contract: (a) Hunt transferred half of the concession to BP; (b) BP undertook to transfer to Hunt certain contributions (called 'farm-in' contributions) in cash and oil; (c) BP undertook to explore the concession for oil and, if oil was found, to develop the field; (d) all funds until the oil came on stream were to be provided by BP; (e) when the oil came on stream, the profits would be shared, but 3/8 of Hunt's share would be paid to BP until the payments covered 125 per cent of the farm-in contributions and 1/2 of the money expended by BP in developing the field. The general thinking behind the contract, therefore, was that BP should bear the risk of there being no oil but that, if an oilfield were found, BP would initially take the 'lion's share' of the profits. In the event, a giant oilfield was found and the field came on stream in 1967. In 1971 the Libyan government was overthrown and the new Revolutionary Command Council, led by Colonel Gaddafi, expropriated BP's half share in the concession. At that time, BP had received approximately one third of their reimbursement entitlement. Two years later, Hunt's share was also expropriated. BP claimed that the contract had been frustrated by the expropriation in 1971 and sought the award of a just sum under section 1(3) of the Law Reform (Frustrated Contracts) Act 1943.

Robert Goff J held that the contract had been frustrated in 1971 and, having closely examined the 1943 Act, he awarded BP around $35.4 million (subject to currency adjustments) plus interest. His decision was upheld with little further analysis of the Act by the Court of Appeal [1983] 1 WLR 232 although his reference to the principle of unjust enrichment as underpinning the Act was regarded as unhelpful: Lawton LJ giving the judgment of the court said at 243, 'We get no help from the use of words which are not in the statute'. A further limited appeal to the House of Lords [1983] 2 AC 352 (on section 2(3) of the 1943 Act and on interest) was dismissed. We here focus on Robert Goff J's examination of section 1(2) and section 1(3) of the 1943 Act.

Robert Goff J:

(1) The principle of recovery

   (a) The principle, which is common to both section 1 (2) and (3), and indeed is the fundamental principle underlying the Act itself, is prevention of the unjust enrichment of either party to the contract at the other's expense. ... [T]he principle [of unjust enrichment] underlying the Act...underlies the right of recovery in very many cases in English law, and indeed is the basic principle of the English law of restitution, of which the Act forms part.

   (b) Although section 1 (2) and (3) is concerned with restitution in respect of different types of benefit, it is right to construe the two subsections as flowing from the same basic principle and therefore, so far as their different subject matters permit, to achieve consistency between them. Even so, it is always necessary to bear in mind the difference between awards of restitution in respect of money payments and awards where the benefit conferred by the plaintiff does not consist of a payment of money. Money has the peculiar character of a universal medium of exchange. By its receipt, the recipient is inevitably benefited; and (subject to problems arising from such matters as inflation, change of position and the time value of money) the loss suffered by the plaintiff is generally equal to the defendant's gain, so that no difficulty arises concerning the amount to be repaid. The same cannot be said of other benefits, such as goods or services. By their nature, services cannot be restored; nor in many cases can goods be restored, for example where they have been consumed or transferred to another. Furthermore the identity and value of the resulting benefit to the recipient may be debatable. From the very nature of things, therefore, the problem of restitution in respect of such benefits is more complex than in cases where the benefit takes the form of a money payment; and the solution of the problem has been made no easier by the form in which the legislature has chosen to draft section 1 (3) of the Act.

(c) The Act is not designed to do certain things: (i) It is not designed to apportion the loss between the parties. There is no general power under either section 1 (2) or section 1 (3) to make any allowance for expenses incurred by the plaintiff (except, under the proviso to section 1 (2), to enable him to enforce pro tanto payment of a sum payable but unpaid before frustration); and expenses incurred by the defendant are only relevant in so far as they go to reduce the net benefit obtained by him and thereby limit any award to the plaintiff. (ii) It is not concerned to put the parties in the position in which they would have been if the contract had been performed. (iii) It is not concerned to restore the parties to the position they were in before the contract was made. A remedy designed to prevent unjust enrichment may not achieve that result; for expenditure may be incurred by either party under the contract which confers no benefit on the other, and in respect of which no remedy is available under the Act.

(d) An award under the Act may have the effect of rescuing the plaintiff from an unprofitable bargain. This may certainly be true under section 1 (2), if the plaintiff has paid the price in advance for an expected return which, if furnished, would have proved unprofitable; if the contract is frustrated before any part of that expected return is received, and before any expenditure is incurred by the defendant, the plaintiff is entitled to the return of the price he has paid, irrespective of the consideration he would have recovered had the contract been performed. Consistently with section 1 (2), there is nothing in section 1 (3) which necessarily limits an award to the contract consideration. But the contract consideration may nevertheless be highly relevant to the assessment of the just sum to be awarded under section 1 (3); this is a matter to which I will revert later in this judgment.

(2) Claims under section 1 (2)

Where an award is made under section 1 (2), it is, generally speaking, simply an award for the repayment of money which has been paid to the defendant in pursuance of the contract, subject to an allowance in respect of expenses incurred by the defendant. It is not necessary that the consideration for the payment should have wholly failed: claims under section 1 (2) are not limited to cases of total failure of consideration, and cases of partial failure of consideration can be catered for by a cross-claim by the defendant under section 1 (2) or section 1 (3) or both. There is no discretion in the court in respect of a claim under section 1 (2), except in respect of the allowance for expenses; subject to such an allowance (and, of course, a cross-claim) the plaintiff is entitled to repayment of the money he has paid. The allowance for expenses is probably best rationalised as a statutory recognition of the defence of change of position. True, the expenses need not have been incurred by reason of the plaintiff's payment; but they must have been incurred in, or for the purpose of, the performance of the contract under which the plaintiff's payment has been made, and for that reason it is just that they should be brought into account. No provision is made in the subsection for any increase in the sum recoverable by the plaintiff, or in the amount of expenses to be allowed to the defendant, to allow for the time value of money. The money may have been paid, or the expenses incurred. many years before the date of frustration; but the cause of action accrues on that date. and the sum recoverable under the Act as at that date can be no greater than the sum actually paid, though the defendant may have had the use of the money over many years, and indeed may have profited from its use. Of course, the question whether the court may award interest from the date of the accrual of the cause of action is an entirely different matter, to which I shall refer later in this judgment.

(3) Claims under section 1 (3)

(a) *General*. In contra[s]t, where an award is made under section 1 (3), the process is more complicated. First, it has to be shown that the defendant has, by reason of something done by the plaintiff in, or for the purpose of, the performance of the contract, obtained a valuable benefit (other than a payment of money) before the time of discharge. That benefit has to be identified, and valued, and such value forms the upper limit of the award. Secondly, the court may award to the plaintiff such sum, not greater than the value of such benefit, as it considers just having regard to all the circumstances of the case, including in particular the matters specified in section 1 (3) (a) and (b). In the case of an award under section 1 (3) there are, therefore, two distinct stages – the identification and valuation of the benefit, and the award of the just sum. The amount to be awarded is the just sum, unless the defendant's benefit is less, in which event the award will be limited to the amount of that benefit. The distinction between the identification and valuation of the defendant's benefit, and the assessment of the just sum, is the most controversial part of the Act. It represents the solution adopted by the legislature of the problem of restitution in cases where the benefit does not consist of a payment of money, but the solution so adopted has been criticised by some commentators as productive of injustice, and it certainly gives rise to considerable problems, to which I shall refer in due course.

(b) *Identification of the defendant's benefit*. In the course of the argument before me, there was much dispute whether, in the case of services, the benefit should be identified as the services themselves, or as the end product of the services. One example canvassed (because it bore some relationship to the facts of the present case) was the example of prospecting for minerals. If minerals are discovered, should the benefit be regarded (as Mr. Alexander [for Hunt] contended) simply as the services of prospecting, or (as Mr. Rokison [for BP] contended) as the minerals themselves being the end product of the successful exercise? Now, I am satisfied that it was the intention of the legislature, to be derived from section 1 (3) as a matter of construction, that the benefit should in an appropriate case be identified as the end product of the services. This appears, in my judgment, not only from the fact that section 1 (3) distinguishes between the plaintiff's performance and the defendant's benefit, but also from section 1 (3) (b) which clearly relates to the product of the plaintiff's performance. Let me take the example of a building contract. Suppose that a contract for work on a building is frustrated by a fire which destroys the building and which, therefore, also destroys a substantial amount of work already done by the plaintiff. Although it might be thought just to award the plaintiff a sum assessed on a quantum meruit basis, probably a rateable part of the contract price, in respect of the work he has done, the effect of section 1 (3) (b) will be to reduce the award to nil, because of the effect, in relation to the defendant's benefit, of the circumstances giving rise to the frustration of the contract. It is quite plain that, in section 1 (3) (b), the word "benefit" is intended to refer, in the example I have given, to the actual improvement to the building, because that is what will be affected by the frustrating event; the subsection therefore contemplates that, in such a case, the benefit is the end product of the plaintiff's services, not the services themselves. This will not be so in every case, since in some cases the services will have no end product; for example, where the services consist of doing such work as surveying, or transporting goods. In each case, it is necessary to ask the question: what benefit has the defendant obtained by reason of the plaintiff's contractual performance? But it must not be forgotten that in section 1 (3) the relevance of the value of the benefit is to fix a ceiling to the award. If, for example, in a building contract, the building is only partially completed, the value of the partially completed building (i.e. the product of the services) will fix a ceiling for the award; the stage of the work may be such that the uncompleted building may be worth less than the value of the work and materials that have gone into it, particularly as completion by another builder may cost more than completion by the original builder would have cost. In other cases, however, the actual benefit to the defendant may be considerably more than the appropriate or just sum to be awarded to the plaintiff, in which event the value of the benefit will not in fact determine the quantum of the award. I should add, however, that, in a case of prospecting, it would usually be wrong to identify the discovered mineral as the benefit. In such a case there is always (whether the prospecting is successful or not) the benefit of the prospecting itself, i.e. of knowing whether or not the land contains any deposit of the relevant minerals; if the prospecting is successful, the benefit may include also the enhanced value of the land by reason of the discovery; if the prospector's contractual task goes beyond discovery and includes development and production, the benefit will include the further enhancement of the land by reason of the installation of the facilities, and also the benefit of in part transforming a valuable mineral deposit into a marketable commodity.

I add by way of footnote that all these difficulties would have been avoided if the legislature had thought it right to treat the services themselves as the benefit. In the opinion of many commentators, it would be more just to do so; after all, the services in question have been requested by the defendant, who normally takes the risk that they may prove worthless, from whatever cause. In the example I have given of the building destroyed by fire, there is much to be said for the view that the builder should be paid for the work he has done, unless he has (for example by agreeing to insure the works) taken upon himself the risk of destruction by fire. But my task is to construe the Act as it stands. On the true construction of the Act, it is in my judgment clear that the defendant's benefit must, in an appropriate case, be identified as the end product of the plaintiff's services, despite the difficulties which this construction creates, difficulties which are met again when one comes to value the benefit.

(c) *Apportioning the benefit*. In all cases, the relevant benefit must have been obtained by the defendant by reason of something done by the plaintiff. Accordingly, where it is appropriate to identify the benefit with an end product and it appears that the defendant has obtained the benefit by reason of work done both by the plaintiff and by himself, the court will have to do its best to apportion that benefit, and to decide what proportion is attributable to the work done by the plaintiff. That proportion will then constitute the relevant benefit for the purposes of section 1 (3) of the Act.

(d) *Valuing the benefit*. Since the benefit may be identified with the product of the plaintiff's performance, great problems arise in the valuation of the benefit. First, how does one solve the problem which arises from the fact that a small service may confer an enormous benefit, and conversely, a very substantial service may confer only a very small benefit? The answer presumably is that at the stage of valuation of the benefit (as opposed to assessment of the just sum) the task of the court is simply to assess the value of the benefit to the defendant. For example, if a prospector after some very simple prospecting discovers a large and unexpected deposit of a valuable mineral, the benefit to the defendant (namely, the enhancement in the value of the land) may be enormous; it must be valued as such, always bearing in mind that the assessment of a just sum may very well lead to a much smaller amount being awarded to the plaintiff. But conversely, the plaintiff may have undertaken building work for a substantial sum which is, objectively speaking, of little or no value – for example, he may commence the redecoration, to the defendant's execrable taste, of rooms which are in good decorative order. If the contract is frustrated before the work is complete, and the work is unaffected by the frustrating event, it can be argued that the defendant has obtained no benefit, because the defendant's property has been reduced in value by the plaintiff's work; but the partial work must be treated as a benefit to the defendant, since he requested it, and valued as such. Secondly, at what point in time is the benefit to be valued? If there is a lapse of time between the date of the receipt of the benefit, and the date of frustration, there may in the meanwhile be a substantial variation in the value of the benefit. If the benefit had simply been identified as the services rendered, this problem would not arise; the court would simply award a reasonable remuneration for the services rendered at the time when they were rendered, the defendant taking the risk of any subsequent depreci-ation and the benefit of any subsequent appreciation in value. But that is not what the Act provides: section 1 (3) (b) makes it plain that the plaintiff is to take the risk of depreciation or destruction by the frustrating event. If the effect of the frustrating event upon the value of the benefit is to be measured, it must surely be measured upon the benefit as at the date of frustration. For example, let it be supposed that a builder does work which doubles in value by the date of frustration. and is then so severely damaged by fire that the contract is frustrated; the valuation of the residue must surely be made on the basis of the value as at the date of frustration. However, does this mean that, for the purposes of section 1 (3), the benefit is always to be valued as at the date of frustration? For example, if goods are trans-ferred and retained by the defendant till frustration when they have appreciated or depreciated in value, are they to be valued as at the date of frustration? The answer must, I think, generally speaking, be in the affirmative, for the sake of consistency. But this raises an acute problem in relation to the time value of money. Suppose that goods are supplied and sold, long before the date of frustration; does the principle that a benefit is to be valued as at the date of frustration require that allowance must be made for the use in the meanwhile of the money obtained by the disposal of the goods, in order to obtain a true valuation of the benefit as at the date of frustration? This was one of the most hotly debated matters before me, for the very good reason that in the present case it affects the valuation of the parties' respective benefits by many millions of dollars. It is very tempting to conclude that an allowance should be made for the time value of money, because it appears to lead to a more realistic valuation of the benefit as at the date of frustration; and, as will appear hereafter, an appropriate method for making such an allowance is available in the form of the net discounted cash flow system of accounting. But I have come to the conclusion that, as a matter of construction, this course is not open to me. First, the subsection limits the award to the value of the benefit obtained by the defendant; and it does not follow that, because the defendant has had the money over a period of time, he has in fact derived any benefit from it. Secondly, if an allowance was to be made for the time value of the money obtained by the defendant, a comparable allowance should be made in respect of expenses incurred by the defendant, i.e. in respect of the period between the date of incurring the expenditure and the date of frustration, and section 1 (3) (a) only contemplates that the court, in making an allowance for expenses, shall have regard to the "amount of [the] expenses." Thirdly, as I have already indicated, no allowance for the time value of money can be made under section 1 (2); and it would be inconsistent to make such an allowance under section 1 (3) but not under section 1 (2).

...

Finally, I should record that the court is required to have regard to the effect, in relation to the defendant's benefit, of the circumstances giving rise to the frustration of the contract. I have already given an example of how this may be relevant, in the case of building contracts; and I have recorded the fact that this provision has been the subject of criticism. There may, however, be circumstances where it would not be just to have regard to this factor – for example if, under a building contract, it was expressly agreed that the work in progress should be insured by the building-owner against risks which include the event which had the effect of frustrating the contract and damaging or destroying the work.

(e) *Assessment of the just sum*. The principle underlying the Act is prevention of the unjust enrichment of the defendant at the plaintiff's expense. Where, as in cases under section 1 (2), the benefit conferred on the defendant consists of payment of a sum of money, the plaintiff's expense and the defendant's enrichment are generally equal; and, subject to other relevant factors, the award of restitution will consist simply of an order for repayment of a like sum of money. But where the benefit does not consist of money, then the defendant's enrichment will rarely be equal to the plaintiff's expense. In such cases, where (as in the case of a benefit conferred under a contract thereafter frustrated) the benefit has been requested by the defendant, the basic measure of recovery in restitution is the reasonable value of the plain-tiff's performance – in a case of services, a quantum meruit or reasonable remuneration, and in a case of goods, a quantum valebat or reasonable price. Such cases are to be contrasted with cases where such a benefit has not been requested by the defendant. In the latter class of case, recovery is rare in restitution; but if the sole basis of recovery was that the defendant had been incontrovertibly benefited, it might be legitimate to limit recovery to the defendant's actual benefit – a limit which has (perhaps inappropriately) been imported by the legislature into section 1 (3) of the Act. However, under section 1 (3) as it stands, if the defendant's actual benefit is less than the just or reasonable sum which would otherwise be awarded to the plaintiff, the award must be reduced to a sum equal to the amount of the defendant's benefit.

A crucial question, upon which the Act is surprisingly silent, is this: what bearing do the terms of the contract, under which the plaintiff has acted, have upon the assessment of the just sum? ...[I]t is likely that in most cases [the contract rate] will impose an important limit upon the sum to be awarded – indeed it may well be the most relevant limit to an award under section 1 (3) of the Act. The legal basis of the limit may be section 2 (3) of the Act; but even if that subsection is inapplicable, it is open to the court, in an appropriate case, to give effect to such a limit in assessing the just sum to be awarded under section 1 (3), because in many cases it would be unjust to impose upon the defendant an obligation to make restitution under the subsection at higher than the contract rate.

(4) The effect of section 2 (3) of the Act

The court has always to bear in mind the provisions of section 2 (3) of the Act. It was submitted by Mr. Rokison that effect should only be given to this subsection where the relevant contractual provision was clearly intended to have effect in the event of the frustrating circumstances. I can see no good reason for so qualifying the express words of the subsection. In my judgment the effect of the subsection depends, as it expressly provides, simply upon applying the ordinary principles of construction. If the contract contains any provision which, upon the true construction of the contract, is intended to have effect in the circumstances specified in the subsection, then the court can only give effect to section 1 of the Act to such extent as is consistent with such provision.

Examples of such provisions may be terms which have the effect of precluding recovery of any award under the Act, or of limiting the amount of any such award, for example, by limiting the award to the contractual consideration or a rateable part thereof. Similarly, the parties may contract upon the terms that the plaintiff shall not be paid until the occurrence of an event, and by reason of the frustration of the contract that event does not or cannot occur, then, if upon a true construction of the contract the court concludes that the plaintiff has taken the risk of non-payment in the event of such frustration the court should make no award by virtue of section 2 (3) of the Act. Such may be the conclusion if the contract contains an express term imposing upon the plaintiff an obligation to insure against the consequences of the frustrating event. Another example considered in argument was a loan of money advanced to a businessman on the terms that it was to be repaid out of the profits of his business. Such a term should not automatically preclude an award in the event of frustration, for example, if the businessman is incapacitated the day after the loan is made; but if the business consists, for example, of a ship, which strikes a reef and sinks, then it may be that the court, having regard to the terms of the contract and the risk taken thereunder by the lender, would make no award. But in such cases the court should only refuse to make an award if it is satisfied that the plaintiff has, by the contract, taken the risk of the consequences of the frustrating event. The principle is the same as in those cases where the contract consideration controls the amount or basis of the award under the Act – the court should not act inconsistently with the contractual intention of the parties applicable in the events which have occurred. But, such cases apart, the court is free to make an award which differs from the anticipated contractual performance of the defendant. I have already referred to the fact that, under section 1 (2) at least, the effect of an award under the Act may be to rescue the plaintiff from a bad bargain. Again, the contract may provide that the plaintiff is to receive goods or services; the court may nevertheless make an award in money. The contract may provide for the plaintiff to receive money at a certain place or in a certain currency; frustration may render that impossible (for example, in a case of supervening illegality), and the court may make an award for payment which takes effect at a different place or in a different currency. Most striking of all, in most frustrated contracts under which the claim is made in respect of a benefit other than money, the time for payment will not yet have come – the contract, or a severable part of it, will be "entire" in the old strict sense of that term; I do not, however, consider that such a provision should automatically preclude an award under section 1 (3). If it were intended to do so, there would be few awards under section 1 (3), and the matter would surely be the subject of an express provision if it was the intention that so fundamental a qualification was to be imposed upon the power of the court under this subsection. Certainly, no such qualification is imposed in section 1 (2), and no such result can be achieved in relation to an award under that subsection since, generally speaking, the plaintiff is entitled to the return of his money. In my judgment, only if upon a true construction of the contract the plaintiff has contracted on the terms that he is to receive no payment in the event which has occurred, will the fact that the contract is "entire" have the effect of precluding an award under the Act.

NOTES AND QUESTIONS

1. The actual application of the principles to the facts of the case was complex. Robert Goff J first worked out the benefit received by the defendant (ie the end product of BP's services which was the enhancement in value of Hunt's concession) taking into account the effect of the frustrating event (the expropriation). The enhanced value of the concession, taking the expropriation into account, was assessed at $84,951,000. This was the ceiling of an award under section 1(3) but was not necessarily the just sum. To value the just sum, his Lordship first looked at the consideration BP was to receive under the contract for the benefits conferred on the defendant. This was in effect the reasonable value of BP's services (equivalent to a standard restitutionary quantum meruit) and was calculated at $98,105,146. Then he removed the value of the benefit actually received by BP which was 33m barrels of oil valued at $62,702,000. This left $35,403,146. As $35,403,146 was well below the ceiling of $84,951,000 that sum did not need to be further modified. $35,403,146 was therefore awarded as the just sum (subject to interest and currency adjustments). As will commonly be the case, valuing the benefit turned out not to be decisive because the just sum was assessed at a lower amount.

2. Despite his eminence as an expert on the English law of restitution (he was co-author with Professor Gareth Jones of the first English book on the subject) it has been argued by several commentators that Robert Goff J's analysis of section 1(3) was flawed. This is essentially because: (i) albeit reluctantly, he identified the benefit under section 1(3) as the end product of the services rather than the services themselves (assuming there is an end product); (ii) he interpreted section 1(3)(b) as meaning that there is no valuable benefit where a building under construction has been destroyed by fire. Yet section 1(3) states that one is concerned with whether a valuable benefit has been obtained *prior* to the frustrating event. Section 1(3)(b) should then come in as a discretionary matter for the court in assessing the just sum. On Robert Goff J's interpretation *Appleby v Myers*, above, 678, would necessarily remain good law. Is the better view that whether one would give any award to the builder in that sort of case

would be a matter for the court's discretion in deciding what was a just sum under section 1(3)(b)?

3.   Robert Goff J saw the proviso to section 1(2) as 'probably best rationalised as a statutory recognition of the defence of change of position' (above, 682). The defence of change of position is the central defence in the law of restitution, albeit that it was not authoritatively recognised by the House of Lords until 1991. Its basic role is to ensure that the recipient of an unjust enrichment does not have to make restitution where it has in good faith been disenriched (eg by suffering a detriment in reliance on its entitlement to the benefit). Some aspects of the proviso are, however, difficult to reconcile with a pure change of position defence (eg there can be compensation for expenses even though no money has been paid provided it was payable) and it may therefore be better to recognise that, while the Act is largely concerned to reverse unjust enrichment, it also permits (eg through the proviso to section 1(2)) some loss apportionment. It will be seen in the next case that Garland J did not derive any assistance from Robert Goff J's suggested rationale of the proviso.

Gamerco SA v ICM/Fair Warning (Agency) Ltd
[1995] 1 WLR 1226, Queen's Bench Division

The claimants, Spanish pop concert promoters, agreed in a contract with the defendants, the company behind the Guns N' Roses rock group, to arrange a concert by the group in the Athletico Madrid football stadium. The claimants paid the defendants $412,500 in advance under the contract. Five days before the concert, use of the stadium was banned by the public authorities because of concerns about the stadium's safety and the permit to hold the event was revoked. The concert therefore had to be cancelled. At the time of the cancellation, another $362,500 was due to be paid to the defendants. Both parties had incurred expenses in preparing for the concert. The claimants' expenses were agreed to be $450,000 and the defendants' expenses were found by Garland J to be $50,000. The claimants alleged that the contract had been frustrated and sought to recover their advance payment. The defendants counterclaimed for damages for breach of contract for the failure to hold the concert. Garland J held that the contract had been frustrated by the ban on the use of the stadium; and that, under section 1(2) of the 1943 Act, the claimants were entitled to restitution of the $412,000 paid without any deduction for the defendants' expenses under the proviso.

Garland J: The onus of establishing [the matters required by the proviso to section 1(2)] must lie on the defendant.

...

Various views have been advanced as to how the court should exercise its discretion [under the proviso] and these can be categorised as follows.

(1) *Total retention*. This view was advanced by the Law Revision Committee in 1939 (Cmd. 6009) on the questionable ground "that it is reasonable to assume that in stipulating for prepayment the payee intended to protect himself from loss under the contract." As the editor of Chitty on Contracts, 27th ed. (1994), vol. 1, p. 1141, para. 23-060, note 51, (Mr. E. G. McKendrick) comments: "He probably intends to protect himself against the possibility of

the other party's insolvency or default in payment." To this, one can add: "and secure his own cash flow."

In *BP Exploration Co (Libya) Ltd v. Hunt (No. 2)*...Robert Goff J. considered the principle of recovery under subsections (2) and (3) *[He set out two passages from Robert Goff J's judgment ((1)(c) and the middle part of (2)) set out above, 682, and continued:]* I do not derive any specific assistance from the *BP Exploration Co* case. There was no question of any change of position as a result of the plaintiffs' advance payment.

(2) *Equal division.* This was discussed by Professor Treitel in *Frustration and Force Majeure*, pp. 555-556, paras. 15-059 and 15-060. There is some attraction in splitting the loss, but what if the losses are very unequal? Professor Treitel considers statutory provisions in Canada and Australia but makes the point that unequal division is unnecessarily rigid and was rejected by the Law Revision Committee in the 1939 report to which reference has already been made. The parties may, he suggests, have had an unequal means of providing against the loss by insurers, but he appears to overlook subsection (5). It may well be that one party's expenses are entirely thrown away while the other is left with some realisable or otherwise usable benefit or advantage. Their losses may, as in the present case, be very unequal. Professor Treitel therefore favours the third view.

(3) *Broad discretion.* It is self-evident that any rigid rule is liable to produce injustice. The words, "if it considers it just to do so having regard to all the circumstances of the case," clearly confer a very broad discretion. Obviously the court must not take into account anything which is not "a circumstance of the case" or fail to take into account anything that is and then exercise its discretion rationally. I see no indication in the Act, the authorities or the relevant literature that the court is obliged to incline towards either total retention or equal division. Its task is to do justice in a situation which the parties had neither contemplated nor provided for, and to mitigate the possible harshness of allowing all loss to lie where it has fallen.

I have not found my task easy. ... In all the circumstances, and having particular regard to the plaintiffs' loss, I consider that justice is done by making no deduction under the proviso.

NOTES AND QUESTIONS

1. The effect of the decision is that the claimants were left to bear $37,500 wasted expenses and the defendants $50,000.

2. In brushing aside Robert Goff J's change of position rationale for the proviso, Garland J was in effect accepting that, within its conferral of a broad discretion to achieve justice, the proviso to section 1(2) encompasses loss apportionment. But while it is correct that the proviso does not equate to a pure change of position defence (see above, 688), it is also correct that any loss apportionment is arbitrarily limited by the requirements of the proviso: eg, it is essential that the party incurring the expenses had been paid in advance or had an entitlement to be paid prior to the frustrating event. The truth seems to be that the proviso is neither one thing nor the other and is the product of muddled thinking.

3. Garland J's reference to the Law Revision Committee is to the *Seventh Interim Report (Rule in Chandler v Webster)* (1939) Cmd 6009 which was the report upon which the 1943 Act was based.

4. **E McKendrick, 'Frustration, Restitution, and Loss Apportionment' in *Essays on the Law of Restitution* (ed A Burrows, 1991) 147,** writing before the *Gamerco* case, analyses the extent to which the 1943 Act conforms with restitutionary principles and considers whether it would be preferable to deal with the

consequences of frustration by loss apportionment rather than restitution. Restitution requires the giving back of a benefit. Loss apportionment looks at the losses of the parties and tries to distribute that loss fairly. Whilst finding that the Act by and large conforms to the former, McKendrick argues that the just solution is the latter. He suggests three arguments in favour of loss apportionment: (i) for each party to bear half the loss will be less economically damaging than for one party to bear all the loss; (ii) judges and legislators often want to take into account the reliance loss as can be seen by their attempts to stretch the concept of benefit (see British Columbian Frustrated Contracts Act section 5(1) for an extreme example); (iii) when a frustrating event has occurred, neither party has foreseen the event, assumed the risk of the event, or is at fault for the occurrence of the event. For the same author's detailed examination of the provisions of the 1943 Act, see also E McKendrick, 'The Consequences of Frustration—The Law Reform (Frustrated Contracts) Act 1943' in *Force Majeure and Frustration of Contract* (ed E McKendrick, 2nd edn, 1995) 223.

5. If you were recommending a reform of the proviso, would you opt for enacting a pure change of position defence or full loss apportionment or both or neither?

6. THE RELATIONSHIP BETWEEN COMMON MISTAKE AND FRUSTRATION

Having considered both common mistake (above, 625–649) and frustration, it will be clear that there are close links between the two doctrines. Both deal with the circumstances being, or becoming, different from what the parties thought; and both doctrines only come into play where the parties have not themselves dealt with the risk of the unexpected. It is therefore not surprising that in *The Great Peace* and other cases on common mistake (above, 629, 635–636), the courts have found it useful to refer to the law on frustration. It is the timing that is crucial in determining whether the relevant law to apply is common mistake or frustration. The former deals with circumstances being different at the time the contract is made; the latter with circumstances becoming different after the contract has been made. This essential difference of timing is made clear in the *Amalgamated Investment* case below.

Yet despite the similarities there are significant differences in the legal treatment of the two situations. The effects are obviously very different. Common mistake makes the contract void whereas frustration automatically terminates the contract. Restitution following a void contract is entirely a matter for the common law of restitution; restitution following a frustrated contract is governed by the 1943 Act. Equitable rectification is possible for common mistake but not for frustration. Moreover, it may be that the doctrine of common mistake is narrower than the doctrine of frustration so that the courts are less willing to allow parties to escape for matters being different at the time of the contract than when they subsequently become different. And in turn this may reflect the belief that, in entering contracts, parties should bear the risk of their mistakes more readily than they should bear the risk of subsequent events. After all, no one can know the future. In terms of legal reasoning, there is also the difference that we debate whether common mistake exists as a doctrine by reference to the same ideas that are used to debate the juristic basis of the accepted doctrine of frustration.

Amalgamated Investment & Property Co v John Walker & Sons Ltd
[1977] 1 WLR 164, Court of Appeal

The claimants bought from the defendants, for £1,700,000, a warehouse, which had originally been purpose-built to be used as a bonded warehouse and bottling factory for the defendants. The property was advertised and purchased on the assumption that it would be redeveloped. During negotiations the claimants inquired of the defendants whether the warehouse had been listed as a 'building of special architectural or historic interest'. The defendants replied in the negative. The day after the contract was made, the Minister for the Environment listed the building as one of special architectural or historic interest. The value of the warehouse dropped to around £200,000. The claimants argued that the contract should be rescinded for equitable common mistake or that it was terminated for frustration. Dismissing the claimants' appeal, it was held by the Court of Appeal that the relevant doctrine was that of frustration, not common mistake. This was because the listing occurred when the list was signed by the Minister and that was after the contract was made. But the listing of the building was not a frustrating event as this was an ordinary risk to be borne by any building owner and did not make the contract radically different.

Buckley LJ: For the application of the doctrine of mutual mistake as a ground for setting the contract aside, it is of course necessary to show that the mistake existed at the date of the contract; and so Mr. Balcombe [counsel for the purchasers] relies in that respect not upon the signing of the list by the officer who alone was authorised to sign it on behalf of the Secretary of State, but upon the decision of Miss Price [the member of staff at the Department of the Environment in charge of drawing up the list] to include the property in the list. That decision, although in fact it led to the signature of the list in the form in which it was eventually signed, was merely an administrative step in the carrying out of the operations of the branch of the ministry. ...The crucial date, in my judgment, is the date when the list was signed. It was then that the building became a listed building, and it was only then that the expectations of the parties (who no doubt both expected that this property would be capable of being developed, subject always of course to obtaining planning permission, without it being necessary to obtain listed building permission) were disappointed. ...In my judgment, there was no mutual mistake as to the circumstances surrounding the contract at the time when the contract was entered into. The only mistake that there was, was one which related to the expectation of the parties. They expected that the building would be subject only to ordinary town planning consent procedures and that expectation has been disappointed. But at the date when the contract was entered into, I cannot see that there is any ground for saying that the parties were then subject to some mutual mistake of fact relating to the circumstances surrounding the contract. Accordingly, for my part, I think that the judge's decision on that part of the case is one which should be upheld.

 ...

 I now turn to the alternative argument which has been presented to us in support of this appeal, which is upon frustration. Mr. Balcombe has relied upon what was said in the speeches in the House of Lords in *Davis Contractors Ltd. v. Fareham Urban District Council* [1956] A.C. 696, and it may perhaps be useful if I refer to what was said by Lord Radcliffe there...[*He cited passages from that speech set out above, 664, and continued:*] ...I have reached the conclusion that there are not here the necessary factual bases for holding that this contract has been frustrated. It seems to me that the risk of property being listed as property of architectural or historical interest is a risk which inheres in all ownership of buildings.

Sir John Pennycuick: [*having delivered a concurring judgment on commom mistake, he went on to discuss frustration and, after referring to Lord Radcliffe's speech in* Davis Contractors Ltd v Fareham UDC, *he concluded:*] The listing struck down the value of the property as might a fire or a compulsory purchase order or a number of other events. It seems to me, however, that the listing did not in any respect prevent the contract from being carried to completion according to its terms; that is to say, by payment of the balance of the purchase price and by conveyance of the property. The property is none the less the same property by reason that listing imposed a fetter upon its use. It seems to me impossible to bring the circumstances of the present case within the test enunciated by Lord Radcliffe. One cannot say that the circumstances in which performance, i.e. completion, will be called for would render that performance a thing radically different from that which was undertaken by the contract. On the contrary, completion, according to the terms of the contract, would be exactly what the purchasers promised to do, and of course the vendors.

Lawton LJ gave a concurring judgment.

NOTES AND QUESTIONS

1. The claimants were relying on *Solle v Butcher* to argue that the contract was voidable for equitable common mistake, the scope of which was wider than common mistake at common law. *Solle v Butcher* has since been overruled by the *Great Peace* case (see above, 643) so that there is now no equitable common mistake.

2. If the listing had taken place before the contract was made, would the contract have been void for common mistake? Even if on these facts, there would have been no difference in result between common mistake and frustration, is it always the case that there is no difference in scope between the two doctrines? In other words, are the tests for common mistake and frustration identical?

J Beatson, *Anson's Law of Contract* (28th edn, 2002) Ch 14
S Smith, *Atiyah's Introduction to the Law of Contract* (6th edn, 2005) 182–92

R Posner and A Rosenfield, 'Impossibility and Related Doctrines in Contract Law: An Economic Analysis' (1977) 6 *Journal of Legal Studies* 83
The authors take as their starting point that the purpose of contract law is to increase efficiency in transactions. Where a frustrating event occurs, the loss either: (i) lands on the promisor, if the contract is not discharged, as he has to perform or pay damages; or (ii) lands on the promisee, if the contract is discharged, as he does not receive what he bargained for. The economics of risk is used to determine which of (i) or (ii) should occur. One asks which of the two parties is the 'superior risk bearer', that is, which is more likely to be able to evade the risk efficiently either through avoidance, or, more importantly, insurance. Essentially, the party who has a cheaper route to evading the risk, should bear the cost if that risk eventuates.

E McKendrick, 'Force Majeure and Frustration—Their Relationship and a Comparative Assessment' in *Force Majeure and Frustration of Contract* (ed E McKendrick, 2nd edn, 1995) 33
McKendrick looks at the relationship between force majeure clauses and frustration; and sets out the limits of the narrow English doctrine. 'Since the doctrine of frustration operates within narrow confines, considerable advantages can be obtained by the incorporation into a contract of a suitably drafted *force majeure* clause' (at 52).

E McKendrick, '*Force Majeure* Clauses: the Gap between Doctrine and Practice' in *Contract Terms* (eds A Burrows and E Peel, 2007) 233
The author points out that force majeure clauses are far more important in practice than is the doctrine of frustration. Having examined two cases (*Thames Valley Power Limited v Total Gas & Power Limited* [2005] EWHC 2208 (Comm) and *The Super Servant Two*, above, 669), in the first of which reliance on a force majeure clause failed, in the second of which it partly succeeded, McKendrick examines the advantages of force majeure clauses. He concludes by exploring some general and specific issues relating to the drafting of force majeure clauses (eg whether it is better to rely on a general clause rather than listing specific events, how one should draft to cover where performance is uneconomic, how one can deal with negligence, and the extent to which UCTA 1977 and the Unfair Terms in Consumer Contracts Regulations 1999 may apply to force majeure clauses).

Principles of European Contract Law (eds O Lando and H Beale, 2000) 322–8, 379–84

Article 6:111: Change of Circumstances
(1) A party is bound to fulfil its obligations even if performance has become more onerous, whether because the cost of performance has increased or because the value of the performance it receives has diminished.

(2) If, however, performance of the contract becomes excessively onerous because of a change of circumstances, the parties are bound to enter into negotiations with a view to adapting the contract or terminating it, provided that:

(a) the change of circumstances occurred after the time of conclusion of the contract,

(b) the possibility of a change of circumstances was not one which could reasonably have been taken into account at the time of conclusion of the contract, and

(c) the risk of the change of circumstances is not one which, according to the contract, the party affected should be required to bear.

(3) If the parties fail to reach agreement within a reasonable period, the court may:

(a) terminate the contract at a date and on terms to be determined by the court ; or

(b) adapt the contract in order to distribute between the parties in a just and equitable manner the losses and gains resulting from the change of circumstances.

In either case, the court may award damages for the loss suffered through a party refusing to negotiate or breaking off negotiations contrary to good faith and fair dealing.

[There is no equivalent in the English law of frustration to this idea that, where subsequent events, outside the risk undertaken, make performance excessively onerous, the parties are bound to renegotiate. But parties may provide for this in 'hardship clauses': see above, 665, note 2.]

Article 8:108: Excuse Due to an Impediment
(1) A party's non-performance is excused if it proves that it is due to an impediment beyond its control and that it could not reasonably have been expected to take the impediment into account at the time of the conclusion of the contract, or to have avoided or overcome the impediment or its consequences.

(2) Where the impediment is only temporary the excuse provided by this article has effect for the period during which the impediment exists. However, if the delay amounts to a fundamental non-performance, the obligee may treat it as such.

(3) The non-performing party must ensure that notice of the impediment and of its effect on its ability to perform is received by the other party within a reasonable time after the non-performing party knew or ought to have known of these circumstances. The other party is entitled to damages for any loss resulting from the non-receipt of such notice.

[In contrast to (2), there is no concept in English law of partial frustration; and the English law on frustration has no equivalent to the requirement in (3) to give notice of the excusing impediment.]

14

Duress

In general terms, duress is concerned with (i) illegitimate pressure (almost always by threats, express or implied) that (ii) causes a person to enter into a contract.

Until relatively recently, the scope of duress was narrow and it was only duress of the person (ie threats of physical violence) that allowed escape from a contract (although, as shown in *Astley v Reynolds* (1731) 2 Stra 915, duress of goods has long triggered the restitution of *non-contractual* payments). However, in the 1970s the picture changed with the recognition that duress of goods and, more wide-ranging still, 'economic duress' renders a contract voidable. As we shall see, this exciting development has spawned a number of cases but several fundamental uncertainties in the law on economic duress remain unresolved. In particular:

(i)   As regards the illegitimacy of the pressure, is a threatened breach of contract always illegitimate? And when, if ever, is it illegitimate to threaten a lawful act (eg to refuse to enter into future contracts)?

(ii)   As regards causation, what is the test of causation and is it the same as for physical duress?

(iii) Is it a third additional requirement for economic duress that the threatened party had no reasonable alternative other than to give in to the threat?

Duress is like misrepresentation in that it renders a contract voidable ie liable to be rescinded. It would appear that bars to rescission (affirmation, lapse of time, counter-restitution being impossible, and third party rights) apply as they do to misrepresentation (see above, 550–555). In contrast to fraudulent and negligent misrepresentation, duress is not a tort and therefore does not trigger a liability in damages (although in some circumstances what is threatened may constitute, eg, the tort of trespass to the person or goods).

We divide our examination of the cases into two main sections. The first is duress of the person. The second, and by far the larger, is economic duress. We include some cases where there has been a *non-contractual* payment so that there is no rescission of a contract involved and one is simply concerned with the restitution of money paid. These are included primarily because what they say about duress appears to apply irrespective of whether one is rescinding a contract or merely seeking restitution of money paid.

Introductory reading: E McKendrick, *Contract Law* (7th edn, 2007) 17.2

1. DURESS OF THE PERSON

Barton v Armstrong [1976] AC 104, Privy Council

This concerned a power struggle for the control of a company called Landmark. The claimant (Barton) agreed in a deed to buy out the defendant's (Armstrong's) interest in Landmark. The claimant sought a declaration that that deed was 'void' on the grounds that he had entered into it because of the defendant's threat to have the claimant murdered. It was held by the trial judge that the defendant had indeed threatened to murder the claimant but that the primary reason the claimant had entered into the agreement was commercial necessity and therefore that duress could not be made out. The Court of Appeal of New South Wales dismissed the claimant's appeal. In allowing the claimant's appeal from that decision, the Privy Council, by a majority, held that it was sufficient to establish duress that the threat was *a reason* for the claimant entering into the contract even though he might well have entered into the contract irrespective of the defendant's threat.

Lord Cross of Chelsea (delivering the judgment on behalf of himself, **Lord Kilbrandon** and **Sir Garfield Barwick**): Their Lordships turn now to consider the question of law which provoked a difference of opinion in the Court of Appeal Division. It is hardly surprising that there is no direct authority on the point, for if A threatens B with death if he does not execute some document and B, who takes A's threats seriously, executes the document it can be only in the most unusual circumstances that there can be any doubt whether the threats operated to induce him to execute the document. But this is a most unusual case and the findings of fact made below do undoubtedly raise the question whether it was necessary for Barton in order to obtain relief to establish that he would not have executed the deed in question but for the threats. ...There is an obvious analogy between setting aside a disposition for duress or undue influence and setting it aside for fraud. ...Had Armstrong made a fraudulent misrepresentation to Barton for the purpose of inducing him to execute the deed of January 17, 1967, the answer to the problem which has arisen would have been clear. If it were established that Barton did not allow the representation to affect his judgment then he could not make it a ground for relief even though the representation was designed and known by Barton to be designed to affect his judgment. If on the other hand Barton relied on the misrepresentation Armstrong could not have defeated his claim to relief by showing that there were other more weighty causes which contributed to his decision to execute the deed, for in this field the court does not allow an examination into the relative importance of contributory causes.

...

Their Lordships think that the same rule should apply in cases of duress and that if Armstrong's threats were "a" reason for Barton's executing the deed he is entitled to relief even though he might well have entered into the contract if Armstrong had uttered no threats to induce him to do so.

...

If Barton had to establish that he would not have made the agreement but for Armstrong's threats, then their Lordships would not dissent from the view that he had not

made out his case. But no such onus lay on him. On the contrary it was for Armstrong to establish, if he could, that the threats which he was making and the unlawful pressure which he was exerting for the purpose of inducing Barton to sign the agreement and which Barton knew were being made and exerted for this purpose in fact contributed nothing to Barton's decision to sign. The judge has found that during the 10 days or so before the documents were executed Barton was in genuine fear that Armstrong was planning to have him killed if the agreement was not signed. His state of mind was described by the judge as one of "very real mental torment" and he believed that his fears would be at end when once the documents were executed. ...It is true that on the facts as their Lordships assume them to have been Armstrong's threats may have been unnecessary, but it would be unrealistic to hold that they played no part in making Barton decide to execute the documents. The proper inference to be drawn from the facts found is, their Lordships think, that though it may be that Barton would have executed the documents even if Armstrong had made no threats and exerted no unlawful pressure to induce him to do so the threats and unlawful pressure in fact contributed to his decision to sign the documents and to recommend their execution by Landmark and the other parties to them.
...

In the result therefore the appeal should be allowed and a declaration made that the deeds in question were executed by Barton under duress and are void so far as concerns him.

Lord Wilberforce and **Lord Simon of Glaisdale** (joint dissenting judgment): The reason why we do not agree with the majority decision is, briefly, that we regard the issues in this case as essentially issues of fact, issues moreover of a character particularly within the sphere of the trial judge bearing, as they do, upon motivation and credibility. On all important issues, clear findings have been made by Street J. and concurred in by the Court of Appeal either unanimously or by majority. Accepted rules of practice and, such rules apart, sound principle should, in our opinion, prevent a second court of appeal from reviewing them in the absence of some miscarriage of justice, or some manifest and important error of law or misdirection. In our view no such circumstance exists in this case.

...

The action is one to set aside an apparently complete and valid agreement on the ground of duress. The basis of the plaintiff's claim is, thus, that though there was apparent consent there was no true consent to the agreement: that the agreement was not voluntary.

This involves consideration of what the law regards as voluntary, or its opposite; for in life, including the life of commerce and finance, many acts are done under pressure, sometimes overwhelming pressure, so that one can say that the actor had no choice but to act. Absence of choice in this sense does not negate consent in law: for this the pressure must be one of a kind which the law does not regard as legitimate. Thus, out of the various means by which consent may be obtained – advice, persuasion, influence, inducement, representation, commercial pressure – the law has come to select some which it will not accept as a reason for voluntary action: fraud, abuse of relation of confidence, undue influence, duress or coercion. In this the law, under the influence of equity, has developed from the old common law conception of duress – threat to life and limb – and it has arrived at the modern generalisation expressed by Holmes J. – "subjected to an improper motive for action": *Fairbanks v. Snow*, 13 N.E. Reporter 596, 598.

In an action such as the present, then, the first step required of the plaintiff is to show that some illegitimate means of persuasion was used. That there were threats to Barton's life was found by the judge...

The next necessary step would be to establish the relationship between the illegitimate means used and the action taken. For the purposes of the present case (reserving our opinion as to cases which may arise in other contexts) we are prepared to accept, as the formula most favourable to the appellant, the test proposed by the majority, namely, that the illegitimate means used was *a* reason (not *the* reason, nor the *predominant* reason nor the *clinching* reason) why the complainant acted as he did. We are also prepared to accept that a decisive answer is not obtainable by asking the question whether the contract would have been made even if there had been no threats because, even if the answer to this question is affirmative, that does not prove that the contract was not made because of the threats.

Assuming therefore that what has to be decided is whether the illegitimate means used was a reason why the complainant acted as he did, it follows that his reason for acting must (unless the case is one of automatism which this is not) be a conscious reason so that the complainant can give evidence of it: "I acted because I was forced." If his evidence is honest and accepted, that will normally conclude the issue. If, moreover, he gives evidence, it is necessary for the court to evaluate his evidence by testing it against his credibility and his actions.

...

We think it important to notice how little of Barton's case was accepted: how much of it – indeed almost the whole of his essential contentions – failed. In general the judge found that his case was reconstructed after the event: it was not until nearly a year after signing the agreement in January 1967 that he brought forward his claim of duress.

...

Street J. had found that Barton was motivated to enter into the agreement by sheer commercial necessity. By this he meant that the company would survive and be profitable without Armstrong, but not with him, and that the likelihood and extent of such profit justified the price to be paid to get rid of Armstrong. He meant also, as his judgment shows, that Barton was motivated by a desire for uncontested control over the business, rather than a sharing of it with Armstrong.

This finding and the evidence supporting it was carefully scrutinised by the Court of Appeal, and, in the end, endorsed. ...

The judge's findings were also accepted, after careful examination by Taylor A.-J.A. – "... the conclusion," he finds, "that Barton entered into this agreement because he wanted to and from commercial motives only is, I think undoubtedly correct."

The appeal cannot succeed unless these most explicit findings are overturned. We consider that no basis exists for doing so.

NOTES AND QUESTIONS

1. On what basis did Lords Wilberforce and Simon dissent? Did they differ from the majority as to the law?
2. There was no difficulty in this case in establishing that the threat was illegit-imate. Rather the importance of the case—apart from it being a rare modern example of duress of the person—is in relation to causation. All their Lordships agreed that it was enough for duress that the murder threat was a reason (or a conscious reason) for entering into the deed. This was contrasted with 'but for' causation which the claimant did not need to satisfy. On whom was the burden of proof in relation to establishing the 'a reason' test?
3. Is the approach in this case consistent with the test for reliance in misrepresen-tation cases (see above, 547–548)?
4. The talk of duress rendering the deed 'void' is confusing. Subsequent cases have clarified that duress renders a contract voidable, not void. Perhaps the best way of interpreting this reference to the deed being void is to say that the declaration sought was that the claimant had validly rescinded the deed so that it had become, by his action, void.

2. ECONOMIC DURESS

(1) Threats to Break (or to Induce Another to Break) a Contract

North Ocean Shipping Co Ltd v Hyundai Construction Co Ltd, The Atlantic Baron [1979] QB 705, Queen's Bench Division

By a shipbuilding contract, the defendant builders agreed to build a ship for the claimant owners for the price of $30,950,000. The price was payable in five instalments and the builders were required to give security for repayment of instalments in the event of their non-performance. Subsequently the US dollar was devalued by 10 per cent and the builders threatened to end the contract unless they were paid an extra 10 per cent. The owners (who were negotiating a favourable charter of the ship with Shell) agreed to this in June 1973 but 'without prejudice' to their rights and provided the builders agreed to increase their repayment security in relation to the extra amount. The ship was completed and delivered in November 1974. In July 1975, the owners demanded the return of the extra 10 per cent paid. They argued that the June 1973 agreement to pay the extra was unsupported by consideration and invalid for duress. Mocatta J held that the June agreement was supported by consideration and that, while economic duress had been made out, the owners had lost the right to rescind the contract for duress by affirming the contract.

Mocatta J: There has been considerable discussion in the books whether, if an agreement is made under duress of goods to pay a sum of money and there is some consideration for the agreement, the excess sum can be recovered. …[In] *Skeate v. Beale* (1841) 11 Ad. & El. 983 [i]t was … said by Lord Denman C.J. that an agreement was not void because made under duress of goods, the distinction between that case and the cases of money paid to recover goods wrongfully seized being said to be obvious in that the agreement was not compulsorily but voluntarily entered into. … Kerr J. in *Occidental Worldwide Investment Corporation v. Skibs A/S Avanti (The Siboen and The Sibotre)* [1976] 1 Lloyd's Rep. 293, 335, gave strong expression to the view that the suggested distinction based on *Skeate v. Beale* would not be observed today. He said, though obiter, that *Skeate v. Beale* would not justify a decision: "For instance, if I should be compelled to sign a lease or some other contract for a nominal but legally sufficient consideration under an imminent threat of having my house burnt down or a valuable picture slashed, though without any threat of physical violence to anyone, I do not think that the law would uphold the agreement."

…

Before proceeding further it may be useful to summarise the conclusions I have so far reached. First, I do not take the view that the recovery of money paid under duress other than to the person is necessarily limited to duress to goods falling within one of the categories hitherto established by the English cases. … Secondly, from this it follows that the compulsion may take the form of "economic duress" if the necessary facts are proved. A threat to break a contract may amount to such "economic duress." Thirdly, if there has been such a form of duress leading to a contract for consideration, I think that contract is a voidable one which can be avoided and the excess money paid under it recovered.

I think the facts found in this ease do establish that the agreement to increase the price by 10 per cent. reached at the end of June 1973 was caused by what may be called "economic duress." The Yard were adamant in insisting on the increased price without having any legal justification for so doing and the owners realised that the Yard would not accept anything other than an unqualified agreement to the increase. The owners might have claimed damages in arbitration against the Yard with all the inherent unavoidable uncertainties of litigation, but in view of the position of the Yard vis-à-vis their relations with Shell it would be unreasonable to hold that this is the course they should have taken: see *Astley v. Reynolds* (1731) 2 Str. 915. The owners made a very reasonable offer of arbitration coupled with security for any award in the Yard's favour that might be made, but this was refused. They then made their agreement, which can truly I think be said to have been made under compulsion, by the telex of June 28 without prejudice to their rights. I do not consider the Yard's ignorance of the Shell charter material. It may well be that had they known of it they would have been even more exigent.

If I am right in the conclusion reached with some doubt earlier that there was consideration for the 10 per cent. increase agreement reached at the end of June 1973, and it be right to regard this as having been reached under a kind of duress in the form of economic pressure, then what is said in *Chitty on Contracts,* 24th ed. (1977), vol. 1, para. 442, p. 207, to which both counsel referred me, is relevant, namely, that a contract entered into under duress is voidable and not void:

> "... consequently a person who has entered into a contract under duress, may either affirm or avoid such contract after the duress has ceased; and if he has so voluntarily acted under it with a full knowledge of all the circumstances he may be held bound on the ground of ratification, or if, after escaping from the duress, he takes no steps to set aside the transaction, he may be found to have affirmed it."

...

The owners were...free from the duress on November 27, 1974, and took no action by way of protest or otherwise between their important telex of June 28, 1973, and their formal claim for the return of the excess 10 per cent. paid of July 30, 1975, when they nominated their arbitrator. ... I have come to the conclusion that the important points here are that since there was no danger at th[e] time [of delivery] in registering a protest, the final payments were made without any qualification and were followed by a delay until July 31, 1975, before the owners put forward their claim, the correct inference to draw, taking an objective view of the facts, is that the action and inaction of the owners can only be regarded as an affirmation of the variation in June 1973 of the terms of the original contract by the agreement to pay the additional 10 per cent.

NOTES AND QUESTIONS

1.   The duress argument failed in this case only because of the owners' affirmation of the contract when free of the duress. What was the illegitimate threat?

2.   This judgment was the first in which an English judge expressly accepted 'economic duress'. However, without using that term, Kerr J in *Occidental Worldwide Investment Corp v Skibs A/S Avanti, The Siboen and The Sibotre* [1976] 1 Lloyd's Rep 293 had in effect accepted economic duress by accepting that a threatened breach of contract could constitute duress, albeit that on the facts there was no duress because there had been no 'coercion of [the] will so as to vitiate...consent' (at 336). Note also that, in the obiter dicta cited by Mocatta J, Kerr J had made clear that, contrary to *Skeate v Beale* (1840) 11 Ad & El, 983, duress of goods (ie threats made in relation to a person's goods) as well as duress to the person can render a contract voidable. Given the acceptance of economic duress, one can regard duress of goods as merely a type of economic duress.

3.   On consideration, Mocatta J applied the traditional rule of *Stilk v Myrick* (above, 104) that a promise to perform a pre-existing contractual duty is not

good consideration for the promise of extra payment. However, the builders had here promised to do more than their pre-existing duty by agreeing to provide repayment security for the extra amount. See also above, 105, note 3.

PaO On v Lau Yiu Long [1980] AC 614, Privy Council

For the facts, see above, 93–94.

Lord Scarman (giving the judgment of himself, **Lord Wilberforce**, **Viscount Dilhorne**, **Lord Simon of Glaisdale** and **Lord Salmon**): Duress, whatever form it takes, is a coercion of the will so as to vitiate consent. Their Lordships agree with the observation of Kerr J. in *Occidental Worldwide Investment Corporation v. Skibs A/S Avanti* [1976] 1 Lloyd's Rep. 293, 336 that in a contractual situation commercial pressure is not enough. There must be present some factor "which could in law be regarded as a coercion of his will so as to vitiate his consent." This conception is in line with what was said in this Board's decision in *Barton v. Armstrong* [1976] A.C. 104, 121 by Lord Wilberforce and Lord Simon of Glaisdale – observations with which the majority judgment appears to be in agreement. In determining whether there was a coercion of will such that there was no true consent, it is material to inquire whether the person alleged to have been coerced did or did not protest; whether, at the time he was allegedly coerced into making the contract, he did or did not have an alternative course open to him such as an adequate legal remedy; whether he was independently advised; and whether after entering the contract he took steps to avoid it. All these matters are...relevant in determining whether he acted voluntarily or not.

In the present case there is unanimity amongst the judges below that there was no coercion of [Lau's] will. In the Court of Appeal the trial judge's finding...that [Lau] considered the matter thoroughly, chose to avoid litigation, and formed the opinion that the risk in giving the guarantee was more apparent than real was upheld. In short, there was commercial pressure, but no coercion. Even if this Board was disposed, which it is not, to take a different view, it would not substitute its opinion for that of the judges below on this question of fact.

It is, therefore, unnecessary for the Board to embark upon an inquiry into the question whether English law recognises a category of duress known as "economic duress." But, since the question has been fully argued in this appeal, their Lordships will indicate very briefly the view which they have formed. At common law money paid under economic compulsion could be recovered in an action for money had and received: *Astley v. Reynolds* (1731) 2 Str. 915. The compulsion had to be such that the party was deprived of "his freedom of exercising his will" (see p. 916). It is doubtful, however, whether at common law any duress other than duress to the person sufficed to render a contract voidable: see *Blackstone's Commentaries*, Book 1, 12th ed. pp. 130-131 and *Skeate v. Beale* (1841) 11 Ad. & E. 983. American law (*Williston on Contracts*, 3rd ed.) now recognises that a contract may be avoided on the ground of economic duress. The commercial pressure alleged to constitute such duress must, however, be such that the victim must have entered the contract against his will, must have had no alternative course open to him, and must have been confronted with coercive acts by the party exerting the pressure: *Williston on Contracts*, 3rd ed., vol. 13 (1970), section 1603. American judges pay great attention to such evidential matters as the effectiveness of the alternative remedy available, the fact or absence of protest, the availability of independent advice, the benefit received, and the speed with which the victim has sought to avoid the contract. Recently two English judges have recognised that commercial pressure may constitute duress the pressure of which can render a contract voidable: Kerr J. in *Occidental Worldwide Investment Corporation v. Skibs A/S Avanti* [1976] 1 Lloyd's Rep. 293 and Mocatta J. in *North Ocean Shipping Co. Ltd. v. Hyundai Construction Co. Ltd.* [1979] Q.B. 705. Both stressed that the pressure must be such that the victim's consent to the contract was not a voluntary act on his part. In their Lordships' view, there is nothing contrary to principle in recognising economic duress as a factor which may render a contract voidable, provided always that the basis of such recognition is that it must amount to a coercion of will, which vitiates consent. It must be shown that the payment made or the contract entered into was not a voluntary act.

NOTES AND QUESTIONS

1. The Privy Council here confirmed the view taken in *Occidental Worldwide Investment Corp v Skibs A/S Avanti* (above, 700 note 2) and *North Ocean Shipping Co Ltd v Hyundai Construction Co Ltd* (above, 699) that 'economic duress' as well as duress of the person can render a contract voidable.
2. Did Lord Scarman ignore or downplay the 'illegitimacy of the pressure' aspect of duress by focussing on whether there had been a 'coercion of the will so as to vitiate consent'?
3. The relevant threat in this case was that, unless the defendants agreed to the guarantee, the claimants would not complete the main contract with Fu Chip. Was that threat illegitimate? Is a threatened breach of contract always illegitimate?

Universe Tankships of Monrovia v International Transport Workers Federation, The Universe Sentinel [1983] 1 AC 366, House of Lords

The claimants' ship, the *Universe Sentinel*, had been 'blacked' by the defendant trade union while it was docked at Milford Haven. The blacking comprised procuring tugmen to refuse to operate their tugs in breach of their contracts of employment with the Harbour Authority. In order to lift the blacking, the claimants, inter alia, agreed to pay and paid $6480 into the defendant's seamen's welfare fund. Having sailed from Milford Haven the claimants sought to recover the money paid on two grounds. The first, which does not here concern us, was that the money had been the subject-matter of a failed trust. The second was that it was paid under economic duress. The defendant admitted that, subject to a trade dispute immunity, it had been paid under economic duress. It argued, however, that it was protected by virtue of the immunity against torts conferred by sections 13 and 29 of the Trade Union and Labour Relations Act 1974 because the threat had been made in connection with a trade dispute. The House of Lords by a majority (Lord Scarman and Lord Brandon dissenting) held that the defendant did not have the immunity it asserted and that the money was therefore recoverable for economic duress.

Lord Diplock: My Lords, I turn to the second ground on which repayment of the $6,480 is claimed, which I will call the duress point. It is not disputed that the circumstances in which I.T.F. demanded that the shipowners should enter into the special agreement and the typescript agreement and should pay the moneys of which the latter documents acknowledge receipt, amounted to economic duress upon the shipowners; that is to say, it is conceded that the financial consequences to the shipowners of the *Universe Sentinel* continuing to be rendered off-hire under her time charter to Texaco, while the blacking continued, were so catastrophic as to amount to a coercion of the shipowners' will which vitiated their consent to those agreements and to the payments made by them to I.T.F. This concession makes it unnecessary for your Lordships to use the instant appeal as the occasion for a general consideration of the developing law of economic duress as a ground for treating contracts as voidable and obtaining restitution of money paid under economic duress as money had and received to the plaintiffs' use. That economic duress may constitute a ground for such redress was recognised, albeit obiter, by the Privy Council in *PaO On v. Lau Yiu Long* [1980] A.C. 614. The Board in that case referred with approval to two judgments at first instance in the commercial court which recognised that commercial pressure may constitute duress: one by Kerr J. in *Occidental Worldwide Investment Corporation v. Skibs A/S Avanti* [1976] 1 Lloyd's Rep. 293, the other by Mocatta J. in *North Ocean Shipping Co. Ltd. v. Hyundai Construction Co. Ltd.* [1979] Q.B. 705, which traces the development of this branch of the law from its origin in the eighteenth and early nineteenth-century cases.

It is, however, in my view crucial to the decision of the instant appeal to identify the rationale of this development of the common law. It is not that the party seeking to avoid the contract which he has entered into with another party, or to recover money that he has paid to another party in response to a demand, did not know the nature or the precise terms of the contract at the time when he entered into it or did not understand the purpose for which the payment was demanded. The rationale is that his apparent consent was induced by pressure exercised upon him by that other party which the law does not regard as legitimate, with the consequence that the consent is treated in law as revocable unless approbated either expressly or by implication after the illegitimate pressure has ceased to operate on his mind. It is a rationale similar to that which underlies the avoidability of contracts entered into and the recovery of money exacted under colour of office, or under undue influence or in consequence of threats of physical duress.

Commercial pressure, in some degree, exists wherever one party to a commercial transaction is in a stronger bargaining position than the other party. It is not, however, in my view, necessary, nor would it be appropriate in the instant appeal, to enter into the general question of the kinds of circumstances, if any, in which commercial pressure, even though it amounts to a coercion of the will of a party in the weaker bargaining position, may be treated as legitimate and, accordingly, as not giving rise to any legal right of redress. In the instant appeal the economic duress complained of was exercised in the field of industrial relations to which very special considerations apply.

...

The use of economic duress to induce another person to part with property or money is not a tort per se; the form that the duress takes may, or may not, be tortious. The remedy to which economic duress gives rise is not an action for damages but an action for restitution of property or money exacted under such duress and the avoidance of any contract that had been induced by it; but where the particular form taken by the economic duress used is itself a tort, the restitutional remedy for money had and received by the defendant to the plaintiff's use is one which the plaintiff is entitled to pursue as an alternative remedy to an action for damages in tort.

In extending into the field of industrial relations the common law concept of economic duress and the right to a restitutionary remedy for it which is currently in process of development by judicial decisions, this House would not, in my view, be exercising the restraint that is appropriate to such a process if it were so to develop the concept that, by the simple expedient of "waiving the tort," a restitutionary remedy for money had and received is made enforceable in cases in which Parliament has, over so long a period of years, manifested its preference for a public policy that a particular kind of tortious act should be legitimised in the sense that I am using that expression.

It is only in this indirect way that the provisions of the Trade Union and Labour Relations Act 1974 are relevant to the duress point. The immunities from liability in tort provided by sections 13 and 14 are not directly applicable to the shipowners' cause of action for money had and received. Nevertheless, these sections, together with the definition of trade dispute in section 29, afford an indication, which your Lordships should respect, of where public policy requires that the line should be drawn between what kind of commercial pressure by a trade union upon an employer in the field of industrial relations ought to be treated as legitimised despite the fact that the will of the employer is thereby coerced, and what kind of commercial pressure in that field does amount to economic duress that entitles the employer victim to restitutionary remedies.

Lord Scarman (dissenting): It is, I think, already established law that economic pressure can in law amount to duress; and that duress, if proved, not only renders voidable a transaction into which a person has entered under its compulsion but is actionable as a tort, if it causes damage or loss: *Barton v. Armstrong* [1976] A.C. 104 and *PaO On v. Lau Yiu Long* [1980] A.C. 614. The authorities upon which these two cases were based reveal two elements in the wrong of duress: (1) pressure amounting to compulsion of the will of the victim; and (2) the illegitimacy of the pressure exerted. There must be pressure, the practical effect of which is compulsion or the absence of choice. Compulsion is variously described in the authorities as coercion or the vitiation of consent. The classic case of duress is, however, not the lack of will to submit but the victim's intentional submission arising from the realisation that there is no other practical choice open to him. This is the thread of principle which links the early law of duress (threat to life or limb) with later developments when the law came also to recognise as duress first the threat to property and now the threat to a man's business or trade. ...

The absence of choice can be proved in various ways, e.g. by protest, by the absence of independent advice, or by a declaration of intention to go to law to recover the money paid or the property transferred...But none of these evidential matters goes to the essence of duress. The victim's silence will not assist the bully, if the lack of any practicable choice but to submit is proved. The present case is an excellent illustration. There was no protest at the time, but only a determination to do whatever was needed as rapidly as possible to release the ship. Yet nobody challenges the judge's finding that the owner acted under compulsion. He put it thus [1981] I.C.R. 129, 143:

> "It was a matter of the most urgent commercial necessity that the plaintiffs should regain the use of their vessel. They were advised that their prospects of obtaining an injunction were minimal, the vessel would not have been released unless the payment was made, and they sought recovery of the money with sufficient speed once the duress had terminated."

The real issue in the appeal is, therefore, as to the second element in the wrong duress: was the pressure applied by the I.T.F. in the circumstances of this case one which the law recognises as legitimate? For, as Lord Wilberforce and Lord Simon of Glaisdale said in *Barton v. Armstrong* [1976] A.C. 104, 121D: "the pressure must be one of a kind which the law does not regard as legitimate."

As the two noble and learned Lords remarked at p. 121D, in life, including the life of commerce and finance, many acts are done "under pressure, sometimes overwhelming pressure": but they are not necessarily done under duress. That depends on whether the circumstances are such that the law regards the pressure as legitimate.

In determining what is legitimate two matters may have to be considered. The first is as to the nature of the pressure. In many cases this will be decisive, though not in every case. And so the second question may have to be considered, namely, the nature of the demand which the pressure is applied to support.

The origin of the doctrine of duress in threats to life or limb, or to property, suggests strongly that the law regards the threat of unlawful action as illegitimate, whatever the demand. Duress can, of course, exist even if the threat is one of lawful action: whether it does so depends upon the nature of the demand. Blackmail is often a demand supported by a threat to do what is lawful, e.g. to report criminal conduct to the police. ...

The present is a case in which the nature of the demand determines whether the pressure threatened or applied, i.e. the blacking, was lawful or unlawful. If it was unlawful, it is conceded that the owner acted under duress and can recover. If it was lawful, it is conceded that there was no duress and the sum sought by the owner is irrecoverable. The lawfulness or otherwise of the demand depends upon whether it was an act done in contemplation or furtherance of a trade dispute. If it was, it would not be actionable in tort: section 13 (1) of the Act. Although no question of tortious liability arises in this case and section 13 (1) is not, therefore, directly in point, it is not possible, in my view, to say of acts which are protected by statute from suit in tort that they nevertheless can amount to duress. Parliament having enacted that such acts are not actionable in tort, it would be inconsistent with legislative policy to say that, when the remedy sought is not damages for tort but recovery of money paid, they become unlawful.

Lords Cross and **Russell** delivered speeches concurring with Lord Diplock. **Lord Brandon** delivered a dissenting speech.

NOTES AND QUESTIONS

1. The difference between the majority and minority (not set out above) turned on matters outside the direct ambit of the law of contract, namely the application of the 'trade dispute' defence which is a statutory defence to certain types of tort.
2. This decision is important for our purposes for what it lays down generally on the law of economic duress. Both Lords Diplock and Scarman stressed the importance of the illegitimacy of the threat; and they indicated that, in one sense, the claimant does consent or choose to give in to the threat. One must, therefore, be careful about 'no consent' or 'overborne will' rationalisations of economic duress.
3. In contrast to most cases on economic duress, the relevant threat in this case was not of a breach of contract by the threatening party. Rather it was a threat to continue the blacking of the ship by inducing the tug men to break their contracts. That was an illegitimate threat in the majority's view because the 'trade dispute' defence was not made out.
4. Was the payment in this case made under a contract? Does the scope of economic duress differ according to whether a payment that the threatened party is seeking to recover was paid under a contract or not?
5. Lord Scarman took the unconventional view that economic duress is itself a tort. This was not supported by Lord Diplock who, more accurately, stated that the form the duress takes may, or may not, be tortious.
6. All their Lordships took the view that the claim here being brought was not a claim in tort. Why, then, was the 'trade dispute' defence relevant?
7. Do not be confused by Lord Diplock's reference to 'waiving the tort'. For explanation of that difficult terminology see A Burrows, *The Law of Restitution* (2nd edn, 2002) 462–3.

B & S Contracts & Design Ltd v Victor Green Publications Ltd
[1984] ICR 419, Court of Appeal

The claimants contracted to erect stands for the defendants at Olympia for an exhibition. There was a 'force majeure' clause in the contract protecting the claimants against the effects of, eg, strikes provided they made every effort to carry out the contract. The claimants' workforce threatened to go on strike unless they were paid

£9000. The claimants offered them half (£4500) but this was rejected. The defendants (represented by Mr Barnes) offered to help by loaning the claimants (represented by Mr Fenech) the balance of £4500 but the claimants rejected this and informed the defendants that they would not be able to perform the contract unless the defendants paid them £4500 outright. The defendants therefore paid £4500 but, after the contract had been performed, deducted it from the contract price and paid the balance only. The claimants sued for the £4500 as money owing under the contract. The Court of Appeal, dismissing the claimants' appeal, held that the £4500 was recoverable by the defendants as having been paid under economic duress.

Eveleigh LJ: The matters that have to be established in order to substantiate a claim for the return of money on the ground that it was paid under duress have been stated in a number of different ways. ... For the purpose of this case it is sufficient to say that if the claimant has been influenced against his will to pay money under the threat of unlawful damage to his economic interest he will be entitled to claim that money back, and as I understand it that proposition was not dissented from.

In this case the plaintiffs say that there was no threat; that Mr. Fenech was really stating the obvious, stating the factual situation, namely, that unless they could retain the workforce they would be unable to perform their contract. I have had some difficulty in deciding whether or not the evidence in this case did disclose a threat, but on a full reading of the evidence of Mr. Fenech and Mr. Barnes and the cross-examination of Mr. Fenech I have come to the conclusion that the judge was right in the way in which he put it. There was here, as I understand the evidence, a veiled threat although there was no specific demand, and this conclusion is very much supported, as I see it, by Mr. Barnes's reaction, which must have been apparent to Mr. Fenech when Mr. Barnes said, "You have got me over a barrel." On 18 April what was happening was this. Mr. Fenech was in effect saying, "We are not going on unless you are prepared to pay another £4,500 in addition to the contract price," and it was clear at that stage that there was no other way for Mr. Barnes to avoid the consequences that would ensue if the exhibition could not be held from his stands than by paying the £4,500 to secure the workforce. But, the plaintiffs now say, "Even so, this was not an unlawful threat or a threat of unlawful action because seeing that there was a strike the strike clause – the force majeure clause – applied and the plaintiffs were entitled to take advantage of that clause and to cancel the contract, and so there was here no threat of unlawful action."... [We] are concerned with the words of the particular clause, and that clause begins, "Every effort will be made to carry out any contract," and the question, to my mind, in this case is whether or not every effort was made to carry out that contract in the face of the strike. ...

...I have come to the conclusion that every effort was not made to perform this contract, and consequently reliance cannot be placed upon that force majeure clause.

Griffiths LJ: I agree. The law on economic pressure creating a situation which will be recognised as duress is in the course of development, and it is clear that many difficult decisions lie ahead of the courts. Many commercial contracts are varied during their currency because the parties are faced with changing circumstances during the performance of the contract, and it is certainly not on every occasion when one of the parties unwillingly agrees to a variation that the law would consider that he had acted by reason of duress. The cases will have to be examined in the light of their particular circumstances. But two recent decisions of the highest authority – the decision of the Privy Council in *PaO On v. Lau Yiu Long* [1980] A.C. 614 and *Universe Tankships Inc. of Monrovia v. International Transport Workers Federation* [1982] I.C.R. 262 – establish that a threatened breach of contract may impose such economic pressure that the law will recognise that a payment made as a result of the threatened breach is recoverable on the grounds of duress.

The facts of this case appear to me to be as follows. The plaintiffs intended to break their contract, subject to the effect of the force majeure clause, by allowing their workforce to walk off the job in circumstances in which they could not possibly replace it with another workforce. The defendants offered to advance the sum of £4,500 on the contract price, which would have enabled the plaintiffs to pay the men a sufficient extra sum of money to induce them to remain on the job. The plaintiffs refused this sum of money. There is no question that they refused to pay as a matter of principle. They refused to pay because they did not want to reduce the sum they would receive for the contract. They said to the defendants, "If you will give us £4,500 we will complete the contract." The defendants, faced with this demand, were in an impossible position. If they refused to hand over the sum of £4,500 they would not be able to erect the stands in this part of the exhibition, which would have clearly caused grave damage to their reputation and I would have thought might have exposed them to very heavy claims from the exhibitors who had leased space from them and hoped to use those stands in the ensuing exhibition. They seem to me to have been placed in the position envisaged by Lord Scarman in the Privy Council decision, *PaO On v. Lau Yiu Long* [1980] A.C. 614, in which they were faced with no alternative course of action but to pay the sum demanded of them. It was submitted to us that there was no overt demand, but it was implicit in negotiations between the parties that the plaintiffs were putting the defendants into a corner and it was quite apparent to the defendants, by reason of the plaintiffs' conduct, that unless they handed over £4,500 the plaintiffs would walk off the job. This is, in my view, a situation in which the judge was fully entitled to find in the circumstances of this case that there was duress. As the defendants' director said, he was over a barrel, he had no alternative but to pay; he had no chance of going to any other source of labour to erect the stands. That being so, the only fall-back position for the plaintiffs was the force majeure clause. Clauses of this kind have to be construed upon the basis that those relying on them will have taken all reasonable efforts to avoid the effect of the various matters set out in the clause which entitle them to vary or cancel the contract: see *Bulman & Dickson v. Fenwick & Co.* [1894] 1 Q.B. 179, in the speech of Lord Esher M.R. at p. 185. Quite apart from that general principle this particular clause starts with the following wording: "Every effort will be made to carry out any contract based on an estimate," which is saying in express terms that which the law will imply when construing such a clause.

There is no doubt that the plaintiffs were faced with a strike situation and the question is, did they behave reasonably when faced with this situation? I, like Eveleigh L.J., am far from saying that whenever a contracting party with such a clause is faced with a strike situation he must give in to it in order to perform his contract. If that were the situation the clause would be absolutely worthless. But the special circumstances of this case, as I see it, are as follows. The plaintiffs were going to close down their subsidiary company; they had already dismissed the workforce and the men were working out their time. There is no question here of any ongoing industrial situation between the plaintiffs' subsidiary company and the workforce. There was no question of principle at stake; the plaintiffs were perfectly prepared to pay what the men were demanding save for the fact, they said, they did not have the money available. Well, then there came the offer of the defendants to make the money available by giving them an advance. In those circumstances I can see no reason why they should not have accepted the money and paid the workforce save their own immediate economic interests, and they chose not to do that but to put pressure on the defendants by refusing the offer and indicating that the only way out was for the defendants to hand over the £4,500 as a gift rather than as an advance.

I think that was thoroughly unreasonable behaviour, and that being so they are not entitled to rely upon the force majeure clause, and for these reasons I agree this appeal fails.

Kerr LJ: I agree that this appeal must be dismissed for the reasons which have been given, and there is little that I wish to add.

...

[T]he plaintiffs were clearly saying in effect, "This contract will not be performed by us unless you pay an additional sum of £4,500." This faced the defendants with a disastrous situation in which there was no way out for them, and in the face of this threat – which is what it was – they paid the £4,500. ...

I ...bear in mind that a threat to break a contract unless money is paid by the other party can, but by no means always will, constitute duress. It appears from the authorities that it will only constitute duress if the consequences of a refusal would be serious and immediate so that there is no reasonable alternative open, such as by legal redress, obtaining an injunction, etc. ...[T]here was no other practical choice open to the defendants in the present case, and accordingly I agree that this is a case where money has been paid under duress, which was accordingly recoverable by the defendants provided they acted promptly as they did, and which they have recovered by deducting it from the contract price. In these circumstances the plaintiffs' claim for this additional sum must fail.

NOTES AND QUESTIONS

1.   Did it matter that there was no *explicit* threat in this case?
2.   Griffiths and Kerr LJ both stressed that there was no (reasonable) alternative open to the defendants other than to give in to the threat. Should that be an important criterion? If a threatened person has given in to an illegitimate threat, should it matter that it was unreasonable to have done so?
3.   Analysis of the illegitimacy of the threat was here complicated by the 'force majeure' clause. On the face of it, the Court of Appeal appeared to accept that a threatened breach of contract is illegitimate so that the only issue on this aspect of duress was whether the 'force majeure' clause gave the defendants a defence to breach.
4.   Was the extra payment a contractual payment or not? Did that matter for the purposes of duress?

Atlas Express Ltd v Kafco (Importers and Distributors) Ltd [1989] QB 833, Queen's Bench Division

The defendants, Kafco, a small company, secured a contract to sell and deliver baskets to branches of the large retailer, Woolworth. In order to fulfil that contract they entered into a contract (referred to as a 'trading agreement') with the claimants (Atlas) for the carriage of the baskets to the Woolworth's branches. The trading agreement was to last for at least six months. After the first delivery, Atlas realised that they had underestimated the size of the cartons to be carried and hence how much it would cost to transport the goods. They unsuccessfully tried to persuade Kafco to vary the price. Atlas then sent an empty trailer to Kafco's premises with a document specifying an amended minimum charge and instructions that, if Kafco did not sign the document, the trailer was to be taken away unloaded. It was vital to Kafco's commercial success and indeed survival that they should meet the delivery dates agreed with Woolworth and at such short notice they would be unlikely to find an alternative carrier. Kafco therefore signed the document. When Atlas later sought to recover money due under that new agreement, Kafco refused to pay arguing that the new agreement had been entered into under economic duress and that, in any event, there was no consideration for that new agreement. Both those arguments were held to be successful.

Tucker J: I find that when Mr. Armiger [on behalf of the defendants] signed that agreement he did so unwillingly and under compulsion. He believed on reasonable grounds that it would be very difficult if not impossible to negotiate with another contractor. He did not regard the fact that he had signed the new agreement as binding the defendants to its terms. He had no bargaining power. He did not regard it as a genuine arm's length re-negotiation in which he had a free and equal say and, in my judgment, that view was fully justified.

...

The issue which I have to determine is whether the defendants are bound by the agreement signed on their behalf on 18 November 1986. The defendants contend that they are not bound, for two reasons: first because the agreement was signed under duress; second because there was no consideration for it.

The first question raises a particularly interesting point of law – whether economic duress is a concept known to English law. Economic duress must be distinguished from commercial pressure, which on any view is not sufficient to vitiate consent. The borderline between the two may in some cases be indistinct. But the authors of *Chitty on Contracts* and of *Goff and Jones, The Law of Restitution* appear to recognise that in appropriate cases economic duress may afford a defence, and in my judgment it does. It is clear to me that in a number of English cases judges have acknowledged the existence of this concept.

[Having discussed the prior cases, Tucker J continued:]

Reverting to the case before me, I find that the defendants' apparent consent to the agreement was induced by pressure which was illegitimate and I find that it was not approbated. In my judgment that pressure can properly be described as economic duress, which is a concept recognised by English law, and which in the circumstances of the present case vitiates the defendants' apparent consent to the agreement.

In any event, I find that there was no consideration for the new agreement. The plaintiffs were already obliged to deliver the defendants' goods at the rates agreed under the terms of the original agreement. There was no consideration for the increased minimum charge of £440 per trailer.

NOTES AND QUESTIONS

1. The judge did not clarify why the pressure was illegitimate. Is it enough that what the claimants were threatening was a breach of contract? Should it have been relevant that the claimants appeared to have made a genuine mistake in quoting too low a price (they had not anticipated, despite inspection of a sample, that the cartons to be carried would be as big as they were and therefore thought that more could be carried in a single load)?
2. Can the 'no consideration' aspect of this case stand in the light of *Williams v Roffey Bros*, below, and above, 106?

Williams v Roffey Bros & Nicholls (Contractors) Ltd
[1991] 1 QB 1, Court of Appeal

For the facts and judgments, see above, 106–111.

NOTES AND QUESTIONS

1. Why was economic duress not made out on the facts of this case? See above, 111 note 4.
2. What is the relationship between the doctrine of consideration and duress? Is duress a better regulator of contractual variations than consideration?

3.   **P Birks, 'The Travails of Duress' [1990]** *LMCLQ* **342**, in examining inter alia
Williams v Roffey, points out that in applying duress to renegotiations, the
courts face a policy choice. They could apply a wide doctrine which would give
priority to the initial bargain and to discipline in bidding; or a narrow doctrine
which would recognise the merits of renegotiations and would rarely unsettle
them. Which is the preferable policy?

Dimskal Shipping Co SA v International Transport Workers Federation, The Evia Luck [1992] 2 AC 152, House of Lords

The claimants were the owners of the *Evia Luck* which was loading at a Swedish port.
They were informed by the defendant trade union that their ship would be blacked
unless they entered into contracts with the trade union. The claimants therefore
entered into those contracts under which they made various payments to the trade
union, totalling some $140,000, the greater part being back-dated pay for the crew.
The contracts were expressed to be governed by English law. The claimants subsequently brought an action seeking a declaration that they had validly avoided the
contracts for duress and restitution of the sums paid to the defendant. The primary
focus in the case was on the 'conflict of laws' point as to whether the illegitimacy of
the pressure should be judged by English law (under which the pressure was illegitimate, statutory reform since *The Universe Sentinel* having removed any possible
trade dispute defence) or by Swedish law (under which the pressure was lawful). The
House of Lords held that the claimants were entitled to rescind the contract and to
restitution of the money paid because the relevant law to apply to such rescission and
restitution was English law. The blacking was unlawful according to the law of
England and constituted duress. In the following extract we confine ourselves to the
general discussion of economic duress and do not examine the specialised 'conflict of
laws' point.

Lord Goff of Chieveley: It was common ground between the parties before your Lordships
that the money in respect of which the owners claimed restitution was paid to the I.T.F. under
a contract, albeit a contract which the owners claim to have been voidable by them, and
indeed to have been avoided by them, on the ground of duress. It follows that, before the
owners could establish any right to recover the money, they had first to avoid the relevant
contract. Until this was done, the money in question was paid under a binding contract and
so was irrecoverable in restitution. ...

We are here concerned with a case of economic duress. It was at one time thought that, at
common law, the only form of duress which would entitle a party to avoid a contract on that
ground was duress of the person. The origin for this view lay in the decision of the Court of
Exchequer in *Skeate v. Beale* (1841) 11 Ad. & El. 983. However, since the decisions of Kerr J. in
*Occidental Worldwide Investment Corporation v. Skibs A/S Avanti (The Siboen and The
Sibotre)* [1976] 1 Lloyd's Rep. 293, of Mocatta J. in *North Ocean Shipping Co. Ltd. v. Hyundai
Construction Co. Ltd* [1979] Q.B. 705, and of the Judicial Committee of the Privy Council in
PaO On v. Lau Yiu Long [1980] A.C. 614, that limitation has been discarded; and it is now
accepted that economic pressure may be sufficient to amount to duress for this purpose,
provided at least that the economic pressure may be characterised as illegitimate and has
constituted a significant cause inducing the plaintiff to enter into the relevant contract (see
Barton v. Armstrong [1976] A.C. 104, 121, *per* Lord Wilberforce and Lord Simon of Glaisdale
(referred to with approval in *PaO On v. Lau Yiu Long* [1980] A.C 614, 635, *per* Lord Scarman)

and *Crescendo Management Pty. Ltd. v. Westpac Banking Corporation* (1988) 19 N.S.W.L.R. 40, 46, *per* McHugh J.A.). It is sometimes suggested that the plaintiff's will must have been coerced so as to vitiate his consent. This approach has been the subject of criticism: see *Beatson, The Use and Abuse of Unjust Enrichment* (1991), pp. 113-117; and the notes by Professor Atiyah in (1982) 98 L.Q.R. 197-202, and by Professor Birks in [1990] 3 L.M.C.L.Q. 342-351. I myself, like McHugh J.A., doubt whether it is helpful in this context to speak of the plaintiff's will having been coerced. It is not however necessary to explore the matter in the present case. Nor is it necessary to consider the broader question of what constitutes illegitimate economic pressure, for it is accepted that blacking or a threat of blacking, such as occurred in the present case, does constitute illegitimate economic pressure in English law, unless legitimised by statute. The question which has fallen for decision by your Lordships is whether, in considering the question whether the pressure should be treated as legitimised, the English courts should have regard to the law of Sweden (where the relevant pressure was exerted on the owners by the agents of the I.T.F.) under which such pressure was lawful.

Lords Keith, Lowry and Ackner concurred with Lord Goff. **Lord Templeman** dissented on the ground that the conduct was lawful under Swedish law.

NOTES AND QUESTIONS

1. Lord Goff here stressed the twin requirements for economic duress of (i) illegitimate pressure which (ii) is a 'significant cause' of the threatened party entering the contract.
2. Is a 'significant cause' different from the 'a reason' test in *Barton v Armstrong*?
3. Lord Goff doubted whether it is helpful to talk of 'coercion of the will'. Why is this unhelpful?

Huyton SA v Peter Cremer
[1999] 1 Lloyd's Rep 620, Queen's Bench Division

Cremer, the defendant seller, contracted to sell to the claimant buyer, Huyton, 30,000 tonnes of wheat, payment to be by cash against the presentation by the seller of certain documents. Although it had received the goods, Huyton rejected the documents and refused to pay the contract price alleging that the documents presented did not comply with the contract. Huyton continued to refuse to pay until eventually, and with reluctance, Cremer, on 6/7 February 1996, agreed to a compromise whereby it gave up any right to go to arbitration (to try to recover all its loss) in return for Huyton paying the contract price. After Huyton had paid, Cremer sought arbitration and alleged that the compromise agreement forbidding it from going to arbitration had been entered into under duress. It was held that duress was not made out so that Huyton was entitled to an injunction preventing Cremer from going to arbitration. Mance J's primary reasoning (not set out below) was that there was no illegitimate pressure as Huyton was not in breach of contract by refusing to pay. But he went on to consider the position even if Huyton had been threatening a breach of contract so that there was illegitimate pressure. Even then he concluded that there was no economic duress because the threatened breach was not a sufficiently significant cause of Cremer entering into the compromise agreement.

Mance J: I start with the requirement that the illegitimate pressure must, in cases of economic duress, constitute "a significant cause" (cf per Lord Goff in *The Evia Luck*, at p 120; p 165, cited above). This is contrasted in Goff and Jones on The Law of Restitution (4th ed) p 251, footnote 59 with the lesser requirement that it should be "a" reason which applies in the context of duress to the person. The relevant authority in the latter context is *Barton v Armstrong*, [1976] AC 104 (a case of threats to kill).

...

The use of the phrase "a significant cause" by Lord Goff in *The Evia Luck*, supported by the weighty observation in the footnote in Goff & Jones, suggests that this relaxed view of causation in the special context of duress to the person cannot prevail in the less serious context of economic duress. The minimum basic test of subjective causation in economic duress ought, it appears to me, to be a "but for" test. The illegitimate pressure must have been such as actually caused the making of the agreement, in the sense that it would not otherwise have been made either at all or, at least, in the terms in which it was made. In that sense, the pressure must have been decisive or clinching. There may of course be cases where a commonsense relaxation, even of a but for requirement is necessary, for example in the event of an agreement induced by two concurrent causes, each otherwise sufficient to ground a claim of relief, in circumstances where each alone would have induced the agreement, so that it could not be said that, but for either, the agreement would not have been made. On the other hand, it also seems clear that the application of a simple "but for" test of subjective causation in conjunction with a requirement of actual or threatened breach of duty could lead too readily to relief being granted. It would not, for example, cater for the obvious possibility that, although the innocent party would never have acted as he did, but for the illegitimate pressure, he nevertheless had a real choice and could, if he had wished, equally well have resisted the pressure and, for example, pursued alternative legal redress.

I turn therefore to consider other ingredients of economic duress. One possibility, harking back for example to a word used by the minority in *Barton*, is that the pressure should represent the "predominant" cause. Professor Birks in An Introduction to the Law of Restitution (1985), pp 182-183 has suggested that, in cases such as *PaO On v Lau Yiu Long*, [1980] AC 614 where relief was refused on the ground that there had been "commercial pressure but no coercion" (p 635), the Court was, in effect, insisting "on a more severe test of the degree of compulsion than is found in *Barton v Armstrong*", securing what he describes as "a concealed discretion to distinguish between reasonable and unreasonable, legitimate and illegitimate applications of this species of independently unlawful pressure". His own preference, he indicated, was for "the simplest and more open course . . . to restrict the right to restitution to cases in which one party sought, mala fide to exploit the weakness of the other". These comments highlight the extent to which any consideration of causation in economic duress inter-acts with consideration of the concept of legitimacy. Mr Males [counsel for Huyton] adopts the same approach as Professor Birks in relation to apparent contractual compromises for good consideration, suggesting that here at least bad faith ought to be a pre-condition to relief. The law will of course be cautious about re-opening an apparent compromise made in good faith on both sides. But it seems, on the one hand, questionable whether a "compromise" achieved by one party who does not believe that he had at least an arguable case is a compromise at all—though it may be upheld if there is other consideration (cf *Occidental Worldwide Investment Corporation v Skibs A/S Avanti (The Siboen and The Sibotre)*, [1976] 1 Lloyd's Rep 293 at p 334, col 2); and, on the other hand, difficult to accept that illegitimate pressure applied by a party who believes bona fide in his case could never give grounds for relief against an apparent compromise. Another commentator, Professor Burrows, in The Law of [Restitution] (1993) pp 181-182, has suggested that the concept of legitimacy is open to some flexibility or at least qualification, so that a threatened or actual breach of contract may not represent illegitimate pressure if there was a reasonable commercial basis for the threat or breach, eg because circumstances had radically changed. This suggestion too, is by no means uncontentious.

As to authority, in *The Siboen and The Sibotre*, one of the early cases on economic duress. Mr Justice Kerr indicated at p 335, col 1—in rejecting a contrary submission by Mr Robert Goff, QC as he was—that he did not think that bad faith had any relevance at all. On the other hand, in McHugh, JA's judgment in the Supreme Court of New South Wales in *Crescendo Management Pty Ltd v Westpac Banking Corporation*, (1988) 19 N.S.W.L.R. 40 at p 46, referred to by Lord Goff in *The Evia Luck*, McHugh, JA said that "Pressure will be illegitimate if it consists of unlawful threats or amounts to unconscionable conduct." It is also clear that illegitimate pressure may exist, although the threat is of action by itself lawful, if in conjunction with the nature of the demand, it involves potential blackmail: see *Thorn v Motor Trade Association*, [1937] AC 797, especially at pp 806-807, cited in Lord Scarman's dissenting judgment in *Universe Tankships Inc v International Transport Workers Federation*, [1982] 1 Lloyd's Rep 537 at p 555 and *CTN Cash and Carry Ltd v. Gallagher Ltd*, [1994] 4 All ER 713. And in this last case, Lord Justice Steyn, as he was, contemplated the possibility that unconscionable conduct might have a yet wider ambit. He said:

> "Outside the field of protected relationships, and in a purely commercial context, it might be a relatively rare case in which 'lawful act duress' can be established. And it might be particularly difficult to establish duress if the defendant bona fide considered that this demand was valid. In this complex and changing branch of the law I deliberately refrain from saying 'never'."

That good or bad faith may be particularly relevant when considering whether a case might represent a rare example of "lawful act duress" is not difficult to accept. Even in cases where the pressure relied on is an actual or threatened breach of duty, it seems to me better not to exclude the possibility that the state of mind of the person applying such pressure may in some circumstances be significant, whether or not the other innocent party correctly appreciated such state of mind. "Never" in this context also seems too strong a word.

In *The Evia Luck*, Lord Goff did not speak in absolute terms. He said, with reference to the previous authorities, that—

> ". . . it is now accepted that economic pressure may be sufficient to amount to duress for this purpose, provided at least that the economic pressure may be characterised as illegitimate and has constituted a significant cause inducing the plaintiff to enter the relevant contract."

This description itself leaves room for flexibility in the characterization of illegitimate pressure and of the relevant causal link. Lord Goff was identifying minimum ingredients, not ingredients which, if present, would inevitably lead to liability. The recognition of some degree of flexibility is not, I think, fairly open to the reproach that it introduces a judicial "discretion". The law has frequently to form judgments regarding inequitability or unconscionability, giving effect in doing so to the reasonable expectations of honest persons. It is the law's function to discriminate, where discrimination is appropriate, between different factual situations—as it does, to take one example, when deciding whether or not to recognize a duty of care. The present context is intervention in relation to bargains or payments in relatively extreme situations. Lord Justice Steyn in *CTN Cash and Carry* cited, albeit in the context of threats involving no unlawful act, an aphorism of Oliver Wendell Holmes "that general propositions do not solve concrete cases" and went on:

> "It may only be a half-truth, but in my view the true part applies to this case. It is necessary to focus on the distinctive features of this case, and then to ask whether it amounts to a case of duress."

A similar approach appears to me to be appropriate in the present context.

In older authorities, relief against economic duress was said to require illegitimate pressure coercing the innocent party's will and vitiating consent (cf *The Siboen and The Sibotre* at p 336 and *PaO On v Lau Yiu Long* at p 635). Lord Goff in *The Evia Luck* doubted whether it was helpful to speak in such terms, and referred to McHugh, JA's comments to that effect in the *Crescendo* case. The approach there adopted by McHugh, JA, at p 45 was based on statements by the House of Lords in *DPP v Lynch*, [1975] AC 653, to the effect that, in cases of duress, "the will [is] deflected, not destroyed". Even on this more generous formulation, a simple enquiry whether the innocent party would have acted as he did "but for" an actual or threatened breach of contract cannot, I think, be the hallmark of deflection of will. Whether because the specific ingredients identified by Lord Goff should be interpreted widely or because it is implicit in the flexibility of Lord Goff's formulation and the underlying rationale of the law's intervention to prevent unconscionability, relief must, I think, depend on the Court's assessment of the qualitative impact of the illegitimate pressure, objectively assessed. It is not necessary to go so far as to say that it is an inflexible third essential ingredient of economic duress that there should be no or no practical alternative course open to the innocent party. But it seems, as I have already indicated, self-evident that relief may not be appropriate, if an innocent party decides, as a matter of choice, not to pursue an alternative remedy which any and possibly some other reasonable persons in his circumstances would have pursued. Relief may perhaps also be refused, if he has made no protest and conducted himself in a way which showed that, for better or for worse, he was prepared to accept and live with the consequences, however unwelcome. Factors such as these are referred to as relevant to relief against duress in both *The Siboen and The Sibotre* and *PaO On*, although in some contexts it may also be possible to rationalize them by reference to other doctrines such as affirmation or estoppel. The emphasis, now to be discarded, in such cases on coercion of will does not, it seems to me, mean that such factors are no longer relevant. Taking, for example, *PaO On*, the complainant there was able, in the face of the illegitimate pressure, to consider its position, to take alternative steps if it wished, and to decide, as it apparently did (and however wrongly with hindsight), that the substitute arrangements proposed were of no real concern or risk to it and that it was preferable to agree to them, rather than become involved in litigation. Although there would have been no re-negotiation at all "but for" illegitimate pressure, the relationship between the illegitimate pressure applied and the substitute arrangements made was not of a nature or quality, or sufficiently significant in objective terms in deflecting the will, to justify relief. Examination of the same relationship may also involve taking into account the extent to which the party applying illegitimate pressure intended or could reasonably foresee that pressure which he applied would lead to the agreement or payment made, or at least the extent to which factors extraneous to that party played any important role.

The onus of proof in respect of economic duress is another relatively unexplored area. McHugh, JA in *Crescendo* assumed that it would be reversed in accordance with the principle applied by the Privy Council in *Barton v. Armstrong*. That was a case of threats to kill, where the Privy Council took as an analogy dispositions induced by fraud. With such threats, as the Privy Council pointed out, it is only in the most unusual circumstances that there can be any doubt whether the threats operated to achieve their intended aim or known effect. The Privy Council's recognition of, not merely the prima facie factual inference, but of an apparent shifting of the legal onus, cannot, I think, be transposed automatically to the context of the more recently developed tort of economic duress. Threats to the person are, by definition, mala fide acts. Economic duress, as this case shows, embraces situations where the party applying what can, at least with hindsight, be shown to have been economic pressure held the view quite reasonably at the time that he was entitled to do so. There is, also, as indicated above, a major difference between the substantive test of causation in cases of threats to the person and in cases of economic duress. Leaving aside cases of fraud and fraudulent misrepresentation, mentioned in *Barton v. Armstrong*, the law normally treats the party seeking relief in respect of a breach of contract or seeking to set aside a bargain on grounds, such as innocent misrepresentation, as under a legal onus to prove his case on causation. The particular facts may give rise to an inference of loss or inducement, which may shift a factual onus to the other party, but the underlying legal onus remains at the end of the day on the party seeking relief (cf eg *Marc Rich & Co v. Portman*, [1996] 1 Lloyd's Rep 430 at p 442, considering *Pan Atlantic Insurance Co Ltd v. Pine Top Insurance Co Ltd*, [1994] 2 Lloyd's Rep 427 on misrepresentation and non-disclosure in relation to insurance contracts). It would seem to me, as presently advised, that this could represent the appropriate general approach in cases of economic duress. I am conscious that the question of onus of proof was only briefly touched on before me without citation of authority from outside the field of economic duress, but in view of my other conclusions I have not felt it necessary or appropriate to call for further submissions on it.

...

I come back to the question whether, assuming that Huyton did commit an actual and threatened breach of contract in refusing to pay the price, the agreement which was reached on Feb 6/7, 1996 was induced, or Cremer's will was deflected, in any significant way by such breach—as opposed, for example, to Cremer's own perception of the merits and demerits of alternative courses open to it, influenced to a major extent by Cremer's mistaken perceptions about Huyton's conduct and intentions. It seems to me, as I have said, that in so far as Cremer felt under pressure into entering into the agreement at all, a major element in the pressure which it perceived came from its own misconceptions about the position...

In the result Cremer's defences to this action fail on the basis that (a) by the agreement dated Feb 6/7, 1996 Cremer agreed irrevocably to withdraw the demands which it now seeks to pursue in arbitration against Huyton and (b) this agreement binds Cremer. It binds Cremer, because there was no illegitimate pressure, since Huyton never owed the price or its equivalent. But, for the reasons I have given, even if there had been illegitimate pressure, Cremer's case on economic duress should still, I believe, have failed, on the ground that there was no sufficient deflection of will or no sufficiently significant causal link—between such pressure and the agreement—to make it unconscionable for Huyton to insist on the agreement. Huyton is in these circumstances entitled to the relief sought.

NOTES AND QUESTIONS

1. Mance J indicated that there is a less stringent test of causation for physical duress than for economic duress. Why should that be so?
2. To what extent did Mance J consider it relevant that, even if in breach of contract, Huyton had acted in good faith?
3. Did Mance J consider that the non-existence of a practical alternative was a third separate requirement for duress?
4. In *DSND Subsea Ltd v Petroleum Geo-Services ASA* [2000] BLR 530 the claimant, DSND, was carrying out construction work for the defendant, PGS, on oil rigs in the North Sea. DSND suspended its work pending the signing of a contractual variation (a Memorandum of Understanding) with more favourable terms for DSND. Subsequently, in an action by DSND, PGS sought to escape from the Memorandum of Understanding on the ground, inter alia, that it had been induced to enter into that agreement by duress. Dyson J rejected that duress argument for three reasons. First, even if DSND was in breach of contract, that pressure was not illegitimate because DSND was acting reasonably in good faith in insisting on the new terms [134]. Secondly, in any event, PGS had not entered into the agreement because of

duress and had had realistic practical alternatives [136]–[142]. Thirdly, in any event, PGS had affirmed the contract when free of the duress [143]–[148]. The case is perhaps particularly significant for Dyson J's succinct statement of the law on duress at [131] in which, controversially, he separated out the lack of a practical choice as a third element and in which he referred to a list of relevant factors in deciding whether the pressure was illegitimate. He said, 'The ingredients of actionable duress are that there must be pressure, (a) whose practical effect is that there is compulsion on, or a lack of practical choice for, the victim, (b) which is illegitimate, and (c) which is a significant cause inducing the claimant to enter into the contract... In determining whether there has been illegitimate pressure, the court takes into account a range of factors. These include whether there has been an actual or threatened breach of contract; whether the person allegedly exerting the pressure has acted in good or bad faith; whether the victim had any realistic practical alternative but to submit to the pressure; whether the victim protested at the time; and whether he affirmed and sought to rely on the contract. These are all relevant factors. Illegitimate pressure must be distinguished from the rough and tumble of the pressures of normal commercial bargaining.'

(2) 'Lawful Act' Duress

The cases that we have so far considered on economic duress have all concerned a threatened breach of contract or a threat to induce a breach of contract by the unlawful 'blacking' of a ship. What was being threatened in those cases was, therefore, to do something unlawful (namely to commit a civil wrong, whether a breach of contract or tort). We now cross the line to threatened lawful acts and the central question being asked is when, if ever, can a threatened lawful act be illegitimate pressure.

As Lord Scarman pointed out in obiter dicta in *The Universe Sentinel* (above, 704) the analogy of the crime of blackmail shows that 'lawful act' duress must in principle exist. He gave the example of demanding money under the threat of reporting criminal conduct to the police. This is supported by cases, such as *Williams v Bayley* (1866) LR 1 HL 200 and *Mutual Finance Ltd v John Wetton and Sons Ltd* [1937] 2 KB 389, in which agreements to pay money, induced by threats to prosecute a member of the threatened person's family, have been held voidable for undue influence. As we shall see in Chapter 15, the equitable doctrine of undue influence extends far beyond illegitimate pressure and threats. However, in those cases, undue influence was responding to illegitimate threats and was therefore playing exactly the same role as the modern common law of duress. Now that duress is no longer confined to duress to the person, those older undue influence threat cases are most rationally viewed as examples of 'lawful act' duress.

In this section, we set out the two leading modern cases on lawful act duress. Both accepted that lawful act duress exists while denying that it had been made out on the particular facts.

CTN Cash and Carry Ltd v Gallaher Ltd
[1994] 4 All ER 714, Court of Appeal

The defendant sellers delivered cigarettes to the claimant buyers. Unfortunately they were mistakenly delivered to the claimants' Burnley warehouse rather than their Preston warehouse. The cigarettes were then stolen. Believing mistakenly that the risk had passed to the claimants, the defendants demanded the £17,000 contract price and made clear that they would withdraw the claimants' credit facilities on future contracts if they failed to pay. The claimants paid the £17,000 but later claimed repayment on the ground that they had paid under duress. The claim failed at first instance and in the Court of Appeal because the threat was not illegitimate.

Steyn LJ: It is necessary to focus on the distinctive features of this case, and then to ask whether it amounts to a case of duress.

The present dispute does not concern a protected relationship. It also does not arise in the context of dealings between a supplier and a consumer. The dispute arises out of arm's length commercial dealings between two trading companies. It is true that the defendants were the sole distributors of the popular brands of cigarettes. In a sense the defendants were in a monopoly position. The control of monopolies is, however, a matter for Parliament. Moreover, the common law does not recognise the doctrine of inequality of bargaining power in commercial dealings. See *National Westminster Bank Plc v. Morgan* [1985] 1 All ER 821, [1985] AC 686. The fact that the defendants were in a monopoly position cannot therefore by itself convert what is not otherwise duress into duress.

A second characteristic of the case is that the defendants were in law entitled to refuse to enter into any future contracts with the plaintiffs for any reason whatever or for no reason at all. Such a decision not to deal with the plaintiffs would have been financially damaging to the defendants, but it would have been lawful. A fortiori it was lawful for the defendants, for any reason or for no reason, to insist that they would no longer grant credit to the plaintiffs. The defendants' demand for payment of the invoice, coupled with the threat to withdraw credit, was neither a breach of contract nor a tort.

A third, and critically important, characteristic of the case is the fact that the defendants bona fide thought that the goods were at the risk of the plaintiffs and that the plaintiffs owed the defendants the sum in question. The defendants exerted commercial pressure on the plaintiffs in order to obtain payment of a sum which they bona fide considered due to them. The defendants' motive in threatening withdrawal of credit facilities was commercial self-interest in obtaining a sum that they considered due to them.

Given the combination of these three features, I take the view that none of the cases cited to us assist the plaintiffs' case. Miss Heilbron [counsel for the claimants] accepted that there is no decision which is in material respects on all fours with the present case. It is therefore unnecessary to disinter all those cases and to identify the material distinctions between each of those decisions and the present case. But Miss Heilbron rightly emphasised to us that the law must have a capacity for growth in this field. I entirely agree.

I also readily accept that the fact that the defendants have used lawful means does not by itself remove the case from the scope of the doctrine of economic duress. Professor Birks, in *An Introduction to the Law of Restitution* (1989), at 177, lucidly explains:

'Can lawful pressures also count? This is a difficult question, because, if the answer is that they can, the only viable basis for discriminating between acceptable and unacceptable pressures is not positive law but social morality. In other words, the judges must say what pressures (though lawful outside the restitutionary context) are improper as contrary to prevailing standards. That makes the judges, not the law or the legislature, the arbiters of social evaluation. On the other hand, if the answer is that lawful pressures are always exempt, those who devise outrageous but technically lawful means of compulsion must always escape restitution until the legislature declares the abuse unlawful. It is tolerably clear that, at least where they can be confident of a general consensus in favour of their evaluation, the courts are willing to apply a standard of impropriety rather than technical unlawfulness.'

And there are a number of cases where English courts have accepted that a threat may be illegitimate when coupled with a demand for payment even if the threat is one of lawful action. See *Thorne v Motor Trade Association* [1937] 3 All ER 157 at 160-161, [1937] AC 797 at 806-807; *Mutual Finance, Limited v John Wetton & Sons, Limited* [1937] 2 All ER 657, [1937] 2 K.B. 389 and *Universe Tankships Inc. of Monrovia v. International Transport Workers Federation* [1982] 2 All ER 67 at 76, 89, [1983] 1 AC 366 at 384 and 401. On the other hand, Goff and Jones, *Law of Restitution* (3rd edn, 1986) p 240 observed that English courts have wisely not accepted any general principle that a threat not to contract with another, except on certain terms, may amount to duress.

We are being asked to extend the categories of duress of which the law will take cognizance. That is not necessarily objectionable, but it seems to me that an extension capable of covering the present case, involving 'lawful act duress' in a commercial context in pursuit of a bona fide claim, would be a radical one with far-reaching implications. It would introduce a substantial and undesirable element of uncertainty in the commercial bargaining process. Moreover, it will often enable bona fide settled accounts to be reopened when parties to commercial dealings fall out. The aim of our commercial law ought to be to encourage fair dealing between parties. But it is a mistake for the law to set its sights too highly when the critical enquiry is not whether the conduct is lawful but whether it is morally or socially unacceptable. That is the enquiry in which we are engaged. In my view there are policy considerations which militate against ruling that the defendants obtained payment of the disputed invoice by duress.

Outside the field of protected relationships, and in a purely commercial context, it might be a relatively rare case in which 'lawful act duress' can be established. And it might be particularly difficult to establish duress if the defendant bona fide considered that his demand was valid. In this complex and changing branch of the law I deliberately refrain from saying 'never'. But as the law stands, I am satisfied that the defendants' conduct in this case did not amount to duress.

It is an unattractive result, inasmuch as the defendants are allowed to retain a sum which at the trial they became aware was not in truth due to them. But in my view the law compels the result.

Sir Donald Nicholls V-C: It is important to have in mind that the sole issue raised by this appeal and argued before us was duress. The plaintiff claims payment was made by it under duress and is recoverable accordingly. I agree, for the reasons given by Steyn L.J., that that claim must fail. When the defendant company insisted on payment, it did so in good faith. It believed the risk in the goods had passed to the plaintiff company, so it considered it was entitled to be paid for them. The defendant company took a tough line. It used its commercial muscle. But the feature underlying and dictating this attitude was a genuine belief on its part that it was owed the sum in question. It was entitled to be paid the price for the goods. So it took the line: the plaintiff company must pay in law what it owed, otherwise its credit would be suspended.

Further, there is no evidence that the defendant's belief was unreasonable. Indeed we were told by the defendant's counsel that he had advised his client that on the risk point the defendant stood a good chance of success. I do not see how a payment demanded and made in those circumstances can be said to be vitiated by duress.

So that must be an end to this appeal. I confess to being a little troubled at the overall outcome. At a late stage of the trial the defendant's counsel accepted that the risk in the goods had not in law passed to the plaintiff. Hence, and this must follow, the defendant company was not, and never had been, entitled to be paid for the goods. The risk remained throughout on the defendant. What also follows is that the basis on which the defendant had sought and insisted on payment was then shown to be false.

In those circumstances I confess to being a little surprised that a highly reputable tobacco manufacturer has, so far, not reconsidered the position. A claim for restitution based on wrongful retention of the money, once the risk point had been established, was not pursued before us, no doubt for good reasons. But on the sketchy facts before us – and I emphasise that we have heard argument only from the plaintiff – it does seem to me that prima facie it would be unconscionable for the defendant company to insist on retaining the money now. It demanded the money when under a mistaken belief as to its legal entitlement to be paid. It only made the demand because of its belief that it was entitled to be paid. The money was then paid to it by a plaintiff which in practical terms had no other option. In broad terms, in the end result the defendant may be said to have been unjustly enriched. Whether a new claim for restitution now, on the facts as they have since emerged, would succeed is not a matter I need pursue. I observe, as to that, only that the categories of unjust enrichment are not closed.

Farquharson LJ concurred.

NOTES AND QUESTIONS

1. The Court of Appeal recognised that duress could be founded on a threat of lawful action, here not to grant credit on future contracts. But the threat was not here illegitimate because the defendants made it bona fide, albeit in the mistaken belief that they were contractually entitled to the money.
2. The judges were clearly uncomfortable with the result. Given that, as a matter of law, the money was not owing under the contract, should it have mattered that the threat was made in good faith?
3. Does good faith have a greater role to play in lawful act economic duress than where what is threatened is a breach of contract?
4. In *Alf Vaughan & Co Ltd v Royscot Trust plc* [1999] 1 All ER (Comm) 856, on the administrative receivership of the claimants, the defendants became contractually entitled to re-take possession of vehicles that the claimants had leased, or taken on hire-purchase, from them. So as to be able to sell the business as a group concern, the receivers offered to buy the vehicles by paying off the balance owing on the hire and hire-purchase agreements (which totalled about £34,000). The defendants threatened to re-take possession of the vehicles unless they were paid £82,000. The receivers reluctantly paid that sum but then sought to avoid the contract and to recover the difference between the two figures (about £48,000) on the ground of duress. Judge Rich QC's essential reasoning was that the defendants' threat to repossess their goods (prior to any relief against forfeiture being applied for, let alone granted) was lawful and not illegitimate. Yet this would appear to have been a case where the defendants were acting in bad faith in the sense that they were concerned to exploit the claimants' financial weakness. This suggests that the circumstances will be very exceptional in which even a bad faith threatened lawful act will constitute economic duress.
5. The normal price of potatoes to retailers is 30p per pound. At a time of acute shortage of food, A and other farmers will only sell potatoes to retailers at £5 per pound. B buys at that price. B is contractually bound to supply C's hotel at 35p per pound. B now refuses to deliver unless C agrees to pay £6 per pound. C

agrees to this and pays the increased sums. When normal conditions return, B and C seek to recover the extra sums paid (from A and B respectively) on the ground of economic duress. Would they succeed?

R v Attorney General for England and Wales
[2003] UKPC 22, Privy Council

The defendant, 'R', was a member of the SAS during the Gulf War. After the war, along with other existing members of the SAS, he was requested—under threat of being demoted out of the SAS back to his ordinary regiment if he did not comply—to sign a confidentiality agreement promising not to disclose any information relating to the work of the SAS. R signed the contract but shortly afterwards left the army. R then returned to New Zealand and entered into a contract with publishers for the publication of his memoirs as a member of the special Bravo Two Zero patrol in the SAS. The Attorney General sought an injunction to prevent publication of his book and, although the New Zealand Court of Appeal refused this, they did make an order against the defendant for an account of profits and an assessment of damages for breach of contract. R appealed to the Privy Council contending as one of a number of grounds that he had entered into the confidentiality contract under duress. The Privy Council held that the Crown had not applied illegitimate pressure to R so that the doctrine of duress did not provide a defence.

Lord Hoffmann (giving the judgment of himself and **Lords Bingham, Steyn, Millett** and **Scott, Lord Scott** dissenting only on a separate undue influence point):

Duress

15 In *Universe Tankships Inc of Monrovia v International Transport Workers Federation* [1983] 1 AC 366, 400 Lord Scarman said that there were two elements in the wrong of duress. One was pressure amounting to compulsion of the will of the victim and the second was the illegitimacy of the pressure. R says that to offer him the alternative of being returned to unit, which was regarded in the SAS as a public humiliation, was compulsion of his will. It left him no practical alternative. Their Lordships are content to assume that this was the case. But, as Lord Wilberforce and Lord Simon of Glaisdale said in *Barton v Armstrong* [1976] AC 104, 121:

> "in life ... many acts are done under pressure, sometimes overwhelming pressure, so that one can say that the actor had no choice but to act. Absence of choice in this sense does not negate consent in law: for this the pressure must be one of a kind which the law does not regard as legitimate."

16 The legitimacy of the pressure must be examined from two aspects: first, the nature of the pressure and secondly, the nature of the demand which the pressure is applied to support: see Lord Scarman in the *Universe Tankships* case, at 401. Generally speaking the threat of any form of unlawful action will be regarded as illegitimate. On the other hand, the fact that the threat is lawful does not necessarily make the pressure legitimate. As Lord Atkin said in *Thorne v Motor Trade Association* [1937] A.C. 797, 806:

> "The ordinary blackmailer normally threatens to do what he has a perfect right to do—namely, communicate some compromising conduct to a person whose knowledge is likely to affect the person threatened ... What he has to justify is not the threat, but the demand of money."

17 In this case, the threat was lawful. Although return to unit was not ordinarily used except on grounds of delinquency or unsuitability and was perceived by members of the SAS as a severe penalty, there is no doubt that the Crown was entitled at its discretion to transfer any member of the SAS to another unit. Furthermore, the judge found, in para 123:

> "The MOD could not be criticised for its motivation in introducing the contracts. They were introduced because of the concerns about the increasing number of unauthorised disclosures by former UKSF personnel and the concern that those disclosures were threatening the security of operations and personnel and were undermining the effectiveness and employability of the UKSF. Those are legitimate concerns for the MOD to have."

18 It would follow that the MOD was reasonably entitled to regard anyone unwilling to accept the obligation of confidentiality as unsuitable for the SAS. Thus the threat was lawful and the demand supported by the threat could be justified. But the judge held that the demand was unlawful because it exceeded the powers of the Crown over a serviceman under military law. It was an attempt to restrict his freedom of expression after he had left the service and was no longer subject to military discipline.

19 The judge's reasoning was that R had signed the contract because he had been ordered to do so. The MOD could not give a serviceman an order which, as a matter of military law, he was obliged to obey after he had left the service and therefore it was an abuse of power for the MOD to try to extend the temporal reach of its orders by ordering the serviceman to sign a contract which could be enforced after he had left.

20 If R had signed the contract because as a matter of military law he had been obliged to do so, their Lordships would see much force in this reasoning. But they agree with the Court of Appeal that this was not the case. There was no order in the sense of a command which created an obligation to obey under military law. Instead, R was faced with a choice which may have constituted "overwhelming pressure" but was not an exercise by the MOD of its legal powers over him. The legitimacy of the pressure therefore falls to be examined by normal criteria and as neither of the courts in New Zealand considered either the threat to be unlawful or the demand unreasonable, it follows that the contract was not obtained by duress.

NOTES AND QUESTIONS

1. The threat was held to be legitimate, being both lawful and reasonable. Is reasonableness the same as good faith?
2. Strictly speaking, the duress in question here was not economic duress. The threat to demote R was not so much a threat to his economic interests as to his reputation and self-esteem.

J Beatson, *Anson's Law of Contract* (28th edn, 2002) 277–84
S Smith, *Atiyah's Introduction to the Law of Contract* (6th edn, 2005) 267–83

P Atiyah, 'Economic Duress and the Overborne Will' (1982) 98 *LQR* 197

Atiyah argues that the 'overborne will' theory of duress (as espoused, eg, by Lord Scarman in the *PaO On* case) should be rejected, as it was in the criminal law case of *Lynch v DPP* [1975] AC 653. In cases of duress the victim does know what he is doing, does choose to submit, and does intend to do so.

D Tiplady, 'Concepts of Duress' (1983) 99 *LQR* 188

Tiplady, in a direct response to Atiyah's article, argues that 'overborne will' language (as with 'vitiation of the will') remains useful shorthand. In the context of duress in contract, that language is consistent with saying that the victim has chosen to succumb and with saying that what matters is whether the pressure is legitimate or not.

S Smith, 'Contracting Under Pressure: A Theory of Duress' [1997] *CLJ* 343

Smith sharply separates out the two central elements of duress—which he terms 'wrongdoing' and 'lack of consent'—and argues that each is a distinct reason for invalidating a contract. A full recognition of 'lack of consent' as an invalidating factor would, however, extend beyond duress, as conventionally understood, to encompass a defence of necessity (on which see below, 767).

[In *Contract Theory* (2004) the author clarified/modified his position by suggesting, at 339, that 'the label "duress" should be reserved to claims based on the wrongdoing principle'.]

E McKendrick, 'The Further Travails of Duress' in *Mapping the Law: Essays in Memory of Peter Birks* (eds A Burrows and Lord Rodger, 2006) 181

The author examines three aspects of duress: the setting aside of a contract for duress, the recovery of a non-contractual benefit because of duress, and the award of compensatory damages for duress. Particularly significant are his acceptance of the view that a threatened breach of contract is always illegitimate pressure for the purposes of economic duress and his rejection of any difference in the causation test to be applied as between duress of the person and economic duress.

Principles of European Contract Law (eds O Lando and H Beale, 2000) 257–61

Article 4:108: Threats
A party may avoid a contract when it has been led to conclude it by the other party's imminent and serious threat of an act:

(a) which is wrongful in itself, or

(b) which it is wrongful to use as a means to obtain the conclusion of the contract, unless in the circumstances the first party had a reasonable alternative.

[It is arguable that this is very similar to English law although the uncertainty as to what the precise English law is on duress makes comparison difficult. It may be thought that the English preference for 'illegitimate' rather than 'wrongful' under (b) is to be preferred, and it may be doubted whether the reasonable alternative proviso deserves its prominence.]

Article 4:116: Partial Avoidance
See above, 589.

Article 4:117: Damages
See above, 589.

[These articles contrast with English law in that rescission in England cannot be partial and duress is not itself a wrong triggering damages: see above, 549, 695.]

15

Undue Influence and Exploitation of Weakness

1. UNDUE INFLUENCE

There is a close link between duress and undue influence. Indeed, as has been pointed out above, 716, until the recent expansion of duress, undue influence was regarded as embracing threats or pressure that fell outside the then narrow doctrine of duress. As recognised by many commentators and some judges, since the acceptance of economic duress it is rational, in order to avoid an overlap between undue influence and duress, to treat cases on illegitimate threats/pressure as examples solely of duress. That excision then leaves undue influence to deal with where one party unacceptably influences another in entering a contract without using illegitimate threats or pressure. So it is influence, as distinct from threats/pressure, that we are here concerned with.

Ever since *Allcard v Skinner* (below, 726), undue influence has been divided into two categories: actual and presumed. In the leading case of *Royal Bank of Scotland v Etridge (No 2)*, below, 737, the House of Lords has recently clarified, or redefined, the difference between the categories. Undue influence is a single concept. It does not have two different forms. The presumption of undue influence is an evidential (not a legal) presumption. It follows that the correct analysis of the categories is that they refer to two different ways of *proving* undue influence. Presumed undue influence refers to where the person alleging undue influence relies on an evidential presumption. Actual undue influence refers to where the person alleging undue influence relies on direct proof and does not raise an evidential presumption. Not surprisingly cases in which a person has sought to establish undue influence (as distinct from duress) by direct proof rather than by relying on an evidential presumption are very rare. In other words, one is almost always concerned with presumed, rather than actual, undue influence.

An additional underlying issue of controversy is why precisely undue influence is regarded as objectionable. Is it because it constitutes bad behaviour by the defendant or is it that the influenced party is unable to exercise a full and free choice or is it both?

While the paradigm case of undue influence has involved the influenced party entering into a contract with the influencing party, in recent years the House of Lords has had to consider very important three-party cases. In *Etridge*, the situation in question was one of a wife having been induced by her husband's undue influence to enter into a contract with a bank by which she guaranteed her husband's, or his company's, debts, and gave the security of a charge over the home, in return for a loan from the bank. The central issue was whether the wife could escape from the contract with the bank because of the husband's undue influence.

Like duress, undue influence leads to the rescission of a contract but does not trigger damages. The standard four bars to rescission apply as they do to misrepresentation (see above, 550–557).

Introductory reading: E McKendrick, *Contract Law* (7th edn, 2007) 17.3

Allcard v Skinner (1887) 36 Ch D 145, Court of Appeal

The claimant, who had inherited her father's wealth, was a nun in a convent run by the defendant, who was the Mother Superior. The claimant had been introduced to the defendant by a Reverend Nihill. According to the rules of the convent, the claimant had to give up all her property. She made various substantial gifts (eg of shares) to the defendant to be used for the purposes of the sisterhood. In accordance with the rules of the convent, she did so without seeking independent outside advice. Some eight years after becoming a sister, the claimant left the convent (in 1879) but made no demand for the return of the gifts until 1885. It was held by the Court of Appeal, in dismissing the claimant's appeal, that the claimant would have been entitled to the return of the gifts still in the hands of the defendant because the gifts had been made under undue influence; but (Cotton LJ dissenting) that her claim was barred by her laches (that is, delay in seeking a remedy) and acquiescence after she had left the sisterhood. We here focus on the reasoning on undue influence.

Cotton LJ: The question is – Does the case fall within the principles laid down by the decisions of the Court of Chancery in setting aside voluntary gifts executed by parties who at the time were under such influence as, in the opinion of the Court, enabled the donor afterwards to set the gift aside? These decisions may be divided into two classes – First, where the Court has been satisfied that the gift was the result of influence expressly used by the donee for the purpose; second, where the relations between the donor and donee have at or shortly before the execution of the gift been such as to raise a presumption that the donee had influence over the donor. In such a case the Court sets aside the voluntary gift, unless it is proved that in fact the gift was the spontaneous act of the donor acting under circumstances which enabled him to exercise an independent will and which justifies the Court in holding that the gift was the result of a free exercise of the donor's will. The first class of cases may be considered as depending on the principle that no one shall be allowed to retain any benefit arising from his own fraud or wrongful act. In the second class of cases the Court interferes, not on the ground that any wrongful act has in fact been committed by the donee, but on the ground of public policy, and to prevent the relations which existed between the parties and the influence arising therefrom being abused.

Both the Defendant and Mr. *Nihill* have stated that they used no influence to induce the Plaintiff to make the gift in question, and there is no suggestion that the Defendant acted from any selfish motive, and it cannot be contended that this case comes under the first class of decisions to which I have referred. The question is whether the case comes within the principle of the second class, and I am of opinion that it does. At the time of the gift the Plaintiff was a professed sister, and, as such, bound to render absolute submission to the Defendant as superior of the sisterhood. She had no power to obtain independent advice, she was in such a position that she could not freely exercise her own will as to the disposal of her property, and she must be considered as being (to use the words of Lord Justice *Knight Bruce* in *Wright v. Vanderplank* 8 D.M. & G. 137) "not, in the largest and amplest sense of the term – not, in mind as well as person – an entirely free agent." We have nothing to do with the Plaintiff's reasons for leaving the sisterhood; but, in my opinion, when she exercised her legal right to do this she was entitled to recover so much of the fund transferred by her as remained in the hands of the Defendant, on the ground that it was property the beneficial interest in which she had never effectually parted with.

...

In my opinion, even if there were evidence that she had, before she joined the sisterhood, advice on the question of how she should deal with her property, that would not be sufficient. The question is, I think, whether at the time when she executed the transfer she was under such influences as to prevent the gift being considered as that of one free to determine what should be done with her property.

Lindley LJ: The result of the evidence convinces me that no pressure, except the inevitable pressure of the vows and rules, was brought to bear on the Plaintiff; that no deception was practised upon her; that no unfair advantage was taken of her; that none of her money was obtained or applied for any purpose other than the legitimate objects of the sisterhood.

...

It is to the doctrines of equity...that recourse must be had to invalidate such gifts, if they are to be invalidated. The doctrine relied upon by the Appellant is the doctrine of undue influence expounded and enforced in *Huguenin v. Baseley* 14 Ves. 273 and other cases of that class. These cases may be subdivided into two groups, which, however, often overlap.

First, there are the cases in which there has been some unfair and improper conduct, some coercion from outside, some overreaching, some form of cheating, and generally, though not always, some personal advantage obtained by a donee placed in some close and confidential relation to the donor. ... The evidence does not bring this case within this group.

The second group consists of cases in which the position of the donor to the donee has been such that it has been the duty of the donee to advise the donor, or even to manage his property for him. In such cases the Court throws upon the donee the burden of proving that he has not abused his position, and of proving that the gift made to him has not been brought about by any undue influence on his part. In this class of cases it has been considered necessary to shew that the donor had independent advice, and was removed from the influence of the donee when the gift to him was made.

...

I have not been able to find any case in which a gift has been set aside on the ground of undue influence which does not fall within one or other or both of the groups above mentioned. Nor can I find any authority which actually covers the present case. But it does not follow that it is not reached by the principle on which the Court has proceeded in dealing with the cases which have already called for decision. They illustrate but do not limit the principle applied to them.

The principle must be examined. What then is the principle? Is it that it is right and expedient to save persons from the consequences of their own folly? or is it that it is right and expedient to save them from being victimised by other people? In my opinion the doctrine of undue influence is founded upon the second of these two principles. Courts of Equity have never set aside gifts on the ground of the folly, imprudence, or want of foresight on the part of donors. The Courts have always repudiated any such jurisdiction. …It would obviously be to encourage folly, recklessness, extravagance and vice if persons could get back property which they foolishly made away with, whether by giving it to charitable institutions or by bestowing it on less worthy objects. On the other hand, to protect people from being forced, tricked or misled in any way by others into parting with their property is one of the most legitimate objects of all laws; and the equitable doctrine of undue influence has grown out of and been developed by the necessity of grappling with insidious forms of spiritual tyranny and with the infinite varieties of fraud.

As no Court has ever attempted to define fraud so no Court has ever attempted to define undue influence, which includes one of its many varieties. The undue influence which Courts of Equity endeavour to defeat is the undue influence of one person over another; not the influence of enthusiasm on the enthusiast who is carried away by it, unless indeed such enthusiasm is itself the result of external undue influence. But the influence of one mind over another is very subtle, and of all influences religious influence is the most dangerous and the most powerful, and to counteract it Courts of Equity have gone very far.

…

[The plaintiff] was absolutely in the power of the lady superior and Mr. *Nihill*. A gift made by her under these circumstances to the lady superior cannot in my opinion be retained by the donee. The equitable title of the donee is imperfect by reason of the influence inevitably resulting from her position, and which influence experience has taught the Courts to regard as undue. Whatever doubt I might have had on this point if there had been no rule against consulting externs, that rule in my judgment turns the scale against the Defendant. In the face of that rule the gifts made to the sisterhood cannot be supported in the absence of proof that the Plaintiff could have obtained independent advice if she wished for it, and that she knew that she would have been allowed to obtain such advice if she had desired to do so. I doubt whether the gifts could have been supported if such proof had been given, unless there was also proof that she was free to act on the advice which might be given to her.

…

Where a gift is made to a person standing in a confidential relation to the donor, the Court will not set aside the gift if of a small amount simply on the ground that the donor had no independent advice. In such a case, some proof of the exercise of the influence of the donee must be given. The mere existence of such influence is not enough… But if the gift is so large as not to be reasonably accounted for on the ground of friendship, relationship, charity, or other ordinary motives on which ordinary men act, the burden is upon the donee to support the gift. So, in a case like this, a distinction might well be made between gifts of capital and gifts of income, and between gifts of moderate amount and gifts of large sums, which a person unfettered by vows and oppressive rules would not be likely to wish to make.

Bowen LJ: [I]t is plain that equity will not allow a person who exercises or enjoys a dominant religious influence over another to benefit directly or indirectly by the gifts which the donor makes under or in consequence of such influence, unless it is shewn that the donor, at the time of making the gift, was allowed full and free opportunity for counsel and advice outside – the means of considering his or her worldly position and exercising an independent will about it. This is not a limitation placed on the action of the donor; it is a fetter placed upon the conscience of the recipient of the gift, and one which arises out of public policy and fair play. If this had been the gift of a chattel, therefore, the property then would have passed in law, and the gift of this stock may be treated upon a similar method of reasoning. Now, that being the rule, in the first place, was the Plaintiff entitled to the benefit of it? She had vowed in the most sacred and solemn way absolute and implicit obedience to the will of the Defendant, her superior, and she was bound altogether to neglect the advice of externs – not to consult those outside the convent. Now I offer no sort of criticism on institutions of this sort; no kind of criticism upon the action of those who enter them, or of those who administer them. In the abstract I respect their motives, but it is obvious that it is exactly to this class of case that the rule of equity which I have mentioned ought to be applied if it exists. It seems to me that the Plaintiff, so long as she was fettered by this vow – so long as she was under the dominant influence of this religious feeling – was a person entitled to the protection of the rule. Now, was the Defendant bound by this rule? I acquit her most entirely of all selfish feeling in the matter. I can see no sort of wrongful desire to appropriate to herself any worldly benefit from the gift; but, nevertheless, she was a person who benefited by it so far as the disposition of the property was concerned, although, no doubt, she meant to use it in conformity with the rules of the institution, and did so use it. ... For these reasons I think that without any interference with the freedom of persons to deal with their property as they please, we can hold but one opinion, that in 1879 the Plaintiff could have set this gift aside.

NOTES AND QUESTIONS

1. This case is best known for Cotton LJ's distinction (see also Lindley LJ's judgment) between the two classes of undue influence, which have since been labelled actual and presumed undue influence; and for Lindley LJ's test, within presumed undue influence, for the sort of gift that will be set aside.

2. Was undue influence here made out because (i) the relationship between the nun and her spiritual adviser was irrebuttably one of influence; (ii) the gift was not to be 'reasonably accounted for ...on ordinary motives' (applying Lindley LJ's test); and (iii) the nun had not received independent advice?

3. Did Cotton LJ (and Lindley LJ) regard the two classes of undue influence as merely two different ways of proving undue influence?

4. The judges indicated that they did not regard the defendant as having acted unfairly or wrongfully. Why then would the undue influence have resulted in the gifts being set aside had the claimant not delayed in seeking to set aside the gifts when free of the influence? Is undue influence based on bad conduct/wrongdoing?

5. This was a case of a gift being set aside. It has been assumed that the same (or very similar) principles apply to the setting aside of contracts.

Barclays Bank plc v O' Brien [1994] 1 AC 180, House of Lords

Mr and Mrs O'Brien, the defendants, agreed to execute a second charge over their home as security for an increased overdraft from the claimant bank for a company in which Mr O'Brien had an interest. The bank manager had instructed that the O'Briens should be made fully aware of the effect of the documentation but those instructions were not carried out. The second defendant, Mrs O'Brien, signed the guarantee without receiving independent advice and having been falsely told by her husband that the liabilities were limited to £60,000 and would only last three weeks. When the company's indebtedness rose to £154,000, the bank sought to enforce the charge. Mrs O'Brien defended the claim on the basis that she had been induced to sign the charge by the undue influence and misrepresentation of her husband. The claim based on undue influence was rejected in the Court of Appeal and was not pursued in the House of Lords, albeit that their Lordships did carefully consider the law on undue influence. The essential issue on misrepresentation (and equally applicable, in principle, to undue influence) was whether the bank, which had entered into the contract with Mrs O'Brien, was caught by the misrepresentation of the husband. It was held that the bank was so caught because it had constructive notice of the husband's misrepresentation. Therefore Mrs O'Brien could rescind the contract as against the bank.

Lord Browne-Wilkinson: A person who has been induced to enter into a transaction by the undue influence of another ("the wrongdoer") is entitled to set that transaction aside as against the wrongdoer. Such undue influence is either actual or presumed. In *Bank of Credit and Commerce International S.A. v. Aboody* [1990] 1 Q.B. 923, 953, the Court of Appeal helpfully adopted the following classification.

Class 1: Actual undue influence

In these cases it is necessary for the claimant to prove affirmatively that the wrongdoer exerted undue influence on the complainant to enter into the particular transaction which is impugned.

Class 2: Presumed undue influence

In these cases the complainant only has to show, in the first instance, that there was a relationship of trust and confidence between the complainant and the wrongdoer of such a nature that it is fair to presume that the wrongdoer abused that relationship in procuring the complainant to enter into the impugned transaction. In Class 2 cases therefore there is no need to produce evidence that actual undue influence was exerted in relation to the particular transaction impugned: once a confidential relationship has been proved, the burden then shifts to the wrongdoer to prove that the complainant entered into the impugned transaction freely, for example by showing that the complainant had independent advice. Such a confidential relationship can be established in two ways, viz.,

Class 2(A)

Certain relationships (for example solicitor and client, medical advisor and patient) as a matter of law raise the presumption that undue influence has been exercised.

Class 2(B)

Even if there is no relationship falling within Class 2(A), if the complainant proves the de facto existence of a relationship under which the complainant generally reposed trust and confidence in the wrongdoer, the existence of such relationship raises the presumption of undue influence. In a Class 2(B) case therefore, in the absence of evidence disproving undue influence, the complainant will succeed in setting aside the impugned transaction merely by proof that the complainant reposed trust and confidence in the wrongdoer without having to prove that the wrongdoer exerted actual undue influence or otherwise abused such trust and confidence in relation to the particular transaction impugned.

As to dispositions by a wife in favour of her husband, the law for long remained in an unsettled state. In the 19th century some judges took the view that the relationship was such that it fell into Class 2(A) i.e. as a matter of law undue influence by the husband over the wife was presumed. It was not until the decisions in *Howes v. Bishop* [1909] 2 K.B. 390 and *Bank of Montreal v. Stuart* [1911] A.C. 120 that it was finally determined that the relationship of husband and wife did not as a matter of law raise a presumption of undue influence within Class 2(A). ...

Although there is no Class 2(A) presumption of undue influence as between husband and wife, it should be emphasised that in any particular case a wife may well be able to demonstrate that de facto she did leave decisions on financial affairs to her husband thereby bringing herself within Class 2(B)...

...

[I]n surety cases the decisive question is whether the claimant wife can set aside the transaction, not against the wrongdoing husband, but against the creditor bank. Of course, if the wrongdoing husband is acting as agent for the creditor bank in obtaining the surety from the wife, the creditor will be fixed with the wrongdoing of its own agent and the surety contract can be set aside as against the creditor. Apart from this, if the creditor bank has notice, actual or constructive, of the undue influence exercised by the husband (and consequentially of the wife's equity to set aside the transaction) the creditor will take subject to that equity and the wife can set aside the transaction against the creditor (albeit a purchaser for value) as well as against the husband: see *Bainbrigge v. Browne* (1881) 18 Ch.D. 188 and *Bank of Credit and Commerce International S.A. v. Aboody* [1990] 1 Q.B. 923, 973. Similarly, in cases such as the present where the wife has been induced to enter into the transaction by the husband's misrepresentation, her equity to set aside the transaction will be enforceable against the creditor if either the husband was acting as the creditor's agent or the creditor had actual or constructive notice.

...

In my judgment, if the doctrine of notice is properly applied, there is no need for the introduction of a special equity in these types of cases. A wife who has been induced to stand as a surety for her husband's debts by his undue influence, misrepresentation or some other legal wrong has an equity as against him to set aside that transaction. Under the ordinary principles of equity, her right to set aside that transaction will be enforceable against third parties (e.g. against a creditor) if either the husband was acting as the third party's agent or the third party had actual or constructive notice of the facts giving rise to her equity. Although there may be cases where, without artificiality, it can properly be held that the husband was acting as the agent of the creditor in procuring the wife to stand as surety, such cases will be of very rare occurrence. The key to the problem is to identify the circumstances in which the creditor will be taken to have had notice of the wife's equity to set aside the transaction.

The doctrine of notice lies at the heart of equity. Given that there are two innocent parties, each enjoying rights, the earlier right prevails against the later right if the acquirer of the later right knows of the earlier right (actual notice) or would have discovered it had he taken proper steps (constructive notice). In particular, if the party asserting that he takes free of the earlier rights of another knows of certain facts which put him on inquiry as to the possible existence of the rights of that other and he fails to make such inquiry or take such other steps as are reasonable to verify whether such earlier right does or does not exist, he will have constructive notice of the earlier right and take subject to it. Therefore where a wife has agreed to stand surety for her husband's debts as a result of undue influence or misrepresentation, the creditor will take subject to the wife's equity to set aside the transaction if the circumstances are such as to put the creditor on inquiry as to the circumstances in which she agreed to stand surety.

...

[I]n my judgment a creditor is put on inquiry when a wife offers to stand surety for her husband's debts by the combination of two factors: (a) the transaction is on its face not to the financial advantage of the wife; and (b) there is a substantial risk in transactions of that kind that, in procuring the wife to act as surety, the husband has committed a legal or equitable wrong that entitles the wife to set aside the transaction.

It follow that unless the creditor who is put on inquiry takes reasonable steps to satisfy himself that the wife's agreement to stand surety has been properly obtained, the creditor will have constructive notice of the wife's rights.

...

Applying those principles to this case, to the knowledge of the bank Mr. and Mrs. O'Brien were man and wife. The bank took a surety obligation from Mrs. O'Brien, secured on the matrimonial home, to secure the debts of a company in which Mr. O'Brien was interested but in which Mrs. O'Brien had no direct pecuniary interest. The bank should therefore have been put on inquiry as to the circumstances in which Mrs. O'Brien had agreed to stand as surety for the debt of her husband. ...

Mrs. O'Brien signed the documents without any warning of the risks or any recommendation to take legal advice. In the circumstances the bank (having failed to take reasonable steps) is fixed with constructive notice of the wrongful misrepresentation made by Mr. O'Brien to Mrs. O'Brien. Mrs. O'Brien is therefore entitled as against the bank to set aside the legal charge on the matrimonial home securing her husband's liability to the bank.

Lords Templeman, Lowry, Slynn of Hadley and **Woolf** concurred.

NOTES AND QUESTIONS

1. Most undue influence cases in recent years have concerned contracts made not between the influencer (X) and the influenced party (C) but between the influenced party and another party (D). The commonest example is where under her husband's (X's) undue influence, a wife (C) guarantees to a bank (D), secured by a charge over the matrimonial home, the debts owed to D by X or X's company. The *O'Brien* case exemplified this pattern, albeit that it directly concerned X's misrepresentation rather than undue influence.

2. The central importance of the *O'Brien* case is in the House of Lords' rationalisation of how D (the bank) is caught by X's (the husband's) undue influence or misrepresentation. Leaving aside the very rare case of X acting as D's agent, their Lordships laid down that it is D's actual or constructive notice of X's undue influence or misrepresentation that is determinative. Lord Browne-Wilkinson spelt out the three main elements required for constructive notice in this situation: (i) D must be aware that C is in a relationship of trust and confidence with X so that there is a substantial risk of undue influence (or misrepresentation); (ii) the transaction on its face must not be to the financial advantage of C; (iii) D must have failed to take reasonable steps to be satisfied that the transaction was entered into by C freely and with knowledge of the full facts. The first two elements go to putting D on inquiry, while the third element goes to what D, who has been put on inquiry, must do to avoid being fixed with constructive notice. This idea of constructive notice, novel in this context, subsequently spawned a mass of case law culminating in a clarification of the law in *Etridge*, below, 737.

3. Is constructive notice an appropriate concept in this situation?

4. Lord Browne-Wilkinson relied on a categorisation of presumed undue influence cases into class 2A and class 2B (presumed undue influence where the relationship is, respectively, irrebuttably/automatically one of influence or is established on the facts to be one of influence). This categorisation was first approved in *Bank of Credit and Commerce International SA v Aboody* [1990] 1 QB 923, CA, and was for many years cited regularly by the courts. Although with careful handling that distinction could still be usefully made, *Etridge* has since clarified that it tends to be misunderstood and is, therefore, best avoided. In particular, it tends to obscure the important points that (i) the presumption of undue influence is an evidential presumption only albeit that (ii) in setting up that evidential presumption, one may be able to rely on an irrebuttable legal presumption that a particular type of relationship is one of influence.

5. In the case accompanying *O'Brien*, *CIBC Mortgages Plc v Pitt* [1994] 1 AC 200, the House of Lords decided that: (i) it is not a necessary element of

(actual) undue influence that the transaction be disadvantageous; (ii) the claimant bank was not put on inquiry, and therefore did not have constructive notice of the husband's undue influence, because, in contrast to the *O'Brien* case, the transaction in question was an ordinary one of a joint loan to a husband and wife secured on their home. In Lord Browne-Wilkinson's words at 211, 'What distinguishes the case of the joint advance from the surety case is that, in the latter, there is not only the possibility of undue influence having been exercised but also the increased risk of it having in fact been exercised because, at least on its face, the guarantee by a wife of her husband's debts is not for her financial benefit. It is the combination of these two factors that puts the creditor on inquiry.'

Cheese v Thomas [1994] 1 WLR 129, Court of Appeal

The claimant (Mr Cheese) contributed £43,000 to the purchase price of a house (for £83,000) by his great-nephew (the defendant), who had taken out a mortgage for £40,000 for his share. The agreement between them was that the claimant was to be entitled to live in the property rent-free for the rest of his life. When the defendant failed to pay off the mortgage instalments, the claimant sought to set aside the transaction and to recover his £43,000 on the ground of presumed undue influence. The house had been sold for only £55,400. It was held by the Court of Appeal that the claimant was entitled to have the contract set aside on the ground of undue influence. However, the claimant was allowed to recover only £11,000 and not the full £43,000 because the loss in value of the house should be borne proportionately by both parties.

Sir Donald Nicholas VC: I approach the matter in this way. Restitution has to be made, not damages paid. Damages look at the plaintiff's loss, whereas restitution is concerned with the recovery back from the defendant of what he received under the transaction. If the transaction is set aside, the plaintiff also must return what he received. Each party must hand back what he obtained under the contract. There has to be a giving back and a taking back on both sides, as Bowen L.J. observed in *Newbigging v. Adam* (1886) 34 Ch.D. 582, 595. If, for this purpose, the transaction in this case is analysed simply as a payment of £43,000 by Mr. Cheese to Mr. Thomas in return for the right to live in Mr. Thomas's house, there is a strong case for ordering repayment of £43,000, the benefit received by Mr. Thomas, regardless of the subsequent fall in the value of the house. In the ordinary way, if a plaintiff is able to return to the defendant the property received from him under the impugned transaction, it matters not that the property has meanwhile fallen in value. This is not surprising. A defendant cannot be heard to protest that such an outcome is unfair when he is receiving back the very thing he persuaded the plaintiff, by undue influence or misrepresentation, to buy from him.

In my view the present case stands differently. Mr. Cheese paid Mr. Thomas £43,000, not outright, but as part of the purchase price of a house in which both would have rights: Mr. Cheese was to have sole use of the house for his life, and then the house would be Mr. Thomas's. ... This is the transaction which has to be reversed. Doing so requires, first, that the house should be sold and, second, that each party should receive back his contribution to the price. There is no difficulty over the first requirement. Mr. Cheese sought an order for sale, the judge so directed, and the sale has taken place. The second requirement is more difficult. Indeed, it cannot be achieved, because under the transaction the money each contributed was spent in buying a house which then lost one third of its value.

This difficulty, rightly in my view, has not been allowed to stand in the way of setting aside the transaction. It is well established that a court of equity grants this type of relief even when it cannot restore the parties precisely to the state they were in before the contract. The court will grant relief whenever, by directing accounts and making allowances, it can do what is practically just: see *Erlanger v. New Sombrero Phosphate Co.* (1878) 3 App.Cas. 1218, 1278-1279, *per* Lord Blackburn. Here justice requires that each party should be returned as near to his original position as is now possible. Each should get back a proportionate share of the net proceeds of the house, before deducting the amount paid to the building society. Thus the £55,400 should be divided between Mr. Cheese and Mr. Thomas in the proportions of 43:40. Mr. Cheese should receive about £28,700 and Mr. Thomas £26,700. To achieve this result Mr. Thomas should pay £11,033 on top of the net proceeds, of £17,667, remaining after discharging the mortgage. This was the view of the judge, and I see no occasion to disturb his conclusion. On the contrary, I agree with him. It is interesting to note that this result accords with the primary relief sought by Mr. Cheese in the action. His primary claim was that the house belonged to them both in the proportions of 43:40. Had the claim succeeded, Mr. Cheese would have borne a proportionate share of the loss on the sale of the house.

...

In the ordinary way, when a sum of money is paid to a defendant under a transaction which is set aside, the defendant will be required to repay the whole sum. There may be exceptional cases where that would be unjust. This may the more readily be so where the personal conduct of the defendant was not open to criticism. Here, having heard the parties give evidence, the judge acquitted Mr. Thomas of acting in a morally reprehensible way towards Mr. Cheese. He described Mr. Thomas as an innocent fiduciary. Here also, and I return to this feature because on any view it was an integral element of the transaction, each party applied money in buying the house. In all the circumstances, to require Mr. Thomas to shoulder the whole of the loss flowing from the problems which have beset the residential property market for the last year or two would be harsh. That is not an outcome a court of conscience should countenance.

Butler-Sloss LJ and **Peter Gibson LJ** concurred.

NOTES AND QUESTIONS

1.   The importance of this case is in showing the flexibility that the courts have when rescinding a contract. Normally on rescission (as we have seen in relation to, eg, misrepresentation: above, 553–555) each party makes restitution to the other of the benefits, or the value of the benefits, it has received under the contract. However here, where the parties had gone into a joint venture, it was held that a simple restoration of the benefits would not have achieved practical justice for the parties. In particular, it would have left the defendant with an unjustified loss.

2.   In passages not extracted above, it was explained that the undue influence was presumed. There was a relationship of influence over the elderly Mr Cheese established on the facts, the transaction was manifestly disadvantageous to Mr Cheese (which was to apply the now discredited test laid down by Lord Scarman in *National Westminster Bank v Morgan*, below, 774), and there had been insufficient independent advice to rebut the presumption.

3.   It should be noted that, as in *Allcard v Skinner*, the conduct of the defendant was expressly said not to be open to criticism. See also below, 775, note 6. What does this tell us about the rationale of undue influence?

4.   In contrast to the flexibility in relation to rescission that is here shown, it appears to be the law that rescission for misrepresentation or undue influence is all or nothing and cannot be granted on the terms of the claimant entering into a new contract: see above, 549.

Credit Lyonnais Nederland NV v Burch
[1997] 1 All ER 144, Court of Appeal

The defendant was a junior employee of a company (API) in which she had no financial interest. She was asked by her boss, Mr Pelosi, the major shareholder in that company, to mortgage her flat as security for an increase in the company's overdraft. She therefore entered into a transaction with the claimant bank under which she gave them an unlimited guarantee of the company's debts secured by a second charge over her flat. The bank did not explain to her the nature of the transaction into which she was entering and, although it advised her to obtain independent advice, she did not do so. The company went into liquidation and the bank sought possession of the defendant's flat. In dismissing the claimant bank's appeal, the Court of Appeal held that the transaction should be set aside for presumed undue influence, of which the bank had had constructive notice.

Nourse LJ: Turning to the case based on undue influence, the recorder found without hesitation that there existed between Mr Pelosi and Miss Burch such a relationship of trust and confidence as to raise a presumption of undue influence; he said that if she had been seeking to set aside the legal charge as against API, she would certainly have succeeded. As between Miss Burch and the bank, he found that the bank knew that she was only an employee of API and, further, that the transaction was manifestly to her disadvantage; it knew that Mr Pelosi was putting forward, as the provider of collateral security for a possible debt of £270,000, an employee of his company who had no interest in it as shareholder or director. He held that that was notice of facts which put the bank on inquiry. I respectfully agree.

. . .

Since it was so manifestly disadvantageous to Miss Burch, the bank could not be said to have taken reasonable steps to avoid being fixed with constructive notice of Mr Pelosi's undue influence over her when neither the potential extent of her liability had been explained to her nor had she received independent advice.

Millett LJ: [This] is an extreme case. The transaction was not merely to the manifest disadvantage of Miss Burch; it was one which, in the traditional phrase, 'shocks the conscience of the court'. Miss Burch committed herself to a personal liability far beyond her slender means, risking the loss of her home and personal bankruptcy, and obtained nothing in return beyond a relatively small and possibly temporary increase in the overdraft facility available to her employer, a company in which she had no financial interest. The transaction gives rise to grave suspicion. It cries aloud for an explanation.

. . .

[I]t was for Miss Burch to prove that the relationship between her and Mr Pelosi had developed into a relationship of trust and confidence. Whether it had done so or not was a question of fact. While she had to prove this affirmatively, she did not have to prove it as a primary fact by direct evidence. It was sufficient for her to prove facts from which the existence of a relationship of trust and confidence could be inferred. In the present case the excessively onerous nature of the transaction into which she was persuaded to enter, coupled with the fact that she did so at the request of and after discussion with Mr Pelosi, is in my judgment quite enough to justify the inference, which is really irresistible, that the relationship of employer and employee had ripened into something more and that there had come into existence between them a relationship of trust and confidence which he improperly exploited for his own benefit.

I do not accept the bank's submission that this conclusion is inconsistent with the authorities. I repeat that the mere fact that a transaction is improvident or manifestly disadvantageous to one party is not sufficient by itself to give rise to a presumption that it has been obtained by the exercise of undue influence; but where it is obtained by a party between whom and the complainant there is a relationship like that of employer and junior employee which is easily capable of developing into a relationship of trust and confidence, the nature of the transaction may be sufficient to justify the inference that such a development has taken place; and where the transaction is so extravagantly improvident that it is virtually inexplicable on any other basis, the inference will be readily drawn.

The bank submitted that in the absence of evidence that there was a sexual or emotional tie between Mr Pelosi and Miss Burch the facts were insufficient to justify the judge's finding that there was a relationship of confidence between them; and that, in the absence of evidence that the bank was aware of such a tie between Mr Pelosi and Miss Burch, the facts known to the bank were insufficient to fix it with notice of the existence of a relationship of trust and confidence between them. I do not accept this. The presence of a sexual or emotional tie would at least make the transaction explicable. A wife might well consider (and be properly advised) that it was in her interest to provide a (suitably limited) guarantee of her husband's business borrowings and to charge it on her interest in the matrimonial home, even if she had no legal interest in the company which owned the business. Her livelihood and that of her family would no doubt depend on the success of the business; and a refusal to entertain her husband's importunity might put at risk the marital relationship as well as the continued prosperity of herself and her family. Similar considerations would no doubt influence a cohabitee and her adviser.

But Miss Burch had no such incentive to induce her to enter into the transaction. No competent solicitor could possibly have advised her to enter into it.

…

I do not, therefore, accept that a bank, in circumstances where it ought to appreciate the possibility that undue influence has been exercised, can escape the consequences by putting forward an unnecessarily onerous form of guarantee and relying on the failure of the guarantor's solicitor to advise her of the possibility of offering a guarantee on less onerous terms and more appropriate to the situation.

Swinton Thomas LJ gave a concurring judgment.

NOTES

1. The case shows that, exceptionally, undue influence can be made out as between employer and employee; that a bank will be put on inquiry as to that undue influence (given that the relationship is non-commercial, albeit not involving a sexual relationship); and that there can be circumstances in which a bank will be bound by constructive notice even where it has advised the other party to take independent advice.
2. The decision was approved by the House of Lords in *Etridge*, below.
3. For Nourse LJ's view that it was 'very well arguable' that the transaction could alternatively have been set aside as an unconscionable bargain, see below, 726, note 3.
4. **M Chen-Wishart, 'The O'Brien Principle and Substantive Unfairness' [1997] *CLJ* 60** argues, with especial reference to *Credit Lyonnais Bank v Burch*, that

substantive unfairness should be given more prominence in undue influence than has traditionally been the case.

Royal Bank of Scotland plc v Etridge (No 2)
[2001] UKHL 44, [2002] 2 AC 773, House of Lords

The House of Lords heard eight appeals, each of which arose out of the same fact scenario. A wife charged her interest in her home in favour of a bank as security for her husband's debts or the debts of his company. In seven of the eight appeals the bank sought to enforce the charge signed by the wife and the wife raised the defence that the bank had notice of the husband's undue influence over her. In the eighth appeal, the wife claimed damages from a solicitor who advised her. In some of the appeals the wife succeeded, in others she lost. We are here concerned purely with the legal principles laid down by the House of Lords—which included a major clarification of the general law on undue influence and of how the concept of constructive notice, established in the *O'Brien* case, above, 729, should be applied—and not with the application of that law to the particular facts.

Lord Bingham of Cornhill:

3 ...While the opinions of Lord Nicholls and Lord Scott show some difference of expression and approach, I do not myself discern any significant difference of legal principle applicable to these cases, and I agree with both opinions. But if I am wrong and such differences exist, it is plain that the opinion of Lord Nicholls commands the unqualified support of all members of the House.

Lord Nicholls of Birkenhead:

6 The issues raised by these appeals make it necessary to go back to first principles. Undue influence is one of the grounds of relief developed by the courts of equity as a court of conscience. The objective is to ensure that the influence of one person over another is not abused. In everyday life people constantly seek to influence the decisions of others. They seek to persuade those with whom they are dealing to enter into transactions, whether great or small. The law has set limits to the means properly employable for this purpose. To this end the common law developed a principle of duress. Originally this was narrow in its scope, restricted to the more blatant forms of physical coercion, such as personal violence.

7 Here, as elsewhere in the law, equity supplemented the common law. Equity extended the reach of the law to other unacceptable forms of persuasion. The law will investigate the manner in which the intention to enter into the transaction was secured: "how the intention was produced", in the oft repeated words of Lord Eldon LC, from as long ago as 1807 (*Huguenin v Baseley* 14 Ves 273, 300). If the intention was produced by an unacceptable means, the law will not permit the transaction to stand. The means used is regarded as an exercise of improper or "undue" influence, and hence unacceptable, whenever the consent thus procured ought not fairly to be treated as the expression of a person's free will. It is impossible to be more precise or definitive. The circumstances in which one person acquires influence over another, and the manner in which influence may be exercised, vary too widely to permit of any more specific criterion.

8 Equity identified broadly two forms of unacceptable conduct. The first comprises overt acts of improper pressure or coercion such as unlawful threats. Today there is much overlap with the principle of duress as this principle has subsequently developed. The second form arises out of a relationship between two persons where one has acquired over another a measure of influence, or ascendancy, of which the ascendant person then takes unfair advantage. ...

9 In cases of this latter nature the influence one person has over another provides scope for misuse without any specific overt acts of persuasion. The relationship between two individuals may be such that, without more, one of them is disposed to agree a course of action proposed by the other. Typically this occurs when one person places trust in another to look after his affairs and interests, and the latter betrays this trust by preferring his own interests. He abuses the influence he has acquired. In *Allcard v Skinner* (1887) 36 Ch D 145, a case well known to every law student, Lindley LJ, at p 181, described this class of cases as those in which it was the duty of one party to advise the other or to manage his property for him. ...

10 The law has long recognised the need to prevent abuse of influence in these "relationship" cases despite the absence of evidence of overt acts of persuasive conduct. The types of relationship, such as parent and child, in which this principle falls to be applied cannot be listed exhaustively. Relationships are infinitely various. Sir Guenter Treitel QC has rightly noted that the question is whether one party has reposed sufficient trust and confidence in the other, rather than whether the relationship between the parties belongs to a particular type: see *Treitel, The Law of Contract*, 10th ed (1999), pp 380-381. For example, the relation of banker and customer will not normally meet this criterion, but exceptionally it may: see *National Westminster Bank plc v Morgan* [1985] AC 686, 707-709.

11 Even this test is not comprehensive. The principle is not confined to cases of abuse of trust and confidence. It also includes, for instance, cases where a vulnerable person has been exploited. Indeed, there is no single touchstone for determining whether the principle is applicable. Several expressions have been used in an endeavour to encapsulate the essence: trust and confidence, reliance, dependence or vulnerability on the one hand and ascendancy, domination or control on the other. None of these descriptions is perfect. None is all embracing. Each has its proper place.

12 In *CIBC Mortgages plc v Pitt* [1994] 1 AC 200 your Lordships' House decided that in cases of undue influence disadvantage is not a necessary ingredient of the cause of action. It is not essential that the transaction should be disadvantageous to the pressurised or influenced person, either in financial terms or in any other way. However, in the nature of things, questions of undue influence will not usually arise, and the exercise of undue influence is unlikely to occur, where the transaction is innocuous. The issue is likely to arise only when, in some respect, the transaction was disadvantageous either from the outset or as matters turned out.

Burden of proof and presumptions

13 Whether a transaction was brought about by the exercise of undue influence is a question of fact. Here, as elsewhere, the general principle is that he who asserts a wrong has been committed must prove it. The burden of proving an allegation of undue influence rests upon the person who claims to have been wronged. This is the general rule. The evidence required to discharge the burden of proof depends on the nature of the alleged undue influence, the personality of the parties, their relationship, the extent to which the transaction cannot readily be accounted for by the ordinary motives of ordinary persons in that relationship, and all the circumstances of the case.

14 Proof that the complainant placed trust and confidence in the other party in relation to the management of the complainant's financial affairs, coupled with a transaction which calls for explanation, will normally be sufficient, failing satisfactory evidence to the contrary, to discharge the burden of proof. On proof of these two matters the stage is set for the court to infer that, in the absence of a satisfactory explanation, the transaction can only have been procured by undue influence. In other words, proof of these two facts is prima facie evidence that the defendant abused the influence he acquired in the parties' relationship. He preferred his own interests. He did not behave fairly to the other. So the evidential burden then shifts to him. It is for him to produce evidence to counter the inference which otherwise should be drawn.

16 Generations of equity lawyers have conventionally described this situation as one in which a presumption of undue influence arises. This use of the term "presumption" is descriptive of a shift in the evidential onus on a question of fact. When a plaintiff succeeds by this route he does so because he has succeeded in establishing a case of undue influence. The court has drawn appropriate inferences of fact upon a balanced consideration of the whole of the evidence at the end of a trial in which the burden of proof rested upon the plaintiff. The use, in the course of the trial, of the forensic tool of a shift in the evidential burden of proof should not be permitted to obscure the overall position. These cases are the equitable counterpart of common law cases where the principle of res ipsa loquitur is invoked. There is a rebuttable evidential presumption of undue influence.

17 The availability of this forensic tool in cases founded on abuse of influence arising from the parties' relationship has led to this type of case sometimes being labelled "presumed undue influence". This is by way of contrast with cases involving actual pressure or the like, which are labelled "actual undue influence": see *Bank of Credit and Commerce International SA v Aboody* [1990] 1 QB 923, 953, and *Royal Bank of Scotland plc v Etridge (No 2)* [1998] 4 All ER 705, 711-712, paras 5-7. This usage can be a little confusing. In many cases where a plaintiff has claimed that the defendant abused the influence he acquired in a relationship of trust and confidence the plaintiff has succeeded by recourse to the rebuttable evidential presumption. But this need not be so. Such a plaintiff may succeed even where this presumption is not available to him; for instance, where the impugned transaction was not one which called for an explanation.

18 The evidential presumption discussed above is to be distinguished sharply from a different form of presumption which arises in some cases. The law has adopted a sternly protective attitude towards certain types of relationship in which one party acquires influence over another who is vulnerable and dependent and where, moreover, substantial gifts by the influenced or vulnerable person are not normally to be expected. Examples of relationships within this special class are parent and child, guardian and ward, trustee and beneficiary, solicitor and client, and medical adviser and patient. In these cases the law presumes, irrebuttably, that one party had influence over the other. The complainant need not prove he actually reposed trust and confidence in the other party. It is sufficient for him to prove the existence of the type of relationship.

19 It is now well established that husband and wife is not one of the relationships to which this latter principle applies. … But there is nothing unusual or strange in a wife, from motives of affection or for other reasons, conferring substantial financial benefits on her husband. Although there is no presumption, the court will nevertheless note, as a matter of fact, the opportunities for abuse which flow from a wife's confidence in her husband. The court will take this into account with all the other evidence in the case. Where there is evidence that a husband has taken unfair advantage of his influence over his wife, or her confidence in him, "it is not difficult for the wife to establish her title to relief": see *In re Lloyds Bank Ltd; Bomze and Lederman v Bomze* [1931] 1 Ch 289, 302, per Maugham J.

Independent advice

20 Proof that the complainant received advice from a third party before entering into the impugned transaction is one of the matters a court takes into account when weighing all the evidence. The weight, or importance, to be attached to such advice depends on all the circumstances. In the normal course, advice from a solicitor or other outside adviser can be expected to bring home to a complainant a proper understanding of what he or she is about to do. But a person may understand fully the implications of a proposed transaction, for instance, a substantial gift, and yet still be acting under the undue influence of another. Proof of outside advice does not, of itself, necessarily show that the subsequent completion of the transaction was free from the exercise of undue influence. Whether it will be proper to infer that outside advice had an emancipating effect, so that the transaction was not brought about by the exercise of undue influence, is a question of fact to be decided having regard to all the evidence in the case.

Manifest disadvantage

21 As already noted, there are two prerequisites to the evidential shift in the burden of proof from the complainant to the other party. First, that the complainant reposed trust and confidence in the other party, or the other party acquired ascendancy over the complainant. Second, that the transaction is not readily explicable by the relationship of the parties.

22 Lindley LJ summarised this second prerequisite in the leading authority of *Allcard v Skinner* 36 Ch D 145, where the donor parted with almost all her property. Lindley LJ pointed out that where a gift of a small amount is made to a person standing in a confidential relationship to the donor, some proof of the exercise of the influence of the donee must be given. The mere existence of the influence is not enough. He continued, at p 185 "But if the gift is so large as not to be reasonably accounted for on the ground of friendship, relationship, charity, or other ordinary motives on which ordinary men act, the burden is upon the donee to support the gift." ...

24 ... The second prerequisite, as expressed by Lindley LJ, is good sense. It is a necessary limitation upon the width of the first prerequisite. It would be absurd for the law to presume that every gift by a child to a parent, or every transaction between a client and his solicitor or between a patient and his doctor, was brought about by undue influence unless the contrary is affirmatively proved. Such a presumption would be too far-reaching. The law would be out of touch with everyday life if the presumption were to apply to every Christmas or birthday gift by a child to a parent, or to an agreement whereby a client or patient agrees to be responsible for the reasonable fees of his legal or medical adviser. The law would be rightly open to ridicule, for transactions such as these are unexceptionable. They do not suggest that something may be amiss. So something more is needed before the law reverses the burden of proof, something which calls for an explanation. When that something more is present, the greater the disadvantage to the vulnerable person, the more cogent must be the explanation before the presumption will be regarded as rebutted.

25 This was the approach adopted by Lord Scarman in *National Westminster Bank plc v Morgan* [1985] AC 686, 703-707. He cited Lindley LJ's observations in *Allcard v Skinner* 36 Ch D 145, 185, which I have set out above. He noted that whatever the legal character of the transaction, it must constitute a disadvantage sufficiently serious to require evidence to rebut the presumption that in the circumstances of the parties' relationship, it was procured by the exercise of undue influence. ...

26 Lord Scarman attached the label "manifest disadvantage" to this second ingredient necessary to raise the presumption. This label has been causing difficulty. It may be apt enough when applied to straightforward transactions such as a substantial gift or a sale at an undervalue. But experience has now shown that this expression can give rise to misunderstanding. The label is being understood and applied in a way which does not accord with the meaning intended by Lord Scarman, its originator.

27 The problem has arisen in the context of wives guaranteeing payment of their husband[s'] business debts. In recent years judge after judge has grappled with the baffling question whether a wife's guarantee of her husband's bank overdraft, together with a charge on her share of the matrimonial home, was a transaction manifestly to her disadvantage.

28 In a narrow sense, such a transaction plainly ("manifestly") is disadvantageous to the wife. She undertakes a serious financial obligation, and in return she personally receives nothing. But that would be to take an unrealistically blinkered view of such a transaction. Unlike the relationship of solicitor and client or medical adviser and patient, in the case of husband and wife there are inherent reasons why such a transaction may well be for her benefit. Ordinarily, the fortunes of husband and wife are bound up together. If the husband's business is the source of the family income, the wife has a lively interest in doing what she can to support the business. A wife's affection and self-interest run hand-in-hand in inclining her to join with her husband in charging the matrimonial home, usually a jointly-owned asset, to obtain the financial facilities needed by the business. The finance may be needed to start a new business, or expand a promising business, or rescue an ailing business.

29 Which, then, is the correct approach to adopt in deciding whether a transaction is disadvantageous to the wife: the narrow approach, or the wider approach? The answer is neither. The answer lies in discarding a label which gives rise to this sort of ambiguity. The better approach is to adhere more directly to the test outlined by Lindley LJ in *Allcard v Skinner* 36 Ch D 145, and adopted by Lord Scarman in *National Westminster Bank plc v Morgan* [1985] AC 686, in the passages I have cited.

30 I return to husband and wife cases. I do not think that, in the ordinary course, a guarantee of the character I have mentioned is to be regarded as a transaction which, failing proof to the contrary, is explicable only on the basis that it has been procured by the exercise of undue influence by the husband. Wives frequently enter into such transactions. There are good and sufficient reasons why they are willing to do so, despite the risks involved for them and their families. They may be enthusiastic. They may not. They may be less optimistic than their husbands about the prospects of the husbands' businesses. They may be anxious, perhaps exceedingly so. But this is a far cry from saying that such transactions as a class are to be regarded as prima facie evidence of the exercise of undue influence by husbands.

31 I have emphasised the phrase "in the ordinary course". There will be cases where a wife's signature of a guarantee or a charge of her share in the matrimonial home does call for explanation. Nothing I have said above is directed at such a case.

A cautionary note

32 I add a cautionary note, prompted by some of the first instance judgments in the cases currently being considered by the House. It concerns the general approach to be adopted by a court when considering whether a wife's guarantee of her husband's bank overdraft was procured by her husband's undue influence. Undue influence has a connotation of impropriety. In the eye of the law, undue influence means that influence has been misused. Statements or conduct by a husband which do not pass beyond the bounds of what may be expected of a reasonable husband in the circumstances should not, without more, be castigated as undue influence. Similarly, when a husband is forecasting the future of his business, and expressing his hopes or fears, a degree of hyperbole may be only natural. Courts should not too readily treat such exaggerations as misstatements.

33 Inaccurate explanations of a proposed transaction are a different matter. So are cases where a husband, in whom a wife has reposed trust and confidence for the management of their financial affairs, prefers his interests to hers and makes a choice for both of them on that footing. Such a husband abuses the influence he has. He fails to discharge the obligation of candour and fairness he owes a wife who is looking to him to make the major financial decisions.

The complainant and third parties: suretyship transactions

34 The problem considered in *O'Brien*'s case and raised by the present appeals is of comparatively recent origin. It arises out of the substantial growth in home ownership over the last 30 or 40 years and, as part of that development, the great increase in the number of homes owned jointly by husbands and wives. More than two-thirds of householders in the United Kingdom now own their own homes. For most home-owning couples, their homes are their most valuable asset. They must surely be free, if they so wish, to use this asset as a means of raising money, whether for the purpose of the husband's business or for any other purpose. Their home is their property. The law should not restrict them in the use they may make of it. … Finance raised by second mortgages on the principal's home is a significant source of capital for the start-up of small businesses.

35 If the freedom of home-owners to make economic use of their homes is not to be frustrated, a bank must be able to have confidence that a wife's signature of the necessary guarantee and charge will be as binding upon her as is the signature of anyone else on documents which he or she may sign. Otherwise banks will not be willing to lend money on the security of a jointly owned house or flat.

36 At the same time, the high degree of trust and confidence and emotional interdependence which normally characterises a marriage relationship provides scope for abuse. One party may take advantage of the other's vulnerability. Unhappily, such abuse does occur. Further, it is all too easy for a husband, anxious or even desperate for bank finance, to misstate the position in some particular or to mislead the wife, wittingly or unwittingly, in some other way. The law would be seriously defective if it did not recognise these realities.

37 In *O'Brien*'s case this House decided where the balance should be held between these competing interests. On the one side, there is the need to protect a wife against a husband's undue influence. On the other side, there is the need for the bank to be able to have reasonable confidence in the strength of its security. Otherwise it would not provide the required money. The problem lies in finding the course best designed to protect wives in a minority of cases without unreasonably hampering the giving and taking of security. The House produced a practical solution. The House decided what are the steps a bank should take to ensure it is not affected by any claim the wife may have that her signature of the documents was procured by the undue influence or other wrong of her husband. Like every compromise, the outcome falls short of achieving in full the objectives of either of the two competing interests. In particular, the steps required of banks will not guarantee that, in future, wives will not be subjected to undue influence or misled when standing as sureties. Short of prohibiting this type of suretyship transaction altogether, there is no way of achieving that result, desirable although it is. What passes between a husband and wife in this regard in the privacy of their own home is not capable of regulation or investigation as a prelude to the wife entering into a suretyship transaction.

38 The jurisprudential route by which the House reached its conclusion in *O'Brien*'s case has attracted criticism from some commentators. It has been said to involve artificiality and thereby create uncertainty in the law. I must first consider this criticism. In the ordinary course a bank which takes a guarantee security from the wife of its customer will be altogether ignorant of any undue influence the customer may have exercised in order to secure the wife's concurrence. In *O'Brien* Lord Browne-Wilkinson prayed in aid the doctrine of constructive notice. In circumstances he identified, a creditor is put on inquiry. When that is so, the creditor "will have constructive notice of the wife's rights" unless the creditor takes reasonable steps to satisfy himself that the wife's agreement to stand surety has been properly obtained: see [1994] 1 AC 180, 196.

39 Lord Browne-Wilkinson would be the first to recognise this is not a conventional use of the equitable concept of constructive notice. The traditional use of this concept concerns the circumstances in which a transferee of property who acquires a legal estate from a transferor with a defective title may nonetheless obtain a good title, that is, a better title than the transferor had. That is not the present case. The bank acquires its charge from the wife, and there is nothing wrong with her title to her share of the matrimonial home. The transferor wife is seeking to resile from the very transaction she entered into with the bank, on the ground that her apparent consent was procured by the undue influence or other misconduct, such as misrepresentation, of a third party (her husband). She is seeking to set aside her contract of guarantee and, with it, the charge she gave to the bank.

40 The traditional view of equity in this tripartite situation seems to be that a person in the position of the wife will only be relieved of her bargain if the other party to the transaction (the bank, in the present instance) was privy to the conduct which led to the wife's entry into the transaction. Knowledge is required... The law imposes no obligation on one party to a transaction to check whether the other party's concurrence was obtained by undue influence. But *O'Brien* has introduced into the law the concept that, in certain circumstances, a party to a contract may lose the benefit of his contract, entered into in good faith, if he ought to have known that the other's concurrence had been procured by the misconduct of a third party.

41 There is a further respect in which *O'Brien* departed from conventional concepts. Traditionally, a person is deemed to have notice (that is, he has "constructive" notice) of a prior right when he does not actually know of it but would have learned of it had he made the requisite inquiries. A purchaser will be treated as having constructive notice of all that a reasonably prudent purchaser would have discovered. In the present type of case, the steps a bank is required to take, lest it have constructive notice that the wife's concurrence was procured improperly by her husband, do not consist of making inquiries. Rather, *O'Brien* envisages that the steps taken by the bank will reduce, or even eliminate, the risk of the wife entering into the transaction under any misapprehension or as a result of undue influence by her husband. The steps are not concerned to discover whether the wife has been wronged by her husband in this way. The steps are concerned to minimise the risk that such a wrong may be committed.

42 These novelties do not point to the conclusion that the decision of this House in *O'Brien* is leading the law astray. Lord Browne-Wilkinson acknowledged he might be extending the law: see [1994] 1 AC 180, 197. Some development was sorely needed. The law had to find a way of giving wives a reasonable measure of protection, without adding unreasonably to the expense involved in entering into guarantee transactions of the type under consideration. The protection had to extend also to any misrepresentations made by a husband to his wife. In a situation where there is a substantial risk the husband may exercise his influence improperly regarding the provision of security for his business debts, there is an increased risk that explanations of the transaction given by him to his wife may be misleadingly incomplete or even inaccurate.

43 The route selected in *O'Brien* ought not to have an unsettling effect on established principles of contract. *O'Brien* concerned suretyship transactions. These are tripartite transactions. They involve the debtor as well as the creditor and the guarantor. The guarantor enters into the transaction at the request of the debtor. The guarantor assumes obligations. On the face of the transaction the guarantor usually receives no benefit in return, unless the guarantee is being given on a commercial basis. Leaving aside cases where the relationship between the surety and the debtor is commercial, a guarantee transaction is one-sided so far as the guarantor is concerned. The creditor knows this. Thus the decision in *O'Brien* is directed at a class of contracts which has special features of its own. ...

The threshold: when the bank is put on inquiry

44 In *O'Brien* the House considered the circumstances in which a bank, or other creditor, is "put on inquiry". Strictly this is a misnomer. As already noted, a bank is not required to make inquiries. But it will be convenient to use the terminology which has now become accepted in this context. The House set a low level for the threshold which must be crossed before a bank is put on inquiry. For practical reasons the level is set much lower than is required to satisfy a court that, failing contrary evidence, the court may infer that the transaction was procured by undue influence. Lord Browne-Wilkinson said [1994] 1 AC 180, 196:

> "Therefore in my judgment a creditor in put on inquiry when a wife offers to stand surety for her husband's debts by the combination of two factors: (a) the transaction is on its face not to the financial advantage of the wife; and (b) there is a substantial risk in transactions of that kind that, in procuring the wife to act as surety, the husband has committed a legal or equitable wrong that entitles the wife to set aside the transaction."

In my view, this passage, read in context, is to be taken to mean, quite simply, that a bank is put on inquiry whenever a wife offers to stand surety for her husband's debts.

46 ...I do not understand Lord Browne-Wilkinson to have been saying that, in husband and wife cases, whether the bank is put on inquiry depends on its state of knowledge of the parties' marriage, or of the degree of trust and confidence the particular wife places in her husband in relation to her financial affairs. That would leave banks in a state of considerable uncertainty in a situation where it is important they should know clearly where they stand. The test should be simple and clear and easy to apply in a wide range of circumstances. I read (a) and (b) as Lord Browne-Wilkinson's broad explanation of the reason why a creditor is put on inquiry when a wife offers to stand surety for her husband's debts. These are the two factors which, taken together, constitute the underlying rationale.

47 The position is likewise if the husband stands surety for his wife's debts. Similarly, in the case of unmarried couples, whether heterosexual or homosexual, where the bank is aware of the relationship: see Lord Browne-Wilkinson in *O'Brien*'s case, at p 198. Cohabitation is not essential. The Court of Appeal rightly so decided in *Massey v Midland Bank plc* [1995] 1 All ER 929: see Steyn LJ, at p 933.

48 As to the type of transactions where a bank is put on inquiry, the case where a wife becomes surety for her husband's debts is, in this context, a straightforward case. The bank is put on inquiry. On the other side of the line is the case where money is being advanced, or has been advanced, to husband and wife jointly. In such a case the bank is not put on inquiry, unless the bank is aware the loan is being made for the husband's purposes, as distinct from their joint purposes. That was decided in *CIBC Mortgages plc v Pitt* [1994] 1 AC 200.

49 Less clear cut is the case where the wife becomes surety for the debts of a company whose shares are held by her and her husband. Her shareholding may be nominal, or she may have a minority shareholding or an equal shareholding with her husband. In my view the bank is put on inquiry in such cases, even when the wife is a director or secretary of the company. Such cases cannot be equated with joint loans. The shareholding interests, and the identity of the directors, are not a reliable guide to the identity of the persons who actually have the conduct of the company's business.

The steps a bank should take

50 The principal area of controversy on these appeals concerns the steps a bank should take when it has been put on inquiry. In *O'Brien* [1994] 1 AC 180, 196-197 Lord Browne-Wilkinson said that a bank can reasonably be expected to take steps to bring home to the wife the risk she is running by standing as surety and to advise her to take independent advice. That test is applicable to past transactions. All the cases now before your Lordships' House fall into this category. For the future a bank satisfies these requirements if it insists that the wife attend a private meeting with a representative of the bank at which she is told of the extent of her liability as surety, warned of the risk she is running and urged to take independent legal advice. In exceptional cases the bank, to be safe, has to insist that the wife is separately advised.

53 My Lords, it is plainly neither desirable nor practicable that banks should be required to attempt to discover for themselves whether a wife's consent is being procured by the exercise of undue influence of her husband. This is not a step the banks should be expected to take. Nor, further, is it desirable or practicable that banks should be expected to insist on confirmation from a solicitor that the solicitor has satisfied himself that the wife's consent has not been procured by undue influence. ...

54 The furthest a bank can be expected to go is to take reasonable steps to satisfy itself that the wife has had brought home to her, in a meaningful way, the practical implications of the proposed transaction. This does not wholly eliminate the risk of undue influence or misrepresentation. But it does mean that a wife enters into a transaction with her eyes open so far as the basic elements of the transaction are concerned.

55 This is the point at which, in the *O'Brien* case, the House decided that the balance between the competing interests should be held. A bank may itself provide the necessary information directly to the wife. Indeed, it is best equipped to do so. But banks are not following that course. Ought they to be obliged to do so in every case? I do not think Lord Browne-Wilkinson so stated in *O'Brien*. I do not understand him to have said that a personal meeting was the only way a bank could discharge its obligation to bring home to the wife the risks she is running. It seems to me that, provided a suitable alternative is available, banks ought not to be compelled to take this course. …

56 I shall return later to the steps a bank should take when it follows this course. Suffice to say, these steps, together with advice from a solicitor acting for the wife, ought to provide the substance of the protection which *O'Brien* intended a wife should have. Ordinarily it will be reasonable that a bank should be able to rely upon confirmation from a solicitor, acting for the wife, that he has advised the wife appropriately.

57 The position will be otherwise if the bank knows that the solicitor has not duly advised the wife or, I would add, if the bank knows facts from which it ought to have realised that the wife has not received the appropriate advice. In such circumstances the bank will proceed at its own risk.

The content of the legal advice

61 [I]t is not for the solicitor to veto the transaction by declining to confirm to the bank that he has explained the documents to the wife and the risks she is taking upon herself. If the solicitor considers the transaction is not in the wife's best interests, he will give reasoned advice to the wife to that effect. But at the end of the day the decision on whether to proceed is the decision of the client, not the solicitor. A wife is not to be precluded from entering into a financially unwise transaction if, for her own reasons, she wishes to do so.

62 That is the general rule. There may, of course, be exceptional circumstances where it is glaringly obvious that the wife is being grievously wronged. In such a case the solicitor should decline to act further. …

64 … In identifying what are the solicitor's responsibilities the starting point must always be the solicitor's retainer. What has he been retained to do? As a general proposition, the scope of a solicitor's duties is dictated by the terms, whether express or implied, of his retainer. … As a first step the solicitor will need to explain to the wife the purpose for which he has become involved at all. He should explain that, should it ever become necessary, the bank will rely upon his involvement to counter any suggestion that the wife was overborne by her husband or that she did not properly understand the implications of the transaction. The solicitor will need to obtain confirmation from the wife that she wishes him to act for her in the matter and to advise her on the legal and practical implications of the proposed transaction.

65 When an instruction to this effect is forthcoming, the content of the advice required from a solicitor before giving the confirmation sought by the bank will, inevitably, depend upon the circumstances of the case. Typically, the advice a solicitor can be expected to give should cover the following matters as the core minimum. (1) He will need to explain the nature of the documents and the practical consequences these will have for the wife if she signs them. She could lose her home if her husband's business does not prosper. Her home may be her only substantial asset, as well as the family's home. She could be made bankrupt. (2) He will need to point out the seriousness of the risks involved. The wife should be told the purpose of the proposed new facility, the amount and principal terms of the new facility, and that the bank might increase the amount of the facility, or change its terms, or grant a new facility, without reference to her. She should be told the amount of her liability under her guarantee. The solicitor should discuss the wife's financial means, including her understanding of the value of the property being charged. The solicitor should discuss whether the wife or her husband has any other assets out of which repayment could be made if the husband's business should fail. These matters are relevant to the seriousness of the risks involved. (3) The solicitor will need to state clearly that the wife has a choice. The decision is hers and hers alone. Explanation of the choice facing the wife will call for some discussion of the present financial position, including the amount of the husband's present indebtedness, and the amount of his current overdraft facility. (4) The solicitor should check whether the wife wishes to proceed. She should be asked whether she is content that the solicitor should write to the bank confirming he has explained to her the nature of the documents and the practical implications they may have for her, or whether, for instance, she would prefer him to negotiate with the bank on the terms of the transaction. Matters for negotiation could include the sequence in which the various securities will be called upon or a specific or lower limit to her liabilities. The solicitor should not give any confirmation to the bank without the wife's authority.

66 The solicitor's discussion with the wife should take place at a face-to-face meeting, in the absence of the husband. It goes without saying that the solicitor's explanations should be couched in suitably non-technical language. It also goes without saying that the solicitor's task is an important one. It is not a formality.

67 The solicitor should obtain from the bank any information he needs. If the bank fails for any reason to provide information requested by the solicitor, the solicitor should decline to provide the confirmation sought by the bank.

Independent advice

69 I turn next to the much-vexed question whether the solicitor advising the wife must act for the wife alone. ...

73 ... A requirement that a wife should receive advice from a solicitor acting solely for her will frequently add significantly to the legal costs. Sometimes a wife will be happier to be advised by a family solicitor known to her than by a complete stranger. Sometimes a solicitor who knows both husband and wife and their histories will be better placed to advise than a solicitor who is a complete stranger.

74 ...The advantages attendant upon the employment of a solicitor acting solely for the wife do not justify the additional expense this would involve for the husband. When accepting instructions to advise the wife the solicitor assumes responsibilities directly to her, both at law and professionally. These duties, and this is central to the reasoning on this point, are owed to the wife alone. In advising the wife the solicitor is acting for the wife alone. He is concerned only with her interests. I emphasise, therefore, that in every case the solicitor must consider carefully whether there is any conflict of duty or interest and, more widely, whether it would be in the best interests of the wife for him to accept instructions from her. If he decides to accept instructions, his assumption of legal and professional responsibilities to her ought, in the ordinary course of things, to provide sufficient assurance that he will give the requisite advice fully, carefully and conscientiously. Especially so, now that the nature of the advice called for has been clarified. If at any stage the solicitor becomes concerned that there is a real risk that other interests or duties may inhibit his advice to the wife he must cease to act for her.

Agency

75 No system ever works perfectly. There will always be cases where things go wrong, sometimes seriously wrong. The next question concerns the position when a solicitor has accepted instructions to advise a wife but he fails to do so properly. He fails to give her the advice needed to bring home to her the practical implications of her standing as surety. What then? The wife has a remedy in damages against the negligent solicitor. But what is the position of the bank who proceeded in the belief that the wife had been given the necessary advice?

77 ...The mere fact that, for its own purposes, the bank asked the solicitor to advise the wife does not make the solicitor the bank's agent in giving that advice.

78 In the ordinary case... deficiencies in the advice given are a matter between the wife and her solicitor. The bank is entitled to proceed on the assumption that a solicitor advising the wife has done his job properly. ...

Obtaining the solicitor's confirmation

79 I now return to the steps a bank should take when it has been put on inquiry and for its protection is looking to the fact that the wife has been advised independently by a solicitor. ...

(1) ...[T]he bank should take steps to check *directly with the wife* the name of the solicitor she wishes to act for her. To this end, in future the bank should communicate directly with the wife, informing her that for its own protection it will require written confirmation from a solicitor, acting for her, to the effect that the solicitor has fully explained to her the nature of the documents and the practical implications they will have for her. She should be told that the purpose of this requirement is that thereafter she should not be able to dispute she is legally bound by the documents once she has signed them. She should be asked to nominate a solicitor whom she is willing to instruct to advise her, separately from her husband, and act for her in giving the necessary confirmation to the bank. She should be told that, if she wishes, the solicitor may be the same solicitor as is acting for her husband in the transaction. If a solicitor is already acting for the husband and the wife, she should be asked whether she would prefer that a different solicitor should act for her regarding the bank's requirement for confirmation from a solicitor. The bank should not proceed with the transaction until it has received an appropriate response directly from the wife.

(2) Representatives of the bank are likely to have a much better picture of the husband's financial affairs than the solicitor. If the bank is not willing to undertake the task of explanation itself, the bank must provide the solicitor with the financial information he needs for this purpose. Accordingly it should become routine practice for banks, if relying on confirmation from a solicitor for their protection, to send to the solicitor the necessary financial information. What is required must depend on the facts of the case. Ordinarily this will include information on the purpose for which the proposed new facility has been requested, the current amount of the husband's indebtedness, the amount of his current overdraft facility, and the amount and terms of any new facility. If the bank's request for security arose from a written application by the husband for a facility, a copy of the application should be sent to the solicitor. The bank will, of course, need first to obtain the consent of its customer to this circulation of confidential information. If this consent is not forthcoming the transaction will not be able to proceed.

(3) Exceptionally there may be a case where the bank believes or suspects that the wife has been misled by her husband or is not entering into the transaction of her own free will. If such a case occurs the bank must inform the wife's solicitors of the facts giving rise to its belief or suspicion.

(4) The bank should in every case obtain from the wife's solicitor a written confirmation to the effect mentioned above.

80 These steps will be applicable to future transactions. In respect of past transactions, the bank will ordinarily be regarded as having discharged its obligations if a solicitor who was acting for the wife in the transaction gave the bank confirmation to the effect that he had brought home to the wife the risks she was running by standing as surety.

A wider principle

82 Before turning to the particular cases I must make a general comment on the *O'Brien* principle. ... Sexual relationships are no more than one type of relationship in which an individual may acquire influence over another individual. The *O'Brien* decision cannot sensibly be regarded as confined to sexual relationships, although these are likely to be its main field of application at present. What is appropriate for sexual relationships ought, in principle, to be appropriate also for other relationships where trust and confidence are likely to exist.

83 The courts have already recognised this. Further application, or development, of the *O'Brien* principle has already taken place. In *Credit Lyonnais Bank Nederland NV v Burch* [1997] 1 All ER 144 the same principle was applied where the relationship was employer and employee. ...

84 The crucially important question raised by this wider application of the *O'Brien* principle concerns the circumstances which will put a bank on inquiry. ...

87 ...[T]here is no rational cut-off point, with certain types of relationship being susceptible to the *O'Brien* principle and others not. Further, if a bank is not to be required to evaluate the extent to which its customer has influence over a proposed guarantor, the only practical way forward is to regard banks as "put on inquiry" in every case where the relationship between the surety and the debtor is non-commercial. The creditor must always take reasonable steps to bring home to the individual guarantor the risks he is running by standing as surety. ...

88 Different considerations apply where the relationship between the debtor and guarantor is commercial, as where a guarantor is being paid a fee, or a company is guaranteeing the debts of another company in the same group. Those engaged in business can be regarded as capable of looking after themselves and understanding the risks involved in the giving of guarantees.

89 By the decisions of this House in *O'Brien* and the Court of Appeal in *Credit Lyonnais Bank Nederland NV v Burch* [1997] 1 All ER 144, English law has taken its first strides in the development of some such general principle. It is a workable principle. It is also simple, coherent and eminently desirable. I venture to think this is the way the law is moving, and should continue to move. ...

Lord Hobhouse of Woodborough:

100 ... I will, in the course of this speech and without qualifying the scope of my agreement with Lord Nicholls, mention certain points in the hope that it will add to the clarity and accuracy of the analysis. ...

103 The division between presumed and actual undue influence derives from the judgments in *Allcard v Skinner*. Actual undue influence presents no relevant problem. It is an equitable wrong committed by the dominant party against the other which makes it unconscionable for the dominant party to enforce his legal rights against the other. It is typically some express conduct overbearing the other party's will. It is capable of including conduct which might give a defence at law, for example, duress and misrepresentation. ... Actual undue influence does not depend upon some preexisting relationship between the two parties though it is most commonly associated with and derives from such a relationship. He who alleges actual undue influence must prove it.

104 Presumed undue influence is different in that it necessarily involves some legally recognised relationship between the two parties. As a result of that relationship one party is treated as owing a special duty to deal fairly with the other. It is not necessary for present purposes to define the limits of the relationships which give rise to this duty. Typically they are fiduciary or closely analogous relationships. ... Such legal relationships can be described as relationships where one party is legally presumed to repose trust and confidence in the other—the other side of the coin to the duty not to abuse that confidence. But there is no presumption properly so called that the confidence has been abused. It is a matter of evidence. ...It will be appreciated that the relevance of the concept of "manifest disadvantage" is evidential. It is relevant to the question whether there is any issue of abuse which can properly be raised. It is relevant to the determination whether in fact abuse did or did not occur. It is a fallacy to argue from the terminology normally used, "presumed undue influence", to the position, not of presuming that one party reposed trust and confidence in the other, but of presuming that an abuse of that relationship has occurred; factual inference, yes, once the issue has been properly raised, but not a presumption.

105 The Court of Appeal in *Aboody* [1990] 1 QB 923 and Lord Browne-Wilkinson classified cases where there was a legal relationship between the parties which the law presumed to be one of trust and confidence as "presumed undue influence: class 2(A)". They then made the logical extrapolation that there should be a class 2(B) to cover those cases where it was proved by evidence that one party had in fact reposed trust and confidence in the other. It was then said that the same consequences flowed from this factual relationship as from the legal class 2(A) relationship. ... Where the relevant question is one of fact and degree and of the evaluation of evidence, the language of presumption is likely to confuse rather than assist and this is borne out by experience.

106 That there is room for an analogous approach to cases concerning a wife's guarantee of her husband's debts is clear and no doubt led to Lord Browne-Wilkinson saying what he did. ... [But if] at the end of the trial the wife succeeds on the issue of undue influence, it will be because that is the right conclusion of fact on the state of the evidence at the end of the trial, not because of some artificial legal presumption that there must have been undue influence.

107 In agreement with what I understand to be the view of your Lordships, I consider that the so-called class 2(B) presumption should not be adopted. It is not a useful forensic tool. The wife or other person alleging that the relevant agreement or charge is not enforceable must prove her case. She can do this by proving that she was the victim of an equitable wrong. This wrong may be an overt wrong, such as oppression; or it may be the failure to perform an equitable duty, such as a failure by one in whom trust and confidence is reposed not to abuse that trust by failing to deal fairly with her and have proper regard to her interests. Although the general burden of proof is, and remains, upon her, she can discharge that burden of proof by establishing a sufficient prima facie case to justify a decision in her favour on the balance of probabilities, the court drawing appropriate inferences from the primary facts proved. Evidentially the opposite party will then be faced with the necessity to adduce evidence sufficient to displace that conclusion. Provided it is remembered that the burden is an evidential one, the comparison with the operation of the doctrine res ipsa loquitur is useful.

Lord Scott of Foscote:

151 Undue influence cases have, traditionally, been regarded as falling into two classes, cases where undue influence must be affirmatively proved (Class 1) and cases where undue influence will be presumed (Class 2). The nature of the two classes was described by Slade LJ in *Bank of Credit and Commerce International SA v Aboody* [1990] 1 QB 923, 953:

> "Ever since the judgments of this court in *Allcard v Skinner*... a clear distinction has been drawn between (1) those cases in which the court will uphold a plea of undue influence only if it is satisfied that such influence has been affirmatively proved on the evidence (commonly referred to as cases of 'actual undue influence' ... 'Class 1' cases); (2) those cases (commonly referred to as cases of 'presumed undue influence' ... 'Class 2' cases) in which the relationship between the parties will lead the court to presume that undue influence has been exerted unless evidence is adduced proving the contrary, e g by showing that the complaining party has had independent advice."

152 This passage provides, if I may respectfully say so, an accurate summary description of the two classes. But, like most summaries, it requires some qualification.

153 First, the Class 2 presumption is an evidential rebuttable presumption. It shifts the onus from the party who is alleging undue influence to the party who is denying it. Second, the weight of the presumption will vary from case to case and will depend both on the particular nature of the relationship and on the particular nature of the impugned transaction. Third, the type and weight of evidence needed to rebut the presumption will obviously depend upon the weight of the presumption itself. ...

154 The onus will, of course, lie on the person alleging the undue influence to prove in the first instance sufficient facts to give rise to the presumption. The relationship relied on in support of the presumption will have to be proved.

155 In *National Westminster Bank plc v Morgan* [1985] AC 686, 704 Lord Scarman, referring to the character of the impugned transaction in a Class 2 case, said: "it must constitute a disadvantage sufficiently serious to require evidence to rebut the presumption that in the circumstances of the relationship between the parties it was procured by the exercise of undue influence." Lord Scarman went on:

"In my judgment, therefore, the Court of Appeal erred in law in holding that the presumption of undue influence can arise from the evidence of the relationship of the parties without also evidence that the transaction itself was wrongful in that it constituted an advantage taken of the person subjected to the influence which, failing proof to the contrary, was explicable only on the basis that undue influence had been exercised to procure it."

With respect to Lord Scarman, the reasoning seems to me to be circular. The transaction will not be "wrongful" unless it was procured by undue influence. Its "wrongful" character is a conclusion, not a tool by which to detect the presence of undue influence. On the other hand, the nature of the transaction, its inexplicability by reference to the normal motives by which people act, may, and usually will, constitute important evidential material.

156 Lord Browne-Wilkinson in *CIBC Mortgages plc v Pitt* [1994] 1 AC 200 pointed out, plainly correctly, that if undue influence is proved, the victim's right to have the transaction set aside will not depend upon the disadvantageous quality of the transaction. Where, however a Class 2 presumption of undue influence is said to arise, the nature of the impugned transaction will always be material, no matter what the relationship between the parties. Some transactions will be obviously innocuous and innocent. A moderate gift as a Christmas or birthday present would be an example. A solicitor who is appointed by a client as his executor and given a legacy of a moderate amount if he consents to act, is not put to proof of the absence of undue influence before he can take the legacy. If the nun/postulant/novice in *Allcard v Skinner* had given moderate Christmas presents to the Mother Superior, or to the Sisterhood, no inference that the gifts had been procured by undue influence could be drawn and no presumption of undue influence would have arisen. It is, in my opinion, the combination of relationship and the nature of the transaction that gives rise to the presumption and, if the transaction is challenged, shifts the onus to the transferee.

161 For my part, I doubt the utility of the Class 2B classification. Class 2A is useful in identifying particular relationships where the presumption arises. The presumption in Class 2B cases, however, is doing no more than recognising that evidence of the relationship between the dominant and subservient parties, coupled with whatever other evidence is for the time being available, may be sufficient to justify a finding of undue influence on the balance of probabilities. The onus shifts to the defendant. Unless the defendant introduces evidence to counteract the inference of undue influence that the complainant's evidence justifies, the complainant will succeed. In my opinion, the presumption of undue influence in Class 2B cases has the same function in undue influence cases as res ipsa loquitur has in negligence cases. It recognises an evidential state of affairs in which the onus has shifted.

162 In the surety wife cases it should, in my opinion, be recognised that undue influence, though a possible explanation for the wife's agreement to become surety, is a relatively unlikely one. *O'Brien* itself was a misrepresentation case. Undue influence had been alleged but the undoubted pressure which the husband had brought to bear to persuade his reluctant wife to sign was not regarded by the judge or the Court of Appeal as constituting undue influence. The wife's will had not been overborne by her husband. Nor was *O'Brien* a case in which, in my opinion, there would have been at any stage in the case a presumption of undue influence.

219 The presumption of undue influence, whether in a category 2A case, or in a category 2B case, is a rebuttable evidential presumption. It is a presumption which arises if the nature of the relationship between two parties coupled with the nature of the transaction between them is such as justifies, in the absence of any other evidence, an inference that the transaction was procured by the undue influence of one party over the other. This evidential presumption shifts the onus to the dominant party and requires the dominant party, if he is to avoid a finding of undue influence, to adduce some sufficient additional evidence to rebut the presumption. In a case where there has been a full trial, however, the judge must decide on the totality of the evidence before the court whether or not the allegation of undue influence has been proved. In an appropriate case the presumption may carry the complainant home. But it makes no sense to find, on the one hand, that there was no undue influence but, on the other hand, that the presumption applies. If the presumption does, after all the evidence has been heard, still apply, then a finding of undue influence is justified. If, on the other hand, the judge, having heard the evidence, concludes that there was no undue influence, the presumption stands rebutted. A finding of actual undue influence and a finding that there is a presumption of undue influence are not alternatives to one another. The presumption is, I repeat, an evidential presumption. If it applies, and the evidence is not sufficient to rebut it, an allegation of undue influence succeeds.

220 As to manifest disadvantage, the expression is no more than shorthand for the proposition that the nature and ingredients of the impugned transaction are essential factors in deciding whether the evidential presumption has arisen and in determining the strength of that presumption. It is not a divining-rod by means of which the presence of undue influence in the procuring of a transaction can be identified. It is merely a description of a transaction which cannot be explained by reference to the ordinary motives by which people are accustomed to act.

Lord Clyde delivered a speech concurring with Lord Nicholls.

NOTES AND QUESTIONS

1. This is by far the most important case in English law on undue influence. Its impact is on both the law of undue influence generally and the specific problems raised by undue influence (or misrepresentation) in three-party cases.
2. *Undue influence generally.*
(i) According to the House of Lords, the difference between the traditional two categories of actual and presumed undue influence has been commonly misunderstood. The presumption of undue influence is not an irrebuttable legal presumption but a rebuttable evidential presumption [16]. One could manage without the two categories (although, not surprisingly, the courts have subsequently continued to use them) by simply saying that it is for the claimant to prove that a transaction was entered into as a result of undue influence and that in some situations the claimant is assisted by a rebuttable evidential presumption of undue influence which shifts the evidential burden of proof to the other party. The categories therefore refer to ways of proving undue influence and are not referring to different types of undue influence. Lord Scott emphasised at [219] that it follows that it is inconsistent and incorrect for a judge to conclude that there was no actual undue influence while at the same time deciding that the claimant succeeds by a presumption of undue influence. To avoid inaccuracy, what a judge should be saying in that situation is that it is only with the benefit of a presumption of undue influence that the claimant succeeds in proving undue influence.
(ii) To establish the (evidential) presumption of undue influence, there are two requirements. First, there must be a relationship of influence. This may be established on the facts. However, in respect of some relationships (eg, parent and child, solicitor and client, doctor and patient, trustee and beneficiary) there is an irrebuttable legal presumption [18] that the relationship is one of influence (but note, in line with what has been said in (i) above, that this is not an irrebuttable legal presumption of *undue* influence). Husband and wife is not such a relationship (that is, it is not automatically a relationship of influence)

[19]. Secondly, the transaction must be 'not readily explicable by the relationship of the parties' [21] or 'not readily explicable on ordinary motives' (as Lindley LJ said in *Allcard v Skinner*) [26] and [29]. In other words, the transaction must make one suspect that undue influence has been exercised. It is no longer regarded as helpful to express the second requirement in terms of whether the transaction was 'manifestly disadvantageous' (the test laid down by the House of Lords in *National Westminster Bank v Morgan*, below, 774) [26]–[29].

(iii) If the presumption of undue influence is established, the (evidential) burden of proof shifts and it is for the party seeking to enforce the contract to rebut the presumption by showing that the other party was free of undue influence in entering into it. The most obvious way of discharging the burden is to show that the other party has taken and acted on independent advice [20].

(iv) Although not a necessary element, see the *Pitt* case above, 732, note 5, it is unlikely that undue influence will be established unless the transaction is disadvantageous. See [12].

3.   *Three-party cases*

(i)   The House of Lords confirmed the validity of the *O'Brien* principle of constructive notice but sought to clarify what is meant by constructive notice. There are two key elements within constructive notice. First, the bank must be put on inquiry of the undue influence. Secondly, the bank must fail to take reasonable steps to ensure that the influenced party fully understands what she is doing.

(ii)   As regards the first element, the House of Lords said that a bank would be put on inquiry whenever a wife offers to stand as surety for her husband's debts or her husband's company's debts or the debts of a company jointly owned by the wife and her husband. But this would not be so where the loan is made jointly to a husband and wife unless the bank knows that the loan is only intended to be used for the husband's purposes. At [87] Lord Nicholls suggested that the underpinning wider principle is that a bank is put on inquiry wherever a person offers to stand as surety for the debts of another and the relationship between the surety and the debtor is non-commercial (eg spouses, cohabitees, father and daughter, or junior employer and employee as in *Credit Lyonnais Bank Nederland v Burch*, above, 735).

(iii)   As regards the second element, the House of Lords laid down, in a code of (future) practice, the reasonable steps the bank should take [79]–[80]:

(a)   The bank should communicate directly with the wife informing her that the bank requires written confirmation from a solicitor acting for her that she understands what she is doing.

(b)   The bank should forward to the wife directly, or to her solicitor, the financial circumstances regarding her husband's application for a loan (eg, his request and the amount of his existing indebtedness).

(c)   The bank should not proceed unless it has received from the wife's solicitor a confirmation that the solicitor has advised her appropriately. It is not a matter for the bank if the wife is improperly advised, unless the bank actually knows of this.

If such steps are not taken, and the bank has been put on inquiry, a wife who can establish undue influence (or misrepresentation) will be able to rescind the contract (guaranteeing her husband's debts) with the bank because the bank has constructive notice. On the other hand, if such steps are taken, the bank will not have constructive notice and, unless it actually knows of undue influence (or misrepresentation), it can enforce the contract.

(iv) The House of Lords also laid down a code of practice for solicitors [64]–[67].

4.   *Questions*

(i)   In the light of *Etridge*, is it helpful to continue to distinguish actual and presumed undue influence?

(ii) Do you agree, and if so why, that for the second requirement of presumed undue influence, Lindley LJ's test of 'not readily explicable on ordinary motives' is preferable to Lord Scarman's test of 'manifest disadvantage'? What will be the likely effect of that change in test?

(iii) Has the House of Lords made it less likely than before that a bank will be held to have constructive notice of a husband's undue influence over his wife?

R v Attorney General for England and Wales
[2003] UKPC 22, Privy Council

For the facts and the decision as regards duress, see above, 720. One of the other grounds on which R argued that he was not bound by the confidentiality agreement was that he had entered into it under undue influence. The Privy Council, Lord Scott dissenting, held that, as there had been no unfair exploitation of its relationship of influence by the Army or its commanding officer, the contract had not been obtained by undue influence.

Lord Hoffmann (giving the judgment of himself and **Lords Bingham, Steyn,** and **Millett**):

Undue influence

21 The subject of undue influence has recently been re-examined in depth by the House of Lords in *Royal Bank of Scotland plc v Etridge (No. 2)* [2002] AC 773. Their Lordships summarise the effect of the judgments. Like duress at common law, undue influence is based upon the principle that a transaction to which consent has been obtained by unacceptable means should not be allowed to stand. Undue influence has concentrated in particular upon the unfair exploitation by one party of a relationship which gives him ascendancy or influence over the other.

22 The burden of proving that consent was obtained by unacceptable means is upon the party who alleges it. Certain relationships – parent and child, trustee and beneficiary, etc – give rise to a presumption that one party had influence over the other. That does not of course in itself involve a presumption that he unfairly exploited his influence. But if the transaction is one which cannot reasonably be explained by the relationship, that will be prima facie evidence of undue influence. Even if the relationship does not fall into one of the established categories, the evidence may show that one party did in fact have influence over the other. In such a case, the nature of the transaction may likewise give rise to a prima facie inference that it was obtained by undue influence. In the absence of contrary evidence, the court will be entitled to find that the burden of proving unfair exploitation of the relationship has been discharged.

23 The absence of independent legal advice may or may not be a relevant matter according to the circumstances. It is not necessarily an unfair exploitation of a relationship for one party to enter into a transaction with the other without ensuring that he has obtained independent legal advice. On the other hand, the transaction may be such as to give rise to an inference of undue influence even if the induced party was advised by an independent lawyer and understood the legal implications of what he was doing.

24 In the present case it is said that the military hierarchy, the strong regimental pride which R shared and his personal admiration for his commanding officer created a relationship in which the Army as an institution or the commanding officer as an individual were able to exercise influence over him. Their Lordships are content to assume that this was the case. But the question is whether the nature of the transaction was such as to give rise to an inference that it was obtained by an unfair exploitation of that relationship. Like the Court of Appeal, their Lordships do not think that the confidentiality agreement can be so described. As in the case of duress, their Lordships think that the finding that it was an agreement which anyone who wished to serve or continue serving in the SAS could reasonably have been required to sign is fatal to such a conclusion. The reason why R signed the agreement was because, at the time, he wished to continue to be a member of the SAS. If facing him with such a choice was not illegitimate for the purposes of duress, their Lordships do not think that it could have been an unfair exploitation of a relationship which consisted in his being a member of the SAS. There seems to their Lordships to be some degree of contradiction between R's claim, in the context of duress, that he signed only because he was threatened with return to his unit and his claim, for the purposes of undue influence, that he signed because of the trust and confidence which he reposed in the Army or his commanding officer.

25 The question which has troubled their Lordships is the absence of legal advice. ...

26 ...[T]he New Zealand courts made a finding that R had not been able to obtain legal advice which their Lordships of course accept. In any event they think it a matter for regret that members of [the] SAS were not told explicitly that arrangements could be made for them to obtain legal advice. They recognise the security problems which would have had to have been overcome; R could not, for example, have consulted an outside solicitor without disclosing that he was a member of the SAS. Nevertheless, as the commanding officer said, suitable arrangements could have been made and it would have avoided suspicion and recrimination to make this known.

27 The legal question, however, is whether failing to provide an opportunity for obtaining legal advice made the transaction one in which the MOD had unfairly exploited its influence over R. Here it is important to note that R does not allege that he did not understand the implications of what he was being asked to do. The contract was in simple terms and the explanatory memorandum even plainer. ...

28 In these circumstances, their Lordships do not think that the absence of legal advice affected the fairness of the transaction. The most that R can say is that a lawyer might have advised him to reflect upon the matter and, as in fact he changed his mind within a fairly short time after signing, that might have led to his not signing at all. But that is a decision which he could have made without a lawyer's advice.

Lord Scott of Foscote (dissenting):

41... It is, in my opinion, entirely artificial to draw sharp distinctions between orders from senior officers that are military orders breach of which will be an offence under military law and may attract court martial sanctions and "orders" from senior officers couched as requests or as recommendations. It has become a music-hall joke for a sergeant-major to say to the troops under him "I want three volunteers; you, you and you". The hierarchical culture of the Armed Services and the deference and obedience to senior officers, both commissioned and non-commissioned, which is part of that culture are the essential background to the circumstances in which the appellant was asked to sign the contract in the present case.

45 In my opinion, the relationship between the appellant and his senior officers and the circumstances, as found by the judge, in which the contract came to be signed by the appellant produced a classic "relationship" case in which undue influence should be presumed. No evidence was introduced to rebut that presumption. Legal advice was not available to the appellant. As in *Allcard v Skinner*, where no suggestion of fraud or indeed any impropriety was made against the lady superior to whom the plaintiff had transferred her assets, no such suggestion has been, or could be, made against any of the appellant's senior officers who play a part in the story. It is the relationship, produced by the background to which I have referred, between a soldier and that part of the Armed Services of which he is a member, that introduces the potentially vitiating element into the contract. If the Ministry of Defence wants to impose contractual obligations on soldiers by which they will be bound when they leave the service, it must, in my opinion, at the least make available to them independent legal advice. Fairness, in my view, requires it and I think the law requires it. In this case it was not done. I would have allowed the appeal.

NOTES AND QUESTIONS

1. Lord Hoffmann's judgment gives a useful succinct summary of the general law on undue influence laid down in *Etridge*. R here failed because, although he could establish the relationship of influence, the confidentiality agreement was one which anyone who wished to serve in the SAS could reasonably have been expected to sign. That is, it was 'reasonably… explained by the relationship' so that there had been no unfair exploitation of that relationship.

2. Lord Hoffmann described the principle underpinning undue influence as being that 'consent has been obtained by unacceptable means' [21]. This indicates that, like misrepresentation and duress, undue influence looks both at the conduct of the defendant and its effect on the claimant. Is that compatible with saying that undue influence is a factor that vitiates consent? See also above, 711, note 3; 722.

3. The majority's approach to the lack of legal advice is confusing. Why was it not simply a case where (i) R was relying on a presumption of undue influence (ii) R had failed to establish that presumption so that (iii) the question of independent advice, which goes to the rebuttal of the presumption, did not arise?

4. In his dissenting reasoning, was Lord Scott accepting that any contract with the Army that a serving officer is asked to enter into is presumptively induced by undue influence?

5. For another example of the Privy Council refusing to set aside a contract for undue influence because, although there was (factually) a relationship of influence (between a bank and its customer), the transaction was not one by which the bank obtained any unfair advantage so that there had been no unfair exploitation, see *National Commercial Bank (Jamaica) Ltd v Hew* [2003] UKPC 51. Although the purpose for which the loan from the bank was sought was commercially imprudent for the customer, it was stressed that it was not for a bank to save its customer from an unwise project.

6. Three other post-*Etridge* cases deserve mention:

(i) In *Pesticcio v Huet* [2004] EWCA Civ 372 Mummery LJ made explicit at [20] his rejection of the view that undue influence depends on wrongdoing. 'Although undue influence is sometimes described as an "equitable wrong" or even as a species of equitable fraud, the basis of the court's intervention is not the commission of a dishonest or wrongful act by the defendant, but that, as a matter of public policy, the presumed influence arising from the relationship of trust and confidence should not operate to the disadvantage of the victim, if the transaction is not satisfactorily explained by ordinary motives... A transaction may be set aside by the court, even though the actions and conduct of the person who benefits from it could not be criticised as wrongful.'

(ii) In *Macklin v Dowsett* [2004] EWCA Civ 904, [2004] 2 EGLR 75 the two requirements for a presumption of undue influence were established so that, as there had been no rebuttal, an option granted to the claimants to buy property in which the defendant had a life interest was held to have been obtained by undue influence. It was also again stressed that bad conduct is not a necessary feature of undue influence. Auld LJ, at [10] said, 'To succeed in such a defence, the prima facie establishment of undue influence, Mr Dowsett, in the light of the ruling of the House of Lords in [the *Etridge* case] had to show two things: (i) that, in entering the option agreement, he had reposed trust and confidence in the Macklins or that they had acquired some ascendency over him; and (ii) that the transaction was not otherwise readily explicable by the relationship between them. Proof of such matters which—I emphasise—did not require him to prove any misconduct by the Macklins or even that he was disadvantaged by the transaction, would, in the absence of satisfactory evidence to rebut his contention, entitle him to have the agreement set aside for undue influence. Further and more recent authorities of this Court [ie *Pesticcio v Huet*] have underlined the rationale of the doctrine of undue influence as the protection of the vulnerable in dealings with their property and also the lack of the need to show misconduct on the part of the transferee.'

(iii) There was a useful discussion in *Turkey v Ahwad* [2005] EWCA Civ 382 of the second requirement for the presumption of undue influence. Buxton LJ at [23] approved the trial judge's approach of asking whether 'the transaction... says to the unbiased observer that, absent explanation, it must represent the beneficiary taking advantage of his position'.

2. EXPLOITATION OF WEAKNESS

This section primarily considers the long-established equitable jurisdiction to set aside (ie rescind) so-called 'unconscionable bargains'. While sometimes linked with duress and, even more commonly, with undue influence, the cases in this section seem sufficiently distinct to merit separate treatment under the general heading of 'exploitation of weakness'. The courts are not here responding to lies, as in misrepresentation cases, nor to illegitimate threats, as in duress cases, nor to unacceptable influence, as in undue influence cases. Rather they seek to protect the claimant against a weakness. On the other hand, the weakness is not so extreme as to constitute incapacity. In the absence of lies, threats or influence, and given that the claimant has capacity, it is not surprising that the courts have generally regarded the weakness alone—the claimant's lack of full and free choice in entering into the contract—as insufficient to allow escape from it. Rather the courts look for exploitation—taking advantage—of the claimant's weakness as evidenced by the terms of the contract being unfair to the claimant. The touchstone for intervention is a combination, therefore, of procedural and substantive unfairness.

It would appear that there are at least three main elements required before a court will set aside (ie rescind) a transaction on this ground. They are: first, that the claimant has a mental weakness or a weakness derived from particular difficult circumstances; secondly, disadvantageous terms; and, thirdly, although the evidential burden of proof may here be on the defendant, a lack of independent advice given to the claimant. It is probably also a requirement—arguably indicated by cases such as *Portman Building Society v Dusangh* (below, 764) and *Alec Lobb Garages Ltd v Total Oil (GB) Ltd* (below, 768)—that the defendant knows of the claimant's weakness and is acting in bad faith (ie dishonestly) in taking advantage of that weakness. The standard four bars to rescission appear to apply as they do to undue influence and misrepresentation (see above, 550–557). As with duress and undue influence, exploitation of weakness does not itself trigger a claim for damages.

It should be stressed that the term 'exploitation of weakness' is not the only, or indeed the usual, way in which this escape from the contract can be described. Judges and commentators have alternatively used the terms 'unconscionability' or 'inequality of bargaining power'. Nothing of real significance should turn on one's chosen label but 'exploitation of weakness' does seem preferable. 'Unconscionability' is vague and wide-ranging and is a term used in several other areas of the law. To use it again here requires careful delineation and may be confusing. 'Inequality' can be misleading in that it is generally no reason in itself for allowing an escape from a contract that the claimant was in a position of inequality with the defendant: it is the abuse of particular positions of strength that the law normally objects to. Moreover, Lord Denning's explicit invocation of a principle of 'inequality of bargaining power' in *Lloyds Bank Ltd v Bundy* (below, 771) was not approved by the House of Lords in *National Westminster Bank v Morgan* (below, 774).

Introductory reading: E McKendrick, *Contract Law* (7th edn, 2007) 17.4, 17.5, 17.7

(1) Exploitation of Mental Weakness

Earl of Aylesford v Morris (1873) 8 Ch App 484, Court of Appeal

The claimant, who was 21 years old and stood to inherit his wealthy father's estates, had run up a large number of debts. In order to pay these off, he entered into a contract of loan with the defendant moneylender (Morris). The claimant received no independent advice and the rate of interest under the loan was 60 per cent. The claimant sought to have the contract of loan set aside. The Court of Appeal held that the defendant had taken advantage of the claimant's weakness of youth, so that the contract should be set aside (and the bills of exchange given by the claimant as security for repayment should be returned) on condition that the claimant repaid the sums advanced plus interest of 5 per cent.

Lord Selborne LC: There is hardly any older head of equity than that described by Lord Hardwicke in *Earl of Chesterfield v. Janssen* 2 Ves Sen 125, 157, as relieving against the fraud "which infects catching bargains with heirs, reversioners, or expectants, in the life of the father," &c. "These (he said) have been generally mixed cases," and he proceeded to note two characters always found in them. "There is always fraud presumed or inferred from the circumstances or conditions of the parties contracting – weakness on one side, usury on the other, or extortion, or advantage taken of that weakness. There has been always an appearance of fraud from the nature of the bargain."

...

Fraud does not here mean deceit or circumvention; it means an unconscientious use of the power arising out of these circumstances and conditions; and when the relative position of the parties is such as *primâ facie* to raise this presumption, the transaction cannot stand unless the person claiming the benefit of it is able to repel the presumption by contrary evidence, proving it to have been in point of fact fair, just, and reasonable.

This is the rule applied to the analogous cases of voluntary donations obtained for themselves by the donees, and to all other cases where influence, however acquired, has resulted in gain to the person possessing at the expense of the person subject to it. Lord Cranworth, in a recent case in the House of Lords (*Smith v. Kay* 7 H L C 750, 771), said that no influence can be more direct, more intelligible, or more to be guarded against than that of a person who gets hold of a young man of fortune, "and takes upon himself to supply him with means, pandering to his gross extravagance during his minority, and extorting from him, or at least obtaining from him, for every advance that he has made, a promise that the moment he comes of age it shall all be ratified, so as to make the securities good." The circumstances of the particular case in which these words were spoken differed widely from those of the case now before us; the element of personal influence is here wanting. But it is sufficient for the application of the principle, if the parties meet under such circumstances as, in the particular transaction, to give the stronger party dominion over the weaker; and such power and influence are generally possessed, in every transaction of this kind, by those who trade upon the follies and vices of unprotected youth, inexperience, and moral imbecility.

In the cases of catching bargains with expectant heirs, one peculiar feature has been almost universally present; indeed, its presence was considered by Lord Brougham to be an indispensable condition of equitable relief, though Lord St. Leonards, with good reason, dissents from that opinion Sug V & P 11th Ed p 316. The victim comes to the snare (for this system of dealing does set snares, not, perhaps, for one prodigal more than another, but for prodigals generally as a class), excluded, and known to be excluded, by the very motives and circumstances which attract him, from the help and advice of his natural guardians and protectors, and from that professional aid which would be accessible to him, if he did not feel compelled to secrecy. He comes in the dark, and in fetters, without either the will or the power to take care of himself, and with nobody else to take care of him. Great Judges have said that there is a principle of public policy in restraining this; that this system of under-mining and blasting, as it were, in the bud the fortunes of families, is a public as well as a private mischief; that it is a sort of indirect fraud upon the heads of families from whom these transactions are concealed, and who may be thereby induced to dispose of their means for the profit and advantage of strangers and usurers, when they suppose themselves to be fulfilling the moral obligation of providing for their own descendants.

Whatever weight there may be in any such collateral considerations, they could hardly prevail, if they did not connect themselves with an equity more strictly and directly personal to the Plaintiff in each particular case. But the real truth is, that the ordinary effect of all the circumstances by which these considerations are introduced, is to deliver over the prodigal helpless into the hands of those interested in taking advantage of his weakness; and we so

arrive in every such case at the substance of the conditions which throw the burden of justifying the righteousness of the bargain upon the party who claims the benefit of it.

Sir G Mellish LJ concurred.

1. What is the precise weakness in issue in the 'expectant heir' cases?
2. An analogy can be drawn with the evidential presumption of undue influence.
   The vulnerability of a young expectant heir plus substantive unfairness gives
   rise to an evidential presumption of exploitation which it is then for the
   defendant to rebut, principally by establishing that independent advice was
   obtained.

Fry v Lane (1888) 40 Ch D 312, Chancery Division

The claimants were two brothers, JB Fry and George Fry. They had poorly paid jobs,
one working for a plumber and the other as a laundryman. They each had a reversionary interest in the estate of their uncle, subject to the life tenancy of their aunt. In
1878, they sold their interests to the defendant, Lane, for £170 and £270 respectively.
In doing so, they were advised by an inexperienced solicitor, who was also acting for
Lane. When the aunt died in 1886, the interests were each worth £730 and an actuary
stated that in 1878 JB Fry's reversionary interest would have been worth £475. The
claimants brought an action to set aside the transactions, and this succeeded on the
basis that the sales had been at an undervalue to men who were poor and ignorant
and had not been independently advised.

Kay J: [*Having cited* Earl of Aylesford v Morris, *Kay J continued:*] The most common case for
the interference of a Court of Equity is that of an expectant heir, reversioner, or remainderman
who is just of age, his youth being treated as an important circumstance. Another analogous
case is where the vendor is a poor man with imperfect education, as in *Evans v. Llewellin* 1
Cox 333; *Haygarth v. Wearing* Law Rep.12 Eq. 320.

In the case of a poor man, in distress for money, a sale, even of property in possession, at
an undervalue has been set aside in many cases... [*He discussed the cases and continued:*]

The result of the decisions is that where a purchase is made from a poor and ignorant man
at a considerable undervalue, the vendor having no independent advice, a Court of Equity will
set aside the transaction. This will be done even in the case of property in possession, and *à
fortiori* if the interest be reversionary.

The circumstances of poverty and ignorance of the vendor, and absence of independent
advice, throw upon the purchaser, when the transaction is impeached, the onus of proving, in
Lord Selborne's words [in *Aylesford v Morris*], that the purchase was "fair, just, and
reasonable."

Upon the evidence before me I cannot hesitate to conclude that the price of £170 in *J. B.
Fry*'s case and £270 in *George Fry*'s case were both considerably below the real value. ...

Both *J. B. Fry* and his brother *George* were poor, ignorant men, to whom the temptation of
the immediate possession of £100 would be very great. Neither of them in the transaction of
the sale of his share, was ... "on equal terms" with the purchaser. Neither had independent
advice. The solicitor who acted for both parties in each transaction seems, from the *Law List*,
to have been admitted in March, 1877. In October, 1878, at the time of completing the sale of
J. B. Fry's share, he had not been much more than a year and a-half on the roll. His inexperience probably in some degree accounts for his allowing himself to be put in the position of

solicitor for both parties in such a case. ... I regret that I must come to the conclusion that, though there was a semblance of bargaining by the solicitor in each case, he did not properly protect the vendors, but gave a great advantage to the purchasers, who had been former clients, and for whom he was then acting. The circumstances illustrate the wisdom and necessity of the rule that a poor, ignorant man, selling an interest of this kind, should have independent advice, and that a purchase from him at an undervalue should be set aside if he has not. The most experienced solicitor, acting for both sides, if he allows a sale at an under-value, can hardly have duly performed his duty to the vendor. To act for both sides in such a case, and permit a sale at an undervalue, is a position in which no careful practitioner would allow himself to be placed.

NOTES AND QUESTIONS

1. As with the expectant heir cases, so in the 'poor and ignorant' cases, we see the combination of mental inadequacy (here ignorance) and substantive unfairness (here undervalue) raising an evidential presumption of exploitation of weakness that will lead to the contract being set aside unless rebutted (by the defendant showing that independent advice was given).
2. Why is it necessary for there to be poverty as well as ignorance?

Cresswell v Potter [1978] 1 WLR 255n, Chancery Division

The claimant was a Post Office telephonist. On her divorce from the defendant, she entered into a contract with him by which she conveyed to him her interest in the matrimonial home ('Slate Hall') in return for being released from liability under the mortgage. A couple of years later, the defendant sold the property for some £3350 which, after deducting costs, was estimated to have made the defendant a profit of £1400. The claimant successfully sought to have the contract with the defendant set aside so that she would be entitled to half of those profits. It was held that she was the modern equivalent of a poor and ignorant person and that the *Fry v Lane* principle applied.

Megarry J: I can go straight to the well-known case of *Fry v. Lane* (1888) 40 Ch. D. 312. In his judgment, Kay J. ...laid down three requirements. What has to be considered is, first, whether the plaintiff is poor and ignorant; second, whether the sale was at a considerable undervalue; and third, whether the vendor had independent advice. I am not, of course, suggesting that these are the only circumstances which will suffice; thus there may be circumstances of oppression or abuse of confidence which will invoke the aid of equity. But in the present case only these three requirements are in point. Abuse of confidence, though pleaded, is no longer relied on; and no circumstances of oppression or other matters are alleged. I must therefore consider whether the three requirements laid down in *Fry v. Lane* are satisfied.

I think that the plaintiff may fairly be described as falling within whatever is the modern equivalent of "poor and ignorant." Eighty years ago, when *Fry v. Lane* was decided, social conditions were very different from those which exist today. I do not, however, think that the principle has changed, even though the euphemisms of the 20th century may require the word "poor" to be replaced by "a member of the lower income group" or the like, and the word "ignorant" by "less highly educated." The plaintiff has been a van driver for a tobac-conist, and is a Post Office telephonist. The evidence of her means is slender. The defendant told me that the plaintiff probably had a little saved, but not much; and there was evidence that her earnings were about the same as the defendant's, and that these were those of a carpenter. The plaintiff also has a legal aid certificate.

In those circumstances I think the plaintiff may properly be described as "poor" in the sense used in *Fry v. Lane,* where it was applied to a laundryman who, in 1888, was earning £1 a week. In this context, as in others, I do not think that "poverty" is confined to destitution. Further, although no doubt it requires considerable alertness and skill to be a good telephonist, I think that a telephonist can properly be described as "ignorant" in the context of property transactions in general and the execution of conveyancing documents in particular. I have seen and heard the plaintiff giving evidence, and I have reached the conclusion that she satisfies the requirements of the first head.

The second question is whether the sale was at a "considerable undervalue."...If Slate Hall was worth no more than it cost, she was giving up her half share in an equity worth £300; and, after all, the mortgage was a recent mortgage to a well-known building society. If she had sought advice it is unlikely in the extreme that she would have been told that there was any real probability that the value of the property would be less than the sum due under the mortgage. There can be little doubt that she was getting virtually nothing for £150.

In fact, as is now known, within a little over two years the property fetched £3,350, so that at the time in question the plaintiff's share of the equity may have been worth appreciably more than £150. ...It seems to me that by the release the plaintiff parted with her interest in Slate Hall at an undervalue which cannot be dismissed as being trifling or inconsiderable. In my judgment the undervalue was "considerable."

As for independent advice, from first to last there is no suggestion that the plaintiff had any. The defendant, his solicitor and the inquiry agent stood on one side: on the other the plaintiff stood alone. This was, of course, a conveyancing transaction, and English land law is notoriously complex. I am certainly not saying that other transactions, such as hire-purchase agreements, are free from all difficulty. But the authorities put before me on setting aside dealings at an undervalue all seem to relate to conveyancing transactions, and one may wonder whether the principle is confined to such transactions, and, if so, why. I doubt whether the principle is restricted in this way; and it may be that the explanation is that it is in conveyancing matters that, by long usage, it is regarded as usual, and, indeed, virtually essential, for the parties to have the services of a solicitor. The absence of the aid of a solicitor is thus, as it seems to me, of especial significance if a conveyancing matter is involved. The more usual it is to have a solicitor, the more striking will be his absence, and the more closely will the courts scrutinise what was done.

... [W]hat matters, I think, is not whether she could have obtained proper advice but whether in fact she had it; and she did not. Nobody, of course, can be compelled to obtain independent advice: but I do not think that someone who seeks to uphold what is, to him, an advantageous conveyancing transaction can do so merely by saying that the other party could have obtained independent advice, unless something has been done to bring to the notice of that other party the true nature of the transaction and the need for advice.

...

At the end of the day, my conclusion is that this transaction cannot stand. In my judgment the plaintiff has made out her case, and so it is for the defendant to prove that the transaction was "fair, just, and reasonable." This he has not done. The whole burden of his case has been that the requirements of *Fry v. Lane*...were not satisfied, whereas I have held that they were.

NOTES AND QUESTIONS

1.   This is an important case in 'breathing new life' into the *Fry v Lane* principle. It may be doubted, however, whether the old insistence on 'poverty' can be sensibly updated in the way suggested by Megarry J. Would it not be preferable to concentrate on the 'ignorance' aspect in relation to which, as Megarry J said, the important point here was that the claimant was ignorant *of property transactions?*

2. In *Backhouse v Backhouse* [1978] 1 WLR 243 a wife, on separation from her husband, had transferred to him for nothing her share in the matrimonial home. Balcombe J cited *Cresswell v Potter* at length but the difficulty in directly applying it was that the claimant was an intelligent woman and could not therefore be classed as 'poor and ignorant'. In obiter dicta, Balcombe J suggested (drawing on Lord Denning's principle of 'inequality or bargaining power' in *Lloyds Bank Ltd v Bundy*, see below, 771) that the law might be developed so as to allow the setting aside of an unfavourable contract entered into without independent advice because of the 'great emotional strain' (at 251) that divorcing parties are under. Is that a preferable analysis of the weakness in question?

3. We have seen that in *Credit Lyonnias Bank Nederland NV v Burch*, above, 735, Miss Burch successfully based her case purely on undue influence. However, Nourse LJ thought that Miss Burch might very well have argued that the legal charge should be set aside against the bank on the basis that the contract was an unconscionable bargain. He said, at 151, that *Cresswell v Potter* demonstrated that the jurisdiction to relieve against such transactions was 'in good heart and capable of adaptation to different transactions entered into in changing circumstances'.

Boustany v Pigott (1995) 69 P & CR 298, Privy Council

The claimant, Miss Pigott, was an elderly landlady. As she had become 'quite slow', her cousin, George Pigott, managed her affairs. One of her tenants, Mrs Boustany, the defendant, persuaded the claimant, while George Pigott was away, to agree to a new lease being drawn up by an independent lawyer. The lease was for 10 years at a monthly rent of $1000 (the existing rent had been $833.35) renewable at the tenant's option for another 10 years at the same rent. The lawyer, Mr Kendall, pointed out to Miss Pigott the disadvantageous aspects of the transaction (that there was no provision for review of the rent) but she insisted on going ahead with it. When George Pigott discovered what had happened, he protested to Mrs Boustany who was unmoved. Acting on Miss Pigott's behalf, he therefore sought a declaration that the lease was an unconscionable bargain, which should be declared rescinded. The Privy Council upheld the decision of the Court of Appeal of the Eastern Caribbean States that the lease was an unconscionable bargain and should be set aside.

Lord Templeman (giving the judgment of himself and **Lords Lowry, Mustill** and **Slynn of Hadley**): In a careful and thoughtful submission, Mr Robertson, who appeared before the Board on behalf of Mrs Boustany, made the following submissions with which their Lordships are in general agreement. (1) It is not sufficient to attract the jurisdiction of equity to prove that a bargain is hard, unreasonable or foolish; it must be proved to be unconscionable, in the sense that "one of the parties to it has imposed the objectionable terms in a morally reprehensible manner, that is to say, in a way which affects his conscience": *Multiservice Bookbinding v Marden* [1979] Ch 84, 110. (2) "Unconscionable" relates not merely to the terms of the bargain but to the behaviour of the stronger party, which must be characterised by some moral culpability or impropriety: *Lobb (Alec) (Garages) Ltd. v Total Oil (Great Britain) Ltd.* [1983] 1 WLR 87, 94. (3) Unequal bargaining power or objectively unreasonable terms provide no basis for equitable interference in the absence of unconscientious or extortionate abuse of power where exceptionally, and as a matter of common fairness, "it was not right that the strong should be allowed to push the weak to the wall": *Lobb (Alec) (Garages) Ltd. v Total Oil (Great Britain) Ltd.* [1985] 1 WLR 173, 183. (4) A contract cannot be set aside in equity as "an unconscionable bargain" against a party innocent of actual or constructive fraud. Even if the terms of the contract are "unfair" in the sense that they are more favourable to one party than the other ("contractual imbalance"), equity will not provide relief unless the beneficiary is guilty of unconscionable conduct: *Hart v O'Connnor* [1985] AC 1000 applied in *Nichols v Jessup* [1986] NZLR 226. (5) "In situations of this kind it is necessary for the plaintiff who seeks relief to establish unconscionable conduct, namely that unconscientious advantage has been taken of his disabling condition or circumstances": per Mason J. in *Commercial Bank of Australia Ltd. v Amadio* (1983) 46 ALR 402, 413.

Mr Robertson submitted that Miss Pigott had received independent advice from Mr Kendall, that she had been made aware by Mr Kendall that the terms of the 1980 lease were disadvantageous to her, that Miss Pigott could not be described as poor or ignorant and that the judge did not find and could not, consistently with the evidence, have found unconscionable behaviour on the part of Mrs Boustany.

The crucial question in this case is – what brought Miss Pigott to the chambers of Mr Kendall in September 1980? That question was not answered by direct evidence because Miss Pigott was not able to give evidence and Mrs Boustany and her husband chose not to do so. The trial judge inferred unconscionable conduct by Mrs Boustany after careful consideration of a number of features which he held were only consistent with unconscientious conduct on the part of Mrs Boustany. The management of the property had been given up by Miss Pigott because of her incapacity. The properties were managed by Mr George Pigott and there was no reason why Miss Pigott should interfere in the management of this one property leased to Mrs Boustany. There was no evidence of any personal attachment between Miss Pigott and her tenant. Mrs Boustany had negotiated with Mr George Pigott and knew that he was the representative of Miss Pigott. No advice was sought by Miss Pigott; she turned up not at her family's solicitors but to Mr Kendall who knew nothing about her save that he had prepared the 1976 lease. Miss Pigott gave to Mr Kendall, according to his evidence, absurd reasons for the grant of a new lease and no reason for the grant of a lease for 20 years on disadvantageous terms.

Miss Pigott must have been under a total misapprehension of the facts when she represented that she might be worried about the property and about the repair of the property while she was away. Mr Kendall forcibly pointed out not only to Miss Pigott but also to Mrs Boustany and her husband the disadvantages of the new lease but Mrs Boustany and her husband gave no explanation and offered no concessions. They were content to allow Miss Pigott ostensibly to insist on the unjustifiable terms which they must already have persuaded her to accept. When a writ was issued Mrs Boustany did not write to the solicitor but sought out Miss Pigott and obtained a disclaimer which the court in due course rejected. The inference which the trial judge drew, and which he was entitled to draw, was that Mrs Boustany and her husband had prevailed upon Miss Pigott to agree to grant a lease on terms which they knew they could not extract from Mr George Pigott or anyone else. When they were summoned by Mr Kendall, and the unfairness of the lease was pointed out to them, they did not release Miss Pigott from the bargain which they had unfairly pressed on her. In short Mrs Boustany must have taken advantage of Miss Pigott before, during and after the interview with Mr Kendall and with full knowledge before the 1980 lease was settled that her conduct was unconscionable.

NOTES

1.   This is an odd decision. It was not suggested that Miss Pigott was senile so as to invalidate the lease on the basis of her incapacity. Nor was it suggested that

Mrs Boustany had undue influence over Miss Pigott. Rather the decision was based on the unconscionable conduct of Mrs Boustany. Yet applying *Fry v Lane* one would have thought that, even if one treated Mrs Pigott as having a mental weakness equivalent to those who are (poor and) ignorant, she had been given firm independent legal advice.

2.   Applying the controversial decision in *Hart v O'Connor* [1985] AC 1000, PC, even if Miss Pigott had no capacity to contract because of senility that would only have invalidated the contract had that incapacity been known about by the other party.

3.   Lord Templeman referred to *Commercial Bank of Australia Ltd v Amadio* (1983) 151 CLR 447. This was the first in a series of radical decisions of the High Court of Australia developing the law on unconscionable bargains. In *Amadio* a doctrine of 'unconscionable dealing' was accepted and applied in setting aside a mortgage and guarantee executed by an elderly and ignorant couple who were unfamiliar with English and had received no independent advice. See also *Louth v Diprose* (1992) 175 CLR 621; *Garcia v National Australia Bank Ltd* (1998) 194 CLR 395.

Portman Building Society v Dusangh
[2000] 2 All ER (Comm) 221, Court of Appeal

The defendant was a 72 year-old man. He could not read English and spoke it poorly and had a low income. He was granted a mortgage by the claimant building society by which he was loaned £33,750 in return for granting a charge over his home. The repayment was guaranteed by the defendant's son to whom the defendant paid over most of the loan to enable him to buy a supermarket. Although the defendant was advised by a solicitor, that same solicitor was also acting for the claimant and the son. When the supermarket failed and the son was unable to repay the loan, the claimant sought to enforce its charge over the defendant's home. The defendant argued that the transaction should be set aside as an unconscionable bargain. In dismissing the defendant's appeal, the Court of Appeal held that there had been no morally reprehensible exploitation of the father so that the bargain was not an unconscionable one.

Simon Brown LJ: As the Recorder here found, the first defendant [the father] entered into this transaction to turn his son from a labourer at Rolls Royce into the owner of a large supermarket. Should he have been prevented from doing so? That is the ultimate question raised by this appeal. In submitting that he should and that the building society were morally bound to refuse this mortgage application, Mr Bedford [counsel for the first defendant] stresses the first defendant's personal circumstances and the essential unwisdom of the transaction from his point of view. The first defendant, submits Mr Bedford, is (and was at the date of this transaction), the modern equivalent of 'poor and ignorant' as explained by Nourse LJ in *Burch*'s case: elderly, illiterate and on a very low income. I agree. And...I would agree too that the transaction was an improvident one, necessarily dependent for its success upon the son's ability to make the monthly repayments and thus upon the success of the supermarket venture. Undoubtedly, therefore, it placed the property at risk. But I simply cannot accept that building societies are required to police transactions of this nature to ensure that parents (even poor and ignorant ones) are wise in seeking to assist their children. Mr Bedford points to the building society's several failures to follow their own policy and safeguards for ensuring that the first defendant would be able to meet his commitments in the future. But these safeguards exist to protect the building society's interests, not their borrowers. That it was commercially unwise for the claimants to put their trust in the first defendant (and his son) is not to say that it was morally culpable for them to do so. It was the first defendant who approached them, not they him. He applied to borrow £33,750 and they agreed to lend it on their normal condition that the loan was secured.

To my mind none of the essential touchstones of an unconscionable bargain are to be found in this case. The first defendant was not at a serious disadvantage to the building society: neither he nor his son had any existing indebtedness towards them. His situation was not exploited by the building society. The building society did not act in a morally reprehensible manner. The transaction, although improvident, was not 'overreaching and oppressive'. In short, the conscience of the court is not shocked.

Ward LJ: The first defendant's case is, or can be, put in two ways, firstly, unconscionable conduct by the son affecting the building society, and, secondly, the unconscionable conduct by the building society itself. Although there is inevitably some overlap, the argument is essentially this. (1) The charge to the property was obtained by the son's exploiting the weaknesses of his father's position in order to benefit from a transaction which was manifestly disadvantageous to the father. Such unconscionable conduct was a vitiating factor, similar to undue influence, of which the building society had notice and by which it is bound on *Barclays Bank plc v O'Brien* [1994] 4 All ER 417, [1994] 1 A.C. 180 principles. (2) The building society itself acted unconscionably in taking a mortgage of the property which was a manifestly disadvantageous transaction for a 'poor and ignorant man' acting without adequate legal advice and which the building society could not show was fair, just and reasonable.

Although I agree with the judgment of Simon Brown L.J., which I have read in draft, the points raised are of sufficient interest for me to add, but add shortly, some reasons of my own.

Unconscionable conduct by the son affecting the building society

...

The salient features here are that the son had committed himself to the purchase of the small supermarket business. There is no reason to think that he did not believe that it would be a profitable venture which would turn out to his advantage. He needed money to complete the purchase. He persuaded his father to lend it. On the findings of the judge there was no undue influence and no misrepresentation. So it was a case of father coming to the assistance of his son. True it is that it was a financially unwise venture because, absent good profit from the business, there was never likely to be the income to service the borrowing and the father's home was at risk. But there was nothing, absolutely nothing, which comes close to morally reprehensible conduct or impropriety. No unconscientious advantage has been taken of the father's illiteracy, his lack of business acumen or his paternal generosity. True it may be that the son gained all the advantage and the father took all the risk, but this cannot be stigmatised as impropriety. There was no exploitation of father by son such as would prick the conscience and tell the son that in all honour it was morally wrong and reprehensible.

...

Unconscionable conduct by the building society itself

...The first defendant's argument derives from an application of the judgment of Kay J. in *Fry v Lane, re Fry, Whittet v Bush* (1888) 40 Ch. D. 312, 322, [1886-90] All ER Rep 1084 at 1089, as modernised by Megarry J. in *Cresswell v Potter* [1978] 1 W.L.R. 255n. The first defendant concentrates on the three elements there referred to: first, the 'poor and ignorant man'; second the considerable undervalue/manifest disadvantage; and third the lack of independent advice.

...

What the first defendant's approach on the facts of this case appears to me to miss is this: for the lending by the building society to be unconscionable, it must, as is implicit in the very word, be against the conscience of the lender – he must act with no conscience, with no moral sense that he is doing wrong. Making all the assumptions in the first defendant's favour of the frailties of the father, the lack of wisdom in taking on this large commitment with limited income, the real risk of foreclosure, the failure by the building society to follow its own rules, even an assumption that the building society in those heady days of rising property prices was lending money almost irresponsibly, none of that, in my judgment, gets near to establishing morally reprehensible conduct on its part. The family wanted to raise money: the building society was prepared to lend it. One shakes one's head, but with sadness and with incredulity at the folly of it all, alas not with moral outrage. I am afraid the moral conscience of the court has not been shocked. That is an end of the matter.

Sedley LJ concurred.

NOTES AND QUESTIONS

1. The reasoning of the Court of Appeal is not entirely clear. One might have expected it to say that two of the three standard elements required for the *Fry v Lane* principle were not present because, in the context of a father wishing to help his son, the transaction was not substantively unfair and the father had taken independent legal advice. But the judges seemed to suggest that, even if those three elements were present, a contract will not be set aside unless the party has acted in a morally reprehensible way. The difficulty with this is in understanding what additional element is needed in order to 'shock the court's conscience'. Arguably the judges are indicating that it is necessary for the party to have been acting in bad faith, dishonestly taking advantage of the other's weakness.
2. Ward LJ thought that undue influence and the *Fry v Lane* principle were similar. As undue influence does not necessitate morally bad conduct (see above, 729, note 4; 755, note 6) is it inconsistent to insist on it in this area?
3. As was made clear at the start of his judgment, Ward LJ looked at the bank's position both as a third party to the son's conduct and, directly, in terms of its own conduct. As regards it being a third party, he held (in a passage not set out above) that, applying *O'Brien*, above, 729, the bank did not have (actual or constructive) notice of the son's unconscionable conduct (even if, contrary to his view, that conduct had been unconscionable).

(2) Exploitation of the Claimant's Circumstantial Weakness

The above cases all concerned claimants who were in a weak position essentially because of their age (young or old) or ignorance or emotional state, albeit that they did not lack capacity. In contrast to such mental weaknesses, we are here concerned with where the claimant is in a weak position because of difficult circumstances.

The Medina (1876) 2 PD 5, Court of Appeal

The *Medina*, on a voyage from Singapore to Jedda, hit Parkin Rock in the Red Sea and was wrecked. There were 550 passengers (all pilgrims) on board who were taken by the ship's lifeboats onto the rocks. The claimants' ship, the *Timor*, answered the distress signals but refused to rescue the pilgrims and take them to Jedda unless the master of the shipwrecked ship agreed to pay £4000, which he reluctantly agreed to do. When the defendants, the owners of the *Medina*, later refused to pay, the claimants brought an action for the £4000. In dismissing the claimants' appeal, it was held that the contract should be set aside as requiring the payment, in desperate circumstances, of a grossly exorbitant sum and £1800 was awarded instead.

James LJ: [A] sum of 4000*l.* was a very exorbitant sum for only a few days' work, coming up to the rock, taking the pilgrims on board, and carrying them on to the point defined. I agree that the conclusion of the judge of the Admiralty Court was right, that the sum exacted was exorbitant, and, having regard to the peculiar circumstances, that pressure was exercised, and that the agreement ought not to stand. But the Court was right in giving a reasonable amount, fixed by the Court below with the assistance of two assessors, at 1800*l.*

Baggallay, JA: [B]y the very fact that we find an amount agreed to be paid which is very large in comparison with the services rendered, we are led to the conclusion that there may have been some unfair dealing in the transaction. And that applies with particular force where persons, who are in an extremity, in order to obtain assistance in their extremity, have been required to pay a large price for the assistance. That appears to have been the case here, and with 550 pilgrims on board the captain of the *Medina* was bound to accept any terms which were pressed upon him by the *Timor*.

Brett, JA: I think the old rule of the Admiralty Court ought not to be lightly encroached upon, viz., that where there is an agreement made by competent persons and there is no misrepresentation of facts, the agreement ought to be upheld, unless there is something very strong to shew that it is inequitable; but I think that this agreement cannot be upheld. The amount claimed by the *Timor* was exorbitant – not merely too large, but, for the services to be rendered, grossly exorbitant – and it was forced upon the captain of the *Medina* by practical compulsion. Now, that the sum was grossly exorbitant, I think, follows from this consideration – that the service was one of no difficulty at all, and, under the circumstances, there was no danger whatever to the salving ship. She could take these people off with perfect facility; the service was not an onerous service; the pretence of a difficulty in going into a known port like Jedda is fallacious; from the beginning to the end there was no difficulty or danger to the salving ship; and at the time the agreement was made there was no probability of any danger to her. But there is more in this case. It was forced upon the captain of the *Medina* by practical compulsion, because his position was this – and that is to be considered – he was the captain of a ship ashore on a rock with 550 pilgrims on board her. If the captain refused to accept the terms, he took upon himself the responsibility of allowing 550 human beings under his care to be left to the danger of being drowned. That is compulsion to the mind of any honest man. Therefore, I think there was a grossly exorbitant sum obtained on practical compulsion. Under all these circumstances I think that by the rules of the Admiralty Court the agreement cannot stand.

NOTES AND QUESTIONS

1. The common law jurisdiction of the Court of Admiralty to set aside extortionate salvage agreements developed separately from the equitable jurisdiction to set aside unconscionable bargains. But they appear to share similar features.

2. It might be argued that, in the light of the judges' reference to practical compulsion, this case is best analysed as a case of duress. One difficulty with that interpretation is that it would require treating threats of lawful omissions as illegitimate. Another difficulty is that the judges regarded it as essential that the terms were substantively unfair: that is, the contract was only set aside to the extent that the price charged was excessive. In contrast, substantive unfairness is, at least normally, irrelevant in the context of duress. It seems preferable therefore to regard this situation as one where the court was responding to the exploitation of the other party's difficult circumstances analogously to the equitable jurisdiction to relieve from an unconscionable bargain.

3. What explains the award of £1800?

4. Another well-known example of an extortionate salvage agreement is *The Port Caledonia and The Anna* [1903] P 184. In a storm, a ship was being dragged towards another ship in a harbour. The master of the distressed ship signalled for a tug but the master of the tug, the claimant, demanded '£1000 or no rope'. The master of the distressed ship objected but agreed to pay the money. The tug then towed the ship back to its berth. In the claimant's action for the £1000, it was held by Bucknill J that the contract should be set aside as 'an inequitable, extortionate and unreasonable agreement' (at 190). The claimant was instead awarded £200 for the services rendered.

Alec Lobb Garages Ltd v Total Oil (GB) Ltd
[1985] 1 WLR 173, Court of Appeal

The claimant (whose managing director was Mr Lobb) was a small company that ran a petrol station and garage. Under a tie agreement, it was bound to buy its petrol from the defendant oil company. In 1969, the claimant was in financial difficulty. To alleviate those problems, it entered into an agreement with the defendant, contrary to the advice of its solicitor, for the lease and lease-back of the petrol station, which included a new tie agreement. The payments received by the claimant allowed it to pay off its debts. Ten years later, the claimant sought to have the contract set aside on the ground that it was an unconscionable bargain (or, which we are not here concerned with, that it was void as being an unreasonable restraint of trade). In dismissing the claimant's appeal, the Court of Appeal held that the contract was not an unconscionable bargain (nor was it an unreasonable restraint of trade) and that, even if it had been, the claimant was barred by laches from setting it aside.

Dillon LJ: The basis of the contention that the transaction of the lease and lease-back ought to be set aside in equity is that it is submitted, and in the court below was accepted on behalf of Total, that during the negotiations for the lease and lease-back the parties did not have equal bargaining power, and it is therefore further submitted that a contract between parties who had unequal bargaining power can only stand and be enforced by the stronger if he can prove that the contract was in point of fact fair, just and reasonable. The concept of unequal bargaining power is taken particularly from the judgment of Lord Denning M.R. in *Lloyds Bank Ltd. v. Bundy* [1975] Q.B. 326. The reference to a contract only standing if it is proved to have been in point of fact fair, just and reasonable is taken from the judgment of Lord Selborne LC in *Earl of Aylesford v. Morris* (1873) L.R. 8 Ch. App. 484, 490-491. Lord Selborne was not there seeking to generalise; he was dealing only with what he regarded as one of the oldest heads of equity, relieving against fraud practised on heirs or expectants, particularly fraud practised on young noblemen of great expectations, considerable extravagance and no ready money. It is none the less submitted that the logic of the development of the law leads to the conclusion that Lord Selborne LC's test should now be applied generally to any contract entered into between parties who did not have equal bargaining power.

In fact Lord Denning MR's judgment in *Lloyds Bank Ltd. v. Bundy* merely laid down the proposition that where there was unequal bargaining power the contract could not stand if the weaker did not have separate legal advice. In the present case Mr Lobb and the company did have separate advice from their own solicitor. On the facts of this case, however, that does not weaken the appellants' case if the general proposition of law which they put forward is valid. Total refused to accept any of the modifications of the transaction as put forward by Total which the company's and Mr Lobb's solicitor suggested, and in the end the solicitor advised them not to proceed. Mr Lobb declined to accept that advice because his and the company's financial difficulties were so great, and, it may be said, their bargaining power was so small, that he felt he had no alternative but to accept Total's terms. Because of the existing valid tie to Total which had ... three to four years to run, he had no prospect at all of raising finance on the scale he required from any source other than Total. There is no suggestion that there was any other dealer readily available who could have bought the property from him subject to the tie. The only practical solutions open to him were to accept the terms of the lease and lease-back as put forward by Total on which Total was not prepared to negotiate, or to sell the freehold of the property to Total and cease trading. In these circumstances, it would be unreal, in my judgment, to hold that if the transaction is otherwise tainted it is cured merely because Mr Lobb and the company had independent advice.

But on the deputy judge's findings can it be said that the transaction is tainted? Lord Selborne LC dealt with the case before him as a case of fraud. [*He cited from Lord Selborne's judgment set out above, 758, and continued:*]

The whole emphasis is on extortion, or undue advantage taken of weakness, an unconscientious use of the power arising out of the inequality of the parties' circumstances, and on unconscientious use of power which the court might in certain circumstances be entitled to infer from a particular – and in these days notorious – relationship unless the contract is proved to have been in fact fair, just and reasonable. Nothing leads me to suppose that the course of the development of the law over the last 100 years has been such that the emphasis on unconscionable conduct or unconscientious use of power has gone and relief will be granted in equity in a case such as the present if there has been unequal bargaining power, even if the stronger has not used his strength unconscionably. I agree with the judgment of Browne-Wilkinson J, in *Multiservice Bookbinding Ltd. v. Marden* [1979] Ch. 84, which sets out that to establish that a term is unfair and unconscionable it is not enough to show that it is, objectively, unreasonable.

In the present case there are findings of fact by the deputy judge that the conduct of Total was not unconscionable, coercive or oppressive. There is ample evidence to support those findings and they are not challenged by the appellants. Their case is that the judge applied the wrong test; where there is unequal bargaining power, the test is, they say, whether its terms are fair, just and reasonable and it is unnecessary to consider whether the conduct of the stronger party was oppressive or unconscionable. I do not accept the appellants' proposition of law. In my judgment the findings of the judge conclude this ground of appeal against the appellants.

Inequality of bargaining power must anyhow be a relative concept. It is seldom in any negotiation that the bargaining powers of the parties are absolutely equal. Any individual wanting to borrow money from a bank, building society or other financial institution in order to pay his liabilities or buy some property he urgently wants to acquire will have virtually no bargaining power; he will have to take or leave the terms offered to him. So, with house property in a seller's market, the purchaser will not have equal bargaining power with the vendor. But Lord Denning M.R. did not envisage that any contract entered into in such circumstances would, without more, be reviewed by the courts by the objective criterion of what was reasonable: see *Lloyds Bank Ltd. v. Bundy* [1975] Q.B. 326, 336. The courts would only interfere in exceptional cases where as a matter of common fairness it was not right that the strong should be allowed to push the weak to the wall. The concepts of unconscionable conduct and of the exercise by the stronger of coercive power are thus brought in, and in the present case they are negatived by the deputy judge's findings.

Even if, contrary to my view just expressed, the company and Mr and Mrs Lobb had initially in 1969 a valid claim in equity to have the lease and lease-back set aside as a result of the inequality of bargaining power, that claim was, in my judgment, barred by laches well before the issue of the writ in this action.

Dunn LJ:

Equitable relief

[Counsel for the appellants] conceded that he could not bring himself within any of the established categories of equitable relief, but relied on the dictum of Lord Denning M.R. in *Lloyds Bank Ltd. v. Bundy* [1975] Q.B. 326, 339 and submitted that the circumstances of this case disclosed a classic case of inequality of bargaining power of which the defendants had taken advantage by entering into the transaction, although he did not suggest any pressure or other misconduct on their part. He submitted that if it was necessary to categorise the grant of relief sought, it was an unconscionable bargain. He reminded us that the categories of unconscionable bargains are not closed (*per* Browne-Wilkinson J. in *Multiservice Bookbinding Ltd. v. Marden* [1979] Ch 84, 110) and sought to distinguish the instant case from that case by submitting that here the plaintiffs were under a compelling necessity to accept the loan, so that misconduct by the defendants was unnecessary. The fact of their impecuniosity, that they were already tied to the defendants by mortgages, that there was no other source of finance, and that they could not sell the equities of redemption under the mortgages without giving up trading, coupled with the knowledge of the defendants of those facts rendered the transaction unconscionable, and placed the onus upon the defendants to show that its terms were fair and reasonable.

I find myself unable to accept those arguments. Mere impecuniosity has never been held a ground for equitable relief. In this case no pressure was placed upon the plaintiffs. On the contrary the defendants were reluctant to enter into the transaction. The plaintiffs took independent advice from their solicitors and accountants. They went into the transaction with their eyes open, and it was of benefit to them because they were enabled to continue trade from the site for a number of years. In my view the judge was right to refuse equitable relief.

Laches

If I am wrong, and the plaintiffs are entitled to equitable relief, I would hold that they are barred by laches ...

Waller LJ concurred.

NOTES AND QUESTIONS

1. In refusing to extend the law by relying on Lord Denning's principle of inequality of bargaining power (see on this, below, 771), what does this case tell us about the requirements for setting aside unconscionable bargains? Might it be interpreted as indicating that it will be very rare indeed that a contract will be set aside for exploitation of another's mere financial weakness?
2. There were problems, in any event, with two of the three elements normally required for an unconscionable bargain: first, it was not entirely clear that the

terms were substantively unfair; and, secondly, the claimant had taken independent legal advice albeit that it had gone ahead contrary to that advice.

3. There are certain statutory provisions, which one can view as based on protecting a claimant against exploitation of his difficult circumstances. For example, sections 140A–140D of the Consumer Credit Act 1974 protect against exploitation of the claimant's need for credit by giving the courts a wide range of remedies to undo credit agreements where the relationship between the creditor and the debtor is unfair to the debtor.

4. To what extent, if at all, can one say that the Unfair Contract Terms Act 1977 and the Unfair Terms in Consumer Contracts Regulations 1999 (Chapter 6 above) allow escape from a contract (or from particular contract terms) because there has been exploitation of weakness?

(3) Rejection of a Principle of 'Inequality of Bargaining Power'

Lloyds Bank Ltd v Bundy [1975] QB 326, Court of Appeal

The defendant was an elderly farmer. He and his son were customers of the claimant bank. The defendant had given a guarantee, with a charge over his farmhouse, to the claimant to secure a loan to his son's company. The son wished to increase the loan and he and the claimant's assistant bank manager visited the defendant to seek his agreement to increase the guarantee and charge. The assistant bank manager knew that the farmhouse was the defendant's only asset and that the defendant was relying on him for advice. The defendant had no independent advice and signed the relevant documents. Six months later, when the company had become insolvent, the bank sought to enforce the charge against the defendant. It was held by the Court of Appeal, allowing the defendant's appeal, that the guarantee and the charge should be set aside. The majority (Sir Eric Sachs, with whom Cairns LJ concurred) reasoned that there was a presumption of undue influence (the relationship of influence by the bank over its customer having been established on the facts) which had not been rebutted. In contrast, Lord Denning preferred to rest the decision on 'inequality of bargaining power' and it is solely with that principle that we are here concerned.

Lord Denning MR: Now let me say at once that in the vast majority of cases a customer who signs a bank guarantee or a charge cannot get out of it. No bargain will be upset which is the result of the ordinary interplay of forces. There are many hard cases which are caught by this rule. Take the case of a poor man who is homeless. He agrees to pay a high rent to a landlord just to get a roof over his head. The common law will not interfere. It is left to Parliament. Next take the case of a borrower in urgent need of money. He borrows it from the bank at high interest and it is guaranteed by a friend. The guarantor gives his bond and gets nothing in return. The common law will not interfere. Parliament has intervened to prevent money-lenders charging excessive interest. But it has never interfered with banks.

Yet there are exceptions to this general rule. There are cases in our books in which the courts will set aside a contract, or a transfer of property, when the parties have not met on equal terms – when the one is so strong in bargaining power and the other so weak – that, as a matter of common fairness, it is not right that the strong should be allowed to push the weak to the wall. Hitherto those exceptional cases have been treated each as a separate category in itself. But I think the time has come when we should seek to find a principle to unite them. I put on one side contracts or transactions which are voidable for fraud or misrepresentation or mistake. All those are governed by settled principles. I go only to those where there has been inequality of bargaining power, such as to merit the intervention of the court.

The categories

The first category is that of "duress of goods." A typical case is when a man is in a strong bargaining position by being in possession of the goods of another by virtue of a legal right, such as by way of pawn or pledge or taken in distress. The owner is in a weak position because he is in urgent need of the goods. The stronger demands of the weaker more than is justly due: and he pays it in order to get the goods. Such a transaction is voidable. He can recover the excess: see *Astley v. Reynolds* (1731) 2 Stra. 915... To which may be added the cases of "colore officii," where a man is in a strong bargaining position by virtue of his official position or public profession. He relies upon it so as to gain from the weaker – who is urgently in need – more than is justly due... In such cases the stronger may make his claim in good faith honestly believing that he is entitled to make his demand. He may not be guilty of any fraud or misrepresentation. The inequality of bargaining power – the strength of the one versus the urgent need of the other – renders the transaction voidable and the money paid to be recovered back: see *Maskell v. Horner* [1915] 3 K.B. 106.

The second category is that of the "unconscionable transaction." A man is so placed as to be in need of special care and protection and yet his weakness is exploited by another far stronger than himself so as to get his property at a gross undervalue. The typical case is that of the "expectant heir." But it applies to all cases where a man comes into property, or is expected to come into it – and then being in urgent need – another gives him ready cash for it, greatly below its true worth, and so gets the property transferred to him: see *Evans v. Llewellin* (1787) 1 Cox 333. Even though there be no evidence of fraud or misrepresentation, nevertheless the transaction will be set aside: see *Fry v. Lane* (1888) 40 Ch.D. 312, 322 where Kay J. said:

> "The result of the decisions is that where a purchase is made from a poor and ignorant man at a considerable undervalue, *the vendor having no independent advice,* a court of equity will set aside the transaction."

This second category is said to extend to all cases where an unfair advantage has been gained by an unconscientious use of power by a stronger party against a weaker...

The third category is that of "undue influence" usually so called. These are divided into two classes as stated by Cotton L.J. in *Allcard v. Skinner*...

The fourth category is that of "undue pressure." The most apposite of that is *Williams v. Bayley* (1866) L.R. 1 H.L. 200 ... Other instances of undue pressure are where one party stipulates for an unfair advantage to which the other has no option but to submit. As where an employer – the stronger party – has employed a builder – the weaker party – to do work for him. When the builder asked for payment of sums properly due (so as to pay his workmen) the employer refused to pay unless he was given some added advantage. Stuart V.-C. said: "Where an agreement, hard and inequitable in itself, has been exacted under circumstances of pressure on the part of the person who exacts it, this court will set it aside": see *Ormes v. Beadel* (1860) 2 Giff. 166, 174 (reversed on another ground, 2 De G.F. & J. 333) and *D. & C. Builders Ltd. v. Rees* [1966] 2 Q.B. 617, 625.

The fifth category is that of salvage agreements. When a vessel is in danger of sinking and seeks help, the rescuer is in a strong bargaining position. The vessel in distress is in urgent need. The parties cannot be truly said to be on equal terms. The Court of Admiralty have always recognised that fact. The "fundamental rule" is

> "if the parties have made an agreement, the court will enforce it, unless it be manifestly unfair and unjust; but if it be manifestly unfair and unjust, the court will disregard it and decree what is fair and just."

See *Akerblom v. Price* (1881) 7 Q.B.D. 129, 133, *per* Brett L.J., applied in a striking case *The Port Caledonia and The Anna* [1903] P. 184, when the rescuer refused to help with a rope unless he was paid £1,000.

...

Gathering all together, I would suggest that through all these instances there runs a single thread. They rest on "inequality of bargaining power." By virtue of it, the English law gives relief to one who, without independent advice, enters into a contract upon terms which are very unfair or transfers property for a consideration which is grossly inadequate, when his bargaining power is grievously impaired by reason of his own needs or desires, or by his own ignorance or infirmity, coupled with undue influences or pressures brought to bear on him by or for the benefit of the other. When I use the word "undue" I do not mean to suggest that the principle depends on proof of any wrongdoing. The one who stipulates for an unfair advantage may be moved solely by his own self-interest, unconscious of the distress he is bringing to the other. I have also avoided any reference to the will of the one being "dominated" or "overcome" by the other. One who is in extreme need may knowingly consent to a most improvident bargain, solely to relieve the straits in which he finds himself. Again, I do not mean to suggest that every transaction is saved by independent advice. But the absence of it may be fatal. With these explanations, I hope this principle will be found to reconcile the cases. Applying it to the present case, I would notice these points:

(1) The consideration moving from the bank was grossly inadequate. ...
(2) The relationship between the bank and the father was one of trust and confidence.
    ...
(3) The relationship between the father and the son was one where the father's natural affection had much influence on him. He would naturally desire to accede to his son's request. ...
(4) There was a conflict of interest between the bank and the father. ...

These considerations seem to me to bring this case within the principles I have stated. But, in case that principle is wrong, I would also say that the case falls within the category of undue influence of the second class stated by Cotton L.J. in *Allcard v. Skinner*, 36 Ch.D. 145, 171.

Sir Eric Sachs: The conclusion that Mr. Bundy has established that as between himself and the bank the relevant transaction fell within the second category of undue influence cases referred to by Cotton L.J. in *Allcard v. Skinner*, 36 Ch.D. 145, 171, is one reached upon the single issue pursued on behalf of the defendant in this court. On that issue we have had the benefit of cogent and helpful submissions on matter plainly raised in the pleadings. As regards the wider areas covered in masterly survey in the judgment of Lord Denning M.R., but not raised arguendo, I do not venture to express an opinion – though having some sympathy with the views that the courts should be able to give relief to a party who has been subject to undue pressure as defined in the concluding passage of his judgment on that point.

Cairns LJ concurred with **Sir Eric Sachs.**

NOTES AND QUESTIONS

1. Lord Denning saw his inequality of bargaining power principle as underpinning five categories of case (duress of goods, unconscionable transactions, undue influence, undue pressure, and salvage agreements). Do you agree that that principle underpins those (or even some of those) categories?
2. Even if accurate, is there any advantage in referring to the principle rather than to the particular category in play? Is the principle too uncertain to be helpful?

Might it be argued that recognition of the principle would make it easier for the law to be developed further? Is further development justified?

3. While in a number of cases litigants relied on Lord Denning's principle (see, eg, *Alec Lobb* above, 768) it was never approved by an appellate court and, as we shall now see, was rejected by the House of Lords.

National Westminster Bank v Morgan [1985] AC 686, House of Lords

Mr and Mrs Morgan, the defendants, had bought their home using a mortgage from the Abbey National Building Society. They fell into arrears in repaying the mortgage and Mr Morgan also had business debts. To save their home, the defendants sought, and obtained, a short-term bridging loan, secured by a charge over the house, from the claimant bank. The bank manager, Mr Barrow, had visited the home of the Morgans to obtain Mrs Morgan's signature for the loan and charge. The defendants failed to repay the loan and the claimant brought proceedings for possession. The wife's defence was that, in obtaining her signature to the charge, the claimant, through its manager Mr Barrow, had exercised undue influence over her. The House of Lords, allowing the claimant's appeal, held that, while a relationship of influence could be established on the facts between a bank and its customer as shown by *Lloyds Bank v Bundy*, there was no such relationship here; in any event, the transaction would not be set aside because it had not been shown to be 'manifestly disadvantageous' to the wife. The terminology of 'manifest disadvantage' has since been disapproved by the House of Lords in *Etridge* (above, 737). We are here solely concerned with what was briefly said about 'inequality of bargaining power'.

Lord Scarman: Lord Denning M.R. believed that the doctrine of undue influence could be subsumed under a general principle that English courts will grant relief where there has been "inequality of bargaining power" (p. 339). He deliberately avoided reference to the will of one party being dominated or overcome by another. The majority of the court did not follow him; they based their decision on the orthodox view of the doctrine as expounded in *Allcard v. Skinner*, 36 Ch.D. 145. The opinion of the Master of the Rolls, therefore, was not the ground of the court's decision, which was to be found in the view of the majority, for whom Sir Eric Sachs delivered the leading judgment.

Nor has counsel for the respondent sought to rely on Lord Denning M.R.'s general principle: and, in my view, he was right not to do so. The doctrine of undue influence has been sufficiently developed not to need the support of a principle which by its formulation in the language of the law of contract is not appropriate to cover transactions of gift where there is no bargain. The fact of an unequal bargain will, of course, be a relevant feature in some cases of undue influence. But it can never become an appropriate basis of principle of an equitable doctrine which is concerned with transactions "not to be reasonably accounted for on the ground of friendship, relationship, charity, or other ordinary motives on which ordinary men act" (Lindley L.J. in *Allcard v. Skinner*, at p. 185). And even in the field of contract I question whether there is any need in the modern law to erect a general principle of relief against inequality of bargaining power. Parliament has undertaken the task – and it is essentially a legislative task – of enacting such restrictions upon freedom of contract as are in its judgment necessary to relieve against the mischief: for example, the hire-purchase and consumer protection legislation, of which the Supply of Goods (Implied Terms) Act 1973, Consumer Credit Act 1974, Consumer Safety Act 1978, Supply of Goods and Services Act 1982 and Insurance Companies Act 1982 are examples. I doubt whether the courts should assume the burden of formulating further restrictions.

Lords Keith of Kinkel, Roskill, Bridge of Harwich and **Brandon of Oakbrook** concurred.

NOTES AND QUESTIONS

1. Do you agree with Lord Scarman that any development of the law on inequality of bargaining power should be a matter for Parliament, not the courts?

2. In obiter dicta in *PaO On v Lau Liu Long* [1980] AC 614, 634 (see generally 93, 103, 701 above, but the extracts do not include these obiter dicta) Lord Scarman said, without referring to *Lloyds Bank v Bundy*, that 'a rule [disallowing unfair use of a dominating bargaining position] would be unhelpful because it would render the law uncertain. It would become a question of fact and degree to determine in each case whether there had been, short of duress, an unfair use of a strong bargaining position'. Is that a valid objection to such a rule?

Additional Reading for Chapter 15

J Beatson, *Anson's Law of Contract* (28th edn, 2002) 284–300
S Smith, *Atiyah's Introduction to the Law of Contract* (6th edn, 2005) 283–306, 308–13

H Beale, 'Inequality of Bargaining Power' (1986) 6 *OJLS* 123
In the course of this article, reviewing a relatively obscure Anglo-Swedish comparative law book on law and the weaker party, Beale examines what is meant in the English law of contract by unfairness and inequality of bargaining power. He looks at various categories (including unconscionable bargains, undue influence, duress and the control of exclusion clauses) and argues (at 125) that while 'most of the traditional doctrines... apply only where there is unfairness in the sense of inadequacy of consideration... more modern rules strike at clauses which leave a party at risk, even if he got value-for-money'; and that inequality of bargaining power can mean 'ignorance, vulnerability to persuasion, desperate need, lack of bargaining skill or simple lack of influence in the market place'.

S Thal, 'The Inequality of Bargaining Power Doctrine: The Problem of Defining Contractual Unfairness' (1988) 8 *OJLS* 17
Thal argues that, despite the rejection of Lord Denning's principle of 'inequality of bargaining power', contracts are struck down on the grounds of 'unfairness' in a

range of situations. Those situations are best understood as concrete examples of bargaining weakness. In line with this, clarity is best achieved if one accepts that it is procedural unfairness (fairness of the bargaining process) rather than substantive unfairness (fairness of the outcome) that should be focussed on.

N Bamforth, 'Unconscionability as a Vitiating Factor' [1995] *LMCLQ* 538

By examining numerous English and Commonwealth authorities, Bamforth argues that unconscionability has emerged as a distinct factor vitiating transactions. He sees there as being four necessary elements: special or serious disadvantage, actual or constructive fraud, lack of independent advice, and disadvantageous terms.

P Birks and C Yin, 'On the Nature of Undue Influence' in *Good Faith and Fault in Contract Law* (eds J Beatson and D Friedmann, 1995) 57

It is argued that, once one has taken out pressure cases as belonging within duress, undue influence is concerned with the claimant's impaired consent ('excessive dependence' on another person) rather than with the defendant's wicked exploitation of the claimant. Undue influence is therefore 'plaintiff-sided' rather than 'defendant-sided'.

R Bigwood, 'Undue Influence: "Impaired Consent" or "Wicked Exploitation"?' (1995) 16 *OJLS* 503

Bigwood disagrees with the Birks/Yin approach. His view is that, in relation to undue influence, impaired consent and exploitation are inextricably linked so that it is a mistake to regard the doctrine as focusing on one to the exclusion of the other.

[For his more recent argument that in some undue influence and unconscionable bargain cases, the best justification for why the law allows escape is a principle of 'transactional neglect' (ie D's failure to take reasonable precautions where exploitation is known to be possible) see 'Contracts by Unfair Advantage: From Exploitation to Transactional Neglect' (2005) 25 *OJLS* 65.]

D Capper, 'Undue Influence and Unconscionability: A Rationalisation' (1998) *LQR* 479

Capper argues that the doctrines of undue influence and unconscionability are so similar that they can, and might profitably, be merged into one (the latter swallowing up the former). He regards the linked common requirements as being relational inequality, transactional imbalance and unconscionable conduct (although he includes within this last requirement, passive receipt of benefits in circumstances where the defendant ought to realise that he should not accept them).

M Chen-Wishart, 'Undue Influence: *Beyond* Impaired Consent and Wrongdoing towards a Relational Analysis' in *Mapping the Law: Essays in Memory of Peter Birks* (eds A Burrows and Lord Rodger, 2006) 201

Both the claimant-sided consent-based view of undue influence and the defendant-sided 'wrongful act' explanation are here rejected. Instead it is suggested that the best explanation lies in a 'relational theory of undue influence'. This goes beyond a 'single factor' explanation but in essence views the doctrine as requiring the defendant to protect the claimant or to ensure that the claimant can protect herself.

Principles of European Contract Law (ed O Lando and H Beale, 2000) 261–5

Article 4:109: Excessive Benefit or Unfair Advantage
(1) A party may avoid a contract if, at the time of the conclusion of the contract:

(a) it was dependent on or had a relationship of trust with the other party, was in economic distress or had urgent needs, was improvident, ignorant, inexperienced or lacking in bargaining skill, and

(b) the other party knew or ought to have known of this and, given the circumstances and purpose of the contract, took advantage of the first party's situation in a way which was grossly unfair or took an excessive benefit.

(2) Upon the request of the party entitled to avoidance, a court may if it is appropriate adapt the contract in order to bring it into accordance with what might have been agreed had the requirements of good faith and fair dealing been followed.

(3) A court may similarly adapt the contract upon the request of a party receiving notice of avoidance for excessive benefit or unfair advantage, provided that this party informs the party who gave the notice promptly after receiving it and before that party has acted in reliance on it.

[This is similar to English law but appears to go beyond it in that: eg, it requires bad faith advantage-taking even where there is undue influence; covers a wider range of weaknesses; and gives the court the power to rewrite the contract.]

Article 4:116: Partial Avoidance
See above, 589.

Article 4:117: Damages
See above, 589.

[These articles contrast with English law in that rescission in England cannot be partial; and undue influence and exploitation of weakness are not in themselves wrongs triggering damages: see above, 549, 726, 757.]

Index